Lecture Notes in Computer Science 13269

More information about this series at https://link.springer.com/bookseries/558

Giuseppe Ateniese · Daniele Venturi (Eds.)

Applied Cryptography and Network Security

20th International Conference, ACNS 2022
Rome, Italy, June 20–23, 2022
Proceedings

Editors
Giuseppe Ateniese ⓘ
Stevens Institute of Technology
Hoboken, NJ, USA

Daniele Venturi ⓘ
Sapienza University of Rome
Rome, Italy

ISSN 0302-9743   ISSN 1611-3349 (electronic)
Lecture Notes in Computer Science
ISBN 978-3-031-09233-6   ISBN 978-3-031-09234-3 (eBook)
https://doi.org/10.1007/978-3-031-09234-3

This Springer imprint is published by the registered company Springer Nature Switzerland AG
The registered company address is: Gewerbestrasse 11, 6330 Cham, Switzerland

Preface

We are pleased to present the proceedings of the 20th International Conference on Applied Cryptography and Network Security (ACNS 2022). ACNS 2022 was held in Rome, Italy. Due to the ongoing COVID-19 crisis, we decided to have a hybrid conference to face any health risks or travel restrictions for attending the conference. The organization was in the capable hands of Mauro Conti (University of Padua, Italy) and Angelo Spognardi (Sapienza University of Rome, Italy) as general co-chairs, and Massimo Bernaschi (National Research Council, IAC-CNR, Italy) and Fabio De Gaspari (Sapienza University of Rome, Italy) as local organizing chairs. We are deeply indebted to them for their tireless work to ensure the success of the conference even in such complex conditions.

For the third time, ACNS had two rounds of submission cycles, with deadlines in September 2021 and January 2022, respectively. We received a total of 185 submissions from authors in 37 countries. This year's Program Committee (PC) consisted of around 150 members with diverse backgrounds and broad research interests. The review process was double-blind and rigorous, and papers were evaluated on the basis of research significance, novelty, and technical quality. In total, 691 reviews were submitted, with four reviews for most papers. Some papers submitted in the first round received a decision of major revision. The revised versions of those papers were further evaluated in the second round and some of them were accepted. After the review process concluded, a total of 44 papers were accepted to be presented at the conference and included in the proceedings, representing an acceptance rate of around 24%.

Among those papers, we awarded the Best Student Paper Award to Narmeen Shafqat (Northeastern University, Boston, MA, USA) for the paper "ZLeaks: Passive Inference Attacks on Zigbee based Smart Homes" (co-authored with Daniel J. Dubois, David Choffnes, Aaron Schulman, Dinesh Bharadia, and Aanjhan Ranganathan). The monetary prize of 1,000 euro was generously sponsored by Springer.

We had a rich program including eight satellite workshops in parallel with the main event, providing a forum to address specific topics at the forefront of cybersecurity research. The papers presented at those workshops were published in separate proceedings.

This year we had two outstanding keynote talks: "Chosen Ciphertext Security from Injective Trapdoor Functions" by Prof. Susan Hohenberger Waters (Johns Hopkins University, USA), and "Secure Computation in Practice" by Prof. Raluca Ada Popa (University of California, Berkeley, USA). To them, our heartfelt gratitude for their outstanding presentations.

The conference was made possible by the untiring efforts of many individuals and organizations. We are grateful to all the authors for their submissions. We sincerely appreciate the outstanding work of all the PC members and the external reviewers, who selected the papers after reading, commenting, and debating them. Finally, we thank all the people who volunteered their time and energy to put together the conference, the speakers and session chairs, and everyone who contributed to the success of the conference. We are also grateful to Riccardo Lazzeretti (Sapienza University of Rome, Italy) for taking care of these proceedings. Last, but certainly not least, we are very grateful to Frontiers for sponsoring the conference, Easychair for the management of the submissions, and Springer for their help in assembling these proceedings.

June 2022   Daniele Venturi
                                                                       Giuseppe Ateniese

Organization

General Chairs

Mauro Conti   University of Padua, Italy
Angelo Spognardi   Sapienza University of Rome, Italy

Program Chairs

Giuseppe Ateniese   Stevens Institute of Technology, USA
Daniele Venturi   Sapienza University of Rome, Italy

Workshop Chair

Jianying Zhou   Singapore University of Technology and Design,
                                Singapore

Poster Chair

Emiliano Casalicchio   Sapienza University of Rome, Italy

Local Organization Chairs

Massimo Bernaschi   National Council of Research, Italy
Fabio De Gaspari   Sapienza University of Rome, Italy

Publicity Chair

Alessandro Brighente   University of Padua, Italy

Publication Chair

Riccardo Lazzeretti   Sapienza University of Rome, Italy

Web Chair

Alicia K. Bidi   Sapienza University of Rome, Italy

Program Committee

Masayuki Abe	NTT, Japan
Mitsuaki Akiyama	NTT, Japan
Cristina Alcaraz	University of Malaga, Spain
Giuseppe Ateniese	George Mason University, USA
Xiaolong Bai	Alibaba Group, China
Lejla Batina	Radboud University, The Netherlands
Carsten Baum	Aarhus University, Denmark
Estuardo Bock	Aalto University, Finland
Matteo Campanelli	Protocol Labs, Denmark
Ignacio Cascudo	IMDEA Software Institute, Spain
Sang Kil Cha	Korea Advanced Institute of Science and Technology, South Korea
Sudipta Chattopadhyay	Singapore University of Technology and Design, Singapore
Sherman S. M. Chow	Chinese University of Hong Kong, Hong Kong
Michele Ciampi	University of Edinburgh, UK
Mauro Conti	University of Padua, Italy
Sandro Coretti	IOHK, Switzerland
Marc Dacier	Qatar Computing Research Institute, Qatar
Roberto Di Pietro	Hamad Bin Khalifa University, Qatar
Josep Domingo-Ferrer	Universitat Rovira i Virgili, Spain
Nico Döttling	Aarhus University, Denmark
Antonio Faonio	EURECOM, France
Prastudy Fauzi	Simula UiB, Norway
Tommaso Gagliardoni	Kudelski Security, Switzerland
Chaya Ganesh	Aarhus University, Denmark
Debin Gao	Singapore Management University, Singapore
Paolo Gasti	New York Institute of Technology, USA
Esha Ghosh	Microsoft, USA
Yong Guan	Iowa State University, USA
Susan Hohenberger	Johns Hopkins University, USA
Hsu-Chun Hsiao	National Taiwan University, China
Hongxin Hu	University at Buffalo, SUNY, USA
Xinyi Huang	Fujian Normal University, China
Sotiris Ioannidis	Technical University of Crete, Greece
Hai Jin	Huazhong University of Science and Technology, China
Stefan Katzenbeisser	University of Passau, Germany
Kwok Yan Lam	Nanyang Technological University, Singapore
Peeter Laud	Cybernetica AS, Estonia
Xiapu Luo	Hong Kong Polytechnic University, Hong Kong

Bernardo Magri   Aarhus University, Denmark
Mark Manulis   Universität der Bundeswehr München, Germany
Giorgia Azzurra Marson   NEC Labs Europe, Germany
Daniel Masny   Meta, USA
Christian Matt   Concordium, Switzerland
Vashek Matyas   Masaryk University, Czech Republic
Veelasha Moonsamy   Ruhr University Bochum, Germany
Pratyay Mukherjee   Hedera Hashgraph/Swirlds, USA
David Naccache   ENS, France
Ariel Nof   Technion, Israel
Sabine Oechsner   University of Edinburgh, UK
Cristina Onete   Université de Limoges, France
Gerardo Pelosi   Politecnico di Milano, Italy
Giuseppe Persiano   Università degli Studi di Salerno, Italy
Thomas Peters   Université catholique de Louvain, Belgium
Josef Pieprzyk   CSIRO/Data61, Australia
Bertram Poettering   IBM Research - Zurich, Switzerland
Divya Ravi   Aarhus University, Denmark
Reihaneh Safavi-Naini   University of Calgary, Canada
Nitesh Saxena   Texas A&M University, USA
Janno Siim   University of Tartu, Finland
Mark Simkin   Ethereum Foundation
Angelo Spognardi   Sapienza Università di Roma, Italy
Purui Su   Institute of Software, CAS, China
Qiang Tang   University of Sydney, Australia
Mehdi Tibouchi   NTT, Japan
Daniel Tschudi   Concordium, Switzerland
Yiannis Tselekounis   University of Edinburgh
Daniele Venturi   Sapienza University of Rome, Italy
Ivan Visconti   University of Salerno, Italy
Cong Wang   City University of Hong Kong, Hong Kong
Zhaoyan Xu   Palo Alto Networks, USA
Chao Zhang   Tsinghua University, China
Fan Zhang   Zhejiang University, China
Kehuan Zhang   Chinese University of Hong Kong, Hong Kong
Yinqian Zhang   Southern University of Science and Technology,
                                China
Hong-Sheng Zhou   Virginia Commonwealth University, USA
Jianying Zhou   Singapore University of Technology and Design,
                                Singapore
Yajin Zhou   Zhejiang University, China

Contents

Cryptographic Primitives

MPC

Blockchain

Block-Cyphers

Post-quantum Cryptography

Encryption

Encryption

Keyed-Fully Homomorphic Encryption Without Indistinguishability Obfuscation

Shingo Sato[1]($\boxtimes$), Keita Emura[2], and Atsushi Takayasu[3]

[1] Yokohama National University, Yokohama, Japan
sato-shingo-zk@ynu.ac.jp
[2] National Institute of Information and Communications
Technology (NICT), Koganei, Japan
k-emura@nict.go.jp
[3] The University of Tokyo, Bunkyo-ku, Japan
takayasu-a@g.ecc.u-tokyo.ac.jp

Abstract. (Fully) homomorphic encryption ((F)HE) allows users to publicly evaluate circuits on encrypted data. Although public homomorphic evaluation property has various applications, (F)HE cannot achieve security against chosen ciphertext attacks (CCA2) due to its nature. To achieve both the CCA2 security and homomorphic evaluation property, Emura et al. (PKC 2013) introduced keyed-homomorphic public key encryption (KH-PKE) and formalized its security denoted by KH-CCA security. KH-PKE has a homomorphic evaluation key that enables users to perform homomorphic operations. Intuitively, KH-PKE achieves the CCA2 security unless adversaries have a homomorphic evaluation key. Although Lai et al. (PKC 2016) proposed the first keyed-fully homomorphic encryption (keyed-FHE) scheme, its security relies on the indistinguishability obfuscation (iO), and this scheme satisfies a weak variant of KH-CCA security. Here, we propose a generic construction of a KH-CCA secure keyed-FHE scheme from an FHE scheme secure against non-adaptive chosen ciphertext attack (CCA1) and a strong dual-system simulation-sound non-interactive zero-knowledge (strong DSS-NIZK) argument system by using the Naor-Yung paradigm. We show that there are a strong DSS-NIZK and an IND-CCA1 secure FHE scheme that are suitable for our generic construction. This shows that there exists a keyed-FHE scheme from simpler primitives than iO.

Keywords: Keyed-homomorphic public key encryption · Keyed-fully homomorphic encryption · Strong DSS-NIZK

1 Introduction

1.1 Background

Homomorphic encryption (HE) allows users to convert encryptions of messages $m_1, \ldots, m_\ell$ into an encryption of $C(m_1, \ldots, m_\ell)$ publicly for some circuit C. In particular, *fully homomorphic encryption (FHE)* can be used to handle arbitrary

© Springer Nature Switzerland AG 2022
G. Ateniese and D. Venturi (Eds.): ACNS 2022, LNCS 13269, pp. 3–23, 2022.
https://doi.org/10.1007/978-3-031-09234-3_1

circuits. The public homomorphic evaluation property is applied to various applications. For example, suppose encryptions of private data are stored in a remote server, delegating computations on the encrypted data to the server without revealing the private data is possible. Thus, users leverage the results of computations on other devices without compromising data privacy. Since Gentry proposed the first FHE scheme [24], the research area has gained widespread attention and many schemes have been proposed (e.g., FHE schemes [5,7–11,19,24,25], identity-based FHE (IBFHE) schemes [15,25], and attribute-based FHE schemes [6,25]), where most schemes are secure under the learning with errors (LWE) assumption. Although the public evaluation property is useful, one downside is that (F)HE schemes are vulnerable against adaptive chosen ciphertext attacks (CCA). (In this paper, we use IND-CCA2 or IND-CCA, IND-CCA1, and IND-CPA as indistinguishability against adaptive chosen ciphertext attacks, non-adaptive chosen ciphertext (i.e., lunchtime) attacks, and chosen-plaintext attacks, respectively). Therefore, several IND-CCA1 secure (F)HE schemes have been proposed. For example, Canetti et al. [11] proposed a generic construction of IND-CCA1 secure FHE from the LWE assumption or a zero-knowledge succinct non-interactive argument of knowledge (zk-SNARK) [3,4] and IND-CPA secure FHE. However, IND-CCA1 security can be inadequate for FHE since Loftus et al. [33] showed that an IND-CCA1 secure FHE scheme is vulnerable against ciphertext validity attacks.

To achieve both CCA2-like security and homomorphic evaluation property, Emura et al. [21,22] introduced *keyed-homomorphic public-key encryption (KH-PKE)*. Contrary to traditional HE, the homomorphic evaluation property of KH-PKE is not public. Specifically, KH-PKE has a homomorphic evaluation key. Thus, only users with the homomorphic evaluation key can perform homomorphic operations. Due to its nature, KH-PKE can achieve CCA2-like security.[1] Suppose adversaries do not have the homomorphic evaluation key, then, KH-PKE satisfies the IND-CCA2 security. Moreover, KH-PKE satisfies stronger security than HE even if adversaries receive a homomorphic evaluation key. Suppose adversaries receive the homomorphic evaluation key before the challenge query, then the strongest security that KH-PKE can satisfy is the IND-CCA1 security as the case of HE. In contrast, KH-PKE can satisfy stronger securities than the IND-CCA1 security if adversaries receive the homomorphic evaluation key after the challenge query since they continue making decryption queries until they receive the homomorphic evaluation key. Moreover, KH-PKE is secure against ciphertext validity attacks [20].

Emura et al. [22] proposed the notion of KH-PKE but their security proofs contain bugs (which have been corrected in [21] and they gave the KH-PKE schemes under the decisional Diffie-Hellman (DDH) assumption or the decisional composite residuosity (DCR) assumption). Libert et al. [32] proposed the first KH-PKE schemes secure in the model given in [22] using the Decision Linear (DLIN) assumption or the symmetric external Diffie-Hellman (SXDH) assumption.

---

[1] Although Desmedt et al. [18] proposed a HE scheme with a designated evaluation called controlled HE, no CCA security was considered unlike the KH-PKE.

Jutla and Roy [29] proposed a KH-PKE scheme based on SXDH assumption. All KH-PKE schemes support either multiplicative or additive homomorphisms. Maeda and Nuida [35] proposed a two-level KH-PKE scheme that supports one multiplication and any number of additions. Lai et al. [30] proposed the first *keyed-fully homomorphic encryption (keyed-FHE)*[2] scheme, which is secure under lattice assumptions and the indistinguishability obfuscation (iO) [1]. However, known candidates of iO [1] remain arguable. Therefore, constructing keyed-FHE schemes without iO has to be an interesting open problem. We remark that the keyed-FHE scheme of [30] satisfies only weaker security than the KH-PKE's security (called KH-CCA security) formalized in [21]. In the case where an adversary receives a homomorphic evaluation key before the challenge query, the security considered in [30] corresponds to the IND-CPA security of (F)HE, while in that case, KH-CCA security corresponds to the IND-CCA1 security of (F)HE.

1.2 Contribution

In this work, we propose a generic construction of the keyed-FHE without iO. This construction uses IND-CCA1 secure FHE and a strong dual-system unbounded simulation-sound NIZK (strong DSS-NIZK) introduced by Jutla and Roy [29] as building blocks, where the strong DSS-NIZK is used for FHE ciphertext. In our security proof, we employ the Naor-Yung paradigm [36,37] to achieve IND-CCA2-like security. Since no strong DSS-NIZK scheme exists for NP, we have to construct the desired scheme. For this purpose, we show that a modification of Jutla and Roy's strong DSS-NIZK scheme [29] satisfies the requirement of our generic construction of keyed-FHE, where the construction of the strong DSS-NIZK scheme uses a smooth projective hash proof system (PHPS) and an unbounded simulation-sound NIZK scheme. We note that there are smooth PHPS [2] secure statistically and unbounded simulation-sound NIZK schemes [12,26,31] whose security depends on lattice assumptions or the security of the commitment schemes used in [12,26]. We remark that for adopting the strong DSS-NIZK scheme above we need to assume that the underlying IND-CCA1 secure FHE schemes are publicly verifiable (but these exists such a scheme [11]). To sum up, we obtain the first keyed-FHE scheme without iO. Note that even if an IND-CPA secure FHE scheme under (a variant of) the approximate GCD assumption (e.g., [13,16,19]) is employed to construct an IND-CCA1 secure FHE scheme, our generic construction gives no keyed-FHE scheme based solely on that assumption because there is no existing HPS for approximate GCD-based ciphertexts. Furthermore, another advantage of our result is that our keyed-FHE scheme satisfies stronger security (i.e., KH-CCA security) than the existing keyed-FHE scheme [30].

1.3 Technical Overview

We give a brief overview of our results. Since Lai et al. [30] constructed the keyed-FHE scheme using iO, the most convincing way to achieve the goal is

---

[2] In this paper, keyed-FHE is a public key setting.

to remove the iO from the construction. However, completing the task seems technically difficult. Thus, we focus on Jutla and Roy's KH-PKE scheme [29] under the SXDH assumption. Their construction used an ElGamal encryption scheme and a stronger version of the dual-system unbounded simulation-sound NIZK (DSS-NIZK) for the Diffie-Hellman language. Due to the nature of one-time simulation-sound NIZK for the Diffie-Hellman language, their construction satisfies IND-CCA2-like security as noted in [27]. Therefore, the remaining task to prove the security is how to simulate the homomorphic key reveal oracle (RevHK) and how to prove the IND-CCA1 security even after the RevHK query. Here, the properties of strong DSS-NIZK resolve the problems. The homomorphic evaluation key of the KH-PKE scheme is a trapdoor of the strong DSS-NIZK. In particular, one-time full zero-knowledge ensures that the strong DSS-NIZK is trapdoor leakage resilient. Moreover, unbounded partial simulation-soundness ensures that their KH-PKE scheme satisfies the IND-CCA1 security even after the RevHK query. To satisfy the required properties, Jutla and Roy constructed the strong DSS-NIZK scheme for the Diffie-Hellman language using quasi-adaptive NIZK for the same language [28] and a hash proof system (HPS) [17] that is smooth projective and universal$_2$.

Using a similar approach, we construct the keyed-FHE without iO by replacing (a variant of) the ElGamal encryption scheme with FHE schemes. For this purpose, we have to overcome three issues. First, Jutla and Roy's KH-PKE scheme used strong DSS-NIZK for the Diffie-Hellman language that is not suitable for FHE. Therefore, we construct strong DSS-NIZK for another language that handles FHE ciphertexts. Thus, we construct the strong DSS-NIZK for NP. Second, Jutla and Roy's KH-PKE scheme satisfies IND-CCA2-like security based on simulation-sound NIZK for the Diffie-Hellman language. That is, just replacing the ElGamal encryption scheme with FHE schemes does not satisfy IND-CCA2-like security. Here, we resolve the issue by employing the Naor-Yung paradigm [36,37]. For simplicity, these modifications enable us to construct a keyed-FHE scheme without iO. We observe whether we can construct strong DSS-NIZK for NP following a similar approach as Jutla and Roy. Jutla and Roy used quasi-adaptive NIZK for the Diffie-Hellman language and an HPS [17] that is smooth projective and universal$_2$. In this step, the last issue occurs since there is no known lattice-based universal$_2$ HPS. We construct the desired strong DSS-NIZK for NP by replacing the universal$_2$ HPS of Jutla-Roy's construction with unbounded simulation-sound NIZK and modifying slightly the construction. Therefore, this completes a brief overview of our generic keyed-FHE scheme.

All building blocks of our generic construction of keyed-FHE do not require iO. We remark that our generic construction of keyed-FHE requires only the IND-CCA1 security for the underlying FHE scheme, but our strong DSS-NIZK system requires public verifiability for the IND-CCA1 secure FHE scheme. There is an IND-CCA1 secure publicly verifiable FHE scheme [11] under zk-SNARK [3, 4]. It is known that there exist zk-SNARK systems in the quantum random oracle model [14]. Hence, there exists an IND-CCA1 secure FHE scheme in the quantum random oracle model. In addition, we can also obtain an IND-CCA1 secure FHE scheme without random oracles if the underlying zk-SNARK is based on a strong assumption such as knowledge assumptions. We can construct strong DSS-NIZK using the following building blocks: (1) the NIZK system for NP in the random oracle model from Σ-protocols (ZKBoo) [26] using the Fiat-Shamir transformation [23], the NIZK system secure in the quantum random oracle model [12], or the NIZK system secure in the standard model [31], and (2) the smooth projective HPS [2] for lattice-based ciphertexts. Therefore, we can obtain a keyed-FHE scheme secure in the standard model or the quantum random oracle model. Notice that Libert et al. proposed a simulation-sound NIZK system for LWE-like relations in the standard model [31], they do not give a security proof that it satisfies the zero-knowledge property after the trapdoor is revealed. Nevertheless, since their zero-knowledge property is statistical, it can be applied to our construction. However, their scheme is not very efficient, and thus it would be interesting to see that the efficiency of their NIZKs could be improved in future work.

2 Preliminaries

We use the following notation: For a positive integer n, let $[n] := \{1, 2, \ldots, n\}$. For n values $x_1, x_2, \ldots, x_n$ and a subset $I \subseteq [n]$ of indexes, let $\{x_i\}_{i \in I}$ be a set of values whose indexes are included in I, and let $(x_i)_{i \in I}$ be a sequence of values whose indexes are included in I. Probabilistic polynomial-time is abbreviated as PPT. If a function $f : \mathbb{N} \to \mathbb{R}$ fulfills $f(\lambda) = o(\lambda^{-c})$ for every constant $c > 0$ and sufficiently large $\lambda \in \mathbb{N}$, then we say that f is negligible in λ and write $f(\lambda) = \mathsf{negl}(\lambda)$. A probability is overwhelming if it is $1 - \mathsf{negl}(\lambda)$. For a probabilistic algorithm A, $y \leftarrow \mathsf{A}(x; r)$ means that A takes as input x and a picked randomness r, and it outputs y.

In addition, we describe the definitions of several cryptographic primitives.

2.1 Non-Interactive Zero-Knowledge Argument

Definition 1. *A non-interactive zero-knowledge argument (NIZK) system for a relation $R \subseteq \{0,1\}^* \times \{0,1\}^*$ consists of three polynomial-time algorithms* (Gen, P, V): *Let $\mathcal{L}(R) = \{x \mid \exists w \text{ s.t. } (x, w) \in R\}$ be the language defined by R.*

- crs $\leftarrow$ Gen(1^λ): *The randomized algorithm* Gen *takes as input a security parameter 1^λ, and it outputs a common reference string (CRS) crs.*
- $\pi \leftarrow$ P(crs, x, w): *The randomized algorithm* P *takes as input a CRS crs, a statement x, and a witness w, and it outputs a proof π.*
- $1/0 \leftarrow$ V(crs, x, π): *The deterministic algorithm* V *takes as input a CRS crs, a statement x, and a proof π, and it outputs 1 or 0.*

We define several properties of NIZKs which are required for constructing strong DSS-NIZK. For removing universal$_2$ property of PHPS, the adversary is allowed to query x such that $x \notin \mathcal{L}(R)$ in the definition of unbounded simulation-soundness. For considering trapdoor leakage in strong DSS-NIZK, the adversary is allowed to obtain a trapdoor td in the definition of composable zero-knowledge.

Definition 2. *In this paper, it is required that a NIZK system* (Gen, P, V) *with a PPT simulator* Sim = (Sim$_0$, Sim$_1$) *satisfies completeness, unbounded simulation-soundness, and (composable) zero-knowledge: Let* Sim$_0$ *be a PPT algorithm which, given* 1^λ, *outputs a CRS* crs *and a trapdoor* td, *and* Sim$_1$ *be a PPT algorithm which, given* crs, td, *and a statement* x, *outputs a simulated proof* π.

Completeness. *For every* $(x, w) \in R$, *it holds that* $\Pr[\text{crs} \leftarrow \text{Gen}(1^\lambda); \pi \leftarrow P(\text{crs}, x, w) : V(\text{crs}, x, \pi) = 1] \geq 1 - \text{negl}(\lambda)$.

Unbounded Simulation-Soundness. *For any PPT adversary* A, *it holds that*

$$\Pr\left[\begin{array}{l} (\text{crs}, \text{td}) \leftarrow \text{Sim}_0(1^\lambda); \mathcal{Q} \leftarrow \emptyset; \\ (x^*, \pi^*) \leftarrow A^{\text{Sim}_1(\text{crs},\text{td},\cdot)}(\text{crs}) \end{array} : \begin{array}{l} (x^*, \pi^*) \notin \mathcal{Q} \wedge \\ x^* \notin \mathcal{L}(R) \wedge \\ V(\text{crs}, x^*, \pi^*) = 1 \end{array}\right] \leq \text{negl}(\lambda),$$

where the Sim$_1$ *oracle on input* x *returns* $\pi \leftarrow \text{Sim}_1(\text{crs}, \text{td}, x)$ *and sets* $\mathcal{Q} \leftarrow \mathcal{Q} \cup \{(x, \pi)\}$. *Notice that* A *is allowed to query* x *such that* $x \notin \mathcal{L}(R)$.

Composable Zero-Knowledge. *For any PPT adversaries* A$_1$ *and* A$_2$, *it holds that*

$$\left|\Pr\left[\text{crs} \leftarrow \text{Gen}(1^\lambda) : 1 \leftarrow A_1(\text{crs})\right] - \Pr\left[(\text{crs}, \text{td}) \leftarrow \text{Sim}_0(1^\lambda) : 1 \leftarrow A_1(\text{crs})\right]\right|$$
$$\leq \text{negl}(\lambda), \text{ and}$$

$$\left|\Pr[(\text{crs}, \text{td}) \leftarrow \text{Sim}_0(1^\lambda) : 1 \leftarrow A_2^{P(\text{crs},\cdot,\cdot)}(\text{crs}, \text{td})]\right.$$
$$\left. - \Pr[(\text{crs}, \text{td}) \leftarrow \text{Sim}_0(1^\lambda) : 1 \leftarrow A_2^{\text{Sim}^*(\text{crs},\text{td},\cdot)}(\text{crs}, \text{td})]\right| \leq \text{negl}(\lambda),$$

where the Sim* *oracle on input* $(x, w) \notin R$ *returns* $\perp$ *if* $(x, w) \notin R$, *and returns* $\pi \leftarrow \text{Sim}_1(\text{crs}, \text{td}, x)$ *otherwise.*

2.2 Dual-System Simulation-Sound NIZK

Following [29], we describe the definition of dual-system (unbounded) simulation-sound NIZK (DSS-NIZK).

Definition 3. *A DSS-NIZK system for a relation* $R \subseteq \{0,1\}^* \times \{0,1\}^*$ *consists of polynomial-time algorithms in three worlds, as follows: Let* $\mathcal{L}(R) = \{x \mid \exists w \text{ s.t. } (x, w) \in R\}$ *be the language defined by* R. *We remark that the witness relation parameter* ρ *is introduced in [29] because it considers quasi-adaptive NIZK. We omit the parameter in this paper.*

Real World. *A DSS-NIZK in* **real world** *consists of three polynomial-time algorithms* (Gen, P, V):

- crs $\leftarrow$ Gen(1^λ): *The randomized algorithm* Gen, *called a generator, takes as input a security parameter* 1^λ, *and it outputs a common reference string (CRS)* crs.
- $\pi \leftarrow$ P(crs, x, w, lbl): *The randomized algorithm* P, *called a prover, takes as input a CRS* crs, *a statement* x, *a witness* w, *and a label* lbl $\in \{0,1\}^*$, *and it outputs a proof* π.

- $1/0 \leftarrow \mathsf{V}(\mathsf{crs}, x, \pi, \mathsf{lbl})$: *The deterministic algorithm* V, *called a verifier, takes as input a CRS* crs, *a statement* x, *a proof* π, *and a label* $\mathsf{lbl} \in \{0,1\}^*$, *and it outputs 1 or 0.*

Partial-Simulation World. *A DSS-NIZK in* **partial-simulation world** *consists of three polynomial-time algorithms* $(\mathsf{sfGen}, \mathsf{sfSim}, \mathsf{pV})$:

- $(\mathsf{crs}, \mathsf{td}_s, \mathsf{td}_v) \leftarrow \mathsf{sfGen}(1^\lambda)$: *The randomized algorithm* sfGen, *called a semi-functional generator, takes as input a security parameter* 1^λ, *and it outputs a semi-functional CRS* crs, *and two trapdoors* td_s *and* td_v.
- $\pi \leftarrow \mathsf{sfSim}(\mathsf{crs}, \mathsf{td}_s, x, \beta, \mathsf{lbl})$: *The randomized algorithm* sfSim, *called a semi-functional simulator, takes as input a CRS* crs, *a trapdoor* td_s, *a statement* x, *a membership-bit* $\beta \in \{0,1\}$, *and a label* $\mathsf{lbl} \in \{0,1\}^*$, *and it outputs a proof* π.
- $1/0 \leftarrow \mathsf{pV}(\mathsf{crs}, \mathsf{td}_v, x, \pi, \mathsf{lbl})$: *The deterministic algorithm* pV, *called a private verifier, takes as input a CRS* crs, *a trapdoor* td_v, *a statement* x, *a proof* π, *and a label* $\mathsf{lbl} \in \{0,1\}^*$, *and it outputs 1 or 0.*

One-time Full Simulation World. *A DSS-NIZK in* **one-time full simulation world** *consists of three polynomial-time algorithms* $(\mathsf{otfGen}, \mathsf{otfSim}, \mathsf{sfV})$:

- $(\mathsf{crs}, \mathsf{td}_s, \mathsf{td}_{s,1}, \mathsf{td}_v) \leftarrow \mathsf{otfGen}(1^\lambda)$: *The randomized algorithm* otfGen, *called a one-time full generator, takes as input a security parameter* 1^λ, *and it outputs a CRS* crs *and three trapdoors* td_s, $\mathsf{td}_{s,1}$, *and* td_v.
- $\pi \leftarrow \mathsf{otfSim}(\mathsf{crs}, \mathsf{td}_{s,1}, x, \mathsf{lbl})$: *The randomized algorithm* otfSim, *called a one-time full simulator, takes as input a CRS* crs, *a trapdoor* $\mathsf{td}_{s,1}$, *a statement* x, *and a label* $\mathsf{lbl} \in \{0,1\}^*$, *and it outputs a proof* π.
- $1/0 \leftarrow \mathsf{sfV}(\mathsf{crs}, \mathsf{td}_v, x, \pi, \mathsf{lbl})$: *The deterministic algorithm* sfV, *called a semi-functional verifier, takes as input a CRS* crs, *a trapdoor* td_v, *a statement* x, *a proof* π, *and a label* $\mathsf{lbl} \in \{0,1\}^*$, *and it outputs 1 or 0.*

Definition 4. *It is required that a DSS-NIZK system for a relation* R *satisfies* completeness, partial zero-knowledge, unbounded partial simulation-soundness, *and* one-time full zero-knowledge:

Completeness. *For every* $(x,w) \in R$ *and every* $\mathsf{lbl} \in \{0,1\}^*$, *it holds that* $\Pr[\mathsf{crs} \leftarrow \mathsf{Gen}(1^\lambda); \pi \leftarrow \mathsf{P}(\mathsf{crs}, x, w, \mathsf{lbl}) : \mathsf{V}(\mathsf{crs}, x, \pi, \mathsf{lbl}) = 1] > 1 - \mathsf{negl}(\lambda)$.

(Composable) Partial Zero-Knowledge. *For any PPT algorithms* A_0 *and* A_1, *it holds that*

$$\big| \Pr[\mathsf{crs} \leftarrow \mathsf{Gen}(1^\lambda) : 1 \leftarrow \mathsf{A}_0(\mathsf{crs})]$$
$$- \Pr[(\mathsf{crs}, \mathsf{td}_s, \mathsf{td}_v) \leftarrow \mathsf{sfGen}(1^\lambda) : 1 \leftarrow \mathsf{A}_0(\mathsf{crs})] \big| \leq \mathsf{negl}(\lambda), \ and$$

$$\big| \Pr[(\mathsf{crs}, \mathsf{td}_s, \mathsf{td}_v) \leftarrow \mathsf{sfGen}(1^\lambda) : 1 \leftarrow \mathsf{A}_1^{\mathsf{P}(\mathsf{crs},\cdot,\cdot,\cdot),\mathsf{sfSim}^*(\mathsf{crs},\mathsf{td}_s,\cdot,\cdot,\cdot),\mathsf{V}(\mathsf{crs},\cdot,\cdot,\cdot)}(\mathsf{crs})]$$
$$- \Pr[(\mathsf{crs}, \mathsf{td}_s, \mathsf{td}_v) \leftarrow \mathsf{sfGen}(1^\lambda) :$$
$$1 \leftarrow \mathsf{A}_1^{\mathsf{sfSim}^*(\mathsf{crs},\mathsf{td}_s,\cdot,\cdot,\cdot),\mathsf{sfSim}^*(\mathsf{crs},\mathsf{td}_s,\cdot,\cdot,\cdot),\mathsf{pV}(\mathsf{crs},\mathsf{td}_v,\cdot,\cdot,\cdot)}(\mathsf{crs})] \big| \leq \mathsf{negl}(\lambda),$$

where $\mathsf{sfSim}^*(\mathsf{crs}, \mathsf{td}_s, x, w, \mathsf{lbl})$ *oracle returns* $\mathsf{sfSim}(\mathsf{crs}, \mathsf{td}_s, x, \beta = 1, \mathsf{lbl})$, *the challenger aborts if either* (x, w, lbl) *such that* $(x, w) \notin R$ *is queried to the first oracle (*sfSim^* *or* P*), or the second oracle* sfSim^* *receives a query* (x, β, lbl) *such that* $\beta = 0$ *or* $x \notin \mathcal{L}(R)$.

Unbounded Partial Simulation-Soundness. *For any PPT algorithm* A, *it holds that*

$$\Pr[(\mathsf{crs}, \mathsf{td}_s, \mathsf{td}_v) \leftarrow \mathsf{sfGen}(1^\lambda); (x, \pi, \mathsf{lbl}) \leftarrow \mathsf{A}^{\mathsf{sfSim}(\mathsf{crs}, \mathsf{td}_s, \cdot, \cdot, \cdot), \mathsf{pV}(\mathsf{crs}, \mathsf{td}_v, \cdot, \cdot, \cdot)}(\mathsf{crs}) :$$
$$((x \notin \mathcal{L}(R) \vee \mathsf{V}(\mathsf{crs}, x, \pi, \mathsf{lbl}) = 0) \wedge \mathsf{pV}(\mathsf{crs}, \mathsf{td}_v, x, \pi, \mathsf{lbl}) = 1] \leq \mathsf{negl}(\lambda).$$

One-time Full Zero-Knowledge. *For any PPT algorithm* $\mathsf{A} = (\mathsf{A}_0, \mathsf{A}_1)$, *it holds that*

$$|\Pr[(\mathsf{crs}, \mathsf{td}_s, \mathsf{td}_v) \leftarrow \mathsf{sfGen}(\lambda);$$
$$(x^*, \beta^*, \mathsf{lbl}^*, \mathsf{st}) \leftarrow \mathsf{A}_0^{\mathsf{sfSim}^*(\mathsf{crs}, \mathsf{td}_s, \cdots, \cdot), \mathsf{pV}(\mathsf{crs}, \mathsf{td}_v, \cdot, \cdot, \cdot)}(\mathsf{crs});$$
$$\pi^* \leftarrow \mathsf{sfSim}(\mathsf{crs}, \mathsf{td}_s, x^*, \beta^*, \mathsf{lbl}^*) : 1 \leftarrow \mathsf{A}_1^{\mathsf{sfSim}^*(\mathsf{crs}, \mathsf{td}_s, \cdot, \cdot, \cdot), \mathsf{pV}(\mathsf{crs}, \mathsf{td}_v, \cdot, \cdot, \cdot)}(\pi^*, \mathsf{st})]$$
$$- \Pr[(\mathsf{crs}, \mathsf{td}_s, \mathsf{td}_{s,1}, \mathsf{td}_v) \leftarrow \mathsf{otfGen}(\lambda);$$
$$(x^*, \beta^*, \mathsf{lbl}^*, \mathsf{st}) \leftarrow \mathsf{A}_0^{\mathsf{sfSim}^*(\mathsf{crs}, \mathsf{td}_s, \cdot, \cdot, \cdot), \mathsf{sfV}(\mathsf{crs}, \mathsf{td}_v, \cdot, \cdot, \cdot)}(\mathsf{crs});$$
$$\pi^* \leftarrow \mathsf{otfSim}(\mathsf{crs}, \mathsf{td}_{s,1}, x^*, \mathsf{lbl}^*) : 1 \leftarrow \mathsf{A}_1^{\mathsf{sfSim}^*(\mathsf{crs}, \mathsf{td}_s, \cdot, \cdot, \cdot), \mathsf{sfV}(\mathsf{crs}, \mathsf{td}_v, \cdot, \cdot, \cdot)}(\pi^*, \mathsf{st})]|$$
$$\leq \mathsf{negl}(\lambda),$$

where st *is state-information, and the challenger aborts if one of the following conditions holds:*

- *The generated* (x^*, β^*) *is not correct for the language* $\mathcal{L}(R)$.[3]
- (x, β, lbl) *such that the membership-bit* β *is not correct for* $\mathcal{L}(R)$ *is queried to the first oracle* sfSim^*.
- *The generated* $(x^*, \pi^*, \mathsf{lbl}^*)$ *is queried to* sfV/pV.

Propositions 1 and 2 were proven in [29]. Here, for a DSS-NIZK system Π_{DN}, let $\mathsf{Adv}_{\Pi_{\mathsf{DN}}}^{\mathsf{pzk}}(\lambda)$ be the maximum probability that any PPT adversary breaks the partial zero-knowledge of Π_{DN}, let $\mathsf{Adv}_{\Pi_{\mathsf{DN}}}^{\mathsf{upss}}(\lambda)$ be the maximum probability that any PPT adversary breaks the unbounded partial simulation-soundness of Π_{DN}, and let $\mathsf{Adv}_{\Pi_{\mathsf{DN}}}^{\mathsf{otzk}}(\lambda)$ be the maximum probability that any PPT adversary breaks the one-time full zero-knowledge of Π_{DN}.

Proposition 1 ([29], Lemma 4 (true simulation-soundness)). *If a DSS-NIZK* Π_{DN} *fulfills both of properties* partial zero-knowledge *and* unbounded partial simulation-soundness, *then for any PPT adversary* A, *it holds that*

$$\Pr\left[\begin{matrix}(\mathsf{crs}, \mathsf{td}_s, \mathsf{td}_v) \leftarrow \mathsf{sfGen}(1^\lambda); \\ (x, \pi, \mathsf{lbl}) \leftarrow \mathsf{A}^{\mathsf{sfSim}^*(\mathsf{crs}, \mathsf{td}_s, \cdot, \cdot, \cdot)}(\mathsf{crs})\end{matrix} : \mathsf{V}(\mathsf{crs}, x, \pi, \mathsf{lbl}) = 1 \wedge x \notin \mathcal{L}(R)\right]$$
$$\leq \mathsf{Adv}_{\Pi_{\mathsf{DN}}}^{\mathsf{pzk}}(\lambda) + \mathsf{Adv}_{\Pi_{\mathsf{DN}}}^{\mathsf{upss}}(\lambda),$$

---

[3] (x, β) is correct for a language $\mathcal{L}(R)$ (or β is correct for x) if $x \in \mathcal{L}(R) \wedge \beta = 1$, or $x \notin \mathcal{L}(R) \wedge \beta = 0$. (x, β) is not correct for $\mathcal{L}(R)$ (or β is not correct for x) otherwise.

where the challenger aborts if A *issues a query* (y, β, lbl) *such that* $y \notin \mathcal{L}(R)$ *or* $\beta = 0$, *to the* sfSim^* *oracle.*

Proposition 2 ([29], Lemma 12 (simulation-soundness of semi-functional verifier)). *If a DSS-NIZK* Π_{DN} *fulfills both of properties* one-time full zero-knowledge *and* unbounded partial simulation-soundness, *then, for any PPT algorithm* $\mathsf{A} = (\mathsf{A}_0, \mathsf{A}_1)$, *it holds that*

$$
\Pr\left[
\begin{array}{l}
(\mathsf{crs}, \mathsf{td}_s, \mathsf{td}_{s,1}, \mathsf{td}_v) \leftarrow \mathsf{otfGen}(1^\lambda); \\
(x^*, \mathsf{lbl}^*, \beta^*, \mathsf{st}) \leftarrow \mathsf{A}_0^{\mathsf{sfSim}^*(\mathsf{crs}, \mathsf{td}_s, \cdot, \cdot, \cdot), \mathsf{sfV}(\mathsf{crs}, \mathsf{td}_v, \cdot, \cdot, \cdot)}(\mathsf{crs}); \\
\pi^* \leftarrow \mathsf{otfSim}(\mathsf{crs}, \mathsf{td}_{s,1}, x^*, \mathsf{lbl}^*); \\
(x, \mathsf{lbl}, \pi) \leftarrow \mathsf{A}_1^{\mathsf{sfSim}^*(\mathsf{crs}, \mathsf{td}_s, \cdot, \cdot, \cdot), \mathsf{sfV}(\mathsf{crs}, \mathsf{td}_v, \cdot, \cdot, \cdot)}(\pi^*, \mathsf{st})
\end{array}
\middle|
\begin{array}{l}
\mathsf{sfV}(\mathsf{crs}, \mathsf{td}_v, x, \pi, \mathsf{lbl}) = 1 \\
\wedge x \notin \mathcal{L}(R)
\end{array}
\right]
$$
$$
\leq \mathsf{Adv}^{\mathsf{otzk}}_{\Pi_{\mathsf{DN}}}(\lambda) + \mathsf{Adv}^{\mathsf{upss}}_{\Pi_{\mathsf{DN}}}(\lambda),
$$

where the challenger aborts if at least one of the following conditions hold:

– *For* (x, β, lbl) *queried to the* sfSim^* *oracle,* (x, β) *is not correct for* $\mathcal{L}(R)$.
– β^* *is not the correct membership-bit of* $\mathcal{L}(R)$.
– $(x^*, \mathsf{lbl}^*, \pi^*)$ *is queried to* sfV.
– *The output of* A *is the same as* $(x^*, \mathsf{lbl}^*, \pi^*)$.

Furthermore, a stronger notion of DSS-NIZK is defined as follows. We call reveal event when td_s is revealed to adversaries where $(\mathsf{crs}, \mathsf{td}_s, \mathsf{td}_v) \leftarrow \mathsf{sfGen}(1^\lambda)$ or $(\mathsf{crs}, \mathsf{td}_s, \mathsf{td}_{s,1}, \mathsf{td}_v) \leftarrow \mathsf{otfGen}(1^\lambda)$.

Definition 5 (Strong DSS-NIZK [29]). *A DSS-NIZK system with partial simulation trapdoor reveal oracle is a strong DSS-NIZK system with the following changes to the DSS-NIZK definition:*

– *The first part of the* composable partial zero-knowledge *continues to hold.*
– *The second part of the* composable partial zero-knowledge *holds under the additional restriction that the adversary cannot invoke the third oracle (i.e.,* V *or* pV *oracle) after the reveal event.*
– *The* unbounded partial simulation-soundness *continues to hold.*
– *The trapdoors* td_s *and* $\mathsf{td}_{s,1}$ *generated by* otfGen *are same and statistically indistinguishable from* td_s *generated by* sfGen.
– *The* one-time full zero-knowledge *holds under the additional restriction that* $(x^*, \beta^*, \mathsf{lbl}^*)$ *is such that* $x^* \in \mathcal{L}(R)$ *and* $\beta^* = 1$ *and the second oracle (i.e.,* pV *or* sfV *oracle) is not invoked after the reveal event.*
– *The* simulation-soundness *of* sfV *(Proposition 2) holds under the additional restriction that* sfV *oracle is not invoked after the reveal event. Notice that there is no restriction that* $(x^*, \beta^*, \mathsf{lbl}^*)$ *is such that* $x^* \in \mathcal{L}(R)$ *and* $\beta^* = 1$.

2.3 (Keyed-)Fully Homomorphic Encryption

Definition 6. *A fully homomorphic encryption (FHE) scheme consists of four polynomial-time algorithms* $(\mathsf{KGen}, \mathsf{Enc}, \mathsf{Dec}, \mathsf{Eval})$: *For a security parameter* λ, *let* $\mathcal{M} = \mathcal{M}(\lambda)$ *be a message space.*

- (pk, sk) ← KGen(1^λ): *The randomized algorithm* KGen *takes as input a security parameter* 1^λ*, and it outputs a public key* pk *and a secret key* sk.
- ct ← Enc(pk, m): *The randomized algorithm* Enc *takes as input a public key* pk *and a message* m ∈ $\mathcal{M}$*, and it outputs a ciphertext* ct.
- m/⊥ ← Dec(sk, ct): *The deterministic algorithm* Dec *takes as input a secret key* sk *and a ciphertext* ct*, and it outputs a message* m ∈ $\mathcal{M}$ *or a rejection symbol* ⊥.
- $\widehat{ct}$ ← Eval(C, (ct$^{(1)}$, ct$^{(2)}$, . . . , ct$^{(\ell)}$)): *The deterministic or randomized algorithm* Eval *takes as input a circuit* C : $\mathcal{M}^\ell \to \mathcal{M}$ *and a tuple of ciphertexts* (ct$^{(1)}$, ct$^{(2)}$, . . . , ct$^{(\ell)}$)*, and it outputs a new ciphertext* $\widehat{ct}$.

We require that an FHE scheme meet both correctness and compactness.

Definition 7 (Correctness). *An FHE scheme* (KGen, Enc, Dec, Eval) *satisfies* correctness *if the following conditions hold:*

- *For every* (pk, sk) ← KGen(1^λ) *and every* m ∈ $\mathcal{M}$*, it holds that* Dec(sk, ct) = m *with overwhelming probability, where* ct ← Enc(pk, m).
- *For every* (pk, sk) ← KGen(1^λ)*, every circuit* C*, and every* (m$^{(1)}$, . . . , m$^{(\ell)}$) ∈ $\mathcal{M}^\ell$*, it holds that* Dec(sk, $\widehat{ct}$) = C(m$^{(1)}$, . . . , m$^{(\ell)}$) *with overwhelming probability, where* $\widehat{ct}$ ← Eval(C, (ct$^{(1)}$, . . . , ct$^{(\ell)}$)) *and for every* i ∈ [ℓ]*,* ct$^{(i)}$ ← Enc(pk, m$^{(i)}$).

Definition 8 (Compactness). *An FHE scheme satisfies* compactness *if there exists a polynomial* poly *such that the output-size of* Eval($\cdot, \cdot$) *is at most* poly(λ) *for every security parameter* λ.

Definition 9 (IND-CCA1 security). *An FHE scheme* Π_{FHE} = (KGen, Enc, Dec, Eval) *is IND-CCA1 secure if for any PPT adversary* A = (A$_0$, A$_1$) *against* Π_{FHE}*, the advantage*

$$\mathsf{Adv}^{\mathrm{ind\text{-}cca1}}_{\Pi_{\mathsf{FHE}},\mathsf{A}}(\lambda) := \left| \Pr\left[\begin{array}{l} (\mathsf{pk}, \mathsf{sk}) \leftarrow \mathsf{KGen}(1^\lambda); \\ (\mathsf{m}_0, \mathsf{m}_1, \mathsf{st}) \leftarrow \mathsf{A}_0^{\mathsf{Dec}(\mathsf{sk}_d, \cdot)}(\mathsf{pk}); \\ b \overset{\$}{\leftarrow} \{0, 1\}; \mathsf{ct}^* \leftarrow \mathsf{Enc}(\mathsf{pk}, \mathsf{m}_b); \\ b' \leftarrow \mathsf{A}_1(\mathsf{ct}^*, \mathsf{st}) \end{array} : b = b' \right] - \frac{1}{2} \right|,$$

is negligible in λ*, where* st *is state information.*

Following the definition of KH-PKE in [21], we describe the definition of keyed-fully homomorphic encryption (keyed-FHE) given by Lai et al. [30], except that the adversaries are allowed to access the decryption oracle until the homomorphic evaluation key is revealed.

Definition 10. *A keyed-FHE scheme consists of four polynomial-time algorithms* (KGen, Enc, Dec, Eval): *For a security parameter* λ*, let* $\mathcal{M}$ = $\mathcal{M}(\lambda)$ *be a message space.*

- (pk, sk$_d$, sk$_h$) ← KGen(1^λ): *The randomized algorithm* KGen *takes as input a security parameter* 1^λ*, and it outputs a public key* pk*, a decryption key* sk$_d$*, and a homomorphic evaluation key* sk$_h$.

– ct ← Enc(pk, m): *The randomized algorithm* Enc *takes as input a public key* pk *and a message* m ∈ $\mathcal{M}$, *and it outputs a ciphertext* ct.

– m/⊥ ← Dec(sk_d, ct): *The deterministic algorithm* Dec *takes as input a decryption key* sk_d *and a ciphertext* ct, *and it outputs a message* m *or a rejection symbol* ⊥.

– $\widehat{ct}$/⊥ ← Eval(sk_h, C, ($ct^{(1)}, ct^{(2)}, \ldots, ct^{(\ell)}$)): *The deterministic or randomized algorithm* Eval *takes as input a homomorphic evaluation key* sk_h, *a circuit* C : $\mathcal{M}^\ell \to \mathcal{M}$, *and a tuple of ciphertexts* ($ct^{(1)}, ct^{(2)}, \ldots, ct^{(\ell)}$), *and it outputs a new ciphertext* $\widehat{ct}$ *or a rejection symbol* ⊥.

We require that a keyed-FHE scheme meet both correctness and compactness.

Definition 11 (Correctness). *A keyed-FHE scheme* (KGen, Enc, Dec, Eval) *satisfies* correctness *if the following conditions hold:*

– *For every* (pk, sk_d, sk_h) ← KGen(1^λ) *and every* m ∈ $\mathcal{M}$, *it holds that* Dec(sk_d, ct) = m *with overwhelming probability, where* ct ← Enc(pk, m).

– *For every* (pk, sk_d, sk_h) ← KGen(1^λ), *every circuit* C : $\mathcal{M}^\ell \to \mathcal{M}$, *and every* ($m^{(1)}, \ldots, m^{(\ell)}$) ∈ $\mathcal{M}^\ell$, *it holds that* Dec(sk_d, $\widehat{ct}$) = C($m^{(1)}, \ldots, m^{(\ell)}$) *with overwhelming probability, where* ct ← Eval(sk_h, C, ($ct^{(1)}, \ldots, ct^{(\ell)}$)) *and for every* i ∈ [$\ell$], $ct^{(i)}$ ← Enc(pk, $m^{(i)}$).

Definition 12 (Compactness). *A keyed-FHE scheme satisfies* compactness *if there exists a polynomial* poly *such that the output-size of* Eval(sk_h, ·, ·, ·) *is at most* poly(λ) *for every security parameter* λ.

Definition 13 (KH-CCA security). *A keyed-FHE scheme* Π_{KFHE} = (KGen, Enc, Dec, Eval) *is KH-CCA secure if for any PPT adversary* A = (A_0, A_1) *against* Π_{KFHE}, *the advantage*

$$\mathsf{Adv}^{\text{kh-cca}}_{\Pi_{\mathsf{KFHE}}, A}(\lambda) := \left| \Pr\left[\begin{array}{l} (\mathsf{pk}, \mathsf{sk}_d, \mathsf{sk}_h) \leftarrow \mathsf{KGen}(1^\lambda); \\ (m_0, m_1, \mathsf{st}) \leftarrow A_0^{\mathsf{Eval}(\mathsf{sk}_h, \cdot, \cdot), \mathsf{RevHK}(\cdot), \mathsf{Dec}(\mathsf{sk}_d, \cdot)}(\mathsf{pk}); \\ b \xleftarrow{\$} \{0,1\}; \mathsf{ct}^* \leftarrow \mathsf{Enc}(\mathsf{pk}, m_b); \\ b' \leftarrow A_1^{\mathsf{Eval}(\mathsf{sk}_h, \cdot, \cdot), \mathsf{RevHK}(\cdot), \mathsf{Dec}(\mathsf{sk}_d, \cdot)}(\mathsf{ct}^*, \mathsf{st}) \end{array} : b = b' \right] - \frac{1}{2} \right|,$$

is negligible in λ, *where* st *is state information, and let* $\mathcal{D}$ *be a list which is set as* $\mathcal{D}$ ← {ct^*} *in* **Challenge** *phase, and the oracles above are defined as follows:*

– *Homomorphic key reveal oracle* RevHK: *Given a request, the* RevHK *oracle returns* sk_h.

– *Evaluation oracle* Eval(sk_h, ·): *Given an* Eval *query* (C, ($ct^{(1)}, \ldots, ct^{(\ell)}$)), *the* Eval *oracle checks whether the* RevHK *oracle has been queried before. If so, it returns* ⊥. *Otherwise, it returns* $\widehat{ct}$/⊥ ← Eval(sk_h, C, ($ct^{(1)}, \ldots, ct^{(\ell)}$)). *In addition, if* $\widehat{ct}$ ≠ ⊥ *and one of ciphertexts* $ct^{(1)}, \ldots, ct^{(\ell)}$ *is in* $\mathcal{D}$, *it sets* $\mathcal{D}$ ← $\mathcal{D}$ ∪ {$\widehat{ct}$}.

– *Decryption oracle* Dec(sk_d, ·): *This oracle is not available if* A *has accessed the* RevHK *oracle and obtained the challenge ciphertext* ct^*. *Given a* Dec *query* ct, *the* Dec *oracle returns* Dec(sk_d, ct) *if* ct ∉ $\mathcal{D}$, *and returns* ⊥ *otherwise.*

3   Generic Construction of Keyed-FHE

Our Construction. We propose a generic construction of a keyed-FHE scheme Π_{KFHE} from two IND-CCA1 secure FHE schemes $\Pi_{\mathsf{FHE},1}, \Pi_{\mathsf{FHE},2}$ and a (strong) DSS-NIZK system Π_{DN}. We briefly explain an overview of the construction whose spirit is similar to Jutla and Roy's KH-PKE scheme [29] except that we use the Naor-Yung paradigm [36]. Let $(\mathsf{pk}_1, \mathsf{sk}_1)$ and $(\mathsf{pk}_2, \mathsf{sk}_2)$ denote two pairs of public/secret keys of $\Pi_{\mathsf{FHE},1}$ and $\Pi_{\mathsf{FHE},2}$. A public key $\mathsf{pk} = (\mathsf{pk}_1, \mathsf{pk}_2, \mathsf{crs})$ of Π_{KFHE} consists of two public keys $(\mathsf{pk}_1, \mathsf{pk}_2)$ of schemes $\Pi_{\mathsf{FHE},1}, \Pi_{\mathsf{FHE},2}$ and the CRS crs of Π_{DN}, while the secret key $\mathsf{sk}_d = \mathsf{sk}_1$ is the secret key of $\Pi_{\mathsf{FHE},1}$. The ciphertext $\mathsf{ct} = (\mathsf{ct}_1, \mathsf{ct}_2, \pi)$ consists of two FHE ciphertexts $(\mathsf{ct}_1, \mathsf{ct}_2)$ both of which are encryptions of m and π is a proof such that $(\mathsf{ct}_1, \mathsf{ct}_2)$ are encryptions of the same message. The decryption algorithm first checks the validity of π by using the real world verification algorithm V_N, then decrypt ct_1 by using $\mathsf{sk}_d = \mathsf{sk}_1$. To complete the overview, we show how to evaluate keyed-FHE ciphertexts $\mathsf{ct}^{(1)}, \ldots, \mathsf{ct}^{(\ell)}$ for a circuit C and obtain $\widehat{\mathsf{ct}}$. A point to note is that we should create a proof $\widehat{\pi}$ without the knowledge of the message $\mathsf{C}(\mathsf{m}^{(1)}, \ldots, \mathsf{m}^{(\ell)})$ of $\widehat{\mathsf{ct}}$. For this purpose, we use the DSS-NIZK system Π_{DN} in *partial-simulation world* as the case of Jutla and Roy's KH-PKE scheme [29]. Then, we set the homomorphic evaluation key $\mathsf{sk}_h = \mathsf{td}_s$ as the trapdoor of Π_{DN}. Therefore, the *(composable)* partial zero-knowledge ensures that $\widehat{\pi}$ can be computed correctly by using the sfSim_N algorithm. Here, we note that the verification algorithm V_N can correctly verify the proof created by the sfSim_N algorithm owing to partial zero-knowledge.

To sum up, we use the following primitives: An FHE scheme $\Pi_{\mathsf{FHE},i} = (\mathsf{KGen}_{F,i}, \mathsf{Enc}_{F,i}, \mathsf{Dec}_{F,i}, \mathsf{Eval}_{F,i})$ for $i \in \{1, 2\}$, and a DSS-NIZK system Π_{DN} in partial-simulation world $(\mathsf{sfGen}_N, \mathsf{sfSim}_N, \mathsf{pV}_N)$ for a relation $R_N = \{(\mathsf{ct}_1, \mathsf{ct}_2)(\mathsf{m}, r_1, r_2) \mid \mathsf{ct}_1 = \mathsf{Enc}_{F,1}(\mathsf{pk}_1, \mathsf{m}; r_1) \wedge \mathsf{ct}_2 = \mathsf{Enc}_{F,2}(\mathsf{pk}_2, \mathsf{m}; r_2)\}$, where $(\mathsf{pk}_1, \mathsf{sk}_1) \leftarrow \mathsf{KGen}_{F,1}(1^\lambda)$ and $(\mathsf{pk}_2, \mathsf{sk}_2) \leftarrow \mathsf{KGen}_{F,2}(1^\lambda)$. We also remark that a proof generated by the sfSim_N algorithm can be verified by the real world verification algorithm V_N owing to the partial zero-knowledge property. Thus, we use the V_N algorithm in our construction.

Our scheme $\Pi_{\mathsf{KFHE}} = (\mathsf{KGen}, \mathsf{Enc}, \mathsf{Dec}, \mathsf{Eval})$ is constructed as follows:

- $(\mathsf{pk}, \mathsf{sk}_d, \mathsf{sk}_h) \leftarrow \mathsf{KGen}(1^\lambda)$:
    1. $(\mathsf{pk}_1, \mathsf{sk}_1) \leftarrow \mathsf{KGen}_{F,1}(1^\lambda)$, $(\mathsf{pk}_2, \mathsf{sk}_2) \leftarrow \mathsf{KGen}_{F,2}(1^\lambda)$.
    2. $(\mathsf{crs}, \mathsf{td}_s, \mathsf{td}_v) \leftarrow \mathsf{sfGen}_N(1^\lambda)$.
    3. Output $\mathsf{pk} = (\mathsf{pk}_1, \mathsf{pk}_2, \mathsf{crs})$, $\mathsf{sk}_d = \mathsf{sk}_1$, and $\mathsf{sk}_h = \mathsf{td}_s$.
- $\mathsf{ct} \leftarrow \mathsf{Enc}(\mathsf{pk}, \mathsf{m})$:
    1. $\mathsf{ct}_1 \leftarrow \mathsf{Enc}_{F,1}(\mathsf{pk}_1, \mathsf{m}; r_1)$, $\mathsf{ct}_2 \leftarrow \mathsf{Enc}_{F,2}(\mathsf{pk}_2, \mathsf{m}; r_2)$.
    2. $\pi \leftarrow \mathsf{P}_N(\mathsf{crs}, (\mathsf{ct}_1, \mathsf{ct}_2), (\mathsf{m}, r_1, r_2), \emptyset)$.
    3. Output $\mathsf{ct} = (\mathsf{ct}_1, \mathsf{ct}_2, \pi)$.
- $\mathsf{m}/\bot \leftarrow \mathsf{Dec}(\mathsf{sk}_d, \mathsf{ct})$: Let $\mathsf{ct} = (\mathsf{ct}_1, \mathsf{ct}_2, \pi)$.
    1. If $\mathsf{V}_N(\mathsf{crs}, (\mathsf{ct}_1, \mathsf{ct}_2), \pi, \emptyset) = 1$, output $\mathsf{m} \leftarrow \mathsf{Dec}_{F,1}(\mathsf{sk}_1, \mathsf{ct}_1)$. Otherwise, output $\bot$.
- $\widehat{\mathsf{ct}}/\bot \leftarrow \mathsf{Eval}(\mathsf{sk}_h, \mathsf{C}, (\mathsf{ct}^{(1)}, \ldots, \mathsf{ct}^{(\ell)}))$: Let $\mathsf{ct}^{(i)} = (\mathsf{ct}_1^{(i)}, \mathsf{ct}_2^{(i)}, \pi^{(i)})$ for $i \in [\ell]$.
    1. Output $\bot$ if $\mathsf{V}_N(\mathsf{crs}, (\mathsf{ct}_1^{(i)}, \mathsf{ct}_2^{(i)}), \pi^{(i)}, \emptyset) = 0$ for some $i \in [\ell]$.

2. $\widehat{\mathsf{ct}}_1 \leftarrow \mathsf{Eval}_{F,1}(\mathsf{C}, (\mathsf{ct}_1^{(1)}, \ldots, \mathsf{ct}_1^{(\ell)}))$, $\widehat{\mathsf{ct}}_2 \leftarrow \mathsf{Eval}_{F,2}(\mathsf{C}, (\mathsf{ct}_2^{(1)}, \ldots, \mathsf{ct}_2^{(\ell)}))$.
3. $\widehat{\pi} \leftarrow \mathsf{sfSim}_N(\mathsf{crs}, \mathsf{td}_s, (\widehat{\mathsf{ct}}_1, \widehat{\mathsf{ct}}_2), 1, \emptyset)$.
4. Output $\widehat{\mathsf{ct}} = (\widehat{\mathsf{ct}}_1, \widehat{\mathsf{ct}}_2, \widehat{\pi})$.

The correctness of Π_{KFHE} follows the correctness of $\Pi_{\mathsf{FHE},1}$ and $\Pi_{\mathsf{FHE},2}$, and the completeness of Π_{DN}. The first condition of the correctness holds since the completeness of Π_{DN} ensures that V_N outputs 1 and the correctness of $\Pi_{\mathsf{FHE},1}$ ensures that $\mathsf{Dec}_{F,1}$ correctly outputs m with overwhelming probability. Similarly, the second condition of the correctness also holds since the composable partial zero-knowledge of Π_{DN} ensures that V_N outputs 1 even if the proof $\widehat{\pi}$ is computed by the semi-functional simulator sfSim_N. In addition, the output-size of sfSim_N used in Eval is equal to that of P_N since the semi-functional simulator sfSim_N simulates the prover P_N. Thus, the compactness of Π_{KFHE} follows the compactness of $\Pi_{\mathsf{FHE},1}$ and $\Pi_{\mathsf{FHE},2}$.

Remark 1. Canetti et al. [11] showed that IND-CCA1 secure FHE can be constructed from IND-CPA secure FHE and zk-SNARK via the Naor-Yung transformation. Here, circuit C to be evaluated is a witness and thus the underlying NIZK system needs to be succinct. On the other hand, in our evaluation algorithm first ciphertexts are evaluated by the evaluation algorithm of the underlying IND-CCA1 secure FHE schemes, and then the underlying NIZK system proves that two ciphertexts $\widehat{\mathsf{ct}}_1$ and $\widehat{\mathsf{ct}}_2$ have the same plaintext using the trapdoor. So, C is not a witness here, and we do not have to directly employ zk-SNARK in our construction.

Security Analysis

Theorem 1 (KH-CCA security). *If both $\Pi_{\mathsf{FHE},1}$ and $\Pi_{\mathsf{FHE},2}$ are IND-CCA1 secure, and Π_{DN} is a strong DSS-NIZK system, then the resulting keyed-FHE scheme Π_{KFHE} is KH-CCA secure.*

Theorem 1 shows the security of our keyed-FHE scheme. The proof of this theorem appears in the full version of this paper. For simplicity, we explain that our scheme satisfies KH-CCA security if the underlying NIZK system Π_{DN} meets the properties of strong DSS-NIZKs. We first give the intuitive explanation. To guarantee security against adaptive chosen ciphertext attacks before a homomorphic evaluation key (a trapdoor of Π_{DN}) is revealed by RevHK oracle access, the underlying DSS-NIZK system must satisfy (one-time) simulation-soundness so that we can return the non-malleable challenge ciphertext correctly. In addition, if the ciphertexts generated by the evaluation oracle are malleable, it is possible to break KH-CCA security by querying such ciphertexts to the decryption oracle. Thus, unbounded (partial) simulation-soundness is required for Π_{DN} in order to return non-malleable ciphertexts for evaluation queries. Moreover, our scheme needs the partial zero-knowledge and one-time full zero-knowledge properties of strong DSS-NIZKs, so that the challenge message can be hidden even if a simulation trapdoor of Π_{DN} is revealed. Since we can assume that the underlying FHE schemes are IND-CCA1 secure, we can simulate decryption queries until the challenge phase.

Remark 2. Although we assume that the underlying FHE schemes are IND-CCA1 secure in Theorem 1, we can prove KH-CCA security even when the underlying FHE schemes are IND-CPA secure. For this purpose, we follow Canetti et al. generic construction [11] and additionally use a zk-SNARK. Nevertheless, we assume IND-CCA1 security of the underlying FHE schemes since it enables us to obtain a much simpler proof.

Table 1. Summary of Games in the Proof of Theorem 1

| Game | Components of ct* | | $C(m_1,\ldots,m_\ell)$ computed for | Verification of | | Msg-Rec. of |
	ct_2^*	π^*	Dep. Eval	Indep. Eval	Dec	Dec
$Game_0$	$Enc_{F,2}(m_b)$	P_N^*	Ordinary	V_N	V_N	$Dec_{F,1}$
$Game_1$	$Enc_{F,2}(m_b)$	$sfSim_N^*$	Ordinary	pV_N	pV_N	$Dec_{F,1}$
$Game_2$	$Enc_{F,2}(m_b)$	$sfSim_N^*$	Random	pV_N	pV_N	$Dec_{F,1}$
$Game_3$	$Enc_{F,2}(m_b)$	$otfSim_N^*$	Random	sfV_N	sfV_N	$Dec_{F,1}$
$Game_4$	$Enc_{F,2}(0^{|m_b|})$	$otfSim_N^*$	Random	sfV_N	sfV_N	$Dec_{F,1}$
$Game_5$	$Enc_{F,2}(0^{|m_b|})$	$otfSim_N^*$	Random	sfV_N	sfV_N	$Dec_{F,2}$

"$C(m_1,\ldots,m_\ell)$ computed for Dep. Eval" denotes a message $C(m_1,\ldots,m_\ell)$ for $\widehat{ct}$ generated by the Eval oracle on input a dependent Eval query. "Ordinary" (resp. "Random") means that $C(m_1,\ldots,m_\ell)$ is a message whose encryption is generated by the Eval algorithm on input encryptions queried by the adversary A (resp. encryptions of random messages). "Verification of Indep. Eval" denotes a verification algorithm in the Eval algorithm run by the Eval oracle on input an independent Eval query. "Verification of Dec" denotes a verification algorithm in the Dec algorithm run by the Dec oracle on input a Dec query. "Msg-Rec. of Dec" denotes an algorithm which recovers a message in the Dec algorithm run by Dec oracle on input a Dec query. For $i \in \{1,2\}$, let $Enc_{F,i}(\cdot) = Enc_{F,i}(pk_i,\cdot)$ and $Dec_{F,i}(\cdot) = Dec_{F,i}(sk_i,\cdot)$. Let $P_N^* = P_N(crs,(ct_1^*,ct_2^*),(m_b,r_1^*,r_2^*),\emptyset)$, $sfSim_N^* = sfSim_N(crs,td_s,(ct_1^*,ct_2^*),1,\emptyset)$, and $otfSim_N^* = otfSim_N(crs,td_{s,1},(ct_1^*,ct_2^*),\emptyset)$.

Next, we give the more concrete explanation. Let a *dependent* Eval query be a query $(C,(ct^{(1)},\ldots,ct^{(\ell)}))$ issued to the Eval oracle, such that at least one of $ct^{(1)},\ldots,ct^{(\ell)}$ are in $\mathcal{D}$, and let an *independent* Eval query be a query issued to the Eval oracle, such that all $ct^{(1)},\ldots,ct^{(\ell)}$ are not in $\mathcal{D}$. In order to prove Theorem 1, we consider security games $Game_0,\ldots,Game_5$ (Table 1 shows the summary of these games). The proof of the indistinguishability between $Game_0$ and $Game_3$ is similar to a part of the security proof of the Jutla and Roy's scheme [29] because this indistinguishability mainly follows the properties of the underlying strong DSS-NIZK (see also Table 2). The remaining proofs are different from the security proof of [29], because our scheme employs the Naor-Yung paradigm while the Jutla and Roy's scheme uses a variant of ElGamal encryption. Furthermore, we describe the important point of our security proof. In $Game_4$, the challenge ciphertext is replaced by an invalid one due to a reduction from the security of the underlying primitives, in the same way as the security proof of the Naor-Yung paradigm [36]. However, when an adversary issues the challenge ciphertext (or derivatives of the challenge ciphertext) to the Eval oracle, this oracle must return a valid ciphertext. In order to simulate the Eval oracle correctly even in this case, the Eval oracle on input a dependent Eval query returns a random and valid ciphertext instead of an ordinary evaluated ciphertext, in $Game_2$. If $Game_2$ is indistinguishable from the previous game, it is possible to replace the ordinary challenge ciphertext by an invalid one in the security games after $Game_2$.

Table 2. Outline of the Proof of Theorem 1

Game	Property
$Game_0 \approx Game_1$	partial zero-knowledge of Π_{DN}, true simulation-soundness of Π_{DN}
$Game_1 \approx Game_2$	one-time full zero-knowledge of Π_{DN}, unbounded partial simulation-soundness of Π_{DN}, IND-CCA1 security of $\Pi_{FHE,1}$ and $\Pi_{FHE,2}$
$Game_2 \approx Game_3$	one-time full zero-knowledge of Π_{DN}, simulation-soundness of sfV_N
$Game_3 \approx Game_4$	simulation-soundness of sfV_N, IND-CCA1 security of $\Pi_{FHE,2}$
$Game_4 \approx Game_5$	one-time full zero-knowledge of Π_{DN}, unbounded partial simulation-soundness of Π_{DN}
$Game_5$	IND-CCA1 security of $\Pi_{FHE,1}$

4 Strong DSS-NIZK from Smooth PHPS and Unbounded Simulation-Sound NIZK

In this section, we show that there exists a strong DSS-NIZK system for NP, constructed from a smooth PHPS and an unbounded simulation-sound NIZK. Although our construction is similar to the generic construction [29] of strong DSS-NIZKs for linear subspaces, the properties of the underlying primitives are different from those of the primitives used in ours. As mentioned in Sect. 1.2, the previous construction assumes the underlying PHPS to be universal$_2$ and uses a true simulation-sound quasi-adaptive NIZK while we assume that the underlying PHPS do not have to satisfy universal$_2$, and the underlying NIZK satisfies the unbounded simulation-soundness (Definition 2).

Furthermore, we modify the generic construction [29] under our assumption, slightly. This is because the languages of existing PHPSs for lattice-based ciphertexts are not necessarily identical to those of existing unbounded simulation-sound NIZKs based on lattice assumptions.

Following [17], we define smooth PHPSs to describe our DSS-NIZK scheme.

Definition 14 (Projective Hash Family [17]). *Let X and Π be finite sets. Let $H = \{H_k\}_{k \in K}$ be a collection of functions indexed by K so that $H_k : X \to \Pi$ is a hash function for every $k \in K$. Then, (H, K, X, Π) is called a hash family. Let L be a non-empty proper subset of X. Let S be a finite set, and $\alpha : K \to S$ be a function. $\mathbf{H} = (H, K, X, \Pi, L, S, \alpha)$ is called a projective hash family (PHF) if for every $k \in K$, the action of H_k on L is determined by $\alpha(k)$.*

Definition 15 ((Smooth) Projective Hash Proof System [17]). *For languages defined by a relation $R \subseteq \{0, 1\}^* \times \{0, 1\}^*$, the PHF $\mathbf{H} = (H, K, X, \Pi, L, S, \alpha)$ constitutes a projective hash proof system (PHPS) if α, H_k, and a public evaluation function $\hat{H}$ are efficiently computable, where $\hat{H}$ takes as input the projection key $\alpha(k)$, a statement $x \in L = \mathcal{L}(R) = \{x \mid \exists w \text{ s.t. } (x, w) \in R\}$, and a witness w such that $(x, w) \in R$, and it computes $H_k(x)$.*

Furthermore, a PHPS constituted by a PHF $\mathbf{H} = (H, K, X, \Pi, L, S, \alpha)$ is called a labeled PHPS if the public evaluation function takes an additional input $\mathsf{lbl} \in \{0, 1\}^*$ which is called a label. A labeled PHPS is ϵ-smooth if the statistical distance between $U(\mathbf{H}) = (x, \alpha(k), \pi')$ and $V(\mathbf{H}) = (x, \alpha(k), H_k(x, \mathsf{lbl}))$ is at most ϵ for all $k \in K$, all $x \in X \backslash L$, all $\mathsf{lbl} \in \{0, 1\}^*$, and all $\pi' \in \Pi$.

In order to construct our DSS-NIZK system Π_{DN}, we assume that the following primitives are used: An ϵ-smooth labeled PHPS Π_{PHPS} with a public evaluation function $\hat{H}$, which is constituted by a PHF $\mathbf{H} = (H, K, X_H, L_H, \Pi, S, \alpha)$, and a NIZK system $\Pi_{\mathsf{N}} = (\mathsf{Gen}_N, \mathsf{P}_N, \mathsf{V}_N)$ for an augmented relation $R_N = \{((x, x_H, \pi_H, \mathsf{lbl}), (w, w_H)) \mid (x, w) \in R \wedge \pi_H = \hat{H}(\alpha(k), (x_H, x\|\mathsf{lbl}), w_H)\}$, with a PPT simulator $(\mathsf{Sim}_{N,0}, \mathsf{Sim}_{N,1})$ (where $R \subseteq X \times W$ is the relation of Π_{DN}).

In addition, we assume that there exist polynomial-time algorithms E_1, E_2, E_3, $\mathcal{G}$, and $\mathcal{E}_{\mathcal{G}}$, which are defined as follows: E_1 samples auxiliary information ψ of R, which can be regarded as witness of R, E_2 given ψ decides whether x is in $\mathcal{L}(R)$, E_3 samples a uniformly random value from Π, and we write $(x_H; w_H) \leftarrow (\mathcal{G}\|\mathcal{E}_{\mathcal{G}})(x, \mathsf{lbl}; w)$ when $\mathcal{G}$ given $(x, \mathsf{lbl}) \in X \times \{0, 1\}^*$ outputs $x_H \in X_H$ (then, we write $x_H \leftarrow \mathcal{G}(x, \mathsf{lbl})$), and $\mathcal{E}_{\mathcal{G}}$ given w outputs a witness w_H by using the internal information of $\mathcal{G}(x, \mathsf{lbl})$. $(\mathcal{G}\|\mathcal{E}_{\mathcal{G}})(x, \mathsf{lbl}; w)$ outputs $(x_H; w_H)$ such that x_H is in the language L_H of Π_{PHPS} (and (x_H, w_H) is in the relation R_H of Π_{PHPS}) if x is in $\mathcal{L}(R)$, but x_H is not in L_H (and $(x_H, w_H) \notin R_H$) otherwise.

Furthermore, there is a gap between the two languages $\mathcal{L}(R)$ and L_H (e.g., $\mathcal{L}(R) \subset L_H$) in general. This may be a problem to construct $\mathcal{G}$. Thus, we assume that a statement x is publicly verifiable for a language L_X such that $\mathcal{L}(R) = L_H \cap L_X$.

We explain that assuming the algorithms E_1, E_2, E_3, $\mathcal{G}$, $\mathcal{E}_{\mathcal{G}}$, and the public verifiability for L_X is reasonable. The algorithms E_1, E_2, and E_3 are the same as the ones assumed in the DSS-NIZK construction of [29]. Thus, we explain that the remaining assumptions are reasonable in some cases (in particular, a case where we apply our DSS-NIZK to our keyed-FHE scheme). For example, we consider the language of the PHPS of [2], which can be simply defined as $L_H = \{\mathsf{ct} \mid \exists w, \mathsf{Enc}_{\mathsf{pk}}(0; w) = \mathsf{ct}\}$, where $\mathsf{Enc}_{\mathsf{pk}}(\cdot)$ is an encryption algorithm of public key encryption. In addition, we suppose that this public key encryption scheme for L_H is an IND-CCA1 secure FHE scheme from IND-CPA secure FHE schemes and a zk-SNARK [11]. Let L_X be the language for the zk-SNARK used in this IND-CCA1 secure FHE scheme [11]. First, assuming the public verifiability for L_X is reasonable because the FHE scheme [11] is based on the Naor-Yung paradigm, and it is clear that the ciphertexts are publicly verifiable for L_X. Next, we show that assuming $\mathcal{G}$ algorithm is reasonable. $\mathcal{G}$ checks whether two FHE ciphertexts are in L_X. If so, $\mathcal{G}$ transforms this pair into a statement in L_H by using the technique of the generic construction [34] of multi-key FHE, starting from an FHE scheme.[4] Otherwise, it samples $x_H \notin L_H$ and outputs this. Hence, if two ciphertexts are in $\mathcal{L}(R)$, then this pair is also in L_H. Otherwise, it is not in L_H due to the public verifiability of the IND-CCA1 secure FHE scheme. Hence, the algorithm $\mathcal{G}$ fulfills the required property. Accordingly, there exits an algorithm which generates the corresponding witness by using the algorithm of this transformation. Hence, there exist algorithms $\mathcal{G}$ and $\mathcal{E}_\mathcal{G}$.

Our DSS-NIZK system Π_{DN} for a relation R is described as follows:

Real World consists of
- crs $\leftarrow$ Gen(1^λ): Sample $k \stackrel{\$}{\leftarrow} K$ and compute $\mathsf{crs}_N \leftarrow \mathsf{Gen}_N(\lambda)$. Output $\mathsf{crs} = (\alpha(k), \mathsf{crs}_N)$.
- $\pi \leftarrow$ P(crs, x, w, lbl): Compute $(x_H; w_H) \leftarrow (\mathcal{G} \| \mathcal{E}_\mathcal{G})(x, \mathsf{lbl}; w)$, $\pi_H \leftarrow \hat{H}(\alpha(k), (x_H, x \| \mathsf{lbl}), w_H)$ and $\pi_N \leftarrow \mathsf{P}_N(\mathsf{crs}_N(x, x_H, \pi_H, \mathsf{lbl})(w, w_H))$. Output $\pi = (x_H, \pi_H, \pi_N)$
- 1/0 $\leftarrow$ V(crs, x, π, lbl): Output 1 if $\mathsf{V}_N(\mathsf{crs}_N, (x, x_H, \pi_H, \mathsf{lbl}), \pi_N) = 1$. Output 0 otherwise.

Partial Simulation World consists of
- $(\mathsf{crs}, \mathsf{td}_s, \mathsf{td}_v) \leftarrow \mathsf{sfGen}(1^\lambda)$: Sample ψ by using E_1. Sample $k \stackrel{\$}{\leftarrow} K$ and compute $(\mathsf{crs}_N, \mathsf{td}_N) \leftarrow \mathsf{Sim}_{N,0}(1^\lambda)$. Output $\mathsf{crs} = (\alpha(k), \mathsf{crs}_N)$, $\mathsf{td}_s = (k, \mathsf{td}_N)$, and $\mathsf{td}_v = (\psi, k)$.
- $\pi \leftarrow \mathsf{sfSim}(\mathsf{crs}, \mathsf{td}_s, x, \beta, \mathsf{lbl})$:
  - If $\beta = 1$, then compute $x_H \leftarrow \mathcal{G}(x, \mathsf{lbl})$, $\pi_H \leftarrow H_k(x_H, x \| \mathsf{lbl})$ and $\pi_N \leftarrow \mathsf{Sim}_{N,1}(\mathsf{crs}_N, \mathsf{td}_N, (x, x_H, \pi_H, \mathsf{lbl}))$.
  - If $\beta = 0$, then sample $\pi_H \stackrel{\$}{\leftarrow} \Pi$ by using E_3 and compute $x_H \leftarrow \mathcal{G}(x, \mathsf{lbl})$ and $\pi_N \leftarrow \mathsf{Sim}_{N,1}(\mathsf{crs}_N, \mathsf{td}_N(x, x_H, \pi_H, \mathsf{lbl}))$.

  Output $\pi = (x_H, \pi_H, \pi_N)$.
- 1/0 $\leftarrow \mathsf{pV}(\mathsf{crs}, \mathsf{td}_v, x, \pi, \mathsf{lbl})$: Output 1 if it holds that $x \in \mathcal{L}(R_N)$ by using E_2 given ψ, $H_k(x_H, x \| \mathsf{lbl}) = \pi_H$, and $\mathsf{V}_N(\mathsf{crs}_N, (x, x_H, \pi_H, \mathsf{lbl}), \pi_N) = 1$. Output 0 otherwise.

One-time Full Simulation World consists of
- $(\mathsf{crs}, \mathsf{td}_s, \mathsf{td}_{s,1}, \mathsf{td}_v) \leftarrow \mathsf{otfGen}(1^\lambda)$: Sample $k \stackrel{\$}{\leftarrow} K$ and compute $(\mathsf{crs}_N, \mathsf{td}_N) \leftarrow \mathsf{Sim}_{N,0}(1^\lambda)$. Output $\mathsf{crs} = (\alpha(k), \mathsf{crs}_N)$, $\mathsf{td}_s = \mathsf{td}_{s,1} = (k, \mathsf{td}_N)$, and $\mathsf{td}_v = k$.

---

[4] Concretely, two FHE ciphertexts $\mathsf{Enc}(\mathsf{pk}_1, \mathsf{m}_1)$ and $\mathsf{Enc}(\mathsf{pk}_2, \mathsf{m}_2)$ can be transformed into a ciphertext $\mathsf{Enc}(\mathsf{pk}_1, \mathsf{Enc}(\mathsf{pk}_2, \mathsf{m}_1 - \mathsf{m}_2))$. If for two FHE ciphertexts $\mathsf{Enc}(\mathsf{pk}_1, \mathsf{m}_1; r_1)$ and $\mathsf{Enc}(\mathsf{pk}_2, \mathsf{m}_2; r_2)$, (m, r_1, r_2) where $\mathsf{m} = \mathsf{m}_1 = \mathsf{m}_2$ is a witness of the Naor-Yung language, then $\mathsf{Enc}(\mathsf{pk}_1, \mathsf{Enc}(\mathsf{pk}_2, \mathsf{m}_1 - \mathsf{m}_2))$ is a statement in L_H.

- $\pi \leftarrow$ otfSim$(\text{crs}, \text{td}_{s,1}, x, \text{lbl})$: Compute $x_H \leftarrow \mathcal{G}(x, \text{lbl})$, $\pi_H \leftarrow H_k(x_H, x\|\text{lbl})$, and $\pi_N \leftarrow \text{Sim}_{N,1}(\text{crs}_N, \text{td}_N, (x, x_H, \pi_H, \text{lbl}))$. Output $\pi = (x_H, \pi_H, \pi_N)$.
- $1/0 \leftarrow$ sfV$(\text{crs}, \text{td}_v, x, \pi, \text{lbl})$: Output 1 if it holds that $H_k(x_H, x\|\text{lbl}) = \pi_H$ and $V_N(\text{crs}_N(x, x_H, \pi_H, \text{lbl}), \pi_N) = 1$. Output 0 otherwise.

Theorem 2. *If Π_{PHPS} is ϵ-smooth, and Π_N is an unbounded simulation-sound NIZK, then the resulting NIZK system Π_{DN} is a strong DSS-NIZK system.*

Theorem 2 shows the properties of Π_{DN}. The proof of this theorem appears in the full version of this paper. The overview of our proof is as follows: The partial zero-knowledge and unbounded partial simulation-soundness of Π_{DN} can be proven in the same way as the proof of [29]. In the one-time full zero-knowledge game, an adversary is allowed to submit $(x^*, \beta^*, \text{lbl}^*)$ such that $x^* \notin \mathcal{L}(R)$ in order to get a proof π^* generated by sfSim or otfSim. The difference between pV and sfV is the verification of $x \in \mathcal{L}(R)$ with E_2. Thus, the outputs of pV and sfV may be different if the adversary issues (x, π, lbl) to the given verifier oracle, such that $x \notin \mathcal{L}(R)$, $(x, \pi, \text{lbl}) \neq (x^*, \pi^*, \text{lbl}^*)$, and the verifier oracle accepts. In the proof of [29], it is proven that this event does not occur due to the universal$_2$ property of Π_{PHPS} and a special property of the underlying NIZK. In our proof, the event occurs with negligible probability, due to the unbounded simulation-soundness of Definition 2. This is because $((x^*, x_H^*, \pi_H^*, \text{lbl}^*), \pi^*)$ is included in the list $\mathcal{Q}$ of the unbounded simulation-soundness game of Π_N, and issuing the query above $(x, \pi = (x_H, \pi_H, \pi_N), \text{lbl})$ corresponds to the adversary's winning condition in Definition 2 (i.e., $(x, x_H, \pi_H, \text{lbl}) \notin \mathcal{L}(R_N)$, $((x, x_H, \pi_H, \text{lbl}), \pi_N) \notin \mathcal{Q}$, and $V_N(\text{crs}_N, (x, x_H, \pi_H, \text{lbl}), \pi_N) = 1$). Therefore, Π_{PHPS} does not need to satisfy universal$_2$ property, and Π_N must fulfill the unbounded simulation-soundness.

5   Feasibility of Our Construction

We show that a keyed-FHE scheme without iO can be constructed from existing schemes. For the FHE used in our generic construction, IND-CCA1 security is required. However, our generic construction of strong DSS-NIZKs requires not only IND-CCA1 security but also public verifiability of ciphertexts (see Sect. 4). Canetti et al. [11] proposed generic constructions of IND-CCA1 secure FHE. They employed the Naor-Yung paradigm [36] with two IND-CPA secure FHE schemes and zk-SNARK [3,4]. This construction satisfies both IND-CCA1 security and public verifiability of ciphertexts, since it is possible to check the validity of ciphertexts owing to the public verifiability of the underlying zk-SNARK. Although they also showed that multi-key IBFHE can be used for constructing IND-CCA1 secure FHE, this IND-CCA1 secure scheme does not necessarily satisfy public verifiability. Thus, we cannot apply this one to our generic construction of keyed-FHE. Although a generic construction of IND-CCA1 secure FHE from iO was also proposed in [11], we emphasis that no iO is required for constructing IND-CCA1 secure FHE from the viewpoint of feasibility.

The remaining part is strong DSS-NIZK. As described in Sect. 1.2, NIZKs used to obtain a strong DSS-NIZK for NP can be constructed from Σ-protocols [26] by using the Fiat-Shamir transformation [23], and there exists such a NIZK in the quantum random oracle model [12] or the standard model [31]. There exists a smooth (approximate) PHPS [2] for lattice-based ciphertexts. Hence, we can obtain a strong DSS-NIZK for NP by using existing schemes.

Acknowledgments. This work was supported by JST CREST Grant Numbers JPMJCR19F6 and JPMJCR2113, Japan, and JSPS KAKENHI Grant Number 19K20267. We would like to thank Prof. Thomas Peters since he gave us insightful suggestion to instantiate our keyed-FHE scheme in the standard model.

References

1. Barak, B., et al.: On the (Im)possibility of obfuscating programs. In: Kilian, J. (ed.) CRYPTO 2001. LNCS, vol. 2139, pp. 1–18. Springer, Heidelberg (2001). https://doi.org/10.1007/3-540-44647-8_1
2. Benhamouda, F., Blazy, O., Ducas, L., Quach, W.: Hash proof systems over lattices revisited. In: Abdalla, M., Dahab, R. (eds.) PKC 2018. LNCS, vol. 10770, pp. 644–674. Springer, Cham (2018). https://doi.org/10.1007/978-3-319-76581-5_22
3. Bitansky, N., et al.: The hunting of the SNARK. J. Cryptol. **30**(4), 989–1066 (2017)
4. Bitansky, N., Canetti, R., Chiesa, A., Tromer, E.: Recursive composition and bootstrapping for SNARKS and proof-carrying data. In: STOC. ACM (2013)
5. Brakerski, Z.: Fully homomorphic encryption without modulus switching from classical GapSVP. In: Safavi-Naini, R., Canetti, R. (eds.) CRYPTO 2012. LNCS, vol. 7417, pp. 868–886. Springer, Heidelberg (2012). https://doi.org/10.1007/978-3-642-32009-5_50
6. Brakerski, Z., Cash, D., Tsabary, R., Wee, H.: Targeted homomorphic attribute-based encryption. In: TCC (B2), pp. 330–360 (2016)
7. Brakerski, Z., Gentry, C., Vaikuntanathan, V.: (Leveled) fully homomorphic encryption without bootstrapping. In: ITCS, pp. 309–325. ACM (2012)
8. Brakerski, Z., Vaikuntanathan, V.: Efficient fully homomorphic encryption from (standard) LWE. In: FOCS, pp. 97–106. IEEE Computer Society (2011)
9. Brakerski, Z., Vaikuntanathan, V.: Fully homomorphic encryption from ring-LWE and security for key dependent messages. In: Rogaway, P. (ed.) CRYPTO 2011. LNCS, vol. 6841, pp. 505–524. Springer, Heidelberg (2011). https://doi.org/10.1007/978-3-642-22792-9_29
10. Brakerski, Z., Vaikuntanathan, V.: Lattice-based FHE as secure as PKE. In: ITCS, pp. 1–12. ACM (2014)
11. Canetti, R., Raghuraman, S., Richelson, S., Vaikuntanathan, V.: Chosen-ciphertext secure fully homomorphic encryption. In: Public Key Cryptography, pp. 213–240 (2017)
12. Chase, M., et al.: Post-quantum zero-knowledge and signatures from symmetric-key primitives. In: CCS, pp. 1825–1842. ACM (2017)
13. Cheon, J.H., et al.: Batch fully homomorphic encryption over the integers. In: Johansson, T., Nguyen, P.Q. (eds.) EUROCRYPT 2013. LNCS, vol. 7881, pp. 315–335. Springer, Heidelberg (2013). https://doi.org/10.1007/978-3-642-38348-9_20

14. Chiesa, A., Manohar, P., Spooner, N.: Succinct arguments in the quantum random oracle model. In: Hofheinz, D., Rosen, A. (eds.) TCC 2019. LNCS, vol. 11892, pp. 1–29. Springer, Cham (2019). https://doi.org/10.1007/978-3-030-36033-7_1
15. Clear, M., McGoldrick, C.: Multi-identity and multi-key leveled FHE from learning with errors. In: Gennaro, R., Robshaw, M. (eds.) CRYPTO 2015. LNCS, vol. 9216, pp. 630–656. Springer, Heidelberg (2015). https://doi.org/10.1007/978-3-662-48000-7_31
16. Coron, J.-S., Mandal, A., Naccache, D., Tibouchi, M.: Fully homomorphic encryption over the integers with shorter public keys. In: Rogaway, P. (ed.) CRYPTO 2011. LNCS, vol. 6841, pp. 487–504. Springer, Heidelberg (2011). https://doi.org/10.1007/978-3-642-22792-9_28
17. Cramer, R., Shoup, V.: Universal hash proofs and a paradigm for adaptive chosen ciphertext secure public-key encryption. In: EUROCRYPT, pp. 45–64 (2002)
18. Desmedt, Y., Iovino, V., Persiano, G., Visconti, I.: Controlled homomorphic encryption: definition and construction. In: Brenner, M., et al. (eds.) FC 2017. LNCS, vol. 10323, pp. 107–129. Springer, Cham (2017). https://doi.org/10.1007/978-3-319-70278-0_7
19. van Dijk, M., Gentry, C., Halevi, S., Vaikuntanathan, V.: Fully homomorphic encryption over the integers. In: Gilbert, H. (ed.) EUROCRYPT 2010. LNCS, vol. 6110, pp. 24–43. Springer, Heidelberg (2010). https://doi.org/10.1007/978-3-642-13190-5_2
20. Emura, K.: On the security of keyed-homomorphic PKE: preventing key recovery attacks and ciphertext validity attacks. IEICE Trans. Fundam. Electron. Commun. Comput. Sci. **104**-A(1), 310–314 (2021)
21. Emura, K., Hanaoka, G., Nuida, K., Ohtake, G., Matsuda, T., Yamada, S.: Chosen ciphertext secure keyed-homomorphic public-key cryptosystems. Des. Codes Crypt. **86**(8), 1623–1683 (2017). https://doi.org/10.1007/s10623-017-0417-6
22. Emura, K., Hanaoka, G., Ohtake, G., Matsuda, T., Yamada, S.: Chosen ciphertext secure keyed-homomorphic public-key encryption. In: Kurosawa, K., Hanaoka, G. (eds.) PKC 2013. LNCS, vol. 7778, pp. 32–50. Springer, Heidelberg (2013). https://doi.org/10.1007/978-3-642-36362-7_3
23. Faust, S., Kohlweiss, M., Marson, G.A., Venturi, D.: On the non-malleability of the fiat-shamir transform. In: Galbraith, S., Nandi, M. (eds.) INDOCRYPT 2012. LNCS, vol. 7668, pp. 60–79. Springer, Heidelberg (2012). https://doi.org/10.1007/978-3-642-34931-7_5
24. Gentry, C.: Fully homomorphic encryption using ideal lattices. In: STOC, pp. 169–178. ACM (2009)
25. Gentry, C., Sahai, A., Waters, B.: Homomorphic encryption from learning with errors: conceptually-simpler, asymptotically-faster, attribute-based. In: Canetti, R., Garay, J.A. (eds.) CRYPTO 2013. LNCS, vol. 8042, pp. 75–92. Springer, Heidelberg (2013). https://doi.org/10.1007/978-3-642-40041-4_5
26. Giacomelli, I., Madsen, J., Orlandi, C.: ZKBoo: faster zero-knowledge for boolean circuits. In: USENIX Security Symposium, pp. 1069–1083. USENIX Association (2016)
27. Jutla, C., Roy, A.: Relatively-sound NIZKs and password-based key-exchange. In: Fischlin, M., Buchmann, J., Manulis, M. (eds.) PKC 2012. LNCS, vol. 7293, pp. 485–503. Springer, Heidelberg (2012). https://doi.org/10.1007/978-3-642-30057-8_29

28. Jutla, C.S., Roy, A.: Switching lemma for bilinear tests and constant-size NIZK proofs for linear subspaces. In: Garay, J.A., Gennaro, R. (eds.) CRYPTO 2014. LNCS, vol. 8617, pp. 295–312. Springer, Heidelberg (2014). https://doi.org/10.1007/978-3-662-44381-1_17

29. Jutla, C.S., Roy, A.: Dual-system simulation-soundness with applications to UC-PAKE and more. In: Iwata, T., Cheon, J.H. (eds.) ASIACRYPT 2015. LNCS, vol. 9452, pp. 630–655. Springer, Heidelberg (2015). https://doi.org/10.1007/978-3-662-48797-6_26

30. Lai, J., Deng, R.H., Ma, C., Sakurai, K., Weng, J.: CCA-secure keyed-fully homomorphic encryption. In: Cheng, C.-M., Chung, K.-M., Persiano, G., Yang, B.-Y. (eds.) PKC 2016. LNCS, vol. 9614, pp. 70–98. Springer, Heidelberg (2016). https://doi.org/10.1007/978-3-662-49384-7_4

31. Libert, B., Nguyen, K., Passelègue, A., Titiu, R.: Simulation-sound arguments for LWE and applications to KDM-CCA2 security. In: Moriai, S., Wang, H. (eds.) ASIACRYPT 2020. LNCS, vol. 12491, pp. 128–158. Springer, Cham (2020). https://doi.org/10.1007/978-3-030-64837-4_5

32. Libert, B., Peters, T., Joye, M., Yung, M.: Non-malleability from malleability: simulation-sound quasi-adaptive NIZK Proofs and CCA2-Secure encryption from homomorphic signatures. In: Nguyen, P.Q., Oswald, E. (eds.) EUROCRYPT 2014. LNCS, vol. 8441, pp. 514–532. Springer, Heidelberg (2014). https://doi.org/10.1007/978-3-642-55220-5_29

33. Loftus, J., May, A., Smart, N.P., Vercauteren, F.: On CCA-secure somewhat homomorphic encryption. In: Miri, A., Vaudenay, S. (eds.) SAC 2011. LNCS, vol. 7118, pp. 55–72. Springer, Heidelberg (2012). https://doi.org/10.1007/978-3-642-28496-0_4

34. López-Alt, A., Tromer, E., Vaikuntanathan, V.: On-the-fly multiparty computation on the cloud via multikey fully homomorphic encryption. In: STOC, pp. 1219–1234. ACM (2012)

35. Maeda, Y., Nuida, K.: Chosen ciphertext secure keyed two-level homomorphic encryption. IACR Cryptol. ePrint Arch. **2021**, 722 (2021). https://eprint.iacr.org/2021/722

36. Naor, M., Yung, M.: Public-key cryptosystems provably secure against chosen ciphertext attacks. In: STOC, pp. 427–437. ACM (1990)

37. Sahai, A.: Non-malleable non-interactive zero knowledge and adaptive chosen-ciphertext security. In: FOCS, pp. 543–553. IEEE Computer Society (1999)

A Performance Evaluation
of Pairing-Based Broadcast Encryption
Systems

Arush Chhatrapati[1], Susan Hohenberger[2]([✉]), James Trombo[3],
and Satyanarayana Vusirikala[4]

[1] Henry M. Gunn High School, Palo Alto, CA, USA
[2] Johns Hopkins University, Baltimore, MD, USA
susan@cs.jhu.edu
[3] George Mason High School, Falls Church, VA, USA
[4] University of Texas at Austin, Austin, TX, USA
satya@cs.utexas.edu

Abstract. In a broadcast encryption system, a sender can encrypt a
message for any subset of users who are listening on a broadcast channel. The goal is to leverage the broadcasting structure to achieve better
efficiency than individually encrypting to each user; in particular, reducing the ciphertext size required to transmit securely, although other factors such as public and private key size and the time to execute setup,
encryption and decryption are also important.

In this work, we conduct a detailed performance evaluation of eleven
public-key, pairing-based broadcast encryption schemes offering different
features and security guarantees, including public-key, identity-based,
traitor-tracing, private linear and augmented systems. We implemented
each system using the MCL Java pairings library, reworking some of
the constructions to achieve better efficiency. We tested their performance on a variety of parameter choices, resulting in hundreds of data
points to compare, with some interesting results from the classic Boneh-
Gentry-Waters scheme (CRYPTO 2005) to Zhandry's recent generalized
scheme (CRYPTO 2020), and more. We combine this performance data
with data we collected on practical usage scenarios to determine which
schemes are likely to perform best for certain applications, such as video
streaming services, online gaming, live sports betting and distributor-
limited applications. This work can inform both practitioners and future
cryptographic designers in this area.

1 Introduction

In a broadcast encryption system [9], a sender can encrypt a message for any
subset of users who are listening on a broadcast channel. We focus on public-key

S. Hohenberger—Supported by NSF CNS-1908181, the Office of Naval Research
N00014-19-1-2294, and a Packard Foundation Subaward via UT Austin.
S. Vusirikala—Supported by a UT Austin Provost Fellowship, NSF CNS-1908611, and
the Packard Foundation.

G. Ateniese and D. Venturi (Eds.): ACNS 2022, LNCS 13269, pp. 24–44, 2022.
https://doi.org/10.1007/978-3-031-09234-3_2

systems, where there is a public system key that allows anyone to encrypt a message to any set S of his choice out of an established set of N users. The public system key is established by a master authority, who also distributes individualized secret keys to each user in the system. If a user is in the set S for a particular broadcast, then she can decrypt that broadcast using her secret key. A critical security property for these systems is collusion resistance, which guarantees that users not in S learn nothing about the broadcast message. Some schemes offer a traitor-tracing functionality that protects against digital piracy; specifically, it guarantees that if one or more malicious users work together to release piracy information (e.g., software or a key) that decrypts on the broadcast channel, then this piracy information can be traced back to at least one of them.

The goal of broadcast encryption is efficiency. In particular, the goal is to leverage the broadcasting structure to achieve better efficiency than individually encrypting to each user. This can result in huge practical savings. To measure the concrete performance benefits offered by various broadcast encryption systems, for several different sizes of system users N and encryption subsets $S \subset N$, we will compare each broadcast encryption scheme in terms of ciphertext size, public and private key size, and the setup, key generation, encryption and decryption times. We focus on pairing-based broadcast systems, since this is the most promising algebraic setting for reducing ciphertext size and obtaining fast runtimes (see [4] for more on pairings). We also compare the broadcast schemes to an optimized "baseline" scheme[1] derived from ElGamal encryption [11] with shared parameters (see Sect. 2) that individually encrypts to each user in the broadcast set S.

Our Contributions and Results. To the best of our knowledge, this work is the only current detailed performance study of public-key, pairing-based broadcast encryption systems. Although schemes can be loosely grouped and compared at the asymptotic level for performance purposes, the tradeoffs, underlying constant factors, scalability and differing system features could significantly impact various applications. To provide the community with a solid foundation for comparisons, this work includes the following:

- We collected eleven public-key, pairing-based broadcast encryption systems, which are detailed in Table 2 of Sect. 3 and which we thought were likely to perform the best. In some cases, we made efficiency-focused alterations to the schemes, such as creating a separate setup and key generation function or finding the most efficient asymmetric pairing implementation for a scheme presented symmetrically. Any change from the original publication is documented herein, with details in the full version [4].
- We implemented the eleven broadcast systems using the MCL pairings library (currently employed by some cutting-edge cryptocurrency companies) and the baseline ElGamal system using OpenSSL. These implementations will be made publicly available. We ran hundreds of tests on these systems for various

---

[1] Because the Sect. 2 baseline scheme will not require the pairing operation, it is implemented using an elliptic curve group, whose elements are even smaller; thus requiring real performance gains from the broadcast systems to overtake it.

parameter choices, reporting on those results in Sect. 3. This is a contribution in terms of providing the community with data and public reference implementations; additionally careful implementation is also important for rooting out any potential issues in prior publications. In the course of our study, we discovered a technical issue in a prior publication; we communicated it to the author(s) and they updated their scheme accordingly. (Details are removed for submission anonymity, but we will be explicit in the final version.) Thus, this implementation effort has also been useful as an additional verification process for prior work.

– In Tables 7 and 8, we document that individual encryption is more efficient than broadcast encryption for systems with 100 users or less. The $100 < N < 10,000$ range is a gray area where there are tradeoffs to be made. But once a system's users exceed 10,000, broadcast encryption dominates the individual encryption (baseline) in overall performance.

– To understand which broadcast system offers the "best" performance, we researched the yearly reports and shareholder letters of companies such as Nvidia [20], Disney [5] and Netflix [6] to understand the performance demands of some interesting applications for broadcast encryption. We summarize our findings in Sect. 4. We start with the classic application of video streaming and then explore the emerging applications of online gaming, live sports betting and more. In a nutshell, if traitor tracing is not required, we found that the classic Boneh-Gentry-Waters system [2, S3.2] provides the best tradeoffs for video streaming and is strong for online gaming too, with [23] also strong for gaming. Zhandry's generalized nonrisky system (see [4] for details) can be tuned to optimize a parameter of interest (e.g., ciphertext size), although this usually results in another parameter (e.g., decryption time) becoming infeasible. For live sports betting, the smaller number of users and the importance of encryption speed make Gentry-Waters [15] the preferred choice. We found the private tracing system of Gentry, Kumarasubramanian, Sahai and Waters [12] to provide the best overall system performance when tracing is needed, but it may not be fast enough for live streaming applications. For peer-to-many applications, we favored Boneh-Gentry-Waters [2, S3.1] when many keys must be generated. Finally, we discovered that none of the identity-based broadcast systems (IBBE) were practical for large user applications, so a practical IBBE remains an interesting open research problem.

The schemes we implemented (as taken from their respective publications), including the ElGamal baseline, achieve security against chosen plaintext attacks [16] (CPA), while NIST recommends that deployed systems achieve a stronger notion of security against chosen ciphertext attacks [8,19,21] (CCA). While efficient general transformations from CPA to CCA exist for public key encryption [10], it is not clear if these can be applied to broadcast encryption systems without compromising some of their functionality (e.g., traitor tracing). This is an exciting area for future research.

We believe this timely implementation study will inform practitioners as they look to harness the performance savings of broadcast encryption, while also providing context for future broadcast encryption designs.

2   An ElGamal Baseline and Other Related Works

We construct a baseline system, which encrypts the same message individually to each privileged user, so that we can contrast its performance with the broadcast systems. This CPA-secure system uses ElGamal encryption [11] with shared parameters. Private key sizes are constant, but the public key size grows linearly with the number of system users.

Setup(λ, N)***:*** Let $\mathbb{G}$ be an elliptic curve group of prime order p for which the DDH assumption holds true. Pick a random generator $g \in \mathbb{G}$. For $i = 1, 2, \ldots, n$ pick a random $x_i \in \mathbb{Z}_p$ and compute $h_i = g^{x_i}$. The master public key is $PK = (g, h_1, ..., h_n)$ and the private key for user i is x_i. Output the public key PK and the N private keys $x_1, x_2, \ldots, x_N$.

Enc(PK, S, m)***:*** To encrypt a message m to a set of users S, first pick a random $y \in \mathbb{Z}_p$. For each user $i \in S$, compute $z_i = (h_i)^y \cdot m$. Output the ciphertext $CT = (g^y, z_1, \ldots, z_S)$.

Dec(i, CT)***:*** Parse the ciphertext as $CT = (c, z_1, \ldots, z_S)$. User i decrypts by computing $m = z_i / (c^{x_i})$.

We implement this baseline scheme and tested it in OpenSSL over the curves NIST P-192, NIST P-224, NIST P-256, NIST P-384, and NIST P-521. Based on the results from our implementation, we use the results over the curve NIST P-256 as a basis of comparison to the pairing-based scheme runtimes over BN254. The runtimes are the fastest over this curve and the 128 bit security provided by NIST P-256 is very close to the 110 bit security provided by BN254.

Table 1. Runtimes for the ElGamal baseline over different curves when $N = 100\mathrm{K}$ and $|S| = 10\mathrm{K}$. Let s denote seconds and ms denote milliseconds.

Curve	Security	Setup Time	Encrypt Time	Decrypt Time
NIST P-192	96 bits	39.27 s	3.78 s	0.51 ms
NIST P-224	112 bits	5.51 s	515.13 ms	0.09 ms
NIST P-256	128 bits	2.40 s	248.08 ms	0.05 ms
NIST P-384	192 bits	145.82 s	14.66 s	2.67 ms
NIST P-521	260.5 bits	37.04 s	3.62 s	0.73 ms

Additional related works are discussed in the full version [4].

3 Broadcast Encryption Implementations and Analysis

We refer to the following for the definitions of broadcast encryption [9], and the identity-based [7,22], trace-and-revoke [18], augmented [1], traitor-tracing [3,17], and private-linear [3] variants.

We provide a reference implementation[2] and comparison of eleven broadcast encryption systems. All schemes are implemented in the asymmetric pairing setting using the MCL pairings library[3] with a Barreto-Naehrig BN254 curve. This curve is conjectured to have approximately 100-bit security. Group elements in $\mathbb{G}_1$, $\mathbb{G}_2$, and $\mathbb{G}_T$ occupy 32 bytes, 64 bytes, and 381 bytes of space in memory, respectively. Elements in $\mathbb{Z}_p$ occupy 254 bits of space. We also compare all of the systems to an ElGamal baseline system in Sect. 2, which was implemented using prime-order elliptic curve groups in OpenSSL since it does not require pairings. The baseline system was implemented using C++ but all the others are in Java. We chose Java for the pairing-based broadcast schemes because the MCL Java library possessed a remarkably simple, flexible software interface which allowed us to easily implement and compare these systems to each other.

We compare the setup, encryption, key generation, and decryption times in each of our systems. The runtimes are tested by setting the size of the subset of privileged users S to be equal to some percent of the total number of users in the system. This ensures that the subset size scales with the number of users in the system. All of the runtimes were tested on a 2014 Macbook Air with a 1.4 GHz Dual-Core Intel Core i5 processor and 4 GB RAM.

We also compare the sizes of the public key, private key, and ciphertext for each of the systems. Table 2 shows how the sizes scale asymptotically. It also provides an overview of the systems that we implement.

3.1 Boneh-Gentry-Waters Scheme Using Asymmetric Pairings

The Boneh-Gentry-Waters-Scheme, [2], refers to a fully collusion resistant public key broadcast system for stateless receivers. In the paper, two schemes are described, and both are secure against static adversaries. In the "special case", [2, S3.1], the public key grows linearly with the total number of users in the broadcast system. Ciphertext sizes and private key sizes are constant. In the general construction [2, S3.2], the public key and ciphertext are both of size $O(\lambda \cdot \sqrt{N})$, and private key sizes are constant. We rewrite both of these schemes using Type-III pairings, strategically placing certain group elements in $\mathbb{G}_1$ and $\mathbb{G}_2$ to optimize the efficiency of our construction. We also add a KeyGen function instead of generating the private keys for all N users in the Setup phase. This facilitates the comparison of this scheme to other public-key broadcast encryption schemes in Sect. 3.4.

In Table 3, we present the encryption times for the BGW special case construction for varying subset sizes. We define the subset size to be some percent

---

[2] https://github.com/ArushC/broadcast.
[3] https://github.com/herumi/mcl.

Table 2. A summary of pairing-based broadcast encryption systems. Let N be the number of users in the broadcast system, ℓ be the maximal size of the subset of users S such that $|S| \leq \ell$, and λ be the security parameter. Note that for the broadcast and trace system [24, $\mathcal{S}9.3$], $a \in [0, 1]$.

Scheme	Type	Ciphertext Size	Private Key Size	Public Key Size	Security
ElGamal baseline	Public Key	$O(\lambda \cdot |S|)$	$O(\lambda)$	$O(\lambda \cdot N)$	CPA-secure
[2, $\mathcal{S}3.1$]	Broadcast	$O(\lambda)$	$O(\lambda)$	$O(\lambda \cdot N)$	static
[2, $\mathcal{S}3.2$]	Broadcast	$O(\lambda \cdot \sqrt{N})$	$O(\lambda)$	$O(\lambda \cdot \sqrt{N})$	static
[23]	Broadcast	$O(\lambda)$	$O(\lambda \cdot N)$	$O(\lambda \cdot N)$	adaptive
[15, $\mathcal{S}3.1$]	Broadcast	$O(\lambda)$	$O(\lambda \cdot N)$	$O(\lambda \cdot N)$	semi-static
[15, $\mathcal{S}4.1$]	IBBE	$O(\lambda \cdot \ell)$	$O(\lambda)$	$O(\lambda \cdot \ell)$	adaptive
[15, $\mathcal{S}4.3.1$]	IBBE	$O(\lambda)$	$O(\lambda)$	$O(\lambda \cdot \ell)$	semi-static
[14, $\mathcal{S}3.1$]	IBBE	$O(\lambda)$	$O(\lambda \cdot N)$	$O(\lambda \cdot N)$	adaptive
[24, $\mathcal{S}9.3$]	Risky Trace	$O(\lambda \cdot N)$	$O(\lambda)$	$O(\lambda)$	adaptive
[13, $\mathcal{S}5.2$]	Trace	$O(\lambda \cdot \sqrt{N})$	$O(\lambda \cdot \sqrt{N})$	$O(\lambda \cdot \sqrt{N})$	adaptive and public tracing
[24, $\mathcal{S}9.3$]	Trace	$O(\lambda \cdot N^{1-a})$	$O(\lambda \cdot N^{1-a})$	$O(\lambda \cdot N^{a})$	adaptive
[12]	PLBE	$O(\lambda \cdot \sqrt{N})$	$O(\lambda)$	$O(\lambda \cdot \sqrt{N})$	private tracing

of the total number of users in the system. Notice a general trend that as the subset size percentage increases, so does the encryption time. This is because even though the ciphertext sizes are constant, $O(|S|)$ multiplications over $\mathbb{G}_1$ are required to compute the product $v \cdot \prod_{j \in S}(h_{n+1-j})$ during encryption.

We implement the general construction by setting $B = \lfloor \sqrt{n} \rfloor$ as the authors of [2] suggest. In this case, B is an arbitrary parameter that scales the public key and ciphertext to the desired size, and setting B to the specified value enables us to achieve the optimal public key and ciphertext sizes of $O(\lambda \cdot \sqrt{N})$. Again, we modify this system to include a KeyGen function instead of generating the private keys for all N users in the Setup phase.

We notice that runtimes increase when we read the table from left to right. However, when we read the table from top to bottom, we see mixed results. To understand the context for the discussion that follows, we ask readers to refer to the bottom of page 7 of [2].

In the encryption algorithm, runtimes are determine by two significant steps. First is the computation of S_ℓ, which is dominated by the number of operations required to calculate $\hat{S}_\ell = S \cap \{\ell B - B + 1, \ell B - B + 2, \ldots, \ell B\}$. In order to compute the intersection of two sets, for each item in the latter set, the system must check if there is a corresponding item in S. Since we use hash sets to compute this intersection, the time that it takes to lookup an item in S is $O(1)$. But we still need to iterate over each item in the original set of size B, so this step will take time $O(B)$. The computation of the subset $\hat{S}_\ell$ is an intermediate step which dominates the computation of S_ℓ for $\ell = 1, 2, \ldots, A$. Therefore, the

Table 3. Encryption times for the Boneh-Gentry-Waters Special Case scheme. Let s denote seconds and ms denote milliseconds.

Subset Size	Encryption time when number of system users $N =$				
	100	1K	10K	100K	1M
1%	1.24 ms	0.88 ms	1.29 ms	6.08 ms	87.24 ms
5%	0.71 ms	1.31 ms	2.16 ms	14.06 ms	340.73 ms
10%	1.26 ms	1.32 ms	2.40 ms	16.35 ms	664.76 ms
20%	1.51 ms	1.69 ms	3.27 ms	30.89 ms	1.13 s
50%	0.75 ms	2.19 ms	8.60 ms	67.59 ms	1.62 s

total time to compute all of these subsets is $O(A \cdot B) = O(N)$. After computing these subsets, there is a second step. The system still has to calculate the product $v_i \cdot \prod_{j \in S_i} (h_{B+1-j})$ for $i \in \{1, 2, \ldots, A\}$. According to our implementation, this takes a total of $|S|$ group multiplications. Hence, the overall time complexity for the encryption algorithm is given by $O(N + \lambda \cdot |S|)$. The $O(N)$ operations in computing the S_ℓ subsets are individually much less costly than each of the $|S|$ group multiplications, but they still influence runtimes to an extent. Reading the table from top to bottom, we keep the total number of users in the system N constant while increasing the subset size $|S|$. For the smaller values of $|S|$ (i.e. $N = 100, 1\,\mathrm{K}, 10\,\mathrm{K}$), the slight increase in the value of $|S|$ does not significantly affect runtimes to an extent that it can be explained by the big-O notation. But reading the table from left to right, we increase both $|S|$ AND the value of N, which causes runtimes to increase as expected.

Table 4. Encryption times for the Boneh-Gentry-Waters general scheme. Let ms denote milliseconds.

Subset Size	Encryption time when number of system users $N =$				
	100	1K	10K	100K	1M
1%	3.67 ms	9.59 ms	29.62 ms	77.61 ms	288.11 ms
5%	3.62 ms	8.14 ms	24.68 ms	83.09 ms	297.83 ms
10%	3.58 ms	8.61 ms	26.60 ms	86.36 ms	306.96 ms
20%	2.77 ms	6.90 ms	30.41 ms	134.18 ms	548.08 ms
50%	4.43 ms	13.09 ms	47.39 ms	145.08 ms	897.48 ms

3.2   Gentry-Waters: A Semi-static Variant of the BGW System

In [15], Gentry and Waters introduce the notion of semi-static security, which is between static security and adaptive security. They construct a semi-statically secure variant of [2]. In their system, the public key and private key both grow linearly with the total number of system users, but the ciphertext sizes are constant. We implemented their semi-static scheme in the asymmetric (Type-III) pairing setting and optimized it for efficiency, with details in the full version. In Table 5, we give the encryption times. We notice a general trend that reading the table from left to right, encryption times increase. For the larger values of N, encryption times also generally increase when reading the table from top to bottom. In both of these scenarios, the subset size is increasing dramatically, which is why we see such a great increase in encryption times. Encryption time is dominated by the time required to calculate $C_2 = (\prod_{j \in S} h_j)^t$, which requires $O(|S|)$ group multiplications over $\mathbb{G}_1$.

Table 5. Encryption times for the Gentry-Waters semi-static variant of the Boneh-Gentry-Waters scheme. Let ms denote milliseconds.

Subset Size	Encryption time when number of system users $N =$				
	100	1K	10K	100K	1M
1%	0.64 ms	0.59 ms	1.51 ms	1.97 ms	13.00 ms
5%	0.65 ms	1.11 ms	1.53 ms	6.21 ms	62.30 ms
10%	1.18 ms	1.37 ms	1.99 ms	12.63 ms	153.56 ms
20%	0.80 ms	0.80 ms	2.95 ms	20.99 ms	200.77 ms
50%	1.04 ms	1.59 ms	5.46 ms	65.02 ms	486.97 ms

3.3 Waters Dual System Broadcast Encryption System

We implement a broadcast encryption system that is secure against adaptive adversaries, described in [23]. We remind readers that the adaptive security provided by this scheme is stronger than the static and semi-static security of the schemes implemented in Sects. 3.1 and 3.2, respectively. In this system, the ciphertext sizes are constant, but the public key and private key sizes grow linearly with the total number of system users. This system, like the others, was originally written in the symmetric pairing setting. In the full version, we describe how we implemented it in the Type-III pairing setting, strategically choosing which group elements to place in $\mathbb{G}_1$ and $\mathbb{G}_2$ to maximize efficiency.

In Table 6, we show the encryption times from our implementation, which are dominated by the computation of $E_1 = (\prod_{i \in S} u_i)^t$, which requires $O(|S|)$ group multiplications over $\mathbb{G}_1$.

Table 6. Encryption times for the Waters Dual Broadcast System. Let ms denote milliseconds.

Subset Size	Encryption time when number of system users $N =$				
	100	1K	10K	100K	1M
1%	2.01 ms	2.23 ms	2.97 ms	3.35 ms	14.22 ms
5%	2.02 ms	2.57 ms	4.39 ms	7.70 ms	73.20 ms
10%	2.03 ms	2.38 ms	3.44 ms	14.55 ms	131.80 ms
20%	2.06 ms	3.26 ms	4.49 ms	22.90 ms	239.53 ms
50%	2.61 ms	3.37 ms	8.22 ms	79.07 ms	494.90 ms

3.4   Comparison of General Broadcast Encryption Systems

We now compare the broadcast encryption systems that we describe in Sects. 3.1, 3.2, and 3.3 to each other, and to the baseline scheme which we describe in Sect. 2. We perform a runtime evaluation based on experimental values for setup, encryption, key generation (when applicable), and decryption. Based on these values, we then count individual operations and construct asymptotic runtime tables for each of the functions in each scheme. We only compare the runtimes based on the runtime tables that we construct in this paper, but we refer the reader to our implementation to view all of the runtimes. We also do a size evaluation based on the actual sizes of the group elements in $\mathbb{G}_1$, $\mathbb{G}_2$, and $\mathbb{G}_T$ over the curve BN254, given in Table 8. We have already given the theoretical sizes of the public key, private key, and ciphertext for each scheme at the beginning of this section in Table 2.

Setup Times. We start by analyzing the setup times presented in Table 7. For all the pairing-based schemes, the setup phase requires computing a public key PK and master secret key MSK. Computing the master secret key takes a negligible, constant amount of time, but the time that it takes to compute the public key varies. The baseline scheme setup phase requires $O(N)$ exponentiations over the elliptic curve group $\mathbb{G}$ to calculate a linear-sized PK. On the other hand, [2, $S3.2$] requires $O(\sqrt{N})$ exponentiations over $\mathbb{G}_1$ to calculate a public key of size $O(\lambda \cdot \sqrt{N})$. All the other pairing-based schemes require on the order of $O(N)$ operations over $\mathbb{G}_1$ to calculate a linear-sized public key. From our implementation, individual group operations over the elliptic curve group $\mathbb{G}$ (NIST P-256) used for the baseline were found to be faster than operations over $\mathbb{G}_1$ used in the pairings-based schemes. This explains why the baseline setup times are faster than those for all of the pairings-based schemes *except* [2, $S3.2$].

Setup times for [2, $S3.2$] appear to be faster than those for the baseline when $N >= 1K$, but not when $N = 100$. This is because when $N = 100$, the difference in the total number of exponentiations computed during setup for the baseline and [2, $S3.2$] is negligible. Hence, faster setup times for the baseline can be attributed the faster time for individual exponentiations over $\mathbb{G}$ compared to

$\mathbb{G}_1$. When $N >= 1K$, though, [2, $S3.2$] has faster setup times because calculating the public key requires much fewer exponentiations than for the baseline. Even though individual exponentiations are still faster over $\mathbb{G}$ in the baseline scheme, the sheer number of exponentiations required to calculate the public key has increased to an extent that it results in slower setup times.

Encryption Times. On a first glance, it might seem surprising that the encryption times for most of the pairing-based schemes appear to be consistently faster than those for the baseline. But then if we look at the baseline construction from Sect. 2, we notice that during encryption, we have to calculate $z_i = (h_i)^y \cdot m$ for each $i \in S$, in addition to g^y. Overall, this takes $|S| + 1$ group exponentiations and $|S|$ multiplications. Just like the baseline, ALL of the pairing-based schemes compute a part of the ciphertext with with $O(|S|)$ group multiplications. But for all of the pairing-based schemes except [2, $S3.2$], the total number of exponentiations computed during encryption is constant. In [2, $S3.1$] and [15, $S3.1$], we only need one group exponentiation each time to compute $C_0 = (g_2)^t$. In [23], we have exactly six exponentiations over $\mathbb{G}_1$ and size over $\mathbb{G}_2$ every time we compute the ciphertext. This makes the total time for encryption for these schemes less than that for the baseline as the value of N increases. We better explain the results in a series of observations:

- When $N = 100$, the baseline encryption is the most efficient, even though it requires computing more group exponentiations than the other schemes. This is because the efficient group operations over the elliptic curve group $\mathbb{G}$ used for the baseline are outweighed by the slower group operations in the pairing-based schemes. However, the number of exponentiations required for the baseline encryption increases linearly with N. So when $N >= 1K$, despite the faster group operations over $\mathbb{G}$, the number of exponentiations increases sharply for the baseline, while it stays constant for all the pairing-based schemes except [2, $S3.2$]. Hence, all of the pairing-based schemes except [2, $S3.2$] have faster encryption times when $N >= 1K$.
- If we compare the baseline to [2, $S3.2$], we notice that [2, $S3.2$] is only more efficient than the baseline when $N \geq 100K$. We recall that encryption in [2, $S3.2$] requires a total of $|S|$ group multiplications over $\mathbb{G}_1$, one exponentiation over $\mathbb{G}_2$, and A exponentiations over $\mathbb{G}_1$, where $A \approx \sqrt{N}$. We also recall that in encryption for [2, $S3.2$], we need to compute S_ℓ for $\ell \in \{1, 2, \ldots, A\}$ by computing the intersection of integer subsets. This technically takes $O(N)$ time to run, but since iterating over and adding integers to subsets is much faster than multiplying/exponentiating group elements, this step in encryption is fairly rapid. When $N = 100, 1K, 10K$, the baseline scheme's faster encryption times can be attributed to the efficiency of group operations over the elliptic curve group $\mathbb{G}$. Combined with the time to compute S_ℓ for $\ell \in \{1, 2, \ldots, A\}$, the $O(\sqrt{N})$ exponentiations in encryption for [2, $S3.2$] take longer to compute than the $O(N)$ exponentiations for the baseline. This changes when $N \geq 100K$. Now, the sheer number of exponentiations required for the

baseline encryption has increased so greatly that the baseline encryption takes longer than that for [2, $S3.2$].
– When we compare the pairing-based schemes to each other, we see that [15, $S3.1$] consistently has the fastest encryption times. For the smaller values of N, the only other scheme that has encryption times nearly as fast is [2, $S3.1$]. As N grows larger, the encryption times for [23] grows closer to those for [15, $S3.1$] and [2, $S3.1$]. We recall that [15, $S3.1$] is actually a semi-static variant of [2, $S3.1$]. The encryption algorithms for both of these schemes are very similar. Hence the similar runtimes. What is significant, though, is that a semi-statically secure broadcast encryption system achieved faster encryption times that its static counterpart. So far, we see that the [15, $S3.1$] appears to be a well-performing system. It has the fastest encryption times, very fast setup times, and a moderately strong level of security. For adaptive security, [23] seems to be a very good option. The only downside to both of these schemes, as we will shortly see, is their large private key sizes.

Key Generation Times. The baseline scheme, [2, $S3.1$], and [2, $S3.1$] are all secure against static adversaries. Private key sizes are constant, and therefore, single-user key generation times are constant. In order to achieve semi-static and adaptive security, though, the private key size must be expanded. The key generation algorithms for [15, $S3.1$] and [23] generate much larger private keys of size $O(\lambda \cdot N)$. The problem that we found in our implementation is that these key generation algorithms take very long to run. In both [15, $S3.1$] and [23], it takes more than 1.5 min to generate a key for a single user when the total number of system users $N = 1M$. For these two schemes, reading the key generation runtimes from left to right, we see that they increase linearly with the number of users in the system. This makes sense because it require $O(N)$ operations over $\mathbb{G}_1$ to generate a single user's linear-sized private key. In [15, $S3.1$], we need $N + 1$ exponentiations over $\mathbb{G}_1$ to calculate the private key for a single user. Key generation for [23] is similar, but slightly slower. In addition to the $N + 1$ exponentiations over $\mathbb{G}_1$, the system needs to calculate $D_1, D_2, \ldots, D_7$. It would take up a lot of time and space to generate and store the private keys for a large subset of privileged users. The keys for all the privileged users in S would take up $O(\lambda \cdot N \cdot |S|)$ space.

Decryption Times. The only two schemes for which the decryption times remained relatively constant as the total number of system users increased were the baseline scheme and [2, $S3.2$]. For the baseline scheme, decryption does not require any pairings. The decryption algorithm runs in constant time because only a single division needs to be computed ($m = z_i / (c^{x_i})$), regardless of the value of N. In [2, $S3.2$], since we break up our broadcast encryption system into $\sqrt{N}$ instances, we only have to use a single one of those instances – which we created during encryption – to decrypt the message. It is a tradeoff: slower encryption times to calculate each of the instances, but approximately constant

Table 7. Time evaluation for general public key broadcast encryption systems. The baseline scheme was implemented using NIST P-256 in OpenSSL, while the pairing-based schemes used curve BN254 in MCL. The KeyGen and Dec times represent the cost for a single user, while the Setup is the cost to initialize the entire system and Enc is the cost to encrypt to an arbitrary 10% of the system users. Let ms denote milliseconds, s denote seconds, and min denote minutes.

Item	Scheme	Time when number of system users $N =$				
		100	1K	10K	100K	1M
Setup	baseline 2	4.46 ms	27.39 ms	252.65 ms	2.40 s	23.21 s
	[2, S3.1] 3.1	51.47 ms	456.97 ms	4.94 s	40.06 s	7.06 min
	[2, S3.2] 3.1	14.09 ms	15.75 ms	58.81 ms	158.08 ms	762.45 ms
	[15, S3.1] 3.2	35.00 ms	69.40 ms	321.98 ms	2.80 s	29.44 s
	[23] 3.3	32.39 ms	34.45 ms	297.71 ms	3.05 s	29.71 s
KeyGen	baseline 2	—	—	—	—	—
	[2, S3.1] 3.1	0.19 ms	0.18 ms	0.09 ms	0.11 ms	0.12 ms
	[2, S3.2] 3.1	0.11 ms	0.10 ms	0.14 ms	0.12 ms	0.16 ms
	[15, S3.1] 3.2	11.07 ms	164.14 ms	954.00 ms	9.75 s	1.77 min
	[23] 3.3	11.05 ms	104.49 ms	954.14 ms	9.78 s	1.60 min
Enc	baseline 2	0.39 ms	2.85 ms	25.52 ms	248.08 ms	2.81 s
	[2, S3.1] 3.1	1.26 ms	1.32 ms	2.40 ms	16.35 ms	664.76 ms
	[2, S3.2] 3.1	3.58 ms	8.61 ms	26.60 ms	86.36 ms	306.96 ms
	[15, S3.1] 3.2	1.18 ms	1.37 ms	1.99 ms	12.63 ms	153.56 ms
	[23] 3.3	2.03 ms	2.38 ms	3.44 ms	14.55 ms	131.80 ms
Dec	baseline 2	0.04 ms	0.03 ms	0.03 ms	0.05 ms	0.07 ms
	[2, S3.1] 3.1	2.60 ms	1.92 ms	2.78 ms	15.36 ms	349.52 ms
	[2, S3.2] 3.1	2.13 ms	1.49 ms	2.12 ms	2.46 ms	1.63 ms
	[15, S3.1] 3.2	2.82 ms	2.82 ms	2.93 ms	16.56 ms	261.98 ms
	[23] 3.3	6.37 ms	6.44 ms	7.49 ms	23.05 ms	157.66 ms

decryption times. All of the pairing-based schemes except [23] required only two pairings to be computed during decryption. [23] required nine pairings. This large number of pairings explains why the decryption times are consistently the slowest for this system for $N <= 100K$. We again see that the decryption times for [2, S3.1] are similar to those of its semi-static counterpart, [15, S3.1]. And this makes sense. For both, decryption times are dominated by a step that requires $|S| - 1$ group multiplications over $\mathbb{G}_1$.

Overall Runtime Comparison. If we consider key generation a step in the decryption process, then [15, S3.1] and [23] by far have the slowest runtimes. But recall that these are the only two systems that are secure against non-static

Table 8. Space evaluation for general public key broadcast encryption systems. In the above, we set $|S|$, the size of the set of users a ciphertext is encrypted to, to be an arbitrary 10% of the total number of system users. The baseline scheme was implemented using NIST P-256 in OpenSSL, while the pairing-based schemes used curve BN254 in MCL. Let B denote bytes, KB denote kilobytes, and MB denote megabytes.

Item	Scheme	Space when number of system users $N =$				
		100	1K	10K	100K	1M
pk	baseline 2	3.23 KB	32.03 KB	320.03 KB	3.20 MB	32.00 MB
	$[2, S3.1]$ 3.1	12.90 KB	128.10 KB	1.28 MB	12.80 MB	128.00 MB
	$[2, S3.2]$ 3.1	1.66 KB	5.09 KB	16.06 KB	50.66 KB	160.06 KB
	$[15, S3.1]$ 3.2	3.68 KB	32.48 KB	320.48 KB	3.20 MB	32.00 MB
	$[23]$ 3.3	4.19 KB	32.99 KB	320.99 KB	3.20 MB	32.00 MB
sk	baseline 2	32.00 B	32.00 B	32.00 B	32.00 B	32.00 B
	$[2, S3.1]$ 3.1	32.00 B	32.00 B	32.00 B	32.00 B	32.00 B
	$[2, S3.2]$ 3.1	32.00 B	32.00 B	32.00 B	32.00 B	32.00 B
	$[15, S3.1]$ 3.2	3.26 KB	32.06 KB	320.06 KB	3.20 MB	32.00 MB
	$[23]$ 3.3	3.49 KB	32.29 KB	320.29 KB	3.20 MB	32.00 MB
ct	baseline 2	352.00 B	3.23 KB	32.03 KB	320.03 KB	3.20 MB
	$[2, S3.1]$ 3.1	96.00 B	96.00 B	96.00 B	96.00 B	96.00 B
	$[2, S3.2]$ 3.1	384.00 B	1.12 KB	3.26 KB	10.21 KB	32.06 KB
	$[15, S3.1]$ 3.2	96.00 B	96.00 B	96.00 B	96.00 B	96.00 B
	$[23]$ 3.3	861.00 B	861.00 B	861.00 B	861.00 B	861.00 B

adversaries. It is a tradeoff: in order to achieve the higher level of security, the decryption will be slower.

The encryption times for $[15, S3.1]$ and $[23]$ were comparable, if not better, than the encryption times for the systems which were secure against static adversaries. The setup times were faster because the n private keys were not computed during the setup phase. The only other downside with both of these systems are the long key generation times and the large private key sizes.

Looking at Table 8, we argue that if the primary goal of the broadcast system is to achieve short public and private key sizes and efficient decryption times, then we recommend using $[2, S3.2]$. This is the only scheme that achieves public key and ciphertext sizes of $O(\lambda \cdot \sqrt{N})$. The private key sizes are constant. Even though the setup times for this scheme are not more efficient than those for $[15, S3.1]$ and $[23]$, they are still very fast in comparison to $[2, S3.1]$. Additionally, the public key and private keys in $[15, S3.1]$ and $[23]$ are all of size $O(\lambda \cdot N)$. This is very large. But we recall that while $[2, S3.1]$ and $[2, S3.2]$ are secure only against static adversaries, $[15, S3.1]$ is secure against semi-static adversaries and $[23]$ is secure against adaptive adversaries. If we judge these schemes only by the efficiency of their decryption times and public/private key sizes, and we desire a stronger level of security, then we recommend $[15]$. In general, the decryption times for [15, $S3.1$] are much faster because they only require two applications of the pairing algorithm, while [23] requires nine pairings in decryption. Nevertheless, as the total number of system users N grows larger, the decryption times for [23] approach the times for [15, $S3.1$]. So if we have a small total number of users in our system, we recommend [15, $S3.1$]. But if the value of N is very large, then [23] will perform equally well during decryption. And because the adaptive security provided by [23] is stronger than the semi-static security provided by [15, $S3.1$], we especially recommend [23] when the total number of system users $N \geq 1M$.

If the primary goal of our broadcast system is to achieve efficient encryption times, then we recommend any pairing-based system *except* [15, $S3.2$]. Then, depending on the desired level of security, we would choose either the statically secure [2, $S3.1$], the semi-statically secure [15, $S3.1$], or the adaptively secure [23] broadcast system.

Further Theoretical Analysis. For further theoretical analysis, we denote λ_1 and λ_2 as a single group multiplication operation over $\mathbb{G}_1$ and $\mathbb{G}_2$, respectively. Exponentiations are denoted by $\lambda_1{}^3$ and $\lambda_2{}^3$. We let e denote a single pairing operation. For the baseline scheme, we simply use λ_0 and $\lambda_0{}^3$ to represent a single multiplication and exponentiation over the elliptic curve group $\mathbb{G}$, respectively. Here, we assume the time taken for a single group multiplication is $O(\lambda)$ and the time for a single exponentiation is $O(\lambda^3)$. As an example, if we write $O(X + \lambda \cdot Y)$, then we mean that the runtime for this algorithm is dominated by $O(Y)$ group multiplications (over $\mathbb{G}_1$ or $\mathbb{G}_2$) and X miscellaneous $O(1)$ operations that individually take much less time than single group multiplications or exponentiations.

In Table 9, there are a few operations that we did not count. We did not count multiplications or exponentiations over $\mathbb{G}_T$ because they did not significantly impact runtimes in any of the schemes. We also did not count any addition/subtraction operations over $\mathbb{Z}_p$ because they were only used to compute $s = s_1 + s_2$ and $r = r_1 + r_2$ in the [23] broadcast system. Additionally, runtimes for the setup phase for [23] and [15, $S3.1$] were dominated by choosing N random generators $\in \mathbb{G}_1$. Since we did not define a symbol for choosing a random generator as an "operation", this is not shown in Table 9. When we use big-O notation to describe the time that the setup phase took for these two schemes (see Table 10), we use δ_1 to denote the time required to choose a single random generator in $\mathbb{G}_1$. Other than for these two setup functions, all of the time complexities for the schemes can easily be derived from Table 9. The big-O notation is best to refer to if we want to know which operation(s) are dominating runtimes, but for total runtime details Table 7 is better.

Table 9. Operation counts, where N is the total number of users in the system.

Scheme	Operation Count			
	Setup	KeyGen	Enc	Dec
baseline 2	$\lambda_0^3 \cdot N$	—	$\lambda_0^3 \cdot (|S|+1) + \lambda_0 \cdot |S|$	$2 \cdot \lambda_0^3 + \lambda_0$
[2, S3.1] 3.1	$\lambda_1^3 \cdot (2N-1) + \lambda_2^3 \cdot N + e$	λ_1^3	$\lambda_1 \cdot |S| + \lambda_1^3 + \lambda_2^3$	$\lambda_1 \cdot (|S|-1) + 2 \cdot e$
[2, S3.2] 3.1	$\lambda_1^3 \cdot (2B+A-1) + \lambda_2^3 \cdot B + e$	λ_1^3	$\lambda_1^3 \cdot A + \lambda_1 \cdot |S| + \lambda_2^3$	$\lambda_1 \cdot |S_a| + 2 \cdot e$
[15, S3.1] 3.2	$2 \cdot e + \lambda_1^3 + \lambda_2^3$	$\lambda_1^3 \cdot N + \lambda_2^3$	$\lambda_1 \cdot |S| + \lambda_1^3 + \lambda_2^3$	$\lambda_1 \cdot (|S|-1) + 2 \cdot e$
[23] 3.3	$7 \cdot \lambda_1^3 + 6 \cdot \lambda_2^3 + 2 \cdot e + 2 \cdot \lambda_1$	$\lambda_1^3 \cdot (N+8) + 2 \cdot \lambda_2^3 + 5 \cdot \lambda_1$	$\lambda_1 \cdot (|S|+2) + 6 \cdot \lambda_1^3 + 6 \cdot \lambda_2^3$	$\lambda_1 \cdot (|S|-1) + 9 \cdot e$

Table 10. Theoretical runtimes, where N is the total number of users in the broadcast system.

Scheme	Theoretical Runtime			
	Setup	KeyGen	Enc	Dec
baseline 2	$O(\lambda^3 \cdot N)$	—	$O(\lambda^3 \cdot |S| + \lambda \cdot |S|)$	$O(\lambda)$
[2, S3.1] 3.1	$O(\lambda^3 \cdot N)$	$O(\lambda^3)$	$O(\lambda \cdot |S|)$	$O(\lambda \cdot |S|)$
[2, S3.2] 3.1	$O(\lambda^3 \cdot \sqrt{N})$	$O(\lambda^3)$	$O(N + \lambda^3 \cdot \sqrt{N} + \lambda \cdot |S|)$	$O(\lambda \cdot |S_a|)$
[15, S3.1] 3.2	$O(\delta_1 \cdot N)$	$O(\lambda^3 \cdot N)$	$O(\lambda \cdot |S|)$	$O(\lambda \cdot |S|)$
[23] 3.3	$O(\delta_1 \cdot N)$	$O(\lambda^3 \cdot N)$	$O(\lambda \cdot |S|)$	$O(\lambda \cdot |S|)$

On Identity-Based and Tracing Broadcast Encryption Systems. In the full version [4], we compare the identity-based broadcast encryption systems from [15, S4.1], [15, S4.3.1], and [14, S3.1]. We also compare a wide-range of systems that support tracing, including a private-linear broadcast encryption (PLBE) system from [12], an augmented broadcast encryption (ABBE) system from [13], and a risky broadcast and trace multi-scheme from [24]. We defer these details to [4] for space reasons.

4   Applications of Broadcast Encryption

Online Video Streaming. The most commonly referenced use case for broadcast encryption is online video streaming services like Disney+, Netflix, and Hulu. This category can also include content streamed by individuals on platforms like Twitch and YouTube, online conferencing services like Zoom and Microsoft Teams and even many social media platforms like Facebook, Instagram and Tik-Tok. Users with permission are given access to a myriad of different videos, and ideally bandwidth usage and client side decryption processing requirements need to be minimized so that users can watch the videos in real time and can watch those videos on any device, regardless of processing capability. The user numbers for these services are vast. During the second quarter of 2020 [6], Netflix and

Hulu had at least 190 million and 30 million users respectively. For these media streaming cases, we would recommend using the classic Boneh-Gentry-Waters [2] scheme as it provides the best combination of short ciphertexts and fast decryption times even for large user sets. For $N = 1$ million users, the [2, S3.1] variant provides the best ciphertext size at 96B per ciphertext while decryption takes 350 ms and the [2, S3.2] variant provides the fastest decryption at 1.6 ms with a 32 KB ciphertext. Either of these are reasonable choices, although if the ciphertext size isn't a problem, we'd recommend [2, S3.2] due to its smaller public key size (of 160 KB, where as [2, S3.1] requires 128 MB for 1 million users). For very large user datasets (e.g., in the 190 million range), using [2, S3.2] instead of [2, S3.1] becomes even more important, as the former's public keys scale with $\sqrt{N}$ while the latter scale with N. Both [2] schemes were proven secure in the static security model; if one wants the stronger adaptive security, Waters [23] offers this and small 861B ciphertexts, although the public key sizes grow to 32 MB for $N = 1$ million. Both of the identity-based systems [14,15] require *hours* to decrypt a single ciphertext when N is 1 million, so they are not contenders.

The performance hit from [12] (the best performing traitor tracing scheme) vs. [2] could be worth it for the chance to combat revenue reducers like piracy. For $N = 1$ million users, the decryption time of [12] doubles (over [2, S3.2]) to 3.2 ms while the ciphertext size grows by a factor of 19 to 605 KB – larger, but reasonable on fast networks. The public key size roughly triples to 477 KB. Zhandry's risky traitor tracing scheme [24, S9.3] provides the best ciphertext size for tracing schemes at only 38 4B, but the decryption time explodes to an infeasible 19 h (for $N = 1$ million). Zhandry's nonrisky, post-user expansion compiler version of his scheme (see [4] for details) has decryption times that are comparable to those for [12] and [13] for $N = 1$ million, but the encryption time balloons to over 1 min and the ciphertext size jumps from roughly 600 KB to almost 4 MB (details in [4] when $a = 2/3$.) One potential benefit is that the public/private key sizes of Zhandry's scheme are smaller, but that likely won't offset the additional encryption and space overhead.

Constraint Summary: Needs to scale to 1 million users or more, with small cipertext size overhead and fast (client side) decryption times. Encryption times less of a concern, but traitor tracing may be needed.

Recommendation: Use [2, S3.2] (for fastest decryption and scalable public key size). See Sect. 3.1. If traitor tracing is required, use [12].

Online Game Streaming. Online game streaming is another form of media streaming that is becoming increasingly prevalent. Users receive high quality (resolution and frames per second) game data and give the server data like their keystrokes and mouse clicks in game. This system allows users to play games that have a performance requirement beyond what their client side device is capable of. Currently the way that online game streaming is done is that a server runs the game program remotely for each individual user. However, if adapted a multiplayer game could feasibly send the same stream out to every user maximizing both server-side and client side efficiency.

In comparison to video streaming, online game streaming has a more stringent data speed requirement, as any wasted time could result in a subpar player experience. The most popular service, Nvidia GeForce Now, has around a million users [20], but it is a growing industry and the ceiling for game streaming services could be having user numbers on par with video streaming services. For this case, we would recommend [2, $S3.2$] or [23]. Both schemes have ciphertexts under 1 KB even for 1 million users, but the primary cost for both is a jump in public key size of 128 MB and 32 MB respectively. The [23] offers stronger provable security and low encryption/decryption times, while [2, $S3.2$] offers decryption times that are two orders of magnitude faster but encryption time is roughly triple that of [23].

While the live traitor tracing functionality could be useful, the difference in performance could make a notable difference for users. Perhaps [12] could be used in situations where most of the game data is preloaded on the client side, and the live data is sent out live and unencrypted or from a faster performing scheme like [2]. This could be a hybrid combination, allowing usage of the traitor tracing functionality, and ensuring fast enough performance. We note that the baseline ElGamal scheme takes almost 3 s to encrypt the payload for 1 million users, which likely rules this out for live gaming applications, highlighting the power of broadcast encryption for this setting.

Constraint Summary: Needs to scale to 1 million users or more, with a combination of ciphertext size overhead and (client side) encryption and decryption times that support live interactions. Need to balance benefits of tracing with impact on user experience.

Recommendation: Use [23] (for strong overall balance of security, low size overhead and fast encryption/decryption times) or if more speed in one component is needed, use [2, $S3.2$] (for fastest decryption) or [2, $S3.1$] (for fastest transmission). See Tables 7 and 8. The overhead required for traitor tracing may frustrate the live gaming experience, but if it is needed, a hybrid approach using [12] may work. See [4] for more details.

Live Sports Betting. A novel use case for broadcast encryption arrives with the emergence of live sports betting. Due to the new developments in wireless data speeds with the emergence of 5G technologies, some major companies are developing capabilities for in-person spectators to make bets on their mobile phones throughout a game, utilizing continually updating betting lines given the events happening within the game. Broadcast encryption could be used to quickly send out information to users about how much current bets are worth to cash out and the current betting lines, all in realtime. Additionally, some of these services may include a live broadcast, which could be different from the public broadcast (i.e. a bettors specific broadcast). In this use case, the total speed is the most important factor (making the encryption time more relevant here), and the total number of users is within a pretty regular range ($N = 30,000$ to $70,000$), which is much smaller than the user amounts in some other use cases. In this use case, the total speed is the most important factor (making the encryption time more relevant here), and the total number of users is within a pretty regular range (N = 30,000 to 70,000), which is much smaller than the user amounts in some other use cases. Like with online game streaming, broadcast encryption offers real performance savings over individually encrypting with ElGamal; when $N = 100,000$ the encryption plus decryption time of ElGamal is roughly 10 times that of [15] or [2, $S3.1$]. For the $N \leq 100,000$ range, the public keys of [2, $S3.1$] are 13 MB, while the public keys of [15] are a more tolerable 3MB. Systems [15] and [2, $S3.1$] tie for the shortest ciphertexts at 96 B. The fastest encryption plus decryption time is [15] for this user level (and this holds over a range of sizes of allowed decrypter sets S from 10% to 50% of N), although the difference (a few milliseonds) isn't likely to be observable by a human.

Constraint Summary: Looking for a sweet spot in the 10,000 to 100,000 user range, with a combination of ciphertext size overhead and (server side) encryption and (client side) decryption times that support real-time interactions.

Recommendation: Use [15] (for best ciphertext size, best sum of encryption and decryption time, and public key size tolerable for $N \leq 100,000$). See Sects. 3.2. The overhead required for traitor tracing may frustrate the live betting experience, but if needed, a hybrid approach using [12] and [15] may work.

Distributor Limited Applications. In the above applications, we assume that the distributor (e.g., Netflix, YouTube) has large computing resources at its disposal. However, we also anticipate use cases where distributor performance becomes a bottleneck (e.g., where a person is streaming video from their smartphone to a group). A distributor limited implementation could be relevant in both the private and public sector. Within the private sector, a company manager who wants to broadcast a specific message to his employees could do so using broadcast encryption. With the presumed post-social-distancing increase in online work, consistent, secure communication between manager and employees could be increasingly important with a decline in face-to-face communication.

Within the public and military sector, these same benefits apply. In the public sector, however, having differing levels of access and the ability to revoke access to messages and live communications is more important. For example, if a broadcast encryption system is used to send out orders to a group, and one of the recipient devices is captured then revocation is necessary. Additionally, traitor tracing functionality could be especially valuable.

Thus, in the case of a direct peer-to-many-peer type of communication, the performance of the distributor system becomes relevant, thus making the times for the Setup, KeyGen and Encrypt function times more critical. In this situation, a simple recommendation is harder to make. [2, $S3.2$] for example, performs the best in the case of online video streaming, but if one person was streaming video from their smartphone directly to many peers, the encryption performance of [2, S3.2] is much worse than [2, S3.1] and [15, S3.1]. Due to that constraint, if there are limited resources for the distributor, using [2, S3.2] isn't a good choice. If peers are less than 100 K, in a situation with a distributor bottleneck we'd recommend either [2, S3.1] or [15, S3.1]. The latter has much better performance in terms of encryption times, but the prior is orders of magnitude faster during KeyGen. In a situation where many keys are regularly generated, [2, S3.1] would be preferable, but in cases where keys are generated less often [15, S3.1] will have the best performance, allowing the fastest encryption.

The same consideration can be made for the traitor tracing schemes. When the amount of users is around 1,000, [13] slightly outperforms [12] in both setup times and encryption times, with roughly the same decryption times and notably worse KeyGen times. In a situation with distributor performance restraints, where many keys are regularly generated, [12] will perform better. In a situation where keys are generated less often and there are less than 1,000 users, [13] can perform better. However, both of these schemes are outperformed by the baseline (individual encryption to each peer) until about about the 10,000 user level.

Constraint Summary: For $N \leq 100,000$ user range, looking to optimize the distributor functions without sacrificing much data transfer time or client performance.

Recommendation: Use [2, S3.1] (if need to generate keys often) or [15, S3.1] (otherwise). See Tables 7 and 8. If traitor tracing is required for under 10,000 users, the baseline (individual encryption) will likely outperform any of the tracing broadcast schemes. If traitor tracing is required for over 10,000 users, use [12]. See [4] for more details.

Acknowledgments. The authors are grateful to Mark Zhandry for helpful interactions regarding his work [24] and Brent Waters for helpful discussions regarding prior work in broadcast encryption.

References

1. Bethencourt, J., Sahai, A., Waters, B.: Ciphertext-policy attribute-based encryption. In: IEEE Symposium on Security and Privacy, pp. 321–334 (2007)
2. Boneh, D., Gentry, C., Waters, B.: Collusion resistant broadcast encryption with short ciphertexts and private keys. In: Shoup, V. (ed.) CRYPTO 2005. LNCS, vol. 3621, pp. 258–275. Springer, Heidelberg (2005). https://doi.org/10.1007/11535218_16
3. Boneh, D., Sahai, A., Waters, B.: Fully collusion resistant traitor tracing with short ciphertexts and private keys. In: Vaudenay, S. (ed.) EUROCRYPT 2006. LNCS, vol. 4004, pp. 573–592. Springer, Heidelberg (2006). https://doi.org/10.1007/11761679_34
4. Chhatrapati, A., Hohenberger, S., Trombo, J., Vusirikala, S.: A performance evaluation of pairing-based broadcast encryption systems. Cryptology ePrint Archive, Report 2021/1526 (2021). https://ia.cr/2021/1526

5. Company, T.W.D.: Fiscal year 2019 annual financial report (2019). https://thewaltdisneycompany.com/app/uploads/2020/01/2019-Annual-Report.pdf
6. Corporation, N.: Netflix Q2 2020 shareholder letter, 16 July 2020. https://s22.q4cdn.com/959853165/files/doc_financials/2020/q2/FINAL-Q2-20-Shareholder-Letter-V3-with-Tables.pdf
7. Delerablée, C.: Identity-based broadcast encryption with constant size ciphertexts and private keys. In: Kurosawa, K. (ed.) ASIACRYPT 2007. LNCS, vol. 4833, pp. 200–215. Springer, Heidelberg (2007). https://doi.org/10.1007/978-3-540-76900-2_12
8. Dolev, D., Dwork, C., Naor, M.: Nonmalleable cryptography. SIAM J. Comput. **30**(2), 391–437 (2000)
9. Fiat, A., Naor, M.: Broadcast encryption. In: Stinson, D.R. (ed.) CRYPTO 1993. LNCS, vol. 773, pp. 480–491. Springer, Heidelberg (1994). https://doi.org/10.1007/3-540-48329-2_40
10. Fujisaki, E., Okamoto, T.: How to enhance the security of public-key encryption at minimum cost. In: Imai, H., Zheng, Y. (eds.) PKC 1999. LNCS, vol. 1560, pp. 53–68. Springer, Heidelberg (1999). https://doi.org/10.1007/3-540-49162-7_5
11. Gamal, T.E.: A public key cryptosystem and a signature scheme based on discrete logarithms. IEEE Trans. Inf. Theory **31**(4), 469–472 (1985). https://doi.org/10.1109/TIT.1985.1057074
12. Garg, S., Kumarasubramanian, A., Sahai, A., Waters, B.: Building efficient fully collusion-resilient traitor tracing and revocation schemes. IACR Cryptol. ePrint Arch. **2009**, 532 (2009). http://eprint.iacr.org/2009/532
13. Garg, S., Kumarasubramanian, A., Sahai, A., Waters, B.: Building efficient fully collusion-resilient traitor tracing and revocation schemes. In: ACM CCS, pp. 121–130. ACM (2010). https://doi.org/10.1145/1866307.1866322
14. Ge, A., Wei, P.: Identity-based broadcast encryption with efficient revocation. In: Lin, D., Sako, K. (eds.) PKC 2019. LNCS, vol. 11442, pp. 405–435. Springer, Cham (2019). https://doi.org/10.1007/978-3-030-17253-4_14
15. Gentry, C., Waters, B.: Adaptive security in broadcast encryption systems (with short ciphertexts). In: Joux, A. (ed.) EUROCRYPT 2009. LNCS, vol. 5479, pp. 171–188. Springer, Heidelberg (2009). https://doi.org/10.1007/978-3-642-01001-9_10
16. Goldwasser, S., Micali, S.: Probabilistic encryption. J. Comput. Syst. Sci. **28**(2), 270–299 (1984)
17. Goyal, R., Koppula, V., Russell, A., Waters, B.: Risky traitor tracing and new differential privacy negative results. In: Shacham, H., Boldyreva, A. (eds.) CRYPTO 2018. LNCS, vol. 10991, pp. 467–497. Springer, Cham (2018). https://doi.org/10.1007/978-3-319-96884-1_16
18. Goyal, R., Koppula, V., Waters, B.: Lockable obfuscation. In: FOCS, pp. 612–621 (2017)
19. Naor, M., Yung, M.: Public-key cryptosystems provably secure against chosen ciphertext attacks. In: STOC, pp. 427–437 (1990)
20. Nvidia: 2020 Nvidia Corporation Annual Review (2020). https://s22.q4cdn.com/364334381/files/doc_financials/2020/ar/2020-nvidia-annualreport-content-r25-web-144dpi-combined.pdf
21. Rackoff, C., Simon, D.R.: Non-interactive zero-knowledge proof of knowledge and chosen ciphertext attack. In: Feigenbaum, J. (ed.) CRYPTO 1991. LNCS, vol. 576, pp. 433–444. Springer, Heidelberg (1992). https://doi.org/10.1007/3-540-46766-1_35

22. Sakai, R., Furukawa, J.: Identity-based broadcast encryption. IACR Cryptol. ePrint Arch. (2007). http://eprint.iacr.org/2007/217
23. Waters, B.: Dual system encryption: realizing fully secure IBE and HIBE under simple assumptions. In: Halevi, S. (ed.) CRYPTO 2009. LNCS, vol. 5677, pp. 619–636. Springer, Heidelberg (2009). https://doi.org/10.1007/978-3-642-03356-8_36
24. Zhandry, M.: New techniques for traitor tracing: Size $N^{1/3}$ and more from pairings. In: Micciancio, D., Ristenpart, T. (eds.) CRYPTO 2020. LNCS, vol. 12170, pp. 652–682. Springer, Cham (2020). https://doi.org/10.1007/978-3-030-56784-2_22

An Optimized GHV-Type HE Scheme: Simpler, Faster, and More Versatile

Liang Zhao[1]($\boxtimes$), Ze Chen[1], Liqun Chen[2], and Xinyi Huang[3]

[1] School of Cyber Science and Engineering, Sichuan University, Chengdu, China
zhaoliangjapan@scu.edu.cn
[2] Surrey Centre for Cyber Security, University of Surrey, Guildford, UK
liqun.chen@surrey.ac.uk
[3] Fujian Provincial Key Laboratory of Network Security and Cryptology, College
of Computer and Cyber Security, Fujian Normal University, Fuzhou, China
xyhuang@fjnu.edu.cn

Abstract. In this paper we present an optimized variant of Gentry, Halevi and Vaikuntanathan (GHV)'s Homomorphic Encryption (HE) scheme. Our scheme is appreciably more efficient than the original GHV scheme without losing its merits of the (multi-key) homomorphic property and matrix encryption property. In this research, we first measure the density for the trapdoor pairs that are created by using Alwen and Peikert's trapdoor generation algorithm and Micciancio and Peikert's trapdoor generation algorithm, respectively, and use the measurement result to precisely discuss the time and space complexity of the corresponding GHV instantiations. We then propose a generic GHV-type construction with several optimizations that improve the time and space efficiency from the original GHV scheme. In particular, our scheme can achieve asymptotically optimal time complexity and avoid generating and storing the inverse of the used trapdoor. Finally, we present an instantiation that, by using a new set of (lower) bound parameters, has the smaller sizes of the key and ciphertext than the original GHV scheme.

Keywords: Homomorphic encryption · LWE · Matrix operations

1 Introduction

Background and Related Work. Homomorphic Encryption (HE) allows running operations on ciphertexts so that decryptions match the results from the corresponding operations on plaintexts. HE has many interesting applications in the real-world, e.g., the computational private information retrieval [6], and the indistinguishability obfuscation [5]. Since introduced by Rivest, Adleman and Dertouzos [24] in 1978, the HE research has a long history in the modern cryptography. Early HE systems focused on evaluating asymmetric encryption and supports only one operation over encrypted data, either addition or multiplication. This type of HE is referred to as partially HE. Typical examples involve the

The full version of this work appears in [28].

© Springer Nature Switzerland AG 2022
G. Ateniese and D. Venturi (Eds.): ACNS 2022, LNCS 13269, pp. 45–64, 2022.
https://doi.org/10.1007/978-3-031-09234-3_3

additively HE schemes: Goldwasser-Micali and Paillier, and the multiplicatively HE schemes: RSA and ElGamal.

Breaking through the single operation homomorphism took a long time. The first step forward was given in 2005 by Boneh, Goh and Nissim (BGN for short) [6], who presented an additively HE scheme supporting one multiplication. An HE scheme that can evaluate two types of operations but only for a subset of operations is referred to as a Somewhat Homomorphic Encryption (SHE) scheme. The BGN scheme is the first SHE scheme. Breaking the security of this scheme is as hard as solving the subgroup-membership problem in composite-order groups that admit bilinear maps. Later Gentry, Halevi and Vaikuntanathan (GHV for short) in 2010 [10] proposed an additively HE scheme supporting one "direct" matrix multiplication. Notably, a "direct" matrix multiplication here means an ordinary matrix multiplication that does not require any extra computation. Security of their scheme is based on the standard Learning With Errors (LWE) assumption (see Sect. 2.1). The GHV scheme can be regarded as an improvement of the BGN scheme and has several inherent advantages (see Sect. 2.3 on details of the GHV scheme). Specifically, one significant advantage is that there is a worst-case/average-case classical reduction from the standard LWE problem to the GHV security. Another important advantage is that the GHV scheme can encrypt messages from a large space (i.e., any matrix ring) and has no restriction for the output size. Moreover, the GHV scheme holds much of the flexibility of the LWE-based cryptosystem, e.g., it can be made identity-based and leakage-resilient. In a nutshell, the GHV cryptosystem is still an outstanding SHE scheme.

The first theoretically feasible construction capable of supporting arbitrary computations over ciphertexts, which is referred to as Fully HE (FHE), was introduced by Gentry in 2009 [9]. Since then, many FHE schemes have been proposed (e.g., [4,7,12,14,25,27]). Generally speaking, the development of FHE until now involves three generations. Typical examples of the first generation are Gentry's initial scheme based on ideal lattices [9] and van Dijk et al.'s proposal employing integer arithmetic [25]. The second generation includes Brakerski and Vaikuntanathan's constructions [4,7] that use new techniques to control the growth of noise. The third generation of FHE originates from the scheme of Gentry, Sahai and Waters (GSW for short) [12], which exhibits a somewhat distinct noise growth pattern. Although there is a great progress for the theoretical and practical improvements of FHE, for many applications, especially the applications requiring a single algebraic operation, this type of encryption is currently impractical because of the big key size, the large ciphertext expansion and the long evaluation time [8,22].

Besides the GHV scheme, there are two asymmetric HE schemes that can encrypt matrices and support homomorphic matrix addition and multiplication. The first one was proposed in 2015 by Hiromasa, Abe, and Okamoto (HAO for short) [14], and their scheme is a matrix extension of the GSW-FHE scheme [12]. Security of the HAO scheme can be reduced from the standard LWE assumption, while an additional special circular security assumption is necessary. The homomorphic matrix multiplication does not correspond to the "direct" matrix multiplication and needs to employ a randomized function. In 2018, Wang, Wang, Xue, and Huang (WWXH for short) [27] presented another FHE scheme for encrypting matrices. Security of their scheme is based on hardness of the standard LWE problem, and the size of ciphertext matrices is smaller than that of the HAO scheme. However, for the WWXH scheme, the tensor product is largely employed to perform the homomorphic matrix multiplication, and the corresponding computational cost is $\Theta(m^4)$ for $m \times m$ input matrices. Thus, the complexity of using this scheme for some homomorphic computations (e.g., homomorphic computations over nondeterministic finite automata and linear algebra) is very large and not lower than that of the HAO scheme for the same computations. Some details of these two matrix-FHE schemes are listed in Table 1. Notably, total computational costs of both schemes are $\mathcal{O}(m^3)$.

Motivation and Our Target: Building a More Efficient GHV-Type HE Scheme. Based on the above descriptions, asymmetric matrix-FHE schemes [14,27] currently do not match with very efficient cloud computing-related applications that only run a single (linear algebra) operation. A typical example is the private and verifiable delegation of linear algebra [17] that only allows a client to run $\mathcal{O}(m^{c'})$ computation for matrices of large size $m \times m$, where $c' \in [2,3[$ is close to 2. SHE schemes are much more efficient and suitable for many applications. In particular, the GHV scheme has a sequence of desirable properties. Allowing encryption of a square matrix from any matrix ring in one operation and supporting the "direct" homomorphic matrix multiplication can make this scheme match with applications requiring the linear algebra computation over any ring, and be a powerful tool for the very efficient verifiable linear algebra computation. Although the construction of the GHV scheme is elegant, it seems that there are some optimizations left in its performance, and these optimizations can make it more versatile. This brings the main question that we want to answer in this work: *Can we create a more efficient GHV-Type HE scheme?* In more detail, this question involves the following three aspects:

- The new GHV-type HE scheme has lower time complexity, and in particular it is suitable for applications only permitting efficient privacy protection and verification (e.g., the private and verifiable delegation of linear algebra).
- The new GHV-type HE scheme has lower space complexity. To achieve this we need to first figure out whether some key employed by the original GHV scheme is not needed for the improved one.
- The new GHV-type HE scheme has smaller key and ciphertext sizes than those of the original GHV scheme.

Our Results. In this work, we propose an efficient GHV-type HE scheme together with optimized parameters. Security of our proposal is still based on the standard LWE assumption. Specifically, our contributions are four folds:

First Result (Sect. 3): Density of Trapdoor Matrix Pairs. Trapdoor generation algorithms (e.g., [1,3,19]) play a big role in advanced lattice-based cryptographic primitives. They generate a pair of matrices $(\mathbf{A}^t, \mathbf{T}^t)$, i.e., $\mathbf{A}^t$ is an (almost) uniformly random matrix and $\mathbf{T}^t$ is the corresponding trapdoor that is in the form of a nonsingular square matrix with short integer vectors. Some significant parameters related to the matrix pair, i.e., the lattice dimension and the quality of the trapdoor, generally have been explored when the corresponding trapdoor construction was given. In an asymmetric encryption scheme, $(\mathbf{A}^t, \mathbf{T}^t)$ can be used as the public and secret keys. In particular, since the short basis $\mathbf{T}^t$ and its inversion $(\mathbf{T}^t)^{-1}$ used in the encryption schemes may multiply by matrices over a matrix ring, a natural question is how to evaluate the corresponding computational cost. To answer this question, we first introduce the concept of the density of a (trapdoor) matrix for matrix multiplication and give its definition. Actually, the density of a (trapdoor) matrix is measured by the number of nonzero elements of a matrix needed for a single matrix multiplication. Then, we take $(\mathbf{T}^t, (\mathbf{T}^t)^{-1})$ respectively generated by Alwen and Peikert's trapdoor sampling algorithm (APTrapSamp for short) [3] and by Micciancio and Peikert's trapdoor sampling algorithm (MPTrapSamp for short) [19] as targets and analyze their concrete density. Notably, the non-deterministically constructed components of these two trapdoor matrix pairs become the hard nut of the corresponding density analyses. Technically, we thus employ the matrix decomposition to simplify the complex components, which makes us simply focus on exploring components with the deterministic distribution. Using our concrete decompositions, for $(\mathbf{T}^t, (\mathbf{T}^t)^{-1})$ generated by APTrapSamp and MPTrapSamp, the analyses give accurate estimates on their density (see Lemma 4 to 7).

Second Result (Sects. 3 and 4): More Accurate Efficiency Analyses. For the GHV-HE scheme, although the approximate result of its computational cost has been given in [10], the more accurate estimate on the computational cost is important, in particular for finding applications which the cryptosystem can be plugged directly into. Hence, we carefully analyze the encryption and decryption procedures of the GHV scheme using APTrapSamp and MPTrapSamp, and present accurate results on their computational cost and space cost (see Theorem 2 to 5). Technically, our analysis for the decryption procedure is based on the idea that multiplying matrices over a matrix ring with $\mathbf{T}^t$ (resp. $(\mathbf{T}^t)^{-1}$) is equivalent to multiplying matrices over a matrix ring with the decomposition form of $\mathbf{T}^t$ (resp. $(\mathbf{T}^t)^{-1}$). This implies that results on the density of $\mathbf{T}^t$ and $(\mathbf{T}^t)^{-1}$ are used for the efficiency analyses of the decryption procedure. We also employ the Hoeffding's inequality to estimate a (near-)lower bound of the computational cost of the decryption procedure. Of course, the same idea is used to give the (time and space) efficiency analyses on our optimized GHV-type scheme (see Theorem 10).

Third Result (Sect. 4): Simpler Construction and Optimizations. Towards addressing the question of the above section in a systematic way, we first propose a generic GHV-type construction that removes the expensive matrix inversion computation for $(\mathbf{T}^t)^{-1}$ and the multiplication by $(\mathbf{T}^t)^{-1}$ on decryption. In our generic construction, a sparse matrix $\tilde{\mathbf{T}}$ that is easily built is employed to recover the plaintext message (see Sect. 4.2 on $\tilde{\mathbf{T}}$). Notice that, $\tilde{\mathbf{T}}$ is constructed deterministically, which means that it actually can be regarded as a "public" key for decryption. Moreover, our generic construction has an additional benefit for the multiplication by $\mathbf{T}^t$ on decryption. That is, a plaintext message can be recovered by multiplying with part of $\mathbf{T}^t$ instead of $\mathbf{T}^t$, which further reduces the computational cost and space cost of decryption. Then we present some simple optimizations on speeding up the matrix multiplication used in our generic construction (see Algorithms 2 and 3). For our optimizations, only element-wise additions are employed to achieve the multiplication by part of $\mathbf{T}^t$ and $\tilde{\mathbf{T}}$ on decryption, and a random, short component of $\mathbf{T}^t$ is used as the unique secret key (i.e., the component matrix $\mathbf{R}$). This implies that our optimizations guarantee that any instantiation of our GHV-type scheme using APTrapSamp-like trapdoor generation algorithms has the asymptotically optimal time complexity and storage size of the secret key. Surprisingly, we achieve these efficiency improvements without having a negative effect on the security of the GHV-type scheme.

Fourth Result (Sect. 4): Tighter Parameters. To ensure that our GHV-type instantiation using APTrapSamp enjoys correctness and the same homomorphism as the original GHV instantiation using APTrapSamp holds, we show new bounds for the modulus q and the lattice dimension m (see Theorems 6 and 7). In particular, the parameter bounds that we establish are lower than those of the original GHV instantiation. Since q has a direct impact on the key and ciphertext sizes, this means that sizes of elements of the public key and ciphertext can be smaller than those of the original GHV instantiation. Specifically, we first give a parameter setting for the case that our GHV-type instantiation only supports polynomially many additions (see Theorem 6). Then we present a parameter setting for the case that our GHV-type instantiation can permit polynomial number of additions and one multiplication (see Theorem 7).

Table 1. Comparisons of asymmetric LWE-based matrix-HE schemes with equal parameters n and m satisfying $n \ll m$.

Scheme	Classification	Homomorphism		Encryption Time	Decryption Time
		$\oplus^\dagger$	$\odot^\dagger$		
GHV(APTrapSamp) [10]	SHE	✓	✓	$\mathcal{O}(nm^2)$	$\mathcal{O}(m^3)$
GHV(MPTrapSamp)*	SHE	✓	✓	$\mathcal{O}(nm^2)$	$\mathcal{O}(m^3)$
HAO [14]	FHE	✓	✗	$\tilde{\mathcal{O}}(nm^2)$	$\mathcal{O}(m^3)$
WWXH [27]	FHE	✓	✗	$\tilde{\mathcal{O}}(nm^2)$	$\mathcal{O}(m^3)$
oGHV(APTrapSamp) [this paper]	SHE	✓	✓	$\mathcal{O}(nm^2)$	$\tilde{\mathcal{O}}(nm^2)$
oGHV(MPTrapSamp) [this paper]	SHE	✓	✓	$\mathcal{O}(nm^2)$	$\tilde{\mathcal{O}}(nm^2)$

* For GHV(MPTrapSamp), MPTrapSamp is used in the original GHV scheme.
† $\oplus$ and $\odot$: "Direct" matrix addition and multiplication between the input ciphertexts

Comparisons and Applications. A comparison of our optimized GHV (oGHV for short) scheme with the GHV scheme and other asymmetric matrix-(F)HE schemes is shown in Table 1, where we assume that all the schemes make use of the same security parameter n and plaintext matrix size $m \times m$. Notice that n and m are not the same; indeed, typically we have $m = \Theta(n \lg q)$, where $q = \mathsf{poly}(n)$.

Clearly, based on the above comparisons, we believe that our oGHV scheme can be plugged in as a "black box" to replace the original GHV scheme and deliver significant efficiency benefits in such applications discussed by Gentry et al. [10], e.g., electronic election protocols, private information retrieval protocols and identity-based encryption. Of course, the oGHV scheme may be used as a drop-in replacement in some other typical applications such as two-party computation protocols [16], graph encryption schemes supporting approximate shortest distance queries [18] and the protocol for private regular-expression searches on encrypted data [26]. Here we want to highlight that, compared with the GHV scheme, our oGHV scheme opens the door to more efficient real-world privacy-preserving applications. A such example is the private and verifiable delegation of linear algebra, which is always an important research subject in cryptography. Although Mohassel [17] has given the GHV scheme based delegation protocols for some linear algebra problems such as matrix multiplication and matrix inversion, as shown in Table 1, the GHV scheme actually should be excluded from consideration due to the "heavy" decryption performing roughly $\mathcal{O}(m^3)$ computations. Since our oGHV scheme achieves the desirable improvements in terms of the efficiency, it can be a natural match for private delegations of some linear algebra problems and even specific computations related to linear algebra.

2   Preliminaries

Notations. Throughout this paper, we use capital letters (e.g., X, Y) for random variables and probability distributions, standard letters (e.g., x, y) for scalars, and calligraphic letters (e.g., $\mathcal{X}$, $\mathcal{Y}$) for sets. We denote (column) vectors by standard bold letters (e.g., $\mathbf{x}$, $\mathbf{y}$) and matrices by capital bold letters (e.g., $\mathbf{X}$, $\mathbf{Y}$). For a matrix $\mathbf{X}$ over any ring, the ith column of $\mathbf{X}$ is denoted by $\mathbf{x}_i$, the ith element of a vector $\mathbf{x}$ is denoted by x_i, and the ith element of the jth column of $\mathbf{X}$ is denoted by $x_{i,j}$. $N_{\mathbf{X}}$ is a random variable (or probability distribution) on the number of nonzero elements of $\mathbf{X}$. We use $\mathbf{X}^t$ to denote the transpose of $\mathbf{X}$. The ith standard basis vector is denoted by $\mathbf{e}_i$. $\lg$ refers to the base 2 logarithm. We use $[x]$ to denote the set $\{1, 2, \cdots, x\}$. $x \xleftarrow{\$} \mathcal{X}$ is considered as sampling an element x from a finite set $\mathcal{X}$ uniformly at random, and $x \leftarrow X$ refers to sampling an element x according to a probability distribution X. For a finite set $\mathcal{X}$, we denote the uniform distribution over $\mathcal{X}$ by $\mathcal{U}(\mathcal{X})$. We denote the binomial distribution with parameters $\rho \in [0, 1]$ and $m \in \mathbb{N}_+$ by $\mathsf{Bin}_{\rho,m}$, where $\Pr[\mathsf{Bin}_{\rho,1} \neq 0] = \rho$ and $\Pr[\mathsf{Bin}_{\rho,1} = 0] = 1 - \rho$. We denote the discrete Gaussian (error) distribution over $\mathbb{Z}_q$ by $\bar{\Psi}_\beta(q)$ that may be generated by sampling $y \leftarrow \frac{1}{\beta} \exp(-\pi(\frac{x}{\beta})^2)$ and outputting $\lfloor q \cdot y \rfloor \pmod{q}$, where $\beta > 0$ and $q \geq 2$. $X \sim D$ denotes that a random variable X follows a probability distribution D. For two distribution ensembles $X \stackrel{\text{def}}{=} \{X_n\}$ and $Y \stackrel{\text{def}}{=} \{Y_n\}$ indexed by $n \in \mathbb{N}_+$, $X \stackrel{s}{\approx} Y$ refers to the statistical indistinguishability between X and Y. $x \pmod{q}$ is considered as mapping x into the interval $]-\frac{q}{2}, \frac{q}{2}]$. Let $\mathbf{x} = (x'_1, x'_2, \ldots, x'_n) \in \{0, 1\}^n$ be the binary representation of x. Then we call $\mathsf{bwt}(x) = \|\mathbf{x}\|_1 = \#\{i \in [n] | x'_i \neq 0\}$ the (Hamming) weight of x. Let t_a, t_m and t_g denote the running time of the (modulo) addition, (modulo) multiplication and discrete Gaussian sampling over the integers, respectively.

We also use the following simplified notations in this paper. Throughout, we denote the security parameter by $n \in \mathbb{N}_+$, and most parameters are functions of n, e.g., $m_1, m_2, m, q = \mathsf{poly}(n)$, $\beta = \frac{1}{\mathsf{poly}(n)}$ and $c = c(n) > 0$, where $\mathsf{poly}(n)$ denotes some polynomial function in n. Thus, we often omit n for the simplified notations. Moreover, overwhelming probability means that the probability is $1 - \psi$, where ψ is negligible in n.

2.1 Cryptographic Problem

We present below a famous hard learning problem, i.e., the Learning with Errors (LWE) problem, which has proven to be a rich and versatile source of many (post-quantum) cryptographic primitives.

Definition 1 (LWE [10,23]). *Let n, m, q be positive integers, $\mathbf{s} \in \mathbb{Z}_q^n$ be a secret vector, and χ be a probability distribution over $\mathbb{Z}_q$. We denote the LWE distribution by $L_{\mathbf{s}, \chi, q}$ that is the probability distribution over $\mathbb{Z}_q^{m \times n} \times \mathbb{Z}_q^m$ given by choosing $\mathbf{A} \xleftarrow{\$} \mathbb{Z}_q^{m \times n}$, sampling a vector $\mathbf{x} \leftarrow \chi^m$ and outputting $(\mathbf{A}, \langle \mathbf{A}, \mathbf{s} \rangle + \mathbf{x}) = (\mathbf{A}, \mathbf{b}) \in \mathbb{Z}_q^{m \times n} \times \mathbb{Z}_q^m$.*

The decision LWE problem $\mathsf{dLWE}(n, m, q, \chi)$ is the problem of distinguishing whether a sample $(\mathbf{A}, \mathbf{b})$ is drawn from $L_{\mathbf{s}, \chi, q}$ or uniformly at random from $\mathbb{Z}_q^{m \times n} \times \mathbb{Z}_q^m$. The search LWE problem $\mathsf{sLWE}(n, m, q, \chi)$ is the problem of finding the secret $\mathbf{s}$ from a sample $(\mathbf{A}, \langle \mathbf{A}, \mathbf{s} \rangle + \mathbf{x})$ drawn according to $L_{\mathbf{s}, \chi, q}$.

In particular, χ is generally the discrete Gaussian distribution $\overline{\Psi}_\beta(q)$ [15]. For the LWE version defined with $\overline{\Psi}_\beta(q)$, it is known as the "standard form". About the hardness of the standard LWE problem, there have been several results, e.g., [21,23]. Specifically, Regev [23] first proved that solving $\mathsf{sLWE}(n, m, q, \beta)$ efficiently is as hard as finding a quantum solution for approximating certain worst-case lattice problems, i.e., the decision version of the Shortest Vector Problem (GAPSVP) and the Shortest Independent Vectors Problem (SIVP). Regev [23] also showed that $\mathsf{dLWE}(n, m, q, \beta)$ can be equivalent to (worst-case) $\mathsf{sLWE}(n, m, q, \beta)$ for a prime modulus $q \in [2, \mathsf{poly}(n)]$, with a loss of up to a $\mathsf{poly}(n) \cdot q$ factor in m. Then, Peikert [21] gave that solving $\mathsf{sLWE}(n, m, q, \beta)$ efficiently is (at least) as hard as approximating GAPSVP (and a GAPSVP variant) in the worst case via a classical (PPT) reduction with similar parameters. Moreover, based on the above Regev's search-to-decision reduction, Peikert [21] provided a classical foundation for the hardness of $\mathsf{dLWE}(n, m, q, \beta)$. Notice that $\mathbf{s}$ can be sampled from the error distribution (i.e., $\overline{\Psi}_\beta(q)^n$) without any loss in security [2]. In what follows, since (post-quantum) cryptographic applications are typically based on $\mathsf{dLWE}(n, m, q, \beta)$, we summarize Regev and Peikert's results for the decision variant.

Lemma 1 (Theorem 1.1 in [23], Theorem 3.3 in [21]). Let n be a positive integer, $\beta > 0$ and $q \in \mathbb{N}_+$ be a product of co-prime numbers, i.e., $q = \prod q_i$, where $\forall i \in \mathbb{N}_+$ $q_i = \mathsf{poly}(n)$. For $\beta q > 2\sqrt{n}$, if there is an efficient algorithm solving $\mathsf{dLWE}(n, m, q, \beta)$, there is an efficient quantum algorithm running in time $\mathsf{poly}(n)$ to approximate GAPSVP and SIVP on n-dimensional lattices in the worst case to within $\tilde{\mathcal{O}}(\frac{n}{\beta})$ factors, and an efficient classical algorithm running in time $\mathsf{poly}(n)$ to approximate a ζ-to-ζ' GAPSVP variant $\mathsf{GAPSVP}_{\zeta,\zeta'}$ on n-dimensional lattices in the worst case to within $\zeta = \tilde{\mathcal{O}}(q\sqrt{n})$ and $\zeta' = \tilde{\mathcal{O}}(\frac{n}{\beta})$ factors.

2.2 Trapdoor Sampling Algorithms

Here we recall two significant trapdoor generation algorithms for cryptographic lattices, which are inspired by Ajtai's initial work [1]. The first proposal is the Alwen and Peikert trapdoor generator [3], denoted by APTrapSamp. This randomized algorithm outputs a hard random lattice $\mathbf{A}^t \in \mathbb{Z}_q^{n \times m}$ together with some short orthogonal basis (i.e., trapdoor) $\mathbf{T}^t \in \mathbb{Z}^{m \times m}$ of the lattice $\Lambda_q^\perp(\mathbf{A}^t)$, where $m = \Theta(n \lg q)$. The block structures of $\mathbf{A}^t$ and $\mathbf{T}^t$ are shown in Fig. 1(a), where $\mathbf{A}_1 \overset{\$}{\leftarrow} \mathbb{Z}_q^{n \times m_1}$ and $m_1 + m_2 = m$. In particular, APTrapSamp involves two concrete algorithms. Compared with Alwen and Peikert's first algorithm, the second algorithm, denoted by APSTrapSamp, can be regarded as an optimized algorithm with respect to the lattice dimension and the quality of the trapdoor. Then, APSTrapSamp is more suitable for efficient cryptographic applications. The second type of trapdoor generator is introduced by Micciancio and Peikert [19], which is the current state of the art in the trapdoor generation. This randomized algorithm, denoted by MPTrapSamp, can output a hard random lattice $\mathbf{A}^t \in \mathbb{Z}_q^{n \times m}$ together with a sufficiently "short" integer matrix $\mathbf{R} \in \mathbb{Z}^{m_1 \times m_2}$ as the gadget-based trapdoor (with tag (e.g., $\mathbf{I}$) over $\mathbb{Z}_q^{n \times n}$), where $m = \Theta(n \lg q)$ and $m_1 + m_2 = m$. MPTrapSamp includes the statistical instantiation, denoted by MPSTrapSamp, and the computational instantiation. In particular, the statistically secure trapdoor construction from MPSTrapSamp is the better choice of cryptographic applications. Moreover, MPSTrapSamp may generate a good basis $\mathbf{T}^t$ for $\Lambda^\perp(\mathbf{A}^t)$ from knowledge of $\mathbf{R}$, which implies that MPSTrapSamp can also serve as a "traditional" trapdoor sampling algorithm. The corresponding block structures of $\mathbf{A}^t$ and $\mathbf{T}^t$ are given in Fig. 1(b), where $\mathbf{A}_1 \overset{\$}{\leftarrow} \mathbb{Z}_q^{n \times m_1}$. Notice that, since the block structure of $\mathbf{T}^t$ generated by MPSTrapSamp is similar to that of the trapdoor from APSTrapSamp, we refer to the "traditional" MPSTrapSamp as the APTrapSamp-type trapdoor sampling algorithm. In what follows, we state some consequences related to APSTrapSamp and MPSTrapSamp. For more details, please refer to [3,19]. In the full version of this paper [28, Appendix A.1], we also present details of component matrices $\mathbf{G} \in \mathbb{Z}^{m_1 \times m_2}(\mathbf{G} \in \mathbb{Z}_q^{n \times m_2}), \mathbf{P} \in \mathbb{Z}^{m_2 \times m_1}, \mathbf{U} \in \mathbb{Z}^{m_2 \times m_2}$ and $\mathbf{R} \in \mathbb{Z}^{m_1 \times m_2}$ generated by APSTrapSamp and MPSTrapSamp, respectively.

Lemma 2 (Theorem 3.2 in [3], Lemma 5.3 in [19]). There are PPT randomized algorithms APTrapSamp and MPSTrapSamp that, on input 1^n, $q \geq 2$ and $m = \Theta(n \lg q)$, can generate matrices $\mathbf{A}^t \in \mathbb{Z}_q^{n \times m}$ and $\mathbf{T}^t \in \mathbb{Z}^{m \times m}$ such that

- $\mathbf{A}^t$ is statistically close to uniform over $\mathbb{Z}_q^{n \times m}$.
- $\mathbf{T}^t$ is a "small" invertible matrix. In particular, the Euclidean norm of all columns of $\mathbf{T}^t$ from APSTrapSamp is bounded by $\mathcal{O}(n \lg q)$, where the constant hidden in the $\mathcal{O}(\cdot)$ is at most 20.
- $\mathbf{TA} = \mathbf{0} \pmod{q}$.

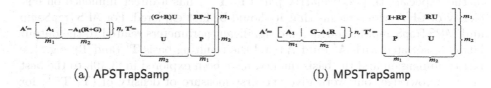

(a) APSTrapSamp   (b) MPSTrapSamp

Fig. 1. Block structures of $\mathbf{A}^t$ and $\mathbf{T}^t$.

2.3 The Gentry-Halevi-Vaikuntanathan Encryption Scheme

The GHV scheme [10] is a public-key encryption scheme for encrypting matrices over any matrix ring $\mathbb{Z}_p^{m \times m}$, where $p \geq 2$. This scheme employs the idea of the trapdoor function given by Gentry, Peikert and Vaikuntanathan in 2008 [11], where a near-uniformly random matrix $\mathbf{A} \in \mathbb{Z}_q^{m \times n}$ is the "public key" and an invertible "small" matrix $\mathbf{T} \in \mathbb{Z}^{m \times m}$ such that $\mathbf{TA} = \mathbf{0} \pmod{q}$ is the used trapdoor, to get the public and secret key pair for the encryption and decryption, and specifically runs the APTrapSamp-type sampling algorithm (e.g., APSTrapSamp and MPSTrapSamp) to output such a key pair $(\mathbf{A}, \mathbf{T})$. The basic construction of the GHV scheme, denoted by GHV, is due to the fact that the trapdoor $\mathbf{T}$ can solve the standard LWE instance relative to $\mathbf{A}$, which implies that security of GHV relies on the hardness of the standard LWE problem $\mathsf{dLWE}(n, m, q, \beta)$ (see Lemma 1). For lack of space, please refer to [10] or the full version of this paper [28, Appendix A.2] on more details of the GHV scheme.

2.4 Other Preliminaries

Definition 2 (Density of a Matrix for Matrix Multiplication). *Let* $\mathbf{X}$ *and* $\mathbf{Y}$ *be matrices over any rings. In a single matrix multiplication* $\mathbf{XY}$ *over a matrix ring, density of* $\mathbf{X}$ *(resp.* $\mathbf{Y}$*) is equal to the number of necessary nonzero elements of* $\mathbf{X}$ *(resp.* $\mathbf{Y}$*) over the ring. These nonzero elements are used in* $\mathbf{XY}$*.*

Lemma 3 (Fact 1 in [10]). *Let positive integers* $n, q \geq 2$, $\beta > 0$ *and* $g = \omega(\sqrt{\lg n})$. *For* $\mathbf{x} \leftarrow \overline{\Psi}_\beta(q)^n$ *and an arbitrary vector* $\mathbf{y} \in \mathbb{Z}^n$, $|\langle \mathbf{x}, \mathbf{y} \rangle| \leq \beta qg \|\mathbf{y}\|$ *with probability* $1 - \psi$, *where* $\|\mathbf{y}\|$ *is the Euclidean norm of* $\mathbf{y}$, *and* ψ *is negligible in* n.

Theorem 1 (Hoeffding Bound [13]). *Let* $X_1, X_2, \ldots, X_\kappa$, *where* $\kappa \in \mathbb{N}_+$, *be a sequence of independent random variables such that* $\forall i \in [1, \kappa]$ $\Pr[X_i \in [a_i, b_i]] = 1$. *Let* $X = \sum_{i=1}^{\kappa} X_i$. *Then, for any* $\tau > 0$, $\Pr[|X - \mathbb{E}[X]| \geq \tau] \leq 2 \exp^{-\frac{2\tau^2}{\sum_{i=1}^{\kappa}(b_i - a_i)^2}}$.

3   Efficiency Analyses of GHV

In this section, we precisely discuss (time and space) efficiency of the original scheme GHV and show why GHV using APSTrapSamp or even MPSTrapSamp is "relatively" inefficient and should be ruled out for some cryptographic applications that only run in time $\mathcal{O}(m^{c'})$, where $c' \in [2,3[$. In particular, the density of the "special" trapdoor matrix pair $(\mathbf{T}, \mathbf{T}^{-1})$ has a direct influence on efficiency of GHV, which means that it should be first explored. For APSTrapSamp and MPSTrapSamp, although some significant parameters related to the output lattice associated with $\mathbf{A}^t$ (and $\mathbf{A}$) and the resulting basis $\mathbf{T}^t$ (and $\mathbf{T}$), e.g., the lattice dimension and the basis quality, have been explored in [3,19], to the best of our knowledge, our work give the first measure of density of $(\mathbf{T}, \mathbf{T}^{-1})$ for matrix multiplication.

3.1   On the Density of Trapdoor Matrix Pair $(\mathbf{T}, \mathbf{T}^{-1})$

We first give the density analysis of the matrix $\mathbf{T}$ generated by APSTrapSamp and MPSTrapSamp (i.e., $N_{\mathbf{T}}$), respectively. Then, we focus on exploring density of the corresponding inverse matrix $\mathbf{T}^{-1}$ over $\mathbb{Z}_p$ for $p \geq 2$ (i.e., $N_{\mathbf{T}^{-1}}$). Interestingly, we obtain $N_{\mathbf{T}}$ and $N_{\mathbf{T}^{-1}}$ based on simple and special decomposition forms of $\mathbf{T}$ and $\mathbf{T}^{-1}$. Notice that, for APSTrapSamp, when the modulus q is a prime, $\mathbf{H}$ can be of the form $[\,_{q}\mathbf{e}_1 \cdots \,_{q}\mathbf{e}_n \hat{\mathbf{H}}\,]$, where $\hat{\mathbf{H}} = [\begin{smallmatrix} \tilde{\mathbf{H}} \\ \mathbf{I} \end{smallmatrix}] \in \mathbb{Z}_q^{m_1 \times (m_1-n)}$ is the column reduction form of the kernel of $\mathbf{A}_1$. Since $\mathbf{A}_1 \xleftarrow{\$} \mathbb{Z}_q^{n \times m_1}$ in APSTrapSamp, we present a mild assumption on $\mathbf{H}$ as follows: if q is a prime, $\forall i \in [n]$ and $\forall j \in [n+1, m_1]$ $h_{i,j} \xleftarrow{\$} \mathbb{Z}_q$, which means $\tilde{\mathbf{H}} \xleftarrow{\$} \mathbb{Z}_q^{n \times (m_1-n)}$.

Lemma 4. *For the trapdoor matrix* $\mathbf{T} \in \mathbb{Z}^{m \times m}$ *generated by APSTrapSamp, it has the decomposition form* $\mathbf{T} = \left([\begin{smallmatrix} \mathbf{GU} & -\mathbf{I} \\ \mathbf{0} & \mathbf{0} \end{smallmatrix}] + [\begin{smallmatrix} \mathbf{R} \\ \mathbf{I} \end{smallmatrix}][\mathbf{U} \;\; \mathbf{P}]\right)^t$. *Then, under the assumption that* $\forall i \in [n]$ *and* $\forall j \in [n+1, m_1]$ $h_{i,j} \xleftarrow{\$} \mathbb{Z}_q$, *where* q *is a prime, we have* $N_{\mathbf{T}} = N_{\mathbf{R}} + N_{\mathcal{P}_{\tilde{\mathbf{H}}}} + m + m_2 + n(w + \mathsf{bwt}(q-1))$, *where* $N_{\mathbf{R}} \sim Bin_{\frac{1}{2}, dm_2}$ *and* $N_{\mathcal{P}_{\tilde{\mathbf{H}}}} \stackrel{s}{\approx} Bin_{\frac{1}{2}, n(m_1-n)w}$, *where* $\mathcal{P}_{\tilde{\mathbf{H}}}$ *is the binary representation of* $\{h'_{i,j} | i \in [n], j \in [n+1, m_1]\}$.

Proof. A proof is given in the full version of this paper [28, Appendix A.3].

Lemma 5. *Let the modulus* q *be a large enough prime. Consider that* $\mathbf{R}$ *is sampled from the distribution over* $\{0, \pm 1\}^{m_1 \times m_2}$ *that outputs 0 with probability* $\frac{1}{2}$ *and* ± 1 *each with probability* $\frac{1}{4}$[1]. *For the trapdoor matrix* $\mathbf{T} \in \mathbb{Z}^{m \times m}$ *generated by MPSTrapSamp, based on its decomposition form* $\mathbf{T} = ([\begin{smallmatrix} \mathbf{I} & \mathbf{R} \\ \mathbf{0} & \mathbf{I} \end{smallmatrix}][\begin{smallmatrix} \mathbf{I} & \mathbf{0} \\ \mathbf{P} & \mathbf{U} \end{smallmatrix}])^t$, *we have* $N_{\mathbf{T}} = N_{\mathbf{R}} + N_{\mathbf{P}} + 2m + n(w - 2 + \mathsf{bwt}(q))$, *where* $N_{\mathbf{R}} \sim Bin_{\frac{1}{2}, m_1 m_2}$ *and* $N_{\mathbf{P}} \stackrel{s}{\approx} Bin_{\frac{1}{2}, nm_1 w}$.

---

[1] We believe that a matrix sampled from the distribution over $\{0, \pm 1\}^{m_1 \times m_2}$ is generally sparser than a matrix from the discrete Gaussian distribution for some $\beta' \geq \eta_v(\mathbb{Z})$.

Proof. A proof is given in the full version of this paper [28, Appendix A.4].

Lemma 6. *For the inverse matrix* $\mathbf{T}^{-1} \in \mathbb{Z}_p^{m \times m}$ *corresponding to* $\mathbf{T}$ *generated by APSTrapSamp, it is of the form* $\left(\begin{bmatrix} \mathbf{U}^{-1}\mathbf{PH}^{-1} & \mathbf{U}^{-1}(\mathbf{I}-\mathbf{PH}^{-1}(\mathbf{G}+\mathbf{R})) \\ -\mathbf{H}^{-1} & \mathbf{H}^{-1}(\mathbf{G}+\mathbf{R}) \end{bmatrix} \right)^t$,
and can be expressed as $\left(\begin{bmatrix} \mathbf{U}^{-1} & 0 \\ 0 & \mathbf{I} \end{bmatrix} \left(\begin{bmatrix} 0 & \mathbf{I} \\ 0 & 0 \end{bmatrix} + \begin{bmatrix} \mathbf{P} \\ -\mathbf{I} \end{bmatrix} \begin{bmatrix} \mathbf{H}^{-1} & -\mathbf{H}^{-1}(\mathbf{G}+\mathbf{R}) \end{bmatrix} \right) \right)^t$, *where*
$\mathbf{U}^{-1} = diag(\mathbf{V}_{w_1}^{-1}, \cdots, \mathbf{V}_{w_{m_1}}^{-1}, \mathbf{I})$ *and in particular* $\forall i \in [w_k]$ *the ith column of*
the $w_k \times w_k$ *matrix* $\mathbf{V}_{w_k}^{-1}$ *(i.e.,* $\mathbf{v}_i^{-1}$*) is* $\sum_{j=1}^{i} 2^{i-j}\mathbf{e}_j$, *where* $k \in [m_1]$. *Then, under*
the assumption that $\forall i \in [n]$ *and* $\forall j \in [n+1, m_1]$ $h_{i,j} \xleftarrow{\$} \mathbb{Z}_q$, *where* q *is a prime,*
we have that $N_{\mathbf{T}^{-1}}$ *is (at least)* $2m + m_1 + nbwt(q-1) + N_{\mathcal{P}_{\tilde{\mathbf{H}}}} + Y_1 + Y_2$ *with*
$Y_1 \overset{s}{\approx} Bin_{\frac{p-1}{p}, n(m-n)}$ *and* $Y_2 \sim Bin_{\frac{1}{2}, (d-n)m_2}$.

Proof. A proof is given in the full version of this paper [28, Appendix A.5].

Lemma 7. *Let the modulus* q *be a large enough prime. Consider that* $\mathbf{R}$ *is*
sampled from the distribution over $\{0, \pm 1\}^{m_1 \times m_2}$ *that outputs 0 with probabil-*
ity $\frac{1}{2}$ *and* ± 1 *each with probability* $\frac{1}{4}$. *For the inverse matrix* $\mathbf{T}^{-1} \in \mathbb{Z}_p^{m \times m}$
corresponding to $\mathbf{T}$ *generated by MPSTrapSamp, it has the decomposition form*
$\mathbf{T}^{-1} = \left(\begin{bmatrix} \mathbf{I} & 0 \\ 0 & \mathbf{U}^{-1} \end{bmatrix} \begin{bmatrix} \mathbf{I} & 0 \\ -\mathbf{P} & \mathbf{I} \end{bmatrix} \begin{bmatrix} \mathbf{I} & -\mathbf{R} \\ 0 & \mathbf{I} \end{bmatrix} \right)^t$, *where* $\mathbf{U}^{-1} = diag(\mathbf{V}_w^{-1}, \cdots, \mathbf{V}_w^{-1}, \mathbf{I})$. *Then,*
we have $N_{\mathbf{T}^{-1}} = N_{\mathbf{R}} + N_{\mathbf{P}} + 3m + Y_3$, *where* $N_{\mathbf{R}} \sim Bin_{\frac{1}{2}, m_1 m_2}$, $N_{\mathbf{P}} \overset{s}{\approx} Bin_{\frac{1}{2}, nm_1 w}$
and $n(w-1) < Y_3 \le \frac{n(w^2+3w-2)}{2}$.

Proof. A proof is given in the full version of this paper [28, Appendix A.6].

3.2 Theoretical Efficiency of GHV

Now we analyze the computational cost and space cost of GHV when encrypting
matrices over $\mathbb{Z}_p^{m \times m}$. In particular, the cases of employing APSTrapSamp and
MPSTrapSamp are discussed, respectively. Using results on the density of trapdoor matrix pair $(\mathbf{T}, \mathbf{T}^{-1})$ in Lemma 4 to 7, we can show accurate estimates of
these two costs. Notice that, we present (near-)lower bounds on these two costs
of the decryption procedure of GHV.

Theorem 2. *For a plaintext matrix* $\mathbf{B} \in \mathbb{Z}_p^{m \times m}$ $(p \ge 2)$ *that is encrypted by*
GHV using APSTrapSamp, Enc($\mathbf{B}$) *takes at most* $m^2((n+1)t_m + (n+2)t_a +$
$t_g)$ *time to generate a ciphertext matrix* $\mathbf{C}$, *and* Dec($\mathbf{C}$) *needs to take at least*
$2m(\frac{p-1}{p}n(m-n) + (d - \frac{n}{2} - 3\sqrt{\frac{n}{2}})m_2 + (m_1 - n)nw + 4m)(t_m + t_a)$ *time (with*
overwhelming probability) to recover $\mathbf{B}$ *from* $\mathbf{C}$.

Proof. A proof is given in the full version of this paper [28, Appendix A.7].

Notice that, letting $m_1 = \frac{101}{100}n \lg q$ and $m_2 = \frac{402}{100}n \lg q$, which means
$m = \frac{503}{100}n \lg q < \lfloor 8n \lg q \rfloor$, from the consequence on Dec($\mathbf{C}$) in Theorem 2, we
see that the computational cost of the decryption procedure of GHV employing
APSTrapSamp is at least $\frac{2}{5}m^3(t_m + t_a)$ $(\approx \mathcal{O}(m^3))$.

Theorem 3. *For a plaintext matrix* $\mathbf{B} \in \mathbb{Z}_p^{m \times m}$ $(p \geq 2)$ *that is encrypted by GHV using MPSTrapSamp, Enc($\mathbf{B}$) takes at most* $m^2((n+1)t_m + (n+2)t_a + t_g)$ *time to generate a ciphertext matrix* $\mathbf{C}$, *and Dec($\mathbf{C}$) needs to take at least* $2m(m_1(nw+m_2) - \sqrt{2n(m_1(nw+m_2)+1)} + 5m + (2w-3)n)(t_m+t_a)$ *time (with overwhelming probability) to recover* $\mathbf{B}$ *from* $\mathbf{C}$.

Proof. A proof is given in the full version of this paper [28, Appendix A.8].

Let us consider $m_1 \approx n \lg q$ and $m_2 = n \lg \lceil q \rceil$, which are used in the "traditional" MPSTrapSamp construction. According to the consequence on Dec($\mathbf{C}$) in Theorem 3, we see that the computational cost of the decryption procedure of GHV employing MPSTrapSamp is about $m^3(t_m + t_a)$ $(\approx \mathcal{O}(m^3))$.

Theorem 4. *For a plaintext matrix* $\mathbf{B} \in \mathbb{Z}_p^{m \times m}$ $(p \geq 2)$ *that is encrypted by GHV using APSTrapSamp, Enc($\mathbf{B}$) takes* $2nm\lceil \lg q \rceil + m^2\lceil \lg p \rceil$ *bits to generate a ciphertext matrix* $\mathbf{C}$, *and Dec($\mathbf{C}$) needs to take at least* $2m^2\lceil \lg q \rceil + n(m - n)\lceil \lg p \rceil + 2dm_2 + n(m_1 - n)w$ *bits to recover* $\mathbf{B}$ *from* $\mathbf{C}$.

Proof. A proof is given in the full version of this paper [28, Appendix A.9].

Theorem 5. *For a plaintext matrix* $\mathbf{B} \in \mathbb{Z}_p^{m \times m}$ $(p \geq 2)$ *that is encrypted by GHV using MPSTrapSamp, Enc($\mathbf{B}$) takes* $2nm\lceil \lg q \rceil + m^2\lceil \lg p \rceil$ *bits to generate a ciphertext matrix* $\mathbf{C}$, *and Dec($\mathbf{C}$) needs to take at least* $2m^2\lceil \lg q \rceil + m_1(2m_2 + nw)$ *bits to recover* $\mathbf{B}$ *from* $\mathbf{C}$.

Proof. A proof is given in the full version of this paper [28, Appendix A.10].

4   Our Optimized GHV-Type Encryption Scheme

The above efficiency analysis confirms that GHV is not suitable for applications (e.g., the private and verifiable delegation of computation) that must use data protection techniques with roughly $\mathcal{O}(m^{c'})$ computational complexity, where $c' \in [2, 3[$ is close to 2. Hence, in this section, we modify the original scheme and are ready to present our optimized variant, denoted by oGHV, for keeping inherent merits of the scheme and making the corresponding running process more efficient, e.g., achieving $\tilde{\mathcal{O}}(nm^2)$ computational overhead. In particular, to make comparisons with the GHV instantiation that employs APSTrapSamp (see [10]), APSTrapSamp is still used in our oGHV instantiation. Of course, MPTrapSamp is also a candidate for oGHV. Notice that the trapdoor $\mathbf{T}^t := [\mathbf{T}_1^t \; \mathbf{T}_2^t]$, where $\mathbf{T}_1^t := \left[\begin{smallmatrix} (\mathbf{G}+\mathbf{R})\mathbf{U} \\ \mathbf{U} \end{smallmatrix} \right]$ and $\mathbf{T}_2^t := \left[\begin{smallmatrix} \mathbf{RP}-\mathbf{I} \\ \mathbf{P} \end{smallmatrix} \right]$, as adopted throughout the whole section.

4.1   Using a Sparse Matrix to Replace $\mathbf{T}^{-1}$

From Theorem 2, we know that GHV takes roughly $\mathcal{O}(nm^2)$ running time to encrypt an $m \times m$ matrix and uses $\mathcal{O}(m^3)$ time to recover this matrix. In particular, the computational cost of the decryption procedure is evidently larger than that of the encryption procedure. This means that we can focus on optimizing the decryption algorithm and reducing the corresponding cost to make the whole cryptosystem more efficient. Notice that there exist two steps in the decryption algorithm, i.e., $\mathbf{C}' = \mathbf{TCT}^t$ (mod q) and $\mathbf{B} = \mathbf{T}^{-1}\mathbf{C}'(\mathbf{T}^t)^{-1}$ (mod p). Specifically, based on the fact that $\mathbf{C}$ is of the form $\mathbf{AS} + p\mathbf{X} + \mathbf{B}$ (mod q), computing $\mathbf{TCT}^t$ (mod q) is an indispensable step, which is used to cancel out $\mathbf{AS}$. $\mathbf{T}^{-1}\mathbf{C}'(\mathbf{T}^t)^{-1}$ (mod p) can be seen as a "supplement" of $\mathbf{TCT}^t$ (mod q). The main purpose of this step is to cancel out $(\mathbf{T}, \mathbf{T}^t)$ and recover $\mathbf{B}$. Although the second step is similar to an additional operation, the corresponding computation is expensive in the decryption procedure and has great influence on the computational cost of the whole cryptosystem.

Thus, let us consider how to reduce the running time of the step $\mathbf{T}^{-1}\mathbf{C}'(\mathbf{T}^t)^{-1}$ (mod p) and improve efficiency of the whole decryption algorithm including the first step. Ideally, we would like to find a sufficiently sparse matrix to replace $\mathbf{T}^{-1}$ and "indirectly" recover $\mathbf{B}$ from $\mathbf{C}'$ by employing some other simple computation. Unfortunately, this is not a computationally feasible operation. However, from the definition of $\mathbf{T}$ in Sect. 2.2 (see Fig. 1(a)), we notice that the $m_2 \times m_2$ invertible component matrix $\mathbf{U}$ is the main part of $\mathbf{T}$ and satisfies $N_{\mathbf{U}} \ll m_2^2 - N_{\mathbf{U}}$. According to Lemma 6, we also know that $\mathbf{U}^{-1} = diag(\mathbf{V}_w^{-1}, \cdots, \mathbf{V}_w^{-1}, \mathbf{I})$ satisfies $N_{\mathbf{U}^{-1}} \ll m_2^2 - N_{\mathbf{U}^{-1}}$. These observations inspire us that we can construct an extremely sparse matrix involving $\mathbf{U}^{-1}$, denoted by $\tilde{\mathbf{T}}$, to decrypt $\mathbf{B}$ from $\mathbf{C}$. Specifically, the original plaintext matrix $\mathbf{B}$ should be first enlarged to $\left[\begin{smallmatrix} 0 & 0 \\ 0 & B \end{smallmatrix}\right]$ by padding zero elements in the encryption algorithm. Notice that, the number of the padded zero elements is far less than that of elements of $\mathbf{B}$. Then, in the decryption algorithm, $\mathbf{C}' = \mathbf{TCT}^t$ (mod q) is executed and, after that, $\tilde{\mathbf{T}} = \left[\begin{smallmatrix} \mathbf{U}^{-1} \\ 0 \end{smallmatrix}\right]$ is used to recover $\mathbf{B}$ by running $\tilde{\mathbf{T}}^t\mathbf{C}'\tilde{\mathbf{T}}$ (mod p). As described above, our optimization for the construction of GHV is very simple but can surprisingly achieve the desired efficiency improvement. In Sects. 4.3 and 4.5, we give the detailed correctness analysis for the optimized scheme oGHV and also present the efficiency exploration of oGHV, which supports our optimization. Moreover, here we highlight another merit of using $\tilde{\mathbf{T}}$ instead of $\mathbf{T}^{-1}$. That is, it is unnecessary to store $\tilde{\mathbf{T}}$ for multiple encryptions. From Lemma 6, we have that $\forall i \in [m_1]$ $\mathbf{V}_{w_i}^{-1}$ can be seen as a deterministically-constructed matrix, which means that $\tilde{\mathbf{T}}$ is also a deterministically-constructed matrix that is easily reconstructed for multiple encryptions, while some components of $\mathbf{T}^{-1}$ must be stored for each GHV encryption. In Sect. 4.4, we introduce a concrete algorithm (i.e., Algorithm 3) to show how to efficiently run the multiplication between $\tilde{\mathbf{T}}$ (resp. $\tilde{\mathbf{T}}^t$) and $\mathbf{C}'$ without using $\tilde{\mathbf{T}}$ (resp. $\tilde{\mathbf{T}}^t$).

4.2 Generic Construction of oGHV

Now we give details on the generic construction of the optimized GHV-type HE scheme oGHV with parameters n, m_1, m_2, m, q, β for plaintext matrices over $\mathbb{Z}_p$ with any integer $p \geq 2$, where q is an odd prime, and β is a Gussian error parameter. In particular, oGHV including a triple of PPT algorithms (oKeyGen, oEnc, oDec) is described below.

- oKeyGen$(1^n) \rightarrow (\mathbf{A}, (\mathbf{T}, \tilde{\mathbf{T}}))$: Run APTrapSamp-type trapdoor sampling algorithm to get a matrix $\mathbf{A} \in \mathbb{Z}_q^{m \times n}$ and its trapdoor matrix $\mathbf{T} \in \mathbb{Z}^{m \times m}$ such that $\mathbf{TA} = \mathbf{0}$ (mod q). Generate a matrix $\tilde{\mathbf{T}} = \begin{bmatrix} \mathbf{U}^{-1} \\ \mathbf{0} \end{bmatrix} \in \mathbb{Z}^{m \times m_2}$, where $\mathbf{U}^{-1} \in \mathbb{Z}^{m_2 \times m_2}$ is defined in Lemma 6. Output $(\mathbf{A}, (\mathbf{T}, \tilde{\mathbf{T}}))$ as the public and secret key pair.
- oEnc$_{\mathbf{A}}(\mathbf{B}) \rightarrow \mathbf{C}$: Given a plaintext matrix $\mathbf{B} \in \mathbb{Z}_p^{m_2 \times m_2}$, build an $m \times m$ matrix $\mathbf{B}' = \begin{bmatrix} \mathbf{0} & \mathbf{0} \\ \mathbf{0} & \mathbf{B} \end{bmatrix}$ using three small zero matrices of respective size $m_1 \times m_1$, $m_1 \times m_2$ and $m_2 \times m_1$, where $m_1 + m_2 = m$. Choose $\mathbf{S} \xleftarrow{\$} \mathbb{Z}_q^{n \times m}$ and $\mathbf{X} \leftarrow \overline{\Psi}_\beta(q)^{m \times m_2}$, and generate a ciphertext matrix $\mathbf{C} \in \mathbb{Z}_q^{m \times m}$ as $\mathbf{C} = \mathbf{AS} + p\mathbf{X} + \mathbf{B}'$ (mod q).
- oDec$_{(\mathbf{T}, \tilde{\mathbf{T}})}(\mathbf{C}) \rightarrow \mathbf{B}$: Given the ciphertext matrix $\mathbf{C}$, run $\mathbf{C}' = \mathbf{TCT}^t$ (mod q) $= \mathbf{T}(p\mathbf{X} + \mathbf{B}')\mathbf{T}^t$ (mod q) and output $\mathbf{B} = \tilde{\mathbf{T}}^t \mathbf{C}' \tilde{\mathbf{T}}$ (mod p).

In the above construction, if APSTrapSamp is employed by oKeyGen, from Sect. 2.2 (cf. the full version of this paper [28, Appendix A.1]), we know that m_1 can be equal to $(1 + \delta)n \lg q$ and $m_2 \geq (4 + 2\delta)n \lg q$, this implies that m_1 and m_2 can satisfy $m_2 \gg m_1$. Then, most of elements of $\mathbf{B}'$ come from $\mathbf{B}$, and we have, in some sense, "oEnc$_{\mathbf{A}}(\mathbf{B}) \approx$ Enc$_{\mathbf{A}}(\mathbf{B})$", where Enc is the encryption algorithm of GHV. About concrete instantiations of the parameters m_1, m_2, m, q and β, which are used to guarantee that oGHV holds correctness, security and homomorphism, please refer to Sect. 4.3. In particular, according to properties of the proposed generic construction, the prime q related to the key and ciphertext sizes can be set to be smaller than that used for GHV. Moreover, some detailed optimizations based on the generic construction are presented in Sect. 4.4, which further reduce the computational cost and memory cost of oGHV and guarantee that the smallest key pair is employed. Notice that, similar to that in GHV, the post-multiplication by $\mathbf{T}^t$ and $\tilde{\mathbf{T}}$ on decryption in oGHV is unnecessary. This means that oDec simply runs $\tilde{\mathbf{T}}^t (\mathbf{TC}$ (mod q)) (mod p) for obtaining $\mathbf{B}$. The post-multiplication can be employed to decrypt product ciphertexts (see Sect. 4.3).

4.3 Homomorphic Operations and Concrete Parameters

Our optimized scheme oGHV enjoys the same homomorphic properties as GHV holds. Specifically, oGHV also supports addition and multiplication homomorphism. In particular, for two ciphertext matrices $\mathbf{C}_1 = \mathbf{AS}_1 + p\mathbf{X}_1 + \mathbf{B}_1'$ (mod q) and $\mathbf{C}_2 = \mathbf{AS}_2 + p\mathbf{X}_2 + \mathbf{B}_2'$ (mod q) corresponding to two plaintext matrices $\mathbf{B}_1$ and $\mathbf{B}_2$, considering the sum ciphertext $\mathbf{C} = \mathbf{C}_1 + \mathbf{C}_2$ (mod q), we have

$$\mathbf{C} = \mathbf{C}_1 + \mathbf{C}_2 \pmod{q} = \mathbf{A}\underbrace{(\mathbf{S}_1 + \mathbf{S}_2)}_{\mathbf{S}} + p\underbrace{(\mathbf{X}_1 + \mathbf{X}_2)}_{\mathbf{X}} + \underbrace{\mathbf{B}_1' + \mathbf{B}_2'}_{\mathbf{B}'} \pmod{q}.$$

---

[2] Clearly, the state-of-the-art discrete Gaussian sampling algorithms over the integers (e.g., [20]) can be considered as candidates used in oGHV to replace the sampling method proposed by Gentry et al. [10]. What is important is that the corresponding parameter setting needs to ensure that oGHV still holds the desired correctness, security and homomorphism.

It is easy to see that $\mathbf{C}_1 + \mathbf{C}_2 \pmod{q}$ can be decrypted to $\mathbf{B}_1 + \mathbf{B}_2 \pmod{p}$ if values of all the elements of $\mathbf{T}(p\mathbf{X} + \mathbf{B}')\mathbf{T}^t$ are smaller than $\frac{q}{2}$, where $\mathbf{B}' = \begin{bmatrix} 0 & 0 \\ 0 & \mathbf{B}_1 + \mathbf{B}_2 \end{bmatrix}$. Moreover, considering the product ciphertext $\mathbf{C} = \mathbf{C}_1 \mathbf{C}_2^t \pmod{q}$, we have

$$\mathbf{C} = \mathbf{C}_1 \mathbf{C}_2^t \pmod{q}$$
$$= \mathbf{A} \underbrace{\left(\mathbf{S}_1 \mathbf{C}_2^t \right)}_{\mathbf{s}} + p \underbrace{\left(\mathbf{X}_1 \left(p\mathbf{X}_2 + \mathbf{B}_2' \right) + \mathbf{B}_1' \mathbf{X}_2^t \right)}_{\mathbf{x}} + \underbrace{\mathbf{B}_1' \left(\mathbf{B}_2' \right)^t}_{\mathbf{B}'} + \underbrace{\left(p\mathbf{X}_1 + \mathbf{B}_1' \right) \mathbf{S}_2^t}_{\tilde{\mathbf{s}}} \mathbf{A}^t \pmod{q}.$$

This naturally implies that $\mathbf{C}_1 \mathbf{C}_2^t \pmod{q}$ can be decrypted to $\mathbf{B}_1 \mathbf{B}_2^t \pmod{p}$ when values of all the elements of $\mathbf{T}(p\mathbf{X} + \mathbf{B}')\mathbf{T}^t$ are smaller than $\frac{q}{2}$, where $\mathbf{B}' = \begin{bmatrix} 0 & 0 \\ 0 & \mathbf{B}_1 \mathbf{B}_2^t \end{bmatrix}$, as discussed above. In what follows, we present our answer on the parameter setting (for q, m_1, m_2, m and β), which guarantees the feasibility of the homomorphic operations.

Notably, according to the above analysis on the additive homomorphism of oGHV, we know that, similar to the case on decryption of the normal ciphertext, the post-multiplication by $\mathbf{T}^t$ is not required for decrypting a sum ciphertext $\mathbf{C} = \sum_{i=1}^{n^c} (\mathbf{A}\mathbf{S}_i + p\mathbf{X}_i + \mathbf{B}_i') \pmod{q}$, where $c > 0$. Moreover, compared with GHV, of which the correctness of decryption must rely on a condition that each element of $\mathbf{T}(p\mathbf{X} + \mathbf{B})\mathbf{T}^t$ is bounded by $\frac{q}{2}$, we want to show that the correctness of decryption of oGHV is able to depend on a more relaxed condition, resulting in the smaller parameters q and m that we can set. Specifically, consider that $\mathbf{C}' = \begin{bmatrix} \mathbf{C}_1' & \mathbf{C}_2' \\ \mathbf{C}_3' & \mathbf{C}_4' \end{bmatrix}$, where block matrices $\mathbf{C}_1' = \mathbf{T}_1 \mathbf{C} \mathbf{T}_1^t \pmod{q}$, $\mathbf{C}_2' = \mathbf{T}_1 \mathbf{C} \mathbf{T}_2^t \pmod{q}$, $\mathbf{C}_3' = \mathbf{T}_2 \mathbf{C} \mathbf{T}_1^t \pmod{q}$ and $\mathbf{C}_4' = \mathbf{T}_2 \mathbf{C} \mathbf{T}_2^t \pmod{q}$ are respective sizes $m_2 \times m_2$, $m_2 \times m_1$, $m_1 \times m_2$ and $m_1 \times m_1$, we have $\tilde{\mathbf{T}}^t \mathbf{C}' \tilde{\mathbf{T}} \pmod{p} = (\mathbf{U}^{-1})^t \mathbf{C}_1' \mathbf{U}^{-1} \pmod{p}$. This means that the final result can be recovered if the absolute value of each element in $\mathbf{T}_1(p\mathbf{X} + \mathbf{B}')\mathbf{T}_1^t$ (instead of $\mathbf{T}(p\mathbf{X} + \mathbf{B}')\mathbf{T}^t$) is bounded by $\frac{q}{2}$. Then, from the relaxed condition, we first set the parameters that simply ensure that oGHV is able to support n^c additions. After that, we establish the concrete parameters that guarantee that oGHV also holds the one-multiplication homomorphism.

Theorem 6. *Consider that APSTrapSamp is employed by oGHV. For the fixed parameters n and $c > 0$, let q, m_1, m_2, m, β be set as $q > 40n^{c+1}p\lg n$, $m = m_1 + m_2 \geq \lceil \frac{101}{100} n \lg q \rceil + \frac{201}{50} n \lg q$, where $m_1 = \lceil \frac{101}{100} n \lg q \rceil$ and $m_2 \geq \frac{201}{50} n \lg q$, and $\beta = \frac{1}{5n^c p \sqrt{m_1 \lg n}}$. Then, oGHV with parameters n, m_1, m_2, m, q, β supports n^c homomorphic addition operations over the matrix ring $\mathbb{Z}_p^{m \times m}$ (and $\mathbb{Z}_p^{m_2 \times m_2}$).*

Proof. A proof is given in the full version of this paper [28, Appendix A.11]. $\square$

Theorem 7. *Consider that APSTrapSamp is employed by oGHV. For the fixed parameters n and $c > 0$, let q, m_1, m_2, m, β be set as $q > 2^{13} n^{3+3c} p^2 \lg^3 n$, $m = m_1 + m_2 \geq \lceil \frac{101}{100} n \lg q \rceil + \frac{201}{50} n \lg q$, where $m_1 = \lceil \frac{101}{100} n \lg q \rceil$ and $m_2 \geq \frac{201}{50} n \lg q$, and $\beta = \frac{1}{2n^{\frac{3}{2}} p \sqrt{mm_1 q \lg n}}$. Then, oGHV with parameters n, m_1, m_2, m, q, β supports n^c homomorphic addition operations and one homomorphic multiplication operation over the matrix ring $\mathbb{Z}_p^{m \times m}$ (and $\mathbb{Z}_p^{m_2 \times m_2}$).*

Proof. A proof is given in the full version of this paper [28, Appendix A.12].

4.4 Computational Optimizations

Generally speaking, the matrix multiplication is a costly operation for cryptographic primitives related to the matrix. Here, according to concrete constructions of $\mathbf{T}^t$ and $\tilde{\mathbf{T}}$ from APSTrapSamp and the generic construction of the cryptosystem presented in Sects. 2.2 and 4.2, some practical optimizations on speeding up the matrix multiplication used in oGHV and further improving efficiency of oGHV are given[3].

Algorithm 1: Ternary-Integer Matrix Product

    Input: $\mathbf{X} \in \{0, \pm 1\}^{m_3 \times m_4}$, $\mathbf{Y} \in \mathbb{Z}_q^{m_4 \times m_5}$, m_3, m_4, and m_5

    Output: $\mathbf{Z} = \mathbf{XY} \in \mathbb{Z}_q^{m_3 \times m_5}$

1 $\mathbf{Z} = \{0\}^{m_3 \times m_5}$;

2 **for** $i \in [m_3]$ **do**

3 | **for** $j \in [m_4]$ **do**

4 | | **for** $k \in [m_5]$ **do**

5 | | | **if** $x_{i,j} == 0$ **then**

6 | | | | $z_{i,k} += 0$;

7 | | | **else if** $x_{i,j} == 1$ **then**

8 | | | | $z_{i,k} += y_{j,k}$;

9 | | | **else if** $x_{i,j} == -1$ **then**

10 | | | | $z_{i,k} -= y_{j,k}$;

11 | | | **end**

12 | **end**

13 | **end**

14 **end**

15 **return** $\mathbf{Z}$;

Accelerating the Multiplication by a Ternary Matrix. Our idea is that, if a ternary matrix is involved in the matrix multiplication, the corresponding element multiplications are eliminated by running selections and additions. More concretely, a product can be obtained based on Algorithm 1.

Decomposing the Multiplication by $\mathbf{T}^t$ and $\mathbf{T}$. According to Algorithm 1, we can get a method to replace the multiplications in $\mathbf{TCT}^t$ by selections and additions. In particular, our technique is based on the decomposition form of $\mathbf{T}^t$ (resp. $\mathbf{T}$) in Lemma 4. Specifically, for $\begin{bmatrix} \mathbf{GU} & -\mathbf{I} \\ \mathbf{0} & \mathbf{0} \end{bmatrix}$ (resp. $\begin{bmatrix} \mathbf{GU} & -\mathbf{I} \\ \mathbf{0} & \mathbf{0} \end{bmatrix}^t$), there is (at most) a 1 in each column of $\mathbf{GU}$, and others are zero elements. Then, (at most) a 1 or -1 is in each column of $\begin{bmatrix} \mathbf{GU} & -\mathbf{I} \\ \mathbf{0} & \mathbf{0} \end{bmatrix}$, which means that the product of $\begin{bmatrix} \mathbf{GU} & -\mathbf{I} \\ \mathbf{0} & \mathbf{0} \end{bmatrix}$ (resp. $\begin{bmatrix} \mathbf{GU} & -\mathbf{I} \\ \mathbf{0} & \mathbf{0} \end{bmatrix}^t$) and some matrix can be achieved by simply employing selections shown in Algorithm 1. For $\begin{bmatrix} \mathbf{R} \\ \mathbf{I} \end{bmatrix}$ (resp. $\begin{bmatrix} \mathbf{R} \\ \mathbf{I} \end{bmatrix}^t$), since values of all elements are from $\{0, \pm 1\}$, Algorithm 1 can be directly used to obtain the product of $\begin{bmatrix} \mathbf{R} \\ \mathbf{I} \end{bmatrix}$ (resp. $\begin{bmatrix} \mathbf{R} \\ \mathbf{I} \end{bmatrix}^t$) and some matrix. For $[\mathbf{U}\ \mathbf{P}]$ (resp. $[\mathbf{U}\ \mathbf{P}]^t$), values of elements

---

[3] The proposed optimizations are not only focus on $\mathbf{T}^t$ and $\tilde{\mathbf{T}}$ from APSTrapSamp. Actually, some extremely similar optimizations can be developed for any APTrapSamp-type trapdoor sampling algorithm (e.g., MPTrapSamp).

are from $\{-2, 0, 1\}$. Then, a modified Algorithm 1, where multiplying by -2 is replaced by two additions, is suitable for generating the product of $[\,\mathbf{U}\ \mathbf{P}\,]$ (resp. $[\,\mathbf{U}\ \mathbf{P}\,]^t$) and some matrix. In Algorithm 2, how to run the multiplication by $\mathbf{T}$ and $\mathbf{T}^t$ is shown. Notice that, as discussed in Sect. 4.3, for $\mathbf{C}' = \begin{bmatrix} \mathbf{C}'_1 & \mathbf{C}'_2 \\ \mathbf{C}'_3 & \mathbf{C}'_4 \end{bmatrix} = \mathbf{T}\mathbf{C}\mathbf{T}^t$, only $\mathbf{C}'_1 = \mathbf{T}_1\mathbf{C}\mathbf{T}_1^t$ is the required matrix corresponding to the final result. According to the decomposition form in Lemma 4, this means that Algorithm 2 simply needs to involve $\mathbf{T}_1^t = \begin{bmatrix} \mathbf{G}\mathbf{U} \\ \mathbf{0} \end{bmatrix} + \begin{bmatrix} \mathbf{R} \\ \mathbf{I} \end{bmatrix}\mathbf{U}$, where $\mathbf{R}$ can be regarded as the only "secret" matrix.

Algorithm 2: Multiplication by $\mathbf{T}^t$ and $\mathbf{T}$

> **Input:** $\mathbf{C} \in \mathbb{Z}_q^{m \times m}$, $\mathbf{R} \in \{0, \pm 1\}^{m_1 \times m}$, n, w, m_1, m_2, and m
> **Output:** $\mathbf{C}'_1 \in \mathbb{Z}_q^{m_2 \times m_2}$

```
 1  Ĉ = C;
 2  for i ∈ [m] do                                    /* Running the multiplication by T₁ᵗ */
 3      for j ∈ [m₂] do
 4          ĉ_{i,j} = ĉ_{i,(j+m₁)};
 5          for k ∈ [m₁] do                           /* Invoking Algorithm 1 */
 6              ĉ_{i,j} = ĉ_{i,j} + r_{k,j} ĉ_{i,k};
 7          end
 8      end
 9      for j ∈ [0, n − 1] do
10          for k ∈ [w − 1] do
11              ĉ_{i,(wj+k+1)} = ĉ_{i,(wj+k+1)} − (ĉ_{i,(wj+k)} + ĉ_{i,(wj+k)});
12          end
13          ĉ_{i,(wj+1)} = c_{i,(j+1)} + ĉ_{i,(wj+1)};
14      end
15  end
16  for i ∈ [m₂] do                                   /* Running the multiplication by T₁ */
17      for j ∈ [n] do
18          ĉ_{j,i} = ĉ_{j,i};
19      end
20      for j ∈ [m₂] do
21          ĉ_{j,i} = ĉ_{(j+m₁),i};
22          for k ∈ [m₁] do                           /* Invoking Algorithm 1 */
23              ĉ_{j,i} = ĉ_{j,i} + r_{k,j} ĉ_{k,i};
24          end
25      end
26      for j ∈ [0, n − 1] do
27          for k ∈ [w − 1] do
28              ĉ_{(wj+k+1),i} = ĉ_{(wj+k+1),i} − (ĉ_{(wj+k),i} + ĉ_{(wj+k),i});
29          end
30          ĉ_{(wj+1),i} = ĉ_{(j+1),i} + ĉ_{(wj+1),i};
31      end
32  end
33  C'₁ = the top-left m₂ × m₂ block of Ĉ;
34  return C'₁;
```

Simplifying the Multiplication by $\tilde{\mathbf{T}}$ and $\tilde{\mathbf{T}}^t$. For $\tilde{\mathbf{T}} = \begin{bmatrix} \mathbf{U}^{-1} \\ \mathbf{0} \end{bmatrix}$, where $\mathbf{U}^{-1} = diag(\mathbf{V}_w^{-1}, \cdots, \mathbf{V}_w^{-1}, \mathbf{I})$, we have $\forall i \in [w]$ $\mathbf{v}_i^{-1} = \sum_{j=1}^{i} 2^{i-j}\mathbf{e}_j$, which implies that $\mathbf{v}_{i'+1}^{-1} = \mathbf{e}_{i'+1} + 2\mathbf{v}_{i'}^{-1}$, where $i' \in [w-1]$. Based on this fact, for the case of multiplying some matrix (e.g., $\mathbf{C}'$) with $\tilde{\mathbf{T}}$ (resp. $\tilde{\mathbf{T}}^t$), elements of the $(wj+i+1)$th column (resp. row) of the corresponding product can be generated from elements of the $(wj + i)$th column (resp. row) of the product by running $2m$ additions, where $i \in [w-1]$ and $j \in [0, n-1]$. Consider that $\mathbf{C}' = \begin{bmatrix} \mathbf{C}'_1 & \mathbf{C}'_2 \\ \mathbf{C}'_3 & \mathbf{C}'_4 \end{bmatrix}$. Since the concrete multiplications can focus on $\mathbf{C}'_1$, the "whole" product of $(\mathbf{U}^{-1})^t \mathbf{C}'_1 \mathbf{U}^{-1} = \tilde{\mathbf{T}}^t \mathbf{C}' \tilde{\mathbf{T}}$

is computed as shown in Algorithm 3. Notice that Algorithm 3 does not need any additional memory except the memory for storing $\mathbf{C}'_1$.

Algorithm 3: Multiplication by $\tilde{\mathbf{T}}$ and $\tilde{\mathbf{T}}^t$

    Input: $\mathbf{C}'_1 \in \mathbb{Z}_q^{m_2 \times m_2}$, n, w, and m_2
    Output: $\mathbf{B} = (\mathbf{U}^{-1})^t \mathbf{C}'_1 \mathbf{U}^{-1} \in \mathbb{Z}_p^{m_2 \times m_2}$
1 **for** $i \in [w-1]$ **do**
2   **for** $j \in [0, n-1]$ **do**
3   **for** $k \in [m_2]$ **do**
4             $c'_{k,(wj+i+1)} = c'_{k,(wj+i+1)} + c'_{k,(wj+i)} + c'_{k,(wj+i)};$
5             $c'_{(wj+i+1),k} = c'_{(wj+i+1),k} + c'_{(wj+i),k} + c'_{(wj+i),k};$
6   **end**
7   **end**
8 **end**
9 **return** $\mathbf{B} = \mathbf{C}'_1;$

4.5   Property Analysis

In this section, we present the analyses on correctness, security and efficiency of the optimized encryption scheme oGHV, respectively.

Theorem 8. *For a plaintext matrix* $\mathbf{B} \in \mathbb{Z}_p^{m_2 \times m_2}$, *oGHV with parameters* n, m_1, m_2, m, q, β *that we can establish has correct encryption and decryption.*

Proof. A proof is given in the full version of this paper [28, Appendix A.13].

Theorem 9. *If there is a distinguishing algorithm with advantage* ϵ *against the* IND-CPA *security of oGHV with parameters* n, m_1, m_2, m, q, *and* β, *then there must be a distinguisher against* dLWE(n, m, q, β) *with roughly the same running time and advantage (at most)* $\frac{\epsilon}{2m}$.

Proof. The security proof follows directly from the proof of IND-CPA security for GHV (see Theorem 2 in [10]).

Theorem 10. *For a plaintext matrix* $\mathbf{B} \in \mathbb{Z}_p^{m_2 \times m_2}$ *that is encrypted by the optimized scheme oGHV using* APSTrapSamp, *oEnc*$(\mathbf{B})$ *takes (at most)* $m^2(n + 1)(t_a + t_m) + m^2 t_g + m_2^2 t_a$ *time and* $2nm\lceil \lg q \rceil + m_2^2 \lceil \lg p \rceil$ *bits to generate a ciphertext matrix* $\mathbf{C}$, *and* oDec$(\mathbf{C})$ *needs to take (at most)* $((\frac{1}{2}d + \sqrt{\frac{n}{2}} + 2)(m + m_2) + 4n(w-1))m_2 t_a$ *time and* $(m^2 + m_2^2)\lceil \lg q \rceil + 2dm_2$ *bits to recover* $\mathbf{B}$.

Proof. A proof can be found in the full version of this paper [28, Appendix A.14].

5   Conclusions

In this paper, we have proposed an optimized GHV-type asymmetric HE scheme, which is more efficient than the original GHV scheme. In particular, it provides a much faster decryption algorithm, and the computational complexity of the decryption is decreased from $\mathcal{O}(m^3)$ to $\tilde{\mathcal{O}}(nm^2)$. As the same as the GHV scheme, security of our new GHV-type scheme is based on the standard LWE problem, and our scheme also supports matrix encryption. We have compared the performance of our scheme with two LWE-based FHE schemes, which support matrix operations, and the comparison result indicates that our scheme is more efficient. We also have discussed the options of using APSTrapSamp or MPSTrapSamp in the GHV scheme, and our optimizations can benefit both of these two options.

Although we have given the optimized GHV-type HE scheme, from the perspective of implementation, how to make this proposal more practical is an interesting open problem.

Acknowledgments. The authors would like to thank the anonymous reviewers for providing their valuable comments. This work was supported in part by the National Natural Science Foundation of China (No. 61302161, No. 61972269, No. 62032005), in part by the Doctoral Fund, Ministry of Education, China (No. 20130181120076), and in part by the European Union's Horizon 2020 research and innovation program under grant agreement No. 952697 (ASSURED) and grant agreement No. 101019645 (SECANT).

References

1. Ajtai, M.: Generating hard instances of the short basis problem. In: Wiedermann, J., van Emde Boas, P., Nielsen, M. (eds.) ICALP 1999. LNCS, vol. 1644, pp. 1–9. Springer, Heidelberg (1999). https://doi.org/10.1007/3-540-48523-6_1

2. Applebaum, B., Cash, D., Peikert, C., Sahai, A.: Fast cryptographic primitives and circular-secure encryption based on hard learning problems. In: Halevi, S. (ed.) CRYPTO 2009. LNCS, vol. 5677, pp. 595–618. Springer, Heidelberg (2009). https://doi.org/10.1007/978-3-642-03356-8_35

3. Alwen, J., Peikert, C.: Generating shorter bases for hard random lattices. Theory Comput. Syst. **48**(3), 535–553 (2011)

4. Brakerski, Z.: Fully homomorphic encryption without modulus switching from classical GapSVP. In: Safavi-Naini, R., Canetti, R. (eds.) CRYPTO 2012. LNCS, vol. 7417, pp. 868–886. Springer, Heidelberg (2012). https://doi.org/10.1007/978-3-642-32009-5_50

5. Brakerski, Z., Döttling, N., Garg, S., Malavolta, G.: Candidate iO from homomorphic encryption schemes. In: Canteaut, A., Ishai, Y. (eds.) EUROCRYPT 2020. LNCS, vol. 12105, pp. 79–109. Springer, Cham (2020). https://doi.org/10.1007/978-3-030-45721-1_4

6. Boneh, D., Goh, E.-J., Nissim, K.: Evaluating 2-DNF formulas on ciphertexts. In: Kilian, J. (ed.) TCC 2005. LNCS, vol. 3378, pp. 325–341. Springer, Heidelberg (2005). https://doi.org/10.1007/978-3-540-30576-7_18

7. Brakerski, Z., Vaikuntanathan, V.: Efficient fully homomorphic encryption from (standard) LWE. SIAM J. Comput. **43**(2), 831–871 (2014)

8. Clear, M., McGoldrick, C.: Additively homomorphic IBE from higher residuosity. In: Lin, D., Sako, K. (eds.) Public-Key Cryptography-PKC 2019, pp. 496–515. Springer, Cham (2019)

9. Gentry, C.: Fully homomorphic encryption using ideal lattices. In: STOC, pp. 169–178. ACM Press (2009)

10. Gentry, C., Halevi, S., Vaikuntanathan, V.: A simple BGN-type cryptosystem from LWE. In: Gilbert, H. (ed.) EUROCRYPT 2010. LNCS, vol. 6110, pp. 506–522. Springer, Heidelberg (2010). https://doi.org/10.1007/978-3-642-13190-5_26

11. Gentry, C., Peikert, C., Vaikuntanathan, V.: Trapdoors for hard lattices and new cryptographic constructions. In: STOC, pp. 197–206. ACM Press (2008)
12. Gentry, C., Sahai, A., Waters, B.: Homomorphic encryption from learning with errors: conceptually-simpler, asymptotically-faster, attribute-based. In: Canetti, R., Garay, J.A. (eds.) CRYPTO 2013. LNCS, vol. 8042, pp. 75–92. Springer, Heidelberg (2013). https://doi.org/10.1007/978-3-642-40041-4_5
13. Hoeffding, W.: Probability inequalities for sums of bounded random variables. J. Am. Statis. Assoc. **58**(301), 13–30 (1963)
14. Hiromasa, R., Abe, M., Okamoto, T.: Packing messages and optimizing bootstrapping in GSW-FHE. In: Katz, J. (ed.) PKC 2015. LNCS, vol. 9020, pp. 699–715. Springer, Heidelberg (2015). https://doi.org/10.1007/978-3-662-46447-2_31
15. Lindner, R., Peikert, C.: Better key sizes (and attacks) for LWE-based encryption. In: Kiayias, A. (ed.) CT-RSA 2011. LNCS, vol. 6558, pp. 319–339. Springer, Heidelberg (2011). https://doi.org/10.1007/978-3-642-19074-2_21
16. López-Alt, A., Tromer, E., Vaikuntanathan, V.: On-the-fly multiparty computation on the cloud via multikey fully homomorphic encryption. In: STOC, pp. 1219–1234. ACM Press (2012)
17. Mohassel, P.: Efficient and secure delegation of linear algebra. Cryptology ePrint Archive, Report 2011/605 (2011). https://eprint.iacr.org/2011/605
18. Meng, X., Kamara, S., Nissim, K., Kollios, G.: GRECS: graph encryption for approximate shortest distance queries. In: CCS, pp. 504–517. ACM Press (2015)
19. Micciancio, D., Peikert, C.: Trapdoors for lattices: simpler, tighter, faster, smaller. Cryptology ePrint Archive, Report 2011/501 (2011). https://eprint.iacr.org/2011/501
20. Micciancio, D., Walter, M.: Gaussian sampling over the integers: efficient, generic, constant-time. In: Katz, J., Shacham, H. (eds.) CRYPTO 2017. LNCS, vol. 10402, pp. 455–485. Springer, Cham (2017). https://doi.org/10.1007/978-3-319-63715-0_16
21. Peikert, C.: Public-key cryptosystems from the worst-case shortest vector problem. In: STOC, pp. 333–342. ACM Press (2009)
22. Pereira, H.V.L.: Efficient AGCD-based homomorphic encryption for matrix and vector arithmetic. In: Conti, M., Zhou, J., Casalicchio, E., Spognardi, A. (eds.) ACNS 2020. LNCS, vol. 12146, pp. 110–129. Springer, Cham (2020). https://doi.org/10.1007/978-3-030-57808-4_6
23. Regev, O.: On lattices, learning with errors, random linear codes, and cryptography. J. ACM **56**(6), 1–40 (2009)
24. Rivest, R.L., Adleman, L., Dertouzos, M.L.: On data banks and privacy homomorphisms. In: Foundations of Secure Computation, pp. 169–180. Academic Press, London (1978)
25. van Dijk, M., Gentry, C., Halevi, S., Vaikuntanathan, V.: Fully homomorphic encryption over the integers. In: Gilbert, H. (ed.) EUROCRYPT 2010. LNCS, vol. 6110, pp. 24–43. Springer, Heidelberg (2010). https://doi.org/10.1007/978-3-642-13190-5_2
26. Wei, L., Reiter, M.K.: Toward practical encrypted email that supports private, regular-expression searches. Int. J. Inf. Secur. **14**(5), 397–416 (2014). https://doi.org/10.1007/s10207-014-0268-3
27. Wang, B., Wang, X., Xue, R., Huang, X.: Matrix FHE and its application in optimizing bootstrapping. Comput. J. **61**(12), 1845–1861 (2018)
28. Zhao, L., Chen, Z., Chen, L., Huang, X.: An optimized GHV-type HE scheme: simpler, faster, and more versatile. Cryptology ePrint Archive, Report 2021/1534 (2021). https://eprint.iacr.org/2021/1534

Attacks

Analyzing the Provable Security Bounds of GIFT-COFB and Photon-Beetle

Akiko Inoue[1], Tetsu Iwata[2], and Kazuhiko Minematsu[1(✉)]

[1] NEC, Kawasaki, Japan
{a_inoue,k-minematsu}@nec.com
[2] Nagoya University, Nagoya, Japan
tetsu.iwata@nagoya-u.jp

Abstract. We study the provable security claims of two NIST Lightweight Cryptography (LwC) finalists, GIFT-COFB and Photon-Beetle, and present several attacks whose complexities contradict their claimed bounds in their final round specification documents. For GIFT-COFB, we show an attack using q_e encryption queries and no decryption query to break privacy (IND-CPA). The success probability is $O(q_e/2^{n/2})$ for n-bit block while the claimed bound contains $O(q_e^2/2^n)$. This positively solves an open question posed in [Khairallah, ePrint 2021/648 (also accepted at FSE 2022)]. For Photon-Beetle, we show an attack using q_e encryption queries (using a small number of input blocks) followed by a single decryption query and no primitive query to break authenticity (INT-CTXT). The success probability is $O(q_e^2/2^b)$ for a b-bit block permutation, and it is significantly larger than what the claimed bound tells, which is independent of the number of encryption queries. We also show a simple tag guessing attack that violates the INT-CTXT bound when the rate $r = 32$. Then, we analyze other (improved/modified) bounds of Photon-Beetle shown in the subsequent papers [Chakraborty et al., ToSC 2020(2) and Chakraborty et al., ePrint 2019/1475]. As a side result of our security analysis of Photon-Beetle, we point out that a simple and efficient forgery attack is possible in the related-key setting.

We emphasize that our results do not contradict the claimed "bit security" in the LwC specification documents for any of the schemes that we studied. That is, we do not negate the claims that GIFT-COFB is $(n/2 - \log n)$-bit secure for $n = 128$, and Photon-Beetle is $(b/2 - \log b/2)$-bit secure for $b = 256$ and $r = 128$, where r is a rate. We also note that the security against related-key attacks is not included in the security requirements of NIST LwC, and is not claimed by the designers.

Keywords: Authenticated Encryption · Lightweight Cryptography · Provable Security · NIST

1 Introduction

NIST Lightweight cryptography[1] aims at standardizing authenticated encryption (AE) schemes for resource-constrained devices. In March 2021, NIST has

---

[1] https://csrc.nist.gov/projects/lightweight-cryptography.

© Springer Nature Switzerland AG 2022
G. Ateniese and D. Venturi (Eds.): ACNS 2022, LNCS 13269, pp. 67–84, 2022.
https://doi.org/10.1007/978-3-031-09234-3_4

announced ten finalists among the 32 second-round candidates. The finalists include GIFT-COFB [3] and Photon-Beetle [6]. GIFT-COFB is a block cipher-based AE that combines a variant of COFB mode [13] and the lightweight 128-bit block cipher GIFT [5]. Photon-Beetle is a permutation-based AE that combines Beetle mode [11] and the lightweight cryptographic permutation Photon [19], which is an ISO standard [1]. This paper studies the provable security bounds of GIFT-COFB and Photon-Beetle, and shows some attacks whose success probabilities are inconsistent with the presented security bounds in the final round specification documents of NIST LwC.

GIFT-COFB. For the original COFB and GIFT-COFB, the security bounds for the combined AE notion of IND-CPA and INT-CTXT were presented in [3,13]. Assuming a nonce-respecting attacker and that the underlying block cipher is a random permutation, GIFT-COFB's AE bound is roughly $\sigma^2/2^n + nq_d/2^{n/2}$ for $\sigma = \sigma_e + \sigma_d + q_e + q_d$, where σ_e (resp. σ_d) denotes the total queried blocks in encryption (resp. decryption) queries, and q_e (resp. q_d) denotes the number of encryption (resp. decryption) queries. This bound suggests that if (1) σ_e reaches $2^{n/2}$, or (2) σ_d reaches $2^{n/2}$, or (3) q_d reaches $2^{n/2}/n$, the bound reaches 1 and hence no security guarantee is possible. The tightness of these conditions has been studied by Khairallah [21–23] and Inoue and Minematsu (IM21) [20]. Khairallah [21–23] showed attacks with $q_d = 2^{n/2}$ with about $\sigma_e = 2^{n/2}$ or $\sigma_e = 2^{n/4}$, called Weak Key attack and Mask collision attack [21,22]. Khairallah finally showed one with $q_e = 1$, $\sigma_e = O(1)$ (a few blocks) and $q_d = 2^{n/2}$, called Mask Presuming attack [23]. The last one implies that the tightness condition (3) has only the small gap of $\log n$ factor. Inoue and Minematsu [20] studied the tightness of (1) and showed an attack with $\sigma_e = 2^{n/2}$ and $q_d = 1$. As in the previous attacks, this attack breaks the authenticity and matches the aforementioned bound. For (2) it remains unsolved, and [20] mentioned that it might be an artifact in the proofs.

We take a closer look at the condition (1). IM21's attack with q_e encryption queries and 1 decryption query has success probability roughly $q_e^2/2^n$. However, we found an improved attack that needs q_e encryption queries to break privacy (hence the combined AE notion) success probability roughly $q_e/2^{n/2}$. The existence of such an attack has been posed as an open problem by Khairallah [23]. We solved this positively. This implies a contradiction with the bound in the NIST LwC document although the bit-level security maintains. We give a brief analysis on the root of this contradiction in Sect. 3.2.

Photon-Beetle. For Photon-Beetle, the security proofs for the original version and the NIST LwC version have been shown in [6,11,12]. For b-bit block permutation with $b = 256$ and rate (which is the length of one message block processed in one permutation call) $r = 128$, the security bounds roughly tell $b/2 - \log b/2 = 121$-bit security for both IND-CPA and INT-CTXT. Dobraunig and Mennink commented on a constant factor related to a key recovery attack [18], and Mège analysed the security of the hash function [27].

We focus the authenticity bound shown in the final round NIST LwC submission document [6], which is roughly $q_p(q + q')/2^b + rq_p/2^{b/2} + q_p^r/2^{(b/2)\cdot(r-1)} + r\sigma'/2^{256-r}$, where q_p, q, q' and σ' denote the number of primitive queries, the number of encryption queries, the number of decryption queries, and the total number of blocks in decryption queries. The rate can be either $r = 128$ or 32, where $r = 128$ is the primary setting. The tag length is 128 bits for both cases. When $r = 128$, we observed that if $q_p = 0$, *i.e.* we do not query the primitive (permutation), the above authenticity bound reduces to the bound that has no contribution from encryption queries. We invalidate this by presenting a simple forgery using $2^{b/2}$ encryption queries and a single decryption query. The success probability is close to 1, while the claimed bound indicates a negligibly small probability with that complexity. This attack shows inconsistency with the claimed bound and implies the lack of the birthday term with respect to the block size, $O(q_e^2/2^b)$, in the claimed bound. Moreover, when $r = 32$, the INT-CTXT bound reduces to the bound that is smaller than $q'/2^{128}$, which is impossible to achieve for any AE of 128-bit tags. Thus, a simple tag guessing attack (*i.e.*, decryption queries with identical nonce, AD, ciphertext, and distinct tags) invalidates the claimed bound. This implies even the break of bit-level security suggested by the bound. However, the bit security shown in [6, Table 4.1] claims 128-bit authenticity. We clarify that we do not break the figure. Moreover, we study other (improved or modified) security bounds for Photon-Beetle shown in the subsequent papers [15,16]. In [16], an improved bound AE bound is presented. The bound claims that the IND-CPA security is maintained beyond $2^{b/2}$ encryption queries, but this is not possible to achieve. The same paper presents a simplified AE bound, and we point out that this cannot be true. We then clarify that the ePrint version [15] of [16] addresses the issue, while we still see an issue in simplification.

As a side result of our security analysis of Photon-Beetle for $r = 128$, we point out that a simple and efficient forgery attack is possible in the related-key setting, in which the attacker can modify the key used in the oracle [7,9,26]. In Photon-Beetle, a fixed constant is xor'ed into the secret key when the input (both AD and a message) is empty, and our forgery makes use of this fact. See [4,17,24] for examples of related-key attacks on some AE schemes. In the domain of public-key authenticated encryption, see [25].

Our attacks do not depend on the primitives and do not break the primitives. The attack against GIFT-COFB does not work against the COFB versions in [13, 14] because of the shorter nonce length than the NIST LwC version. Our attacks show some inconsistencies in the claimed security bounds of GIFT-COFB and Photon-Beetle. At the same time, we would like to emphasize that these results do not negate the claimed bit security levels of GIFT-COFB and Photon-Beetle. We also note that the security against related-key attacks is not included in the security requirements of NIST LwC, and is not claimed by the designers.

2 Preliminaries

2.1 Notations

Our notations largely follow the specifications of GIFT-COFB and Photon-Beetle [3,6]. Let $[i] := \{1, \ldots, i\}$ and $[\![i]\!] := \{0, 1, \ldots, i\}$. Let $\{0,1\}^*$ denote the set of all bit strings. The set of bit strings whose length is a multiple of n is denoted as $(\{0,1\}^n)^*$. For $X \in \{0,1\}^*$, $|X|$ denotes its bit length. An empty string ε is a bit string of length zero; we have $|\varepsilon| = 0$. The block length of $X \in \{0,1\}^*$ in n-bit blocks is denoted as $|X|_n := \lceil |X|/n \rceil$. A concatenation of two bit strings X and Y is written as $X \parallel Y$ or simply XY. Let $\mathsf{Trunc}_t(X)$ denote the first $t \in [\![|X|]\!]$ bits of X, where $\mathsf{Trunc}_0(X) = \varepsilon$. For two integers a and b, we write $a|b$ if a divides b. For a bit string X, $X \ll c$ denotes the left-shift of X by c bits. Bit rotation of X by c bits to the left (right) is denoted by $X \lll c$ ($X \ggg c$).

For $X \in \{0,1\}^*$, the parsing operation of X into n-bit blocks is denoted by $(X[1], \ldots, X[x]) \xleftarrow{n} X$. Here, if $X \neq \varepsilon$, $X[1] \parallel X[2] \parallel \ldots \parallel X[x] = X$ and $|X[i]| = n$ for $i < |X|_n$ and $|X[x]| \in [n]$ for $x = |X|_n$. By writing $X_1 \parallel X_2 \xleftarrow{a_1, a_2} X$ we mean the parsing such that $X_1 \parallel X_2 = X$ and $|X_1| = a_1$ and $|X_2| = a_2$. If $X = \varepsilon$, $x = 1$ and $|X[x]| = 0$ (i.e., the parsing yields the same empty string). The sequence of i zeros is denoted by 0^i. We may use an integer $i \in \{0, 1, \ldots, 2^n - 1\}$ to mean an element of $\{0,1\}^n$, assuming the standard encoding, e.g., for $n = 4$, 3 denotes 0011.

Galois Field of 2^n Elements. An element a in the Galois extension field $\mathrm{GF}(2^n)$ will be interchangeably denoted as an n-bit string $a_{n-1} \ldots a_1 a_0$ or an integer $\sum_{i=0}^{n-1} a_i 2^i$. Hence, by writing $2 \cdot a$ or $2a$ when no confusion is possible, we mean the multiplication of a by $2 = \mathsf{x}$. This operation is called *doubling* and has been frequently used by various modes for the "domain separation" task. See [28] for example. For $n = 64$ (that will be used for GIFT-COFB), we use the primitive polynomial $\mathsf{x}^{64} + \mathsf{x}^4 + \mathsf{x}^3 + \mathsf{x} + 1$ to define the field $\mathrm{GF}(2^n)$. In this case, the doubling $2 \cdot a$ is $(a \ll 1)$ if $\mathsf{msb}_1(a) = 0$ and $(a \ll 1) \oplus (0^{59}11011)$ if $\mathsf{msb}_1(a) = 1$, and the tripling $3 \cdot a$ means $2 \cdot a \oplus a$. Combined expressions such as $2^i \cdot 3^j \cdot a$ are defined analogously, namely i doublings and j triplings of a.

2.2 Cryptographic Components

A keyed function with key space $\mathcal{K}$, domain $\mathcal{X}$, and range $\mathcal{Y}$ is a function $F : \mathcal{K} \times \mathcal{X} \to \mathcal{Y}$. We may write $F_K(X)$ for $F(K, X)$. If Mode is a mode of operation for F using a single key $K \in \mathcal{K}$ for F, we write $\mathsf{Mode}[F_K]$ instead of $\mathsf{Mode}[F]_K$. A block cipher is a keyed function $E : \mathcal{K} \times \mathcal{T} \times \mathcal{M} \to \mathcal{M}$ such that for each $K \in \mathcal{K}$, $E(K, \cdot)$ is a permutation over $\mathcal{M}$. A cryptographic permutation $P : \mathcal{M} \to \mathcal{M}$ is simply a (keyless) permutation. GIFT-COFB is based on a block cipher, while Photon-Beetle is based on a cryptographic permutation.

Let $\mathcal{A}$ be an adversary that queries c oracles, $O_1, \ldots, O_c$ in an arbitrarily order and outputs a certain final output. By writing $\mathcal{A}^{O_1, O_2, \cdots}$, we mean the final output of $\mathcal{A}$. Let $\mathrm{Perm}(n)$ be the set of all permutations over $\{0,1\}^n$. For block cipher $E : \mathcal{K} \times \mathcal{M} \to \mathcal{M}$, the PRP advantage is defined as

$$\mathbf{Adv}_E^{\mathrm{prp}}(\mathcal{A}) := \Pr\left[K \xleftarrow{\$} \mathcal{K} : \mathcal{A}^{E_K(*)} \Rightarrow 1\right] - \Pr\left[\pi \xleftarrow{\$} \mathrm{Perm}(n) : \mathcal{A}^{\pi(*)} \Rightarrow 1\right].$$

The PRP advantage represents the indistinguishability of E_K from the uniform random permutation of the same message space for adversaries performing queries to encryption oracles (either $E_K(*)$ or $\pi(*)$).

2.3   Authenticated Encryption

We briefly describe the syntax and security notions about authenticated encryption (AE). Our targets are both nonce-based AEs [8,29], which requires nonce to be unique for each encryption. Let Π denote a nonce-based AE scheme consisting of an encryption function $\Pi.\mathcal{E}_K$ and a decryption function $\Pi.\mathcal{D}_K$, for key $K \xleftarrow{\$} \mathcal{K}$. For plaintext M with nonce N and associated data (AD) A, $\Pi.\mathcal{E}_K$ takes (N, A, M) and returns ciphertext C (typically $|C| = |M|$) and tag T. Here, AD is a part of the input that is not encrypted but must be authenticated (e.g., a protocol header). The tuple (N, A, C, T) will be sent to the receiver. For decryption, $\Pi.\mathcal{D}_K$ takes (N, A, C, T) and returns a decrypted plaintext M if the authentication check is successful, and otherwise an error symbol, $\perp$.

Security Notions. The security of AEs can be defined by two notions. The privacy[2] notion is the indistinguishability of encryption oracle $\Pi.\mathcal{E}_K$ from the random-bit oracle \$ which returns random $|M| + \tau$ bits for any query (N, A, M). The adversary is assumed to be nonce-respecting, i.e., nonces can be arbitrarily chosen but must be distinct for encryption queries. The privacy advantage is defined as

$$\mathbf{Adv}_\Pi^{\mathrm{priv}}(\mathcal{A}) := \Pr\left[K \xleftarrow{\$} \mathcal{K} : \mathcal{A}^{\Pi.\mathcal{E}_K(\cdot,\cdot,\cdot)} \Rightarrow 1\right] - \Pr\left[\mathcal{A}^{\$(\cdot,\cdot,\cdot)} \Rightarrow 1\right],$$

which measures the hardness of breaking the privacy notion for $\mathcal{A}$. This notion corresponds to IND-CPA [8].

The authenticity notion is the probability of successful forgery via queries to $\Pi.\mathcal{E}_K$ and $\Pi.\mathcal{D}_K$ oracles. We define the authenticity advantage as

$$\mathbf{Adv}_\Pi^{\mathrm{auth}}(\mathcal{A}) := \Pr\left[K \xleftarrow{\$} \mathcal{K} : \mathcal{A}^{\Pi.\mathcal{E}_K(\cdot,\cdot,\cdot),\Pi.\mathcal{D}_K(\cdot,\cdot,\cdot,\cdot)} \text{ forges}\right],$$

where $\mathcal{A}$ forges if it receives a value $M' \neq \perp$ from $\Pi.\mathcal{D}_K$. Here, to prevent trivial wins, if $(C, T) \leftarrow \Pi.\mathcal{E}_K(N, A, M)$ is obtained earlier, $\mathcal{A}$ cannot query (N, A, C, T) to $\Pi.\mathcal{D}_K$. The adversary must be nonce-respecting for encryption queries, but has no restriction on decryption queries. It corresponds to INT-CTXT notion [8].

---

[2] Following the literature (e.g., [28]), we conventionally refer to it as privacy, but in practice, it may be more intuitive to call it confidentiality.

It is also common to use a combined notion, sometimes called AE advantage, define as

$$\mathbf{Adv}_{\Pi}^{ae}(\mathcal{A}) := \Pr\left[K \xleftarrow{\$} \mathcal{K} : \mathcal{A}^{\Pi.\mathcal{E}_K(\cdot,\cdot,\cdot),\Pi.\mathcal{D}_K(\cdot,\cdot,\cdot,\cdot)} \Rightarrow 1\right] - \Pr\left[\mathcal{A}^{\$(\cdot,\cdot,\cdot),\perp} \Rightarrow 1\right],$$

where $\perp$ oracle denotes the oracle that always returns the rejection symbol. It is know that the sum of Privacy and Authenticity advantages is a bound of AE advantage [30], thus it compactly represents the security of an AE scheme as a whole.

3 Analysis of GIFT-COFB

Specification. For reference, the specification of GIFT-COFB is shown in Appendix A (Figs. 4 and 5). The padding function pad : $\{0,1\}^* \to (\{0,1\}^n)^*$ is a variant of so-called one-zero padding and defined as $\mathsf{pad}(X) = X$ if $X \neq \varepsilon$ and $|X| \bmod n = 0$, and otherwise $\mathsf{pad}(X) = X \parallel 10^{(n-(|X| \bmod n)-1)}$. The G in Fig. 4 denotes a matrix such that $G \cdot X := (X[2], X[1] \lll 1)$ for $X[1], X[2] \xleftarrow{n/2} X$, $X \in \{0,1\}^n$. We also write $G(X)$ to mean $G \cdot X$.

We show our attack against GIFT-COFB that contradicts the claimed security bound. As mentioned earlier, this does not invalidate the claimed bit security levels, namely 64-bit IND-CPA security and 58-bit INT-CTXT security in the specification document.

3.1 Our Attack

The security bound shown in the latest NIST LwC specification document is as follows (with minor changes in notations):

Theorem 1 (Chapter 4 in [3]).

$$\mathbf{Adv}_{\mathsf{GIFT\text{-}COFB}}^{ae}(\mathcal{A}) \leq \mathbf{Adv}_{\mathsf{GIFT}}^{prp}(q',t') + \frac{\binom{q'}{2}}{2^n} + \frac{1}{2^{n/2}} + \frac{q_d(n+4)}{2^{n/2+1}}$$
$$+ \frac{3\sigma_e^2 + q_d + 2(q_e + \sigma_e + \sigma_d) \cdot \sigma_d}{2^n},$$

where $q' = q_e + q_d + \sigma_e + \sigma_d$, which corresponds to the total number of block cipher calls through the game, and $t' = t + O(q')$. Note that the advantage has been taken by the maximum advantage over all the adversaries making q_e encryption queries, q_d decryption queries and running in time t, such σ_e, σ_d are the total number of blocks queried in the encryption and decryption queries, respectively.

The term $\mathbf{Adv}_{\mathsf{GIFT}}^{prp}(q',t')$ denotes the maximum of PRP advantage for any adversary of q' queries and t' time complexity. When we only use encryption queries, the above bound effectively reduces to about $\sigma_e^2/2^n$ and hence about $q_e^2/2^n$ if each message is short. We present an attack using q_e encryption queries (where

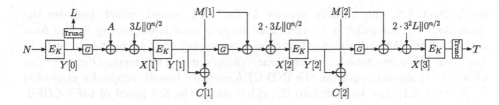

Fig. 1. The first encryption query of the attack against GIFT-COFB.

each message is short) with success probability about $q_e/2^{n/2}$. This contradicts the bound of Theorem 1, since $q_e^2/2^n \leq q_e/2^{n/2}$ necessarily holds when $1 \leq q_e \leq 2^{n/2}$. The attack proceeds as follows.

1. The attacker makes a query (N, A, M) to the encryption oracle such that $|A| = n$, $|M| = 2n$ and $M = M[1] \parallel M[2]$ (for arbitrarily chosen N, single-block A and two-block M), and it obtains corresponding (C, T), where $C = C[1] \parallel C[2]$, as shown in Fig. 1.
2. The attacker computes $Y[1]$, $Y[2]$, and $\mathtt{lsb}_{n/2}(X[2]) = \mathtt{lsb}_{n/2}(G(Y[1]) \oplus M[1])$. Note that $\mathtt{msb}_{n/2}(X[2])$ is unknown; nevertheless, the attacker can mount a privacy attack by using *the guessed* $X[2]$ as the nonce of the next encryption query.
3. For $0 \leq i \leq 2^{n/2}-1$, the attacker queries (N_i, A_i, M_i), where $|A_i| = |M_i| = n$, to the encryption oracle such that

$$N_i = (i)_{n/2} \parallel \mathtt{lsb}_{n/2}(X[2]), \quad L_i := \mathsf{Trunc}_{n/2}(Y[2]),$$
$$A_i = N_i \oplus G(Y[2]) \oplus 3L_i \parallel 0^{n/2},$$
$$M_i = N_i \oplus G(Y[2]) \oplus 3^2 L_i \parallel 0^{n/2},$$

where $(i)_{n/2}$ denotes $n/2$-bit string of a binary representation of i. The attacker obtains corresponding (C_i, T_i). In the real world, there always exists i such that $M_i \oplus C_i = Y[2]$ and $T_i = \mathsf{Trunc}_\tau(Y[2])$, where i fulfilling $N_i = X[2]$. In the ideal world, $\Pr[M_i \oplus C_i - Y[2], T_i - \mathsf{Trunc}_\tau(Y[2])] - 1/2^{n+\tau}$ holds for all i, and thus the attacker can find i such that $M_i \oplus C_i = Y[2]$ and $T_i = \mathsf{Trunc}_\tau(Y[2])$ holds with a negligibly small probability, $1/2^{n/2+\tau}$.

In the real world, the above attack fails when $N = X[2]$ accidentally holds because it prevents the attacker from using $X[2]$ for the next nonce. To prevent such a case, the attacker can query a longer plaintext in Step 1, and it can find $X[\cdot]$ s.t. $\mathtt{lsb}_{n/2}(X[\cdot]) \neq \mathtt{lsb}_{n/2}(N)$ with a sufficiently high probability.

We remark that this attack does not work against versions of COFB in TCHES 2017 [13] and Journal of Cryptology [14] because the nonce length of these versions is $n/2$ bits.

3.2   Brief Analysis on Security Proof

As we mentioned in the previous section, the security bound shown in [3, Chapter 4] does not include the term $O(q_e/2^{n/2})$ nor $O(\sigma_e/2^{n/2})$. However, in [3, Sect. 4.2], the authors provide INT-CTXT bound, which includes the term $3\sigma_e/2^{64}$ assuming $n = 128$. This term is somehow missing in the final bound of the AE advantage that combines privacy and authenticity. Still, in any case, since our attack uses only encryption queries, the terms $O(q_e/2^{n/2})$ or $O(\sigma_e/2^{n/2})$ should appear in the IND-CPA security bound, originally presented in [3, Sect. 4.1]. Let us look into [2] which shows the full proof of GIFT-COFB. The authors define the following two events as the bad events.

B1: $X_{i_1}[j_1] = X_{i_2}[j_2]$ for some $(i_1, j_1) \neq (i_2, j_2)$ where $j_1, j_2 > 0$.
B2: $Y_{i_1}[j_1] = Y_{i_2}[j_2]$ for some $(i_1, j_1) \neq (i_2, j_2)$ where $j_1, j_2 > 0$.

Here, $X_i[j]$ and $Y_i[j]$ denote input and output of the j-th underlying block cipher call in the i-th encryption query. Also, $X_i[0] := N_i$, where N_i is the nonce value in the i-th encryption query. As our attack shows, the attacker can produce a collision between $X_i[0]$ and $X_1[2]$ with probability $q_e/2^{n/2}$. One can speculate that this inconsistency could be fixed by setting $j_1, j_2 \geq 0$ in the above events (then it covers the presented attack), rather than $j_1, j_2 > 0$.

4 Analysis of Photon-Beetle

Specification. For reference, we present the AEAD specification of Photon-Beetle almost verbatim in Appendix A (Figs. 6 and 7). In the specification, $\mathsf{ozs}_r(X)$ for any X such that $|X| < r$, is another variant of one-zero padding, defined as $\mathsf{ozs}_r(X) = X \parallel 10^{r-|X|-1}$. The expression $\mathbf{E}?a : b$ evaluates to a if $\mathbf{E}$ holds and b otherwise. Similarly, $(\mathbf{E_1} \text{ and } \mathbf{E_2}?a : b : c : d)$ evaluates to a if $\mathbf{E_1} \wedge \mathbf{E_2}$ holds, b if $\mathbf{E_1} \wedge \overline{\mathbf{E_2}}$ holds, c if $\overline{\mathbf{E_1}} \wedge \mathbf{E_2}$, and d otherwise. The Shuffle in the ρ and ρ^{-1} functions is a function: $\{0,1\}^r \to \{0,1\}^r$. It is defined as $\mathsf{Shuffle}(S) = (S[2] \parallel S[1] \ggg 1)$, where $(S[1], S[2]) \xleftarrow{r/2} S$.

We show our attacks against Photon-Beetle that violate its claimed security bound in NIST LwC documentation [6]. We emphasize that our attacks do not violate the claimed "bit security" levels of Photon-Beetle, which are 121-bit IND-CPA and INT-CTXT security when $r = 128$, and 128-bit IND-CPA and INT-CTXT security when $r = 32$.

4.1 Claimed Security Bound and Our Attack

In [6], Photon-Beetle is claimed to be provably secure, with the security bound of

$$O\left(\frac{\sigma^2}{2^{256}} + \frac{q_p}{2^{256-r}} + \frac{q \cdot q_p}{2^{256}} + \frac{rq_p}{2^{128}} + \frac{\sigma_e^r}{2^{128(r-1)}}\right)$$

for privacy (IND-CPA), where σ is the total number of blocks in encryption queries, q_p is the number of offline queries, r is the rate ($r = 32$ or 128), q is the number of encryption queries, and σ_e is the total number of blocks in encryption queries [6, Sect. 4.1][3]. For authenticity (INT-CTXT), the claimed bound is

$$O\left(\frac{q_p(q+q')}{2^{256}} + \frac{rq_p}{2^{128}} + \frac{q_p^r}{2^{128(r-1)}} + \frac{r\sigma'}{2^{256-r}} \right), \qquad (1)$$

where q_p is the number of offline queries, q is the number of encryption queries, q' is the number of decryption queries, r is the rate ($r = 32$ or 128), and σ' is the total number of blocks in decryption queries [6, Sect. 4.2].

We present two attacks that invalidate the bound in (1). The observation is that, when $q_p = 0$, i.e., when the attacker does not make offline queries, then the bound (1) is simplified into

$$O\left(\frac{r\sigma'}{2^{256-r}} \right). \qquad (2)$$

We observe that the bound (2) claims that the authenticity security is maintained even if the attacker makes an unlimited number of encryption queries and that the success probability is smaller than $\sigma'/2^{128}$ when $r = 32$. In what follows, we present attacks based on these observations.

Birthday Forgery Against Photon-Beetle. The attack is as follows.

1. Let $q = 2^{b/2}$, and fix q distinct nonces $N_1, \ldots, N_q$, q distinct AD $A_1, \ldots, A_q$ with $|A_i| = b$, and q distinct messages $M_1, \ldots, M_q$ with $|M_i| = b + r$. The attacker chooses $M_1, \ldots, M_q$ of the form $M_i = M' \| M_i'$, where $|M'| = b$, $|M_i'| = r$, and $M_1', \ldots, M_q'$ take q distinct values. That is, the first b bits of $M_1, \ldots, M_q$ take the same value M', and the corresponding portions of ciphertexts are used to detect a full-state collision.
2. Make q encryption queries $(N_1, A_1, M_1), \ldots, (N_q, A_q, M_q)$ and obtain $(C_1, T_1), \ldots, (C_q, T_q)$, where $|C_i| = b + r$.
3. Find (i, j) such that $C_i' = C_j'$, where C_i' is the first b bits of C_i, and the same for C_j'.
4. Output (N_i, A_i, C_j, T_j) (or (N_j, A_j, C_i, T_i)) as the forgery.

See Fig. 2 for the process of (N_i, A_i, M_i) and (N_j, A_j, M_j) when $r = 128$. With a high probability, we have a full-state collision, i.e., we have (i, j) such that $S_i = S_j$ in the figure. The collision can be detected from C_i' and C_j', which are the first b bits of C_i and C_j. If this happens, we see that the forgery in Step 4 succeeds.

The bound (2) claims that the success probability of the attack is negligibly small and at most $O(7r/2^{256-r})$ when $r = 128$ (or at most $O(6r/2^{256-r})$ depending on the interpretation of σ'), while the attack succeeds with an overwhelming probability. Therefore, the bound (1) is invalidated.

---

[3] We do not know the difference between σ and σ_e.

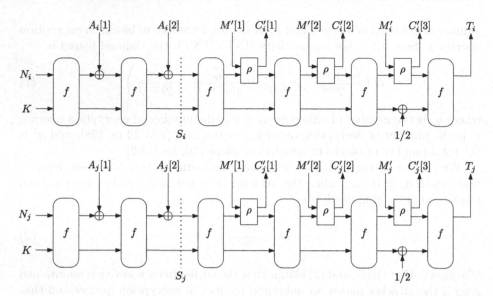

Fig. 2. Two encryption queries (N_i, A_i, M_i) and (N_j, A_j, M_j) when $r = 128$. Here, $A_i = A_i[1] \| A_i[2]$ and $M_i = M'[1] \| M'[2] \| M_i'$.

Tag Guessing Attack Against Photon-Beetle with $r = 32$. When $r = 32$, the above setting of $q_p = 0$ makes the INT-CTXT bound (1) reduces to $32\sigma'/2^{256-32} = \sigma'/2^{219}$ which is smaller than $\sigma'/2^{128}$. When σ' is close to q', this implies a bound that is not possible to achieve with 128-bit tags. A simple tag guessing attack invalidates this bound, that is, q' decryption queries using identical (nonce, AD, ciphertext) tuple with distinct tags will succeed with probability about $q'/2^{128}$.

Discussion and Implication. In [6, Sect. 4.2], the designers outline the proof of the bound (1). To quote:

> Also, if an adversary can obtain a state collision among the input/output of a permutation query with the state of an encryption query or decryption query, it can use the fact to mount an forgery attack.

The argument here ignores a full-state collision among encryption queries, resulted in the first attack. Here is another quote from the same document:

> The trivial solution for forging is to guess the key or the tag which can be bounded by $\frac{q+q'}{2^{128}}$.

We do not find an issue here, while for $r = 32$, the bound (1) makes a stronger security claim than this argument.

We note that the above two attacks need 2^{128} complexity, and thus do not violate the claimed 121-bit security (when $r = 128$) or 128-bit security (when $r = 32$). However, our attacks show that the theoretical reasoning for the bit security in the NIST LwC document [6] is inaccurately mentioned.

4.2 Analysis of the Bound in [16]

There are various provable security claims related to Beetle [6,11,12,15,16]. We do not consider the bound in [11,12] for the difference in the specification.

For Photon-Beetle, we write the combined AE advantage as $\mathbf{Adv}^{\text{ae}}_{\text{Photon-Beetle}}$, which is the same as the case of combined AE notion defined in Sect. 2, except that the attacker has additional oracles to compute the forward and inverse directions of the permutation that is modeled as a public random permutation. In [16], improved provable security bounds of Photon-Beetle are presented. Corollary 1 in [16] claims that, in the combined AE notion, the success probability of the attacker for the case $r = 128$ is

$$\mathbf{Adv}^{\text{ae}}_{\text{Photon-Beetle}}(\mathcal{A}) \leq \frac{4\tau\sigma_d}{2^c} + \frac{4r\sigma_d}{2^c} + \frac{4b\sigma_d}{2^c} + \frac{q_p}{2^\kappa} + \frac{2q_d}{2^\tau} + \frac{2\sigma_d(\sigma + q_p)}{2^b}$$
$$+ \frac{6\sigma_e q_p}{2^b} + \frac{8rq_p}{2^c} + \frac{4\tau q_p}{2^{b-\tau}} + \frac{\sigma_e + q_p}{2^b} + \frac{4rq_p\sigma_d}{2^{2c}}, \qquad (3)$$

where τ is the tag length, c is the capacity, r is the rate, $b = r + c$, κ is the key length, q_e is the number of encryption queries, q_d is the number of decryption queries, σ_e is the total number of blocks in encryption queries, σ_d is the total number of blocks in decryption queries, q_p is the number of offline queries, and $\sigma = \sigma_e + \sigma_d$.

When $q_p = 0$ and $q_d = \sigma_d = 0$, the bound (3) is

$$\mathbf{Adv}^{\text{ae}}_{\text{Photon-Beetle}}(\mathcal{A}) \leq \frac{\sigma_e}{2^b},$$

i.e., it claims IND-CPA security up to $\sigma_e = 2^b$, which is flawed as we show below.

We note that the birthday forgery attack in Sect. 4.1 implies a distinguishing attack with a comparable complexity as follows:

1. Let $q_e = 2^{b/2}$, and fix q_e distinct nonces $N_1, \ldots, N_{q_e}$, q_e distinct AD $A_1, \ldots, A_{q_e}$ with $|A_i| = b$. We also fix a message M with $|M| = b$.
2. Make q_e encryption queries $(N_1, A_1, M), \ldots, (N_{q_e}, A_{q_e}, M)$ and obtain $(C_1, T_1), \ldots, (C_{q_e}, T_{q_e})$, where $|C_i| = b$.
3. If there exists (i, j) such that $(C_i, T_i) = (C_j, T_j)$, then output 1 (real world). Otherwise, output 0 (ideal world).

Since the b-bit state collision can be expected in the real world, the attacker finds (i, j) in Step 3 with a high probability. The attack makes $q_e = 2^{b/2}$ encryption queries, no primitive query ($q_p = 0$), and no decryption query ($q_d = \sigma_d = 0$), violating the bound (3).

In [16, Sect. 7.2], the following AE bound is claimed for $r = 128$:

$$\mathbf{Adv}^{\text{ae}}_{\text{Photon-Beetle}}(\mathcal{A}) \leq \frac{q_p}{2^\kappa} + \frac{13rq_p}{2^c} \qquad (4)$$

When $q_p = 0$, the bound claims perfect security both in IND-CPA and INT-CTXT. Even the ideal AE scheme cannot have a perfect security bound in authenticity, and our birthday forgery in Sect. 4.1 invalidates the INT-CTXT claim, and the above distinguishing attack invalidates the IND-CPA claim.

The bound (4) is obtained from the bound (3) by using the relation

$$\sigma \leq q_p, \tag{5}$$

which is not the case in our attacks. We do not see how the relation (5) can be ensured, as our attacks demonstrate that there are attackers with $q_p = 0$.

We clarify that the ePrint version [15] of [16] addresses the issue in the bound (3) with the following revised bound for $r = 128$:

$$\mathbf{Adv}^{\mathsf{ae}}_{\mathsf{Photon\text{-}Beetle}}(\mathcal{A}) \leq \frac{8r\sigma_d}{2^c} + \frac{8b^3 q_p^2 \sigma_d}{2^{b+c}} + \frac{q_p}{2^\kappa} + \frac{2q_d}{2^r} + \frac{2\sigma(2\sigma + q_p)}{2^b}$$
$$+ \frac{q_p^2}{2^b} + \frac{6\sigma_e q_p}{2^b} + \frac{12rq_p}{2^c} + \frac{\sigma_e + q_p}{2^b} + \frac{4rq_p\sigma_d}{2^{2c}}, \tag{6}$$

i.e., the revised bound contains a term $\sigma^2/2^b$. A full-state collision in encryption queries is covered in the analysis of [16], and the above attack no longer applies. The source of the gap seems to be an error in the final step of the proof in [16] to take the summation of various terms, where a term $2\sigma_e^2/2^b$ has been somewhat missing.

In the ePrint version [15, Sect. 7.3.1], a simplified bound is presented. For $r = 128$, the bound is

$$\mathbf{Adv}^{\mathsf{ae}}_{\mathsf{Photon\text{-}Beetle}}(\mathcal{A}) \leq \frac{q_p}{2^\kappa} + \frac{2\sigma}{2^r} + \frac{10b^2 q_p^2}{2^b} + \frac{24rq_p}{2^c} + \frac{12\sigma q_p}{2^b}, \tag{7}$$

which is obtained from the bound (6) by using the relation (5). We do not have an attack for this, but we do not know its correctness, as there are attackers outside of the relation (5).

On SCHWAEMM. A NIST LwC finalist Sparkle [10] adopts Beetle. More specifically, the AE member of Sparkle, SCHWAEMM, uses Beetle with minor modifications. The specification document [10] does not present security bounds of SCHWAEMM nor mention the relationship with the original bounds of Beetle. Thus our analysis above does not have any implications to SCHWAEMM beyond the fact that it is based on Beetle. Moreover, as with the case of Photon-Beetle, we do not negate the bit security claims of SCHWAEMM.

4.3   Related-Key Attack

We present an efficient forgery attack against Photon-Beetle for $r = 128$ in the related-key setting [7,9,26]. In this setting, we consider the security notion as in Sect. 2, where we additionally assume that the adversary can modify the secret key. The encryption oracle $\Pi.\mathcal{E}_K(\cdot, \cdot, \cdot)$ takes (N, A, M) and returns $(C, T) = \Pi.\mathcal{E}_K(N, A, M)$. In the related-key setting, it additionally takes $\Delta \in \{0, 1\}^k$, where k is the bit length of the secret key K. The related-key encryption oracle

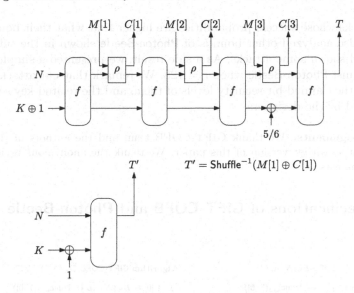

Fig. 3. The adversary makes a single encryption query with key $K \oplus 1$. This immediately allows a forgery for empty message and AD.

returns $(C, T) = \Pi.\mathcal{E}_{K \oplus \Delta}(N, A, M)$ for a query (Δ, N, A, M). The decryption oracle can also be defined to take additional input to modify the key, but we do not use this in our attack.

Our attack goes as follows:

1. Fix (Δ, N, A, M), where $\Delta = 1$, N can be any nonce, A is empty, and M can be any message such that $|M| \geq r$.
2. Make a related-key encryption query (Δ, N, A, M) and obtain (C, T). Let $M[1]$ be the first r bits of M, and $C[1]$ be the first r bits of C.
3. Return (N, A', C', T') as the forgery, where A' and C' are empty, and $T' = \mathsf{Shuffle}^{-1}(M[1] \oplus C[1])$.

See Fig. 3. We see that the encryption query with key $K \oplus 1$ simulates the process for the empty message and AD, and the forgery in Step 3 succeeds with probability 1. The attack makes one related-key encryption query, one decryption query, and the success probability is 1.

We remark that the impact is limited, as the attack only forges the empty AD and message. We also remark that the security against related-key attacks is not included in the security requirements of NIST LwC, and is not claimed by the designers. However, this type of weakness is avoided, *e.g.*, in SCHWAEMM.

5   Conclusions

We have investigated the provable security bounds in the specification documents of two NIST LwC finalists, GIFT-COFB and Photon-Beetle, and reported some attacks whose success probabilities are higher that what their bounds tell. We have also analyzed other bounds of Photon-Beetle shown in the subsequent papers and shown some attacks. As a side result, we presented a simple forgery attack against Photon-Beetle when $r = 128$. We remark that our attacks do not invalidate the claimed bit security levels of them, and the related-key security is not claimed by the designers.

Acknowledgements. We thank GIFT-COFB team and the authors of [15,16] for feedback on an earlier version of this paper. We thank the anonymous reviewers for helpful comments.

A   Specifications of **GIFT-COFB** and **Photon-Beetle**

Algorithm GIFT-COFB-$\mathcal{E}_K(N, A, M)$

1. $Y[0] \leftarrow E_K(N)$, $L \leftarrow \mathsf{Trunc}_{n/2}(Y[0])$
2. $(A[1], \ldots, A[a]) \xleftarrow{n} \mathsf{pad}(A)$
3. **if** $M \neq \epsilon$ **then**
4. $\quad (M[1], \ldots, M[m]) \xleftarrow{n} \mathsf{pad}(M)$
5. **for** $i = 1$ **to** $a - 1$
6. $\quad L \leftarrow 2 \cdot L$
7. $\quad X[i] \leftarrow A[i] \oplus G \cdot Y[i-1] \oplus L\|0^{n/2}$
8. $\quad Y[i] \leftarrow E_K(X[i])$
9. **if** $|A| \bmod n = 0$ **and** $A \neq \epsilon$ **then** $L \leftarrow 3 \cdot L$
10. **else** $L \leftarrow 3^2 \cdot L$
11. **if** $M = \epsilon$ **then** $L \leftarrow 3^2 \cdot L$
12. $X[a] \leftarrow A[a] \oplus G \cdot Y[a-1] \oplus L\|0^{n/2}$
13. $Y[a] \leftarrow E_K(X[a])$
14. **for** $i = 1$ **to** $m - 1$
15. $\quad L \leftarrow 2 \cdot L$
16. $\quad C[i] \leftarrow M[i] \oplus Y[i+a-1]$
17. $\quad X[i+a] \leftarrow M[i] \oplus G \cdot Y[i+a-1] \oplus L\|0^{n/2}$
18. $\quad Y[i+a] \leftarrow E_K(X[i+a])$
19. **if** $M \neq \epsilon$ **then**
20. $\quad$ **if** $|M| \bmod n = 0$ **then** $L \leftarrow 3 \cdot L$
21. $\quad$ **else** $L \leftarrow 3^2 \cdot L$
22. $\quad C[m] \leftarrow M[m] \oplus Y[a+m-1]$
23. $\quad X[a+m] \leftarrow M[m] \oplus G \cdot Y[a+m-1] \oplus L\|0^{n/2}$
24. $\quad Y[a+m] \leftarrow E_K(X[a+m])$
25. $\quad C \leftarrow \mathsf{Trunc}_{|M|}(C[1]\|\ldots\|C[m])$
26. $\quad T \leftarrow \mathsf{Trunc}_\tau(Y[a+m])$
27. **else** $C \leftarrow \epsilon$, $T \leftarrow \mathsf{Trunc}_\tau(Y[a])$
28. **return** (C, T)

Algorithm GIFT-COFB-$\mathcal{D}_K(N, A, C, T)$

1. $Y[0] \leftarrow E_K(N)$, $L \leftarrow \mathsf{Trunc}_{n/2}(Y[0])$
2. $(A[1], \ldots, A[a]) \xleftarrow{n} \mathsf{pad}(A)$
3. **if** $C \neq \epsilon$ **then**
4. $\quad (C[1], \ldots, C[c]) \xleftarrow{n} \mathsf{pad}(C)$
5. **for** $i = 1$ **to** $a - 1$
6. $\quad L \leftarrow 2 \cdot L$
7. $\quad X[i] \leftarrow A[i] \oplus G \cdot Y[i-1] \oplus L\|0^{n/2}$
8. $\quad Y[i] \leftarrow E_K(X[i])$
9. **if** $|A| \bmod n = 0$ **and** $A \neq \epsilon$ **then** $L \leftarrow 3 \cdot L$
10. **else** $L \leftarrow 3^2 \cdot L$
11. **if** $C = \epsilon$ **then** $L \leftarrow 3^2 \cdot L$
12. $X[a] \leftarrow A[a] \oplus G \cdot Y[a-1] \oplus L\|0^{n/2}$
13. $Y[a] \leftarrow E_K(X[a])$
14. **for** $i = 1$ **to** $c - 1$
15. $\quad L \leftarrow 2 \cdot L$
16. $\quad M[i] \leftarrow Y[i+a-1] \oplus C[i]$
17. $\quad X[i+a] \leftarrow M[i] \oplus G \cdot Y[i+a-1] \oplus L\|0^{n/2}$
18. $\quad Y[i+a] \leftarrow E_K(X[i+a])$
19. **if** $C \neq \epsilon$ **then**
20. $\quad$ **if** $|C| \bmod n = 0$ **then**
21. $\quad\quad L \leftarrow 3 \cdot L$
22. $\quad\quad M[c] \leftarrow Y[a+c-1] \oplus C[c]$
23. $\quad$ **else**
24. $\quad\quad L \leftarrow 3^2 \cdot L$, $c' \leftarrow |C| \bmod n$
25. $\quad\quad M[c] \leftarrow \mathsf{Trunc}_{c'}(Y[a+c-1] \oplus C[c])\|10^{n-c'-1}$
26. $\quad X[a+c] \leftarrow M[c] \oplus G \cdot Y[a+c-1] \oplus L\|0^{n/2}$
27. $\quad Y[a+c] \leftarrow E_K(X[a+c])$
28. $\quad M \leftarrow \mathsf{Trunc}_{|C|}(M[1]\|\ldots\|M[c])$
29. $\quad T' \leftarrow \mathsf{Trunc}_\tau(Y[a+c])$
30. **else** $M \leftarrow \epsilon$, $T' \leftarrow \mathsf{Trunc}_\tau(Y[a])$
31. **if** $T' = T$ **then return** M, **else return** $\perp$

Fig. 4. Algorithms of GIFT-COFB [3, Fig. 2.3]

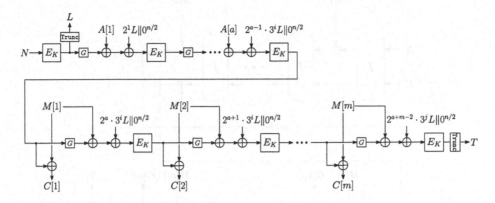

Fig. 5. GIFT-COFB.

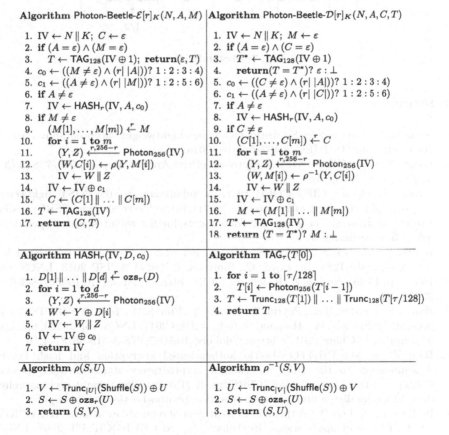

Algorithm Photon-Beetle-$\mathcal{E}[r]_K(N, A, M)$

1. $IV \leftarrow N \| K; \ C \leftarrow \varepsilon$
2. **if** $(A = \varepsilon) \wedge (M = \varepsilon)$
3. $\quad T \leftarrow TAG_{128}(IV \oplus 1); \ \textbf{return}(\varepsilon, T)$
4. $c_0 \leftarrow ((M \neq \varepsilon) \wedge (r| \, |A|))? \ 1:2:3:4$
5. $c_1 \leftarrow ((A \neq \varepsilon) \wedge (r| \, |M|))? \ 1:2:5:6$
6. **if** $A \neq \varepsilon$
7. $\quad IV \leftarrow HASH_r(IV, A, c_0)$
8. **if** $M \neq \varepsilon$
9. $\quad (M[1], \dots, M[m]) \xleftarrow{r} M$
10. $\quad$ **for** $i = 1$ **to** m
11. $\qquad (Y, Z) \xleftarrow{r,256-r} Photon_{256}(IV)$
12. $\qquad (W, C[i]) \leftarrow \rho(Y, M[i])$
13. $\qquad IV \leftarrow W \| Z$
14. $\qquad IV \leftarrow IV \oplus c_1$
15. $\quad C \leftarrow (C[1] \| \dots \| C[m])$
16. $T \leftarrow TAG_{128}(IV)$
17. **return** (C, T)

Algorithm Photon-Beetle-$\mathcal{D}[r]_K(N, A, C, T)$

1. $IV \leftarrow N \| K; \ M \leftarrow \varepsilon$
2. **if** $(A = \varepsilon) \wedge (C = \varepsilon)$
3. $\quad T^* \leftarrow TAG_{128}(IV \oplus 1)$
4. $\quad$ **return**$(T = T^*)? \ \varepsilon : \bot$
5. $c_0 \leftarrow ((C \neq \varepsilon) \wedge (r| \, |A|))? \ 1:2:3:4$
6. $c_1 \leftarrow ((A \neq \varepsilon) \wedge (r| \, |C|))? \ 1:2:5:6$
7. **if** $A \neq \varepsilon$
8. $\quad IV \leftarrow HASH_r(IV, A, c_0)$
9. **if** $C \neq \varepsilon$
10. $\quad (C[1], \dots, C[m]) \xleftarrow{r} C$
11. $\quad$ **for** $i = 1$ **to** m
12. $\qquad (Y, Z) \xleftarrow{r,256-r} Photon_{256}(IV)$
13. $\qquad (W, M[i]) \leftarrow \rho^{-1}(Y, C[i])$
14. $\qquad IV \leftarrow W \| Z$
15. $\qquad IV \leftarrow IV \oplus c_1$
16. $\quad M \leftarrow (M[1] \| \dots \| M[m])$
17. $T^* \leftarrow TAG_{128}(IV)$
18. **return** $(T = T^*)? \ M : \bot$

Algorithm $HASH_r(IV, D, c_0)$

1. $D[1] \| \dots \| D[d] \xleftarrow{r} ozs_r(D)$
2. **for** $i = 1$ **to** d
3. $\quad (Y, Z) \xleftarrow{r,256-r} Photon_{256}(IV)$
4. $\quad W \leftarrow Y \oplus D[i]$
5. $\quad IV \leftarrow W \| Z$
6. $IV \leftarrow IV \oplus c_0$
7. **return** IV

Algorithm $TAG_r(T[0])$

1. **for** $i = 1$ **to** $\lceil \tau/128 \rceil$
2. $\quad T[i] \leftarrow Photon_{256}(T[i-1])$
3. $T \leftarrow Trunc_{128}(T[1]) \| \dots \| Trunc_{128}(T[\tau/128])$
4. **return** T

Algorithm $\rho(S, U)$

1. $V \leftarrow Trunc_{|U|}(Shuffle(S)) \oplus U$
2. $S \leftarrow S \oplus ozs_r(U)$
3. **return** (S, V)

Algorithm $\rho^{-1}(S, V)$

1. $U \leftarrow Trunc_{|V|}(Shuffle(S)) \oplus V$
2. $S \leftarrow S \oplus ozs_r(U)$
3. **return** (S, U)

Fig. 6. Algorithms of Photon-Beetle [6, Fig. 3.6]

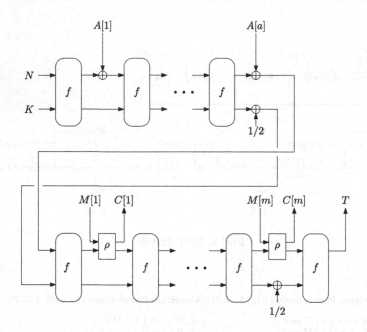

Fig. 7. Photon-Beetle.

References

1. Information technology-Security techniques-Lightweight cryptography-Part 5: Hash-functions. ISO/IEC 29192–5:2016 (2016)
2. Banik, S., et al.: GIFT-COFB. Cryptology ePrint Archive, Report 2020/738 (2020). https://ia.cr/2020/738
3. Banik, S., et al.: GIFT-COFB v1.1. A submission to the NIST lightweight cryptography standardization process (2021). https://csrc.nist.gov/CSRC/media/Projects/lightweight-cryptography/documents/finalist-round/updated-spec-doc/gift-cofb-spec-final.pdf
4. Banik, S., Maitra, S., Sarkar, S., Meltem Sönmez, T.: A chosen IV related key attack on grain-128a. In: Boyd, C., Simpson, L. (eds.) ACISP 2013. LNCS, vol. 7959, pp. 13–26. Springer, Heidelberg (2013). https://doi.org/10.1007/978-3-642-39059-3_2
5. Banik, S., Pandey, S.K., Peyrin, T., Sasaki, Y., Sim, S.M., Todo, Y.: GIFT: a small present. In: Fischer, W., Homma, N. (eds.) CHES 2017. LNCS, vol. 10529, pp. 321–345. Springer, Cham (2017). https://doi.org/10.1007/978-3-319-66787-4_16
6. Bao, Z., et al.: PHOTON-beetle authenticated encryption and hash family. A submission to the NIST lightweight cryptography standardization process (2021). https://csrc.nist.gov/CSRC/media/Projects/lightweight-cryptography/documents/finalist-round/updated-spec-doc/photon-beetle-spec-final.pdf
7. Bellare, M., Kohno, T.: A theoretical treatment of related-key attacks: RKA-PRPs, RKA-PRFs, and applications. In: Biham, E. (ed.) EUROCRYPT 2003. LNCS, vol. 2656, pp. 491–506. Springer, Heidelberg (2003). https://doi.org/10.1007/3-540-39200-9_31

8. Bellare, M., Namprempre, C.: Authenticated encryption: relations among notions and analysis of the generic composition paradigm. In: Okamoto, T. (ed.) ASIACRYPT 2000. LNCS, vol. 1976, pp. 531–545. Springer, Heidelberg (2000). https://doi.org/10.1007/3-540-44448-3_41

9. Biham, E.: New types of cryptanalytic attacks using related keys. In: Helleseth, T. (ed.) EUROCRYPT 1993. LNCS, vol. 765, pp. 398–409. Springer, Heidelberg (1994). https://doi.org/10.1007/3-540-48285-7_34

10. Biryukov, C.B.A., et al.: SPARKLE (SCHWAEMM and ESCH). A submission to the NIST lightweight cryptography standardization process (2021). https://csrc.nist.gov/CSRC/media/Projects/lightweight-cryptography/documents/finalist-round/updated-spec-doc/sparkle-spec-final.pdf

11. Chakraborti, A., Datta, N., Nandi, M., Yasuda, K.: Beetle family of lightweight and secure authenticated encryption ciphers. IACR TCHES **2018**(2), 218–241 (2018). https://doi.org/10.13154/tches.v2018.i2.218-241, https://tches.iacr.org/index.php/TCHES/article/view/881

12. Chakraborti, A., Datta, N., Nandi, M., Yasuda, K.: Beetle family of lightweight and secure authenticated encryption ciphers. Cryptology ePrint Archive, Report 2018/805 (2018). https://eprint.iacr.org/2018/805

13. Chakraborti, A., Iwata, T., Minematsu, K., Nandi, M.: Blockcipher-based authenticated encryption: how small can we go? In: Fischer, W., Homma, N. (eds.) CHES 2017. LNCS, vol. 10529, pp. 277–298. Springer, Cham (2017). https://doi.org/10.1007/978-3-319-66787-4_14

14. Chakraborti, A., Iwata, T., Minematsu, K., Nandi, M.: Blockcipher-based authenticated encryption: how small can we go? J. Cryptol. **33**(3), 703–741 (2019). https://doi.org/10.1007/s00145-019-09325-z

15. Chakraborty, B., Jha, A., Nandi, M.: On the security of sponge-type authenticated encryption modes. Cryptology ePrint Archive, Report 2019/1475 (2019). https://eprint.iacr.org/2019/1475

16. Chakraborty, B., Jha, A., Nandi, M.: On the security of sponge-type authenticated encryption modes. IACR Trans. Symmetric Cryptol. **2020**(2), 93–119 (2020). https://doi.org/10.13154/tosc.v2020.i2.93-119

17. Dobraunig, C., Eichlseder, M., Mendel, F.: Related-key forgeries for Prøst-OTR. In: Leander, G. (ed.) FSE 2015. LNCS, vol. 9054, pp. 282–296. Springer, Heidelberg (2015). https://doi.org/10.1007/978-3-662-48116-5_14

18. Dobraunig, C., Mennink, B.: Key recovery attack on PHOTON-Beetle. OFFICIAL COMMENT: PHOTON-Beetle (2020). https://csrc.nist.gov/CSRC/media/Projects/lightweight-cryptography/documents/round-2/official-comments/photon-beetle-round2-official-comment.pdf

19. Guo, J., Peyrin, T., Poschmann, A.: The PHOTON family of lightweight hash functions. In: Rogaway, P. (ed.) CRYPTO 2011. LNCS, vol. 6841, pp. 222–239. Springer, Heidelberg (2011). https://doi.org/10.1007/978-3-642-22792-9_13

20. Inoue, A., Minematsu, K.: GIFT-COFB is tightly birthday secure with encryption queries. Cryptology ePrint Archive, Report 2021/737 (2021). https://ia.cr/2021/737

21. Khairallah, M.: Weak keys in the rekeying paradigm: Application to COMET and mixFeed. IACR Trans. Symmetric Cryptol. **2019**(4), 272–289 (2019). https://doi.org/10.13154/tosc.v2019.i4.272-289

22. Khairallah, M.: Observations on the tightness of the security bounds of GIFT-COFB and HyENA. Cryptology ePrint Archive, Report 2020/1463 (2020). https://eprint.iacr.org/2020/1463

23. Khairallah, M.: Security of COFB against chosen ciphertext attacks. Cryptology ePrint Archive, Report 2021/648 (2021). https://eprint.iacr.org/2021/648, (also accepted at FSE 2022)

24. Lee, Y., Jeong, K., Sung, J., Hong, S.: Related-key chosen IV attacks on Grain-v1 and Grain-128. In: Mu, Y., Susilo, W., Seberry, J. (eds.) ACISP 2008. LNCS, vol. 5107, pp. 321–335. Springer, Heidelberg (2008). https://doi.org/10.1007/978-3-540-70500-0_24

25. Lu, X., Li, B., Jia, D.: KDM-CCA security from RKA secure authenticated encryption. In: Oswald, E., Fischlin, M. (eds.) EUROCRYPT 2015. LNCS, vol. 9056, pp. 559–583. Springer, Heidelberg (2015). https://doi.org/10.1007/978-3-662-46800-5_22

26. Lucks, S.: Ciphers secure against related-key attacks. In: Roy, B., Meier, W. (eds.) FSE 2004. LNCS, vol. 3017, pp. 359–370. Springer, Heidelberg (2004). https://doi.org/10.1007/978-3-540-25937-4_23

27. Mège, A.: OFFICIAL COMMENT: PHOTON-Beetle (2021). https://csrc.nist.gov/CSRC/media/Projects/lightweight-cryptography/documents/round-2/official-comments/photon-beetle-round2-official-comment.pdf

28. Rogaway, P.: Efficient instantiations of tweakable blockciphers and refinements to modes OCB and PMAC. In: Lee, P.J. (ed.) ASIACRYPT 2004. LNCS, vol. 3329, pp. 16–31. Springer, Heidelberg (2004). https://doi.org/10.1007/978-3-540-30539-2_2

29. Rogaway, P.: Nonce-based symmetric encryption. In: Roy, B., Meier, W. (eds.) FSE 2004. LNCS, vol. 3017, pp. 348–358. Springer, Heidelberg (2004). https://doi.org/10.1007/978-3-540-25937-4_22

30. Rogaway, P., Shrimpton, T.: A provable-security treatment of the key-wrap problem. In: Vaudenay, S. (ed.) EUROCRYPT 2006. LNCS, vol. 4004, pp. 373–390. Springer, Heidelberg (2006). https://doi.org/10.1007/11761679_23

Beware of Your Vibrating Devices! Vibrational Relay Attacks on Zero-Effort Deauthentication

Prakash Shrestha[1(✉)] and Nitesh Saxena[2]

[1] Equifax, Atlanta, GA, USA
prakash.shrestha@equifax.com
[2] Texas A&M University, College Station, TX, USA
nsaxena@tamu.edu

Abstract. Zero-effort deauthentication (ZED) aims to log out a user from a computer terminal, if not in use, without any user intervention. A representative instance of such an approach is ZEBRA, which makes use of a wrist-worn wearable device (e.g., smartwatch) to deauthenticate the user if the activities on the computer terminal (e.g., typing) do not match with the user's wrist movements.

In this paper, we present VibRaze (VibRaze stands for Vibration-enabled Relay Attacks on Zero-EffoRt deauthenticaton.), a new class of potentially devastating relay attacks against ZED (specifically, a prominent ZED instance ZEBRA) based on the ubiquitous and inconspicuous vibration capability of the underlying wrist-wearable. Since merely launching a ghost-and-leech relay attack against these schemes is not going to bypass their security, VibRaze additionally creates vibrations on the wrist-wearable remotely (e.g., through a phone call) while the attacker attempts to defeat the deauthentication functionality of the ZEBRA system. This serves to defeat ZEBRA since the vibration-triggered movements at the wrist-wearable highly correlate with the typing events at the terminal. We design and evaluate VibRaze against ZEBRA's machine learning design demonstrating that it can allow the attacker to remain logged into the terminal and perform typing activity at will, while the user remains oblivious to the ongoing attack. VibRaze represents a significantly powerful and challenging threat to address due to its remote and inconspicuous nature. Nevertheless, we provide some potential mitigation strategies that may be used to reduce the impact of VibRaze.

1 Introduction

Any usable authentication system should consist of a *deauthentication* mechanism, i.e., a means for promptly detecting when to log out a previously authenticated user from an ongoing session at a computer terminal. To improve the usability of deauthentication, it is crucial to make it *oblivious* to users by eliminating the cognitive effort required of them. Although such *zero-effort* deauthentication (ZED) schemes are compelling, designing them correctly can be a challenge in practice given the obvious tension between the underlying usability and security requirements.

A concrete representative ZED approrach is ZEBRA, a zero-effort bilateral deauthentication method, proposed by Mare et al. [21]. ZEBRA is geared for scenarios where users authenticate to computer terminals (such as desktop computers in a collaborative setting). In such scenarios, users typically have to either manually deauthenticate

© Springer Nature Switzerland AG 2022
G. Ateniese and D. Venturi (Eds.): ACNS 2022, LNCS 13269, pp. 85–104, 2022.
https://doi.org/10.1007/978-3-031-09234-3_5

themselves by logging out or locking the terminal, or the terminal can deauthenticate a user automatically after a sufficiently long period of inactivity. The former approach requires explicit user effort while the latter approach reduces promptness of log out. ZEBRA makes the process of deauthentication both prompt and transparent: once a user is authenticated to a terminal (using say a password), it continuously, yet transparently re-authenticates the user so that prompt deauthentication is possible without explicit user action. In ZEBRA, the user is required to wear a device on her wrist (e.g., a smartwatch or bracelet) equipped with motion sensors on his mouse-holding hand. The bracelet is wirelessly connected and paired to the terminal, which compares the sequence of events it observes (e.g., keyboard/mouse interactions) with the sequence of events predicted using measurements from the device's motion sensors. The logged-in user is deauthenticated when the two sequences no longer match. The application scenarios for ZEBRA can very well extend beyond the shared-space setting and may include (de)authentication to a personal computer or a laptop, or even a mobile phone, like to enhance the security of Google Smart Lock [9].

In this paper, we present a new class of potentially devastating relay attack against ZED (specifically a prominent ZED instance ZEBRA) based on the ubiquitous and inconspicuous vibration capability of the underlying wrist-worn wearable device. VibRaze involves mounting a *ghost-and-leech relay attack*, and crucially *creating vibrations* on the wearable device of the user located remotely (e.g., through a phone call or notifications) (can be visualized in Fig. 1b) The leech is installed at the remote location where the user's wearable device resides (e.g., home, office, or cafeteria), and the ghost is installed near the terminal. Once the ghost and leech pairs have been installed, the attacker does not need to be in close proximity of the remote user. To break the security of ZEBRA, while creating vibrations on the wearable device, the attacker performs typing activity at will on the terminal unbeknownst to the victim. The vibration functionality serves to defeat ZEBRA since vibration creates subtle movements on the device that match the characteristics of a typing activity being applied at the terminal.

Ghost-and-leech relay attacks have already been demonstrated to be practical for various short range wireless communication technologies like Bluetooth [18], RFID [7, 14] and NFC [8], making this vulnerability a serious threat. We also implemented and tested the ghost-and-leech relay attack over the Bluetooth channel, the wireless medium used in ZEBRA. However, such *standard relay attacks* do not work to defeat ZEBRA because ZEBRA involves correlating user's hand movements captured by the wearable with activities on the terminal (as shown in Fig. 1a). Therefore, simply relaying the wireless communication between two end points as in standard attacks is not sufficient to bypass the security of ZEBRA. We address this challenge by introducing the notion of *vibration-based relay attacks*.

Since the attack is triggered by a simple and random spam call/notification, the user remains unaware of the ongoing attack. For instance, a call ring/vibration typically lasts for roughly 20 s (if the call is not picked up), during which an attacker can type in 60–65 characters (given the typing speed of an average person is 190–200 characters per minute [20]). Even with these limited characters, the attacker can swiftly perform various nefarious activities on the terminal, such as deleting important files, uploading private files to the attacker's server, changing dosage and making fake prescriptions in a hospital setting, and leave to evade the detection. Due to the zero-effort nature of the underlying schemes, the user can not determine if the spam call/notification was received as part of attacking these schemes. On the contrary, if the user is required to be diligently present in the loop to detect such attacks, the schemes will no longer be zero-effort.

Our Contributions: We believe that our work makes the following novel contributions:

1. **A Fundamental New Vulnerability in Zero-Effort Deauthentication (ZED):** We introduce VibRaze, a new vulnerability associated with ZED based on bilateral activity correlations. It takes the form of a standard ghost and leech relay attack augmented with remote vibrations triggered with simple phone calls/notifications that allows the attacker to remain logged into an authentication terminal.
2. **VibRaze Design based on Vibration Triggers:** We design VibRaze as a significant extension to the standard relay attacks based on two types of remote vibration triggers – *Call-Vib*, the vibration created on the watch/bracelet when there is a call on the phone (a companion device of the watch), and *Notif-Vib*, the vibration generated on the watch when there is a notification (e.g., a message, an email) for the user. We observed that the motion sensor readings associated with the vibration mostly (88.31%) match with those of typing activity, which enables VibRaze to launch a relay attack enhanced with vibration against ZEBRA when the user is located remotely doing other activities.
3. **Evaluation of VibRaze:** We evaluate VibRaze against ZEBRA's machine learning design demonstrating that it can allow the attacker to remain logged into the terminal (with 100% of probability in most of the cases) and perform typing activity at will, during which it can perform malicious activities on the terminal (such as deleting important files, uploading private files to the attacker's server, or changing dosage and writing new prescriptions in a hospital setting). Since the attack is triggered by a simple spam call/notification, the user remains unaware of the ongoing attack.

The rest of the paper is organized as follows. In Sect. 2, we review ZEBRA, proximity attacks against it, and recently proposed defensive system. In Sect. 3, we introduce our remote attack system, VibRaze, against ZEBRA, followed by Sect. 4, where we provide details on the design of VibRaze. Next, in Sect. 5, we present data collection procedures. We evaluate VibRaze against ZEBRA in Sect. 6. Finally, in Sect. 7, we discuss potential mitigation strategies against VibRaze, review related literatures in Sect. 8, and conclude our work in Sect. 9.

2 Background: ZEBRA Review

In ZEBRA, the user, once authenticated, is continuously and transparently reauthenticated making the deauthentication process prompt without any explicit user interaction.

System Architecture: ZEBRA considers a terminal with keyboard and mouse, and a watch equipped with motion sensors (i.e., accelerometer and gyroscope). The readings recorded by the watch's embedded sensors capture the wrist movement of the wearer. The terminal keeps track of the watch associated with each authorized user. Once a user is authenticated to the terminal, ZEBRA continuously re-authenticates the user by correlating his interactions at the terminal with the interactions predicted based on the motion signal captured by the watch. If they do not correlate, ZEBRA promptly deauthenticates the current user.

ZEBRA considers three types of interactions: typing on the keyboard, mouse scrolling, and keyboard-to-mouse and mouse-to-keyboard hand movements (termed as "MKKM"). When comparing interactions, ZEBRA considers three parameters – *window size* (w), *threshold* (m), and *grace period* (g). ZEBRA compares a sequence of w interactions (a window) at a time. A window is marked '1' if the fraction of matching interactions exceeds a threshold m, otherwise, it is marked '0'. If ZEBRA marks '0' for 'g' consecutive windows, it outputs "different" and instantly deauthenticate the user.

In ZEBRA, the wrist-wearable can be a wrist-band, such as those from Fitbit [6] and Xiaomi [28], or a general-purpose smartwatch, such as LG G Watch R that we have used in our implementation. Typically, being constrained devices, these wrist-bands need, and always remain connected with a companion device, the smartphone in particular, for its proper functionality. Similar to the smartwatch, these wrist-bands offer a vibration feature to alert the user when the user's phone rings or gets notifications.

Adversary Model: ZEBRA considers the threat of unauthorized access to the terminal when a user leaves the terminal without logging out and remains in its proximity doing other tasks. Specifically, ZEBRA considers two types of adversaries. First, *an innocent adversary*, a user who uses an unattended terminal for his own purposes without realizing that another user ('victim') is logged in or because she does not want to go through the login process. Second, a malicious adversary who deliberately uses the already logged-in terminal with the intent to perform some action impersonating the victim. The malicious individual may observe and mimic the actions of the victim user using another nearby terminal to fool the terminal into falsely authenticating himself as the victim user. Mare et al. [21] have demonstrated that their system was able to detect and deauthenticate both *innocent* and *malicious* adversaries in a reasonable time while maintaining low false negative rates.

3   Overview and Threat Model

VibRaze represents a new threat, potentially a devastating one, to ZEBRA that can compromise the system's security when victim user is located remotely, far away from the authentication terminal in question. VibRaze involves mounting a *ghost-and-leech relay attack*, and creating *vibrations* on the wearable device of the user located remotely (e.g., through a phone call/notifications) while the attacker performs the typing activity on the terminal unbeknownst to the victim. VibRaze assumes a malicious adversary who attempts to access an already logged-in terminal (similar to ZEBRA) or who has compromised the user's credentials (via phishing attacks, password databases leakage or other mechanisms) and attempts to access the terminal on behalf of the user. Specifically, to compromise the security of the ZEBRA system, VibRaze follows below-mentioned steps. Figure 1 presents the visualization of VibRaze.

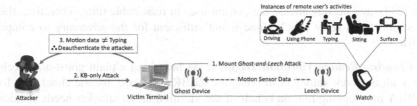

(a) A plain ghost-and-leech relay attack againt ZEBRA. This attack alone cannot succeed due to matching of hand movements with terminal activity in ZEBRA.

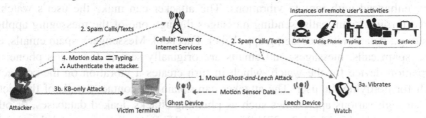

(b) VibRaze: A ghost-and-leech relay attack enhanced with remote vibration. This attack can succeed to defeat ZEBRA as vibrational motions on the wearable device match with keyboard activity on most occasions.

Fig. 1. VibRaze Attack Model with and without vibration. "KB-only Attack": the attacker interacts with victim terminal using only keyboard.

(1) Mounting Ghost-and-Leech Attack: To defeat ZEBRA, VibRaze mounts a ghost-and-leech relay attack that enables the watch to remain connected with the terminal even after the wearable goes out of the terminal's proximity. Ghost-and-leech relay attacks have already been demonstrated to be practical for various short-range wireless communication technologies like Bluetooth [18], RFID [7,14] and NFC [8]. VibRaze can employ a ghost-and-leech attack following the approach similar to any of these works. In fact, we implemented and tested the ghost-and-leech relay attack on Bluetooth channel, the wireless medium utilized in ZEBRA, as described in Sect. 4.2. In VibRaze, an adversary implants a *ghost* near the terminal, and a *leech* at the location where the watch of the user has a high chance to be present, e.g., at home or on a car (such as hidden in the exterior of the car somewhere). The leech emulates the terminal and receives the stream of motion sensor data from the watch and relays it to the ghost. The ghost emulates the watch and transfers the stream of motion data received from the leech to the terminal. Thus, launching the relay attack enables the terminal to remain connected to the watch and allows it to continuously receive the motion sensor data from the watch. Figure 1a shows this plain ghost-and-leech relay attack against ZEBRA.

When the adversary launches the relay attack, the user at the remote location may perform various wrist activities that are different from the user-terminal interactions. To continuously and transparently re-authenticate the user, ZEBRA correlates the wrist movements with the terminal activities. Mare et al. have demonstrated that ZEBRA can correctly detect the non-terminal activities with high accuracy (as shown in Figs. 5 and

6 in [21]), and deauthenticate the current user in reasonable time. Therefore, the plain ghost-and-leech relay attack alone is not sufficient for the adversary to compromise ZEBRA.

(2) Creating Remote Vibration Triggers: As launching a plain ghost-and-leech relay attack alone is not sufficient to break the ZEBRA system, for the attacker to fool the ZEBRA into logging him on behalf of the victim user, an attacker needs an additional step of vibrating the watch to make the motion signal match the typing activity at the terminal. Figure 1b shows the VibRaze attack consisting of the ghost-and-leech relay attack enhanced with remote vibrations. The attacker can make the user's watch to vibrate through spam calls, sending messages through one of the messaging applications (e.g., default text messaging app, Viber, Facebook Messenger), spam emails, etc. These spam calls, messages, and emails are originally sent to the user's phone, the companion device for the watch, which in turn creates a vibration on the connected watch for notifying the user. The attacker can obtain the contact details of the victim user through various approaches such as phishing attacks, leaked databases, or other mechanisms [10, 15–17, 24, 25, 27]. We note that VibRaze does not need the attacker to continuously ring/vibrate the victim's watch. The attacker can devise a strategy to periodically and randomly ring the watch such that it does not alert the victim while he can accomplish his intended task. In fact, VibRaze can be launched for a duration of a single call (or a couple of messages), and wait for a certain time, perhaps for a sufficiently long time, and repeat the attack, thereby making it inconspicuous to the victim user. One may assume that the victim can block a phone number if he receives spam calls/messages from it. However, the attacker can use different phone numbers over the duration of the attack to generate spam calls and messages.

We note that the first step in VibRaze, i.e., mounting the relay attack, is performed only once while the second step of creating a vibration on the user's watch can be performed multiple times as per attacker's choice such that the undergoing attack remains oblivious to the victim user. Further, VibRaze considers a *keyboard-only attack* where the attacker interacts with the terminal using only the keyboard at the time when there is a vibration on the user's watch due to an ongoing call or a message notification. Since motion signals associated with vibrations are mostly classified to typing interaction (explained next), employing a keyboard-only attack enables the attacker to successfully compromise the ZEBRA system.

Why Vibration?: ZEBRA considers three types of interactions – typing, scrolling, and MKKM. When a motion segment corresponding to an interaction is fed to *Interaction Classifier*, it is always classified to one of the classes/interactions. Therefore, a keyboard-only attacker can succeed to fool the ZEBRA into logging him as a legitimate user if he can enforce the user's watch to create a motion that is close to the typing interaction. In VibRaze, the attacker utilizes the vibrator motor available on the watch to create such motion on the watch. Specifically, as mentioned earlier, the attacker makes the user's watch to vibrate by making a spam phone call or sending a bunch of messages. When the watch vibrates, it creates certain motion on the device, which when fed to ZEBRA, it gets mapped to one of the interactions considered in ZEBRA (mostly to typing as detailed below).

To find out what class the motion corresponding to vibration is classified to by the *Interaction Classifier* of ZEBRA, we mismatched all the actual interaction from 45 user samples (collected in our study as explained in Sect. 5) with the vibration-triggered motion sample. While mismatching, the starting point of the vibration-triggered motion sensor sample was aligned with the starting point of interaction samples. Since we are interested in the keyboard-only attack, we removed all the mouse-related interactions (scrolling and MKKM) from the actual interaction sequence during mismatching. Vibration motion data was then segmented into blocks based on the timestamps of actual interactions, features were extracted from each block, and were fed to already trained *Interaction Classifier*. The result shows that most (88.31%, 8687/9836) of the vibration motion sensor data are classified as typing, and rest (11.68%, 1151/8685) are classified as scrolling. Since, for *Interaction Classifier*, vibration on the watch closely matches with the typing, enforcing the user's watch to vibrate can enable VibRaze to compromise the security of ZEBRA.

Further, the user study of [22] with 113 Amazon Mechanical Turk workers has shown that the majority of the users keep their smartphones either in ringer or vibration mode most of the time at home and while asleep. We note that ringer mode generally includes vibration on it. We believe that similar results would apply in the case of smartwatches. Since the majority of smartwatches (e.g., LG G Watch R, Sony Smartwatch 3) do not come with built-in speakers that leave the user with only two options, either to set the watch in vibration mode or in silent mode. As in the case of the phone, it is reasonable to assume that the majority of users would keep their watches in vibration mode, the *default* mode. Given that the users would mostly keep their watches in the vibration mode, and the motion segments corresponding to vibration are mostly mapped to typing in ZEBRA, we design VibRaze by carefully considering different vibration patterns such that they match with the typing activities.

Broader Implications – Extension to VibRaze: VibRaze can further be extended to launch an attack against various other security schemes, particularly against authorization schemes based on motion sensors. For instance, the vibration-based attack notion underlying VibRaze may be applied to defeat *OpenSesame* [29], a lock/unlock system for smartphones based on the hand waving pattern of the users. VibRaze may be designed to generate the vibration pattern on the phone that matches the hand waving pattern of the user, thereby fooling the system to unlock the device. The accelerometer-based tapping mechanism proposed in *Tap-Wave-Rub* [19] geared for NFC applications may also be defeated by carefully updating VibRaze. The vibration pattern generated in such a modified VibRaze may match with the tapping gesture of the user. Several other schemes that rely on motion sensors may also be vulnerable to VibRaze. Further investigation is needed to measure the extent that the vibration pattern matches with gesture activities used in security schemes.

4 Design and Implementation

4.1 Implementation of ZEBRA

Software: We designed and developed two applications – *Wear-app* (Android), and *Desktop-app* (Java). Wear-app runs on the LG watch and captures the wearer's wrist motion measurements while Desktop-app runs on the terminal and captures the actual keyboard-mouse interaction observed on the terminal. The watch synchronizes its clock with the terminal and transmits the motion sensor data to the terminal at the sampling rate 200 Hz through Bluetooth. We utilized MATLAB to implement the rest of the components of ZEBRA with the functionalities as described in [21].

Feature Set and Classifier: Similar to [21], we used the same set of 12 features from each of the accelerometer and gyroscope. The list of features is shown in Table 1. We also used a RandomForest classifier with 100 weak-learners. Each weak-learners consider $sqrt(n)$ features, where 'n' (=24) is the total number of features. All the classes under consideration were weighted to account for any imbalances in the training dataset. Further, the exact parameters (as shown in Table 2) as provided in [21] were used in our implementation.

Table 1. List of features used in our implementation.

Feature	Description
Mean	mean value of signal
Median	median value of signal
Variance	variance of signal
Standard Deviation	standard deviation of signal
MAD	median absolute deviation
IQR	inter-quartile range
Power	power of signal
Energy	energy of signal
Peak-to-peak	peak-to-peak amplitude
Autocorrelation	similarity of signal
Kurtosis	peakedness of signal
Skewness	asymmetry of signal

Table 2. Parameters and their values used in our implementation of ZEBRA.

Parameter	Value	Parameter	Value
Minimum duration	25 ms	Window size (w)	5-30
Maximum duration[a]	1 s	Match threshold (m)	50-70 %
Idle threshold[a]	1 s	Overlap fraction (f)	0
		Grace period (g)	1, 2

[a]For MKKM, idle threshold and maximum duration is 5s.

4.2 Implementation of Relay Attack

As a prerequisite to launch the attack, we implemented and tested a ghost-and-leech relay attack against the Bluetooth channel (the wireless channel used in ZEBRA) utilizing Python-Bluez and socket libraries. The relay attack consists of two attacking devices – ghost (or the attacker's watch $\mathcal{G}$) and leech (or the attacker's terminal $\mathcal{L}$), each with a reprogrammable Bluetooth device. They communicate with each other through a network connection. We developed two python scripts using Python-Bluez and socket libraries for these two attacking devices. Unlike the attacking devices, the terminal (T) and the watch (W) have fixed mac addresses. The ghost device (G) and the leech device (L) clone the mac addresses of original W and T, respectively. With this setup, G appears to be W to T while L appears to be T to W. Initially, G and L establish a network socket connection to forward messages between them. Once they are connected, L starts the Bluetooth Socket server to accept the incoming connection request from W, and G establishes a Bluetooth connection to T. Upon establishing a Bluetooth connection between $G–T$ and $L–W$, all the messages including challenge-response messages and motion sensor measurements are relayed through G and L from W to T (and vice-versa). Thus, the relay attack was performed successfully. Since the ghost-and-leech attack can be launched stealthily installing G and L devices at their respective locations and following the approaches similar to [7, 8, 14, 18], or our implementation as described earlier, in our study, we mainly focus on designing and analyzing the additional step of creating the remote vibrations on victim's watch.

4.3 Design of VibRaze's Attack Scenarios

To evaluate the effectiveness of VibRaze against ZEBRA, we consider various scenarios based on the vibration type and the watch position as described below.

Vibration Type: We consider two types of vibrations on the user's watch – *Call-Vib* and *Notif-Vib*. *Call-Vib* is the vibration generated on the watch due to a call. In *Call-Vib*, the watch vibrates for approximately 20 s, assuming the call is not picked up, or is dropped. The watch may vibrate for a shorter period if the user picks up the call or disconnects it. However, an attacker can call the victim user multiple times after a certain time gap so that the attack remains oblivious to the user. *Notif-Vib* is the vibration created on the watch due to the notification of a text message, or an email. In *Notif-Vib*, the watch vibrates for a very short duration (approximately 500 ms). Similar to *Call-Vib*, the attacker can send multiple messages making the watch vibrate for a longer duration.

To evaluate VibRaze against ZEBRA with these two vibration setups, we updated/programmed the Wear-app to create *Call-Vib* and *Notif-Vib*. Since the vibration on the watch when its companion device (i.e., the phone) rings, specifically *Call-Vib*, generally follows a *vibration-pause-vibration* pattern, we simulated *Call-Vib* with the duration of (1000-2000-1000) ms based on the vibration pattern generated on the LG G watch when its companion device rings. Similarly, we simulated *Notif-Vib*, i.e., the vibration generated when the watch receives a text message or an email with a short vibration of 500 ms. To simulate multiple calls, Wear-app plays the *Call-Vib* repeatedly with an inter-*Call-Vib* gap of (2000–3000) ms while it plays the *Notif-Vib* repeatedly with an inter-*Notif-Vib* gap of 1000 ms to simulate multiple text messages.

Watch Position: We consider VibRaze with two settings – *On-Wrist*, where the watch is worn by the user, and *Off-Wrist*, where the watch is not worn. In the *On-Wrist* setting, we consider various scenarios based on the real-life activities of the users. For instance, we consider a *driving* scenario that reflects the attack setting where the victim user is driving his car, or riding a bus/train. We also consider a *using-phone* scenario, where the victim user is using his phone for various purposes such as for typing/reading a text/email, or surfing the internet. Next, we consider the *writing* scenario where the user performs a hand-writing task. Further, we consider the attack setting with the *typing* scenario where the user uses his personal computer or his laptop at home or other places. In daily life, the users should also perform walking activities so we consider the attack setting with the *walking* scenario. Moreover, we consider *miscellaneous* wrist-activities that represents an attack scenario where the user is resting by sitting on a sofa or a chair and moving his hand for random activities. Apart from these activities, users may do several other activities in day-to-day life. Covering all day-to-day real-life activities of the user to evaluate the performance of VibRaze is not possible in the study. However, we try to cover all the user's activities by categorizing them into the following classes – *driving, using phone, writing, typing and miscellaneous.* "Miscellaneous" represents all the random activities that the user performs while sitting on a sofa or a chair. During all these activities, we assume that users are wearing the watch designated for authentication.

While at home, users may take off their watches and keep them on the desk, or on other surface for charging or for other reasons. Users are most likely to take off their watches before they go to the bed. We refer to such a non-worn setting as *Off-Wrist*. Unlike a table/desk, some surfaces where users keep their watches may dampen the vibration. Therefore, we consider two types of surfaces – (a) a smooth surface that does not dampen the vibration, e.g., wooden table surface, and (b) a surface that can dampen the vibration, e.g. sofa, pillow, etc.

5 Data Collection

To evaluate the performance of our implementation of ZEBRA (in benign and adversarial settings) and that of VibRaze, we recruited 15 participants (mostly graduate students, 18 - 35 years old, 11 males and 4 females). All participants were right-handed. Participants were told that the purpose of the study was to evaluate the feasibility of using wrist-motion while interacting with the terminal to authenticate the user. Before starting the experiment, they were asked about their general demographics. During the experiment, participants performed three 10-minute tasks of filling a web form similar to [21]. From each task, two sets of data were collected – (i) motion data, i.e., accelerometer and gyroscope sensor readings, from the user's watch, and (ii) user's activities on the terminal, i.e., actual interaction identified by *Interaction Extractor* on the terminal. The 15 user sessions thus resulted in a total of 45 samples. All the experiments were conducted in the lab settings. Our experiment and the data collection followed the IRB procedures at our institution.

To evaluate VibRaze against ZEBRA, we collected the motion sensor data for each of the attack settings detailed in Sect. 4.3. For the *Off-Wrist* setting, the watch was placed on the top of three different surfaces – the surface of a wooden table, a soft pillow, and a sofa. Since, unlike the wooden table, the soft pillow and the sofa can dampen the intensity of the vibration on the watch, they emulate the scenario where the watch is placed on top of a vibration absorber. In our work, one of the researchers involved in the study played the role of the victim, and data was collected corresponding to this user in different scenarios of the *On-Wrist* setup. For the *On-Wrist* setting, motion sensor data was recorded when the victim was performing various regular activities while wearing the watch on his right hand. We collected motion data when the victim was walking at his regular pace, and when he was writing some text from a random wiki link on a sheet of paper. Motion data were also collected when the victim was using his phone. On the phone, the victim performed the following tasks – typing the provided text, browsing Facebook/Instagram, and checking email. Further, motion sensor data was collected when the victim was filling a simple web-form similar to the one used earlier. Moreover, motion sensor data was collected when the victim was driving a car at a speed ranging between 20–60 mph. We also collected motion data when the victim was sitting on a chair and communicating with other people. In this setting, the victim moves his hand at random. We term the wrist-activity of this setting as "miscellaneous". All these activities were performed for 10 min. We note that only motion data was collected when the victim was performing these activities. In total, we collected 16 motion samples, eight samples (3 samples with *Off-Wrist* and 5 with *On-Wrist* setup) for each of *Call-Vib* and *Notif-Vib* settings. This pool of motion samples represents various attack settings of VibRaze with different activities of the users, and the watch placement.

6   Analysis and Results

In this section, we evaluate the performance of our implementation of ZEBRA and that of VibRaze against ZEBRA in various scenarios.

6.1   Performance of ZEBRA

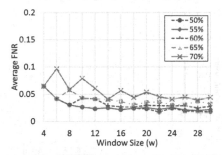
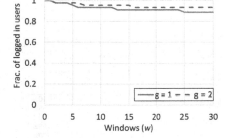

(a) Average FNR vs. window size (w) for different threshold (m) values. Fraction of windows that are incorrectly classified as mismatching.

(b) Fraction of users remaining logged after 'n' authentication windows (with $w = 20$, $m = 60\%$) for different grace periods (g).

Fig. 2. Legitimate users.

Performance with Legitimate Users: To evaluate the performance of our implementation of ZEBRA with legitimate users, we employ the same approach as in [21] on the data samples collected from 15 users. Specifically, we compute False Negative Rate (FNR) as the fraction of interaction windows from a user that the *Authenticator* outputs incorrectly as from "different user". Similarly, we employ the *leave-one-out* cross-validation approach – for a given user, we train the classifier using 42 data samples collected from all the other 14 user sessions, and three data samples from the current user are used to test the model. Thus, we build 15 different classifiers and report the aggregate classification results of 45 samples.

With our implementation of ZEBRA, we achieved FNRs in the range between 0–10% (as shown in Fig. 2a) which is in line with [21] (0–18)%. We achieved FNRs below 6% for window sizes above 15. Similar to [21], we fixed $w = 20$ and $m = 60\%$ to estimate the length of time (in terms of the number of windows) for which a legitimate user remained logged in. Figure 2b shows the fraction of users remaining logged in after 'n' authentication windows for a grace period (g) of 1 and 2. With $g = 1$, ZEBRA recognizes 89% of the users as a legitimate user for the entire session while with $g = 2$, this fraction increases to 94%. These results are in line with those reported in [21].

Table 3. Confusion matrix of *Interaction Classifiers* for 15 legitimate user samples.

		Predicted		
		Typing	Scrolling	MKKM
Actual	Typing	9662	69	403
	Scrolling	118	1127	3
	MKKM	622	36	5829

Table 3 shows the confusion matrix of 15 *Interaction Classifiers* for classification performance. We achieved overall precision of 93.01%, recall of 93.00%, and F-Measure of 92.98%. These results are in line with those reported in [12,23] and show that similar to their classifiers, our classifiers are very good at correctly recognizing the interactions.

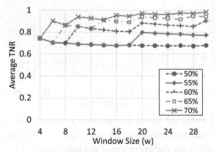
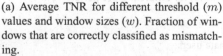

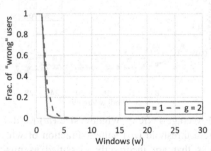

(a) Average TNR for different threshold (m) values and window sizes (w). Fraction of windows that are correctly classified as mismatching.

(b) Fraction of "wrong" (mismatched) users remaining logged in after 'n' authentication windows (with $w = 20$, $m = 60\%$) for different grace periods (g).

Fig. 3. Simulated *innocent* adversaries.

Security against Innocent Adversaries: To evaluate the security of our implementation of ZEBRA against innocent adversaries, we compute True Negative Rate (TNR). Specifically, we compute TNR as the fraction of windows that *Authenticator* correctly outputs as from "different user". We simulated the innocent adversary by *mismatching* the sequences where an actual interaction sequence from one sample is compared against the predicted interaction sequence from a different sample. During this simulation, the sequences were synchronized by aligning the starting point of the sequence being compared. For the threshold of (60–70)%, most (>85%) of the authentication windows were correctly identified as *mismatching* windows for window size above 20 (as shown in Fig. 3a). Figure 3b shows the fraction of innocent adversaries remaining logged in to ZEBRA system for a given number of authentication windows. As shown in the figure, all the innocent adversaries or "wrong" users were quickly deauthenticated within 5 authentication windows. This shows that our implementation of the ZEBRA system is robust against such innocent adversaries. Thus, it serves as a valid implementation to test the effectiveness of the VibRaze attack.

6.2 Performance of VibRaze Against ZEBRA

To evaluate the performance of VibRaze against ZEBRA, we consider the interaction sequence from 45 samples collected from 15 user sessions as the *attack-sample* and the motion data collected from the victim (or the researcher) with different attack settings as a *victim-sample*. Considering the regular user's interaction sample as an attack-sample reflects that a non-expert individual is playing the role of an attacker who attacks the victim at a random point in time, i.e., *non-opportunistic attack*. Further, taking the motion data from different attack settings as a victim-sample indicates that the victim user is performing various regular activities, or has placed his watch on different surfaces. Since VibRaze considers a *keyboard-only attack*, we discard all the mouse-related interactions including MKKM from each of the attack-samples. In our attack analysis, we map the interaction sequences from each of the attack-samples with the motion signals from the victim-sample by aligning the starting point of these two samples. This mapping represents the scenario where an attacker attempts to access the already logged-in terminal when the victim user is performing his routine activities. Below we present the performance of VibRaze against ZEBRA in different *On-Wrist* and *Off-Wrist* settings.

On-Wrist **Setting:** Figure 4 shows the fraction of attackers remaining logged in to ZEBRA for given 'n' authentication windows with the *On-Wrist* setting. Figure 4a shows this result with *Call-Vib* setting when the user is executing five different activities When the victim was driving his car, all the attackers were incorrectly recognized as legitimate users and were able to remain logged in for the entire experiment session with the grace period (g) of both 1 and 2. Similar results were achieved when the victim was using his phone (typing, browsing, playing game), and writing some random text on a sheet of paper while wearing the watch on his wrist. With the user's typing activities at the remote location, 98% of the attackers succeeded to remain logged in when using $g = 2$ while when using $g = 1$, 72% of attackers succeeded. Further, with the regular wrist movement while sitting on a chair or a sofa, nearly 75% of the attackers were able to remain logged in on behalf of the user when using $g = 2$. Even with the strict

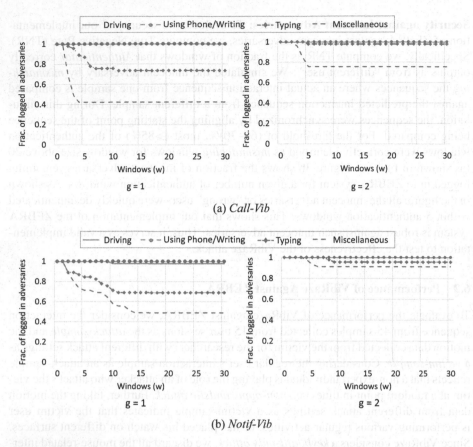

(a) *Call-Vib*

(b) *Notif-Vib*

Fig. 4. *On-Wrist* Setting. Fraction of attackers remaining logged in to ZEBRA after '*n*' authentication windows (with $w = 20$, $m = 60\%$) when user is undergoing different wrist-activities.

grace period of 1, more than 40% of the attackers were able to remain logged in for the entire session of the experiment.

Figure 4b shows the fraction of attackers remaining logged in for given '*n*' authentication windows with the *Notif-Vib* setting. 100% of attackers were able to remain logged in when the victim was performing the following three activities – driving, using the phone, and writing on a paper – at the remote location. With the typing activities of the user, 96% of the attackers succeeded to remain logged in when using $g = 2$ while 68% succeeded when using $g = 1$. Compared to the *Call-Vib* setting, when the user was executing regular wrist activities, a larger fraction (90%) of the attackers were able to remain logged in for the entire session when using $g = 2$. With $g = 1$, nearly 50% of the attackers remained logged in for the entire session. We also tested VibRaze with the walking scenario. However, the attack in this setting did not succeed potentially because the wrist-motion generated while walking may have dominated the vibration motion on the watch. Fortunately, if the VibRaze attack does not succeed at a given time, the attacker can wait and repeat the attack at a later point of time when the victim user may be performing other activities.

Thus, these results indicate that in the *On-Wrist* setup, VibRaze can completely compromise (i.e., 100% attackers can remain logged in) the security of ZEBRA in most of the scenarios such as driving, using the phone, and writing.

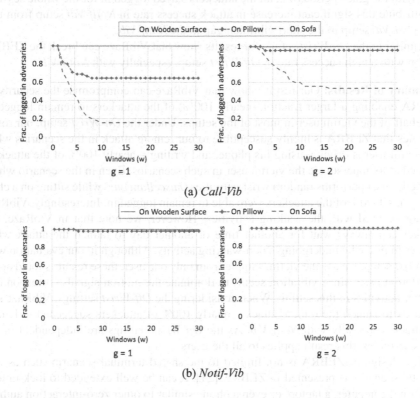

Fig. 5. *Off-Wrist* Settings. Fraction of attackers remaining logged in to ZEBRA after 'n' authentication windows (with $w = 20$, $m = 60\%$) when watch is placed on different surfaces.

Off-Wrist Setting: Figure 5 shows the fraction of attackers who succeeded to remain logged in to ZEBRA for 'n' authentication windows with the *Off-Wrist* setting. As shown in Fig. 5a, with *Call-Vib* and watch on wooden surface setup, all the attackers were incorrectly recognized as legitimate users and were able to remain logged in for the entire session at grace period (g) of both 1 and 2. When the watch was placed on the top of a pillow or on a sofa, we found that the attack success rate decreases potentially because of the vibration absorbent nature of these surfaces. With the pillow setup, the fraction of attackers who succeeded to remained logged decreases slightly to 95% with $g = 2$. This fraction further decreases to 55% with the sofa setup. When the grace period $g = 1$, 65% of the attackers succeeded to remain logged in with the pillow setup, and only 15% with the sofa setup.

In line with the *Call-Vib* setup, Fig. 5b shows the attack success rate with *Notif-Vib*. *Notif-Vib* also resulted in a 100% attack success rate with the watch on the wooden surface setting similar to *Call-Vib*. With *Notif-Vib*, the attack success rate increases significantly for the watch on the pillow and on the sofa setup. For both setups, 98% of the attackers were able to remain logged in for the entire session with the grace period of 1. With the grace period of 2, all the attackers stayed logged in for the whole session. We attribute this significant increase in attack success rate in *Notif-Vib* setup from that with *Call-Vib* setup to the short vibration gap in the *Notif-Vib*.

Similar to the *On-Wrist* setup, our results show that VibRaze can break the ZEBRA system with a high success rate in *Off-Wrist* setup, especially with *Notif-Vib*.

Summary of Results: Our results show that VibRaze can compromise the security of ZEBRA enabling a larger fraction (nearly 100%) of the attackers to remain logged in on behalf of the victim user in most of the setups. Under the *On-Wrist* setup, our result indicates that ZEBRA is highly susceptible to our remote attack in the scenarios when the victim user is driving, using his phone, and writing – nearly 100% of the attackers succeeded to impersonate the victim user in such scenarios. Even in the scenario where the victim user performs random wrist-activities (*miscellaneous*) while sitting on a chair or a sofa, 40–90% of the attackers were able to remain logged in. Interestingly, VibRaze did not succeed with the walking activities. However, we note that in VibRaze, the attacker can always wait for another time or another day to launch the attack when the victim might be undergoing a non-walking activity. Although in our evaluation with *On-Wrist* setup, we use the victim sample from only one user, these results should apply to different users since vibration seems to dominate the motion signals corresponding to other activities in this setting. When considering the *Off-Wrist* settings, VibRaze still succeeds to launch the remote attack – nearly 100% of attackers succeeded to launch the attack, especially with *Notif-Vib*. As the *Off-Wrist* settings are independent of the user's activities, this result applies to all the users.

The design of ZEBRA is not limited to the shared terminal scenario such as in a hospital scenario as presented in ZEBRA [21]. It can be well extended to lock-unlock a personal computer, a laptop, or even a phone similar to other zero-interaction authentication schemes. Even with such extensions of ZEBRA, VibRaze can still break the scheme. For instance, considering the use case of ZEBRA to lock-unlock a home computer, VibRaze can be launched while the victim is in the office. For this relay attack to work, the leech can be installed stealthily at the office location and the ghost near the home computer, and the vibration triggers can be sent the same way as we demonstrated in this section.

7   Potential Mitigations

In this section, we discuss various potential technical mitigation strategies against VibRaze and their limitations. We note that designing mitigation strategies and evaluating their effectiveness against VibRaze is beyond the scope of our study.

Disabling the Apps during Vibration: A natural, and perhaps a non-technical, defense against our attacks would be to disable the ZEBRA system in the scenario when a call or a notification is received. Alternatively, the calls, notifications could be disabled when the ZEBRA system is running. However, such mitigation will prevent the user from receiving calls/notifications while interacting with ZEBRA implemented system, and could possibly degrade the usability of the wearable system.

Re-Design of Classifier: In ZEBRA, *Interaction Classifier* is trained in such a way that it always classifies the motion segment to one of the three interactions – typing, scrolling, and MKKM, even if the motion segment corresponds to a different activity. The consideration of only three interactions in ZEBRA could be the reason behind the success of VibRaze. Therefore, one potential mitigation strategy to defeat VibRaze may be the addition of a fourth interaction class ("other") in the *Interaction Classifier*. The "other" class will represent the activities other than the already considered interactions, including the ones corresponding to vibration. The addition of the fourth interaction may defeat the VibRaze attack since the motion associated with the vibration and any other activities now will be classified as "other". However, the additional class for classification may degrade the performance of the classifier, and hence the usability of ZEBRA. Further investigation is needed to explore the effect of increasing the classes/interactions on ZEBRA, and its performance against VibRaze.

Distance Bounding Protocols: Several approaches exist to bound the distance between two devices that can thwart the relay attacks, and eventually VibRaze. Such distance bounding protocols can utilize Received Signal Strength (RSS) [4], and Time-of-the-Flight (ToF) for distance estimation between two devices. RSS is a measurement that shows the strength of the radio signal received by the device. Since the strength of the radio signal decreases over the distance from its source, the variation of RSS measurement can be used to estimate the distance. However, the signal strength of the radio signal can be manipulated using a signal amplifier or an attenuator [1]. Therefore, RSS is not a reliable and secure method for distance estimation. ToF based protocols employ the time elapsed, either Time-of-Arrival (ToA) [11] or Round-Trip-Time (RTT), during a message exchange to estimate the distance. Since ToA uses only the propagation time of single message exchange, it requires two devices to share a synchronized and high-precision clock. This requirement makes ToA infeasible to implement in the real-world scenario where devices would have different clocks. RTT measures the time elapsed during message exchange, i.e., the time between the transmission of a message to the reception of its response. However, a small error on timing measurement (estimating processing or transmission delay) at one node can result in a large deviation on distance estimation [3].

Attack Detection via Logs: The ZEBRA system may be designed to keep the log of users accessing the shared terminal. By reviewing the recorded logs, the victim user may find out that his system has been compromised, and someone else has used his terminal on his behalf. Further, the VibRaze attack may leave long term traces (e.g., messages, call logs) on the companion device, the phone, that can be correlated with the attack based on their time. However, by the time users realize that the system has been compromised, the attacker might have already fulfilled his malicious intention. Moreover, users might not be concerned about the security or be diligent enough to review the logs carefully and frequently. Several research studies (e.g., [5,26]) on user-centered security have shown that the users may not pay attention to security notifications or heed to security warnings and messages. Moreover, relying upon the users to detect such attacks will break the zero-effort property of ZEBRA.

8 Related Work

One work that is closely related to our VibRaze attack is Sound-Danger [22]. Sound-Danger is an attack system against Sound-Proof [13], a zero-effort two-factor authentication system that leverages ambient sounds to detect the proximity between the second-factor device (phone) and the login terminal (browser). Similar to VibRaze, Sound-Danger attack system is based on making a phone call and sending a message to create predictable or previously known sounds. However, the design of VibRaze is completely different from Sound-Danger. Sound-Danger is based on the creation of predictable *sounds* on the *phone* while VibRaze is based on creation of *vibration* on the *watch* to match the wrist-motion of the user with typing. Further, Sound-Danger relies on the predictable sound creation on the *phone* while VibRaze relies on vibration creation on the *watch*.

Similar to ZEBRA, WACA [2] is also a wearable-assisted continuous authentication system, which is based on sensor-based keystroke dynamics. WACA operates by deriving users' keystroke dynamics profile via the built-in sensors of a wrist-wearable, and periodically and transparently comparing the derived keystroke dynamics with the registered profile of the initially logged-in user. Rigorous future research would be needed to explore whether WACA is vulnerable to VibRaze.

Extensive research literature has shown the feasibility of the ghost-and-leech relay attacks in various short-range wireless channels. For instance, Francillon et al. [7] and Kfir et al. [14] have shown how a relay attack can be mounted against the system using RFID communication channel. Specifically, the relay attack in [7] is mounted against *Passive Keyless Entry and Start (PKES)* system used in modern cars to open and start the cars. In [14], the relay attack is executed against contactless smartcard system that provides low cost "no-touch" authentication. Francis et al. [8] have demonstrated the relay attacks against the system that uses NFC communication. Further, with the aim of impersonation, Levi et al. [18] have shown a relay attack on Bluetooth authentication protocol.

9 Conclusion and Future Work

As a representative instance of zero-effort deauthentication, ZEBRA is an appealing and useful proposition. In this paper, we presented VibRaze, a new attack vector against ZEBRA, that can compromise the security of the system even when the attacker is located remotely, far away from the victim user. VibRaze comprises launching a *ghost-and-leech* relay attack and creating vibrations (e.g., through a phone call or notification) on the wearable device located remotely. We evaluated this attack system against ZEBRA considering various real-life potential activities that the user may perform at a remote location and demonstrated that ZEBRA is highly susceptible to the attack (succeeding with a 100% success probability in most of the cases). Our work shows how vibration, a seemingly innocuous and highly ubiquitous means of device-to-user interaction, can be exploited for offensive purposes. Although this remote attack is fundamental in nature and challenging to address, we presented some potential mitigation approaches that may be used to alleviate the threat of the exposed vulnerability.

Since the first step of VibRaze, i.e., mounting the relay attack, can be easily and stealthy performed, in this study, we mainly focused on the second step of VibRaze, i.e., creating remote vibrations on the user's watch. Further, we evaluated VibRaze by closely simulating *Call-Vib* and *Notif-Vib* via a programmatic method, rather than leveraging actual vibration when call and notification are received. Rigorous future work would be needed to have an end-to-end implementation of VibRaze with actual in-device vibration and to evaluate the performance of such an implementation against ZEBRA. Since the success of VibRaze relies on the duration of vibration on the victim's watch, future work is needed to quantify how often (or long) and what kind of calls/notifications (e.g., from known vs. unknown caller) that the users do not pay attention and leave their devices vibrating.

References

1. Abu-Mahfouz, A., Hancke, G.P.: Distance bounding: a practical security solution for real-time location systems. IEEE Trans. Ind. Inf. **9**(1), 16–27 (2013)
2. Acar, A., Aksu, H., Uluagac, A.S., Akkaya, K.: WACA: wearable-assisted continuous authentication. In: 2018 IEEE Security and Privacy Workshops (SPW), pp. 264–269. IEEE (2018)
3. Avoine, G., et al.: Security of distance-bounding: a survey. ACM Comput. Surv. (2017)
4. Bahl, P., Padmanabhan, V.N.: Radar: an in-building RF-based user location and tracking system. In: INFOCOM 2000. Nineteenth Annual Joint Conference of the IEEE Computer and Communications Societies. Proceedings. IEEE, vol. 2, pp. 775–784. IEEE (2000)
5. Felt, A.P., Chin, E., Hanna, S., Song, D., Wagner, D.: Android permissions demystified. In: Proceedings of the 18th ACM Conference on Computer and Communications Security, pp. 627–638. ACM (2011)
6. Fitbit: Fitbit official site for activity trackers (2019). https://www.fitbit.com/. Accessed 02 Mar 2019
7. Francillon, A., Danev, B., Čapkun, S.: Relay attacks on passive keyless entry and start systems in modern cars. In: Proceedings of the Network and Distributed System Security Symposium (NDSS) (2011)
8. Francis, L., Hancke, G., Mayes, K., Markantonakis, K.: Practical NFC peer-to-peer relay attack using mobile phones. In: Ors Yalcin, S.B. (ed.) RFIDSec 2010. LNCS, vol. 6370, pp. 35–49. Springer, Heidelberg (2010). https://doi.org/10.1007/978-3-642-16822-2_4
9. Google Inc.: Smart lock (2018). https://get.google.com/smartlock/
10. Gutman, M.: Snapchat hacked: 4.6 million user names, partial phone numbers leaked-ABC15 Arizona (2015). https://goo.gl/5aM36K
11. Hancke, G.P., Kuhn, M.G.: An RFID distance bounding protocol. In: Security and Privacy for Emerging Areas in Communications Networks, 2005. SecureComm 2005. First International Conference on, pp. 67–73. IEEE (2005)
12. Huhta, O., Shrestha, P., Udar, S., Juuti, M., Saxena, N., Asokan, N.: Pitfalls in designing zero-effort deauthentication: opportunistic human observation attacks. In: Network and Distributed System Security Symposium (NDSS) (2016)

13. Karapanos, N., Marforio, C., Soriente, C., Capkun, S.: Sound-proof: usable two-factor authentication based on ambient sound. In: USENIX Security, pp. 483–498 (2015)
14. Kfir, Z., Wool, A.: Picking virtual pockets using relay attacks on contactless smartcard. In: Proceedings of the First International Conference on Security and Privacy for Emerging Areas in Communications Networks. pp. 47–58. SECURECOMM 2005, IEEE Computer Society, Washington, DC, USA (2005). https://doi.org/10.1109/SECURECOMM.2005.32, http://dx.doi.org/10.1109/SECURECOMM.2005.32
15. Kumar, M.: Coalition of law enforcement hacked & agents information leaked (2011). https://goo.gl/8EtvTx. Accessed 28 Sep 2018
16. Kumar, M.: Anonymous leaks database from Israeli musical act magazine site #opisrael (2012). https://goo.gl/hRczbu. Accessed 28 Sep 2018
17. Kumar, M.: Bulgarian torrent tracker forum hacked and accused of collecting user IP (2012). https://goo.gl/iVPWwv. Accessed 28 Sep 2018
18. Levi, A., Cetintas, E., Aydos, M., Koc, C., Caglayan, M.: Relay attacks on bluetooth authentication and solutions. In: Computer and Information Sciences (ISCIS) (2004)
19. Li, H., Ma, D., Saxena, N., Shrestha, B., Zhu, Y.: Tap-wave-rub: lightweight malware prevention for smartphones using intuitive human gestures. In: Proceedings of the Sixth ACM Conference on Security and Privacy in Wireless and Mobile Networks, pp. 25–30. ACM (2013)
20. LiveChat Inc. (2020). https://www.livechat.com/typing-speed-test/#/. Accessed 9 Oct 2020
21. Mare, S., Markham, A.M., Cornelius, C., Peterson, R., Kotz, D.: Zebra: Zero-effort bilateral recurring authentication. In: Security and Privacy (SP), 2014 IEEE Symposium on, pp. 705–720. IEEE (2014)
22. Shrestha, B., Shirvanian, M., Shrestha, P., Saxena, N.: The sounds of the phones: dangers of zero-effort second factor login based on ambient audio. In: Proceedings of the 2016 ACM SIGSAC Conference on Computer and Communications Security, pp. 908–919. ACM (2016)
23. Shrestha, P., Anand, S.A., Saxena, N.: Yelp: masking sound-based opportunistic attacks in zero-effort deauthentication. In: Proceedings of the 10th ACM Conference on Security and Privacy in Wireless and Mobile Networks, pp. 195–206. ACM (2017)
24. Sonnad, N.: What's in the Ashley Madison database that hackers released online (2015). https://goo.gl/kqk95v. Accessed 28 Sep 2018
25. Souza, R.D.: Hacker leaks 250GB of NASA data, another group claims to hijack NASA drone (2016). https://goo.gl/bx7XEd. Accessed 28 Sep 2018
26. Sunshine, J., Egelman, S., Almuhimedi, H., Atri, N., Cranor, L.F.: Crying wolf: an empirical study of SSL warning effectiveness. In: USENIX Security Symposium, pp. 399–416 (2009)
27. Wisniewski, C.: Sony Europe hacked by Lebanese hacker... again-naked security (2011). https://goo.gl/v5KbsU. Accessed 28 Sep 2018
28. Xiaomi: Mi global home (2019). https://www.mi.com/global/miband/. Accessed 02 Mar 2019
29. Yang, L., et al.: Unlocking smart phone through handwaving biometrics. IEEE Trans. Mob. Comput. 14(5), 1044–1055 (2015)

ZLeaks: Passive Inference Attacks on Zigbee Based Smart Homes

Narmeen Shafqat[1]([⊠]) [iD], Daniel J. Dubois[1] [iD], David Choffnes[1] [iD],
Aaron Schulman[2] [iD], Dinesh Bharadia[2] [iD], and Aanjhan Ranganathan[1] [iD]

[1] Northeastern University, Boston, MA, USA
{shafqat.n,d.dubois,d.choffnes,aanjhan}@northeastern.edu
[2] University of California San Diego (UCSD), California, USA
schulman@cs.ucsd.edu, dinesh@ucsd.edu

Abstract. Zigbee is an energy-efficient wireless IoT protocol that is increasingly being deployed in smart home settings. In this work, we analyze the privacy guarantees of Zigbee protocol. Specifically, we present ZLeaks, a tool that passively identifies in-home devices or events from the encrypted Zigbee traffic by 1) inferring a single application layer (APL) command in the event's traffic, and 2) exploiting the device's periodic reporting pattern and interval. This enables an attacker to infer user's habits or determine if the smart home is vulnerable to unauthorized entry. We evaluated ZLeaks' efficacy on 19 unique Zigbee devices across several categories and 5 popular smart hubs in three different scenarios; controlled RF shield, living smart-home IoT lab, and third-party Zigbee captures. We were able to i) identify unknown events and devices (without a-priori device signatures) using command inference approach with 83.6% accuracy, ii) automatically extract device's reporting signatures, iii) determine known devices using the reporting signatures with 99.8% accuracy, and iv) identify APL commands in a public capture with 91.2% accuracy. In short, we highlight the trade-off between designing a low-power, low-cost wireless network and achieving privacy guarantees. We have also released ZLeaks tool for the benefit of the research community.

Keywords: Zigbee · IoT · Device identification · Passive inference

1 Introduction

Smart home products (e.g., bulbs, outlets, sensors, etc.) allow users to control and monitor their smart home's environment wirelessly, but unfortunately, pose a significant risk to users' privacy. Prior studies have demonstrated that by intercepting the IP traffic of a smart home, the attacker can determine in-home devices [1–3], events [4,5], and user's habits [6]. In practice, these attacks are difficult to carry out, as the attacker must find a vulnerability to capture the user's IP network traffic (e.g., by gaining root access to the home router). Yet, there exists an easy privacy violation attack, i.e., simply sniffing the Internet of Things (IoT) wireless protocol (e.g., Zigbee) transmissions that are unintentionally emitted to up to hundreds of feet. Although the IoT traffic is encrypted to

© Springer Nature Switzerland AG 2022
G. Ateniese and D. Venturi (Eds.): ACNS 2022, LNCS 13269, pp. 105–125, 2022.
https://doi.org/10.1007/978-3-031-09234-3_6

prevent eavesdropping, researchers recently showed that the attacker can still identify events using a-priori device signatures [7,8] and infer a few encrypted Zigbee (Network layer) commands by exploiting the payload lengths [9].

In this work, we analyze the privacy guarantees of one of the most popular IoT wireless protocols, Zigbee [10], that is increasingly being used in smart hubs such as Amazon Echo Plus, Samsung SmartThings, and Philips Hue. With the launch of more than 500 new Zigbee-certified devices in 2020 alone and the expected sale of nearly four billion Zigbee chipsets by 2023 [11], Zigbee continues to be the preferred choice of device manufacturers.

Our key insight is that design optimizations incorporated into Zigbee to enable low-latency communication on low-cost resource-constrained devices fundamentally leak information, e.g., to keep the frame length small, Zigbee performs encryption transformation [10] on AES encrypted output to match the message length. This enables an eavesdropper to exploit unpadded payload lengths and discrepancies in traffic metadata to infer *every* encrypted network layer (NWK) and application layer (APL) command. Moreover, to prevent device timeout, Zigbee devices periodically report attributes like battery level, temperature, etc., to the smart hub. The distinct reporting patterns and intervals inadvertently serve as device fingerprints. In this work, we exploit device's unique reporting patterns and the possibility of inferring APL commands to passively determine devices and events in the target network. Specifically, we make following contributions.

Device and Event Identification Using Inferred APL Command: We demonstrate that the event traffic of a device always includes at least one functionality-specific APL command (such as *Door Lock/Unlock*), which alone specifies the triggered event (i.e., lock/unlock) and the functional device type (i.e., door lock). Zigbee Cluster Library (ZCL) specification [12] inherently leaks information about all such APL commands. We attempt to infer a single functionality specific APL command in the encrypted event traffic to determine event and device type and combine manufacturer's identity obtained from the Organizationally Unique Identifier (OUI) of the device's MAC address to identify a particular Zigbee device. Unlike prior works [7,8], this approach does not require device's event signatures and can even identify unknown events and devices[1].

In practice, inferring functionality-specific APL commands is extremely challenging, and so far, no study has attempted it. This is because the metadata of functionality-specific APL commands is immensely similar to a hundred other generic APL commands. Few APL commands are also manufacturer configurable, which prevent us from exploiting only the payload length, packet direction, and radius (hops) to infer APL commands using prior NWK command inference approach [9]. We utilize frame format guidelines [12] to identify all possible APL commands with payload lengths overlapping with the functionality-specific APL commands and their response commands (if any), e.g., *door unlock request and response*. The discrepancies in the traffic's metadata, together with the device's logical type (electricity-powered or battery-powered), are used to construct inference rules for each target functionality-specific APL command.

---

[1] Zigbee Devices not previously observed, i.e., no a-priori access to their traffic.

Device Identification Using Periodic Reporting Patterns: Zigbee devices periodically report attributes to the smart hub. We exploit reporting patterns and intervals to create unique device fingerprints. This approach is useful for identifying a known device with unpatched vulnerability (e.g., to spread malware) in the Zigbee network, which has minimal user activity. Unlike prior works [7,8] that analyze Zigbee traffic generated due to event occurrence only: this approach can identify devices even when no event is triggered. Given that every device's current consumption varies based on its communication pattern and hardware, the periodic reporting time is not trivial to modify as it directly impacts device certification requirement of minimum 2-years battery life [13].

Automating Event and Device Identification with ZLeaks Tool: We developed a comprehensive privacy analysis tool for Zigbee protocol, named ZLeaks [14], that automates the aforementioned identification techniques. ZLeaks takes the Zigbee traffic as input and passively determines events and devices in the smart home. It can also extract devices' reporting signatures automatically.

We experimentally evaluated ZLeaks on by far the most extensive device set used in privacy analysis of Zigbee protocol including 5 popular smart hubs (SmartThings, Amazon Echo Plus, Philips Hue, OSRAM Lightify, and Sengled) and 27 commercial off-the-shelf Zigbee devices, out of which 19 devices were unique. The experiments were performed in 1) an isolated RF shield and 2) a living smart-home "Mon(IoT)r Lab" [15] with multiple IoT and non-IoT networks operating simultaneously. Furthermore, we validated the findings on third-party capture files available on Wireshark [16] and Crawdad [17] forums. Our results indicate that ZLeaks identified event and device information using inferred APL commands with 83.6% accuracy and devices using reporting patterns with 99.8% accuracy. Also, we inferred functionality-specific APL commands in a public Zigbee capture, using our command inference rules, with 91.2% accuracy.

2   Background and Motivation

2.1   Zigbee Overview

Zigbee is one of the most popular low-cost, low-power, wireless protocols specifically designed for battery-powered applications in smart ecosystems such as smart homes and industries. Zigbee is built on top of the low data-rate IEEE 802.15.4 wireless personal area networking (PAN) standard and implements the physical (PHY) and medium access control (MAC) layers as defined by the IEEE standard. Most commercial Zigbee devices operate at a data rate of 250 kbps in the 2.4 GHz band (divided into 16 channels, each 5 MHz apart). Some Zigbee devices also operate in the unlicensed frequency bands of 784, 868, and 915 MHz.

Network Architecture: Zigbee supports both centralized and distributed network architectures. Centralized networks comprise of three logical device types; Zigbee coordinator (ZC), Zigbee router (ZR), and Zigbee end-device (ZED),

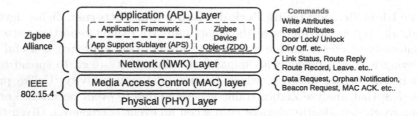

Fig. 1. Zigbee's Protocol Stack comprising of PHY, MAC, NWK and APL layers

while the distributed networks have ZR and ZED only. ZEDs do not route traffic and may sleep to conserve battery, making them appropriate for battery-powered devices (e.g., sensors, door locks). ZRs are responsible for routing traffic between nodes and storing messages intended for ZEDs until they are requested. Every Zigbee network has one ZC that is responsible for network formation, issuing network identifiers, and logical network addresses. ZC also acts as a trust center to authenticate new nodes and distribute keys. ZRs and ZCs are powered devices (e.g., bulbs, smart hubs) and do not sleep during the network's lifetime. Besides, Zigbee supports connectivity in star, mesh, and tree topologies. Zigbee does not implement MAC address randomization. Each Zigbee node has a manufacturer-assigned 64-bit MAC (extended) address that is mapped to a unique 16-bit network (logical) address by the ZC during device pairing. The logical address is used for routing, while the extended address is used for authentication.

Zigbee Protocol Stack (Fig. 1): Zigbee standard [10] defines the functionalities of the Network and Application layers. The Network layer is responsible for network formation and management, routing and address allocation. There are 12 NWK commands, such as *Link Status, Route Record, Route Reply*, etc. Zigbee's Application layer comprises of Application Support (APS) sublayer, Zigbee Device Object (ZDO), and Application Framework. APS sublayer maintains binding tables and address mappings, and ZDO implements the device in one of the three logical roles (ZC, ZR, or ZED). The application framework offers pre-defined profiles (e.g., home automation, health care, etc.) and functional domains called clusters (e.g., lighting, security, etc.) for end-manufacturers to support device interoperability. Broadly, APL commands are either functionality specific or generic (such as *Read Attributes, Report Attributes* etc.).

Security and Privacy: Zigbee uses 128-bit AES encryption to provide payload confidentiality and message authentication. The standard also has the provision for integrity-protection using 128-bit AES CCM* block cipher and replay protection using a 32-bit frame counter. Each Zigbee device has a pre-installed global trust center link key, which is used if the manufacturer does not provide any unique link key or QR install code. The Network (encryption) key is randomly generated by ZC during network formation and is common to all Zigbee nodes.

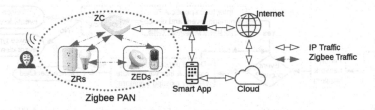

Fig. 2. Communication Flow in a Zigbee Home Network.

2.2   System and Threat Model

We assume a Zigbee home network, similar to Fig. 2, where a smart hub (ZC) is paired with several popular Zigbee devices (ZRs and ZEDs). The hub is connected to an IP gateway to update devices' states on the cloud and the user's smart app. The smart home's occupants carry out routine activities and can control devices via the smart app from virtually anywhere. We assume that a passive attacker is collecting Zigbee transmissions using a wireless Zigbee sniffer from within the wireless communication range of the victim network. We use TI CC2531 Zigbee sniffer [18], equipped with the standard omnidirectional antenna, to receive Zigbee transmissions at a distance of $20\,\mathrm{m}^2$. The attacker does not need access to the smart app or physical presence inside the smart home; he can even implant a Zigbee sniffer nearby and observe the traffic remotely.

The attacker analyses the captured Zigbee traffic to passively identify the events and devices using either command inference or periodic reporting patterns, irrespective of the network or link keys, device's QR code, or specific events like device pairing or rejoining, which aid the attacker to extract the Network key. In other words, we assume a fully operational Zigbee network with subject devices (door locks, bulbs, outlets, and various types of sensors) configured and commissioned a-priori. The attacker only requires some background knowledge of the Zigbee standard. There is no need to collect event signatures for each device. Only when a specific device is required to be identified in the target smart home with zero user activity, the attacker needs the device's reporting signatures. Note that Zigbee packets are exchanged between the hub and end-devices only; so even having access to the user's smart app and reverse engineering it would not leak information regarding the Zigbee commands.

Challenges: The AES-128 algorithm used by Zigbee has proven confusion and diffusion properties and prevents eavesdropping. The attacker can resort to using the existing NWK command inference scheme [9] based on payload size, radius, and actively determined logical device type to infer NWK frames. Unfortunately, the events and device information is embedded in APL commands where the radius is insignificant. Also, unlike the 12 NWK commands, which have defined payload lengths [10], there are more than a hundred APL commands, most of

---

[2] Range can be extended with a high gain directional antenna.

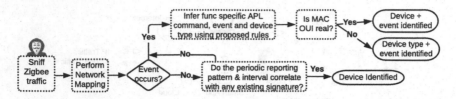

Fig. 3. Inference Strategy: If event occurs, infer functionality specific APL command and combine MAC identifier to identify the device and event. If there's no event, identify device using periodic signature correlation. If it fails, wait for an event.

which are manufacturer configurable (e.g., Report Attributes, Read Attributes, etc.). Hence there exist several overlappings at each payload length. These factors make the existing approach [9] insufficient to *passively* infer APL commands.

The unencrypted IEEE 802.15.4 frames in the Zigbee traffic also provide negligible information regarding the devices and events, e.g., the frequently exchanged IEEE 802.15.4 ACK does not mention network or MAC address for the source or destination, and the incremental frame sequence numbers roll back after 256, making it extremely challenging to trace the communicating nodes.

Moreover, existing research studies rely on a-priori event signatures for the identification of events [7,8]. In practice, user events are infrequent, e.g., during nighttime. In this idle state, the devices and hub exchange periodic reports only and do not leak any device information. Hence, identifying a device without event signatures or in the absence of events are still open problems for the attacker.

3   Passive Inference Attacks on Zigbee

3.1   Attack Overview

As illustrated in Fig. 3, our fundamental goal is to invade the smart home's privacy by determining Zigbee devices, triggered events, and encrypted commands exchanged in the home. We use a low-cost wireless Zigbee receiver, TI-CC2531 [18], to identify and tune to the target network's communication frequency channel and sniff the Zigbee traffic. To maximize the amount of information extracted from the sniffed traffic, we first perform network mapping, whereby the logical device type of each node (ZC, ZR, or ZED) is determined.

If an event occurs, we use proposed inference rules (Sect. 3.3) to identify the functionality-specific APL command in the event's traffic, which further reveals event and device type. The manufacturer is revealed from the device's MAC identifier. Specifically, we exploit the device's logical type and metadata variations in APL commands, that stem from power consumption optimizations incorporated into Zigbee. Unlike prior works [7,8], we do not require a-priori event signatures for every device and can infer unknown devices and events.

In addition, we leverage the device's reporting pattern and interval to create unique reporting signatures (Sect. 3.4). Whenever a known device with unpatched vulnerability needs to be identified in the target network with no event triggers, we correlate the device's reporting signature with the reporting pattern and interval of every device in the target's Zigbee traffic. If the reporting signatures are unavailable, we wait for an event to identify the device using command inference. To the best of our knowledge, no prior work has demonstrated device identification, using APL commands, without collecting event signatures or through periodic reporting patterns. Below we explain the attack phases.

3.2 Passive Network Mapping

To keep the frame length small, Zigbee uses logical address for routing, the source's MAC address for authentication, and excludes the destination's MAC address. Thus, to identify the type and model of the target device, it is essential to keep a mapping of logical address, MAC address, and logical type (ZC, ZED, or ZR) for each logical address (i.e., node) in the traffic. Zigbee specification [10] identifies ZC as the node having 0x0000 logical address. We observed that for IEEE 802.15.4 Data Requests specifically, the source node is ZED and the destination node (other than 0x0000) is ZR. In addition, we recognized ZRs as the destination node of any Zigbee frame that has source routing information in the metadata, and that node does not send IEEE 802.15.4 Data Requests. ZR can also be identified as the source of NWK commands namely *Link Status, Rejoin Response, and Network Report*, provided the node address is not 0x0000 [9].

3.3 Device and Event Identification Using Inferred APL Command

Although devices exhibit unique event patterns, the event traffic of same functional devices always includes same functionality-specific APL command, e.g., bulbs use *color control* command for color change. It happens because device manufacturers use defined Zigbee clusters to support vendor interoperability. This is validated from the official Zigbee compliance documents, e.g., Lightify [19] and Sengled [20] bulbs use same APL commands. Below we describe our scheme to devise and use command inference rules to identify events and devices.

Inference Algorithm: The functionality-specific APL commands of interest (*OnOff, Color Control, Level Control, Lock/Unlock,* and *Zone Status* (short for *IAS Zone Status Change*) have fixed payload lengths. However, there exist overlappings with several generic APL commands within the encrypted traffic. This happens because there are more than hundred APL commands, many of which are manufacturer configurable and only have minimal payload and attribute size specified in the standard [12]. Thus, command xyz with a minimum 10-byte payload and 3-byte attribute size has a payload subset of 10, 13, 16 bytes etc.

As shown in Fig. 4, to devise inference rule for a functionality-specific APL command, we utilize APL frame formats [12] to first identify all APL commands that have overlapping payload lengths and packet direction with the target command and its response command (if any), e.g., *Door Lock/unlock request* and *response*. Next, a test event is triggered, and overlapping commands are differentiated based on the logical device type and metadata variations (e.g., network

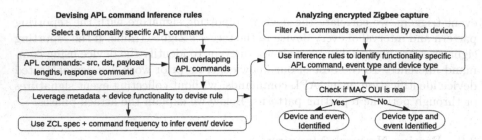

Fig. 4. Strategy to identify devices and events from inferred APL commands.

Table 1. Identifying devices and events from Inferred commands. (Resp = Response, D = ZED/ZR, ND = NWK discovery, * = burst repeats, ** = broadcast, (x) = payload len)

Target	Inference Rule	Command	Device Type	Event
ZC-ZED(11)	Resp = (12 ∥ 21)	Lock/unlock	Door lock	Lock/unlock
ZC - D(11)	Resp=13∥15 != 12**	OnOff	Outlet/ bulb	On/ off
ZC - D(14)	ND = 1 Resp != 11 Prec != 17**	Level Control	Smart Bulb	Level changed
ZC - D(15)	ND = 1 Resp != 12	Color Control		Color Changed
ZED-ZC(17)	Preceding Packet (Prec) != 13	Zone Status (1*)	Motion Sensor	Motion
		Zone Status (1)	Door Sensor	Open/ close
		Zone Status (2)	Flood sensor	Water leakage
		Zone Status (3)	Audio sensor	Audio detected

discovery, end device initiator, etc.). As seen in Table 1, a command inference rule specifies properties of APL commands that must be present in the event burst (traffic). For instance, an APL command of payload length 11 bytes, sent from ZC to ZED is *Lock/unlock* command if the response packet (ZED to ZC) is 12 or 21 bytes. Since same functional devices use same functionality-specific commands, the inference rules constructed for a certain device also hold true for other manufacturers' devices. We stress-checked the rules against 200 MBs of Zigbee capture from our devices and third-party sources [17,21]. Note that most APL commands (like *color control*), directly reflect the event and device type. However, for outlets and bulbs, that use same *OnOff* command, the device type is indistinguishable until an additional event, e.g., color change is triggered. For *Zone Status* command, we observed behavioral consistencies that allowed us to differentiate various types of sensors; e.g., *Zone Status* appears twice in the event burst for flood sensor and thrice for the audio sensor. For motion and door sensor, *Zone Status* appears once only. However, we noticed that for motion sensors, the same burst pattern repeats after few seconds.

Identifying Events and Devices: We first filter all APL commands in the event's traffic sent to or received by the target logical address (e.g., 0xabcd)

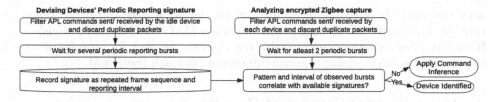

Fig. 5. Strategy to identify devices using periodic reporting patterns.

and discard any duplicate packet. We observed that the functionality-specific command is generally the first APL command of the event burst; hence we also discard bursts that do not have any frame with target payload lengths (11–17 bytes) in the initial half of the burst. If a command with target payload length exists, we use Table 1 to identify the APL command, event, and device type. Finally, we combine the manufacturer's identity extracted from the device's MAC OUI (e.g., PhilipL) to identify the device. Note that the exact device's identification depends on the MAC OUI showing real manufacturer, rather than system-on-chip (SOC) manufacturer, e.g., SiliconL. In essence, we can passively identify unknown events and devices from the target functional domains (bulbs, outlets, door locks, and sensors) without the Network key or event signatures.

3.4 Device Identification Using Periodic Reporting Patterns

Zigbee devices periodically report their status (battery level, firmware upgrades, etc.) to ZC. Since every functional device has varied power consumption, the manufacturers manipulate periodic reporting frequency, and specific frame attributes to comply with the Zigbee certification requirement of minimum 2 years battery life [13]. The discrepancies in reporting patterns and intervals allow us to devise unique device fingerprints and identify devices even when no event occurs (e.g., during office hours). Unlike event bursts, reporting bursts have no functionality-specific APL command and do not directly reveal device's identity.

Devising Periodic Reporting Signatures: As shown in Fig. 5, to devise a device's periodic reporting signature, we put the device in the idle state and filter all APL commands exchanged between the device and ZC. After discarding duplicate packets, we analyze the traffic to determine at least three bursts with same reporting pattern and interval. Thus, the signature $sign_i$ is a sequence of APL frames f_i defined using logical device type of source (src) and destination (dst), payload length (pl), and reporting interval (RI) and is represented as:

$$sign_i = \{f_1, f_2, f_3, ...\} \text{ where } f_i = \{src_i, dst_i, pl_i, RI_i\} \tag{1}$$

Identifying Devices: We first filter APL commands from the traffic and discard duplicate packets or bursts with any functionality-specific command. Next, we look for two similar bursts and correlate the observed pattern and interval with the available signature set to identify the device. Rarely, but if two signature sets collide, we use additional attributes like MAC OUI to make a decision. If no reporting signatures are available for a device, we wait for an event burst to identify the device using command inference approach (Sect. 3.3).

4   Experimental Setup and Results

4.1   Automating Passive Inference Attacks with ZLeaks Tool

To automate the inference attacks depicted in Fig. 3, we developed a command-line tool in Python, named ZLeaks. ZLeaks takes Zigbee PCAP capture as input and determines the event occurrences and devices in the network. While in the vicinity of the target network, the attacker can run ZLeaks on his laptop or embedded board like Raspberry Pi with a single command. ZLeaks extracts all APL commands from the captured traffic and uses Pyshark library [22] to parse required frame attributes (e.g., payload length, logical types of nodes, etc.) in a temporary CSV file for analysis. ZLeaks then attempts to identify events and devices using either proposed APL inference rules (Sect. 3.3) or available reporting signatures (Sect. 3.4). Note that the attacker can automatically extract reporting signatures of an idle Zigbee device using ZLeaks Signature Extractor.

4.2   Experimental Setup

Our device set comprised of 27 commercial off-the-shelf Zigbee devices (ranging from bulbs, locks, outlets, to various sensors) that were selected based on Amazon's popularity and manufacturer diversity. Amongst 27 devices, 19 devices were unique, while a few non-unique devices were purchased from a different source and tested to ensure that the evaluation results for a particular device and model remain consistent. Furthermore, while we used 11 unique devices to formulate inference strategy, we set aside 8 unique devices, at least one from each functional domain as the unknown devices for the sole purpose of evaluation. The known and unknown devices are listed for reference in Table 3 and Table 4 respectively. The tests were conducted with 2 universal (manufacturer-independent) hubs; SmartThings and Amazon Echo Plus and 3 vendor-specific hubs; Philips Hue Bridge 2.1, Sengled Z02-hub, and Lightify Gateway. This is by far the most extensive Zigbee device set used to evaluate Zigbee protocol.

We evaluated ZLeaks identification techniques in following three settings;

RF Shield: It was used to i) study devices' response to event triggers while devising command inference rules, ii) collect the device's reporting pattern, and iii) perform a controlled evaluation of ZLeaks by simultaneously pairing multiple devices with each hub. As depicted in Fig. 6; the RF shield was connected to the gateway to provide continued Internet access to ZC placed inside the shield. To sniff the Zigbee communication, a standard omnidirectional antenna (inside the shield) was connected via an SMA cable to a low-cost TI CC2531 wireless Zigbee sniffer [18] plugged into the laptop (outside the shield).

Fig. 6. Experimental Setup for analyzing Zigbee Devices: SMA cable connects sniffer's antenna (inside RF shield) with TI CC2531 sniffer connected to the laptop outside.

IoT "Living Lab": It is a realistic noisy IoT lab named "Mon(IoT)r Lab" at Northeastern University [15], which has more than 100 smart devices already connected over several wireless networks, along with various non-IoT networks.

Public Captures: We used Zigbee captures from; i) Wireshark forum [16], and ii) Prior captures [9] available on Crawdad [17] to show that ZLeaks is independent of evaluation testbed, device set, and works for unknown devices. We verified the results using the Network keys available with the capture files. Both the captures contained only event bursts and did not include enough reporting patterns to evaluate the periodic reporting approach.

4.3 Evaluation Metrics

We evaluated ZLeaks using three parameters; 1) Inferred APL commands, 2) Event and device type extracted from APL command, and 3) Correlated periodic reporting patterns. We used traditional accuracy metrics to evaluate parameters 1 and 3. As a particular inferred APL command always yields same results for event and device, we evaluated parameter 2 using proposed *Device Score* scheme.

Traditional Metrics: We use True Positive Rate (TPR) and False Negative Rate (FNR) to specify the rate of correct and missed (or out-of-order) observations, respectively. As evaluation results indicate, there are no False Positives (FP) or True Negative (TN) outcomes, hence, we calculate *accuracy*, i.e., the ratio of correctly inferred observations to the total number of observations, as:

$$TPR \text{ (recall)} = \frac{TP}{TP + FN}, \tag{2}$$

$$FNR = \frac{FN}{TP + FN}, \tag{3}$$

$$Accuracy = \frac{TP+TN}{TP + TN + FP + FN}, \tag{4}$$

Score (*Short for Device Score*): It determines the amount of device and event information extracted from the inferred APL command and device OUI. We calculate Score as a sum of device type (DT), event type (ET) and manufacturer's identity (M), with weights of each attribute defined in Table 2.

$$Score = M + DT + ET \tag{5}$$

Table 2. Score Table for Evaluating Command Inference Approach

Attributes	Score	Example
Manufacturer (M)	0 = SOC OUI	SiliconL, Ember, TexasIns, NordiacSE ..
	1 = Real MAC OUI	PhilipsL, OSRAM, SmartThi, Zhejiang ..
Device Type (DT)	0 = Unidentified	-
	1 = Uncertain	door lock or bulb (different commands)
	1.5 = Indistinct	either outlet or bulb? (same command)
	2 = Identified	Outlet, door lock, motion sensor, bulb ..
Event Type (ET)	0 = Unidentified	-
	1 = Uncertain	lock/unlock or on/off (different commands)
	1.5 = Indistinct	either door lock or unlock? (same commands)
	2 = Identified	motion detected, color change, etc ..

To understand Score, consider switching on a bulb that triggers a functionality-specific APL command from ZC to ZED of payload size 11 bytes. The highest Score is 5 when all attributes are correctly inferred, and lowest is 0 when nothing is inferred. As per Table 1, the command is either *Lock/unlock or On/off*. From Table 2, DT and ET are 1 if these two commands are indistinguishable. For *On/off* command, DT (bulbs or outlet) and ET (on or off) are 1.5, whereas for *Lock/unlock* command, DT is 2 (lock) while ET is 1.5 (lock or unlock).

4.4   Device and Event Identification Using Inferred APL Command

Controlled Evaluation in RF Shield: We simultaneously paired all compatible devices with one hub at a time inside the RF shield and generated events randomly. From the sniffed traffic, ZLeaks inferred functionality-specific APL commands and MAC OUI for each device to determine triggered events and devices. Since the inferred APL command and MAC OUI remain same for a particular device-event pair (e.g., color change for Sengled bulb), the Score remains same for every event prompt irrespective of the hub. Therefore, Table 3 reports findings of each device once. We see that distinct events like color change, motion detected, etc., are easy to infer than binary events (e.g., on/off). Philips bulb is an exception here as it uses distinct commands to represent on and off events. Furthermore, we identified various sensors from a single *Zone Status* command based on behavioral consistencies (refer to rules in Table 1). To conclude, the Score is dependent on the correct identification of the APL command and the MAC OUI showing the real manufacturer e.g., PhilipsL (Philips), SmartThi/Samjin (SmartThings), Ledvance (OSRAM), Zhejiang (Sengled), Jennic (Aqara), etc. ZLeaks identified all devices with an average Score of 4.3 out of 5 (i.e., 86.3% information was successfully extracted).

Realistic Evaluation in an IoT "Living Lab": Next, we shifted all these devices, hubs, and 8 unknown (unseen) devices to the IoT lab. Again, we simultaneously paired all devices to one hub at a time, generated random events, and analyzed the traffic with ZLeaks. Despite the noisy environment, the known

Table 3. Controlled Evaluation: Identifying Devices and Events using Inferred APL Commands. Here, SMT= SmartThings, M = Manufacturer, DT = Device Type, ET = Event type, and * = burst repeats after few seconds

Device (Model)	Event	OUI	Command (#)	M	DT	ET	Score
Philips Hue Color Bulb (LCA-003)	Off	PhilipsL	Off with effect	1	2	2	5
	On	PhilipsL	On/off: On	1	2	2	5
	Color change	PhilipsL	Color Control	1	2	2	5
	Dim	PhilipsL	Level Control	1	2	2	5
Sengled Color Bulb (E11-N1EA)	Color change	Zhejiang	Color Control	1	2	2	5
	Dim	Zhejiang	Level Control	1	2	2	5
	On/off	Zhejiang	On/Off	1	1.5	1.5	4
Sengled White Bulb G14	On/Off	Zhejiang	On/Off	1	1.5	1.5	4
Centralite Outlet (Mini)	On/Off	siliconL	On/Off	0	1.5	1.5	3
Sonoff Outlet (S31 Lite)	On/Off	texasIns	On/Off	0	1.5	1.5	3
SMT Outlet (US-2)	On/Off	Smartthi	On/Off	1	1.5	1.5	4
SMT Motion sensor (IM)	Motion	Smartthi	Zone Status (1*)	1	2	2	5
SMT Multisensor (250)	Open/close	samjin	Zone Status (1)	1	2	1.5	4.5
Ecolink Water Sensor	water leak	ember	Zone Status (2)	0	2	2	4
Ecolink Sound Sensor	Sound	ember	Zone Status (3)	0	2	2	4
Yale Door lock (YRD226)	Lock/unlock	ember	Lock/Unlock	0	2	1.5	3.5

Table 4. Realistic Evaluation: Identifying Unknown Devices and Events using Inferred Commands. (M= Manufacturer, DT = Device Type, ET = Event type, * = repeats)

Device (Model)	Event	OUI	Command (#)	M	DT	ET	Score
Philips White Bulb	Off	PhilipsL	Off with effect	1	2	2	5
	On		On/off: On	1	2	2	5
OSRAM Color Bulb (Sylvania Smart+)	On/off	ledvance	On/Off	1	2	1	4
	Color change	ledvance	Color Control	1	2	2	5
	Dim	ledvance	Level Control	1	2	2	5
SmartThings (SMT) Bulb	On/off	SiliconL	On/Off	0	1.5	1.5	3
Aqara Outlet (US)	On/off	jennic	On/Off	1	1.5	1.5	4
Ewelink Outlet (SA-003)	On/off	TexasIns	On/Off	0	1.5	1.5	3
SMT Motion Sensor IRM	Motion	samjin	Zone Status (1*)	1	2	2	5
Visonic Door sensor MCT	Open/close	ember	Zone Status (1)	0	2	1.5	3.5
Schlage Lock (Connect)	Lock/unlock	siliconL	Lock/Unlock	0	2	1.5	3.5

devices exhibited the same Score as reported in Table 3. The experimental results for unknown devices are presented in Table 4. Unknown devices with real MAC OUI and distinct event types, e.g., color change for Sengled bulb, were accurately identified by ZLeaks. Overall, ZLeaks identified unknown devices with an average Score of 4.2 out of 5 (i.e., identified 83.6% devices and events). We conclude that despite devices exhibiting unique event signatures across different hubs, the functionality-specific APL command remains same and can be used to effectively identify any unknown device with a single event trigger.

Table 5. Public Evaluation: Identifying Unknown Devices and Events using Inferred Commands. (M= Manufacturer, DT = Device Type, ET = Event type, * = repeats)

Source	Unknown Device	MAC OUI	Command (#)	M	DT	ET	Score
Wireshark ZCL log [16]	Motion Sensor 1	private	Zone Status (1*)	0	2	2	4
	Motion Sensor 2	none	Zone Status (1*)	0	2	2	4
Zigator [17] Sth2-duos	SmartThings Outlet (IM6001)	samjin	On/off	1	1.5	1.5	4

Table 6. Evaluating APL Command Inference rules on Public Zigbee Capture [17]. Note: * implies that the command is identified, but not the state.

APL Commands	Total Packets	Inferred Packets	Accuracy (%)
Zone Status Change	2916	2712	93.0
ZCL On || ZCL Off	2423	2175*	89.8
Door lock || Unlock Request	676	596*	88.1
Door lock || Unlock Response	403	370*	91.8
Color Control, Level Control	0	0	0

Open World Evaluation on Public Captures: We evaluated ZLeaks over public Zigbee captures and reported results in Table 5. In capture 1 [16], we found 2 unknown devices that were recognized as motion sensors due to the presence of repetitive *Zone Change* commands. Capture 2 [17] had 1 unknown device which used *On/Off* for events. Note that we removed device commissioning traffic (including Network key) from both files to comply with our threat model.

As device identification is dependent on the correct inference of functionality-specific APL commands, we also evaluated ZLeaks inference rules on capture 2 [17]. The results in Table 6 indicate that ZLeaks inferred functionality-specific APL commands with 91.2% accuracy. We used our command inference strategy on generic APL commands and were able to infer *Device Announcement, Bind Request and Response (RR), Link Quality RR, NWK Address RR, Parent Announcement RR,* etc., with 100% accuracy. Most of all, the 6 NWK commands that Zigator [9] could not identify, were inferred with 85.7% accuracy.

4.5 Device Identification Using Periodic Reporting Patterns

Controlled Evaluation in RF Shield: We simultaneously paired all known devices with one hub at a time in an RF shield and left them in the idle state for at least 3 h. This way, devices reporting the attributes every 5 or 10 min yielded 36 and 18 reporting patterns, respectively, which are sufficient to evaluate two main features; reproducibility and uniqueness of periodic signatures. Table 7 summarizes the results of this experiment, with reporting intervals in second, minute, and hour represented using letters s, m, and h. Note that several devices exhibited more than one reporting pattern, e.g., for battery, temperature, etc., while few devices showed a different number of reporting patterns across different hubs, e.g., SMT and Sonoff outlet. This essentially helped identify both the

Table 7. Controlled Evaluation of Periodic Reporting scheme. Here, SMT = SmartThings, RI = Reporting interval, TPR = True positive rate, FNR = False negative rate

Device	SMT v2 Hub			Amazon Echo+			Philips/Sengled		
	RI	TPR	FNR	RI	TPR	FNR	RI	TPR	FNR
Centralite Outlet	5, 10m	1	0	5, 9m	0.982	0.018	N/A		
Sonoff Outlet	5m	1	0	5, 10m	1	0	N/A		
SMT Outlet	5, 10m	1	0	10m	1	0	N/A		
Sengled White Bulb	5m	1	0	10m	1	0	5,20,25m	1	0
Sengled Color Bulb	10m, 1h	1	0	10m, 1h	1	0	5,20,25m	1	0
Philips Hue Color Bulb	1s, 2m	1	0	1s, 2m	1	0	1s, 2m	1	0
SMT Motion sensor (IM)	5m	1	0	5m	1	0	N/A		
SMT Multisensor	5m, 1h	0.975	0.025	5m, 1h	1	0	N/A		
Ecolink water sensor	30, 30m	1	0	N/A			N/A		
Ecolink sound sensor	27, 30m	1	0	N/A			N/A		
Yale Door Lock	1h	1	0	10m	1	0	N/A		

Table 8. Realistic Evaluation of Periodic Reporting scheme. (● = successful device identification, ◑ = success using additional info, and ○ = resembled other device)

Device	SMT v2 Hub				Amazon Echo+				Vendor Hub			
	15m	30m	1h	3h	15m	30m	1h	3h	15m	30m	1h	3h
Centralite Outlet	●	●	●	●	●	●	●	●				
Sonoff Outlet	●	●	●	●	●	●	●	●				
SmartThings (SMT) Outlet	●	●	●	●	●	●	●	●				
Sengled (White) Bulb	●	●	●	●	●	●	●	●	●	●	●	●
Sengled (Color) Bulb	●	●	●	●	●	●	●	●	●	●	●	●
Philips Hue (Color) Bulb	●	●	●	●	●	●	●	●	●	●	●	●
SMT Motion sensor (IM)	◑	●	●	●	◑	●	●	●				
SMT Multi sensor	○	○	●	●	◑	●	●	●				
Ecolink water sensor		●	●	●	Not compatible							
Ecolink sound sensor		●	●	●	Not compatible							
Yale Door Lock			◑	◑	●	●	●	●				

device and the smart hub from the encrypted traffic. It is evident from a high average TPR of 0.998 and low FNR of 0.002 that the periodic signatures were identifiable and consistent over time, except once when the Centralite outlet and SMT Multisensor showed two out-of-order packets and were not identified.

Realistic Evaluation in IoT "Living Lab": Next, we shifted all the hubs, and known and unknown devices to the Mon(IoT)r lab. We paired all compatible devices to one target hub at a time and used the remaining devices as background Zigbee noise sources. The devices were left in the idle state for 3 h, and ZLeaks analyzed traffic after specific time intervals (15 min, 30 min, 1 h, and 3 h). In Table 8, devices that were distinctively identified after the specified time are marked with a full circle, e.g., all outlets had reporting intervals of 5 and/or 10 min; and were successfully identified within 15 min. Half-circle indicates identical reporting pattern and interval for two devices, e.g., both Yale and Schlage lock (unknown device) reported the same pattern after 1 h. In such a case, we used additional parameters (e.g., MAC OUI or logical device type) to identify the device. Finally, an empty circle depicts a complete resemblance between two devices, e.g., SMT motion sensor IRM (an unknown device) and SMT multisensor showed same patterns until the latter device reported its second pattern after 1 h. In essence, it is quite concerning that the device and manufacturer identity is leaked even in the device's idle state. Note that we could not evaluate this approach on public captures due to the absence of periodic reporting patterns.

5   Discussion and Related Work

5.1   Security Implications of Leaked Data

The know-how of devices in the smart home and their states (e.g., door unlocked or bulb off) is crucial to the smart home's security. A burglar can use this information to get insight into users' affluence and determine when the house is vulnerable to intrusion. In addition, an attacker can use Common Vulnerabilities and Exposures (CVE) database [23] to find and exploit unpatched vulnerabilities in the identified devices. The vulnerable devices can be weaponized to spread malware to the network [24], create IoT botnets [25] or carry out denial of service attacks. The attacker may also use side-channel attack to hijack the vulnerable hub [26]. From a business perspective, the leaked information can help Zigbee manufacturers gain deep insights into users' usage and activity patterns. This information can be sold to advertisers for interest-based advertisements, online tracking, or used in business decisions on future products. In short, our study provides deep insights into potential information leakages right at the source.

5.2   Potential Countermeasures

ZLeaks demonstrates the significance of unencrypted metadata (MAC OUI, frame, and payload lengths) in identifying functionality specific commands, events, and devices in the Zigbee network. Although exponential padding [27] effectively disguises payload lengths, it adds transmission overhead and increases power consumption for low-power Zigbee devices. We suggest padding random bytes in each payload (e.g., 0, 1, 2 or 3 bytes) and using the reserved field in the Zigbee security header to denote the number of padded bytes. This way, even same APL commands will have four different payload sizes, which will add enough entropy to make the Zigbee commands indistinguishable. Secondly, Zigbee Alliance can mandate the use of chipset manufacturer's identifier as MAC OUI to hide the real manufacturer's identity. This alone reduces the average Score calculated for unknown devices using the APL inference approach from 4.0 (80%) to 3.1 (62%).

Table 9. Privacy Implications of Leaked Information and Suggested Countermeasures.

Info	Privacy Implication	Countermeasure to disguise info
Device	- Hijack vulnerable devices/network	Use SOC MAC OUI to hide vendor
	- Insight regarding user's affluence	Use random payload padding to complicate command inference
	- Online advertising	
Event	- Reveals user's presence/absence daily routine	Attribute Pipelining **OR** similar request-response patterns to hide events

The volumetric analysis also provides significant hints regarding the occurrence of an event or periodic reporting. To make events indistinguishable, prior research [28,29] leverage mains-powered ZR or ZC to inject decoy packets in the traffic at pseudo-random intervals. However, decoy injector requires continuous training to avoid detection by the attacker. An efficient way to disguise events is to have similar event responses and reporting patterns for all devices. Alternatively, all attributes can be pipelined in a single packet instead of a series of packets. The suggested countermeasures, as summarized in Table 9 require significant design and implementation changes in the Zigbee protocol, as it is hard to prevent proposed inference attacks with a simple workaround like using a secure network or link key. We believe this is why the Zigbee Alliance is involved in new smart home technology, Matter [30], which has security as the fundamental design tenet and does not use Zigbee as the underlying IoT protocol.

5.3   Related Work

Privacy Analysis of Smart Home's IP Traffic: Several research studies have analysed the encrypted IP network traffic of smart homes to predict devices' events [4,5], user's habits [6], device types [1–3,31,32], and network anomalies [33,34]. Few studies [8,35] also analyzed the IP traffic between the smart app and cloud to detect misbehaving smart apps. Although these studies yield promising results, there are a few limitations; 1) attacker requires physical access to the network or mobile app, and 2) these approaches exploit traffic metadata (i.e., payload length, DNS responses, etc.); hence their effectiveness is questionable under realistic network conditions like Virtual Private Networks and Network Address and Port Translation enabled. Although recent studies have leveraged packet-level signatures and temporal packet relations to identify events [5] and devices [36] despite traffic shaping in place, these machine learning (ML) approaches require re-training after firmware upgrades to extract new signatures.

Privacy analysis of Zigbee (non-IP) Traffic: Unlike IP traffic patterns, Zigbee traffic patterns are challenging to obfuscate using conventional traffic shaping, as it directly impacts power consumption and battery life. Still, very few studies [7,8,37–39] have analyzed Zigbee traffic with the intent to study information leakages right at the source. Zigator [9] exploited unencrypted attributes

Table 10. ZLeaks vs. existing Zigbee based schemes for identifying Event Type (ET), Device Type (DT), Device Identity (DI) and applicability on Unknown devices (UD)

Research Work	Unique		Technique (Feature)	Identified			
	Hubs	Devices		ET	DT	DI	UD
Peekaboo [7]	1	3	ML (traffic profiling)	✓	✓		
Z-IoT [37]	1	8	ML (inter-arrival-times)		✓		✓
IoTGaze [38]	1	5	ML (event pattern)	✓			
IoTSpy [39]	1	5	NLP (frame len (fl), direction)	✓			
Homonit [8]	1	7	Levenshtein Distance (fl, direction)	✓			
ZLeaks	5	19	Command Inference (metadata)	✓	✓	✓	✓
			Correlation (periodic reporting)		✓	✓	

of Zigbee frames, notably packet length, directions, radius, and logical device type, to infer 6 out of 12 encrypted NWK commands. However, this inference approach does not apply to APL commands. Peekaboo [7] exploited traffic rate variations, and IoTSpy [39] leveraged packet sequence features to fingerprint known IoT events of merely 3 and 5 Zigbee devices, respectively. In addition, Homonit [8] and IoTGaze [38] analyzed Zigbee event patterns to detect malicious smart home apps. However, all these studies are confined to the identification of known events using a-priori event fingerprints. In contrast, ZLeaks infers event as well as device information without collecting event fingerprints for every device. Another study, Z-IoT [37] employed ML to identify device type by exploiting inter-arrival-time of NWK frames and IEEE 802.15.4 Data requests of the idle device. In contrast, ZLeaks exploits the device's periodic reporting interval and pattern (based on APL commands) to identify the device type and the *device* with 99.8% accuracy. As evident from Table 10, our study was conducted on the largest device set spanning 5 hubs and 19 unique Zigbee devices.

Security of Zigbee Protocol: Several attacks have been demonstrated against Zigbee protocol so far, such as selective jamming [9], worm chaining [24], command injection [40], replaying [41], etc., with an aim to recover the Network key or make the target devices malfunction. Unlike ZLeaks, these attacks either rely on leaked global link key, install (QR) codes or require attacker's presence during the device's setup to identify key material.

6   Conclusion

This work highlighted that the power optimization-oriented design of Zigbee protocol has destroyed the legal concept of privacy in smart homes. We presented ZLeaks [14], a privacy analysis tool that employs two inference techniques to demonstrate how easily a passive eavesdropper can determine in-home devices and events from the encrypted traffic, using a low-cost wireless Zigbee sniffer (TI CC2531). The evaluation conducted on an exhaustive set of 19 unique Zigbee devices and 5 smart hubs indicates that the ZLeaks command inference technique identified unknown events and devices with 83.6% accuracy, without using event signatures. In addition, ZLeaks periodic reporting technique identified known devices in the absence of any user activity with 99.8% accuracy. Finally, we evaluated our command inference rules on a third-party capture file and identified functionality-specific APL commands with 91.2% accuracy, irrespective of the secret keys. We conclude that the proposed inference attacks are impossible to prevent without making significant design changes in the Zigbee protocol.

References

1. Marchal, S., Miettinen, M., Nguyen, T.D., Sadeghi, A.-R., Asokan, N.: AuDI: toward autonomous IoT device-type identification using periodic communication. IEEE J. Sel. Areas Commun. **37**(6), 1402–1412 (2019). https://doi.org/10.1109/JSAC.2019.2904364
2. Meidan, Y., et al.: ProfilIoT: a machine learning approach for iot device identification based on network traffic analysis. In: Proceedings of the Symposium on Applied Computing, Morocco, pp. 506–509. ACM (2017)
3. Miettinen, M., Marchal, S., Hafeez, I., Asokan, N., Sadeghi, A.R., Tarkoma, S.: IoT sentinel: automated device-type identification for security enforcement in IoT. In: 37th International Conference on Distributed Computing Systems, USA, pp. 2177–2184. IEEE (2017)
4. Pierre Marie Junges, J.F., Festor, O.: Passive inference of user actions through IoT gateway encrypted traffic analysis. In: IEEE Symposium on Integrated Network and Service Management, USA. IEEE (2019)
5. Trimananda, R., Varmarken, J., Markopoulou, A., Demsky, B.: Packet-level signatures for smart home devices. In: Network and Distributed System Security Symposium, NDSS, USA, vol. 10, no. 13, p. 54 (2020)
6. Copos, B., Levitt, K., Bishop, M., Rowe, J.: Is anybody home? Inferring activity from smart home network traffic. In: IEEE Security and Privacy Workshops (SPW), USA, pp. 245–251. IEEE (2016)
7. Acar, A., et al.: Peek-a-Boo: i see your smart home activities, even encrypted! In: 13th ACM Conference on Security and Privacy in Wireless and Mobile Networks, Austria, WiSec 2020. ACM (2020)
8. Zhang, W., Meng, Y., Liu, Y., Zhang, X., Zhang, Y., Zhu, H.: HoMonit: monitoring smart home apps from encrypted traffic. In: Proceedings of the SIGSAC Conference on Computer and Communications Security, Canada, pp. 1074–1088. ACM (2018)
9. Akestoridis, D.G., Harishankar, M., Weber, M., Tague, P.: Zigator: analyzing the security of zigbee-enabled smart homes. In: 13th ACM Conference on Security and Privacy in Wireless and Mobile Networks, Austria, WiSec 2020. ACM (2020)
10. Zigbee Alliance: ZigBee Specification, 05-3474-21 (2015)
11. Zigbee Alliance: 2020 and Beyond. https://zigbeealliance.org/news_and_articles/zigbee-momentum/. Accessed June 2021
12. Zigbee Alliance: Zigbee Cluster Library Specification, 07-5123-06 (2016)
13. Smart Home Enthusiast's Guide to ZigBee (2019). https://linkdhome.com/articles/what-is-zigbee-guide. Accessed June 2021
14. ZLeaks. https://github.com/narmeenshafqat1/ZLeaks
15. Mon(IoT)r Lab. https://moniotrlab.ccis.neu.edu/. Accessed June 2021

16. Wireshark bug. https://bugs.wireshark.org/bugzilla/show_bug.cgi?id=9423
17. Zigator CRAWDAD dataset CMU. (v. 2020-05-26). https://crawdad.org/cmu/zigbee-smarthome/20200526. Accessed May 2021
18. TI CC2531 zigbee. https://www.ti.com/product/CC2531. Accessed June 2021
19. Zigbee Compliance Document of Lightify bulb (2014). https://zigbeealliance.org/zigbee_products/lightify-classic-a60-rgbw/. Accessed June 2021
20. Zigbee Compliance Document of Sengled Bulb (2018). https://zigbeealliance.org/zigbee_products/sengled-element-3/. Accessed July 2021
21. Tshark captures. https://tshark.dev/search/pcaptable/. Accessed May 2021
22. Pyshark. https://github.com/KimiNewt/pyshark. Accessed June 2021
23. US-CERT: CVE. http://cve.mitre.org/. Accessed May 2021
24. Ronen, E., Shamir, A., Weingarten, A.O., OFlynn, C.: IoT goes nuclear: creating a ZigBee chain reaction. In: IEEE Symposium on Security and Privacy, USA (2017)
25. Herwig, S., Harvey, K., Hughey, G., Roberts, R., Levin, D.: Measurement and analysis of Hajime, a peer-to-peer IoT botnet. In: Network and Distributed Systems Security Symposium (NDSS), USA (2019)
26. Sugawara, T., Cyr, B., Rampazzi, S., Genkin, D., Fu, K.: Light commands: laser-based audio injection attacks on voice-controllable systems. In: 29th USENIX Security Symposium, USA, pp. 2631–2648. USENIX (2020)
27. Sun, Q., Simon, D.R., Wang, Y.M., Russell, W., Padmanabhan, V.N., Qiu, L.: Statistical identification of encrypted web browsing traffic. In: IEEE Symposium on Security and Privacy, USA, pp. 19–30. IEEE (2002)
28. Leu, P., Puddu, I., Ranganathan, A., Čapkun, S.: I send, therefore i leak: information leakage in low-power wide area networks. In: Proceedings of 11th ACM Conference on Security & Privacy in Wireless and Mobile Networks, Sweden (2018)
29. Liu, X., Zeng, Q., Du, X., Valluru, S.L., Fu, C., Fu, X.: SniffMislead: non-intrusive privacy protection against wireless packet sniffers in smart homes. In: 24th International Symposium on Research in Attacks, Intrusions and Defenses (2021)
30. Matter. https://buildwithmatter.com/. Accessed May 2021
31. Anantharaman, P., et al.: IoTHound: environment-agnostic device identification and monitoring. In: 10th International Conference on Internet of Things. ACM (2020)
32. Thangavelu, V., Divakaran, D.M., Sairam, R., Bhunia, S.S., Gurusamy, M.: DEFT: a distributed IoT fingerprinting technique. IEEE Internet Things J. 6(1), 940–952 (2019)
33. Cho, K.T., Shin, K.G.: Fingerprinting electronic control units for vehicle intrusion detection. In: USENIX Security Symposium, USA, pp. 911–927 (2016)
34. Salman, O., Elhajj, I.H., Chehab, A., Kayssi, A.: A machine learning based framework for IoT device identification and abnormal traffic detection. Trans. Emerg. Telecommun. Technol. 33, e3743 (2019)
35. Earlence Fernandes, J.J., Prakash, A.: Security analysis of emerging smart home applications. In: 37th IEEE Symposium on Security and Privacy, USA (2016)
36. Perdisci, R., Papastergiou, T., Alrawi, O., Antonakakis, M.: IoTFinder: efficient large-scale identification of IoT devices via passive DNS traffic analysis. In: European Symposium on Security and Privacy (EuroS&P), virtual, pp. 474–489. IEEE (2020)
37. Babun, L., Aksu, H., Ryan, L., Akkaya, K., Bentley, E.S., Uluagac, A.S.: Z-IoT: passive device-class fingerprinting of ZigBee and Z-Wave IoI devices. In: IEEE International Conference on Communications (ICC), Ireland, pp. 1–7. IEEE (2020)

38. Gu, T., Fang, Z., Abhishek, A., Fu, H., Hu, P., Mohapatra, P.: IoTGaze: IoT security enforcement via wireless context analysis. In: IEEE Conference on Computer Communications (INFOCOM), virtual, pp. 884–893. IEEE (2020)
39. Gu, T., Fang, Z., Abhishek, A., Mohapatra, P.: IoTSpy: uncovering human privacy leakage in IoT networks via mining wireless context. In: IEEE 31st Annual International Symposium on Personal, Indoor and Mobile Radio Communications, virtual, pp. 1–7. IEEE (2020)
40. Brown, F., Gleason, M.: ZigBee hacking: smarter home invasion with ZigDiggity. In: Black Hat, USA (2019)
41. Olawumi, O., Haataja, K., Asikainen, M., Vidgren, N., Toivanen, P.: Three practical attacks against ZigBee security: attack scenario definitions, practical experiments, countermeasures, and lessons learned. In: 14th International Conference on Hybrid Intelligent Systems, Kuwait, pp. 199–206. IEEE (2014)

Passive Query-Recovery Attack Against Secure Conjunctive Keyword Search Schemes

Marco Dijkslag[1](✉), Marc Damie[3](✉), Florian Hahn[1](✉),
and Andreas Peter[1,2](✉)

[1] University of Twente, Enschede, The Netherlands
m.dijkslag@alumnus.utwente.nl, {f.w.hahn,a.peter}@utwente.nl
[2] University of Oldenburg, Oldenburg, Germany
andreas.peter@uni-oldenburg.de
[3] Univ. Lille, Inria, CNRS, Centrale Lille, UMR 9189 - CRIStAL, Lille, France
marc.damie@inria.fr

Abstract. While storing documents on the cloud can be attractive, the question remains whether cloud providers can be trusted with storing private documents. Even if trusted, data breaches are ubiquitous. To prevent information leakage one can store documents encrypted. If encrypted under traditional schemes, one loses the ability to perform simple operations over the documents, such as searching through them. Searchable encryption schemes were proposed allowing some search functionality while documents remain encrypted. Orthogonally, research is done to find attacks that exploit search and access pattern leakage that most efficient schemes have. One type of such an attack is the ability to recover plaintext queries. Passive query-recovery attacks on single-keyword search schemes have been proposed in literature, however, conjunctive keyword search has not been considered, although keyword searches with two or three keywords appear more frequently in online searches.

We introduce a generic extension strategy for existing passive query-recovery attacks against single-keyword search schemes and explore its applicability for the attack presented by Damie et al. (USENIX Security '21). While the original attack achieves up to a recovery rate of 85% against single-keyword search schemes for an attacker without exact background knowledge, our experiments show that the generic extension to conjunctive queries comes with a significant performance decrease achieving recovery rates of at most 32%. Assuming a stronger attacker with partial knowledge of the indexed document set boosts the recovery rate to 85% for conjunctive keyword queries with two keywords and achieves similar recovery rates as previous attacks by Cash et al. (CCS '15) and Islam et al. (NDSS '12) in the same setting for single-keyword search schemes.

Keywords: Searchable encryption · Conjunctive keyword search · Passive query-recovery attack

© Springer Nature Switzerland AG 2022
G. Ateniese and D. Venturi (Eds.): ACNS 2022, LNCS 13269, pp. 126–146, 2022.
https://doi.org/10.1007/978-3-031-09234-3_7

1 Introduction

With increasing number of enterprises storing their documents in the cloud the question arises how to cope with storing sensitive documents on the cloud without the cloud provider learning information about the stored documents or information being leaked when a data breach occurs. One solution for this problem would be to encrypt the documents to hide its contents to the cloud provider. However, this prevents users from using the (often available) computational resources cloud providers offer, since searching through the documents is no longer possible without first downloading and decrypting it.

Searchable symmetric encryption schemes can be a solution to this problem that offer constructions for search functionalities over encrypted documents. The first practical solution towards searchable encryption has been proposed by Song et al. [22]. Proposers of searchable encryption schemes need to find a trade-off in efficiency, security, and functionality. With this trade-off in terms of security comes information leakage such as possible *search pattern* leakage (revealing which queries concerned the same underlying, but unknown, keyword) and *access pattern* leakage (revealing the identifiers of all documents matching the search query). Most of the efficient searchable encryption schemes that allow for keyword search leak information in the access pattern for efficiency.

Searchable encryption is an active line of research for finding efficient schemes that allow for search in encrypted documents with well-defined security in terms of a leakage function. Orthogonally, research is performed on finding attacks against proposed searchable encryption schemes. One such type of attack is a query-recovery attack, i.e. the ability for an adversary to recover the plaintexts from performed queries. In general two kinds of query-recovery attacks exist: (1) a *passive* attack where an adversary only has access to the information leaked by a scheme and (2) an *active* attack in which an adversary is able to inject tailored documents into the to-be-searched dataset.

Active query-recovery attacks on conjunctive keyword search do exist [18, 28] which are described as an extension on the proposed single-keyword search attack. Currently, all existing *passive* query-recovery attacks against searchable symmetric encryption that allow for keyword searches only focuses on single-keyword search schemes. However, these attacks do not reflect a realistic scenario, since single-keyword searches are limited and statistics show that the number of keywords used by people online in the US peaks at two keywords [5]. Also, three keyword searches are still more frequent than searches for a single keyword. The frequency of searches using seven or more keywords becomes negligible.

Note that the recovery of conjunctive keyword queries is more difficult with respect to the recovery of single-keyword queries using similar vocabulary sizes. This difficulty stems from the fact that the space for keyword conjunctions is combinatorial in the number of conjunction terms compared to single-keywords, therefore an attacker needs to consider more possible candidates of keyword conjunctions for each observed query.

In this work, we explore a passive query-recovery attack against secure conjunctive keyword search (CKWS) schemes. We propose a generic extension strategy for query-recovery attacks against single-keyword search to recover conjunctive queries using the same attack. Our extension strategy is based on the use of trapdoors created from a keyword-conjunction set as a generalization of trapdoors created from single-keywords. Replacing keywords with keyword conjunction sets. Our attack is static and does also work on forward and backward private schemes [17].

We introduce an adaptation of the query-recovery attack proposed by Damie et al. [6] to achieve keyword conjunction recovery. We explore the applicability of the attack in two setups: (1) a *similar-documents* attack, where the attacker only has access to a set of documents that is similar, but otherwise different, from the indexed documents and (2) a *known-documents* attack, where the attacker has (partial) knowledge of the indexed documents. In both setups it is assumed the attacker knows the keyword conjunctions for a small set of queries a priori. We experimentally show that our attack can work for a relatively small vocabulary size (500) in an attack setup allowing only conjunctive keyword search using 2 keywords. However, we show that in an attack setup using similar-documents the attack performs poorly unless many known queries are assumed to be part of the attacker's knowledge. Furthermore, we demonstrate limitations of our generic extension posed by the combinatorial complexity increase for larger conjunctions.

2   Related Work

Most attacks against searchable symmetric encryption that have been described in the literature are query-recovery attacks. Islam et al. [10] were the first to propose a passive query-recovery attack in which they are exploiting the *access pattern* leakage, i.e. leaked document identifiers from observed queries. In their attack, the adversary needs to know all the documents indexed on the server to be successful. They introduced the idea of computing (word-word and trapdoor-trapdoor) co-occurrences to attack SSE. This idea being reused by other the passive attacks. The attack works by finding the closest mapping between the word-word co-occurrence matrix and trapdoor-trapdoor co-occurrence matrix in which they use meta heuristic simulated annealing. Also, the attack requires a number of known queries to work, i.e. trapdoors from which the attacker knows the underlying plaintext value.

Cash et al. [3] proposed another passive query-recovery attack. Their attack first exploits that keywords with high frequency have unique keyword document counts to initialize their set of known queries. Then for keywords that do not have a unique keyword document occurrence count they construct a co-occurrence matrix of their known documents and observed queries, similar to Islam et al. They try to recover more queries by constructing for every unknown query their candidate set (i.e. keywords having the same document occurrence count) and remove candidates from the set that do not have the same co-occurrence with a known query in the known queries set. If after iterating over every known query only one candidate is left, the last candidate is appended to the known queries set. This process is repeated for all unknown queries until the set of known queries stops increasing.

Both [3,10] rely on the attacker knowing a large part of the indexed documents, where the count attack performs better than the attack by Islam et al. However, their query recovery rate roughly only increases when the attacker knows at least 80% of the indexed documents.

The query-recovery attack proposed by Pouliot et al. [21] uses weighted graph matching where the attacker needs to find mapping of keyword graph G and trapdoor graph H. The attack achieves recovery rates above 90% when the attacker knows the entire set of indexed documents, but fails as similar-documents attack unless having a smaller set of documents and vocabulary size. Also, the runtime of the attack increases rapidly, where for a vocabulary size of 500 the attack runs in less than one hour, whereas it takes more than 16 h for a vocabulary size of 1000. The attack in [10] has a runtime of a maximum of 14 h, whereas attacks from [3,6] run in seconds.

Ning et al. [15] introduced a query-recovery attack that works when the attacker knows a percentage of the indexed documents. Keywords and trapdoors are represented as a binary string where the i-th bit is 1 if the keyword (resp. trapdoor) occurs in document i. Recovery is done by converting the bit strings to integers, where it is considered that a keyword corresponds to a trapdoor if they have the same integer value.

The proposed attack outperforms the attack by Cash et al. [3], where in their scenario [3] achieves a recovery rate of roughly 28% and their proposed attack around 56% when the attacker knows 80% of the indexed documents. However, they do not report a recovery rate for an attacker having knowledge of more than 80% of the indexed documents.

Blackstone et al. [2] proposed a "sub-graph" attack requiring much less known documents to be successful and also works on co-occurrence hiding schemes. Their experiments show that an attacker only needs to know 20% of the indexed documents to succeed in her attack.

In [6], Damie et al. proposed their refined score attack that works in a setting where the attacker only knows a similar, but otherwise different and non-indexed, set of documents for query-recovery. A mathematical formalization of the similarity is proposed in their paper. In [3] they showed that both the attack proposed by Islam et al. [10] and their proposed count attack do not work using similar documents. In [6], the query-recovery attack uses similar techniques as used by [3,10], i.e. constructing co-occurrence matrices from the document set known by the attacker and a trapdoor-trapdoor co-occurrence matrix from the assumed access pattern leakage. By starting with a few known (keyword, trapdoor)-pairs their attack iteratively recovers queries where previous recovered queries with high confidence scores are added to the set of known queries. Using this approach their attack reaches recovery rates around 85%.

Other Types of Attacks. Zhang et al. [28] proposed an effective active document injection attack to recover keywords. Furthermore, they proposed an extension of their attack to a conjunctive keyword search setting which was experimentally verified for queries with 3 keywords.

In [18], Poddar et al. proposed several attacks that uses volume pattern as auxiliary information in combination with the attacker's ability to replay queries and inject documents. Moreover, they also gave an extension of their attack for queries with conjunctive keywords which is based on the extension from [28] using a document injection approach.

Liu et al. [14] proposed a query-recovery attack which makes use of the search pattern leakage as auxiliary information. In particular, they exploit the query frequency. However, they simulated their queries by applying Gaussian noise to keyword search frequency from Google Trends[1] because of the lack of a query dataset. The attacker has access to the original frequencies.

Another attack introduced by Oya and Kerschbaum [16] combines both volume information derived from the access pattern leakage and query frequency information derived from the search pattern leakage as auxiliary information.

Conjunctive Keyword Search Schemes. Passive query-recovery attacks against single-keyword search schemes already work for some conjunctive keyword search schemes where the server performs search for each individual keyword in a query independently and returns the intersection of document identifiers of each single-keyword search, i.e. leaking the *full* access pattern for each individual keyword in the conjunction. However, these attacks cannot be applied on conjunctive keyword search schemes with less or *common* access pattern leakage, where *common* refers to the scheme only leaking the document identifiers for the documents containing all keywords from a conjunctive keyword query. Hence, in this work we explore one extension strategy for conjunctive keywords that can be applied to most passive query-recovery attacks against single-keyword search using only common access pattern leakage.

[19,23] both proposed such a conjunctive keyword search scheme that returns the intersection of document identifiers for each individual keyword in a conjunctive keyword query, thus leaking the *full* access pattern. However, we would like to emphasize that in this scenario only an *honest-but-curious* server that is able to observe the result set for each intermediate keyword can be considered an attacker, since an *eavesdropper* on the communication channel would not be able to observe the document identifiers for each intermediate single-keyword search. Furthermore, it should be noted that both schemes also offer more functionality than conjunctive keyword search alone. Where [19] allows for phrase searches and [23] offers result set verifiability and index updatability.

Other proposed conjunctive keyword search schemes exist [4,7–9,11,13,24, 26,27]. However, all of them leak at least the common access pattern, where [4,9,25] have more than common access pattern leakage. To the best of our knowledge there do not exist efficient conjunctive keyword search schemes that have no access pattern leakage.

3   Preliminaries

We first introduce some notations that are used throughout this work. Let document set $\mathcal{D}$ consist of documents $\{D_1, ..., D_n\}$. Let keyword set $\mathcal{W}$ consist of

---

[1] https://trends.google.com/trends.

Table 1. Notation

Notation	Meaning	Size notation
Q	Set of observed trapdoors by the adversary	l
R_Q	Document identifiers for each observed $td \in Q$	l
$KnownQ$	Known (td, ckw)-pairs by the adversary	k
ckw_q	Set of distinct keywords used in a conjunctive keyword query q	d
C_{ckw}	ckw-ckw co-occurrence matrix created from $\mathcal{D}_{similar}$ or $\mathcal{D}_{p-known}$	$m_{similar} \times m_{similar}$ or $m_{known} \times m_{known}$
C_{td}	td-td co-occurrence matrix created from R_Q	$l \times l$
$\mathcal{D}_{real}$	Real (indexed) document set	n_{real}
$\mathcal{D}_{similar}$	Similar document set	$n_{similar}$
$\mathcal{D}_{p-known}$	p-Known document set $(0 < p \leq 1)$	n_{known} ($= p \cdot n_{real}$)
$\mathcal{W}_{real}$	Vocabulary of keywords extracted from $\mathcal{D}_{real}$	v_{real}
$\mathcal{W}_{similar}$	Vocabulary of keywords extracted from $\mathcal{D}_{similar}$	$v_{similar}$
$\mathcal{W}_{known}$	Vocabulary of keywords extracted from $\mathcal{D}_{p-known}$	v_{known}
$\mathcal{K}_{real}$	Set containing possible conjunctions of keyword combinations generated from $\mathcal{W}_{real}$	$m_{real} = \binom{v_{real}}{d}$
$\mathcal{K}_{similar}$	Set containing possible conjunctions of keyword combinations generated from $\mathcal{W}_{similar}$	$m_{similar} = \binom{v_{similar}}{d}$
$\mathcal{K}_{known}$	Set containing possible conjunctions of keyword combinations generated from $\mathcal{W}_{known}$	$m_{known} = \binom{v_{known}}{d}$

keywords $\{w_1, ..., w_m\}$. Document D_i consists of keywords that form a subset of keyword set $\mathcal{W}$. Let $id(D_i) = i$ return the identifier for document D_i. We denote $x \in D_i$ if keyword x ($\in \mathcal{W}$) occurs in document D_i. A summary of all notations and their meaning used throughout this work is given in Table 1.

3.1 Searchable Symmetric Encryption

A searchable encryption scheme allows a user to search in encrypted documents and is often described in a client-server setting. The client can search through encrypted documents stored on the server, without the server learning information about the plaintext documents. Often a searchable encryption scheme can be divided in four algorithms:

- KeyGen(1^k): takes security parameter k and outputs a secret key K.
- BuildIndex($K, \mathcal{D}$): takes document set $\mathcal{D}$ and secret key K and produces an (inverted) index I.
- Trapdoor(K, q): takes query q and secret key K and outputs a trapdoor td_q.
- Search(I, td_q): takes trapdoor td_q and index I and outputs the documents that match with query q.

In single-keyword search schemes q corresponds to a keyword w, whereas in conjunctive keyword search schemes q would correspond to a query for documents containing d keywords, i.e., the conjunction of keywords $w_1 \wedge ... \wedge w_d$ of keywords $w_1, ..., w_d$. Then, td_q would correspond to the conjunction of d keywords.

3.2   Considered Conjunctive Keyword Search Model

We assume a fixed number of keywords (d) that are allowed to be searched for in a conjunctive keyword search. For instance if $d = 2$, only trapdoors with 2 distinct keywords are allowed. We denote such a fixed-d scheme as *secure d-conjunctive keyword search scheme*.

For simplicity, we assume a fixed number of d distinct keywords, however one could consider d as a maximum number of keywords in the conjunctive search by reusing the same keyword for non-used keyword entries in the conjunction. For instance, when $d = 2$, $kw \land kw$ for the same keyword kw would be equivalent to a single-keyword search for kw.

We consider ckw to be the set of d different keywords that are used to construct a trapdoor (td_{ckw}). For instance, if we consider a conjunctive keyword search scheme that allows search for $d = 3$ conjunctive keywords, we would create a keyword set ckw for every possible combination of 3 keywords, where $ckw_1 = \{kw_1, kw_2, kw_3\}$.[2]

First, in the BuildIndex algorithm, the client encrypts every document in the document set locally. Then creates an encrypted index of the document set (locally). Given a trapdoor td_{ckw}, the server can find the documents containing keywords in ckw using such a created index. The encrypted document set and index are then uploaded by the client to the server.

Although in literature different methods for constructing such an index were proposed, here we do not fix which index is used. We only require the model to have at least *common* access pattern leakage, where *common* refers to the scheme only leaking the document identifiers for the documents containing all keywords in a conjunctive keyword query. All conjunctive search schemes described in Sect. 2 leak at least the common access pattern.

The client can search documents by constructing trapdoors. The client constructs a trapdoor by picking d keywords she wants to search for. In our model, she constructs a trapdoor using the function $td_q = \mathsf{Trapdoor}(K, ckw_i = \{kw_1, ..., kw_d\})$, for the keywords she wants to search for. By sending the trapdoor td_q to the server, the server responds with a set of document identifiers R_{td_q} for documents that contain all keywords in ckw_i.

3.3   Attacker Model

Like in [6], we consider two types of passive attackers which both can observe trapdoors sent by a user and its response including the document identifiers. The first type of attacker is an *honest-but-curious* server. The server is considered to be an honest entity meaning it follows the protocol. Hence, it always returns the correct result for each query. However, such curious server tries to learn as much information as possible using the scheme leakage. Secondly, we consider an *eavesdropper* that is able to observe pairs of trapdoor and document identifiers from the communication channel between client and server as an attacker.

---

[2] Note: $d = 1$ refers to a single-keyword search scheme.

For both attackers an *observation*$_i$ is a tuple (td_q, R_{td_q}) considering conjunctive keyword queries where trapdoor td corresponds to d conjunctive keywords.

3.4 Attacker Knowledge

It is assumed the attacker knows the number of keywords d that are allowed to construct trapdoors. Moreover, it can be assumed that an *honest-but-curious* attacker knows the byte size of the stored documents and the number of documents stored (e.g. from the index). However, an *eavesdropper* does not. In that case we make use of the proposed formula by [6] that approximates the number of documents stored on the server (n_{real}) derived from the attacker's knowledge.

We consider two types of attack setups, i.e. a *similar-documents* attack setup where the attacker has access to a set of similar documents (as formalized in [6]) and a *known-documents* attack setup where the attacker has (partial) knowledge of the documents stored on the server.

Similar-Documents Attack. In our similar-documents attack we assume the attacker has a document set $\mathcal{D}_{similar}$ that is ϵ-similar to the real indexed document set $\mathcal{D}_{real}$. However, we assume ϵ-similarity (as formalized in [6]) over the possible keyword conjunctions rather than keywords, where smaller ϵ means more similar. Also, $\mathcal{D}_{similar} \cap \mathcal{D}_{real} = \emptyset$, thus do not have overlapping documents.

Known-Documents Attack. Like in [3,10], for our known-documents attack setup we assume that the attacker has a p-known document set $\mathcal{D}_{p-known}$, where $0 < p \leq 1$ defines the known-documents rate. Meaning, the attacker knows a fraction p of the real indexed document set $\mathcal{D}_{real}$ stored on the server.

It should be noted that a similar-documents attack can be considered more realistic than a known-documents attack as discussed by Damie et al. [6]. Since a known-documents attack will most likely only be possible on a data breach, whereas documents that are only similar to the actual indexed documents maybe even publicly available. Moreover, the user could remove the leaked documents that are used in a known-documents attack from the index.

The assumption that the attacker knows (a subset of) the documents stored on the server is rather strong, but is based on what is done in previous work [3,10].

4 CKWS-Adapted Refined Score Attack

In this section we describe our conjunctive keyword search (CKWS) adaptation of the *refined score attack*. Our adaptation builds upon the *score attacks* that were introduced by Damie et al. [6]. We have chosen to use their query-recovery attack against single-keyword search schemes, since it is, to the best of our knowledge, the most accurate similar-documents attack that has been described yet. Furthermore, the matching algorithm used in their attack only has a runtime of 20 s while considering a vocabulary size of 4000 keywords. Since the space of possible queries increases combinatorial, we have to consider many possible keyword conjunctions and thus faster runtimes is desired. Moreover, their attack can use either known documents or similar documents as adversary's knowledge. We describe how one can transform their query-recovery attack to an attack on conjunctive keyword search schemes, i.e. considering the (abstract) secure d-conjunctive keyword search scheme described in Sect. 3.2, using similar terminology as in [6].

In addition, the code for the score attacks has been made publicly available online by Damie et al. This allowed us to verify their results first before adapting it to our conjunctive keyword setting.

4.1   Score Attacks

Damie et al. [6] first propose the *score attack* based on the idea of ranking potential keyword-trapdoor mappings according to a *score* function. To run the score attack an attacker calculates the word-word co-occurrence matrix from its auxiliary document set and constructs a trapdoor-trapdoor co-occurrence matrix from observed queries and their result sets. Assuming some known queries, the attacker removes the columns from both matrices that do not occur in their set of known queries (i.e. word-trapdoor pairs) to obtain so-called sub-matrices. Then for every (observed) trapdoor, it goes through all possible keywords extracted from the auxiliary document set and returns the keyword for which their score function is maximized.

Secondly, their proposed *refined score attack* builds upon previously described score attack. Instead of returning a prediction for all trapdoors, they define a *certainty* function for each prediction and only keep the $RefSpeed$ best predictions according to this certainty function. These predictions are then added to the set of known queries and the attacker recomputes the co-occurrence sub-matrices. This procedure is repeated until there are no predictions left to make, i.e. no unknown queries left.

4.2   Generic Extension

In short, our generic extension proposes to replace single keywords with keyword conjunction sets. The extension consists of five steps, highlighted by the next five subsections to adapt a passive query-recovery attack against single-keyword search to conjunctive keyword search, i.e. attacks that try to find a mapping between co-occurrences of keywords and trapdoors to recover queries. We describe our extension in a similar-documents attack setup using $\mathcal{D}_{similar}$, but the same steps can be taken in a known-documents attack setup using $\mathcal{D}_{p-known}$ as the attacker's auxiliary document set.

Extract Vocabulary. First, the attacker extracts keywords from the set of documents $\mathcal{D}_{similar}$ to vocabulary $\mathcal{W}_{similar}$. As in query-recovery attacks on single-keyword search [3,6,10], we also assume that the keyword extraction method used by the attacker is the same as the one used by the user when she created the encrypted index.

Construct Set of Possible Keyword Conjunctions. The attacker creates the set of all possible keyword conjunctions $\mathcal{K}_{similar} = \{ckw_i \in \mathcal{P}(\mathcal{W}_{similar}) \mid |ckw_i| = d\}$, where $m_{similar} = |\mathcal{K}_{similar}| = \binom{v_{similar}}{d}$ and $\mathcal{P}(X)$ denotes the power set of set X.

Compute Co-occurrence Matrix for Keyword Conjunctions. From $\mathcal{D}_{similar}$ and derived keyword conjunctions set $\mathcal{K}_{similar}$ the attacker creates the $m_{similar} \times m_{similar}$ matrix $ID_{similar}$. Here $ID_{similar}[i, j] = 1$ if the i-th document in $\mathcal{D}_{similar}$ contains the keywords that are in keyword conjunction ckw_j and is otherwise 0. Then the attacker computes the ckw-ckw co-occurrence matrix $C_{ckw} = ID_{similar}^T \cdot ID_{similar} \cdot \frac{1}{n_{similar}}$.[3]

Compute the Trapdoor-Trapdoor Co-occurrence Matrix. We define $Q = \{td_1, ..., td_l\}$ to be the set of observed queries by the attacker containing trapdoors that have been queried by the user. These trapdoors were created by the user from keyword conjunctions in $\mathcal{K}_{real} = \{ckw_i \in \mathcal{P}(\mathcal{W}_{real}) \mid |ckw_i| = d\}$. Let $R_{td} = \{id(D)|(ckw \in \mathcal{K}_{real}) \wedge (td = \mathsf{Trapdoor}(K, ckw)) \wedge (D \in \mathcal{D}_{real}) \wedge \forall_{kw_t \in ckw}(kw_t \in D)\}$ be the set of document identifiers that were observed by the attacker for trapdoor td. Then we define the set of document identifiers $DocumentIDs = \bigcup_{td \in Q} R_{td}$ of size s, where $s \le n_{real}$. Similar to the construction of the matrix $ID_{similar}$, we construct $s \times l$ trapdoor-document matrix ID_{real}, where $ID_{real}[i, j] = 1$ if i-th document identifier occurs in R_{td_j} (and td_j refers to j-th trapdoor from Q). Otherwise, $ID_{real}[i, j] = 0$. Then trapdoor-trapdoor co-occurrence matrix $C_{td} = ID_{real}^T \cdot ID_{real} \cdot \frac{1}{n_{real}}$.

Apply Attack. The last step is to apply a passive query-recovery attack using the set of keyword conjunctions and the co-occurrence matrices.

4.3   Transform Key Steps of Refined Score Attack

As in [3,6,10], our attack also requires the attacker to have knowledge of a set of known queries. However, our set of known queries is slightly different because of the keyword conjunctions. In a similar-documents attack setup our set of known queries $KnownQ = \{(ckw_i, td_{known})|(ckw_i \in \mathcal{K}_{similar} \cap \mathcal{K}_{real}) \wedge (td_{known} \in Q) \wedge (td_{known} = \mathsf{Trapdoor}(K, ckw_i)\}$. For our known-documents attack setup, $KnownQ$ is similarly defined by replacing $\mathcal{K}_{similar}$ with $\mathcal{K}_{known}$.

We recall key steps in the score attack w.r.t. the projection of the keyword-keyword co-occurrence and trapdoor-trapdoor co-occurrence matrix to sub-matrices using the set of known queries. These steps are important because they are different for our CKWS-adapted refined score attack. In short, the projection is done by only keeping the columns of known queries in C_{ckw} and C_{td}.

---

[3] A^T denotes the transpose of matrix A.

Our goal is to generate sub-matrices C^s_{ckw} and C^s_{td} from C_{ckw} and C_{td} respectively. We describe the projection step for C_{ckw} using $\mathcal{K}_{similar}$, but the same holds for $\mathcal{K}_{known}$. Recall that $\mathcal{K}_{similar} = \{ckw_1, ..., ckw_{m_{similar}}\}$.

We define $pos(ckw)$, which returns the position of $ckw \in \mathcal{K}_{similar}$. That is, $pos(ckw_i) = i$. Similarly, $pos(td)$ returns the position of td in $Q = \{td_1, ..., td_l\}$.

Let $C_{ckw} = (..., \vec{c}_i, ...)_{i \in [m_{similar}]}$ be the $m_{similar} \times m_{similar}$ co-occurrence matrix, where the column vector $\vec{c}_i$ denotes its i-th column. Then the $m_{similar} \times k$ sub-matrix $C^s_{ckw} = (..., \vec{c}_{pos(ckw_j)}, ...)_{(ckw_j, td_j) \in KnownQ}$, where $\vec{c}_{pos(ckw_j)}$ is the $pos(ckw_j)$-th column vector of C_{ckw}.

Let $C_{td} = (..., \vec{u}_i, ...)_{i \in [l]}$ be the $l \times l$ trapdoor-trapdoor co-occurrence matrix, where the column vector $\vec{u}_i$ denotes its i-th column. Then $l \times k$ sub-matrix C^s_{td} can be constructed as follows: $C^s_{td} = (..., \vec{u}_{pos(td_j)}, ...)_{(ckw_j, td_j) \in KnownQ}$, where $u_{pos(td_j)}$ is the $pos(td_j)$-th column vector of C_{td}.

Superscript s emphasizes that C^s_{ckw} and C^s_{td} are sub-matrices of C_{ckw} and C_{td} respectively. Also, we denote $C^s_{ckw}[ckw_i]$ to be the i-th row vector for keyword conjunction set ckw_i and $C^s_{td}[td_j]$ to be the j-th row vector for trapdoor td_j, where $|C^s_{ckw}[ckw_i]| = |C^s_{td}[td_j]| = k$.

Additionally, we revise the *scoring algorithm* for which the score is higher if a trapdoor corresponds to a certain keyword conjunction, i.e. the distance between two vectors $C^s_{td}[td_j]$ and $C^s_{ckw}[ckw_i]$ is small. Using keyword conjunctions the score function is defined as: $Score(td_j, ckw_i) = -ln(||C^s_{ckw}[ckw_i] - C^s_{td}[td_j]||)$, for all $ckw_i \in \mathcal{K}_{similar}$ (or $\mathcal{K}_{known}$) and all $td_j \in Q$, where $ln(\cdot)$ is the natural log and $|| \cdot ||$ is a vector-norm (e.g. L2 norm).

4.4 Revised Algorithm

We substitute C^s_{kw} for C^s_{ckw} in [6] to transform the refined score attack to the *CKWS-adapted refined score attack*. Algorithm 1 contains its pseudocode, where a step is highlighted blue if it is different from the *refined score attack* proposed by Damie et al. [6]. Note that this algorithm is described using $\mathcal{K}_{similar}$, but also works for $\mathcal{K}_{known}$ as input.

One iteration of the algorithm can be defined by the three key phases. First remove known queries from the observed queries set Q. Secondly, find the best scoring keyword conjunction candidate for each unknown query and compute the certainty of this candidate. Using keyword conjunctions the certainty of a keyword conjunction candidate ckw_i for trapdoor td is defined by: $Certainty(td, ckw_i) = Score(td, ckw_i) - \max_{j \neq i} Score(td, ckw_j)$

Using this definition the certainty of a correct match of keyword conjunction with a trapdoor is higher when the score of the match is much higher than all other possible candidate scores.

The algorithm defines a notion of refinement speed ($RefSpeed$) which defines the number of most certain predictions that will be added each iteration of the algorithm to the set of known queries. Which describes the third and last key step of an iteration, i.e. adding the most certain predictions to the known queries and

---

Algorithm 1: CKWS-adapted refined score attack.

Input: $\mathcal{K}_{similar}$, C^s_{ckw}, Q, C^s_{td}, $KnownQ$, $RefSpeed$

Result: List of keyword conjunctions as predictions for trapdoors with certainty

$final\_pred \leftarrow []$;

$unknownQ \leftarrow Q$;

while $unknownQ \neq \emptyset$ **do**

    // Set remaining unknown queries.

    $unknownQ \leftarrow \{td : (td \in Q) \wedge (\nexists ckw \in \mathcal{K}_{similar} : (td, ckw) \in KnownQ)\}$;

    $temp\_pred \leftarrow []$;

    // Propose a prediction for each unknown query.

    forall $td \in unknownQ$ **do**

        $cand \leftarrow []$;

        forall $ckw \in \mathcal{K}_{similar}$ **do**

            $s \leftarrow -ln(||C^s_{ckw}[ckw] - C^s_{td}[td]||)$;

            Append $\{$ "kw": ckw, "score": s $\}$ to $cand$;

        end

        Sort $cand$ in descending order according to the score;

        $certainty \leftarrow score(cand[0]) - score(cand[1])$;

        Append $(td, cand[0], certainty)$ to $temp\_pred$;

    end

    // Stop refining or keep refining.

    if $|unknownQ| < RefSpeed$ **then**

        $final\_pred \leftarrow KnownQ \cup temp\_pred$;

        $unknownQ \leftarrow \emptyset$;

    else

        Add $RefSpeed$ most certain predictions $temp\_pred$ to $KnownQ$;

        Add the columns corresponding to the new known queries to C^s_{ckw} and C^s_{td}

    end

end

return $final\_pred$

---

recompute sub-matrices C^s_{ckw} and C^s_{td}. Thereafter, either start a new iteration or stop the algorithm if the number of unknown queries is less than $RefSpeed$.

4.5 Complexity

As in [6], a higher refinement speed will result in a faster runtime, but less accurate predictions. However, due to our use of keyword conjunctions the number of candidates for a trapdoor increases for larger d. Therefore, the runtime of the *CKWS-adapted refined score attack* grows combinatorial. The time complexity of the attack is given by $\mathcal{O}(f(v) + g(v))$, where $f(v) = \frac{v!}{d!(v-d)!} \cdot (d - 1)$ corresponds to the time complexity of the generic extension, where we assume multiplying two vectors takes constant time. Further, $g(v) = \frac{|Q|}{RefSpeed} \cdot |Q| \cdot \frac{v!}{d!(v-d)!} \cdot k$ is the time complexity of the attack. For both f and g, input v is either $v_{similar}$ or v_{known} depending on the attack setup.

Besides the increase in runtime, having $d > 1$ also the space complexity of the algorithm increases faster relative to the vocabulary size. Since co-occurrence matrix C_{ckw} in the similar-documents attack setup is $m_{similar} \times m_{similar}$, in terms of vocabulary size is $\frac{v_{similar}!}{d!(v_{similar}-d)!} \times \frac{v_{similar}!}{d!(v_{similar}-d)!}$ thus increasing faster with larger $v_{similar}$.

This increase in time and space complexity led us to first further optimize the revised algorithm for our implementations. Moreover, we use a GPU to decrease runtimes through computing expensive matrix operations on it.

5 Experiments

5.1 Setup

Documents. As described previously, in our experiments we simulate our attack using the publicly available Enron email document set introduced by Klimt & Yang [12]. We chose this document set since this one is also used in most attack papers requiring a set of documents. Similarly, we constructed the same corpus of emails from the folder _sent_mail_ which results in a set of 30109 documents.

Keyword Extraction. We extract keywords from solely the contents of the emails in the dataset, i.e. we do not consider email addresses or email subjects to be part of the document set. For keyword extraction we use the Porter Stemmer algorithm [20] to obtain stemmed words, moreover we remove stop words in the English language like 'the' or 'a'. Using this method results in a total of 62976 unique keywords in our entire considered document set.

Number of Keywords in Conjunction. Throughout our experiments we fix d, i.e. the number of keywords allowed in one conjunction, to either 1, 2 or 3. This means that no mixture of number of keywords is allowed in search. For instance, when the $d = 3$ only queries with 3 distinct keywords are allowed, i.e. queries that contain either 1 or 2 keywords are not allowed.

Testing Environment. We implemented the attack on an Ubuntu 20.04 server with Intel Xeon 20-core processor (64 bits, 2.2 GHz), 512 GB of memory, and NVIDIA Tesla P100 GPU (16GB). We used Python 3.7 and the Tensorflow library [1] to accelerate matrix operations on a GPU.[4]

Limitations. Running experiments with larger vocabulary sizes requires a lot of memory, since a vocabulary size of 150 and $d = 2$ means a document-keyword-conjunction matrix size of 18065×11175 (already 1.5 GiB) and a maximum co-occurrence matrix size of 11175×11175 (0.9 GiB) which both have to fit in the memory of the GPU for fast calculations. Therefore, having similar vocabulary

---

[4] Our code is available at https://github.com/marcowindt/passive-ckws-attack.

sizes as used in the score attack is unrealistic in our generic extension strategy setting without having sufficient resources. However, we propose an extrapolation strategy to have approximate results for larger vocabularies.

5.2 Results

In our experiments where similar-documents are used as the attacker's knowledge, we use the same ratio in similar (40%) and real (60%) documents as in [6]. Similar to [3,6,10], we define the accuracy to be the number of correct predictions divided by the number of unknown queries excluding the initial known queries, i.e. the $accuracy = \frac{|CorrectPredictions(unknownQ)|}{|Q|-|KnownQ|}$.

If not specified otherwise, each accuracy result corresponds to the average accuracy over 50 experiments. Also, the vocabulary used in experiments is always created from the most frequently occurring keywords in the document set. From this vocabulary the keyword conjunctions set is generated. In each experiment it is assumed the attacker has observed 15% of queries that can be performed by the user, i.e. $|Q| = 0.15 \cdot m_{real}$, where queries are sampled u.a.r. from $\mathcal{K}_{real}$ to construct trapdoors.

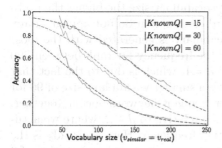
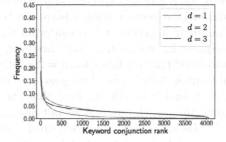

Fig. 1. Score attack using similar-documents for varying vocabulary sizes and initially known queries with $d = 2$, $|\mathcal{D}_{real}| = 18K$, $|\mathcal{D}_{similar}| = 12K$, $|Q| = 0.15 \cdot m_{real}$.

Fig. 2. Frequency of keyword conjunctions ordered from most frequent to least frequent occurring keyword conjunction in $\mathcal{D}_{similar}$.

Result Extrapolation

Figure 1 shows the accuracy of the score attack from [6] where the attacker has access to similar-documents for varying vocabulary size and $d = 2$. We show these results to highlight that we can extrapolate the accuracy of the attack in a similar-documents setting closely, where the extrapolation is depicted by the dashed line and measured results are the solid line. We obtain this extrapolation by first transforming the accuracies using the logit[5] function. Using this transformation, we obtain a space in which we seem to have a linear relationship such that $logit(acc) = b \cdot v_{similar} + a$. We then perform a linear regression to obtain

---

[5] $logit(x) = log(\frac{x}{1-x})$.

these coefficients using our experimental results. Lastly, we use the inverse logit function to transform it back to the original scale. We make use of this extrapolation where running experiments becomes infeasible (i.e. experiments with $d = 2$ and $v_{real} > 500$) to extrapolate the accuracy for larger vocabulary sizes.

In our linear regressions, we do not provide the coefficient of determination R^2 and the p-value since they are based on the assumption that results are independent which is not true in our experiments as they all use the same document set. Hence, these values should not be used to evaluate the quality of the model even if they are high (e.g. $R^2 \approx 0.95$ in Fig. 1) but the linear regression is still valid. Although there may exist more precise extrapolation techniques, our intention is to have a simple yet realistic approximation of the accuracy for larger vocabularies for the sake of our discussion.

Frequency of Keyword Conjunctions. Figure 2 shows the frequency of a keyword conjunction occurring in $\mathcal{D}_{similar}$ for $d \in \{1, 2, 3\}$, where keyword conjunction rank is lowest for the most frequent keyword conjunction. We observe the behavior of using keyword conjunctions instead of a single-keyword, i.e. the frequency of the most frequent keyword conjunction becomes smaller with higher d and the frequency of the least frequent keyword conjunction reaches almost zero. This is to be expected, since the larger vocabulary size the higher the probability that certain keywords from a keyword conjunction do not appear in any document together, i.e. considering the vocabulary is generated with the most frequent keywords first. Note however, that the frequency for rank between 200 and 3600 part is higher for $d = 2$ relative to $d = 1$, which is due to the fact that obtaining 4000 keyword conjunctions requires a smaller vocabulary size of 90 for $d = 2$, and it is still the case that the most frequent keywords occur together. Nevertheless, the same does not hold for $d = 3$ relative to $d = 2$, where we actually observe a decrease in keyword conjunction frequency. Here it already is the case that the most frequent keywords used to create a keyword conjunction of 3 keywords do not have to necessarily occur together in a document.

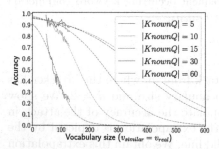

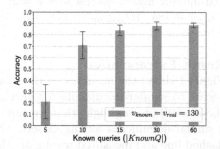

Fig. 3. Accuracy plot of the CKWS-adapted refined score attack with $d = 2$ extrapolated and varying vocabulary size. With $|\mathcal{D}_{real}| = 18K$, $|\mathcal{D}_{similar}| = 12K$, $|Q| = 0.15 \cdot m_{real}$.

Fig. 4. Accuracy plot of the CKWS-adapted refined score attack with $d = 2$ and varying number of known queries. With $|\mathcal{D}_{real}| = 18K$, $|\mathcal{D}_{similar}| = 12K$, $|Q| = 0.15 \cdot m_{real}$.

CKWS-Adapted Refined Score Attack Using Similar-Documents.
Figure 3 shows the accuracy of the CKWS-adapted refined score attack using
similar-documents with $d = 2$ and varying vocabulary size. Also, the plot shows
an extrapolation of the accuracies for vocabulary sizes larger than 130 (and
smaller than 50). From the extrapolation of the accuracies for varying vocabulary sizes we clearly see a rapid decrease in accuracy with larger vocabulary
sizes. We conclude that, when we consider the results with 30 known queries we
can still reach a reasonable recovery rate above 50% for vocabulary size 300 to
400 keywords. However, the results are far from the single-keyword search set up
presented in [6] achieving up to 85% recovery rate for vocabulary size of 1000.

In [6], they discussed how the 'quality' of a known query influences the accuracy. A known query is more qualitative if the underlying keyword occurs more
frequently. We remind that in the CKWS-adapted setting, it is a way to reduce
the number of known queries needed. A lower rank of a keyword conjunction in
Fig. 2 the query for the keyword-conjunction is considered more qualitative.

Figure 4 shows the accuracy of the CKWS-adapted refined score attack using
similar-documents with $d = 2$ and varying number of known queries. The plot
shows that the standard deviation of the accuracy, assuming 5 or 10 known
queries, is relatively high compared to the standard deviation for 15, 30, or 60
known queries. For 5 known queries the standard deviation is 0.15, which is at
least 3 times higher than the standard deviation for 15 known queries (≈ 0.05).
The accuracy increases and standard deviation decreases with a higher number
of known queries, since it becomes more likely to pick more qualitative queries
(u.a.r.). This also explains why we observe this noisy behavior of the accuracy
in the plot.

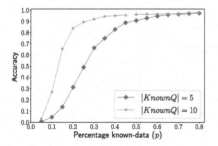
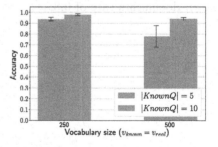

Fig. 5. Accuracy of the CKWS-adapted
refined score attack using known-data for
varying known-data rates p with $d = 2$
and $v_{known} = v_{real} = 130$.

Fig. 6. Accuracy of the extended refined
score known-documents attack with $d = 2$ and $p = 0.7$, i.e. $n_{known} = p \cdot n_{real}$.

CKWS-Adapted Refined Score Attack Using p-Known-Documents.
Since we have shown in Sect. 5.2 that the CKWS-adapted refined score attack
does provide limited scaling with having $d > 1$, we explore how well the attack
performs assuming known-documents as the attacker's knowledge. Figure 5

shows the accuracy of the attack using known-documents with varying known-documents rates of $0.05 \leq p \leq 0.8$ and steps of 0.05. We observe that with the initial $|KnownQ| = 10$ setting the attack achieves higher accuracies faster for lower known-documents rates compared to an attack setting having $|KnownQ| = 5$ initially. Also, with known-documents rates $p \geq 0.7$ the accuracy of the attack becomes constant and reaches near 100% accuracy for both 5 and 10 known queries. However, we do note that having a vocabulary size of $v_{real} = 130$ is a rather limited setting. In the next section we explore the attack using known-documents with larger vocabularies.

CKWS-Adapted Refined Score Attack Using 0.7-Known-Documents. In the previous result with varying known-documents rates we observed that the accuracy of the attack using known-documents reaches near 100% for known-documents rate $p = 0.7$ for both 5 and 10 known queries. Here we explore the accuracy of the attack by fixing the known-documents rate to $p = 0.7$ with vocabulary sizes 250 and 500. Figure 6 shows a bar plot for both these results with error bar describing the standard deviation of the accuracy over 50 experiments. We observe that for vocabulary size 250 the difference with an attack using 5 known queries compared to 10 known queries is small. Also, the standard deviation in both settings is small. However, for the 500 keyword setting we clearly see a decrease in accuracy using 5 known queries and a large standard deviation. Whereas for 10 known queries the attack still reaches above 93% accuracy and standard deviation is small. We do note however that in this case an attacker has great advantage, since it knows at least 70% of the whole indexed dataset and 10 known queries. In comparison, previous passive query-recovery attacks [3,10] on single-keyword search did not exceed 40% accuracy assuming known-documents rate of 0.8.

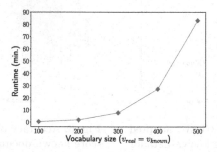

Fig. 7. Runtime of the CKWS-adapted refined score attack using known-documents w.r.t. to vocabulary size, with $d = 2$ and $p = 0.7$.

Runtime and Memory Usage. Figure 7 describes the average runtime of the attack using known-documents over 50 repetitions in function of v_{real} for $d = 2$. We observe that the runtime is high for considerably small vocabulary sizes, which is to be expected considering the time complexity described in Sect. 4.5.

We only show the runtime of the attack using known-documents, however, runtime of the attack using similar-documents is similar. Although our runtime can further benefit from using multiple GPUs and even our code is written in such fashion, we found that using two GPUs does not necessarily speed up our attack due to large overhead.

The overall memory usage is dominated by the size of co-occurrence matrices C_{ckw} and C_{td}. Therefore, we can define the main memory usage of the attack by the size of these two matrices as a function of the vocabulary size and the number of queries observed. In our experiments we always assume the attacker observes $|Q| = 0.15 \cdot m_{real}$ queries. As a result an accurate estimation of the bytes used by one experiment is given by $\mathsf{numberOfBytes}(v_{real}, d) = 2 \cdot (0.15 + 0.15^2) \cdot \left(\binom{v_{real}}{d}\right)^2 \cdot$ $\mathsf{sizeof}(\mathsf{float})$, where $\mathsf{sizeof}(\cdot)$ returns the number of bytes used by the system to store a certain data type. Filling in for $v_{real} = 500$, $d = 2$ and using 64 bit float, $\mathsf{numberOfBytes}(500, 2) \approx 40$ GiB, whereas the GPU used in our experiments fits at most 16 GB, meaning batching intermediate results is already required.

6   Discussion

Runtime. Although requiring large co-occurrence matrices for the extended refined score attack is cumbersome, if the adversary has sufficient memory resources these large matrices will not be her only concern. Her main concern will be the runtime of the attack because without being able to parallelize our attack to multiple GPUs our attack is difficult to run for vocabulary sizes > 500 and becomes infeasible for vocabulary sizes > 1000, whereas the added time complexity using our extension strategy is relatively small.

Observed Queries. Furthermore, the question arises whether it is realistic for an attacker to observe 15% of all possible queries. With only single-keyword search we believe this can be achieved. However, with $d = 2$ the number of keyword conjunctions to be observed is big, i.e. $0.15 \cdot \binom{v_{real}}{d}$. Although a smaller percentage could be considered more realistic and would even decrease the runtime of the attack, larger $|Q|$ is still desired, since it will result in better estimators for prediction and thus higher accuracies.

Query Distribution. In our experiments we only sampled queries using a uniform distribution. However, it is likely that this is unrealistic for keyword conjunctions, since certain keywords might be more likely to be used in a query together whereas other possible conjunctions might not be queried at all. Having knowledge of whether certain keywords are more likely to be searched for in conjunction would decrease the complexity of the attack, since one can then only consider the top most likely keyword conjunctions.

Countermeasure. Previous query-recovery attacks on single-keyword search also describe a countermeasure against their attack. In our work we focus on the question if a generic extension is possible. However, because of our generic extension strategy, countermeasures tested in [6] will be applicable but were not explored. Also, most introduced countermeasures do not actually leak less information, they make the leakage unusable by the attack proposed in the corresponding work (e.g. adding false positives in the result set).

Generic Extension. Although we described an adapted version of the refined score attack by [6] to a conjunctive keyword setting since it is good performing with low runtimes for single-keywords, our generic extension strategy using keyword conjunction sets is also valid for other attacks [2,3,10] and even other types of attacks (e.g. attacks using query frequency [14,16]). However, we expect similar runtime issues due to the large query space. Blackstone et al. [2] has a particular algorithm using cross-filtering that could be helpful to be an attack specifically against conjunctive keyword search.

7   Conclusion

In this work we presented a generic extension strategy to adapt any passive query-recovery attack to a conjunctive keyword search setting. We specifically explored its applicability using the refined score attack proposed by Damie et al. [6] to a conjunctive keyword search setting. It is the first study of passive query-recovery attacks in the conjunctive keyword search setting. We showed that our attack using documents that are similar, but otherwise different from the indexed documents on the server, does only achieve accuracy of 32% as attack on conjunctive keyword search. However, applying the adapted attack using known-documents can still perform with a low number of known queries and vocabulary size of 500 and achieves a recovery rate similar to previous passive query-recovery attacks [3,10,15] against single-keyword search.

Further, we discussed that the time complexity of the adapted attack grows combinatorial with the number of keywords in the conjunctive search query. Also, the storage required to perform the attack is dominated by the size of the co-occurrence matrices computed from the attacker's knowledge which also increases combinatorial.

References

1. Abadi, M., et al.: TensorFlow: a system for large-scale machine learning. In: 12th {USENIX} Symposium on Operating Systems Design and Implementation ({OSDI} 2016) (2016)
2. Blackstone, L., Kamara, S., Moataz, T.: Revisiting leakage abuse attacks. IACR Cryptol. ePrint Arch. **2019**, 1175 (2019)
3. Cash, D., Grubbs, P., Perry, J., Ristenpart, T.: Leakage-abuse attacks against searchable encryption. In: Proceedings of the 22nd ACM SIGSAC Conference on Computer and Communications Security (2015)

4. Cash, D., Jarecki, S., Jutla, C., Krawczyk, H., Roşu, M.-C., Steiner, M.: Highly-scalable searchable symmetric encryption with support for Boolean queries. In: Canetti, R., Garay, J.A. (eds.) CRYPTO 2013. LNCS, vol. 8042, pp. 353–373. Springer, Heidelberg (2013). https://doi.org/10.1007/978-3-642-40041-4_20
5. Clement, J.: U.S. online search query size in 2020, August 2020. https://www.statista.com/statistics/269740/number-of-search-terms-in-internet-research-in-the-us/
6. Damie, M., Hahn, F., Peter, A.: A highly accurate query-recovery attack against searchable encryption using non-indexed documents. In: 30th USENIX Security Symposium (USENIX Security 21). USENIX Association, August 2021
7. Fairouz, S.A., Lu, S.F.: Symmetric key encryption with conjunctive field free keyword search scheme. J. Adv. Math. Comput. Sci. 16(6), 1–11 (2016)
8. Golle, P., Staddon, J., Waters, B.: Secure conjunctive keyword search over encrypted data. In: Jakobsson, M., Yung, M., Zhou, J. (eds.) ACNS 2004. LNCS, vol. 3089, pp. 31–45. Springer, Heidelberg (2004). https://doi.org/10.1007/978-3-540-24852-1_3
9. Hu, C., et al.: Forward secure conjunctive-keyword searchable encryption. IEEE Access 7, 35035–35048 (2019)
10. Islam, M.S., Kuzu, M., Kantarcioglu, M.: Access pattern disclosure on searchable encryption: ramification, attack and mitigation. In: NDSS, vol. 20. Citeseer (2012)
11. Jho, N.S., Hong, D.: Symmetric searchable encryption with efficient conjunctive keyword search. KSII Trans. Internet Inf. Syst. 7(5), 1328–1342 (2013)
12. Klimt, B., Yang, Y.: Introducing the Enron corpus. In: CEAS (2004)
13. Lai, S., et al.: Result pattern hiding searchable encryption for conjunctive queries. In: Proceedings of the 2018 ACM SIGSAC Conference on Computer and Communications Security (2018)
14. Liu, C., Zhu, L., Wang, M., Tan, Y.A.: Search pattern leakage in searchable encryption: attacks and new construction. Inf. Sci. 265, 176–188 (2014)
15. Ning, J., Xu, J., Liang, K., Zhang, F., Chang, E.C.: Passive attacks against searchable encryption. IEEE Trans. Inf. Forensics Secur. 14(3), 789–802 (2018)
16. Oya, S., Kerschbaum, F.: Hiding the access pattern is not enough: exploiting search pattern leakage in searchable encryption. In: 30th {USENIX} Security Symposium ({USENIX} Security 21) (2021)
17. Patranabis, S., Mukhopadhyay, D.: Forward and backward private conjunctive searchable symmetric encryption. Cryptology ePrint Archive (2020)
18. Poddar, R., Wang, S., Lu, J., Popa, R.A.: Practical volume-based attacks on encrypted databases. In: 2020 IEEE European Symposium on Security and Privacy (EuroS&P). IEEE (2020)
19. Poon, H.T., Miri, A.: An efficient conjunctive keyword and phase search scheme for encrypted cloud storage systems. In: 2015 IEEE 8th International Conference on Cloud Computing. IEEE (2015)
20. Porter, M.F.: An algorithm for suffix stripping. Program (1980)
21. Pouliot, D., Wright, C.V.: The shadow nemesis: inference attacks on efficiently deployable, efficiently searchable encryption. In: Proceedings of the 2016 ACM SIGSAC Conference on Computer and Communications Security (2016)
22. Song, D.X., Wagner, D., Perrig, A.: Practical techniques for searches on encrypted data. In: Proceeding 2000 IEEE Symposium on Security and Privacy, S&P 2000. IEEE (2000)
23. Sun, W., Liu, X., Lou, W., Hou, Y.T., Li, H.: Catch you if you lie to me: efficient verifiable conjunctive keyword search over large dynamic encrypted cloud data. In: 2015 IEEE Conference on Computer Communications (INFOCOM). IEEE (2015)

24. Wang, S., Poddar, R., Lu, J., Popa, R.A.: Practical volume-based attacks on encrypted databases. IACR Cryptol. ePrint Arch. **2019**, 1224 (2019)
25. Wang, Y., Wang, J., Sun, S., Miao, M., Chen, X.: Toward forward secure SSE supporting conjunctive keyword search. IEEE Access **7**, 142762–142772 (2019)
26. Wu, Z., Li, K.: VBTree: forward secure conjunctive queries over encrypted data for cloud computing. VLDB J. **28**(1), 25–46 (2018). https://doi.org/10.1007/s00778-018-0517-6
27. Zhang, L., Zhang, Y., Ma, H.: Privacy-preserving and dynamic multi-attribute conjunctive keyword search over encrypted cloud data. IEEE Access **6**, 34214–34225 (2018)
28. Zhang, Y., Katz, J., Papamanthou, C.: All your queries are belong to us: the power of file-injection attacks on searchable encryption. In: 25th {USENIX} Security Symposium ({USENIX} Security 16) (2016)

Gummy Browsers: Targeted Browser Spoofing Against State-of-the-Art Fingerprinting Techniques

Zengrui Liu[1]([envelope]), Prakash Shrestha[2], and Nitesh Saxena[1]

[1] Texas A&M University, College Station, TX 77843, USA
{lzr,nsaxena}@tamu.edu
[2] University of Florida, Gainesville, FL 32611, USA
prakash.shrestha@ufl.edu

Abstract. We present a simple yet potentially devastating and hard-to-detect threat, called *Gummy Browsers* (Named after "Gummy Fingers" that can impersonate a user's fingerprint biometrics.), whereby the browser fingerprinting information can be collected and spoofed without the victim's awareness, thereby compromising the privacy and security of any application that uses browser fingerprinting.

We design and implement the Gummy Browsers attack using three orchestration methods based on script injection, browser settings and debugging tools, and script modification, that can successfully spoof a wide variety of fingerprinting features to mimic many different browsers (including mobile browsers and the Tor browser). We then evaluate the attack against two state-of-the-art browser fingerprinting systems, *FPStalker* and *Panopticlick*. Our results show that A can accurately match his own manipulated browser fingerprint with that of any targeted victim user U's fingerprint for a long period of time, without significantly affecting the tracking of U and when only collecting U's fingerprinting information only once. The TPR (true positive rate) for the tracking of the benign user in the presence of the attack is larger than 0.9 in most cases. The FPR (false positive rate) for the tracking of the attacker is also high, larger than 0.9 in all cases. We also argue that the attack can remain completely oblivious to the user and the website, thus making it extremely difficult to thwart in practice.

Keywords: Web security · Browser fingerprinting · Spoofing attack

1 Introduction

Many websites and web services leverage browser fingerprinting techniques to track their users for various purposes, including targeted advertisements [33] based on browsing history and habits, user authentication [1,5,7], and fraud detection [6,30]. Browser fingerprinting aims to uniquely identify web browsers. Specifically, browser fingerprinting uses a stateless identifier for web browsers composed of a set of browser and system attributes, including browser vendor and version,

© Springer Nature Switzerland AG 2022
G. Ateniese and D. Venturi (Eds.): ACNS 2022, LNCS 13269, pp. 147–169, 2022.
https://doi.org/10.1007/978-3-031-09234-3_8

plugins and extensions, canvas rendering, available fonts, performance characteristics, platform, clock skews and screen resolutions. These attributes are collected through JavaScript APIs and HTTP headers.

Based on different combinations of browser and system attributes, and their uniqueness to the browser, researchers and practitioners have proposed a myriad of browser fingerprinting techniques [9,10,13,14,17,21,23,26,29,41–43,45–48]. However, the uniqueness of the fingerprint alone is not sufficient for prolonged user tracking because the browser fingerprint changes over time, potentially when the browsers are updated or configured differently [52]. For a successful long-term user tracking, changes to the fingerprints need to be tracked to link the current fingerprint with previously recorded fingerprints [27,52], using what is referred to as a *tracking technique*.

The fingerprint linking algorithm *Panopticlick*, proposed by Eckersley, [27], and *FP-Stalker* developed by Vastel et al. [52], are representative instantiations of such tracking techniques. Panopticlick showed that its visitors can be uniquely identified from a fingerprint composed of only eight browser and system attributes. It follows a very simple heuristic based on the comparison of the string representation of browser characteristics. FP-Stalker consists of two variants of fingerprint linking algorithms – a *rule-based variant* and a *hybrid variant*, which leverage ruleset and machine learning algorithms. These algorithms aim to link browser fingerprint evolutions for tracking the user. The experiment conducted in the FP-Stalker paper [52] showed that its linking algorithm, especially the hybrid variant, can track a given browser instance for a long period of time, significantly better than Panopticlick.

In this paper, we closely investigate the potential privacy leakage and security vulnerability associated with state-of-the-art browser fingerprint linking algorithms, Panopticlick and FP-Stalker to be specific, motivated by their very appealing applications and practicality features. Unfortunately, we identify a significant threat vector against such linking algorithms. Specifically, we find that an attacker can capture and spoof the browser characteristics of a victim's browser, and hence can "present" its own browser as the victim's browser when connecting to a website. The browser attributes can be easily captured (one-time or frequently based on the application) by luring the victim into visiting a benign-looking website controlled by the attacker (or a malicious website). Then, all (or most of) these attributes can be spoofed (once, or continually based on the intended level of adversarial impact on the victim), for example, by injecting a web script, modifying the existing web script, or utilizing the browser's built-in settings and debugging tools. By spoofing the victim's browser characteristics, which are used to construct its fingerprint, the attacker's browser would be recognized as the victim's browser when visiting a targeted website.

Exploiting this general threat, we introduce *Gummy Browsers*, an attack system that can fully compromise the security and privacy of the schemes that leverage browser fingerprinting techniques. For instance, if the browser fingerprinting is employed for personalized and targeted ads, the web server, hosting a benign website, would push the same or similar ads to the attacker's browser like the ones that would have been pushed to the victim's browser because the web server considers the attacker's browser as the victim's browser. Based on the personalized ads (e.g., related to pregnancy products, medications and brands), the attacker can infer various sensitive information about the victim (e.g., gender, age group, health condition, interests, salary level, etc.), even build a personal behavioral profile of the victim. Leakage of such personal and private information can raise a frightful privacy threat to the user. The study of Castelluccia et al. [25] has demonstrated that the knowledge of the ads the user is provided in targeted advertising can indeed leak significant sensitive information about the user. Similarly, if browser fingerprinting is used for security purposes, such as user authentication and fraud detection (e.g., clickbot detection), our fingerprint spoofing attacker can circumvent the security functionality of such defensive schemes. The authentication system may be based on some other factors beyond browser fingerprinting. In this paper, we only show how to defeat the fingerprinting factor.

Gummy Browsers can remain hidden and invisible to the targeted user and the targeted website. Since the capturing and spoofing of the browser attributes is done fully transparently and remotely, Gummy Browsers can be launched easily and effectively without being noticed by the user or the website. In this light, given the fact that browser fingerprinting techniques are getting deployed widely in the real world, Gummy Browsers can have a devastating and lasting impact on the online privacy and security of the users. Capturing the victim's fingerprinting information just once allows the attacker to spoof the victim for a long period of time. The process can be repeated for further impact. Given the fundamental nature of the attack, it would be very difficult to defeat.

Our experiments consider that the website only uses browser fingerprinting for tracking, and does not employ cookies (or cookies are blocked by the user). Therefore our attacks and implications of our attacks are only limited to fingerprint spoofing.

Our Contributions: We believe that our work makes the following contributions:

1. *A Novel Threat of Spoofing Browser Fingerprints:* We introduce a novel and serious threat raised due to the use of browser fingerprinting techniques to track the user, referred to as *Gummy Browsers*. Specifically, this attacker with the ability to capture and spoof the browser fingerprint can learn various personal and sensitive information about the user based on personalized ads and compromise the security of browser-fingerprinting based defensive applications, such as user authentication and fraud detection. The ease with which this threat can be perpetrated is a strength of our work since it can be deployed in real world by even naive attackers.
2. *Design and Implementation of Gummy Browsers:* We provide the design and implementation of Gummy Browsers that enable an attacker to glean sensitive information about the user and compromise the browser fingerprinting based defensive schemes. Gummy Browsers leverages a benign-looking fake website to capture the victim's browser characteristics (could also be a malicious, attacker-controlled website). Gummy Browsers then utilizes spoofing methods, such as *script injection, script modification,* or *browser's*

built-in setting and debugging tool to orchestrate its browser to appear as the victim's browser.

3. ***Evaluation against Notable Fingerprinting Techniques:*** We employ state-of-the-art browser fingerprinting algorithms, specifically *Panopticlick* [27] and *FP-Stalker* [52], and evaluate the performance of Gummy Browsers against them. Based on a dataset of 200+ users, our results show that the attacker can successfully spoof the fingerprint of the browser instance to match with that of the targeted victim's browser instance for a long period of time without any significant impact on the tracking of the victim.

2 Background and Related Work

2.1 Browser Fingerprinting

Different combinations of the browser and system attributes can be used to generate a unique identifier for a given browser, referred to as the *browser fingerprint*. Based on different combinations of attributes, various browser fingerprinting techniques have been proposed [17, 23, 26, 41–43, 46, 47]. These attributes can be grouped into three different categories [20] as presented in Table 1.

(C1) Browser-Provided Information: JavaScript API can be used to extract a wide range of system information, referred to as browser-provided information, that can be employed to fingerprint a device. A set of such features are listed in the first row of Table 1. The feature set in this category includes software and hardware details (e.g., browser/OS vendor and version, system language [21], platform [13], user-agent string [23], resolution, etc.), device timezone and clock drift [23] from Coordinated Universal Time (UTC), battery information [47] (e.g., battery charge level, discharge rate), and password autofill [45] (e.g., the password is user-typed or auto-filled by a browser or password manager). The information corresponding to *WebGL* [17], a JavaScript API for rendering graphics within web browsers, and *WebRTC* [22], a set of W3C standards that supports browser-to-browser applications, e.g., voice and video chat, can also be used to fingerprint a browser. WebGL information includes the WebGL vendor and version, maximum texture size, supported WebGL extensions, renderer strings, etc. WebRTC information includes connected media devices (e.g., webcam and microphones) information. The support for *local storage*, which enables the browser to store data without any expiration [18], and the status of *do not track*, which blocks (or allows) the website from tracking [14] are also often used in browser fingerprinting.

(C2) Inference based on Device Behavior: The device information can also be extracted by executing a specially crafted JavaScript code on the browser and observing the resulting effect. This category of the fingerprinting features is based on the fact that the execution of JavaScript code creates different effects based on the software and hardware configuration of the device, and hence can be used to infer various characteristics of the device. For instance, HTML5 canvas renders the text and graphics differently based on OS, available fonts, and the

Table 1. Three different categories of browser fingerprinting features [20], and a summary of how they can be spoofed via our attack.

Category	Feature name	Spoofable	Spoofing approach	Detectable by targeted websites
C1	1. User-agent + - * [23]	Yes	a, b, c	Hard
	2. WebGL information - * [17]		b	
	3. System time + - *[23]		a, b	
	4. Battery information [47]		a, b	
	5. Cookie enabled + - * [10]		a, b, c	
	6. WebRTC [22]		b	
	7. Password autofill [45]		b	
	8. Platform - * [13]		a, b	
	9. Language + - * [21]		a, b, c	
	10. Local storage + - * [48]		b	
	11. Resolution + - * [9]		a, b	
	12. Do Not Track - * [14]		a, b, c	
C2	1. HTML5 canvas fingerprinting - * [43]	Yes	b	Hard
	2. System performance [42]		b	
	3. Font detection [29]		b	
	4. Scroll wheel fingerprinting [46]		b	
	5. CSS feature detection [41]		b	
C3	1. Browser plugin fingerprinting + - * [28]	Yes	a, b	Hard
	2. Browser extension fingerprinting [34]		b	

I. +: Features used in Panopticlick [27]. -: Features used in Rule-based Linking Algorithm [52]. *: Features used in Hybrid Linking Algorithm [52].
II. C1: Browser-provided information. C2: Inference based on device behavior. C3: Extensions and plugins.
III. a: Script Injection. b: Script Modification. c: Browser Setting and Debugging Tool.

video driver [43]. The elapsed time to execute the JavaScript code can be used to infer the performance characteristics of the device [42]. Various aspects of a pointing device can be inferred by monitoring the scroll events generated by the mouse wheel or touchpad [26]. The browser vendor and version can be inferred by testing CSS features [41]. The presence (or absence) of different fonts can be inferred by rendering a text with a predefined list of fonts [29].

(C3) Browser Extensions and Plugins: The aforementioned approaches can be used to extract information about the browser extensions and plugins to build a browser fingerprint. Various browser plugins, e.g., Java, Flash and Silverlight, can be queried through JavaScript APIs to reveal system information [28]. For instance, Flash can provide the OS kernel version. Both Java and Flash can provide an enumerated list of system fonts. Installed NoScript (that disables JavaScript) and its blacklisted website can be detected by loading a large set of websites. Similarly, AdBlocker can be detected by monitoring if fake ads are loaded on the websites [34] or not. Other extensions can also be detected by other methods.

2.2   Representative Fingerprinting Techniques

As mentioned earlier, various browser fingerprinting approaches have been proposed in the literature, each utilizing a different set of device characteristics. Panopticlick [27] and FP-Stalker [52], specifically its Rule-based Linking Algorithm and Hybrid Linking Algorithm, are representative browser fingerprint linking techniques.

Panopticlick: Panopticlick [27] leverages eight different browser and system attributes to track the user through browser fingerprinting. It categorizes these attributes into two groups. The first group contains cookies enabled (C1-5), screen resolution (C1-11), time zone (C1-3), and partial supercookie test (e.g., local storage, session storage and IE userData) (C1-10). The second group contains user-agent (C1-1), HTTP ACCEPT headers (C1-9), system fonts (C2-3), and browser plugins information (C3-1). To learn the identity of an unknown fingerprint 'F_u', Panopticlick compares F_u with each of the pre-stored fingerprints 'F_k'. If F_u has all the eight attributes the same as that of F_k, Panopticlick marks them as the same fingerprint, i.e., generated from the same browser instance. If any of the attributes in the first group and more than one attribute from the second group differs, Panopticlick marks F_u and F_k as different fingerprints. In the case where there is only one difference in the attribute set from the first group, Panopticlick estimates the similarity score of that attribute between F_u and F_k. If the similarity score is higher than a set threshold (say 0.85), F_u is marked the same as F_k. In the rest of the scenarios, F_u is marked differently from F_k.

Rule-based Linking Algorithm (RLA): This approach for browser fingerprinting categorizes the fingerprinting attributes under consideration into three sets. The first attribute set consists of operating system (C1-1), platform (C1-8), browser name (C1-1), local storage (C1-10), do not track (C1-12), cookies enable (C1-5), and canvas (C2-1). The second set consists of user-agent (C1-1), GPU vendor (C1-2), renderer (C1-2), browser plugins (C3-1), system language (C1-9) and HTTP accept headers (C1-9). The third feature set consists of the resolution (C1-11), time zone (C1-3) and encoding (HTTP header). Similar to Panopticlick, RLA compares the aforementioned attributes of an unknown fingerprint F_u with each of the stored fingerprint F_k. If all the attributes of both the fingerprints are the same, RLA marks them as *exact* fingerprints. If F_u and F_k have differences in at least one of the attributes in the first set, RLA marks them as different. if F_u has an older version of the browser, the algorithm will mark them as different. Otherwise, it estimates the similarity between the remaining attributes from the second and third sets. If the similarity score is greater than the set threshold (say 0.75), the algorithm counts the number of features that are different between F_u and F_k. All the F_ks that have less than one different attribute from the first set and less than two different attributes from the first and second sets are marked as *candidate* fingerprints. If all the F_k-s that have been marked as *exact* fingerprints correspond to the same user, F_k is assigned to that particular user. Similarly, if all the F_k-s that have been marked as *candidate* fingerprints belong to the same user, F_u is assigned to that particular user. In the rest of the cases, F_u is recognized as a new user.

Hybrid Linking Algorithm (HLA): This approach enhances RLA with the machine learning technique. HLA divides the browser attributes into two sets. The first set consists of the operating system (C1-1), device platform (C1-8), browser information (C1-1), local storage (C1-10), do not track (C1-12), cookies enable (C1-5), and canvas (C2-1). The second set contains the following nine features – number of changes, system languages (C1-9), HTTP based user-agent (C1-1), canvas (C2-1), created time (C1-3), browser plugins (C3-1), fonts (C2-3), renderer (C1-2) and resolution (C1-11). HLA compares an unknown fingerprint 'F_u' with each of the known fingerprints 'F_k' to give an identity to F_u. F_k is assigned to the set "*exact*" if these two fingerprints have the exact same first attribute set, otherwise, to the set "F_{k_sub}". If all the fingerprints in the set *exact* have the same id, this id is assigned to F_u, otherwise, a new id is given to F_u. If there are no fingerprints in the set *exact*, HLA compares the first attribute set of F_u with that of each of the F_k in F_{k_sub}. Each attribute comparison results in '1' if the attribute is the same in both F_k and F_u, otherwise, '0'. If there are less than five different attributes, HLA feeds the results to the machine learning model, Random Forest to be specific, resulting in a similarity score (in the range of 0 and 1). The F_k having a score higher than 0.994 is assigned to the set '*candidates*'. The F_k-s in the candidate set are sorted in descending order of the score. If the first score is larger than the second one plus 0.1, the id of F_u ID becomes the top-one id. If the top-one and top-two ids have the same id, this id is assigned to F_u, otherwise, a new ID is given to F_u.

2.3   Applications of Browser Fingerprinting

Targeted Advertising: The browser fingerprinting can be employed to provide targeted and personalized ads on the user devices (e.g., general desktop PC, handheld mobile device) [33]. When a user visits a website, the web server (or the online service provider) extracts and stores the browser fingerprint along with the user's browsing behavior. When the user revisits the same website, the web server looks for his fingerprint in its repository and pushes the relevant ads based on the user's prior browsing behavior. Besides browser fingerprinting, there exist other approaches for targeted advertisements, such as account-based targeted ads [50] and cookie-based targeted ads [51]. Unlike these approaches, the browser fingerprinting neither requires the user to log into his online account, nor requires the user to enable the cookie, rather it works transparently.

User Authentication: Various services, such as Oracle [1], Inauth [7] and SecureAuth IdP [5] are leveraging the browser fingerprinting technique to enhance the overall security and usability of their authentication mechanisms [39]. The browser fingerprinting is usually integrated with existing authentication schemes, such as two-factor authentication (2FA) schemes [5]. On successful login, the web server captures and stores the browser fingerprint of the device that the user has used to login. Next time, when the user attempts to login to the same web service using the same device, the current browser fingerprint is matched against the stored fingerprints. If they match with a high score, the second-factor of 2FA process is dropped (i.e., no need to provide the PIN), merely typing in the password is sufficient to login. Thus, browser fingerprinting approach for authentication lowers the user-effort during the authentication process, and hence improves the system's usability.

Fraud Detection: Several security services, e.g., Seon [30] and IPQualityScore [6], are leveraging browser fingerprinting for the purpose of fraud detection and prevention in the online setting. The fraud detection techniques can be

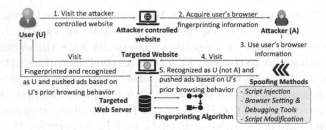

Fig. 1. A high-level overview of the Gummy Browsers attack model.

categorized into two groups – *supervised* and *unsupervised* methods [24]. The supervised method leverages the information from the prior fraud behavior (i.e., already marked as fraud) to build a model to infer if the current behavior is fraud or non-fraud. The unsupervised method does not rely on the prior fraudulent behavior, rather it sets a baseline for normal behavior. If the current behavior significantly deviates from the baseline behavior, the unsupervised method marked the behavior as fraudulent. The browser fingerprinting can be used to mark the user as a fraudster or a legitimate user. When any of these methods find the user's behavior fraudulent, the service provider captures and flags the browser fingerprint as fraudulent. Since the browser fingerprint changes over time, a risk level can be estimated by comparing the browser fingerprint against the flagged fingerprints. If the risk level is significantly high, the current user is flagged as a fraudster.

3   Attack Model and Spoofing Methods

3.1   Attack Model

Gummy Browsers consider a remote adversary who can spoof the victim's browser to a target remote web service. The main goal of Gummy Browsers is to fool the web server into believing that a legitimate user is accessing its services so that it can learn sensitive information about the user (e.g., interests of the user based on the personalized ads), or circumvent various security schemes (e.g., authentication and fraud detection) that rely on the browser fingerprinting. A high-level overview of the attack is shown in Fig. 1.

We assume that the attacker has obtained the browser fingerprint of the victim. The adversary can easily capture the victim's fingerprinting information by designing a benign-looking website and luring the victim into visiting his website. The adversary can leverage the exact mechanism as that of any fingerprinting website to acquire the browser fingerprint, i.e., via JavaScript APIs. It is also possible that a compromised web service, running a malicious script, could acquire the victim's browser fingerprint when the victim visits the attacker-owned website.

We also assume that before accessing a target web service, the attacker spoofs (or injects) previously acquired victim's browser information into his own fully controlled device to present it as the victim's device. When the attacker visits the target website, the target web server would receive the victim's fingerprint from the attacker's device. Therefore, for the target web service, it looks like the victim is accessing its services, and can not really recognize the malicious attacker.

We consider three different modes of executing the attack. An adversary can retrieve and spoof the victim's browser fingerprint only once, referred to *Acquire-Once-Spoof-Once*. *Acquire-Once-Spoof-Once* can be used to bypass the security of the user authentication scheme. Alternatively, to increase the impact of the attack, the attacker can spoof the same browser fingerprint instance multiple times over a few days gap, referred to *Acquire-Once-Spoof-Frequently*. Leveraging *Acquire-Once-Spoof-Frequently*, the attacker can track the personalized ads associated with the victim for a long period of time, and can infer various sensitive information about the user, even build a personal profile of the victim. Since the browser fingerprint changes over time, to increase the attack success rate, the attacker can also retrieve and spoof the browser fingerprint multiple times, and is referred to *Acquire-Frequently-Spoof-Frequently*. With this approach, the attacker could always obtain the latest browser fingerprint of the victim. This can enable the attacker to compromise the security of the fraud detection mechanism.

3.2   Spoofing Methods

The key component of Gummy Browsers is the ability of the attacker to spoof the victim's browser fingerprint so that the attacker can present its own browser as if it is the victim's browser in front of the web service. Our spoofing methods are only focusing on the features which are listed in Table 1, and we did not spoof network level features like IP address. The attacker can leverage the following methods to spoof the fingerprint.

3.2.1   Script Injection

In browser fingerprinting, when the browser loads a website, the website executes scripts consisting of various JavaScript API calls to extract the browser information. To spoof the browser fingerprint, the values extracted by the JavaScript API calls should be changed before the browser executes the scripts embedded in the website. The objects where these extracted values are stored can be overwritten by creating a new object with the same name and constructor as that of the original JavaScript APIs. To implement this method, a browser extension, a specialized and independent software module for customizing a web browser, and/or Selenium [16], a portable framework for testing web applications, can be utilized. The browser always loads and executes the website scripts in the browser extension prior to loading and executing it to the client machine. Those scripts would not change any scripts contents that are loaded from the visited websites. In the case of Selenium, pre-designed scripts are executed, which is followed by launching the browser, loading the website, and executing the embedded scripts. The feature of the browser extension and Selenium to execute the scripts prior to loading the website allows the adversary to overwrite the browser properties extracted through JavaScript API calls. An example is listed in [37].

3.2.2   Browser Setting and Debugging Tool

Many of the browsers offer a mechanism in the form of the *browser setting* and the *debugging tool* that enables its users (the attacker in our case) to change various attributes of the client device and the browser. For instance, cookies, local storage and "do not track" options can be enabled or disabled simply through the browser setting in the Google Chrome browser [40] and the "about:config" page in the Firefox browser [4]. Further, about:config page in the Firefox browser allows the user to design his own APIs that can overwrite the browser's pre-defined APIs. This approach can completely change the browser's attributes.

The browser also offers a *debugging tool* intended for web application developers that allows them to debug and improve their web application functionality [3]. Using the debugging tool, various browser attributes, such as user-agent, geolocation, and caches disabled can be easily changed. The changes affect both the JavaScript API (e.g., `navigator.userAgent`) and the corresponding value in the HTTP header (e.g., the value of user-agent field). The debugging tool allows the changes on the browser's attributes to any custom value, whether it is a pre-defined valid string, or a random text.

3.2.3   Script Modification

The browser properties can also be changed by modifying the scripts embedded in the website. Once the embedded scripts have extracted the browser information, they can be changed before the website sends it to the web server. Utilizing the developer debugging tool (mentioned earlier), a breakpoint can be set at the beginning of each script of the website so that the scripts' execution gets paused at the set breakpoint. By inspecting the embedded scripts, the JavaScript API expression can be replaced with the spoofed values. For instance, `platform = navigator.platform` can be replaced with `platform = `"Win32" that exposes the underlying platform of the device as Win32, instead of the actual platform. However, each API expression should be changed very carefully as the use of an incorrect expression (i.e., its value and format) can alert the web service, and the changes can fail.

A more convenient method to spoof the browser information is to leverage the fact that JavaScript always uses *Ajax* (Asynchronous JavaScript And XML) to transfer the data to the remote server [31]. Since Ajax employs JSON (JavaScript Object Notation) [11,12] format when transferring data to the web server, the browser information can be changed by checking the variable in the JSON object. Given that the debugging tool shows current variables and their values at each breakpoint, the values can be changed easily. Once the changes on the scripts are completed, the breakpoints are removed allowing the execution of the modified scripts. With this approach, the remote web service would receive the spoofed browser attributes. As the executed scripts are never sent outside the client machine, the approach remains oblivious to the remote web server.

Most websites or web services use JavaScript obfuscation on the scripts, instead of the native ones. The purpose of using obfuscation is to make the scripts difficult to understand. JavaScript Obfuscator Tool [2] is an example of such obfuscation methods. JavaScript obfuscation can indeed make script modification harder than native scripts. However, there are JavaScript deobfuscation methods that can help us to get native scripts. A previous study [38] and deobfuscation service [19] have proved that deobfuscation can work. So obfuscated scripts will not pose a problem in script modification.

We have listed all spoofing approaches for each feature in Table 1. More details for spoofing all features are listed in [37].

4   Attack Implementation

4.1   Acquiring User Browser Fingerprint

To impersonate as the victim in front of the target website, Gummy Browsers needs to acquire the device fingerprinting information from the victim's device. Gummy Browsers employ the following two methods to capture the victim's browser fingerprint.

With JavaScript: JavaScript provides a variety of APIs that can be utilized to extract the device information. The execution of these APIs does not require any permission from the users [44]. For instance, the API `navigator.platform` retrieves the details on the platform (e.g., MacIntel, Win32, Linux, etc.) of the device that the user is using. The `cookieEnabled` API tells if the browser has disabled cookies or not. These methods are exactly the same as deployed by the web service that uses browser fingerprinting. All these APIs are completely transparent to the user.

Without JavaScript: Some device fingerprinting attributes can also be extracted through methods other than JavaScript APIs. For instance, user-agent, supported languages and their order can be retrieved from the HTTP header [36], fonts can be extracted using Flash and CSS. Although JavaScript has `navigator.userAgent` API, the use of HTTP header is preferred to retrieve user-agent because the user can disable the JavaScript, thereby failing the retrieval of user-agent through JavaScript API. Fortunately, in such a situation, the HTTP header can still provide the user-agent attribute of the browser. For some of the attributes, such as the list of fonts in the device, JavaScript does not offer any APIs. Flash and CSS are used to list the available fonts in the device.

4.2   Visual Attack

We utilize the Panopticlick website [15] and the FingerprintJS demo website [8] to assess the effectiveness of various spoofing methods, referred to as the *visual attack*.

Attacking Panopticlick Site: Panopticlick provides a dashboard for displaying the browser information, which we leverage to assess our spoofing methods. Figure in [37] presents a snapshot of the Panopticlick dashboard showing fingerprint information when a (victim) user uses a Firefox browser on a Windows machine, i.e., "Win+Firefox". By visually inspecting the information displayed

Table 2. The attacks executed for each user in our evaluation methodology.

Attack Number	1	2	3	4	5	6	7	8	9
Time Gap (day)	1	7	15	30	60	90	180	270	365

on the dashboard, we validated if the spoofing methods succeed in injecting spoofed attributes. We use the browser setting and debugging tool to modify the following attributes – user-agent, HTTP accept header, cookie enabled, and local storage, used in Panopticlick. Specifically, we use the debugging tool to change the user-agent and the browser's setting option to change the language attribute found in HTTP accept header. We change the language category and its order in the Google Chrome browser to meet target languages combination. To modify the *cookie enabled* and *local storage*, we use corresponding options in the privacy setting of the Google Chrome browser. To change the remaining attributes used in Panonpticlick, either the script injection or the script modification approach is used. Due to the convenience of using script modification, we use this approach for the said purpose. Specifically, we change the attributes' value in the JSON file of the script such that the Panopticlick would receive the modified values.

Attacking FingerprintJS Site and Real-Life Fingerprint Service: We also successfully did the visual attack against FingerprintJS website and the Fingerprintjs pro service. We listed full details in [37].

4.3   Algorithm Attack: Attacking Prominent Fingerprinting Based Techniques

We emulate the attack against the browser fingerprinting algorithms by simply copying the entire fingerprint, referred to as the *algorithm attack*. To evaluate the performance of our algorithm attack, we employ three prominent browser fingerprinting algorithms – *Panopticlick, RLA, HLA* and launch the algorithm attack against them. We utilize the dataset from [49], referred to as the *original dataset*, to evaluate the performance of the algorithm attack. Details on the dataset are provided in Sect. 5.1. Each fingerprint in the dataset has following three timestamps: *created_date, updated_date* and *expired_date*, which denote the timestamps when the fingerprint is created/recorded, updated, and expired, respectively. Utilizing the original dataset, various datasets are generated based on different collect frequency, referred to as the *benign dataset*.

In a real-world setting, an adversary can capture the victim's browser fingerprint at any point in time. Given this, we consider that the attacker can spoof any of the fingerprints in the original dataset. Therefore, we copy one fingerprint instance of the given user at a time, update the creation date and order, consider it as a spoofed fingerprint, and inject it back into the original dataset, forming the *attack dataset*. Such an injection of copied fingerprint simulates the scenario where an adversary acquires the victim's fingerprint, and then tries to impersonate the victim by spoofing the fingerprint. The fingerprinting algorithms are executed on the attack dataset to link together the browser fingerprints from the same user. The attack succeeds if the fingerprinting algorithm incorrectly marks the spoofed fingerprint as from the victim.

Since the browser fingerprint changes over time, the impact of the algorithm attack may vary based on the gap between the time when the fingerprint is acquired and the time when the attack is launched, referred to as *"time gap"*. In terms of the dataset, the time gap refers to the difference in the *created_date* between two fingerprints from the same user. To measure the effectiveness of the time gap in our algorithm attack, we design and build nine different attacks based on nine different time gaps. The attack number and corresponding time gaps are presented in Table 2.

In the original dataset, each user has more than one fingerprint collected over a long period of time. To execute the aforementioned nine different attacks, we assume that the adversary captures the oldest of the fingerprints (the first one) of the user and spoofs after each of the 'n' days considered in nine different attacks, referred to as spoofed/copied fingerprint. Thus, we consider Acquire-Once-Spoof-Frequently setting for our nine attacks. The *created_date* of the spoofed fingerprint is set as 'n' days after its original *created_date*. Similarly, the *expired_date* is set to 5 days after its *created_date*. Since none of the three algorithms uses the *updated_date*, we set its value to "NULL". Although we employ Acquire-Once-Spoof-Frequently approach for all our attacks, the results are also applicable to Acquire-Once-Spoof-Once, where the fingerprint is spoofed only once. If the fingerprint is acquired frequently over a period of time, our attack would have a higher chance to succeed.

To evaluate our algorithm attack, we utilize the exact same code as that of FP-Stalker, which is made publicly available in the GitHub repository by its authors [49]. They have implemented all three algorithms, namely Panopticlick, RLA, and HLA, considered in our study, and can be found in their code repository. For each user in the dataset, we run these algorithms in two different settings – i) the benign setting without any spoofed fingerprints, and ii) the attack setting with nine different spoofed (or attack) fingerprints.

5   Dataset and Evaluation Methodology

5.1   FP-Stalker Dataset

We use the FP-Stalker dataset [49] to evaluate the performance of Gummy Browsers against browser fingerprinting techniques. The authors of FP-Stalker designed and built two extensions, one for the Firefox browser and the other for the Chrome browser, and used the AmIUnique website to collect the browser fingerprints. Although they noted that their dataset consists of 98598 browser fingerprints from 1905 users collected over a period of two years in their paper, their public dataset contains only 15000 fingerprints collected from 1819 users. Each fingerprint in the dataset contains 40 variables. 38 of them correspond to browser fingerprinting attributes. The remaining two variables are "Counter" and "ID". The counter denotes the order of the fingerprint based on the created date of the fingerprint. ID uniquely represents an individual user, referred to as "*original ID*" in our analysis.

We observed that the fingerprints in the dataset have inconsistency, i.e., the fingerprints from the given user do not have consistent browser attributes, e.g., different operating systems, the newer fingerprint having older browser version/vendor than the older fingerprint. As such inconsistency in the dataset may impact the performance of the browser fingerprint algorithms as well as that of our attack, we removed all inconsistent fingerprints resulting in the dataset with the fingerprints from 275 users. Further, we remove the user having less than seven fingerprints, which is considered insufficient for the three fingerprint algorithms, dropping the user counts in the dataset from 275 to 239. This dataset is what we use to evaluate our attack.

Collect Frequency: We sample the dataset using a configurable collect frequency similar to FP-Stalker. Collect frequency indicates how often a browser is fingerprinted. The lesser the fingerprinting frequency (or the higher collect frequency), the harder it would be to track the user. We use 11 different collect frequencies – 1, 2, 3, 4, 5, 6, 7, 8, 10, 15, and 20, in terms of days. To generate a dataset for a given collect frequency, we employ the approach as suggested in FP-Stalker. When a dataset is sampled using a collect frequency, the approach usually extends the dataset by copying (or replicating) the fingerprints at missing dates, therefore, we refer to it as the *expansion algorithm*. The expansion algorithm iterates in time with a step of collect frequency days and creates (or recovers) the browser fingerprint at each time step $(t \pm f_c * i)$, where t is the fingerprint creation date, f_c is collect frequency, and i is a natural number. The iteration continues until the expired date of the previous and the current fingerprint is reached. The process is repeated for each of the fingerprints collected from the given user. Thus, the expansion algorithm generates a new dataset with the fingerprints sampled at a consistent frequency of collect frequency days.

5.2   Evaluation Methodology

5.2.1   Visual Attack

We leverage the Panopticlick website and the FingerprintJS demo website and use various combinations of the terminal and the browser that the victim user may use to visually assess the spoofing methods. We employ a Mac laptop running macOS 10.14 Mojave, an Android phone running Android OS Pie 9.0, a Windows desktop running Windows 10 OS as the terminal, while we use Google Chrome, Mozilla Firefox, Microsoft Edge, and Tor as the browser. Using the Panopticlick website, we note all the fingerprinting features when using different terminal-browser combinations.

For the purpose of our evaluation, we consider that the attacker uses the Google Chrome browser on the Mac laptop, i.e., "Mac+Chrome" to launch the attack. We believe that this is a very standard setup, and the attacker can just use this setup to launch the spoofing attack. Since the user may use different combinations of the terminal and the browser to access the target website, we consider the browser fingerprint obtained from all the remaining combinations of the terminal and the browser as the victim's browser fingerprint. We spoof each of the victim's fingerprints on the attacker's Mac+Chrome setup using various spoofing methods detailed in Sect. 3.2. To validate if the spoofing methods have indeed succeeded or not, we compare the fingerprint shown on the attacker's browser after spoofing with the previously noted victim's fingerprint.

5.2.2   Algorithm Attack Evaluation Scenarios

As mentioned earlier, to emulate our attack against the three fingerprinting algorithms, we insert nine spoofed fingerprints, each corresponding to our nine different attacks, to the original dataset. We inject the spoofed fingerprint after the latest fingerprint in the dataset that has the smaller (or same) created date as that of the spoofed fingerprint. As the counter in the dataset represents the order of the fingerprint based on its created date, when injecting the spoofed fingerprint, the dataset is re-organized for the counter. Thus, after injecting all our nine spoofed fingerprints, the new dataset would contain 15009 fingerprints (the original dataset had 15000 fingerprints), with a different and corrected order in terms of the counter.

In our evaluation, we choose one user as a victim at a time and evaluate our attack against the three fingerprinting algorithms, i.e., nine spoofed fingerprints corresponding to the chosen user are injected into the original dataset generating the attack dataset. The attack dataset is then reverted back to the original dataset. We repeat the process for each user in the dataset, resulting in a total of 239 attacks (for 239 users).

FP-Stalker uses 40% of the total fingerprints as a training dataset and the remaining fingerprints as the testing dataset. The fingerprint dataset is extended leveraging the expansion algorithm (which is based on the collect frequency provided in FP-Stalker) resulting in a sufficiently large fingerprint dataset.

Evaluation Metrics: To evaluate the performance of fingerprinting algorithms in the benign setting (using benign dataset), we use true positive rate (TPR), whereas, to evaluate the performance of our attack against fingerprinting algorithms, we use false positive rate (FPR). TPR measures how often the legitimate fingerprints have been correctly identified as belonging to the correct user's device. FPR measures how often the spoofed fingerprints are incorrectly identified as belonging to the victim.

In our evaluation, since we consider the tracking of the user over a period of time, we compute TPR and FPR for each day separately. When computing TPR and FPR for a given day, we consider only the fingerprints from that particular day. We expect the TPR to be high, close to 1, which indicates the benign user is being tracked well even in the presence of the Gummy Browsers attack. We also expect FPR to be close to 1, which denotes the attack is highly successful.

6   Results

6.1   Visual Attack Results

We have successfully spoofed all the fingerprinting information on Panopticlick and FingerprintJS website. The full details of spoofing results are listed in [37].

6.2   Algorithm Attack Results

6.2.1   Benign Setting

To validate the implementation of the three algorithms (obtained from FP-Stalker repository), similar to FP-Stalker, we plot various graphs on the performance of these algorithms for tracking the users. Figure 2 shows the average tracking duration (and Figure in [37] shows the average of *maximum* tracking duration) as a function of collect frequency for the three different fingerprinting algorithms. The tracking duration indicates the time duration (in terms of days) that the fingerprinting algorithm can track the user. The higher value of average tracking duration is considered good for user tracking. Figure 2 (and Figure in [37]) shows that the HLA outperforms Panopticlick and RLA at tracking the user, which is inline with the one reported in FP-Stalker. Further, we achieved similar results as those reported in FP-Stalker for each of the three fingerprinting algorithms.

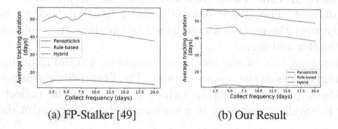

(a) FP-Stalker [49]   (b) Our Result

Fig. 2. Average tracking duration as a function of collect frequency for three different algorithms.

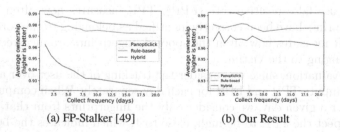

(a) FP-Stalker [49]   (b) Our Result

Fig. 3. Average ownership as a function of collect frequency for three fingerprinting algorithms.

Figure 3 shows the average ownership as a function of collect frequency. Ownership indicates how often the fingerprints were correctly associated with their actual users by the fingerprinting algorithms. The higher the ownership score, the better would be the performance of the fingerprinting algorithms. We achieved average ownership of above 0.95 for all the three fingerprinting algorithms, which is inline with that reported in FP-Stalker [49]. Figure in [37] shows the number of new IDs assigned to each user as a function of collect frequency for three different fingerprinting algorithms. If the number of new IDs assigned to a user is '1', this means all his fingerprints have been identified as from the original user (the best result). If the number of new assigned IDs is larger than '1', say 'n', this means the user's fingerprints are still tracked correctly, but as 'n' separate tracking durations, which can be seen as from three different users. Although we used the exact same implementation of the three algorithms from FP-Stalker, we achieved slightly different results compared to those in FP-Stalker. We attribute this difference to the difference in the volume of our dataset (239 users) compared to that used in FP-Stalker (1905 users).

Figure 4a, 4b, and 4c show the performance of the tracking algorithms in the benign setting. Specifically, they show the TPRs as a function of tracking days (when the collect frequency was set as 1) for Panopticlick, RLA, and HLA, respectively. Like earlier, RLA and HLA perform better than Panopticlick.

6.2.2 Attack Setting

To evaluate the performance of our attack and its impact on the tracking of legitimate users, we compute the average of TPRs and the average of FPRs over 239 attacks. Figure 5a, 5b, and 5c show the average TPRs as a function of tracking days in the attack setting for Panopticlick, RLA, and HLA, respectively, when collect frequency is set to 1. When comparing these TPRs with those in the benign setting, we see only a very minor difference in the TPR scores, potentially because of the addition of the spoofed fingerprints in the attack setting. This indicates that our attack does not have any significant impact on the performance of fingerprinting algorithms.

Similarly, Fig. 6a, 6b and 6c show the average FPRs as a function of tracking days in the attack setting for Panopticlick, RLA, and HLA, respectively, when the collect frequency is set to 1. We achieved average FPRs of greater than 0.95, mostly close to 1.00, which indicates that most of the spoofed fingerprints were misrecognized as the legitimate ones. In other words, these results show that our attacks were highly successful in fooling the fingerprinting algorithms into believing the spoofed fingerprints as the legitimate fingerprints. We note that similar results were achieved in both the benign and attack settings when the collect frequency was set to values other than 1.

7   Implications of Our Attack

As the browser fingerprinting is processed at the backend (i.e., the remote server) of the website and no web services are claiming that they are using any browser

164   Z. Liu et al.

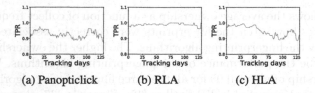

Fig. 4. True positive rate (TPR) as a function of tracking days in the benign setting when the collect frequency is set as 1.

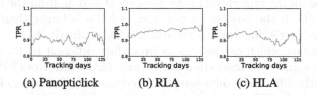

Fig. 5. True positive rate (TPR) as a function of tracking days in the attack setting when the collect frequency is set as 1.

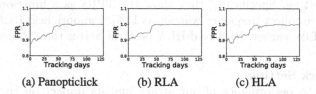

Fig. 6. False positive rate (FPR) as a function of tracking days in the attack setting when the collect frequency is set to 1.

fingerprinting approaches, we could not verify the actual impact of our attacks without inspecting the backend codes of the website. However, our results show that if they were to implement only fingerprinting techniques (without integration with any of the cookies, caches, or authentication mechanisms), our attack can have a significant impact on the user's privacy and security applications as described below.

Compromising Ad Privacy: A prior study [26] has shown that by simply monitoring the user's personalized ads, one can build the user's personal profile. In our attack, the attacker is successful at presenting his device to a target website as if it is the victim user's device through various spoofing methods. If the target website only uses browser fingerprinting to track the user and for personalized ads, the same or similar ads, or the ads from the same category would show up on the attacker's device. Given this, the attacker may learn various sensitive information about the user, including his gender, age group, the potential location of the user, his habits, and many more. Further, the attacker can sell such user's information for the purpose of personal and financial gain.

Defeating User Authentication: The purpose of browser fingerprinting in authentication is to remember the old device and enhance the security of traditional authentication methods such as passwords. For account login, since the attacker exposes his device as the victim's device in our attack, the target website will misrecognize the attacker as the victim who is using an old device, assuming that the attacker has obtained the victim's login credentials (i.e., the user's username and password). The authentication mechanisms only based on browser fingerprinting cannot block such an attack.

Bypassing Fraud Detection: Given the fact that many of the fraud detection techniques use browser fingerprinting information, the attacker can circumvent the detection by exposing his device as the victim's device leveraging various spoofing methods. Unless the victim user does not make any major big changes on his device (e.g., changing to a different operating system, downgrading system version, or replacing hardware) the attacker can impersonate the victim and bypass the detection. Generally, the attacker would be unaware of such big changes. However, the attacker can always pull the most recent browser fingerprint by simply fooling the user into visiting an attacker designed website. Given this, the fraud-detection algorithm cannot thwart our attack solely based on browser fingerprinting. It needs some additional metrics to detect fraud.

8   Discussion

Potential Attack Detection: The web service may detect our attack if the adversary does not follow the correct data format, provides invalid data, or takes time longer than the set time limit. However, the attack can remain undetected if the adversary carefully provides the correct and valid spoofed data within the set time limit. To use the script injection approach, the attacker should use a valid value to replace the Javascript API values, e.g., in the `Date()` object, 'year' should be replaced with 'year' (not 'month'). When employing the script modification approach, the attacker has to use the correct data format in the return value, e.g., '2020-04-12' can be replaced with '2020-03-29', but not with '2020.04.12'. We note that the spoofed date should not be older than the current date. To detect our attack, the web service may periodically request a response from the website running in the client machine, e.g., request the current time for every 5 s. When modifying the script, the adversary needs to stop all the scripts on the website, and thus prevent the website from sending the response to the web service. When the web service does not receive the expected response from the client machine in a timely manner, it can detect the potential attack. However, the attacker can use a pre-designed script to overwrite the existing scripts in the targeted website. The use of such a pre-designed script automates the script modification process, thereby defeating the above detection approach.

Limitations and Future Work: Although the fingerprinting techniques, considered in our study, utilize many of the attributes, they exclude several attributes used in other fingerprinting algorithms, such as the ones related to network and protocols (e.g., TCP/IP stack fingerprinting [32], DNS resolver [35]), and the hardware sensors [26] on the performance of our attack. The impact of these attributes on the performance of our attack has not been assessed in our study. Further investigation is needed to explore this direction. As noted earlier, the current dataset is insufficient to evaluate the performance of fingerprinting algorithms and that of our attacks after 130 tracking days. Further study with a larger dataset would be needed to assess the performance of our attack for a longer tracking period. Our study assumes that the attacker can fully spoof all browser information obtained from the victim's device. In some scenarios, the spoofed information may be outdated. In such a scenario, only partial browser information is correctly spoofed that may impact our attack. Future work would be needed to evaluate the impact of partial spoofing on the performance of our attack. Furthermore, an ethically-sound study of attacking personalized ads, authentication and fraud detection schemes that use fingerprinting in the real world via Gummy Browsers should be conducted in future work. Our spoofing methods (detailed in Sect. 4.2) can also be extended as an evasion technique that can obfuscate the true user's identity by creating and supplying a fake browser fingerprint to the visiting website. Similar to Gummy Browsers, the evasion can be oblivious to the target website. The impact of such evasion and subtle difference between Gummy Browsers and the evasion technique should be evaluated and discussed further in future work.

9   Conclusion

In this paper, we identified a novel and serious threat akin to the well-studied and popular notion of browser fingerprinting. Specifically, we showed that an attacker can make its own browser appear as the victim's browser by simply capturing (through an attacker-controlled or a malicious website) and mimicking the browser fingerprint (through script injection/modification or the leveraging browser's built-in settings and debugging tools). By exploiting this threat, we introduced and designed *Gummy Browsers*, an attack system that would enable a malicious entity to subvert any web application that uses browser fingerprinting, for example, to glean various sensitive information about the user in a targeted advertising application and to compromise the security of online defensive schemes, such as user authentication and fraud detection. We employed state-of-the-art browser fingerprinting techniques, Panopticlick and FP-Stalker, and evaluated the performance of Gummy Browsers against these algorithms. Our results showed that Gummy Browsers can successfully impersonate the victim's browser transparently almost all the time without affecting the tracking of legitimate users. Since acquiring and spoofing the browser characteristics is oblivious to both the user and the remote web-server, Gummy Browsers can be launched easily while remaining hard to detect. The impact of Gummy Browsers can be devastating and lasting on the online security and privacy of the users, especially given that browser-fingerprinting is starting to get widely adopted in the real world. In light of this attack, our work raises the question of whether browser fingerprinting is safe to deploy on a large scale.

References

1. Fusion middleware administrator's guide for oracle adaptive access manager (2015). https://docs.oracle.com/cd/E40329_01/admin.1112/e60557/finger.htm#AAMAD6186. Accessed 17 Apr 2020
2. Javascript obfuscator tool (2016). https://obfuscator.io/. Accessed 13 June 2021
3. Chrome DevTools — tools for web developers — google developers (2020). https://developers.google.com/web/tools/chrome-devtools. Accessed 23 Apr 2020
4. Configuration editor for firefox (2020). https://support.mozilla.org/en-US/kb/about-config-editor-firefox. Accessed 17 Apr 2020
5. Device/browser fingerprinting - heuristic-based authentication (2020). https://docs.secureauth.com/pages/viewpage.action?pageId=37225209. Accessed 15 Apr 2020
6. Device fingerprinting (2020). https://www.ipqualityscore.com/device-fingerprinting. Accessed 23 Apr 2020
7. Device intelligence | prevent fraud | accertify (2020). https://www.accertify.com/products/device-intelligence/. Accessed 1 May 2020
8. Fraud detection API demo (2020). https://fingerprintjs.com/demo. Accessed 6 June 2020
9. How to detect screen resolution with javascript (2020). https://www.tutorialrepublic.com/faq/how-to-detect-screen-resolution-with-javascript.php. Accessed 30 Apr 2020
10. How to detect that Javascript and/or cookies are disabled? (2020). https://stackoverflow.com/questions/4603289/how-to-detect-that-javascript-and-or-cookies-are-disabled. Accessed 29 Apr 2020
11. Introducing JSON (2020). https://www.json.org/json-en.html. Accessed 29 Apr 2020
12. The JSON data interchange syntax (2020). https://www.ecma-international.org/publications/files/ECMA-ST/ECMA-404.pdf. Accessed 1 May 2020
13. Navigator platform property (2020). https://www.w3schools.com/jsref/prop_nav_platform.asp. Accessed 27 Apr 2020
14. Navigator.donottrack (2020). https://developer.mozilla.org/en-US/docs/Web/API/Navigator/doNotTrack. Accessed 22 Apr 2020
15. Panopticlick (2020). https://panopticlick.eff.org/. Accessed 8 June 2020
16. Selenium automates browsers. That's it! (2020). https://www.selenium.dev/. Accessed 18 Apr 2020
17. WebGL: 2D and 3D graphics for the web (2020). https://developer.mozilla.org/en-US/docs/Web/API/WebGL_API. Accessed 30 Apr 2020
18. Window.localstorage (2020). https://developer.mozilla.org/en-US/docs/Web/API/Window/localStorage. Accessed 21 Apr 2020
19. Javascript deobfuscator and unpacker (2021). https://github.com/lelinhtinh/de4js. Accessed 13 June 2021
20. Alaca, F., Van Oorschot, P.C.: Device fingerprinting for augmenting web authentication: classification and analysis of methods. In: Proceedings of the 32nd Annual Conference on Computer Security Applications (2016)
21. Alvestrand, H.: Content language headers. Technical report, RFC 3282, May 2002
22. Beltran, V., Bertin, E., Crespi, N.: User identity for webRTC services: a matter of trust. IEEE Internet Comput. **18**, 18–25 (2014)

23. Boda, K., Földes, Á.M., Gulyás, G.G., Imre, S.: User tracking on the web via cross-browser fingerprinting. In: Laud, P. (ed.) NordSec 2011. LNCS, vol. 7161, pp. 31–46. Springer, Heidelberg (2012). https://doi.org/10.1007/978-3-642-29615-4_4

24. Bolton, R.J., Hand, D.J.: Statistical fraud detection: a review. Stat. Sci. **17**, 235–255 (2002)

25. Castelluccia, C., Kaafar, M.A., Tran, M.D.: Betrayed by your ads! In: International Symposium on Privacy Enhancing Technologies Symposium (2012)

26. Das, A., Borisov, N., Caesar, M.: Tracking mobile web users through motion sensors: attacks and defenses. In: National Down Syndrome Society (2016)

27. Eckersley, P.: How unique is your web browser? In: International Symposium on Privacy Enhancing Technologies Symposium (2010)

28. FaizKhademi, A., Zulkernine, M., Weldemariam, K.: FPGuard: detection and prevention of browser fingerprinting. In: Samarati, P. (ed.) DBSec 2015. LNCS, vol. 9149, pp. 293–308. Springer, Cham (2015). https://doi.org/10.1007/978-3-319-20810-7_21

29. Fifield, D., Egelman, S.: Fingerprinting web users through font metrics. In: Böhme, R., Okamoto, T. (eds.) FC 2015. LNCS, vol. 8975, pp. 107–124. Springer, Heidelberg (2015). https://doi.org/10.1007/978-3-662-47854-7_7

30. Florian: Device fingerprinting for fraud reduction - how and why does it work? (2019). https://seon.io/resources/device-fingerprinting/. Accessed 23 Apr 2020

31. Garrett, J.J., et al.: Ajax: a new approach to web applications (2005)

32. Glaser, T.: TCP/IP stack fingerprinting principles (2000). https://www.giac.org/paper/gsec/159/tcp-ip-stack-fingerprinting-principles/100625. Accessed 20 Apr 2020

33. Hoofnagle, C.J., Soltani, A., Good, N., Wambach, D.J.: Behavioral advertising: the offer you can't refuse. Harv. L. Pol'y Rev. **6**, 273 (2012)

34. Iqbal, U., Shafiq, Z., Qian, Z.: The ad wars: retrospective measurement and analysis of anti-adblock filter lists. In: Proceedings of the 2017 Internet Measurement Conference (2017)

35. Kim, T., Ju, H.: Effective DNS server fingerprinting method. In: 2011 13th Asia-Pacific Network Operations and Management Symposium (2011)

36. Kristol, D., Montulli, L.: HTTP state management mechanism. Technical report (2000)

37. Liu, Z., Shrestha, P., Saxena, N.: Gummy browsers: targeted browser spoofing against state-of-the-art fingerprinting techniques. arXiv preprint arXiv:2110.10129 (2021)

38. Lu, G., Coogan, K., Debray, S.: Automatic simplification of obfuscated Javascript code (extended abstract). In: Dua, S., Gangopadhyay, A., Thulasiraman, P., Straccia, U., Shepherd, M., Stein, B. (eds.) ICISTM 2012. CCIS, vol. 285, pp. 348–359. Springer, Heidelberg (2012). https://doi.org/10.1007/978-3-642-29166-1_31

39. Martherus, R.E., Ramamurthy, S.: User authentication (2007). https://patentimages.storage.googleapis.com/cb/d5/f8/e9d54ed4a44f0c/US7194764.pdf. Accessed 29 Apr 2020

40. Melicher, W., Sharif, M., Tan, J., Bauer, L., Christodorescu, M., Leon, P.G.: (Do not) track me sometimes: users' contextual preferences for web tracking. In: Proceedings on Privacy Enhancing Technologies (2016)

41. Mesbah, A., Mirshokraie, S.: Automated analysis of CSS rules to support style maintenance. In: 2012 34th International Conference on Software Engineering (ICSE) (2012)

42. Mowery, K., Bogenreif, D., Yilek, S., Shacham, H.: Fingerprinting information in JavaScript implementations. In: Proceedings of W2SP (2011)

43. Mowery, K., Shacham, H.: Pixel perfect: fingerprinting canvas in HTML5. In: Proceedings of W2SP (2012)

44. Mulazzani, M., et al.: Fast and reliable browser identification with Javascript engine fingerprinting. In: Web 2.0 Workshop on Security and Privacy (W2SP) (2013)

45. Neal, J.: Detect autofill in Chrome, Edge, Firefox, and Safari (2020). https://gist.github.com/jonathantneal/d462fc2bf761a10c9fca60eb634f6977. Accessed 25 Apr 2020

46. Norte, J.C.: Advanced tor browser fingerprinting, March 2016. http://jcarlosnorte.com/security/2016/03/06/advanced-tor-browser-fingerprinting.html. Accessed 22 Apr 2020

47. Olejnik, Ł., Acar, G., Castelluccia, C., Diaz, C.: The leaking battery. In: Data Privacy Management, and Security Assurance (2015)

48. Roesner, F., Kohno, T., Wetherall, D.: Detecting and defending against third-party tracking on the web. In: Presented as part of the 9th USENIX Symposium on Networked Systems Design and Implementation (NSDI 2012) (2012)

49. Spirals-Team: Spirals-team/FPStalker (2020). https://github.com/Spirals-Team/FPStalker. Accessed 23 Apr 2020

50. Taylor, D.G., Lewin, J.E., Strutton, D.: Friends, fans, and followers: do ads work on social networks?: how gender and age shape receptivity. J. Advert. Res. **51**, 258–275 (2011)

51. Tucker, C.E.: The economics of advertising and privacy. Int. J. Ind. Organ. **30**, 326–329 (2012)

52. Vastel, A., Laperdrix, P., Rudametkin, W., Rouvoy, R.: FP-STALKER: tracking browser fingerprint evolutions. In: 2018 IEEE Symposium on Security and Privacy (SP) (2018)

Identifying Near-Optimal Single-Shot Attacks on ICSs with Limited Process Knowledge

Herson Esquivel-Vargas[1]([⊠]), John Henry Castellanos[2], Marco Caselli[3],
Nils Ole Tippenhauer[4], and Andreas Peter[1,5]

[1] University of Twente, Enschede, The Netherlands
{h.esquivelvargas,a.peter}@utwente.nl
[2] Singapore University of Technology and Design, Singapore, Singapore
john_castellanos@mymail.sutd.edu.sg
[3] Siemens AG, Munich, Germany
marco.caselli@siemens.com
[4] CISPA Helmholtz Center for Information Security, Saarbrücken, Germany
tippenhauer@cispa.de
[5] University of Oldenburg, Oldenburg, Germany

Abstract. Industrial Control Systems (ICSs) rely on insecure protocols and devices to monitor and operate critical infrastructure. Prior work has demonstrated that powerful attackers with detailed system knowledge can manipulate exchanged sensor data to deteriorate performance of the process, even leading to full shutdowns of plants. Identifying those attacks requires iterating over all possible sensor values, and running detailed system simulation or analysis to identify optimal attacks. That setup allows adversaries to identify attacks that are most impactful when applied on the system for the first time, before the system operators become aware of the manipulations.

In this work, we investigate if constrained attackers without detailed system knowledge and simulators can identify comparable attacks. In particular, the attacker only requires abstract knowledge on general information flow in the plant, instead of precise algorithms, operating parameters, process models, or simulators. We propose an approach that allows single-shot attacks, i.e., near-optimal attacks that are reliably shutting down a system on the first try. The approach is applied and validated on two use cases, and demonstrated to achieve comparable results to prior work, which relied on detailed system information and simulations.

1 Introduction

Attacks on Industrial Control Systems (ICSs) have been thoroughly investigated in the post-Stuxnet era. Different initiatives such as Mitre's *ATT&CK for ICS* and SANS Institute's *ICS Cyber Kill Chain* have emerged to systematically analyze ICS attacks [6,23]. After a decade of research, it became clear that the

---

The full version of this paper can be found at https://arxiv.org/abs/2204.09106.

© Springer Nature Switzerland AG 2022
G. Ateniese and D. Venturi (Eds.): ACNS 2022, LNCS 13269, pp. 170–192, 2022.
https://doi.org/10.1007/978-3-031-09234-3_9

difficulty of ICS attacks is not the execution itself but the preparation [12]. The latter stages of an ICS attack are considered easy because most industrial protocols lack security services such as message encryption and authentication, Programmable Logic Controllers (PLCs) remain operational for years without software updates, unprotected Human-Machine Interfaces (HMIs), and many more. The difficulty about preparing an ICS attack is due the complexity of ICSs that can have hundreds of components (e.g., sensors, setpoints, actuators) and knowing *what to target* and *how to target it* is considered far from trivial.

Most research on ICSs security argues, or simply assumes, that detailed knowledge about the system is a requirement for a successful compromise. In this work, we challenge such a claim by considering an attacker whose goal is to destabilize the physical process using only limited process knowledge. Despite this preparation constraint, the attack (1) must target one component only once (single-shot); and (2) must have a fast effect after the attack execution (near-optimal). The first requirement aims at executing stealthy and hard to detect attacks. The second requirement discards attacks whose impact take a long time, increasing the chance of detection and defensive reaction. More precisely, we call 'near-optimal' the top-3 fastest attacks under the same system and attack conditions.

Previous research has identified the data sources required by an attacker to prepare a successful attack against ICSs [12]. For instance, PLC configuration, HMI/Workstation configuration, historian configuration, network traffic, system/component constraints, and piping and instrumentation diagrams (P&IDs). The main argument being that only through the combination of multiple data sources, an attacker is able to reach the level of "process comprehension" required to launch an attack. Previous works confirm this claim. We analyzed the attack preparation phase of several papers and categorized their requirements according to the data sources presented in [12]. Table 1 shows that previous works use multiple data sources to prepare an ICS attack.

In this work, we propose a new approach that only requires limited knowledge of the system's architecture, and still allows to identify *near-optimal single-shot* attacks. Our approach requires an abstract representation of the information flow in the system - which sensors and setpoints influence which control decision, which actuators are controlled by which control function. We show how to obtain this information (e.g., from P&IDs), and how to express it in an abstract graph representation. We then leverage the accumulated knowledge on IT software weaknesses and apply it to the ICSs domain. In particular, we use weaknesses from Mitre's Common Weakness Enumeration (CWE) database, and translate them to specific graph patterns. Our goal is to look for these patterns in the ICS graph to identify suitable targets. From this set of targets, the attacker picks one (e.g., randomly) and executes his 'one-shot' attack.

We evaluate our approach using a simulated ICS known as the Tennessee Eastman Plant (TEP). We used two different implementations of the TEP and build the corresponding CCL graphs. Our analysis of the graphs reveals weaknesses which we hypothesize are the components in best capacity to compromise the availability of the plant. We then execute simulations to test our hypotheses. We found out that there is a correlation between the targets automatically

Table 1. Comparison of the required attacker knowledge in previous works. Data sources are based on the process knowledge data source taxonomy from [12]. P&ID: Piping and Instrumentation Diagram, PLC: Programmable Logic Controller, HMI: Human-Machine Interface, WS: Workstation.

Data source	Work										
	[2]	[3]	[7]	[8]	[9]	[13]	[15]	[16]	[19]	[28]	**Our**
PLC configuration	✓							✓			
HMI/WS configuration		✓	✓			✓	✓				
Historian configuration	✓	✓	✓	✓	✓	✓			✓	✓	
Network traffic					✓	✓					
P&ID	✓			✓		✓	✓	✓	✓	✓	✓

chosen by our approach and the components that, according to the simulations, are prone to cause a shutdown of the plant. Although different security aspects of the TEP have been studied in the past, most of them have run simulations under very limited conditions [13,15]. To gain more confidence in our results, we executed 748 individual simulations under 14 different conditions that account for 2.52 years of simulated time.

Summarizing, our two main contributions are as follows. (1) We present a novel method to identify near-optimal single-shot attacks on ICSs. Unlike previous offensive approaches, our work uses limited process knowledge, thus, offering new insights about the actual security risks in ICSs. (2) To validate our approach, we executed, documented, and published the most extensive set of simulated attacks on the TEP to date. The code, results of each simulation, and screenshots are provided in the corresponding repositories.

2 Background

2.1 Closed Control Loops

Closed Control Loops (CCLs) constitute a basic programming pattern for ICSs. A CCL is comprised of four basic components, namely, a setpoint, a sensor, a control function, and an actuator (e.g., valve, heater, light, etc.). The CCL's control function receives inputs from the environment through sensors, compares them with pre-established setpoints, and reacts with a compensatory action intended to minimize the difference. The compensatory action is executed by an actuator in order to control the physical variable measured by the sensor (e.g., pressure, temperature, illumination, etc.). Figure 1 depicts the simplest form of a CCL.

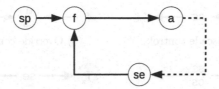

Fig. 1. A CCL comprised of a setpoint (sp), a sensor (se), a control function (f), and an actuator (a). Solid lines represent communication in the *cyber* domain whereas the dashed line represents interaction in the *physical* realm.

The control function is a software component typically running in high availability embedded systems such as Programmable Logic Controllers (PLCs). Control functions implement the control logic; for example, arithmetic operations, rate limiters, and other kinds of data processing functions. From the function's perspective, hardware devices such as sensors and actuators are abstracted simply as variables to be read and written. It is worth noting that in distributed control systems these variables might not necessarily reside on the same PLC. Therefore, communication to and from the control function might require network transmissions.

Advanced CCL configurations are often needed, e.g., to cope with system disturbances. One of such configurations is called *cascade control*, where one control function adjusts the setpoint of another control function [32]. This dynamically computed setpoint is called a *calculated setpoint*. In contraposition, we denote user-defined setpoints as *static setpoints*. Although we typically make an explicit distinction between static setpoints and calculated setpoints, in what follows, we use the word *setpoint* to refer to either of them when such a distinction is irrelevant. Graphically, an example of cascade control is shown in Fig. 2a.

Another advanced CCL configuration is called *override control*. In this setting, one control function manipulates one variable during normal operation, however, a second control function can take over during abnormal operation to prevent some safety, process, or equipment limit from being exceeded [32]. The notion of normal and abnormal operation is dependent on the physical process under control. The variable under control by two or more control functions is typically used to manipulate one actuator or calculated setpoint. Figure 2b shows a graphical representation of the override control technique.

It is also common to find setpoints and sensors shared between two or more control functions, as shown in Fig. 2c and Fig. 2d, respectively. Shared setpoints provide a convenient centralized configuration for multiple control functions at once. The motivation behind shared sensors is similar to that of shared setpoints, which in addition reflects the fact that typically there are limited instances of physical sensors in the system under control. An arbitrary number of the CCL configurations shown in Fig. 2 can be used to control ICSs [29].

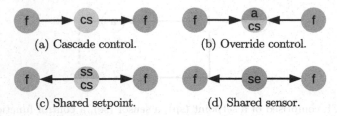

(a) Cascade control.   (b) Override control.

(c) Shared setpoint.   (d) Shared sensor.

Fig. 2. Advanced CCL configurations. Color code: gray: static setpoint (ss), blue: controlling function (f), red: actuator (a), purple: sensor (se), and yellow: calculated setpoint (cs). (Color figure online)

2.2   Process Knowledge Data Sources

Process comprehension is the main challenge attackers need to overcome to design successful and efficient attack strategies. Based on their capabilities, attackers can access different data sources of the targeted system, from collecting network captures to full access to an operator's workstation. Each data source provides a different view of the system. Depending on the attacker's interests, they could find some data sources more useful than others. We follow the data source taxonomy presented in [12] and describe the information that can be derived from them. The data sources explored in their work include:

PLC Configuration. PLCs are one of the most valuable components of ICSs. As they run the control logic that governs the process, they contain all the mechanisms to manipulate the system's physical properties. An attacker can learn the system's control logic and understand what sensors and network messages could jeopardize the system more quickly.

HMI/Workstation Configuration. HMIs are a valuable target for attackers because they typically run on Windows-based machines and have a comprehensive view of the system, as it was shown in the Ukraine power grid incident [18]. Attackers with access to HMIs have a larger view of the system than individual PLCs. Attackers with access to HMIs could infer a more general view of the system, such as the type of industry they control [28].

Historian Configuration. Historian data is also a valuable data source for attackers. As historians store previous traces of the system, they provide helpful information for attackers to understand the nominal behavior of the system. Historians are particularly valuable for model learning and the design of stealthy attacks [19].

Network Traffic. Network flows describe how devices interact with each other. Attackers can sneak into the system's network and passively learn patterns of the system's behavior. Networks provide a source of realistic attack vectors that can drive the system into unsafe states [8,9].

Piping and Instrumentation Diagram (P&ID). P&IDs show the functional relationship between the main components of the system, including piping, instrumentation and control devices. Attackers could learn valuable information about operational equipment and deduce which computing devices are worth being attacked.

3   Identifying Near-Optimal Single-Shot Attacks

3.1   System Model

In this work, we focus on generic Industrial Control Systems (ICSs) implemented using a common programming pattern known as *Closed Control Loop* (CCL). The structure of CCLs is typically comprised of 4 components: a control function, a setpoint, a sensor, and an actuator. Control functions run in high availability embedded systems such as PLCs. Setpoints, sensors, and actuators are abstracted as variables that serve as inputs and outputs for control functions. The system might be distributed, meaning that the components of a single CCL reside on different PLCs but are interconnected through a communication network and exchange messages using standard ICS protocols (e.g., Modbus, EtherNet/IP, BACnet).

3.2   Attacker Model

Attacker Goal. We consider an attacker that aims to lead to process damage (e.g., an emergency process shutdown) as fast as possible (as with longer attacks, the likelihood of detection rises).

Attacker Capabilities. To achieve this goal, the attacker will manipulate the values reported by a specific sensor (which simplifies the analysis, consistent with related work [13,15], and also limits the discussion to attacks on single sensors). Exactly how the sensor is manipulated is out of scope. Prior work has demonstrated many ways to achieve this via physical-layer manipulations [30], traffic manipulations [15], or direct attacks on the PLCs or other hosts [1]. In prior work, a number of approaches to select values to spoof have been discussed. In this work we use the *constant* and *minimum/maximum* value attack from [7,31].

Attacker Knowledge. As obtaining information on the target process is costly (e.g., reconnaissance effort, bribes, industrial espionage), the attacker aims to minimize the type of information required to successfully run an attack. In particular, we assume an attacker that only has access to an abstract P&ID. We will show later how from this diagram a CCL graph can be derived.

Lack of Simulation. In particular, the attacker does not have access to detailed physical process simulation environments. This implies (combined with the lack of detailed knowledge on the attacked process) that the effect of the attacker's manipulations cannot be reliably predicted in advance.

3.3   Research Questions and Challenges

Given this system and attacker model we address the following research question:

Given the set of all ICS sensors in the target system, how can the attacker identify the sensor to manipulate to achieve a near-optimal single-shot attack, with limited knowledge on the attacked process and system (i.e., a CCL graph)?

Here we motivate the single-shot and near-optimal attack requirements in detail.

Need for Single-Shot Attacks. While the system under attack does not use process-aware attack detection systems [31], the human operators will eventually detect anomalous system conditions. Once anomalous system conditions are detected, a full-scale forensic investigation would be launched, which would remove the attacker's ability to launch further attacks. This means that the attacker will have to ideally perform an efficient attack on their first try. We call such attacks *single-shot* attacks.

Near-Optimal Attacks. Out of a large set of possible attacks within our attacker model, we expect there to be an attack that is optimal in the sense that its sensor manipulation leads to the fastest possible intended effect (i.e., shutdown of the process). But there might be other attacks that are nearly as fast. For the purpose of our evaluation, we introduce the concept of *near-optimal* attacks. In particular, when ranking all possible attacks by their expected shutdown time, we call the three best attacks *near-optimal*. We will also discuss alternative efficiency comparisons later in our discussion.

Challenge. We note that prior ICS security research argues (or simply assumes) that *detailed knowledge* about the system under attack is a requirement for a successful compromise [12]. So the main challenge we will have to solve is to leverage the limited process knowledge (i.e., high-level CCL graph) to identify suitable sensors to attack—without using attacker-side simulations to predict the outcome of process manipulations. If a near-optimal attack is reliably conducted on the first shot (even with limited knowledge on the system), our solution is considered successful.

3.4   Identifying Near-Optimal Single-Shot Attacks in CCL Graphs

We model ICSs as graph data structures that abstract the configuration of their closed control loops (CCLs). The graph abstraction of a single ICS might consist of multiple subgraphs. There are 5 types of nodes in our graphs that match the 5 components of CCLs: *static setpoints*, *sensors*, *control functions*, *actuators*, and *calculated setpoints*.

Formally, an ICS is modeled as a directed graph $G(V, E)$ where V is a nonempty set of vertices (or nodes) and E is a set of edges. Every edge has exactly two vertices in V as endpoints. The direction of every edge $e \in E$ models the way information flows in the graph. There are 5 partitions SS, SE,

F, A and CS in V, that segregate the 5 types of nodes (*static setpoint, sensor, control function, actuator,* and *calculated setpoint,* respectively), such that $SS \cup SE \cup F \cup A \cup CS = V$. It is worth noting that although we assume knowledge about the type of the nodes (e.g., sensor), we do not require further details about them (e.g., temperature sensor, pressure sensor, etc.).

There are different options to create CCL graphs. It is possible to extract the CCL graph of ICSs from P&IDs. These diagrams show interconnected physical instruments and might contain information about the CCLs used in the ICS. Figure 3 shows an example of a P&ID in Fig. 3a, and its corresponding CCL graph abstraction in Fig. 3b. Moreover, there are other options to create CCL graphs. For instance, it is possible to create a CCL graph exclusively from network traffic in the BACnet protocol [11]. A use case from a real BACnet system is discussed and exemplified in Sect. 6.

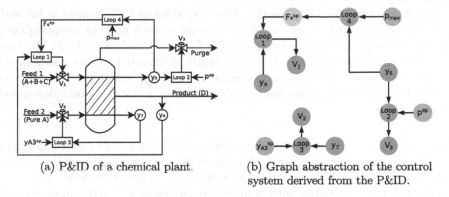

(a) P&ID of a chemical plant.   (b) Graph abstraction of the control system derived from the P&ID.

Fig. 3. Piping and instrumentation diagram (P&ID) of an ICS and its corresponding graph abstraction.

The proposed approach starts by searching for specific patterns in CCL graphs. These patterns relate to well understood weaknesses originally analyzed in IT systems. After that, a post-processing step is needed to filter out non-sensor targets. This is important since according to our attacker model only sensor nodes will be targeted. Finally, the attacker has to choose among the pre-selected sensors and has only one opportunity to compromise its integrity. In the next sections, we explain how to execute near-optimal single-shot attacks and exemplify the proposed approach using the system presented in Fig. 3.

Pattern Matching. We propose to use the accumulated knowledge about software weaknesses in the IT domain and transfer it to the ICSs domain. In particular, we leverage Mitre's Common Weakness Enumeration (CWE) database, which specifies common IT weaknesses. While we later use several of those CWE patterns in our implementation, here we focus on two entries which proved particularly useful experimentally. Our goal is to provide an intuitive comprehension of the proposed approach without limiting its applicability to a specific subset of weaknesses. More formally, we identify each pattern P_i with an index $i = 1, \ldots, n$. Each pattern matching query on the graph returns a subset $S_i \subseteq V$ of matching nodes using pattern P_i.

CWE-1108: Excessive Reliance on Global Variables. "*The code is structured in a way that relies too much on using or setting global variables throughout various points in the code, instead of preserving the associated information in a narrower, more local context.*" [22].

Global variables are generally considered a bad software engineering practice. Their main disadvantage is that malicious or benign-but-buggy changes to them will propagate and possibly disrupt many parts of the code. Global variables can be observed in CCL graphs mainly due to shared setpoints and/or sensors. As explained in Sect. 2, these are typical ways to combine CCLs in ICSs (see e.g., Fig. 2c and Fig. 2d).

A suitable algorithm to identify global variables in CCL graphs is the *out-degree* centrality. This algorithm assigns a score to each node by counting their number of outgoing edges. More formally, for every node $v \in V \backslash F$, the out-degree of v is denoted as $d^+(v)$. We explicitly disregard *function* nodes in set F since this particular weakness is exclusively about variables. We select as potential targets those nodes whose value $d^+(v) \geq \tau$, for a context dependent threshold τ.

CWE-1109: Use of Same Variable for Multiple Purposes. "*The code contains a callable, block, or other code element in which the same variable is used to control more than one unique task or store more than one instance of data.*" [22].

Overloading a variable with multiple responsibilities might unnecessarily increase the complexity of the code around it. Such complexity becomes an indirect security issue since it can hide potential vulnerabilities.

In control engineering, the usage of *override controllers* deliberately creates a pattern in which two or more control functions manipulate a single variable (see Sect. 2, Fig. 2b). The manipulated variable is commonly of type *actuator* or *calculated setpoint*. Due to the widespread implementation of override controllers in ICSs, it is possible to find this pattern in real CCL graphs.

The automated identification of override controllers in a CCL graph can be done by computing the in-degree centrality of every node $v \in V \backslash F$. This algorithm assigns a score to each node by counting their number of incoming edges. As in the previous case, we explicitly disregard *function* nodes in set F since this particular weakness is exclusively about variables. We denote the number of incoming edges of a node as $d^-(v)$. Thus, we look at nodes whose $d^-(v) \geq \tau$, where typically $\tau = 2$.

Post-processing. According to our attacker model, it is a requirement to target nodes of type *sensor* only. Although some of the nodes that satisfy a weakness-related pattern might be of type *sensor* other node types could be chosen too. In fact, it is common to find *setpoint* nodes as global variables and *actuator* nodes as multi-purpose variables.

For each node $v \in S_i$, we first check whether $v \in SE$. If v is of type *sensor* then v is added to the result set $R_i \subseteq SE$. Else, we search for every sensor $u \in SE$, such that there is a path from u to v, and add u to the result set R_i. The pseudocode of this algorithm is listed in Algorithm 1.

Algorithm 1. Pattern matching post-processing.

---

input: set $S_i \subseteq V$ of nodes identified using P_i.
output: set $R_i \subseteq SE$ of candidate sensor targets according to P_i.
$R_i = \emptyset$
for all $v \in S_i$ do
  if $v \in SE$ then
    $R_i = R_i \cup \{v\}$
  else
    for all $u \in SE$ do
      if exist_path(from:u, to:v) then
        $R_i = R_i \cup \{u\}$
      end if
    end for
  end if
end for

Single-Shot Attacks. After the pattern matching phase, the attacker has to choose one target from all the result sets obtained. To choose one target from $\cup_{i=1}^{n} R_i$, we assign each sensor a score depending on how many result sets R_i they occur in. The reasoning behind this scoring system is that the sensors that have been identified by more weakness-related patterns have a greater chance of attack success. This selection criteria creates a subset of targets $T \subseteq \cup_{i=1}^{n} R_i$ among which only one has to be selected. Without further insights about the targeted infrastructure besides the CCL graph, it is hard to provide a meaningful sensor selection strategy from T. However, we hypothesize that T (1) will be smaller that the original sensor set; and (2) will contain only sensors capable of causing near-optimal shutdown times (SDTs). A smaller subset to choose sensors from, gives the attacker a probabilistic advantage over, e.g., an attacker that has to choose a sensor from the whole sensor set SE. Moreover, since we hypothesize that *all* sensors in T are capable of causing near-optimal SDTs, a simple (e.g., random) selection strategy is suitable from the attacker's perspective.

To compromise the integrity of a sensor, the attacker overwrites legitimate sensor readings in such a way that all linked control functions will take the attacker's desired value instead. This value is fixed throughout the whole period of the attack, however, the attacker is free to choose the value at will.

3.5 Motivating Example

Figure 3a shows the model of a chemical plant originally described in [25]. Four chemical components referred to as A, B, C, and D, are part of the process. The first three components are combined in the reactor to create the final product D. The goal of the software controlling the plant is to keep a stable high quality production rate while minimizing the waste of raw material. There are four control functions that take as input the values coming from three sensors and four setpoints (1 calculated setpoint and 3 static setpoints). The output of the functions aims to control three valves in the plant.

From a security perspective, there are several details of the plant that a potential attacker would like to know to execute an attack. For example, the types of sensors (i.e., pressure, temperature), the chemical reaction carried out by the plant (i.e., $A + C \xrightarrow{B} D$), the maximum pressure supported by the reactor (3,000 kPa), etc. Detailed process knowledge has been used in previous works to exemplify simulated attacks against this chemical plant [7,13]. Our approach, however, assumes limited process knowledge. More precisely, we only assume access to the CCL graph of the targeted infrastructure (Fig. 3b), which lacks all of the previously mentioned details.

Figure 3b depicts the CCL graph of the chemical plant, which can be easily derived from its piping and instrumentation diagram. This graph shows two kinds of CCL combinations: (1) a shared sensor y_5 between control functions *Loop 4* and *Loop 2*; and (2) a cascade control in which control function *Loop 4* sets a calculated setpoint $F_{4^{sp}}$ to control function *Loop 1*.

The proposed approach looks for weakness patterns in the chemical plant's CCL graph that could identify suitable sensors to target. The search for multi-purpose variables (functions excluded) aims at nodes whose in-degree is greater or equal than two; no results are produced in this case. The search for global variables (functions excluded) looks for nodes whose out-degree is greater than a predefined threshold τ. All setpoints have an out-degree of one which makes them unfit to be labeled as global variables. However, the three sensors y_4, y_5, and y_7 have an out-degree of 1, 2, and 1, respectively. This small sensors sample shows an average out-degree of 1.33 with standard deviation of 0.58. Defining τ as the sum of the average and one standard deviation ($\tau = 1.91$) sets node y_5 as a potential target according to the proposed approach. The result set would have sensor y_5 as an ideal candidate to target in this particular infrastructure. This result is concordant with previous works which state that "[i]n general we found that the plant is very resilient to attacks on y_7 and y_4... If the plant operator only has enough budget to deploy advanced security mechanisms for one sensor (e.g., tamper resistance, or TPM chips), y_5 should be the priority" [7].

4 Implementation

We implement the proposed approach on top of Neo4j version 4.1.2 [24]. Neo4j is a noSQL database engine specialized in graph data structures. Neo4j offers a natural way to store CCL graphs and a high level query language that allows to perform complex queries in just a few lines of code.

We assume that the attacker already has access to the CCL graph of the targeted infrastructure and has persisted it in a Neo4j database. Without any further knowledge, the selection of the sensors to attack is done through a set of queries on the graph. Such queries must be written in Neo4j's query language called *Cypher Query Language*. Figure 4 depicts the overall process to obtain a subset R_i of candidate sensor targets according to a pattern P_i.

Our implementation includes a *pre-processing* stage that pre-computes information required in the *pattern matching* phase. Since both weakness-related patterns discussed in Sect. 3.4 are based on the in- and out-degree centrality algorithms, the *pre-processing* stage consists of queries that assign the in- and out-degree to every node in the graph.

The *pattern matching* phase consists in finding nodes that satisfy a specific condition in the graph's topology. These particular conditions pinpoint nodes of interest from the attacker's perspective. For the sake of brevity, here we discuss two weaknesses, namely, global variables and multi-purpose variables. Global variables are nodes whose out-degree is greater than a context dependent threshold τ. In our implementation, we define τ as the average plus one standard deviation of the out-degree of nodes segregated per type.

The second *pattern matching* query looks for multi-purpose variables (e.g., override controllers). This pattern is simpler since we only need to find nodes with an in-degree greater or equal than 2.

Lastly, the *post-processing* phase replaces non-sensor nodes found during the *pattern matching* phase, with sensor nodes that have a path to them, thus, influencing their behavior. This ensures that the list of targets for each weakness-related pattern is comprised exclusively of sensor nodes.

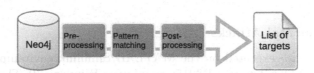

Fig. 4. Implementation of the proposed approach.

5 Experimental Evaluation

We evaluate the proposed approach in a realistic industrial control system. We use this environment to perform experimental attacks against *all* relevant sensors to obtain a ground-truth about the severity of the attacks in terms plant availability. Due to the large number of attacks required to obtain the ground-truth, we opted for a simulated environment where the attacks can be executed without safety concerns. The simulated plant is known as the Tennessee Eastman Plant and has been extensively used in previous cybersecurity research [7,13,15,16,28].

5.1 Tennessee Eastman Plant

The seminal 1993 paper by Downs and Vogel describes the Tennessee Eastman Plant (TEP) [10]. Their description includes, among other details, the expected input and output of the plant, each step of the process from start to end, and the hardware available to control the process. The control hardware includes

41 sensors and 12 actuators. Their paper describes 20 disturbances commonly found in real chemical plants. For instance, sticky valves, changes in chemical reaction kinetics, and random variations in the composition of input streams. Each disturbance has a unique numeric identifier in the range [1–20]. Finally, there are process operating constraints (e.g., maximum reactor temperature, maximum reactor pressure, etc.) that must be satisfied at all times or the plant shuts down. Downs and Vogel present the challenge of implementing a control strategy for the TEP. To ease engagement in the challenge, the authors provide software source code to simulate the core components of the TEP such as the sensors, actuators, disturbances, and process operating constraints, leaving space for the missing control strategy.

Several authors have proposed control strategies for the TEP [17,20,21,26]. The main difference between control strategies are the robustness against external disturbances, the optimization objectives, and the mechanisms to set the production rate. The TEP challenge is considered an open-ended problem without a unique correct solution [20].

In this work, we perform an extensive analysis of two control strategies for the TEP in terms of plant *availability* upon sensor integrity attacks. The first strategy, proposed by Larsson et al. [17], is available in the MATLAB/Simulink environment [27].[1] The second strategy, proposed by Luyben et al., is available in the Fortran programming language [20]. We translated it to the MATLAB/Simulink environment and published it.[2]

5.2 Experimental Attacks

All simulations are executed on the MATLAB/Simulink environment. Specifically, we use MATLAB version R2015a running on Windows 10. The simulations are configured to run for 72 h under attack. However, some of the attacks cause violations in the process operating constraints. As a consequence, some simulations stop earlier than expected. We refer to the time elapsed since the beginning of the attack and until the simulation stops as the shutdown time (SDT).

An *experiment* is a set of simulations using the same environmental conditions (i.e., disturbances) and attack strategy. In our experiments, we execute simulations with and without disturbances. The disturbances considered are those in the range [1–13] and are executed one at a time. According to the original TEP paper, disturbances in the range [14–20] should be used in conjunction with other disturbances [10]. The combinatorial explosion of such constraint deters us from executing simulations with disturbances in the range [14–20]. The attack strategy is the way in which the attacker chooses the value used to compromise the integrity of sensors. We use three different attack strategies. First, assuming that the attacker does not have any knowledge about the targeted sensor, we choose the constant 127. This number is small enough to fit in 1 byte (signed int) which ensures that most industrial protocols will deliver the malicious value

---

[1] Simulation and results available at https://gitlab.com/eastman_tennessee/larsson.

[2] Simulation and results available at https://gitlab.com/eastman_tennessee/luyben.

in a single packet, thus, executing a stealthy attack. For the second and third attack strategies, we assume that the attacker knows historic sensor readings, in which case we choose the minimum and maximum values observed per sensor. Although this additional knowledge is not required by our approach, we use these attack strategies to compare our results with previous works.

After the experimental setup has been defined, we execute the attacks against each sensor, one at a time, and record its SDT (or 72 h if no shutdown happens). If a simulation finishes at 72 h, we assume that the attack does not cause a shutdown. The experiment finishes when all sensors used by the control strategy have been attacked. We rank the targets according to their SDT to identify the fastest SDT in the experiment and the sensor that causes it. We refer to them as the *optimal SDT* and the *optimal target*, respectively. In general, we refer to the top-3 fastest attacks as *near-optimal attacks*.

To put our results in perspective, we compare the chances of achieving a near-optimal attack of an attacker using our approach (with the capabilities described in Sect. 3.2) and an attacker who picks, uniformly at random, one sensor to target (we assume that both attackers use the same attack strategy). Hereafter, we refer to the latter simply as the *random attacker*.

Control Strategy #1. The control strategy by Larsson et al. [17], uses only 9 actuators and 16 sensors out of the 12 actuators and 41 sensors available in the TEP. Additionally, there are 20 control functions, 9 static setpoints, and 12 calculated setpoints. The CCL graph of this control strategy is comprised of 66 nodes divided in 3 subgraphs. An illustration of the graph is shown in Fig. 5.

We use the queries detailed in Sect. 4 to identify potential targets. First, we compute the in- and out-degree centrality for all the sensors, setpoints, and actuators. Then, we run the pattern matching queries that aim at finding global variables and multi-purpose variables. The first query identifies the calculated setpoint number 12 (located in the middle of the largest subgraph) as a *global variable*. Although there are 16 sensors used in this control strategy, the post-processing phase identifies that only one of them has a path to the global variable: *sensor 17* (i.e., $R_1 = \{17\}$). Such a path can be visually confirmed following the direction of the edges in Fig. 5. No *multi-purpose variables* are identified in this control strategy (i.e., $R_2 = \emptyset$) Thus, the final target set $T = \{17\}$ contains only one sensor, which makes the target selection easier for a single-shot attack.

We hypothesize that sensor 17 is a near-optimal target for control strategy #1. To test our hypothesis we execute 28 experiments comprised of 448 individual simulations that account for 11,047.465 simulated hours (∼1.26 years). For the first two experiments we use the constant value attack strategy. In one of the experiments we set ideal environmental conditions (no disturbance) and in the other experiment we enable disturbance #8. We choose disturbance #8 because previous works have used exclusively this disturbance for their experiments. The results of the first two experiments are shown in Table 2. Regardless of the environmental conditions, the results are consistent in the top half of the table with greater variations in the bottom half. In these two experimental settings, a *random attacker* would have 1/16 chances (≈6%) of choosing sensor 40 (which does not cause a shutdown), and 3/16 ($\approx$18%) of choosing a near-optimal target. Considering only the 15 sensors that do cause a shutdown, a *random attacker* would achieve an average SDT of 2.66 h without disturbance and 2.52 h under disturbance #8. On the other hand, an attacker using our approach has to choose one sensor from $T = \{17\}$, thus, ensuring 100% chance of finding a near-optimal target with a SDT of 0.192 h in both cases ($\approx$11 min) and a difference of about 5 min behind the optimal target (sensor 9 with SDT of 0.101 h.).

Previous works have used the minimum and maximum value attack strategies against this control strategy. Unlike previous works that have used only one environmental condition to execute their experiments (disturbance #8), we execute our experiments under 13 different environmental conditions (including disturbance #8) to gather data from more diverse scenarios and gain more confidence in our results. Disturbance #6 is excluded because it is not supported by this particular control strategy, which means that a shutdown happens even without any attacks [17]. Due to space constraints, we summarize our results per attack strategy, which shows the average SDT and standard deviation for each sensor among all the simulations. The results, detailed in Tables 3 and 4, show that sensor 17 is a near-optimal target with an average SDT of 1.21 h and 1.07 h, respectively. For the minimum value attack strategy, a random attacker would achieve an average SDT of 24.23 h, whereas in the maximum value attack strategy an average SDT of 24.87 (excluding sensor 1). Finally, for both the minimum and maximum attack strategies, sensor 17 is ranked in the second position. This confirms that sensor 17 is a near-optimal target not only during specific plant conditions, but in many different situations.

Table 2. Experiments using the constant value attack strategy under two different environmental conditions. Sensor 17, identified as a near-optimal target, is highlighted.

No disturbance		Disturbance 8	
Sensor	SDT (h) ▲	Sensor	SDT (h) ▲
9	0.101	9	0.101
14	0.181	14	1.181
17	0.192	17	0.192
11	0.426	11	0.427
8	0.431	8	0.430
4	0.526	4	0.526
31	0.557	31	0.560
12	0.569	12	0.567
3	1.604	3	1.607
2	1.757	2	1.614
15	2.126	15	2.052
1	7.335	5	5.644
5	7.609	7	6.971
10	8.182	10	7.249
7	8.297	1	9.691
40	72 (no shutdown)	40	72 (no shutdown)

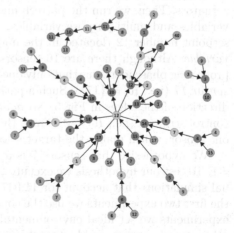

Fig. 5. CCL graph of control strategy #1. The color of each node represents its type, as described in Fig. 2. (Color figure online)

Table 3. Summary of experiments considering the minimum value attack strategy under 13 different environmental conditions. Sensor 17, identified as a near-optimal target, is highlighted.

Sensor	Avg. SDT (h) ▲	Std. Deviation
4	0.79	0.67
17	1.21	0.76
9	2.06	0.73
8	2.66	0.41
3	4.11	0.35
2	4.55	0.75
7	7.70	2.19
12	7.97	2.25
14	8.94	2.39
15	11.18	3.96
5	14.53	17.49
31	55.15	27.74
11	66.64	19.31
40	66.69	19.14
10	66.73	19.02
1	66.78	18.82

Table 4. Summary of experiments considering the maximum value attack strategy under 13 different environmental conditions. Sensor 17, identified as a near-optimal target, is highlighted.

Sensor	Avg. SDT (h) ▲	Std. Deviation
9	0.57	0.19
17	1.07	0.14
4	1.27	0.21
3	2.60	0.42
8	2.83	0.46
2	3.32	0.66
12	5.44	1.36
14	8.79	2.45
15	11.10	4.36
5	12.64	17.91
31	56.78	27.62
11	66.59	19.50
10	66.64	19.34
40	66.70	19.10
7	66.73	19.00
1	72 (no shutdown)	0.00

Control Strategy #2. The second control strategy, proposed by Luyben et al. [20], uses 10 sensors and 10 actuators from those available in the plant. This control strategy requires 13 static setpoints, 13 control functions, and 1 calculated setpoint. In total, the CCL graph is comprised of 47 nodes.

As in the previous control strategy, we use the queries detailed in Sect. 4 to identify sensor targets, starting with the computation of the in- and out-degree centrality for all the sensors, setpoints, and actuators. The query regarding global variables identifies sensors 8, 12, and 15 (i.e., $R_1 = \{8, 12, 15\}$). The query regarding multi-purpose variables identifies actuators 1, 2, 7, and 11. The post-processing phase looks for sensor nodes that have a path to these actuators and identifies sensors 8, 12, 15, and 29 (i.e., $R_2 = \{8, 12, 15, 29\}$). As described in Sect. 3.4, the final targets subset T contains those sensors identified by most weakness-related patterns. In this particular case, $T = \{8, 12, 15\}$ because these sensors occur in both R_1 and R_2. Finally, the attacker selects one target $t \in T$ at random.

We hypothesize that sensors 8, 12, and 15 are near-optimal targets against control strategy #2. To test our hypotheses we execute 30 experiments comprised of 300 individual simulations that account for 11,079.163 simulated hours (~1.26 years). As in the previous control strategy, we begin with two experiments using the constant value attack strategy under two different environmental conditions. The first experiment without any disturbance and the second experiment under disturbance #8. The results of the first two experiments, detailed in Table 5, show no significant differences between both plant conditions. In these environmental conditions, the *random attacker* has a 30% chance of choosing a near-optimal target (3 out of 10 sensors), and the same chances of choosing a sensor that do not cause a shutdown. On the other hand, an attacker using our approach has a 66% chance of finding a near-optimal target (2 out of 3 sensors) since sensors 12 and 15 are near-optimal but not sensor 8. The *random attacker* can achieve an average SDT of 1.59 h without disturbance and 1.51 h under disturbance #8 (excluding the 3 sensors that do not cause a shutdown). On the other hand, an attacker using our approach achieves an average SDT of about 0.50 h in both cases; more than 1 h faster (Fig. 6).

As for control strategy #1, we execute additional experiments using the minimum and maximum attack strategies. This time we use all disturbances in the range [1–13] because this control strategy is able to handle all of them. Thus, we execute two attack strategies over 14 environmental conditions (no disturbance + 13 disturbances), which adds up to 28 additional experiments. Again, due to space constraints, we summarize our results per attack strategy. Tables 6 and 7 show the average SDT and standard deviation for each sensor attack throughout all the simulations. As in the first two experiments, for the minimum and maximum attacks, the *random attacker* has 30% chance to find a near-optimal target but also 30% chance of finding a target that does not cause a shutdown. For our attacker, however, the chances of finding a near-optimal target differ per attack strategy. The minimum value attack gives our attacker only 1 out of 3 chances of finding the near-optimal sensor 15 (33%); a marginal benefit with respect to the *random attacker*. However, our attacker does not have the 30% risk of a no-shutdown attack. After excluding the 3

Table 5. Experiments using the constant value attack strategy under two different environmental conditions. The 3 sensors identified as near-optimal targets are highlighted.

No disturbance		Disturbance 8	
Sensor	SDT (h) ▲	Sensor	SDT (h) ▲
7	0.144	7	0.144
15	0.161	15	0.161
12	0.311	12	0.311
9	0.440	9	0.440
8	1.031	8	1.032
11	2.486	11	2.647
23	6.549	23	5.844
18	72 (no shutdown)	18	72 (no shutdown)
29	72 (no shutdown)	29	72 (no shutdown)
30	72 (no shutdown)	30	72 (no shutdown)

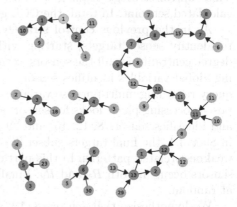

Fig. 6. CCL graph of control strategy #2. The color of each node represents its type, as described in Fig. 2. (Color figure online)

Table 6. Summary of experiments considering the minimum value attack strategy under 14 different environmental conditions. The 3 sensors identified as near-optimal targets are highlighted.

Sensor Id.	Avg. SDT (h) ▲	Std. Deviation
15	0.65	0.20
9	1.28	0.51
7	1.72	0.79
12	4.25	1.72
8	8.29	1.98
23	63.03	22.83
30	66.01	16.82
29	72 (no shutdown)	0.00
11	72 (no shutdown)	0.00
18	72 (no shutdown)	0.00

Table 7. Summary of experiments considering the maximum value attack strategy under 14 different environmental conditions. The 3 sensors identified as near-optimal targets are highlighted.

Sensor Id.	Avg SDT (h) ▲	Std. Deviation
12	0.69	0.16
15	0.70	0.07
9	1.09	0.40
8	4.48	0.55
23	52.01	29.46
7	55.30	27.60
29	67.46	16.97
30	72 (no shutdown)	0.00
11	72 (no shutdown)	0.00
18	72 (no shutdown)	0.00

sensors that do not cause a shutdown, the average SDT of the *random attacker* is 20.75 h; significantly larger than the average SDT of 4.4 h for our attacker. For the maximum value attack, our attacker has 2 out of 3 chances of picking a near-optimal target After excluding the 3 sensors that do not cause a shutdown, the average SDT of the *random attacker* is 25.96 h. On the contrary, an attacker using our approach achieves an average SDT of 1.96 h.

6   Discussion

CCL Graphs. The first challenge faced by graph-based studies is the creation of the graph itself. There are different possibilities to create CCL graphs like those used in this work. Piping and Instrumentation Diagrams (P&IDs) are a suitable alternative because ICS documentation can be obtained through a variety of illegal means (e.g., phishing, social engineering, bribes) or simply downloaded from public repositories [14]. The creation of a CCL graph from a P&ID could even be automated using diagram digitization techniques such as [5].

Another way to create CCL graphs leverages the rich semantics of some industrial communication protocols. A concrete example is the BACnet protocol (ISO 16484-5), commonly used to automate diverse services in hospitals, airports, and other buildings [4]. In these environments, the CCL programming pattern is extensively used. For that reason, the BACnet protocol implements an application layer object called *Loop*, which eases the implementation of CCLs. This object contains properties that point to other BACnet objects abstracting CCL components such as sensors, setpoints, and actuators. Since BACnet objects are regularly exchanged through the network, it is possible to create CCL graphs in a fully automated way simply by sniffing the traffic [11]. We used this method to create the CCL graph of a real BACnet system comprised of more that 20 buildings located at the University of Twente. We can confirm that this method is capable of creating large CCL graphs (4,771 nodes) just by passively listening the network traffic. In general, we note similar structures in the BACnet graphs and the TEP graphs, which suggests the possibility to apply the proposed approach to other systems besides ICSs.

Additional CWE Weaknesses. To describe the proposed approach, we elaborate on two weaknesses from Mitre's CWE database, in particular, global variables (CWE-1108) and multi-purpose variables (CWE-1109) [22]. We emphasize these two because they proved particularly useful to find weaknesses in both TEP implementations analyzed in our evaluation. Although it is not our goal to provide an exhaustive list of software weaknesses that can be mapped to ICSs, here we discuss additional weaknesses that could be observed in CCL graphs.

Circular dependencies (CWE-1047) happen when *"[t]he software contains modules in which one module has references that cycle back to itself."* [22]. In ICSs, circular dependencies can occur, for example, through control functions that write their output to a calculated setpoint node that, in turn, is the input of another control function node and so on, until at some point the sequence of references return to the initial node. Although none of the CCL graphs analyzed showed a circular dependency pattern, we found a similar structure in the BACnet system previously discussed.

Deep nesting (CWE-1124) manifests in software that *"contains a callable or other code grouping in which the nesting/branching is too deep."* [22]. The software implementation of ICSs might contain a deep nesting weakness whenever a long sequence of closed control loops are chained together. For example, several cascade controllers concatenated. In this setting, the precise definition of 'long sequence' is determined by a context dependent threshold.

Countermeasures. The most promising way to thwart our described approach to identify near-optimal single-shot attacks would be by preventing the attacker's ability to gain knowledge of the CCL graph representation of the targeted infrastructure in the first place. However for many ICSs, P&IDs are publicly available, which an attacker can use to generate a corresponding CCL graph as we described before. Therefore, it would be necessary to keep such P&IDs secret and to protect them from being leaked to attackers. We stress here that further protective measures might be needed to prevent an attacker from being able to generate the CCL graph through possibly other information such as, in the case of building automation systems, using the BACnet protocol, for which eavesdropping on the traffic is already sufficient to automatically generate CCL graphs [11].

Our approach relies on identifying specific weakness patterns in the CCL graph which can be matched with well-known software weaknesses in the IT domain (e.g., via Mitre's CWE database). Therefore, if a CCL graph does not contain any of these matching weaknesses, then our approach would fail in identifying near-optimal single-shot attacks with a better probability than by simply picking any sensor from the set of all sensors at random. This means that if an attacker cannot be prevented from creating the CCL graph, then another way to thwart our method would be by ensuring that the CCL graph contains no weakness patterns. One option to achieve this would be by performing a re-engineering on the software controlling the ICS (as we saw, several control strategies are possible for ICSs such as the TEP). However, designing security-aware control strategies that also meet operational and economic requirements is cumbersome [15] and completely avoiding certain weakness patterns could even be impossible in certain settings.

If all of the above fails and the attacker is able to perform the identified near-optimal single-shot attack, then an operator can try to detect the attack as soon as possible by using monitoring systems to detect manipulated sensor values [7]. However, the detection time of such systems can be in the order of hours, which would be too slow to detect near-optimal attacks which, depending on the concrete case, can potentially bring down the ICS within minutes. An idea to improve the detection would be to tighten the monitoring specifically at those components in the ICS that our CCL-graph based attack method matches with known software weaknesses.

7   Related Work

Several researchers have analyzed different security aspects of the TEP. Here we focus in a subset of those works that have studied diverse attacks against the TEP. In [15], the goal was to get insights on the resilience of the physical process under attack. Similar to our attacker model, they focused on compromising sensors and identifying those in best capacity to cause a shutdown on the targeted infrastructure. In this particular case, the targeted infrastructure was Larsson's implementation of the TEP, described in our evaluation as control strategy #1. Aligned with our results, they found out that sensors 4, 9, and 17 are the best targets under the minimum and maximum value attack strategies. However, they reached that conclusion by using much more knowledge than our approach, i.c., a fully-fledged simulation of the targeted infrastructure. For an attacker to be able to build an accurate simulation of the targeted infrastructure, he would need access to at least, full PLC(s) configuration, P&IDs, and documentation about the system's constraints.

In another work, the goal was to find out the right time to launch an attack on individual sensor signals to cause a shutdown of the targeted infrastructure [16]. In this case, again, the target was Larsson's implementation of the TEP. The authors focused on DoS attacks on sensor signals, which forces control functions to use a stale value from the sensor. Under the assumption that launching sensor attacks at minimum or maximum peaks is the fastest way to cause a shutdown of the plant, the goal was to identify such peaks in real time. They approached this challenge using the Best Choice Problem (BCP) methodological framework. Using different learning windows, they identified sensors 4, 9, and 17 as the best candidate targets (i.e., fastest SDT). To execute this approach a potential attacker might need at least network traffic access, a notion about the physical process and its potential disturbances (e.g., from P&IDs), and ideally, some historic data. Moreover, this approach has three main disadvantages besides the increased attacker knowledge about the plant. First, it is focused on identifying the right time to launch an attack but does not indicate the optimal target. Launching an attack on the wrong target might not cause any impact whatsoever on the plant. Only after executing attacks on all sensors it becomes clear which of them are optimal, which is unrealistic. Second, the time to attack is lengthy (this includes the learning window and the selection of the moment to launch the attack), ranging from 9.61 h to 27.17 h in their experiments. Third, in some circumstances their approach might not reach a conclusion, in which case the attacker "has to choose a clearly suboptimal candidate (last sample in the attack window) or decide to not launch an attack." [16].

The works in [7] and [13], analyze diverse attacks against a simplified version of the TEP. Both works incorporate detailed knowledge from the process dynamics to execute optimal attacks. An attacker leveraging the techniques proposed in these 2 works would require at least access to the PLC(s) configuration, historic data, and documentation about the system's constraints. We deem the simplified version of the TEP so small that we use it only in our motivating example (Sect. 3.5). However, as we showed, our approach is also applicable to this plant and our results match the results obtained by previous works, but using limited knowledge.

8   Conclusion

In this work, we investigated if constrained attackers without detailed system knowledge and simulators can identify near-optimal attacks. In contrast to attacks in prior work (that require precise algorithms, operating parameters, process models or simulators), in our approach the attacker only requires abstract knowledge on general information flow in the plant. Based on that information, we construct a CCL graph, and apply graph-based pattern matching based on several weakness patterns from the CWE database.

Our resulting approach provides us with one (or more) sensors to attack. Experimentally, we applied and validated our approach on two use cases, and demonstrated that the approach successfully generates single-shot attacks, i.e., near-optimal attacks that are reliably shutting down a system on the first try.

Our positive results in finding near-optimal targets with limited knowledge suggest that the difficulty of preparing ICS attacks is lower than previously thought. We not only showed that the graph analysis can be automated, but that the graph creation can be automated too (e.g., using BACnet network traffic). This significantly lowers the bar for ICS attacks and calls for a reassessment of the actual security risks in ICSs.

References

1. Abbasi, A., Hashemi, M.: Ghost in the PLC designing an undetectable programmable logic controller rootkit via pin control attack. Black Hat Europe **2016**, 1–35 (2016)
2. Adepu, S., Mathur, A.: Distributed detection of single-stage multipoint cyber attacks in a water treatment plant. In: AsiaCCS (2016)
3. Ahmed, C.M., Zhou, J., Mathur, A.P.: Noise matters: using sensor and process noise fingerprint to detect stealthy cyber attacks and authenticate sensors in CPS. In: ACSAC (2018)
4. ANSI/ASHRAE STANDARD 135–2016: A data communication protocol for building automation and control networks (2016)
5. Arroyo, E., Fay, A., Hoernicke, M.: A method of digitalizing engineering documents (2016)
6. Assante, M.J., Lee, R.M.: The industrial control system cyber kill chain, vol. 1. SANS Institute InfoSec Reading Room (2015)
7. Cárdenas, A.A., Amin, S., Lin, Z.S., Huang, Y.L., Huang, C.Y., Sastry, S.: Attacks against process control systems: risk assessment, detection, and response. In: AsiaCCS, pp. 355–366. ACM (2011)
8. Chen, Y., Poskitt, C.M., Sun, J., Adepu, S., Zhang, F.: Learning-guided network fuzzing for testing cyber-physical system defences. In: ASE (2019)
9. Chen, Y., Xuan, B., Poskitt, C.M., Sun, J., Zhang, F.: Active fuzzing for testing and securing cyber-physical systems. In: ISSTA (2020)
10. Downs, J.J., Vogel, E.F.: A plant-wide industrial process control problem. Comput. Chem. Eng. **17**(3), 245–255 (1993)
11. Esquivel-Vargas, H., Caselli, M., Peter, A.: BACgraph: automatic extraction of object relationships in the BACnet protocol. In: DSN (Industry Track). IEEE (2021)
12. Green, B., Krotofil, M., Abbasi, A.: On the significance of process comprehension for conducting targeted ICS attacks. In: CPS-SPC. ACM (2017)
13. Huang, Y., Cárdenas, A.A., Amin, S., Lin, Z., Tsai, H., Sastry, S.: Understanding the physical and economic consequences of attacks on control systems. Int. J. Crit. Infrastruct. Prot. **2**(3), 73–83 (2009). https://doi.org/10.1016/j.ijcip.2009.06.001
14. Konstantinou, C., Sazos, M., Maniatakos, M.: Attacking the smart grid using public information. In: LATS, pp. 105–110. IEEE (2016). https://doi.org/10.1109/LATW.2016.7483348
15. Krotofil, M., Cárdenas, A.A.: Resilience of process control systems to cyber-physical attacks. In: Riis Nielson, H., Gollmann, D. (eds.) NordSec 2013. LNCS, vol. 8208, pp. 166–182. Springer, Heidelberg (2013). https://doi.org/10.1007/978-3-642-41488-6_12
16. Krotofil, M., Cárdenas, A.A., Manning, B., Larsen, J.: CPS: driving cyber-physical systems to unsafe operating conditions by timing DoS attacks on sensor signals. In: ACSAC, pp. 146–155. ACM (2014). https://doi.org/10.1145/2664243.2664290
17. Larsson, T., Hestetun, K., Hovland, E., Skogestad, S.: Self-optimizing control of a large-scale plant: the Tennessee Eastman process. Ind. Eng. Chem. Res. **40**(22), 4889–4901 (2001)
18. Lee, R.M., Assante, M.J., Conway, T.: Analysis of the cyber attack on the ukrainian power grid table of contents (2016). https://media.kasperskycontenthub.com/wp-content/uploads/sites/43/2016/05/20081514/E-ISAC_SANS_Ukraine_DUC_5.pdf

19. Lin, Q., Adepu, S., Verwer, S., Mathur, A.: TABOR: a graphical model-based approach for anomaly detection in industrial control systems. In: AsiaCCS (2018)
20. Luyben, W.L., Tyréus, B.D., Luyben, M.L.: Plantwide Process Control. McGraw-Hill, New York (1999)
21. Lyman, P.R.: Plant-wide control structures for the Tennessee Eastman process. Master's thesis, Lehigh University (1992)
22. Mitre: Common Weakness Enumeration: A Community-Developed List of Software & Hardware Weakness Types (2020). https://cwe.mitre.org/. Accessed 08 Sept 2020
23. Mitre: ATT&CK® for Industrial Control Systems (2021). https://collaborate.mitre.org/attackics/. Accessed 04 Jan 2021
24. Neo4j: Neo4j Graph Platform - The Leader in Graph Databases (2021). https://neo4j.com/. Accessed 09 Jan 2021
25. Ricker, N.L.: Model predictive control of a continuous, nonlinear, two-phase reactor. J. Process Control 3(2), 109–123 (1993)
26. Ricker, N.L.: Decentralized control of the Tennessee Eastman challenge process. J. Process Control 6(4), 205–221 (1996)
27. Ricker, N.L.: Tennessee Eastman Challenge archive (2020). https://depts.washington.edu/control/LARRY/TE/download.html. Accessed 25 July 2020
28. Sarkar, E., Benkraouda, H., Maniatakos, M.: I came, I saw, I hacked: automated generation of process-independent attacks for industrial control systems. In: AsiaCCS. ACM (2020)
29. Sharma, K.: Overview of Industrial Process Automation. Elsevier, Amsterdam (2016)
30. Tu, Y., Rampazzi, S., Hao, B., Rodriguez, A., Fu, K., Hei, X.: Trick or heat?: manipulating critical temperature-based control systems using rectification attacks. In: CCS, pp. 2301–2315. ACM (2019). https://doi.org/10.1145/3319535.3354195
31. Urbina, D.I., Giraldo, J.A., Tippenhauer, N.O., Cárdenas, A.A.: Attacking fieldbus communications in ICS: applications to the swat testbed. In: SG-CRC. IOS Press (2016)
32. Wade, H.L.: Basic and Advanced Regulatory Control - System Design and Application, 3rd edn. ISA (2017)

RSA Key Recovery from Digit Equivalence Information

Chitchanok Chuengsatiansup[1(✉)], Andrew Feutrill[1,2],
Rui Qi Sim[1], and Yuval Yarom[1]

[1] The University of Adelaide, Adelaide, Australia
chitchanok.chuengsatiansup@adelaide.edu.au

[2] CSIRO, Data61, Sydney, Australia

Abstract. The seminal work of Heninger and Shacham (Crypto 2009) demonstrated a method for reconstructing secret RSA keys from partial information of the key components. In this paper we further investigate this approach but apply it to a different context that appears in some side-channel attacks. We assume a fixed-window exponentiation algorithm that leaks the *equivalence* between digits, without leaking the value of the digits themselves.

We explain how to exploit the side-channel information with the Heninger-Shacham algorithm. To analyse the complexity of the approach, we model the attack as a Markov process and experimentally validate the accuracy of the model. Our model shows that the attack is feasible in the commonly used case where the window size is 5.

1 Introduction

One of the roles of a cryptographer is to ensure that implementations of cryptographic primitives are secure. In recent decades, side-channel attacks have been identified as a major threat to the security of cryptographic implementations. These attacks observe the effects that executing implementation of a cryptographic primitive has on the environment in which it executes. Such effects include the power the device consumes [18,19], its electromagnetic emissions [10,32], timing [1,5,29], micro-architectural components [11,23], and even acoustic and photonic emanations [12,20]. By measuring these effects, an attacker can obtain information on the internal state of the cryptographic algorithm, which can lead to compromising the security of the primitive.

In many cases, there is a gap between the information obtained through the side channel and secret information, such as plaintexts or keys, which the attacker may wish to recover [8]. Techniques to bridge this gap have been developed for multiple cryptographic schemes [3,6,7,16,24,25].

For RSA [33], in many cases the side-channel information provides the private key directly, requiring no further analysis [18,31,35]. When only partial information on the private key is available, there are two main approaches for key recovery. The Coppersmith method factors the RSA public modulus $N = pq$ given

© Springer Nature Switzerland AG 2022
G. Ateniese and D. Venturi (Eds.): ACNS 2022, LNCS 13269, pp. 193–211, 2022.
https://doi.org/10.1007/978-3-031-09234-3_10

enough consecutive bits of the private prime p [7]. The Heninger-Shacham (HS) algorithm [16] exploits algebraic relationships among the two private primes p and q, the private exponent d, and the two partial private exponents d_p and d_q, which are used in some implementations of RSA. Past works have used the HS algorithm to correct errors when the attacker obtains a degraded version of the key [15,16,30], to correct errors in side-channel information [15,17,21,26–28,30], and to recover information that is not obtained through the side channel [2,4,36].

In this work we consider the case that an attacker obtains knowledge of *digit equivalence* of the partial private exponents d_p and d_q. Specifically, we assume that the exponents are represented as digits in radix 2^ω and that the attacker can find which digits of the representation are the same without knowing the values of the digits themselves. Past works showed that such information can be obtained through side-channel attacks on fixed-window implementations [13] and that similar information can be obtained for sliding window implementations [17,22,34].

A naive approach for recovering the key from the digit equivalence information is to brute force the values of each of the 2^ω digits. However, such approach requires testing $2^\omega!$ combinations, or an expected complexity of $2^\omega!/2$. This complexity requires significant resources even for $\omega = 4$ and is prohibitive for the commonly used case of $\omega = 5$. Past works overcome this limitation by relying on additional information from the precomputation stage of the fixed-window and sliding window algorithms. Since hardening modular exponentiation against side-channel attacks requires additional resources, it may be tempting to harden the precomputation stage and rely on the complexity of recovering the key from the digit equivalence for side-channel protection.

Our Contribution

In this work we show how to apply the HS algorithm to the problem of recovering RSA private keys given digit equivalence. Specifically, we show how to use guesses for low significant digits to prune the search space of the HS algorithm when processing higher significant digits.

To analyse the complexity of our algorithm, we develop a theoretical model based on Markov chains. We use the model to calculate the probability of success and the number of operations required to recover the RSA key. Using this model we show that for the case of $\omega = 4$, more than 99% of the keys can be broken with a search space of size 2^{25}, well within the means of modestly resourced adversaries. For the common case of $\omega = 5$, the model predicts that 65% of the keys can be broken with a search space of 2^{40}, which is within the means of well resources adversaries.

We complement the theoretical analysis with concrete experiments, applying our algorithm to randomly generated RSA-2048 keys. We find that the model is highly accurate, correctly predicting the success and complexity of the attack. Specifically, for the case of $\omega = 4$, we can break 987 out of the 1000 keys we experiment, with a search space of 2^{25}.

2   Background

2.1   RSA

RSA [33] is a public key system that can be used for encryptions and for digital signatures. To generate an RSA key, Alice picks two random primes, p and q. The public key is (N, e), where $N = pq$, and e is chosen such that it is co-prime with $\varphi(N) = (p-1)(q-1)$. The private key is (p, q, d) where $d = e^{-1} \bmod \varphi(N)$. Most modern implementations use $e = 65537 = 2^{16} + 1$, and choose p and q to match the requirement.

We use $n = \lfloor \log_2 N \rfloor + 1$ to denote the bit length of the public modulus N. We further assume that the bit length of p and q is $n/2$.

To encrypt a message m, Bob calculates $c = m^e \bmod N$. To decrypt, Alice calculates $m = c^d \bmod N$. Signing a message m is done by calculating $s = m^d \bmod N$, and the signature is verified by testing that $m = s^e \bmod N$.

CRT-RSA. Alice can reduce the complexity of the private key operations using the Chinese Remainder Theorem (CRT). Specifically, Alice precomputes the CRT-RSA private key $(p, q, d, d_p, d_q, q_{inv})$, where $d_p = d \bmod (p-1)$, $d_q = d \bmod (q-1)$, and $q_{inv} = q^{-1} \bmod p$. To calculate $c^d \bmod N$, Alice then computes:

$$m_p = m^{d_p} \bmod p$$
$$m_q = m^{d_q} \bmod q$$
$$h = q_{inv}(m_p - m_q) \bmod p$$
$$m = m_q + hq.$$

2.2   Fixed-Window Exponentiation

The fixed-window exponentiation algorithm, shown in Algorithm 1, calculates $B^E \bmod M$. The algorithm, parameterised by a window size ω, represents the exponent E as a number in radix 2^ω. We use the notation $E[\![i]\!]$ to refer to the ith digit of E. That is, E is represented as a sequence of digits $0 \le E[\![i]\!] < 2^\omega$, such that $E = \sum E[\![i]\!]2^{\omega i}$.

To perform the exponentiation, the algorithm first precomputes 2^ω values $B_i = B^i \bmod M$. It then initialises an intermediate result r to 1 and proceeds to scan the exponent E digit by digit from the most significant to the least significant. For each digit $E[\![i]\!]$, the algorithm raises r to the power of 2^ω modulo M using squaring ω times, each time reducing the result modulo M. It then multiplies the result by the precomputed value $B_{E[\![i]\!]} = B^{E[\![i]\!]} \bmod M$, again reducing modulo M. At the end of the algorithm we have $r = B^{\sum E[\![i]\!]2^{\omega i}} \bmod M = B^E \bmod M$.

2.3   Attacks on Fixed-Window Exponentiation

While the fixed-window algorithm is fairly regular and does not use secret-dependent control flow, implementations may still leak information about the

---

Algorithm 1: Fixed-window exponentiation

---

input : window size ω, base B, modulo M,
         exponent $E = \sum E[\![i]\!]2^{\omega i}$ with $0 \le E[\![i]\!] < 2^{\omega}$.
output: B^E mod M

//*Precomputation*
$B_0 \leftarrow 1$
for j *from* 1 *to* $2^{\omega} - 1$ **do**
  | $B_j \leftarrow B_{j-1} \cdot B$ mod M
end

//*Exponentiation*
$r \leftarrow 1$
for i *from* $|E| - 1$ *downto* 0 **do**
  for j *from* 1 *to* ω **do**
    | $r \leftarrow r^2$ mod M
  end
  $r \leftarrow r \cdot B_{E[\![i]\!]}$ mod M
end
return r

---

digit being processed in each iteration. In some cases, the attacker can recover (some of) the bits of each digit $E[\![i]\!]$ [36]. However, a common leakage identifies digit equivalence, i.e. detecting when two digits $E[\![i]\!]$ and $E[\![j]\!]$ are the same without identifying the digits themselves [13,34]. Specifically, Genkin et al. [13] uses a cache attack [22] to detect victim access patterns to the same digit, and Walter [34] exploits a differential power analysis [19] to identify repeating patterns in power traces. Several works recover similar information from sliding window implementations of modular exponentiation [17,22]. All these works exploit leakage during the precomputation phase to recover the key. Specifically, when computing B_{i+1}, Algorithm 1 uses B_i. The order of precomputation is known, thus an attacker that identifies the use of B_i in the exponentiation phase can tie to its use in the precomputation phase and recover the digit value.

2.4 The Heninger-Shacham Algorithm

The Heninger-Shacham (HS) algorithm [16] uses a branch-and-prune approach for recovering an RSA private key from partial information on the bits of the components of the private key. Specifically, let (N, e) be an RSA public key and (p, q, d, d_p, d_q) be components of the corresponding private key, such that $N = pq$ is an n-bit RSA modulus with p and q primes, $e = 2^{16} + 1$ is the public exponent, $d = e^{-1}$ mod $(p - 1)(q - 1)$ is the private exponent, and $d_p = d$ mod $p - 1$, $d_q = d$ mod $q - 1$ are the CRT-RSA private exponents.

As Heninger and Shacham [16] note, there exist k, k_p, and k_q with $0 < k < e$ such that

$$N = pq$$
$$ed = k(N - p - q + 1) + 1$$
$$ed_p = k_p(p - 1) + 1$$
$$ed_q = k_q(q - 1) + 1.$$

Moreover, Inci et al. [17] show that $0 < k_p, k_q < e$ and that given k_p we can find k_q and vice versa.

Let $\tau(x)$ be the exponent of the largest power of two that divides x. We note that because e is odd, $\tau(ed) = \tau(d)$, $\tau(ed_p) = \tau(d_p)$, and $\tau(ed_q) = \tau(d_q)$. Heninger and Shacham [16] first show how to find $d \bmod 2^{\tau(k)+2}$, $d_p \bmod 2^{\tau(k_p)+1}$, and $d_q \bmod 2^{\tau(k_q)+1}$. They then define a *slice* of the private key as

$$\text{slice}(i) = (p[i], q[i], d[i + \tau(k)], d_p[i + \tau(k_p)], d_q[i + \tau(k_q)]).$$

where i indicates the bit index starting from the least significant bit. Therefore $p[i]$ is the ith bit of p and $p[0]$ refers to the least significant bit of p. Finally, they show that if we have a partial solution (p', q', d', d'_p, d'_q) for $\text{slice}(0)$ to $\text{slice}(i-1)$, the following four congruences hold.

$$p[i] + q[i] = (N - p'q')[i] \pmod 2 \tag{1}$$
$$d[i + \tau(k)] + p[i] + q[i] = (k(N+1) + 1 - k(p' + q') - ed')[i + \tau(k)] \pmod 2 \tag{2}$$
$$d_p[i + \tau(k_p)] + p[i] = (k_p(p' - 1) + 1 - ed'_p)[i + \tau(k_p)] \pmod 2 \tag{3}$$
$$d_q[i + \tau(k_q)] + q[i] = (k_q(q' - 1) + 1 - ed'_q)[i + \tau(k_q)] \pmod 2 \tag{4}$$

Note that because p and q are primes and by the definition of $\tau(\cdot)$, we have that $\text{slice}(0) = (1, 1, 1, 1, 1)$.

The HS algorithm has been proposed in the context of cold boot attacks [14], where most of the errors are that bits containing 1 may decay into 0. Further work has investigated the HS algorithm with unbalanced bidirectional errors [15, 30]. The HS algorithm has been further applied in the context of side-channel attacks which can have noisy measurements [21, 26–28]. The HS algorithm can be used to complete partial information obtained through cache attacks [2, 4, 36]

2.5   Markov Chains

This section introduces terminologies and relevant facts that we use in our analysis. We start with the definition of a Markov chain.

Definition 1. *A discrete-time stochastic process $\{X_n\}_{n \in \mathbb{Z}^+}$ on a countable state space Ω is called a Markov chain if for every n*

$$Pr(X_n = x_n | X_{n-1} = x_{n-1}, \dots, X_1 = x_1) = Pr(X_n = x_n | X_{n-1} = x_{n-1}).$$

The intuition for the definition is that the history of a Markov chain is only considered through the current state, and the knowledge of the previous states has no impact on the movement to the next state.

An additional property that we use in the modelling is *time-homogeneity*. This refers to the fact that the probabilities of transitioning to the next state, with knowledge of the current state, do no change over time. That is,

$$Pr(X_{n+1} = j | X_n = i) = Pr(X_n = j | X_{n-1} = i).$$

Using the property of time-homogeneity, we then define the probabilities of transitioning between two states as

$$p_{ij} = Pr(X_n = j | X_{n-1} = i).$$

These can be generalised to the k-step transition probabilities by considering the probability of transitioning between states in k steps. That is,

$$p_{ij}^k = Pr(X_{n+k} = j | X_n = i).$$

The analysis of Markov chains is greatly simplified knowing these properties. For example, we create a matrix P of the transition probabilities of each of the possible transitions where each entry of the matrix $[P]_{i,j} = p_{ij}$. This forms a stochastic matrix, where each row sums to 1, since each state has its own probability distribution. The advantage of creating this matrix is that we can easily compute the k-step transition probabilities by taking powers of the matrix P [9, Theorem 1.1]. Then we have that the k-step transition probabilities can be calculated as

$$p_{ij}^k = [P^k]_{i,j}.$$

Therefore, describing a problem in this way enables us to convert a potentially computationally difficult problem of calculating the probabilities of moving between two states in k steps, from a combinatorial problem, whose complexity grows quickly in the number of steps, to a linear algebra problem of taking matrix powers.

3   Attacker Model

Recall that the aim is to recover the secret exponent E, where E represents d_p and d_q, used during the RSA exponentiation routine. The attacker knows that the victim performs the exponentiation using a fixed-window method whose width ω is publicly known.

We assume that the attacker can observe, via the side channel, the digit equivalence of the secret exponent. Note that the attacker does not know the values of those digits; the attacker only knows whether, for example, $E[\![i]\!]$ equals $E[\![i]\!]$ for $i \neq j$.

Figure 1 illustrates digit equivalence for $\omega = 4$. The attacker *does know* that $E[\![2]\!] = E[\![4]\!] = E[\![7]\!]$ but *does not know* that they are 1010. Similarly, the

···	1010	0111	0001	1010	1100	1010	1100	0111
	$E[\![7]\!]$	$E[\![6]\!]$	$E[\![5]\!]$	$E[\![4]\!]$	$E[\![3]\!]$	$E[\![2]\!]$	$E[\![1]\!]$	$E[\![0]\!]$

Fig. 1. A visualisation of digit equivalence for exponent E with $\omega = 4$.

attacker knows that $E[\![0]\!] = E[\![6]\!]$ but does not know their value. Moreover, the attacker also knows that $E[\![0]\!] \neq E[\![1]\!] \neq E[\![2]\!] \neq E[\![5]\!]$.

Continuing with this example, $\omega = 4$ has $2^\omega = 2^4 = 16$ possible different values of the digits. This means that the naive approach of determining the digits requires $16! \approx 2^{44}$. With well funded organisations, this attack is feasible. However, commonly used ω is usually larger than this.

Consider $\omega = 5$ as used in OpenSSL [36], there are a total of $2^5 = 32$ different digit values. The naive approach would require $32! \approx 2^{118}$, rendering this attack infeasible, even for well funded organisations such as the NSA.

4   Our Approach

We apply the HS algorithm with a branch-and-bound strategy together with pruning from our knowledge of digit equivalence. Recall that the HS algorithm reconstructs the CRT-RSA private components by looking at slices of the private key (p, q, d, d_p, d_q). At every slice(i), the algorithm builds the key by satisfying the four congruence relations described in Eqs. (1) to (4).

4.1   Algorithm Overview

In addition to the HS algorithm, we take advantage of side-channel information regarding digit equivalence. This allows us to further prune the solution space by removing any solutions that do not agree with our knowledge of digit equivalence. As a consequence, we significantly reduce the solution space and can reconstruct the key for larger window widths.

Our algorithm follows the HS algorithm and starts building the solution space from the least significant bit denoted by bit 0. When considering d_p and d_q (hence k_p and k_q), recall that slice(i) considers the bits $d_p[i + \tau(k_p)]$ and $d_q[i + \tau(k_q)]$. This results in two scenarios. One is where $\tau(k_p)$ and $\tau(k_q)$ are zero, which we denote as the *aligned case*. The other one is where $\tau(k_p)$ and $\tau(k_q)$ are not zero, which we denote as the *unaligned case*. We begin our analysis with the aligned case. The unaligned case is discussed in Sect. 4.4

4.2   Complexity Analysis of the Aligned Case

Assume the RSA fixed-window exponentiation uses a window width ω. This means that there are 2^ω different digits. Recall that we consider slice(i) and build bit i for p, q, d, d_p and d_q. Furthermore, recall that slice(0) is known. Because we assume $\tau(k_p) = \tau(k_q) = 0$, we know exactly one bit of the first (least significant) digit of each of d_p and d_q. Consequently, for the first digit, there remain $2^{\omega-1}$ possible partial solutions. Because we do not know any further information about the first digit, we cannot prune any possible solution at this step.

In the subsequent slices, there are two possibilities for pruning.

1. The first case is where the value of the current digit of d_p (or d_q) is equivalent to one of the previously observed digits. We can compare the current partial solution at each bit slice of the current digit and reject the solutions that do not match the bits of the equivalent digit seen previously.
2. The second case is where the value of the current digit is not equivalent to any of the previously observed digits. In this case, we can eliminate solutions where the value of its current digit equals a value of a previously seen digit.

In our algorithm, we model the search space as a search tree. The starting partial solution at slice(0) is at the root. Each level of the tree is a slice of the partial solution. The tree width reflects the number of solutions kept after pruning that level. For the purpose of the statistical analysis we make two assumptions about the statistical distributions of digits in the keys.

Assumption 1 (digit independence)
No correlation between lower and higher significant key bits. That is, given the knowledge of lower significant bits observed in the past, we do not gain further information regarding higher significant bits to be explored in the future.

Assumption 2 (key independence)
No dependency between p and q, thus d_p and d_q. This means that the knowledge of d_p (resp. d_q) does not provide additional information to infer d_q (resp. d_p).

We note that neither assumption hold in practice—Coppersmith [7] likely implies that Assumption 1 is invalid and Heninger and Shacham [16] invalidates Assumption 2. Hence, we only use them to facilitate the statistical analysis. The agreement between our model and the experiments indicates that violations of the assumptions do not result in significant statistical differences. We further note that any violation of these assumptions is likely to facilitate attacks on RSA.

We now consider slice(i). For the aligned case, slice(i) contains bits $d_p[i]$ and $d_q[i]$, which fall in digits $d_p[\lfloor i/\omega \rfloor]$ and $d_q[\lfloor i/\omega \rfloor]$, respectively. The side-channel information regarding the digit equivalence of $d_p[\lfloor i/\omega \rfloor]$ and $d_q[\lfloor i/\omega \rfloor]$ is categorised into four possibilities

(P1) Both $d_p[\lfloor i/\omega \rfloor]$ and $d_q[\lfloor i/\omega \rfloor]$ have been seen;
(P2) $d_p[\lfloor i/\omega \rfloor]$ has been seen, but $d_q[\lfloor i/\omega \rfloor]$ has not;
(P3) $d_q[\lfloor i/\omega \rfloor]$ has been seen, but $d_p[\lfloor i/\omega \rfloor]$ has not;
(P4) Neither $d_p[\lfloor i/\omega \rfloor]$ nor $d_q[\lfloor i/\omega \rfloor]$ has been seen.

Figure 2 illustrates seen and unseen digits of d_p and d_q, in the aligned case, where $\omega = 4$. Each box represents a digit whose value is printed within the box along with colors used to represent its value. The bit positions are given below

···	0111	0001	1010	1101	1010	1101
	$d_p[5]$	$d_p[4]$	$d_p[3]$	$d_p[2]$	$d_p[1]$	$d_p[0]$

···	0101	0011	1000	1110	1000	0011
	$d_q[5]$	$d_q[4]$	$d_q[3]$	$d_q[2]$	$d_q[1]$	$d_q[0]$

Fig. 2. An example of seen and unseen digits in the aligned case, $\omega = 4$.

the boxes. Recall that the attacker does not know the values of the digits; they only know the digit equivalence. Considering this scenario, where $\omega = 4$, there would be 2^3 solutions at the end of the first digit at slice(3). The subsequent digits for d_p and d_q are both unseen, corresponding to **(P4)**, so pruning can only occur at the end of the digit at slice(7). Using the notation introduced previously, any solution where $E[1] = E[0]$ in either d_p or d_q are pruned. Moving on to the next digit, we get scenario **(P2)**. The digit $d_p[2]$ has been seen previously in $d_p[0]$ and thus pruning could occur at each slice(8) to slice(11), i.e. solutions where $E[2] \neq E[0]$ for d_p are pruned. Additional pruning could occur from the unseen digit of $d_q[2]$ at slice(11). The search continues on and the pruning at each slice depends on whether the current digit has been seen.

Because the side-channel information only applies to full digits, i.e. groups of ω bits, we only perform the pruning at a digit boundary. That is, we combine ω steps of the HS algorithm. To simplify notation, we use γ to refer to the digit number where bit i falls, i.e. $\gamma = \lfloor i/\omega \rfloor$.

Let y_γ and z_γ be the numbers of unique digits that have been observed at $d_p[0], \ldots, d_p[\gamma]$ and $d_q[0], \ldots, d_q[\gamma]$, respectively. We now make the concept of a previously seen digit more concrete by saying that a digit $d_p[\gamma]$ (resp. $d_q[\gamma]$) has been seen before if $y_\gamma = y_{\gamma-1}$ (resp. $z_\gamma = z_{\gamma-1}$).

Define two random variables Y_γ and Z_γ from the space $\{0, \ldots, 2^\omega - 1\}$ for the number of *unique* digits observed after reading γ digits. Hence, the four possibilities above, i.e., **(P1)**–**(P4)**, correspond to the four possibilities in Eq. 5 for moving to observe the next slice. That is, given the previous value $(y_{\gamma-1}, z_{\gamma-1})$, we obtain the following probabilities:

$$Pr\left((Y_\gamma, Z_\gamma) = (y_\gamma, z_\gamma)|(Y_{\gamma-1}, Z_{\gamma-1}) = (y_{\gamma-1}, z_{\gamma-1})\right)$$

$$= \begin{cases} \left(\dfrac{y_{\gamma-1}}{2^\omega}\right)\left(\dfrac{z_{\gamma-1}}{2^\omega}\right) & \text{if } y_\gamma = y_{\gamma-1} \text{ and } z_\gamma = z_{\gamma-1} \\[2mm] \left(\dfrac{y_{\gamma-1}}{2^\omega}\right)\left(\dfrac{2^\omega - z_{\gamma-1}}{2^\omega}\right) & \text{if } y_\gamma = y_{\gamma-1} \text{ and } z_\gamma = z_{\gamma-1} + 1 \\[2mm] \left(\dfrac{2^\omega - y_{\gamma-1}}{2^\omega}\right)\left(\dfrac{z_{\gamma-1}}{2^\omega}\right) & \text{if } y_\gamma = y_{\gamma-1} + 1 \text{ and } z_\gamma = z_{\gamma-1} \\[2mm] \left(\dfrac{2^\omega - y_{\gamma-1}}{2^\omega}\right)\left(\dfrac{2^\omega - z_{\gamma-1}}{2^\omega}\right) & \text{if } y_\gamma = y_{\gamma-1} + 1 \text{ and } z_\gamma = z_{\gamma-1} + 1 \end{cases} \quad (5)$$

We derive these probabilities by utilising the independence of the two keys, d_p and d_q. Therefore, we consider each contribution to the probability separately and the contribution is either the proportion of seen digits or the proportion of unseen digits, depending on whether the current digit has been seen in the key stream. Therefore, we can calculate the probability of a particular key sequence by multiplying the probability of the individual components. In Sect. 4.3 we discuss the formulation of these probabilities into two independent Markov chains to model the key recovery.

Note that the complexity of our attack depends on the size of the search space, i.e. the number of nodes in the search tree. Let W_γ be a random variable that denotes the search space (the number of possible candidate keys) or tree width after γ digit steps. The change of the width at each step is defined as follows.

$$
\begin{cases}
\dfrac{1}{2^\omega} & \text{if } y_\gamma = y_{\gamma-1} \text{ and } z_\gamma = z_{\gamma-1} \\[2mm]
\dfrac{2^\omega - z_\gamma}{2^\omega} & \text{if } y_\gamma = y_{\gamma-1} \text{ and } z_\gamma = z_{\gamma-1} + 1 \\[2mm]
\dfrac{2^\omega - y_\gamma}{2^\omega} & \text{if } y_\gamma = y_{\gamma-1} + 1 \text{ and } z_\gamma = z_{\gamma-1} \\[2mm]
\dfrac{(2^\omega - y_\gamma)(2^\omega - z_\gamma)}{2^\omega} & \text{if } y_\gamma = y_{\gamma-1} + 1 \text{ and } z_\gamma = z_{\gamma-1} + 1
\end{cases}
$$

Observe that the change in the width only depends on the number of unique digits that have been seen and the number of digits scanned, γ. In other words, the width *is not* dependent upon the sequence of Y_γ or Z_γ but the value at γ. Since we know that the first digit must be odd (due to being prime), the first bit must be one. This means that there are fewer possibilities for the first digit. Consequently, this gives a factor of $2^{\omega-1}$ for the first width since we have one fewer binary choice for the first bit. Therefore, the width after reading in γ digits from each of d_p and d_q is

$$
\frac{2^{\omega-1}}{2^{\gamma\omega}} \prod_{m=1}^{y_\gamma} (2^\omega - m) \prod_{m=1}^{z_\gamma} (2^\omega - m). \tag{6}
$$

As noted previously, the width is independent of the order of the sequence. The expression takes the product of the y_γ and z_γ numerators of the change in widths and the initial width $2^{\omega-1}$, then divides by the number of 2^ω for γ digits scanned. Assume the threshold of 2^t, we have

$$
\frac{2^{\omega-1}}{2^{\gamma\omega}} \prod_{m=1}^{y_\gamma} (2^\omega - m) \prod_{m=1}^{z_\gamma} (2^\omega - m) \geq 2^t
$$

and therefore to exceed the threshold we need

$$
\prod_{m=0}^{y_\gamma} (2^\omega - m) \prod_{m=0}^{z_\gamma} (2^\omega - m) \geq 2^{t-1+(\gamma-1)\omega}.
$$

4.3 Independent Markov Chains

Recall the two assumptions in our analysis, namely, digit independence (i.e. previously observed digits do not determine unexplored digits) and key independence (i.e. knowing d_p does not infer d_q or vice versa). We use these properties to create identical distributed Markov chains and analyse these chains operating on d_p and d_q independently. Each Markov chain has the state space $\Omega = \{0, \ldots, 2^\omega - 1\}$ whose transitions have two possibilities:

1. Sample a digit that has previously been seen, or
2. Sample a digit that has not been seen.

Therefore, we define the probability transitions as

$$y_\gamma \rightarrow \begin{cases} y_{\gamma-1} & \text{with probability } \dfrac{y_{\gamma-1}}{2^\omega} \\ y_{\gamma-1} + 1 & \text{with probability } \dfrac{2^\omega - y_{\gamma-1}}{2^\omega}. \end{cases}$$

Using this formulation, we construct a probability transition matrix P. An example for $\omega = 4$ state chain is given below. Notice that the matrix has non-zero probabilities on the main diagonal and the diagonal above only.

$$P = \begin{bmatrix} \frac{1}{4} & \frac{3}{4} & 0 & 0 \\ 0 & \frac{1}{2} & \frac{1}{2} & 0 \\ 0 & 0 & \frac{3}{4} & \frac{1}{4} \\ 0 & 0 & 0 & 1 \end{bmatrix}$$

Let Y_γ be a random variable for the number of unique digits observed at digit γ. Thus, the Markov chain tracking the evolution of either d_p or d_q is

$$\mathcal{I} = \{Y_\gamma\}_{\gamma \in \{0, \ldots, 2^\omega - 1\}}.$$

Given the Markov chain structure, we can calculate the probabilities of having observed y_γ unique digits, after observing γ digits.

Note that this Markov chain is time-homogeneous since the transition probabilities do not change with the number of digits that have been read. This allows the calculation of the probabilities at each number of digit γ read as the γth power of the probability transition matrix. That is,

$$Pr(Y_\gamma = y_\gamma | Y_1 = y_1) = [P^k]_{y_1, y_\gamma}$$

since both d_p and d_q are independent and identically distributed.

The probability transition matrix P and its powers completely determine the system. Note also that we consider the initial state of beginning the first digit with a single unique value. This means that we will always consider the top row of the matrix P for calculation of the relevant probabilities.

To finalise this discussion, thanks to the independence assumptions, we can calculate the transition probabilities for random variables Y_γ and Z_γ, the number of unique digits observed by digit γ of d_p and d_q respectively,

$$Pr(Y_\gamma = l, Z_\gamma = m) = Pr(Y_\gamma = l)Pr(Z_\gamma = m) = [P^\gamma]_{1,y_\gamma}[P^\gamma]_{1,z_\gamma}.$$

Note that the index of the starting state is 1, as we consider the probability of moving from state 1 to j in γ steps.

Regarding computational complexity, the naive calculation seen previously required that at each step, ω probabilities are calculated, thus resulting in the complexity $O(\omega^\gamma)$. Utilising the Markov chain approach, the calculation is reduced to taking the γ powers of P where each matrix multiplication is $O((2^\omega)^{2.37}) = O(2^{2.37\omega})$. This means that our approach has the computational complexity of $O(\gamma 2^{2.37\omega})$.

4.4 Unaligned Case

As previously mentioned, many real examples do not begin scanning digits from the least significant bit, i.e. $\tau(k_p)$ and $\tau(k_q)$ are not zero. Our analysis suggests modelling these offsets as independent geometric random variables. That is, each bit stream of d_p and d_q, the offset O has probability of occurring of

$$Pr\left(O = o\right) = \frac{1}{2^{o+1}}, o \in \{0, 1, \ldots\}.$$

We calculate the change in width by taking the assumption that all bits before the offset are known and we retain knowledge of their values. This has no impact on the evolution of the Markov chain. Therefore, we can utilise the same probability transitions while adjusting the weight by the offset. As a result, given the offsets o_p and o_q, we have that the width can be calculated as

$$\left(\frac{1}{2^{o_p}}\right)\left(\frac{1}{2^{o_q}}\right)\left(\frac{2^{\omega-1}}{2^{k\omega}}\right) \prod_{m=1}^{y_\gamma} (2^\omega - m) \prod_{m=1}^{z_\gamma} (2^\omega - m). \tag{7}$$

That is, we derive this expression from Eq. 6 and adjusting for the known bits, which are those before the offset. Note that this means that any offset provided will lower the width for the same digit γ, and number of digits observed, y_γ and z_γ. Therefore, the case with no offsets for scanning digits will have the largest width, for identical keys.

We calculate the expected width at each digit γ by summing over widths of the offset Eq. 7 and the probabilities of being in a state (y_γ, z_γ) from Eq. 5. Explicitly, this gives the expected width for a digit γ of

$$E[W_\gamma] = \sum_{y_\gamma \leq \gamma} \sum_{z_\gamma \leq \gamma} \sum_{o_p} \sum_{o_q} [P^\gamma]_{1,y_\gamma}[P^\gamma]_{1,z_\gamma} \frac{1}{2^{o_p}} \cdot \frac{1}{2^{o_q}} \cdot \frac{2^{\omega-1}}{2^{\gamma\omega}} \prod_{m=1}^{y_\gamma} (2^\omega - m) \prod_{m=1}^{z_\gamma} (2^\omega - m).$$

5   Results and Comparisons

We theoretically and experimentally evaluate our approach of reconstructing RSA private keys given side-channel information of digit equivalence. For the former, we use our derived formulas to estimate the search space and success probability. For the latter, we run our algorithm on a high-performance cluster and observe the convergence to the solution. In both cases, we also set threshold on the space complexity.

5.1   Theoretical Results

For the theoretical evaluation, we consider the RSA fixed-window exponentiation with $\omega = 4$ and 5. For each ω, we use three different thresholds corresponding to three computation budgets. These three thresholds are $2^{25}, 2^{40}$ and 2^{60} which represent resource-constrained attackers, well-funded organisations, and nation-state organisations such as the NSA.

The results for $\omega = 4$ are shown in Fig. 3. This suggests that the algorithm can recover the majority of the key before reaching the lowest resource-constrained attackers threshold of 2^{25}. To be more precise, 99.9% of the key can successfully be recovered. Further analysis shows that the keys that exceed the maximum width have many consecutive unique digits at the beginning of the key. Thus, this allows the width to grow much quicker than the ability to prune infeasible keys.

The results for $\omega = 5$ is shown in Fig. 4. As expected, the percentiles, median and mean all increase as the window width increases from $\omega = 4$ to $\omega = 5$. Even though it becomes more challenging for resource-constrained attackers, it is feasible for well-funded organisations.

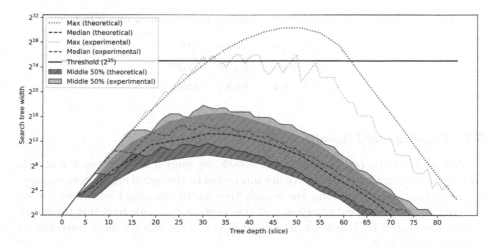

Fig. 3. Distribution of width seen at each slice for $\omega = 4$ for both the theoretical and experimental results.

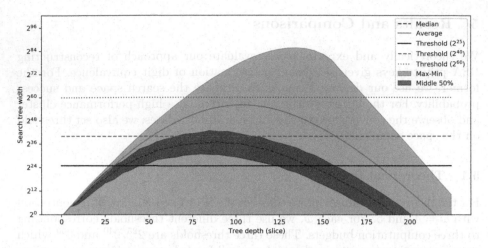

Fig. 4. Distribution of width seen at each slice of the Markov chain model, $\omega = 5$.

These plots give insight into how the key recovery behaves. Most of the typical behaviour of keys is contained within a relatively small band demonstrated by the middle 50%. The mean is higher than the 75th percentile, which highlights that the maxima tend to be much higher than the middle values. The influence of the unaligned keys lowers the width in general, as the resulting reduction in width is a power-of-two offset. This has a large impact in lowering the median and percentile ranges, since many combinations of unaligned keys still occur with high probability, while have large reductions to the size of the width. Table 1 summarises the success probability and the threshold for window width $\omega = 4$ and 5.

Table 1. Success rate in reconstructing keys for different ω and thresholds

	2^{25}	2^{40}	2^{60}
$\omega = 4$	99.9%	100.0%	100.0%
$\omega = 5$	8.2%	64.8%	99.9%

5.2   Experimental Results

To demonstrate the practicality of our attack, we implement and run the attack on a high-performance cluster. We are interested in the behaviour of convergence to a solution before reaching the search tree width threshold which we set to 2^{25} (resource-constrained attackers). If the solution space exceeds this threshold width, the search is abandoned as it would be too computationally intensive to continue the search.

The distribution of the search tree width at each bit slice for $\omega = 3$ and 4 are shown in Fig. 5 and Fig. 3 respectively. It shows the widths up to slice(85). The widths at the subsequent layers fluctuate between 1 and 2. One of these solution is the key in which we want to recover. These results are generated with 1000 samples with randomly generated secret values. The key is randomly generated with $e = 65537$ and with 2048-bit RSA modulus.

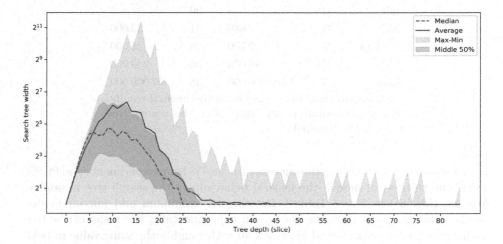

Fig. 5. Distribution of width seen experimentally at each slice, $\omega = 3$.

The success rate for $\omega = 4$ is 98.7%. From these results, we can observe that the search widths follow a general pattern of an exponential-like increase before an exponential-like decrease. This aligns with our understanding. Initially, building the key with no seen digits, we expect there to be a growing number of possibilities for the digit string. As we move further along the slices of the key, at some point, we would have enough information of the key to narrow the search space.

Table 2 lists the values of the widths seen when $\omega = 4$ and threshold is 2^{25}. Note that the maximum and minimum width seen in the experimental results is not the true maximum and minimum as it is affected by the attacker-imposed threshold. The search is abandoned when the tree width exceeds the threshold, so we would get that the tree width drops to zero when an experiment passes the threshold, and the maximum width captured will be the width right before the run was abandoned. The theoretical results also accounts for extremely low probability events; thus a higher theoretical maximum is expected.

Table 2. Comparison of the width seen when $\omega = 4$ and threshold 2^{25}

	Theoretical		Experimental	
	bit index	maximum	bit index	maximum
mean	39	570 000	38	790 000
min*	3	8	20	3
25%	31	880	31	33 000
median	31	9 700	26	26 000
75%	35	98 000	30	240 000
max*	47	1 400 000 000	38	67 000 000

* Expect different theoretical and experimental results. The experimental results stop after the search tree exceeds the threshold.

Despite the differences of the success rate, 98.7% from experiments and 99.9% using the theoretical model, the general behaviour of the search tree is similar. We see this in Fig. 3 and Table 2. Ignoring the minimum and maximum due to the difference in performing the search experimentally, the mean of the tree width reaches its peak around bit index 40 with roughly the same value in both theoretical and experimental results. The middle 50% range occurs roughly at bit index 32, although the ranges of this value is much lower in the theoretical results. Again, this could be due to the modelling accounting for extremely low probability events.

6   Conclusions

In this work we apply the Heninger-Shacham algorithm in a new context. We assume a side-channel adversary that can observe the equivalence of digits in the private exponents of CRT-RSA. We show how to apply the algorithm given such information and develop a theoretical model that allows us to analyse the complexity of the attack. The model shows that the attack is feasible for a suitably funded organisation with a window size of 5 bits. We further validate the model through experimentation with randomly chosen RSA keys.

Our model assumes that the digit equivalence information is complete. A potential extension of this work is to evaluate cases where we have partial information. For example, when there are errors in the digit equivalence information or when we only know the class of the digits (e.g. the Hamming weight). The work could also be extended to consider cases that use sliding window exponentiation.

The results presented here has, once again, made apparent the importance of using constant-time implementations against side-channel attacks.

Acknowledgements. We would like to thank all reviewers for providing insightful feedback, which has improved the paper.

This work was supported by an ARC Discovery Early Career Researcher Award (project number DE200101577); an ARC Discovery Project (project number DP210102670); The Blavatnik ICRC at Tel-Aviv University; the Phoenix HPC service at the University of Adelaide; and gifts from Google and Intel.

References

1. Bernstein, D.J.: Cache-timing attacks on AES (2005). Preprint available at http:// cr.yp.to/papers.html#cachetiming
2. Bernstein, D.J., Breitner, J., Genkin, D., Bruinderink, L.G., Heninger, N., Lange, T., van Vredendaal, C., Yarom, Y.: Sliding right into disaster: left-to-right sliding windows leak. In: Fischer, W., Homma, N. (eds.) CHES 2017. LNCS, vol. 10529, pp. 555–576. Springer, Cham (2017). https://doi.org/10.1007/978-3-319-66787-4_27
3. Boneh, D., Venkatesan, R.: Hardness of computing the most significant bits of secret keys in Diffie-Hellman and related schemes. In: Koblitz, N. (ed.) CRYPTO 1996. LNCS, vol. 1109, pp. 129–142. Springer, Heidelberg (1996). https://doi.org/ 10.1007/3-540-68697-5_11
4. Breitner, J.: More on sliding right. Cryptology ePrint Archive 2018/1163 (2018). http://eprint.iacr.org/2018/1163/
5. Brumley, B.B., Tuveri, N.: Remote timing attacks are still practical. In: Atluri, V., Diaz, C. (eds.) ESORICS 2011. LNCS, vol. 6879, pp. 355–371. Springer, Heidelberg (2011). https://doi.org/10.1007/978-3-642-23822-2_20
6. Chuengsatiansup, C., Genkin, D., Yarom, Y., Zhang, Z.: Side-channeling the Kalyna key expansion. In: Galbraith, S.D. (ed.) CT-RSA 2022. LNCS, vol. 13161, pp. 272–296. Springer, Cham (2022). https://doi.org/10.1007/978-3-030-95312-6_12
7. Coppersmith, D.: Finding a small root of a bivariate integer equation; factoring with high bits known. In: Maurer, U. (ed.) EUROCRYPT 1996. LNCS, vol. 1070, pp. 178–189. Springer, Heidelberg (1996). https://doi.org/10.1007/3-540-68339-9_16
8. De Micheli, G., Heninger, N.: Recovering cryptographic keys from partial information, by example. Cryptology ePrint Archive, Report 2020/1506 (2020). http:// eprint.iacr.org/2020/1506/
9. Durrett, R., Durrett, R.: Essentials of Stochastic Processes, vol. 1. Springer, New York (1999)
10. Gandolfi, K., Mourtel, C., Olivier, F.: Electromagnetic analysis: concrete results. In: Koç, Ç.K., Naccache, D., Paar, C. (eds.) CHES 2001. LNCS, vol. 2162, pp. 251–261. Springer, Heidelberg (2001). https://doi.org/10.1007/3-540-44709-1_21
11. Ge, Q., Yarom, Y., Cock, D., Heiser, G.: A survey of microarchitectural timing attacks and countermeasures on contemporary hardware. J. Cryptogr. Eng. 8(1), 1–27 (2016). https://doi.org/10.1007/s13389-016-0141-6
12. Genkin, D., Pachmanov, L., Tromer, E., Yarom, Y.: Drive-by key-extraction cache attacks from portable code. In: Preneel, B., Vercauteren, F. (eds.) ACNS 2018. LNCS, vol. 10892, pp. 83–102. Springer, Cham (2018). https://doi.org/10.1007/ 978-3-319-93387-0_5
13. Genkin, D., Shamir, A., Tromer, E.: RSA key extraction via low-bandwidth acoustic cryptanalysis. In: Garay, J.A., Gennaro, R. (eds.) CRYPTO 2014. LNCS, vol. 8616, pp. 444–461. Springer, Heidelberg (2014). https://doi.org/10.1007/978-3-662-44371-2_25

14. Halderman, J.A., Schoen, S.D., Heninger, N., Clarkson, W., Paul, W., Calandrino, J.A., Feldman, A.J., Appelbaum, J., Felten, E.W.: Lest we remember: cold boot attacks on encryption keys. In: USENIX Security, pp. 45–60 (2008)

15. Henecka, W., May, A., Meurer, A.: Correcting errors in RSA private keys. In: Rabin, T. (ed.) CRYPTO 2010. LNCS, vol. 6223, pp. 351–369. Springer, Heidelberg (2010). https://doi.org/10.1007/978-3-642-14623-7_19

16. Heninger, N., Shacham, H.: Reconstructing RSA private keys from random key bits. In: Halevi, S. (ed.) CRYPTO 2009. LNCS, vol. 5677, pp. 1–17. Springer, Heidelberg (2009). https://doi.org/10.1007/978-3-642-03356-8_1

17. İnci, M.S., Gulmezoglu, B., Irazoqui, G., Eisenbarth, T., Sunar, B.: Cache attacks enable bulk key recovery on the cloud. In: Gierlichs, B., Poschmann, A.Y. (eds.) CHES 2016. LNCS, vol. 9813, pp. 368–388. Springer, Heidelberg (2016). https://doi.org/10.1007/978-3-662-53140-2_18

18. Kocher, P.C.: Timing attacks on implementations of Diffie-Hellman, RSA, DSS, and other systems. In: Koblitz, N. (ed.) CRYPTO 1996. LNCS, vol. 1109, pp. 104–113. Springer, Heidelberg (1996). https://doi.org/10.1007/3-540-68697-5_9

19. Kocher, P., Jaffe, J., Jun, B.: Differential power analysis. In: Wiener, M. (ed.) CRYPTO 1999. LNCS, vol. 1666, pp. 388–397. Springer, Heidelberg (1999). https://doi.org/10.1007/3-540-48405-1_25

20. Krämer, J., Nedospasov, D., Schlösser, A., Seifert, J.-P.: Differential photonic emission analysis. In: Prouff, E. (ed.) COSADE 2013. LNCS, vol. 7864, pp. 1–16. Springer, Heidelberg (2013). https://doi.org/10.1007/978-3-642-40026-1_1

21. Kunihiro, N., Honda, J.: RSA meets DPA: recovering RSA secret keys from noisy analog data. In: Batina, L., Robshaw, M. (eds.) CHES 2014. LNCS, vol. 8731, pp. 261–278. Springer, Heidelberg (2014). https://doi.org/10.1007/978-3-662-44709-3_15

22. Liu, F., Yarom, Y., Ge, Q., Heiser, G., Lee, R.B.: Last-level cache side-channel attacks are practical. In: IEEE SP, pp. 605–622 (2015)

23. Lou, X., Zhang, T., Jiang, J., Zhang, Y.: A survey of microarchitectural side-channel vulnerabilities, attacks and defenses in cryptography. CoRR, abs/2103.14244 (2021)

24. Nguyen, P.Q., Shparlinski, I.E.: The insecurity of the digital signature algorithm with partially known nonces. J. Cryptol. **15**(3), 151–176 (2002). https://doi.org/10.1007/s00145-002-0021-3

25. Nguyen, P.Q., Shparlinski, I.E.: The insecurity of the elliptic curve digital signature algorithm with partially known nonces. Des. Codes Cryptogr. **30**(2), 201–217 (2003)

26. Oonishi, K., Kunihiro, N.: Attacking noisy secret CRT-RSA exponents in binary method. In: Lee, K. (ed.) ICISC 2018. LNCS, vol. 11396, pp. 37–54. Springer, Cham (2019). https://doi.org/10.1007/978-3-030-12146-4_3

27. Oonishi, K., Kunihiro, N.: Recovering CRT-RSA secret keys from noisy square-and-multiply sequences in the sliding window method. In: Liu, J.K., Cui, H. (eds.) ACISP 2020. LNCS, vol. 12248, pp. 642–652. Springer, Cham (2020). https://doi.org/10.1007/978-3-030-55304-3_34

28. Oonishi, K., Huang, X., Kunihiro, N.: Improved CRT-RSA secret key recovery method from sliding window leakage. In: Seo, J.H. (ed.) ICISC 2019. LNCS, vol. 11975, pp. 278–296. Springer, Cham (2020). https://doi.org/10.1007/978-3-030-40921-0_17

29. Page, D.: Theoretical use of cache memory as a cryptanalytic side-channel. Cryptology ePrint Archive, Report 2002/169 (2002). http://eprint.iacr.org/2002/169/

30. Paterson, K.G., Polychroniadou, A., Sibborn, D.L.: A coding-theoretic approach to recovering noisy RSA keys. In: Wang, X., Sako, K. (eds.) ASIACRYPT 2012. LNCS, vol. 7658, pp. 386–403. Springer, Heidelberg (2012). https://doi.org/10.1007/978-3-642-34961-4_24

31. Percival, C.: Cache missing for fun and profit. In: BSDCan 2005 (2005). http://css.csail.mit.edu/6.858/2014/readings/ht-cache.pdf

32. Quisquater, J.-J., Samyde, D.: ElectroMagnetic Analysis (EMA): measures and counter-measures for smart cards. In: Attali, I., Jensen, T. (eds.) E-smart 2001. LNCS, vol. 2140, pp. 200–210. Springer, Heidelberg (2001). https://doi.org/10.1007/3-540-45418-7_17

33. Rivest, R.L., Shamir, A., Adleman, L.M.: A method for obtaining digital signatures and public-key cryptosystems. Commun. ACM **21**(2), 120–126 (1978)

34. Walter, C.D.: Sliding windows succumbs to big mac attack. In: Koç, Ç.K., Naccache, D., Paar, C. (eds.) CHES 2001. LNCS, vol. 2162, pp. 286–299. Springer, Heidelberg (2001). https://doi.org/10.1007/3-540-44709-1_24

35. Yarom, Y., Falkner, K.: Flush+reload: a high resolution, low noise, L3 cache side-channel attack. In: USENIX Security, pp. 719–732 (2014)

36. Yarom, Y., Genkin, D., Heninger, N.: CacheBleed: a timing attack on OpenSSL constant time RSA. In: Gierlichs, B., Poschmann, A.Y. (eds.) CHES 2016. LNCS, vol. 9813, pp. 346–367. Springer, Heidelberg (2016). https://doi.org/10.1007/978-3-662-53140-2_17

Practical Seed-Recovery of Fast Cryptographic Pseudo-Random Number Generators

Florette Martinez[✉]

Sorbonne Université, CNRS, LIP6, 75005 Paris, France
`florette.martinez@lip6.fr`

Abstract. Trifork is a family of pseudo-random number generators described in 2010 by Orue *et al.* It is based on Lagged Fibonacci Generators and has been claimed as cryptographically secure. In 2017 was presented a new family of lightweight pseudo-random number generators: Arrow. These generators are based on the same techniques as Trifork and designed to be light, fast and secure, so they can allow private communication between resource-constrained devices. The authors based their choices of parameters on NIST standards on lightweight cryptography and claimed these pseudo-random number generators were of cryptographic strength.

We present practical implemented algorithms that reconstruct the internal states of the Arrow generators for different parameters given in the original article. These algorithms enable us to predict all the following outputs and recover the seed. These attacks are all based on a simple guess-and-determine approach which is efficient enough against these generators.

We also present an implemented attack on Trifork, this time using lattice-based techniques. We show it cannot have more than 64 bits of security, hence it is not cryptographically secure.

Keywords: Pseudo-random number generators · Guess-and-determine · Cryptanalysis · Lattices

1 Introduction

Randomness is a fundamental tool in cryptography. All key generation algorithms use randomness to generate the keys and it is used in several well-known cryptographic protocols such as DSA, ECDSA, Schnorr signature scheme, etc. A pseudo-random number generator (PRNG) is an efficient deterministic algorithm that stretches a small random seed into a longer pseudo-random sequence of numbers. It is an efficient way to create pseudo-randomness to be used in cryptography protocols. A PRNG used in a cryptographic protocol needs to produce a sequence of bits indistinguishable from "truly" random bits by efficient adversaries or the whole protocol might become insecure. PRNGs of cryptographic strength exist, some of them have been approved by NIST [7].

© Springer Nature Switzerland AG 2022
G. Ateniese and D. Venturi (Eds.): ACNS 2022, LNCS 13269, pp. 212–229, 2022.
https://doi.org/10.1007/978-3-031-09234-3_11

Because of the miniaturization of components and the emergence of the Internet of Things, we face a new cryptographic challenge in which highly-constrained devices must wirelessly and securely communicate with one another. The standardized available PRNGs do not fit into these constrained devices, this is the reason why we are looking for lighter PRNGs. In [9], NIST presented several generally-desired properties that they would use to evaluate the design of future lightweight cryptographic protocols. They strongly underline the fact that the security should be of at least 112 bits.

The lagged Fibonacci generators (LFG) are a class of linear generators. A LFG is defined by four parameters: (r, s, N, m) and an initial internal state composed of r words of size N: $(x_{-r}, \ldots, x_{-1})$. At step n, the internal state of the generator is $(x_{n-r}, \ldots, x_{n-1})$. The generator computes x_n as $x_n \equiv x_{n-r} + x_{n-s} \bmod m$, outputs x_n and update its internal state to $(x_{n-r+1}, \ldots, x_n)$. These generators are light and fast, as needed for lightweight cryptography, but highly insecure. They have poor statistical properties, which make them easily distinguishable from the uniform distribution, and they are easily predictable (as we can obtain the full internal state by clocking the generator enough times).

The goal of Arrow, presented by Lopez et al. [11] was to use two of these LFGs to keep their lightweight properties by combining them in a way that would make the resulting PRNG more secure. To improve the security of these new PRNGs, the authors used two LFGs of different lengths and combined them using both modular arithmetic over $\mathbb{Z}/m\mathbb{Z}$ and modular arithmetic over $\mathbb{Z}/2\mathbb{Z}$, as combining two moduli tends to break the linearity of the operations. The sequences generated by Arrow pass successfully all the Marsaglia's Diehard randomness tests suite and the randomness tests of NIST. The statistical randomness distribution of the outputs of Arrow has been studied further in [5], by Blanco et al. in 2019.

The idea behind Arrow derives from an older family of PRNGs: Trifork. Trifork has been presented in 2010 by Orue *et al.* [12]. The generators in Trifork combine three Lagged Fibonacci Generators together, again mixing modular arithmetic over $\mathbb{Z}/m\mathbb{Z}$ and over $\mathbb{Z}/2\mathbb{Z}$. They also use a Linear Congruential Generator to initialise their large internal states. These large internal states are the main reason Trifork is not suited for lightweight cryptography. These PRNGs have a key of 192 bits and a claimed security of 192 bits.

The Linear Congruential Generators (LCG) are an other class of linear generators. A LCG is defined by three (often) public parameters a, c, m and a secret seed x_0. At step $i > 0$ the generator outputs $x_i = ax_{i-1} + c \bmod m$. These generators are well studied and generally not cryptographically secure.

Contribution. We show that Arrow, even if it has good statistical properties, is insecure. We present several practical algorithms to attack different versions of Arrow presented in the original paper, using the same choice of parameters they made for their tests. These algorithms reconstruct the full internal state of the PRNG. This allows to predict the pseudo-random stream deterministically and clock the generator backwards. For those attacks we choose a "guess-and-determine" approach: some bits of the internal state are guessed; assuming the guesses are correct, some other information is computed; a consistency check discards bad guesses early on; then candidate internal states are computed and fully tested. Unfortunately, our attack is not general and the choice of bits to guess depends on the parameters of the underlying FLGs. This is why we need a different algorithm for each version of Arrow we want to attack. We will attack three different versions of Arrow.

	words size	key length	Claimed security	attack complexity
Arrow-I	8 bits	96(128) bits	96(128) bits	38 bits
Arrow-II	16 bits	96(128) bits	96(128) bits	48 bits
Arrow-III	N bits	$32N$ bits	$32N$ bits	$7 \times N$ bits

For Arrow-I and Arrow-II, the key length is 128 bits but can be shortened to 96 bits using an IV. For Arrow-III, the attack is practical on a laptop for $N = 8$.

We also present an attack against Trifork. The generators in Trifork have keys of length 192 bits but we show they cannot have more than 64 bits of security. Even if the two families of generators are close, the strategies to attack them greatly differ. As the internal state of Trifork is composed of several words of size 64 bits, we cannot use a "guess-and-determine" approach. As this internal state is large, it cannot be directly initialized with the key. This is why a Linear Congruential Generator is used. The LCG will be the breach we will use to attack Trifork. We will guess a third of the key (64 bits) and use lattice-based techniques to recover the rest of the seed. All the codes are available on my personal website.

Related Work. Linear Congruential Generators (LCGs) have been largely studied through the years. The main attack against them was presented by Frieze *et al.* in 1984 [8]. In this attack, a Euclidean lattice related to the public parameters is built. Then outputs of the LCG are used to create a vector T1, not in the lattice but close to a vector T2 such that T2 is in the lattice and contains the seed of the generator. The lattice is reduced thanks to the LLL-algorithm -a polynomial-time reduction algorithm presented by Lenstra, Lenstra, and Lovász in 1982- and its new basis is used to solve integer linear equations to retrieve the seed of the generator. In 1985, Knuth [10] studied a variant of the LCG: the secret LCG, where the usually public parameters are now secret. This variant was attacked by Stern in 1987 [14].

Guess-and-determine (GD) techniques are mainly used to attack stream ciphers. The stream cipher SOBER was presented by Rose in 1998 [13]. In 1999, Bleichenbacher et al. presented a first GD attack against SOBER-II [6] and in 2003 Baggage et al. presented another GD attack against SOBER-t32 [3]. Several generators from the NESSIE competition [1] (including SOBER-t32) have been attacked with a "guess-and-determine" approach. It is also the case for the cipher stream algorithms candidate in eSTREAM [2]. You can find a quick summary of other GD uses in this survey [4], paragraph 3.10.

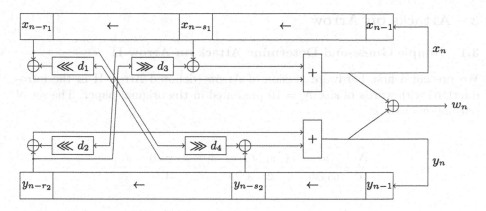

Fig. 1. Description of Arrow

2   Description of Arrow

The lagged Fibonacci generators (LFG) are a class of linear generators. A LFG is defined by four parameters: (r, s, N, m) and an initial internal state composed of r words of size N: $(x_{-r}, \ldots, x_{-1})$. At step n, the internal state of the generator is $(x_{n-r}, \ldots, x_{n-1})$. Then it computes x_n as $x_n \equiv x_{n-r} + x_{n-s} \bmod m$, outputs x_n and update its internal state to $(x_{n-r+1}, \ldots, x_n)$.

Arrow is a more elaborated architecture, its structure is described in Fig. 1. It is composed of two LFGs of respective parameters (r_1, s_1, N, m) and (r_2, s_2, N, m). The internal states of the first LFG are denoted (x_i), the internal states of the second one (y_i) and the outputs (w_i). The values $(x_i)_{-r_1 \leq i \leq -1}$ and $(y_i)_{-r_2 \leq i \leq -1}$ are the seed of this generator. The parameters r_1, r_2, s_1, s_2, N, m are public.

Instead of having $x_n = x_{n-s_1} + x_{n-r_1} \bmod m$ and $y_n = y_{n-s-2} + y_{n-r_2} \bmod m$ we scramble the two generators to obtain at step $n \geq 0$:

$$x_n = ((x_{n-r_1} \oplus (y_{n-s_2} \lll d_1)) + (x_{n-s_1} \oplus (y_{n-r_2} \ggg d_3))) \bmod m \qquad (1)$$

$$y_n = ((y_{n-r_2} \oplus (x_{n-s_1} \lll d_2)) + (y_{n-s_2} \oplus (x_{n-r_1} \ggg d_4))) \bmod m \qquad (2)$$

where d_1, d_2, d_3 and d_4 are four public constant satisfying $0 < d_i < N$; $\oplus$ is the bitwise exclusive-or; $\ggg$ and $\lll$ are the right-shift and left-shift operators (as defined in C, not as rotations). The output at step n is:

$$w_n = x_n \oplus y_n.$$

The security of Arrow is based on the secrecy of the internal states. If we clock r_2 times the generator, then for all $i \in \{0, \ldots, r_2 - 1\}$, we know the value $x_i \oplus y_i$ (which is equal to w_i). This is the main weakness we are going to exploit in the following attacks.

3   Attacks on Arrow

3.1   Simple Guess-and-Determine Attack on Arrow-II

We present a first hardware version of Arrow (denoted Arrow-II in the introduction) with words of size $N = 16$ presented in the original paper. The set of parameters used is

N	m	r_1	s_1	r_2	s_2	$d_1 = d_2 = d_3 = d_4$
16	65536	5	2	3	1	4

and the claimed security is 128 bits (96 bits if a public IV is used).

If we decide to split all the relevant words of size 16 into four sub-words of 4 bits, we can represent the internal state of this variant of Arrow as follows:

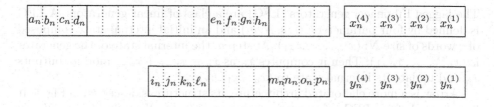

We also split the outputs w_n of size 16 into four sub outputs of 4 bits: $w_n^{(1)}$, $w_n^{(2)}$, $w_n^{(3)}$ and $w_n^{(4)}$ with $w_n^{(1)}$ being the least significant bits of w_n and $w_n^{(4)}$ the most significant bits.

The Eq. (1) and (2) become:

$$x_n^{(1)} = d_n + (h_n \oplus k_n) \bmod 16 \tag{3}$$

$$c_x^{(1)} = (d_n + (h_n \oplus k_n)) \mathrm{div} 16 \tag{4}$$

$$x_n^{(2)} = (c_n \oplus p_n) + (g_n \oplus j_n) + c_x^{(1)} \bmod 16 \tag{5}$$

$$c_x^{(2)} = ((c_n \oplus p_n) + (g_n \oplus j_n) + c_x^{(1)}) \mathrm{div} 16 \tag{6}$$

$$x_n^{(3)} = (b_n \oplus o_n) + (f_n \oplus i_n) + c_x^{(2)} \bmod 16 \tag{7}$$

$$c_x^{(3)} = (b_n \oplus o_n) + (f_n \oplus i_n) + c_x^{(2)} \mathrm{div} 16 \tag{8}$$

$$x_n^{(4)} = ((a_n \oplus n_n) + e_n + c_x^{(3)}) \bmod 16 \tag{9}$$

$$y_n^{(1)} = \ell_n + (c_n \oplus p_n) \bmod 16 \tag{10}$$

$$c_y^{(1)} = (\ell_n + (c_n \oplus p_n)) \mathrm{div} 16 \tag{11}$$

$$y_n^{(2)} = (h_n \oplus k_n) + (b_n \oplus o_n) + c_y^{(1)} \bmod 16 \tag{12}$$

$$c_y^{(2)} = ((h_n \oplus k_n) + (b_n \oplus o_n) + c_y^{(1)}) \mathrm{div} 16 \tag{13}$$

$$y_n^{(3)} = (g_n \oplus j_n) + (a_n \oplus n_n) + c_y^{(2)} \bmod 16 \tag{14}$$

$$c_y^{(3)} = (g_n \oplus j_n) + (a_n \oplus n_n) + c_y^{(2)} \mathrm{div} 16 \tag{15}$$

$$y_n^{(4)} = ((f_n \oplus i_n) + m_n + c_y^{(3)}) \bmod 16 \tag{16}$$

$$x_n^{(1)} \oplus y_n^{(1)} = w_n^{(1)} \tag{17}$$

$$x_n^{(2)} \oplus y_n^{(2)} = w_n^{(2)} \tag{18}$$

$$x_n^{(3)} \oplus y_n^{(3)} = w_n^{(3)} \tag{19}$$

$$x_n^{(4)} \oplus y_n^{(4)} = w_n^{(4)} \tag{20}$$

were "div" denotes the *integer division*. The $c_x^{(i)}$ and $c_y^{(i)}$ are the carries we must work with. Their value is either 0 or 1. The (w_i) are *known* as they are the outputs.

Our attack will be based on a classical "guess-and-determine" approach. The guessed bits will appear in red, the derived bits at the first step in blue, and the derived bits at the second step in olive. In this case, the attack is very simple: we start by clocking 3 times our generator.

Step 1 We guess $a_3, b_3, c_3, d_3, e_3, f_3, g_3, h_3, i_3, j_3, k_3, \ell_3$ (hence 48 bits). With d_3, h_3 and k_3 we compute $x_3^{(1)}$ and $c_x^{(1)}$(Eq. 3 and 4). Then we compute $y_3^{(1)}$ with $x_3^{(1)}$ and $w_3^{(1)}$ (Eq. 17) and retrieve p_3 as we know ℓ_3 and c_3 (Eq. 10). The knowledge of c_3 allows us to compute $x_3^{(2)}$ (Eq. 5), recover $y_3^{(2)}$(Eq. 18) and then o_3 (Eq. 12). With o_3 we can compute $x_3^{(3)}$ (Eq. 7), recover $y_3^{(3)}$ (Eq. 19) and then n_3 (Eq. 14). And finally, with n_3 we can compute $x_3^{(4)}$ (Eq. 9) and recover $y_3^{(4)}$ (Eq. 20) as well as m_3 (Eq. 16). As we know w_0, w_1, w_2, we can fill up the internal states above i_3, j_3, k_3, ℓ_3 and m_3, n_3, o_3, p_3 and under e_3, f_3, g_3, h_3 (Eq. 17, 18, 19 and 20).

Step 2 We clock the generator twice. As explained above, we have derived a_5, b_5, c_5, d_5 from i_3, j_3, k_3, ℓ_3 and w_0. The values e_5, f_5, g_5, h_5 are $x_3^{(4)}$, $x_3^{(3)}, x_3^{(2)}, x_3^{(1)}$ and i_5, j_5, k_5, ℓ_5 are m_3, n_3, o_3, p_3. We remark that we are in a similar situation as step 1, hence we use the same equations to derive m_5, n_5, o_5, p_5 as well as $x_5^{(1)}, x_5^{(2)}, x_5^{(3)}, x_5^{(4)}, y_5^{(1)}, y_5^{(2)}, y_5^{(3)}$ and $y_5^{(4)}$.

The values above m_5, n_5, o_5, p_5 can be computed thanks to w_4.

At this point, we know the full internal state of the generator.

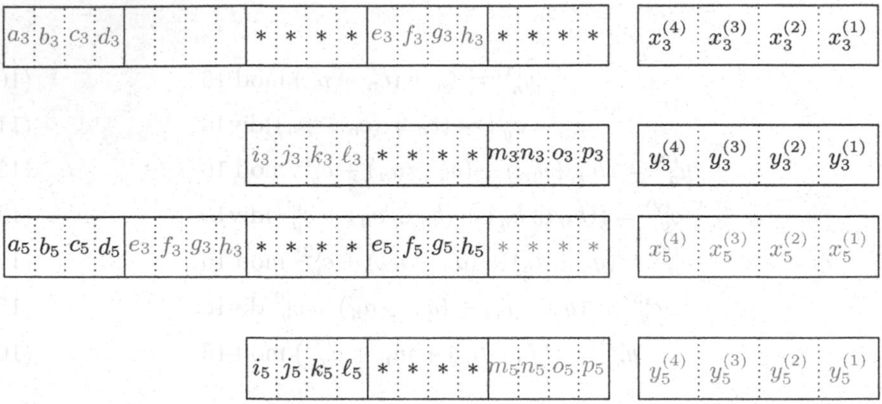

Step 3 We compute the five following outputs using the internal states we have and we compare them with the true outputs given by the generator. If they are equal it means we have recovered the full internal state of the generator with overwhelming probability. We notice that the generator is easily invertible, hence we can recover the seed.

This particular version of Arrow was supposed to have between 96 and 128 bits of security (depending on whether or not an IV was used) and with this attack, we show it cannot have more than 48 bits of security which is far from the 112 bits of security recommended by NIST for lightweight cryptography. This attack had been implemented in C but is not practical on a standard laptop: a Dell Latitude 7400, running on Ubuntu 18.04 (the same laptop will be used for the rest of this paper). If we only test a hundred sets of guesses, the algorithm runs in 0.000144 s. To retrieve the full internal state of the generator, the algorithm should run for approximately 12 years.

3.2 Longer Guess-and-Determine Attack on Arrow-I

Arrow-I is another hardware version of Arrow presented in the original paper, this time with words of size $N = 8$. The set of parameters used is

N	m	r_1	s_1	r_2	s_2	$d_1 = d_2 = d_3 = d_4$
8	256	9	4	7	3	4

and the claimed security is 128 bits (96 bits if a public IV is used).

If we decide to split all the relevant words of 8 bits into four sub-words of 4 bits, we can represent the internal state of this variant of Arrow as follows:

We also split the outputs w_n of 8 bits in two sub words of 4 bits: $w_n^{(1)}$ and $w_n^{(2)}$, with $w_n^{(1)}$ being the least significant bits of w_n and $w_n^{(2)}$ the most significant bits.

The Eqs. (1) and (2) become:

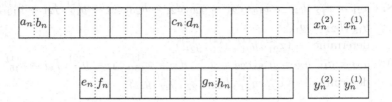

$$x_n^{(1)} = b_n + (e_n \oplus d_n) \bmod 2^{N/2} \qquad (21)$$
$$c_x = (b_n + (e_n \oplus d_n))\mathrm{div}2^{N/2} \qquad (22)$$
$$y_n^{(1)} = f_n + (a_n \oplus h_n) \bmod 2^{N/2} \qquad (23)$$
$$c_y = (f_n + (a_n \oplus h_n))\mathrm{div}2^{N/2} \qquad (24)$$
$$x_n^{(2)} = (c_n + (a_n \oplus h_n) + c_x) \bmod 2^{N/2} \qquad (25)$$
$$y_n^{(2)} = (g_n + (e_n \oplus d_n) + c_y) \bmod 2^{N/2} \qquad (26)$$

We start the attack by clocking the generator seven times. Then, for every $n \geq 7$, $e_n, f_n = y_{n-7}^{(2)}, y_{n-7}^{(1)}$, $c_n, d_n = x_{n-4}^{(2)}, x_{n-4}^{(1)}$ and $g_n, h_n = y_{n-3}^{(2)}, y_{n-3}^{(1)}$. If we denote $\bar{e}_i, \bar{f}_i$ the values above e_i, f_i, we see that we can easily derive them from e_i, f_i and w_{i-7}. We also denote $\bar{g}_i, \bar{h}_i$ the values above g_i, h_i and $\bar{c}_i, \bar{d}_i$ the values under c_i, d_i

Step 0: guess $b_7, g_7, (e_7 \oplus d_7), (a_7 \oplus h_7)$
determine $\rightarrow (x_7^{(1)}, y_7^{(1)}, f_7, y_7^{(2)}, x_7^{(2)}, c_7)$

Step 1: $b_9 = \bar{f}_7$
guess $g_9, (c_9 \oplus d_9), (a_9 \oplus h_9)$
determine $\rightarrow (x_9^{(1)}, y_9^{(1)}, f_9, y_9^{(2)}, x_9^{(2)}, c_9)$

Step 2: $b_{11} = \bar{f}_9, c_{11} = x_7^{(2)}, d_{11} = x_7^{(1)}, e_{11} = g_7$
guess f_{11}
determine $\rightarrow (x_{11}^{(1)}, y_{11}^{(1)}, x_{11}^{(2)}, y_{11}^{(2)}, g_{11})$

Step 3: $a_{12} = c_7, c_{12} = \bar{g}_{11}, e_{12} = \bar{c}_9, g_{12} = y_9^{(2)}, h_{12} = y_9^{(1)}$
guess b_{12}, c_x, c_y
determine $\rightarrow (x_{12}^{(2)}, y_{12}^{(2)}, d_{12}, x_{12}^{(1)}, y_{12}^{(1)}, f_{12})$

Step 4: $a_{15} = \bar{g}_9, c_{15} = x_{11}^{(2)}, d_{15} = x_{11}^{(1)}, e_{15} = g_{11}, g_{15} = y_{12}^{(2)}, h_{12} = y_{12}^{(1)}$
determine $\rightarrow (y_{15}^{(1)}, x_{15}^{(1)}, b_{15}, x_{15}^{(2)}, y_{15}^{(2)})$

Step 5: $a_{16} = x_7^{(2)}, b_{16} = x_7^{(1)}, c_{16} = x_{12}^{(2)}, d_{16} = x_{12}^{(1)}, e_{16} = y_9^{(2)}, f_{16} = y_9^{(1)}$
determine $\rightarrow (x_{16}^{(1)}, y_{16}^{(1)}, h_{16}, x_{16}^{(2)}, y_{16}^{(2)}, g_{16})$

Step 6: $a_{18} = x_9^{(2)}, b_{18} = x_9^{(1)}, e_{18} = y_{11}^{(2)}, f_{18} = y_{11}^{(1)}, g_{18} = y_{15}^{(2)}; h_{18} = y_{15}^{(1)}$
determine $\rightarrow (y_{18}^{(1)}, x_{18}^{(1)}, d_{18}, y_{18}^{(2)}, x_{18}^{(2)}, c_{18})$

Step 7: $a_{20} = x_{11}^{(2)}, b_{20} = x_{11}^{(1)}, c_{20} = x_{16}^{(2)}, d_{20} = x_{16}^{(1)}, e_{20} = g_16, f_{20} = h_16$
determine $\rightarrow (x_{20}^{(1)}, y_{20}^{(1)}, h_{20}, \bar{x}_{20}^{(2)}, y_{20}^{(2)}, g_{20})$

Step 8: $a_{21} = x_{12}^{(2)}, b_{21} = x_{12}^{(1)}, c_{21} = g_{20}^-, d_{21} = h_{20}^-, e_{21} = y_{12}^{(2)}, f_{21} = y_{12}^{(1)}, g_{21} = y_{18}^{(2)}, h_{21} = y_{18}^{(1)}$
determine $\rightarrow (x_{21}^{(1)}, y_{21}^{(1)}, x_{21}^{(2)}, y_{21}^{(2)})$

Step 9: $a_{22} = g_{16}^-, b_{22} = h_{16}^-, c_{22} = x_{18}^{(2)}, d_{22} = x_{18}^{(1)}, e_{22} = y_{15}^{(2)}, f_{22} = y_{15}^{(1)}$
determine $\rightarrow (x_{22}^{(1)}, y_{22}^{(1)}, h_{22}, x_{22}^{(2)}, y_{22}^{(2)}, g_{22})$

At the end of Step 9, we have derived from our guesses the whole internal state of the generator. We use these values to compute the five following outputs and compare them to the five "true" outputs given by the original generator to know if our guesses were correct or not with overwhelming probability. As we guess 16 bits in Step 0, 12 bits in Step 1, 4 bits in Step 2, and 6 bits in Step 3, our time complexity will be approximately (2^{38}). We recall that the security of this generator was supposed to be of at least 96 bits. This attack had been implemented in C and is running in 20 min over 8 threads and with the -O3 option on a standard laptop.

3.3 An Attack Against Arrow-III, the Software Version of Arrow

The software version of Arrow with words of size N is using the following set of parameters

N	m	r_1	s_1	r_2	s_2	$d_1 = d_2 = d_3 = d_4$
N	2^N	31	3	17	3	$N/2$

with $N = 8$ or $N = 32$.

If we decide to split all the relevant words of N bits into two sub-words of N/2 bits, we can represent the internal state of this variant of Arrow as follows:

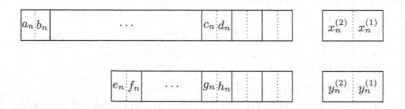

We obtain the same equations as in the previous case.
This version of Arrow has two specificities:

– The values c_i, d_i are above g_i, h_i. Hence if the generator has been clocked enough times and if we know g_i and h_i, then we know c_i and d_i.

– The two lagged Fibonacci generator used in this version of Arrows are more or less synchronized (which is something that should have been avoided). If we call t the difference between r_1 and r_2, we notice that $t = r_1 - r_2 = s_2 - r_2$. Hence, if we know e_i, f_i, c_i, d_i we will know $a_{i+14}, b_{i+14}, e_{i+14}, f_{i+14}$. It will ease our guess-and-determine attack;

Because of that, in our attack we will only face three cases:

Case gh We know a_i, b_i, e_i, f_i, we guess g_i, h_i and derive c_i, d_i, x_i, y_i with the help of w_{i-3} and w_i. We compare $x_i^{(2)} \oplus y_i^{(2)}$ to $w_i^{(2)}$.

Case a We know e_i, f_i, g_i, h_i, we guess a_i and derive x_i, y_i with the help of w_i. We compare $x_i^{(2)} \oplus y_i^{(2)}$ to $w_i^{(2)}$.

Case 0 We know all the relevant values, we derive x_i, y_i from them and compare $x_i \oplus y_i$ to the output w_i.

We start by clocking the generator 17 times to know all the xor between x_i and y_i for i in $\{0, \ldots, 16\}$.

Step 0: guess $a_{17}, e_{17}, f_{17}, g_{17}, h_{17}$
determine $\rightarrow (c_{17}, d_{17}, x_{17}^{(1)}, x_{17}^{(2)}, y_{17}^{(1)}, y_{17}^{(2)})$
assert $x_{17}^{(2)} \oplus y_{17}^{(2)} = w_{17}^{(2)}$

Step 1 (case gh): $a_{31} = e_{17}, b_{31} = f_{17}, e_{31} = g_{17}, f_{31} = h_{17}$
guess g_{31}, h_{31}
determine $\rightarrow (c_{31}, d_{31}, x_{31}, y_{31})$
assert $x_{31}^{(2)} \oplus y_{31}^{(2)} = w_{31}^{(2)}$

Step 2 (case a): $c_{34} = x_{31}^{(2)}, d_{34} = x_{31}^{(1)}, e_{34} = y_{17}^{(2)}, f_{34} = y_{17}^{(1)}, g_{34} = y_{31}^{(2)}, h_{34} = y_{31}^{(1)}$
guess a_{34}
determine $\rightarrow (x_{34}, y_{34})$
assert $x_{34}^{(2)} \oplus y_{34}^{(2)} = w_{34}^{(2)}$

Step 3 (case gh): $a_{45} = c_{17}, b_{45} = d_{17}, e_{45} = g_{31}, f_{45} = h_{31}$
guess g_{45}, h_{45}
determine $\rightarrow (c_{45}, d_{45}, x_{45}, y_{45})$
assert $x_{45}^{(2)} \oplus y_{45}^{(2)} = w_{45}^{(2)}$

Step 4 (case 0): $a_{48} = x_{17}^{(2)}, b_{48} = x_{17}^{(1)}, c_{48} = x_{45}^{(2)}, d_{48} = x_{45}^{(1)}, e_{48} = y_{31}^{(2)}, f_{48} = y_{31}^{(1)}, g_{48} = y_{45}^{(2)}, h_{48} = y_{45}^{(1)}$
determine $\rightarrow (x_{48}, y_{48})$
assert $x_{48} \oplus y_{48} = w_{48}$

In step 0, there are $2^{5N/2}$ possibilities for the set of values $\{a_{17}, e_{17}, f_{17}, g_{17}, h_{17}\}$. Thanks to the first filter, on average only $2^{4N/2}$ possibilities are still on course for step 1.

In step 1, there are $2^{6N/2}$ possibilities for the set of values $\{a_{17}, e_{17}, f_{17}, g_{17}, h_{17}, g_{31}, h_{31}\}$ ($2^{4N/2}$ from step 0 and $2^{2N/2}$ for g_{31}, h_{31}). Thanks to the filter, on average only $2^{5N/2}$ possibilities remains for step 2.

In step 2, there are $2^{6N/2}$ possibilities for the set of values $\{a_{17}, e_{17}, f_{17}, g_{17},$ $h_{17}, g_{31}, h_{31}, a_{34}\}$ ($2^{5N/2}$ from step 1 and $2^{N/2}$ for a_{34}). Thanks to the filter, on average only $2^{5N/2}$ possibilities remains for step 2.

In step 3 we consider $2^{5N/2} \times 2^{2N/2}$ possibilities, on average only $2^{6N/2}$ of them pass the filter.

In step 4 we consider $2^{6N/2}$ possibilities, on average only $2^{4N/2}$ of them pass the filter.

Step 5 (case a): $c_{51} = x_{48}^{(2)}, d_{51} = x_{48}^{(1)}, e_{51} = y_{34}^{(2)}, f_{51} = y_{34}^{(1)}, g_{51} = y_{48}^{(2)}, h_{51} = y_{48}^{(1)}$

guess a_{51}

determine $\rightarrow (x_{51}, y_{51})$

assert $x_{51}^{(2)} \oplus y_{51}^{(2)} = w_{51}^{(2)}$

Step 6 (case gh): $a_{59} = c_{31}, b_{59} = d_{31}, e_{59} = g_{45}, f_{59} = h_{45}$

guess g_{59}, h_{59}

determine $\rightarrow (c_{59}, d_{59}, x_{59}, y_{59})$

assert $x_{59}^{(2)} \oplus y_{59}^{(2)} = w_{59}^{(2)}$

Step 7 (case 0): $a_{62} = x_{31}^{(2)}, b_{62} = x_{31}^{(1)}, c_{62} = x_{59}^{(2)}, d_{62} = x_{59}^{(1)}, e_{62} = y_{45}^{(2)}, f_{62} = y_{45}^{(1)}, g_{62} = y_{59}^{(2)}, h_{62} = y_{59}^{(1)}$

determine $\rightarrow (x_{62}, y_{62})$

assert $x_{62} \oplus y_{62} = w_{62}$

Step 8 (case 0): $a_{65} = x_{34}^{(2)}, b_{65} = x_{34}^{(1)}, c_{65} = x_{62}^{(2)}, d_{65} = x_{62}^{(1)}, e_{65} = y_{48}^{(2)}, f_{65} = y_{48}^{(1)}, g_{65} = y_{62}^{(2)}, h_{65} = y_{62}^{(1)}$

determine $\rightarrow (x_{65}, y_{65})$

assert $x_{65} \oplus y_{65} = w_{65}$

Step 9 (case a): $c_{68} = x_{65}^{(2)}, d_{68} = x_{65}^{(1)}, e_{68} = y_{51}^{(2)}, f_{68} = y_{51}^{(1)}, g_{68} = y_{65}^{(2)}, h_{68} = y_{65}^{(1)}$

guess a_{68}

determine $\rightarrow (x_{68}, y_{68})$

assert $x_{68}^{(2)} \oplus y_{68}^{(2)} = w_{68}^{(2)}$

Step 10 (case gh): $a_{73} = c_{45}, b_{73} = d_{45}, e_{73} = g_{59}, f_{73} = h_{59}$

guess g_{73}, h_{73}

determine $\rightarrow (c_{73}, d_{73}, x_{73}, y_{73})$

assert $x_{73}^{(2)} \oplus y_{73}^{(2)} = w_{73}^{(2)}$

Step 11 (case 0): $a_{76} = x_{45}^{(2)}, b_{76} = x_{45}^{(1)}, c_{76} = x_{73}^{(2)}, d_{76} = x_{73}^{(1)}, e_{76} = y_{59}^{(2)}, f_{76} = y_{59}^{(1)}, g_{76} = y_{73}^{(2)}, h_{76} = y_{73}^{(1)}$

determine $\rightarrow (x_{76}, y_{76})$

assert $x_{76} \oplus y_{76} = w_{76}$

Step 12 (case 0): $a_{79} = x_{48}^{(2)}, b_{79} = x_{48}^{(1)}, c_{79} = x_{76}^{(2)}, d_{79} = x_{76}^{(1)}, e_{79} = y_{62}^{(2)}, f_{79} = y_{62}^{(1)}, g_{79} = y_{76}^{(2)}, h_{79} = y_{76}^{(1)}$

determine $\rightarrow (x_{79}, y_{79})$

assert $x_{79} \oplus y_{79} = w_{79}$

Step 13 (case 0): $a_{82} = x_{51}^{(2)}, b_{82} = x_{41}^{(1)}, c_{82} = x_{79}^{(2)}, d_{82} = x_{79}^{(1)}, e_{82} =$
$y_{65}^{(2)}, f_{82} = y_{65}^{(1)}, g_{82} = y_{79}^{(2)}, h_{82} = y_{79}^{(1)}$
determine $\rightarrow (x_{82}, y_{82})$
assert $x_{82} \oplus y_{82} = w_{82}$

We keep repeating these three steps (case a, case gh, and case 0) until we reach $n = 243$. It takes another 110 steps to go there. At this point, we will have derived the full internal state of the generator and only one guess would have passed all the filters with overwhelming probability. This attack had been fully implemented in C. For $N = 8$ the attack is practical as it runs in 20 s over 8 threads on a standard laptop: a Dell Latitude 7400, running on Ubuntu 18.04.

In each step, there are never more than $2^{7N/2}$ possibilities tested (the maximum is in step 3). We can assume that the complexity is roughly $2^{7N/2}$. For $N = 8$, we obtain 2^{28}, which is coherent with our experimental results. For $N = 32$, it would give 112 bits of security, which is enough for NIST's standards, but far lower than the claim of 1024 bits of security.

4   Description of Trifork

Trifork's structure is described in Fig. 2.

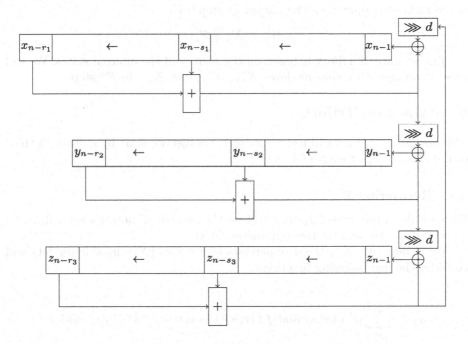

Fig. 2. Description of Trifork

A Trifork generator is going to use three LFGs of respective parameters (r_1, s_1, N, m), (r_2, s_2, N, m) and (r_3, s_3, N, m). The internal states of the first

LFG are denoted (X_i), the internal states of the second one (Y_i), the ones of the third (Z_i) and the outputs (w_i).

The seed of the generator is $(X_{-r_1}, Y_{-r_2}, Z_{-r_3})$. To fill its internal states, it will use a Linear Congruential Generator of public parameters a, c, m with a odd and where m is the same as the one used by the LFGs.

For $i \in \{-r_1 + 1, \ldots, -1\}, X_i = aX_{i-1} + c \bmod m$
For $i \in \{-r_2 + 1, \ldots, -1\}, Y_i = aY_{i-1} + c \bmod m$
For $i \in \{-r_3 + 1, \ldots, -1\}, Z_i = aZ_{i-1} + c \bmod m$

A step i, the generator computes

$$X_i' = X_{i-r_1} + X_{i-s_1} \bmod m$$
$$Y_i' = Y_{i-r_2} + Y_{i-s_2} \bmod m$$
$$Z_i' = Z_{i-r_3} + Z_{i-s_3} \bmod m$$

$$X_i = X_i' \oplus (Z_i' \ggg d) \tag{27}$$
$$Y_i = Y_i' \oplus (X_i' \ggg d) \tag{28}$$
$$Z_i = Z_i' \oplus (Y'i \ggg d) \tag{29}$$

where d is a constant satisfying $0 < d < N$; $\oplus$ is the bitwise exclusive-or and $\ggg$ is the right-shift operator. The output at step n is:

$$W_n = X_n \oplus Z_n.$$

The security of Trifork is based on the secrecy of the internal states. We will present an algorithm that retrieves X_{-r_1}, Y_{-r_2} and Z_{-r_3} in 2^{64} steps.

5   Attack on Trifork

The reason this attack will use 2^{64} steps is because we start by guessing a third of the seed: X_{-r_1} of length 64 bits.

5.1   Recovering Z_{-r_3}

We consider a parameter f_1 that will be the number of outputs we will use to recover Z_{-r_3}. We will set this parameter later.

We denote by $\lceil X \rceil_d$ the d upper bits of a value, $\lfloor X \rfloor_d$ its d lower bits and consider the two following functions :

$$g : i \to \sum_{j=0}^{i-1} a^j \bmod m \text{ and } f : (r, s, i) \to g(r - s + i) + g(i) \bmod m$$

The first step is to compute an approximation of the d upper bits of the values $\{X_0, \ldots, X_{f_1-1}\}$. If $i < 0$, $X_i = a(\ldots a(aX_{-r_1} + c) + c \ldots) + c \bmod m$, that we conveniently rewrite $X_i = a^{r_1+i}X_{-r_1} + g(r_1 + i) \times c \bmod m$. If $i \geq 0$, by Eq. (27), $\lceil X_i \rceil_d = \lceil X_{i-s_1} + X_{i-r_1} \bmod m \rceil_d$.

- if $i < s_1$, then $\lceil X_i \rceil_d = \lceil a^i(1 + a^{r_1 - s_1})X_{-r_1} + f(r_1, s_1, i) \times c \bmod m \rceil_d$ and we can compute this value correctly.
- if $i \geq s_1$, then $\lceil X_i \rceil_d \simeq \lceil X_i - r_1 \rceil_d + \lceil X_{i-s_1} \rceil_d = \lceil a^i X_{-r_1} + g(i) \times c \bmod m \rceil_d + \lceil X_{i-s_1} \rceil_d$ and we can only compute the $d - (i - s_1)$ upper bits correctly.

With that we obtain an approximation of the d upper bits of $\{Z_0, \ldots, Z_{f_1 - 1}\}$ knowing that $Z_i = W_i \oplus X_i$. We call these approximations $\bar{Z}_i$.

- if $i < s_3$, then $\lceil Z_i \rceil_d = \lceil a^i(1 + a^{r_3 - s_3})Z_{-r_3} + f(r_3, s_3, i) \times c \rceil_d$. We set $t_i = \bar{Z}_i 2^{n-d} - f(r_3, s_3, i) \times c$.
  - If $i < s_1$ then $\bar{Z}_i = \lceil Z_i \rceil_d$ and $a^i(1 + a^{r_3 - s_3})Z_{-r_3} - t_i \bmod m = \lfloor Z_i \rfloor_{n-d}$. Hence $|a^i(1 + a^{r_3 - s_3})Z_{-r_3} - t_i| < 2^{n-d}$.
  - If $i \geq s_1$, $\bar{Z}_i$ and $\lceil Z_i \rceil_d$ are only equal on the $d - (i - s_1)$ upper bits. Hence $|a^i(1 + a^{r_3 - s_3})Z_{-r_3} - t_i| < 2^{n-d+i-s_1}$.
- if $i \geq s_3$, then $\lceil Z_i \rceil_d = \lceil a^i Z_{-r_3} + Z_{i-s_3} + g(i) \times c \rceil_d$. We set $t_i = (\bar{Z}_i - Z_{i-s_3})2^{n-d} - g(i) \times c$.
  - If $i < s_1$ then $\bar{Z}_i = \lceil Z_i \rceil_d$ and $\overline{Z_{i-s_3}} = \lceil Z_{i-s_3} \rceil_d$, so

$$
\begin{aligned}
a^i Z_{-r_3} - t_i &= a^i Z_{-r_3} - (\lceil Z_i \rceil_d - \lceil Z_{i-s_3} \rceil_d)2^{n-d} - g(i) \times c \bmod m \\
&= Z_{i-r_3} - (\lceil Z_i \rceil_d - \lceil Z_{i-s_3} \rceil_d)2^{n-d} \bmod m \\
&= (\lceil Z_{i-r_3} \rceil_d + \lceil Z_{i-s_3} \rceil_d - \lceil Z_{i-s_3} + Z_{i-r_3} \rceil_d)2^{n-d} \\
&\quad + \lfloor Z_{i-r_3} \rfloor_{n-d} \bmod m'
\end{aligned}
$$

Hence $|a^i Z_{-r_3} - t_i| < 2^{n-d+1}$.
  - If $i \geq s_1$, $\bar{Z}_i$ and $\lceil Z_i \rceil_d$ are only equal on the $d - (i - s_1)$ upper bits. Hence $|a^i(1 + a^{r_3 - s_3})Z_{-r_3} - t_i| < 2^{n-d+i-s_1+1}$.

Remark 1. *As we use few outputs we will not treat the case were $i - r_3 > 0$.*

Case 1: If $s_3 \geq f_1$, we construct

$$T = (T_i)_{i < f_1},$$

which is close to

$$(1 + a^{r_3 - s_3})Z_{-r_3} \times (1, a, a^2, \ldots, a^{f_1 - 1}) \bmod m.$$

We can see T as the outputs of a *Truncated Linear Congruential Generator* of seed $(1 + a^{r_3 - s_3})Z_{-r_3}$ and known multiplier a. So we search for the closest vector to T in the lattice: $\{X \times (1, a, a^2, \ldots, a^{f_1 - 1}) \bmod m | X \in \mathbb{Z}\}$. This lattice is spanned by the line of the following matrix:

$$
\begin{pmatrix}
1 & a & a^2 & \ldots & a^{f_1 - 1} \\
0 & m & 0 & \ldots & 0 \\
0 & 0 & m & \ldots & 0 \\
& & & \ddots & \\
0 & 0 & 0 & \ldots & m
\end{pmatrix}.
$$

The Closest Vector Problem (CVP) is finding, in a given lattice, the closest vector to a vector target T. This is usually a hard problem and we could have used the attack described in [8]. But here the matrix is of small dimension and we can solve exactly the CVP thanks to a CVP solver/We use the CVP solver of the fpylll library [15] for python.
If f_1 is large enough the CVP solver returns

$$(1 + a^{r_3 - s_3})Z_{-r_3} \times (1, a, a^2, a^3, \ldots) \bmod m.$$

We obtain $(1 + a^{r_3 - s_3})Z_{-r_3}$ but not Z_{-r_3} because $(1 + a^{r_3 - s_3})$ is not invertible mod m.

Case 2: If $s_3 < f_1$, we set $b = a^{-1} \bmod m$ and $\alpha_3 = (1 + a^{r_3 - s_3})$. We construct

$$T = (t_{s_3}, \ldots, t_{f_1 - 1}, t_0, \ldots, t_{s_3 - 1})$$

which is close to

$$a^{s_3} Z_{-r_3} \times (1, a, a^2, \ldots, a^{f_1 - 1 - s_3}, b^{s_3} \alpha_3 \ldots, b\alpha_3) \bmod m.$$

We search for the closest vector to T in the lattice:

$$\{X \times (1, a, a^2, \ldots, a^{f_1 - 1 - s_3}, b^{s_3} \alpha_3 \ldots, b\alpha_3) \bmod m | X \in \mathbb{Z}\}.$$

This lattice is spanned by the line of the following matrix:

$$\begin{pmatrix} 1 & a & \ldots & a^{f_1 - 1 - s_3} & b^{s_3}\alpha_3 & b^{s_3 - 1}\alpha_3 & \ldots & b\alpha_3 \\ 0 & m & \ldots & 0 & 0 & 0 & 0 & \ldots \\ \multicolumn{8}{c}{\ldots\ldots\ldots\ldots} \\ 0 & 0 & \ldots & m & 0 & 0 & 0 & \ldots \\ 0 & 0 & \ldots & 0 & m & 0 & 0 & \ldots \\ \multicolumn{8}{c}{\ldots\ldots\ldots\ldots} \end{pmatrix}.$$

If f_1 is large enough the CVP solver returns

$$a^{s_3} Z_{-r_3} \times (1, a, a^2, \ldots, a^{f_1 - 1 - s_3}, b^{s_3} \alpha_3 \ldots, b\alpha_3) \bmod m$$

and we compute Z_{-r_3}.

The value f_1 is large enough when we have n bits of correct information. If $n/d < s_1$, then we set $f_1 = n/d + 1$ and the $d - 1$ upper bits of the $n/d + 1$ computed approximation of X_i are correct. If $n/d \geq s_1$ the we set f_1 such that $f_1 - 1 \times (d - f_1 - s_1) \geq n$.

If we set X_{-r_1}, we compute Z_{-r_3} or $\alpha_3 Z_{-r_3}$ by solving one CVP on a matrix of size $f_1 \times f_1$.

5.2   Recovering Y_{-r_2}

We consider a parameter f_3 that will be the number of outputs we will use to recover Y_{-r_2}. We will set this parameter as we set f_1. If $n/d < s_3$, then we set

$f_3 = n/d + 1$ and the $d - 1$ upper bits of the n/d computed approximation of Z_i are correct. If $n/d \geq s_3$ the we set f_3 such that $f_3 - 1 \times (d - f_3 - s_3) \geq n$.

Firstly we will compute an approximation of the $n - d$ upper bits of the values $\{Z_0, \ldots, Z_{f_3-1}\}$.

- if $i < s_3$, then $\lceil Z_i \rceil_d = \lceil a^i(1 + a^{r_3 - s_3})Z_{-r_3} + f(r_3, s_3, i) \times c \bmod m \rceil_d$ and we can compute this value correctly.
- if $i \geq s_3$, then $\lceil Z_i \rceil_d \simeq \lceil a^i Z_{-r_3} + g(i) \times c \bmod m \rceil_d + \lceil Z_{i-s_3} \rceil_d$ and only the $d - (i - s_3)$ upper bit are computed correctly.

Remark 2. *If we do not know Z_{-r_3} but only $(1 + a^{r_3 - s_3})Z_{-r_3}$, it means $s_3 \geq f_1 \geq n/d$. So $f_3 = n/d$ and $s_3 \geq f_3$ and we never need Z_{-r_3}.*

Secondly we will compute an approximation of the $n - d$ lower bits of the values $\{X_0, \ldots, X_{f_3-1}\}$.

- if $i < s_1$, then $X_i = (a^i(1 + a^{r_1 - s_1})X_{-r_1} + f(r_1, s_1, i) \times c \bmod m) \oplus (Z_i \ggg d)$.
- if $i \geq s_1$, then $X_i = (a^i X_{-r_1} + g(i) \times c + X_{i-s_1} \bmod m) \oplus (Z_i \ggg d)$.

With the lower bits of the (X_i) we can compute an approximation of the $n - d$ lower bits of the values $\{Z_0, \ldots, Z_{f_3-1}\}$ knowing that $Z_i = W_i \oplus X_i$.

Then we obtain an approximation of the $n - d$ upper bits of $\{Y_0, \ldots, Y_{f_3-1}\}$ knowing that $Z_i = (Z_{i-r_3} + Z_{i-s_3} \bmod m) \oplus (Y_i \ggg d)$. We call these new values $\bar{Y}_i$.

Remark 3. *When we computed the upper bits of (Z_i), we only had the d upper bits, not the $n - d$. This lack of information impacts the rest of the calculation and at the final step, we know there is no information in the $n - 2d$ lower bits of the $(\bar{Y}_i)$.*

- if $i < s_2$, then $\lceil Y_i \rceil_d = \lceil a^i(1 + a^{r_2 - s_2})Y_{-r_2} + f(r_2, s_2, i) \times c \bmod m \rceil_d$. We set $t_i = \bar{Y}_i 2^d - f(r_2, s_2, i) \times c$.
- if $i \geq s_2$, then $\lceil Y_i \rceil_d = \lceil a^i Y_{-r_2} + Y_{i-s_2} + g(i) \times c \bmod m \rceil_d$. We set $t_i = (\bar{Y}_i - Y_{i-s_2})2^d - g(i) \times c$.

Here the dependences between the different values are harder to make explicit. For example, in the case where $i < min(s_1, s_2, s_3)$, we can compute the d upper bits of Z_i correctly. Thank to that we can compute the d upper bits of $\lfloor X_i \rfloor_{n-d}$ correctly. We obtain directly the d upper bits of $\lfloor Z_i \rfloor_{n-d}$ with $Z_i = W_i \oplus X_i$. The last step is obtaining the d upper bits of $Y_i \ggg d$. At this point there is an addition so we might loose one bit of precision because of a carry. We obtain that $|a^i(1 + a^{r_2 - s_2})Y_{-r_2} - t_i| < 2^{n-d+1}$.

Case 1: If $s_2 \geq f_3$, we construct

$$T = (T_i)_{i < f_3}$$

which is close to $(1 + a^{r_2 - s_2})Y_{-r_2} \times (1, a, a^2, \ldots) \bmod m$. We search for the closest vector to T in the lattice:

$$\{X \times (1, a, a^2, \ldots) \bmod m | X \in \mathbb{Z}\}.$$

This lattice is spanned by the lines of the following matrix:

$$\begin{pmatrix} 1 & a & a^2 \dots \\ 0 & m & 0 \dots \\ 0 & 0 & m \dots \\ \dots\dots\dots \end{pmatrix}$$

The CVP solver returns $(1 + a^{r_2 - s_2})Y_{-r_2} \times (1, a, a^2, \dots) \bmod m$. We cannot compute Y_{-r_2} because $(1 + a^{r_2 - s_2})$ is not invertible mod m.

Case 2: If $s_2 < f_3$, we set $b = a^{-1} \bmod m$ and $\alpha_2 = (1 + a^{r_2 - s_2})$. We construct

$$T = (t_{s_2}, \dots, t_{f_3 - 1}, t_0, \dots, t_{s_2 - 1})$$

which is close to

$$a^{s_2} Y_{-r_2} \times (1, a, a^2, \dots, a^{f_3 - 1 - s_2}, b^{s_2}\alpha_2 \dots, b\alpha_2) \bmod m.$$

and we search for the closest vector to T in the lattice:

$$\{X \times (1, a, a^2, \dots, a^{f_3 - 1 - s_2}, b^{s_2}\alpha_2 \dots, b\alpha_2) \bmod m | X \in \mathbb{Z}\}.$$

This lattice is spanned by the lines of the following matrix:

$$\begin{pmatrix} 1 & a & \dots a^{f_3 - 1 - s_2} & b^{s_2}\alpha_2 & b^{s_2 - 1}\alpha_2 & \dots & b\alpha_2 \\ 0 & m & \dots 0 & 0 & 0 & 0 & \dots \\ \dots\dots\dots\dots & & \dots & & \dots & & \dots\dots \\ 0 & 0 & \dots m & 0 & 0 & 0 & \dots \\ 0 & 0 & \dots 0 & m & 0 & 0 & \dots \\ \dots\dots\dots\dots & & \dots & & \dots & & \dots\dots \end{pmatrix}$$

We CVP solver returns $a^{s_2} Y_{-r_2} \times (1, a, a^2, \dots, a^{f_3 - 1 - s_2}, b^{s_2}\alpha_2 \dots, b\alpha_2) \bmod m \bmod m$ and we can compute Y_{-r_2}.

Once again, for a set X_{-r_1} we only solve one CVP to compute Y_{-r_2} or $\alpha_2 Y_{-r_2}$.

Remark 4. *We will not detail here how we recover Z_{-r_3} and/or Y_{-r_2} in the cases where we only have $(1 + a^{r_3 - s_3})Z_{-r_3}$ and/or $(1 + a^{r_2 - s_2})Y_{-r_2}$ because it does not make appears interesting techniques. It only use modular arithmetic and does not need other guess or resource-consuming operation.*

This attack is fully implemented in sagemath but cannot run on a laptop as it needs to solve $2^{64} \times 2$ CVPs.

References

1. NESSIE, the new european schemes for signatures, integrity and encryption (2000). https://www.cosic.esat.kuleuven.be/nessie/
2. eStream, the ECRYPT stream cipher project (2004). https://www.ecrypt.eu.org/stream/project.html
3. Babbage, S., De Cannière, C., Lano, J., Preneel, B., Vandewalle, J.: Cryptanalysis of SOBER-t32. In: Johansson, T. (ed.) FSE 2003. LNCS, vol. 2887, pp. 111–128. Springer, Heidelberg (2003). https://doi.org/10.1007/978-3-540-39887-5_10
4. Banegas, G.: Attacks in stream ciphers: A survey. Cryptology ePrint Archive, Report 2014/677 (2014). https://eprint.iacr.org/2014/677
5. Blanco Blanco, A., et al.: On-the-fly testing an implementation of arrow lightweight PRNG using a LabVIEW framework. In: Martínez Álvarez, F., Troncoso Lora, A., Sáez Muñoz, J.A., Quintián, H., Corchado, E. (eds.) CISIS/ICEUTE -2019. AISC, vol. 951, pp. 175–184. Springer, Cham (2020). https://doi.org/10.1007/978-3-030-20005-3_18
6. Bleichenbacher, D., Patel, S.: SOBER Cryptanalysis. In: Knudsen, L. (ed.) FSE 1999. LNCS, vol. 1636, pp. 305–316. Springer, Heidelberg (1999). https://doi.org/10.1007/3-540-48519-8_22
7. Elaine Barker, J.K.: Recommendation for random number generation using deterministic random bit generators. Tech. Rep. NIST Special Publication (SP) 800–90A, Rev. 1, National Institute of Standards and Technology, Gaithersburg, MD (2015). https://doi.org/10.6028/NIST.SP.800-90Arl
8. Frieze, A.M., Kannan, R., Lagarias, J.C.: Linear congruential generators do not produce random sequences. In: 25th FOCS, pp. 480–484. IEEE Computer Society Press, October 1984. https://doi.org/10.1109/SFCS.1984.715950
9. Keery A. McKay, L.B.: Report on lightweight cryptography. Tech. Rep. NISTIR 8114, National Institute of Standards and Technology, Gaithersburg, MD (2017). https://doi.org/10.6028/NIST.IR.8114
10. Knuth, D.: Deciphering a linear congruential encryption. IEEE Trans. Inf. Theory $31(1)$, 49–52 (1985)
11. López, A.B.O., Encinas, L.H., Muñoz, A.M., Vitini, F.M.: A lightweight pseudorandom number generator for securing the internet of things. IEEE Access 5, 27800–27806 (2017)
12. Orue, A., Montoya, F., Hernández Encinas, L.: Trifork, a new pseudorandom number generator based on lagged fibonacci maps. J. Comput. Sci. Eng. 2, 46–51 (2010)
13. Rose, G.: A stream cipher based on linear feedback over $GF(2^8)$. In: Boyd, C., Dawson, E. (eds.) ACISP 1998. LNCS, vol. 1438, pp. 135–146. Springer, Heidelberg (1998). https://doi.org/10.1007/BFb0053728
14. Stern, J.: Secret linear congruential generators are not cryptographically secure. In: 28th FOCS, pp. 421–426. IEEE Computer Society Press, October 1987. https://doi.org/10.1109/SFCS.1987.51
15. Development team, T.F.: fpylll, a lattice reduction library for python (2016). https://github.com/fplll/fpylll, available at https://github.com/fplll/fpylll

Autoguess: A Tool for Finding Guess-and-Determine Attacks and Key Bridges

Hosein Hadipour[✉] and Maria Eichlseder

Graz University of Technology, Graz, Austria
{hossein.hadipour,maria.eichlseder}@iaik.tugraz.at

Abstract. The guess-and-determine technique is one of the most widely used techniques in cryptanalysis to recover unknown variables in a given system of relations. A subset of the unknown variables is guessed such that the remaining unknowns can be deduced using the relations. Applications include state recovery for stream ciphers and key-bridging in key-recovery attacks on block ciphers. Since the attack complexity depends on the number of guessed variables, it is essential to find small guess bases.

In this paper, we present *Autoguess*, an easy-to-use tool to search for a minimal guess basis. We propose several new modeling techniques to harness SAT/SMT, MILP, and Gröbner basis solvers. We demonstrate their usefulness in guess-and-determine attacks on stream ciphers and block ciphers, as well as finding key-bridges for block ciphers. Moreover, integrating our CP models for the key-bridging technique into the previous CP-based frameworks to search for distinguishers, we propose a unified and general CP model to find key-recovery-friendly distinguishers for both linear and nonlinear key schedules.

Keywords: Guess & determine · CP · MILP · SAT · Gröbner basis

1 Introduction

The practical security of symmetric-key cryptographic primitives with respect to known attacks is ensured by extensive cryptanalysis. There is a wide variety of different cryptanalytic techniques, including differential, linear, and integral cryptanalysis, and more. Many of these involve tracing the propagation of certain cryptographic properties at the bit-level, which can be highly nontrivial. From a designer's perspective, designing a primitive requires the analysis with all these known techniques. Thus, the design and cryptanalysis of symmetric-key primitives is a time-consuming and error-prone process. Therefore, it is of significant importance for the community to develop automatic methods and tools.

One of the most widely used techniques in cryptanalysis is the guess-and-determine (GD) technique, especially when only low amounts of data are available to the attacker. GD recovers the unknown variables in a given system of relations on a set of variables: A subset of the unknown variables is guessed such

© Springer Nature Switzerland AG 2022
G. Ateniese and D. Venturi (Eds.): ACNS 2022, LNCS 13269, pp. 230–250, 2022.
https://doi.org/10.1007/978-3-031-09234-3_12

that the remaining unknowns can be deduced using the information from the guessed variables. The correctness of the guesses also can be checked using the given relations since it is assumed that the incorrect guesses yield inconsistency.

This approach can be used in various areas of cryptanalysis. For instance, it can be applied to recover the internal state of a stream cipher from a sufficient amount of output data, or the state and secret key of a block cipher from plaintext/ciphertext pairs. Another important application is the key-bridging technique in key recovery attacks on block ciphers, where the attacker aims to find the involved sub-keys based on the relations induced by the key schedule. Beyond these cryptanalytic uses, the GD technique also finds application in a broader mathematical context, for example in its links to uniquely restricted matching problems in graph theory [14]. In these applications, the complexity of the GD technique is directly dependent on the number of guessed variables. It is thus essential to find the smallest possible subset of guessed variables from which the remaining variables can be determined efficiently.

In this paper, we provide a general tool to search for a suitable set of guessed variables with minimum size. This tool allows designers of symmetric-key primitives to easily and thoroughly analyze their designs from the GD attack point of view. Additionally, our tool can help designers to optimize their key schedule algorithms with respect to the key-bridging technique.

Our contributions can be summarized as follows:

1. We present *Autoguess*, an easy-to-use open-source tool which integrates a wide range of CP/SMT/SAT/MILP solvers as well as the Gröbner basis algorithm to automate GD attacks and the key-bridging technique. Autoguess is publicly available at https://github.com/hadipourh/autoguess.
2. We introduce new encodings in CP and SAT/SMT to formulate the GD attack which achieves a better performance compared to MILP encoding [3] in many cases, particularly when searching for feasible solutions. In contrast to previous models [3,7] where all variables should be deduced from the guessed variables, our reformulation takes an arbitrary subset of variables as the target variables into account. This enables us to extend the application to the key bridging technique, where only an arbitrary subset of variables needs to be deduced. Additionally, we adapt the method introduced by Danner et al. [7] to translate GD attacks to the problem of computing the Gröbner basis of a Boolean ideal, and extend it for key-bridging technique as well.
3. Using Autoguess to search for key-bridges in bit-oriented block ciphers with nonlinear keyschedule, we reduce the time complexity of the analysis phase in linear attack on 26-round PRESENT-80 presented at EUROCRYPT 2020 [11] from 2^{65} to 2^{64}. In addition we show that our tool can automatically re-discover many of the best results obtained with the key-bridging technique, which previously had to be generated either manually or with dedicated, cipher-specific tools. For example, we successfully automatically re-discovered the integral attack on 24-round LBlock [6].
4. To show the application of our tool in the analysis of stream ciphers, we use it to reduce the computational complexity of the GD attack on ZUC from 2^{392} [10] to 2^{390} while using the same amount of 9 keystream output words.

Table 1. Summary of our Attacks on SKINNY-128-256, SKINNY-64-192, SKINNY-64-128 and TWINE-80, where $\mathcal{DS}$-MITM denote Demirci-Selçuk Meet-in-the-Middle cryptanalysis and ST stands for single-tweakey setting.

Cipher	#Rounds	Data	Memory	Time	Attack	Setting	Reference
SKINNY-128-256	19	2^{96} CP	$2^{210.99}$	$2^{238.26}$	$\mathcal{DS}$-MITM	ST	Sect. 9.1
SKINNY-64-192	21	2^{60} CP	$2^{133.99}$	$2^{186.63}$	$\mathcal{DS}$-MITM	ST	Sect. 9.1
SKINNY-64-128	18	2^{32} CP	$2^{61.91}$	$2^{126.32}$	$\mathcal{DS}$-MITM	ST	Sect. 9.1
TWINE-80	20	2^{32} CP	$\mathbf{2^{62.91}}$	$2^{76.92}$	$\mathcal{DS}$-MITM	-	Sect. 9.2
TWINE-80	20	2^{32} CP	$2^{82.91}$	$2^{77.44}$	$\mathcal{DS}$-MITM	-	[18]

5. To show the versatility of our tool, we also used it for finding low-data-complexity attacks on block ciphers. More precisely, we used it to find GD attacks on AES, CRAFT, and SKINNY. For example concerning AES, we could rediscover the best previous GD attack on 3 rounds with data complexity of merely one known plaintext/ciphertext pair.
6. We show that our CP-based approaches for the key-bridging technique are consistent with the previous CP-based frameworks to search for distinguishers. Hence, we integrate it into the previous CP-based frameworks for automatic search of distinguishers to build a general CP-model to find the key recovery friendly distinguishers taking the key-bridging into account for both linear and nonlinear key schedules. To show the usefulness of this new method, as it can be seen in Table 1 we could improve the memory complexity of the best previous $\mathcal{DS}$-MITM attack on 20-rounds of TWINE-80 by a factor of 2^{20}. We also utilized this new framework to find the $\mathcal{DS}$-MITM attacks on SKINNY-64-128, SKINNY-64-192 and SKINNY-128-256 for the first time.

Full Version. The full version of this paper [12] provides details on all applications.

Outline. In Sect. 2, we recall the preliminaries on GD attacks and the key-bridging technique. In Sect. 3, we propose the constraint programming model of these two techniques, and in Sect. 4, we discuss an alternative model using Gröbner bases. In Sect. 5, we introduce our tool Autoguess with its preprocessing and early-abort techniques. We apply it to find key bridges for different ciphers in Sect. 6 as well as GD attacks on block ciphers in Sect. 7 and stream ciphers in Sect. 8. Finally, we provide a discussion in Sect. 10.

2   Preliminaries

In this section, we provide a brief overview of the cryptanalytic background.

We denote the integer range i to j by $i \sim j$. We use $\neg, \wedge, \vee, \oplus$ to denote bitwise NOT, AND, OR, XOR and $\|$ for concatenation. For a fixed wordsize, $\lll i, \ggg i$ denote left rotation and right rotation by i bits, and $\boxplus, \boxminus$ denote modular addition and subtraction, respectively. In SMT models, $\texttt{BVZExt}(x, n)$

is zero-extension of x by n bits as $0||\cdots||0||x$, BVAdd(x,y) is bit-vector addition of x and y, and BVULE(x,y) is an unsigned $\leq$ comparison of two bit-vectors x and y. In the GD context, we use $x \Rightarrow y$ to indicate y can be deduced from x.

2.1 Guess-and-Determine Technique

The GD technique is a general method to solve a system of equations, given as a set of variables linked by relations. In this method, the values of a subset of the variables are guessed first. Next, using the relations, one may find the values of a subset of the remaining unknown variables, which is called knowledge propagation. If all of the remaining unknown variables are determined from the guessed variables, we call the set of guessed variables a guess basis [2].

For systems of equations obtained from cryptographic primitives, the GD technique is often used when data is very scarce, and statistical attacks are therefore impossible. The main challenges of a GD attack are to find a suitable guess basis and to effectively propagate knowledge. Since the complexity of GD attacks depends crucially on the size of the guess basis, the main goal is finding a guess basis of minimal size to addressing which several improvements and approaches have been proposed. For instance, Ahmadi and Ehglidos [1] proposed a heuristic approach based on dynamic programming to automatically find GD attack for classes of stream ciphers.

2.2 Key-Bridging Technique

Key-bridging is a technique to optimize the key-recovery process in attacks on block ciphers. In such attacks, a core distinguisher can often be extended by additional initial and final key-recovery rounds, where an attacker guesses selected round key bits to verify the distinguisher. Key-bridging attempts to minimize the number of guessed key bits using dependencies in the key schedule.

An interesting automated approach to search for key-bridging was introduced by Lin et al. at FSE 2016 [16]. However, their approach cannot handle certain cryptographic operations like modular addition and provides only a limited output: It only derives a bound on the number of solutions, but not the actual guess basis or determination flow. Moreover, their tool is based on a dedicated linear algebraic method and hence not consistent with the CP-based approaches to search for distinguishers, whereas as we will show in Sect. 9, our CP-based approaches for key-bridging can be merged into the previous CP-based tools.

2.3 Connection Relations

We can describe the GD technique using two types of connection relations [3].

Definition 1 (Implication Relation). *Let $x_0, \ldots, x_{n-1}, y$ denote some variables. If y can be uniquely determined from $x_0, \ldots, x_{n-1}$, we say they have an implication relation r and denote LHS$(r) = \{x_0, \ldots, x_{n-1}\}$ and RHS$(r) = \{y\}$:*

$$r : x_0, \ldots, x_{n-1} \Rightarrow y.$$

Table 2. Modeling a cipher using connection relations, where $x_0, x_1 \ldots, x_{n-1}, y \in \mathbb{F}_2^n$

Equation or prerequisite	Connection relation
Xor: $y = \bigoplus_{i=0}^{n-1} x_i$	$[x_0, \ldots, x_{n-1}, y]$
And: $y = \bigwedge_{i=0}^{n-1} x_i$	$x_0, \ldots, x_{n-1} \Rightarrow y$
Modular Addition: $y = \boxplus_0^{n-1} x_i$	$[x_0, \ldots, x_{n-1}, y]$
S-Box: $y = F(x)$ with $F : \mathbb{F}_2^n \to \mathbb{F}_2^n$	$[x, y]$
Concatenation: $x = x_0 \| \ldots \| x_{n-1}$	$x_0, \ldots, x_{n-1} \Rightarrow x; \ \forall \ 0 \le i \le n - 1 : x \Rightarrow x_i$
Elimination: If $[x_0, \ldots, x_{n-1}, x] \wedge [x, y_0, \ldots, y_{n-1}]$, then $[x_0, \ldots, x_{n-1}, y_0, \ldots, y_{n-1}]$	

Definition 2 (Symmetric relation). *Let $x_0, \ldots, x_{n-1}$ denote n variables. We say they have a symmetric relation r with $|r| = n$ if and only if each variable x_i can be uniquely deduced when the remaining $n - 1$ variables are all known:*

$$r : [x_0, x_2, \ldots, x_{n-1}].$$

We can model a cipher using a combination of implication and symmetric relations by applying rules such as those illustrated in Table 2.

2.4 A Naive Guess-and-Determine Approach

Assume we have a system of connection relations involving n unknown variables and are looking for a guess basis of minimum size. A naive approach is exhaustive search, i.e., checking each possible subset of each possible size k, $1 \le k \le n$, to discover a minimal subset that is a guess basis. To check whether a subset K of size k can be a guess basis, we assume that all variables in K are known and apply knowledge propagation through the given connection relations to update the set of known variables. A minimal guess basis is found as soon as a set of known variables is found which deduces all of the remaining variables. The complexity of the exhaustive search for a guess basis of size less than or equal to m (if it exists) is roughly $\sum_{k=1}^{m} \binom{n}{k}$, which is exponential in both n and m. Thus, this approach is infeasible when m or n are large enough.

3 Constraint Programming for GD and Key-Bridging

3.1 Modelling Knowledge Propagation

Two main challenges of the GD technique are knowledge propagation and finding a minimal guess basis [2]. Finding a minimal guess basis is an optimization problem, but can be transformed into a sequence of decision problems whether a guess basis of a specified size exists. We thus need to model knowledge propagation. We consider variables which can either be unknown or known, and their state may change from unknown to known during the guessing sequence.

Let $(X, \mathcal{R})$ be a system of connection relations, where $X = \{x_0, \ldots, x_{n-1}\}$ and $\mathcal{R} = \{r_0, \ldots, r_{m-1}\}$. Assuming that a subset of variables such as $K_0 \subseteq X$ is initially known, the known/unknown status of each single variable $x \in X$ in each step can be represented by a new binary decision variable, the *state variable*.

Definition 3 (State variables). *For a given system of connection relations* $(X, \mathcal{R})$, *where* $X = \{x_0, \ldots, x_{n-1}\}$, *let the set of binary decision variables* $S_j = \{x_{0,j}, \ldots, x_{n-1,j}\}$ *represent the status of variables in the jth step of knowledge propagation, where* $x_{i,j} = 1$ *if* x_i *is known at step j and* $x_{i,j} = 0$ *otherwise, for* $0 \leq i \leq n-1$ *and* $j \in \mathbb{Z}_{\geq 0}$.

For a given initial subset $K_0 \subseteq X$ of known variables, the knowledge propagation can be represented as a chain $S_0 \to S_1 \to \cdots \to S_j \to \cdots$.

Given that a variable can be involved in more than one connection relation, we define *path variables* to link each variable to its corresponding relations.

Definition 4 (Path variables). *Let* $(X, \mathcal{R})$ *be a system of connection relations with* $R = \{r_0, \ldots, r_{m-1}\}$. *Assume* $x_i \in X$ *appears in* λ *relations* $\{r_0^i, \ldots, r_{\lambda-1}^i\}$, *where for each* $0 \leq k \leq \lambda-1$, r_k^i *is either a symmetric relation or an implication relation with* $x_i \in RHS(r_k^i)$. *Then, for each step j of knowledge propagation, λ new binary decision variables* $\mathtt{Path}(x_{i,j}) := \{x_{i,j,k} : 0 \leq k \leq \lambda - 1\}$ *are defined as*

$$
x_{i,j,k} = \begin{cases} 1 & x_i \text{ can be determined from the relation } r_k^i \text{ at step } j - 1 \\ 0 & \text{otherwise,} \end{cases}
$$

where $0 \leq i \leq n-1$ *and* $j \in \mathbb{Z}_{\geq 1}$. $\mathtt{Path}(x_{i,j})$ *is called the set of path variables corresponding to* $x_i \in X$ *at the jth step of knowledge propagation. For $j = 0$ and all* $0 \leq i \leq n-1$, $\mathtt{Path}(x_{i,0}) = \emptyset$.

Proposition 1 (Knowledge propagation). *Let* $(X, \mathcal{R})$ *be a system of connection relations and* $\mathtt{Path}(x_{i,j}) = \{x_{i,j,k} : 0 \leq k \leq \lambda - 1\}$ *as defined above. Then* $x_{i,j} = 1$ *if and only if at least one of the following conditions holds:*

- **Already known:** $x_{i,j-1} = 1$, *i.e., x_i has been known since the previous steps,*
- **Determined:** *There exists* $x_{i,j,k} \in \mathtt{Path}(x_{i,j})$ *such that* $x_{i,j,k} = 1$, *i.e., $x_{i,j}$ can be determined from the previously known variables.*

For a given system of connection relations $(X, \mathcal{R})$ and a subset of known variables, any assignment for the state and path variables satisfying the definitions of state and path variables as well as Proposition 1 corresponds to a valid knowledge propagation. For a valid assignment of state and path variables, let $K_j := \{x_{i,j} \in S_j : x_{i,j} = 1\}$. According to the first condition in Proposition 1, if $x_{i,j} = 1$, then for all $j' \geq j$, $x_{i,j'} = 1$, where $0 \leq i \leq n-1$, since a variable remains known after it becomes known once. As a consequence, $K_0 \to \cdots \to K_j \to \cdots$, where $j \in \mathbb{Z}_{\geq 0}$ is an ascending chain. On the other hand, the number of known variables is upper bounded by $|X| = n$. Therefore, according to the ascending chain condition, there exists a positive integer β such that $K_\beta = K_{\beta+1} = \cdots$.

While in the GD technique one usually looks for a minimal guess basis to deduce all of the remaining variables, in the key-bridging technique we are looking for a minimal set of guessed variables to determine a certain subset of variables, which are the sub-keys involved in the key-recovery. Accordingly, we define the concept of guess basis for a subset $T \subseteq X$ as the target variables.

Definition 5 (Guess basis). *Let $(X, \mathcal{R})$ be a system of connection relations and $T \subseteq X$. The subset $K \subseteq X$ is called a guess basis for T if there exists some positive integer β such that all variables in T can be deduced from K after β steps of knowledge propagation.*

Using the following proposition, one can characterize the guess basis for a given system of connection relations and a subset of target variables.

Proposition 2 (Characterizing guess basis). *Let $(X, \mathcal{R})$ be a system of connection relations and $S_0 \rightarrow \cdots \rightarrow S_j \rightarrow \cdots$ be its chain of state variables. $K_0 \subseteq X$ is a guess basis for $T \subseteq X$ if there exists a positive integer β and an assignment of state and path variables for which the following conditions hold:*

- *For all $x_{i,0} \in S_0$, if $x_i \in K_0$, then $x_{i,0} = 1$, and $x_{i,0} = 0$ otherwise.*
- *The assignment satisfies the definition of state and path variables and Proposition 1.*
- *For all $x_{i,\beta} \in S_\beta$, if $x_i \in T$, then $x_{i,\beta} = 1$, i.e., all target variables should be known in the final step of knowledge propagation.*

3.2   Encoding Using CP

Proposition 3 (Link from path to state variables in CP encoding). *Let $x_{i,j,k}$ be a path variable corresponding to the state variable $x_{i,j}$ in connection relation r_k^i. Assume that the variables of r_k^i are x_i and $x_{i_0}, \ldots, x_{i_{p-1}}$ for some $p \in \mathbb{Z}_{\geq 1}$. Then, the link between $x_{i,j,k}$, and the state variables $x_{i_0,j-1}, \ldots, x_{i_{p-1},j-1}$, is encoded as follows, where $j \in \mathbb{Z}_{\geq 1}$, and r_k^i is either a symmetric relation, or an implication relation such that $x_i \in RHS(r_k^i)$:*

$$x_{i,j,k} = x_{i_0,j-1} \wedge \cdots \wedge x_{i_{p-1},j-1}.$$

Proposition 4 (Link from state to path variables in CP encoding). *Let $\mathtt{Path}(x_{i,j})$ be the set of path variables $\{x_{i,j,k} : 0 \leq k \leq \lambda - 1\}$ corresponding to the state variable $x_{i,j}$. The link between $x_{i,j}$ and $\mathtt{Path}(x_{i,j})$ can be encoded as*

$$x_{i,j} = x_{i,j-1} \vee x_{i,j,0} \vee \cdots \vee x_{i,j,\lambda-1}.$$

For a given system of connection relations $(X, \mathcal{R})$, let $T \subseteq X$ be the set of target variables for which we are looking for a minimal guess basis. To encode this problem into a CP model, we firstly consider a fixed positive integer value for β as the depth of knowledge propagation and then generate the state and path variables corresponding to β steps of knowledge propagation. Assume that the chain $S_0 \to \cdots \to S_\beta$, represents the knowledge propagation through β steps where $S_j = \{x_{i,j} : 0 \le i \le n-1\}$. Then, we set the objective function as follows:

$$\min \sum_{i=0}^{n-1} x_{i,0},$$

such that $x_{i,\beta} = 1$ for all $x_i \in \mathcal{T}$, and all CP constraints linking the state and path variables (Propositions 3 and 4) are satisfied. If the constructed CP model is satisfiable, then the set $\mathcal{M} := \{x_i \in X : x_{i,0} = 1\}$ is a guess basis for $\mathcal{T}$. By the ascending chain rule, the set $\mathcal{M}$ converges to a minimal guess basis for $\mathcal{T}$ when β is large enough. Algorithm 1 summarizes the CP encoding. With a similar approach, we show in the long version of our paper how to encode the search for guess bases in SMT/SAT languages.

Algorithm 1: CP Encoding (Sect. 3.2)

Input: System of connection relations $(X, \mathcal{R})$, where $X = \{x_0, \ldots, x_{n-1}\}$, a set of target variables $\mathcal{T} \subseteq X$, the depth $\beta \in \mathbb{Z}_{\ge 1}$ of knowledge propagation
Output: A sufficient subset $\mathbb{G} \subseteq X$ for $\mathcal{T}$

1   Initialize a dictionary Deriver with $keys(\mathtt{Deriver}) = X$ and a CP model $\mathcal{M}$;
2   **for** $i = 0 \to n-1$ **do**
3     $\mathtt{Deriver}[x_i] \leftarrow [\{x_i\}]$;
4   **for** $r \in \mathcal{R}$ **do**
5   **if** r *is a symmetric relation* **and** $x_i \in r$ **then**
6         $\mathtt{Deriver}[x_i] \leftarrow \mathtt{Deriver}[x_i] \cup [\{v \in r : v \ne x_i\}]$;
7   **if** r *is an implication relation* **and** $x_i \in RHS(r)$ **then**
8         $\mathtt{Deriver}[x_i] \leftarrow \mathtt{Deriver}[x_i] \cup [\mathrm{LHS}(r)]$;
9   **for** $j = 0 \to \beta - 1$ **do**
10   **for** $i = 0 \to n-1$ **do**
11       $\mathcal{M}.var \leftarrow \{x_{i,j+1}\}$;
12       $\lambda \leftarrow |\mathtt{Deriver}[x_i]|$;
13   **for** $k = 0 \to \lambda - 1$ **do**
14   Let $\mathtt{Deriver}[x_i][k] = \{x_{i_0}, \ldots, x_{i_{p-1}}\}$;
15         $\mathcal{M}.var \leftarrow \{x_{i,j+1,k}\} \cup \{x_{i_0,j}, \ldots, x_{i_{p-1},j}\}$;
16         $\mathcal{M}.con \leftarrow x_{i,j+1,k} = \bigwedge_{l=0,\ldots,p-1} x_{i_l,j}$ ▷ Link path to state variables;
17       $\mathcal{M}.con \leftarrow x_{i,j+1} = \bigvee_{k=0,\ldots,\lambda-1} x_{i,j+1,k}$ ▷ Link state to path variables;
18   **for** $x_i \in \mathcal{T}$ **do**
19     $\mathcal{M}.con \leftarrow x_{i,\beta} = 1$ ▷ Target variables must be known in final step ;
20   $\mathcal{M}.obj \leftarrow \min. \sum_{i=0}^{n-1} x_{i,0}$ ▷ Objective function;
21   $\mathtt{solution} \leftarrow \mathcal{M}.solve$ ▷ Call a CP solver;
22   **return** $\mathbb{G} = \{x_i \in X | x_{i,0} = 1\}$;

---

4   From Guess Basis to Gröbner Basis

In this section, we briefly recall the method introduced in [7] to translate the GD problem to the problem of computing the reduced Gröbner basis of a Boolean polynomial ideal, and also modify it to take the target variables and known variables into account, allowing us to model the key-bridging problem as well.

Given a system of connection relations $(X, \mathcal{R})$, where $X = \{x_0, \ldots, x_{n-1}\}$, without loss of generality we can assume that all relations are implication relations. For each implication relation $x_{i_0}, \ldots, x_{i_{m-2}} \Rightarrow x_{i_{m-1}}$, we replace each variable x_{i_k} with a Boolean variable X_{i_k} representing whether it is known. This yields the logical formula $(\neg X_{i_0} \vee \ldots \vee \neg X_{i_{m-2}} \vee X_{i_{m-1}})$. Accordingly, a system of connection relations is translated to a CNF formula. Let $\mathcal{C}$ be the derived CNF with n binary variables, and let $Sat(\mathcal{C})$ be a subset of $\{0,1\}^n$ including all solutions of $\mathcal{C}$. It is well-known that $\mathcal{C}$ can be represented via a set of Boolean polynomials $\mathcal{F}$ such that $Sat(\mathcal{C}) = \mathcal{Z}(\mathcal{F})$, where $\mathcal{Z}(\mathcal{F})$ denotes the solution set of $\mathcal{F}$. To do so, every Horn clause $(\neg X_{i_0} \vee \ldots \vee \neg X_{i_{m-2}} \vee X_{i_{m-1}})$ is translated to a binomial $x_{i_0} \cdots x_{i_{m-2}} \cdot (x_{i_{m-1}} + 1)$ in the Boolean polynomial ring $\frac{\mathbb{F}_2[x_0,\ldots,x_{n-1}]}{\langle x_0^2+x_0,\ldots,x_{n-1}^2+x_{n-1}\rangle}$. Thus, every system of connection relations can be translated to a set of Boolean binomials. The following theorem represents the relation between a minimal guess basis for a system of connection relations and the reduced Gröbner basis of its algebraic representation. While the CP approaches require specifying the depth of knowledge propagation, this is not necessary in the Gröbner basis approach.

Proposition 5 (Link between a guess basis and Gröbner basis [7]). *Let* $(X, \mathcal{R})$ *be a system of connection relations where* $X = \{x_0, \ldots, x_{n-1}\}$, *and* $\mathcal{K}, \mathcal{T} \subseteq X$ *include the known and target variables respectively. Let* $\mathcal{F}$ *be the set of Boolean binomials in* $\frac{\mathbb{F}_2[x_0,\ldots,x_{n-1}]}{\langle x_0^2+x_0,\ldots,x_{n-1}^2+x_{n-1}\rangle}$ *as the algebraic representation of* $(X, \mathcal{R})$. *Besides, assume that* σ *is a degree-compatible term ordering and* J *is the ideal generated by* $\mathcal{F} \cup \{k+1 : \text{for all } k \in \mathcal{K}\}$. *Next, compute the reduced* σ-*Gröbner basis of* $J + \langle t \mid \text{for all } t \in \mathcal{T}\rangle$. *Then every monomial* $x_{i_0} \cdots x_{i_{m-1}}$ *of smallest degree in this reduced Gröbner basis corresponds to a guess basis* $G = \{x_{i_0}, \ldots, x_{i_{m-1}}\}$ *of minimal length.*

5   Autoguess

We developed *Autoguess*, an easy-to-use tool that implements these techniques to find GD attacks and key bridges. It receives a text file including the system of relations, target and known variables, and if applicable the depth of knowledge propagation as input, and outputs a guess basis of minimum size. Autoguess supports all encoding methods including CP, MILP, SMT, and SAT and allows the user to choose from many state-of-the-art solvers. It also supports the Gröbner encoding method, which has the advantage that the user does not need to specify the depth of knowledge propagation. The output of Autoguess not only represents the guessed variables but also includes the determination flow which illustrates how the target variables can be determined from the guessed variables. Autoguess uses `graphviz` to generate a directed graph visualizing the determination flow.

Figure 1 gives a high-level overview of the program flow in Autoguess. For Gröbner bases, we use SageMath's direct interface to efficient algorithms like PolyBoRi and Singular. For the CP model, we use MiniZinc as a CSP modeling language to support many state-of-the-art CP solvers like Or-Tools, Gecode, and Choco. For MILP encoding, Autoguess has a direct interface to Gurobi. For SMT, we apply PySMT to support many solvers, like Z3, CVC4, Boolector, MathSAT, and Yices. For direct access to SAT solvers, we use PySAT, which supports many modern SAT solvers like CaDiCaL, Lingeling, Minisat, and MapleSAT. Additionally, PySAT supports a variety of cardinality constraint encodings.

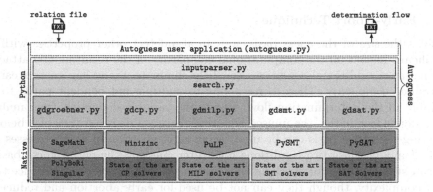

Fig. 1. The program flow of Autoguess

5.1   Preprocessing Phase

When translating a system of equations to connection relations, we only consider the connectivity relations between the variables and not the algebraic structure of the original system of equations. This is why neither the CP-based nor the Gröbner basis-based method can exploit such an algebraic structure. However, by taking the algebraic structure into account and adding new equations, we might be able to achieve a better result. Following the algebraic approaches to solve multivariate polynomial equations over finite field such as the Gröbner basis and XL algorithms [5,9,13], we can even derive further equations. To do so, we use reduced row echelon form of the degree-D Macaulay matrix which is defined as follows.

Definition 6 [13]. *For any integer k, let T_k be the set of monomials of degree smaller than or equal to k, in $\mathbb{F}_2[x_0, \ldots, x_{n-1}]$. The degree-$D$ Macaulay matrix of a system of equation F, denoted by $Mac_D(F)$, is the matrix with coefficients in $\mathbb{F}_2$ whose columns are indexed by T_D and rows by the set $\{(u, f_i) \mid i \in [1; m], u \in T_{D - \deg(f_i)}\}$, and whose coefficients are those of the products $u\, f_i$ in the basis T_D.*

According to our observations, using the new algebraic equations derived with the reduced Macaulay matrix can result in a smaller guess basis. Although reduced row echelon form of the Macaulay matrix can be used to compute the Gröbner basis if the degree D is large enough [15], we use relatively small D ($D \leq 3$) to derive further relations as a preprocessing phase when there are some algebraic equations over finite field $\mathbb{F}_2$ among the given original equations. We include the Macaulay matrix preprocessing phase into Autoguess. This feature allows the user to include the algebraic equations into the input text file for a hybrid relation file with connection relations as well as algebraic relations. Autoguess applies the preprocessing phase with a specified degree on the algebraic equations and converts the derived equations into connection relations before encoding the GD attack.

5.2 Early-Abort Technique

Besides the size of the guess basis, we can also detect other properties with a significant impact on the computational complexity of the resulting GD attack. For instance, additional conditions can help eliminate wrong key guesses early to reduce complexity. These corresponds to multiple independent paths to a variable in the determination flow. Beside the variable deduction from multiple independent paths, the unused equations between deduced variables before guessing the entire basis can be used for an early abortion of wrong guesses as well. If any of these two conditions hold after guessing the entire guess basis, we can still use them for checking the correctness of our guesses and reduce the data complexity, though they can not be used for early abortion and reducing the time complexity. To guide the user to simply detect the unused equations and the variables deduced from multiple paths, Autoguess returns all unused equations as well as those variables deducing from multiple paths, in addition to the determination flow.

6 Application to Automatic Search for Key Bridges

6.1 Application to PRESENT

PRESENT is an ISO-standard ultra-lightweight SPN block cipher with 64-bit blocksize and 80-bit (or 128-bit) key $K = \kappa_0 \ldots \kappa_{79}$ (or $K = \kappa_0 \ldots \kappa_{127}$) as input.

The key schedule of PRESENT includes bit-wise rotation, constant addition and an S-box. To model the S-box we assume that the output bits are deduced if all input bits are known, and vice versa. Let $k_{0,r}, \ldots, k_{79,r}$ represent whether the key bits $\kappa_0, \ldots, \kappa_{79}$ are known in round r, where $0 \leq r \leq 31$, and $k_{0,0}, \ldots, k_{79,0}$ the master key bits. The connection relations for R rounds of key schedule are

$$k_{r+1,i} + k_{r,(i+61 \bmod 80)}, \tag{1}$$
$$k_{r,0}, k_{r,1}, k_{r,2}, k_{r,3} \Rightarrow k_{r+1,i}; \ k_{r+1,0}, k_{r+1,1}, k_{r+1,2}, k_{r+1,3} \Rightarrow k_{r,i}; \ 0 \leq i \leq 3,$$

where $0 \leq r \leq R - 1$. Similarly, to model R rounds of key schedule of PRESENT-128, it is sufficient to use the following relations alongside those in Eq. 1:

$$k_{r,4}, k_{r,5}, k_{r,6}, k_{r,7} \Rightarrow k_{r+1,i}; k_{r+1,4}, k_{r+1,5}, k_{r+1,6}, k_{r+1,7} \Rightarrow k_{r,i} \text{ for } 4 \leq i \leq 7. \tag{2}$$

The best attacks on PRESENT so far are the linear attacks on 28 rounds of both variants of this cipher proposed at EUROCRYPT 2020 [11]. They try to use the dependencies between sub-key bits involved in the key recovery to reduce the time complexity of their general key recovery algorithms. However, the authors admit that they have been unable to provide an efficient general algorithm which takes account of all dependency relationships between the key-bits. In total, 96 key bits need to be guessed in the 26-round attack on PRESENT-80 in [11]:

$$T = \{k_{0,16\sim47}, k_{1,20\sim27}, k_{1,36\sim43}, k_{25,0}, k_{25,2}, k_{25,8}, k_{25,10}, k_{25,16}, k_{25,18}, k_{25,24}, k_{25,26},$$
$$k_{25,32}, k_{25,34}, k_{25,40}, k_{25,42}, k_{25,48}, k_{25,50}, k_{25,56}, k_{25,58}\} \cup \{k_{26,2\cdot i} : 0 \leq i \leq 31\}.$$

Exploiting the dependencies between the involved key bits, the authors showed that all can be deduced from 61 bits. However, using Autoguess running on a single core of Intel Core i9 processor at 3.6 GHz, we can find the minimal guess basis K_T of size 60 in less than 3 s with the Gröbner basis approach, which includes the following variables:

$$\{k_{26,2 \cdot i} : 0 \le i \le 7\} \cup \{k_{6,42}, k_{26,15 \sim 22}, k_{26,24}, k_{26,26 \sim 63}, k_{26,67}, k_{26,69}, k_{26,75}, k_{26,77}\}.$$

According to [11], the cost of computing the multiple linear cryptanalysis statistic throughout the analysis phase of the multiple linear attack on 26 rounds of PRESENT is $M_2 \cdot 2^{|K_T|}$, where $M_2 = 16$. Consequently, our finding reduces the time complexity of the analysis phase from 2^{65} in [11] to 2^{64}.

Moreover, to compute the time complexity of the analysis phase in the 28-round multiple linear attack on PRESENT-128 [11], it is claimed that all relevant key bits can be deduced from 114 bits, whereas the minimum-size guess basis we could discover with our tool would include 115 bits. Contacting the authors of [11], they confirmed that it is a typo, and they also discovered a guess basis of size 115 in their analysis. Thus, the time complexity of the analysis phase in this attack is more than $2^{121.58}$, whereas [11] claimed less than 2^{121}. The total time complexity of attack remains at 2^{122}, as the analysis phase is not the bottleneck.

6.2 Application to LBlock with Nonlinear Key Schedule

Application to Integral Attack on 24 Rounds of LBlock The best known single-key attack on LBlock [20], except for biclique attacks [19], is the 24-round integral attack in [6]. We follow the same notations as [6]. To mount a key-recovery attack on 24 rounds of LBlock, they use a 17-round integral distinguisher based on which the correctness of $\bigoplus Z^{17}[4]\{3,2\} = \bigoplus X_L^{18}[4]\{3,2\}$ must be checked. Thanks to the meet-in-the-middle technique, they compute $\bigoplus Z^{17}[4]$ and $\bigoplus X_L^{18}$ independently to reduce the time complexity further. To calculate the $\bigoplus Z^{17}[4]$, 80 key bits are involved, but our tool automatically detects in less than a second that they can be determined from 55 key bits. On the other hand, 48 key bits are involved in calculation of $\bigoplus X_L^{18}[4]$ whereas our tool automatically detects they can be determined from 47 key bits. Lastly, our tool detected that all involved key bits can be deduced from 69 variables: $G = \{k_{24,0 \sim 8}, k_{24,17 \sim 30}, k_{24,34 \sim 79}\}$, where $k_{r,i}$ is the ith sub-key bit in round r.

Application to Impossible Differential Attack on 23 Rounds of LBlock. Applying our tool to find key bridges for the impossible differential attack on 23-round LBlock, we can reproduce the same result as [16] in a few seconds with the Gröbner basis method. While [16] only detects the number of independent relations between the key bits, our tool not only finds a guess basis of 73 bits for 144 involved sub-key bits, but also produces a precise determination flow.

7 Application to GD Attack on Block Ciphers

We now show the usefulness of our tool to find GD attacks on block ciphers. The full version [12] includes further applications to CRAFT and SKINNY.

7.1 Automatic GD Attack on AES

Let $w_{r,i,j}, x_{r,i,j}, y_{r,i,j}$, and z_i denote whether the jth byte at the ith row before AK, SB, SR, and MC is known in round r of AES. Given that $x_{r,i,j}$ is known if and only if $y_{r,i,j}$ is known for all $0 \le i, j \le 15$, we can assume that $x_{r,i,j} = y_{r,i,j}$. Assuming that M is the 4×4 MDS matrix of AES, if $w = M \times z$, then knowing four bytes of (z, w) is sufficient to uniquely determine the remaining four bytes. Furthermore, $z_{r,i,j} = y_{r,i,(j+i) \bmod 4}$ and $y_{r,i,j} = x_{r,i,j}$ for all $0 \le i, j \le 15$. Hence, each matrix multiplication $(w_{r,0,j}, w_{r,1,j}, w_{r,2,j}, w_{r,3,j})^t = M \times (z_{r,0,j}, z_{r,1,j}, z_{r,2,j}, z_{r,3,j})^t$ with $0 \le j \le 3$ in the MC layer can be modeled via $\binom{8}{5} = 56$ symmetric relations, each of which including five variables from the following set: $\{w_{r,0,j}, w_{r,1,j}, w_{r,2,j}, w_{r,3,j}, x_{r,0,j}, x_{r,1,j+1}, x_{r,2,j+2}, x_{r,3,j+3}\}$. In total, $4 \times \binom{8}{5} = 224$ symmetric relations are required to model the MC layer.

Let $k_{r,i,j}$ denote whether the jth byte in the ith row of the sub-key in round r is known, where $0 \le i, j \le 3$, and $0 \le r \le 10$. Since round constant c_i is known, we can model the key schedule of AES via linear algebraic relations: For each key variable $k_{r,i,3}$ in the third column of the key state, we define a new variable $sk_{r,i,3}$ as well as the new symmetric relation $[k_{r,i,3}, sk_{r,i,3}]$, since $k_{r,i,3}$ can be uniquely determined from $sk_{r,i,3}$ and vice versa. Thus, we can model the key schedule as

$$k_{r,i,j} \oplus k_{r+1,i,j-1} \oplus k_{r+1,i,j} = 0, \qquad 0 \le i \le 3, 1 \le j \le 3,$$
$$k_{r,3,0} \oplus sk_{r,0,3} \oplus k_{r+1,3,0} = 0, \qquad k_{r,1,0} \oplus sk_{r,2,3} \oplus k_{r+1,1,0} = 0,$$
$$k_{r,2,0} \oplus sk_{r,3,3} \oplus k_{r+1,2,0} = 0, \qquad k_{r,0,0} \oplus sk_{r,1,3} \oplus k_{r+1,0,0} = 0.$$

In the AK layer, 16 bytes of sub-key are XORed to the internal state, which can be modeled via the connection relation $[w_{r-1,i,j}, k_{r,i,j}, x_{r,i,j}]$ for all $0 \le i, j \le 15$.

Consider an adversary who seeks to break 3 rounds of AES where only a single known plaintext is available. Given the 3-round connection relations and the known and target variables, (with or without preprocessing) Autoguess finds a minimal guess basis of 15 bytes. It means there is a GD attack with time complexity of 2^{120} on 3 rounds of AES. As Autoguess yields the variables determined from multiple paths as well as relations not used during the determination flow, we can ensure that only one known plaintext/ciphertext pair is sufficient to uniquely determine the unknown variables.

Running Autoguess on a single core Intel Core i9 processor at 3.6 GHz with the SAT-based method (CaDiCal), it took less than a minute, to find the GD attack on 3 rounds of AES, whereas it took about 10 h when we used the Gröbner basis approach (PolyBoRi). The MILP-based methods (Gurobi) is also much slower, even if we want to find only a feasible solution. For the 3-round GD attack on AES, Autoguess gives the same result as the dedicated AES tool in [2] when only one plaintext/ciphertext pair is known.

8   Application to GD Attack on Stream Ciphers

8.1   Automatic GD Attack on ZUC

ZUC is a word-based stream cipher with two versions, ZUC-128 [8] and ZUC-256 [21], both performing exactly the same keystream generation phase (Fig. 2).

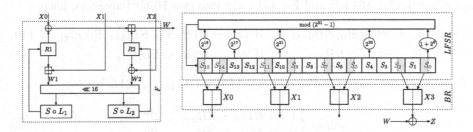

Fig. 2. The keystream generation phase of ZUC stream cipher

The LFSR consists of 16 cells $S_t, \dots, S_{t+15}$ at clock t, each a 31-bit element from the finite field $GF(p)$, $p = 2^{31} - 1$. The LFSR rule is

$$S_{16+t} = 2^{15}S_{15+t} + 2^{17}S_{13+t} + 2^{21}S_{10+t} + 2^{20}S_{4+t} + (1 + 2^8)S_t \mod p. \quad (3)$$

If $S_{16+t} = 0$, then $S_{16+t} = p$. If we denote the value of registers $X0, \dots, X4$ at clock t as $X0_t, X1_t, X2_t, X3_t$, then we have $X0_t = SH_{15+t}||SL_{14+t}, X1_t = SL_{11+t}||SH_{0+t}, X2_t = SL_{7+t}||SH_{5+t}$, and $X3_t = SL_{2+t}||SH_t$, where SH_t and SL_t represent the high and low 16 bits of register S_t, i.e., $SH_t = S_t[30\dots15]$ and $SL_t = S_t[15\dots0]$. Note that, in this representation, $SL_t[15] = SH_t[0]$. We have:

$$Z_t = ((R1_t \oplus X0_t) \boxplus_{32} R2_t) \oplus X3_t, \quad (4)$$

$$W1_t = R1_t \boxplus_{32} X1_t, \qquad\qquad W2_t = R2_t \oplus X2_t, \quad (5)$$

$$R1_{t+1} = S(L_1(W1L_t||W2H_t)), \qquad R2_{t+1} = S(L_2(W2L_t||W1H_t)), \quad (6)$$

where $R1_t$ and $R2_t$ represent the value of 32-bit registers $R1$ and $R2$ at clock t, and $W1H_t$, and $W1L_t$ represent the high and low 16 bits of $W1$ at clock t, respectively. $W2L_t$, and $W2H_t$ are defined in the same way. Here S is a 32×32 one-to-one S-box, and L_1, L_2 are two 32×32 linear functions.

The best previous GD attack on ZUC proposed in [10] has a computational complexity of 2^{392} while requiring 9 keystream outputs. Here, assisted by Autoguess, we propose a GD attack on ZUC with a computational complexity of 2^{390}, using the same amount of 9 keystream outputs as [10].

To find GD attacks on ZUC, we use a half-word-based model. Let $R1H_t, R1L_t$ be the high and low 16 bits of $R1$ at clock t, and $R2H_t, R2L_t$ of $R2$. Using (4):

$$ZL_t = ((SL_{14+t} \oplus R1L_t) \boxplus_{16} R2L_t) \oplus SH_t, \quad (7)$$

$$ZH_t = ((SH_{15+t} \oplus R1H_t) \boxplus_{16} R2H_t \boxplus_{16} c1_t) \oplus SL_{2+t}, \quad (8)$$

where ZL_t and ZH_t denote the high and low 16 bits of output word Z at clock t, and cl_t the carry bit in modular addition $(SL_{14+t} \oplus R1L_t) \boxplus_{16} R2L_t$:

$$cl_t = \begin{cases} 1 & \text{if } (SL_{14+t} \oplus R1L_t) + R2L_t \geq 2^{16} \\ 0 & \text{if } (SL_{14+t} \oplus R1L_t) + R2L_t < 2^{16}. \end{cases} \tag{9}$$

Splitting the Eq. (5) left and Eq. (5) right into two 16-bit halves, we have:

$$W1L_t = R1L_t \boxplus_{16} SH_{9+t}, \qquad W1H_t = R1H_t \boxplus_{16} SL_{11+t} \boxplus_{16} c2_t, \tag{10}$$

$$W2L_t = R2L_t \oplus SH_{5+t}, \qquad W2H_t = R2H_t \oplus SL_{7+t}., \tag{11}$$

where $c2_t$ is the carry bit of modular addition $(SL_{14+t} \oplus R1L_t)$:

$$c2_t = \begin{cases} 1 & \text{if } R1L_t + SH_{9+t} \geq 2^{16} \\ 0 & \text{if } R1L_t + SH_{9+t} < 2^{16}. \end{cases} \tag{12}$$

All of the derived relations can be simply modeled via symmetric relations, except for Eqs. (9) and (12) which can be modeled via the implication relations. Besides the main equations, we add trivial implications to link each 32-bit word to its two half-words. For example, to link S_t to SH_t and SL_t, we include $S_t \Rightarrow SH_t$, $S_t \Rightarrow SL_t$, and $SH_t, SL_t \Rightarrow S_t$ into the model.

Therefore, we can generate the system of connection relations modeling the knowledge propagation through to the given number of clock cycles of ZUC based on half-words. In contrast to our previous models, where all variables have the same size, the relations for ZUC use variables with different lengths. For the length of each variable, we use a weighted objective function in Line 20 of Algorithm 1, such that each variable is multiplied by its length. Consequently, solving the generated model yields a guess basis of minimum weight, which corresponds to the minimum number of guessed bits to derive the internal state of ZUC.

Applying Autoguess to the connection relations for 9 clock cycles of ZUC, we see that finding a minimal guess basis is very time consuming and state-of-the-art MILP or CP solvers cannot solve the problem in a reasonable time. However, we are still able to find feasible solutions which result in some guess basis smaller than that in [10] by two bits. One of the guess bases of size 391 bits we found is

$$G = \{S_5, R1_5, S_{19}, SH_{13}, S_6, S_7, S_9, S_{10}, SL_{13}[14...0], S_{15}, S_{16}, S_{18}, S_{20}, c2_5, SH_{12}, c1_3\}.$$

Here, Z_t and thus ZL_t, ZH_t are known for $0 \leq t \leq 8$. Thanks to the output of Autoguess, which provides the full determination flow, we see that two halves SL_{11} and SH_{11} of S_{11} can be deduced from two independent paths. Furthermore, Autoguess shows that SL_{11} and SH_{11} are independent of $c1_3, SH_{12}$. To find this, we simply consider $G \backslash \{c1_3, SH_{12}\}$ as the known variables and $T = \{SL_{11}, SH_{11}\}$ as the target variable and run Autoguess to see whether there is a guess basis of size zero and thus SL_{11}, SH_{11} can be uniquely deduced from $G \backslash \{c1_3, SH_{12}\}$. As a consequence, we can check the condition $SH_{11}[0] = SL_{11}[15]$, before guessing $c1_3, SH_{12}$ as an early abortion technique to filter out half of the wrong guesses. Algorithm 2 precisely describes our GD attack on ZUC more. Before Line 14 of

Algorithm 2, 374 bits are guessed in total. Since the condition in Line 14 holds with a probability of 2^{-1}, the lines after Line 14 will be performed 2^{373} times on average, where there is a loop enumerating 2^{17} possible cases for (SH_{12}, cl_3). Hence, the total computational complexity of our GD attack on ZUC is 2^{390}, in which we use 9 output keystream to determine the whole internal state.

9   Key-Recovery-Friendly Distinguishers

Most automatic CP-based methods to search for distinguishers are blind to the key recovery phase and only describe the distinguishing part. Very recently, some authors attempted a unified CP-model combining the distinguisher and key recovery phases to directly find a key-recovery attack, but they are limited to linear key schedules [4,17,18]. To the best of our knowledge, no general CP-based model integrating both phases that finds key bridges for both linear and nonlinear key schedules has been introduced so far. We now show that our CP-based key-bridge search is consistent with previous CP-based methods to search for distinguishers, and hence they can be merged to directly find a key-recovery-friendly distinguisher. To do so, we extend the CP model of [18] with key recovery using key-bridging while searching for $\mathcal{DS}$-MITM distinguishers for ciphers with linear and nonlinear key schedules.

Algorithm 2: GD attack on ZUC with time complexity 2^{390}

Input: Output keystream derived from 9 clock cycles of ZUC: $(Z_0, \ldots, Z_8)$

1 **forall** $(S_5, R1_5, S_{19}, SH_{13}) \in \mathbb{F}_2^{110}$ **do**

2 $\quad$ $W1L_4, W2H_4 \Leftarrow (6); R1L_4 \Leftarrow (10); R2L_5 \Leftarrow (7); cl_5 \Leftarrow (9); c2_4 \Leftarrow (12);$

3 $\quad$ **forall** $(S_{20}, S_7) \in \mathbb{F}_2^{62}$ **do**

4 $\quad\quad$ $X0_5 \Leftarrow SH_{20}||SL_{19}; X3_5, X2_0 \Leftarrow SL_7, SH_5; R2_5 \Leftarrow (4); W1H_4, W2L4 \Leftarrow (6);$

5 $\quad\quad$ **forall** $(S_{16}, S_{10}, c2_5, S_9, S_{15}, S_{18}, S_6) \in \mathbb{F}_2^{178}$ **do**

6 $\quad\quad\quad$ $W1H_5 \Leftarrow (10); W2L_5 \Leftarrow (11); R2_6 \Leftarrow (6); X1_4, X2_8 \Leftarrow SL_{15}||SH_{13}; S2_1 \Leftarrow (3);$

7 $\quad\quad\quad$ $R1_4 \Leftarrow (5); R2L_4 \Leftarrow (11); R1L_6 \Leftarrow (7); S_{22} \Leftarrow (3); X0_4 \Leftarrow SH_{19}||SL_{18};$

8 $\quad\quad\quad$ $SH_4 \Leftarrow (7); cl_4 \Leftarrow (9); R2H_4 \Leftarrow (8); X3_4 \Leftarrow SL_6||SH_4, W1L_3, W2H_3 \Leftarrow (6);$

9 $\quad\quad\quad$ $cl_6 \Leftarrow (9); X2_2, X3_7 \Leftarrow SL_9||SH_7; c2_6 \Leftarrow (12); W1L_3, W2H_3 \Leftarrow (6);$

10 $\quad\quad\quad$ $W1L_6 \Leftarrow (10); SL_{11} \Leftarrow (11); R2_4 \Leftarrow (4); X0_7 \Leftarrow SH_{22}||SL_{21}; R2H_3 \Leftarrow (11);$

11 $\quad\quad\quad$ **forall** $SL_{13}[14 \ldots 0] \in \mathbb{F}_2^{15}$ **do**

12 $\quad\quad\quad\quad$ $W2H_6 \Leftarrow (11); R1_7 \Leftarrow (6); S_3 \Leftarrow (3); R2_7 \Leftarrow (4); W2L_6, W1H_6 \Leftarrow (6);$

13 $\quad\quad\quad\quad$ $SH_{11} \Leftarrow (11); X1_0 \Leftarrow SL_{11}||SH_9; X1_2 \Leftarrow SL_{13}||SH_{11};$

14 $\quad\quad\quad\quad$ **if** $SH_{11}[0] = SL_{11}[15]$ **then**

15 $\quad\quad\quad\quad\quad$ **forall** $(SH_{12}, cl_3) \in \mathbb{F}_2^{17}$ **do**

16 $\quad\quad\quad\quad\quad\quad$ $W1H_3, W2L_3 \Leftarrow (6); c2_3 \Leftarrow (12); R1H_3 \Leftarrow (8); R1L_3 \Leftarrow (10);$

17 $\quad\quad\quad\quad\quad\quad$ $SL_{14} \Leftarrow (10); X1_7 \Leftarrow SL_{18}||SH_{16}; W1_7 \Leftarrow (5); W2H_7 \Leftarrow (11);$

18 $\quad\quad\quad\quad\quad\quad$ $R1_8 \Leftarrow (6); W2L_7 \Leftarrow (11); R2_8 \Leftarrow (6); SH_8 \Leftarrow (7); R2L_3 \Leftarrow (11);$

19 $\quad\quad\quad\quad\quad\quad$ $SL_{17} \Leftarrow (7); R1H_6 \Leftarrow (10); SL_8 \Leftarrow (8); X2_1 \Leftarrow SL_8||SH_6;$

20 $\quad\quad\quad\quad\quad\quad$ $W1L_2, W2H_2 \Leftarrow (6); W1H_2, W2L_2 \Leftarrow (6); R1L_2 \Leftarrow (10); R1_2 \Leftarrow (5);$

21 $\quad\quad\quad\quad\quad\quad$ $W1L_1, W2H_1 \Leftarrow (6); R2_2 \Leftarrow (5); W2L_1, W1H_1 \Leftarrow (6);$

22 $\quad\quad\quad\quad\quad\quad$ $X1_6 \Leftarrow SL_{17}||SH_{15}; R1_6 \Leftarrow (5); W1L_5, W2H_5 \Leftarrow (6); SL_{12} \Leftarrow (11);$

23 $\quad\quad\quad\quad\quad\quad$ $X1_1 \Leftarrow SL_{12}||SH_{10}; R1_1 \Leftarrow (5); R2_1 \Leftarrow (5); W1L_0, W2H_0 \Leftarrow (6);$

24 $\quad\quad\quad\quad\quad\quad$ $R1_0 \Leftarrow (5); W2L_0, W1H_0 \Leftarrow (6); R2_0 \Leftarrow (5); X0_0 \Leftarrow SH_{15}||SL_{14};$

25 $\quad\quad\quad\quad\quad\quad$ $X3_0 \Leftarrow (4); SL_2 \Leftarrow X3_0; R2L_2 \Leftarrow (11); SH_2 \Leftarrow (7);$

26 $\quad\quad\quad\quad\quad\quad$ $SH_{14} \Leftarrow (10); S_{17}(3); S_1 \Leftarrow (3); S_4 \Leftarrow (3); S_0 \Leftarrow (3);$

27 $\quad\quad\quad\quad\quad\quad$ **if** $\text{ZUC}^{18\text{clks}}(S_0, \ldots, S_{15}, R1_0, R2_0) = (Z_0, \ldots, Z_{17})$ **then**

28 $\quad\quad\quad\quad\quad\quad\quad$ **return** $(S_0, \ldots, S_{15}, R1_0, R2_0)$

29 $\quad\quad\quad\quad\quad\quad$ **else**

30 $\quad\quad\quad\quad\quad\quad\quad$ Go to step 1 and try another guesses.

Our strategy to integrate the key-bridging technique into the CP-based frameworks for automatic search of distinguishers is summarized as follows:

1. We generate constraints for the distinguisher using previous CP models.
2. Next, we generate the constraints modeling the active cell propagation before and after the distinguisher to determine the involved sub-keys.
3. To model the key-schedule including the key-bridging technique, we generate the constraints for the key-bridging technique based on our approach.
4. We add constraints to link the variables for the last step of knowledge propagation in key-bridging to the variables for the involved sub-keys.
5. Finally, we look for a feasible solution minimizing the actual number of guessed sub-key variables such that all involved sub-keys can be deduced.

Modeling the distinguisher part as well as the active cells propagation through the outer rounds (Item 1 and Item 2) are discussed in previous works [17,18]. We already described Item 3, so we now explain Item 4.

Among the variables defined in Item 2, let $ISK_{r,i}$ be a binary variable indicating whether the ith word (bit) of sub-key in round r is involved. Assuming that wk sub-key words (bits) are used in each round, as illustrated in Fig. 3, suppose that $B = \{ISK_{r,i} : 0 \leq r \leq r_b - 1, \ 0 \leq i \leq wk - 1\}$, and $F = \{ISK_{r,i} : r_b + r_m \leq r \leq r_b + r_m + r_f - 1, \ 0 \leq i \leq wk - 1\}$ include the indicator variables corresponding to the involved sub-key words in the rounds before and after the distinguisher. Moreover, assuming that $\beta \in \mathbb{Z}_{\geq 0}$ denotes the depth of knowledge propagation in key-bridging, let $SK_{r,i,j}$ specify whether the ith word of the sub-key in round r is known at the jth step of knowledge propagation. While our previous models specified the target sub-keys in advance, in our new model we include constraints to dynamically determine the target sub-key variables:

$$\{SK_{r,i,\beta} \geq ISK_{r,i} : \ 0 \leq r \leq r_b - 1 \ \lor \ r_b + r_m \leq r \leq r_b + r_m + r_f - 1, \ 0 \leq i \leq wk - 1\}.$$

Thus, if $ISK_{r,i} = 1$ then $SK_{r,i,\beta} = 1$, so each sub-key variable is deduced after β steps. Hence, we can minimize the guessed variables at the first step of knowledge propagation, $\sum_{r,i} SK_{r,i,0}$. To model the distinguisher part and the active cells propagation, we use the same method as [18], and follow their notations. Although we demonstrate the application of our method only for $\mathcal{DS}$-MITM attacks, it can be straightforwardly applied to find key-recovery-friendly distinguishers in linear or differential cryptanalysis as well.

9.1 $\mathcal{DS}$-MITM Attack on SKINNY-{64-192, 64-128, 128-256}

To show the usefulness of our method, we apply it to different SKINNY variants. For SKINNY-64-192, we discover a 21-round $\mathcal{DS}$-MITM attack in the single-tweakey setting with a 8.5-round distinguisher. Although there is a 9.5-round $\mathcal{DS}$-MITM distinguisher for SKINNY-64-192 which can be used to construct a 21-round attack, thanks to our new model we noticed that building the attack on an 8.5-round distinguisher results in an attack with lower complexity.

Figure 4 illustrates the distinguisher of our attack on 21 rounds of SKINNY-64-192, where 31 nibbles should be guessed in the offline phase. Hence, the time complexity of the offline phase is $2^{4\times31} \times 2^{4\times2} \times \frac{31}{21\times16} C_E \approx 2^{128.56} C_E$, and the memory complexity is $(2^{4\times2} - 1) \times 4 \times 2^{4\times31} \approx 2^{133.99}$ bits. As it is shown in Fig. 5, 15 nibbles are active in the input state in the first round, which shows that the data complexity of our attack is $2^{4\times15} = 2^{60}$ chosen plaintexts. Figure 5 shows that 63 sub-key nibbles are involved in the key recovery attack, but they can be deduced from only 45 sub-key nibbles. As a result, the time complexity of the online phase is $2^{45\times4} \times 2^{4\times2} \times \frac{29+101}{21\times16} C_E \approx 2^{186.63} C_E$.

In the same way, we find a 19-round $\mathcal{DS}$-MITM attack on SKINNY-128-256 and an 18-round attack on SKINNY-64-128, relying on 8.5-round and 7.5-round distinguishers. The complexity of our attacks is summarized in Table 1. The full version [12] includes more details about our $\mathcal{DS}$-MITM attacks on SKINNY.

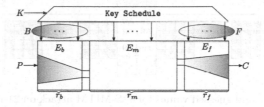

Fig. 3. A high level view of the involved key materials in a key recovery attack.

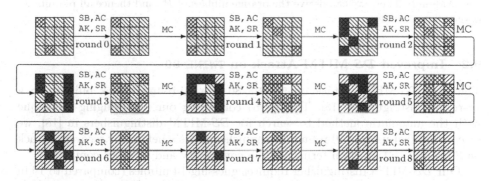

Fig. 4. Distinguisher for $\mathcal{DS}$-MITM attack on 21-round SKINNY-64-192: A 8.5-round $\mathcal{DS}$-MITM distinguisher for SKINNY-64-192 such that $\mathcal{A} = [0, 13]$ (crosshatches in round 0), $\mathcal{B} = [12]$ (crosshatch at the end), and $\text{Deg}(\mathcal{A}, \mathcal{B}) = 31$ (in red). The blue cells can be determined from the red cells via the connection relations from the linear layer. (Color figure online)

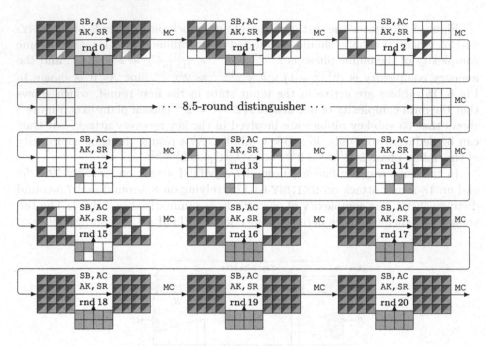

Fig. 5. Key recovery and guessed values for $\mathcal{DS}$-MITM attack on 21-round SKINNY-64-192: Backward differential and forward determination relationship in the outer rounds using the distinguisher in Fig. 4 as E_1. Cells in Guess(E_0) and Guess(E_2) are marked in red. Derive k_{E_0} and k_{E_2} from these. The orange sub-keys must be guessed (without key-bridging). Then, we can derive the orange nibbles of P^0 and thence all red nibbles (Color figure online).

9.2 Improved $\mathcal{DS}$-MITM Attack on TWINE-80

The best $\mathcal{DS}$-MITM attack on TWINE-80 is a 20-round attack built upon a 11-round distinguisher [18]. Thanks to combining our key-bridging technique with the automatic method to search for $\mathcal{DS}$-MITM distinguishers in [18], we discovered that using a 10-round distinguisher yields a better key recovery attack on 20-round TWINE-80 in terms of time complexity and memory complexity.

Our $\mathcal{DS}$-MITM distinguisher requires guessing 14 nibbles (compared to 19 in [18]), so the time complexity of the offline phase is $2^{4\times14}\times2^{4\times1}\times\frac{14}{20\times8}C_E \approx 2^{56.48}$ ($2^{76.93}C_E$ in [18]), where C_E is the runtime of 20-round TWINE-80. The memory complexity is $(2^4-1)\times4\times2\times2^{4\times14} \approx 2^{62.91}$ bits ($2^{82.91}$ in [18]). 26 sub-key nibbles are involved in the key recovery phase of our attack. With key-bridging, all 26 sub-key nibbles can be deduced from 19 sub-key nibbles. $7+12=19$ S-boxes are involved in the outer rounds, so the time complexity of the online phase is $2^{4\times19}\times2^{4\times1}\times\frac{7+12}{20\times8} \approx 2^{76.92}$, slightly lower than in [18]. The 76-bit subkey space is reduced by 4 bits. The data complexity is $2^{4\times8}=2^{32}$, since 8 input nibbles are active. To see more details about our $\mathcal{DS}$-MITM attack on TWINE-80 see the full version of our paper [12].

10   Conclusion

In this paper, we introduced the CP and SAT/SMT encoding of the GD problem and integrated them with MILP- and Gröbner basis-based methods in one tool to automate GD and key-bridging techniques. Moreover, we managed to integrate our CP-based approach for key-bridging technique into the previous CP-based frameworks for finding distinguishers and introduced a general CP model to search for key-recovery-friendly distinguishers supporting both linear and nonlinear key schedules for the first time.

In our experiments, we observed that the SAT-based method often outperforms the others when we want to find only a feasible solution. For instance, executing the SAT method on a single core Intel Core i9 processor at 3.6 GHz, it takes less than a second to reproduce the GD attack on Enocoro-128v2 in [3], whereas finding the same result via the MILP-based method takes minutes. We had the same observation in applying Autoguess to reproduce the best previous GD attacks on SNOW1, SNOW2, SNOW3, KCipher2, etc. However, in some other applications, using the Gröbner basis approach performs better. For instance, we observed that the Gröbner basis-based method performs very well in our applications for the key-bridging technique, while it also ensures the optimum output. Thus, it makes sense to integrate different encoding methods in one tool.

Acknowledgments. The authors would like to thank Mohammad Ali Orumiehchiha and Siwei Sun for motivating discussions and helpful comments on an earlier version of the tool.

References

1. Ahmadi, H., Eghlidos, T.: Heuristic guess-and-determine attacks on stream ciphers. IET Inf. Secur. **3**(2), 66–73 (2009)
2. Bouillaguet, C., Derbez, P., Fouque, P.-A.: Automatic search of attacks on round-reduced AES and applications. In: Rogaway, P. (ed.) CRYPTO 2011. LNCS, vol. 6841, pp. 169–187. Springer, Heidelberg (2011). https://doi.org/10.1007/978-3-642-22792-9_10
3. Cen, Z., Feng, X., Wang, Z., Cao, C.: Minimizing deduction system and its application. arXiv preprint (2020). https://arxiv.org/abs/2006.05833
4. Chen, Q., Shi, D., Sun, S., Hu, L.: Automatic Demirci-Selçuk meet-in-the-middle attack on SKINNY with key-bridging. In: Zhou, J., Luo, X., Shen, Q., Xu, Z. (eds.) ICICS 2019. LNCS, vol. 11999, pp. 233–247. Springer, Cham (2020). https://doi.org/10.1007/978-3-030-41579-2_14
5. Courtois, N., Klimov, A., Patarin, J., Shamir, A.: Efficient algorithms for solving overdefined systems of multivariate polynomial equations. In: Preneel, B. (ed.) EUROCRYPT 2000. LNCS, vol. 1807, pp. 392–407. Springer, Heidelberg (2000). https://doi.org/10.1007/3-540-45539-6_27
6. Cui, Y., Xu, H., Qi, W.: Improved integral attacks on 24-round LBlock and LBlock-s. IET Inf. Secur. **24**, 505–512 (2020)
7. Danner, J., Kreuzer, M.: A fault attack on KCipher-2. Int. J. Comput. Math. Comput. Syst. Theory **6**, 291–312 (2020)

8. ETSI/SAGE: Specification of the 3gpp confidentiality and integrity algorithms 128-EEA3 and 128-EIA3: ZUC specification. Document 2, Version 1.6 (2011)
9. Faugere, J.C.: A new efficient algorithm for computing Gröbner bases without reduction to zero (F5). In: ISSAC 2002, pp. 75–83 (2002)
10. Guan, J., Ding, L., Liu, S.: Guess and determine attack on SNOW3G and ZUC. J. Softw. 24(6), 1324–1333 (2013)
11. Flórez-Gutiérrez, A., Naya-Plasencia, M.: Improving key-recovery in linear attacks: application to 28-round PRESENT. In: Canteaut, A., Ishai, Y. (eds.) EURO-CRYPT 2020. LNCS, vol. 12105, pp. 221–249. Springer, Cham (2020). https://doi.org/10.1007/978-3-030-45721-1_9
12. Hadipour, H., Eichlseder, M.: Autoguess: a tool for finding guess-and-determine attacks and key bridges (full version). IACR Cryptology ePrint Archive, Report 2021/1529 (2021). https://ia.cr/2021/1529
13. Joux, A., Vitse, V.: A crossbred algorithm for solving boolean polynomial systems. In: Kaczorowski, J., Pieprzyk, J., Pomykała, J. (eds.) NuTMiC 2017. LNCS, vol. 10737, pp. 3–21. Springer, Cham (2018). https://doi.org/10.1007/978-3-319-76620-1_1
14. Khazaei, S., Moazami, F.: On the computational complexity of finding a minimal basis for the guess and determine attack. ISeCure 9(2), 101–110 (2017)
15. Lazard, D.: Gröbner bases, Gaussian elimination and resolution of systems of algebraic equations. In: van Hulzen, J.A. (ed.) EUROCAL 1983. LNCS, vol. 162, pp. 146–156. Springer, Heidelberg (1983). https://doi.org/10.1007/3-540-12868-9_99
16. Lin, L., Wu, W., Zheng, Y.: Automatic search for key-bridging technique: applications to LBlock and TWINE. In: Peyrin, T. (ed.) FSE 2016. LNCS, vol. 9783, pp. 247–267. Springer, Heidelberg (2016). https://doi.org/10.1007/978-3-662-52993-5_13
17. Qin, L., Dong, X., Wang, X., Jia, K., Liu, Y.: Automated search oriented to key recovery on ciphers with linear key schedule: applications to boomerangs in SKINNY and ForkSkinny. IACR Trans. Symmetric Cryptol. 2021(2), 249–291 (2021)
18. Shi, D., Sun, S., Derbez, P., Todo, Y., Sun, B., Hu, L.: Programming the Demirci-Selçuk meet-in-the-middle attack with constraints. In: Peyrin, T., Galbraith, S. (eds.) ASIACRYPT 2018. LNCS, vol. 11273, pp. 3–34. Springer, Cham (2018). https://doi.org/10.1007/978-3-030-03329-3_1
19. Wang, Y., Wu, W., Yu, X., Zhang, L.: Security on LBlock against biclique cryptanalysis. In: Lee, D.H., Yung, M. (eds.) WISA 2012. LNCS, vol. 7690, pp. 1–14. Springer, Heidelberg (2012). https://doi.org/10.1007/978-3-642-35416-8_1
20. Wu, W., Zhang, L.: LBlock: a lightweight block cipher. In: Lopez, J., Tsudik, G. (eds.) ACNS 2011. LNCS, vol. 6715, pp. 327–344. Springer, Heidelberg (2011). https://doi.org/10.1007/978-3-642-21554-4_19
21. ZUC Design Team: The ZUC-256 stream cipher (2018). http://www.is.cas.cn/ztzl2016/zouchongzhi/201801/W020180126529970733243.pdf

Cryptographic Protocols

KEMTLS with Delayed Forward Identity Protection in (Almost) a Single Round Trip

Felix Günther[1], Simon Rastikian[1,2], Patrick Towa[1(✉)], and Thom Wiggers[3]

[1] ETH Zurich, Zurich, Switzerland
mail@felixguenther.info, patrick.towa@inf.ethz.ch
[2] IBM Research Europe, Zurich, Switzerland
sra@zurich.ibm.com
[3] Radboud University, Nijmegen, Netherlands
thom@thomwiggers.nl

Abstract. The recent KEMTLS protocol (Schwabe, Stebila and Wiggers, CCS'20) is a promising design for a quantum-safe TLS handshake protocol. Focused on the web setting, wherein clients learn server public-key certificates only during connection establishment, a drawback of KEMTLS compared to TLS 1.3 is that it introduces an additional round trip before the server can send data, and an extra one for the client as well in the case of mutual authentication. In many scenarios, including IoT and embedded settings, client devices may however have the targeted server certificate pre-loaded, so that such performance penalty seems unnecessarily restrictive.

This work proposes a variant of KEMTLS tailored to such scenarios. Our protocol leverages the fact that clients know the server public keys in advance to decrease handshake latency while protecting client identities. It combines medium-lived with long-term server public keys to enable a delayed form of forward secrecy even from the first data flow on, and full forward secrecy upon the first round trip. The new protocol is proved to achieve strong security guarantees, based on the security of the underlying building blocks, in a new model for multi-stage key exchange with medium-lived keys.

Keywords: Key Exchange · Post-Quantum · Identity Protection · KEMTLS

1 Introduction

The Transport Layer Security (TLS) protocol is among the most widely deployed cryptographic protocols. It is used to securely access web pages, email servers, Internet-of-Things (IoT) gateways or even servers in Cooperative Intelligent

S. Rastikian—Part of the work was completed while the second author was affiliated with DIENS, École Normale Supérieure, PSL University, Paris, France.

© Springer Nature Switzerland AG 2022
G. Ateniese and D. Venturi (Eds.): ACNS 2022, LNCS 13269, pp. 253–272, 2022.
https://doi.org/10.1007/978-3-031-09234-3_13

Transport Systems [40] (C-ITSs). In the TLS *handshake* sub-protocol, a client and a server authenticate each other (at least the server to the client) and jointly establish a symmetric key that is then used in the *record* sub-protocol to privately communicate authenticated application data. The latest version of the protocol, standardized in 2018, is TLS 1.3 [35] and uses an ephemeral Diffie–Hellman key exchange to establish keys that remain secure even after a potential compromise of the parties' long-term keys, i.e., enabling so-called *forward secrecy*.

Post-quantum TLS. In anticipation of large-scale quantum computers, several candidates for a post-quantum version of the TLS handshake protocol have emerged. These for instance include the CECPQ2 experiment [29,30] by Google that combines X25519 ECDH with the NTRU-HRSS lattice-based key exchange in the TLS 1.3 handshake, or the Open Quantum Safe initiative [42] with prototype integrations in the OpenSSL library of TLS 1.3 key exchange with hybrid security.

A promising candidate in this area is the KEMTLS protocol recently proposed by Schwabe, Stebila, and Wiggers [38]. It is free of handshake signatures and only relies on key encapsulation to provide both key establishment and authentication in a quantum-safe way. The main idea is reminiscent of the OPTLS protocol [28] (which in turn inspired the TLS 1.3 handshake design): at its core are encapsulations against the respective partner's public key, using the resulting secrets to establish a shared key. As the resulting shared key can only be recovered with the partner's secret key, this approach implicitly authenticates the partner. Besides, to enable forward secrecy, the client also sends at the beginning of the protocol an ephemeral public key that the server encapsulates against to obtain an ephemeral contribution. The prototype implementation of KEMTLS showed that its bandwidth was over 50% lighter than that of a size-optimized post-quantum instantiation of TLS 1.3, and that it reduces the amount of CPU cycles by almost 90% compared to a speed-optimized post-quantum instantiation of TLS 1.3.

However, the KEMTLS protocol only treats the classical web scenario in which the client has no prior knowledge of the server public key, although the client could in practice cache the server certificate during an initial handshake. In IoT or embedded-device settings, the server public key is often even hardcoded, e.g., in firmware. The client therefore knows the server public key ahead of time in many practical scenarios. This knowledge not only has the benefit of allowing the client to verify the server certificate only once before any handshake (thereby speeding handshakes and saving power for IoT devices), but could potentially lead to a protocol with fewer message round trips, which is in practice crucial to reduce network latency (also in the web setting) and power consumption.

Indeed, in the KEMTLS protocol, the server cannot send application data before the client does, and the client can only send data after two round trips in the case of mutual authentication, i.e., it is a two-Round-Trip-Time or 2-RTT protocol. This contrasts with TLS 1.3, where the server can send data (e.g., a server banner or an IoT-hub certificate) from its first message flow and the client can do so after a single round trip even in the case of mutual authentication.

The underlying reason is that each party must wait for the other's public key to then encapsulate against it, thereby implicitly authenticating the latter, since there are no handshake signatures as in TLS 1.3. Scenarios in which the client knows the server public key from the beginning of the protocol hence promise to enable substantial performance improvements.

No Forward Identity Protection in 1-RTT. In case the client must also authenticate herself to the server, as it is for instance necessary for IoT devices or vehicles in C-ITSs, the TLS protocol is expected to also provide *identity protection* [26], namely that the client's identity should only be recoverable by a server that is already authenticated. The client can of course leverage the server public key that it already knows to encrypt her certificate, but since there is no ephemeral contribution from the server yet, an adversary that compromises the server's key could recover the client's identity even *after* the handshake completed. In other words, there would be no *forward(-secure)* identity protection.

Despite the efficiency benefits of a 1-RTT protocol, forgoing forward identity protection altogether might be too great of a compromise, especially when privacy is a primary concern. For instance, the European Telecommunications Standards Institute identifies the high risk of user profiling as a main privacy challenge in IoT [16]. The US National Institute of Standards and Technology considers as a high-level risk mitigation "safeguarding the confidentiality ... of data ... collected by, stored on, processed by, or transmitted to or from the IoT device" [17] and stated that an IoT device should have "the ability to use demonstrably secure cryptographic modules for standardized cryptographic algorithms ... to prevent the confidentiality ... of the device's stored and transmitted data from being compromised" [18]; here, the client identity belongs to such transmitted data.

Nevertheless, to maintain client privacy (in a protocol using only key encapsulation) even if the server long-term keys are later compromised, the client cannot send her certificate before the server has made an ephemeral contribution in a first round trip. This means the client cannot be authenticated before the server encapsulates against her public key in a second round trip. There seems to be no way of fully leveraging the knowledge of the server public key to have a 1-RTT protocol while maintaining forward identity protection.

1.1 Contributions

The core contribution of this paper is a protocol (in Sect. 3) that bridges the gap between forward identity protection and a 1-RTT protocol solely based on key encapsulation, under the assumption that the client knows the server public key at the start of the protocol (see Fig. 1 for a sketch). The main idea is to introduce semi-static public keys on the server side which the client also knows at the start of the protocol. These semi-static keys are periodically refreshed (e.g., once every other day), and if the corresponding secret key is not compromised before it expires, the client's identity can no longer be recovered, even if the server long-term secret key is later compromised. In this sense, the protocol satisfies a *delayed* form of forward identity protection [8] without any extra round compared to a 1-RTT protocol without forward identity protection. As a side-effect, the protocol also allows for optional zero round-trip time (0-RTT) data with the same delayed forward secrecy, which the client can already send within its first flight without having to wait for the server. Since the semi-static keys are not assumed to be certified (the protocol would otherwise be impractical), they must be transmitted during an initial handshake that then consists of two round trips. The protocol takes care of this mechanism, and allows for semi-static keys to roll over between two time periods, so that servers can serve clients using both the key for the current and the next time periods.

Section 4 presents a model that formalizes the properties expected from a protocol involving semi-static keys, and Sect. 5 proves (in the reductionist framework and in exact-security terms) that the protocol does satisfy them under standard assumptions. The model in Sect. 4 is closely related to the multi-stage key exchange model [19] proposed for TLS 1.3 [13,14] and that for KEMTLS [38], but it also accounts for the semi-static keys and their lifetime. Section 5 then shows that the protocol achieves the intended security levels across the various stages of the handshake, relying only on standard-model assumptions. Section 6 compares the protocol to alternative approaches and highlights its advantages. Section 7 discusses implementation choices as well as a prototype implementation and Sect. 8 discusses benchmarking results. As expected, caching certificates incurs significant performance gains as it reduces the handshake time by at least 45%, and the privacy gains from semi-static keys come at negligible performance costs.

Concurrent Work. In concurrent work, Schwabe, Stebila, and Wiggers [39] also consider a variant of the KEMTLS protocol, called KEMTLS-PDK, that leverages prior knowledge of peer public keys. Similarly to this work, they show how pre-distributed public keys can lead to reduced round trips and bandwidth for the handshake. Their work further explores the performance characteristics for various NIST post-quantum KEM candidates. This work in contrast focuses on identity privacy and forward secrecy: beyond leveraging pre-distributed long-term keys, our protocol additionally employs in-band-distributed, semi-static keys to achieve (delayed) forward secrecy for the first data flow including the client's identity and, optionally, 0-RTT data.

2 Preliminaries

Notation. The security parameter is denoted λ and is encoded in unary when given as input to algorithms. For an integer $n \geq 1$, $[\![n]\!]$ denotes the set $\{1, \ldots, n\}$. The notation $y \leftarrow \mathsf{A}(x)$ or $\mathsf{A}(x) \to y$ means that a deterministic algorithm A runs on input x and returns y; for probabilistic algorithms the notation $\leftarrow_\$$ resp. $\to_\$$ is used instead.

Symmetric Primitives. The presented protocols rely on classical symmetric primitives, including collision-resistant hash functions, pseudorandom functions,

Client		Server

$(pk_e, sk_e) \leftarrow_\$ \mathsf{KEM}_e.\mathsf{KeyGen}\left(1^\lambda\right)$

$(K_s, C_s) \leftarrow_\$ \mathsf{KEM}_s.\mathsf{Encaps}(pk_s); \left(K_s^t, C_s^t\right) \leftarrow_\$ \mathsf{KEM}_s.\mathsf{Encaps}\left(pk_s^t\right)$

$K_0 \leftarrow \mathsf{KDF}\left(K_s^t\right)$

$K_1, K_1', K_2 \leftarrow \mathsf{KDF}\left(K_s, K_s^t\right)$

$pk_e, \mathsf{AEAD}_{K_0}(C_s), C_s^t, \mathsf{AEAD}_{K_1}\left(cert[pk_c]\right), \mathsf{AEAD}_{K_1'}$ (opt. 0-RTT data)

⟶

$K_s^t \leftarrow \mathsf{KEM}_s.\mathsf{Decaps}\left(sk_s^t, C_s^t\right)$

$K_0 \leftarrow \mathsf{KDF}(K_s^t)$

$K_s \leftarrow \mathsf{KEM}_s.\mathsf{Decaps}\left(sk_s, C_s\right)$

$K_1, K_1', K_2 \leftarrow \mathsf{KDF}\left(K_s, K_s^t\right)$

$(K_e, C_e) \leftarrow_\$ \mathsf{KEM}_e.\mathsf{Encaps}\left(pk_e\right); (K_c, C_c) \leftarrow_\$ \mathsf{KEM}_c.\mathsf{Encaps}\left(pk_c\right)$

$K_{3,c}, K_{3,c}', K_{3,s}, K_{3,s}' \leftarrow \mathsf{KDF}\left(K_s, K_s^t, K_e, K_c\right)$

$C_e, \mathsf{AEAD}_{K_2}(C_c), \mathsf{AEAD}_{K_{3,s}}$ (key confirmation), $\mathsf{AEAD}_{K_{3,s}'}$ (app. data)

⟵

$K_e \leftarrow \mathsf{KEM}_e.\mathsf{Decaps}\left(sk_e, C_e\right); K_c \leftarrow \mathsf{KEM}_c.\mathsf{Decaps}\left(sk_c, C_c\right)$

$K_{3,c}, K_{3,c}', K_{3,s}, K_{3,s}' \leftarrow \mathsf{KDF}\left(K_s, K_s^t, K_e, K_c\right)$

$\mathsf{AEAD}_{K_{3,c}}$ (key confirmation), $\mathsf{AEAD}_{K_{3,c}'}$ (app. data)

⟶

Fig. 1. Sketch of the main protocol.

message-authentication codes, and key derivation functions, formally defined in the full version [23].

Key Encapsulation Mechanisms. The protocol further relies on key encapsulation mechanisms (KEMs), a public-key primitive which allows a party to send a symmetric key to another party encrypted under the public key of the latter. It consists of a key generation algorithm $\mathsf{KeyGen}\left(1^\lambda\right) \to_\$ (pk, sk)$ that generates a pair of public and secret keys, an encapsulation algorithm $\mathsf{Encaps}(pk) \to_\$ (K, C)$ which computes a symmetric key in a set $\mathcal{K}$ and a ciphertext, and a decapsulation algorithm $\mathsf{Decaps}(sk, C) \to K$ that computes a symmetric key on the input of a secret key and a ciphertext.

3   Protocol

This section presents a key-exchange protocol, specified in Fig. 2, with mutual authentication that solely relies on KEMs for key establishment and authentication between a client and a server. The protocol assumes the client to have prior knowledge of the server certificate, as it is often the case for embedded or IoT devices and other applications of TLS. This, together with novel insights, allows the client to send forward-secret and fully authenticated application data after a single round trip, and the server from its first flow, as in TLS 1.3. It also allows (optional) zero round-trip time (0-RTT) to be send by the client along with its first flight of messages. In comparison, in the KEMTLS protocol [38] the client can only send application data after two round trips in the case of mutual authentication, and the server can only do so from its second flow regardless of client authentication.

Building Blocks. The protocol involves three KEMs: KEM_e for establishing ephemeral secrets and enabling forward secrecy, KEM_c for implicit client authentication, and KEM_s for implicit server authentication. All three could be instantiated with the same scheme or be chosen differently depending on various optimization factors. For instance, KEM_e could be chosen so as to minimize the key-generation time and alleviate client computation, whereas KEM_c and KEM_s could be selected as schemes with fast encapsulation even though key generation might be long, with an even stronger computational-efficiency requirement for the client than for the server.

Besides, the protocol also uses Krawczyk's hash-based key derivation function HKDF [27] as keystone of the key schedule to extract (via HKDF.Extract) randomness from the KEM-generated secrets and derive (via HKDF.Expand) stage keys, HMAC [4] as message authentication code for explicit party authentication and a hash function H, e.g., SHA-256, to compute expansion labels for HKDF as well as compress the handshake messages before explicit authentication.

Outline. The protocol shares similarities with the KEMTLS protocol, which is itself modeled after the OPTLS protocol [28]. However, it goes beyond prior work to reconcile client privacy (even if server long-term keys are later compromised) and a 1-RTT handshake: it leverages *server semi-static KEM keys* which the client encapsulates against and mixes the result into the key schedule at the beginning of the protocol, so that only a party privy to the semi-static secret key can decipher the client identity.

Key Lifetime. A pair of semi-static keys is only to be used in a given time period, e.g., a duration of two days, after which the server refreshes the pair. Though the privacy guarantees are not as strong as those of a 2-RTT handshake which uses fully ephemeral secrets to protect client certificates, they are still relevant in practice and it is a fair compromise for the efficiency benefits.

Clocks. The server keeps track of time periods with an integer counter. Only the server must maintain a clock, just to know when to refresh the keys. The client need only store the latest semi-static public key it received from the server along with the corresponding time period, which is indicated by the server. This means that the protocol can even be used with clients that may not have a clock as it is the case for some IoT devices.

Time-Period Transition. The server generates the keys for a time period before its beginning and sends the public key to the client as part of a handshake during

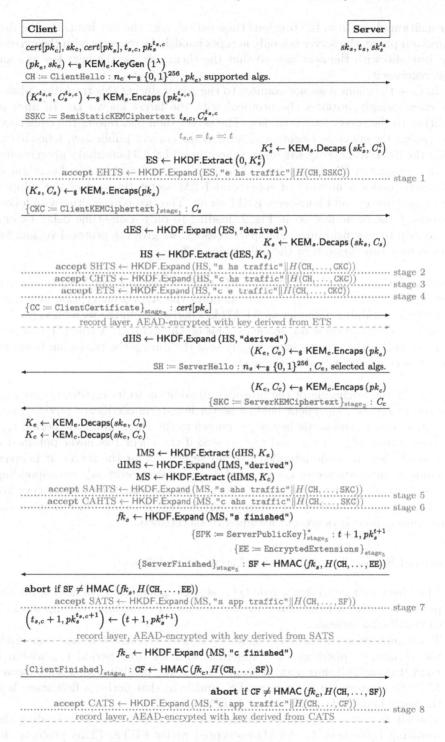

Fig. 2. Protocol in the case of matching time periods.

a transition phase from the previous time period, e.g., the last hour. During this transition phase, the server not only accepts handshake requests with the current key, but also with the next one, so that the client can use the next key as soon as it receives it.

In case the client does not connect to the server during this transition phase, the client simply initiates the protocol with the latest known key (if any) in addition to the server long-term key. The server then just rejects the ciphertext encrypting the client certificate and returns the current public key; following in spirit the `HelloRetryRequest` message sent in a TLS 1.3 handshake upon configuration mismatch [35, Sect. 4.1.4]. The client can now send its certificate anew, encrypted under a mixture of ephemeral KEM secret (instead of the skipped semi-static secret) and long-term KEM secret. The two parties otherwise follow essentially the same flow as in Fig. 2, leading to only a one-time delay by one round trip to re-synchronize. For space reasons, we give the protocol version for unmatching time periods in the full version [23].

Protocol Notation. In Figs. 2, "$\mathrm{MSG} : M$" denotes that message MSG is sent and contains M, and "$\{\mathrm{MSG}\}_{\mathrm{stage}_k} : M$" denotes the AEAD encryption of a message MSG containing M under an AEAD key derived from the secret accepted at stage k (the derivation is not made explicit on the figures). A star (*) as superscript indicates that the message is only sent the during the transition from the current server time period to the next.

Inputs. At the beginning of the protocol, in addition to its certificate $cert[pk_c]$ and secret key sk_c, the client holds a server long-term certificate $cert[pk_s]$ and the latest server semi-static key $pk_s^{t_{s,c}}$ known to the client in a time period $t_{s,c}$. By convention, $pk_s^{t_{s,c}} := \perp$ and $t_{s,c} := -\infty$ if the client has never obtained a semi-static key from the intended partner server. As for the server, it is given as input a long-term secret key sk_s and a semi-static secret $sk_s^{t_s}$ corresponding to the current server time period t_s. Note that the long-term public keys are certificated out of band by an external certification authority. In constrast, the semi-static public keys are *not* assumed to be certified.

Protocol Steps. The main protocol steps are as follows.

- The client first generates a pair (pk_e, sk_e) of ephemeral keys, and sends the public key with a fresh nonce n_c and the list of algorithms it supports in a `ClientHello` message.
- The client then encapsulates against the server semi-static key and sends the resulting ciphertext $C_s^{t_{s,c}}$ together with its time period $t_{s,c}$ within a `SemiStaticKEMCiphertext` message. It uses the resulting semi-static secret $K_s^{t_{s,c}}$ to compute an early secret ES, and from that derive a first stage key, the early handshake traffic secret EHTS.
- The client next encapsulates against the server long-term key, sending the resulting ciphertext C_s AEAD-encrypted under EHTS. (This protects the

certified identity of the server from an active adversary with delayed forward secrecy, in case C_s may leak such information.) The resulting key K_s is mixed into the key schedule to obtain a handshake secret HS, which implicitly authenticates the server.

– The handshake secret HS is used to compute server and client handshake traffic secrets SHTS and CHTS. The client uses CHTS to AEAD-encrypt its certificate in a `ClientCertificate` message. (This ensures that only a party knowing both the server long-term and semi-static secret keys used can infer information about the client's identity.)

Additionally, an early traffic secret ETS is derived to optionally send protected 0-RTT application data.

– When the server receives the `ClientHello`, `SemiStaticKEMCiphertext` and `ClientCertificate` messages from the client, two cases arise: either the client time period $t_{s,c}$ matches the current server time period t_s or not.

Matching time periods. If $t_{s,c} = t_s =: t$ (or $t_{s,c} = t_s + 1$ during the transition from t_s to $t_s + 1$) as in Fig. 2, the server has the semi-static secret key sk_s^t and can thus compute EHTS, SHTS, CHTS, and ETS, and recover C_s, the client certificate and potential early application data.

* The server encapsulates against pk_e and sends in a `ServerHello` message the resulting ciphertext C_e, together with a fresh nonce and the algorithms selected from the algorithms that the client supports.
* Next, the server encapsulates against the client public key pk_c and encrypts the resulting ciphertext C_c under SHTS. (This prevents information about the client's identity to leak through C_c.)
* Both parties now compute a master secret by mixing in the ephemeral and client long-term KEM secrets K_e and K_c. Secret K_c enables forward secrecy, K_c implicitly authenticates the client.
* From MS, both parties compute (mutually) authenticated handshake traffic secrets SAHTS and CAHTS for the server and the client, used to derive AEAD keys to encrypt the remaining handshake.
* From MS, MAC "finished" keys fk_s and fk_c are further derived for explicit authentication as well as application transport secrets SATS and CATS for application data encryption.
* The server explicitly authenticates by sending a "finished" message, a MAC over the transcript under key fk_s and can then send application data.

  During a transition phase to the next time period, it also sends the public key pk_s^{t+1} for the next time period.[1] The client saves this key (and discards pk_s^t) only after verifying the server MAC.
* Upon receiving the server "finished" message, the client explicitly authenticates by also sending a MAC over the transcript under key fk_c, and can then send application data.

---

[1] The server does so once per client; the client will then switch to the next key for subsequent handshakes.

Unmatching Time Periods. If $t_{s,c} \neq t_s$ (and $t_{s,c} \neq t_s + 1$ during the transition from t_s to $t_s + 1$), the server does not hold $sk_s^{t_{s,c}}$ and cannot compute the early handshake-traffic, the server/client handshake traffic or the early traffic secrets (denoted EHTS', SHTS', CHTS', and ETS'), and therefore cannot recover K_s, the client certificate or any potential early application data. The server thus rejects the first four stages.

The main idea in this case is close to that of a `HelloRetryRequest` in TLS 1.3 [35]. The server's response to the client does not contain a KEM_c ciphertext, indicating that their time periods did not match, but however contains an ephemeral KEM ciphertext. The client can then decapsulate the ciphertext, recover an ephemeral secret, and restart as in the case of matching time periods; the now-established ephemeral secret essentially takes the place of the semi-static one. The protocol is thereby delayed by a single round trip. The details are given in the full version [23].

4   Security Model

This section introduces the model to capture security of the key-exchange protocol presented in Sect. 3. It is close to the model for authenticated key exchange proposed by Dowling, Fischlin, Günther and Stebila [13,14] and that for KEMTLS by Schwabe, Stebila, and Wiggers [38]. Their models follow a line of work [19,22] concerned with *multi-stage* key exchange protocols in which keys are computed at multiple stages of each single protocol execution. Session-key indistinguishability originates from the seminal Bellare–Rogaway model [5]. Due to space restrictions, only the key properties captured by the model are presented here; the technical details are given in the full version [23].

In the security model, the adversary controls the network and can passively eavesdrop, modify and orchestrate the communication across several concurrent sessions of the protocol. The adversary can further expose long-term and semi-static secrets of honest parties as well as the keys established during protocol runs (individually per stage). The protocol is then deemed *multi-stage secure* if such an adversary cannot distinguish a key established at a stage of a non-compromised (*"fresh"*) session from a uniformly random key.

Authentication. The model supports *mutual* authentication, as required in the scenario of IoT or embedded devices. For the authentication of each stage key, *implicit* and *explicit* authentication are distinguished. Implicit authentication refers to the property that the stage key can only be recovered by the intended partner, whereas explicit authentication guarantees that the partner actively participated in the protocol and also established a stage key. The authentication of a stage key can further be lifted from unauthenticated or implicit to explicit once a later stage of the protocol is accepted: a stage key can be *retroactively* explicitly authenticated.

Forward Secrecy. The model further covers forward secrecy, the notion that stage keys remain secret even if the long-term keys involved in its computation are later compromised. As the protocol in Sect. 3 introduces server semi-static keys (i.e., keys that are periodically refreshed) for servers in addition to long-term keys, the notion of forward secrecy is here refined to also take the compromise of such keys into account.

More precisely, the model considers two types of forward secrecy determined by whether the semi-static key used to compute a stage key may be corrupted. A stage key satisfies *(full) forward secrecy* if the adversary remained passive until the stage is accepted or did not corrupt the long-term key of the intended communication partner before the latter was explicitly authenticated. The semi-static key used to compute the stage key may be corrupted at any time. A stage key satisfies *delayed forward secrecy* if, in addition to the previous conditions, the adversary did not corrupt the semi-static key used to compute the stage key. In particular, if the long-term key of the intended partner is not corrupted before the semi-static key expires, the secrecy of the stage key is equivalent to that of a key satisfying full forward secrecy. This (informal) definition of delayed forward secrecy is related to Boyd and Gellert's [8].

Key Usage. The use of stage keys is also specified, i.e., whether a key is meant to be used internally within the protocol (e.g., to encrypt handshake traffic) or externally (for example to protect application messages).

Replays. The model further captures that the initial, first-flight keys are *replayable*: an attacker may copy the client's initial messages and send them to the server (again), leading to multiple server sessions sharing the same keys with that one original client. This is due to the key being derived without interaction (in zero round-trip time) and hence with no active contribution from the server side. Following [14,20], the model distinguishes between replayable and non-replayable stages, catering for this situation (which would otherwise lead to a violation of partnering uniqueness), while still demanding that keys remain indistinguishable from random, even when replayable.

5 Security Analysis

This section discusses the security of the Sect. 3 protocol in the model from Sect. 4, and shows that it achieves multi-stage security based on the IND-CCA security of the involved KEMs, PRF security of the key derivation functions, EUF-CMA security of HMAC, and collision resistance of the hash function. Only a summary of the results in the case of matching time periods is given here due to space constraints.

Properties. The protocol satisfies the following properties in the case of matching time periods (Fig. 2). It has 8 stages, of which the first four satisfy delayed forward secrecy, the others full forward secrecy. Server and client are implicitly authentication from stage 2 resp. stage 5 on and explicitly authenticated from stage 7 resp. stage 8 on. The keys of stages 1–3 and 5–6 are used internally, to encrypt handshake traffic. The first four stage keys, without active server contribution, are replayable; all other keys are not.

Theorem 51 (Multi-stage Security – Matching Time Periods). *Let $\mathscr{A}$ be an adversary against the multi-stage security of the protocol in Fig. 2. There exist explicit reduction algorithms to the respective security of each protocol building block such that the advantage of $\mathscr{A}$ in the multi-stage security game in the case of matching time periods is at most*

$$2^{-257}n_\sigma^2 + \varepsilon_H^{\mathrm{Coll}} + (2\delta_s + \delta_e + \delta_c)n_\sigma$$

$$+ 8n_\sigma \left(\begin{array}{c} n_{id} \left(\begin{array}{c} \varepsilon_{\mathsf{KEM}_c}^{\mathrm{IND\text{-}CCA}} + \varepsilon_{\mathsf{KEM}_s}^{\mathrm{IND\text{-}CCA}} \\ + 3\varepsilon_{\mathsf{HKDF.Extract}}^{\mathrm{PRF}} + \varepsilon_{\mathsf{HKDF.Extract}}^{\mathrm{dual\text{-}PRF}} \\ + 4\varepsilon_{\mathsf{HKDF.Expand}}^{\mathrm{PRF}} + \varepsilon_{\mathsf{HMAC}}^{\mathrm{EUF\text{-}CMA}} \end{array} \right) \\ + n_{id}\cdot n_{period}\cdot n_\sigma \left(\begin{array}{c} \varepsilon_{\mathsf{KEM}_s}^{\mathrm{IND\text{-}CCA}} + 3\varepsilon_{\mathsf{HKDF.Extract}}^{\mathrm{PRF}} \\ + \varepsilon_{\mathsf{HKDF.Extract}}^{\mathrm{dual\text{-}PRF}} + 4\varepsilon_{\mathsf{HKDF.Expand}}^{\mathrm{PRF}} \\ + \varepsilon_{\mathsf{HMAC}}^{\mathrm{EUF\text{-}CMA}} \end{array} \right) \\ + n_\sigma\cdot\varepsilon_{\mathsf{KEM}_e}^{\mathrm{IND\text{-}1CCA}} \end{array} \right),$$

with n_{id}, n_{period}, and n_σ being the number of users, time periods used across all servers, resp. sessions, $\varepsilon_H^{\mathrm{Coll}}$ being the probability that an algorithm given in the proof finds a collision for H by running $\mathscr{A}$ as subroutine, and KEM_s, KEM_e, and KEM_c being δ_s-, δ_e-, and δ_c-correct.

Proof (Sketch, cf. full version [23]). The proof proceeds via a sequence of games, initially ruling out nonce collisions (via the birthday bound $2^{-257}n_\sigma^2$) and hash collisions in honest sessions (based on the hash-function collision resistance). It then applies a hybrid argument, reducing the number of tests to a single one, losing a factor of at most the total number of stages across all sessions, i.e., $8n_\sigma$.

The proof then branches into several sub-cases based on the freshness conditions necessary to test a session (cf. the formal definition in the full version [23]). The main steps in each branch essentially consist in proving the following.

1. One of the KEM-encapsulated secrets K_s, $K_s^{t_{s,c}}$, K_e or K_c used in the tested session remains secret due to encapsulation being done by an honest session and the corresponding KEM secret key remaining uncompromised. This allows to replace that KEM key K with a uniformly random value based via a reduction to the IND-CCA security of the corresponding KEM. Based on the KEM type, this step first requires guessing the corresponding peer, time period, and/or partner session holding the KEM public key, inducing factors involving n_{id}, n_{period}, resp. n_σ.
2. This allows to replace all keys derived from the secret KEM key K all the way up to the master secret MS and the keys derived from MS. These steps can be

argued via the PRF (or dual-PRF) security of the involved HKDF.Extract and HKDF.Expand calls, replacing derived keys at on level at a time with random values. After these steps, tested keys are indistinguishable from random ones, preventing the adversary from winning by testing a fresh session key.

3. As a result, any received HMAC value ensuring explicit authentication cannot have been forged, as this would result in a valid MAC forgery under the (now random) MAC keys fk_s/fk_c, contradicting the EUF-CMA security of HMAC. This guarantees that the adversary cannot make a session maliciously accept.

An upper-bound over all sub-cases then yields the theorem statement.   □

The multi-stage security bound for the protocol with unmatching time periods is derived similarly to that in Theorem 51, except that there are twelve stages to consider (implying a hybrid factor loss of $12n_\sigma$ instead of $8n_\sigma$) and four more keys (EHTS' on the one hand, and SHTS', CHTS' and ETS' on the other hand) derived (adding an extra $2\varepsilon_{\mathsf{HKDF.Expand}}^{\mathsf{PRF}}$ term in the bound). Due to space constraints, the full proof and the detailed theorem statement for the unmatching case are deferred to the full version [23].

6 Discussion

Identity Protection. TLS 1.3 protects parties' identities by following the SIGMA-I key exchange pattern of Krawczyk [26]. More specifically, it protects the server identity against passive attackers and the client identity against active attackers, the latter identity being revealed only after having seen a valid server signature. The KEMTLS protocol [38] carefully mimics these properties, achieving identity protection for the server against passive attackers and for the client against active attackers. Client identity protection in KEMTLS comes with an additional half or full round trip (depending on the targeted authentication properties). The KEMTLS-PDK protocol [39], in reducing roundtrips, sends the KEM encapsulation against the server's static key in cleartext. Unless an anonymous KEM [3,21,32] is deployed, this value might leak information about the server's identity.

Our protocol leverages the pre-loaded server certificate to reduce handshake round trips *while* achieving stronger identity protection: it protects both server and client identities against *active* attackers, both with delayed forward secrecy through encrypting the client certificate and ClientKEMCiphertext C_s under the server's semi-static key (authenticated in a previous handshake).

On the Security Proofs. The security proofs are similar to those of the KEMTLS protocol, are given in the standard model and do not rely on any form of adversary rewinding. Existing techniques in the literature (e.g., Song's "lifting lemma" [41]) can thus be used to prove the protocol secure against quantum adversaries as long as the underlying primitives are.

However, the proofs are non-tight (with the precise losses spelled out in exact-security terms) as they require to guess the test session as well as, depending on the proof case, the contributive session or the identity of the intended peer. The proofs can thus be understood as heuristic arguments for the soundness of the protocol design. It is worth noting that except for very recent work on TLS 1.3 [11,12], most proofs of deployed authenticated key-exchange protocols are also non-tight.

Downgrade Resilience. The model in Sect. 4 does not capture algorithm negotiation although any practical deployment of the protocol would support multiple instantiations for each primitive. However, one can still informally argue that the downgrade resilience properties of the protocol in Sect. 3 are similar to those of the KEMTLS protocol. More precisely, an active adversary could in principle make a party choose an algorithm other than the one it would have used if the adversary were passive, but the adversary cannot make a party use an unsupported algorithm. Moreover, assuming that the security of the building blocks is not breached before the confirmation messages are received, the client and the server are guaranteed to share the same transcript which includes negotiation messages. In other words, full downgrade resilience [6,15] is satisfied once the other party is explicitly authenticated.

Comparison with KEMTLS. The assumption that the client knows the server public key from the onset of the protocol is precisely what allows to have the server send application data from its first message flow and to reduce the handshake by a full round-trip compared to the KEMTLS protocol. It also implies that the client need not verify the server certificate during the handshake, which speeds up the handshake even further and reduces power consumption.

However, as explained in the introduction, in a KEM-based protocol that achieves mutual authentication in a single round trip, an adversary could a priori recover the client's identity by corrupting the long-term key of the server even after the handshake is completed (no forward identity protection), as it is for instance the case of the KEMTLS-PDK protocol [39]. The semi-static keys introduced in this paper mitigate this privacy loss and ensure, without extra round trip, that the client's identity cannot be recovered once the semi-static keys have expired. The lifetime of the semi-static keys now depends on the desired trade-off between efficiency and privacy: the shorter the lifetime is, the stronger the privacy guarantees are for the client and the heavier the computational burden is on (mainly) the server.

Comparison with Session Resumption and Forward-Secret 0-RTT. TLS 1.3 specifies a session resumption (pre-shared key/"PSK") handshake, bootstrapping from symmetric secret keys that have been established in a prior connection and also enabling a 0-RTT mode. As also discussed in [39], the PSK handshake has efficiency advantages (e.g., for relying purely on symmetric cryptography) but also downsides wrt. key management of symmetric keys which need to be frequently changed (requiring additional communication) and securely stored in client memory. Our approach in contrast only stores (semi-static and long-term) *public* keys of the server at the client, reducing the risk for compromise as well as communication overhead.

The 0-RTT mode of TLS 1.3 enables clients to send application data in the first message flow, and thus reduce the handshake by a round trip compared to the standard mode. This requires servers to reconstruct secrets from previous sessions when receiving the clients' first messages, i.e., the 0-RTT mode is a resumption mechanism.

The standard resumption technique to achieve forward-secrecy and resilience to replay attacks consists in having servers store session caches (resumption secrets from all recent sessions) in local databases and issuing clients unique lookup keys that they use for their next connections. Similar techniques could a priori be used to reduce the KEMTLS handshake while maintaining forward identity protection, provided that the resumption handshake uses a KEM to achieve post-quantum security. The presented approach with semi-static keys in contrast obviates the need for extra secure updatable storage on the client side for resumption keys. It also allows the server to save storage by re-using $sk_s^{t_s}$ with many clients; session caches can easily grow huge.

Aviram, Gellert, and Jager [1,2] proposed a different approach to forward secrecy based on puncturing techniques, improving over session caches in terms of server storage. Yet, at a 128-bit security level this easily requires tens of MB of server storage, compared to, e.g., a 2.342 kB single Kyber key pair with our protocol.

The main benefits of our protocol over forward-secret session resumption are therefore in small storage overhead (mainly on the server side), not needing (expensive) updatable secure client storage, and reliance on standardized post-quantum KEM components.

7   Implementation

This section discusses the implementation choices for the handshake protocol in Sect. 3. Since certificates are pre-distributed and need not be verified during handshakes, the main performance bottleneck depends on the choice of underlying KEMs. The main protocol is subsequently denoted PDK-SS (pre-distributed keys with semi-static contributions) for simpler referencing.

Choice of Primitives. The KEMs considered for implementation are among the finalists and alternates in the third round of the NIST Post-Quantum Standardization Process [33], with parameters chosen at security level 1 (roughly equivalent to the security of AES-128). The criteria of particular relevance in the IoT use case include the speed of cryptographic operations, the size of ciphertexts that may impact the handshake latency, and the size of the keys stored on devices and transmitted during the handshake.

We compare three of the NIST Round 3 finalist KEMs that rely on hardness assumptions over structured lattices and achieve good performance in terms of speed and size. These are Kyber512 [37] with security relying on the Module

Learning with Errors (MLWE) problem, LightSABER [10] relying on the Module Learning with Rounding (MLWR) problem and NTRU-HPS-2048-509 [9] with security relying on the NTRU problem. We also include Round 3 Alternate candidate SIKE [24] which is based on supersingular isogeny Diffie–Hellman, using parameter set SIKEp434-compressed. Despite slower operations compared to its lattice-based counterparts, SIKE benefits from the smallest key and ciphertext sizes of remaining candidates in the NIST process.

To verify (client) certificates, we combined these KEMs with Dilithium-II [31] (with Kyber512 and LightSABER) and Falcon512 [34] (with NTRU) based on the similar assumptions. For the smallest size instantiation based on SIKE, we used Falcon, which has the smallest signatures of the finalists.

Prototype Implementation. To experimentally evaluate PDK-SS, we implemented it by modifying the prototype implementation of the KEMTLS protocols [38,39] based on Rustls [7], a TLS library written in Rust. The prototype integrates implementations of the post-quantum primitives from PQClean [25] and the Open Quantum Safe (OQS) library [42]. For all implementations we used AVX2-accelerated code. The implementation is available under permissive licences at https://github.com/AbuLSim/1RTT-KEMTLS.

8   Benchmarking

Table 1 compares the main protocol with other mutually authenticated handshake protocols, some of which also leverage cached leaf certificates. Even though these experiments were run on a powerful server and not on IoT devices, they clearly demonstrate the performance benefits of the main protocol.

Methodology. We compare PDK-SS to TLS with cached certificates [36] (both TLS 1.3 using X25519/RSA2048 and post-quantum variants), and to KEMTLS, with [39] and without [38] pre-distributed keys (the former is denoted PDK in Table 1). Cached TLS is included for the sake of comparison to a real-world Internet protocol.

We analyze the performance of the PDK-SS protocol in three cases:

- the synchronized case PDK-SS, where the client and server share the same semi-static key;
- the asychronized case PDK-SS async, where the client and server have out-of-sync copies of the semi-static key and so the server must send its key to the client;
- the PDK-SS update case, where the client and server share the same semi-static server key but an update to the next semi-static epoch key is available.

The numbers in each column of Table 1 represent the average time to reach the corresponding stage of the protocol, measured in milliseconds over 60,000 handshakes for each scheme and each set of network parameters. The handshakes were performed on an emulated network; the experiment code is included in the

Table 1. Average time in ms for mutually authenticated handshakes with cached leaf certificates.

Mutually authenticated	30.9 ms RTT, 1000 Mbps				195.5 ms RTT, 10 Mbps			
	Client send req.	Client recv. resp.	Server expl. auth.	Server recv CFIN.	Client send req.	Client recv. resp.	Server expl. auth.	Server recv CFIN.
kemtls								
SIKE-c	196.8	228.0	**228.0**	165.9	697.0	893.3	**893.2**	500.9
MLWE/MSIS	95.0	126.2	**126.2**	64.1	598.1	794.2	**794.2**	401.6
NTRU	95.1	126.3	**126.2**	64.2	594.8	791.0	**790.9**	398.4
Cached TLS								
TLS 1.3	68.8	100.3	**66.0**	38.2	399.2	596.6	**396.5**	204.6
SIKE-c	103.0	134.8	**101.6**	72.8	431.7	630.5	**430.3**	238.1
MLWE/MSIS	64.3	95.9	**63.7**	33.8	400.3	619.4	**399.7**	224.7
NTRU	66.0	97.8	**64.6**	35.7	397.9	596.7	**396.5**	204.2
PDK								
SIKE-c	130.6	161.7	**130.5**	99.7	466.6	662.7	**466.5**	269.3
Kyber	63.3	94.4	**63.2**	32.3	400.5	596.5	**400.4**	200.6
NTRU	63.3	94.5	**63.3**	32.4	396.7	592.7	**396.6**	198.8
SABER	63.4	94.5	**63.3**	32.5	399.3	595.3	**399.2**	200.4
PDK-SS								
SIKE-c	126.8	157.8	**126.7**	91.9	474.1	670.2	**474.0**	276.5
Kyber	63.5	94.6	**63.4**	32.5	402.0	598.3	**401.9**	201.5
NTRU	63.5	94.7	**63.5**	32.6	397.6	593.6	**397.5**	199.4
SABER	63.6	94.7	**63.5**	32.7	401.5	597.7	**401.5**	201.1
PDK-SS async								
SIKE-c	170.6	201.7	**170.6**	129.7	672.6	868.7	**672.5**	475.1
Kyber	94.7	125.9	**94.7**	63.8	614.7	810.8	**614.7**	403.0
NTRU	94.8	125.9	**94.7**	63.8	597.5	793.5	**597.5**	398.0
SABER	94.9	126.0	**94.8**	63.9	604.0	800.0	**603.9**	401.1
PDK-SS update								
SIKE-c	127.5	158.5	**127.4**	92.5	474.1	670.2	**474.0**	276.5
Kyber	63.5	94.7	**63.5**	32.6	402.1	598.4	**402.0**	202.2
NTRU	63.6	94.7	**63.5**	32.6	398.1	594.1	**398.1**	200.0
SABER	63.7	94.8	**63.6**	32.7	401.5	597.7	**401.5**	201.7

source code repository. The server running the simulations was equipped with two Intel Xeon Gold 6230 CPUs, each with 20 cores. The left hand columns were computed over a low-latency, high-bandwidth (30.9 ms round trip and 1000 Mbps) connection, with the right hand over a high-latency, low-bandwidth (195.5 ms round trip and 10 Mbps) connection. For each handshake, we measured the time taken for the client to send its first request in the form of application data, the client to receive the server response, the server to be explicitly authenticated, and finally the server to receive the client finished message. The time taken for the server to be explicitly authenticated is in bold font as we view it as the most important metric for our use case.

Analysis. Table 1 shows that the performances of PDK-SS (in the synchronized case), PDK and cached TLS are similar. That is because they are all 1-RTT, and the handshake time is dominated by the number of round trips since computation and transmission times are dwarfed by the network latency. The only exception is with SIKE as KEM, as its operations are an order of magnitude (milliseconds versus microseconds) slower than those of the other KEMs.

As for the asynchronized case, PDK-SS async compares most closely with the original KEMTLS handshake (PDK-SS async is somewhat faster as clients do not verify server certificates); their additional round trip clearly impacts the overall handshake time as expected. More precisely, PDK-SS is 50 to 55% faster than KEMTLS in the low-latency setup, and 50 to 53% faster in the high-latency setup.

Overall, our experiments confirm that the privacy benefits of introducing semi-static keys come at a negligible performance cost.

Acknowledgments. The authors thank Kenny Paterson and Cédric Fournet for helpful discussions. This work was supported by the Eurostars ZERO-TOUCH Project (E113920) and the European Research Council under Grant Agreement No. 805031 (EPOQUE). Felix Günther was supported in part by German Research Foundation (DFG) Research Fellowship grant GU 1859/1-1.

References

1. Aviram, N., Gellert, K., Jager, T.: Session resumption protocols and efficient forward security for TLS 1.3 0-RTT. In: Ishai, Y., Rijmen, V. (eds.) EUROCRYPT 2019. LNCS, vol. 11477, pp. 117–150. Springer, Cham (2019). https://doi.org/10.1007/978-3-030-17656-3_5
2. Aviram, N., Gellert, K., Jager, T.: Session resumption protocols and efficient forward security for TLS 1.3 0-RTT. J. Cryptol. **34**(3), 1–57 (2021). https://doi.org/10.1007/s00145-021-09385-0
3. Bellare, M., Boldyreva, A., Desai, A., Pointcheval, D.: Key-privacy in public-key encryption. In: Boyd, C. (ed.) ASIACRYPT 2001. LNCS, vol. 2248, pp. 566–582. Springer, Heidelberg (2001). https://doi.org/10.1007/3-540-45682-1_33
4. Bellare, M., Canetti, R., Krawczyk, H.: Keying hash functions for message authentication. In: Koblitz, N. (ed.) CRYPTO 1996. LNCS, vol. 1109, pp. 1–15. Springer, Heidelberg (1996). https://doi.org/10.1007/3-540-68697-5_1
5. Bellare, M., Rogaway, P.: Entity authentication and key distribution. In: Stinson, D.R. (ed.) CRYPTO 1993. LNCS, vol. 773, pp. 232–249. Springer, Heidelberg (1994). https://doi.org/10.1007/3-540-48329-2_21
6. Bhargavan, K., Brzuska, C., Fournet, C., Green, M., Kohlweiss, M., Zanella-Béguelin, S.: Downgrade resilience in key-exchange protocols. In: 2016 IEEE Symposium on Security and Privacy, pp. 506–525. IEEE Computer Society Press, May 2016. https://doi.org/10.1109/SP.2016.37
7. Birr-Pixton, J.: A modern TLS library in rust. https://github.com/ctz/rustls
8. Boyd, C., Gellert, K.: A modern view on forward security. Cryptology ePrint Archive, Report 2019/1362 (2019). https://eprint.iacr.org/2019/1362
9. Chen, C., et al.: NTRU. Technical report, National Institute of Standards and Technology (2020). https://csrc.nist.gov/projects/post-quantum-cryptography/round-3-submissions
10. D'Anvers, J.P., et al.: SABER. Technical report, National Institute of Standards and Technology (2020). https://csrc.nist.gov/projects/post-quantum-cryptography/round-3-submissions
11. Davis, H., Günther, F.: Tighter proofs for the SIGMA and TLS 1.3 key exchange protocols. Cryptology ePrint Archive, Report 2020/1029 (2020). https://eprint.iacr.org/2020/1029

12. Diemert, D., Jager, T.: On the tight security of TLS 1.3: theoretically-sound cryptographic parameters for real-world deployments. Cryptology ePrint Archive, Report 2020/726 (2020). https://eprint.iacr.org/2020/726
13. Dowling, B., Fischlin, M., Günther, F., Stebila, D.: A cryptographic analysis of the TLS 1.3 handshake protocol candidates. In: Ray, I., Li, N., Kruegel, C. (eds.) ACM CCS 2015, pp. 1197–1210. ACM Press, October 2015. https://doi.org/10.1145/2810103.2813653
14. Dowling, B., Fischlin, M., Günther, F., Stebila, D.: A cryptographic analysis of the TLS 1.3 handshake protocol. J. Cryptol. **34**(4), 1–69 (2021). https://doi.org/10.1007/s00145-021-09384-1
15. Dowling, B., Stebila, D.: Modelling ciphersuite and version negotiation in the TLS protocol. In: Foo, E., Stebila, D. (eds.) ACISP 2015. LNCS, vol. 9144, pp. 270–288. Springer, Cham (2015). https://doi.org/10.1007/978-3-319-19962-7_16
16. Smartm2m; guidelines for security, privacy and interoperability in IoT system definition; a concrete approach. Technical report. ETSI SR 003 680, ETSI (2020)
17. Fagan, M., Megas, K., Scarfone, K., Smith, M.: Foundational cybersecurity activities for IoT device manufacturers. Technical report. NISTIR 8259, NIST (2020)
18. Fagan, M., Megas, K., Scarfone, K., Smith, M.: IoT device cybersecurity capability core baseline. Technical report. NISTIR 8259A, NIST (2020)
19. Fischlin, M., Günther, F.: Multi-stage key exchange and the case of Google's QUIC protocol. In: Ahn, G.J., Yung, M., Li, N. (eds.) ACM CCS 2014, pp. 1193–1204. ACM Press, November 2014. https://doi.org/10.1145/2660267.2660308
20. Fischlin, M., Günther, F.: Replay attacks on zero round-trip time: the case of the TLS 1.3 handshake candidates. In: 2017 IEEE European Symposium on Security and Privacy, EuroS&P 2017, pp. 60–75. IEEE, April 2017
21. Grubbs, P., Maram, V., Paterson, K.G.: Anonymous, robust post-quantum public key encryption. Cryptology ePrint Archive, Report 2021/708 (2021). https://eprint.iacr.org/2021/708
22. Günther, F.: Modeling advanced security aspects of key exchange and secure channel protocols. Ph.D. thesis, Technische Universität, Darmstadt (2018). http://tuprints.ulb.tu-darmstadt.de/7162/
23. Günther, F., Rastikian, S., Towa, P., Wiggers, T.: KEMTLS with delayed forward identity protection in (almost) a single round trip. Cryptology ePrint Archive, Report 2021/725 (2021). https://eprint.iacr.org/2021/725
24. Jao, D., et al.: SIKE. Technical report, National Institute of Standards and Technology (2020). https://csrc.nist.gov/projects/post-quantum-cryptography/round-3-submissions
25. Kannwischer, M., Rijneveld, J., Schwabe, P., Stebila, D., Wiggers, T.: PQClean: clean, portable, tested implementations of post quantum cryptography. https://github.com/pqclean/pqclean
26. Krawczyk, H.: SIGMA: the 'SIGn-and-MAc' approach to authenticated Diffie-Hellman and its use in the IKE protocols. In: Boneh, D. (ed.) CRYPTO 2003. LNCS, vol. 2729, pp. 400–425. Springer, Heidelberg (2003). https://doi.org/10.1007/978-3-540-45146-4_24
27. Krawczyk, H.: Cryptographic extraction and key derivation: the HKDF scheme. In: Rabin, T. (ed.) CRYPTO 2010. LNCS, vol. 6223, pp. 631–648. Springer, Heidelberg (2010). https://doi.org/10.1007/978-3-642-14623-7_34
28. Krawczyk, H., Wee, H.: The OPTLS protocol and TLS 1.3. Cryptology ePrint Archive, Report 2015/978 (2015). https://eprint.iacr.org/2015/978
29. Kwiatkowski, K., Valenta, L.: The TLS post-quantum experiment (2019). https://blog.cloudflare.com/the-tls-post-quantum-experiment/

30. Langley, A.: Cecpq2 (2018). https://www.imperialviolet.org/2018/12/12/cecpq2.html
31. Lyubashevsky, V., et al.: Crystals-Dilithium. Technical report, National Institute of Standards and Technology (2020). https://csrc.nist.gov/projects/post-quantum-cryptography/round-3-submissions
32. Mohassel, P.: A closer look at anonymity and robustness in encryption schemes. In: Abe, M. (ed.) ASIACRYPT 2010. LNCS, vol. 6477, pp. 501–518. Springer, Heidelberg (2010). https://doi.org/10.1007/978-3-642-17373-8_29
33. NIST: Submission requirements and evaluation criteria for the post-quantum cryptography standardization process. Technical report (2016)
34. Prest, T., et al.: FALCON. Technical report, National Institute of Standards and Technology (2020). https://csrc.nist.gov/projects/post-quantum-cryptography/round-3-submissions
35. Rescorla, E.: The Transport Layer Security (TLS) Protocol Version 1.3. RFC 8446 (Proposed Standard), August 2018. https://doi.org/10.17487/RFC8446, https://www.rfc-editor.org/rfc/rfc8446.txt
36. Santesson, S., Tschofenig, H.: Transport Layer Security (TLS) Cached Information Extension. RFC 7924, July 2016. https://doi.org/10.17487/RFC7924, https://rfc-editor.org/rfc/rfc7924.txt
37. Schwabe, P., et al.: CRYSTALS-Kyber. Technical report, National Institute of Standards and Technology (2020). https://csrc.nist.gov/projects/post-quantum-cryptography/round-3-submissions
38. Schwabe, P., Stebila, D., Wiggers, T.: Post-quantum TLS without handshake signatures. In: Ligatti, J., Ou, X., Katz, J., Vigna, G. (eds.) ACM CCS 2020, pp. 1461–1480. ACM Press, November 2020. https://doi.org/10.1145/3372297.3423350
39. Schwabe, P., Stebila, D., Wiggers, T.: More efficient post-quantum KEMTLS with pre-distributed public keys. In: Bertino, E., Shulman, H., Waidner, M. (eds.) ESORICS 2021. LNCS, vol. 12972, pp. 3–22. Springer, Cham (2021). https://doi.org/10.1007/978-3-030-88418-5_1
40. Sjöberg, K., Andres, P., Buburuzan, T., Brakemeier, A.: C-ITS deployment in Europe - current status and outlook. CoRR abs/1609.03876 (2016). http://arxiv.org/abs/1609.03876
41. Song, F.: A note on quantum security for post-quantum cryptography. In: Mosca, M. (ed.) PQCrypto 2014. LNCS, vol. 8772, pp. 246–265. Springer, Cham (2014). https://doi.org/10.1007/978-3-319-11659-4_15
42. Stebila, D., Mosca, M.: Post-quantum key exchange for the internet and the open quantum safe project. In: Avanzi, R., Heys, H. (eds.) Selected Areas in Cryptography – SAC 2016, SAC 2016. LNCS, vol. 10532, pp. 14–37. Springer, Cham (2016). https://doi.org/10.1007/978-3-319-69453-5_2

Improving the Privacy of Tor Onion Services

Edward Eaton, Sajin Sasy, and Ian Goldberg$^{(\boxtimes)}$

University of Waterloo, Waterloo, ON, Canada
{eeaton,ssasy,iang}@uwaterloo.ca

Abstract. Onion services enable bidirectional anonymity for parties
that communicate over the Tor network, thus providing improved privacy properties compared to standard TLS connections. Since these services are designed to support server-side anonymity, the entry points
for these services shuffle across the Tor network periodically. In order
to connect to an onion service at a given time, the client has to resolve
the .onion address for the service, which requires querying volunteer
Tor nodes called Hidden Service Directories (HSDirs). However, previous
work has shown that these nodes may be untrustworthy, and can learn
or leak the metadata about which onion services are being accessed. In
this paper, we present a new class of attacks that can be performed by
malicious HSDirs against the current generation (v3) of onion services.
These attacks target the *unlinkability* of onion services, allowing some
services to be tracked over time.

To restore unlinkability, we propose a number of concrete designs that
use Private Information Retrieval (PIR) to hide information about which
service is being queried, even from the HSDirs themselves. We examine
the three major classes of PIR schemes, and analyze their performance,
security, and how they fit into Tor in this context. We provide and evaluate implementations and end-to-end integrations, and make concrete
suggestions to show how these schemes could be used in Tor to minimize
the negative impact on performance while providing the most security.

Keywords: Tor · Onion Services · Unlinkability · PIR

1 Introduction

Tor provides anonymity to millions of users accessing the Internet every day [28].
However, Tor can also be used to provide this same protection to *hosts* of content,
resulting in bidirectional anonymity (or pseudonymity). This is achieved through
the use of Tor *onion services*[1] [11]. Communication over Tor is done using Tor
circuits. A circuit is a chain of typically three relay nodes through which traffic,

---

[1] Onion services were originally called hidden services, and hence some of the related
nomenclature still uses the word "hidden" instead of "onion" (for example, "HSDir").

An extended version of this paper is available [12].

G. Ateniese and D. Venturi (Eds.): ACNS 2022, LNCS 13269, pp. 273–292, 2022.
https://doi.org/10.1007/978-3-031-09234-3_14

encrypted in layers, is sent. The first node in a circuit is a client's *guard* node. In order to prevent certain attacks, a client will try to use the same guard node for every circuit it builds over the course of several months [10]. In order to communicate with an onion service, the client must learn the location of a Tor relay that has an open circuit to the onion service, called an *introduction point*. Each onion service typically has multiple introduction points distributed across the Tor network, which maintain circuits that connect to the onion service. Clients use these introduction points to inform the onion service of a *rendezvous point* that the onion service and client can communicate through via Tor circuits. In order to start this process the client must first obtain a list of the introduction points an onion service uses. This is done by querying the *hidden service directories*, or HSDirs. HSDirs assist the client in the task of translating the `.onion` address of an onion service into its list of introduction points. Onion addresses are encodings of the long-term identity public key owned by the onion service. For example, an onion address looks like: vww6ybal4bd7szmgncyruucpgfkqahzddi37ktceo3ah7ngmcopnpyyd.onion. How this address is distributed to users varies according to the onion service in question.

In version 3 of the onion services protocol, which we focus on in this paper, the onion address is used to query the HSDirs by first translating the original public key to a new 'blinded' public key, which changes at a regular interval (currently one day). The client uses the blinded public key to query the HSDirs, who provide the client with the *descriptor* associated with that blinded public key. These descriptors are encrypted under a symmetric key that can be derived from the onion address and contain a list of the introduction points. Each descriptor is held by a pseudorandom subset of Tor relays with the HSDir flag enabled. The mapping of which relays hold which descriptors changes over time, and is determined by a variety of inputs and system parameters, including the blinded public key of the onion service, the identity of the relay, and a shared random value distributed across the network; this shared randomness makes it hard for a malicious adversary that intends to censor an onion service to a priori compute and target the relays that will be used for serving the descriptors of an onion service in the future. We describe this process in detail in Sect. 2.1.

Tor has deprecated version 2 of the onion service protocol as of July 2021. An explicit goal of version 3 of the onion services protocol is that it should be difficult for the HSDirs to know i) which onion services they hold descriptors for, and ii) which onion services are being accessed when they are queried [32]. In version 2 of the protocol, the permanent public key associated with the onion service was contained within the descriptor, allowing HSDirs to identify the onion services they hold descriptors for. To protect against this, in version 3 the HSDirs hold descriptors indexed by a blinded public key, and since the identity public key (the onion address) cannot be recovered from the blinded key, the HSDirs cannot link an onion service descriptor with the underlying onion service unless it already knows the identity public key for the onion service. This process of keyblinding provides the security property of "unlinkability", which states that for an adversary who only observes blinded public keys and signatures under those keys, it is cryptographically impossible to pair two blinded keys as having the same underlying identity key.

However, in many cases it is reasonable to expect that the HSDir may know the identity public key. For example, many onion services widely distribute their `.onion` address so that anyone can access them, or a malicious adversary trying to deanonymize an onion service may get the public keys in some other way. Any HSDir can check if they hold the descriptor for an onion service that they know the identity public key for, simply by deriving the blinded public key and checking the descriptors they hold. In this work we consider how an HSDir's ability to connect incoming descriptor queries to blinded public keys impacts the privacy of onion services in Tor. We find that the information HSDirs have access to puts them in an advantageous position for launching attacks that can harm the anonymity of both onion services and clients connecting to those services. In particular we find that for onion services that wish to remain unknown, but are relatively popular within a community, it may be possible to violate unlinkability. To prevent this source of information being available, we explore the integration of Private Information Retrieval (PIR) into the descriptor lookup process.

1.1 Related Work

The idea of using PIR to mask the relative popularity of onion service queries from (version 2) HSDirs was mentioned in a blog post by Kadianakis in 2013 [18]. This blog post outlined various deficiencies in the way onion services worked (at the time), as well as proposing research directions for the scientific community to investigate to address these problems. In particular, while the post suggested using PIR as a possible solution to this problem, it did not investigate what kinds of PIR would be ideal or propose how the PIR schemes would actually be integrated into Tor. Ours is the first work that characterizes attacks against the newer version 3 onion services, explores the design space of a PIR-based solution to address it, and provides an implementation to demonstrate the effectiveness of those designs.

Other integrations of PIR into Tor have been explored before [23,26], but the focus in those works was on using PIR for finding nodes to build circuits, and not for onion service queries, although the two do share similar interests. Consideration of the possibility and the ramifications of malicious HSDirs has been addressed in some works before [16,22,25], but no work has yet explored whether knowledge of the distribution of queries made to an HSDir could be used to aid attacks that deanonymize clients or onion services.

Our Contributions.

1. We provide a description of the v3 onion service lookup process, which is key to the remainder of the text in Sect. 2. We then analyze the leakage induced by the descriptor lookup mechanism of v3 onion services, and propose attacks targeting both clients and onion services that leverage this leakage.
2. In Sect. 3 we discuss the variants of PIR that could solve this problem, and address the challenges of integrating them into a complete end-to-end solution for Tor's onion services, while also highlighting a network-level optimization

that saves an additional network round-trip that PIR would otherwise introduce.
3. We analyze the different PIR schemes proposed to compare the privacy guarantees provided by each in the context of Tor, using enumerative techniques to provide an upper bound on the probability an adversary is able to compromise our multi-server PIR system in Sect. 4.
4. Finally, in Sect. 5 we provide microbenchmarks for all of the defences we propose. Additionally, we also implement and evaluate an end-to-end integration for the best solution from our microbenchmarks on the live Tor network. Our results demonstrate that the performance overhead (or effect on time to load an onion service for clients) of our proposed defence is negligible.

2   Attacks

In this section we describe various avenues of attack enabled by the metadata currently provided by query lookups. We start with an overview of the lookup process, so that we can motivate our adversarial model and explain the attacks. Next we consider two broad classes of attacks: those targeting clients, and those targeting hidden services. For each class, we argue how a malicious HSDir may leverage the information of the distribution of query lookups to gain information on a target or track them over time.

2.1   Tor and Hidden Service Directories

The Tor network is run by thousands of volunteer nodes, called *relays*. As of January 2022, there are roughly 7000 relays that forward traffic for the Tor network [28]. These relays are listed in the Tor *network consensus*, which is a document generated by the nine Tor network directory authorities once per hour [29]. This consensus lists some global *parameters* conveying information about how Tor clients and relays should behave, and each relay listed in the consensus can also have *flags* indicating what properties the relay has. Currently, roughly 4000 relays have the "HSDir" flag, indicating that the relay will hold descriptors for onion services and deliver them to clients. Time is divided into *epochs*, with the size of the epoch being a consensus parameter of the Tor network. Currently, the length of an epoch is one day.

The HSDirs collectively store the onion service descriptors in a distributed hash table. Each epoch, each node has a separate index value, denoted hsdir_index. These indices are unpredictable and uncontrollable by the HSDirs. By ordering these indices, and looping back at the end, we can form a ring of the HSDirs. For redundancy, each descriptor is held by multiple HSDirs. To determine which HSDirs hold which descriptors, we can calculate hs_index_i values for the onion service, where i ranges from 1 to hsdir_n_replicas (a parameter given in the consensus, currently 2). These hs_index_i values are determined by the blinded public key of the onion service for that epoch, as well as the index i and a few consensus parameters. The descriptor is uploaded to the `hsdir_spread_store` (currently 4) HSDirs whose `hsdir_index` values come directly after the hs_index_i values in the HSDir ring. In this way, the descriptor is replicated across the hash ring multiple times (currently 8) in each epoch, so that a client wishing to access the descriptor has a variety of HSDirs that may be queried, improving the privacy and availability of the onion service.

The Tor metrics site [28] provides some sense of the current scale of onion service usage. It reports around 4000 HSDirs (Tor nodes with the HSDir flag) in the network. Since their deprecation, the number of v2 onion services has dwindled to around 25 thousand, while the number of v3 onion services has steadily increased since tracking began (in September 2021), to around 700 thousand today. Given the number of HSDirs, the number of unique services, and the number of times a descriptor is replicated, we arrive at a rough estimate of $700000 \times 8/4000 = 1400$ descriptors on average per HSDir.

For the remainder of this section, we want to consider the capabilities of a malicious entity willing to act as an HSDir. To model this, we consider that the Tor network has n relays with the HSDir flag. We envision that our adversary controls a of these relays. This adversary can see all incoming HS lookup queries on the HSDirs that they control. As we will see, even with this simple model, the adversary can draw conclusions and make inferences about both clients and onion services that go beyond what Tor allows for from other nodes in the network.

2.2 Attacks Targeting Clients

An adversary hoping to deanonymize a Tor user who uses onion services is placed in a relatively powerful position in the network. When a client resolves an onion service descriptor lookup, they connect to the HSDir via a circuit. Hence if an adversary in addition to controlling the HSDir, controls even the middle node of this circuit to the HSDir, they learn both the client's guard relay and the blinded public key of the service being connected to.[2]

For a service that widely distributes their .onion address, this gives the adversary the client's entry point to the network (the guard relay) and their final destination (the onion service). As clients maintain their guard node for a long period of time (currently up to six months) [13,30], the guard relay itself provides substantial information that can allow a malicious actor to trace a client over time. Combined with the information of the final destination, this can lead to powerful epistemic attacks [7,8].

---

[2] Of course if the adversary controls the guard relay, they have an even stronger attack vector, and will learn the client's true IP address. However it is easier for an adversary to control middle nodes, since attaining guard status for a relay requires uptime on the order of several weeks, and clients do not often select new guards.

2.3   Attacks Targeting Onion Services

The introduction of blinded public keys in version 3 of the onion services protocol intended to provide better anonymity properties for onion services against malicious HSDirs. Blinded public keys cannot be traced back to the identity public key, and the blinded public key changes with each epoch; therefore, in theory onion services cannot be tracked by HSDirs across epochs. Cryptographically, this is formulated as *unlinkability*, which states that after observing many public keys and many signatures under those public keys, an adversary cannot do better than guessing to link two blinded public keys as being derived from the same identity key. In this subsection, we argue that while the cryptography used for blinded key schemes is solid, these guarantees do not extend to all onion services in practice because of how descriptor lookups are resolved.

To track an onion service over time, an HSDir can consider the *distribution* of queries made to each service over time. Different services are likely to have radically different distributions of queries. By identifying two blinded public keys that received a similar distribution of queries over the course of an epoch, an adversary can ascertain with a reasonable degree of confidence that the two blinded keys correspond to the same identity public key. The challenge in this setting is that the database is distributed, and hence the adversary's view is limited to a fraction of the total set of queries made within an epoch. This fraction is defined by the adversarial power a and the total number of nodes n. This notion of building a 'profile' for an onion service based on the query distribution is simply the starting point of our attack, and we will refer to it as the *weak variant* of the attack. A truly malicious adversary has several other sources of information available to them that strengthens the profiles constructed. For a given onion service, additional sources of metadata that a malicious HSDir could leverage include (i) the set of guard nodes that make the HSDir lookup requests, (ii) the frequency distribution of lookup requests from the aforementioned set of guard nodes, or (iii) the timings of lookup requests within an epoch.

There are other information channels possibly available to an adversary as well, such as considering correlations between the timing of queries to cross-linked onion services. Nonetheless, the common underlying element that makes the attack feasible is *the ability of an adversarial HSDir to infer which of its onion service descriptors is being looked up in a request, allowing them to link the metadata of the request to that particular onion service.* The solutions that we propose in Sect. 3 will prevent these attacks we outlined.

3   PIR for Descriptor Lookups

To prevent the kinds of attacks established in Sect. 2, we need to prevent malicious HSDirs from learning which descriptor is being queried by a user. As a general approach, the obvious tool for this requirement is Private Information Retrieval (PIR). However, there is a large research gap between the simple idea of using PIR and its actual integration into the descriptor lookup process. We consider the three approaches of multi-server PIR, single-server PIR using computational assumptions (CPIR), and single-server PIR using hardware assumptions.

For the remainder of the paper, we show how these different PIR schemes can be integrated into Tor to prevent the statistical attacks we have shown. Single-server PIR does not change how clients decide which HSDir to query from. The structure of the hash ring, how the client decides where to query from, and the logic the onion service uses to decide where to upload can all stay the same, while multi-server PIR does introduce significant changes to this structure. We provide a complete system design for how to integrate each of these into Tor, and explore the advantages and disadvantages of each approach. Integrating a PIR scheme into any application context poses several challenges of bridging the rigid semantics of a PIR scheme with the underlying architecture:

1. Commonly, records in PIR schemes are stored as logical arrays and are indexed by an integer; in order to retrieve a particular record the client has to query for the corresponding index of this record. However in our context of onion service descriptors, the data to be queried privately is a key-value store, and we discuss later in this section how to bridge this gap.

2. PIR schemes are computationally expensive and hence in order to ensure that integrating PIR guarantees into queries does not impact the performance of the entire application we need to ensure that PIR queries are handled asynchronously. In the extended version of this paper [12, App. A] we give the technical details of how we extend Tor's program architecture to support asynchronous PIR queries on both the client and server side.

3. In order to even construct a PIR query, the client needs to a priori know the parameters of the PIR scheme it is interacting with; this will induce a performance penalty of an additional round trip of communication for learning those parameters. Note that the delay introduced by the additional round trip directly impacts the time for an onion service's page to start rendering, which is an important user-experience metric to minimize. We provide an optional optimization that can remove this additional round trip in the extended version [12, App. B] by leveraging the fact that these parameters can be publicly published.

Single-server PIR. In a single-server scheme, a client queries a database by sending an encrypted version of the index that they want to retrieve data for. The server performs some computation over the database, and returns an encrypted response without learning any information about the index. This goal can be accomplished either by using encryption with strong mathematical properties like fully homomorphic encryption, as in XPIR [1] or SealPIR [2], or by using secure hardware, as in ZeroTrace [27].

Multi-server PIR. Multi-server schemes instead have the database distributed across several servers. The client must query these servers to obtain some data that can be recombined to obtain the query result. These schemes rely on non-collusion assumptions; if the queried servers collude with each other, they can determine what a client has queried. In a multi-server PIR scheme, there are ℓ servers that can be queried. Each holds the same data, indexed in the same way. Clients query each one with a separate query, and can then recombine the responses to extract the desired data. In simple PIR schemes, such as Chor's [6], the client only succeeds if each of the ℓ servers responds correctly. However, more robust schemes, such as those of Goldberg [15] and of Devet et al. [9], have since been developed that generalise this. In these schemes, only k of the ℓ servers need respond, and up to v of the servers may deviate from the protocol, and the client will still be successful in extracting their desired query.

We next sketch a design for a process to distribute a descriptor across ℓ servers so that multi-server PIR schemes are possible. Our system needs to allow for a single database to be distributed (identically) across multiple servers. When a client wishes to query for a descriptor, they must be able to figure out which servers can serve their query. We calculate the hsdir_index$_i$ values as in the current Tor specification; however, previously these values pointed to the start of a sequence of hsdir_spread_store nodes, any of which could be queried for the desired descriptor. To support ℓ-server PIR, these will instead point to the start of the sequence of ℓ servers that will be used for the protocol.

When a circuit is constructed in Tor, basic precautions are taken to try and ensure that the routers in the path actually represent distinct, non-colluding entities. Specifically, the Tor Path Specification [31] outlines several constraints for building a path, which include the following:

- If two routers list each other in the "family" entry of their descriptors, they are in the same family and should not be in the same path.
- Two routers in the same /16 subnet should not be in the same path.
- Non-running and non-valid routers should not be in a path.

We can employ the same principles for path selection for the purpose of choosing the ℓ servers for multi-server PIR. Of course, any malicious adversary can simply ensure that routers they control do not list each other and are not in the same /16 subnet. These restrictions do not stop such adversaries, but take precautions to prevent incidental collusion by routers. We can take the exact same approach for choosing the HSDirs that will process a multi-server PIR query.

When a client wants to fetch a descriptor using multi-server PIR, it chooses a random index i from $\{1, \ldots, \text{hsdir\_n\_replicas}\}$ and computes hsdir_index$_i$ for the hidden service. It then locates the ℓ next valid HSDirs who are all in different families and /16 subnets whose dir_index values come after hsdir_index$_i$. The client can then engage in the multi-server PIR protocol with these ℓ servers. If this protocol fails for any reason, such as too many of the servers being unavailable, the client simply selects a new i and tries again.[3]

HSDirs keep their collection of descriptors separated into logical databases, according to their position in the sequence of ℓ servers in the hash ring; that is, the 'one' database held by an HSDir is identical to the 'two' database held by

---

[3] Currently, the number of times the descriptor is replicated (and thus the number of places it can be accessed from) is hsdir_n_replicas times hsdir_spread_store, which is currently 8. To ensure that there are the same number of logical databases where a descriptor can be accessed from, hsdir_n_replicas would have to be increased.

the next server, and so on. When a client makes their PIR query to each server, they must also indicate which logical database they are querying from, so that each database they query from is the same.

Note that for PIR schemes, it is crucial that all of the databases distributed across the ℓ servers are identical. Ensuring the consistency of replicated data across servers is of course a fundamental problem in the study of distributed systems. For this reason, specific solutions to the problem are largely orthogonal to this work. However, in the extended version [12, App. C.1] we outline some of the general approaches that can be used in Tor in order to address this issue.

Perfect Hashing. In most PIR schemes, clients look up a particular *index* in a database without revealing that index to the server [6,21]. Chor et al. [5] propose a number of ways to use a PIR scheme such that clients can look up records by a *string* instead of a record index. One of their techniques uses a construction called *perfect hashing*. Given a set of D keys (which are arbitrary strings), a perfect hash function (PHF) maps these D keys *injectively* into integers in the range $[0, \ldots, r-1]$, where $r = \mathsf{c} \cdot D$ and c is a small constant, typically in the range of 1 to 2. In our application, we choose to maintain a small c so as to maintain a smaller-sized PIR database. Ideally, we would like $\mathsf{c} = 1$, which results in a variant of perfect hash functions known as *minimal perfect hash functions* (MPHF). The information needed to evaluate an MPHF requires slightly more bits per key (D) to describe than a general PHF, but in our context this results in us being able to maintain a smaller PIR database size, which would intuitively result in overall gain. Therefore an MPHF seems like the ideal solution to our indexing challenge.

We discuss the details of the MPHF we use, provide benchmarks for it, as well as discuss why this does not entail any concerning leakages in the extended version [12, App. D]. Later in Sect. 5.1 we give optimizations to resolve indexing in hardware-assisted PIR schemes *without the use of MPHFs*, thus eliminating these leakages entirely in the hardware-assisted PIR case.

4   Privacy Analysis for PIR Schemes

To evaluate candidate PIR schemes, we must discuss what underlying assumptions give a scheme its privacy properties, and how these assumptions hold up in Tor. The Tor context in no way affects schemes that make only computational assumptions, This means that single-server computational PIR schemes can be trusted to the extent that the underlying cryptographic assumptions are trusted. For XPIR and Seal-PIR, this corresponds to the Learning With Errors assumption, widely believed to be secure by cryptographers. The problem has received increased scrutiny and cryptanalysis due to post-quantum cryptography standardization efforts by NIST [24] and other standardizing bodies.

For hardware-based schemes, privacy guarantees depend on the security of trusted enclaves. In our implementation we leverage Intel SGX as the secure hardware module for our hardware-aided PIR scheme. Trusting the hardware in this case boils down to being able to verify that an HSDir that claims to support hardware-aided PIR does in fact run on a processor with such hardware prowess. In Intel SGX, this is done via *remote attestation* [17], towards which Intel issues certificates that validate the claims made by its processors with SGX support. In the event of Intel "going rogue", they can at most misissue future certificates. This would not affect the security of PIR lookups that happened before misissuance. Additionally, we implicitly trust these modules to deliver the confidentiality and integrity guarantees they claim. However, recently researchers have demonstrated side-channel vulnerabilities of SGX that attack its confidentiality. These works have also demonstrated defences which are actively being incorporated by Intel, and this is a natural part of a new hardware component's lifecycle. In both of these classes of trust violations, our design still has *forward secrecy* in that the privacy of past queries cannot be compromised by future violations. Furthermore, even in such a worst-case event, the security of our scheme would simply reduce to the current status quo. We also note that while we used SGX to prototype our work, the underlying techniques can be adapted onto any of the other existing processors with secure hardware capabilities such as ARM TrustZone [3], AMD SEV [19], or their open-source sibling Keystone [20].

The privacy guarantees provided by multi-server ITPIR schemes are based on *non-collusion* assumptions made about the servers involved in servicing the queries. To guarantee the privacy of a query made by a client, we must assume that the ℓ servers involved in the query do not collude to break the privacy of this query. For non-robust schemes like Chor et al.'s, this assumption holds as long as at least one server does not collude to break a client's privacy. For robust schemes like Goldberg's [15], this is generalised so that as long as no more than t servers collude, privacy is still guaranteed. To analyze this assumption, we imagine an adversary who controls a Tor HSDirs, and then ask various questions about the probability they are able to break the non-collusion assumption. Remember that the position of a HSDir in the hash ring is determined by random values that the nodes have no control over, so that an adversary cannot adaptively position themselves in a hash ring to compromise security.

In addition to analyzing the probability an adversary can compromise privacy, we need to analyze the robustness of these schemes and the probability that the adversary can disrupt the availability of descriptors by behaving in a malicious way. In this section we will present our analysis on privacy compromise of queries, and in the extended version [12, App. C] we provide an in-depth analysis of availability compromise in the multi-server ITPIR model. With a multi-server scheme, the privacy can be compromised if the adversary is able to control at least $t + 1$ out of the ℓ servers involved in the PIR query (with the value of t depending on the particular scheme). In order to evaluate how much more difficult this makes the adversary's task, we assume the adversary controls some number a of the n Tor HSDirs overall. We then ask the probability that when the hash ring is constructed, there is a consecutive sequence of ℓ servers in the hash ring (an "ℓ-block") where the adversary controls at least $t + 1$ of them.

We can estimate how often this may happen using a combination of experimental and enumerative techniques. An exact enumeration is a somewhat

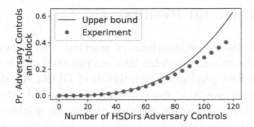

Fig. 1. Comparing our provided upper bound with experimental results for the probability an adversary is able to control *any* ℓ-block and violate query privacy in an ITPIR setting. Here $n = 4000$, $\ell = 5$, and $t = 2$. Experiments were performed by simulating 100,000 hash rings independently. Again recall that in the current Tor setup without PIR, this query privacy is *always* violated.

challenging combinatorial problem, but we can establish an upper bound. We provide an upper bound for the number of configurations of a hash ring with n nodes, of which a subset of size a are controlled by an adversary, such that at least one set of consecutive ℓ nodes contains at least $t + 1$ adversarial nodes:

$$U(n, a, \ell, t) := a \cdot \binom{a - 1}{t} \cdot \binom{\ell - 1}{t} \cdot (t)! \cdot (n - t - 1)!$$

This equation does not perfectly enumerate the number of hash rings where the adversary controls an ℓ-block. It overcounts this number of hash rings, because hash rings where the adversary controls multiple blocks are counted once per block. However, since it strictly overcounts, the equation can be used as an upper bound. We leave a tighter bound as future work.

Lemma 1. *The number of hash rings of size n in which an adversary controlling a nodes controls at least $t+1$ of a sequence of ℓ consecutive nodes is upper bounded by $U(n, a, \ell, t)$.*

The combinatorial proof can be found in the extended version [12, App. E]. We can upper bound the probability that an adversary can compromise at least one database by dividing $U(n, a, \ell, t)$ by $(n - 1)!$, the total number of hash rings on n nodes. To see how this upper bound compares to the actual probability, we perform a series of experiments, varying the number of adversaries in the hash ring and observing the frequency with which the adversaries control an ℓ-block. With $n = 4000$, $\ell = 5$, and $t = 2$, we varied the number of adversaries from 0 to 120. Our results are shown in Fig. 1. Notably, the lower a is, the better our upper bound performs compared to the true probability. This is not surprising, as our upper bound overcounts hash rings where the adversary controls multiple ℓ-blocks, which occurs more frequently when a is higher.

5   Benchmarking and Results

In this section, we discuss evaluations of selected PIR schemes we proposed earlier in Sect. 3. All our microbenchmarks are run on a single server-grade Intel Xeon E3-1270, with four physical cores, 64 GB of DDR4 RAM, and support for Intel SGX. Our server machine runs Ubuntu 16.04, and all our experimental results for the systems we measure are for a single core without any parallelism. For the end-to-end integration experiments we reuse the same server as the HSDir node, and use a 1.8 GHz i7-8565U laptop as the client. The source code to reproduce our experiments is available on our website.[4]

In order to get a more complete picture of how many lookup requests an HSDir handles at a time, as well as the sizes those descriptors, we monitored the activity on an HSDir for around eight months.[5] In terms of sizes, about 81% of the v3 descriptors we observed were <16 KiB, 7% were between 16 and 32 KiB, and 12% between 32 and 48 KiB. Hence for all of the PIR schemes we evaluate, we are concerned with large record sizes (approximately 16 KiB) since hidden service descriptors are about that size.[6] Larger v3 descriptors correspond to onion services that have a large encrypted list of authorized clients. To avoid leaking whether, and how many, authorized clients there are, hidden services may add fake lines to the descriptor to pad the length [32]. For microbenchmarks on multi-server PIR, we refer to Devet et al. [9], which provides a comprehensive picture on implementation details of many different configurations of multi-server PIR. Multi-server PIR schemes are fast, and we do not foresee the performance of these schemes being a bottleneck.

5.1   Hardware-Assisted PIR Benchmarks

For hardware-assisted PIR schemes, we leverage ZeroTrace and benchmark four different variants of PIR flavours using it. Specifically, two variants of linear scan (one where the data is stored in the Processor Reserved Memory (PRM) pages, and the other where it is stored outside the PRM), Path ORAM, and Circuit ORAM. The linear scan variants do not face the indexing challenge, unlike the other PIR schemes. However, Circuit ORAM and Path ORAM do have the indexing problem to address. Instead of using an MPHF however, notice that in this context, indexing for the ORAM scheme can be achieved more simply by performing a linear scan over an array that maps blinded public keys of the hidden service descriptors to indices in the ORAM scheme. The overheads induced by this linear scan is minimal since each record in this array is a 32-byte key and an 8-byte index, and is significantly faster than scanning the entire

---

[4] https://crysp.uwaterloo.ca/software/piros/.

[5] For privacy reasons, we only gathered bucketized numbers and sizes of descriptors, and never the actual descriptors themselves. In the extended version [12, App. F] we give more information on how we followed Tor research safety guidelines.

[6] The smallest v3 descriptors are 14200 bytes; descriptors of this size are the overwhelming majority of descriptors in the < 16 KiB pool.

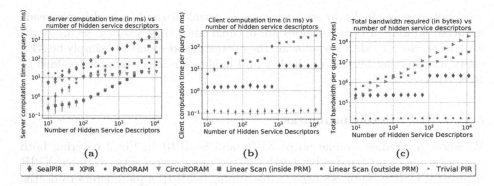

(a)   (b)   (c)

| ◆ SealPIR | ✕ XPIR | ● PathORAM | ▼ CircuitORAM | ■ Linear Scan (inside PRM) | ● Linear Scan (outside PRM) | ▶ Trivial PIR |

Fig. 2. Detailed microbenchmarks evaluating server computation time, client computation time, and total bandwidth overheads as a function of the number of descriptors held by the server. Trivial PIR requires no computation and is hence omitted from (a). For (b) and (c) we only display the line corresponding to ZeroTrace's Linear Scan with data stored outside PRM as representative of all the ZeroTrace variants since the client computation and bandwidth overheads of all the ZeroTrace variants are identical.

collection of hidden service descriptors. Our microbenchmarks for both ORAMs are hence inclusive of this online cost of index resolution via linear scanning.

We note that the PIR parameters for such a hardware-assisted ORAM scheme is simply a public key, under which the queries are encrypted by a client, such that only the SGX enclave can decrypt it. Hence these constructions also have the additional benefit that the tiny parameter size means they can forego the extra round trip required to fetch the PIR parameters, for example by simply including the public key in the Tor consensus directly. We observe later in Sect. 5.3 that doing so results in almost no perceivable overheads in the end-to-end latencies experienced by a user loading an onion service.

Our microbenchmarks in Fig. 2a show that among the two linear scan variants, storing the data outside of the PRM scales better. Although counterintuitive, this arises from the fact that on Intel SGX, the PRM is limited to about 90 MB and thus when the data to be stored crosses this threshold, it leads to significant overheads induced by page faults. From our rough estimate in Sect. 2.1, the total number of v3 onion services that an HSDir server holds today is close to 1500. Hence for the remainder of this section we compare the schemes at the datapoint of 1702.[7] However, we note that both the linear scan variants of PIR in fact provide the best server computation time of 7.04±0.04 ms for 1702 descriptors. In comparison, the ORAM schemes are slightly more computationally expensive as seen in the figure with server computation times of 33.2±0.4 ms and 14.2±0.5 ms for Path ORAM and Circuit ORAM respectively at the same number of descriptors; however, as the number of descriptors increases, they

---

[7] For the microbenchmarks in Fig. 2 we chose data points evenly across the exponentially increasing x-axis, resulting in the odd data point of 1702 as closest to (but exceeding) 1500.

soon outperform the linear scan variants. In terms of the bandwidth overheads induced, all four of these schemes are optimal since they leverage secure hardware at the server side, thus allowing the queries and responses to simply be AES encryptions of the blinded public key and hidden service descriptor (padded to 16 KiB) respectively.

5.2   CPIR Microbenchmarks

We show a detailed evaluation of XPIR and SealPIR in Fig. 2 covering both computational and bandwidth overheads. In our experiments, we force XPIR to use LWE with 80-bit security, while tuning SealPIR's parameters to do the same. We allow XPIR's optimizer module to select the parameters d (recursion levels) and α (aggregation factor), for the best overall time for performing a PIR request. SealPIR's implementation is currently limited to small data record sizes; specifically, the implementation expects that a single data record will fit into a single plaintext polynomial, which limits an individual data record size to 1.5 × N, where N is the degree of the underlying polynomial. (The 1.5 × N arises from the fact that with plaintext modulus t = 12 bits, a completely filled degree-N plaintext polynomial can store exactly 1.5 bytes per coefficient.)

For large data records, one would store the data over multiple plaintext polynomials. Hence in our evaluations, we extrapolate SealPIR results by assuming that the costs of query processing and reply extraction will increase by a factor of K, where K is the number of plaintext polynomials required to store a single hidden service descriptor. To this end, we run our SealPIR experiments with a record size of 3000 bytes. (For N = 2048, 3072 B is the maximum data size that a plaintext polynomial can store.) The query processing time (excluding the time for expansion) and reply extraction are then multiplied by K = 6 to meet our required 16 KiB descriptor size. Figures 2a and 2b highlight the server computation time and client computation time induced by these schemes respectively. SealPIR and XPIR scale computationally poorly at the server side as well as the client side due to the underlying computation overheads of the FHE schemes (FV [14] and BV [4] respectively) that they use. The XPIR and SealPIR points in our graphs show irregularities since we allow the optimizer to select optimal parameters for each problem size. For all of our experiments we note that the XPIR optimizer chose to not use recursion, but instead heavily aggregate data blocks using high values of α (in the range of 8 to 60). In order to choose the optimal recursion point for SealPIR for a given problem size, we evaluate SealPIR with both choices of d and present the one corresponding to minimum total time in our graphs. The break in SealPIR points in these graphs correspond to switching the number of recursion levels (d) from 1 to 2.

At 1702 records of 16 KiB, XPIR induces a server computation overhead of 31±3 ms, and SealPIR 451±1 ms. These overheads induced by these CPIR schemes are barely practical today and higher than their ZeroTrace counterparts by about an order of magnitude. However the client-side overheads at the same datapoint (158±12 ms and 13.32±0.03 ms for XPIR and SealPIR respectively)

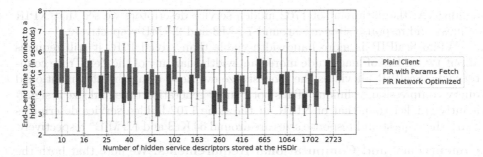

Fig. 3. Comparison of end-to-end latencies for connecting to an onion service with a plain Tor client vs. a Tor client with PIR support (with and without our optional optimization that saves the network round trip for fetching the PIR parameters). Our optimization saves approximately one second as we see from the difference in medians for the two PIR modes across the data points we collected. Moreover, end-to-end latencies for a user are barely impacted by incorporating PIR as the overheads of PIR are hidden by the noise of Tor network costs.

are more concerning as it may be much higher for lightweight clients like mobile users that would have weaker CPUs.

Queries in XPIR are encryptions of a bit vector of length corresponding to the number of records stored at the PIR server, with the bit at the index being queried being 1 (and 0s elsewhere). SealPIR introduces the notion of a compressed query, where the query is just an encryption of the queried index itself. In terms of reply extraction time, SealPIR and XPIR are quite close, and the difference in total client computation time arises from the fact that client query generation time is much smaller for SealPIR than XPIR, due to this query compression technique, but in total ZeroTrace is about two orders of magnitude better in terms of client computational overheads as seen in Fig. 2b.

However this query compression technique has its own costs; first, it induces additional server-side computation for expanding this compressed query. Second, it limits the size of data that can be stored in a single underlying FV plaintext. Specifically, SealPIR has to force a plaintext modulus of $t = 12$ bits out of its coefficient modulus of $q = 60$ bits (as detailed by Angel et al. [2, §6] and seen in their implementation), so that after expansion and query processing the underlying plaintext is still decryptable with very high probability. The impact of this is not obvious from SealPIR's original evaluations, as they limit themselves to a small record size of 288 bytes, which fit within a single FV plaintext polynomial even with such low values of t. Ultimately this technique makes SealPIR perform well in the context of large numbers of small records; however, this is the opposite of our context, where each HSDir has only a relatively small number of descriptors but of fairly large size, and this is reflected in our benchmarking.

Finally in Fig. 2c, we see the total bandwidth overhead imposed by these schemes. Here we also include trivial PIR (clients download *all* descriptors whenever they make a query) as a baseline to compare the proposed PIR schemes against. At the datapoint of 1702 hidden service descriptors we see that XPIR request and response sizes are around 7.5 MB and 2.5 MB respectively.

While SealPIR is more bandwidth-viable than trivial PIR, it still requires about two orders of magnitude more bandwidth than any of the ZeroTrace counterparts. SealPIR alleviates the request size overhead using the aforementioned query compression technique. Thus both query generation time and size is significantly smaller than that of XPIR, at the same 1702 hidden service descriptors mark the request and response sizes are around 64 KiB and 1.9 MiB[8] respectively.

Concurrency and Computational Requirements. We note that both the CPIR schemes are parallelizable, and so are the linear scan variants of Zero-Trace, but not the ORAM counterparts. Hence multiple queries can be handled concurrently for these schemes. Even for the sequential ORAM schemes, multiple cores on the machine can be used to run several instances of the ORAM enclaves allowing it to serve concurrent queries.

We also collected the number of v2 and v3 lookups that our HSDir received during the months of April to June 2020. During this period, typically the HSDir served approximately 1500 queries in an hour. From the server computation microbenchmarks above and in the event that just a single core is used by the server to serve PIR, this would take less than 10.6 s in an hour to serve all these queries using the linear scan variant of ZeroTrace, while the XPIR and SealPIR require close to 46 s and 11.3 min respectively to serve 1500 requests. However, some days we note spikes up to a maximum of 766,000 requests in an hour,[9] at which point the load cannot be supported by a single core alone; however, as we mention in Sect. 3, PIR operations should be handled asynchronously in a separate thread anyway. Using two cores on these HSDir machines asynchronously, even these peak loads can still be handled smoothly for the ZeroTrace variants. However, XPIR and SealPIR would require more than 7 and 96 cores respectively to handle such peak loads, making it prohibitive for deployment.

5.3 Tor Integration Results

Finally, we also implemented and evaluated the impact on end-to-end latencies induced in Tor to connect to a hidden service when using PIR. For evaluating

---

[8] Above ≈1000 descriptors, the SealPIR size jumps to about 1.9 MiB due to recursion, as seen in Fig. 2c. Recursion in CPIR schemes increases the response size by a factor of f at each level, where f is the *ciphertext expansion factor*. Since the SealPIR compression technique reduces the effective plaintext modulus, it increases f from the expected ≈ 7 to 10. The expected f ≈ 7 arises from the fact that the underlying FV scheme can use a plaintext modulus $t = 23$ for 80-bit security with a coefficient modulus q of 60 bits, but since SealPIR uses an effective plaintext modulus $t = 12$ and $q = 60$, and ciphertexts contain two polynomials, the total ciphertext expansion f is 10.

[9] These spikes were for v3 descriptors, and were presumably due to the HSDir holding an extremely *popular* descriptor, as we did not observe a corresponding spike in the *number* of v3 descriptors held.

our proposal on the live Tor network, we ran a Tor relay that would serve as an HSDir, instrumented with modifications to support asynchronous PIR querying. Specifically, in addition to handling incoming HS descriptor stores as a normal Tor relay would, it also inserted the incoming HS descriptor into the PIR scheme's store. Full details of this are included in the extended version [12, App. A]. Similarly, we instrumented a Tor client to make PIR requests to this relay, and finally we created yet another Tor process that was modified to upload hidden service descriptors only to our HSDir with PIR support. In our experiments, we used this hidden service generator to generate several hidden services to a local web server, and then timed the curl requests for our client to perform a HS descriptor lookup and establish a connection with these hidden services. For privacy reasons, we only queried for the descriptors we ourselves uploaded.

With the above described setup, we evaluate three different clients; a standard Tor client, a Tor client that uses ZeroTrace's linear scan PIR (with the underlying data stored outside the PRM), and an optimized client that does not perform an additional round trip for the parameter fetch, assuming that the parameters were already available to the client as we describe in Sect. 5.1. We use the linear scan variant of ZeroTrace, since we know this to be the appropriate choice with the current scale of hidden services from our microbenchmarks in Fig. 2a. We note that end-to-end latencies are subject to a lot of variance due to variability of several factors such as choice of relays for constructing circuits, and unpredictable network conditions encountered by different requests. Hence we present our findings in the form of a boxplot in Fig. 3.

For each of the datapoints in Fig. 3, we collected the timing reported for 100 curl requests to a hidden service that was not in the client's cache. The impact of our proposed optimization for compressing the additional round trip is immediately evident from this figure, as the medians for these two conditions seem to differ by almost an entire second across a majority of the datapoints we collected. Furthermore, we notice that deploying PIR in practice does not drastically impact the end-to-end latencies experienced by a user connecting to a hidden service, as the PIR overheads are completely hidden within the noise of overheads of using the Tor network.

6   Conclusion

HSDirs serve a unique purpose in the Tor network, acting as a DNS server for .onion addresses. For this reason it is important to make sure we can completely characterize the information HSDirs are privy to in their roles. We have shown that HSDirs have access to a relatively high amount of information in the Tor network. We find that the property of unlinkability, which is intended to guarantee that onion services cannot be tracked by HSDirs over time, is not provided to all onion services due to the HSDir's ability to count the number of queries made for each service in an epoch.

Table 1. Summarizing the results of all schemes that were considered

Scheme	Sec Guarantee	Required Changes	BW Overhead	Availability
Current	None	None	None	Unchanged
CPIR [1,2]	LWE	Minimal	Large	Unchanged
ZeroTrace [27]	Hardware	Minimal	Minimal	Unchanged
ITPIR [6,15]	Probabilistic	Major Changes	$\times \ell$	Increased with v

To prevent this information leakage in the future, we investigate the integration of PIR into Tor. This integration is a complex problem due to the large design space and many PIR options, each with their own requirements, guarantees, and drawbacks. In this work we have thoroughly explored these options, explaining their strengths and weaknesses, and show how to integrate them into Tor. We conclude by discussing the options we have investigated and their suitability for our purpose. Our results are summarized in Table 1.

XPIR and SealPIR are attractive options because of their well-understood security assumptions (LWE) and the minimal changes needed to the structure of the hash ring. Clients would still only query a single HSDir in the hash ring, and the availability of the descriptors would be unaffected. However, the heavy computational and bandwidth burden incurred by XPIR is too high. SealPIR on the other hand alleviates the bandwidth overhead due its small query size, but worsens the computational overhead.

In contrast, Multi-server PIR schemes are very efficient, and the extra bandwidth used mainly comes from the fact that ℓ queries are made, instead of one. However, their security guarantees are probabilistic, and in each epoch, there is a possibility that enough adversarial HSDirs will be placed into an ℓ-block to compromise the privacy or availability of a query. Furthermore, multi-server PIR schemes require major changes to how descriptors are stored and queried.

Hardware-based PIR schemes are attractive in some senses, but challenging in others. Like XPIR and SealPIR, they require only minimal changes to the structure of the hash ring and process by which descriptors are queried. Availability is unchanged compared to the current state of the network. As well, these schemes perform very well, and add minimal bandwidth costs. The drawback with these schemes is that they depend on the security and availability of the hardware used. The security of trusted execution environments like Intel SGX is still being actively explored and improved.

Any use of PIR for retrieving descriptors improves privacy over the current state of Tor. Currently all queries (made by querying a blinded public key) are readable by an HSDir, allowing them to selectively deny queries and correlate incoming queries with the descriptors they hold to gather conclusions that erode the privacy of both clients and onion services. PIR can thus provide a significant improvement to the privacy of Tor onion services.

Acknowledgements. We thank the reviewers for their helpful feedback. We thank Hobbes, Luna, and Maple for their helpful purr-review. This work benefitted from the use of the CrySP RIPPLE Facility at the University of Waterloo. Edward Eaton was supported by a Natural Sciences and Engineering Research Council of Canada (NSERC) Alexander Graham Bell Canada Graduate Scholarship. Sajin Sasy was supported by an Ontario Graduate Scholarship and NSERC grant CRDPJ-534381. This research was undertaken, in part, thanks to funding from the Canada Research Chairs program.

References

1. Aguilar Melchor, C., Barrier, J., Fousse, L., Killijian, M.: XPIR : private information retrieval for everyone. In: Proceedings on Privacy Enhancing Technologies (PoPETs). Sciendo (2016)
2. Angel, S., Chen, H., Laine, K., Setty, S.: PIR with compressed queries and amortized query processing. In: Proceedings of the IEEE Symposium on Security and Privacy (S&P) (2018)
3. ARM. ARM Security Technology: Building a Secure System using TrustZone Technology (2015). https://developer.arm.com/documentation/PRD29-GENC-009492/c/TrustZone-Hardware-Architecture?lang=en
4. Brakerski, Z., Vaikuntanathan, V.: Fully homomorphic encryption from ring-LWE and security for key dependent messages. In: Rogaway, P. (ed.) CRYPTO 2011. LNCS, vol. 6841, pp. 505–524. Springer, Heidelberg (2011). https://doi.org/10.1007/978-3-642-22792-9_29
5. Chor, B., Gilboa, N., Naor, M.: Private Information Retrieval by Keywords. Cryptology ePrint Archive, Report 1998/003 (1998). https://eprint.iacr.org/1998/003
6. Chor, B., Goldreich, O., Kushilevitz, E., Sudan, M.: Private information retrieval. In: Proceedings of the 36th Annual Symposium on Foundations of Computer Science (FOCS). IEEE (1995)
7. Danezis, G., Clayton, R.: Route fingerprinting in Anonymous Communications. In: Sixth IEEE International Conference on Peer-to-Peer Computing (P2P). IEEE (2006)
8. Danezis, G., Syverson, P.: Bridging and fingerprinting: epistemic attacks on route selection. In: Borisov, N., Goldberg, I. (eds.) PETS 2008. LNCS, vol. 5134, pp. 151–166. Springer, Heidelberg (2008). https://doi.org/10.1007/978-3-540-70630-4_10
9. Devet, C., Goldberg, I., Heninger, N.: Optimally robust private information retrieval. In: Proceedings of the 21st USENIX Security Symposium (2012)
10. Dingledine, R.: Improving Tor's anonymity by changing guard parameters (2013). https://blog.torproject.org/improving-tors-anonymity-changing-guard-parameters. Accessed Mar 2022
11. Dingledine, R., Mathewson, N., Syverson, P.: Tor: the second-generation onion router. In: Proceedings of the 13th USENIX Security Symposium (2004)
12. Eaton, E., Sasy, S., Goldberg, I.: Improving the Privacy of Tor Onion Services. Cryptology ePrint Archive, Report 2022/407 (2022). https://eprint.iacr.org/2022/407
13. Elahi, T., Bauer, K., AlSabah, M., Dingledine, R., Goldberg, I.: Changing of the guards: a framework for understanding and improving entry guard selection in Tor. In: Proceedings of the ACM Workshop on Privacy in the Electronic Society (WPES) (2012)

14. Fan, J., Vercauteren, F.: Somewhat practical fully homomorphic encryption. Cryptology ePrint Archive, Report 2012/144 (2012). https://eprint.iacr.org/2012/144
15. Goldberg, I.: Improving the robustness of private information retrieval. In: IEEE Symposium on Security and Privacy (S&P) (2007)
16. Hopper, N.: Proving Security of Tor's Hidden Service Identity Blinding Protocol. Tech. Rep., The Tor Project (2013). https://www-users.cs.umn.edu/~hoppernj/basic-proof.pdf
17. Intel: Software Guard Extensions (Intel® SGX) Data Center Attestation Primitives: ECDSA Quote Library API (2018). https://sgx101.gitbook.io/sgx101/sgx-bootstrap/attestation
18. Kadianakis, G.: Hidden Services need some love (2013). https://blog.torproject.org/hidden-services-need-some-love. Accessed Mar 2022
19. Kaplan, D., Powell, J., Woller, T.: AMD Memory Encryption (2016). https://developer.amd.com/wordpress/media/2013/12/AMD_Memory_Encryption_Whitepaper_v7-Public.pdf
20. Karandikar, S., et al.: Keystone Open-source Secure Hardware Enclave (2018). https://keystone-enclave.org/. Accessed Mar 2022
21. Kushilevitz, E., Ostrovsky, R.: Replication is not needed: single database, computationally-private information retrieval. In: 38th Annual Symposium on Foundations of Computer Science (FOCS) (1997)
22. Loesing, K.: Distributed Storage of Tor Hidden Service Descriptors (2007)
23. Mittal, P., Olumofin, F.G., Troncoso, C., Borisov, N., Goldberg, I.: PIR-Tor: scalable anonymous communication using private information retrieval. In: 20th USENIX Security Symposium Proceedings (2011)
24. National Institute of Standards and Technology. Post-Quantum Cryptography (2019). https://csrc.nist.gov/projects/post-quantum-cryptography. Accessed Mar 2022
25. Sanatinia, A., Noubir, G.: Honey onions: a framework for characterizing and identifying misbehaving Tor HSDirs. In: IEEE Conference on Communications and Network Security (CNS) (2016)
26. Sasy, S., Goldberg, I.: ConsenSGX: scaling anonymous communications networks with trusted execution environments. In: Proceedings on Privacy Enhancing Technologies (PoPETs) (2019)
27. Sasy, S., Gorbunov, S., Fletcher, C.W.: ZeroTrace : Oblivious memory primitives from Intel SGX. In: 25th Annual Network and Distributed System Security Symposium (NDSS) (2018)
28. The Tor Project Inc: Tor Metrics (2020). https://metrics.torproject.org/. Accessed Mar 2022
29. The Tor Project Inc: Tor directory protocol, version 3 (2021). https://gitweb.torproject.org/torspec.git/tree/dir-spec.txt. Accessed March 2022
30. The Tor Project Inc: Tor Guard Specification (2021). https://gitweb.torproject.org/torspec.git/tree/guard-spec.txt. Accessed Mar 2022
31. The Tor Project Inc: Tor Path Specification (2021). https://gitweb.torproject.org/torspec.git/tree/path-spec.txt. Accessed Mar 2022
32. The Tor Project Inc: Tor Rendezvous Specification - Version 3 (2021). https://gitweb.torproject.org/torspec.git/tree/rend-spec-v3.txt. Accessed Mar 2022

Privacy-Preserving Authenticated Key Exchange for Constrained Devices

Loïc Ferreira[✉]

Orange Labs, Applied Crypto Group, Caen, France
loic.ferreira@orange.com

Abstract. In this paper we investigate the field of privacy-preserving authenticated key exchange protocols (PPAKE). First we make a cryptographic analysis of a previous PPAKE protocol. We show that most of its security properties, including privacy, are broken, despite the security proofs that are provided. Then we describe a strong security model which captures the security properties of a PPAKE: entity authentication, key indistinguishability, forward secrecy, and privacy. Finally, we present a PPAKE protocol in the symmetric-key setting which is suitable for constrained devices. We formally prove the security of this protocol in our model.

Keywords: Authenticated key agreement · Internet of Things · Cryptanalysis · Privacy · PPAKE · Security model

1 Introduction

Entity authentication and indistinguishability for the session key are the primary goals that a key exchange protocol aims at achieving. With the growth of social networks, and virtual communications, privacy-preserving techniques have gained interest in the design of real-world protocols (e.g., TLS 1.3 [32]). With the development of the Internet of Things (IoT) and its novel use cases interest in privacy is revived.

IoT provides applications in many fields: patient remote monitoring, energy consumption, air pollution control, traffic management, retail and logistics, etc. IoT technologies deal with and combine sets of data which makes increasingly difficult to distinguish between information that enable identification and information which do not [38]. For instance, smartphones gather critical amount of private data about their owner (identifiers, location, activity) that bear privacy risks. The diversity of connected objects form a large intelligent network that can serve as a medium for the leakage of personal data [29]. Rather soon the threats induced by the distributed nature of the IoT have been highlighted [23], among which one can cite identification, tracking, and profiling.

Devising a security protocol for the IoT is a challenging task since the devices that must implement and execute the protocol are constrained in terms of energy,

© Springer Nature Switzerland AG 2022
G. Ateniese and D. Venturi (Eds.): ACNS 2022, LNCS 13269, pp. 293–312, 2022.
https://doi.org/10.1007/978-3-031-09234-3_15

computation, and memory in particular. Consequently, the protocols are often built on symmetric-key functions for efficiency reasons. In turn, these "symmetric" protocols do not achieve the same security properties as "asymmetric" protocols (i.e., based on public-key schemes). Adding yet another security property (privacy) is not a trivial task.

In this paper we focus our attention on the SAKE protocol proposed by Avoine, Canard, and Ferreira [5]. Built solely upon symmetric-key functions, SAKE is an efficient protocol for constrained devices. It provides mutual authentication, key exchange, and forward secrecy. Its security is proved in a strong model (roughly the same type of model as those used to analyse protocols based on asymmetric algorithms). Moreover, with a suitable choice of symmetric functions, SAKE is quantum-secure. This raised the attention of the French National Cybersecurity Agency (ANSSI) which indicates that SAKE is a possible alternative to current "classical" authenticated key exchange (AKE) protocols in a quantum world [2]. Our goal is to turn SAKE into a privacy-preserving protocol, while keeping all its security properties, and to formally prove the security of the resulting protocol in a model at least as strong as that of used to analyse the original protocol.

1.1   Related Work

Most of the privacy-preserving protocols for low-resource devices, and the corresponding adversarial models are related to the RFID field (e.g., [7,16–18,25,27,28,36] to cite a few). Privacy-preserving mechanisms have also been investigated in other IoT contexts such as smart homes [31,35] or low-power wide area networks (LPWAN) [4,37]. However most of these works consider the privacy property only, focus on a specific setting (LPWAN), require a specific hardware (physically unclonable functions), or are built on questionable techniques with respect to security and efficiency (chaotic maps).

In [1], Aghili, Jolfaei, and Abidin propose a privacy-preserving authenticated key exchange protocol (PPAKE) with forward secrecy dedicated to IoT. This protocol builds upon Avoine et al.'s proposal [5]. Aghili et al. propose a variant of this protocol that aims in particular at guaranteeing privacy. However, and despite the security proofs they provide, their proposal is flawed (see Sect. 3).

Restarting from Avoine et al.'s protocol, we fix the issues of Aghili et al.'s protocol, and devise a clean and proper security model that we use to formally prove the security of the corrected PPAKE protocol.

1.2   Contributions

In this paper we investigate the field of privacy-preserving authenticated protocols. First we make a security analysis of a previous PPAKE protocol [1]. Then we describe a new security model which captures privacy (among other security properties) for authenticated key exchange protocols. Finally, we present a PPAKE protocol secure in our model.

Cryptanalysis. In [1], Aghili et al. propose a PPAKE protocol dedicated to IoT. Built upon a previous work by Avoine et al. [5], their proposal aims at keeping the same security properties as Avoine et al.'s protocol: entity authentication, key indistinguishability, and forward secrecy, and at being resistant to several attacks: "replay attacks", "time-based attack", and "tracking" (cf. [1, Sects. 6.1 and 9]). We make a cryptographic analysis of Aghili et al.'s protocol and show that most of the claimed security properties are broken (we respect the same attack settings that are considered in [1], in particular the powers granted to the adversary).

Security Model. We present a security model that captures strong guarantees for authenticated key exchange protocols. We extend the security model used by Avoine et al. [5] to prove the security of their protocol by introducing a criterion for indistinguishability of identities. That is, in order to define the privacy property, we borrow the concept of *virtual identifier* from Hermans, Pashalidis, Vercauteren, and Preneel [24], which appears also in Ouafi and Phan [30]. This concept allows hiding the identity of the party the adversary interacts with. The privacy property guarantees not only that the identity of an end-device is hidden, but that two different protocol runs are *unlinkable*. We also follow the paradigm proposed by Schwenk, Schäge, and Lauer [33], and incorporate the privacy property together with the other security properties. This approach guarantees that the different security properties are independent of each other. More specifically, our resulting model requires that, say, the key indistinguishability property holds even in the presence of attacks that adaptively unmask identities. Conversely, confidentiality of identities is ensured even in the presence of queries that let the attacker reveal session keys. This yields a strong security model which can serve as a tool to analyse other authenticated key exchange protocols that implement mechanisms to guarantee privacy.

Privacy-Preserving AKE. Starting anew from the SAKE protocol proposed by Avoine et al., we take another look at the concept of PPAKE for constrained devices. To the security properties guaranteed by SAKE, we add privacy. This results in a PPAKE protocol suitable for constrained devices that we naturally call Privacy-Preserving SAKE (PPSAKE). We formally prove that PPSAKE is secure in our strong security model.

2 Description of the SAKE Protocol

2.1 SAKE

SAKE [5] is a two-party AKE based on symmetric-key functions and pre-shared keys (see Fig. 2). The two parties A and B share a derivation master key K and an authentication master key K'. In order to mutually authenticate, each party exchanges a pseudo-random value (r_A, r_B). A MAC tag is computed over this challenge and returned to the sender (messages m_B and m_A). The session key is computed from the two pseudo-random values r_A and r_B and the derivation master key: $sk \leftarrow \mathsf{KDF}(K, r_A, r_B)$. Forward secrecy is guaranteed by using a key evolving scheme. That is, once both parties are mutually authenticated and the session key is computed, the derivation master key is updated with a one-way function: $K \leftarrow \mathsf{update}(K)$. Therefore the previous session keys remain safe even if (updated) K is disclosed.

As soon as two parties make a shared (symmetric) key evolve, a synchronisation problem arises: one of the parties has to make the first move whereas the other remains late, at least temporarily. This issue is solved with the authentication master key. The initiator A in SAKE stores the authentication keys corresponding to three consecutive epochs: previous (K'_{j-1}), current (K'_j), and future (K'_{j+1}) (see Fig. 1). Upon reception of the MAC-ed challenge computed by B (message m_B), A detects which epoch B belongs to by checking its MAC tag. Then, in the subsequent message (m_A), A indicates B if it must catch up (with the bit ϵ). Likewise, if A is late, it updates its master keys and then proceeds with the regular operations (upon reception of message τ'_B). Eventually, both parties update the authentication master keys the same way they do for the derivation master key. Only the initiator needs to keep the authentication master keys of three consecutive epochs. Avoine et al. have proved that the initiator A can only be either *one step* behind, or in sync, or *one step* ahead to B (hence the figure of three keys K'_{j-1}, K'_j, K'_{j+1}). That is $\delta_{AB} \in \{-1, 0, 1\}$ where δ_{AB} is the gap between A and B. Since the derivation master key and the authentication master key are independent, keeping previous authentication master keys does not jeopardise forward secrecy.

Once a correct and complete session ends, three goals are achieved in the same protocol run: (i) the two parties have updated their master keys, (ii) their master keys are synchronised, and (iii) they share a new session key. Therefore mutual authentication, key exchange (with forward secrecy), and resynchronisation are done in the continuity of a single session. Moreover, there is no need for an additional procedure (e.g., resynchronisation phase) or functionality (e.g., shared clock). The protocol is made of five messages at most, and can be reduced to four messages if the two parties are synchronised at the beginning of the session.

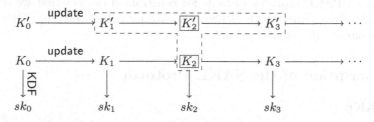

Fig. 1. Party A stores authentication master keys corresponding to three consecutive epochs $(j - 1, j, j + 1)$, and one derivation master key (illustration with $j = 2$ with the blue dashed box). Party B stores one sample of each master key (boxed in blue). (Color figure online)

A	B
$(K, K'_{j-1}, K'_j, K'_{j+1})$	(K, K')

$r_A \overset{\$}{\leftarrow} \{0,1\}^\lambda$

$$\xrightarrow{\quad \boxed{id_A\|r_A} \quad}$$

$r_B \overset{\$}{\leftarrow} \{0,1\}^\lambda$
$\tau_B \leftarrow \mathsf{Mac}(K', id_B\|id_A\|r_B\|\boxed{r_A})$
$m_B \leftarrow \boxed{id_B}\|r_B\|\tau_B$

$$\xleftarrow{\quad m_B \quad}$$

if $(\mathsf{Vrf}(K'_j, id_B\|id_A\|r_B\|\boxed{r_A}, \tau_B) = \mathtt{true})$
    $\delta_{AB} \leftarrow 0$
    $K' \leftarrow K'_j$; kdf; upd$_A$; $\epsilon \leftarrow 0$
else if $(\mathsf{Vrf}(K'_{j-1}, id_B\|id_A\|r_B\|\boxed{r_A}, \tau_B) = \mathtt{true})$
    $\delta_{AB} \leftarrow 1$
    $K' \leftarrow K'_{j-1}$; $\epsilon \leftarrow 1$
else if $(\mathsf{Vrf}(K'_{j+1}, id_B\|id_A\|r_B\|\boxed{r_A}, \tau_B) = \mathtt{true})$
    $\delta_{AB} \leftarrow -1$
    $K' \leftarrow K'_{j+1}$; upd$_A$; kdf; upd$_A$; $\epsilon \leftarrow 0$
else
    abort

$\tau_A \leftarrow \mathsf{Mac}(K', \epsilon\|id_A\|id_B\|r_A\|r_B)$
$m_A \leftarrow \epsilon\|\boxed{r_A}\|\tau_A$

$$\xrightarrow{\quad m_A \quad}$$

if $(\mathsf{Vrf}(K', \epsilon\|id_A\|id_B\|r_A\|r_B, \tau_A) = \mathtt{false})$
    abort
if $(\epsilon = 1)$
    upd$_B$

kdf; upd$_B$
$\tau'_B \leftarrow \mathsf{Mac}(K', \boxed{id_B\|id_A}\|r_B\|r_A)$

$$\xleftarrow{\quad \tau'_B \quad}$$

if $(\epsilon = 0)$
    $K' \leftarrow K'_j$
    if $(\mathsf{Vrf}(K', \boxed{id_B\|id_A}\|r_B\|r_A, \tau'_B) = \mathtt{false})$
      abort
else if $(\epsilon = 1)$
    $K' \leftarrow K'_{j+1}$
    if $(\mathsf{Vrf}(K', \boxed{id_B\|id_A}\|r_B\|r_A, \tau'_B) = \mathtt{false})$
      abort
    kdf; upd$_A$

$\tau'_A \leftarrow \mathsf{Mac}(K', r_A\|r_B)$

$$\xrightarrow{\quad \tau'_A \quad}$$

if $(\mathsf{Vrf}(K', r_A\|r_B, \tau'_A) = \mathtt{false})$
    abort

Fig. 2. The SAKE/SAKE-AM protocol. Elements surrounded by a blue dashed box appear only in SAKE. Elements boxed in blue appear only in SAKE-AM. (Color figure online)

Notations. For the sake of clarity, we use the following notation in Fig. 2:

- kdf corresponds to: $sk \leftarrow \mathsf{KDF}(K, r_A, r_B)$
- upd$_A$ corresponds to
   1. $K \leftarrow \mathsf{update}(K)$
   2. $K'_{j-1} \leftarrow K'_j$

3. $K'_j \leftarrow K'_{j+1}$
4. $K'_{j+1} \leftarrow \mathsf{update}(K'_{j+1})$

- upd_B corresponds to: 1. $K \leftarrow \mathsf{update}(K)$, 2. $K' \leftarrow \mathsf{update}(K')$.

Moreover, $\mathsf{Vrf}(k, m, \tau)$ denotes the MAC verification function that takes as input a secret key k, a message m, and a tag τ. It outputs $\mathtt{true}$ if τ is a valid tag on message m with respect to k. Otherwise, it returns $\mathtt{false}$.

2.2 SAKE-AM

From SAKE a complementary mode can be derived: SAKE-AM (which stands for "agressive mode"). Compared to SAKE, the first message $(id_A \| r_A)$ is skipped. Hence, in SAKE-AM, B is the initiator (and stores two master keys K, K'). What becomes the first message is computed as $m_B = id_B \| r_B \| \tau_B$ with $\tau_B = \mathsf{Mac}(K', id_B \| id_A \| r_B)$. The second message is computed as $m_A = \epsilon \| r_A \| \tau_A$ (with τ_A computed as in SAKE). The other messages and calculations are essentially the same as in SAKE.

Used together, SAKE and SAKE-AM allow any party to be either initiator or responder in a protocol run. Moreover the smallest amount of calculation is always done by the same party (irrespective of its role). This is particularly convenient in the context of a set of end-devices communicating with a back-end server. When the end-device wants to initiate a communication, protocol SAKE-AM is launched. Otherwise (the server is initiator), SAKE is used. Therefore, the end-device always does the lightest computations.

3   A Flawed Proposal

In [1] Aghili et al. propose to modify SAKE/SAKE-AM in order to turn the protocol into a privacy-preserving scheme. They consider a setting where party A is a server communicating with a set of end-devices (many parties B). They modify the SAKE and SAKE-AM protocols in order to achieve three main goals:

1. Forbidding identification and tracking of a party B (in particular with id_B).
2. Forbidding the replay of the first message (m_B) in SAKE-AM. In SAKE-AM, a message m_B corresponding to the previous epoch (i.e., computed with the authentication master key K'_{j-1}) can be replayed multiple times to A (until a new session is completed), and A computes and responds with a message m_A. Although this is not sufficient for the responder A to "accept" and to authenticate the initiator B (eventually the session aborts), Aghili et al. aim at preventing such a possibility. In contrast, in TLS 1.3 with 0-RTT mode [32] the server must deem the initial message (Client Hello) as authentic, and execute the request herein included [21]. Consequently, mitigations are necessary in TLS 1.3 (cf. [32, Sect. 8]).
3. Forbidding recognition of a party B based on the amount of calculations done by A. In some cases (see below), when party A receives a message m_B in Aghili et al.'s version of SAKE and SAKE-AM, A must try all authentication

master keys it stores in its database in order to verify the message, until a match is found. Therefore the time spent by A to find the correct key allows an adversary to recognise which party B communicates with A (the measurement done by the adversary is used as an index that designates B).

3.1 Issues

Aghili et al. modify the SAKE/SAKE-AM protocol as follows. First they add identifiers in the messages in order for two communicating parties A and B to distinguish which messages are intended to them, among the flow of messages sent by all parties. That is, they necessarily mix the communication and the application (cryptographic) layers since the former may include parameters (identifier) that contradict the goals they want to achieve.[1] In addition, upon reception of m_A, id_B is updated by B (A does also the same): $id_B \leftarrow \mathsf{update}(id_B \| K')$. This new identifier value is transmitted in the subsequent message sent by B and also in the first message of the next protocol run. We can see that there is a first issue since the same identifier id_B is used in two consecutive sessions. Therefore it is trivial to track party B (this contradicts goal 1.).

Moreover, id_B is replaced with a pseudo-random value r_α in m_B if message m_A was not received by B during the previous session. The purpose is to avoid that the same identifier id_B be used in two consecutive messages m_B (a correct message m_A triggers the update of id_B, hence id_B remains the same in the absence of such a message). In Aghili et al.'s version of SAKE-AM, this means that $m_B = x \| r_B \| \tau_B$ with $x \in \{id_B, r_\alpha\}$ and $\tau_B = \mathsf{Mac}(K', id_B \| id_A \| r_B)$. When $x = r_\alpha$, party A tries all the authentication master keys K' (corresponding to different communicating parties B) it stores in its database until a match is found. The issue here is that r_α is not included in the computation of τ_B even when it replaces id_B in m_B. Therefore an adversary can alter m_B without A being able to notice the change. This breaks entity authentication because, in the adopted security model, partnership is based on the notion of "matching conversations" (i.e., equality of transcript of messages) [26].

Furthermore this invalidates goal 3. Indeed when the adversary modifies id_B in m_B this compels A to try all the authentication master keys, which helps the adversary to recognise which party B has sent the message m_B, hence to track that party (defeating goal 1. again).

In order to achieve goal 2. (which concerns SAKE-AM only), A stores the pseudo-random value r_B received in the *two previous* sessions. This countermeasure is not enough and can easily be bypassed. The adversary merely intercepts three times consecutively an initial message m_B sent by the initiator B, and not received by A (dropped by the adversary). Next the adversary lets A and B complete successfully one protocol run. The three messages m_B highly likely carry pairwise distinct values r_B. When the adversary sends any of these messages, they are accepted by A because they carry an unknown value r_B, and

---

[1] In [5], Avoine et al. describe the message flow of a cryptographic protocol. Consequently, they indicate only the parameters that are necessary on a cryptographic point of view.

because they all correspond to the previous epoch from A's perspective (i.e., computed with K'_{j-1}). Therefore A computes and sends a message m_A. Alternatively sending these three messages "flushes" A's memory of r_B values. Hence A keeps sending messages m_A in response.

The issues raised above break the security properties claimed in [1, Sects. 6.1 and 9] (respecting the same security experiments and adversarial model considered by Aghili et al.): replay, time-based attack, tracking, entity authentication.

3.2   Countermeasures

The vulnerabilities in Aghili et al.'s proposal can be thwarted as follows. In order to fix the issue in the entity authentication, the pseudo-random value r_α must also be involved in the computation of the MAC tag τ_B of message m_B.

To thwart the replay attack, A must detect *all* values r_B previously received. This can be done efficiently with a Bloom filter [14] or a Cuckoo filter [19].

The time-based attack can be mitigated by equalising the time spent to explore the set of authentication keys (e.g., all keys are tried even when the correct one is found), or by randomly exploring this set [6].

To forbid any tracking, a value id_B must be used once only per session.

The vulnerabilities we describe question also the correctness of the security proofs provided in [1], made in the computational model (using the game-based methodology [11,34]), and with the ProVerif verification tool [13]. In particular, the privacy property is not captured by the security model used in [1]. This highlights the importance of devising and using a suitable security model.

The relevance of the countermeasures that we succinctly present due to lack of space is shown in the security proofs (see the full version of the paper [20]) for our privacy-preserving AKE protocol described in Sect. 5.

4   Security Model

In this section, we present our security model for PPAKE protocols. We use the model for authenticated key exchange protocols described by Avoine et al. [5] to prove the security of their SAKE and SAKE-AM protocols, which is based on the model of Brzuska, Jacobsen, and Stebila [15]. This model captures entity authentication, key indistinguishability, and forward secrecy in the symmetric-key setting.

We extend this model by introducing a criterion for indistinguishability of identities. That is, in order to define the privacy property, we borrow the concept of virtual identifier from Ouafi et al. [30] and Hermans et al. [24]. This concept allows hiding the identity of the party the adversary is interacting with. The privacy property guarantees not only that the identity of an end-device is hidden, but that two different protocol runs are *unlinkable*. Given the two-party protocol which we want to prove the security, and its deployment context, we aim at guaranteeing the end-device's privacy only. However our model can be extended in a straightforward manner to provide privacy to any party involved in a protocol run (end-device and server).

Finally, we follow the paradigm proposed by Schwenk et al. [33], and incorporate the privacy property together with the other security properties. This approach guarantees that the different security properties are independent of each other. More specifically, our resulting model requires that, say, the key indistinguishability property holds even in the presence of attacks that adaptively unmask identities. Conversely, confidentiality of identities is ensured even in the presence of queries that let the attacker reveal session keys. Hence our model is stronger than models where security properties are considered separately (e.g., privacy and key indistinguishability), and not all the adversarial queries are available in all the security experiments (e.g. [3,22]).

In our model, the long-term symmetric keys shared by the two communicating parties can not be given to the adversary before the session is completed (i.e., our security model does not capture key compromise impersonation attacks [14]). However these keys can be disclosed once one of the two instances accepts (this captures forward secrecy). This makes our model stronger than other models used in the symmetric-key setting (e.g., [22]), and comparable in terms of powers granted to the adversary to security models used in the asymmetric setting (e.g., [15,26]).

We do think that this security model can serve as a tool to analyse other authenticated key exchange protocols that implement mechanisms to guarantee privacy.

4.1   Execution Environment

Parties. Let $\mathcal{E}$ be a set of end-devices, and $\mathcal{S}$ a set of servers. The type of a party P_i is denoted $\mathsf{type}(P_i) \in \{\mathsf{end\text{-}device}, \mathsf{server}\}$.

A two-party protocol is carried out by an end-device and a server. Each party $P_i \in \mathcal{E} \cup \mathcal{S}$ has an associated long-term key $P_i.\mathsf{ltk}$, and is identified with two parameters: its permanent identifier which we also denote by P_i, and its current identifier $P_i.\mathsf{id}$. The same long-term key is shared by a unique pair of parties (P_i, P_j). That is: $P_i.\mathsf{ltk} = P_j.\mathsf{ltk}$.

In addition, a party $P_i \in \mathcal{S}$ stores a database which each entry corresponds to the long-term key of an end-device party $P_j.\mathsf{ltk}$, its current identifier $P_j.\mathsf{id}$, along with its permanent identifier P_j.

Instances. Each party can take part in multiple sequential executions of the protocol. We prohibit *parallel* executions of the protocol. Indeed, since the protocol we propose is based on shared *evolving* symmetric keys, running multiple instances in parallel may cause some executions to abort.[2] This is the only restriction we demand compared to AKE security models used in the public-key setting.

---

[2] This is a technical feature of the SAKE and SAKE-AM protocols, which our PPSAKE protocol is based on. In this regard, we refer the reader to [5, Sect. 6].

Each run of the protocol is called a session. To each session of a party P_i, an instance π_i^s is associated which embodies this (local) session's execution of the protocol, and has access to the long-term key and current identifier of the party. P_i is called the *parent* of π_i^s, and the type of an instance is the type of its parent: type(π_i^s) = type(P_i) $\in$ {end-device, server}. In addition, each instance maintains the following state specific to the session.

- ρ: the role $\rho \in$ {initiator, responder} of the session in the protocol execution, being either the initiator or the responder.
- pid: the identity pid $\in \mathcal{P}$ of the intended communication partner of π_i^s.
- α: the state $\alpha \in \{\perp, \text{running}, \text{accepted}, \text{rejected}\}$ of the instance.
- sk: the session key derived by π_i^s.
- κ: the status $\kappa \in \{\perp, \text{revealed}\}$ of the session key π_i^s.sk.
- sid: the identifier of the session.
- b: a random bit b $\in \{0, 1\}$ sampled at initialisation of π_i^s.

We use the notion of initiator and responder on the one hand, and end-device, server on the other hand. An initiator instance sends the first message of the protocol, whereas a responder instance responds to it. An end-device party hides its "real" identity, whereas a server party does not. In Sect. 5, we present two protocols that allow an end-device party to behave either as initiator or responder, and conversely a server can be either responder or initiator. Therefore the notion of end-device and server is mainly used in the privacy experiment in order to indicate which party the adversary's goal is to find the identity.

We put the following correctness requirements on the variables α, sk, sid and pid. For any two instances π_i^s, π_j^t, the following must hold:

$$\pi_i^s.\alpha = \text{accepted} \Rightarrow \pi_i^s.\text{sk} \neq \perp \wedge \pi_i^s.\text{sid} \neq \perp \tag{1}$$

$$\pi_i^s.\alpha = \pi_j^t.\alpha = \text{accepted} \wedge \pi_i^s.\text{sid} = \pi_j^t.\text{sid} \Rightarrow \begin{cases} \pi_i^s.\text{sk} = \pi_j^t.\text{sk} \\ \pi_i^s.\text{pid} = P_j \\ \pi_j^t.\text{pid} = P_i \end{cases} \tag{2}$$

Virtual identifier. In order to hide to the adversary which end-device party it is interacting with, the notion of virtual identifier is used. A virtual identifier $vid = P_i | P_j$ refers to two parties $P_i, P_j \in \mathcal{E}$, which are known to the adversary. The real involved party is designated by realvid(vid), depending on a secret bit b $\in \{0, 1\}$. This bit is sampled at initialisation of vid. If vid.b = 0, then realvid(vid) = P_i. If vid.b = 1, then realvid(vid) = P_j. In addition, type(vid) = end-device.

Adversarial Queries. The adversary $\mathcal{A}$ is assumed to control the network, and interacts with the instances by issuing the following queries to them.

- DrawParty(P_i, P_j): this query creates a virtual identifier $vid = P_i | P_j$, adds vid to the list $\mathcal{L}_{\text{vid}}$, and returns vid. If $P_i \notin \mathcal{E}$ or $P_j \notin \mathcal{E}$, then it returns $\perp$. If P_i or P_j are used in a virtual identifier already in $\mathcal{L}_{\text{vid}}$, then it returns $\perp$.

- NewSession(id, ρ, id'): this query creates a new instance π_i^s at party id, having role ρ, and intended partner id'. If type(id) = type(id'), the query aborts. If id is a virtual identifier, then the parent of π_i^s is realvid(id). If id' is a virtual identifier, then π_i^s.pid = realvid(id'). $\pi_i^s.\alpha$ is set to running. If ρ = initiator, it produces the first message of the protocol which is returned to the adversary.
- Send(π_i^s, m): this query allows the adversary to send any message m to π_i^s. If $\pi_i^s.\alpha \neq$ running, it returns $\bot$. Otherwise π_i^s responds according to the protocol specification.
- Corrupt(P_i): if type(P_i) = end-device, this query returns the long-term key P_i.ltk of P_i. If type(P_i) = server, this query returns all long-term keys P_j.ltk, $P_j \in \mathcal{E}$, stored by P_i. If Corrupt(P_i) is the ν-th query issued by the adversary, then we say that P_i is ν-corrupted. For a party that has not been corrupted, we define $\nu = +\infty$. Moreover we say that a virtual identifier $vid = P_i | P_j$ is corrupted if either P_i or P_j is corrupted.
- Reveal(π_i^s): this query returns the session key π_i^s.sk, and $\pi_i^s.\kappa$ is set to revealed.
- Unmask(π_i^s): this query returns the permanent identifier P_i of π_i^s's parent.
- Test(π_i^s): this query may be asked only once throughout the game. If $\pi_i^s.\alpha \neq$ accepted, then it returns $\bot$. Otherwise it samples an independent key $sk_0 \xleftarrow{\$} \mathcal{K}$, and returns sk_b with $b = \pi_i^s$.b, where $sk_1 = \pi_i^s$.sk. The key sk_b is called the Test-*challenge-key*.
- Free(vid): this query removes vid from $\mathcal{L}_{vid}$. Moreover, for any instance π_i^s such that either vid is the parent of π_i^s or π_i^s.pid = vid, if $\pi_i^s.\alpha \in \{\bot,$running$\}$, then it sets $\pi_i^s.\alpha =$ rejected.

The adversary is an active Man-in-the-Middle which can interact with parties, and adaptively issue queries. The adversary is granted the ability to query the used identities of arbitrary session partners (with the Unmask query). Our goal is to consider a strong adversary, in the sense that we allow as far as possible all queries (Corrupt, Reveal, Send, Unmask, etc.) except the queries that allow trivial attacks (i.e., attacks that allow the adversary to win, regardless of the design of the protocol).

Definition 1 (Partnership). *Two instances π_i^s and π_j^t are partners if π_i^s.sid = π_j^t.sid.*

A *privacy-preserving authenticated key exchange protocol* (PPAKE) is a two-party protocol satisfying the correctness requirements 1 and 2, and where the security is defined in terms of a PPAKE experiment played between a challenger and an adversary. This experiment uses the execution environment described above. The adversary can win the PPAKE experiment in one of three ways: (i) by making an instance accept maliciously, (ii) by guessing the secret bit of the Test-instance, or (iii) by guessing the secret bit of the privacy experiment.

Definition 2 (Entity Authentication (EA)). *An instance π_i^s of a protocol Π is said to have accepted maliciously in the PPAKE security experiment with intended partner P_j, if*

1. $\pi_i^s.\alpha =$ accepted and $\pi_i^s.$pid $= P_j$ when $\mathcal{A}$ issues its ν_0-th query,
2. P_i and P_j are ν- and ν'-corrupted with $\nu_0 < \nu$, $\nu_0 < \nu'$, and
3. there is no unique instance π_j^t such that π_i^s and π_j^t are partners.

The adversary's advantage is defined as its winning probability:

$$\text{adv}_\Pi^{\text{ent-auth}} = \Pr[\mathcal{A} \text{ wins the EA game}].$$

Definition 3 (Key Indistinguishability). An adversary $\mathcal{A}$ against a protocol Π, that issues its Test-query to instance π_i^s during the PPAKE security experiment, answers the Test-challenge-key correctly if it terminates with output b', such that

1. $\pi_i^s.\alpha =$ accepted and $\pi_i^s.$pid $= P_j$ when $\mathcal{A}$ issues its ν_0-th query,
2. $\pi_i^s.\kappa \neq$ revealed and P_i is ν-corrupted with $\nu_0 < \nu$,
3. for any partner instance π_j^t of π_i^s, we have that $\pi_j^t.\kappa \neq$ revealed and P_j is ν'-corrupted with $\nu_0 < \nu'$, and
4. $\pi_i^s.b = b'$.

The adversary's advantage is defined as

$$\text{adv}_\Pi^{\text{key-ind}} = \left| \Pr[\pi_i^s.b = b'] - \frac{1}{2} \right|.$$

Note that the definition of key indistinguishability incorporates a requirement for forward secrecy.

Definition 4 (Privacy). An adversary $\mathcal{A}$ against a protocol Π, wins the privacy game during the PPAKE security experiment, if it terminates with output (π_i^s, b'), such that

- type$(\pi_i^s) \neq$ type$(\pi_i^s.$pid$)$
- If type$(\pi_i^s) =$ server, let vid be the (virtual) identifier of $\pi_i^s.$pid:
  1. $\pi_i^s.\alpha =$ accepted when $\mathcal{A}$ issues its ν_0-th query,
  2. $\pi_i^u.\alpha =$ accepted when $\mathcal{A}$ issues its ν_1-th query, where π_i^u is the instance created after π_i^s such that its parent and intended partner are the same as those of π_i^s,
  3. the parents of π_i^s and vid are ν- and ν'-corrupted with $\nu_1 < \nu$, $\nu_0 < \nu'$,
  4. $\mathcal{A}$ did not issue an Unmask query to π_j^t for any instance π_j^t such that π_j^t is partnered with π_i^s and type$(\pi_j^t) =$ end-device, and
  5. vid.b $= b'$.
- If type$(\pi_i^s) =$ end-device, let vid be the (virtual) identifier of the parent of π_i^s:
  1. $\pi_i^s.\alpha =$ accepted when $\mathcal{A}$ issues its ν_0-th query,
  2. $\pi_j^v.\alpha =$ accepted when $\mathcal{A}$ issues its ν_1-th query, where π_j^v is created after π_j^t for any partner π_j^t of π_i^s, such that $\pi_j^v.$pid is π_i^s's parent and π_j^v's parent is $\pi_i^s.$pid,
  3. vid and $\pi_i^s.$pid are ν- and ν'-corrupted with $\nu_0 < \nu$, $\nu_1 < \nu'$,
  4. $\mathcal{A}$ did not issue an Unmask query to π_i^s, and
  5. vid.b $= b'$.

The adversary's advantage is defined as

$$\mathsf{adv}_\Pi^{\mathsf{privacy}} = \left| \Pr[vid.b = b'] - \frac{1}{2} \right|.$$

Definitions 2, 3, and 4 allow the adversary to corrupt an instance involved in the security experiment (after some time, in order to exclude trivial attacks). Therefore, protocols secure with respect to Definition 5 below provide *forward secrecy*. We do not allow the targeted instance to be corrupted before it accepts. That is, this security model does not capture key-compromise impersonation attacks (KCI) [12] since that would allow trivially breaking key exchange protocols solely based on shared symmetric keys.

Definition 5 (PPAKE Security). *We say that a two-party protocol Π is a secure PPAKE protocol if Π satisfies the correctness requirements 1 and 2, and for all probabilistic polynomial time adversary $\mathcal{A}$, $\mathsf{adv}_\Pi^{\mathsf{ent-auth}}$, $\mathsf{adv}_\Pi^{\mathsf{key-ind}}$, and $\mathsf{adv}_\Pi^{\mathsf{privacy}}$ are a negligible function of the security parameter.*

4.2 Security Definitions of the Building Blocks

In our proofs, we rely upon standard security definitions. The security definition of a pseudo-random function (PRF) is taken from Bellare, Desai, Jokipii, and Rogaway [8], and that of a MAC strongly unforgeable under chosen-message attacks from Bellare and Namprempre [9]. We rely also on the definition of matching conversations initially proposed by Bellare and Rogaway [10], and modified by Jager, Kohlar, Schäge, and Schwenk [26].

5 Privacy-Preserving SAKE/SAKE-AM

In this section we present the protocol obtained when applying to [1] the mitigations described in Sect. 3. We call these corrected versions respectively Privacy-preserving SAKE (PPSAKE) and Privacy-preserving SAKE-AM (PPSAKE-AM).

Description. The protocol PPSAKE is depicted by Fig. 3. It illustrates the generic case when party A is a server communicating with a set of end-devices (parties B). As in [1], B uses either an ephemeral identity parameter id_B (which evolves the same way as its master keys K and K') or a pseudo-random value, depending if the previous protocol run has completed successfully (this is tracked with the flag ϕ, initialised to 0). $\bar{id}_B = id_B$ allows A to retrieve the set of parameters corresponding to B in its database db. For each party B, A stores the identity parameter of three consecutive epochs, as it is done with the authentication master key (each *entry* in db is of the form: $K, (id_{B,j}, K'_j), (id_{B,j-1}, K'_{j-1}), (id_{B,j+1}, K'_{j+1})$).

A	B
$(id_A,\ \mathsf{db},\ \boxed{\mathsf{htable}})$	$(id_B,\ K,\ K',\ \phi)$

$r_A \xleftarrow{\$} \{0,1\}^\lambda$

$$\xrightarrow{\quad \boxed{id_A \| r_A} \quad}$$

if $(\phi = 0)$
   $i\bar{d}_B \leftarrow id_B$
   $\phi \leftarrow 1$
else if $(\phi = 1)$
   $i\bar{d}_B \xleftarrow{\$} \{0,1\}^\lambda$

$r_B \xleftarrow{\$} \{0,1\}^\lambda$
$\tau_B \leftarrow \mathsf{Mac}(K', i\bar{d}_B \| id_A \| r_B \| \boxed{r_A})$
$m_B \leftarrow i\bar{d}_B \| r_B \| \tau_B$

$$\xleftarrow{\quad m_B \quad}$$

if $(i\bar{d}_B \in \mathsf{db.id})$
   $entry \leftarrow$ get corresponding entry
   ┌─────────────────────────────────────┐
   │ if $(\mathsf{verif\text{-}table}(\mathsf{htable}, m_B) = \mathtt{true})$ │
   └─────────────────────────────────────┘
      abort
   if $(\mathsf{verif\text{-}entry}(entry, m_B) = \mathtt{false})$
      abort
else
   $entry \leftarrow \mathsf{find\text{-}entry}(m_B)$
   if $(entry = \emptyset)$
      abort
   ┌─────────────────────────────────────┐
   │ if $(\mathsf{verif\text{-}table}(\mathsf{htable}, m_B) = \mathtt{true})$ │
   └─────────────────────────────────────┘
      abort

┌────────────────────────────┐
│ $\mathsf{insert\text{-}table}(\mathsf{htable}, m_B)$ │
└────────────────────────────┘
$\tau_A \leftarrow \mathsf{Mac}(K', \epsilon \| id_A \| i\bar{d}_B \| r_A \| r_B)$
$m_A \leftarrow \epsilon \| i\bar{d}_B \| \boxed{r_A} \| \tau_A$

$$\xrightarrow{\quad m_A \quad}$$

if $(\mathsf{Vrf}(K', \epsilon \| id_A \| i\bar{d}_B \| r_A \| r_B, \tau_A) = \mathtt{false})$
   abort
if $(\epsilon = 1)$
   upd_B

$\mathsf{kdf};\ \mathsf{upd}_B$
$\phi \leftarrow 0$
$\tau'_B \leftarrow \mathsf{Mac}(K', i\bar{d}_B \| \boxed{id_A} \| r_B \| r_A)$
$m'_B \leftarrow i\bar{d}_B \| \tau'_B$

$$\xleftarrow{\quad m'_B \quad}$$

if $(\epsilon = 0)$
   $K' \leftarrow K'_j$
   if $(\mathsf{Vrf}(K', id_B \| \boxed{id_A} \| r_B \| r_A, \tau'_B) = \mathtt{false})$
      abort
else if $(\epsilon = 1)$
   $K' \leftarrow K'_{j+1}$
   if $(\mathsf{Vrf}(K', id_B \| \boxed{id_A} \| r_B \| r_A, \tau'_B) = \mathtt{false})$
      abort
   $\mathsf{kdf};\ \mathsf{upd}_A$

$\tau'_A \leftarrow \mathsf{Mac}(K', id_B \| r_A \| r_B)$
$m'_A \leftarrow i\bar{d}_B \| \tau'_A$

$$\xrightarrow{\quad m'_A \quad}$$

if $(\mathsf{Vrf}(K', i\bar{d}_B \| r_A \| r_B, \tau'_A) = \mathtt{false})$
   abort

Fig. 3. The PPSAKE/PPSAKE-AM protocol. Elements surrounded by a blue dashed box appear only in PPSAKE. Elements boxed in blue appear only in PPSAKE-AM. (Color figure online)

When B transmits a pseudo-random value $i\bar{d}_B$ (instead of id_B), A must explore (in constant time) the database (function find-entry) in order to find the matching authentication master key (i.e., which allows verifying the MAC tag τ_B). This happens only if the previous session was not successful.

The same value $i\bar{d}_B$ is used in a given session, and a new value is used in the next session (see Fig. 4). The identity parameter $i\bar{d}_B$ appears in all messages (but the first one in PPSAKE). The purpose is to allow A to recognise which keys to use (when $i\bar{d}_B$ is output by the update function), but also to allow B detecting which messages sent by A are intended to it. Likewise, with $i\bar{d}_B$ (equal to id_B or pseudo-random), A can correlate the messages m_B, m'_B and the corresponding parameters in database. The identity parameter id_A used by A is explicit, and never changed as the privacy property aims at protecting B.

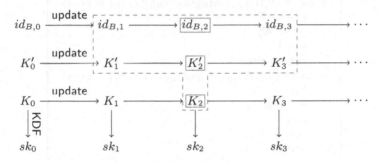

Fig. 4. Party A stores authentication master keys and identifiers corresponding to three consecutive epochs $(j - 1, j, j + 1)$, and one derivation master key (illustration with $j = 2$ with the blue dashed box). Party B stores one sample of each master key, and identifier (boxed in blue). (Color figure online)

In PPSAKE-AM, party A stores efficiently (e.g., using a Bloom or a Cuckoo filter) the messages m_B it receives (this is not necessary in PPSAKE). Upon reception of a message m_B, A verifies if it has already been received (these operations are done respectively with functions insert-table and verif-table). This prevents A from responding to a replayed message m_B. We use a global table. Note that using one table per entry in the database db (i.e., one table per end-device party) may lead to privacy breaches depending on how the privacy experiment is defined (in particular if the table can be revealed).

We observe that, depending on the communication layer, it may not be necessary to include $i\bar{d}_B$ in all messages. For instance, if the messages are sent through a radio link, A and B can negotiate a specific radio frequency they will use during the session. Likewise, if the messages are sent through a wired link, some ephemeral per-session identifier (e.g., IP address or any equivalent) can be used by A and B to discriminate the messages intended to them. Nonetheless, in order to make the protocol agnostic with respect to the communication layer, we opt for an ephemeral identifier $i\bar{d}_B$ in the messages.

As in [5], using PPSAKE-AM together with PPSAKE (both protocols are based on the same inner functions) allows any party to be either initiator or responder of a session, such that the smallest amount of calculation is always done by the same party (i.e., the low-resource end-device).

```
if (Vrf(K'_j, id̄_B‖id_A‖r_B‖⌈r_A⌉, τ_B) = true)
    δ_AB ← 0
    K' ← K'_j
    kdf
    upd_A
    ε ← 0
    return true
else if (Vrf(K'_{j-1}, id̄_B‖id_A‖r_B‖⌈r_A⌉, τ_B) = true)
    δ_AB ← 1
    K' ← K'_{j-1}
    ε ← 1
    return true
else if (Vrf(K'_{j+1}, id̄_B‖id_A‖r_B‖⌈r_A⌉, τ_B) = true)
    δ_AB ← -1
    K' ← K'_{j+1}
    upd_A
    kdf
    upd_A
    ε ← 0
    return true
else
    return false
```

Fig. 5. Pseudo-code of function verif-entry. Elements surrounded by a blue dashed box appear only in PPSAKE (not in PPSAKE-AM). (Color figure online)

Notations. The notations upd_A, and upd_B are defined as follows:

- upd_A corresponds to
    1. $K \leftarrow \mathsf{update}(K)$
    2. $id_{B,j-1} \leftarrow id_{B,j}$
    3. $id_{B,j} \leftarrow id_{B,j+1}$
    4. $id_{B,j+1} \leftarrow \mathsf{update}(K'_{j+1}, id_{B,j+1})$
    5. $K'_{j-1} \leftarrow K'_j$
    6. $K'_j \leftarrow K'_{j+1}$
    7. $K'_{j+1} \leftarrow \mathsf{update}(K'_{j+1})$
- upd_B corresponds to
    1. $K \leftarrow \mathsf{update}(K)$
    2. $id_B \leftarrow \mathsf{update}(K', id_B)$
    3. $K' \leftarrow \mathsf{update}(K')$

The function verif-entry (see Fig. 5) takes as input an entry $entry \in$ db, and a message m_B (we assume that the other values used in verif-entry are "global" parameters). It outputs **true** if $entry$ allows verifying correctly m_B.

The function find-entry (see Fig. 6) takes as input a message $m_B = i\bar{d}_B \| r_B \| \tau_B$, and outputs either an entry $entry \in$ db or $\emptyset$.

The function verif-table takes as input a hash table htable, and a value x, and outputs **true** if x is present in htable. Otherwise it returns **false**.

The function insert-table takes as input a hash table htable, and a value x, and inserts x into htable.

```
foreach entry ∈ db
    if (verif-entry(entry, mB) = true)
        return entry
return ∅
```

Fig. 6. Pseudo-code of function find-entry

6   Security of Privacy-Preserving SAKE/SAKE-AM

In this section we prove that PPSAKE and PPSAKE-AM are secure PPAKE protocols according to Definition 5. We refer the reader to [5] regarding the *soundness* of PPSAKE and PPSAKE-AM (the proof is the same as that of SAKE and SAKE-AM in this regard).

In order to prove that the protocol PPSAKE/PPSAKE-AM is a secure PPAKE protocol, we use the execution environment described in Sect. 4.1. We define the partnering between two instances with the notion of *matching conversations*. That is, we define sid to be the transcript, in chronological order, of all the (valid) messages sent and received by an instance during the key exchange, but, possibly, the last one. Furthermore, we choose the function update to be a keyed PRF, that is update : $(k, x) \mapsto \mathsf{PRF}(k, x)$, and we define:

- update$(k) = \mathsf{PRF}(k, c)$ if k is a derivation (K) or authentication (K') master key, and c is some (constant) value
- update$(K', id_B) = \mathsf{PRF}(K', id_B)$

Theorem 1. *The protocol* $\Pi \in \{PPSAKE, PPSAKE\text{-}AM\}$ *is a secure PPAKE protocol, and for any probabilistic polynomial time adversary* $\mathcal{A}$ *in the PPAKE security experiment against* Π

$$\mathsf{adv}_\Pi^{\mathsf{ent\text{-}auth}} \leq nq \left((nq-1)2^{-\lambda} + (n_\mathsf{E}(q-1)+2)\mathsf{adv}_{\mathsf{update}}^{\mathsf{prf}} + (n_\mathsf{E}+1)\mathsf{adv}_{\mathsf{Mac}}^{\mathsf{suf\text{-}cma}} \right)$$

$$\mathsf{adv}_\Pi^{\mathsf{key\text{-}ind}} \leq nq \left((q-1)\mathsf{adv}_{\mathsf{update}}^{\mathsf{prf}} + \mathsf{adv}_{\mathsf{KDF}}^{\mathsf{prf}} \right) + \mathsf{adv}_\Pi^{\mathsf{ent\text{-}auth}}$$

$$\mathsf{adv}_\Pi^{\mathsf{privacy}} \leq nq \left(q \cdot \mathsf{adv}_{\mathsf{update}}^{\mathsf{prf}} + 2\mathsf{adv}_{\mathsf{Mac}}^{\mathsf{prf}} + 2^{-\kappa} \right) + \mathsf{adv}_\Pi^{\mathsf{ent\text{-}auth}}$$

where n_E is the number of end-device *parties, n_S the number of* server *parties, $n = n_E + n_S$, q the maximum number of instances (sessions) per party, κ the size of the derivation master key K, λ the size of the pseudo-random values (r_A, r_B), and* $\mathsf{adv}^{prf}_{\mathsf{update}}$, $\mathsf{adv}^{suf\text{-}cma}_{\mathsf{Mac}}$, $\mathsf{adv}^{prf}_{\mathsf{KDF}}$, *and* $\mathsf{adv}^{prf}_{\mathsf{Mac}}$ *are the advantage of an adversary to break respectively the PRF-security of* update, *the SUF-CMA-security of* Mac, *the PRF-security of* KDF, *and the PRF-security of* Mac.

The extended proof of Theorem 1 is presented in the full version of the paper [20].

7   Conclusion

In this paper we have investigated the field of privacy-preserving authenticated key exchange protocols (PPAKE).

First we have made a cryptographic analysis of a previous PPAKE protocol intended to the IoT [1], and shown that most of its security properties, including privacy, are broken. Furthermore we have described countermeasures that allow preventing these vulnerabilities. The attacks that we exhibit question the correctness of the security proofs provided in [1], and highlight the importance of using a suitable security model.

Secondly, we have presented a security model which captures the security properties of a PPAKE protocol: entity authentication, key indistinguishability, forward secrecy, and privacy. The approach that we take guarantees that the different security properties are independent of each other, which yields a strong security model. We do think that this security model can serve as a tool to analyse other authenticated key exchange protocols that implement mechanisms to guarantee privacy.

Finally, we have described a PPAKE protocol in the symmetric-key setting which is suitable for constrained devices. We have formally proved the security of this protocol in our strong model.

References

1. Aghili, S.F., Jolfaei, A.A., Abidin, A.: SAKE$^+$: strengthened symmetric-key authenticated key exchange with perfect forward secrecy for IoT. Cryptology ePrint Archive, Report 2020/778, 20200714:112142 (2020)
2. ANSSI. Should Quantum Key Distribution be Used for Secure Communications? (2020)
3. Arfaoui, G., Bultel, X., Fouque, P.A., Nedelcu, A., Onete, C.: The privacy of the TLS 1.3 protocol. PoPETs 2019(4), 190–210 (2019)
4. Ashur, T., et al.: A privacy-preserving device tracking system using a low-power wide-area network. In: Capkun, S., et al. (eds.) CANS 2017. LNCS, vol. 11261, pp. 347–369. Springer, Cham (2018). https://doi.org/10.1007/978-3-030-02641-7_16

5. Avoine, G., Canard, S., Ferreira, L.: Symmetric-key authenticated key exchange (SAKE) with perfect forward secrecy. In: Jarecki, S. (ed.) CT-RSA 2020. LNCS, vol. 12006, pp. 199–224. Springer, Cham (2020). https://doi.org/10.1007/978-3-030-40186-3_10
6. Avoine, G., Coisel, I., Martin, T.: Time measurement threatens privacy-friendly RFID authentication protocols. In: Yalcin, O., Berna, S. (ed.) RFIDSec 2010. LNCS, vol. 6370, pp. 138–157. Springer, Heidelberg (2010). https://doi.org/10.1007/978-3-642-16822-2_13
7. Avoine, G., Coisel, I., Martin, T.: Untraceability model for RFID. IEEE Trans. Mob. Comput. 13(10), 9 (2014)
8. Bellare, M., Desai, A., Jokipii, E., Rogaway, P.: A concrete security treatment of symmetric encryption. In: 38th FOCS, pp. 394–403. IEEE Computer Society Press (1997)
9. Bellare, M., Namprempre, C.: Authenticated encryption: relations among notions and analysis of the generic composition paradigm. J. Cryptol. 21(4), 469–491 (2008)
10. Bellare, M., Rogaway, P.: Entity authentication and key distribution. In: Stinson, D.R. (ed.) CRYPTO 1993. LNCS, vol. 773, pp. 232–249. Springer, Heidelberg (1994). https://doi.org/10.1007/3-540-48329-2_21
11. Bellare, M., Rogaway, P.: The security of triple encryption and a framework for code-based game-playing proofs. In: Vaudenay, S. (ed.) EUROCRYPT 2006. LNCS, vol. 4004, pp. 409–426. Springer, Heidelberg (2006). https://doi.org/10.1007/11761679_25
12. Blake-Wilson, S., Johnson, D., Menezes, A.: Key agreement protocols and their security analysis. In: Darnell, M. (ed.) Cryptography and Coding 1997. LNCS, vol. 1355, pp. 30–45. Springer, Heidelberg (1997). https://doi.org/10.1007/BFb0024447
13. Blanchet, B., Smyth, B., Cheval, V., Sylvestre, M.: ProVerif 2.01: automatic cryptographic protocol verifier, user manual and tutorial (2020)
14. Bloom, B.H.: Space/time trade-offs in hash coding with allowable errors. Commun. ACM 13(7), 422–426 (1970)
15. Brzuska, C., Jacobsen, H., Stebila, D.: Safely exporting keys from secure channels. In: Fischlin, M., Coron, J.-S. (eds.) EUROCRYPT 2016. LNCS, vol. 9665, pp. 670–698. Springer, Heidelberg (2016). https://doi.org/10.1007/978-3-662-49890-3_26
16. Canard, S., Coisel, I.: Data synchronization in privacy-preserving RFID authentication schemes. In: Radio Frequency Identification: Security and Privacy Issues - 4th International Workshop, RFIDSec 2008 (2008)
17. Canard, S., Coisel, I., Etrog, J., Girault, M.: Privacy-preserving RFID systems: model and constructions. Cryptology ePrint Archive, Report 2010/405 (2010)
18. Dimitriou, T.: Key evolving RFID systems. Ad Hoc Netw. 37(P2), 195–208 (2016)
19. Fan, B., Andersen, D.G., Kaminsky, M., Mitzenmacher, M.: Cuckoo filter: practically better than bloom. In: Seneviratne, A., Diot, C., Kurose, J., Chaintreau, A., Rizzo, L. (eds.) Proceedings of the 10th ACM International on Conference on emerging Networking Experiments and Technologies, CoNEXT 2014, pp. 75–88. ACM (2014)
20. Ferreira, L.: Privacy-preserving authenticated key exchange for constrained devices. Cryptology ePrint Archive, Report 2021/1647 (2021)
21. Fischlin, M., Günther, F.: Replay attacks on zero round-trip time: the case of the TLS 1.3 handshake candidates. In: 2017 IEEE European Symposium on Security and Privacy (EuroS&P), pp. 60–75. IEEE (2017)

22. Fouque, P.A., Onete, C., Richard, B.: Achieving better privacy for the 3GPP AKA protocol. PoPETs **2016**(4), 255–275 (2016)
23. Hedbom, H.: A survey on transparency tools for enhancing privacy. In: Matyáš, V., Fischer-Hübner, S., Cvrček, D., Švenda, P. (eds.) Privacy and Identity 2008. IAICT, vol. 298, pp. 67–82. Springer, Heidelberg (2009). https://doi.org/10.1007/978-3-642-03315-5_5
24. Hermans, J., Pashalidis, A., Vercauteren, F., Preneel, B.: A new RFID privacy model. In: Atluri, V., Diaz, C. (eds.) ESORICS 2011. LNCS, vol. 6879, pp. 568–587. Springer, Heidelberg (2011). https://doi.org/10.1007/978-3-642-23822-2_31
25. Huang, H.F., Yu, P.K., Liu, K.C.: A privacy and authentication protocol for mobile RFID system. In: International Symposium on Independent Computing - ISIC 2014 (2014)
26. Jager, T., Kohlar, F., Schäge, S., Schwenk, J.: On the security of TLS-DHE in the standard model. In: Safavi-Naini, R., Canetti, R. (eds.) CRYPTO 2012. LNCS, vol. 7417, pp. 273–293. Springer, Heidelberg (2012). https://doi.org/10.1007/978-3-642-32009-5_17
27. Juels, A.: RFID security and privacy: a research survey. IEEE J. Sel. A. Commun. **24**(2), 381–394 (2006)
28. Juels, A., Weis, S.A.: Defining strong privacy for RFID. In: Fifth Annual IEEE International Conference on Pervasive Computing and Communications Workshops (PerComW'07), pp. 342–347 (2007)
29. Malina, L., Srivastava, G., Dzurenda, P., Hajny, J., Ricci, S.: A privacy-enhancing framework for Internet of Things services. In: Liu, J.K., Huang, X. (eds.) NSS 2019. LNCS, vol. 11928, pp. 77–97. Springer, Cham (2019). https://doi.org/10.1007/978-3-030-36938-5_5
30. Ouafi, K., Phan, R.C.-W.: Traceable privacy of recent provably-secure RFID protocols. In: Bellovin, S.M., Gennaro, R., Keromytis, A., Yung, M. (eds.) ACNS 2008. LNCS, vol. 5037, pp. 479–489. Springer, Heidelberg (2008). https://doi.org/10.1007/978-3-540-68914-0_29
31. Ray, A.K., Bagwari, A.: Study of smart home communication protocol's and security privacy aspects. In: 7th International Conference on Communication Systems and Network Technologies (CSNT), pp. 240–245 (2017)
32. Rescorla, E.: The transport layer security (TLS) protocol version 1.3 (2018)
33. Schäge, S., Schwenk, J., Lauer, S.: Privacy-preserving authenticated key exchange and the case of IKEv2. In: Kiayias, A., Kohlweiss, M., Wallden, P., Zikas, V. (eds.) PKC 2020. LNCS, vol. 12111, pp. 567–596. Springer, Cham (2020). https://doi.org/10.1007/978-3-030-45388-6_20
34. Shoup, V.: Sequences of games: a tool for taming complexity in security proofs. Cryptology ePrint Archive, Report 2004/332 (2004)
35. Song, T., Li, R., Mei, B., Yu, J., Xing, X., Cheng, X.: A privacy preserving communication protocol for IoT applications in smart homes. IEEE Internet Things J. **4**(6), 1844–1852 (2017)
36. Vaudenay, S.: On privacy models for RFID. In: Kurosawa, K. (ed.) ASIACRYPT 2007. LNCS, vol. 4833, pp. 68–87. Springer, Heidelberg (2007). https://doi.org/10.1007/978-3-540-76900-2_5
37. You, I., Kwon, S., Choudhary, G., Sharma, V., Seo, J.T.: An enhanced LoRaWAN security protocol for privacy preservation in IoT with a case study on a smart factory-enabled parking system. Sensors **18**(6) (2018)
38. Ziegeldorf, J.H., Morchon, O.G., Wehrle, K.: Privacy in the Internet of Things: threats and challenges. Secur. Commun. Netw. **7**(12), 2728–2742 (2014)

Relations Between Privacy, Verifiability, Accountability and Coercion-Resistance in Voting Protocols

Alisa Pankova$^{(\boxtimes)}$ and Jan Willemson

Cybernetica AS, Narva mnt 20, 51009 Tartu, Estonia
{alisa.pankova,jan.willemson}@cyber.ee

Abstract. This paper studies quantitative relationships between privacy, verifiability, accountability, and coercion-resistance of voting protocols. We adapt existing definitions to make them better comparable with each other and determine which bounds a certain requirement on one property poses on some other property. It turns out that, in terms of proposed definitions, verifiability and accountability do not necessarily put constraints on privacy and coercion-resistance. However, the relations between these notions become more interesting in the context of particular attacks. Depending on the assumptions and the attacker's goal, voter coercion may benefit from a too weak as well as too strong verifiability.

Keywords: Security and privacy metrics · Privacy · Anonymity · Verifiability · Voting

1 Introduction

Voting is a complex process subject to a number of requirements such as eligibility, generality, uniformity, freedom of choice, tally integrity, accessibility, etc. [4,10,19,24]. In order to implement these requirements, a number of measures can be applied. For example, in order to express one's preference freely and withstand coercion, voting privately is often required. Tally integrity, on the other hand, can be achieved via various verification procedures.

Even though both the privacy and verifiability of voting are well-motivated, they are at least partially contradictory. Intuitively, when targeting full public verifiability without any trust assumptions, it seems necessary to also open all the personalised votes, but this causes privacy loss and potential coercion issues. Of course, this intuition is very informal and the situation becomes more complicated when we consider particular definitions for privacy and verifiability.

In order to study the connections between the two notions, the corresponding definitions must be given in comparable terms. However, it is far from being clear which terms are the best suited for this comparison. Working towards definitions that can be quantitatively compared to each other, and coming up with some comparison results, are the main aims of the current paper.

© Springer Nature Switzerland AG 2022
G. Ateniese and D. Venturi (Eds.): ACNS 2022, LNCS 13269, pp. 313–333, 2022.
https://doi.org/10.1007/978-3-031-09234-3_16

2 Related Work

There are many definitions of privacy in the context of voting, and an extensive survey discussing their advantages and drawbacks can be found in [3]. Relations between privacy and coercion-resistance for certain formal definitions of these notions have been shown in [9]. In this work, we are using definitions of privacy and coercion-resistance that originate from [16]. The benefit of these definitions is that they allow to measure the corresponding properties quantitatively. We instantiate our definitions of verifiability and accountability in the KTV framework [7,15,17]. This framework provides generic definitions for verifiability and accountability, and many other, more specific definitions of verifiability can be instantiated in this framework. Among other results, [16] shows the relation between privacy and coercion resistance, and [15] shows the relation between verifiability and accountability. In all these works, the agents (i.e. the voters and the authorities) of a voting protocol are modeled as some processes, typically specified in pi-calculus.

The KTV framework relies on the notion of end-to-end (E2E, global) verifiability, where voters and external observers are able to check whether the final result corresponds to the actual choices of honest voters. An alternative is to consider *universal* and *individual* verifiability as separate properties [23]. Previous research has established the following:

- There can be no unconditional privacy if there *is* universal verifiability [5].
- There can be no privacy if there *is no* individual verifiability [8].

In addition, [5] proves that universal verifiability and receipt-freeness cannot be achieved simultaneously unless private channels are available. A receipt is a witness which allows verifying in an unambiguous way the vote of a certain voter. Intuitively, the existence of a receipt may lead to voter coercion. Different types of realistic coercion methods, both legal and illegal, are discussed in [11].

It has been noted in [14] that universal and individual verifiability are not *sufficient* for E2E verifiability [12]. Indeed, by definition, universal verifiability only checks that the final result corresponds to the submitted votes, but it does not require that the votes are well-formed (e.g. that there are no negative votes). Also by [14], universal verifiability is not *necessary* for E2E verifiability.

In [8], it is shown how manipulation of even one vote may break privacy by observing the change that it caused in the tally. It is important that the attacker knows whose vote he is trying to change, so privacy requires *individual* verifiability. The proposed attack breaks a particular privacy definition, which says that the attacker should not be able to distinguish two protocol transcripts where some honest voters Alice and Bob have decided to swap their votes. The attacker may drop Alice's vote in both transcripts, and observe the difference in the tally of the two transcripts to determine what Alice's vote actually was. Such a privacy definition is very strong, and in practice, the attacker does not actually have access to two alternative voting transcripts. If there are many voters, dropping a single vote does not help much in actually guessing some other votes. Nevertheless, if the attacker has a strong prior knowledge of the other voters' choices, such an attack may allow learning the vote of the victim. In this work, we consider similar attacks w.r.t. the privacy definition of [16], which allows assessing the severity of the attack quantitatively.

An interesting approach to estimate voting systems in terms of *distributional differential privacy* has been proposed in [18]. While differential privacy is often achieved by adding noise to the system, which is unacceptable for voting, DDP is achieved by considering the distribution of votes as a source of randomness.

3 Preliminaries

3.1 Protocols

In this section, we present a generic framework for the definitions considered in this paper. The framework originates from [7,15,16] and is provided with some simplifications, excluding details that are not relevant for this paper.

First of all, we need the notion of a process that can perform internal computation and can communicate with other processes by sending messages via (external) input/output channels.

Definition 1 (Process). *A process is a set of probabilistic polynomial-time interactive Turing machines (also named programs) that are connected via named tapes (also called channels). We denote by $\Pi(I, O)$ the set of all processes with external input channels I and external output channels O. A process defines a family of probabilistic distributions over runs, indexed by the security parameter η. The concurrent composition of processes π and π' is denoted by $\pi\|\pi'$.*

A protocol is not a process by itself, but rather a collection of building blocks that will be used to define a process. As noted in [16], since the quantitative level of privacy, coercion-resistance, and verifiability of a voting protocol depends on several parameters such as the number of voters and the number of choices, we consider a protocol *instantiation* for which these parameters are fixed.

Definition 2 (Protocol instantiation). *A protocol instantiation is a tuple $P = (\Sigma, \mathsf{Ch}, \mathsf{In}, \mathsf{Out}, \{\Pi_a\}_{a \in \Sigma})$ where*

- *Σ is a set of protocol agents.*
- *Ch is a set of protocol channels.*
- *In and Out are functions from Σ to 2^{Ch} (i.e. assignments of input and output channels for each protocol agent) such that $\mathsf{In}(a) \cap \mathsf{In}(b) = \emptyset$ and $\mathsf{Out}(a) \cap \mathsf{Out}(b) = \emptyset$ for all $a, b \in \Sigma$, $a \neq b$.*
- *$\Pi_a \subseteq \Pi(\mathsf{In}(a), \mathsf{Out}(a))$ for $a \in \Sigma$ is the set of honest programs that can be run by the agent a.*

The randomness of agent behaviour, such as the probabilistic distribution of choices of an honest voter, is covered by Π_a. Particular probability distributions are not relevant for the results of this paper.

A protocol *instance* is the process that will actually be executed.

Definition 3 (Protocol instance, run). *Let* $P = (\Sigma, \mathsf{Ch}, \mathsf{In}, \mathsf{Out}, \{\Pi_{a_1}, \ldots, \Pi_{a_n}\})$ *for* $\Sigma = \{a_1, \ldots, a_n\}$ *be a protocol instantiation.*

- *An* instance *of* P *is a process* $\pi_P = \pi_{a_1} \| \ldots \| \pi_{a_n}$ *where* $\forall a \in \Sigma : \pi_a \in \Pi_a$,
- *A* run *of* P *is a run of some instance of* P.

Similarly to [7,16], we have not included processes of dishonest parties into the definitions of P and π_P. Instead, the dishonest parties are subsumed by a special *adversary* process.

Definition 4 (Adversary). *A protocol instance* π_P *is typically run in parallel with an adversary process* π_A *as a process* $\pi := \pi_P \| \pi_A$.

There is a bidirectional channel between the adversary A *and each protocol agent* $a_i \in \Sigma$. *The adversary can corrupt an agent* $a_i \in \Sigma$ *by sending a special message* corrupt. *Upon receiving such a message,* a_i *reveals its internal state to* A *and from then on is controlled by* A, *i.e. runs a dummy process* dum *which simply forwards all messages between* A *and the interface of* a_i *in* π_P. *Some agents (honest users and incorruptible authorities) ignore* corrupt *messages. Public information (such as the election result) is output to* A *even without corruption.*

At the end of a run, π_A *produces some output* y. *We use the notation* $\pi \overset{A}{\mapsto} y$ *to say that the output of* π_A *in a run of* π *is* y.

We say that an agent $a \in \Sigma$ is *honest* in a run of $\pi := \pi_A \| \pi_P$ if a has not been corrupted in this run, i.e. has not accepted the message corrupt. We use notation $\pi \vDash \mathsf{dis}(a)$ to denote an event (viewing π as a probabilistic distribution over runs) that the agent a has been corrupted.

The condition $\mathsf{dis}(a)$ can be viewed as a certain *property* of a protocol P. A property is a function that takes as input a run of a process π and returns a boolean value, telling whether that property is satisfied. For a fixed protocol instantiation P, a property can be viewed as a subset of runs of P.

Definition 5 (Protocol property). *A property* γ *of* P *defines a subset of the set of all runs of* P. *By* $\neg\gamma$ *we denote the complement of* γ, *i.e. the set of runs that do not satisfy* γ.

In order to reason about probability distributions of protocol runs taking into account the privacy parameter η, we will need the following definition.

Definition 6 (negligible, overwhelming, δ-bounded [7,15–17]). *A function* $f : \mathbb{N} \to [0,1]$ *is* negligible *if, for every* $c > 0$, *there exists* η_0 *such that* $f(\eta) \leq \frac{1}{\eta^c}$ *for all* $\eta > \eta_0$. *The function* f *is* overwhelming *if the function* $1 - f$ *is negligible. A function* f *is* δ-bounded *if, for every* $c > 0$, *there exists* η_0 *such that* $f(\eta) \leq \delta + \frac{1}{\eta^c}$ *for all* $\eta > \eta_0$.

The summary of process-related notation used in this paper is given in Table 1.

Table 1. Table of notations. For events, π is viewed as a distribution of runs.

Notation	Type	Meaning
$\pi^{(\eta)}$	process	A process π where all programs use the security parameter η.
$\pi_1 \| \pi_2$	process	Concurrent composition of processes π_1 and π_2.
$\pi(\vec{x})$	process	A process π running with inputs $\vec{x}$.
$\pi_{P \setminus \Sigma'}$	process	Concurrent composition of all subprocesses of π_P, excluding subprocesses π_a of agents $a \in \Sigma' \subseteq \Sigma$.
$\pi_{P \setminus \vec{i}}$	process	Same as $\pi_{P \setminus \Sigma'}$ for $\Sigma' = \{v_{i_1}, \ldots, v_{i_k}\}$, where $\vec{i} \subseteq \{1, \ldots, |V|\}$.
$\pi \mapsto (a : y)$	event	The final output of the agent $a \in \Sigma$ in the run of π is y.
$\pi \overset{A}{\mapsto} y$	event	The final output of the adversary π_A in the run of π is y.
$\pi \vDash \gamma$	event	A run of π satisfies a property γ.
$\mathsf{dis}(a)$	property	The agent $a \in \Sigma$ has been corrupted.
$\mathsf{voted}(i, c)$	property	The voter $v_i \in V$ cast a vote c.
$\mathcal{F}_{dis}$	set	The set of boolean formulae over literals $\mathsf{dis}(a)$ for $a \in \Sigma$.

3.2 Notation Related to Voting Protocols

We will use V to denote the set of voters, C the set of possible choices to select from by the voters (a choice does not necessarily represent a single candidate), and R the set of possible election results. Let $V = V_H \cup V_D$ for $V_H \cap V_D = \emptyset$, where V_H are honest voters, and V_D are dishonest voters (controlled by the adversary). Let $|V| = n = n_h + n_d$ be the total number of voters, where $n_h = |V_H|$ and $n_d = |V_D|$. We assume that the voters are somehow ordered, and the voter with index $i \in \{1, \ldots, n\}$ is denoted by v_i. The votes are combined using a result function $\rho : C^n \to R$ whose exact definition depends on the used voting rule.

3.3 Verifiability and Accountability

We start from a generic definition of verifiability from [7]. First of all, we need to state what exactly we are verifying. We assume a certain property γ (Definition 5) that we want to achieve in each protocol run, e.g. that each voter votes at most once, or that all ballots are well-formed. If γ is achieved, then everything is fine. If γ is not achieved, then we at least want to detect such a case.

The definitions of verifiability and accountability used in this paper will be based on the particular γ for quantitative verifiability proposed in [7]. First, let us define the protocol runs covered by γ. The idea of the following definition is that the final tally (i.e. the multiset of ballots before applying ρ) of a voting protocol may differ from the true tally in at most k votes.

Definition 7 (k-correctness of the protocol run [7]). *A protocol run r, where $c_1, \ldots, c_{n_h}$ are the choices of honest voters, is called k-correct if there exist valid choices $c'_1, \ldots, c'_{n_d}$ (representing possible choices of dishonest voters) and some choices $\tilde{c}_1, \ldots, \tilde{c}_n$, such that:*

- *an election result is published in r and it is equal to $\rho(\tilde{c}_1, \ldots, \tilde{c}_n)$;*
- *$d((c_1, \ldots, c_{n_h}, c'_1, \ldots, c'_{n_d}), (\tilde{c}_1, \ldots, \tilde{c}_n)) \leq k$;*

where the distance d is defined as $d(\vec{c}_0, \vec{c}_1) = \sum_{c \in C} |f_{count}(\vec{c}_0)[c] - f_{count}(\vec{c}_1)[c]|$, where C is the set of possible choices, and $f_{count} : C^n \to \mathbb{N}^C$ counts how many times each choice occurs in a vector.

The set of all k-correct runs of a protocol is denoted by γ_k.

In [7], verifiability w.r.t. a property γ is quantified by an upper bound on the probability that:

1. γ is not achieved; and
2. this fact remains undetected by a certain designated party J called the Judge.

The particular definition of γ can be very different, and various choices of γ provide different flavours of verifiability. In this paper, we instantiate the generic verifiability property of [7] on γ_k. This leads to the following definition.

Definition 8 ((k, δ)-verifiability). *Let π_P be an instance of a voting protocol P with the set of agents Σ. Let $\delta \in [0, 1]$ be the tolerance, $J \in \Sigma$ be the Judge, and γ_k be the set of runs of P such that, for all runs $r \in \gamma_k$, r is k-correct according to Definition 7. We say that π_P is (k, δ)-verifiable w.r.t. J if for all adversaries π_A and $\pi = \pi_P \| \pi_A$, the probability*

$$\Pr[(\pi^{(\eta)} \vDash \neg\gamma_k) \wedge (\pi^{(\eta)} \mapsto (J : accept))]$$

is δ-bounded as a function of η, and

$$\Pr[\pi^{(\eta)} \mapsto (J : reject)] = 0$$

if $\pi \nvDash \mathsf{dis}(a)$ for all $a \in \Sigma$.

We do not want the attacker to be able to abort the elections, so we need to specify what actually happens after the Judge rejects. As proposed in [15], in general verifiability is not enough, and in practice, we want *accountability*. This property assumes that, if the Judge rejects, he needs to come up with a certain *verdict*, which states which parties have potentially misbehaved. A verdict is a boolean formula over statements $\mathsf{dis}(a)$ for $a \in \Sigma$. Let $\mathcal{F}_{dis}$ be the set of all boolean formulae of such a form. It is possible that a verdict has a form of disjunction, e.g. $\mathsf{dis}(v_i) \vee \mathsf{dis}(a)$, for a voter v_i and a voting authority $a \in \Sigma$, which could mean that it is not clear whether a has dropped the message of the voter v_i, or the voter v_i has not sent a valid message. An *accountability constraint* of a protocol P consists of a property α that we want to be satisfied, and a set of possible verdicts $\phi_1, \ldots, \phi_\ell$ the Judge J must come out in the case when α is not satisfied.

Definition 9 (Accountability constraint [15]). *An accountability constraint of a protocol P is a tuple $(\alpha, \phi_1, \ldots, \phi_\ell)$ where α is a property of P (i.e. a subset of runs of P) and $\phi_1, \ldots, \phi_\ell \in \mathcal{F}_{dis}$.*

In this paper, we will be working with the property $\alpha := \gamma_k$ as in Definition 8. This means that we require accountability if the tally error is at least k, and we agree to accept smaller errors in the tally.

Definition 10 ((k, δ)-**accountability**). *Let π_P be an instance of a voting protocol P with the set of agents Σ, and let $J \in \Sigma$ be the Judge. Let $\Phi = (\gamma_k, \phi_1, \ldots, \phi_\ell)$ be an accountability constraint where γ_k is set of runs of P such that, for all runs $r \in \gamma_k$, r is k-correct according to Definition 7.*

We say that π_P is (k, δ)-accountable w.r.t. Φ and J if for all adversaries π_A and $\pi = \pi_P \| \pi_A$, the probability

$$\Pr[(\pi^{(\eta)} \models \neg \gamma_k) \wedge \neg \exists i (\pi^{(\eta)} \mapsto (J : \phi_i))]$$

is δ-bounded as a function of η, and, for all $i \in \{1, \ldots, n\}$,

$$\Pr[\pi^{(\eta)} \mapsto (J : \phi_i)] = 0$$

if $\pi \not\vdash \phi_i$.

Ideally, we would like to have *individual accountability* where every verdict blames a particular agent. However, as shown in [15], individual accountability is typically not achieved by voting protocols, and in [2] it was shown that resolving a dispute between two agents requires certain assumptions such as undeniable channels or trusted authorities. The problem is the communication between the voter and the voting system, where a voter may always say that "the system does not respond", and the system may always argue that "the voter has not attempted to communicate". In this work, we will consider general accountability.

3.4 Privacy and Coercion-Resistance

We take the definition of voter privacy from [16], defined as the inability to distinguish whether the voter $v \in V$ under observation made the choice $c \in C$ or $c' \in C$. The parameter k quantifies the number of voters under observation.

Definition 11 ((k, δ)-**privacy**). *Let π_P be an instance of a voting protocol P with n voters. Let $\delta \in [0, 1]$ be the tolerance. For all $i \in \{1, \ldots, n\}$, let π_{v_i} be the honest process of the voter v_i. Let $\vec{i} = \{i_1, \ldots, i_k\} \subseteq \{1, \ldots, n\}$ be the indices of honest voters under observation, and let $\vec{c}, \vec{c'} \in C^k$ be two assignments of choices to the voters $\vec{i}$. Denote $\pi_{\vec{i}, \vec{c}} := \pi_A \| \pi_{v_{i_1}}(c_1) \| \ldots \| \pi_{v_{i_k}}(c_k) \| \pi_{P \setminus \vec{i}}$ for an adversary process π_A. We say that π_P is (k, δ)-private if the difference of probabilities*

$$\left| \Pr[\pi_{\vec{i}, \vec{c}}^{(\eta)} \overset{A}{\mapsto} 1] - \Pr[\pi_{\vec{i}, \vec{c'}}^{(\eta)} \overset{A}{\mapsto} 1] \right|$$

is δ-bounded as a function of the security parameter η for all $\vec{i}$, $\vec{c}, \vec{c'}$ and for all adversaries π_A.

Differently from Definition 8, here a larger k means stronger privacy guarantees. The larger k is, the easier it is to distinguish between the two distributions.

Let us now consider the definition of coercion-resistance from [16]. A protocol is called coercion-resistant if the coerced voter, instead of running the dummy strategy dum (which simply lets all messages be chosen by the coercer), can run some counter-strategy $\pi_{\tilde{v}}$ such that:

1. by running this counter-strategy, the coerced voter achieves their own goal, e.g., votes for a specific candidate; and
2. the coercer is not able to distinguish whether the coerced voter followed coercer's instructions or tried to achieve their own goal (by running $\pi_{\tilde{v}}$).

Similar to the privacy definition, we extend the coercion-resistance of [16] to k voters, where we allow that up to k voters can be coerced simultaneously. Here the coerced voters may share a common goal γ. For example, if the goal of k coerced voters is to give at least $\ell < k$ votes to Alice, then it does not matter who exactly gave a vote to Alice, and only the total multiset of votes in the group matters.

Definition 12 ((k, δ)-**coercion-resistance**). *Let π_P be an instance of a voting protocol P with n voters. Let $\delta \in [0, 1]$ be the tolerance. Let $\vec{i} = \{i_1, \ldots, i_k\} \subseteq \{1, \ldots, n\}$ be the indices of honest voters under observation. Let γ be the joint goal of the voters $\vec{i}$. We say that π_P is (k, δ)-coercion-resistant w.r.t. γ, if the exists a joint strategy $\pi_{\tilde{v}}$ of coerced voters such that the following conditions are satisfied for any adversary π_A connected to $v_{i_1}, \ldots, v_{i_k}$ via the interface of* dum:

- $\Pr[(\pi_A \| \pi_{\tilde{v}} \| \pi_{P \setminus \vec{i}})^{(\eta)} \vDash \gamma]$ *is overwhelming as a function of η.*
- $\Pr[(\pi_A \| \mathsf{dum} \| \pi_{P \setminus \vec{i}})^{(\eta)} \overset{A}{\mapsto} 1] - \Pr[(\pi_A \| \pi_{\tilde{v}} \| \pi_{P \setminus \vec{i}})^{(\eta)} \overset{A}{\mapsto} 1]$ *is δ-bounded as a function of η.*

Note that the counter-strategy does not necessarily belong to the set of honest voter processes, and e.g. in order to give k votes to Alice, it is allowed that one of the coerced voters submits a malformed ballot with k votes, while the other $k - 1$ coerced voters abstain from voting.

4   Relations Between Definitions

In this paper, we study relations between the definitions of Sects. 3.3 and 3.4, all of which are quantitative. A summary of relations considered in this paper is depicted in Fig. 1. We note that it does not cover *all* possible relationships between definitions, and that each relation holds under certain assumptions. Theorem 1 and Theorem 2 are based on [16] and [15], and are slightly adapted to match the definitions of Sect. 3.4 which use an additional parameter k. An analogue of Theorem 1 has also been proven in [9], but it is based on non-quantitative definitions. Theorem 3 shows that privacy implies verifiability, and the main difference from [8] is again that we are considering quantitative definitions. Theorem 4 demonstrates incompatibility between verifiability and coercion-resistance. A similar theorem of [5] considers *unconditional* privacy instead of *quantitative* coercion-resistance. Another difference is that [5] considers *universal* verifiability, while we are considering *end-to-end* verifiability. Theorem 5 demonstrates incompatibility of privacy and individual accountability. We have applied some ideas of [2] which lists necessary conditions for fair dispute resolution in voting protocols, but does not discuss the relation between accountability and privacy directly. In this section, we formally state the corresponding theorems and provide proof sketches. The full proofs can be found in [20].

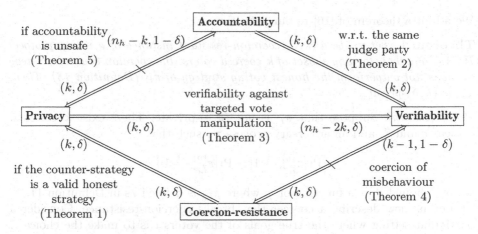

Fig. 1. Summary of the results of this paper (informal, simplified). Here n_h is the total number of honest voters, and k and δ are parameters. The graph depicts relations between these parameters for different properties of a voting protocol. A unidirectional arrow $\Rightarrow$ denotes implication, and a negated bidirectional arrow $\not\Leftrightarrow$ denotes properties that cannot be achieved simultaneously. The arrows can be composed, but one must be careful that the assumptions of corresponding theorems are all taken into account.

4.1   Coercion-Resistance and Privacy

Relationships of coercion-resistance and privacy have been studied in [9,16]. An interesting outcome of [16] is that, while intuitively coercion-resistance is a stronger notion than privacy, for some protocols it is possible that the level of privacy is *lower* than the level of coercion resistance. The reason is that the counter-strategy of a voter in Definition 12 does not necessarily belong to the set of valid strategies of honest voters, and may protect the vote in a better way than following the protocol honestly. However, coercion-resistance is nevertheless stronger than privacy if we assume that the counter-strategy does not *outperform* an honest strategy, defined as follows.

Definition 13 (non-outperforming counter-strategy [16]). *Let π_P be an instance of a voting protocol P. Let $\vec{i} = \{i_1, \ldots, i_k\}$ be the indices of honest voters under observation. Let $\pi_A^{\vec{c}}$ be a process that is only connected to the agents $v_{i_1}, \ldots, v_{i_k}$ using the interface of dum, and acts on their behalf according to an honest strategy $\pi_v(\vec{c'}) := \pi_{v_{i_1}}(c_1') \| \ldots \| \pi_{v_{i_k}}(c_k')$. Let $\pi_v(\vec{c}) := \pi_{v_1}(c_1) \| \ldots \| \pi_{v_k}(c_k)$. Let $\pi_{\tilde{v}}(\vec{c})$ be a joint counter-strategy of the honest voters $\vec{i}$ whose goal is to make choices $\vec{c} = \{c_1, \ldots, c_k\}$. We say that the counter-strategy $\pi_{\tilde{v}}$ does not outperform the honest voting strategy of π_P if, for any adversary process π_A that is not connected to $\pi_A^{\vec{c}}$, and any choices $\vec{c}$ and $\vec{c'}$,*

$$\Pr[(\pi_A \| \pi_A^{\vec{c'}} \| \pi_{\tilde{v}}(\vec{c}) \| \pi_{P \setminus \vec{i}})^{(\eta)} \overset{A}{\mapsto} 1] - \Pr[(\pi_A \| \pi_v(\vec{c}) \| \pi_{P \setminus \vec{i}})^{(\eta)} \overset{A}{\mapsto} 1]$$

is negligible as a function in the security parameter η.

We adapt a theorem of [16] to our definitions.

Theorem 1. *Let π_P be a (k, δ)-coercion-resistant instance of a voting protocol P. Assume that, for any subset of k coerced voters, the coercion counter-strategy $\pi_{\tilde{v}}$ does not outperform the honest voting strategy of π_P (Definition 13). Then, π_P is (k, δ)-private.*

Proof (Sketch). Suppose that π_P is not (k, δ)-private. There exist k voters $\vec{i}$, choices $\vec{c}$ and $\vec{c}'$, and an adversary process π_A such that

$$\left| \Pr[\pi_{\vec{i},\vec{c}}^{(\eta)} \overset{A}{\mapsto} 1] - \Pr[\pi_{\vec{i},\vec{c}'}^{(\eta)} \overset{A}{\mapsto} 1] \right|$$

is not δ-bounded as a function of η, where $\pi_{\vec{i},\vec{c}}$ is defined as in Definition 11.

Let us now describe a coercer that breaks coercion-resistance. Consider a particular setting where the true goals of the voters $\vec{i}$ is to make the choice $\vec{c}$. Let $\pi_A^{\vec{c}'}$ be a coercer that selects for the voters the input $\vec{c}'$, and otherwise acts as an honest voter would. By construction of $\pi_A^{\vec{c}'}$,

$$\Pr[(\pi_A \| \pi_A^{\vec{c}'} \| \mathsf{dum} \| \pi_{P \setminus \vec{i}})^{(\eta)} \overset{A}{\mapsto} 1] = \Pr[\pi_{\vec{i},\vec{c}'}^{(\eta)} \overset{A}{\mapsto} 1] \ .$$

Let $\pi_v = \pi_{v_{i_1}} \| \ldots \| \pi_{v_{i_k}}$. By definition of $\pi_{\vec{i},\vec{c}}$,

$$\Pr[(\pi_A \| \pi_v(\vec{c}) \| \pi_{P \setminus \vec{i}})^{(\eta)} \overset{A}{\mapsto} 1] = \Pr[\pi_{\vec{i},\vec{c}}^{(\eta)} \overset{A}{\mapsto} 1] \ .$$

Since $\pi_{\tilde{v}}$ does not outperform $\pi_v = \pi_{v_{i_1}} \| \ldots \| \pi_{v_{i_k}}$, and there are no direct connections between π_A and $\pi_A^{\vec{c}}$,

$$\Pr[(\pi_A \| \pi_v(\vec{c}) \| \pi_{P \setminus \vec{i}})^{(\eta)} \overset{A}{\mapsto} 1] - \Pr[(\pi_A \| \pi_A^{\vec{c}} \| \pi_{\tilde{v}}(\vec{c}) \| \pi_{P \setminus \vec{i}})^{(\eta)} \overset{A}{\mapsto} 1]$$

is negligible as a function of η. We get that

$$\Pr[(\pi_A \| \pi_A^{\vec{c}'} \| \mathsf{dum} \| \pi_{P \setminus \vec{i}})^{(\eta)} \overset{A}{\mapsto} 1] - \Pr[(\pi_A \| \pi_A^{\vec{c}} \| \pi_{\tilde{v}}(\vec{c}) \| \pi_{P \setminus \vec{i}})^{(\eta)} \overset{A'}{\mapsto} 1]$$

is not δ-bounded as a function of η. Let $\pi_{A'} := \pi_A \| \pi_A^{\vec{c}}$ be an adversary that outputs the final output of π_A. Such $\pi_{A'}$ breaks (k, δ)-coercion-resistance. Since π_A does not interact with $\vec{i}$ (as they are honest), and $\pi_{A'}^{\vec{c}}$ interacts only with $\vec{i}$ using interface of dum, $\pi_{A'}$ satisfies Definition 12.   □

4.2   Accountability and Verifiability

It has been proven in [15] that verifiability can be treated as a special case of accountability. We adapt a theorem of [15] to our definitions.

Theorem 2. *Let an instance π_P of a voting protocol P be (k, δ)-accountable w.r.t. a Judge J and a property $\Phi = (\gamma_k, \phi_1, \ldots, \phi_\ell)$ where $\forall i : \phi_i \in \mathcal{F}_{dis}$. Then, π_P is (k, δ)-verifiable w.r.t. a Judge J' who is defined similarly to J, accepting those runs where J does not output any verdict ϕ_i, and rejecting all the other runs.*

Proof (Sketch). Let $\pi := \pi_A \| \pi_P$. Suppose that π_P is not (k, δ)-verifiable w.r.t. J. The verifiability may fail due to one of the following reasons:

1. There is a run where J' outputs *reject*, but all parties are honest. Then, there is a run where J outputs a verdict ϕ_i while all parties are honest. This violates accountability requirement that $\Pr[\pi^{(\eta)} \mapsto (J : \phi_i)] = 0$ if $\pi \not\vdash \phi_i$.
2. Suppose that there exists an adversary process π_A such that

$$\Pr[(\pi^{(\eta)} \vDash \neg\gamma_k) \wedge (\pi^{(\eta)} \mapsto (J' : accept))]$$

is not δ-bounded as a function of η.

Let us show that π_A breaks accountability as well. By assumption, J' outputs *reject* iff J outputs a verdict ϕ_i. Hence, the event $\pi^{(\eta)} \mapsto (J' : accept)$ is as likely as the event $\neg\exists i(\pi^{(\eta)} \mapsto (J : \phi_i))$, hence,

$$\Pr[(\pi^{(\eta)} \vDash \neg\gamma_k) \wedge \neg\exists i(\pi^{(\eta)} \mapsto (J : \phi_i))]$$

is also not δ-bounded as a function of η.   □

4.3   Privacy and Verifiability

Without additional assumptions, the verifiability of Definition 8 is neither essential for the privacy formalized in Definition 11, nor contradicts it. It is not *essential* since e.g. if the adversary violates the property γ_k by directly interacting with the final tally, when the ballots are not linked to the identities of voters anymore, it will not help in breaking privacy. It does not *contradict* privacy e.g. if the Judge's verdict only depends on inputs of dishonest parties.

Considered Attacks. The importance of verifiability for privacy has been demonstrated in [8]. The necessity of avoiding duplicate ballots in order to preserve privacy is mentioned in [3]. While our results and definitions are formally different, the considered actual attacks are of similar nature, and are related to manipulating the ballots which the attacker can link to identities of particular voters. We consider verifiability against particular types of attacks that could be applied to violate the goal γ_k. Let us briefly summarize our results.

- *Add ballots:* suppose that the attacker is capable of ballot stuffing.
  - If the added ballots *do* depend on the votes of honest voters (e.g. some ballot of an honest voter is replayed), then the attack reduces the privacy of voters whose ballots are replayed.
  - If the added ballots *do not* depend on the votes of honest voters (e.g. are chosen by the attacker or are sampled randomly), then the attack does not directly help in breaking privacy.
- *Drop ballots:* suppose that the attacker is capable of ballot dropping.
  - If the attacker drops ballots of some *honest* voters, it reduces the privacy of the remaining voters who are still counted.

- If the attacker drops ballots of some *dishonest* voters, it does not directly help in breaking privacy.
- *Substitute ballots:* This attack can be viewed as a combination of ballot adding and dropping. The privacy can be reduced in the following two cases:
  - The inserted ballot *does* depend on the votes of honest voters.
  - The replaced ballot *does not* depend on the votes of honest voters.

It is important that the attacker knows whether ballot manipulation has succeeded or not. We need the notion of a *detectable* protocol property.

Definition 14 (detectable property). *Let* $\pi := \pi_A \| \pi_P$ *be a voting protocol instance* π_P *running in parallel with an adversary* π_A. *Let* γ *be a property of* π. *We say that* γ *is detectable in* π *if*

$$\Pr[(\pi_O \| \pi)^{(\eta)} \overset{O}{\mapsto} 1 \mid \gamma] - \Pr[(\pi_O \| \pi)^{(\eta)} \overset{O}{\mapsto} 1 \mid \neg\gamma] = 1$$

for a passive observer process π_O *who has access to the internal state of* π_A, *but does not directly interact with* π_P.

We could quantify the probability in Definition 14 as δ, introducing an extra parameter into relations between privacy and verifiability.

Considered Voting Rules. Many voting systems reveal not just the voting result, but also the full tally, which shows the exact number of votes per candidate. Revealing such information can lead to high privacy leakage. For that reason, some voting systems like Ordinos [13] ensure that only the final result is revealed, e.g. the identity of the winner, and it has been shown in [13] that doing this may reduce privacy leakage significantly. In this work, we want to quantify attacks on privacy that are possible even if only the final result is revealed.

The main idea is that, even if we do not know the particular distribution of votes and cannot compute privacy parameter δ precisely, we can apply the attack on verifiability to change the number of votes that are "known in advance" to the attacker and thus switch between (k, δ_k) and $(k', \delta_{k'})$-privacy. This can be useful for certain kinds of voting rules, satisfying the following definition.

Definition 15 (majority-determined voting rule). *Let* n *be the total number of voters. A voting rule is called* majority-determined *if it is sufficient to cast* $n' = \lfloor \frac{n}{2} \rfloor + 1$ *identical votes to determine the election outcome.*

While Definition 15 is trivially satisfied in the case where the election result is a counting histogram of votes, it actually holds for a greater variety of widely used voting rules. The following descriptions of voting rules are taken from [6].

- **Plurality rule.** Each voter votes for one favorite candidate, and the winner is the candidate with the most votes.
- **Borda rule.** Each voter orders candidates by preference and each candidate j gets $m - i$ points in each vote, where i is the rank of j in the vote, and m is the number of candidates; the winner is the candidate with the highest total points.

More examples of suitable rules satisfying Definition 15 can be found in [20]. While these voting rules guarantee success for an attacker who controls a majority of votes, in practice it is unlikely that all honest voters prefer the same candidate, and the attacker may be successful even controlling way less than half of the votes. This is closely related to the notion of *manipulability* of voting. The authors of [21] have estimated asymptotic bounds for the fraction of voters that are being manipulated to make switching the election outcome hard in the average case. It would be interesting to consider such bounds in future research.

There are some standard voting rules for which Definition 15 does not hold. E.g. in a *veto rule*, each voter gives a score of 0 to one least favorite candidate, and 1 to every other candidate, and the winner is the candidate with the most votes. Here it is possible that all voters that are not controlled by the attacker will veto the particular candidate chosen by the attacker, but the attacker does not have enough votes to veto each of the other candidates.

Results. We now show how privacy implies certain types of *targeted* attacks on votes, i.e. where the attacker is able to link manipulated ballots to the identities of corresponding voters who cast these ballots. We will also assume that the attacker *knows* whether the attack has succeeded or not. The main idea is that, for majority-determined voting rules, if $k > n_h/2$, the attacker can always win in the distinguishability game of Definition 11 by taking choices $\vec{c}$ and $\vec{c'}$ that produce different election outcomes. We cannot get a better result without taking into account a particular vote distribution, since it is possible that there is a candidate whom the remaining $n_h - k$ voters will choose with overwhelming probability, resulting in a constant election result r that does not say anything about the victim's choice.

Proposition 1. *Let π_P be an instance of a voting protocol P that uses a majority-determined voting rule, with n_h honest voters V_H. If π_P is (k, δ)-private w.r.t. a subset of voters $V_{pr} \subseteq V_H$ of size k, then π_P is $(n_h - 2k, \delta)$-verifiable against an attacker π_A who has access to $\mathsf{Out}(J)$ who is only able to drop votes of $V_H \setminus V_{pr}$ from the tally, whose success does not depend on the choices of V_H, and the property γ_{n_h-2k} is detectable in $\pi_A \| \pi_P$.*

Proof (Sketch). Regardless of the prior distribution of votes, if a protocol uses a majority-determined voting rule, if $k > n_h/2$, the attacker may always choose votes $c_1, \ldots, c_k$ and $c'_1, \ldots, c'_k$ that determine some election results $r \neq r'$. If $k \leq n_h/2$, the attacker can use the attack on verifiability to drop some of the $n_h - k$ ballots of voters that are not under observation, until a majority of ballots belongs to voters under observation. Suppose that the attacker has managed to drop ℓ ballots. He will control k out of $n - \ell$ ballots. In order to control a majority, he needs $k > (n_h - \ell)/2$, which means $\ell > n_h - 2k$ dropped ballots. If dropping ℓ ballots has failed, the attacker will detect it and output a constant bit, which will be the same regardless of the choices of V_{pr}. Since the protocol is by assumption (k, δ)-private, the attacker should not be able to drop these ℓ ballots with probability larger than δ. $\square$

Proposition 2. *Let π_P be an instance of a voting protocol P that uses a majority-determined voting rule, with n_h honest voters V_H. If π_P is (k, δ)-private w.r.t. a subset of voters $V_{pr} \subseteq V_H$, then P is $(n_h - 2k, \delta)$-verifiable against an attacker π_A who has access to $\mathsf{Out}(J)$, who is only able to duplicate votes of V_{pr} in the tally, whose success does not depend on the choices of V_H, and the property γ_{n_h-2k} is detectable in $\pi_A \| \pi_P$.*

Proof (Sketch). Regardless of the prior distribution of votes, if a protocol uses a majority-determined voting rule, if $k > n_h/2$, the attacker may always choose votes $c_1, \ldots, c_k$ and $c'_1, \ldots, c'_k$ that determine some election results $r \neq r'$. If $k \leq n_h/2$, the attacker can use the attack on verifiability to duplicate some of the k ballots of voters under observation, until a majority of ballots belongs to voters under observation. Suppose that the attacker has managed to produce ℓ duplicates. He will control $k + \ell$ out of $n_h + \ell$ ballots. In order to control a majority, he needs $k + \ell > (n_h + \ell)/2$, which is $\ell > n_h - 2k$ additional ballots. Since the protocol is by assumption (k, δ)-private, the attacker should not be able to get these additional ℓ ballots with probability larger than δ. □

Propositions 1 and 2 put the same constraint on verifiability, which does not depend on whether the attacker adds or drops the votes. This leads to the following theorem, which is an immediate consequence of the propositions above.

Theorem 3. *Let π_P be an instance of a voting protocol P that uses a majority-determined voting rule, with n_h honest voters V_H. If π_P is (k, δ)-private w.r.t. a subset of voters $V_{pr} \subseteq V_H$, then π_P is $(n_h - 2k, \delta)$-verifiable against an attacker π_A capable of duplicating votes of V_{pr} and dropping votes of $V_H \setminus V_{pr}$, assuming that success of the attack does not depend on the particular choices of the voters V_H, and the property γ_{n_h-2k} is detectable in $\pi_A \| \pi_P$.*

The attacks of Theorem 3 are mostly oriented to small-scale elections with few voters. Suppose that the attacker is interested in a vote of a particular single voter, i.e. $k = 1$. Let there be n_h honest voters for an even n_h. The attacker attempts to drop $\frac{n_h}{2}$ ballots belonging to the remaining $n_h - 1$ voters, and introduces $\frac{n_h}{2}$ copies of the ballot of the vote under observation instead. There are still n_h votes in the final tally, but $\frac{n_h}{2} + 1$ of them are copies of the ballot under observation, so the winner of the election is the main preference of the victim. It is interesting that when the attacker combines vote adding and dropping, in the end, the protocol run may still satisfy γ_{n_h-2k} if the dropped votes occasionally turn out to be the same as the added votes. Such an attack is formally treated as unsuccessful, and in practice, we may get tighter bounds if we measure "success of substituting k votes" instead of "violating γ_{k-1}".

Such types of attack are more interesting in terms of coercion. Suppose that the attacker already controls n_d dishonest voters, and in addition, is able to manipulate ℓ ballots with a high probability of success. If $n_d + \ell < \frac{n}{2}$, then it is not enough to switch the election result and make a certain candidate j the winner. The attacker tries to convince $k = (n_h - \ell)/2$ voters to vote for j. If in the end, j is not the winner, the attacker learns that at least some voters of the coerced group have not obeyed, and may punish them.

4.4   Verifiability and Coercion-Resistance

Suppose that the attacker is trying to convince a subset of k voters to misbehave. It can be viewed as a variant of coercing abstention from voting (since bad votes are not supposed to be counted), or even an attempt to halt the elections, in the case when Judge's rejection does not allow proceeding with publishing the result. Such kind of attacks, called *fault attacks*, have been considered in [9], and the attacker can apply them to test the loyalty of a voter (or a subset of voters) in a probabilistic way. The following definition allows the attacker to break k-correctness by taking control of a certain number of dishonest voters.

Definition 16 (ballot-corruptible protocol). *An instance π_P of a voting protocol P is called ballot-corruptible if, for all $k \in \mathbb{N}$, there exists a subset of voters $V' := \{v_{i1}, \ldots, v_{i\ell}\}$ of size $\ell \leq k+1$, and a joint strategy* bad *for these ℓ voters, such that*

$$\Pr[(\pi_{P \backslash V'} \| \mathsf{bad})^{(\eta)} \vDash \neg \gamma_k] = 1$$

where γ_k is defined as in Definition 7.

We could quantify the probability in Definition 16 as δ, introducing an extra parameter into relations between coercion-resistance and verifiability.

Definition 16 allows the attacker to interact with the protocol in such a way that γ_k will actually be violated and the judging procedure triggered. In practice, the bad voting strategy may correspond to submitting corrupted paper ballots, or malformed digital ballots that e.g. encode several votes in a single ballot. In practice, $\ell \leq k+1$ voters can be sufficient to break γ_k-correctness, e.g. by submitting multiple votes in a single corrupted ballot.

The following theorem estimates a relation between verifiability and coercion-resistance for ballot-corruptible protocols. The idea is that, even if the corrupted final result is not published, the fact that the cheating was detected may already leak something. Since the Judge's decision cannot leak more than a single bit, the attacker needs to encode information into that bit in such a way that it tells whether the inputs of the victim voter(s) are $\vec{c}$ or $\vec{c'}$.

Theorem 4. *Let π_P be an instance of ballot-corruptible voting protocol P with n_h honest voters. Then the following statements cannot be true at once:*

- π_P *is (k, δ)-coercion-resistant (Definition 12) against an attacker who has access to $\mathsf{Out}(J)$;*
- *The instance $\pi_{P'}$ of P with $n_h - k$ honest voters is $(k-1, 1-\delta)$-verifiable (Definition 8).*

Proof (Sketch). Let V' be the k voters of π_P to be coerced. Consider the protocol instance $\pi_{P'}$ where V' are treated as corrupted. Let $\pi_{A'}$ be an adversary who sends corrupt message to V' and follows the strategy bad on their behalf, but does not corrupt any other agents. Let π_A be an adversary that behaves similarly to $\pi_{A'}$, except that it does not send corrupt message to V', but is just connected to them via the interface of dum. Such π_A satisfies Definition 12. The processes $\pi_{A'} \| \pi_{P'}$ and $\pi_A \| \mathsf{dum} \| \pi_{P \backslash V'}$ differ only in the interface between the protocol and the adversary, but the output of J is the same in these processes.

- If the voters V' obey the attacker in $\pi_A \| \pi_P$, they follow the strategy dum, and since P is ballot-corruptible, the goal γ_{k-1} will be violated. Since $\pi_{P'}$ is $(k-1, 1-\delta)$-verifiable, the Judge will *accept* with probability at most $1-\delta$ in $\pi_{A'} \| \pi_{P'}$, and hence also in $\pi_A \| \mathsf{dum} \| \pi_{P \setminus V'}$.
- While the definition of coercion-resistance does not prohibit that the counter-strategy may violate γ_{k-1}, it is reasonable to assume that the goal of the coerced voters is that the elections end up successfully and the Judge will *accept*. Hence, if the voters V' do not obey the attacker, the Judge will *accept* with a probability 1.

The difference between the probabilities of Judge accepting is at least δ. The attacker outputs 1 iff the Judge accepts, breaking (k, δ)-coercion-resistance. □

In practice, Theorem 4 could be applied by an attacker who coerces k voters to put corrupted ballots into the ballot box. The attacker then looks into the ballot box and sees whether it contains at least k corrupted ballots. In the real world, however, it is not excluded that the "bad" vote can occasionally be cast as well by voters who are not controlled by the attacker, even though it is not intended behaviour. Such voters add certain randomness to the experiment.

If the voting protocol is accountable, the coerced voters might not want that the Judge would accuse them of misbehaviour, so they might not agree to follow the strategy bad unless the attacker threatens them by a more severe punishment than the Judge. However, accountability may in turn provide other means of coercion, as discussed in the following section.

4.5 Privacy and Accountability

If the Judge's verdict is independent of the choices of honest participants, it will not harm the privacy of an honest voter in any way. However, as shown in [2], if we want to get a stronger kind of accountability (the *individual accountability*) that allows pinpointing the cheater directly, we may need stronger assumptions. In order to resolve all possible disputes between a voter v_i and a non-voter agent a (such as a voting machine), we need to either assume a semi-trusted a (who processes all received ballots honestly), or the existence of reliable and/or undeniable channels between the voter and the machine, such as voting authorities who actually saw that the voter indeed has interacted with the machine. While an undeniable channel does not leak the exact choice of a voter, it would still at least leak the fact that a voter has voted. Let us formally define an accountability property Φ that does not threaten the privacy of honest voters.

Definition 17 (safe-evidence accountability property). *Let P be a voting protocol instantiation. Let $\delta \in [0, 1]$ be the tolerance. Let $\pi_{\vec{i}, \vec{c}}$ and $\pi_{\vec{i}, \vec{c}'}$ be defined as in Definition 11. We say that the accountability property $\Phi = (\alpha, \phi_1, \dots, \phi_\ell)$ of P w.r.t. a Judge $J \in \Sigma$ is (k, δ)-safe-evidence if*

$$\left| \Pr[\pi_{\vec{i}, \vec{c}}^{(\eta)} \overset{A}{\mapsto} 1 \mid \exists j : \ \pi \mapsto (J : \phi_j)] - \Pr[\pi_{\vec{i}, \vec{c}'}^{(\eta)} \overset{A}{\mapsto} 1 \mid \exists j : \ \pi \mapsto (J : \phi_j)] \right|$$

is δ-bounded as a function of the security parameter η for all indices of honest voters $\vec{i}$, choices $\vec{c}, \vec{c}'$ and for all adversary processes π_A that have access to the channels $\ln(J)$.

Definition 17 says that the evidence for a verdict, based on all inputs that J has received through the channels $\ln(J)$, does not depend (much) on the choices of honest voters. The condition $\exists i : \pi \mapsto (J : \phi_i)$ ensures that we only consider protocol runs where the Judge has actually made a verdict, which excludes possible attacks that come due to failure of accountability, e.g. leakage via the final result. The definition allows an arbitrary property α.

In order to break privacy, the attacker should first of all be able to violate the condition α, so that the judging procedure would be triggered. Then, in order that the Judge would learn anything interesting, the evidence should depend on the vote of an honest voter under observation, at least telling whether the voter has voted or abstained from voting. The following definition characterizes protocols for which accountability has a direct impact on privacy.

Definition 18 (unsafe accountability property). *Let π_P be an instance of a voting protocol P, Σ the agents of P, $\Phi = (\gamma_k, \phi_1, \ldots, \phi_\ell)$ an accountability property, and $J \in \Sigma$ the Judge. The property Φ is called unsafe in π_P w.r.t J if there exists an adversary π_A such that:*

1. $\Pr[(\pi_P \| \pi_A)^{(\eta)} \vDash \neg\gamma_k] = 1$.
2. There is a choice $c \in C$ such that, in every run r of π satisfying $\exists i : (J : \phi_i)$, there is a subset $\vec{i}_r$ of $k+1$ honest voters (which can be different in each run) such that $(\pi_P \| \pi_A)^{(\eta)}$ outputs a boolean value $\mathsf{voted}(i, c)$ for all $i \in \vec{i}_r$ to $\ln(J)$.

Intuitively, the second point of Definition 18 says that, whenever the Judge makes a verdict, he learns something about a subset of voters somehow involved in a dispute. The parameter k could be e.g. the minimal number of complaints required to start the dispute resolution procedure. A particular example of an unsafe accountability property would be individual accountability that relies on undeniable channels, assuming that the Judge makes the verdict based on access to these channels. In that case, c would be an abstention vote. Let us show how Definition 18. is related to Definition 17.

Proposition 3. *Let π_P be an instance of a voting protocol P with n_h honest voters. Let Σ be the agents of P, $\Phi = (\gamma_{k'}, \phi_1, \ldots, \phi_\ell)$ an accountability property, and $J \in \Sigma$ the Judge. Let Φ be unsafe in π_P w.r.t J. Then, Φ is not (k, δ)-safe-evidence w.r.t. J and π_A for any $\delta < 1 - \prod_{j=0}^{k'} \left(1 - \frac{k}{n_h - j}\right)$ and any η.*

Proof (Sketch). Let π_A be an adversary that satisfies Definition 18. Consider the runs of $(\pi_P \| \pi_A)^{(\eta)}$ that satisfy $\exists i : (J : \phi_i)$. In each such run r, there is a subset $\vec{i}_r$ of k' voters such that messages $\mathsf{voted}(i, c)$ are sent to a channel of $\ln(J)$ for all $i \in \vec{i}_r$. The idea is that the same attacker π_A chooses $\vec{c} = (c, \ldots, c)$ and $\vec{c}' = (c', \ldots, c')$ for $c \neq c'$ to break the safe-evidence property. However, the problems is that $\vec{i}_r$ can be different in each run, but we need a single $\vec{i}$ for all runs. The simplest solution would be to take $k' = n_h - k$, when any subset of size $k' + 1$ always covers at least one victim. However, we can do better since the adversary may choose the $\vec{i}$ itself. In the worst case (from attacker perspective), no subset of voters is preferable, and all voters are equally likely to be exposed to $\ln(J)$. The probability that all $k' + 1$ leaked votes are "not interesting" is $\binom{n_h-k}{k'+1}/\binom{n_h}{k'+1}$, which equals $\prod_{j=0}^{k'} \frac{n_h-k-j}{n_h-j} = \prod_{j=0}^{k'} \left(1 - \frac{k}{n_h-j}\right)$. $\square$

The following theorem estimates the relation between privacy and accountability for an unsafe accountability property.

Theorem 5. *Let π_P be an instance of a voting protocol P with n_h honest voters. Let Σ be the agents of P. Let $\Phi = (\gamma_k, \phi_1, \ldots, \phi_\ell)$ and $J \in \Sigma$ be such that Φ is unsafe in π_P w.r.t. J. Then the following statements cannot be true at once:*

- *π_P is (k, δ)-private (Definition 11);*
- *π_P is $\left(k', 1 - \delta/\left(1 - \prod_{j=0}^{k'}\left(1 - \frac{k}{n_h-j}\right)\right)\right)$-accountable w.r.t. Φ, J (Definition 10).*

Proof (Sketch). Assume that π_P is (k, δ_{acc})-accountable. The condition $\exists i : \pi \mapsto (J : \phi_i) \vee \pi \vDash \gamma_{k'}$ is satisfied with probability at least $1 - \delta_{acc}$. Since Φ is by assumption unsafe in π_P w.r.t. J, there exists an adversary π_A such that $\Pr[(\pi_A\|\pi_P)^{(n)} \vDash \neg\gamma_{k'}] = 1$, so $\exists i : \pi \mapsto (J : \phi_i)$ is satisfied with probability at least $1 - \delta_{acc}$. Assume that Φ is (k, δ_{ev})-safe-evidence w.r.t. J and π_A. The success of π_A in distinguishing whether the voters $\vec{i}$ have voted or not equals $\delta_{ev} \cdot (1 - \delta_{acc})$. Assuming that the protocol is (k, δ_{pr})-private, we have $\delta_{ev} \cdot (1 - \delta_{acc}) < \delta_{pr}$, so $\delta_{ev} < \delta_{pr}/(1 - \delta_{acc})$. Now, since Φ is unsafe w.r.t. J, by Proposition 3, it can only be (k, δ_{ev})-safe-evidence w.r.t. J for $\delta_{ev} \geq 1 - \prod_{j=0}^{k'}\left(1 - \frac{k}{n_h-j}\right)$, which gives us $\delta_{acc} > 1 - \delta_{pr}/\left(1 - \prod_{j=0}^{k'}\left(1 - \frac{k}{n_h-j}\right)\right)$, and any smaller δ_{acc} is not suitable. $\square$

In practice, Theorem 5 could be applied by an attacker who takes control over a voting machine that issues receipts for later verification, such as Wombat [1], ThreeBallot, and VAV [22]. The idea is that the corrupted machine will nicely output to all voters appropriate receipts. However, it excludes at least k ballots when displaying information on the bulletin board. With probability at most δ_{acc}, the attack will not be detected, and the Judge does not do anything. Otherwise, there are several outcomes possible.

- The cheating is detected directly by auditors.
- Sufficiently many voters complain after looking at the bulletin board.

In the first case, the Judge does not learn anything interesting from the evidence. In the second case, a subset of voters whose ballots have been dropped come to complain, and the attacker who has corrupted the voting machine can now match the complainer's identity with an affected ballot. If the ballots are not encrypted, the attacker will not only detect that the voter has voted, but also match the corrupted ballot to the complainer's identity and learn the vote.

5   Conclusions and Future Work

In this paper, we have proposed a selection of quantitative definitions of privacy, verifiability, coercion-resistance, and accountability, which are adapted versions of the definitions of the KTV framework. We have shown how these metrics are related to each other, exploring some generic relations that do not depend on the actual distribution of votes. In practice, the quantitative degree of privacy of voting protocols strongly depends on the way in which the voters make their choices. As the next step, it will be natural to analyse particular distributions.

Assuming that the votes are independent, the privacy definition that we have considered in this paper can be viewed as a variant of distributional differential privacy (DDP), albeit DDP estimates the ratio of probabilities instead of the difference. Related work [18] has estimated DDP bounds for various voting rules, and we could study how their definitions of privacy can be combined with verifiability and accountability of the KTV framework.

Acknowledgements. The authors are grateful to the anonymous reviewers for their valuable comments. The paper has been supported by the Estonian Research Council under the grant number PRG920.

References

1. Wombat voting system (2011). http://www.wombat-voting.com/
2. Basin, D.A., Radomirovic, S., Schmid, L.: Dispute resolution in voting. In: 33rd IEEE Computer Security Foundations Symposium, CSF 2020. pp. 1–16. IEEE (2020). https://doi.org/10.1109/CSF49147.2020.00009
3. Bernhard, D., Cortier, V., Galindo, D., Pereira, O., Warinschi, B.: SoK: a comprehensive analysis of game-based ballot privacy definitions. In: 2015 IEEE Symposium on Security and Privacy, SP 2015, pp. 499–516. IEEE Computer Society (2015). https://doi.org/10.1109/SP.2015.37
4. Cetinkaya, O.: Analysis of security requirements for cryptographic voting protocols (extended abstract). In: Proceedings ARES 2008, pp. 1451–1456. IEEE Computer Society (2008)
5. Chevallier-Mames, B., Fouque, P.-A., Pointcheval, D., Stern, J., Traoré, J.: On some incompatible properties of voting schemes. In: Chaum, D., et al. (eds.) Towards Trustworthy Elections. LNCS, vol. 6000, pp. 191–199. Springer, Heidelberg (2010). https://doi.org/10.1007/978-3-642-12980-3_11
6. Conitzer, V., Sandholm, T.: Nonexistence of voting rules that are usually hard to manipulate. In: Proceedings of the 21st National Conference on Artificial Intelligence and the 18th Innovative Applications of Artificial Intelligence Conference, pp. 627–634 (2006). http://www.aaai.org/Library/AAAI/2006/aaai06-100.php
7. Cortier, V., Galindo, D., Küsters, R., Müller, J., Truderung, T.: SoK: verifiability notions for e-voting protocols. In: Proceedings of Symposium on Security and Privacy, SP 2016, pp. 779–798. IEEE Computer Society (2016)
8. Cortier, V., Lallemand, J.: Voting: you can't have privacy without individual verifiability. In: Proceedings of ACM CCS 2018, pp. 53–66. ACM (2018)

9. Delaune, S., Kremer, S., Ryan, M.: Coercion-resistance and receipt-freeness in electronic voting. In: 19th IEEE Computer Security Foundations Workshop, (CSFW-19 2006), pp. 28–42. IEEE Computer Society (2006). https://doi.org/10.1109/CSFW.2006.8

10. Heiberg, S., Willemson, J.: Modeling threats of a voting method. In: Design, Development, and Use of Secure Electronic Voting Systems, pp. 128–148. IGI Global (2014)

11. Jonker, H., Pieters, W.: Anonymity in voting revisited. In: Chaum, D., et al. (eds.) Towards Trustworthy Elections. LNCS, vol. 6000, pp. 216–230. Springer, Heidelberg (2010). https://doi.org/10.1007/978-3-642-12980-3_13

12. Kiayias, A., Zacharias, T., Zhang, B.: End-to-end verifiable elections in the standard model. In: Oswald, E., Fischlin, M. (eds.) EUROCRYPT 2015. LNCS, vol. 9057, pp. 468–498. Springer, Heidelberg (2015). https://doi.org/10.1007/978-3-662-46803-6_16

13. Küsters, R., Liedtke, J., Müller, J., Rausch, D., Vogt, A.: Ordinos: a verifiable tally-hiding e-voting system. In: IEEE European Symposium on Security and Privacy, EuroS&P 2020, pp. 216–235. IEEE (2020). https://doi.org/10.1109/EuroSP48549.2020.00022

14. Küsters, R., Müller, J.: Cryptographic security analysis of E-Voting systems: achievements, misconceptions, and limitations. In: Krimmer, R., Volkamer, M., Braun Binder, N., Kersting, N., Pereira, O., Schürmann, C. (eds.) E-Vote-ID 2017. LNCS, vol. 10615, pp. 21–41. Springer, Cham (2017). https://doi.org/10.1007/978-3-319-68687-5_2

15. Küsters, R., Truderung, T., Vogt, A.: Accountability: definition and relationship to verifiability. In: Proceedings of ACM CCS 2010, pp. 526–535. ACM (2010)

16. Küsters, R., Truderung, T., Vogt, A.: Verifiability, privacy, and coercion-resistance: new insights from a case study. In: Proceedings of IEEE S&P 2011, pp. 538–553. IEEE Computer Society (2011)

17. Küsters, R., Truderung, T., Vogt, A.: Clash attacks on the verifiability of e-voting systems. In: IEEE Symposium on Security and Privacy, SP 2012, pp. 395–409. IEEE Computer Society (2012). https://doi.org/10.1109/SP.2012.32

18. Liu, A., Lu, Y., Xia, L., Zikas, V.: How private are commonly-used voting rules? Cryptology ePrint Archive, Report 2021/392 (2021). https://eprint.iacr.org/2021/392

19. Mitrou, L., Gritzalis, D., Katsikas, S.: Revisiting legal and regulatory requirements for secure E-Voting. In: Ghonaimy, M.A., El-Hadidi, M.T., Aslan, H.K. (eds.) Security in the Information Society. IAICT, vol. 86, pp. 469–480. Springer, Boston, MA (2002). https://doi.org/10.1007/978-0-387-35586-3_37

20. Pankova, A., Willemson, J.: Relations between privacy, verifiability, accountability and coercion-resistance in voting protocols. Cryptology ePrint Archive, Report 2021/1501 (2021). https://eprint.iacr.org/2021/1501

21. Procaccia, A.D., Rosenschein, J.S.: Average-case tractability of manipulation in voting via the fraction of manipulators. In: Durfee, E.H., Yokoo, M., Huhns, M.N., Shehory, O. (eds.) 6th International Joint Conference on Autonomous Agents and Multiagent Systems (AAMAS 2007), p. 105. IFAAMAS (2007). https://doi.org/10.1145/1329125.1329255

22. Rivest, R.L., Smith, W.D.: Three voting protocols: ThreeBallot, VAV, and twin. In: Martinez, R., Wagner, D.A. (eds.) 2007 USENIX/ACCURATE Electronic Voting Technology Workshop, EVT 2007. USENIX Association (2007). https://www.usenix.org/conference/evt07

23. Sako, K., Kilian, J.: Receipt-free mix-type voting scheme. In: Guillou, L.C., Quisquater, J.-J. (eds.) EUROCRYPT 1995. LNCS, vol. 921, pp. 393–403. Springer, Heidelberg (1995). https://doi.org/10.1007/3-540-49264-X_32
24. Schryen, G.: Security aspects of internet voting. In: Proceedings of HICSS-37. IEEE Computer Society (2004)

System Security

An Approach to Generate Realistic HTTP Parameters for Application Layer Deception

Merve Sahin[✉], Cédric Hébert[✉], and Rocio Cabrera Lozoya[✉]

SAP Security Research, Sophia Antipolis, France
{merve.sahin,cedric.hebert,rocio.cabrera.lozoya}@sap.com

Abstract. Deception is a form of active defense that aims to confuse and divert attackers who try to tamper with a system. Deceptive techniques have been proposed for web application security, in particular, to enrich a given application with deceptive elements such as honey cookies, HTTP parameters or HTML comments. Previous studies describe how to automatically add and remove such elements into the application traffic, however, the elements themselves need to be decided manually, which is a tedious task (especially for large-scale applications) and makes the adoption of deception more cumbersome.

In this paper, we aim to automate the generation of deceptive HTTP parameter names for a given web application. Such parameters should seamlessly blend into application context and be indistinguishable from the rest of the parameters, in order to maximize the deception effect. To achieve this, we propose to use word embeddings trained with a domain-specific corpus obtained from existing web application source code. We evaluate our method through a survey, where we ask the participants to identify the deceptive parameters in two different web applications' APIs. Moreover, the survey is composed of two variants in order to further experiment with the impact of the quantity and enticement of deceptive parameters.

The results confirm the effectiveness of our method in generating indistinguishable honey parameter names. We also find that the participants' expectation of the ratio of honey parameters remains constant, regardless of the actual number. Thus, a higher number of honeytokens can provide a stronger defense. Moreover, making attackers aware of deception can help to obfuscate the real attack surface, e.g., by masquerading more than 10% of the real application elements to look like traps. Finally, although our work focuses on the generation of parameter names, we also discuss other related challenges in a holistic way, and provide multiple directions for future research.

Keywords: Web application security · Deception · Active defense

1 Introduction

As part of a defense-in-depth strategy, deception works by confusing and misleading the adversary with false information, while *masking* the real nature of a

© Springer Nature Switzerland AG 2022
G. Ateniese and D. Venturi (Eds.): ACNS 2022, LNCS 13269, pp. 337–355, 2022.
https://doi.org/10.1007/978-3-031-09234-3_17

system, or *repackaging* it to look like something else [14,16]. Various studies have shown that deception can be an effective defense mechanism, not only for attack detection [17,34,47], but also for impeding the attack progress and disrupting attackers' emotional and cognitive state in various ways [26,28,29]. Moreover, deception technology market has been growing in recent years [6,7], with several commercial solutions providing data, network, application or endpoint layer deception [18,37,50].

The focus of this study is on web application layer deception. So far, the main idea has been to augment the application with deceptive elements (also called *honeytokens*, which can be in the form of HTTP parameters, cookies, HTML elements, permissions, or user accounts) in order to showcase a fake attack surface [30–32,34,35,42,45]. Monitoring the modifications to the values of such deceptive elements allows to detect attackers who are tampering with the application in order to find vulnerabilities. For instance, a common attack vector is called *web parameter tampering*, where the attacker manipulates the application parameters exchanged between the server and client, in an attempt to modify privileges, get access to unauthorized information, exploit business logic vulnerabilities, or disrupt the integrity of the application data [20,41]. The attacker may tamper with an object ID in the URL parameter to exploit an improper access control mechanism (known as the Insecure Direct Object Reference vulnerability [46]); or try to modify, e.g., the price of a product sent in a hidden form field, which was assumed to be immutable by the developer [41]. The use of deceptive elements provide a reliable source of warning in such cases, as the regular users of the application are not likely to intercept the communication and try to tamper with application data.

Most of the previous work on application layer deception focuses on how to add the deceptive elements with minimal effort. They use a reverse-proxy in front of the application that adds and removes the deceptive elements on the fly, seamlessly, so that the application itself will not require any modifications [30, 32,34]. Previous work also conducts CTF based experiments to measure the effectiveness of application layer deception [34], including when the attackers are aware of the presence of deception [47].

While these studies focus on automating the injection of deceptive elements into the application, they do not really address the challenges related to the generation of such elements, leaving this as an open research problem. In fact, a survey on deception techniques in computer security [35] draws attention to the lack of proper honey-token generation strategies for web applications and cloud images. Other studies emphasize the need to create "content-oriented deceptions to deceive skilled attackers in the long term" [26] and draw attention to the difficulty of creating such context-specific elements [34]. Previous work also finds that deceptive elements should be well intertwined with the application functionality and logic, to be robust against the deception awareness of the attacker [47]. In this paper, we address this research area of automatically generating realistic deceptive elements for web applications. In particular, we focus on the automated generation of *deceptive HTTP parameters*, as they can be effectively used in every API endpoint, covering a large attack surface of parameter tampering.

Deceptive HTTP parameters can be any type of HTTP parameter (such as the query, path, body or form parameters). However, coming up with context-specific deceptive parameters and embedding them into the application seamlessly accompany multiple challenges:

- How to choose realistic names for the parameters?
- How to make sure that the parameters are enticing enough?
- How to assign them plausible values?
- Where to place the parameters within an API?
- What is the optimal number of deceptive parameters?
- What should be the proper response when a certain parameter is tampered with?

We focus on the first challenge, which is to automatically generate plausible deceptive parameter names that are difficult to distinguish from the real parameters. For this, *we implement a machine learning method to generate parameter names that will blend well into the context of a given application (Sect. 3)*. In particular, we use word embeddings (a Natural Language Processing technique) trained with the source code of publicly available web applications.

Then *we evaluate the effectiveness of our method via a questionnaire with 42 participants (Sect. 4)*. We ask the participants to identify the deceptive parameters in two different web applications' APIs. *Our questionnaire also experiments with two additional challenges: the amount and enticement of deceptive parameters (Sect. 5)*.

In addition to showing that our method successfully generates indistinguishable parameter names, we make several other observations: First, we find that the participants anticipate a certain ratio of parameters to be deceptive, regardless of the actual quantity of deceptive elements. Thus, adding a larger number of deceptive elements would mean that more of them will go undetected. Second, the addition of very obvious (conspicuous) deceptive parameters does not really help to hide the existence of realistic ones. Third, we find that the participants mislabel at least 10% of genuine parameters as deceptive, on average. This provides another evidence on the benefit of informing attackers about the use of deception.

2   Method

As mentioned earlier, we aim to automate the generation of deceptive HTTP parameters that are in agreement with the context of the web application to be protected. For such tasks, the Natural Language Processing (NLP) domain offers different techniques, such as specialized lists, lexical dictionaries and word embeddings.

Specialized lists have the drawback of needing to be handcrafted, a process which can be time-consuming and requires domain-specific knowledge. Lexical dictionaries have been used in traditional NLP approaches. They are networks of meaningfully and semantically related words and concepts (synsets) and provide graph representations of the relationships of a vocabulary. Nevertheless, lexical dictionaries might not be able to keep up with the quick evolution of the language, as well as with domain-specific jargon.

Finally, *embeddings* are vectorial representations of words mapped onto a reduced dimensionality space where similar words (embeddings) are close to each other. The distance between these embeddings is often measured using the cosine similarity or any other distance between vectors. Due to their data-driven nature, embeddings are able to capture the relationships between words in specific contexts. They were initially popularized in the recent years due to their applications in NLP by using rather simple neural network architectures, such as the ones proposed by word2vec [38] and GloVe [43]. More complex language models have been developed in the last years (e.g. ELMo [44], BERT [27]). Nevertheless, these models are often trained on vast English text corpus coming from natural language sources as varied as news articles, Wikipedia entries, literary and web content, among others. While they are useful for generic language understanding tasks, they can struggle with applications which contain a big domain-specific vocabulary.

Outside the realm of natural languages, embeddings have also been used to model programming languages both in a sequence-of-tokens fashion (supported by the *naturalness hypothesis* [13]) or by embedding elements in graph representations of code (e.g., abstract syntax trees or control flow graphs) [15,23,25].

In this paper, we propose the use of embeddings of source code by treating it in a sequence-of-tokens fashion. The choice was made to use the smaller and simpler models like *word2vec* due to their less data-hungry nature and their ease to train them compared to more complex models. Due to the very specific nature of our application, we train our language model with a dataset specifically created for this task.

2.1   Data Collection and Training

In order to create a domain-specific dataset that will capture the terminology and technical context of web applications, we use the source code of web applications available at public GitHub repositories. We start with a list of public GitHub Java repositories with more than 5 stars (watchers), which was made available by Chen et al. [24] and includes 83,082 repository URLs collected from GHTorrent [33] database (last updated on 2019-06-01). Among these, we remove the repositories that include `android` or `mobile` keywords in the repository name, and focus on the repositories with at least 15 stars, which reduces the list to 38,376 URLs.

As our purpose is to generate HTTP parameters for web APIs, we try to limit the training data to the repositories with web application relevant source code. We do this in a coarse-grained way, by pruning the dataset to only contain the repositories that include web related libraries: We download each repository and look for "import" statements for library names such as `org.springframework`.

web, javax.servlet, org.apache.http, httpcomponents and okhttpclient. Finally, we end up with the source code from 10,324 repositories, which corresponds to 4,002,776 Java files.

We further refine the Java files according to their name: The files that are likely to not have a context related to the functionality of the application (e.g., util, filter, exception, config, parser, test) and the files that might have a too specific context (e.g., coin, blockchain, droid, Activity) are removed.

For each project, for each remaining Java file, we parse the file (using the JavaLangParser Python library) to extract the relevant input to train the *word2vec* model. While *word2vec* is normally trained with sentences from natural language, we construct the sentences as sequence-of-tokens collected from the source code. In particular, each of the following items forms a separate sentence by appending the relevant tokens together:

- Each method name (MethodDeclaration) and the names of method parameters
- Each class constructor (ConstructorDeclaration) and the names of constructor parameters
- The names of the class fields (FieldDeclaration)
- All the variable names in the class (VariableDeclaration)

The motivation is that each of these sentences includes tokens that are likely to belong to the same context. Note that, each token (method, parameter, variable, or constructor name) is split by underscore or camel case (if such naming convention was used), and then converted to lower case.

Post-processing: In each sentence, we remove the tokens that are specific to the Java language, and tokens that do not carry any contextual meaning.[1] Finally, we train the *word2vec* model using the Python *gensim.models* library, with the default parameters.

Independently from this process, we also save all the variable names with built-in types (e.g., String, boolean, int, array) for each project in a separate csv file. This corresponds to 8,844,562 variables. We later use this data to find the most suitable parameter type for the generated deceptive parameter names.

2.2 Generation of Parameter Names

To generate deceptive parameters for a target application, we assume to obtain the API specification of the application to start with. In particular, we assume to have an *OpenAPI specification* [40] as input. OpenAPI (formerly known as *Swagger* [49]) specification aims to standardize the descriptions of RESTful APIs. In addition, the Swagger project provides various tools for testing and development,

---

[1] These words are has, have, init, start, stop, get, set, main, create, delete, update, read, add, remove, is, on, by, to, test, parse, write, initialize, string, int, boolean, char.

together with a specific user interface to view and try out the API (called Swagger UI [12]). In our experiments, we use an alternative Swagger user interface called Bootprint [8], as it outputs a static HTML page with a simpler design that is more appropriate for our purpose.

Once we have the Swagger specification (which is often in json or yaml format), we flatten [48] the file and convert it to the csv format, where we have each HTTP parameter and the related information (endpoint, HTTP method, name and type) in one row. Note that, endpoints may pair with multiple different HTTP methods, and each endpoint-method pair is likely to have multiple parameters. Figure 1 shows an example API specification of an endpoint-method pair in json format (a), together with how it looks on Bootprint-Swagger UI (b) and our conversion to csv format (c).

```
"/carts/{id}/entries": {
  "post": {
    "operationId": "
      postCartEntry",
    "parameters": [{
      "type": "string",
      "name": "id",
      "in": "path"},
    {
      "type": "string",
      "name": "
        productVariantId",
      "in": "formData"},
    {
      "type": "integer",
      "name": "quantity",
      "in": "formData"
  }]}}
```

(a) Swagger json file for the endpoint-method pair

POST /carts/{id}/entries

Name	Type	Data type
id	path	string
productVariantId	formData	string
quantity	formData	integer (int32)

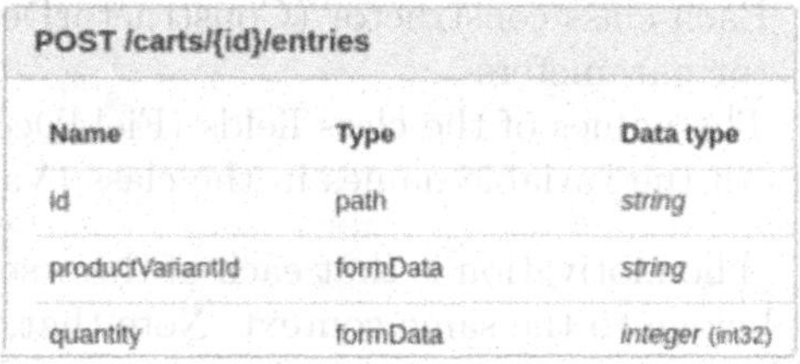

(b) Swagger UI

Endpoint	Method	Location	Name	Type
/carts/id/entries	post	path	id	string
/carts/id/entries	post	formData	productVariantId	string
/carts/id/entries	post	formData	quantity	integer

(c) API endpoint converted to csv

Fig. 1. Example Swagger input for the *POST* method of */carts/{id}/entries* endpoint.

Next, we use our *word2vec* model to generate deceptive elements for the endpoint-method pairs in the API. In particular, we use the `most_similar()` method of *word2vec* library to get the top n words that are the most similar to a list of *existing elements*. We form the *existing elements* list depending on the location of the HTTP parameter:

- **Path parameters:** Path parameters are located in the URL path of an endpoint, and often point to a specific resource [9]. We only attempt to embed a deceptive path parameter to the endpoints that already have at least one path parameter. First, we group the endpoints up to their very first path parameter. Next, within each group, we collect all the endpoint URLs, split the words by underscore or camel case if necessary, and form our *existing elements* list. If this approach does not yield any proper output (due to the thresholds that we will explain later), an alternative approach is to collect the first level URL components of all endpoints as the *existing elements* list. Note that, the generated deceptive path parameter will be added to all the endpoints in this group, to keep the consistency of parameters between endpoints.

- **Query or body parameters:** Query parameters are located at the end of the URL, after a question mark (e.g., '?name1=value1&name2=value2' format). Describing the body parameters, on the other hand, is a bit more complex: The earlier version of OpenAPI (v2) differentiates between the `formData` parameters that describe the payload of a request, and the `body` parameters that describe an object with a data structure [10]. However, the last version (OpenAPI v3) categorizes both of them under the `RequestBody` type [11].

  We process the query and body parameters, for each of the endpoint-method pairs: We take the existing query or body parameter names, in addition to the tokens from the URL path of the related endpoint (again splitted by underscore or camel case, if necessary). Note that, as our *word2vec* model is deterministic once it is trained, it will generate the same output for the same set of *existing elements*. This allows us to preserve the consistency between different endpoints: For instance, two different endpoints that update an address object with the same body parameters will also be assigned the same deceptive parameter.

Finally, our algorithm aims to insert deceptive parameters only if it has a high 'confidence' that the generated element will fit in the context of the endpoint-method pair. For this, we implement the following four steps:

(i) *Making sure that the existing elements list contains sufficient input:* For query and body/form parameters, we set a threshold for the minimum number of *existing elements*: If there are fewer elements than this threshold, we choose to not generate a deceptive parameter for the given endpoint-method pair and parameter location. For path parameters, we also require a certain *number of endpoints* per group, to be able to assign a deceptive parameter to this group.

(ii) *Making sure that the input words are known to the model:* It is possible that some of the *existing elements* will not be present in the vocabulary of our *word2vec* model, as our training dataset may not contain them. Thus, our second threshold becomes the minimum *known_words_ratio*: the ratio of *existing elements* that are present in the vocabulary. If these two thresholds are met, we take the top n most similar words as our *candidate deceptive parameters*.

(iii) *Post-processing to check if the candidate parameters have sufficient similarity to existing elements:* We compute the average similarity score of candidate parameters to the *existing elements*. (The similarity scores are returned by the `most_similar()` method.) If this value is less than our *average_similarity_score* threshold, we choose to not insert any deceptive parameter for this endpoint-method pair and parameter location.

(iv) *Post-processing to avoid repeating parameters:* Finally, we remove the candidate deceptive parameters that are morphologically too close to any of the existing elements. For example if "paymentid" is an existing element and our model generates "paymentnum", we remove "paymentnum" from the candidate list. For this, we use the `ratio()` method from the `difflib.SequenceMatcher` [3] class in Python, to compute a measure of similarity between two sequences. We set a *sequence_matching_score* threshold to decide whether a candidate should be removed. After all these steps, the final deceptive parameter becomes the first element in the *candidate deceptive elements* list, having the highest similarity score value.

Fine Tuning the Algorithm: We tried our algorithm on 17 real-world Swagger API documentations that we collected online (using Google dorks such as intitle: "swagger.json" site:github.com). Note that, we make sure that the collected APIs do not overlap with the GitHub repositories used in our training. By experimenting with these APIs to generate deceptive elements, we come up with a set of threshold values that provide a good starting point. Table 1 gives these threshold values, which we also use for evaluating the performance of our method in the next section.

On a final note, we also assign a type (e.g., int, boolean, string) to the generated deceptive elements using the dataset of more than 8 Million variables collected in Sect. 2.1. To infer a type, we first look for an exact match between the generated parameter name and the variable names dataset. If it does not exist, we again use the `SequenceMatcher` class with a similarity score threshold of 0.8. This algorithm was able to infer a type for almost all of the parameter names in our initial experiments.

Table 1. Thresholds and values that affect the generation of parameters.

Threshold	Value	Threshold	Value
n	5	known_words_ratio	>0.7
number of endpoints	≥2	average_similarity_score	>0.6
number of existing elements	≥2	sequence_matching_score	>0.5

3   Evaluation

In this section we aim to evaluate the performance of our method in generating indistinguishable deceptive parameters. A common evaluation method that

is also used in previous work [21,45] is to ask human subjects to differentiate deceptive elements from genuine elements. However, while in the previous
work the human subjects were informed upfront that 50% of elements they will
evaluate are deceptive, we do not give any tips about the number of deceptive
parameters. Moreover, we present the subjects with real-world APIs using the
Bootprint Swagger UI, so that they can get a sense of the application and thoroughly observe all the endpoint-method pairs, parameters and their types. We
use a separate questionnaire where we list all the distinct parameter names (categorized by location such as query, form, path), and ask the subjects to mark
the parameters that they think are deceptive.

Although this evaluation method does not allow participants to interact with
a running instance of the application, it allows them to really focus on the names
of the parameters. In fact if they were able to interact with the application,
they could rely on additional criteria (e.g. value of the parameter, response to
tampering) to decide if a parameter is deceptive or not. Thus, presenting the
participants with a static API specification better fits our purpose of evaluating
the indistinguishability of parameter names.

3.1 Preparation of the API Specifications

For this experiment, we choose two APIs among the set of 17 real-world APIs
mentioned in the previous section, following the below criteria:

- The APIs should have more or less equal number of endpoints and parameters
  to achieve more reliable results in statistical tests.
- The applications' context should be easy to grasp so that the participants
  can make more informed decisions (i.e., reducing the randomness that might
  emerge from not understanding the API).
- The number of API parameters should be reasonable for manual evaluation;
  to not overwhelm and distract the human subjects, and to make the survey
  feasible to complete in a reasonable amount of time.

In particular, the two APIs we choose include (i) a cloud integration API
for an e-commerce application [1], and (ii) a community based laboratory platform for various professions [4]. The first one has 63 distinct parameters and 38
endpoint-method pairs, and the second one has 74 distinct parameters and 33
endpoint-method pairs.

To prepare the APIs for the experiment, we first anonymize the specification,
removing the application name, all descriptions, and fields ignored by our study
such as response status[2]. Then we generate the deceptive parameters using the
method described in previous section. We insert the generated parameters back
into the Swagger specification, so that the Bootprint Swagger UI can display

---

[2] Full list of fields removed from Swagger: "info", "description", "host", "tags", "summary", "responses", "definitions", "enum" , "example", "security", "securityDefini-
tions", "x-example", "minimum" , "maximum", "readOnly", "maxLength", "min-
Length" , "pattern", "required".

them. Our algorithm generates 8 deceptive parameters for e-commerce and 9 for the laboratory platform. We will call this the *default mode*, and will denote the APIs as $E\text{-}Commerce_D$ and $Lab\text{-}Platform_D$, respectively.

In addition, our experiment also aims to measure the effect of (i) high quantity and (ii) conspicuous (i.e., easily visible, obvious, attracting attention [22]) deceptive parameters. For this, we decide to divide the participants into two groups: Each group is presented 2 applications, one of it with the default mode, and the other with one of the additional characteristics (either higher quantity of parameters, or very conspicuous parameters added). Table 2 shows various statistics on the number of distinct deceptive parameters and affected endpoint-method pairs for the API variants used in our experiment.

High Quantity of Deceptive Parameters: We apply this variant to the e-commerce application, denoted with $E\text{-}Commerce_Q$. To have a significantly higher number of deceptive parameters compared to the default mode (which is $E\text{-}Commerce_D$), we first use the additional results generated by our model (i.e., more parameter names from the *candidate deceptive parameters* list). With this, we obtain 6 more parameters in addition to the 8 parameters generated in default mode. However, while we want this API variant to have statistically significantly higher number of deceptive elements, our model was not able to generate that many parameter names, as we apply several thresholds to choose the best candidates. Thus, we have added 15 additional, manually chosen realistic parameters.

To show that $E\text{-}Commerce_Q$ has significantly more deceptive parameters compared to $E\text{-}Commerce_D$, we employ two-proportions Z-tests: Looking at the ratio of (the number of distinct deceptive parameters)/(the total number of distinct parameters), we find a z-score of -3.0609 and p-value of .00222. Thus, the result is significant at a confidence level of 95%. Moreover, in terms of the ratio of (the number of endpoint-method pairs with deceptive elements)/(the total number of endpoint-method pairs), we also show a statistically significant difference (z-score $= -1.9742$, p-value $= .02442$, significant at $p < .05$).

Conspicuousness of Deceptive Parameters: We use this API variant in the laboratory platform application, denoted as $Lab\text{-}Platform_C$. To manually add conspicuous deceptive parameters to the API (in addition to the realistic ones), we use two different strategies:

- Parameters that look too enticing and do not follow the naming convention of the application (e.g., use of camelcase instead of underscore, uppercase letters): Examples are MakeAdmin, FullPrivileges, ADMIN_PERM, cl4ssifi3d_ID.
- Parameters that do not have any meaning or that are out-of-context of the application: Examples are yoyo, pysantx, vv, disclosed.

To make sure that the parameters are indeed conspicuous, we made an initial evaluation on 7 participants, presenting them a preliminary version of the survey and asking them to mark the parameters that they think are deceptive. All participants marked the conspicuous parameters as deceptive. Note that these participants who were involved in the initial evaluation were not invited to the real experiment.

Table 2. Breakdown of the API variants: showing the distinct number of honeytokens, affected endpoint-method pairs, and their ratios to the total number of parameters and endpoint-method pairs.

	# distinct honeytokens → # endpoint-method pairs				# dist. parameters: honeytokens/total	# endpoint-method pairs: with honeytokens/total
	Path	Query	Form	Body		
$E\text{-}Commerce_D$ (Survey I)	1 → 19	-	5 → 4	2 → 2	8 / 71 (11%)	22 / 38 (58%)
$E\text{-}Commerce_Q$ (Survey II)	2 → 19	3 → 3	14 → 11	10 → 4	29 / 92 (32%)	30 / 38 (79%)
$Lab\text{-}Platform_D$ (Survey II)	2 → 10	1 → 1	2 → 3	4 → 8	9 / 83 (11%)	19 / 33 (57%)
$Lab\ Platform_C$ (Survey I)	5 → 10	1 → 1	4 → 3	7 → 8	17 / 91 (19%)	19 / 33 (57%)

3.2   Preparation of the Surveys

Our experiment consists of two survey versions. Survey I contains $E\text{-}Commerce_D$ and $Lab\text{-}Platform_C$ APIs, and Survey II contains $E\text{-}Commerce_Q$ and $Lab\text{-}Platform_D$. Note that participants were not aware that there were two different versions of the survey. We advertised the survey with a single URL that redirects to a different version of the survey each time it is requested. We changed the redirection rules from time to time, to ensure that both versions will have the same number of participants.

Both surveys start with a section that describes the purpose of the survey. In particular, it states the following:

> In this experiment, you will be presented with 2 different application APIs that include a number of honey parameters. We will ask you to identify the parameters that you think are deceptive (i.e., if you were to attack this application, you would avoid tampering those parameters to avoid being detected).

Although we anonymize the APIs beforehand, we inform the participants that they are real-world APIs, and ask them to not search for the original APIs online for the sake of the validity of the study.

The first three questions of the survey aim to learn about participants' profile (current job title) and their experience on information security and deception technology. Then we have a different section for each application, where we first give a link to the Bootprint Swagger UI of the API. We then ask participants to identify the purpose of the API, and to rate their overall understanding of the purpose of the endpoints. Finally, we list all the distinct parameter names categorized by their location (path, query, form, body) and ask the participants to mark if it is *deceptive* or *genuine*. Note that, by default all answers are set to *genuine*, to save the participants from clicking too many times.

3.3 Participants

We used snowball sampling to reach security experts. We advertise the survey mainly in two communities: First, among the security researchers, experts and enthusiasts in a large software company and second, among the computer security PhD students of a graduate school. Additionally, we advertise it on social media (Twitter).

Note that the survey description warns the participants about an estimated duration of 30 min, which was determined during the initial evaluation phase. Participation is completely on a voluntary basis, without any compensation. Overall, our advertisement is estimated to reach at least a few hundred people and the survey received answers between April 6 and May 24, 2021.

4   Results

We received 42 responses, which correspond to 21 participants for each version of the survey (Survey I & II). This number of responses allows us to show the effectiveness of our method and to make interesting observations.

4.1   Participants' Profile

Majority of participants consist of software/web developers (19%), security researchers working in industry (17%) and MSc students doing internships (17%). Moreover, some PhD students (11%), postdocs, and professors (10%) have also answered the survey. 5 participants did not answer the question about their job title. Participants rate their information security experience as 3.5 ± 1.1 on a scale from 1 to 5. Moreover, they rate their knowledge on deception technology as 2.4 ± 0.9. Overall, the participants seem to have an above average experience in information security, and an average level of familiarity with deception technology.

4.2   Participants' Understanding of the APIs

In a multi-choice question, we first ask participants to identify the purpose of the API. All participants correctly identified both the e-commerce and the laboratory platform applications. Then, we ask participants to rate their understanding of the purpose of API endpoints on a scale from 1 to 5. Participants seem to have a good understanding of the e-commerce endpoints (on average 4 ± 0.6 for *E-Commerce$_D$* and 4 ± 0.5 for *E-Commerce$_Q$*) and a fair to good understanding of the endpoints of the laboratory platform (on average 3.6 ± 0.6 for *Lab-Platform$_D$* and 3.4 ± 0.9 for *Lab-Platform$_C$*).

4.3   Indistinguishability of Deceptive Parameters

To see if our method was able to generate deceptive parameters that are indistinguishable from the genuine application parameters, we analyze the results from *E-Commerce*$_D$ (Survey I) and *Lab-Platform*$_D$ (Survey II). In particular, we compute a *detection rate* for each parameter, that is the ratio of participants that marked this parameter as deceptive. Then, we compare the detection ratios of the group of deceptive parameters and the group of genuine parameters: We use Welch's t-test as the groups have unequal sample sizes and unequal variances [5].

Table 3. Detection rate statistics for deceptive and genuine parameters for the APIs in default mode.

	Detection rate statistics		Welch's t-test ($p < .05$)
	Deceptive	Genuine	
E-Commerce$_D$ (Survey I)	24±13	18±14	$t = 1$, $p=.34$ (Not significant)
Lab-Platform$_D$ (Survey II)	26±22	12±10	$t=1.8$, $p=.1$ (Not significant)

Table 3 shows the detection rate statistics and the results of Welch's t-tests for both applications. **Although detection rates of deceptive elements are slightly higher, we do not observe a statistically significant difference in comparison to the detection rates of genuine parameters**, at a confidence level of 95%. This shows that our method is able to generate indistinguishable deceptive parameters.

Previous work suggests that a "high-quality honeytoken" cannot be distinguished from a real token, even by the experts in relevant field [21]. Thus, the fact that 71% of our participants are security professionals or web developers increases confidence in the reliability of our results.

4.4   Impact of the Quantity of Deceptive Parameters

In this section we aim to answer the following question: Do participants mislabel (i.e., fail to detect) more deceptive parameters, when there are significantly more of them?

For each participant, we compute the ratio of deceptive parameters that they correctly labeled. We also compute the ratio of parameters that they label as deceptive, among all parameters. This second metric refers to participants' expectation (or assumption) on the quantity of deceptive elements.

Table 4. Average ratios of parameters that are labeled as deceptive, among (i) honeytokens and (ii) all parameters.

	Ratio of labeled honeytokens	Ratio of labeled parameters in total
$E\text{-}Commerce_D$ (Survey I)	23±16 %	19±8 %
$E\text{-}Commerce_Q$ (Survey II)	25±19 %	17±13 %

Table 4 shows that **regardless of the quantity of honeytokens, participants label more or less the same percentage of honeytokens as deceptive** (~23 to 25%). Thus, in $E\text{-}Commerce_D$ on average 6 of the 8 deceptive parameters remain undetected by participants, while in $E\text{-}Commerce_Q$, 22 of 29 are undetected. Moreover, **participants' expectation of the ratio of deceptive parameters (among all parameters) remains rather constant even when there are statistically significantly more honeytokens** (~17 to 19%). This means that, when there is a larger quantity of realistic deceptive elements, there will be more elements that will remain undetected. On the other hand, generating a very large number of realistic deceptive elements remains a challenge. As discussed in Sect. 3.1, we used a semi-manual approach, as our model was able to generate a limited number of high quality deceptive elements.

Finally, we also compare the detection rates of deceptive parameters in $E\text{-}Commerce_Q$ that were automatically generated by our model (14 parameters) and that were manually created by us (15 parameters), to see how our approach compares to manual selection. Average detection rate is found to be $21 \pm 9\%$ for automated honeytokens, and $23 \pm 11\%$ for manual honeytokens. Applying a Welch's t-test, we do not see a significant difference between detection rates ($t = -0.44$, $p = .66$). Thus, we can conclude that **automatically generated parameter names were as realistic as manually selected ones.**

4.5 Impact of the Conspicuous Deceptive Parameters

In this section we aim to answer the following question: Do participants mislabel (i.e., fail to detect) more deceptive parameters, when there are some very obvious (conspicuous) honeytokens added as extra? The idea is that conspicuous honeytokens might help to hide realistic honeytokens, by attracting participants' attention.

Table 5. Average ratios of parameters that are labeled as deceptive, among (i) honeytokens and (ii) all parameters.

	Ratio of labeled honeytokens	Ratio of labeled parameters in total
$Lab\text{-}Platform_D$ (Survey II)	26±16 %	13±10 %
$Lab\text{-}Platform_C$ (Survey I) (excluding conspicuous)	25±14 %	12±7 %

Table 5 shows that, if we exclude the conspicuous parameters in *Lab-Platform$_C$*, participants label more or less the same percentage of honeytokens as deceptive ($\sim$25 to 26%) in both *Lab-Platform$_D$* and *Lab-Platform$_C$*. Moreover, participants' expectation of the ratio of deceptive parameters again remains more or less constant ($\sim$12 to 13%). Thus, **we do not observe any significant impact of adding conspicuous honeytokens on further disguising the realistic honeytokens**.

On the other hand, a significantly higher number of participants label the conspicuous honeytokens as deceptive (on average, $72 \pm 11\%$), in comparison to the realistic honeytokens (on average, $24 \pm 30\%$) in *Lab-Platform$_C$* (Welch's t-test: $p = .001$). Thus, we believe that **conspicuous honeytokens can be used to tip off the attacker about the presence of deception**, in order to enable the deception awareness effect that we will discuss next.

4.6 Deception Awareness Effect

In this section, we look at the ratio of genuine parameters that are labeled as deceptive by the participants. On average, *E-Commerce$_D$* and *E-Commerce$_Q$* have $18 \pm 8\%$ and $15 \pm 11\%$ of the genuine parameters mislabeled, respectively. These ratios are $12 \pm 10\%$ and $11 \pm 7\%$ for *Lab-Platform$_D$* and *Lab-Platform$_C$*. Thus, **we observe that at least 10% of genuine parameters were marked as deceptive across all APIs**, which means that participants would avoid tampering with those parameters in an attack scenario. We can interpret this as the effect of deception awareness. Previous studies already observe various benefits of informing attackers about the presence of deception, such as compelling them to modify their attack behavior, impeding the attack progress, and deteriorating attackers' cognitive and psychological state [29,47]. Our results demonstrate yet another benefit of deception awareness, that is, to masquerade the real application elements to look like traps.

5 Limitations and Discussion

Method: In this study we only considered the source code of Java web applications from public GitHub repositories to train the model. However, it is possible to enrich the model with other codebases and projects using different web technologies (e.g., PHP, Node.js). Note that, the number of high quality parameters that can be generated by the model depends on the richness of the training data. Another limitation of our approach is that it is not able to generate compound parameter names. This can be done as a manual post-processing step (e.g., by adding a common prefix or suffix to some parameter names), or it would require to train a model using the compound words as single words, if a proper training set is available. In addition, although we only used *word2vec*, combining it with other NLP approaches (discussed in Sect. 2) is also possible.

Evaluation: The results of our evaluation survey only provide insights about whether the participants were able to distinguish between the generated parameter names and the names of genuine application parameters. *Thus, these results* *should not be considered as a measurement of the effectiveness of deceptive elements in attack detection.* On the other hand, it is important to note that the deceptive parameters mainly aim to detect attacks via attackers' interaction (e.g., tampering the parameter), as opposed to the traditional honeypots that aim to waste attackers' time and resources. This means that, *as soon as an attacker interacts with a deceptive parameter (e.g., with a fuzzing tool), he will be detected and the application will respond accordingly (e.g., by blocking the request or routing to a clone system).* Thus, having realistic deceptive parameters becomes a first requirement to ensure the effectiveness of deception.

As mentioned in Sect. 3.2, in the evaluation survey we only have *deceptive* and *genuine* options to choose between. Thus, participants are forced to make a choice even when they are not sure about the answer. In fact, we have received a few post-survey comments where the participants found some parameters to be implausible, but they were not sure if it was just due to bad API design practices, or due to deception. For instance, one participant stated that:

> Some of these APIs look off from a programming perspective. Why would you include < variable > as a query string when it might be more efficient to use it elsewhere?

Another participant said:

> I would be extra careful in a situation like this and mark things [that maybe are not deceptive] as deceptive just in case. Taking into account that programmers are not perfect, they may create parameters that are not needed. So I think this is not needed, but is it because it is deceptive or it was done like this in reality... My general approach when doing tampering is, just touch what you are sure of.

These comments imply a few points: First, it is likely that there will always be a suspicion about implausible-looking elements. Second, it is important to keep the coherence between API endpoints and imitate realistic functionality for the generated deceptive elements. Finally, we believe that obliging participants to take a decision is a more realistic approach, as in a real attack scenario they would need to make a decision to tamper or not. In fact, previous work observes via a CTF-based experiment that, although most participants are initially very careful to not touch the suspicious-looking elements, they give up on such precautions after some time, if they cannot find an attack vector to progress [47].

6 Related Work

While there are many studies that aim to generate various deceptive content or honey elements, we focus on the ones that relate to web application security.

HoneyGen [21] aims to create relational database with fake entries, based on the rules extracted from a real database. For evaluation, the method is applied on a database from a real-world dating website, to create fake profiles with different personal information attributes. The experiment involved 30 pairs of profiles, each pair having one real and one fake persona. The 109 participants who joined the experiment were unable to distinguish the fake profiles that have high similarity to the real profiles. B.Hive [45] aims to generate honey form field names using a dataset of form fields collected from top websites. While this approach is limited to form parameters from pre-authentication pages, our approach targets all types of HTTP parameters and a wide range of application contexts. A more recent study [19] proposes to allow the user to enrich the UI of a web application with custom honey HTML elements (e.g., link, button, icon), via a browser extension. The idea is that the genuine users would be aware of these 'tripwires' (and not interact with them), but an attacker could easily click on them once he gains access to the account. While the names of the honey HTML elements are ideally chosen by the user, authors also implement a suggestion tool based on a Markov model of URLs gathered from the Common Crawl [2] dataset. However, the paper does not provide an evaluation on the quality of the suggested names.

BogusBiter [51] proposes to generate honey credentials that will be fed into phishing pages to conceal the real credentials of the user. The idea is to start with an initial set of credentials, and generate additional credentials by substituting certain characters of the username and password with different characters, each time. Other relevant studies propose different approaches for password guessing, based on a combination of specialized lists, lexical dictionaries and word embeddings [39] or deep learning techniques [36].

7   Conclusion

This work automates the generation of realistic deceptive parameter names for different types of HTTP parameters. We demonstrate the effectiveness of our method via a survey based experiment, and find that the participants anticipate a certain ratio of elements to be deceptive, regardless of the actual quantity or enticement level of the honeytokens. Additionally, we observe that at least 10% of genuine API parameters were marked as deceptive by the participants, which demonstrates the potential benefit of informing the attackers about the presence of honeytokens. Finally, we provide various directions for future work by looking into the challenges that needs to be addressed for a complete automation of API layer deception.

References

1. Adobe CIF REST API and data model. https://github.com/adobe/commerce-cif-api/tree/deprecated
2. Common Crawl. https://commoncrawl.org/the-data/get-started/
3. difflib - Helpers for computing deltas. https://docs.python.org/3/library/difflib.html
4. Fablabs.io Developer Guide. https://docs.fablabs.io/swagger/index.html
5. Scipy stats ttest reference. https://docs.scipy.org/doc/scipy/reference/generated/scipy.stats.ttest_ind.html#scipy.stats.ttest_ind

6. Deception Technology Market, February 2017. https://www.marketsandmarkets.com/Market-Reports/deception-technology-market-129235449.html
7. Global Deception Technology Market: Growth, Trends and Forecast to 2025 - ResearchAndMarkets.com, April 2020. https://www.businesswire.com
8. bootprint-swagger (2021). https://github.com/karlvr/bootprint-swagger
9. Describing Parameters (2021). https://swagger.io/docs/specification/describing-parameters/
10. Describing Request Body (2021). https://swagger.io/docs/specification/2-0/describing-request-body/
11. Describing Request Body (2021). https://swagger.io/docs/specification/describing-request-body/
12. Swagger UI (2021). https://swagger.io/tools/swagger-ui/
13. Allamanis, M., Barr, E.T., Devanbu, P., Sutton, C.: A survey of machine learning for big code and naturalness. ACM Comput. Surv. (CSUR) **51**, 1–37 (2018)
14. Almeshekah, M., Spafford, E.: Planning and integrating deception into computer security defenses. In: NSPW 2014 (2014)
15. Alon, U., Zilberstein, M., Levy, O., Yahav, E.: code2vec: learning distributed representations of code (POPL) (2019)
16. Anderson, P.: Deception: a healthy part of any defense in-depth strategy, March 2002. sans.org/reading-room/whitepapers/policyissues/deception-healthy-defense-in-depth-strategy-506
17. Araujo, F., Hamlen, K.W., Biedermann, S., Katzenbeisser, S.: From patches to honey-patches: lightweight attacker misdirection, deception, and disinformation. In: CCS 2014 (2014)
18. Attivo Networks: Threat detection (2019). https://attivonetworks.com/solutions/threat-detection/
19. Barron, T., So, J., Nikiforakis, N.: Click this, not that: extending web authentication with deception. In: ASIA CCS 2021 (2021)
20. Beagle Security: Parameter Tampering (2021). https://beaglesecurity.com/blog/vulnerability/parameter-tampering.html
21. Bercovitch, M., Renford, M., Hasson, L., Shabtai, A., Rokach, L., Elovici, Y.: HoneyGen: an automated honeytokens generator. In: Proceedings of 2011 IEEE International Conference on Intelligence and Security Informatics, July 2011
22. Bowen, B.M., Hershkop, S., Keromytis, A.D., Stolfo, S.J.: Baiting inside attackers using decoy documents. In: Chen, Y., Dimitriou, T.D., Zhou, J. (eds.) SecureComm 2009. LNICST, vol. 19, pp. 51–70. Springer, Heidelberg (2009). https://doi.org/10.1007/978-3-642-05284-2_4
23. Cabrera Lozoya, R., Baumann, A., Sabetta, A., Bezzi, M.: Commit2vec: learning distributed representations of code changes (2019). arXiv:1911.07605
24. Chen, B., Jiang, Z.M.: Studying the use of java logging utilities in the wild. In: ICSE (2020)
25. Chen, Z., Monperrus, M.: A literature study of embeddings on source code. arXiv:1904.03061 (2019)
26. Cohen, F., Marin, I., Sappington, J., Stewart, C., Thomas, E.: Red teaming experiments with deception technologies (2001). http://all.net/journal/deception/RedTeamingExperiments.pdf
27. Devlin, J., Chang, M.W., Lee, K., Toutanova, K.: BERT: pre-training of deep bidirectional transformers for language understanding (2018). arXiv:1810.04805
28. Ferguson-Walter, K., et al.: The Tularosa study: an experimental design and implementation to quantify the effectiveness of cyber deception. In: HICSS (2019)

29. Ferguson-Walter, K.J., Major, M.M., Johnson, C.K., Muhleman, D.H.: Examining the efficacy of decoy-based and psychological cyber deception. In: USENIX Security (2021)
30. Fraunholz, D., Schotten, H.D.: Defending web servers with feints, distraction and obfuscation. In: ICNC 2018, March 2018
31. Fraunholz, D., et al.: Demystifying deception technology: a survey. CoRR abs/1804.06196 (2018)
32. Fraunholz, D., Reti, D., Duque Anton, S., Schotten, H.D.: Cloxy: a context-aware deception-as-a-service reverse proxy for web services. In: MTD 2018 (2018)
33. Gousios, G.: The GHTorrent dataset and tool suite. In: MSR 2013, May 2013. pub/ghtorrent-dataset-toolsuite.pdf
34. Han, X., Kheir, N., Balzarotti, D.: Evaluation of deception-based web attacks detection. In: MTD 2017 (2017)
35. Han, X., Kheir, N., Balzarotti, D.: Deception techniques in computer security: a research perspective. ACM Comput. Surv. **51**, 1–36 (2018)
36. Hitaj, B., Gasti, P., Ateniese, G., Perez-Cruz, F.: PassGAN: a deep learning approach for password guessing. In: Deng, R.H., Gauthier-Umaña, V., Ochoa, M., Yung, M. (eds.) ACNS (2019)
37. Illusive Networks: Attack detection system (2019). https://www.illusivenetworks.com/technology/platform/attack-detection-system
38. Mikolov, T., Chen, K., Corrado, G., Dean, J.: Efficient estimation of word representations in vector space. arXiv preprint arXiv:1301.3781 (2013)
39. Ocanto-Dávila, C., Cabrera-Lozoya, R., Trabelsi, S.: Sociocultural influences for password definition: An AI-based study. In: ICISSP, pp. 542–549 (2021)
40. OpenAPI Initiative: OpenAPI Specification v3.1.0 (2021). https://spec.openapis.org/oas/v3.1.0.html
41. OWASP: Web Parameter Tampering (2021). https://owasp.org/www-community/attacks/Web_Parameter_Tampering
42. OWASP Foundation: Appsensor detection points (2015). https://www.owasp.org
43. Pennington, J., Socher, R., Manning, C.D.: Glove: Global vectors for word representation. In: EMNLP (2014)
44. Peters, M.E., et al.: Deep contextualized word representations (2018). arXiv:1802.05365
45. Pohl, C., Zugenmaier, A., Meier, M., Hof, H.-J.: B.Hive: a zero configuration forms honeypot for productive web applications. In: Federrath, H., Gollmann, D. (eds.) SEC 2015. IAICT, vol. 455, pp. 267–280. Springer, Cham (2015). https://doi.org/10.1007/978-3-319-18467-8_18
46. PortSwigger: Insecure direct object references (IDOR) (2021). https://portswigger.net/web-security/access-control/idor
47. Sahin, M., Hebert, C., Oliveira, A.: Lessons learned from sundew: a self defense environment for web applications. In: MADWeb (2020)
48. Swagger: Flatten a swagger spec. https://goswagger.io/usage/flatten.html
49. Swagger: OpenAPI Specification Version 2.0. https://swagger.io/specification/v2/
50. ThinkstCanary: Canarytokens (2019). https://canarytokens.org
51. Yue, C., Wang, H.: BogusBiter: a transparent protection against phishing attacks. ACM Trans. Internet Technol. **10**, 1–31 (2010)

IPSpex: Enabling Efficient Fuzzing via Specification Extraction on ICS Protocol

Yue Sun[1,2], Shichao Lv[1], Jianzhou You[1,2], Yuyan Sun[1], Xin Chen[1(✉)], Yaowen Zheng[3], and Limin Sun[1,2]

[1] Beijing Key Laboratory of IOT Information Security Technology, Institute of Information Engineering, CAS, Beijing, China
{sunyue0205,lvshichao,youjianzhou,sunyuyan,chenxin1990, sunlimin}@iie.ac.cn
[2] School of Cyber Security, University of Chinese Academy of Sciences, Beijing, China
[3] Nanyang Technological University, Singapore, Singapore
yaowen.zheng@ntu.edu.sg

Abstract. Industrial Control System (ICS) protocols are essential to establish communications between system components. Recent cyber-attacks have shown that the vulnerabilities in ICS protocols pose enormous threats to ICS security. However, the efficiency of traditional black-box fuzzing technique is constrained when the protocol specifications are not publicly available.

In this paper, we introduce ICS Protocol Specification Extraction (IPSpex) method to improve black-box fuzzing efficiency via analyzing the network packet construction in industrial software. We extract message field semantics from network traffic, collect execution traces from network packet construction and extract message format using backward data flow tracking and sequence alignment algorithms. Our evaluation shows that compared to Wireshark, IPSpex achieves high correctness and perfection on three common ICS protocols, including Modbus/TCP, S7Comm and FINS. We further combine IPSpex with boofuzz to test an undocumented ICS protocol, UMAS. Totally we have found five 1-day vulnerabilities and two 0-day vulnerabilities.

Keywords: ICS protocol reverse engineering · Memory trace · Black-box fuzzing

1 Introduction

Industrial Control System (ICS) are systems used to monitor and control industrial real-time processes in critical national infrastructures, including power grid, water treatment and chemical industry. Stability and reliability are of paramount importance to ICS. With the ongoing convergence between Operational Technology (OT) and Information Technology (IT), the emerging cyber-attacks against

© Springer Nature Switzerland AG 2022
G. Ateniese and D. Venturi (Eds.): ACNS 2022, LNCS 13269, pp. 356–375, 2022.
https://doi.org/10.1007/978-3-031-09234-3_18

industrial components have become potential threats to ICS, which can result in significant economic impacts, severe environmental disasters and even casualties [2,3,9,11].

Over the past few years, the extensive application of Ethernet in the industrial environment has raised widespread public concern about the security of proprietary ICS protocols [8]. Historically, because the industrial engineering stations were trusted in closed networks, these domain-specific protocols were initially designed with little attention to security [26,41]. However, recent research has shown that the improper input caused by the vulnerabilities in ICS protocols to ICS components has become the most common architectural weaknesses of ICS [22]. With the increasing number of ICS components connecting to external networks [40], the unawareness of this attack surface may lead to unpredictable security breaches.

A common alternative to discover the vulnerabilities in ICS protocols is to conduct a fuzz testing. Since most ICS devices are built on closed operation systems, it is infeasible to use widely used grey-box fuzzing methods. Current fuzzing methods towards ICS protocols mostly use the protocol specification extracted from network packets to facilitate black-box fuzzing [12,25,28]. However, the performance is limited by the diversity of available network packets. In practice, due to the privacy and complexity of ICS protocols, it is hard to obtain sufficient ICS network packets from open-source warehouse or real-world industrial environment, which limits the efficiency of black-box fuzzing [21].

Inspired by IOTFuzzer [18] and DIANE [37], we shift focus to industrial engineering software, which provides hardware and software configuration, program development and real-time process monitoring for ICS devices. Actually, the construction of the network packets *sent* by industrial engineering software reveals abundant information about ICS protocol specifications. However, traditional methods on binary analysis are constrained due to the following reasons: (1) Commercial industrial engineering software usually only supports online operation with connection to ICS devices, which continuously brings a large number of network packets in a few seconds. The frequent network behaviours make it troublesome to analyze the network packet construction in industrial engineering software. (2) Most ICS protocols are designed in binary format without keywords and separators in traditional network protocols such as HTTP. Identifying the field boundaries from execution traces without these prior knowledge is also challenging.

In this paper, we introduce ICS Protocol Specification Extraction (IPSpex) method to improve the efficiency of black-box fuzzing via analyzing the network packet construction in industrial engineering software. To overcome aforementioned difficulties, we use field semantics to locate the target message during program execution, which are extracted from network traffic in advance. And then we apply a novel mechanism specified for industrial engineering software to capture the execution traces. Finally, we combine backward data flow tracking with sequence alignment algorithms to extract message format from execution traces. For evaluation, we compare our results with Wireshark. In general, IPSpex achieves high correctness and perfection on three widely used ICS protocols, including Modbus/TCP, S7Comm and FINS. To show how IPSpex can benefit black-box fuzzing, we use IPSpex to extract the protocol specification of a real-world undocumented ICS protocol, UMAS, and then we build a fuzzer based on boofuzz [4]. Totally we find five 1-day vulnerabilities that have been published on Talos [6], and two 0-day vulnerabilities.

Contributions. In summary, we make the following main contributions.

- We develop IPSpex, a protocol specification extraction method for ICS protocols, which automatically extract the field semantics and message format to facilitate fuzzing.
- We evaluate IPSpex on three widely used ICS protocols based on three open-source software libraries. The results shows that it achieves high correctness and perfection compared to Wireshark.
- We use IPSpex to find the vulnerabilities of a real-world undocumented ICS protocol, UMAS. Totally we find five 1-day vulnerabilities and two 0-day vulnerabilities.

2   Background

2.1   ICS Protocols

ICS protocols are widely used by industrial engineering stations, field devices and systems such as Programmable Logic Controller (PLC), Remote Terminal Unit (RTU), Distributed Control System (DCS) and Industrial Communication Device (ICD) [39], as shown in Fig. 1. As Industrial Ethernet continues to expand, it has recently surpassed traditional field bus architectures to become the leading connection methodology in plants around the world [1]. Industrial Ethernet mainly uses domain-specific ICS protocols such as Modbus/TCP and S7Comm, encapsulated within the Ethernet protocol. However, due to the convergence between industrial Ethernet and traditional Ethernet, this convenience also creates new external threat vectors such as eavesdropping, denial of service and unauthorized device control.

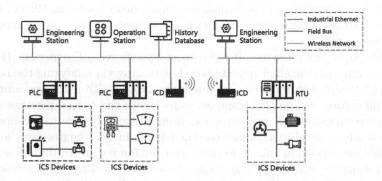

Fig. 1. Typical Application Scenarios of ICS Protocols

ICS devices, such as PLC and RTU, commonly use proprietary ICS protocols to communication with ICS engineering software and other ICS devices. A common alternative to discover the vulnerabilities in ICS protocols is to conduct a penetration test towards ICS devices. Fuzzing has approved to be very effective in finding vulnerabilities on real-world software [31]. Specifically, grey-box fuzzing leverages the coverage information collected from the target software to achieve higher performance when source code is not available [45]. However, a majority of ICS devices run on closed real-time operation systems (e.g., VxWorks [10], ADONIS [7]) or customized runtime system (e.g., CODESYS [5]). As current embedded firmware emulation techniques are not competent for these complex operating systems [19,24], it is infeasible to employ grey-box fuzzing tools based on dynamic binary instrumentation.

2.2   ICS Protocol Reverse Engineering

Protocol reverse engineering is an effective method to extract protocol specification. Due to the challenges to employ binary instrumentation on the firmware of ICS devices, most work use network-based protocol reverse engineering methods on ICS protocols. IPART applies an extended voting expert algorithm to infer the boundaries of industrial protocol fields. It then classifies messages into sub-clusters for protocol message format inference [42]. A full process has been proposed for ICS protocol analysis including fixed position field inference, assembling of fragmented packets, variable-length field inference and client-server relationship field inference [17]. The structure of a read-world private ICS protocol used by Schneider Modicon M580 is analyzed in [38], including message extraction and clustering, field extraction and message format inference.

However, these methods only focused on static network traffic analysis, which cannot achieve high performance on undocumented ICS protocols because they are severely limited by the diversity of available network packets For instance, a message usually consists of several static and dynamic fields indicating different physical meanings. The scarcity in the diversity of network packets can mislead these methods to regard the dynamic fields as static fields, which will cause wrong classification on field types. Therefore, there is a strong possibility that the protocol messages in network traffic only cover a small set of entire definitions and cannot provide a full-scale description on ICS protocol specifications.

2.3   ICS Protocol Fuzzing

Recently, some grey-box fuzzing methods towards ICS protocols have been proposed to guide the generation of new inputs. Peach* collects the coverage information during the testing procedure, saves those valuable packets that trigger new path coverage and breaks them into pieces, which are used to construct higher-quality new packets for further testing [30]. Polar combines static analysis and dynamic taint analysis on software libraries to identify the function code and related information, which can guide the generation of test cases [29]. GANFuzz uses generative adversarial network to learn protocol grammar and produces fake but plausible messages for fuzzing [25]. PropFuzz uses Ratcliff/Obershelp pattern recognition algorithm to analyse the valid process of connection establishment and then send protocol-specific commands [34].

However, because these efforts only focus on open source software libraries such as libmodbus, lib60870 and libiec61850, they fail to provide the impact of the vulnerabilities in these libraries on ICS devices. In fact, these vulnerabilities found by these methods are not sufficient to reflect the weakness of real-world ICS devices, which limits the further application in practice.

3   Problem Statement

To efficiently facilitate black-box fuzzing towards ICS devices, both message format and field semantics should be carefully defined in fuzzing template. The message format is the foundation for protocol reverse engineering, which defines the boundary between different fields. Our goal is to design a method to extract the message format from the network packet construction in industrial engineering software. Previous research [27] also focuses on message format, which recovers the message format by monitoring the message parsing process in open source software libraries. In practice, the parsing process of these messages are implemented in a much complex way in ICS devices so that the results are not competent to facilitate fuzzing towards these devices.

As for field semantics in ICS protocols, we focus on length field and function code field. The length field must be correctly calculated so that the followed bytes are valid. And it is necessary to infer the function code field because ICS devices will not process the data following an undefined function code. Therefore, it is extensively used in ICS protocol fuzzing [29,30]. In addition, we infer the field type from execution traces, namely, whether a field is constant, which can decrease the unnecessary mutation in black-box fuzzing.

4   Methodology

4.1   Overview

For most industrial software, operation commands are only accepted by industrial devices when they are converted to online mode, which continuously brings a large number of network packets in a few seconds. It is hard to locate the specific message in network traffic for an undocumented ICS protocol because the field semantics are unknown. Moreover, the frequent generation of network packets makes it troublesome to capture the execution trace that reflects target packet construction because the memory layouts of these network packets are overlapped.

To address these problems, we propose to use a buffer to store the execution traces. And only if the target message is detected by monitoring *send* function, we output the execution traces and exit the software. If not, the buffer will be cleared. The target message can be identified by the field semantics extracted from network traffic. After obtaining execution traces, we use a backward data flow tracking algorithm to extract the memory trace for each byte in a message. And then we leverage a sequence alignment algorithm to extract message format from these memory traces. Field types are inferred from memory traces.

Figure 2 depicts the architecture of IPSpex that comes with three main modules: ❶ field semantic extractor, ❷ context-aware execution monitor and ❸ protocol specification analyzer.

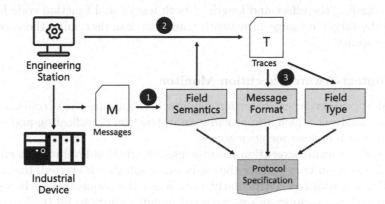

Fig. 2. IPSpex: An Architectural Overview

4.2   Field Semantic Extractor

The field semantic extractor aims to automatically identify the length and function code field from network traffic, which are used to locate specific message in the next step.

Length Field. The length field in most ICS protocols is variable, which indicates part or all of the length of a single message. Generally, we divide the fields in one message into fixed-length fields and variable-length fields, and only the latter contribute to the length of message. Since the changes of length field and the length of the message are both caused by variable-length fields, we could eliminate these changes using the difference between the value of length field and the length of the message. The results are the total length of fixed-length field, which is a *statistical constant*. Based on this observation, we combine n-gram analysis and statistical frequency analysis to identify the offset and length of length field (n is generally 2 or 4). If the frequency of the constant exceeds a given threshold (e.g. 0.95), we could demonstrate that it is the length field. In addition, there should be some messages whose length is greater than 0xff to determine the length of the length field.

Function Code Field. The function code of ICS protocols represents the domain-specific function of a single message. Since the values of function code field are always different between different functions, the number of functions in network traffic should be equal to the number of distinct values in function code field. Based on this insight, we manually generate several different function messages (at least 2 for each function) using industrial software, filter the heartbeat packets, and label the messages of these functions. And then for the messages of each function, we conduct byte frequency statistics and reserve the *invariant fields* for this function among these messages. Finally, we collect all the invariant fields, count the number of distinct values of them and regard the field whose number equals the number of functions as the function code field.

After finding the offset and length of both length and function code field to identify the target message in network traffic, we can determine the execution trace to capture.

4.3   Context-Aware Execution Monitor

The goal of context-aware execution monitor is to capture the execution traces for further analysis, which also provides an instruction classification and records the address of real-time memory access.

The context-aware execution monitor uses instruction-level instrumentation to record execution traces. Once the engineering software is started, the instruction buffer is initialized. Particularly, only when the connection to ICS device is established, the context-aware execution monitor starts to fill the instruction buffer with a tuple. We can intercept the network functions such as *send*, and decide if the message in socket buffer has the same field feature as the target message including the length and function code field. If not, the instruction buffer are cleared. After identifying the target message in network traffic, we can output the execution traces in the buffers and exit the software.

To conduct precise data dependency analysis later, each tuple in the instruction buffer consists of four elements: type, instruction, operands and memory address (e.g. {R|mov|esi, dword ptr [rbp + 8]|0x163f200}). For further memory trace construction, we divide the instructions into three categories: memory read (R), memory write (W) and others (X). For memory read and write instructions, we record the real-time address of memory access. At the same time, the address and size of socket buffer are recorded.

4.4   Protocol Specification Analyzer

The protocol specification analyzer aims to find the message format and field type using backward data flow tracking and sequence alignment algorithms. At the first step, we construct memory traces through backward data steam tracing for each byte in a single message, based on which we extract message format using sequence alignment algorithm. In addition, the function and field types are also inferred from execution traces.

After obtaining the address and length of socket buffer, we build a memory trace for each byte in this address space using a backward data flow tracking algorithm, which mainly processed different types of instructions to recognize corresponding memory region. The details are presented in Algorithm 1. IPSpex

---

Algorithm 1. Memory Trace Construction

Input: The address and length of socket buffer, instructions
Output: $[mt_1, mt_2,...,mt_n]$: one memory trace mapping one byte
1: $insList \leftarrow$ INVERT($instructions$)
2: $MemTraceList \leftarrow \emptyset$
3: **for** each $offset \in [0, BufferLength]$ **do**
4:    $MemTrace \leftarrow \emptyset$
5:    $BufAddr \leftarrow BufferAddress + offset$
6:    $DepChain \leftarrow$ GenDepChain($BufAddr$)
7:    $StackTag \leftarrow 0$
8:    **for** each $ins \in insList$ **do**
9:      **if** ISMEMACCESS(ins) **then**
10:        $addr \leftarrow$ INSPARSE(ins)
11:        $type \leftarrow$ GETTYPE(ins)
12:        $DataLoc \leftarrow$ GENPLOC($DepChain, addr, type, StackTag$)
13:      **else**
14:        $DataLoc \leftarrow$ GENDATALOC($ins, DepChain$)
15:        $stack \leftarrow$ UPDATESTACK($ins, StackTag$)
16:      **end if**
17:      $DepChain \leftarrow DepChain \cup DataLoc$
18:      $MemTrace \leftarrow$ ADDDATALOC($MemTrace, DataLoc$)
19:    **end for**
20:    $MemTraceList \leftarrow MemTraceList \cup MemTrace$
21: **end for**
22: **return** $MemTraceList$

---

supports a subset of x86 instructions that are divided into six categories including derived move instructions (e.g., *mov*, and *movzx*), stack operation instructions (e.g., *push*, *pop* and *ret*), explicit calculation instructions (e.g., *add*, *xor*, *shl* and *inc*), implicit calculation instructions (e.g., *imul* and *idiv*) and data exchange instructions (*xchg*) and byte swap instructions (*bswap*). These instructions supported by IPSpex are enough to extract message format and stop the construction of memory trace.

It is worth noting that the same memory address may store values of different fields. For example, the stacks can be reused using push and pop instructions. If there are different fields on the stack, their memory addresses will be overlapped, which may cause wrong results in message format inference later. Therefore, we use a stack tag (a sequence number) to record these operations to identify different fields.

Figure 3 shows an example of memory trace for write area function in S7Comm protocol, which illustrates the address sequence of the memory access for each byte in a message. According to the memory traces the corresponding field semantics are also presented.

Message Format. The message format of a single message can be extracted using a sequence alignment algorithm, which determines whether the memory traces of two adjacent bytes are spatially continuous. We present some strategies

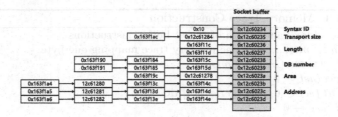

Fig. 3. Memory Trace of Write Area Function in S7Comm Protocol

to determine this spatial continuity. Firstly, different types of program locations in memory trace are divided into different fields. Secondly, if the two locations are both immediate locations and the values of them are equal, we merge them into the same field. Thirdly, if these two program locations are both memory locations, we check if they are in continuous memory region and if their stack tags are the same, so as to decide whether to merge them. These strategies are implemented in Algorithm 2.

Algorithm 2. Message Format Extraction

Input: $[mt_1, mt_2,...,mt_n]$: one memory trace mapping one byte
Output: $[offset_1, offset_2,...,offset_n]$: field offsets for each byte
1: $MemTraceLen \leftarrow$ GETSIZE$(MemTraceList)$
2: $MsgFormat \leftarrow$ INITIALIZE$(MemTraceLen)$
3: **for** each $i \in [1, MemTraceLen - 1]$ **do**
4:     $MemTrace1 \leftarrow MemTrace_i$
5:     $MemTrace2 \leftarrow MemTrace_{i+1}$
6:     $MinSize \leftarrow$ GETMINSIZE$(MemTrace1, MemTrace2)$
7:     **for** each $j \in [0, MinSize]$ **do**
8:         $type \leftarrow$ TYPECOMP$(MemTrace1_j, MemTrace2_j)$
9:         **if** SEQCOMP$(MemTrace1_j, MemTrace2_j, type)$ **then**
10:             $MsgFormat \leftarrow$ MERGE$(MsgFormat, i)$
11:         **end if**
12:     **end for**
13: **end for**
14: **return** $MsgFormat$

Field Type. We can generally classify the fields to constant or non-constant according to their values, or whether the addresses of them fall in the data section of the corresponding module, which are recorded when the programs are loaded. The immediate values in memory traces indicate that the fields in specific functions are constant, which may be checked on the target devices. Therefore, in order to send valid commands these fields can not be changed, which are especially important for test case generation in fuzzing.

5   Evaluation

5.1   Experimental Setup

We implement IPSpex using pin-3.16 and python 3.7.4. Respectively, we use three public software libraries including libmodbus v3.1.6 [35], snap7 v1.4.2 [33] and libfins [13] to collect execution traces. We select these software because they use typical ICS protocols to communicate with industrial devices. And we compare IPSpex with Wireshark like previous work [15, 16, 20].

5.2   Overview

Although Wireshark supports a variety of protocol parsers for ICS protocols, sometimes it is not reliable. Therefore, to completely evaluate the effectiveness of IPSpex, we compare our results with the latest Wireshark v3.2.7 based on the message format extracted from the source codes in libmodbus, snap7 and libfins. We use *correctness and perfection* derived from other indicators for a message to reflect their effectiveness as previous studies [44].

Indicators. For one network message, we use F_s to denote the message field set defined in the source codes. And we use F_i and F_w for those identified by IPSpex and Wireshark. Respectively, the size of them are denoted by $|F_s|$, $|F_i|$ and $|F_w|$.

If the *offset* of the fields identified by IPSpex or Wireshark are the same with those in F_s, we define those fields as a *correct set*, which is denote by S_c. Otherwise, we define those fields as a false set, which is denote by S_f. For the fields in a correct set, if the *length* identified by IPSpex is also identical with the length of those in F_s, we group these fields into a *perfect set* and denote them as S_p. Otherwise, we group them into a incorrect set and denote them as S_e. Respectively, the size of them are denoted by $|S_p|$, $|S_e|$ and $|S_f|$. Generally, for one message we have (x equals i or w):

$$|F_x| = |S_p| + |S_e| + |S_f| \tag{1}$$

The overall performance of IPSpex on one protocol derived from above indicators are defined as follows, where N is the number of tested functions. Correspondingly, we also use these indicators to measure the performance of Wireshark, where N is the number of the functions to evaluate for one protocol, and j is the index of the function.

- **Correctness.** We define the correctness as the ratio from the number of the correct fields identified by IPSpex or Wireshark to the number of fields identified by them (x equals i or w):

$$R = \frac{1}{N} \sum_{j=1}^{N} \frac{|S_{pj}| + |S_{ej}|}{|F_{xj}|} \tag{2}$$

- **Perfection.** We define the perfection as the ratio from the number of the identical fields identified by IPSpex or Wireshark to the number of fields defined in source codes:

$$R = \frac{1}{N} \sum_{j=1}^{N} \frac{|S_{pj}|}{|F_{sj}|} \tag{3}$$

Summary. We have evaluated 11, 15 and 20 different functions for Modbus/TCP, S7Comm and FINS, which has almost covered all of the functions supported by them. Table 1 shows the detailed results for each protocol. As for Modbus/TCP and S7Comm, Wireshark has a better performance than IPSpex because these protocols are used more widely and their formats are elaborately defined in Wireshark. However, the FINS protocol, only used by OMRON controllers, is less known to the public, especially for some seldom used functions, which are not well parsed by the latest Wireshark but IPSpex works. Therefore, IPSpex can provide an alternative to obtain the protocol specifications of undocumented ICS protocols. The deep analysis of eval result is performed as follows.

Table 1. Statistical Results of Indicators

Protocol	Func.	$|F_s|$	Wireshark					IPSpex				
			$|S_p|$	$|S_e|$	$|S_f|$	Corr.	Perf.	$|S_p|$	$|S_e|$	$|S_f|$	Corr.	Perf.
Modbus/TCP	11	8.00	8.00	0.00	0.00	1.00	1.00	7.63	0.18	0.00	1.00	0.96
S7Comm	15	20.0	20.0	0.00	0.00	1.00	1.00	17.6	1.53	1.46	0.94	0.88
FINS	20	14.1	13.25	0.35	0.00	1.00	0.94	14.0	0.01	0.01	0.99	0.99

5.3   Modbus/TCP

We evaluate 11 functions for Modbus/TCP supported by libmodbus v3.1.6. IPSpex tests all the functions of libmodbus, as shown in Fig. 4, with high correctness of 100% and perfection of 96%. After inspecting the memory traces, we find the fields identified in S_e are caused by the semantically fields segmentation and correlation.

Semantically fields segmentation refers to the situation that one field is parsed based on another field in one message. For example, the fields in S_e in "write registers" function is the list of the values of the registers to write. After checking the memory trace of the write register function, we find that these values are in a continuous buffer, which causes IPSpex to aggregate them into one field. However, the list of values are separately defined in specific number of fields based on the "Word Count" field. The implicit semantic-aware way for field segmentation is hard for IPSpex to recognize.

Semantically fields correlation means that some fields represent related physical meanings such as the message length. For instance, we find the fields in S_e

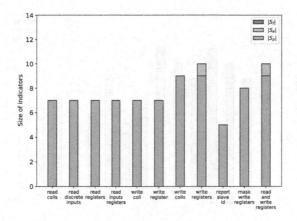

Fig. 4. Indicators for Functions Defined in Libmodbus

in "read and write registers" function are the length to write, which are identified as two-bytes "Write Word Count" and one-byte "Byte Count". Figure 5 shows the instruction trace for calculating the value of these fields. The register "edx" is the source of the value of length, and "dl" stores the low byte while "cl" stores the high byte. However, "al" is equal with "dl" and is doubled before being written to the "Byte Count" field. These two fields are merged because they come from the same memory location. The binary-based methods can not recognize this semantics-aware difference, which leads to the unexpected result.

```
mov   edx, dword ptr [ebp + 0x10]
mov   ecx, edx
sar   ecx, 8
mov   al, dl
mov   byte ptr [ebp + esi - 0x106], cl   ⎫
add   al, al                             ⎬  Write Word Count
mov   byte ptr [ebp + esi - 0x105], dl   ⎭
xor   ecx, ecx
mov   byte ptr [ebp + esi - 0x104], al   ⎬  Byte Count
```

Fig. 5. Assemble Code of Read and Write Registers Function

5.4   S7Comm

We evaluate 15 functions of S7Comm supported by snap7 v1.4.2. For S7Comm protocol, Wireshark defines 12 main functions and there are many sub-functions of userdata under "CPU services" function. IPSpex has tested *all* of the main functions supported in snap7 and some sub-functions under "CPU services" function, as shown in Fig. 6, with high correctness of 94% and perfection of 88%. The main reasons for IPSpex to improperly identify the fields include irregular function code and strings.

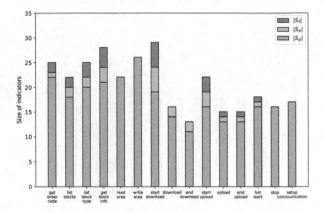

Fig. 6. Indicators for Functions Defined in Snap7

The function code of "CPU services" is irregular that its length is 3 bytes while others are 1 bytes. From the memory trace we find these three bytes are separately assigned with different constant values separately, which leads IPSpex to tell them apart.

The other common fields in S_f and S_e come from the printable strings in messages such as the name and number of block, the length of program and the command of program invocation services. The memory trace shows that the program sets part of a string to constant values while others as variable values, which leads IPSpex to set different types of program locations for them and divide them into different fields. Nevertheless, printable strings are easy to identify with explicable meanings and correct manually.

5.5 FINS

Libfins defines more than 60 functions and some are similar. We manually select some of them to analyze those with abundant information in these fields. For instance, we drop functions such as "finslib_link_unit_reset" that have a body of zero length. We also drop some functions that have the same parameters such as "finslib_access_log_read". In addition, libfins sends FINS/TCP header and FINS body separately, because the former header has a fixed format. Totally we have selected 20 functions for evaluation, as shown in Fig. 7, with high correctness of 99% and perfection of 99%.

The only two functions that are not well parsed by IPSpex include "read file" and "write file". After checking the source code of libfins, we discover that the filename parameter is encoded as an expanded 8.3 filename format with spaces padded where necessary. Indeed, from the memory trace we discover that the filename is divided two part. The first part is 8-bytes variable bytes while the second part is 4-bytes spaces. Therefore, IPSpex regard it as two fields, which leads to the wrong results.

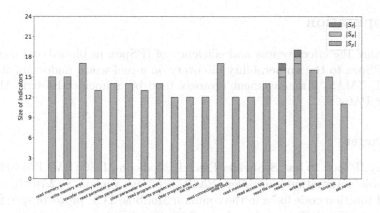

Fig. 7. Indicators for Functions Defined in Libfins

In addition, we discover that some functions are not completely dissected by the latest Wireshark. On one hand, the function code of "read access log" 0x2140 is not defined in the omron-fins dissector in Wireshark, which is unable to identify the subsequent bytes after function code. However, IPSpex can identify the parameter fields in access log reading message such as the start address and the number of bytes to read. On the other hand, although most of the function codes in FINS are well defined by Wireshark, the parameters of some functions are partially absent. IPSpex has recognized these parameter fields, which are consistent with the field semantic information provided by the source code of libfins. Table 2 lists these functions and the semantics of their parameters that Wireshark did not recognize.

Table 2. The Fields Semantics for FINS

Function Description	Parameters
read message	message mask
read file name	disk identifier, path, length of path, number of files, start number of file
read file	disk identifier, file name path, length of path, start position of file, number of bytes
write file	path, length of path, data to write
delete files	path, length of path
force bit	area, main-address, sub-address

6 Application

To measure the effectiveness and efficiency of IPSpex in black-box fuzzing, we apply IPSpex to the vulnerability discovery on a real-world undocumented ICS protocol, UMAS, a management protocol used by Schneider Electric Modicon PLCs or PACs.

6.1 Target

We apply IPSpex to test Schneider Electric Modicon M580 (BMEP584020) programmable automation controller (PAC), firmware version SV2.70. It uses the reserved function code 0x5a in the common Modbus/TCP protocol specification as shown in Fig. 8. The engineering software we use to communicate with the PAC is Unity Pro, which enables various actions such as obtaining the CPU status and reading the program running on device.

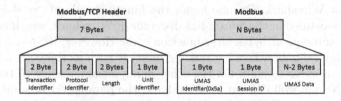

Fig. 8. UMAS Message Encapsulated in Modbus/TCP

6.2 Procedure

According to our protocol specification extraction method, firstly, we use Unity Pro to send specific command and capture the UMAS network traffic using Wireshark. The length and function code field can be identified by comparing the distribution of each byte using the aforementioned method. Secondly, we capture the execution traces that record the target massage construction and extract the message format. Note that the target message is saved for next stage. Finally, we use *boofuzz*, an open-source network protocol fuzzing framework, to generate test cases for fuzzing UMAS protocol. The UMAS message is encapsulated on the Modbus/TCP message. And we use *boofuzz-byte* (i.e., we treat each byte as a single field and perform mutations) as comparison. The default "full_range" option is set to "False" for all dynamic fields.

Although it is efficient to choose an algorithm to select seeds from many UMAS target messages for fuzzing [36], it is hard to trigger Unity Pro to generate a large amount of UMAS network packets in great diversity because some fields in these messages are also dependent in the hardware device (e.g., the default memory address for input). Therefore, we use only one target message as the seed of fuzzing for each function code. And the constant values in the results of protocol specification are set as constants in message template.

Table 3. Description of Vulnerable Functions

Name	Code	Length	Fields	CVE ID	IPSpex	Byte
GetRawAppliInfo	0x20	13	7	CVE-2018-7843	4s	7s
StartRestoreData	0x21	14	8	CVE-2018-7856	1min2s	None
StartSaveData	0x24	13	8	CVE-2019-6828	1min8s	None
StartRestoreData	0x25	18	10	CVE-2018-7857	1min15s	None
WriteSync	0x50	38	26	Confirmed	10s	None
Unknown	0x50	27	19	None	8s	None
SetBreakPoint	0x60	20	11	CVE-2018-7855	6s	8s

6.3   Result

Totally, we have found five 1-day vulnerabilities and two 0-day vulnerabilities, including six ones that lead M580 PAC to enter a non-recoverable fault state, and one that can cause the I/O module into error. However, after searching for related information on public vulnerability report [6], we find similar vulnerability descriptions on five functions of them, which only differs in product name. The detailed descriptions of vulnerable functions are shown in Table 3. The function names are identified from call-stack traces, while the CVE ID refers to the similar description with corresponding functions. The length and number of fields are the attributes of the test cases that trigger the vulnerabilities. The 'None' in Byte column means testcases are exhausted without finding a vulnerability.

Although existing smart black-box fuzzers support some mutation strategies to improve efficiency, the vulnerabilities discovered are largely limited without message format. The root cause is that it is extremely hard to locate the offset and length of the vulnerable field in advance. In our experiment, the CVE-2018-7843, CVE-2018-7855 and the two 0-day vulnerabilities we have found are all caused by one vulnerable field. But the length of the vulnerable field for the latter two is 4, rather than 1 for the former two, which makes boofuzz-byte fuzzer unable to find these two vulnerabilities. According to the public report, CVE-2018-7843 is caused because the PAC does not check the offset parameter when receiving a block reading command. CVE-2018-7855 is caused because the PLC does not verify the invalid program address.

Particularly, some vulnerabilities can only be triggered when more than one fields equal specific values. According to the message format, we sample 4-byte length fields to some boundary values in advance and test other fields. CVE-2018-7856, CVE-2018-7857, CVE-2019-6828 all belong to this type. CVE-2018-7856 is caused when the PAC does check the address parameter with specific object type. Similarly, the PAC does check the offset parameter with specific block number, which result in CVE-2018-7857. CVE-2019-6828 is caused when the PAC does not check one undocumented field with specific type of position variable.

7   Discussion

In this section, we discuss the limitations in our method and present several improvements for future work.

Stability. As IPSpex uses Pintool that only supports the executable written in C or C++ to capture execution traces, it is can not be applied to the engineering software written in other languages such as .NET. Another limitation lies in the complexity of engineering software, which may use multiple process to deal with network data transmission. Under this circumstance, the construction and sending (or receiving) of network packet are processed in different modules. We consider to use dynamic binary instrumentation to recognize the core component of communication, and combine the results with under-constrained symbolic execution to drive the execution of the component. After obtaining the execution traces, we can use IPSpex to extract the protocol specification.

Another issue on ICS protocols is encryption. To the best of our knowledge, ICS protocols use various authentication mechanisms such as session id in Siemens S7CommPlus P2 Version [14], SHA 1 algorithm and RSA in Rockwell CIP [23] and customized algorithm in Mitsubishi MELSEC protocol [32]. But data encryption is rarely adapted due to the inevitable overhead for data encryption and decryption. And we can identify these authentication process through open source software library [23] or the statistics of arithmetic and bitwise instructions [43]. So that we can pass the authentication before fuzzing process.

Robustness. IPSpex uses backward data flow tracking and sequence alignment algorithms to extract the message format from instruction traces. In fact, there are usually slightly differences in instruction traces with different compiler options. These may lead to incorrect results on the identification of strings and continuous constant values. The influence in our experiment is relatively small. Nevertheless, we think this problem needs a comprehensive explanation, and we will further explore it in the future.

8   Conclusion

In this paper, we present IPSpex method to improve the efficiency of blackbox fuzzing. From the execution traces such as instruction trace and call-stack, IPSpex can extract the message format sent by engineering software using a backward data flow tracking and sequence alignment algorithm. And we combine IPSpex with boofuzz to improve the efficiency of fuzzing. We have evaluated IPSpex on Modbus/TCP, S7Comm and FINS, which all achieve high correctness, conciseness and coverage compared to Wireshark. For vulnerability discovery on undocumented UMAS protocol, totally we find five 1-day vulnerabilities and two 0-day vulnerabilities in minutes. Our future work focuses on two aspects including the improvement of IPSpex for higher stability and robustness, and other application of IPSpex.

References

1. Things you need to know about industrial ethernet. https://www.fluke.com/en-us/learn/blog/electrical/industrial-ethernet
2. Analysis of the cyber attack on the Ukrainian power grid. https://ics.sans.org/media/E-ISAC_SANS_Ukraine_DUC_5.pdf
3. Attackers deploy new ICS attack framework "triton" and cause operational disruption to critical infrastructure. https://www.fireeye.com/blog/threat-research/2017/12/attackers-deploy-new-ics-attack-framework-triton.html
4. Boofuzz: network protocol fuzzing for humans. https://boofuzz.readthedocs.io/en/stable/
5. Customize your PLC applications using CODESYS . https://www.deif.us/blog/posts/2019/11/customise-your-plc-applications-using-codesys?sgm=marine+and+offshore
6. Disclosed vulnerabilities. https://talosintelligence.com/vulnerability_info
7. Doors of Durin: the veiled gate to Siemens S7 silicon. https://www.blackhat.com/eu-19/briefings/schedule/#doors-of-durin-the-veiled-gate-to-siemens-s-silicon-18023
8. ICS/SCADA protocol vulnerabilities: CIP (common industrial protocol). https://www.cyberbit.com/blog/ot-security/scada-vulnerabilities-cip-protocol/
9. Industroyer: biggest malware threat to critical infrastructure since Stuxnet. https://www.eset.com/int/industroyer/
10. PLC security risk: controller operating systems. https://www.tofinosecurity.com/blog/plc-security-risk-controller-operating-systems
11. W32.Stuxnet Dossier. https://en.wikipedia.org/wiki/Stuxnet
12. Bai, S., Wen, H., Fang, D., Sun, Y., Liu, P., Sun, L.: DSS: discrepancy-aware seed selection method for ICS protocol fuzzing. In: Sako, K., Tippenhauer, N.O. (eds.) ACNS 2021. LNCS, vol. 12727, pp. 27–48. Springer, Cham (2021). https://doi.org/10.1007/978-3-030-78375-4_2
13. Bies, L.: LibFINS - multi platform MIT licensed FINS library in C. https://github.com/lammertb/libfins
14. Biham, E., Bitan, S., Carmel, A., Dankner, A., Malin, U., Wool, A.: Rogue 7: Rogue engineering-station attacks on S7 Simatic PLCs. In: Black Hat USA (2019)
15. Caballero, J., Poosankam, P., Kreibich, C., Song, D.: Dispatcher: enabling active botnet infiltration using automatic protocol reverse-engineering. In: Proceedings of the 16th ACM Conference on Computer and Communications Security, CCS 2009, New York, NY, USA, pp. 621–634. Association for Computing Machinery (2009)
16. Caballero, J., Yin, H., Liang, Z., Song, D.: Polyglot: automatic extraction of protocol message format using dynamic binary analysis. In: Proceedings of the 14th ACM Conference on Computer and Communications Security, CCS 2007, New York, NY, USA, pp. 317–329. Association for Computing Machinery (2007)
17. Chang, Y., Choi, S., Yun, J.H., Kim, S.: One step more: automatic ICS protocol field analysis. In: D'Agostino, G., Scala, A. (eds.) Critical Information Infrastructures Security, CRITIS 2017. LNCS, vol. 10707. Springer, Cham (2018). https://doi.org/10.1007/978-3-319-99843-5_22
18. Chen, J.: IoTFUZZER: discovering memory corruptions in IoT through app-based fuzzing. In: 25th Annual Network and Distributed System Security Symposium, NDSS 2018, San Diego, California, USA, 18–21 February 2018 (2018)
19. Clements, A.A., et al.: HALucinator: firmware re-hosting through abstraction layer emulation. In: 29th USENIX Security Symposium (USENIX Security 20), pp. 1201–1218. USENIX Association (August 2020)

20. Cui, W., Peinado, M., Chen, K., Wang, H.J., Irun-Briz, L.: Tupni: automatic reverse engineering of input formats. In: Proceedings of the 15th ACM Conference on Computer and Communications Security, CCS 2008, New York, NY, USA, pp. 391–402. Association for Computing Machinery (2008)

21. Gascon, H., Wressnegger, C., Yamaguchi, F., Arp, D., Rieck, K.: PULSAR: stateful black-box fuzzing of proprietary network protocols. In: Thuraisingham, B., Wang, X.F., Yegneswaran, V. (eds.) SecureComm 2015. LNICST, vol. 164, pp. 330–347. Springer, Cham (2015). https://doi.org/10.1007/978-3-319-28865-9_18

22. Gonzalez, D., Alhenaki, F., Mirakhorli, M.: Architectural security weaknesses in industrial control systems (ICS) an empirical study based on disclosed software vulnerabilities. In: IEEE International Conference on Software Architecture, ICSA 2019, Hamburg, Germany, 25–29 March 2019, pp. 31–40. IEEE (2019)

23. Grandgenett, R., Mahoney, W., Gandhi, R.: Authentication bypass and remote escalated i/o command attacks. In: Proceedings of the 10th Annual Cyber and Information Security Research Conference, CISR 2015, New York, NY, USA. Association for Computing Machinery (2015)

24. Gustafson, E., et al.: Toward the analysis of embedded firmware through automated re-hosting. In: 22nd International Symposium on Research in Attacks, Intrusions and Defenses, RAID 2019, Chaoyang District, Beijing, September 2019, pp. 135–150. USENIX Association (2019)

25. Hu, Z., Shi, J., Huang, Y., Xiong, J., Bu, X.: GANFuzz: A GAN-based industrial network protocol fuzzing framework. In: Proceedings of the 15th ACM International Conference on Computing Frontiers, CF 2018, New York, NY, USA, pp. 138–145. Association for Computing Machinery (2018)

26. Irvene, C., Shekari, T., Formby, D., Beyah, R.: If i knew then what i know now: on reevaluating DNP3 security using power substation traffic. In: Proceedings of the 5th Annual Industrial Control System Security (ICSS) Workshop, ICSS, New York, NY, USA, pp. 48–59 (2019)

27. Kai, C., Ning, Z., Liming, W., Zhen, X.: Automatic identification of industrial control network protocol field boundary using memory propagation tree. In: Naccache, D., et al. (eds.) ICICS 2018. LNCS, vol. 11149, pp. 551–565. Springer, Cham (2018). https://doi.org/10.1007/978-3-030-01950-1_32

28. Kim, S., Shon, T.: Field classification-based novel fuzzing case generation for ICS protocols. J. Supercomput. 74, 4434–4450 (2017)

29. Luo, Z., Zuo, F., Jiang, Yu., Gao, J., Jiao, X., Sun, J.: Polar: function code aware fuzz testing of ICS protocol. ACM Trans. Embed. Comput. Syst. 18(5s), 1–22 (2019)

30. Luo, Z., Zuo, F., Shen, Y., Jiao, X., Chang, W., Jiang, Y.: ICS protocol fuzzing: coverage guided packet crack and generation. In: 2020 57th ACM/IEEE Design Automation Conference (DAC), pp. 1–6 (2020)

31. Manes, V.M., et al.: The art, science, and engineering of fuzzing: a survey. IEEE Trans. Softw. Eng. 47(11), 2312–2331 (2021)

32. Yang, S., Cheng, M.: Taking apart and taking over ICS-SCADA ecosystems a case study of Mitsubishi electric. In: DEF CON 29 (2021)

33. Nardella, D.: Step7 open source ethernet communication suite. http://snap7.sourceforge.net/

34. Niedermaier, M., Fischer, F., von Bodisco, A.: PropFuzz - an IT-security fuzzing framework for proprietary ICS protocols. CoRR, abs/1910.07883 (2019)

35. Raimbault, S.: A groovy Modbus library. https://github.com/stephane/libmodbus

36. Rebert, A., et al.: Optimizing seed selection for fuzzing. In: Proceedings of the 23rd USENIX Conference on Security Symposium, SEC 2014, USA, pp. 861–875. USENIX Association (2014)
37. Redini, N., et al.: Diane: identifying fuzzing triggers in apps to generate under-constrained inputs for IoT devices. In: 2021 IEEE Symposium on Security and Privacy (SP), pp. 484–500 (2021)
38. Shim, K.-S., Goo, Y.-H., Lee, M.-S., Kim, M.-S.: Clustering method in protocol reverse engineering for industrial protocols. Int. J. Netw. Manage. **30**, e2126 (2020)
39. Stouffer, K., Falco, J., Scarfone, K.: Guide to Industrial Control Systems (ICS) Security (2015)
40. Volkova, A., Niedermeier, M., Basmadjian, R., de Meer, H.: Security challenges in control network protocols: a survey. IEEE Commun. Surv. Tut. **21**, 619–639 (2019)
41. Volkova, A., Niedermeier, M., Basmadjian, R., de Meer, H.: Security challenges in control network protocols: a survey. IEEE Commun. Surv. Tut. **21**(1), 619–639 (2019)
42. Wang, X., Lv, K., Li, B.: IPART: an automatic protocol reverse engineering tool based on global voting expert for industrial protocols. Int. J. Parallel Emergent Distrib. Syst. **35**, 376–395 (2020)
43. Wang, Z., Jiang, X., Cui, W., Wang, X., Grace, M.: ReFormat: automatic reverse engineering of encrypted messages. In: Backes, M., Ning, P. (eds.) ESORICS 2009. LNCS, vol. 5789, pp. 200–215. Springer, Heidelberg (2009). https://doi.org/10.1007/978-3-642-04444-1_13
44. Ye, Y., Zhang, Z., Wang, F., Zhang, X., Xu, D.: NetPlier: probabilistic network protocol reverse engineering from message traces. In: 28th Annual Network and Distributed System Security Symposium, NDSS 2021, virtually, 21–25 February 2021. The Internet Society (2021)
45. Zheng, Y., Davanian, A., Yin, H., Song, C., Zhu, H., Sun, L.: FIRM-AFL: high-throughput greybox fuzzing of IoT firmware via augmented process emulation. In: 28th USENIX Security Symposium, USENIX Security 19, Santa Clara, CA, August 2019, pp. 1099–1114. USENIX Association (2019)

Probing for Passwords – Privacy Implications of SSIDs in Probe Requests

Johanna Ansohn McDougall$^{(\boxtimes)}$ ⓘ, Christian Burkert ⓘ, Daniel Demmler ⓘ,
Monina Schwarz ⓘ, Vincent Hubbe, and Hannes Federrath

University of Hamburg, Hamburg, Germany
{johanna.ansohn.mcdougall,christian.burkert,daniel.demmler,
monina.schwarz,vincent.hubbe,hannes.federrath}@uni-hamburg.de

Abstract. Probe requests help mobile devices discover active Wi-Fi networks. They often contain a multitude of data that can be used to identify and track devices and thereby their users. The past years have been a cat-and-mouse game of improving fingerprinting and introducing countermeasures against fingerprinting.

This paper analyses the content of probe requests sent by mobile devices and operating systems in a field experiment. In it, we discover that users (probably by accident) input a wealth of data into the SSID field and find passwords, e-mail addresses, names and holiday locations. With these findings we underline that probe requests should be considered sensitive data and be well protected. To preserve user privacy, we suggest and evaluate a privacy-friendly hash-based construction of probe requests and improved user controls.

Keywords: Probe Requests · Wi-Fi Tracking · Privacy Preserving Technologies

1 Introduction

To establish a Wi-Fi connection, mobile devices can transmit so-called *probe requests* to receive information about nearby Wi-Fi networks. An access point observing a probe request is led to reply with a probe response, thereby initiating a connection between both devices. While probe requests are used to establish a connection between a mobile device and an AP, they also serve as a means to track, trilaterate and identify devices for attackers who passively sniff network traffic. They can contain identifying information about the device owner depending on the age of the device and its OS. One of those is the preferred network list (PNL), which contains networks identified by their so called Service Set Identifier (SSIDs). Around 23% of the probe requests contain SSIDs of networks the devices were connected to in the past, according to our measurements. There exist online mapping services like WiGLE[1], which provide

---

[1] https://www.wigle.net.

© Springer Nature Switzerland AG 2022
G. Ateniese and D. Venturi (Eds.): ACNS 2022, LNCS 13269, pp. 376–395, 2022.
https://doi.org/10.1007/978-3-031-09234-3_19

information about geographical locations where SSIDs have been observed. A casual observation of the networks available in any given residential area returns a multitude of personalised, often descriptive SSIDs used for private networks. Therefore, a query for an SSID might reveal home or work addresses, or other visited locations where users connected to Wi-Fi, and can thereby reveal very personal information about them.

Another application in which probe requests are frequently used is tracking of devices in stores or cities: as probe requests are sent rather frequently, they can be used to trilaterate the location of a device with an accuracy of up to 1.5 m [24]. Trilateration can also be used to follow the movements of a device and thereby its user over a longer period of time, and track them through a store or city [23]. This is in fact employed in 23% of the stores already [1]. Companies and cities that conduct Wi-Fi tracking take the legal position that only the MAC address contained in probe request is considered personal data according to GDPR Article 4(1) [8,10], which protects personal data from unlawful collection and processing. They therefore maintain that if the MAC address is anonymised before storage, the collection and evaluation of probe requests is GDPR compliant [29]. The randomisation of MAC addresses mitigates linkability via this element. Instead, we focus on looking at what privacy risks originate from probe requests related to the list of SSIDs stored in the PNL. We provide empirical evidence that probe requests should also be considered personal data on the basis of their SSID field, which we find can even contain directly identifying information. We hope to thereby stress the need for a more thorough legal evaluation. We additionally propose changes to the handling of SSID field and mobile OS behaviour to enhance the privacy of users and decrease their trackability to passive sniffers.

To this end, we contribute the following:

- We conduct a field experiment in a German city, recording probe requests of passersby.
- We evaluate their content, with special regard for SSIDs and identifying information.
- We summarise the state of probe requests for different OS versions.
- We propose a hashing of non-wildcard SSIDs in probe request to protect their confidentiality against passive observers.
- We propose changes to the UI design of Wi-Fi selection and PNL management.

This paper is structured as follows: in the next section, we first provide a background on network discovery and privacy implications of MAC addresses. Here, we also compare the privacy features of various Android and iOS versions. Thereafter, we present related work in Section 3. Section 4 explains the experimental setup and our handling of ethical and privacy concerns. We then present the results of our data analysis in Section 5. Section 6 proposes mitigation approaches on both protocol and user interface level. In Section 7, we discuss the findings. Finally, Section 8 concludes the paper.

2   Background

In this section we define the underlying technological background of our work.

2.1   Network Discovery in 802.11

To establish a Wi-Fi connection between a mobile device and an access point (AP), both devices have to discover each other; either via active or passive discovery:

In a passive discovery, an AP advertises itself by sending out *beacons* containing its SSID, MAC address, the cipher suites it supports and a few other elements [17]. These beacons are sent at an interval of approximately every 100 ms [12], and mobile devices can respond with Wi-Fi association frames.

In an active discovery, mobile devices broadcast *probe requests* to find APs they have previously associated with. Active discovery is also required to connect to so-called hidden networks, for which the AP does not advertise the network, i.e., does not send out beacons. Probe requests sent by most modern devices are typically broadcast and contain the empty wildcard in the SSID field. APs receiving a probe request respond with a *probe response* directed at the sender of the probe request. The probe response contains the SSID of the AP and additional information like supported rates and various capabilities.

The reason both active and passive discovery mechanisms are used is that while APs advertise themselves constantly, scanning for beacons can be rather energy consuming and slow. Additionally, a mobile device scanning for beacons on one channel with a certain frequency might miss beacons sent on another channel. A device actively probing for APs just has to turn on the Wi-Fi radio until it receives the probe response, which typically takes only a few milliseconds [12]. On the other hand, active discovery requires the transmission of packets containing information about the mobile device. While probe requests sent by devices running older OS might contain SSIDs of one or more APs the device has previously been connected to, newer devices transmit only the SSIDs of hidden networks to improve user privacy and make the device less traceable (cf. Section 2.3). Additionally, they omit the real MAC address of the device, instead sending a randomised MAC address.

Probe Requests are sent in bursts, every burst containing several probe requests sent via some or all of the 14 channels of the 2.4 GHz spectrum (and additionally the 5 GHz spectrum if applicable) within a short time span of just a few milliseconds. Whether MAC address randomisation is employed or not, all packets in a burst are sent from the same MAC address.

2.2   Privacy Implications

A MAC address consists of 6 bytes typically represented in hexadecimal notation, separated by colons, e.g. 01:23:45:ab:cd:ef. The first three bytes are called the Organizationally Unique Identifier (OUI) and are typically assigned to the manufacturer of the devices. The last three bytes identify the Network Interface

```
wlan.fc.type_subtype==0x0004

No.      Time            Source             Info
       2284 874.747357275 46:8e:45:03:1c:02  Probe Request, SN=1954, SSID=WootWootKarneval
       2285 874.781384907 46:8e:45:03:1c:02  Probe Request, SN=1955, SSID=Wildcard (Broadcast)
       2286 874.782041635 46:8e:45:03:1c:02  Probe Request, SN=1956, SSID=TestingThisCrazyIdea
       2287 874.782770066 46:8e:45:03:1c:02  Probe Request, SN=1957, SSID=alalalalalong
       2288 874.787660806 46:8e:45:03:1c:02  Probe Request, SN=1958, SSID=WootWootKarneval
       2294 881.989862003 3e:15:5a:f5:1f:74  Probe Request, SN=404, SSID=Wildcard (Broadcast)
       2296 882.031938926 3e:15:5a:f5:1f:74  Probe Request, SN=408, SSID=Wildcard (Broadcast)
       2297 882.032516694 3e:15:5a:f5:1f:74  Probe Request, SN=409, SSID=TestingThisCrazyIdea
       2298 882.033237567 3e:15:5a:f5:1f:74  Probe Request, SN=410, SSID=alalalalalong
       2299 882.038153435 3e:15:5a:f5:1f:74  Probe Request, SN=411, SSID=WootWootKarneval
       2300 882.072168931 3e:15:5a:f5:1f:74  Probe Request, SN=412, SSID=Wildcard (Broadcast)
       2302 882.074146595 3e:15:5a:f5:1f:74  Probe Request, SN=413, SSID=TestingThisCrazyIdea
       2303 882.074876650 3e:15:5a:f5:1f:74  Probe Request, SN=414, SSID=alalalalalong
       2306 882.079439335 3e:15:5a:f5:1f:74  Probe Request, SN=415, SSID=WootWootKarneval
       2313 887.911035684 12:19:a8:58:f5:39  Probe Request, SN=1100, SSID=Wildcard (Broadcast)
       2315 887.913045924 12:19:a8:58:f5:39  Probe Request, SN=1101, SSID=TestingThisCrazyIdea
       2316 887.913747853 12:19:a8:58:f5:39  Probe Request, SN=1102, SSID=alalalalalong
       2318 887.917433850 12:19:a8:58:f5:39  Probe Request, SN=1103, SSID=WootWootKarneval
       2323 887.951525908 12:19:a8:58:f5:39  Probe Request, SN=1104, SSID=Wildcard (Broadcast)
```

Fig. 1. Three bursts of probe requests sent from the same device. Three different SSIDs and the wildcard SSID, an empty string, are broadcast. Note that the starting sequence number (SN) in the info field is randomised per burst as well.

Controller (NIC), produced and assigned by the manufacturer. The OUI contains additional information encoded in the two least significant bits (U/L and I/G) of the most significant byte (01 in our example): The I/G-bit is the least significant bit and specifies whether the recipient is unicast or a multicast. The second-least significant bit, the U/L bit, clarifies whether the address is locally or globally administered, with a globally administered address being a unique identifier for the physical device, while a locally administered address temporarily overwrites the unique global one in software [34]. Older devices use their universal address to broadcast probe request, which makes them easily trackable. To protect the privacy of users and prevent device tracking, probe requests are often sent from locally administered addresses, employing a technique called MAC address randomisation. Here, the MAC address commonly changes between two bursts, such that each burst will be sent from a new, random MAC address. This behaviour was first introduced in iOS 8 in 2014 [11] and in Android 8 [13] in 2017, albeit the first implementations suffered from information leaks: it was often possible to track devices despite the use of MAC address randomisation [32], for example by the SSIDs they contained. If SSIDs are present in a probe request, either all of them or a subset is contained in a burst, with every packet requesting one SSID. Figure 1 shows the capture of three bursts of probe requests sent from the same device employing MAC address randomisation but transmitting SSIDs.

While omitting SSIDs and employing MAC address randomisation renders a device less trackable, other fields included in probe requests can spoil the effect: if the sequence number (SN) is not randomised, it is trivial to still follow a device over time. Therefore, a lot of devices randomise their sequence number with the start of every burst, as can also be observed in Fig. 1.

The newer a device and its OS is, the more information is omitted and fields randomised in the probe requests. All the same, various papers still describe how even modern devices can be fingerprinted due to other information contained in them, e.g. in the Information Elements (IE): These non-mandatory parameters contain information on supported rates, network capabilities, and more. Combining the IE parameters, the signal strength and, in some cases, the sequence number, allows to fingerprint individual devices despite MAC address randomisation. [30, 32] While efforts are made to reduce the fingerprint of modern devices, the owners of older devices that don't receive patches introducing MAC address randomisation, sequence number randomisation and SSID omission can easily be tracked.

2.3   Differences Between Android and iOS Versions

Table 1 shows the differences between iOS and Android in supporting Wi-Fi-related privacy features. We compare iOS versions 8, 10, 14 and 15 and Android 8 to 12. Their combined market share comprises about 90% of the devices [26, 27], which makes them representative and provides a good overview over the changes within the last years. In the following, we elaborate on the various features comprised in Table 1.

Table 1. Privacy features for probe requests in different mobile OSs.

	Apple iOS				Android				
	8	10	14	15	8	9	10	11	12
Market Share in %	< 0.1	1.0	35.9	53.4	10.2	13.5	27.0	35.4	1.9
Randomised MAC ...									
- while probing	✓	✓	✓	✓	✓	✓	✓	✓	✓
- per connected SSID	-	-	✓	✓	-	(-)*	✓	✓	✓
- after resetting settings	-	-	✓	✓	-	-	(-)*	(-)*	(-)*
New random MAC after ...	-	-	-	6w	-	-	-	(-)†	(-)†
Private Address by default	-	-	✓	✓	-	-	✓	✓	✓
Modify distant Network	-	-	-	-	✓	✓	✓	✓	✓
Manually added == hidden	Automatic detection of hidden				✓	-	-	-	-
Probe with SSID	Only if hidden detected				if man. added	If explicitly declared hidden			

*: Only choosable via Developer Options
†: If use of non-persistent MAC is chosen via Developer Options, a new MAC is set (a) for every new connection establishment (b) every 24 hours, unless a connection is still established or (c) if both the DHCP lease has expired and the device has been disconnected for 4 hours

All listed versions use MAC address randomisation while probing [13, 19, 34]. In Android 9 devices, users can choose via Developer Options whether a randomised MAC address should be used while connected. Since Android 10 and iOS 14, private addresses are used by default: They all employ persistent random MAC addresses while connected. Starting with Android 11, one can choose via Developer Options to use non-persistent randomisation per stored SSID during connection. If non-persistent MAC addresses are used in Android, the MAC address is re-randomised either (a) with every new connection establishment, (b) every 24 h, but without disrupting the network connection to switch to a new MAC address or (c) if the DHCP lease has expired and the device has been disconnected for at least 4 h. Nevertheless, up to this date, there are no Android devices that automatically receive a new random MAC address after a certain amount of time by default, without having to modify the Developer Options. Additionally, with persistent private MAC addresses in Android, the default behaviour is to persist a MAC address per SSID even after resetting network settings. This is different in iOS: Starting with iOS 14, removing and adding a network again causes a reset of the network persistent address. In iOS 15, the devices additionally receive a new address when not connected for more than 6 weeks [2,14,34].

All of the listed Android versions offer to remove any saved network at any given time. This is not the case in iOS: Here, a network can only be removed from the device while in physical proximity of it or by modifying the iCloud Keychain from a MacBook. Without access to a MacBook or physical proximity to the network, it can not be removed without resetting the entire network settings [21].

When adding a network manually, iOS verifies whether it is a hidden network or not, whereas Android 8 (and earlier) automatically assumes that manually added networks are hidden networks. Therefore, if a network was manually added, Android 8 devices send the SSID in probe requests, while newer Android versions only do so if the added networks were explicitly declared hidden (cf. Fig. 2b in Section 6.2). In iOS, the SSID is only used in probe requests if the network is detected to be a hidden network [3,20].

3   Related Work

In 2013, Cunche et al. showed how to link various devices by their transmitted SSIDs and inferred relationships between users [5]. This work was published before MAC address randomisation was deployed and free transmittal of SSIDs the typical means of network discovery. The authors propose the use of a geolocation-based service discovery instead of active discovery via probe requests. In 2014, MAC address randomisation was first discussed [34] and subsequently tested and published [4]. It was meant as a means to increase privacy, but since it lacked standardisation, all implementations were vulnerable to attacks [32]. Since then, extensive work has been published on probe requests, MAC address randomisation and fingerprinting devices despite MAC address randomisation: 2015, Freudiger et al. gave an overview over the amount of probe requests sent by different devices and analysed the effectiveness of the MAC address randomisation employed in different devices [12]. On a positive note, Freudiger pointed out that recent mobile operating systems only probe for SSIDs of hidden networks. In another influential publication, Vanhoef et al. investigated how well devices can be tracked by combining various fields in probe requests [32]. They also present two attacks that can be used to reveal the real MAC address of a device and summarise that MAC address randomisation is insufficient to impede tracking.

Various other papers in the field attempt to associate probe requests from randomised MAC addresses: Gu et al. use deep learning methods and suggest to encrypt probe requests using the symmetric stream cipher ChaCha20 to protect them from attackers [16]. Tan et al. use minimum-cost flow optimisation to associate frames and reach an accuracy of more than 80% [30]. As the use of hidden networks and the amount of devices broadcasting SSIDs are decreasing, both papers put only a minor focus on the transmitted SSIDs.

In 2019, Dagelić et al. [6] observe the occurrence of SSIDs in probe requests at a music festival between 2014 and 2018 and present how easy devices are trackable via probe requests if the devices are fingerprintable. Over the years, the number of MAC addresses they observe increases while the number of SSIDs decreases. They conclude that the use of MAC address randomisation is increasing, as is the number of probe requests that contain the empty wildcard SSID.

An attempt at localisation of criminal groups via probe requests was published by Zhao et al. in 2019 [33]. They build a database of SSIDs like WiGLE and monitor probe requests in different locations in search for specific SSIDs. This methodology allows them to find and track devices belonging to a targeted group.

With respect to protecting the content of probe requests, Pang et al. [22] published an architecture called Tryst in 2007 to conceal confidential information during service discovery. Tryst makes use of access control primitives using symmetric encryption, with which it reveals information to the correct access point while concealing all information not directed at it. It remains unclear how exactly the various SSIDs present in the SEND primitive are concealed from everyone except for the intended recipient. They underline the privacy risks of both APs transmitting SSIDs and mobile devices transmitting probe requests by analysing geoinformation on SSIDs collected in a 2004 data set: they find that about a quarter of the devices probe for SSIDs that uniquely appear in just one city. While Pang et al. also perform geolocalisation of SSIDs like we do, to the best of our knowledge, there has been no publication analysing the content of SSIDs of probe requests as we do in this paper and neither one proposing hash-based anonymisation of probe requests to this date.

In the following, we first introduce the experiment and then strive to demonstrate the privacy implications of the use of such verbose devices on their users.

4 Experimental Setup

In this field experiment performed in November 2021, we recorded probe requests in a busy pedestrian zone in the centre of a German city, over the period of one hour, three times in total. We used six off-the-shelf antennae: three for channels 1, 6 and 11 in the 2.4 GHz spectrum and three for channels 36, 40 and 48 in the 5 GHz spectrum. Since our particular focus lies on privacy violations arising from the information contained in the SSID field, we evaluate it with respect to the following:

- The amount of probe requests containing non-empty SSIDs.
- The amount of SSIDs sent per burst.
- Privacy implications of transmitted SSIDs: what potentially personal data can be gleaned from the data set?
- The use of MAC address randomisation.

We calculate an intersection between the data sets of two different days and remove all probe requests by devices that appear in both of them. That way, we strive to isolate the permanent devices in the vicinity of the measurement to have a clearer view on devices more likely to represent human passersby.

4.1 Potential Ethical and Privacy Concerns

A modern smartphone might use MAC address randomisation and refrain from transmitting SSIDs and thereby protect the identity of its user and render itself less trackable. Older devices are often less privacy sensitive, transmit their real MAC address and maybe even known SSIDs. This data can be considered personal data and should therefore only be collected and stored with particular care for the device owner's privacy. To ensure ethical data aggregation, we submitted our study for approval to the ethics committee of the Informatics department of the University of Hamburg under case number 002/2021. The steps taken to protect the peoples privacy as observed and in accordance with the ethics committee can be found in Appendix A.1.

5 Data Analysis

Our field data set contains 252 242 probe requests. We found that overall, 23.2% of the probe requests contained SSIDs. Prior measurements done by Dagelić [6] between 2014 (46.7%) and 2018 (12.9%), and also Vanhoef [32] in 2016 (29.9% to 36.4%), revealed higher numbers in 2014 and 2016, from which a decline is absolutely expected. At the same time, the records of 2018 and our measurements do not match up. One explanation might be, that while a measurement at a music festival might record the probe requests of younger people with more recent devices that already omit SSIDs in probe requests, our measurements were taken in the city centre of a touristic city around noon, where perhaps a larger percentage of people kept their (older) devices over a longer period of time. Our numbers do however correlate with the market share of Android devices [26]: 10.2% of Android devices use Android 8, and devices older than Android 8 amount up to 12%. In these devices, manually added networks are considered hidden networks [20] and they are therefore probed for with SSID. Seeing that Android devices make up approximately 70% of the market share, while iOS devices make up around 29% [28], the percentage of SSIDs in the data set is slightly higher than expected.

During our measurement, 116 961 probes (46.4%) were captured in the 2.4 GHz spectrum, of which 28 836 (24.7%) contained at least one SSID. In the

Table 2. Distribution of the number of SSIDs per cluster.

# SSIDs	1	2	3	4	5	6	7	8	> 8
Share	67.8%	8.2%	4.0%	6.5%	2.7%	2.2%	0.9%	6.6%	1.1%

5 GHz spectrum, we recorded 135 281 probes (53.6%), of which 29 653 (21.9%) contained an SSID.

To prepare the probe requests for analysis, we first grouped all requests that were sent from the same MAC address within a period of four seconds into bursts. We then grouped all bursts into clusters of bursts, likely belonging to a single device, if their PNL was equal. We explicitly did not group requests into the same cluster if their PNL matched only partly to avoid misclassification of distinct devices with partly overlapping PNLs. At the same time, a cluster with only one SSID might contain requests from distinct devices. As can be seen in Table 2, 67.8% of the bursts contain just one SSID, while the remaining 32.2% contain more than one SSID and are unique enough to track devices with it. This is considerably less than Vanhoef et al. recorded in 2016 [32]: In their data set, 53% to 64.8% of the bursts contained a unique PNL.

Of the probe requests containing an SSID, we identified at least 362 devices sending requests from multiple randomised MAC addresses. 542 devices used only one MAC address, and did not employ MAC address randomisation.

In an additional evaluation, we found that the average amount of probe requests sent per unique MAC address was 4.8. This is, again, a legitimate decline in comparison to the capture by Dagelić [6] et al. in 2014 (24.1), 2015 (29.2) and 2017 (6.1) respectively, but is, again, higher than their 2018 count (2.6). For packages including SSIDs, the average amount of probe requests sent per MAC address was 11.2, which confirms that these are likely older devices of which less employ MAC address randomisation.

In the following, we analyse the values contained in the SSID field of probe requests in order to estimate the privacy violations that occur in their commercial collection and analysis.

5.1   SSID Contents

As mentioned in Section 2.3, devices running Android 8 and lower treat manually added networks like hidden networks [20]. We conjecture that a lot of the SSIDs in our record originate from users trying to set up a network connection manually by entering both SSID and password through the advanced network settings, and, apparently mistakenly, enter the wrong strings as the SSIDs. The devices then retransmit the PNL with every probe burst. This results in significant additional information for fingerprinting devices compared to the empty wildcard SSID that would be transmitted otherwise.

In the following, we elaborate on our findings of a manual, as well as automated inspection of the encountered SSIDs.

Password Leaks in SSID Broadcasts. A small but significant amount of probe requests containing SSIDs potentially broadcast passwords in the SSID field: We identified that 11.8% of the transmitted probe requests contain numeric strings with 16 digits or more, which are likely the initial passwords of popular German home routers (e.g., FritzBox or Telekom home router). This hypothesis is supported by various cases, in which the numeric strings follow a PW:, WPA: or (WPA/WPA2:). Also, we repeatedly found both a 16- or 20-digit string and in the same burst additionally the same string, but separated by a space, a dot or a comma every four digits (e.g. 1234567812345678 and 1234 5678 1234 5678), which is a typical way of improving readability of the initial password on the router case. The multitude of similar spellings support our assumption that the users tried the same way of logging in multiple times with different spellings of the same credentials.

Leaking passwords in SSIDs is especially critical if, along with the password, the device also broadcasts the true SSID either correctly or with a mistype that can be used to infer the true SSID. Only 2.8% of the transmitted SSIDs classified as probable passwords were the only entry in the corresponding PNL. All other probable passwords were transmitted in bursts with other SSIDs that might contain the actual SSID belonging to the password. The assumption that the sniffed passwords correspond to SSIDs that were also transmitted could additionally be verified by setting up fake access points on the fly using the potential credentials we observed. As that would constitute an active attack on the devices and since we are determined to improve user security, not undermine it, we decided against employing fake-AP attacks.

Moreover, Wi-Fi locations can often be gathered using Wi-Fi mapping services like WiGLE, as we demonstrate in Section 5.2. Additionally and with enough criminal energy, an attacker could follow the owner of a talkative device to their home and try out the password in their home network.

Broadcasts of SSID Mistypes. In a manual analysis of the data set, we found various devices that broadcast multiple different spellings of presumably the same SSID. We assume that users manually entered them into their devices while trying out for different spelling and capitalisation variations, e.g., my network, MY_NETWORK, MyNetwork. We quantify the amount of mistyped SSIDs by calculating the normalised edit distance between all SSIDs in a burst stemming from a single device. The edit distance defines the minimum amount of operations (insertions, deletions or substitutions of characters) needed to transform one string into another. Since the edit distance can also be calculated over strings of different length, we normalise the result with respect to the longer string length, i. e., we divide the edit distance by the maximum length of the two SSIDs. Similar strings have an edit distance close to 0, while the edit distance is closer to 1 the more strings differ. Before calculating the edit distance, all input strings are transformed to lowercase, as otherwise, the normalised edit distance between SSIDs like NETWORK and network would evaluate to 1. We set the threshold at which the strings are considered similar and thus treated as mistyped to 0.3.

This way, strings that differ in less than 30% of their letters are considered similar. We decided on such a high threshold to accommodate short SSIDs as well as long ones. A manual inspection verified that the results fulfill the typo criteria and nevertheless do not contain distinct network names like "Fritz!Box 7490" and "Fritz!Box 7590".

We found that 19.9% of the transmitted SSIDs, stemming from 138 distinct bursts, are similar enough to another SSID in the same burst to be considered a typo. Such a set of constantly transmitted misspelled SSIDs increases the fingerprint of a device drastically and makes tracking it easy.

Additional Findings. We found at least one string that corresponds to a store and the Wi-Fi password of the store's internal Wi-Fi. We deem this highly likely as it began with the letters "PW:" and contained the name of the store in the password. We identified 106 distinct first and/or last names, which were propagated 3339 times over the course of the experiment. We found three e-mail addresses that were propagated 36 times. We identified 92 distinct holiday homes or accommodations whose SSIDs users had added to their list of known networks, which were propagated 1257 times. In addition, we found the name of a local hospital broadcast in two different spelling variations 15 times. It is particularly shocking to see such sensitive information like an e-mail address being transmitted openly, let alone the hospital name, from which a potential stay at the hospital can be inferred. At the same time, the name of a person or the hotels and holiday homes in which they have stayed can also be used to draw conclusions about the person.

5.2   Geolocation Discoverability and Uniqueness

To provide a better estimate of whether an SSID exists or not, we ran all observed SSIDs trough the geolocation lookup API of WiGLE. This way, we were able to find out whether the captured SSIDs correspond to actual APs catalogued by WiGLE. Of course, this approach has one limitation: Mobile devices should, in a perfect scenario, only transmit SSIDs of hidden networks. Those should not be included in the WiGLE map at all, as the service only maps the transmitted SSIDs.

To evaluate the uniqueness of location of the SSIDs we found, we performed an analysis on the coordinates that WiGLE returned. To reduce the accuracy of the location estimation, we limited the amount of decimal places of the coordinates to 2, thereby providing an approximate 1-kilometre radius in which the actual network can be found. This also removed artifacts like multiple networks with the same SSID found within a radius of a few metres, that most likely belonged to the same network. Our input consisted of 1478 unique SSIDs. We had to limit our evaluation to a subset of 1440 SSIDs, as the remaining 38 contained special characters, which WiGLE can't resolve. We were able to pinpoint 334 SSIDs to one unique location and 377 SSIDs returned multiple locations. 729 (50.6%) of the SSIDs could not be localised anywhere in the world. The latter are either hidden networks that weren't mapped by WiGLE due to being hidden or mistyped SSIDs.

Password Evaluation. To provide an estimate of how many SSIDs contained passwords, we filtered the list for

- strings that contain 16 or more numeric digits and
- strings that contain "pass", "pw", "kennwort" (the German word for password) or "wpa".

Our input consisted of 77 unique strings classified as passwords. The WiGLE evaluation resolved only a single one of the strings to a unique location. We infer that this is strong evidence that the identified strings are in fact actual passwords.

Typo Evaluation. We performed the same evaluation on the potential typos we identified. In this analysis, we inserted all spelling variations we found of an SSID into our evaluation, which amounted to 296 unique strings. The hypothesis in this case was that at least half of the SSIDs we identified were in fact typos and would not resolve to an existing SSID. We assumed that it would be more than 50% since quite a few of the potential typos had more than one spelling variation. We assumed that the remaining SSIDs would contain the correct and actual spelling that could resolve to an access point.

Our analysis showed that of the 296 strings classified as potential typos, we were able to resolve approximately 41.9% of the SSIDs and identified 47 unique locations and 66 cases of multiple locations. These results support our hypothesis.

Limitations. The evaluation of networks contained in WiGLE is severely limited: Only networks that are *not* hidden appear in it, while probe requests of current devices target *only* hidden networks. Nevertheless, we found a large percentage of the networks do in fact exist. This can have several explanations: (1) multiple networks with the same name exist, and the one in question is in fact a hidden one, (2) the network has been set to hidden recently, and the map still contains the result of a scan from before, (3) the network was manually added in WiGLE.

6 Mitigations for Increased Privacy

Our experiments detailed in the previous section suggest that users, presumably mostly by accident or unwillingly, add items to their list of preferred networks, including credentials and sensitive information. Together with legitimately added hidden networks, those threaten user privacy by being sent in plain, making this information observable and the users traceable. To mitigate the issue, we first present a proposal to avoid plain text transmission and then show approaches to limit and control traceable SSIDs through the user interface.

6.1   Hashing SSIDs in Probe Requests

Recall that the introduction of the wildcard SSID in probe requests makes active scanning with specific SSIDs only necessary for hidden networks. While some publications consider hidden networks obsolete and no longer recommended [15], a recent study [25] revealed that in some areas, up to 44% of the detected networks were hidden. While the WPA3 standard contains improvements to the confidentiality management frames (802.11w) [9], this standard only applies to frames transmitted after a 4-way handshake, and not to frames transmitted without handshakes. Consequently, probe requests are not protected. To rectify this, we propose the following mitigation.

SSID Hashing. To circumvent the need to send cleartext SSIDs, we propose to send them in a hashed and salted manner instead. The device emitting the probe request would first salt the SSID using its randomised sender MAC address and the sequence number of the packet and then hash it. It would then send the hash, but omit both salt components as they are included in the frame anyway like so:

$$send(hash(MAC\|SN\|SSID))$$

Access points of hidden networks would then, upon receiving the probe request, prepend the MAC address and sequence number as salt to their own SSID, hash it, and compare the result with the received hash. If they match, the client was probing for their hidden network. As the MAC address should be chosen randomly and the sequence number changes with every packet, they introduce sufficient entropy and variability in combination to be suitable as salt to make sure the sent information can not be used to track and identify devices through a constant hash value. This mitigation could be employed regardless of whether or not a connection to the network has ever been established before, as it does not require the previous exchange of secrets. Another advantage of this mitigation is that potentially sensitive SSIDs (e.g., containing names or passwords) can only be distinguished from other SSIDs (e.g., generic home router names) with significant effort of brute-forcing the cleartext, thereby improving the privacy of clients and AP operators.

Attack Model. We consider an attacker that can monitor all probe requests and has bounded computational power, which makes it impractical for her to find preimages (SSIDs) of the hashes she observes. Introducing the combined MAC address and sequence number salt makes pre-computing hashes impractical, provided that MAC addresses are randomised and sequence numbers are also randomly chosen within their full 12 bit value range. If the randomised MAC address contributes 24 bit of entropy, leaving out the EUI/CID parts as a lower estimate, this totals to 36 bit of salt entropy. Attackers with a priori knowledge of used SSIDs can however, reduce costs significantly compared to true brute-forcing, depending on the number of likely used SSIDs. Consequently, tracking a device whose SSID set is known is therefore feasible.

To determine the practical feasibility of a hash-based mitigation, we first evaluate the computational cost and then calculate the additional bandwidth requirement.

Computational Overhead. Using the SHA-256 hash from Python's `hashlib` library, we prototyped the hashing and comparison that an AP would have to perform: first hashing a received SSID and then comparing it to a known hash (the AP's SSID). For baseline reference, we implemented the current string comparison of SSIDs. We performed one million computations in three runs on a Raspberry Pi Model 3, which is likely a good lower estimate of computational power of most routers. A single computation with hashing required on average 11.7 microseconds pure CPU time, while the baseline required an average of 4.6 ms. Using hashing therefore increases the time by 153.7%. Considering that the Raspberry Pi does not have cryptographic hardware acceleration, which professional Wi-Fi routers might have, we additionally ran the experiment on a laptop with an Intel i5, where hashing only added an average overhead of 53%.

In our experiment in a busy pedestrian zone, we captured around 23 probe requests per second, of which only 23.2% contained an SSID. Therefore, following these figures, an AP would have to hash approximately 5.3 probe requests per second. As a Raspberry Pi can perform around 85 200 hashing operations per second, we deduce that hashing and comparing should be well within the available resources for similarly equipped APs even in much more frequented deployment locations.

Bandwidth Overhead. Our proposal may also introduce a bandwidth overhead by always occupying the full 32 bytes available for SSIDs in a probe request frame [18, Sect. 9.4.2.2], whose length would otherwise vary with the actual SSID length. The average length of all packets in our city centre capture is 133.3 bytes, while the average length of packets containing SSIDs is 147.0 bytes. In our capture, the average length of SSIDs was 11.4 bytes. If all SSIDs were transmitted as hashes, it would increase the size by 20.6 bytes, leading to an average size of packets with SSID of 167.6 bytes, which is an increase of 14.01%. Considering that probe requests make up a tiny fraction of the actual transmitted traffic, we consider this an acceptable trade-off for more privacy and less fingerprintability.

6.2 Mitigations Through User Interface Design

Current iOS and Android version already employ mechanisms to prevent users from accidentally adding items to their PNL, to maintain that list and to change the connection behaviour for individual networks on this list. In the following, we briefly summarise the status quo and suggest further improvements for more accessible and effective controls.

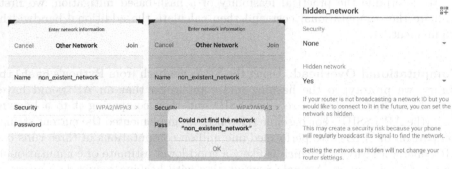

(a) Attempting a connection to a hidden network on iOS
15. Contrary to Android devices, iPhones only allow to
manually add networks to which a connection can be
established.

(b) Warning message when
adding a hidden network on
Android 9 or newer.

Fig. 2. User dialogues mitigating unwanted SSID entry.

SSID Entry Safeguards. Both iOS and Android have safeguards against accidentally adding hidden networks: iOS will only add networks to which a connection can be established at the time of entry (see Fig. 2a). In Android, a manually added network is no longer automatically considered a hidden network. Instead, to enter a hidden network, users have to explicitly select it and then receive a warning about the privacy risks (see Fig. 2b). We suggest to combine both measures for manually adding SSIDs.

Known SSID Removal. Being able to remove entries from the list of preferred networks should be possible to reduce traceability and susceptibility for fake AP attacks [32]. However, as mentioned in Section 2.3, removing a known network from proximity is not straightforward in iOS. On Android, in contrast, the list of known networks can be modified directly and at all times.

PNL Entry Expiry. In order to maintain its usability, user-facing lists of preferred networks should implement measures against cluttering, which result from steadily adding new SSIDs over time. To avoid cluttering with no longer needed SSIDs, e.g., added during temporary stays, we propose an expiration date for SSID entries: Upon adding a new SSID, the user is prompted to choose when the SSID should be forgotten again. The default expiry date would be *never*, but for SSIDs that are knowingly only in use for a limited period of a few days or weeks, users can choose accordingly. By limiting the life span of a network entry, its negative effects on traceability and the chance to exploit them using fake AP attacks are at least temporally limited. To the best of our knowledge, there is no such mechanism in any OS, but to implement it could significantly reduce the amount of SSIDs accumulated over time.

Adjustable Auto-Joining. In addition to networks of limited temporal relevance that benefit from expiry, there are also networks users use only occasionally but regularly, e.g., once every few months or years. While it is convenient to keep them in the PNL, this again increases the risk of fake AP attacks. Instead of removing such networks, preventing the automatic connection to them already effectively reduces the fake AP attack risk. Both iOS and Android offer ways to disable auto-joining on a per network basis. To make this option more visible and broadly realise privacy gains, we suggest to again prompt users when initially joining a network, whether they want to automatically or manually connect in the future.

Silencing Probe Requests. For particularly high privacy demands, disabling probe requests altogether might be an acceptable trade-off. We therefore suggest an advanced network setting, where users are able to choose that their devices do not send active probe requests *at all*, knowing that (a) connection establishment relies only on passive AP announcements and might be slower, (b) the battery usage might be higher, and (c) the connection to hidden networks would be impossible. Such behaviour could also be part of a *reduced visibility* mode that user, e.g., activate in the control center, when they pass through an untrusted area like a shopping centre known for extensive visitor analytics, similar to a do-not-disturb switch.

7 Discussion

Legal Consideration of SSIDs. As mentioned in the introduction, Wi-Fi tracking is also used to measure pedestrian flow and count in cities. In two German cities, such measurements have been conducted until the responsible authority started investigations [31]. The authority's reasoning was that MAC addresses are personal data and it is therefore not legal to record them without legal basis. In both cases, the measurements were ceased. Especially as the continued roll-out of MAC address randomisation might give renewed support to the legal positions that (randomised) MAC addresses should no longer be considered identifying information, we argue that this assessment can and should not be limited to the sender address of probe requests. Considering the wealth of personal and sensitive information we observed in SSID fields, they can constitute identifying information as well and thus require due consideration. For instance, for 334 of the SSIDs we measured, we were able to identify a unique location the SSID originated from. We therefore argue that at least for as long as there are still devices broadcasting SSIDs, probe requests should be considered personal data and not be used for monitoring without legal basis.

Intentional Password Broadcast. Some APs might intentionally broadcast their password as SSID to allow visitors an unrestricted yet encrypted Wi-Fi connection, as an alternative to unprotected Wi-Fi. It is a limitation of our password leakage evaluation that we cannot distinguish those intentional from unintentional cases. However, the fact that we could only resolve one of these SSIDs in our geo-lookup suggest that the ratio of SSIDs to actual APs is rather low. Additionally, the notion of intentionally storing passwords in the SSID field should have been superseded by the introduction of OWE (Opportunistic Wireless Encryption): OWE describes the unauthenticated but encrypted connection between two devices, and is contained in the Wi-Fi specification under the name *Wi-Fi CERTIFIED Enhanced Open*^{TM} [7].

Deployment of Hashed SSID Scheme. Our proposed hash-based scheme requires modifications to the Wi-Fi implementations: The mobile device has to apply the hashing algorithm to its temporary MAC address, sequence number, and the SSID of the sought-after network before transmission. The AP, upon receiving a probe request, has to apply hashing to the MAC address and sequence number as salt to its own SSID. On one hand, these changes are easy to implement, on the other hand they require a widespread deployment to be effective. While the privacy gain would be worth the deployment effort, it is unfortunately likely that only newer devices would profit from the scheme, while older devices would remain unpatched.

Limiting Bandwidth Overhead. Our proposed method of salting and hashing the SSIDs of hidden networks to improve user privacy introduces a bandwidth overhead, (cf. Section 6.1): The average length of a packet containing an SSID would be increased by 14%. This could be addressed by truncating the hash to, e.g., 16 bytes before inserting it into the SSID field. That way, the average packet length would be reduced to 151.6 bytes, which results in an overhead of only 3.2%. At the same time, this reduces the security of the system, as hash collisions become more likely.

Impact of OS Support Lifespans. A contributor of non-wildcard probe requests in the wild, besides hidden networks, are legacy devices. While devices running Android 10 or newer use MAC address randomisation and omit SSIDs, older devices do not receive updates long enough to benefit from this improvement. This especially disadvantages people with budgetary constraints or sustainability in mind, who keep their devices longer. This can only be rectified by longer support lifespans that should be legally mandated if manufacturers do not move voluntarily. Such changes with significance to user privacy should be considered like critical security patches and be back-ported to older versions.

8   Conclusion

Probe requests are plainly observable to everyone around a sending device. Since they can contain sensitive data, they should be sent more carefully and with privacy in mind. We have collected and analyzed data in a pedestrian zone to gather insight into the status quo of probe requests in the wild. We identified a wealth of personal information in transmitted SSIDs such as potential passwords, holiday homes and e-mail addresses, which should be considered personal and sensitive data. For 334 SSIDs, we were even able to resolve their unique geographic location.

In the area of anonymisation of probe requests, some progress has been made in the last few years, with the latest mobile operating system updates. Nevertheless, we are still facing problems in terms of user privacy. To minimise the amount of personal data that can be sent accidentally, we propose mitigations for both the network layer and the user interface. The first consists of hash-based concealment of SSIDs using a salt constructed from the MAC address and the sequence number of the request. To demonstrate its feasibility we provide estimates of the computational overhead and additional bandwidth requirements. For the latter, we propose to remodel the Wi-Fi handling of mobile devices to add only existing networks in range and to empower their users to take more control over their PNL and minimise the amount of potentially exploitable data.

Acknowledgements. We would like to thank our reviewers for their valuable and constructive feedback.

A   Appendix

A.1   Ethical collection of probe requests

Following approval and in coordination with the ethics committee of the informatics faculty of the University of Hamburg, we conformed to the following measures to observe and protect users' privacy rights:

- During the time of the experiment, we set up a well visible sign declaring the undergoing probe request monitoring, including information on how to contact the person in charge.
- We informed and obtained consent from building management to conduct the experiment.
- We provided an option to remove recorded probe requests should participants state their non-consent.
- We used off-the-shelf wireless USB antennae with a limited range to narrow the radius of our measurement
- In case the data set contains personal information, we either anonymise it before storing, or delete it directly after analysing it.
- Any personal data is stored securely, both technically as well as organisationally, to prevent misuse.
- To preserve location privacy, we limit the amount of decimal places of the coordinates returned by WiGLE to 2, thereby providing an approximate 1-kilometre radius in which the actual network can be found.

References

1. Acar, C.: Whitepaper: Smart Store (2018). https://www.ehi.org/de/studien/whitepaper-smart-store/
2. Apple Inc.: Use private Wi-Fi addresses on iPhone, iPad, iPod touch, and Apple Watch. https://support.apple.com/en-us/HT211227
3. Apple Inc.: Apple Platform Security (2021). https://manuals.info.apple.com/MANUALS/1000/MA1902/en_US/apple-platform-security-guide.pdf
4. Bernardos, C.J., Zuniga, J.C., O'Hanlon, P.: Wi-Fi internet connectivity and privacy: hiding your tracks on the wireless Internet. In: IEEE Conference on Standards for Communications and Networking (CSCN), pp. 193–198. IEEE (2015). https://doi.org/10.1109/CSCN.2015.7390443, http://ieeexplore.ieee.org/document/7390443/
5. Cunche, M., Kaafar, M.A., Boreli, R.: Linking wireless devices using information contained in Wi-Fi probe requests. Pervas. Mobile Comput. **11**, 56–69 (2018)
6. Dagelić, A., Perković, T., Čagalj, M.: Location privacy and changes in WiFi probe request based connection protocols usage through years. In: International Conference on Smart and Sustainable Technologies (SpliTech), pp. 1–5. IEEE (2019)
7. Harkins, D.: Wi-Fi CERTIFIED Enhanced Open^{TM}: Transparent Wi-Fi® protections without complexity. https://www.wi-fi.org/beacon/dan-harkins/wi-fi-certified-enhanced-open-transparent-wi-fi-protections-without-complexity
8. Deutscher Bundestag: Datenschutzrechtliche Zulässigkeit des WLAN-Trackings (2021). https://www.bundestag.de/resource/blob/538890/3dfae197d2c930693aa16d1619204f58/WD-3-206-17-pdf-data.pdf
9. Ebbecke, P.: Protected Management Frames enhance Wi-Fi Network Security (2020). https://www.wi-fi.org/beacon/philipp-ebbecke/protected-management-frames-enhance-wi-fi-network-security
10. European Union: Regulation (EU) 2016/679 - general data protection regulation. Official J. Eur. Union **L119**, 1–88 (2016). http://eur-lex.europa.eu/legal-content/EN/TXT/?uri=OJ:L:2016:119:TOC
11. Fenske, E., Brown, D., Martin, J., Mayberry, T., Ryan, P., Rye, E.C.: Three years later: a study of MAC address randomization in mobile devices and when it succeeds. In: PETS 2021, pp. 164–181 (2021)
12. Freudiger, J.: How talkative is your mobile device? An experimental study of Wi-Fi probe requests. In: WiSec 2015. ACM (2015). https://doi.org/10.1145/2766498.2766517
13. Google Android Documentation: Implementing MAC Randomization (2021). https://source.android.com/devices/tech/connect/wifi-mac-randomization
14. Google Android Documentation: MAC Randomization Behavior (2022). https://source.android.com/devices/tech/connect/wifi-mac-randomization-behavior
15. Goovaerts, F., Acar, G., Galvez, R., Piessens, F., Vanhoef, M.: Improving privacy through fast passive Wi-Fi scanning. In: Askarov, A., Hansen, R.R., Rafnsson, W. (eds.) NordSec 2019. LNCS, vol. 11875, pp. 37–52. Springer, Cham (2019). https://doi.org/10.1007/978-3-030-35055-0_3
16. Gu, X., Wu, W., Gu, X., Ling, Z., Yang, M., Song, A.: Probe request based device identification attack and defense. Sensors **20**(16), 4620 (2020). https://doi.org/10.3390/s20164620, https://www.mdpi.com/1424-8220/20/16/4620
17. Harkins, D., Kumari, W.A.: Opportunistic Wireless Encryption. RFC 8110, March 2017. https://doi.org/10.17487/RFC8110, https://rfc-editor.org/rfc/rfc8110.txt

18. IEEE: IEEE STD 802.11 - Wireless LAN Medium Access Control (MAC) and Physical Layer (PHY) Specifications (2020). https://ieeexplore.ieee.org/stamp/stamp.jsp?tp=&arnumber=9363693

19. Martin, J., et al.: A study of MAC address randomization in mobile devices and when it fails. In: PETS 2017, vol. 4, pp. 268–286 (2017)

20. Martinez, S.: Update add network dialog to not make networks hidden by default (2018). https://android.googlesource.com/platform/packages/apps/Settings/+/8bc3fa0649a3ecff5e42fb0d14ddb8ff6f7f7507

21. McElhearn, K.: How to Remove Wi-Fi Networks from Your Mac and iOS Device. The Mac Security Blog (2021). https://www.intego.com/mac-security-blog/how-to-remove-wi-fi-networks-from-your-mac-and-ios-device/

22. Pang, J., Seshan, S.: Tryst: the case for confidential service discovery. In: HotNets 2007 (2007)

23. Post, T.: Scharfe Kritik an Frequenzmessung. Kieler Nachrichten (2017). https://www.kn-online.de/Lokales/Eckernfoerde/Datenschutz-Diskussion-um-WLAN-Tracking-in-Eckernfoerder-Innenstadt

24. Redondi, A.E., Cesana, M.: Building up knowledge through passive WiFi probes. Comput. Commun. **117**, 1–12 (2018)

25. Schepers, D., Ranganathan, A., Vanhoef, M.: Let numbers tell the tale: measuring security trends in Wi-Fi networks and best practices. In: WiSec 2021, pp. 100–105. ACM (2021). https://doi.org/10.1145/3448300.3468286

26. statcounter: Mobile & Tablet Android Version Market Share Worldwide - December 2021 (2021). https://gs.statcounter.com/os-version-market-share/android/mobile-tablet/worldwide#monthly-202112-202112-bar

27. statcounter: Mobile & Tablet iOS Version Market Share Worldwide - December 2021 (2021). https://gs.statcounter.com/ios-version-market-share/mobile-tablet/worldwide/#monthly-202112-202112-bar

28. statcounter: Mobile operating system market share worldwide (2021). https://gs.statcounter.com/os-market-share/mobile/worldwide

29. Struever, A.: Vorteile und Nachteile WLAN-Tracking - Ist WLAN-Tracking DSGVO-Konform? (2019). https://www.expocloud.com/de/blog/vorteile-und-nachteile-wlan-tracking-wifi-tracking

30. Tan, J., Chan, S.H.G.: Efficient association of Wi-Fi probe requests under MAC address randomization. In: INFOCOM 2021, pp. 1–10. IEEE (2021)

31. Unabhängiges Landeszentrum für Datenschutz: 5.4.8 - Offline-Tracking/Ortung von Mobiltelefonen in Fußgängerzone. Unabhängiges Landeszentrum für Datenschutz (2021). https://www.datenschutzzentrum.de/tb/tb37/kap05.html

32. Vanhoef, M., Matte, C., Cunche, M., Cardoso, L.S., Piessens, F.: Why MAC address randomization is not enough: an analysis of Wi-Fi network discovery mechanisms. In: Asia CCS 2016, pp. 413–424. ACM (2016). https://doi.org/10.1145/2897845.2897883

33. Zhao, F., Shi, W., Gan, Y., Peng, Z., Luo, X.: A localization and tracking scheme for target gangs based on big data of Wi-Fi locations. Clust. Comput. **22**(1), 1679–1690 (2018). https://doi.org/10.1007/s10586-018-1737-7

34. Zúñiga, J.C., Bernardos, C.J., Andersdotter, A.: MAC address randomization. Technical report, IETF, July 2021. https://datatracker.ietf.org/doc/html/draft-zuniga-mac-address-randomization-01

Cryptographic Primitives

A Cryptographic View of Deep-Attestation, or How to Do Provably-Secure Layer-Linking

Ghada Arfaoui[1], Pierre-Alain Fouque[2], Thibaut Jacques[1,2,4],
Pascal Lafourcade[3], Adina Nedelcu[1,2], Cristina Onete[4], and Léo Robert[3(✉)]

[1] Orange Labs, Lannion, France
[2] IRISA, University of Rennes 1, Rennes, France
[3] Université Clermont-Auvergne, CNRS, Mines de Saint-Étienne, LIMOS, Saint-Étienne, France
leo.robert@uca.fr
[4] XLIM, University of Limoges, Limoges, France

Abstract. Deep attestation is a particular case of remote attestation, *i.e.*, verifying the integrity of a platform with a remote verification server. We focus on the remote attestation of hypervisors and their hosted virtual machines (VM), for which two solutions are currently supported by ETSI. The first is single-channel attestation, requiring for each VM an attestation of that VM and the underlying hypervisor through the physical TPM. The second, multi-channel attestation, allows to attest VMs via virtual TPMs and separately from the hypervisor – this is faster and requires less overall attestations, but the server cannot verify the *link* between VM and hypervisor attestations, which comes for free for single-channel attestation.

We design a new approach to provide linked remote attestation which achieves the best of both worlds: we benefit from the efficiency of multi-channel attestation while simultaneously allowing attestations to be linked. Moreover, we formalize a security model for deep attestation and *prove* the security of our approach. Our contribution is agnostic of the precise underlying secure component (which could be instantiated as a TPM or something equivalent) and can be of independent interest. Finally, we implement our proposal using TPM 2.0 and vTPM (KVM/QEMU), and show that it is practical and efficient.

Keywords: deep attestation · layer linking · TPM · vTPM

This study was partially supported by the French ANR, grants 16-CE39-0012 (SafeTLS) and 18-CE39-0019 (MobiS5). There are also the French government research program "Investissements d'Avenir" through the IDEX-ISITE initiative 16-IDEX-0001 (CAP 20-25), the IMobS3 Laboratory of Excellence (ANR-10-LABX-16-01), the French ANR project DECRYPT (ANR-18-CE39-0007) and SEVERITAS (ANR-20-CE39-0009). The research leading to these results partly received funding from the European Union's Horizon 2020 research and innovation programme under grant agreement no. 871808 (5GPPP project INSPIRE-5Gplus). The article reflects only the authors' views. The Commission is not responsible for any use that may be made of the information it contains.

© Springer Nature Switzerland AG 2022
G. Ateniese and D. Venturi (Eds.): ACNS 2022, LNCS 13269, pp. 399–418, 2022.
https://doi.org/10.1007/978-3-031-09234-3_20

1   Introduction

Network Function Virtualization (NFV) is a technology that promises to provide better versatility and efficiency in large-scale networks. The core idea is to move from architectures in which physical machines are set up to perform various roles in a network, to a design in virtual configuration. As such, a machine could be configured and re-configured at distance, and, by judicious use of virtual machines, it could perform a variety of roles within the network infrastructure.

Virtualized platforms are set up in layers, including the following basic components: physical resources, the virtualization layer and infrastructures, *virtualized network functions* (VNFs), and the NFV management and orchestration module. At the bottom of the infrastructure are real, physical components, meant for computations, storage, and physical network functions. The virtualization layer (also called *hypervisor*) manages the mapping between those physical components and virtual equivalents. As such, the NFVs – hosted by virtual machines running inside the NFV infrastructure– never have direct access to the physical resources. Instead, the VNFs access the virtual resources. The NFV management and orchestration module runs the combined infrastructure, including: the lifecycle of the instantiated VNFs, resource allocation for VNFs, or overall management in view of particular, given network services.

Deep Attestation (DA). Virtualization enables efficient, versatile remote network configuration and administration; however, the fact that multiple virtual processes share resources can introduce hazards to security. One way to ensure that a component runs correctly is by using *attestation*. Attestation is a process complementary to authentication: whereas the latter allows a platform to prove that it is the entity it claims to be, the former ensures that the platform runs a trustworthy code, *i.e.*, it has not been breached. As described in [13], *"Attestation is the process through which a remote challenger can retrieve verifiable information regarding a platform's integrity state."* A property can be for instance software integrity, geolocalisation, access control, etc.

Attestation relies on a *root of trust* (RoT), usually instantiated through a *trusted platform module* (TPM) – or an equivalent mechanism. The root of trust is responsible, amongst other things, for protecting sensitive cryptographic materials (such as private keys) and for running cryptographic operations in an isolated way. The virtualization layer (hypervisor) has direct access to the RoT, but the virtual machines it manages do not; instead they will have access to the RoT by means of *virtual Roots of Trust* (vRoTs). Virtual Roots of Trust are a combination of resources, some provided by the physical RoT, and other managed by the hypervisor, which directs and mediates access to the RoT.

In a nutshell, attestation is a process which allows an independent, remote verifier to check that a target platform still behaves in the desired way. This is done by first authenticating the RoT, then by comparing a measurement of the current state of the component to a presumably-correct state, as indicated in a *Root of Trust for Storage* (RTS). In addition, a guarantee must be given of the correctness of the RTS, which is done by means of a *Root of Trust for Reporting*

(RTR). Functionalities of RTS and RTR can be provided by a TPM. A TPM is an example of implementation that could provide RTR and RTS by leveraging the specific tampering detection properties of its Platform Configuration Registers (PCR) and issuing signed reports, or *quotes*, of their content.

We consider the attestation of two types of components: virtual machines (VMs), such as VNFs, and the hypervisor managing them, whose underlying physical component includes a RoT providing an RTR and an RTS. This architecture is depicted in Fig. 1.

To verify that the VMs and the hypervisor are running correctly, both these types of components must undergo remote attestation. First, each component must attest in isolation; then we must attest the *layer-binding* between VMs running on the same hypervisor. This is known as *deep attestation* (DA). There are two typical ways of achieving deep attestation (as described by ETSI standardization documents [13]): single- and multi-channel VM-Based Deep Attestation.

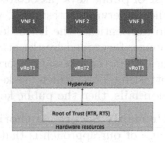

Fig. 1. The setup for DA.

Single/Multi-channel Deep Attestation. In single-channel deep attestation the attestation is run only between the remote verifier and the virtual machines. At each attestation, the VM (by querying its associated virtual TPM, or vTPM) provides not only an attestation for itself, but also the hypervisor it runs on.

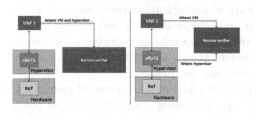

Fig. 2. Single vs multi-channel DA

Specifically the response forwarded by the VM to the remote verifier includes the (independent) attestation of the hypervisor, and the layer-binding attestation between the VM and its hypervisor. This is depicted in Fig. 2, on the left-hand-side. Note that the quotes in this case are both obtained from the (slow) physical TPM. From the point of view of security, this solution is optimal; however, it scales poorly. Given as few as 1000 VMs running on top of the hypervisor, we would require that the hypervisor be attested 1000 times, once for each VM.

By contrast, in multi-channel deep attestation, the VMs are attested separately and independently from the hypervisor. In this scenario, the VMs attest to the remote verifier, thus proving they were not tampered with. Separately, the hypervisor also attests to the remote verifier. This can be seen on the right hand side of Fig. 2. In this case, the efficiency is optimal: for 1000 VMs, we have 1000 VM-attestations and 1 hypervisor attestation. However, there is virtually no layer-binding between the VMs and their hypervisor: there is no guarantee that the VMs are really managed by the hypervisor. An attacker could therefore "convince" a party (such as the owner of the infrastructure) that a VM still exists on a given physical machine when it has, in fact, been removed.

Our Solution. We take the middle path between single- and multi-channel deep attestation to obtain layer-binding between VMs and hypervisors with reasonable efficiency. Our solution is simple, yet elegant, using standard cryptography to ensure that a hypervisor's single attestation is linkable to any number of attestations of VMs managed by it. We give three contributions:

A Cryptographic Scheme. Our scheme ensures secure and efficient linked DA. The hypervisor and VMs each attest only once. However, we also embed a list of public keys (associated with the VMs managed by the hypervisor) *within* the hypervisor attestation, which is established by the root of trust. In order to authenticate the list of forwarded keys, we embed them into the attestation nonce, forwarded by the attestation server. If the hypervisor's attestation verifies, then the attestation server can link that hypervisor with the (subsequently attesting VMs) which use keys in the forwarded list. If the hypervisor's attestation fails, then the public keys cannot be trusted.

Provably Secure Authorized Linked Attestation. An important advantage of our approach is that we have a fully-formalized provable-security guarantee. We use a composition-based approach, constructing primitives that are increasingly stronger out of weaker ones. Our goal is to ultimately obtain *authorized linked attestation* (ALA): a primitive which allows components to individually attest (to an authorized entity), and to have their attestations linked. This primitive solves the problem outlined in the introduction, since VMs sharing the same hypervisor will attest in isolation and together with their hypervisor.

ALA schemes will have three properties: *authorization* (only an authorized server can query an attestation quote); *indistinguishability* (no Person-in-the-Middle adversary can know even a bit of a quote exchanged during a legitimate protocol with probability significantly better than $\frac{1}{2}$); and *linkability* (an attestation server can detect if two components are not linked)

We choose to formalize AKA security as the last of a sequence of primitives, each potentially of independent interest and providing gradually stronger properties. This approach has two virtues: first, we are able to use weaker primitives as black-box components in stronger primitives; and second, the individual proof steps are shorter and smoother.

At the basis of our construction is a yea-or-nay *basic attestation scheme*, which is "secure" by assumption. Its functionality is simple: the basic attestation scheme outputs a faulty attestation whenever a component is compromised, and a correct one for honest components. In other words, this basic attestation scheme is a compromise-oracle: when queried it (indirectly) produces a proof of whether a component has been tampered with or not.

Based on this assumption, we build a sequence of cryptographic mechanisms that add security against stronger adversaries. A first step is to build *authenticated attestation*: a scheme which allows us to authenticate the component that provides the attestation, and additionally ensures that this component's attestations always verifies prior to corruption, but fails to verify as soon as a compromise occurs. We can think of authorized attestation as the minimum provided (and required) by multi-channel attestation. Then, we consider *linked attestation*: a scheme that introduces the hypervisor-VM relationship described above, and permits not only the verification of individual attestations, but also (publicly) linking attestations.

Implementation. We used a regular laptop equipped with TPM 2.0 (as a root of trust). We set up an architecture with one hypervisor and multiple VMs. The VMs used full virtual TPM as a virtual root of trust. We made over 100 experiments. This showed that our solution is more efficient that single channel approach and adds only insignificant charge (a hash function computation) compared to traditional multi-channel DA.

Our work is, to our best knowledge, the first that attempts to provide a sound cryptographic treatment of deep attestation. In many ways, this is much harder than designing the scheme that we present, because attestation is a generic term comprising an entire class of algorithms that have different goals. As such, we are only scratching the surface here, and believe that –aside from the real, and practical advantages of our presented construction– our cryptographic treatment, primitives, and proofs, may be of independent interest to this line of research.

Limitations. A first fundamental limitation is the fact that we assume, in our constructions, the existence of a basic attestation primitive that works infallibly like an oracle, telling us if a component is compromised or not. In reality, this primitive is based on the Platform Configuration Registers (PCRs) of a TPM. A PCR can store hash digests into a register of the length of the hash function output. Typically a TPM will have multiple banks corresponding to various hash functions (*e.g.*, a sha1 bank and a sha256 bank) with 24 registers for each bank. PCR are reset at each boot and are only updateable through an extension operation $PCR_1 \leftarrow H(PCR_1 \mid H(measurement))$. We assume the attacker has no physical access to the component and thus cannot tamper with TPM measurements by using hardware attacks. In practice, this is somewhat limiting since we do not account for runtime corruption; thus, the primitive is vulnerable to Time of Check Time of Use (TOCTOU) attacks. Several proposed mechanisms were introduced to monitor runtime integrity, *e.g.*, LKIM [19] or DynIMA [12]; moreover, in recent years several advancements were made towards verifying runtime integrity for IoT devices [15,17]. Yet, these solutions are not as widely spread at the present day as TPM-based attestation at startup.

We treat the existence of basic attestation as an assumption because we do not see a way of constructing it with cryptographic tools. The cryptography we put on top adds a lot of new properties: authenticity, confidentiality, authorization, linkability, but *not* the simple fact of distinguishing a compromised component from an honest one. Our result should therefore be interpreted as a need for such a scheme to exist, as in fact required by ETSI [13].

Another limitation of our scheme lies in our model of linked-attestation component. We consider classes of components which can be linked. At registration of each piece of hardware, a number of subcomponents of each type is indicated – and (unique) keys are given to those components. As a result, we cannot account for having two hypervisors that manage the same VM on a given infrastructure. A future work could be to consider *multi-hypervisor VM* as introduced in [14].

Related Work. Many attacks have been recently reported on remote attestation mechanism [10] or 5G standards [16]. Many tools such as formal methods or cryptography can be used to model and prove the security of such standards. However, this lack of formalization must be now addressed otherwise we will have more and more attacks. Provable cryptography is a nice solution to solve this problem since it allows to better understand the security model, what is the adversary goal and its means, which oracle can he query. Some cryptographic primitives have already be nicely formalized such as Direct Anonymous Attestation (DAA) which enables remote authentication of a trusted computer (TPM for instance) while preserving the privacy of the platform's user in [9] by Brickell et al. It is a group signature without the feature that a signature can be opened, *i.e.*, the anonymity is not revocable. Such primitive are well described using cryptography as a variant of signature scheme. However, provable cryptography has also been used successfully to formalize security protocols as authenticated key exchange [7,11]. This is precisely our goal to model the different security components independently and to compose them to prove the security of a new security mechanism. Indeed, the attestation server must authenticate the whole platform, *i.e.*, the hypervisor and the NFV running on top. This problem has been addressed by others in the context of secure boot or for instance in [6], where the authors propose an attestation mechanism for swarms of device softwares in IoT and embedded environment. Software attestation is different from remote attestation, as said in [5] since it cannot rely on cryptographic secrets to authenticate the prover device. The first to have taken into account deep attestation are Lauer and Kuntze in [18] but their solution misses a security proof and a rigorous analysis.

2 Towards Authorized Linked Attestation

Our core contribution provides layer-binding in deep attestation. Cryptographically, we view this as a new primitive, which we call *authorized linked attestation*, built in steps from increasingly-stronger primitives. Each of these intermediate steps plays a double role: on the one hand, it formalizes security guarantees that are of independent interest for attestation (if, for instance, layer-linking is not required); on the other hand, it provides an intuition of the guarantees which specific cryptographic primitives can help achieve.

The first, and basic-most step in our architecture is *basic attestation*. This primitive is an abstraction of the algorithm by which a single party (like a component of a virtualized platform) generates an attestation of its state, given a fresh, honestly-generated nonce. Importantly, basic attestation does not employ cryptography to achieve this feature, but rather, the attestation of registers at startup, using a RoT.[1]

---

[1] To ease notation, we assume that all the registers are attested, and that the property we are attesting is that the entire component has not been compromised.

Authenticated attestation builds on basic attestation by associating parties with identities. The attestation must now no longer indicate whether the party is compromised: it must also authenticate the component. Here, thus, we enhanced basic attestation with a cryptographic component, which is in fact sufficient to guarantee the basic functionality required by multi-channel attestation. One step further, the linked-attestation primitive built from authenticated attestation will allow two different components to (a) attest their own states; (b) provide auxiliary material that will make two separate attestations linkable. While this primitive has no immediate parallel in real-world attestation, we use it as a handy way of dividing the security proof of our ultimate result into two: linked-attestation will focus on proving the fact that two attestations can be securely linked; whereas authorized linked attestation models attestation as a protocol, using fresh randomness and a secure channel using an honest attestation server.

We also add a new party into the system: the attestation server that serves as a verifier. We then *compose* the linked-attestation primitive with a unilaterally-authenticated authenticated key-exchange protocol, which will authenticate the attestation server and permit the attestation itself to remain confidential with respect to a Person-in-the-Middle (PitM) adversary.

2.1   Basic Attestation

During basic attestation a single honest party is generated. This party can be later compromised. A quote-generation algorithm will output a quote if the party is still honest at that time, or a special symbol if it is not. Finally a (public) verification algorithm will yield 1 (the component is honest) or 0 (otherwise).

Note that a party such as the one we describe could correspond in practice to a combination of two parties: a virtual entity (like a VM or the hypervisor) and an underlying, uncorruptible, secure part (the TPM), which actually generates the quote. At this stage, we importantly do not associate these entities with keys as authentication will only appear in our next step (Sect. 2.2).

What we want to capture, formalized by the security of basic attestation, is the minimal assumption that a compromised component will always yield an attestation that will fail the verification. This is why, when basic attestation is run for a compromised component, it will yield the special symbol $\aleph$. We also demand correctness: when a non-$\aleph$ quote is generated, the latter will automatically verify. Our basic attestation component thus becomes the minimal non-cryptographic assumption that we need to make to prove our scheme secure.

Formalization. We consider an environment parametrized by a security parameter λ, in which we have a single party P. This party keeps track of a single *attribute*, namely a *compromise bit* γ originally set to 0. Once this bit is flipped to 1, it can never go back to 0. We define a primitive BasicAtt as a tuple of algorithms: (aBSetup, aBAttest, aBVerif):

- aBSetup(1^λ) $\rightarrow$ ppar: on input the security 1^λ (in unary), this algorithm outputs some public parameters ppar.

- aBAttest(ppar) → quote: on input the public parameters ppar, if P.$\gamma = 0$, then this algorithm outputs an attestation quote quote $\neq \aleph$ for P, and if P.$\gamma = 1$, then it outputs $\aleph$.
- aBVerif(ppar, (quote $\cup \aleph$)) → 0 $\cup$ 1: on input public parameters ppar and a value that is either a quote denoted quote or a special symbol $\aleph$, this algorithm outputs a bit. By convention, an output of 0 means the attestation fails, while if the output is 1, the attestation succeeds. We require by construction that for all ppar: aBVerif($\cdot, \cdot, \aleph$) = 0.

This primitive is also depicted in Fig. 3. We assume that if P.$\gamma = 0$ and quote → aBAttest(ppar), then aBVerif(ppar, quote) = 1.

Security. The only security we demand from this primitive is that, if a party is compromised, then its attestation will always fail. This will happen by construction (since this is an assumed primitive) and is embedded in the security model. The adversary $\mathcal{A}$ will play a game against a challenger $\mathcal{G}$. Initially, the challenger sets the system up by running aBSetup to output ppar which is given to $\mathcal{A}$. The unique party is generated, such that its corrupt bit is set to 1 (P.$\gamma = 0$).

Since $\mathcal{A}$ now has ppar, it can now run the aBAttest and aBVerif algorithms. In addition, it has access to the OBAttest oracle: OBAttest() → (quote$\cup \aleph$). This oracle calls the aBAttest() algorithm for the (corrupted) party P and returns the output to the adversary $\mathcal{A}$. The challenger stores the result in a database DB. The adversary wins if, and only if, there exists a quote in DB (possibly with quote = $\aleph$) such that aBVerif(ppar, quote) = 1. Note that by construction our basic attestation primitive is secure, since once the compromise bit is set, the output is $\aleph$, which always yields aBVerif(ppar, $\aleph$) = 0.

Basic Attestation in Reality. One may wonder at this point what our purpose might be in constructing a security model for a primitive that is by definition correct and secure. We need that security model in our reductions: we will use the attestation primitive to build stronger, linked attestation, and then we will want to make the argument that if an attacker can break the larger primitive, it will also break the smaller primitive. As the smaller primitive is secure by design, this is not possible, and hence, the larger primitive is also secure.

2.2 Authenticated Attestation

Basic attestation acts as a foolproof way of telling whether a device is compromised or not. However, the security it provides is very weak. For one thing, it has

Target T		Appraiser
	Setup phase: aBSetup(1^λ) → ppar	
aBAttest(ppar) → quote $\xrightarrow{\text{quote}}$		aBVerif(ppar, quote) → 0 if T compromised (T.$\gamma = 1$)
		→ 1 if T uncompromised (T.$\gamma = 0$)

Fig. 3. Basic attestation description with an honestly-generated target. Notice that there is no authentication involved.

no authentication guarantees, so potentially one could use a quote that was honestly generated for an honest component to attest a compromised one. Another problem that is more subtle concerns the way components are compromised. Because the basic quotes described in the previous section have no timestamp, nor specific freshness, we cannot take into account adaptive tampering. In the security notion, the party generating the quote is either honest or compromised from the beginning. Yet, ideally we would like a primitive that ensures that a party can start out as honest (and all the quotes generated at that time verify as correct), and later be compromised (and all the quotes generated after that moment will fail). We can do this by deploying cryptographic solutions.

A relevant question is why we did not include these security aspects in the basic attestation primitive considered above. To answer this, recall that we have constructed the basic attestation tool to be secure by design. As such, it is an assumption, rather than a solution. If we also assume authentication, it would go against the principle of using minimal assumptions.

Correctness. The correctness of our construction depends on the detection of a compromised component. There are three cases to consider. Assume first that the component is compromised. In that case, the output attestation is $\aleph$. The component can try to authenticate this quote, but the verification will fail. In the second case, the component (VM or hypervisor) is not compromised, and so will receive a valid attestation quote, authenticated by the TPM. This authenticated quote will verify. Finally, in the third case, the component is not compromised, and receives a valid authentication quote. At this point, the adversary might try to forward the authenticated quote and pass it off as someone else's attestation, but this will fail as long as the authentication primitive is EUF-CMA secure.

Formalization. The precise formalization of this primitive is in the full version of our paper [4]. We consider an environment containing up to N parties. The parties keep track of the compromise bit γ used also for basic attestation, and a pair of public and secret keys denoted, for each party P, P.pk (the public key) and P.sk (the private key). Intuitively, the security we require for this primitive will be that a valid authenticated quote for a party P and fresh auxiliary information (used as nonce) is hard to forge by an adversary which knows all the the public information, can register and compromise users, and query an attestation oracle that returns a valid quote or $\aleph$. In particular, in a secure scheme, verification should fail if either the authentication or the attestation fails.

Construction. We construct an authenticated attestation scheme out of basic authentication, a large set of nonces $\mathcal{N} := \{0,1\}^{\ell}$ (with ℓ chosen as a function of the security parameter λ), and an EUF-CMA-secure signature scheme $\mathtt{Sig} = (\mathtt{aSigKGen}, \mathtt{aSigSign}, \mathtt{aSigVerif})$. We thus instantiate $\mathcal{AUX} := \mathcal{N}$, and our $\mathtt{AuthAtt}$ scheme is as follows:

- $\mathtt{aAuthSetup}(1^{\lambda}) \to$ ppar: this algorithm runs $\mathtt{aBSetup}(1^{\lambda})$ a number N of times, outputting $\mathsf{ppar}_1, \mathsf{ppar}_2, \ldots, \mathsf{ppar}_N$. Each time ppar_i is created, a party handle P_i is also created (it will be the party associated with the instance of

Target T	Appraiser
Setup phase: aAuthSetup(1^λ) → ppar	
aAuthKGen → (T.pk, T.sk)	
aAuthAttest(ppar, T.sk, aux) → (quote, σ) $\xrightarrow{\text{authQuote}=(\text{quote},\sigma)}$	aAuthVerif(ppar, T.pk, aux, (quote, σ))
	→ 0 if T compromised (authQuote = ℵ or σ invalid)
	→ 1 if T uncompromised (authQuote ≠ ℵ and σ valid)

Fig. 4. Authenticated attestation built upon basic attestation (Fig. 3).

BasicAtt run for those parameters). It sets ppar := (ppar$_1$, ppar$_2$, ..., ppar$_N$, N), and outputs this value (Fig. 4).

- aAuthKGen(P$_i$) → (P$_i$.pk, P$_i$.sk): it keeps a counter (starting from 0), which indicates how many times this algorithm has been run. If at the time this algorithm is queried counter < N, then aAuthKGen runs aSigKGen as a black box and outputs the resulting (pk, sk) (public and private) keys. It sets P$_i$.pk := pk and P$_i$.sk := sk. Party P$_i$ is then initialized with these keys.
- aAuthAttest(ppar, P.sk, R) → authQuote∪ℵ: on input the public parameters ppar, a private key P.sk of a party P (which has already been registered), and a value $R \xleftarrow{\$} \mathcal{N}$, this algorithm first runs quote ← aBAttest(ppar), then the algorithm signs σ ← aSigSign(P.sk, (quote, R)), that is, it signs a concatenation of the nonce and the obtained quote. The output of this algorithm is authQuote := (quote, σ). If the required party or key does not exist, the value ℵ is output by default. If quote = ℵ, then we instantiate authQuote = ℵ.
- aAuthVerif(ppar, P.pk, R, (authQuote ∪ ℵ)) → 0 ∪ 1: on input public parameters ppar, a public key P.pk of a party P, an auxiliary value $R \in \mathcal{N}$, this algorithm first checks if the last input is ℵ; if so, the algorithm outputs 0 by default. Else, the algorithm parses authQuote = (quote, σ) (with quote ≠ ℵ by construction), then runs b ← aSigVerif(P.pk, quote, σ) and d ← aBVerif(ppar, quote). The algorithm outputs $b \wedge d$. Notably, 1 is output if, and only if, signature and basic attestation verify concomitantly.

Theorem 21 (Secure Authenticated Attestation). *The* AuthAtt *scheme is secure assuming that (1)* BasicAtt *scheme is secure (2) the size of* $\mathcal{N}$ *is large and (3) the* Sig *signature scheme is EUF-CMA secure.*

The proof is given in the full version of our paper [4]

2.3 Linked Attestation

Authenticated attestation allows the attestation of one (out of many) components, based on that component's unique secret key. If we define now parties as being either VMs or hypervisors, the notion of authenticated attestation suffices to capture the basic guarantees of multi-channel deep-attestation. However, in this paper our goal is to allow parties to *link* their attestations (a hypervisor's attestation should, *e.g.*, , be linkable to various VMs hosted on that platform).

In this section we describe our next primitive: linked attestation. The latter takes place in an environment where several parties are registered in a linked way – this corresponds to a single platform. A first step is platform registration, by which several parties are linked on the same underlying hardware. Each entity later generates a linkable attestation – verifiable on its own, and linkable with other linkable attestations.

Although our application scenario is that of linking VM and hypervisor attestations, we make our framework more generic than that. Instead of just two types of components, we consider linkable sets $S_1, S_2, \ldots, S_L$, which resemble equivalence classes. These sets are defined such that any party in one set (say P_{S_1}) can produce an attestation that is linked to attestations produced by parties in sets $S_2, \ldots, S_L$. We write $P \diamond Q$ to say that two parties are linked. The relation is reflexive ($P \diamond P$), symmetric (if $P \diamond Q$, then $Q \diamond P$), and transitive (if $P \diamond Q$ and $Q \diamond R$, then $P \diamond R$).

We formalize a linked-attestation scheme LinkedAtt as a tuple of algorithms LinkedAtt = (aLSetup, aLReg, aLAttest, aLVerif, aLLink), defined for some auxiliary set $\mathcal{AUX}$. The detailed formalization is given in the full version [4].

The setup algorithm outputs public parameters ppar, including the maximal number L of sets considered for linking. One can register platforms including subsets of components of each type: this algorithm generates keys for each party. A linked attestation algorithm produces a linked quote linkedQuote and an auxiliary linking value lkaux. Finally, the verification algorithm checks the attestation in each individual linkedQuote and the linking algorithm outputs 1 if several linked attestations seem to belong to the same registered platform, and 0 otherwise. This syntax is also depicted in Fig. 5.

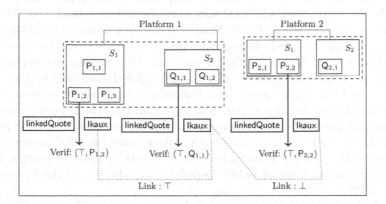

Fig. 5. Linked attestation primitive. Dashed lines indicate platform under the same registration. Here, both platforms are composed of two subsets (S_1, S_2). There are a total of three quote verifications $(P_{1,2}, Q_{1,1}, P_{2,2})$. The link verification outputs true for devices registered on the same platform and false otherwise.

The security of linked attestation informally states that an adversary, which has Person-in-the-Middle capabilities and can compromise devices at will, cannot make it appear that two devices are linked when they are not, in fact, so.

A significant limitation on the adversary's capabilities is that compromising a device will not leak its private keys (which are assumed to be held by a TPM). However, the adversary will gain a limited oracle access to those keys upon compromising the device. The limitations to those queries follow rules of access to an actual TPM.

More formally, we define the security of *linked attestation* as a game $\mathsf{LinkSec}_{\lambda,\mathsf{F}}$ parametrized by a security parameter λ and a set of functions F, which we call the *permitted key-access functions*. The adversary wins if it is able to make attestations stored in $\mathcal{L}_{\mathsf{Att}}$ for parties registered on different platforms (P and Q) link. However, at this point the adversary is constrained to a change-one-change-all kind of game: it cannot, for instance, append an lkaux component of its choice to an honestly-generated linkedQuote, nor vice-versa.

In the security game, the adversary registers platforms and can compromise some of their components. When a component is compromised, the adversary gets oracle access to a set of permitted functions of the component's private key. As a result, the strength of the security proof depends on the function space F. The more functions the adversary is able to query once it compromises a component, the more security our primitive is able to provide. However, note that we cannot give the adversary access to *some* functions, such as the identity function on the component's private key.

Construction. We provide a construction for platforms that have two types of components: virtual machines (VMs) and their managing hypervisor. Thus, in our instantiation, $L = 2$. We use an authenticated attestation scheme (aAuthSetup, aAuthKGen, aAuthAttest, aAuthVerif) as a black box. The basic construction is depicted in Fig. 6. During setup, our linked-attestation scheme first runs aAuthSetup and outputs ppar and $L = 2$. Note that by construction aAuthSetup must output a number N, denoting the maximal number of parties that can be set up. This counter will represent a global maximum to parties of all types that will exist in our ecosystem. Following setup, one can register a subset of VMs together with a hypervisor. The algorithm runs the key-generation algorithm aAuthKGen of the underlying authenticated attestation scheme for each party, independently (note that this also ensures that the total number of parties remains at most N). Finally, keys are grouped by types of parties: keys of VMs are output in a set of public keys PK_1 and the key of the hypervisor is output as PK_2.

The VMs and hypervisor generate linked attestations differently. The hypervisor first fetches the public keys of all the components registered with it on the same platform. It computes a new nonce as the hash of two concatenated values: the original auxiliary value aux and the list of the public keys. The component then runs aAuthAttest on the public parameters, this new nonce, and its private key, outputting the authenticated quote. By contrast, when a VM attests,

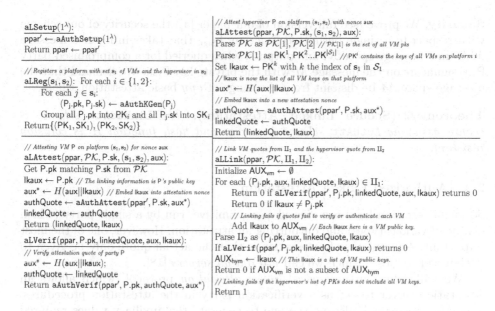

Fig. 6. Our linked attestation scheme for platforms with 2 types of components: VMs (stored in $\mathcal{S}_1$) and hypervisors (stored in $\mathcal{S}_2$). Each type of component attests via a different aLAttest algorithm, the main difference between them being that the hypervisor embeds a list of public keys in its nonce.

it computes a new nonce from the original auxiliary value aux and (only) its own public key. The authenticated quote is provided as the VM's linked quote.

A VM (or a set of VMs) are considered to be linked to a hypervisor if, and only if, the following conditions hold simultaneously: (1) the attestations of all the purportedly-linked parties verify individually (if we run aAuthVerif it returns 1 for each individual attestation); (2) the public key that was successfully used to verify each of the VMs' attestation is part of the auxiliary value lkaux forwarded by the hypervisor.

Correctness. The LinkedAtt scheme is built upon the AuthAtt scheme. There are two types of component to consider, VM and hypervisor. When a component is registered on a platform, its public key is appended in a list (PK_1 for VMs, and PK_2 for the hypervisor). The public key of a VM is appended to the quote in aLAttest and can be retrieved by the hypervisor. The latter can link the attestation to a public key via algorithm aLLink. We consider two cases to verify the correctness (1) a VM (not compromised) is not registered on the platform, and (2) a component (VM or hypervisor) is compromised. For (1) the attestation will be correct since the component is not compromised, but the linking process will abort since the public key does not belong to PK_1. For (2) if a VM (or the hypervisor) is compromised then the attestation will fail since the authenticated attestation is supposed to be correct (the aAuthAttest algorithm is executed to generate the quote).

Security. We prove (see full version of our paper [4]) the security of our scheme with respect to a single permitted function, F_{Sign} that takes in input a message M from a message space $\mathcal{M}$ and outputs, when queried for a compromised party P, a signature on the message M with the private key P.sk. We demand that the message space $\mathcal{M}$ be disjoint from the range of *any* basic attestation scheme.

Theorem 22 (Secure Linked Attestation). *The* LinkedAtt *scheme is secure assuming* AuthAtt *scheme is secure and hash function H is collision resistant.*

2.4   Authorized Linked Attestation

So far, attestation has been viewed as a primitive, run by a single party (which can be of various types) and outputting an attestation. However, one of the most important requirements of attestation is that the actual quote only be given to authorized parties – which we call *attestation servers* [18].

We will define an *authorized linked attestation* protocol, which allows an attestation server to act as a verification party in the attestation procedures. The same server will also be the one to generate the auxiliary values required for the attestation (this provides freshness to the protocol). The server will also be responsible for linking multiple attestations.

Intuition. We provide a full formalization of authorized linked attestation below. However, we also believe it is useful to first give an intuitive understanding of what this primitive *is* and the security it wants to achieve.

In authorized linked attestation we consider a (single) attestation server S and platforms consisting of several types of components (as shown for linked attestation). The server will keep track of an evolving state, which is initially empty. However, as the server starts to attest various components, at every execution of the authorized attestation protocol, the server will output a verdict (indicating whether the component's individual attestation has failed or succeeded) and may – or may not – update its internal state. Intuitively, the state is meant to contain the *linking information* provided by each of the attesting components. After a number of attestations, the server might have enough information in its state to decide if some of the components are linked or not.

The security notion we require for authorized linked attestation is threefold: (1) we require that parties only provide attestation guarantees to the actual attestation server; (2) we require that the contents of the attestation be actually indistinguishable from random for all unauthorized parties; (3) we require a similar kind of linking security as demanded in linked attestation see Sect. 2.3. However, as opposed to linked attestation, the adversary in this case can also play a Person-in-the-Middle role between honest components and the honest server, or it may attempt to replay messages or impersonate one or both parties. Finally, the adversary will be able to have oracle access which returns the secret key of any compromised component (this oracle access is parametrized in terms of a function space F of allowed functions).

Formalization. The complete formalization of authorized linked attestation is given in the full version [4]. Components on platforms are either VMs or hypervisor. In addition, we consider a S, which stores a tuple consisting of a public and a private key $S.pk = pk$ and $S.sk = sk$ respectively, and a state $S.st$. Parties interact with each other in sessions, which are run by an *instance* of the server and an *instance* of a given component. Instances of each party use that party's long-term public and private keys, as well as potential local randomness, such as instance-specific nonces. An instance of a component and an instance of the server are *partnered* if they essentially run the same session (formally, if they share a session identifier, which consists of the concatenation of a number of session-specific values).

Authorized linking attestation is defined as the tuple $ALA = (ASetup, AReg, AAttest, aALink)$. The first, second, and last of these are algorithms, while AAttest is a protocol. The setup algorithm generates parameters (keys and public system values) for all the involved parties. The registration algorithm allows the VMs and hypervisor on a single platform (defined as sets s_1 for the VMs on the platform and s_2 for the hypervisor) to be associated with each other. For administration purposes, the public keys of all VMs on a platform (*i.e.*, , all VMs in some s_1) and respectively the public key of the platform's hypervisor (the hypervisor in the corresponding s_2) are stored respectively in subsets PK_1, PK_2 ($i = 1$ for VMs and $i = 2$ for the hypervisor). Together all the subsets PK_i for all the components form a set $\mathcal{PK}[i]$ (for $i = 1, 2$).

The authorized attestation protocol is run by an instance of a component and an instance of the server, yielding, for the component, an acceptance bit (corresponding to the authentication of its partner as the authorized server) and for the server, a tuple $verdict, S.st$: the verdict verdict is 1 or 0 depending on whether the component attested successfully or not, and the state is an update of the server's current internal state. Finally, the server state can be used on a subset of components in the aALink algorithm, yielding either 1 (the components are linked) or 0 otherwise.

Construction. Our construction of the ALA primitive can be seen in the Fig. 7. We consider the existence on an underlying LinkedAtt scheme that we use for the aLSetup, aLReg and aLLink in a straightforward manner. However, the aLAttest algorithm is no longer a primitive, but a protocol between two

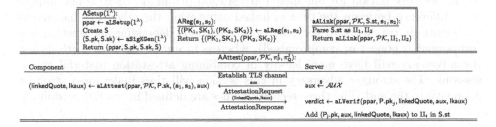

Fig. 7. Our authorized linked attestation scheme for 2 types of components.

instances of two parties, P and Q. For simplicity of exposition, we assume that the instance of Q is the server attesting the component identified by P.

The protocol proceeds as follows. First, P and Q execute the TLS protocol, with P playing the role of the client and Q playing the role of the server. The role of the TLS protocol is two-fold: first, P authenticates the server, so that they can determine whether this party is allowed to obtain attestation data. Second, it leads to the establishment of a secure channel, such that the following messages can be passed on in a secure manner. Once the traffic key(s) established, the protocol continues as follows. First, the server uniformly randomly samples a nonce aux, which is embedded in the first message of the protocol, AttestationRequest. In response, the party P executes the aLAttest algorithm and the output, consisting of a linkedQuote and the linkage information lkaux, is then sent to the server. The server will subsequently update his state.

In order for two components to be linked by the server successfully, the following conditions have to be met. First, the two components' attestation must be valid (their associated verdicts equals 1). Second, the two lkaux must be subsets of each other; essentially, the key that the VM used as part of its attestation must be found in the lkaux provided by the hypervisor.

We note that if the server has at some point accepted the attestation of a component (thus updating its state to add the linking information), and if later a failed attestation occurs with respect to that component, the server updates state as follows: it ignores the linking information provided in the second attestation; and it removes prior linking information provided by that component.

Security. There are three fundamental properties we want ALA schemes to have: an authenticity guarantee for the attestation server (authorization); a confidentiality guarantee for the contents of the attestation (indistinguishability); and a linkability guarantee for honestly-behaving components (linking-security). The first notion, authorization, captures the fact that before reaching an accepting state, a (non-server) party must be sure that it is speaking to the legitimate server (game $\text{AuthSec}_{\lambda,F}$). The second notion, indistinguishability, essentially covers Person-in-the-Middle confidentiality for the attestation protocol (game $\text{AuthInd}_{\lambda,F_{\text{Sign}}}$). The last property, linking-security, refers to the fact that no PitM adversary with the ability to compromise components can convince an attestation server that a component is linked to another if that is not the case in reality (game $\text{AuthLink}_{\lambda,F}$). Although this last property might seem similar to the security notion for our linked attestation primitive, there is one important difference between the two: in linked attestation the adversary has access to essentially two ways to generate an attestation (depending on whether the component is honest or compromised), whereas in *authorized linked attestation* the adversary will have more leeway in combining attestation material across sessions. The stronger adversary in this section will thus make for a stronger primitive in the end. The three security games are defined in the full version [4].

Theorem 23. *Our construction is* AuthSec$_{\lambda,\mathsf{F_{Sign}}}$ *secure if the TLS protocol provides server authentication:* $\Pr[\mathcal{A} \text{ wins } \mathsf{AuthSec}_{\lambda,\mathsf{F}}] \leq \varepsilon_{TLS\text{-}auth}.$

Theorem 24. *Our construction is* AuthLink$_{\lambda,\mathsf{F_{Sign}}}$ *secure if the underlying primitive* LinkedAtt *is* LinkSec$_{\lambda,\mathsf{F_{Sign}}}$ *and TLS is at least (s)ACCE secure.*

Theorem 25. *Our construction is* AuthInd$_{\lambda,\mathsf{F_{Sign}}}$ *secure if the TLS channel provides (minimally) (s)ACCE security. Let* $q_{sessions}$ *be the number of sessions.*

$$\Pr[\mathcal{A} \text{ wins } \mathsf{AuthInd}_{\lambda,\mathsf{F_{Sign}}}] \leq \frac{1}{q_{sessions}} \varepsilon_{TLS\text{-}sACCE}.$$

3   Implementation

We provide a proof of concept implementation of our authorized linked attestation scheme. The implementation consists of three parts, a client for the hypervisor, a client for the Virtual Machines, and an attestation server written in Python 3. We do not consider the underlying NFV or cloud infrastructure, since our scheme abstracts those environments and can be used in any kind deep-attestation scenario. Therefore, any computer equipped with a TPM 2.0 (which can also be emulated) and which has virtualization capacities suffices for the purposes of our implementation. We provide our code as well as a detailed tutorial on how to install and configure both the infrastructure [3].

The Infrastructure. We summarize our testing architecture in Fig. 8 (note that some of our tests use more than 2 VMs – up to 55).

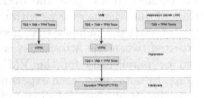

Our *hypervisor* is a laptop running Ubuntu 20.04.3 (kernel version 5.11.0-40) with an Intel i7-10875H CPU, 32 GB RAM and a STMicro-electronics TPM. We used KVM to turn this laptop into a hypervisor. For high attestation performance, we used full *virtual TPM implementation*, using QEMU [1] with libtpms 0.7 [8] and swtpm 0.5 [20].

Fig. 8. Architecture for tests.

All *virtual machines* are QEMU virtual machines (version 4.2.1) with 1 core and 512 RAM running Fedora 35 Cloud. The VM as well as the virtual TPM instances are managed using Vagrant and Vagrant-Libvirt plugin.

The hypervisor, server, and VMs communicate through a private network created with Vagrant. Thus, connection time is not considered in our tests.

To communicate with the TPM we used tpm2-tss, tpm2-abrmd and tpm2-tools from the tpm2-software [2]. Note that the tpm2-tss project implements the TPM software stack (TSS), which is an API specified by the Trusted Computing Group to interact with a TPM. The tpm2-abrmd implements the access broker and resources to manage concurrent access to the TPM and manage memory of the TPM by swapping in and out of the memory as needed (hardware TPM have limited memory).

Table 1. Minimum, median, mean and maximum time in second for attestation of a hypervisor and a virtual machine for 100 trials.

	min	median	mean	max
Hypervisor	3.801	11.940	13.896	40.762
VM	0.337	0.416	0.422	0.572

The *attestation server* is also a virtual machine, with the same characteristics as those above. This allows us to test our implementation on a single machine. We establish a secure connection between the client and the server by using Python's SSL library.

Tests. We perform three types of experiments. The first is a comparison of hypervisor attestation time and VM attestation time. Although both those processes have some (very small) amount of noise, our values faithfully show the difference between attesting a component through the physical TPM – hypervisor attestation – and attesting it by using a virtual TPM – VM attestation.

We ran 100 attestations for the hypervisor and 100 attestations for a virtual machine. The results have high variance so Table 1 presents the minimum, the maximum, mean, and median value of those 100 trials. As expected, time for an attestation using a hardware TPM is much higher than using a vTPM.

As our second and third experiments we wanted to see how the overall runtime of our scheme evolves with the number of virtual machines that need to be attested, when the attestation is sequential or parallelized for the VM attestations. In both cases, each experiment first runs the attestation of the hypervisor, and then (sequentially or in parallel) the attestation of a varying number of VM (up to a maximum of 55). The results are plotted in Fig. 9. We note that the runtime is not entirely linear. This is because in experiments 2 and 3 the initial attestation of the

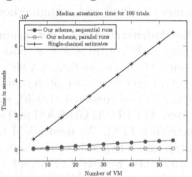

Fig. 9. Attestation time.

hypervisor (which only occurs once) takes larger time than the subsequent VM run-times.

Comparison to Single-Channel Attestation. We did not implement single-channel attestation. However, since we have implemented hypervisor and VM attestations, we can theoretically estimate the run-time of single-channel attestation for a varying number of VMs – which we plot in Fig. 9. Indeed, a single-channel attestation process for a single VM includes a VM attestation *and* a hypervisor attestation. If we want to run it for 2 VMs, then we need to perform 2 hypervisor attestations and 2 VM attestations. This cannot be easily parallelized either, because the same TPM has to run the attestations. This yields a much higher run-time, as depicted in Fig. 9.

Comparison to Multi-channel Attestation. Although our method follows basic multi-channel attestation approaches, we do add an extra computation (a hash function computation) compared to traditional multi-channel attestation. In addition, we require a little extra memory overhead for both the attestation server and for each platform, so that the additional attestation keys are stored for each VM. There is also a slight transmission overhead, since those keys are also sent upon attestation. However, the transmission overhead is negligible since it only appears for the hypervisor attestation (which occurs only once).

4   Conclusions and Future Work

We proposed a layer-binding in deep-attestation without running into the complexity of single-channel attestation. Our construction achieves the best of both worlds, with a complexity similar to that of multi-channel attestation, but with the strong linkage properties provided in single-channel attestation.

We accompany our construction by a proof-of-concept implementation that clearly shows the viability and scalability of our solution, especially if VM attestations are run in parallel.

In addition, we are the first to present a full, formal treatment of our new protocol, which we call *authorized linked attestation*. Our construction of authorized linked attestation is modular, built on primitives which have increasingly stronger properties. Our underlying assumption is a primitive called basic attestation. We show that in order to be able to prove security, we need that attestations be able to reflect compromise of the component. In addition, we rely on a collision-resistant hash function, an EUF-CMA-secure signature scheme, and the sACCE security of a TLS protocol (having AKE properties would be better).

However, our model (and scheme) does not immediately account for other features of virtual infrastructures, such as privacy CAs, migrating VMs, multiple hypervisors managing the same VM, or even replacing TPMs. These aspects are left as future work.

References

1. The Qemu machine emulator. https://www.qemu.org/
2. TPM2_tools. https://github.com/tpm2-software
3. Arfaoui, G., et al.: Implementation. https://github.com/AnonymousDeepAttestation/deep-attestation
4. Arfaoui, G., et al.: A cryptographic view of deep-attestation, or how to do provably-secure layer-linking. Cryptology ePrint Archive, Report 2021/1487 (2021). https://ia.cr/2021/1487
5. Armknecht, F., Sadeghi, A., Schulz, S., Wachsmann, C.: A security framework for the analysis and design of software attestation. In: 2013 ACM SIGSAC Conference on Computer and Communications Security, CCS 2013, Berlin, Germany, 4–8 November 2013, pp. 1–12. ACM (2013)

6. Asokan, N., et al.: SEDA: scalable embedded device attestation. In: Proceedings of the 22nd ACM SIGSAC Conference on Computer and Communications Security, Denver, CO, USA, 12–16 October 2015, pp. 964–975. ACM (2015)
7. Bellare, M., Rogaway, P.: Entity authentication and key distribution. In: Stinson, D.R. (ed.) CRYPTO 1993. LNCS, vol. 773, pp. 232–249. Springer, Heidelberg (1994). https://doi.org/10.1007/3-540-48329-2_21
8. Berger, S.: Library for TPM tools. https://github.com/stefanberger/libtpms
9. Brickell, E.F., Camenisch, J., Chen, L.: Direct anonymous attestation. In: Atluri, V., Pfitzmann, B., McDaniel, P.D. (eds.) Proceedings of the 11th ACM Conference on Computer and Communications Security, CCS 2004, Washington, DC, USA, 25–29 October 2004, pp. 132–145. ACM (2004)
10. Buhren, R., Werling, C., Seifert, J.: Insecure until proven updated: analyzing AMD SEV's remote attestation. In: Cavallaro, L., Kinder, J., Wang, X., Katz, J. (eds.) Proceedings of the 2019 ACM SIGSAC Conference on Computer and Communications Security, CCS 2019, London, UK, 11–15 November 2019, pp. 1087–1099. ACM (2019)
11. Canetti, R., Krawczyk, H.: Universally composable notions of key exchange and secure channels. In: Knudsen, L.R. (ed.) EUROCRYPT 2002. LNCS, vol. 2332, pp. 337–351. Springer, Heidelberg (2002). https://doi.org/10.1007/3-540-46035-7_22
12. Davi, L., Sadeghi, A., Winandy, M.: Dynamic integrity measurement and attestation: towards defense against return-oriented programming attacks. In: Proceedings of the ACM STC, pp. 49–54. ACM (2009)
13. ETSI: Network functions virtualisation (NFV); trust; report on attestation technologies and practices for secure deployments (2017)
14. Gopalan, K., Kugve, R., Bagdi, H., Hu, Y., Williams, D., Bila, N.: Multi-hypervisor virtual machines: enabling an ecosystem of hypervisor-level services. In: Proceedings of the 2017 USENIX Annual Technical Conference, USENIX ATC 2017, pp. 235–249 (2019)
15. Hristozov, S., Heyszl, J., Wagner, S., Sigl, G.: Practical runtime attestation for tiny IoT devices. In: Proceedings of NDSS DISS (2018)
16. Hussain, S.R., Echeverria, M., Karim, I., Chowdhury, O., Bertino, E.: 5GReasoner: a property-directed security and privacy analysis framework for 5G cellular network protocol. In: Cavallaro, L., Kinder, J., Wang, X., Katz, J. (eds.) Proceedings of the 2019 ACM SIGSAC Conference on Computer and Communications Security, CCS 2019, London, UK, 11–15 November 2019, pp. 669–684. ACM (2019)
17. Kuang, B., Fu, A., Zhou, L., Susilo, W., Zhang, Y.: DO-RA: data-oriented runtime attestation for IoT devices. Comput. Secur. 97, 101945 (2020)
18. Lauer, H., Kuntze, N.: Hypervisor-based attestation of virtual environments. In: 2016 IEEE UIC/ATC/ScalCom/CBDCom/IoP/SmartWorld, pp. 333–340 (2016)
19. Loscocco, P.A., Wilson, P.W., Pendergrass, J.A., McDonell, C.D.: Linux kernel integrity measurement using contextual inspection. In: Proceedings of ACM STC, pp. 21–29. ACM (2007)
20. Safford, D., Berger, S.: Software TPM emulator - swtpm. https://github.com/stefanberger/swtpm

Don't Tamper with Dual System Encryption
Beyond Polynomial Related-Key Security of IBE

Tsz Hon Yuen[1], Cong Zhang[2], and Sherman S. M. Chow[3]

[1] University of Hong Kong, Pok Fu Lam, Hong Kong
thyuen@cs.hku.hk
[2] University of Maryland, College Park, MD, USA
czhang20@umd.edu
[3] Department of Information Engineering, Chinese University of Hong Kong,
Sha Tin, NT, Hong Kong
sherman@ie.cuhk.edu.hk

Abstract. In related-key attacks (RKA), an attacker modifies a secret key stored in a device by tampering or fault injection and observes the evaluation output of the cryptographic algorithm based on this related key. In this work, we show that the dual system encryption methodology of Waters (Crypto 2009) fits well with RKA security. We apply simple modifications to a regularly-secure identity-based encryption (IBE) scheme (TCC 2010) constructed through dual system to achieve RKA security for *rational functions*, which is beyond the polynomial barrier of Bellare *et al.*'s framework (Asiacrypt 2012). We achieve security by pushing the complexity of RKA directly down to the underlying intractability assumption. We also discuss how to extend it to a hierarchical IBE scheme that remains secure against RKA over identity-based secret keys beyond the master secret, albeit under some structural constraints.

Keywords: Identity-based encryption · Related-key attacks · Dual system encryption

1 Introduction

Related-key attacks (RKA) are useful in attacking cryptosystems. One of the earliest targets is blockciphers [4,5]. Under RKA, an adversary can obtain input-output samples under not only the target key but also some related keys. Security against RKA is a popular design goal since a key stored in memory could be modified by tampering and fault injection. RKA against public-key primitives could cause broader damage to many users, *e.g.*, RKA could be mounted on a signing key of a certificate authority or SSL server or a master key for an

Sherman S. M. Chow is supported by General Research Fund (CUHK 14209918) from Research Grant Council, and CUHK Project Impact Enhancement Fund (3133292). The authors would like to thank S. M. Yiu for his early support and comments.

© Springer Nature Switzerland AG 2022
G. Ateniese and D. Venturi (Eds.): ACNS 2022, LNCS 13269, pp. 419–439, 2022.
https://doi.org/10.1007/978-3-031-09234-3_21

identity-based encryption (IBE) system. Similarly, the identity-based secret keys of hierarchical IBE (HIBE) will affect the security of all other descendent users.

Bellare *et al.* [2] showed how to construct Φ-RKA secure signatures, public-key encryption, and IBE from Φ-RKA secure blockcipher or pseudorandom functions (PRF). The parameter Φ is a function family that the adversary can choose a related-key derivation function from, which the function will be applied to the secret key, and its output is used to execute the keyed function of the cryptographic primitive. The RKA resilience of the resulting IBE is thus subjected to that of the underlying blockcipher/PRF. Many existing (H)IBE schemes are not linear-RKA-secure [3]. Bellare *et al.* [3] proposed a framework to convert regularly-secure IBE schemes into Φ-RKA secure ones. Their framework requires expanding the identity space since the master public key mpk is appended to the user's identity. So, it is only applicable to schemes that treat the size of the identity space as a tunable system parameter. The same applies to the recent result of Fujisaki and Xagawa [18], which achieves RKA security for efficiently invertible related-key derivation functions[1]. Their best instantiation is from an extension of Waters IBE [29] for Φ being the class of polynomials with degree d, which increases the number of multiplications during encryption and key generation by $\log(|\mathbb{G}|)/2$ times on average since mpk is a group $\mathbb{G}$ element, and the public parameter is of size $O(d)$ for the modularity of the framework [3].

This work provides affirmative answers to a few unsolved problems.

– Is it possible to establish the Φ-RKA security of an IBE scheme for different Φ under a family of assumptions instead of following prior frameworks [3,18]?
– Is there any practical IBE scheme in the standard model that "natively" attains Φ-RKA security, for Φ being more general than the class of degree-d polynomials, with a short public keys and short ciphertexts?
– Can such an RKA-secure IBE scheme be extended to RKA-secure HIBE?
– Can we achieve RKA security when the adversary can modify not only the master secret key but also the identity-based secret keys?

Technical Overview. Our core technique is dual system encryption (DSE) proposed by Waters [30], a paradigm for constructing adaptively secure IBE in the standard model with short public parameters. To our knowledge, its potential in establishing RKA security is yet to be explored. We propose a Φ-RKA-secure IBE scheme in the standard model, where Φ is a general class of rational functions. It is almost as efficient as the underlying standard (H)IBE schemes [24] in the famous commutative-blinding framework (featuring many extensions [9]). They are practically efficient (purely pairing-based without heavyweight tools or any bit-level cryptographic processing) and feature a short public key and short ciphertexts (independent of the length of an identity string).

RKA in IBE allows the adversary to adaptively issue polynomially many queries to a tampered key extraction oracle, namely, Extract(ϕ(msk), ID) for identity ID and function $\phi \in \Phi$, where msk is the master secret. When ϕ is an identity

---

[1] Fujisaki and Xagawa [19] provided a counterexample refuting the security proof of Qin *et al.* [26] for their RKA-secure IBE scheme in the split-state model (*i.e.*, tampering can only be applied to the two parts of the encoded secret state independently).

map and ID is the challenge identity, no scheme can remain secure. We observe that enforcing this natural restriction is all we need, without further restrictions on Φ, to transit from normal to semi-functional (SF) output, a core ingredient for a typical security proof using DSE. In this sense, DSE fits nicely with RKA security (beyond its applications in a related field of leakage resilience [23, 31]).

Implication. Our observation allows us to achieve RKA security beyond *state-of-the-art* polynomial RKA, particularly rational functions. We directly relate the class of RKA functions Φ to an intractability assumption related to Φ. We can then formulate the Φ-assumption to accept functions beyond polynomials, *e.g.*, any functions based on group operations. It is easier to analyze whether a specific function is allowed by checking the validity of the related Φ-assumption. For the existing Φ-RKA secure IBE framework [3], there seems no easy way to check if it remains secure for ϕ' outside of Φ. We also hope that our approach can inspire generalizations, *e.g.*, investigating more exotic classes of RKA functions[2].

Another notable benefit of our direct approach is that the "artifacts" required for key malleability just stay in the security proof but do not manifest in the actual construction. This helps the extensibility of our scheme, especially when IBE is shown to be versatile [9]. As a showcase, we extend our scheme to HIBE.

HIBE. HIBE features a Delegate algorithm taking in a parent secret key $\mathsf{sk_p}$ to generate a child secret key with id_j appended at the end of the parent identity. There are two classes of RKA functions, Φ_e, and Φ_d, one for Extract and one for Delegate. Non-trivial RKAs can be launched over *the identity-based secret keys* beyond the master secret, *i.e.*, giving the value Delegate($\phi(\mathsf{sk_p})$, id_j) to the adversary. Our result for HIBE does not reduce Φ_d to the underlying intractability assumption; however, it comes with some structural restrictions[3]. Removing them may require techniques beyond DSE, which we leave as an open problem.

2 Our Φ-Oracle Bilinear Diffie-Hellman Assumption

2.1 Composite Order Bilinear Groups and Existing Assumptions

Let $\mathcal{G}$ be a bilinear group generator, which takes a parameter 1^λ as input where $\lambda \in \mathbb{N}$, outputs a description of bilinear group context ($N = p_1 p_2 p_3, \mathbb{G}, \mathbb{G}_T, \hat{e}$), where p_1, p_2, p_3 are distinct λ-bit primes, $\mathbb{G}$ and $\mathbb{G}_T$ are cyclic groups of order N, and $\hat{e} : \mathbb{G} \times \mathbb{G} \to \mathbb{G}_T$ is a bilinear map such that $\forall g, h \in \mathbb{G}$ and $a, b \in \mathbb{Z}_N$, $\hat{e}(g^a, h^b) = \hat{e}(g, h)^{ab}$; and $\hat{e}(g, g)$ generates $\mathbb{G}_T$ if g is a generator of $\mathbb{G}$.

We use $\mathbb{G}_{p_i}$ to denote the subgroup of order p_i in $\mathbb{G}$ ($i = 1, 2, 3$). Let g_i be a generator of the subgroup $\mathbb{G}_{p_i}$. Note that for all $h_i \in \mathbb{G}_{p_i}$ and $h_j \in \mathbb{G}_{p_j}$, if $i \neq j$,

---

[2] In the most optimistic case, our construction might turn out to remain secure against an even broader class of RKA attacks, but just no one has explicitly analyzed the hardness of the corresponding version of the assumption so far.

[3] Special restrictions may also apply to existing schemes. For example, Goyal *et al.* [20] proposed *selectively* secure Φ-RKA secure signatures, where Φ are the set of polynomials which are distinct even "ignoring the constant term" (*i.e.*, the difference between any two polynomials should not just be in the constant term).

$\hat{e}(h_i, h_j) = 1$. We use $\mathbb{G}_{p_1 p_2}$ to denote the subgroup of order $p_1 p_2$ in $\mathbb{G}$. For all $T \in \mathbb{G}_{p_1 p_2}$, T can be written uniquely as the product of an element of $\mathbb{G}_{p_1}$ and an element of $\mathbb{G}_{p_2}$. We refer to these elements as the "$\mathbb{G}_{p_1}$ part of T" and the "$\mathbb{G}_{p_2}$ part of T" respectively. We also define $\mathbb{G}_{p_1 p_3}$ and $\mathbb{G} = \mathbb{G}_{p_1 p_2 p_3}$ similarly.

Below are two complexity assumptions to be used in our security proofs.

Assumption 1 [24]. For the bilinear group generated by $\mathcal{G}(1^\lambda)$, given $g \xleftarrow{\$} \mathbb{G}_{p_1}$, $X_3 \xleftarrow{\$} \mathbb{G}_{p_1}$, and T, any probabilistic polynomial-time (PPT) algorithm $\mathcal{A}$ can only distinguish whether $T \in \mathbb{G}_{p_1 p_2}$ or $T \in \mathbb{G}_{p_1}$ with negligible probability in λ.

Assumption 2 [24]. For the bilinear group generated by $\mathcal{G}(1^\lambda)$, given $g \xleftarrow{\$} \mathbb{G}_{p_1}$, $X_3 \xleftarrow{\$} \mathbb{G}_{p_1}$, $X_1 X_2 \xleftarrow{\$} \mathbb{G}_{p_1 p_2}$, $Y_2 Y_3 \xleftarrow{\$} \mathbb{G}_{p_2 p_3}$, and T, any PPT algorithm $\mathcal{A}$ can only distinguish whether $T \in \mathbb{G}_{p_1 p_3}$ or $T \in \mathbb{G}$ with negligible probability in λ.

2.2 Φ-Oracle Decisional Bilinear Diffie-Hellman Assumption

We introduce a non-static[4] assumption based on the decisional bilinear Diffie-Hellman (DBDH) problem. It features an oracle taking a function f that outputs values embedding $f(\alpha)$, where α is a secret exponent in the problem instance.

Φ-**Oracle DBDH Assumption.** Given a group generator $\mathcal{G}$, we define

Experiment Φ-**ODBDH**$_{\mathcal{G},\mathcal{A},\beta}(1^\lambda)$

$$(N = p_1 p_2 p_3, \mathbb{G}, \mathbb{G}_T, \hat{e}) \xleftarrow{\$} \mathcal{G}(1^\lambda), \quad \alpha, s \xleftarrow{\$} \mathbb{Z}_N, \quad g, v \xleftarrow{\$} \mathbb{G}_{p_1},$$

$$X_2, Y_2, Z_2 \xleftarrow{\$} \mathbb{G}_{p_2}, \quad X_3 \xleftarrow{\$} \mathbb{G}_{p_3}, \quad T_0 = \hat{e}(g,g)^{\alpha s}, \quad T_1 \xleftarrow{\$} \mathbb{G}_T.$$

$$\text{Return } \beta' \leftarrow \mathcal{A}^{\mathcal{O}(f)}(N, \mathbb{G}, \mathbb{G}_T, \hat{e}, g, g^\alpha X_2, X_3, g^s Y_2, Z_2, v, v^\alpha, v^{\alpha s}, T_\beta),$$

where on input $f \in \Phi$, the oracle $\mathcal{O}$ outputs $(g^{f(\alpha)} W_2, v^{f(\alpha)} V_2)$ for $W_2, V_2 \in \mathbb{G}_{p_2}$ freshly chosen uniformly at random. We define the advantage of an algorithm $\mathcal{A}$ in breaking the Φ-oracle DBDH assumption to be

$$Adv_{\mathcal{G},\mathcal{A}}(\lambda) := \left| \Pr[\Phi\text{-}\mathbf{ODBDH}_{\mathcal{G},\mathcal{A},1}(1^\lambda) = 1] - \Pr[\Phi\text{-}\mathbf{ODBDH}_{\mathcal{G},\mathcal{A},0}(1^\lambda) = 1] \right|.$$

We say that the bilinear group context from $\mathcal{G}$ satisfies the Φ-oracle DBDH assumption if $Adv_{\mathcal{G},\mathcal{A}}(\lambda)$ is a negligible function of λ for any PPT algorithm $\mathcal{A}$.

The non-interactive part of our assumption is similar to Assumption 3 in the literature [24], with elements $v, v^\alpha, v^{\alpha s}$ added (and elements from $\mathbb{G}_{p_2}$ and $\mathbb{G}_{p_3}$ are samplable). Intuitively, this would not help much in deciding $\hat{e}(g,g)^{\alpha s}$ since the discrete logarithm between g and v is unknown. See Sect. 2.4 for details.

Looking ahead, α will serve as the master secret msk in our scheme. The simulator does not know α only in the last transition (from an SF ciphertext to a random ciphertext). To simulate an SF key for RKA of $f \in \Phi$, we only need $g^{f(\alpha)} W_2$, which is "protected" by W_2, a random $\mathbb{G}_{p_2}$ element. Therefore, Φ can include a large class of functions based on group operations in $\mathbb{Z}_N$.

---

[4] Obviously, static assumptions are weaker than non-static counterparts.

2.3 Turning it into a Non-interactive Assumption

Our Φ-oracle DBDH assumption can be *non-interactive* for specific Φ. For example, if Φ is the class of affine functions, $g^\alpha X_2$ and v^α in the problem instance suffice to derive $(g^{f(\alpha)} W_2, v^{f(\alpha)} V_2)$ for $f \in \Phi$, where $W_2, V_2 \in \mathbb{G}_{p_2}$.

For Φ being the class of polynomials with maximum degree d, we can simply answer all queries if the problem instance also contains $g^{\alpha^2}, \ldots, g^{\alpha^d}, v^{\alpha^2}, \ldots, v^{\alpha^d}$. This assumption is similar to the d-extended decision bilinear Diffie-Hellman assumption[5] used for an existing polynomial-RKA secure IBE scheme [3]. For Φ being the class of rational functions $f(\alpha) := \frac{P(\alpha)}{Q(\alpha)}$, where P, Q are polynomials of degree at most d, $f(\alpha)$ can be computed using group operations on α.

2.4 Generic Security from the Uber-Assumption Family

Boyen [10] offered an exposition of Boneh, Boyen, and Goh's "uber-assumption" family [7] for analyzing the validity and strength of pairing assumptions in the generic-group model (GGM). GGM was introduced by Shoup [28] to study generic-group algorithms that act independently of the group representation. In GGM, algorithms are given access to group elements via a randomly selected representation. In the abstract computation model of Maurer [25], the model this paper uses, an algorithm interacts with a black box via interfaces capturing the real-world atomic computations (*e.g.*, group operation and pairing). The box only reports when any two computed elements are equal (*i.e.*, "collide").

We recall the following master theorem (for a product of three primes) [22].

Theorem 1. *Let* $(N = p_1 p_2 p_3, \mathbb{G}, \mathbb{G}_T, \hat{e}) \overset{\$}{\leftarrow} \mathcal{G}(1^\lambda)$. *Let* $\{A_i\}$ *be random variables over* $\mathbb{G}$, *and let* $\{B_i\}, T_0, T_1$ *be random variables over* $\mathbb{G}_T$, *where all random variables have a degree[6] at most* t. *Consider the below experiment in the GGM:*

Algorithm $\mathcal{A}$ *is given* $N, \{A_i\}, \{B_i\}$ *and* T_b *for a random bit* b, *and outputs* b'. $\mathcal{A}$*'s advantage is the absolute value of the difference between* $\Pr[b' = b]$ *and* $1/2$.

Suppose T_0 *and* T_1 *are independent of* $\{B_i\} \cup \{\hat{e}(A_i, A_j)\}$. *Given a PPT (in* λ*) algorithm* $\mathcal{A}$ *performed at most* q *group operations and has advantage* δ, *we can output a non-trivial factor of* N *in PPT with a probability at least* $\delta - O(q^2 t / 2^\lambda)$.

Appendix A will argue the generic security of our Φ-oracle DBDH assumption when Φ is the class of polynomial and rational functions.

2.5 Beyond Group Operations

Generalizing, one can consider versions of Φ that contain bitwise operations, such as bitwise XOR with a random Gaussian white noise, bit-shifting, or bitwise one-way permutation of α (*cf.*, auxiliary input model in leakage-resilient

---

[5] This belongs to q-type assumptions, commonly known for more than a decade.

[6] A random variable expressed in this way has degree t if the maximum degree of any variable is t [22].

cryptography [16]). The class of functions Φ can also be a combination of any function described above, together with affine or polynomial functions. Of course, the class of functions Φ should be chosen carefully such that for all $f \in \Phi$, $(g^{f(\alpha)} W_2, v^{f(\alpha)} V_2)$ should not help any PPT adversary decide if $T = \hat{e}(g, g)^{\alpha s}$. However, it is more difficult to analyze the validity of the Φ-oracle DBDH assumption if the class of functions Φ involves bitwise operations. An obstacle is that these bitwise operations do not naturally match the group operations. One should be very careful about checking the validity of the assumption if bitwise operations are involved. Meanwhile, we note that RKA security against these kinds of attacks generally appears to require some novel techniques. For example, in the case of pseudorandom functions, the latest results for establishing RKA-security for XOR rely on post-zeroizing multilinear maps [1].

3   Security Model for (Hierarchical) ID-Based Encryption

An IBE scheme consists of four PPT algorithms:

- Setup: On input of a security parameter 1^λ, it generates a public system parameter (an implicit input of all other algorithms) that defines a message space $\mathcal{M}$, a master public key mpk, and a master secret key msk.
- Extract: On input of msk and an identity ID, it outputs an identity-based secret key sk_{ID}.
- Enc: On input of mpk, an identity ID, and a message M from the message space $\mathcal{M}$, it outputs a ciphertext $\mathfrak{C}$.
- Dec: On input of mpk, the identity-based secret key sk_{ID} for the identity ID and $\mathfrak{C}$, it outputs a message M or $\perp$ symbolizing decryption failure.

HIBE is an IBE scheme where the identity ID can be a vector of strings $id_1, \ldots, id_i$, possibly with a bound H over i, with an extra delegation algorithm:

- Delegate: On input of mpk, $sk_{id_1,\ldots,id_j}$, and id_{j+1}, it outputs $sk_{id_1,\ldots,id_{j+1}}$.

Confidentiality is modeled via an indistinguishability-based game against adaptive chosen-plaintext attacks (IND-ID-CPA) between the challenger and the adversary $\mathcal{A}$. For saving space, we give a single definition capturing either Φ_e-RKA security for IBE [2] or (Φ_e, Φ_d)-RKA security for HIBE. The act of tampering or fault injection is applied to the secret used for deriving the output of the corresponding oracle. In particular, a tampered key extraction oracle should not be confused with getting keys for "fake" or "related" identities.

1. *Setup.* The challenger runs $(mpk, msk) \leftarrow$ Setup(1^λ) and gives mpk to $\mathcal{A}$.
2. *Phase 1.* $\mathcal{A}$ can issue queries to the following oracle.
   - Extraction oracle $\mathcal{EO}(\phi, ID)$: On input of a function $\phi \in \Phi_e$ and an identity ID, it returns a secret key $sk_{ID} \leftarrow$ Extract$(\phi(msk), ID)$.
   - Delegation oracle $\mathcal{DO}(\phi, ID_p = (id_1, \ldots, id_{j-1}), id_j)$: For the case of HIBE, on input of a function $\phi \in \Phi_d$, a parent identity ID_p, and a child identity id_j, it returns a secret key $sk_{ID} \leftarrow$ Delegate$(mpk, \phi(\text{Extract}(msk, ID_p)), id_j)$.

3. *Challenge.* $\mathcal{A}$ sends two messages $M_0^*, M_1^* \in \mathcal{M}$ and an identity ID^* to the challenger. The challenger picks a random bit b' and computes $\mathfrak{C}^* \leftarrow \mathsf{Enc}(\mathsf{mpk}, \mathsf{ID}^*, M_{b'}^*)$. The challenger sends $\mathfrak{C}^*$ to $\mathcal{A}$.
4. *Phase 2.* $\mathcal{A}$ can keep issuing queries as in phase 1.
5. *Output.* $\mathcal{A}$ returns a guess b^* of b'.

$\mathcal{A}$ wins the game if $b' = b^*$. We require that the followings are true:

1. There was no query to $\mathcal{EO}$ with input (ϕ, ID) such that $\phi(\mathsf{msk}) = \mathsf{msk}$ while ID equals to ID^* for IBE, or ID is a prefix of ID^* for HIBE;
2. For $\mathcal{DO}$ that is only available for HIBE, there was no query $(\phi, \mathsf{ID_p}, \mathsf{id}_j)$ where $\mathsf{ID_p}$ is a prefix of ID^*, such that $\phi(\mathsf{sk_{ID_p}})$ allows a "trivial break," *e.g.*, $\mathsf{Dec}(\mathsf{mpk}, \mathsf{Delegate}(\mathsf{mpk}, \phi(\mathsf{Extract}(\mathsf{msk}, \mathsf{ID_p})), \mathsf{id}_j), \mathfrak{C}^*) \in \{M_0^*, M_1^*\}$.

The advantage of $\mathcal{A}$ is $\left| \Pr[\mathcal{A} \text{ wins}] - \frac{1}{2} \right|$. If there is no PPT $\mathcal{A}$ with a non-negligible advantage in the game above, we say the IBE scheme is Φ_e-RKA secure, or the HIBE scheme is (Φ_e, Φ_d)-RKA secure.

Complications in HIBE. The definition of the class Φ_d is much more complicated than Φ_e. The culprit is that the master secret key msk is often "less structured." To illustrate, msk in many pairing-based constructions is just an exponent "protected" by the discrete logarithm assumption, restricting the adversary from exploiting the output derived from a related key. Meanwhile, different from Extract, there can be many valid inputs to the Delegate algorithm even for the same identity, since identity-based secret keys are often generated probabilistically, making it tricky to exclude all possible "trivial" RKAs. For many schemes, they consist of group elements that can be considered as a randomized version of the parent identity-based secret key. We thus leave the definition of "trivial break" as a placeholder and define specific structural restrictions for our HIBE scheme.

4 Security Against Related-Key Attack from Dual System Encryption

4.1 Our RKA-Secure IBE Scheme

Lewko and Waters [24] used DSE to lift the selective security of Boneh-Boyen IBE [6] and Boneh-Boyen-Goh HIBE [7] to the composite order setting to obtain adaptive security. At a high level, we make the following modification to the dual system IBE scheme of Lewko and Waters [24]. Let α be the master secret. Both ciphertexts and user secret keys now include randomized copies of v_1^α for some element v_1 of order p_1. Related keys will then be randomized and hence do not help much in decrypting the challenge ciphertext. This is conceptually different from the collision-resistant identity renaming of the Bellare *et al.* [3] framework, which rules out the collision of two user secret keys for different identities when one originated from a related master secret key with the ϕ function applied.

Setup(1^λ): The private key generator (PKG) runs the bilinear group generator $\mathcal{G}(1^\lambda)$ to get $(N = p_1p_2p_3, \mathbb{G}, \mathbb{G}_T, \hat{e})$ as defined in Sect. 2. Suppose $\mathcal{G}$ also gives generators g_1 and g_3 of the subgroups $\mathbb{G}_{p_1}$ and $\mathbb{G}_{p_3}$, respectively. The PKG randomly picks $\alpha \in \mathbb{Z}_N$, $h_1, u_1, v_1 \in \mathbb{G}_{p_1}$. The public system parameter is

$$(N, \mathbb{G}, \mathbb{G}_T, \hat{e}, g_1, h_1, u_1, v_1, g_3).$$

The master public key is $(\hat{e}(g_1, g_1)^\alpha, v_1^\alpha)$. The master secret key is α.

Extract(msk, ID): The PKG randomly picks $r \in \mathbb{Z}_N$, $X_3, X_3' \in \mathbb{G}_{p_3}$ and computes

$$K_1 = g_1^\alpha(h_1 u_1^{\text{ID}} v_1^\alpha)^r X_3, \quad K_2 = g_1^r X_3'.$$

As in existing RKA-secure IBE schemes [3], K_1 is computed by α every time, and the PKG does not reuse g_1^α or v_1^α from past computations.

Enc(mpk, ID, M): To encrypt a message M in the message space $\mathcal{M} = \mathbb{G}_T$ for ID, the sender randomly picks $s \in \mathbb{Z}_N$ and outputs $\mathfrak{C} = (C_0, C_1, C_2)$ where

$$C_0 = M \cdot \hat{e}(g_1, g_1)^{\alpha s}, \quad C_1 = g_1^s, \quad C_2 = (h_1 u_1^{\text{ID}} v_1^\alpha)^s.$$

Dec(mpk, sk$_{\text{ID}}$, $\mathfrak{C}$): Given a ciphertext $\mathfrak{C} = (C_0, C_1, C_2)$ and a secret key sk$_{\text{ID}} = (K_1, K_2)$, the recipient outputs $M = C_0 \cdot \hat{e}(C_2, K_2)/\hat{e}(C_1, K_1)$.

Security. The main ingredients of DSE are semi-functional (SF) keys and SF ciphertexts. An SF key can decrypt a normal ciphertext, and a normal key can decrypt an SF ciphertext. However, an SF key cannot decrypt an SF ciphertext. The security proof goes by a sequence of transformations: from normal ciphertext to SF ciphertext, and then from normal keys to SF keys, one by one at a time. In the end, the adversary got a number of SF keys, which cannot help decrypt the SF challenge ciphertext. This allows the last transition from the SF challenge to an encryption of a random message, in which no adversary has any advantage.

We define the following SF structures used only in the security proofs. They are like their normal version in the actual scheme but "perturbed" by a $\mathbb{G}_{p_2}$ generator, denoted by either $\bar{g}_2$ or $\hat{g}_2$ below.

An *SF secret key* (or just *SF key*) is in the form of $(K_1' = K_1 \cdot \bar{g}_2^\gamma, K_2' = K_2 \cdot \bar{g}_2)$, where $\gamma \in \mathbb{Z}_N$, and (K_1, K_2) is a normal secret key. Naturally, γ is random.

An *SF ciphertext* is in the form of $(C_0' = C_0, C_1' = C_1 \cdot \hat{g}_2, C_2' = C_2 \cdot \hat{g}_2^\delta)$, where $\delta \in \mathbb{Z}_N$ and (C_0, C_1, C_2) is a normal ciphertext. Likewise, δ is also random.

Decrypting an SF ciphertext by an SF secret key will result in a message "blinded" by $\hat{e}(\bar{g}_2, \hat{g}_2)^{\gamma-\delta}$. In case the exponents in these extra blinding factors are zeros, decryption still works, which leads us to the notion of *nominally semi-functional (NSF) secret keys*. An NSF secret key is a special kind of SF key that can decrypt some corresponding SF ciphertexts, which means $\gamma = \delta$. If an SF secret key is not nominally semi-functional, it is *truly semi-functional*.

Theorem 2. *Our IBE scheme is Φ-RKA IND-ID-CPA secure under Assumptions 1, 2, and the Φ-oracle DBDH assumption.*

The security proof is given in Appendix B. Its resemblance with the existing proof of Lewko and Waters [24] demonstrates our point that the DSE framework fits well with the RKA security. Here, we explain some of the intuitions for our security proof. Firstly, our scheme exploits different subgroups for building the SF objects. Like the usual DSE approach, we need to establish a nominally semi-functional secret key (which can always decrypt the corresponding semi-functional ciphertext) to avoid the paradox that the simulator can use the semi-functional ciphertext to check if a user secret key is also semi-functional.

Nevertheless, to ensure this remains unnoticeable to the adversary, we want to avoid the collision of the function values governing the γ and δ factors modulo one of the prime factors. This can be resolved easily as in existing DSE-based proofs since one can factor the order of the composite group when such a collision is found. For our case, we also need to ensure the same holds true when the ϕ function is involved, which can be easily done with another similar hybrid.

For an $\mathsf{Extract}(\phi(\mathsf{msk}), \mathsf{ID})$ oracle query, to avoid the adversary from winning trivially, ϕ cannot be an identity map, and ID cannot be the challenge identity. This restriction is exactly what we need for the above transition to go through in the security proof regarding the γ and δ factors. Also, there is no further restriction on the ϕ function, and hence we can support a wider class of Φ.

Our last transition (from an SF ciphertext to a random ciphertext) is the only transition where the simulator does not know the master secret key α, which we resort to the Φ-oracle DBDH assumption to answer the related-key queries. This is the only place relying on this assumption in our entire security proof.

4.2   Our RKA-Secure Hierarchical IBE Scheme

Our system can be extended to Lewko-Waters HIBE [24]. A complication of allowing RKA attacks on the Delegate algorithm of HIBE is that the identity-based secret key of the parent may be composed of several group elements, and the adversary may apply different RKA functions to different group elements.

$\mathsf{Setup}(1^\lambda)$: We let H denote the maximum depth of the HIBE. The PKG runs the bilinear group generator $\mathcal{G}(1^\lambda)$ to get $(N = p_1 p_2 p_3, \mathbb{G}, \mathbb{G}_T, \hat{e})$. Suppose $\mathcal{G}$ also gives generators g_1 and g_3 of the subgroups $\mathbb{G}_{p_1}$ and $\mathbb{G}_{p_3}$, respectively. The PKG randomly picks $\alpha \in \mathbb{Z}_N$, $u_1, \ldots, u_H, h_1 \in \mathbb{G}_{p_1}$. The public system parameter is

$$(N, \mathbb{G}, \mathbb{G}_T, \hat{e}, g_1, h_1, u_1, \ldots, u_H, v_1, g_3).$$

The master public key is $(\hat{e}(g_1, g_1)^\alpha, v_1^\alpha)$. The master secret key is α.

$\mathsf{Extract}(\mathsf{msk}, \mathsf{ID} = (\mathsf{id}_1, \ldots, \mathsf{id}_j))$: The PKG randomly picks $r \in \mathbb{Z}_N$, X_3, X_3', $X_{3,j+1}, \ldots, X_{3,H} \in \mathbb{G}_{p_3}$ and computes $\mathsf{sk}_{\mathsf{ID}} = (K_1, K_2, D_{j+1}, \ldots, D_H)$, where

$$K_1 = g_1^\alpha (h_1 u_1^{\mathsf{id}_1} \cdots u_j^{\mathsf{id}_j} v_1^\alpha)^r X_3, \quad K_2 = g_1^r X_3', \quad \{D_i = u_i^r X_{3,i}\}_{\forall i \in \{j+1, \ldots, H\}}.$$

Note that the PKG does not reuse g_1^α and v_1^α from past computations.

Delegate(mpk, $sk_{id_1,\ldots,id_j}$, id_{j+1})): On input $sk_{id_1,\ldots,id_j} = (\bar{K}_1, \bar{K}_2, \bar{D}_{j+1}, \ldots, \bar{D}_H)$, it randomly picks $r' \in \mathbb{Z}_N$, $Y_3, Y_3', Y_{3,j+2}, \ldots, Y_{3,H} \in \mathbb{G}_{p_3}$ and computes

$$K_1 = \bar{K}_1(h_1 u_1^{id_1} \cdots u_j^{id_j} u_{j+1}^{id_{j+1}} v_1^\alpha)^{r'} \bar{D}_{j+1}^{id_{j+1}} Y_3, \quad K_2 = \bar{K}_2 g_1^{r'} Y_3',$$

$$D_{j+2} = \bar{D}_{j+2} u_{j+2}^{r'} Y_{3,j+2}, \quad \cdots, \quad D_H = \bar{D}_H u_H^{r'} Y_{3,H}.$$

Enc(mpk, ID = $(id_1, \ldots, id_j)$, M): To encrypt a message $M \in \mathbb{G}_T$ for $(id_1, \ldots, id_j)$, the sender randomly picks $s \in \mathbb{Z}_N$ and outputs $\mathfrak{C} = (C_0, C_1, C_2)$ where

$$C_0 = M \cdot \hat{e}(g_1, g_1)^{\alpha s}, \quad C_1 = g_1^s, \quad C_2 = (h_1 u_1^{id_1} \cdots u_j^{id_j} v_1^\alpha)^s.$$

Dec(mpk, sk_{ID}, $\mathfrak{C}$): Given a ciphertext $\mathfrak{C} = (C_0, C_1, C_2)$ and a secret key $sk_{ID} = (K_1, K_2, \ldots)$, the recipient outputs $M = C_0 \cdot \hat{e}(C_2, K_2)/\hat{e}(C_1, K_1)$.

Security. We define the following SF structures used in the security proofs only. An *SF key* for an identity ID = $(id_1, \ldots, id_j)$ is in the form of

$$K_1' = K_1 \cdot \bar{g}_2^\gamma, \quad K_2' = K_2 \cdot \bar{g}_2, \quad D_{j+1}' = D_{j+1} \cdot \bar{g}_2^{\gamma_{j+1}'}, \quad \ldots, \quad D_H' = D_H \cdot \bar{g}_2^{\gamma_H'},$$

where $\gamma, \gamma_{j+1}', \ldots, \gamma_H' \in \mathbb{Z}_N$, and $(K_1, K_2, D_{j+1}, \ldots, D_H)$ is a normal secret key. An *SF ciphertext* is in the form of $(C_0' = C_0, C_1' = C_1 \cdot \hat{g}_2, C_2' = C_2 \cdot \hat{g}_2^\delta)$, where $\delta \in \mathbb{Z}_N$ and (C_0, C_1, C_2) is a normal ciphertext. Decrypting an SF ciphertext using an SF secret key will result in a message "blinded" by $\hat{e}(\bar{g}_2, \hat{g}_2)^{\gamma-\delta}$. An NSF secret key is a special kind of SF key that can decrypt the SF ciphertext, which means $\gamma = \delta$. Except for this key, other SF keys are truly semi-functional.

Theorem 3. *Our HIBE scheme is (Φ_e, Φ_d)-RKA IND-ID-CPA secure under Assumptions 1, 2, and Φ_e-oracle DBDH assumption, where for all delegation oracle query $\phi = (\varphi_1, \varphi_2, \varphi_{j+1}', \ldots, \varphi_H') \in \Phi_d$ applied to the identity-based secret key $(K_1, K_2, D_{j+1}, \ldots, D_H)$ of an identity ID component-wise, we require that:*

1. $\varphi_1 = \varphi_{j+1}'$.
2. $\varphi_1 : \mathbb{G} \to \mathbb{G}$ *and* $\varphi_2 : \mathbb{G} \to \mathbb{G}$ *are isomorphic functions.*
3. *If* ID *is a prefix of the challenge identity, for all $g \in \mathbb{G}$, the value $\log_{\varphi_2(g)} \varphi_1(g)$ (which is well defined given the isomorphic property) is randomly distributed.*

The security proof is given in Appendix B. An intuitive explanation for the first two restrictions is that not all combinations of group elements constitute a well-formed identity-based secret key. To illustrate the last one, the adversary might supply φ_2 as a trapdoor permutation (*cf.*, auxiliary leakage, *e.g.*, [16,31]), for which the adversary could recover the original term while there is no easy way for the security reduction to identify that. Without upgrading the underlying IBE schemes "too much" beyond the application of DSE techniques, we chose to enforce some random behavior for one of the component functions φ_2.

5   Extensions

Bellare *et al.* [2] showed the relationship between different RKA-secure cryptosystems. It is well-known that IBE implies signatures. Bellare *et al.* [2] demonstrated that Naor's transform preserves RKA security. Similarly, the transform of Boneh, Canetti, Halevi, and Katz [8] using one-time signatures (trivially implied by IBE) turns a Φ-RKA secure IBE scheme into a Φ-RKA secure public-key encryption scheme against chosen-ciphertext attacks (CCA). So, our Φ-RKA secure IBE can be transformed into CCA-secure encryption and signature schemes.

Our (H)IBE schemes described in composite order groups are very similar to the existing ones [24], which have been translated into prime order groups.

Recently, tightly-secure IBE schemes [21] have been constructed from the matrix Diffie-Hellman assumption. The security reduction switches the keys to semi-functional by adding some kernel matrix. The ciphertext is also switched to semi-functional similarly. The main difference from the DSE is that the game hopping is done in $\log(\lambda)$ times, and hence the security reduction is tighter. We leave it as a future work to apply our approach to these IBE schemes.

6   Conclusion and Future Works

Existences of trapdoors can be hard to detect [14,15]. There are growing interests in protecting cryptographic systems from tampering attacks such as related-key attacks (RKA), which apply a function to modify the key before it is used. Existing works mostly propose solutions tailor-made for resilience against a specific form of functions. We propose a design methodology that reduces the set of allowed functions to the underlying assumption, leading to an RKA-secure identity-based encryption (IBE) scheme and its hierarchical IBE extension.

We hope our work can inspire follow-up in devising RKA-secure cryptosystems for a wide class of RKA functions instead of custom-made solutions for each kind of function. We also hope the rather direct correspondence between the real-world RKA security over a function family and the intractability of the related assumptions can stimulate more cryptanalysis. Other future directions include investigating the applicability of our methodology to related/generalized notions, such as security against related-randomness attacks [32], complete non-malleability [13], addressing non-trivial copy attacks in RKA security, possibly through the lens of non-malleable function [11], and investigating RKA-security for escrow-free IBE [12] (existing constructions include full-domain-hash and exponent-inversion IBE schemes [12], and a lattice-based one [17]).

A   Generic Security of Specific Cases of Our Assumption

This section justifies the security of our Φ-oracle DBDH assumption in the variant abstraction of Maurer [25]. This variant GGM model internally stores tuples denoting group elements. We consider the order of the generic group N is a composite of three distinct primes $p_1 p_2 p_3$, which Boyen [10] has discussed a few caveats or justifications. The model internally stores two types of tuples, (μ_1, μ_2, μ_3) and $[\nu_1, \nu_2, \nu_3]$, where $\mu_i, \nu_i \in [1, p_i]$, to represent an element in the base group and the target group, respectively. This computational model provides two types of operations, add and mul, which adds and multiplies the tuples, representing the group operation and the pairing, respectively.

The Φ-oracle DBDH problem can be formalized as one to distinguish two black-box accesses $\mathbf{B}$ and $\mathbf{B}'$ of the same type but with a different distribution of the initial state. Specifically, for $\mathbf{B}$, the model stores tuples

$$(1,0,0), (0,1,0), (0,0,1), (\alpha, x, 0), (s, y, 0), (v, 0, 0), (v\alpha, 0, 0), (v\alpha s, 0, 0), [\alpha s, 0, 0],$$

and for $\mathbf{B}'$, the model stores tuples

$$(1,0,0), (0,1,0), (0,0,1), (\alpha, x, 0), (s, y, 0), (v, 0, 0), (v\alpha, 0, 0), (v\alpha s, 0, 0), [t_1, t_2, t_3].$$

The computational model offers an additional oracle $\mathcal{O}$, which takes a polynomial f_i of degree at most d from Φ as input and stores $(f_i(\alpha), w_{i,1}, 0)$ and $(v f_i(\alpha), w_{i_2}, 0)$ in its state, where $w_{i,1}, w_{i,2}$ are sampled uniformly from $[1, p_2]$. The adversary can only make at most q add, mul, or $\mathcal{O}$ queries to the model.

If no collision occurs in both $\mathbf{B}$ and $\mathbf{B}'$, the views of the adversary are trivially identical. Next, we bound the collision probability. In the former case of accessing $\mathbf{B}$, the collision occurs in either the base group or the target group.

For the base group, it is obvious that the collision probability is bounded by q^2/p (based on an existing analysis [25]), where p is the minimal of (p_1, p_2, p_3).

For the target group, when a collision occurs, the values in all three positions must be identical, which means the values in the second position (mod p_2) must be identical. Note that any value in the second position is in the form of

$$c_0 + c_1 x + c_2 y + c_3 w_{i,1} + c_4 w_{i,2}$$
$$+ d_{1,2} xy + d_{1,3} x w_{i,1} + d_{1,4} x w_{i,2} + d_{2,3} y w_{i,1} + d_{2,4} y w_{i,2} + d_{3,4} w_{i,1} w_{i,2},$$

i.e., a multivariate polynomial of variables $(x, y, w_{1,1}, w_{1,2}, \ldots, w_{q,1}, w_{q,2})$, and their degree is bounded by 2. Therefore, using a lemma due to Schwartz [27], no collision occurs, except a probability of $2q^2/p$.

Conditioned on that no collision on the value in the second position, we have any value in the first position being in the form of

$$c_0 + c_1 \alpha + c_2 s + c_3 v + c_4 v\alpha + c_5 v\alpha s + c_6 v^2 \alpha + c_7 v\alpha^2 + c_8 v\alpha s + c_9 v^2 \alpha s$$

$$+ c_{10} v\alpha^2 s^2 + \sum_{i=1}^{q} a_i f_i(\alpha) + \sum_{i=1}^{q} b_i v f_i(\alpha) + \sum_{i=1}^{q} d_i v\alpha f_i(\alpha) + \sum_{i=1}^{q} e_i v\alpha s f_i(\alpha)$$

$$+ \sum_{i=1}^{q} a_i' v f_i(\alpha) + \sum_{i=1}^{q} b_i' v^2 f_i(\alpha) + \sum_{i=1}^{q} d_i' v^2 \alpha f_i(\alpha) + \sum_{i=1}^{q} e_i' v^2 \alpha s f_i(\alpha) + h_i \alpha s,$$

which is a multivariate polynomial of (α, s, v), and the degree is bounded by $d + 1$. Similarly [27], no collision occurs except for probability $\frac{(d+1)(q^2+q)+2q^2}{p}$.

It is also evident that the collision probability in the latter case (accessing $\mathbf{B}'$) is bounded by the former one (the black-box access to $\mathbf{B}$). Thus, the advantage of our assumption above is bounded by $\frac{(d+1)(q^2+q)+3q^2}{p}$, which is negligible.

The non-interactive version of the assumption can be analyzed in this GGM similarly. Applying an analogous analysis (which we skip due to the space limit), the function family Φ can be easily extended to rational functions, as long as the degrees of their denominators are also bounded. This stems from an idea of Boyen [10], which notationally replaces a rational exponent with a polynomial multiplied with the (non-zero) least common multiple of all denominators.

B Security Proofs

B.1 Proof of Theorem 2

Proof. We prove by a hybrid argument using a sequence of games. The first game Game_{real} is the real Φ-RKA IND-ID-CPA game. We denote the challenge identity to be ID^*. The second game Game_{res} is the same as Game_{real}, except that the adversary cannot ask for the secret key of identity $\text{ID} = \text{ID}^* \bmod p_2$. This restriction will be retained throughout the subsequent games. Let q be the number of extraction oracle queries. For $k = 0$ to q, we define Game_k as:

Game_k: It is the same as Game_{res}, except that the challenge ciphertext is semi-functional (SF), and the keys used to answer first k oracle queries are SF. The keys for the rest of the queries are normal.

As a result, in Game_0, all keys are normal and the challenge ciphertext is SF. In Game_q, all keys and the challenge ciphertext are SF. We defer to the lemmas below to prove the indistinguishability between these games.

The last game is Game_{final}, which is the same as Game_q except that the challenge ciphertext is a semi-functional ciphertext encrypting a random message instead of one of the two challenge messages. In Game_{final}, the value of b' is information-theoretically hidden from $\mathcal{A}$. Hence $\mathcal{A}$ has no advantage in winning Game_{final}. We will prove below that if Assumptions 1, 2, and the Φ-oracle DBDH assumption hold, then Game_{real} is indistinguishable from Game_{final}. $\qquad\square$

Lemma 1. *We can construct an algorithm $\mathcal{B}$ with a non-negligible advantage in breaking Assumption 1 or Assumption 2 if there exists an adversary $\mathcal{A}$ such that $Adv_{\mathcal{A}}(\text{Game}_{real}) - Adv_{\mathcal{A}}(\text{Game}_{res}) = \epsilon$.*

The proof of Lemma 1 is easy (*e.g.*, see [24, 30]) and is omitted.

Lemma 2. *We can construct an algorithm $\mathcal{B}$ with advantage ϵ in breaking Assumption 1 if there exists $\mathcal{A}$ such that $Adv_{\mathcal{A}}(\text{Game}_{res}) - Adv_{\mathcal{A}}(\text{Game}_0) = \epsilon$.*

Proof. Given (g, X_3, T) from Assumption 1, $\mathcal{B}$ can simulate Game_{res} or Game_0. $\mathcal{B}$ chooses random $a, b, c, \alpha \in \mathbb{Z}_N$, $h_1 \in \mathbb{G}_{p_1}$. $\mathcal{B}$ sets $g_1 = g, h_1 = g^a, u_1 = g^b, v_1 = g^c, g_3 = X_3$. $\mathcal{B}$ generates the rest of mpk according to Setup and sets msk $= \alpha$.

For the RKA-extraction oracle queries (ϕ, ID), $\mathcal{B}$ returns $\mathsf{Extract}(\phi(\mathsf{msk}), \mathsf{ID})$. Note that $\mathcal{B}$ can check if $\phi(\alpha) = \alpha$ using the knowledge of α.

In the challenge phase, $\mathcal{A}$ sends $\mathcal{B}$ two messages M_0^*, M_1^*, and an identity ID^*. $\mathcal{B}$ randomly picks a bit $b' \in \{0, 1\}$. $\mathcal{B}$ calculates the challenge ciphertext as:

$$C_0^* = M_{b'}^* \cdot \hat{e}(T, g_1)^\alpha, \quad C_1^* = T, \quad C_2^* = T^{a + b\mathsf{ID}^* + c\alpha}.$$

If $T = g^s$, this is a normal ciphertext, and hence $\mathcal{B}$ simulates Game_{res}. If $T = g^s Y_2$, this is an SF ciphertext with $\hat{g}_2 = Y_2, \hat{g}_2^\delta = Y_2^{a + b\mathsf{ID}^* + c\alpha}$; and $\mathcal{B}$ simulates Game_0 with $\delta = a + b\mathsf{ID}^* + c\alpha$. The values of $a, b, c, \alpha \bmod p_2$ are not correlated with the corresponding values modulo p_1 by the Chinese remainder theorem. If $\mathcal{A}$ can distinguish between Game_{res} and Game_0, $\mathcal{B}$ can break Assumption 1. $\square$

Lemma 3. *We can construct an algorithm $\mathcal{B}$ which breaks Assumption 2 with advantage ϵ if there exists $\mathcal{A}$ such that $Adv_{\mathcal{A}}(\mathsf{Game}_{\ell-1}) - Adv_{\mathcal{A}}(\mathsf{Game}_\ell) = \epsilon$.*

Proof. Given $(g, X_1 X_2, X_3, Y_2 Y_3, T)$ from Assumption 2, $\mathcal{B}$ can simulate $\mathsf{Game}_{\ell-1}$ or Game_ℓ. $\mathcal{B}$ chooses random $a, b, c, \alpha \in \mathbb{Z}_N$, sets $g_1 = g, h_1 = g^a, u_1 = g^b, v_1 = g^c$, and $g_3 = X_3$, and generates the rest of mpk and $\mathsf{msk} = \alpha$ according to Setup.

For the k-th distinct RKA-extraction oracle query on ID_k and ϕ_k, $\mathcal{B}$ can compute $\phi_k(\alpha)$ and check if $\phi_k(\alpha) = \alpha$ using the knowledge of α.

- If $k < \ell$, $\mathcal{B}$ returns $\mathsf{Extract}(\phi_k(\mathsf{msk}), \mathsf{ID}_k)$.
- If $k > \ell$, $\mathcal{B}$ calculates $(K_1, K_2) \leftarrow \mathsf{Extract}(\phi_k(\mathsf{msk}), \mathsf{ID}_k)$ using msk. $\mathcal{B}$ randomly picks $\gamma_1, \gamma_2 \in \mathbb{Z}_N$ and returns the (related) SF-key:

$$K_1' = K_1 \cdot (Y_2 Y_3)^{\gamma_1}, \quad K_2' = K_2 \cdot (Y_2 Y_3)^{\gamma_2}.$$

  This is semi-functional. By the Chinese remainder theorem, the values of γ_1, γ_2 modulo p_2 and modulo p_3 are not correlated.
- If $k = \ell$, $\mathcal{B}$ chooses random $X_3', X_3'' \in \mathbb{G}_{p_3}$ and returns the (related) key:

$$K_1 = g_1^{\phi_\ell(\alpha)} \cdot T^{a + b \cdot \mathsf{ID}_\ell + c \cdot \phi_\ell(\alpha)} \cdot X_3', \quad K_2 = T \cdot X_3''.$$

If $T = Z_1 Z_3 \in \mathbb{G}_{p_1 p_3}$ where $Z_i \in \mathbb{G}_{p_i}$; it is a normal key with $g^r = Z_1$. Hence $\mathcal{B}$ simulates $\mathsf{Game}_{\ell-1}$. If $T = Z_1 Z_2 Z_3 \in \mathbb{G}$, it is an SF key with $\bar{g}_2^\gamma = Z_2^{a + b \cdot \mathsf{ID}_\ell + c \cdot \phi(\alpha)}$ and $\bar{g}_2 = Z_2$. Hence $\mathcal{B}$ simulates Game_ℓ. Note that the value of $\gamma \bmod p_2$ is not correlated with the values of a, b, c, and α modulo p_1.

In the challenge phase, $\mathcal{A}$ sends $\mathcal{B}$ two messages M_0^*, M_1^*, and an identity ID^*. $\mathcal{B}$ chooses a random bit $b' \in \{0, 1\}$ and calculates the challenge ciphertext:

$$C_0^* = M_{b'}^* \cdot \hat{e}(X_1 X_2, g_1)^\alpha, \quad C_1^* = (X_1 X_2), \quad C_2^* = (X_1 X_2)^{a + b \cdot \mathsf{ID}^* + c \cdot \alpha}.$$

It is an SF ciphertext with $\hat{g}_2 = X_2$ and $\hat{g}_2^\delta = X_2^{a + b \cdot \mathsf{ID}^* + c \cdot \alpha}$. If the ℓ-th SF key is created for decrypting the challenge ciphertext, *i.e.*, $\mathsf{ID}_\ell = \mathsf{ID}^*$ and $\phi_\ell(\alpha) = \alpha$, its γ factor becomes $\delta = a + b \cdot \mathsf{ID}^* + c \cdot \alpha$, so it is a nominally semi-functional key which will always decrypt the challenge ciphertext.

Finally, we have to consider the view of the adversary in the Game_ℓ. The value of $\delta = a + b \cdot \mathsf{ID}^* + c \cdot \alpha \bmod p_2$ is uncorrelated to $\gamma = a + b \cdot \mathsf{ID}_\ell + c \cdot \phi_\ell(\alpha)$ since a, b, c, α are only known in modulo p_1 and:

– Case 1: $\mathsf{ID}^* \neq \mathsf{ID}_\ell$. Then $a + b \cdot \mathsf{ID}_\ell$ is uncorrelated[7] to $a + b \cdot \mathsf{ID}^*$ modulo p_2. It implies γ is uncorrelated to δ since a, b, c, α are randomly chosen from $\mathbb{Z}_N$.
– Case 2: $\mathsf{ID}^* = \mathsf{ID}_\ell$ and $\phi_\ell(\alpha) \neq \alpha$. Then $a + c \cdot \phi_\ell(\alpha)$ is uncorrelated[8]. It implies γ is uncorrelated to δ since a, b, c, α are randomly chosen from $\mathbb{Z}_N$.

By definition, the adversary query with $\mathsf{ID}^* = \mathsf{ID}_\ell$ and $\phi_\ell(\alpha) = \alpha$.

So, $\mathcal{B}$ can break Assumption 2 if $\mathcal{A}$ can distinguish $\mathrm{Game}_{\ell-1}$ and Game_ℓ. □

Lemma 4. *Given an adversary $\mathcal{A}$ such that $Adv_\mathcal{A}(\mathrm{Game}_q) - Adv_\mathcal{A}(\mathrm{Game}_{final}) = \epsilon$, we can construct an algorithm $\mathcal{B}$ with advantage ϵ in breaking the Φ-oracle DBDH assumption.*

Proof. Given $(g, g^\alpha X_2, X_3, g^s Y_2, Z_2, v, v^\alpha, v^{\alpha s}, T)$ and accesses to an oracle $\mathcal{O}$ from the Φ-oracle DBDH assumption, $\mathcal{B}$ chooses random $a, b \in \mathbb{Z}_N$ and sets

$$g_1 = g, \quad h_1 = g^a, \quad u_1 = g^b, \quad v_1 = v, \quad \hat{e}(g_1, g_1)^\alpha = \hat{e}(g, g^\alpha X_2).$$

$\mathcal{B}$ implicitly sets $\mathsf{msk} = \alpha$. $\mathcal{B}$ sends the master public key mpk to $\mathcal{A}$.

$\mathcal{B}$ can calculate the semi-functional secret key as follows. $\mathcal{B}$ randomly picks $r \in \mathbb{Z}_N$, $R_2, R_2' \in \mathbb{G}_{p_3}$, and $R_3, R_3' \in \mathbb{G}_{p_3}$, and returns:

$$K_1' = (g^\alpha X_2) \cdot (h_1 u_1^{\mathsf{ID}} v_1^\alpha)^r \cdot R_2 \cdot R_3, \quad K_2' = g^r \cdot R_2' \cdot R_3',$$

If it is a related key query with input ϕ, then $\mathcal{B}$ asks $\mathcal{O}(\phi)$ for obtaining the related key $(g^{\phi(\alpha)} W_2, v_1^{\phi(\alpha)} V_2)$. $\mathcal{B}$ can answer all extraction oracle queries by:

$$K_1' = (g^{\phi(\alpha)} W_2) \cdot (h_1 u_1^{\mathsf{ID}} \cdot v_1^{\phi(\alpha)} V_2)^r \cdot R_2 \cdot R_3, \quad K_2' = g^r \cdot R_2' \cdot R_3',$$

Note that $\mathcal{B}$ can check if $\phi(\alpha) = \alpha$ by checking if $\frac{g^{\phi(\alpha)} W_2}{g^\alpha X_2}$ is in the subgroup $\mathbb{G}_{p_2}$ but not $\mathbb{G}_{p_1}$ and $\mathbb{G}_{p_3}$. This is easily doable using $g \in \mathbb{G}_{p_1}$ and $X_3 \in \mathbb{G}_{p_3}$.

Finally, $\mathcal{B}$ picks a random bit b and calculates the SF challenge ciphertext:

$$C_0' = M_b^* \cdot T, \quad C_1' = (g^s Y_2), \quad C_2' = (g^s Y_2)^{a + b \cdot \mathsf{ID}^*} \cdot v_1^{\alpha s}.$$

If $T = \hat{e}(g, g)^{\alpha s}$, $\mathcal{B}$ simulates Game_q; Game_{final} otherwise. If $\mathcal{A}$ can distinguish between these two, $\mathcal{B}$ can break the Φ-oracle DBDH assumption. □

B.2   Proof of Theorem 3

Proof. We prove by a hybrid argument using a sequence of games. The first game Game_{real} is the real (Φ_e, Φ_d)-RKA IND-ID-CPA game, and we denote the challenge identity to be $\mathsf{ID}^* = (\mathsf{id}_1^*, \ldots, \mathsf{id}_{j^*}^*)$.

The second game Game_{res} is the same as Game_{real}, except that the adversary cannot ask for keys for identities which are prefixes of ID^* modulo p_2, for both

---

[7] The case that $\mathsf{ID}^* \neq \mathsf{ID}_\ell$ and $\mathsf{ID}^* = \mathsf{ID}_\ell \bmod p_2$ is eliminated by Game_{res}.
[8] The case that $\phi_\ell(\alpha) \neq \alpha$ and $\phi_\ell(\alpha) = \alpha \bmod p_2$ can be eliminated by an extra game similar to Game_{res} considering $a + c \cdot \alpha$ modulo p_2. We omit the repetitive details.

extraction oracle $\mathcal{EO}$ and delegation oracle $\mathcal{DO}$. This restriction will be retained throughout the subsequent games. After that, we use q to denote the number of distinct ID queries to $\mathcal{EO}$ and $\mathcal{DO}$. For $k = 0$ to q, we define Game_k as:

Game_k: It is the same as Game_{res}, except that the challenge ciphertext is SF, and the keys used to answer first k oracle queries are SF. The keys for the rest of the queries are normal.

As a result, in Game_0, all keys are normal and the challenge ciphertext is SF. In Game_q, all keys and the challenge ciphertext are SF.

The last game is Game_{final}, which is the same as Game_q except that the challenge ciphertext is an SF encryption of a random message.

The following lemmas prove the indistinguishability between these games.

Lemma 5. *When given an adversary $\mathcal{A}$ with $Adv_{\mathcal{A}}(\text{Game}_{real}) - Adv_{\mathcal{A}}(\text{Game}_{res})$ $= \epsilon$, we can construct an algorithm $\mathcal{B}$ with a non-negligible advantage in breaking Assumptions 1 or 2.*

The proof of Lemma 5 is easy and is omitted.

Lemma 6. *We can construct an algorithm $\mathcal{B}$ with advantage ϵ in breaking Assumption 1 if there exists $\mathcal{A}$ such that $Adv_{\mathcal{A}}(\text{Game}_{res}) - Adv_{\mathcal{A}}(\text{Game}_0) = \epsilon$.*

Proof. Given (g, X_3, T) from Assumption 1, $\mathcal{B}$ can simulate Game_{res} or Game_0 with $\mathcal{A}$. $\mathcal{B}$ uses the bilinear group context from the assumption for the public system parameters, and chooses random $a, b_1, \ldots, b_H, c, \alpha \in \mathbb{Z}_N$, $h_1 \in \mathbb{G}_{p_1}$. $\mathcal{B}$ sets $g_1 = g, h_1 = g^a, u_1 = g^{b_1}, \ldots, u_H = g^{b_H}, v_1 = g^c, g_3 = X_3$. $\mathcal{B}$ generates the rest of mpk according to Setup and sets $\text{msk} = \alpha$.

For the RKA-extraction oracle queries (ϕ, ID), $\mathcal{B}$ returns $\text{Extract}(\phi(\text{msk}), \text{ID})$. Note that $\mathcal{B}$ can check if $\phi(\alpha) = \alpha$ using the knowledge of α.

In the challenge phase, $\mathcal{A}$ sends $\mathcal{B}$ two messages M_0^*, M_1^*, and an identity $\text{ID}^* = (\text{id}_1^*, \ldots, \text{id}_{j^*}^*)$. $\mathcal{B}$ picks a random bit b' and derives the challenge ciphertext:

$$C_0^* = M_{b'}^* \cdot \hat{e}(T, g_1)^{\alpha}, \quad C_1^* = T, \quad C_2^* = T^{a + \sum_{i=1}^{j^*} b_i \text{id}_i^* + c\alpha}.$$

If $T = g^s$, this is a normal ciphertext, and hence $\mathcal{B}$ simulates Game_{res}. If $T = g^s Y_2$, this is an SF ciphertext with $\hat{g}_2 = Y_2, \hat{g}_2^{\delta} = Y_2^{a + \sum_{i=1}^{j^*} b_i \text{id}_i^* + c\alpha}$; and hence $\mathcal{B}$ simulates Game_0 with $\delta = a + \sum_{i=1}^{j^*} b_i \text{id}_i^* + c\alpha$. By the Chinese remainder theorem, the values of $a, b_1, \ldots, b_j, c, \alpha \mod p_2$ are not correlated with the corresponding values modulo p_1. Therefore, if $\mathcal{A}$ can distinguish between Game_{res} and Game_0, $\mathcal{B}$ can break Assumption 1 with the same probability. ☐

Lemma 7. *We can construct an algorithm $\mathcal{B}$ with advantage ϵ in breaking Assumption 2 if there exists $\mathcal{A}$ such that $Adv_{\mathcal{A}}(\text{Game}_{\ell-1}) - Adv_{\mathcal{A}}(\text{Game}_{\ell}) = \epsilon$.*

Proof. Given $(g, X_1 X_2, X_3, Y_2 Y_3, T)$ from Assumption 2, $\mathcal{B}$ can simulate $\text{Game}_{\ell-1}$ or Game_{ℓ} with $\mathcal{A}$. $\mathcal{B}$ chooses random $a, b_1, \ldots, b_H, c, \alpha \in \mathbb{Z}_N$. Like in the proof of the last lemma, $\mathcal{B}$ sets $g_1 = g, h_1 = g^a, u_1 = g^{b_1}, \ldots, u_H =$

$g^{b_H}, v_1 = g^c$, and $g_3 = X_3$. $\mathcal{B}$ generates the rest of mpk according to Setup and sets msk $= \alpha$.

For the k-th distinct RKA-extraction oracle query on $\mathsf{ID}_k = (\mathsf{id}_1, \ldots, \mathsf{id}_j)$ and ϕ_k, $\mathcal{B}$ can check if $\phi_k(\alpha) = \alpha$ by the knowledge of α.

- If $k < \ell$, $\mathcal{B}$ returns $\mathsf{Extract}(\phi_k(\mathsf{msk}), \mathsf{ID}_k)$.
- If $k > \ell$, $\mathcal{B}$ derives $(K_1, K_2, D_{j+1}, \ldots, D_H) \leftarrow \mathsf{Extract}(\phi_k(\mathsf{msk}), \mathsf{ID}_k)$ by msk. $\mathcal{B}$ randomly picks $\gamma_1, \gamma_2, \gamma'_{j+1}, \ldots, \gamma'_H \in \mathbb{Z}_N$ and returns the (related) SF key:

$$K'_1 = K_1 \cdot (Y_2 Y_3)^{\gamma_1}, \quad K'_2 = K_2 \cdot (Y_2 Y_3)^{\gamma_2}, \quad \{D'_i = D_i \cdot (Y_2 Y_3)^{\gamma'_i}\}_{\forall i \in \{j+1,\ldots,H\}}.$$

This is semi-functional. By the Chinese remainder theorem, the values of $\gamma_1, \gamma_2, \gamma'_{j+1}, \ldots, \gamma'_H$ modulo p_2 and modulo p_3 are not correlated.
- If $k = \ell$, $\mathcal{B}$ chooses random $X'_3, X''_3, X_{3,j+1}, \ldots, X_{3,H} \in \mathbb{G}_{p_3}$ and returns the (related) key:

$$K_1 = g_1^{\phi_\ell(\alpha)} T^{a + \sum_{i=1}^{j} b_i \mathsf{id}_i + c\phi_\ell(\alpha)} X'_3, \; K_2 = T X''_3, \{D_i = T^{b_i} X_{3,i}\}_{\forall i \in \{j+1,\ldots,H\}}.$$

If $T = Z_1 Z_3 \in \mathbb{G}_{p_1 p_3}$ where $Z_i \in \mathbb{G}_{p_i}$; it is a normal key with $g^r = Z_1$. Hence $\mathcal{B}$ simulates $\mathsf{Game}_{\ell-1}$. If $T = Z_1 Z_2 Z_3 \in \mathbb{G}$, it is an SF key with $\bar{g}_2 = Z_2$, $\bar{g}_2^\gamma = Z_2^{a + \sum_{i=1}^{j} b_i \mathsf{id}_i + \phi_\ell(\alpha)}$, $\bar{g}_2^{\gamma'_{j+1}} = Z_2^{b_{j+1}}, \ldots, \bar{g}_2^{\gamma'_H} = Z_2^{b_H}$. Hence $\mathcal{B}$ simulates Game_ℓ. Again, note that the values of $\gamma, \gamma'_{j+1}, \ldots, \gamma'_H \bmod p_2$ are not correlated with the values of $a, b_1, \ldots, b_H, c$ and α modulo p_1.

For the k-th distinct RKA-delegation query on $\mathsf{ID}_k = (\mathsf{id}_1, \ldots, \mathsf{id}_{j-1}, \mathsf{id}_j)$ and $\phi_k = (\varphi_1, \varphi_2, \varphi'_j, \ldots, \varphi'_H)$:

- if $k < \ell$, $\mathcal{B}$ calculates $(K_1, K_2, D_j, \ldots, D_H) \leftarrow \mathsf{Extract}(\mathsf{msk}, (\mathsf{id}_1, \ldots, \mathsf{id}_{j-1}))$. $\mathcal{B}$ returns $\mathsf{Delegate}(\mathsf{mpk}, (\varphi_1(K_1), \varphi_2(K_2), \varphi'_j(D_j), \ldots, \varphi'_H(D_H)), \mathsf{id}_j)$.
- if $k > \ell$, $\mathcal{B}$ calculates $\mathsf{sk}'_{\mathsf{ID}_k}$ as above. Denote $\mathsf{sk}'_{\mathsf{ID}_k} = (\tilde{K}_1, \tilde{K}_2, \tilde{D}_{j+1}, \ldots, \tilde{D}_H)$. $\mathcal{B}$ randomly picks $\gamma_1, \gamma_2, \gamma'_{j+1}, \ldots, \gamma'_H \in \mathbb{Z}_N$ and returns the (related) SF key:

$$K'_1 = \tilde{K}_1 \cdot (Y_2 Y_3)^{\gamma_1}, \quad K'_2 = \tilde{K}_2 \cdot (Y_2 Y_3)^{\gamma_2}, \quad \{D'_i = \tilde{D}_i \cdot (Y_2 Y_3)^{\gamma'_i}\}_{\forall i \in \{j+1,\ldots,H\}}.$$

- if $k = \ell$, $\mathcal{B}$ picks $X'_3, X''_3, X_{3,j}, \ldots, X_{3,H} \in \mathbb{G}_{p_3}$ and returns the (related) key:

$$K_1 = g_1^{\alpha} \cdot T^{a + \sum_{i=1}^{j-1} b_i \mathsf{id}_i + c\alpha} \cdot X'_3, \; K_2 = T \cdot X''_3, \; \{D_i = T^{b_i} \cdot X_{3,i}\}_{\forall i \in \{j,\ldots,H\}}.$$

$\mathcal{B}$ returns $\mathsf{Delegate}(\mathsf{mpk}, (\varphi_1(K_1), \varphi_2(K_2), \varphi'_j(D_j), \ldots, \varphi'_H(D_H)), \mathsf{id}_j)$. If $T = Z_1 Z_3 \in \mathbb{G}_{p_1 p_3}$ where $Z_i \in \mathbb{G}_{p_i}$; it is a normal key with $g^r = Z_1$. Hence $\mathcal{B}$ simulates $\mathsf{Game}_{\ell-1}$. If $T = Z_1 Z_2 Z_3 \in \mathbb{G}$, it is a related SF key with $\bar{g}_2 = \varphi_2(Z_2)$ due to the isomorphic property of φ_2, $\bar{g}_2^\gamma = \varphi_1(Z_2^{a + \sum_{i=1}^{j-1} b_i \mathsf{id}_i + c \cdot \alpha})$. $\varphi'_j(Z_2^{\mathsf{id}_j b_j})$, $\bar{g}_2^{\gamma'_{j+1}} = \varphi'_{j+1}(Z_2^{b_{j+1}})$, and $\bar{g}_2^{\gamma'_H} = \varphi'_H(Z_2^{b_H})$. Hence $\mathcal{B}$ simulates Game_ℓ. Again, note that the values of $\gamma, \gamma'_{j+1}, \ldots, \gamma'_H \bmod p_2$ are not correlated with the values of $a, b_1, \ldots, b_H, c$, and α modulo p_1.

$\mathcal{A}$ sends $\mathcal{B}$ two messages M_0^*, M_1^* and an identity $\mathsf{ID}^* = (\mathsf{id}_1^*, \ldots, \mathsf{id}_{j*}^*)$ in the challenge phase. $\mathcal{B}$ picks a random bit b' and derives the challenge ciphertext:

$$C_0^* = M_{b'}^* \cdot \hat{e}(X_1 X_2, g_1)^\alpha, \quad C_1^* = (X_1 X_2), \quad C_2^* = (X_1 X_2)^{a + \sum_{i=1}^{j^*} b_i \mathsf{id}_i^* + c \cdot \alpha}.$$

It is an SF ciphertext with $\hat{g}_2 = X_2$ and $\hat{g}_2^\delta = X_2^{a + \sum_{i=1}^{j^*} b_i \mathsf{id}_i^* + c \cdot \alpha}$. Recall that the γ factor for the ℓ-th SF key will be equal to δ for the same identity vector and when $\phi_\ell(\alpha)$ is an identity function (*i.e.*, a key that can decrypt the challenge ciphertext), so it is a nominally semi-functional key that will always decrypt the challenge ciphertext. If the ℓ-th oracle query is for the extraction oracle, the value of $\delta = a + \sum_{i=1}^{j} b_i \mathsf{id}_i^* + c \cdot \alpha \bmod p_2$ is uncorrelated to $\gamma = a + \sum_{i=1}^{j} b_i \mathsf{id}_i + c \cdot \phi_\ell(\alpha)$ since $a, b_1, \ldots, b_H, c, \alpha$ are only known in modulo p_1 and:

- Case 1: ID_ℓ is not a prefix of ID^*. There exists some $i \in [1, j^*]$ such that $\mathsf{id}_i^* \neq \mathsf{id}_i$. Then $a + b_i \cdot \mathsf{id}_i$ is uncorrelated[9] to $a + b_i \cdot \mathsf{id}_i^*$ modulo p_2. It implies γ is uncorrelated to δ since a and b_i are randomly chosen from $\mathbb{Z}_N$.
- Case 2: ID_ℓ is a prefix of ID^* and $\phi_\ell(\alpha) \neq \alpha$. Then $a + c \cdot \phi_\ell(\alpha)$ is uncorrelated[10], and γ is uncorrelated to δ since a, c are random elements of $\mathbb{Z}_N$.

By the definition of the security model, the adversary cannot ask for any extraction oracle query with $\mathsf{ID}^* = \mathsf{ID}_\ell$ and $\phi_\ell(\alpha) = \alpha$.

If the ℓ-th oracle query is for delegation, since $\varphi_1 = \varphi_j'$, and φ_1 is isomorphic,

$$\bar{g}_2^\gamma = \varphi_1(Z_2^{a + \sum_{i=1}^{j-1} b_i \mathsf{id}_i + c\alpha}) \cdot \varphi_j'(Z_2^{\mathsf{id}_j b_j}) = \varphi_1(Z_2^{a + \sum_{i=1}^{j} b_i \mathsf{id}_i + c\alpha}),$$

- Case 1: If ID_ℓ is not a prefix of ID^*, it is also uncorrelated to the value of $\hat{g}_2^\delta = X_2^{a + \sum_{i=1}^{j^*} b_i \mathsf{id}_i^* + c \cdot \alpha}$, due to a distribution analysis similar to the case of the extraction oracle.
- Case 2: If ID_ℓ is a prefix of ID^*, we have $\bar{g}_2 = \varphi_2(Z_2)$. Hence

$$\gamma = (a + \sum_{i=1}^{j} b_i \mathsf{id}_i + c\alpha) \cdot \log_{\varphi_2(Z_2)} \varphi_1(Z_2).$$

γ is correctly distributed as $\log_{\varphi_2(Z_2)} \varphi_1(Z_2)$ is randomly distributed in $\mathbb{Z}_N$.

So, $\mathcal{B}$ can break Assumption 2 if $\mathcal{A}$ can distinguish $\mathrm{Game}_{\ell-1}$ and Game_ℓ. $\square$

Lemma 8. *Given an adversary $\mathcal{A}$ such that $Adv_\mathcal{A}(\mathrm{Game}_q) - Adv_\mathcal{A}(\mathrm{Game}_{final}) = \epsilon$, we can construct an algorithm $\mathcal{B}$ with advantage ϵ in breaking the Φ_e-oracle DBDH assumption.*

---

[9] The case that $\mathsf{id}_i^* \neq \mathsf{id}_i$ and $\mathsf{id}_i^* = \mathsf{id}_i \bmod p_2$ is eliminated by Game_{res}.

[10] The case that $\phi_\ell(\alpha) \neq \alpha$ and $\phi_\ell(\alpha) = \alpha \bmod p_2$ can be eliminated by an extra game similar to Game_{res} considering $a + c \cdot \alpha$ modulo p_2. We omit the repetitive details.

Proof. Given $(g, g^\alpha X_2, X_3, g^s Y_2, Z_2, v, v^\alpha, v^{\alpha s}, T)$ and accesses to an oracle $\mathcal{O}$ from the Φ_e-oracle DBDH assumption, $\mathcal{B}$ chooses random $a, b \in \mathbb{Z}_N$ and sets

$$g_1 = g, \quad h_1 = g^a, \quad u_1 = g^b, \quad v_1 = v, \quad \hat{e}(g_1, g_1)^\alpha = \hat{e}(g, g^\alpha X_2).$$

$\mathcal{B}$ implicitly sets $\mathsf{msk} = \alpha$. $\mathcal{B}$ sends the master public key mpk to $\mathcal{A}$.

To compute the semi-functional secret key, $\mathcal{B}$ randomly picks $r \in \mathbb{Z}_N$ and $R_2, R_3, R_2', R_3', R_{2,j+1}, R_{3,j+1}, \dots, R_{2,H} R_{3,H} \in \mathbb{G}_{p_3}$, then returns:

$$K_1 = (g^\alpha X_2) \cdot (h_1 u_1^{\mathsf{id}_1} \cdots u_j^{\mathsf{id}_j} v_1^\alpha)^r \cdot R_2 R_3, \quad K_2 = g^r \cdot R_2' R_3',$$

$$D_{j+1} = u_{j+1}^r \cdot R_{2,j+1} R_{3,j+1}, \quad \dots, \quad D_H = u_H^r \cdot R_{2,H} R_{3,H}.$$

If it is an RKA-delegation oracle query with input $\phi_d = (\varphi_1, \varphi_2, \varphi_j', \dots, \varphi_H')$, $\mathcal{B}$ returns $\mathsf{sk}_{\mathsf{ID}_k}' \leftarrow \mathsf{Delegate}(\mathsf{mpk}, (\varphi_1(K_1), \varphi_2(K_2), \varphi_j'(D_j), \dots, \varphi_H'(D_H)), \mathsf{id}_j)$.

If it is a related key query with input ϕ_e, then $\mathcal{B}$ asks $\mathcal{O}(\phi_e)$ and obtains $(g^{\phi_e(\alpha)} W_2, v_1^{\phi_e(\alpha)} V_2)$. $\mathcal{B}$ returns

$$K_1 = (g^{\phi_e(\alpha)} W_2) \cdot (h_1 u_1^{\mathsf{ID}} \cdot v_1^{\phi_e(\alpha)} V_2)^r \cdot R_2 \cdot R_3, \quad K_2 = g^r \cdot R_2' \cdot R_3'.$$

Therefore, $\mathcal{B}$ can answer all extraction oracle queries. Note that $\mathcal{B}$ can check if $\phi_e(\alpha) = \alpha$ by checking if $g^{\phi_e(\alpha)} W_2 / (g^\alpha X_2)$ is in the subgroup $\mathbb{G}_{p_2}$ but not $\mathbb{G}_{p_1}$ and $\mathbb{G}_{p_3}$. This is easily doable with the help of $g \in \mathbb{G}_{p_1}$ and $X_3 \in \mathbb{G}_{p_3}$.

Finally, $\mathcal{B}$ picks a random bit b' and computes the SF challenge ciphertext:

$$C_0' = M_{b'}^* \cdot T, \quad C_1' = (g^s Y_2), \quad C_2' = (g^s Y_2)^{a + b \cdot \mathsf{ID}^*} \cdot v_1^{\alpha s}$$

If $T = \hat{e}(g, g)^{as}$, $\mathcal{B}$ simulates Game$_q$. Otherwise, $\mathcal{B}$ simulates Game$_{final}$. If $\mathcal{A}$ can distinguish, $\mathcal{B}$ can break the Φ_e-oracle DBDH assumption. □

References

1. Abdalla, M., Benhamouda, F., Passelègue, A.: Algebraic XOR-RKA-secure pseudorandom functions from post-zeroizing multilinear maps. In: Galbraith, S.D., Moriai, S. (eds.) ASIACRYPT 2019. LNCS, vol. 11922, pp. 386–412. Springer, Cham (2019). https://doi.org/10.1007/978-3-030-34621-8_14
2. Bellare, M., Cash, D., Miller, R.: Cryptography secure against related-key attacks and tampering. In: Lee, D.H., Wang, X. (eds.) ASIACRYPT 2011. LNCS, vol. 7073, pp. 486–503. Springer, Heidelberg (2011). https://doi.org/10.1007/978-3-642-25385-0_26
3. Bellare, M., Paterson, K.G., Thomson, S.: RKA security beyond the linear barrier: IBE, encryption and signatures. In: Wang, X., Sako, K. (eds.) ASIACRYPT 2012. LNCS, vol. 7658, pp. 331–348. Springer, Heidelberg (2012). https://doi.org/10.1007/978-3-642-34961-4_21
4. Biham, E.: New types of cryptanalytic attacks using related keys. J. Cryptol. **7**(4), 229–246 (1994)
5. Biryukov, A., Khovratovich, D., Nikolić, I.: Distinguisher and related-key attack on the full AES-256. In: Halevi, S. (ed.) CRYPTO 2009. LNCS, vol. 5677, pp. 231–249. Springer, Heidelberg (2009). https://doi.org/10.1007/978-3-642-03356-8_14

6. Boneh, D., Boyen, X.: Efficient selective-ID secure identity-based encryption without random oracles. In: Cachin, C., Camenisch, J.L. (eds.) EUROCRYPT 2004. LNCS, vol. 3027, pp. 223–238. Springer, Heidelberg (2004). https://doi.org/10.1007/978-3-540-24676-3_14
7. Boneh, D., Boyen, X., Goh, E.-J.: Hierarchical identity based encryption with constant size ciphertext. In: Cramer, R. (ed.) EUROCRYPT 2005. LNCS, vol. 3494, pp. 440–456. Springer, Heidelberg (2005). https://doi.org/10.1007/11426639_26
8. Boneh, D., Canetti, R., Halevi, S., Katz, J.: Chosen-ciphertext security from identity-based encryption. SIAM J. Comput. 36(5), 1301–1328 (2007)
9. Boyen, X.: General ad hoc encryption from exponent inversion IBE. In: Naor, M. (ed.) EUROCRYPT 2007. LNCS, vol. 4515, pp. 394–411. Springer, Heidelberg (2007). https://doi.org/10.1007/978-3-540-72540-4_23
10. Boyen, X.: The uber-assumption family. In: Galbraith, S.D., Paterson, K.G. (eds.) Pairing 2008. LNCS, vol. 5209, pp. 39–56. Springer, Heidelberg (2008). https://doi.org/10.1007/978-3-540-85538-5_3
11. Chen, Y., Qin, B., Zhang, J., Deng, Y., Chow, S.S.M.: Non-malleable functions and their applications. J. Cryptol. 35(11), 1–41 (2022)
12. Chow, S.S.M.: Removing escrow from identity-based encryption. In: Jarecki, S., Tsudik, G. (eds.) PKC 2009. LNCS, vol. 5443, pp. 256–276. Springer, Heidelberg (2009). https://doi.org/10.1007/978-3-642-00468-1_15
13. Chow, S.S.M., Franklin, M., Zhang, H.: Practical dual-receiver encryption. In: Benaloh, J. (ed.) CT-RSA 2014. LNCS, vol. 8366, pp. 85–105. Springer, Cham (2014). https://doi.org/10.1007/978-3-319-04852-9_5
14. Chow, S.S.M., Russell, A., Tang, Q., Yung, M., Zhao, Y., Zhou, H.-S.: Let a non-barking watchdog bite: cliptographic signatures with an offline watchdog. In: Lin, D., Sako, K. (eds.) PKC 2019. LNCS, vol. 11442, pp. 221–251. Springer, Cham (2019). https://doi.org/10.1007/978-3-030-17253-4_8
15. Dauterman, E., Corrigan-Gibbs, H., Mazières, D., Boneh, D., Rizzo, D.: True2F: backdoor-resistant authentication tokens. In: IEEE Symposium on Security and Privacy (S&P), pp. 398–416. IEEE (2019)
16. Dodis, Y., Goldwasser, S., Tauman Kalai, Y., Peikert, C., Vaikuntanathan, V.: Public-key encryption schemes with auxiliary inputs. In: Micciancio, D. (ed.) TCC 2010. LNCS, vol. 5978, pp. 361–381. Springer, Heidelberg (2010). https://doi.org/10.1007/978-3-642-11799-2_22
17. Emura, K., Katsumata, S., Watanabe, Y.: Identity-based encryption with security against the KGC: a formal model and its instantiation from lattices. In: Sako, K., Schneider, S., Ryan, P.Y.A. (eds.) ESORICS 2019. LNCS, vol. 11736, pp. 113–133. Springer, Cham (2019). https://doi.org/10.1007/978-3-030-29962-0_6
18. Fujisaki, E., Xagawa, K.: Efficient RKA-secure KEM and IBE schemes against invertible functions. In: Lauter, K., Rodríguez-Henríquez, F. (eds.) LATINCRYPT 2015. LNCS, vol. 9230, pp. 3–20. Springer, Cham (2015). https://doi.org/10.1007/978-3-319-22174-8_1
19. Fujisaki, E., Xagawa, K.: Note on the RKA security of continuously non-malleable key-derivation function from PKC 2015. Crypto. ePrint 2015/1088 (2015)
20. Goyal, V., O'Neill, A., Rao, V.: Correlated-input secure hash functions. In: Ishai, Y. (ed.) TCC 2011. LNCS, vol. 6597, pp. 182–200. Springer, Heidelberg (2011). https://doi.org/10.1007/978-3-642-19571-6_12
21. Hofheinz, D., Jia, D., Pan, J.: Identity-based encryption tightly secure under chosen-ciphertext attacks. In: Peyrin, T., Galbraith, S. (eds.) ASIACRYPT 2018. LNCS, vol. 11273, pp. 190–220. Springer, Cham (2018). https://doi.org/10.1007/978-3-030-03329-3_7

22. Katz, J., Sahai, A., Waters, B.: Predicate encryption supporting disjunctions, polynomial equations, and inner products. In: Smart, N. (ed.) EUROCRYPT 2008. LNCS, vol. 4965, pp. 146–162. Springer, Heidelberg (2008). https://doi.org/10.1007/978-3-540-78967-3_9

23. Lewko, A., Rouselakis, Y., Waters, B.: Achieving leakage resilience through dual system encryption. In: Ishai, Y. (ed.) TCC 2011. LNCS, vol. 6597, pp. 70–88. Springer, Heidelberg (2011). https://doi.org/10.1007/978-3-642-19571-6_6

24. Lewko, A., Waters, B.: New techniques for dual system encryption and fully secure HIBE with short ciphertexts. In: Micciancio, D. (ed.) TCC 2010. LNCS, vol. 5978, pp. 455–479. Springer, Heidelberg (2010). https://doi.org/10.1007/978-3-642-11799-2_27

25. Maurer, U.: Abstract models of computation in cryptography. In: Smart, N.P. (ed.) Cryptography and Coding 2005. LNCS, vol. 3796, pp. 1–12. Springer, Heidelberg (2005). https://doi.org/10.1007/11586821_1

26. Qin, B., Liu, S., Yuen, T.H., Deng, R.H., Chen, K.: Continuous non-malleable key derivation and its application to related-key security. In: Katz, J. (ed.) PKC 2015. LNCS, vol. 9020, pp. 557–578. Springer, Heidelberg (2015). https://doi.org/10.1007/978-3-662-46447-2_25

27. Schwartz, J.T.: Fast probabilistic algorithms for verification of polynomial identities. J. ACM 27(4), 701–717 (1980)

28. Shoup, V.: Lower bounds for discrete logarithms and related problems. In: Fumy, W. (ed.) EUROCRYPT 1997. LNCS, vol. 1233, pp. 256–266. Springer, Heidelberg (1997). https://doi.org/10.1007/3-540-69053-0_18

29. Waters, B.: Efficient identity-based encryption without random oracles. In: Cramer, R. (ed.) EUROCRYPT 2005. LNCS, vol. 3494, pp. 114–127. Springer, Heidelberg (2005). https://doi.org/10.1007/11426639_7

30. Waters, B.: Dual system encryption: realizing fully secure IBE and HIBE under simple assumptions. In: Halevi, S. (ed.) CRYPTO 2009. LNCS, vol. 5677, pp. 619–636. Springer, Heidelberg (2009). https://doi.org/10.1007/978-3-642-03356-8_36

31. Yuen, T.H., Chow, S.S.M., Zhang, Y., Yiu, S.M.: Identity-based encryption resilient to continual auxiliary leakage. In: Pointcheval, D., Johansson, T. (eds.) EUROCRYPT 2012. LNCS, vol. 7237, pp. 117–134. Springer, Heidelberg (2012). https://doi.org/10.1007/978-3-642-29011-4_9

32. Yuen, T.H., Zhang, C., Chow, S.S.M., Yiu, S.: Related randomness attacks for public key cryptosystems. In: Bao, F., Miller, S., Zhou, J., Ahn, G. (eds.) ACM AsiaCCS, pp. 215–223. ACM (2015)

Progressive and Efficient Verification for Digital Signatures

Cecilia Boschini[1,2], Dario Fiore[3], and Elena Pagnin[4(✉)]

[1] Technion, Haifa, Israel
cecilia.bo@cs.technion.ac.il
[2] Reichman University, Herzliya, Israel
[3] IMDEA Software Institute, Madrid, Spain
dario.fiore@imdea.org
[4] Lund University, Lund, Sweden
elena.pagnin@eit.lth.se

Abstract. Digital signatures are widely deployed to authenticate the source of incoming information, or to certify data integrity. Common signature verification procedures return a decision (accept/reject) only at the very end of the execution. If interrupted prematurely, however, the verification process cannot infer any meaningful information about the validity of the given signature. We notice that this limitation is due to the algorithm design solely, and it is not inherent to signature verification.

In this work, we provide a formal framework to handle interruptions during signature verification. In addition, we propose a generic way to devise alternative verification procedures that progressively build confidence on the final decision. Our transformation builds on a simple but powerful intuition and applies to a wide range of existing schemes considered to be post-quantum secure including the NIST finalist Rainbow.

While the primary motivation of progressive verification is to mitigate unexpected interruptions, we show that verifiers can leverage it in two innovative ways. First, progressive verification can be used to intentionally adjust the soundness of the verification process. Second, progressive verifications output by our transformation can be split into a computationally intensive offline set-up (run once) and an efficient online verification that is progressive.

Keywords: Digital Signatures · Amortized Efficiency · Flexible Verification · Progressive Verification · Post-Quantum Security

1 Introduction

Digital signatures allow one party (the signer) to use her secret key to authenticate a message in such a way that, at any later point in time, anyone holding the corresponding public key (the verifiers) can check its validity. The typical nature of signature verification procedures is monolithic: the validity of a signature is

© Springer Nature Switzerland AG 2022
G. Ateniese and D. Venturi (Eds.): ACNS 2022, LNCS 13269, pp. 440–458, 2022.
https://doi.org/10.1007/978-3-031-09234-3_22

determined only *after* a sequence of tests is completed. In particular, if the execution is interrupted *in media res* (Latin for "in the midst of things"), no conclusive answer can be drawn from the outcomes of the partial tests. Although this monolithic nature is not a burden in many application scenarios, e.g., validating financial transactions (Bitcoin protocol), installing certified software updates (Android OS), or delivering e-services (e-Health, electronic tax systems), it is a major limitation to the adoption of digital signatures in cyber-physical systems [24] and in secure eager or speculative executions [19], where the speed at which verification is performed plays a crucial role.

Le et al. [18] proposed to address unexpected interruptions using a new cryptographic primitive called *signatures with flexible verification*. In a nutshell, such schemes admit a verification algorithm that increasingly builds confidence on the validity of the signature while it performs more steps. In this way, at the moment of an interrupt, the verifier is left with a value $\alpha \in [0,1] \cup \bot$ that probabilistically quantifies the validity of the signature, or rejects it. While the primary motivation of flexible verifications is to mitigate unexpected interruptions; we observe that the overarching idea of *progressive verification* has further impacts. In particular, progressive verification can be used to customize the soundness of the verification process. For example, a smart device may decide to verify at a 30-bit security level, if the signatures come from specific sources or the battery is below 30%. From the theoretical perspective, progressive verification (as introduced in this work later on) draws interesting connections between classical, information-theoretic and post-quantum security notions.

1.1 Our Contribution

This work sets out to dismantle the monolithic nature of signature verification by designing *new* verification methods for *existing* signature schemes. Concretely, we investigate two approaches. The first one is to speed-up the verification process for polynomially many signatures by the same signer leveraging a one-time computation on the public key (efficient verification). The second approach is to re-design the verification process so that it allows one to extract sensible information even when the algorithm is executed only partially (progressive verification). In this setting it is of particular interest to investigate the security implications of this new model and what additional features it may bring.

In detail, we introduce formal definitions and security models for both efficient (Sect. 2) and progressive (Sect. 3) verification. In terms of realizations, we focus on a specific family of schemes that we call with **Mv**-style verification (in brief, the verification includes matrix-vector multiplications). For schemes in this class, we propose two compilers, i.e., two information-theoretic transformations that turn monolithic **Mv**-style verifications into provably-secure efficient (Sect. 4.1), or progressive (Sect. 4.2) ones. Our compilers apply to multi-variate polynomials based schemes including the NIST finalist Rainbow [10,11] and LUOV [4]; and lattice-based schemes including GPV [15] (hash & sign), MP [20] (Boyen/BonsaiTree), and GVW [16] (homomorphic). A large part of the security proof is devoted to a detailed analysis of the leakage due to verification queries (that now involve secret randomness). We consider this leakage analysis a result of independent interest as it can be used to estimate leakage in similar information-theoretic approaches to provably secure algorithmic speed-ups or eager executions. Our models for efficient and progressive verification can easily be extended to include signatures with advanced properties including: ring, threshold, homomorphic multi-key, attribute-based and constrained.

1.2   Related Work

The problem of trading security for less computation during a verification has been considered first by Fischlin [13] and Armknecht et al. [1] in the context of message authentication codes (MACs). Le et al. [18] and by Taleb and Vergnaud [23] consider the same question for digital signatures.

Le et al. [18] introduce the notion of flexible signatures and a construction based on the Lamport-Diffie one-time signature [17] with Merkle trees. Taleb and Vergnaud [23] put forth realizations of progressive verification for three specific signature schemes (RSA, ECDSA and GPV). Differently from us, both works demand a modification of the signing or key generation algorithm of the original signature scheme and also a time variable be input to the progressive or flexible verification.

One main difference between our model and those of [13,18,23] is that we aim to capture progressive verification as an independent feature that can enhance existing schemes, rather than a standalone primitive that requires one to change some of the core algorithms of a signature scheme. This is in a way more challenging as it leaves less design freedom when crafting these algorithms. In addition, we define progressive verification as a *stateful* algorithm in contrast to stateless [13,18,23]: although this makes our model slightly more involved, it is comparably more general and can capture more (existing) schemes.

Our model for efficient verification is close the offline-online paradigm used in homomorphic authentication [2,9] and verifiable computation [14]; where a preprocessing is done with respect to a function f, and its result can be used to verify computation results involving the same f. An early instantiation of this technique for speeding up the verification of Rabin-Williams signatures appears in [3]. More recently, Sipasseuth et al. [22] investigate how to speed up lattice-based signature verification while reducing the memory (storage) requirements. The overall idea in [22] is similar to ours (and inspired to Freivalds' Algorithm): to replace the inefficient matrix multiplication in the verification with a probabilistic check via an inner product computation. However, [22] focuses on the DRS signature [21], and investigates the trade-off between pre-computation time for verification and memory storage for this scheme only. Moreover, the work lacks a formal, abstract analysis of the security impact of such a shift in the verification procedure. In contrast, we devise a general framework to model 'more efficient' and 'partial' signature verification. Albeit we developed our approach independently of [22], our techniques can be seen as a generalization of what presented in [22].

Notation. In what follows, λ denotes the parameter for computational security and $\Sigma = (\mathsf{KeyGen}, \mathsf{Sign}, \mathsf{Ver})$ a tuple of algorithms identifying a digital signature scheme that satisfies the syntax and the properties of correctness and existential unforgeability as defined in [23].

2 Efficient Verification for Digital Signatures

The core idea of efficient signature verification is to split the verification process into two steps. The first step is a one-time and signature-independent setup called 'offline verification'. Its purpose is to produce randomness to derive a (short, secret) verification key svk from the signer's public key pk. Note that the offline verification does not change the signature, which remains publicly verifiable; instead it 'randomizes' pk to obtain a concise verification key svk that essentially enables one to verify signatures with (almost) the same precision as the standard verification, but in a more efficient way. We remark that for secure efficient verification svk should be hidden to the adversary, yet, the knowledge of svk gives no advantage in forging signatures verified in the standard way using just pk. The second verification step consists of an 'online verification' procedure. It takes as input svk and can verify an unbounded number of message-signature pairs performing significantly less computation than the standard verification algorithm. For security, it is fundamental svk remains unknown to the adversary. We remark that generating svk during the offline phase achieves efficient online verification with no impact on the original signing or key generation algorithms, which was a drawback of previous work [18,23].

2.1 Syntax for Efficient Verification

Our definition of efficient verification lets the verifier set the confidence level k at which she wishes to carry out the signature verification. Notably k determines the amount of computation to be performed and thus plays a central role in the security and the efficiency of the new verification.

Definition 1 (Efficient Verification). *A signature scheme Σ admits efficient verification if there exist two PPT algorithms $(\mathsf{offVer}, \mathsf{onVer})$ with the following syntax:*[1]

$\mathsf{offVer}(\mathsf{pk}, k)$*: this is a randomized algorithm that on input a public verification key pk, and a positive integer $k \in \{1, \dots, \lambda\}$ (where λ is the security parameter of Σ), returns a secret verification key svk.*

$\mathsf{onVer}(\mathsf{svk}, \mu, \boldsymbol{\sigma})$*: on input a secret verification key svk, a message μ, and a signature $\boldsymbol{\sigma}$, the efficient online verification algorithm outputs 0 (reject) or 1 (accept).*

For convenience we will refer to the signature scheme augmented with the efficient verification algorithms as $\Sigma^E = (\Sigma, \mathsf{offVer}, \mathsf{onVer})$, and to the integer value k as confidence level.

---

[1] Here pk denotes a public verification key output by KeyGen.

To be meaningful, a realization of efficient verification needs to satisfy the properties of correctness, concrete atomized efficiency and security.

Definition 2 (Correctness of Efficient Verification). *A scheme $\Sigma^E = (\Sigma, \mathsf{offVer}, \mathsf{onVer})$ realizes efficient verification correctly if the following conditions hold. For a given security parameter λ, for any honestly generated key pair $(\mathsf{sk}, \mathsf{pk}) \leftarrow \mathsf{KeyGen}(\lambda)$, for any message μ , for any signature σ such that $\mathsf{Ver}(\mathsf{pk}, \mu, \sigma) = 1$, and for any confidence level $k \in \{1, \dots, \lambda\}$; it holds that $\Pr[\mathsf{onVer}(\mathsf{svk}, \mu, \sigma) = 1 \mid \mathsf{svk} \leftarrow \mathsf{offVer}(\mathsf{pk}, k)] = 1$ for any choice of randomness used in offVer.*

Amortized efficiency relies on the fact that running offVer once and reuse its output to run onVer r times is computationally less demanding than running the standard verification Ver r times. To formalize this, we will use the function $\mathrm{cost}(\cdot)$ that given as input an algorithm returns its computational cost (in some desired computational model). In addition, we parameterize concrete amortized efficiency with two intertwined variables: r_0 (number of instances of verification), and e_0 (ratio between the cost of r_0 efficient verifications over r_0 standard verifications). The lower the value of r_0 the sooner Σ^E amortizes the computational cost of offVer. The lower the value of e_0 the more efficient Σ^E is with respect to the standard verification.

Definition 3 (Concrete Amortized Efficiency). *A scheme Σ^E realizes (r_0, e_0)-concrete amortized efficient verification for Σ if given a security parameter λ and a confidence level k; for any key pair $(\mathsf{sk}, \mathsf{pk}) \leftarrow \mathsf{KeyGen}(\lambda)$, for any pair (μ, σ) with $\mu \in \mathcal{M}$ and σ such that $\mathsf{Ver}(\mathsf{pk}, \mu, \sigma) = 1$; there exist a non-negative integer r_0, and a real constant $0 < e_0 < 1$ such that:*

$$\forall \, r \geq r_0 \, , \qquad \frac{\mathrm{cost}(\mathsf{offVer}(\mathsf{pk}, k)) + r \cdot \mathrm{cost}(\mathsf{onVer}(\mathsf{svk}, \mu, \sigma))}{r \cdot \mathrm{cost}(\mathsf{Ver}(\mathsf{pk}, \mu, \sigma))} < e_0 \qquad (1)$$

2.2   Security Model for Efficient Verification

Intuitively, Σ^E realizes efficient verification in a secure way if onVer accepts a signature that would be rejected by Ver only with negligible probability. In the security game (see Fig. 1), the adversary $\mathcal{A}$ has access to the signing oracle $O\mathsf{Sign}$ as well as the efficient verification oracle $O\mathsf{onVer}$. The goal of the adversary is to produce a signature σ^* for a message μ^* that was never queried to $O\mathsf{Sign}$ and for which Ver returns 0 (reject) and onVer returns 1 (accept).

cmvEUF (λ, Σ, k)	$\mathsf{Exp}_{\mathcal{A},\Sigma}^{\mathsf{cmvEUF}}(\lambda, k)$
1: $\mathsf{L}_S \leftarrow \varnothing$	1: $(\mu^*, \sigma^*) \leftarrow \mathsf{cmvEUF}(\lambda, \Sigma, k)$
2: $(\mathsf{pk}, \mathsf{sk}) \leftarrow \mathsf{KeyGen}(1^\lambda)$	2: if $\mu^* \in \mathsf{L}_S$
3: $\mathsf{svk} \leftarrow \mathsf{offVer}(\mathsf{pk}, k)$	3: return 0
4: $(\mu^*, \sigma^*) \leftarrow \mathcal{A}^{O\mathsf{Sign}, O\mathsf{onVer}}(\mathsf{pk}, k)$	4: if $\mathsf{Ver}(\mathsf{pk}, \mu^*, \sigma^*) = 1$
5: return (μ^*, σ^*)	5: return 0
	6: $b \leftarrow \mathsf{onVer}(\mathsf{svk}, \mu^*, \sigma^*)$
	7: return b
$O\mathsf{Sign}_{\mathsf{sk}}(\mu)$	
1: $\mathsf{L}_S \leftarrow \mathsf{L}_S \cup \{\mu\}$	$O\mathsf{onVer}_{\mathsf{svk}}(\mu, \sigma)$
2: $\sigma \leftarrow \mathsf{Sign}(\mathsf{sk}, \mu)$	1: $b \leftarrow \mathsf{onVer}(\mathsf{svk}, \mu, \sigma)$
3: return σ	2: return b

Fig. 1. Security model for efficient verification of signatures: existential unforgeability under adaptive chosen message and verification attack (security game, experiment and oracles). $\mathcal{A}$ is a PPT algorithm that can query the oracles in an adaptive and parallel way. L_S is the list of messages queried to the signing oracle.

Definition 4 (Security of Efficient Verification). *A scheme Σ^E realizes a secure efficient verification for Σ if for a given security parameter λ and for any confidence level $k \in \{1, \ldots, \lambda\}$, for all PPT adversaries $\mathcal{A}$ the success probability in the* cmvEUF *experiment reported in Fig. 1 is negligible, i.e.:* $Adv_{\mathcal{A},\Sigma}^{\mathsf{cmvEUF}}(\lambda, k) = \Pr\left[\mathsf{Exp}_{\mathcal{A},\Sigma}^{\mathsf{cmvEUF}}(\lambda, k) = 1\right] \le \varepsilon(\lambda, k).$

Line 5 of the cmvEUF experiment excludes forgeries against the original signature scheme. This is justified by the correctness of efficient verification and by the fact that Σ is existentially unforgeable. Notably, both the security game and the advantage depend on the confidence level k and assume all algorithms are entirely executed.

3 Progressive Verification for Digital Signatures

The goal of progressive verification is to incrementally increase the confidence on the validity of a signature, for a given message against a public key. Intuitively, the "confidence" should be proportional to the amount of computation invested: the further in the execution we go, the higher the accuracy of the decision, and thus the confidence of the final outcome (accept/reject).

3.1   Signatures with Progressive Verification

Taleb and Vergnaud give a very intuitive definition of progressive verification for digital signatures [23]. They model digital signatures with progressive verification as a 4-tuple of PPT algorithms (KeyGen, Sign, Ver, ProgVer) such that: $\Sigma = $ (KeyGen, Sign, Ver) is a correct digital signature scheme; and ProgVer takes in input a public verification key pk, a message μ, a signature σ, and some timing parameter t, and outputs $\alpha \in \{[0,1] \cap \mathbb{R}\} \cup \{\perp\}$, interpreted as an estimate on the accuracy of its decision whether the signature be valid. Moreover, the scheme satisfies the following properties:

Correctness If for some tuple of inputs ProgVer(pk, μ, σ, t) outputs $\perp$, then Ver(pk, μ, σ) = 0.

Security If for some tuple of inputs ProgVer(pk, μ, σ, t) outputs $\alpha \in [0,1]$, then $\Pr[\text{Ver}(\text{pk}, \mu, \sigma) = 0] \leq 1 - \alpha$ (where the probability is taken over the random coins of ProgVer).

In a nutshell, if $\alpha = \perp$, the progressive verification deems the signature to be invalid (with 100% accuracy). If $\alpha \in [0,1]$, the algorithm considers the signature valid, and α tells how accurate this statement is. Since progressive verification may be interrupted at any arbitrary point t during its execution, in practice α is (the output of) a function $\alpha_{\text{prog}}(t)$ that "converts" the progress in the verification process into a value representing the accuracy of a positive outcome.

Shortcomings. First, similarly to [18], also [23] sees signatures with progressive verification as a stand alone primitive. In contrast we view progressive verification as a feature that can augment existing schemes without requiring change to the core algorithms. Second, the definition lacks a precise notion of time complexity and does not model how unexpected interrupts are handled. The model we introduce in the remainder of this section takes care of these aspects. In addition, we generalize progressive verification to be (possibly) stateful, which can capture more signature schemes as well as reuse the same syntax to model both efficient and progressive verification (details in the full version [6]).

3.2   Syntax for Progressive Verification

In order to model progressive verification as an add-on algorithm we need to derive from Ver an alternative algorithm ProgVer (as introduced in Sect. 3.1), that builds confidence on the final verification outcome in an increasing way. Without loss of generality, this task boils down to identifying a sequence of $T + 1$ atomic instructions that we call ProgStep with the following properties. Each ProgStep performs a check of some sort on the input it receives. If one step fails, the progressive verification returns $\alpha = \perp$. If none of the initial t steps fails, the progressive verification returns the output of a function $\alpha_{\text{prog}}(t) \in [0,1]$ that measures the probability the input will be accepted by Ver. The fact of increasingly building confidence is reflected by functions α_{prog} that are non-decreasing in t, the number of instructions checked before returning the answer. Figure 1 in [23] provides an intuitive and graphical representation of this statement.

Definition 5 (Stateful Progressive Verification). *Let $T \in \mathbb{Z}_{>0}$ and α_{prog} : $\{0, \ldots, T\} \rightarrow [0, 1]$ be an efficiently computable function. A signature scheme Σ admits $(T, \alpha_{\text{prog}})$-progressive verification if there exists a stateful PPT algorithm* ProgVer *that takes in input* pk, μ, σ *and some interruption parameter* $t \in \mathbb{Z}_{>0}$, *outputs* $\alpha \in \{[0, 1] \cap \mathbb{R}\} \cup \{\bot\}$, *and satisfies the following syntax:*

ProgVer(st, pk, μ, σ, t)	4 :	**for** $j = 0, \ldots, t$
1 : $\quad \alpha \leftarrow \bot$	5 :	$\quad (b, \text{st}) \leftarrow \text{ProgStep}_j(\text{st}, \text{pk}, \mu, \sigma)$
2 : $\quad$ **if** $t < 0$: **return** $\bot$	6 :	$\quad$ **if** $(b = 0)$: **return** $\bot$
3 : $\quad$ **if** $t > T$: **set** $t \leftarrow T$	7 :	$\quad$ **else** $(b = 1)$: $\alpha \leftarrow \alpha_{\text{prog}}(j)$
	8 :	**return** α

For convenience we will refer to the signature scheme augmented with progressive verification as $\Sigma^P = (\Sigma, \text{ProgVer}, T, \alpha_{\text{prog}})$.

Concretely, ProgVer is made of $T + 1$ algorithms ProgStep_j, for $j = 0$ to T, that progressively update the state st. We remark that the formalization into steps is without loss of generality: Ver realizes a trivial progressive verification for $T = 0$ where the only step is Ver itself. Finally, the interruption value t is input to ProgVer only, and it is *not* given to each ProgStep_j. Thus our syntax models the fact that the steps are agnostic of the interruption value and must work without knowing when to stop, which is essential to capture arbitrary interruptions.

Correctness essentially states that signatures accepted by the standard verification should also be accepted by the progressive one, with the highest confidence allowed by the number of steps performed.

Definition 6 (Progressive Verification Correctness). *Let Σ^P be a signature scheme with progressive verification;* ProgVer *satisfies progressive verification correctness if, for any value* $t \in \{0, \ldots, T\}$, *for any given security parameter* λ, *for any key pair* $(\text{sk}, \text{pk}) \leftarrow \text{KeyGen}(\lambda)$, *for any admissible state* st *generated by* ProgVer, *for any admissible message, given a signature* σ *such that* $\text{Ver}(\text{pk}, \mu, \sigma) = 1$ *it holds that:* $\Pr[\text{ProgVer}(\text{st}, \text{pk}, \mu, \sigma, t) = \alpha_{\text{prog}}(t)] = 1$.

Efficient vs. Progressive Verification. At a first glance, efficient verification and progressive verification seem to have the common goal of reducing the computational cost of a signature verification. However the way this objective is achieved in the two models is quite different. In progressive verification, the verifier (and thus each ProgVer_i) is unaware of when the computation will be interrupted, and *its execution is independent of* t. In contrast, in efficient verification the verifier (running offVer) determines the confidence level k prior to any actual verification (running onVer). In the latter, the (online) verification is aware of the confidence level k (seen as interruption value), and *adapts its execution to* k.

Stateful vs Stateless Verification. We define progressive verification as stateful. This allows us to keep the framework as general as possible. Stateless progressive verification, á la [18,23], can be obtained setting st to $\varnothing$, this also removes the need for analyzing any cross-query leakage due to state reuse.

3.3   Security Model for Progressive Verification

Our notion of unforgeability states that signatures rejected by the standard verification should also be rejected by the progressive one, except for an inaccuracy factor due to interruptions. More formally, Ver and ProgVer should have the same behavior (accept/reject) with discrepancies happening with probability negligibly close to $\alpha_{\text{prog}}(t)$.

Our security game has three main differences compared to [18]:

State in order to take into account that ProgVer maintains a possibly nontrivial state we allow the adversary $\mathcal{A}$ to interact with the progressive verification oracle OProgVer during the query phase, as well as the signing oracle OSign, in a concurrent manner.

Interruption queries to OProgVer have the form $(\mu, \boldsymbol{\sigma}, t')$, where t' is the desired interruption value submitted by $\mathcal{A}$ (and chosen adaptively).

Output instead of a single bit, our experiment returns a pair (b, t^*). The bit $b \in \{0, 1\}$ flags the absence or the potential presence of a forgery, while $t^* \in \{0, \ldots, T\}$ reports the interruption position used in the final progressive verification. Including t^* in the output of the experiment allows us to measure security in terms of *how close* the probability of $\mathcal{A}$ wining the experiment is from the expected accuracy value $1 - \alpha_{\text{prog}}(t^*)$.

progEUF(Σ^P, λ)	Exp$^{\text{progEUF}}_{\mathcal{A}, \Sigma^P}(\lambda)$
1 : $\mathsf{L}_S \leftarrow \varnothing$	1 : $(\mu^*, \boldsymbol{\sigma}^*, t') \leftarrow \text{progEUF}(\Sigma, \lambda)$
2 : $\mathsf{st} \leftarrow \varnothing$	2 : $\beta \leftarrow \text{Ver}(\mathsf{pk}, \mu^*, \boldsymbol{\sigma}^*)$
3 : $(\mathsf{pk}, \mathsf{sk}) \leftarrow \text{KeyGen}(1^\lambda)$	3 : $t^* \leftarrow O\text{Int}(t')$
4 : $(\mu^*, \boldsymbol{\sigma}^*, t') \leftarrow \mathcal{A}^{O\text{Sign}, O\text{ProgVer}}(\mathsf{pk}, \lambda)$	4 : $\alpha \leftarrow \text{ProgVer}(\mathsf{st}, \mathsf{pk}, \mu^*, \boldsymbol{\sigma}^*, t^*)$
5 : **return** $(\mu^*, \boldsymbol{\sigma}^*, t')$	5 : **if** $\mu^* \in \mathsf{L}_S \vee \alpha = \bot \vee \beta = 1$
	6 : **return** $(0, t^*)$
	7 : **return** $(1, t^*)$
$O\text{Sign}_{\mathsf{sk}}(\mu)$	$O\text{ProgVer}_{\mathsf{st}, \mathsf{pk}}(\mu, \boldsymbol{\sigma}, t')$
1 : $\mathsf{L}_S \leftarrow \mathsf{L}_S \cup \{\mu\}$	1 : $t \leftarrow O\text{Int}(t')$
2 : $\boldsymbol{\sigma} \leftarrow \text{Sign}(\mathsf{sk}, \mu)$	2 : $\alpha \leftarrow \text{ProgVer}(\mathsf{st}, \mathsf{pk}, \mu, \boldsymbol{\sigma}, t)$
3 : **return** $\boldsymbol{\sigma}$	3 : **return** α

Fig. 2. Security model for progressive verification of signatures: existential unforgeability under adaptive chosen message and progressive verification attack (security game, experiment and oracles). $\mathcal{A}$ can query the oracles adaptively, in parallel and polynomially many times in λ. L_S is the list of messages queried to the signing oracle.

Definition 7 (Security of Progressive Verification (progEUF)). *Let Σ be a signature scheme that admits a progressive verification realization Σ^P. Σ^P realizes a secure progressive verification for Σ if for any given security parameter*

λ, *for all PPT adversaries $\mathcal{A}$ the success probability in the* progEUF *experiment in Fig. 2 is negligible, i.e.,:*

$$Adv^{\mathsf{progEUF}}_{\mathcal{A},\Sigma^P}(\lambda) = \Pr\left[\mathsf{Exp}^{\mathsf{progEUF}}_{\mathcal{A},\Sigma^P}(\lambda) = (1,t^*)\right] - (1 - \alpha_{\mathsf{prog}}(t^*)) = \varepsilon \leq \varepsilon(\lambda).$$

Intuitively, Definition 7 states that an adversary has only negligible probability to make ProgVer output a confidence value α^* higher than the expected one. Let $\mathsf{bad}(t)$ denote the probability of accepting a forgery after t verification steps. Then by setting $\alpha_{\mathsf{prog}}(t) = 1 - \mathsf{bad}(t)$, we get $Adv^{\mathsf{progEUF}}_{\mathcal{A},\Sigma^P}(\lambda) = \Pr\left[\mathsf{Exp}^{\mathsf{progEUF}}_{\mathcal{A},\Sigma^P}(\lambda) = (1,t^*)\right] - \mathsf{bad}(t^*) \leq \varepsilon(\lambda)$.

Modelling Interruptions. In [18], unexpected interruptions are modeled via an interruption oracle iOracle(λ) that returns a value $t \in \{0,\ldots,T\}$ used by the progressive verification. However, it is not clear whether $\mathcal{A}$ may control iOracle or not. We overcome these ambiguities by letting $\mathcal{A}$ output t' with every progressive verification query. For the purpose of this work, we consider the strongest security model in which the interruption oracle returns the adversary's value, i.e., $t \leftarrow O\mathsf{Int}(t')$ with $t = t'$. This resembles side-channel attack settings, where $\mathcal{A}$ may try to freeze the execution of the verification. It is possible to relax and generalize our model by setting a different interruption oracle $O\mathsf{Int}$, programmed at the beginning of the game. At each verification query, $O\mathsf{Int}$ takes as input the adversary's suggestion for an interruption position t' and outputs the value t to be used by the progressive verification. In case $t = t'$, we are modelling side channel attacks, but we can also let t be independent of t'. A realistic definition of $O\mathsf{Int}$ is outside the scope of this work.

4 Constructions

In this section, we present generic transformations (compilers) that augment a signature scheme Σ with either efficient (Sect. 4.1) or progressive verification (Sect. 4.2).

Our technique works for a specific class of signature schemes that we call *with* **Mv**-*style verification*. In such schemes, Ver can be seen as the combination of two types of verification checks: a matrix-vector multiplication (referred to as **Mv** = **0**, for appropriate matrix **M** and vector **v**) and other generic checks (collected in the Check subroutine), see Fig. 3 for details and an explanatory example. Among the schemes with **Mv**-style verification we highlight some of the seminal lattice-based signatures [7,8,15,20], homomorphic signatures [5,12,16], and multivariate signatures [4,11].

4.1 A Compiler for Efficient Mv-Style Verifications

We present a generic way to realize efficient verification for signatures with **Mv**-style verification, whenever the computational complexity of Ver is dominated

Ver(pk, μ, σ)

// INITIALIZE ACCEPTANCE BITS
1 : $b_1 \leftarrow 0, b_2 \leftarrow 0$

// SPLIT pk INTO MARTIX - AUX. DATA
2 :   **parse** pk $= (PK, PK.\text{aux})$

// ADDITIONAL VERIFICATION CHECKS
3 : $b_1 \leftarrow \text{Check}(PK.\text{aux}, \mu, \sigma)$

// FORMATTING Mv-STYLE CHECK
4 : $(\mathbf{M}, \mathbf{v}) \leftarrow \text{GetMv}(\text{pk}, \mu, \sigma)$

// MATRIX-VECTOR MULT. CHECK
5 :   **if** $(\mathbf{M} \cdot \mathbf{v} = \mathbf{0})$
6 : $b_2 \leftarrow 1$
7 :   **return** $(b_1 \wedge b_2)$

Example: Ver(pk, μ, σ) for GPV08 [15]

1 : $b_1 \leftarrow 0, b_2 \leftarrow 0$
2 :   **parse** pk $= (PK, PK.\text{aux})$
        set $PK \leftarrow \mathbf{A}$
        set $PK.\text{aux} \leftarrow (\mathcal{H}, \beta)$
3 : $\text{Check}(PK.\text{aux}, \mu, \sigma)$:
        if $\|\sigma\| < \beta$ **set** $b_1 \leftarrow 1$
4 : $\text{GetMv}(\text{pk}, \mu, \sigma)$:
        set $\mathbf{M} \leftarrow [\mathbf{A}| - \mathbf{I}_{rows(\mathbf{A})}]$
        set $\mathbf{u} \leftarrow \mathcal{H}(\mu) \in \mathbb{Z}_q^{rows(\mathbf{A}) \times 1}$
        set $\mathbf{v} \leftarrow [\sigma^T | \mathbf{u}^T]^T$
5 :   **if** $(\mathbf{M} \cdot \mathbf{v} = \mathbf{0}_{rows(\mathbf{A}) \times 1} \mod q)$
6 :   **set** $b_2 \leftarrow 1$
7 :   **return** $(b_1 \wedge b_2)$

Fig. 3. General structure of a signature with Mv-style verification (on the left); an instructive example: the GPV08 [15] signature verification (on the right).

by the matrix-vector multiplication, i.e., $\text{cost}(\text{Check}) \ll \text{cost}(\text{Mv}) \sim mn$ field multiplications (for $\mathbf{M} \in \mathbb{Z}_q^{n \times m}$).

Our compiler for efficient verification is detailed in Fig. 4 with a sketch of instantiation for the LBS scheme GPV08 [15] as a running example. Further details on this scheme as well as instantiations and details on the concrete efficiency estimates for MP12 [20], Rainbow [11] and LUOV [4], are deferred to the full version [6]. Table 1 summarizes the efficiency results. We obtain secure efficient online verification using as little as 0.4% (resp. 50%) of the computational cost of the standard verification for lattice-based signatures on exponentially large fields (resp. for Rainbow).

Overview of Our Technique. Our transformation takes as input Σ, a signature scheme with Mv-style verification; and it returns $\Sigma^E = (\Sigma, \text{offVer}, \text{onVer})$ that securely instantiates efficient verification for Σ. The heart of our compiler leverages the fact that for any pair of vectors σ and $\mathbf{u}$ (often derived from the message μ), and for any matrix $\mathbf{A}$ (of opportune dimensions) if $\mathbf{A} \cdot \sigma = \mathbf{u}$ then for any random vector $\mathbf{c}$ (of opportune dimension) it holds that $\mathbf{c} \cdot (\mathbf{A} \cdot \sigma) = \mathbf{c} \cdot \mathbf{u}$. Collecting variables on the left hand yields $(\mathbf{c} \cdot [\mathbf{A}| - \mathbf{I}_n]) \cdot \begin{bmatrix} \sigma \\ \mathbf{u} \end{bmatrix} = 0$. Thus one can precompute the vector $\mathbf{z} \leftarrow \mathbf{c} \cdot [\mathbf{A}| - \mathbf{I}_n]$ and run the efficient online verification check $\mathbf{z} \cdot \mathbf{v} \overset{?}{=} 0$, where $\mathbf{v} \leftarrow (\sigma, \mathbf{u})$. In a nutshell the idea is to replace the matrix-vector multiplication with a vector-vector multiplication in a sound way. Correctness and efficiency are immediate. Soundness essentially comes from the

offVer(pk, k)	onVer(svk, $\mu, \boldsymbol{\sigma}$)
1: **parse** pk = $(PK, PK.\text{aux})$	// LIGHTWEIGHT CHECKS
// e.g., in GPV08 $PK = \mathbf{A}$, $PK.\text{aux} = (\mathcal{H}, \beta)$	1: **if** Check$(PK.\text{aux}, \mu, \boldsymbol{\sigma}) = 0$
2: $\mathbf{M} \leftarrow \text{GetM}(PK)$	// e.g., in GPV08 this is $\|\boldsymbol{\sigma}\| < \beta$
// e.g., in GPV08 $\mathbf{M} = (\mathbf{A}\| - \mathbf{1}_{n \times n})$	2: **return** 0
3: **if** $(k > rows(\mathbf{M}) \vee k < 1)$ **return** $\perp$	// FORMATTING FOR EFF. VER.
// GENERATE RANDOMIZED KEY	3: $(\mathbf{Z}', \mathbf{v}) \leftarrow \text{GetZV}(\text{svk}, \mu, \boldsymbol{\sigma})$
4: $\mathbf{Z} \leftarrow \text{GetZ}(\mathbf{M}, k)$	4: **parse** $\mathbf{Z}' = [\mathbf{z}_1'^T | \ldots | \mathbf{z}_k'^T]^T$
i: $\mathbf{z}_0 \leftarrow \mathbf{0}_{1 \times cols(\mathbf{M})}$ // for good indexing	// $\mathbf{z}' \in \mathbb{Z}_q^{k \times cols(\mathbf{Z}')}$
ii: **for** $j = 1, \ldots, k$	5: **parse** $\mathbf{v} = [\mathbf{v}_1^T | \ldots | \mathbf{v}_k^T]^T$
iii: $\mathbf{c} \xleftarrow{\$} \mathbb{Z}_q^{1 \times rows(\mathbf{M})}$	// $\mathbf{v} \in \mathbb{Z}_q^{k \times cols(\mathbf{Z}')}$
iv: $\mathbf{z} \leftarrow \mathbf{cM} \in \mathbb{Z}_q^{1 \times cols(\mathbf{M})}$	// LINE-BY-LINE INNER PRODUCTS
v: **if** $\mathbf{z} \in \langle \mathbf{z}_0, \ldots, \mathbf{z}_{j-1} \rangle_q$ **go to** iii.	6: **for** $j = 1, \ldots, k$
vi: $\mathbf{z}_j \leftarrow \mathbf{z}$ // store new lin.indep. vect.	7: **if** $\mathbf{z}_j' \cdot \mathbf{v}_j \neq 0 \mod q$
vii: **set** $\mathbf{Z} \leftarrow [\mathbf{z}_1^T | \ldots | \mathbf{z}_k^T]^T \in \mathbb{Z}_q^{k \times cols(\mathbf{M})}$	8: **return** 0
5: **return** svk $\leftarrow (k, \mathbf{Z}, PK.\text{aux})$	9: **return** 1

(a) The offline verification algorithm.	(b) The online verification algorithm.

Fig. 4. Our compiler for efficient verification of signatures with $\mathbf{Mv}$-style verification. The four scheme-dependent subroutines are: **parse** pk and GetZ (in offVer); Check and GetZV (in onVer). The computational complexity of onVer is linear in k, the chosen confidence level.

fact that if $\mathbf{z} \cdot \mathbf{v} = 0$, then with all but negligible probability the original system of linear equations $\mathbf{A} \cdot \boldsymbol{\sigma} = \mathbf{u}$ is satisfied too, as proven in Theorem 1.

Security Analysis. Despite the construction being intuitive, analysing the leakage due to verification queries that reuse the same svk is not trivial and is one main technical contribution of this result.

Theorem 1. *Let Σ be an existentially unforgeable signature scheme with $\mathbf{Mv}$-style verification (as in Fig. 3). The scheme $\Sigma^E = (\Sigma, \text{offVer}, \text{onVer})$ obtained via our compiler depicted in Fig. 4 is existentially unforgeable under adaptive chosen message and efficient verification attacks. Concretely, the advantage is $Adv_{A,\Sigma}^{CMVA}(\lambda, k) \leq \frac{q_V + 1}{q^k - q_V}$ where $k \in \{1, \ldots, rk(\mathbf{M})\}$ denotes the chosen confidence level that grows up to the rank of the matrix $\mathbf{M}$, $q_V = \text{poly}(\lambda) << q^k$ is a bound on the total number of verification queries and q is the modulo of the algebraic structure on which Σ is built.*

Remark. For simplicity, Theorem 1 considers only existential unforgeability. The statement and the proof actually adapt with ease to other security models such as strong and selective unforgeability.

Table 1. A summary of the concrete efficiency achieved by various instatiations of our compiler for efficient verification. In the table, k_0 denotes the minimum accuracy level that ralizes efficient verification with 128 bits of security, i.e., for which $\Pr[\mathsf{Bad}] \leq 2^{-128}$ is negligible (cf. proof of Theorem 1, with $q_V = 2^{30}$); r_0 is the smallest positive integer for which $\frac{\mathsf{cost}(\mathsf{offVer}(\mathsf{pk},k_0))+r\cdot\mathsf{cost}(\mathsf{onVer})}{r\cdot\mathsf{cost}(\mathsf{Ver})} < 1$, and e_0 is a (tight) upperbound on this ratio.

Ring or field size (representative schemes)	Min. accuracy level for 128-bit security	Concrete amortized efficiency (see Definition 3)	Online efficiency $\frac{\mathsf{cost}(\mathsf{onVer})}{\mathsf{cost}(\mathsf{Ver})} = \frac{k_0}{n}$
exponential: $q = 2^{128}$ FMNP [12]; GVW [16]	$k_0 = 1$	$(r_0 = 2, e_0 = 0.51)$	$\frac{1}{256} < 0.4\%$
large poly.: $q = 2^{30}$ Boyen[7];GPV[15];MP[20]	$k_0 = 5$	$(r_0 = 6, e_0 = 0.86)$	$\frac{5}{256} < 2\%$
small poly.: $q = 16$ Rainbow [11] $\mathbb{F}_{2^4}$-$(32, 32, 32)$	$k_0 = 32$	$(r_0 = 65, e_0 = 0.99)$	$\frac{32}{64} = 50\%$

Proof. Let Win be the event $\{\mathsf{Exp}_{\mathcal{A},\Sigma}^{\mathsf{cmvEUF}}(\lambda, k) = 1\}$. Let $i = 1$ to q_V be the index of the queries $(\mu_i, \boldsymbol{\sigma}_i)$ submitted by $\mathcal{A}$ to the $\mathcal{O}$onVer oracle. Define the family of events bad_i (for $i = 1$ to $q_V + 1$) as:

$$\mathsf{bad}_i := \{\mathsf{Ver}(\mathsf{pk}, \mu_i, \boldsymbol{\sigma}_i) = 0 \wedge \mathsf{onVer}(\mathsf{svk}, \mu_i, \boldsymbol{\sigma}_i) = 1\}$$

where bad_{q_V+1} corresponds to $\mathcal{A}$ returning a valid forgery $(\mu^*, \boldsymbol{\sigma}^*) := (\mu_{q_V+1}, \boldsymbol{\sigma}_{q_V+1})$ at the end of the experiment. We can rewrite the winning condition of the security experiment as $\mathsf{Win} = \{\mathsf{bad}_{q_V+1} \wedge \mu^* \notin L_S\}$. Consider the event Bad defined as "there exists at least one query index i in the game execution for which bad_i occurs". It is clear that

$$Adv_{\mathcal{A},\Sigma}^{\mathsf{cmvEUF}}(\lambda, k) = \Pr[\mathsf{Win} \wedge \mathsf{Bad}] + \Pr[\mathsf{Win} \wedge \neg\mathsf{Bad}]$$
$$\leq \Pr[\mathsf{Bad}] + \Pr[\mathsf{Win} \mid \neg\mathsf{Bad}]$$

where the inequality comes from applying the definition of conditional probability and upperbounding $\Pr[\mathsf{Win} \mid \mathsf{Bad}]$ and $\Pr[\neg\mathsf{Bad}]$ by 1.

We notice that $\Pr[\mathsf{Win} \mid \neg\mathsf{Bad}]$ is essentially the probability that the event bad_i occurs only for $i = q_V + 1$ and never before, i.e.,

$$\Pr[\mathsf{Win} \mid \neg\mathsf{Bad}] \leq \Pr\left[\mathsf{bad}_{q_V+1} \mid \bigwedge_{i=1}^{q_V} \neg\mathsf{bad}_i\right]$$

In order to bound $\Pr[\mathsf{Bad}]$, we define events Bad_i^* (for $i = 1$ to q_V) as "bad_i occurs *for the first time* at query i", namely $\mathsf{Bad}_i^* = \mathsf{bad}_i \wedge \left(\bigwedge_{j=1}^{i-1} \neg\mathsf{bad}_j\right)$. Then we have

$$\Pr[\mathsf{Bad}] = \Pr\left[\bigvee_{i=1}^{q_V} \mathsf{Bad}_i^*\right] = \sum_{i=1}^{q_V} \Pr[\mathsf{Bad}_i^*] \leq \sum_{i=1}^{q_V} \Pr\left[\mathsf{bad}_i \mid \bigwedge_{j=1}^{i-1} \neg\mathsf{bad}_j\right]$$

where the second equality holds because the events Bad_i^* are all disjoint, and the inequality follows from applying the definition of conditional probability and upperbounding $\Pr\left[\bigwedge_{j=1}^{i-1} \neg\mathsf{bad}_j\right]$ by 1, for all i. Thus:

$$Adv_{\mathcal{A},\Sigma}^{\mathsf{cmvEUF}}(\lambda, k) \leq \sum_{i=1}^{q_V+1} \Pr\left[\mathsf{bad}_i \mid \bigwedge_{j=1}^{i-1} \neg\mathsf{bad}_j\right]. \tag{2}$$

Lemma 1. *For every $i = 1$ to $q_V + 1$, it holds that*

$$\Pr\left[\mathsf{bad}_i = 1 \mid \bigwedge_{j=1}^{i-1} \neg\mathsf{bad}_j\right] \leq \frac{1}{q^k - (i-1)}.$$

The proof of Lemma 1 is deferred momentarily to let us complete the reasoning that proves the theorem. Using the inequality provided by Lemma 1, it is easy to see that $\sum_{i=1}^{q_V+1} \Pr\left[\mathsf{bad}_i = 1 \mid \bigwedge_{j=1}^{i-1} \neg\mathsf{bad}_j\right] \leq \sum_{i=1}^{q_V+1} \frac{1}{q^k-(i-1)}$. Indeed, $\frac{1}{q^k-(i-1)} \leq \frac{1}{q^k-q_V}$ for all integers i in $[1, q_V+1]$ and for all $q_V, q, k \in \mathbb{N}$ satisfying $q_V < q^k$. Thus $\sum_{i=1}^{q_V+1} \frac{1}{q^k-(i-1)} \leq \frac{q_V+1}{q^k-q_V}$, which proves the bound on the advantage. $\qquad\square$

Proof of Lemma 1. The goal of this proof is to give a generic structure for estimating the leakage of infromation due to reuse of svk (i.e., probabilities in Equation (2)); due to space constraints details appear only in [6].

To upperbound $\Pr\left[\mathsf{bad}_i = 1 \mid \bigwedge_{j=1}^{i-1} \neg\mathsf{bad}_j\right]$ we need to analyze the information leakage due to verification queries. First of all, by correctness on$\mathsf{Ver}(\mathsf{svk}, \mu_i, \sigma_i) = 0 \Rightarrow \mathsf{Ver}(\mathsf{pk}, \mu_i, \sigma_i) = 0$ and $\mathsf{Ver}(\mathsf{pk}, \mu_i, \sigma_i) = 1 \Rightarrow$ on$\mathsf{Ver}(\mathsf{svk}, \mu_i, \sigma_i) = 1$ for every possible svk generated by offVer from pk. Leakage about svk happens in two cases: when an event bad_i occurs ($\mathcal{O}$onVer accepts where the standard verification would reject); and when $\mathcal{O}$onVer rejects a query (here $\mathcal{A}$ may learn that some combination of rows of pk must appear in svk). Equation (2) gives us a way to bound the adversary's advantage (and thus, the magnitude of this leakage) in terms of the events bad_i and $\neg\mathsf{bad}_i$.

Consider the i-th query (μ_i, σ_i) to $\mathcal{O}$onVer. If the oracle returns 0, the adversary learns that $\mathbf{C} \cdot (\mathbf{M}_i \cdot \mathbf{v}_i) \neq \mathbf{0} \mod q$. In other words, there is *at least one* row of $\mathbf{C} \in \mathcal{C} := \{\mathbf{C} \in \mathbb{Z}_q^{k \times n} : rk(\mathbf{C}) = k\}$, say $\mathbf{c}_j$, that is *not* in the hyperplane orthogonal to $\mathbf{w}_i := \mathbf{M}_i \cdot \mathbf{v}_i$, i.e., $\mathbf{c}_j \cdot \mathbf{w}_i \neq 0 \mod q$. Note that $\mathcal{A}$ knows $\mathbf{w}_i$ since $(\mathbf{M}_i, \mathbf{v}_i)$ can be computed from the pk, μ_i and σ_i. Let us introduce the sets $\mathcal{H}_i \subseteq \mathcal{C}$ of full-rank matrices $\mathbf{C} \in \mathcal{C}$ whose rows are *all orthogonal* to $\mathbf{w}_i$, formally:

$$\mathcal{H}_i := \left\{ \mathbf{C} \in \mathcal{C} \ : \ \mathbf{C} = \begin{bmatrix} \mathbf{c}_1 \\ \dots \\ \mathbf{c}_k \end{bmatrix} \wedge \ \mathbf{c}_j \cdot \mathbf{w}_i = 0 \mod q \ \forall \, j = 1, \dots, k \right\}.$$

We assume $\mathcal{A}$ be able to pick the vectors $\mathbf{w}_i \in \mathbb{Z}_q^n \smallsetminus \{0\}$ of her choosing (e.g., by generating suitable pairs (μ_i, σ_i)). This assumption is generous as it gives the adversary a large amount of power and freedom in the game. The restriction $\mathbf{w}_1 \neq \mathbf{0}$ is technical, as otherwise $\mathsf{Ver}(\mathsf{pk}, \mu_1, \boldsymbol{\sigma}_1) = 0$, which is a necessary condition for $\mathcal{O}$onVer leaking information about svk.

At the first verification query $(\mu_1, \boldsymbol{\sigma}_1)$, $\mathcal{A}$ has no information about $\mathbf{C}$ beyond the fact that it was uniformly sampled from the set $\mathcal{C} := \{\mathbf{C} \in \mathbb{Z}_q^{k \times n} : rk(\mathbf{C}) = k\}$. Therefore, for any choice of $\mathbf{w}_1 \neq \mathbf{0}$, if the event bad_1 occurs, then $\mathsf{bad}_1 = \{\mathbf{C} \cdot \mathbf{w}_1 = \mathbf{0} \mod q \wedge \mathbf{C} \xleftarrow{\$} \mathcal{C}\}$, thus $\Pr[\mathsf{bad}_1] = \Pr[\mathbf{C} \cdot \mathbf{w}_1 = \mathbf{0} \mod q \wedge \mathbf{C} \xleftarrow{\$} \mathcal{C}] = \frac{|\mathcal{H}_1|}{|\mathcal{C}|}$. The first (rejected) verification query leaks the fact that $\mathbf{C} \in \mathcal{C} \backslash \mathcal{H}_1$.

For the second verification query, without loss of generality let $\mathbf{w}_2$ be linearly independent from $\mathbf{w}_1$, i.e., $\mathbf{w}_2 \notin \langle \mathbf{w}_1 \rangle_q$. In this case, we have

$$
\begin{aligned}
\Pr[\mathsf{bad}_2 \mid \neg\mathsf{bad}_1] &= \Pr[\mathbf{C} \cdot \mathbf{w}_2 = \mathbf{0} \mod q \mid \mathbf{C} \xleftarrow{\$} \mathcal{C} \wedge \mathbf{C} \in (\mathcal{C} \backslash \mathcal{H}_1)] \\
&= \frac{\Pr[\mathbf{C} \cdot \mathbf{w}_2 = \mathbf{0} \mod q \wedge \mathbf{C} \xleftarrow{\$} \mathcal{C} \wedge \mathbf{C} \in (\mathcal{C} \backslash \mathcal{H}_1)]}{\Pr[\mathbf{C} \xleftarrow{\$} \mathcal{C} \wedge \mathbf{C} \in (\mathcal{C} \backslash \mathcal{H}_1)]} \\
&\leq \frac{\Pr[\mathbf{C} \cdot \mathbf{w}_2 = \mathbf{0} \mod q \wedge \mathbf{C} \xleftarrow{\$} \mathcal{C}]}{\Pr[\mathbf{C} \xleftarrow{\$} \mathcal{C} \wedge \mathbf{C} \in (\mathcal{C} \backslash \mathcal{H}_1)]} \\
&= \frac{\frac{|\mathcal{H}_2|}{|\mathcal{C}|}}{\frac{|\mathcal{C} \backslash \mathcal{H}_1|}{|\mathcal{C}|}} = \frac{|\mathcal{H}_1|}{|\mathcal{C} \backslash \mathcal{H}_1|}
\end{aligned}
$$

where the inequality follows from the fact that, given three events E_1, E_2, E_3, it always holds that $\Pr[E_1 \wedge E_2 \wedge E_3] \leq \min\{\Pr[E_1 \wedge E_2], \Pr[E_1 \wedge E_3], \Pr[E_2 \wedge E_3]\}$; and the last equality follows since the hyperplanes $\mathcal{H}_1$ and $\mathcal{H}_2$ have the same dimension.

The same reasoning applies to the generic i-th verification query, where, w.l.o.g., $\mathcal{A}$ chooses $\mathbf{w}_i$ outside the space generated by the previous $\mathbf{w}_j$'s, i.e., $\mathbf{w}_i \notin \langle \mathbf{w}_1, \ldots, \mathbf{w}_{i-1} \rangle_q$. At such query, $\mathcal{A}$ knows that $\mathbf{C} \in \mathcal{C} \backslash \left(\bigcup_{j=1}^{i-1} \mathcal{H}_j \right)$. Analogously as before we get that

$$
\begin{aligned}
\Pr\left[\mathsf{bad}_i = 1 \mid \bigwedge_{j=1}^{i-1} \neg\mathsf{bad}_j\right] &\leq \frac{\Pr[\mathbf{C} \cdot \mathbf{w}_i = \mathbf{0} \mod q \wedge \mathbf{C} \xleftarrow{\$} \mathcal{C}]}{\Pr\left[\mathbf{C} \in \mathcal{C} \backslash \left(\bigcup_{j=1}^{i-1} \mathcal{H}_j \right) \wedge \mathbf{C} \xleftarrow{\$} \mathcal{C}\right]} \\
&= \frac{|\mathcal{H}_1|}{\left|\mathcal{C} \backslash \left(\bigcup_{j=1}^{i-1} \mathcal{H}_j \right)\right|} .
\end{aligned}
\tag{3}
$$

The proof concludes using the results in [6] and showing that

$$
\left|\mathcal{C} \backslash \left(\bigcup_{j=1}^{i-1} \mathcal{H}_j \right)\right| \geq |\mathcal{H}_1| \cdot \left(\frac{q^n - q}{q^{n-k} - 1} - (i-1) \right) \quad \forall i = 2, \ldots, q_V + 1 .
$$

Substituting this value into Equation (3) returns:

$$
\Pr[\mathsf{bad}_i = 1 \mid \bigwedge_{j=1}^{i-1} \neg\mathsf{bad}_j] \leq \frac{1}{q^k \cdot \frac{1 - q^{1-n}}{1 - q^{k-n}} - (i-1)} \leq \frac{1}{q^k - (i-1)}
$$

where the last bound follows from the chain:

$$q^{n-1} > q^{n-k} \Leftrightarrow \frac{1}{q^{n-1}} < \frac{1}{q^{n-k}} \Leftrightarrow 1 - \frac{1}{q^{n-1}} > 1 - \frac{1}{q^{n-k}} \Leftrightarrow \frac{1 - \frac{1}{q^{n-1}}}{1 - \frac{1}{q^{n-k}}} > 1 \,,$$

as $1 < k < n$ and $q > 1$. □

4.2 A Compiler for Progressive Mv-Style Verification

Our compiler for progressive verification builds on the result presented in Sect. 4.1. Given a signature scheme Σ with **Mv**-style verification, we define the T steps of a progressive verification Σ^P for Σ as shown in Fig. 5.

The value T sets the upper bound on the number of linear constraints the verifier wants to check, hence $T = rows(\mathbf{M})$, where $\mathbf{M}$ is the matrix employed in the original signature verification of Σ. The set of admissible states $\mathcal{S}$ includes $\emptyset$ and any possible state output by some $\mathsf{ProgVer}_i$, specifically $\mathcal{S} = \{0,1\} \times \mathbb{Z}_q^{rows(\mathbf{Z}') \times cols(\mathbf{Z}')} \times \mathbb{Z}_q^{rows(\mathbf{v}) \times cols(\mathbf{v})} \times \{0,1\}^\lambda \cup \emptyset$. We extract the confidence level from the probability of a progressive forgery (as motivated by the proof of security given in Theorem 1). It is easy to see that the probability that an adversary creates a progressive forgery for an interruption step t is at most $\frac{q^{n-t}-1}{q^n-1}$, this follows from the same reasoning as in the proof of Theorem 1 for efficient verification. Concretely, the bound is derived from [6], where we only consider $\Pr[\mathsf{bad}_1]$ as svk is refreshed with every new efficient verification query, and so there is no useful cross-query leakage, and we replace the confidence level k of the efficient verification with the interruption parameter t. If the size of the underlying algebraic structure is $q = 2^{\mathsf{poly}(\lambda)}$ this probability is negligible already for $t = 1$. In other words, for signatures with **Mv**-style verification

$\mathsf{ProgStep}_0(\mathsf{st}, \mathsf{pk}, \mu, \boldsymbol{\sigma})$	$\mathsf{ProgStep}_j(\mathsf{st}, \mathsf{pk}, \mu, \boldsymbol{\sigma})$
1 : svk $\leftarrow$ offVer(pk, T)	1 : $b \leftarrow 0$
2 : **parse** svk $= (T, \mathbf{Z}, PK.\mathsf{aux})$	2 : **parse** st $= (\mathbf{Z}', \mathbf{v})$
3 : $b \leftarrow$ Check($PK.\mathsf{aux}, \mu, \boldsymbol{\sigma}$)	3 : **if** $\mathbf{Z}'[i, *] \cdot \mathbf{v}[*, i] = 0 \bmod q$
4 : st $\leftarrow$ GetZV(svk, $\mu, \boldsymbol{\sigma}$)	4 : **return** $(b \leftarrow 1, \mathsf{st})$
5 : **return** (b, st)	5 : **return** $(b \leftarrow 0, \mathsf{st})$

$$\alpha_{\mathsf{prog}} : \{0, \dots, T\} \to [0, 1], \qquad \alpha_{\mathsf{prog}}(t) = \left(1 - \tfrac{1}{q^t}\right)$$

Fig. 5. Our compiler for progressive verification of signatures with **Mv**-style verification. The algorithms offVer, Check and GetZV are precisely as defined in Fig. 4, and $T = rows(\mathbf{M})$. The notation $\mathbf{Z}'[i, *]$ describes the i-th row of the matrix $\mathbf{Z}'$, similarly $\mathbf{v}[*, i]$ describes the i-th column of $\mathbf{v}$ (which is usually a vector $\mathbf{v}$, but may be a matrix in some constructions).

defined on *exponentially large* algebraic structures *efficient verification and progressive verification coincide*, trivially. The interesting case is $q = \mathsf{poly}(\lambda)$, as the adversary could create a progressive forgery with non-negligible probability. We remark that in this section we are not targeting efficiency, and our instantiations of progressive verification refresh the svk produced by offVer at every verification query. This way, $\mathcal{A}$ cannot exploit the information possibly leaked by a progressive forgery in future forgery attempts.

Theorem 2. *Let Σ be an existentially unforgeable signature scheme with* **Mv**-*style verification (as of Fig. 3). Then the scheme Σ^P obtained via our compiler (in Fig. 5) is a secure realization of progressive verification for Σ.*

Proof. Following Definition 7, we can realize secure progressive verification by setting $\alpha_{\mathsf{prog}}(t) = 1 - \Pr\left[\mathsf{Exp}_{\mathcal{A},\Sigma}^{\mathsf{progEUF}}(\lambda) = (1,t)\right] + \varepsilon(\lambda)$ for all $t = 0, \ldots, T$. The core part of the proof is to estimate this probability.

Recall that our compiler for efficient **Mv**-style verification (in Fig. 5) runs offVer at every verification query (line 1 in $\mathsf{ProgVer}_0$). This means that every verification query is answered using a freshly generated svk. In particular, the final verification (line 4 in the $\mathsf{Exp}_{\mathcal{A},\Sigma^P}^{\mathsf{progEUF}}(\lambda)$ in Fig. 2) checks $\mathcal{A}$'s output using independent randomness from the previous queries. So, whatever information the adversary may have collected from previous queries is useless to win the experiment. As a consequence, the probability that the adversary wins the game equals the probability that the adversary outputs a valid forgery *without querying* $O\mathsf{ProgVer}$. The latter is precisely the probability of the event bad_1 defined in the proof of Theorem 1, where now we consider the matrix $\mathbf{C}$ to have t^* rows instead of k. Hence from Lemma 1 it follows that $\Pr\left[\mathsf{Exp}_{\mathcal{A},\Sigma}^{\mathsf{progEUF}}(\lambda) \leq (1,t^*)\right] = \frac{1}{q^{t^*}}$ and: $Adv_{\mathcal{A},\Sigma}^{\mathsf{progEUF}}(\lambda) = \Pr\left[\mathsf{Exp}_{\mathcal{A},\Sigma}^{\mathsf{progEUF}}(\lambda) = (1,t^*)\right] - (1 - \alpha_{\mathsf{prog}}(t^*)) \leq \frac{1}{q^{t^*}} - \left(1 - \left(1 - \frac{1}{q^{t^*}}\right)\right) = 0$. $\square$

4.3   Combining Progressive and Efficient Verification

We observe that progressive verifications obtained with our transformation can be split into two parts: a one-time, computationally intensive, setup ($\mathsf{ProgStep}_0$); and an efficient online verification ($\mathsf{ProgStep}_1$ to $\mathsf{ProgStep}_T$). This gives rise to custom (intentionally adjustable) verification soundness, which from the application perspective makes post-quantum secure verification accessible to a larger range of devices, and from the theoretical perspective draws interesting connections between classical, information-theoretic and post-quantum security notions. We include a more detailed discussion on this in the full version [6].

Acknowledgments. This work was partly funded by: ELLIIT, the Swedish Foundation for Strategic Research (RIT17-0035), the Swiss National Science Foundation under the SNSF project number 182452 and the Postdoc.Mobility grant number 203075, the European Research Council (ERC) under the European Union's Horizon 2020 research and innovation program under project PICOCRYPT (grant agreement No.

101001283), by the Spanish Government under projects SCUM (ref. RTI2018-102043-B-I00), CRYPTOEPIC (ref. EUR2019-103816), and RED2018-102321-T, and by the Madrid Regional Government under project BLOQUES (ref. S2018/TCS-4339). Part of this work was made while C.B. was at IBM Research - Zurich (CH) and visiting the University of Aarhus (DK).

References

1. Armknecht, F., Walther, P., Tsudik, G., Beck, M., Strufe, T.: Promacs: progressive and resynchronizing macs for continuous efficient authentication of message streams. In: Proceedings of the 2020 ACM SIGSAC Conference on Computer and Communications Security, pp. 211–223 (2020)
2. Backes, M., Fiore, D., Reischuk, R.M.: Verifiable delegation of computation on outsourced data. In: 2013 ACM SIGSAC CCS, pp. 863–874. ACM (2013)
3. Bernstein, D.J.: A secure public-key signature system with sxtremely fast verification
4. Beullens, W., Szepieniec, A., Vercauteren, F., Preneel, B.: Luov: signature scheme proposal for NIST PQC project (2019)
5. Boneh, D., Freeman, D.M.: Linearly homomorphic signatures over binary fields and new tools for lattice-based signatures. In: Catalano, D., Fazio, N., Gennaro, R., Nicolosi, A. (eds.) PKC 2011. LNCS, vol. 6571, pp. 1–16. Springer, Heidelberg (2011). https://doi.org/10.1007/978-3-642-19379-8_1
6. Boschini, C., Fiore, D., Pagnin, E.: Progressive and efficient verification for digital signatures. Cryptology ePrint Archive, 2021/832 (2021)
7. Boyen, X.: Lattice mixing and vanishing trapdoors: a framework for fully secure short signatures and more. In: Nguyen, P.Q., Pointcheval, D. (eds.) PKC 2010. LNCS, vol. 6056, pp. 499–517. Springer, Heidelberg (2010). https://doi.org/10.1007/978-3-642-13013-7_29
8. Cash, D., Hofheinz, D., Kiltz, E., Peikert, C.: Bonsai trees, or how to delegate a lattice basis. In: Gilbert, H. (ed.) EUROCRYPT 2010. LNCS, vol. 6110, pp. 523–552. Springer, Heidelberg (2010). https://doi.org/10.1007/978-3-642-13190-5_27
9. Catalano, D., Fiore, D., Warinschi, B.: Homomorphic signatures with efficient verification for polynomial functions. In: Advances in Cryptology - CRYPTO (2014)
10. Ding, J., Chen, M.-S., Petzoldt, A., Schmidt, D., Yang, B.-Y.: Rainbow. https://csrc.nist.gov/projects/post-quantum-cryptography/round-2-submissions. Accessed 21 Sept 2020
11. Ding, J., Schmidt, D.: Rainbow, a new multivariable polynomial signature scheme. In: Ioannidis, J., Keromytis, A., Yung, M. (eds.) ACNS 2005. LNCS, vol. 3531, pp. 164–175. Springer, Heidelberg (2005). https://doi.org/10.1007/11496137_12
12. Fiore, D., Mitrokotsa, A., Nizzardo, L., Pagnin, E.: Multi-key homomorphic authenticators. In: ASIACRYPT (2016)
13. Fischlin, M.: Progressive verification: the case of message authentication. In: Johansson, T., Maitra, S. (eds.) INDOCRYPT 2003. LNCS, vol. 2904, pp. 416–429. Springer, Heidelberg (2003). https://doi.org/10.1007/978-3-540-24582-7_31
14. Gennaro, R., Gentry, C., Parno, B.: Non-interactive verifiable computing: outsourcing computation to untrusted workers. In: CRYPTO (2010)
15. Gentry, C., Peikert, C., Vaikuntanathan, V.: Trapdoors for hard lattices and new cryptographic constructions. In: ACM STOC (2008)
16. Gorbunov, S., Vaikuntanathan, V., Wichs, D.: Leveled fully homomorphic signatures from standard lattices. In: STOC, pp. 469–477. ACM (2015)

17. Lamport, L.: Constructing digital signatures from a one-way function. Technical report, Technical Report CSL-98. SRI International (1979)
18. Le, D.V., Kelkar, M., Kate, A.: Flexible signatures: making authentication suitable for real-time environments. In: ESORICS. Springer, Cham (2019). https://doi.org/10.1007/978-3-030-29959-0_9
19. Loveless, A., Dreslinski, R., Kasikci, B., Phan, L.T.X.: Igor: accelerating byzantine fault tolerance for real-time systems with eager execution. In: IEEE Real-Time and Embedded Technology and Applications Symposium (RTAS) (2021)
20. Micciancio, D., Peikert, C.: Trapdoors for lattices: simpler, tighter, faster, smaller. In: EUROCRYPT (2012)
21. Plantard, T., Sipasseuth, A., Dumondelle, C., Susilo, W.: DRS: diagonal dominant reduction for lattice-based signature. In: PQC Standardization Conference (2018)
22. Sipasseuth, A., Plantard, T., Susilo, W.: Using Freivalds' algorithm to accelerate lattice-based signature verifications. In: ISPEC. Springer, Cham (2019)
23. Taleb, A.R., Vergnaud, D.: Speeding-up verification of digital signatures. J. Comput. Syst. Sci. (2020)
24. Wang, Q., Khurana, H., Huang, Y., Nahrstedt, K.: Time valid one-time signature for time-critical multicast data authentication. In: IEEE INFOCOM (2009)

Revocable Hierarchical Attribute-Based Signatures from Lattices

Daniel Gardham[1](✉) and Mark Manulis[2]

[1] Surrey Centre for Cyber Security, University of Surrey, Guildford, UK
daniel.gardham@surrey.ac.uk
[2] Research Institute CODE, Universität der Bundeswehr München,
Munich, Germany
mark@manulis.eu

Abstract. Attribute-based Signatures (ABS) allow users to obtain attributes from issuing authorities, and sign messages whilst simultaneously proving compliance of their attributes with a verification policy. ABS demands that both the signer and the set of attributes used to satisfy a policy remain hidden to the verifier. Hierarchical ABS (HABS) supporting roots of trust and delegation were recently proposed to alleviate scalability issues in centralised ABS schemes.

An important yet challenging property for privacy-preserving ABS is revocation, which may be applied to signers or some of the attributes they possess. Existing ABS schemes lack efficient revocation of either signers or their attributes, relying on generic costly proofs. Moreover, in HABS there is a further need to support revocation of authorities on the delegation paths, which is not provided by existing HABS constructions.

This paper proposes a direct HABS scheme with a Verifier-Local Revocation (VLR) property. We extend the original HABS security model to address revocation and develop a new attribute delegation technique with appropriate VLR mechanism for HABS, which also implies the *first* ABS scheme to support VLR. Moreover, our scheme supports inner-product signing policies, offering a wider class of attribute relations than previous HABS schemes, and is the first to be based on lattices, which are thought to offer post-quantum security.

Keywords: Attribute-based Signatures · Revocation · Delegation · Lattices

1 Introduction

(Hierarchical) Attribute-Based Signatures. To provide privacy-preserving authentication, Attribute-based Signatures (ABS), introduced in [25,32], allow users to collect attributes from authorities and produce signatures showing attribute-compliance with some signing policy. A core security property of ABS

D. Gardham—Some of this work was carried out whilst the author was at the Information Security Group, Royal Holloway, University of London, UK.

G. Ateniese and D. Venturi (Eds.): ACNS 2022, LNCS 13269, pp. 459–479, 2022.
https://doi.org/10.1007/978-3-031-09234-3_23

schemes is that they are attribute-hiding, and for schemes that consider multiple users, it is often required that they also remain anonymous. A second security property, unforgeability, prevents users from generating signatures for policies for which they do not have a satisfying set of attributes.

Most constructions for ABS schemes [14,15,17,34,35] are based on bilinear groups and make use of the flexible Groth-Sahai proof system [21] to provide anonymity guarantees. Notable exceptions include constructions from RSA [22] and recent work in the lattice setting [16,38,40,41], which are in the random oracle model. Originally, ABS schemes were proposed in the centralised model, that is, one central authority is responsible for all attribute issuance, but to allow for larger scalability, decentralised schemes [15] have also been developed.

More recently, Hierarchical Attribute-Based Signatures (HABS) [13,18,19] overcome the shortcomings of previous schemes by allowing attribute delegation to intermediate authorities. In particular, a central *Root Authority (RA)* delegates issuing rights of a subset of attributes to lower tier *Intermediate Authorities (IA)* who can delegate further, or issue directly to a user. This overcomes the bottleneck of requiring a single authority to issue all attributes in a scheme with either a large number of users or attributes, and also allows a verifier to trust a signature without having to trust each authority in the scheme, as is the case in decentralised constructions.

Revocation. A desirable property of any privacy-preserving signature is the support for user revocation. This would enable a trusted authority to prevent users from producing signatures that pass verification, without compromising the anonymity of honest participants. Revocation for a hierarchical structure of authorities would require the ability to check that a revoked authority does not appear anywhere in the delegation path of an attribute. This brings new challenges and any HABS construction would have to perform these additional checks when verifying the HABS signature. Specific to attribute-based protocols, it may also be desirable to revoke an attribute itself, rather than issuing authorities. For example, this maybe be required in the setting where attributes may depend on the time period or can be changed dynamically.

Revocation techniques typically follow one of few approaches. Firstly, it can be achieved by requiring signers to update their secret credentials in order to produce a valid signature. Another approach is to use a public revocation list, which is updated with some information about revoked users. When a signature is formed, the signer typically proves in zero-knowledge that its information does not appear in the list. Finally, we have *verifier-local* revocation which puts the onus on the verifier to check that signatures have not been generated by a revoked signer. This approach still requires up-to-date revocation information but has more semblance to traditional public key infrastructure that typically use Certificate Revocation Lists, and can allow for more efficient constructions as it bypasses the need for costly zero-knowledge proofs when generating signatures. Previously, VLR as a means of revocation has appeared in group signatures (introduced in [7]) but it remains an open problem for an ABS scheme to support *any* revocation technique[1]. We note that Herranz [22] proposed a scheme called Revocable Attribute-based Signatures, however revocation here refers to the revocation of anonymity.

Contribution. In this paper we improve upon security and functionality of existing HABS constructions by proposing a lattice-based scheme which supports revocation and a wider range of signing policies. Our scheme is based on the widely used LWE and SIS assumptions over integer lattices, and supports inner-product relations which allow for conjunctive, disjunctive and threshold policies as well as polynomial evaluations of attributes [23]. Revocation in our HABS schemes uses a novel VLR mechanism to revoke signers and attributes as well as intermediate authorities. We model HABS security and use an integration of techniques from identity-based encryption, trapdoor delegation and signature schemes as well as novel techniques to realise our construction. This work also implies the *first* lattice-based (non-hierarchical) ABS scheme with the aforementioned properties.

Related Work. In this section we review related works on VLR, lattice-based signatures and signing policies in ABS schemes.

Revocation. VLR was first suggested in [3] and formalised in [6] and has been widely researched since then, for example, improving efficiency (e.g. [42]), functionality (e.g. [12]), stronger security properties (e.g. [8]) or basing on different hardness assumptions (e.g. lattices [24], bilinear groups [42]). The first scheme secure in the standard model that supported VLR was a group signature scheme by Libert and Vergnaud [26], based on the DLIN and variants of Diffie-Hellman type assumptions. In the recent lattice-based VLR group signature scheme from Langlois et al. [24], signing requires knowledge of a secret revocation token. We note that this technique cannot be transferred to the HABS setting as a signature must also include tokens for intermediate authorities, which are part of the secret, thus a new approach is needed.

Post-Quantum Security. Most ABS schemes are based on bilinear groups [14,15, 17,34,35], or RSA [22] and do not offer post-quantum security. As some lattice-based hardness assumptions are believed to be resistant to quantum adversaries, this area has attracted significant research interest. As a result, there have been many privacy-preserving signature schemes, such as group signature schemes (e.g. [24,28–30]), ring signatures (e.g. [5,11]), anonymous attribute tokens [9] and even ABS schemes (e.g. [16,38,40,41]). However, whilst ABS have been proposed from lattices, current literature falls short of the delegation offered by HABS.

Signing Policies in (H)ABS. Constructing schemes with more expressive signing policies is an active area of research for ABS, as it allows for a wider range of use-cases and offers signers more flexibility. Despite this, many schemes

---

[1] We note here the work [37] of Su et al. that claims to propose a revocable ABS scheme, however we note that their scheme does not hide the attributes (nor takes a signing policy) so does not meet traditional definitions of ABS.

[15,32], including all known HABS constructions [13,19], utilise span programs that result in restrictive monotone boolean policies. Wang et al. [40] provide a different construction for threshold policies but benefit from shorter private key sizes over comparable schemes. There are notable exceptions that support even unbounded circuits [16]. In particular, [4] offers a lattice construction for a threshold scheme in a centralised setting, and then shows how to transform this to support more expressive $(\wedge, \vee)$-policies. ABS from lattices supporting inner-product policies [41] have been proposed, yet without distinguishing between signers, which prevents any meaningful definition for delegation or revocation.

2   Preliminaries

We denote vectors by lower-case bold letters $(\mathbf{a})$, and use capital bold font for matrices $(\mathbf{A})$. The transpose of a matrix $\mathbf{A}$ (or vector) is denoted by $\mathbf{A}^T$, and the concatenation of matrices (or vectors) $\mathbf{A}$ and $\mathbf{B}$ by $[\mathbf{A}||\mathbf{B}]$. We use $\mathbf{I}$ to denote the identity matrix, and if we wish to be clear on the dimension then we write $\mathbf{I}_{n \times m}$, for some naturals n and m. The interval $[a, b]$ is used to denote all *integer* values x in the range $a \leqslant x \leqslant b$. Sampling a random variable $\mathbf{x}$ from a distribution $\mathcal{X}$ is written $\mathbf{x} \hookleftarrow \mathcal{X}$. The maximum number of users in the scheme is given by $N = 2^d$, and we denote the security parameter by λ. The number of levels in the hierarchy is l, and denote a signing policy by Ψ, and set $\delta := |\Psi|$, i.e. the number of attributes that form the signing policy.

Lattices. Let $n, m, q \geqslant 2$ be integers. For a matrix $\mathbf{A} \in \mathbb{Z}_q^{n \times m}$, define the m-dimensional lattice $\Lambda^{\perp}(\mathbf{A}) = \{\mathbf{z} \in \mathbb{Z}^m : \mathbf{A} \cdot \mathbf{z} = \mathbf{0} \mod q\} \subseteq \mathbb{Z}^m$. For a vector $\mathbf{u}$ in the preimage of $\mathbf{A}$, define the coset $\Lambda_{\mathbf{u}}^{\perp} = \{\mathbf{z} \in \mathbb{Z}^m : \mathbf{A} \cdot \mathbf{z} = \mathbf{u} \mod q\}$.

LWE. The (Decisional) Learning With Errors ($\mathsf{LWE}_{n,m,q,\chi}$) problem is as follows. Let $n, m \geqslant 1$, $q \geqslant 2$ and χ be a probability distribution over $\mathbb{Z}$. Let $\mathbf{s} \in \mathbb{Z}_q^n$, then $\mathcal{D}_{\mathbf{s},\chi}$ is a distribution obtained by sampling $\mathbf{a} \leftarrow \mathbb{Z}_q^n$ and $e \leftarrow \chi$ and computing $(\mathbf{a}, \mathbf{a}^T\mathbf{s} + e) \in \mathbb{Z}_q^n \times \mathbb{Z}_q$. Then the $\mathsf{LWE}_{n,m,q,\chi}$ requires an adversary to distinguish m samples chosen from χ and m uniform samples from $\mathbb{Z}_q^n \times \mathbb{Z}_q^n$.

SIS. The Short Integer Solution problem ($\mathsf{SIS}_{n,m,q,\beta}$), introduced in [1], requires an adversary who, given a uniformly matrix $\mathbf{A} \in \mathbb{Z}_q^{n \times m}$, to find a non-zero vector $\mathbf{z} \in \mathbb{Z}_q^m$ such that $||\mathbf{z}||_{\infty} \leqslant \beta$ and $\mathbf{Az} = \mathbf{0} \mod q$. We define the *Inhomogenous Short Integer Solution* ($\mathsf{ISIS}_{n,m,q,\beta}$) as SIS but for a non-zero syndrome, i.e. $\mathbf{Az} = \mathbf{u} \mod q$.

3   VLR-HABS Model: Entities and Definitions

We start with the description of entities for the VLR-HABS ecosystem.

Attribute Authorities. The set of Attribute Authorities (AA) comprises the Root Authority (RA) and Intermediate Authorities (IAs). As the name suggests, the RA is the root of the hierarchy, and upon setup defines the universe of attributes $\mathbb{A}$. With its key pair $(\mathsf{skd}_0, \mathsf{pkd}_0)$, the RA can delegate a subset of attributes to IAs which hold their own key pairs $(\mathsf{skd}_i, \mathsf{pkd}_i)$, $i > 0$. IAs can further delegate/issue attributes to other IAs or to any end user. This allows for a dynamically expandable VLR-HABS hierarchy to be established.

Users. With key pair $(\mathsf{usk}, \mathsf{upk})$, a user joins the scheme by being issued attributes from potentially many AAs. Then, a user can use usk to create a VLR-HABS signature, provided their issued set of attributes A satisfies the policy, i.e. $\Psi(A') = 1$ for some $A' \subseteq A$ and a signing policy Ψ. Users are prevented from delegating attributes further and thus can be viewed as the lowest tier of the hierarchy. We realise this in our scheme by requiring users to obtain public keys in a different space to that of authorities.

Warrants. A warrant is used to store delegated attributes for each IA or user. It contains the attribute, the delegation information, and a list of identities that comprise the delegation path of the attribute. Warrants are updated any time a new attribute is issued by appending a new entry. We use the notation $|\mathsf{warr}|$ to denote the size of the warrant, i.e. the number of attributes stored in the warrant warr, and we use $|\mathsf{warr}[\mathsf{a}]|$ to denote the length of the delegation path of the attribute $\mathsf{a} \in \mathbb{A}$. During the signing phase, the user submits a reduced warrant for an attribute set $A' \subseteq A$ that satisfies $\Psi(A') = 1$. We fix the maximum depth of the delegation path to be $l \in \mathsf{poly}(\lambda)$ and stress this is not a restriction on the *minimum*.

Tracing Authority. The tracing authority (TA), independent of the hierarchy, is responsible for removing anonymity in the case of misuse. It can identify the signer and all authorities on the delegation paths for attributes that the signer used to satisfy the signing policy, and proves correctness of these identities by producing a publicly verifiable proof.

Revocation Authority. The Revocation Authority (RevA) is a trusted third party that acts independently of the hierarchy. The role of the RevA is to publish a list of revoked IDs that cause any signature generated with a corresponding revoked identity to fail verification. The RevA, with a secret key, would require input of a user or AA identity in order to execute its function, which given the anonymity of VLR-HABS, could require extraction from a signature by the TA. In practice, it might be likely that the TA and RevA would be instantiated as a single authority whose role covers both functions, however, we present them as independent parties to cover a more general scheme.

Definition 1 (VLR-HABS). *A* VLR-HABS $:=$ (Setup, UKGen, AKGen, AttIssue, Revoke, Sign, Verify, Trace, Judge) *consists of nine processes:*

- Setup(1^λ) *is the initialisation process. Based on some security parameter $\lambda \in \mathbb{N}$, the public parameters pp of the scheme are defined. In this phase, the root, tracing and revocation authorities independently generate their own key pairs, i.e. RA's $(\mathsf{skd}_0, \mathsf{pkd}_0)$, TA's $(\mathsf{sk}_{\mathsf{TA}}, \mathsf{pk}_{\mathsf{TA}})$ and RevA's $(\mathsf{sk}_{\mathsf{RevA}}, \mathsf{pk}_{\mathsf{RevA}})$. In addition, RA defines the universe of attributes $\mathbb{A}$, and initialises an empty list*

RevokeList. *We stress that due to dynamic hierarchy, the system can be initialised by publishing (*pp, pkd_0, pk_{TA}, pk_{RevA}) *with* $\mathbb{A}$ *and* RevokeList *contained in* pp.

- UKGen(pp, skd_0) *is a key generation algorithm executed by the root authority for users and issued to users as* (usk, upk, id).
- AKGen(pp) *is a key generation algorithm executed independently by intermediate authorities. Each IA generates its own public key, i.e.,* pkd_i, id_i $(i > 0)$.
- AttIssue($warr_i$, a, $\{pkd_j|upk_j\}$) *is an algorithm that is used to delegate attributes to an authority* id_j *with* pkd_j *or issue them to the user* uid *with* upk. *On input of an authority's warrant* $warr_i$, *an attribute* a *from* $warr_i$, *and the public key of the entity to which attributes are delegated or issued, it outputs a new warrant* warr *for that entity.*
- Revoke(sk_{RevA}, id) *is an algorithm executed by the Revocation Authority. Using* RevokeList *from the implicit input* pp, *and on input of a User or AA ID* (uid, id), *it outputs an updated* RevokeList.
- Sign((usk, warr), m, Ψ) *is the signing algorithm. On input of the signer's* usk *and (possibly reduced)* warr, *a message* m *and a predicate* Ψ *it outputs a signature* σ.
- Verify(pkd_0, (m, Ψ, σ)) *is a deterministic algorithm that outputs 1 if a candidate signature* σ *on a message* m *is valid with respect to the predicate* Ψ *and revocation list* RevokeList *from* pp, *and 0 otherwise.*
- Trace(sk_{TA}, pkd_0, (m, Ψ, σ)) *is an algorithm executed by the TA on input of its private key* sk_{TA} *and a VLR-HABS signature* σ, *it outputs either a triple* (upk, warr, $\hat{\pi}$) *if the tracing is successful or* $\perp$ *to indicate its failure. Note that* warr *contains attributes and delegation paths that were used by the signer.*
- Judge(pk_{TA}, pkd_0, (m, Ψ, σ), (upk, warr, $\hat{\pi}$)) *is a deterministic algorithm that checks a candidate triple* (upk, warr, $\hat{\pi}$) *from the tracing algorithm and outputs 1 if the triple is valid and 0 otherwise.*

A VLR-HABS scheme satisfies the *correctness* property if any signature σ generated based on an honestly issued warrant that satisfies the signing policy, will verify and trace correctly, if and only if identities used in the warrant have not been revoked. The output (upk, warr, $\hat{\pi}$) of the tracing algorithm on such signatures will be accepted by the public judging algorithm with overwhelming probability. Formally, we have:

Definition 2 (Correctness). *A VLR-HABS scheme is correct if the following condition holds:*

If $\Psi(A) = 1$ *and* $\forall a \in A$, $\exists warr[a] \in warr$ *s.t.* warr[a] *is valid, then:*

Verify(pkd_0, (m, Ψ, Sign((usk, warr), m, Ψ))) = 1 $\iff$ $\forall id \in warr$, id $\notin$ RevokeList

and Judge((pk_{TA}, pkd_0, (m, Ψ, σ), Trace(sk_{TA}, pkd_0, (m, Ψ, σ)))) = 1

3.1 Security Properties of VLR-HABS

Our security definitions are closely related to *path anonymity, path traceability,* and *non-frameability* from [13] but with modifications to allow for revocation functionality. We give new game-based definitions assuming probabilistic polynomial time (PPT) adversaries interacting with VLR-HABS entities through a set of oracles given below and formally described in Fig. 1.

- O_{RegU} : $\mathcal{A}$ registers new users through this oracle, for which a key pair will be generated and added to List. The public key is given to the adversary. Initially, the entity is considered honest, and so the public key is also added to the list HUList.
- O_{RegA} : $\mathcal{A}$ registers new IAs through this registration oracle, for which an identity will be generated and added to AList, which is given to the adversary.
- O_{CorrU} : This oracle allows $\mathcal{A}$ to corrupt registered users. Upon input of a public key, the corresponding private key is given as output if it exists in List. The public key is removed from HUList so the oracle keeps track of corrupt entities.
- O_{CorrA} : This oracle allows $\mathcal{A}$ to corrupt registered IAs and User attribute keys. Upon input of a public key and an attribute, the corresponding private key is given as output the if the pair exists in AList. The identity is removed from HAList so the oracle keeps track of corrupt delegations.
- O_{Att} : $\mathcal{A}$ uses this oracle to invoke an attribute authority to delegate attributes to either an IA or to a user. In particular, the adversary has control over which attributes are issued and the oracle outputs a warrant warr if both parties are registered, otherwise it outputs $\perp$. The public key and attribute are added to a list HAList, that is initialised with $\{0, \perp, \perp, \perp, a\}, \forall a \in A$.
- O_{Sig} : $\mathcal{A}$ uses this oracle to obtain a VLR-HABS signature from a registered user. The adversary provides the warrant (and implicitly the attributes used), signing policy, message and the public key of the signer. If the attribute set satisfies the policy, and the public key is contained in HUList then the signature will be given to $\mathcal{A}$, otherwise $\perp$ is returned.
- O_{Tr} : $\mathcal{A}$ uses the Trace oracle on a VLR-HABS signature (provided by the adversary) to extract the attributes and identities. The TA does verification checks and upon failure, will return $\perp$, otherwise it outputs warr.
- O_{RevID} : $\mathcal{A}$ uses this oracle to revoke a user. The adversary has control over which IDs (both Users and AAs) are revoked. The oracle outputs an updated revocation list RevokeList if the entity exists in List or AList, otherwise it outputs $\perp$.

Path Anonymity. This property guarantees anonymity of the signer as well as all intermediate authorities involved in attribute-delegation for attributes used to satisfy the signing policy. The definition for path anonymity for a VLR-HABS scheme is closely related to that given in [13], however we make adjustments to allow for the revocation feature. Our definition captures unlinkability for unrevoked signers. The experiment for path anonymity, defined in Fig. 2, requires a two-stage PPT adversary $(\mathcal{A}_1, \mathcal{A}_2)$ to distinguish which warrant and private key were used in the generation of the challenge VLR-HABS signature σ_b. Initially, $\mathcal{A}_1$ generates the authority and user hierarchy, utilising the registration and delegation oracles. A challenge VLR-HABS signature σ_b according to the predefined challenge bit b, using warrants and keys provided by the adversary. Then, with access to the tracing oracle, the adversary $\mathcal{A}_2$ guesses b'. We note that the game returns 0 if $\mathcal{A}$ revokes the identity in either of the warrants warr_0 and warr_1 that it provides the experiment. Since it does not have access to the revoke oracle in the second phase of the experiment, it cannot use this to help determine the challenge bit.

Definition 3 (Path Anonymity). *A VLR-HABS scheme offers path anonymity if no PPT adversary $\mathcal{A}$ can distinguish between* $\mathsf{Exp}^{pa-0}_{\mathsf{VLR\text{-}HABS},\mathcal{A}}$ *and* $\mathsf{Exp}^{pa-1}_{\mathsf{VLR\text{-}HABS},\mathcal{A}}$ *defined in Fig. 2, i.e., the following is negligible in λ:*

$$\mathsf{Adv}^{pa}_{\mathsf{VLR\text{-}HABS},\mathcal{A}}(\lambda) = |\Pr[\mathsf{Exp}^{pa-0}_{\mathsf{VLR\text{-}HABS},\mathcal{A}}(\lambda) = 1] - \Pr[\mathsf{Exp}^{pa-1}_{\mathsf{VLR\text{-}HABS},\mathcal{A}}(\lambda) = 1]|$$

$\mathcal{O}_{\mathrm{RegU}}(\,i\,),\ i \notin \mathsf{List}$

1: $(\mathsf{id}, \mathsf{usk}_i, \mathsf{upk}_i) \leftarrow \mathsf{UKGen}(\mathsf{pp})$
2: $\mathsf{List} \leftarrow \mathsf{List} \cup \{(i, \mathsf{id}, \mathsf{upk}_i, \mathsf{usk}_i)\}$
3: $\mathsf{HUList} \leftarrow \mathsf{HUList} \cup \{i\}$
4: **return** $(\mathsf{id}, \mathsf{upk}_i)$

$\mathcal{O}_{\mathrm{RegA}}(\,i\,),\ i \notin \mathsf{AList}$

1: $\mathsf{id} \leftarrow \mathsf{AKGen}(\mathsf{pp})$
2: $\mathsf{AList} \leftarrow \mathsf{AList} \cup \{(i, \mathsf{id}, \perp, \perp, \perp)\}$
3: **return** id

$\mathcal{O}_{\mathrm{CorrU}}(\,i\,)$

1: $\mathsf{HUList} \leftarrow \mathsf{HUList} \setminus \{i\}$
2: **return** skd_i from List

$\mathcal{O}_{\mathrm{CorrA}}(i, \mathsf{pkd}_{i,a}, a)$

1: $\mathsf{HAList} \leftarrow \mathsf{HAList} \setminus \{i, \mathsf{pkd}_{i,a}, a\}$
2: **return** $\mathsf{skd}_{i,a}$ from AList

$\mathcal{O}_{\mathrm{Tr}}(\mathsf{m}, \Psi, \sigma)$

1: $\mathsf{warr} \leftarrow \mathsf{Trace}(\mathsf{sk}_{\mathsf{TA}}, \mathsf{pkd}_0, (\mathsf{m}, \Psi, \sigma))$
2: **return** warr

$\mathcal{O}_{\mathrm{Att}}(i, \mathsf{warr}_i, a, \{\mathsf{id}_j | \mathsf{uid}_j\})$

1: $L := \{(i, \mathsf{pkd}_{i,a}, a) | \{i, \mathsf{id}, \mathsf{pkd}_{i,a},$
2: $\qquad\qquad\qquad \mathsf{skd}_{i,a}, a\} \in \mathsf{AList}\}$
3: **if** $(i, \mathsf{warr}_i, a) \notin L \vee j \notin \mathsf{List} \vee \mathsf{AList}$
4: **then** , **return** $\perp$
5: $(\mathsf{skd}_{i,a}, \mathsf{pkd}_{i,a}) \leftarrow \mathsf{AttIssue}(\mathsf{skd}_{i,a},$
6: $\qquad\qquad\qquad \mathsf{warr}_i, a, \{\mathsf{id}_j | \mathsf{uid}_j\})$
7: $\mathsf{warr}_j[a] \leftarrow \mathsf{warr}_i[a] \cup \{\mathsf{pkd}_{i,a}, \mathsf{id}_j, a\}$
8: $\mathsf{AList} \leftarrow \mathsf{AList} \cup \{j, \mathsf{id}_j, \mathsf{pkd}_{j,a}, \mathsf{skd}_{j,a}, a\}$
9: $\mathsf{HAList} \leftarrow \mathsf{HAList} \cup \{j, \mathsf{pkd}_{j,a}, a\}$
10: **return** warr

$\mathcal{O}_{\mathrm{Sig}}(i, \mathsf{warr}, \mathsf{m}, \Psi)$

1: $A \leftarrow \{a | \ a \in \mathsf{warr}\}$
2: **if** $i \in \mathsf{HUList} \wedge \Psi(A)$ **then**
3: $\quad \sigma \leftarrow \mathsf{Sign}((\mathsf{usk}_i, \mathsf{warr}), \mathsf{m}, \Psi)$
4: **return** σ
5: **return** $\perp$

$\mathcal{O}_{\mathrm{RevID}}(i, \mathsf{id}, \mathsf{RevokeList})$

1: **if** $(i, \mathsf{id}, \star, \star, [\star]) \in \mathsf{List} \vee \mathsf{AList}$ **then**
2: $\quad \mathsf{tok} \leftarrow \mathsf{Revoke}(\mathsf{sk}_{\mathsf{RevA}}, \mathsf{id})$
3: $\quad \mathsf{RevokeList} \leftarrow \mathsf{RevokeList} \cup \{\mathsf{tok}\}$
4: **return** $\mathsf{RevokeList}$

Fig. 1. Oracles for VLR-HABS security experiments.

$\mathsf{Exp}^{\mathsf{pa}\text{-}b}_{\mathsf{VLR}\text{-}\mathsf{HABS},\mathcal{A}}(\lambda)$

---

1 : $(\mathsf{pp}, \mathsf{skd}_0, \mathsf{sk}_{\mathsf{TA}}) \leftarrow \mathsf{Setup}(1^\lambda)$

2 : $((\mathsf{usk}_0, \mathsf{warr}_0), (\mathsf{usk}_1, \mathsf{warr}_1), \mathsf{m}, \Psi) \leftarrow \mathcal{A}_1(\mathsf{pp}, \mathsf{skd}_0 :$

$\mathcal{O}_{\mathsf{RegU}}, \mathcal{O}_{\mathsf{RegA}}, \mathcal{O}_{\mathsf{CorrU}}, \mathcal{O}_{\mathsf{CorrA}}, \mathcal{O}_{\mathsf{Tr}}, \mathcal{O}_{\mathsf{RevID}})$

3 : **if** $|\mathsf{warr}_0| = |\mathsf{warr}_1|$ **then**

4 : $\sigma_0 \leftarrow \mathsf{Sign}((\mathsf{usk}_0, \mathsf{warr}_0), \mathsf{m}, \Psi), \ \sigma_1 \leftarrow \mathsf{Sign}((\mathsf{usk}_1, \mathsf{warr}_1), \mathsf{m}, \Psi)$

5 :   **if** $\mathsf{Verify}(\mathsf{pkd}_0, (\mathsf{m}, \Psi, \sigma_0)) = 1$ and $\mathsf{Verify}(\mathsf{pkd}_0, (\mathsf{m}, \Psi, \sigma_1)) = 1$ **then**

6 : $b' \leftarrow \mathcal{A}_2(\sigma_b : \mathcal{O}_{\mathsf{Tr}})$

7 :   **return** $b' \ \wedge \ \mathcal{A}_2$ did not query $\mathcal{O}_{\mathsf{Tr}}(\mathsf{sk}_{\mathsf{TA}}, (\mathsf{m}, \Psi, \sigma_b))$

8 : **return** 0

Fig. 2. Path Anonymity Experiment for VLR-HABS

Non-frameability. Defined in Fig. 3, and based on the definition in [13], this property captures traditional unforgeability notions, i.e., that no PPT adversary can create a VLR-HABS signature without having an honestly issued warrant for a set of attributes that satisfies the policy. It also forbids an adversary from framing another user. The adversary wins if either it produces a valid VLR-HABS signature that verifies against a challenge key, or is able to perform delegation for at least one attribute on behalf of any honest authority that is not 'below' a corrupt authority. This trivially implies that the root authority must also remain honest. We also modify the original definition to include extra winning conditions that capture the scenario the adversary is able to produce a signature that verifies despite using an ID that was revoked. This can be seen in line 10 of Fig. 3. Finally, $\mathcal{A}$ also wins if it can generate a signature for which its attributes do not satisfy the policy.

Definition 4 (Non-frameability). *A VLR-HABS scheme is non-frameable if no PPT adversary $\mathcal{A}$ wins the experiment $\mathsf{Exp}^{nf}_{\mathsf{VLR}\text{-}\mathsf{HABS},\mathcal{A}}$ defined in Fig. 3, i.e., the following advantage is negligible in λ:*

$$\mathsf{Adv}^{nf}_{\mathsf{VLR}\text{-}\mathsf{HABS},\mathcal{A}}(\lambda) = \Pr[\mathsf{Exp}^{nf}_{\mathsf{VLR}\text{-}\mathsf{HABS},\mathcal{A}}(\lambda) = 1]$$

Path Traceability. This property, defined in Fig. 4, provides accountability for authorities in the delegation path. It ensures that any valid VLR-HABS signature can be traced (by the tracing authority) to the signer and the path of authorities that were involved in the issuance of the attributes. To win this game, the adversary $\mathcal{A}$ is required to satisfy one of two conditions. Firstly, it can output a VLR-HABS signature that verifies but cannot be traced (that is, the tracing algorithm fails), or secondly, one in which the tracing algorithm outputs a warrant containing at least one unknown IA or user, i.e., were not previously registered in List or AList. To prohibit trivial attacks, we require the attribute-issuing oracle to check that both entities are registered (are in List or AList) before returning a delegated attribute.

$\mathsf{Exp}^{\mathsf{nf}}_{\mathsf{VLR\text{-}HABS},\mathcal{A}}(\lambda)$

---

1 : $(\mathsf{pp}, \mathsf{skd}_0, \mathsf{sk}_{\mathsf{TA}}) \leftarrow \mathsf{Setup}(1^\lambda)$

2 : $((\sigma, m, \Psi), (\mathsf{upk}_j, \mathsf{warr}, \hat{\pi})) \leftarrow \mathcal{A}(\mathsf{pp}, \mathsf{pkd}_0, \mathsf{sk}_{\mathsf{TA}} :$

$\mathcal{O}_{\mathsf{Att}}, \mathcal{O}_{\mathsf{Sig}}, \mathcal{O}_{\mathsf{RegU}}, \mathcal{O}_{\mathsf{RegA}}, \mathcal{O}_{\mathsf{CorrU}}, \mathcal{O}_{\mathsf{CorrA}}, \mathcal{O}_{\mathsf{RevID}})$

3 :   **if** $\mathsf{Verify}(\mathsf{pkd}_0, (m, \Psi, \sigma)) \,\wedge\, \mathsf{Judge}(\mathsf{pk}_{\mathsf{TA}}, \mathsf{pkd}_0, (m, \Psi, \sigma), (\mathsf{upk}_j, \mathsf{warr}, \hat{\pi}))$ **then**

4 :   **if** $j \in \mathsf{HUList} \wedge \mathcal{A}$ did not query $\mathcal{O}_{\mathsf{Sig}}((\mathsf{usk}_j, \mathsf{warr}), m, \Psi)$ **then** , **return** 1

5 :   **if** $\exists \mathsf{a} \in \mathsf{warr} \implies (\mathsf{pkd}_0, \mathsf{pkd}_1, \dots, \mathsf{pkd}_{l-1}, \mathsf{upk}_j) = \mathsf{warr}[\mathsf{a}] \,\wedge$

6 : $\forall j \in [0, l] : (j, \mathsf{pkd}_j, \mathsf{a}) \in \mathsf{HAList} \vee$

7 : $((\exists i \in [0, l-2].\ \mathcal{A}$ didn't query $\mathcal{O}_{\mathsf{Att}}(i, \cdot, \mathsf{a}, \mathsf{pkd}_{i+1})$

and $\forall j \in [0, i] : (j, \mathsf{pkd}_j, \mathsf{a}) \in \mathsf{HAList}) \vee$

8 : $(\mathcal{A}$ did not query $\mathcal{O}_{\mathsf{Att}}(l-1, \cdot, \mathsf{a}, \mathsf{upk}_j)$

$\wedge \forall j \in [0, i] : (j, \mathsf{pkd}_j, \mathsf{a}) \in \mathsf{HAList})$) **then** , **return** 1

9 :   **if** $\Psi(A) \neq 1$, where $A := \{\mathsf{a} | \mathsf{a} \in \mathsf{warr}\}$ **then** , **return** 1

10 :   **if** $\exists i$ s.t. $\mathsf{id}_i \in \mathsf{RevokeList} \cap \mathsf{warr}$ **then** , **return** 1

11 :   **return** 0

Fig. 3. Non-Frameability Experiment for VLR-HABS

Definition 5 (Path Traceability). *A VLR-HABS scheme offers path traceability if no PPT adversary $\mathcal{A}$ can win the experiment $\mathsf{Exp}^{\mathsf{tr}}_{\mathsf{VLR\text{-}HABS},\mathcal{A}}$ defined in Fig. 4, i.e., the following advantage is negligible in λ:*

$$\mathsf{Adv}^{\mathsf{tr}}_{\mathsf{VLR\text{-}HABS},\mathcal{A}}(\lambda) = |\Pr[\mathsf{Exp}^{\mathsf{tr}}_{\mathsf{VLR\text{-}HABS},\mathcal{A}}(\lambda) = 1]|$$

4   VLR-HABS Scheme

In this section we detail the core contributions. Firstly we introduce the VLR mechanism in Sect. 4.1, then the zero-knowledge protocol in Sect. 4.2, and present the scheme itself in Sect. 4.3. Our construction makes use of a number of building blocks. Due to space limitations, we defer details to the full version [20] where we also provide descriptions of how to make them compatible with our zero knowledge proof.

4.1   New VLR Mechanism

We introduce a novel verifier-local revocation scheme that relies on the LWE and SIS hardness assumptions. For our scheme, a central authority (RevA) maintains a list of revoked identities in a list RevokeList. A user is required to produce and publish privacy-preserving revocation tokens during the signing phase of the signature scheme. As part of verification, values from RevokeList are used to check whether the revocation tokens pass or fails verification.

$\mathsf{Exp}^{\mathsf{tr}}_{\mathsf{VLR\text{-}HABS},\mathcal{A}}(\lambda)$

---

1 : $(\mathsf{pp}, \mathsf{skd}_0, \mathsf{sk}_{\mathsf{TA}}) \leftarrow \mathsf{Setup}(1^\lambda)$

2 : $((\sigma, \mathsf{m}, \Psi), (\mathsf{upk}, \mathsf{warr}, \hat{\pi})) \leftarrow \mathcal{A}(\mathsf{pp}, \mathsf{sk}_{\mathsf{TA}}$:

3 : $\mathcal{O}_{\mathrm{Att}}, O_{\mathrm{RegU}}, O_{\mathrm{RegA}}, \mathcal{O}_{\mathrm{CorrU}}, \mathcal{O}_{\mathrm{CorrA}}, O_{\mathrm{RevID}})$

4 :   **if** $\mathsf{Verify}(\mathsf{pkd}_0, (\mathsf{m}, \Psi, \sigma))$ **then**

5 :   **if** $\mathsf{Trace}(\mathsf{sk}_{\mathsf{TA}}, (\mathsf{m}, \Psi, \sigma)) = \perp$ **then** , **return** 1

6 :   **if** $\mathsf{Judge}(\mathsf{pk}_{\mathsf{TA}}, \mathsf{pkd}_0, (\mathsf{m}, \Psi, \sigma), (\mathsf{upk}, \mathsf{warr}, \hat{\pi})) \wedge$

7 : $(\exists \mathsf{a} \in \mathsf{warr} \implies (\mathsf{pkd}_0, \mathsf{pkd}_1, \dots, \mathsf{pkd}_{l-1}, \mathsf{upk}) = \mathsf{warr}[\mathsf{a}] \wedge$

8 : $((\exists i \in [0, l-2].\ i \in \mathsf{HAList} \wedge i+1 \notin \mathsf{AList}) \vee$

9 : $(l-1 \in \mathsf{HUList} \wedge (\ \cdot\ , \mathsf{upk}, \mathsf{usk}) \notin \mathsf{List})\ )\ )$ **then** , **return** 1

10 :   **return** 0

Fig. 4. Path Traceability Experiment for VLR-HABS

To create a revocation token, the user samples a uniform binary matrix $\mathbf{B} \leftarrow \mathbb{B}^{k_3 \times m_3}$ ($m_3 = m_3'(ld + 1)$) and computes the LWE instance $\mathbf{C} = \mathbf{BR}_{\mathsf{id}} + \mathbf{E}$ for each id in the delegation paths, where $\mathbf{R}_{\mathsf{id}}$ is the encodes id of the entity and $\mathbf{E}$ is an error matrix of size $k_3 \times m_3$. This is repeated for each identity contained in the delegation paths of the obtained attributes, i.e. $\mathsf{id} \in \mathsf{warr}$. In this work, we compute $\mathbf{R}_{\mathsf{id}} = [\mathbf{R} \| \mathbf{R}_1^{\mathsf{id}[1]} \| \dots \| \mathbf{R}_d^{\mathsf{id}[d]}]$ where $\mathsf{id}[i]$ is the ith bit of id and $\mathbf{R}_i^b$ are uniformly sampled matrices in $\mathbb{Z}_q^{n \times m_3'}$, and are published in the public parameters. Finally, $\mathbf{R}$ is the public key of the RevA, whose corresponding secret key is a trapdoor $\mathbf{T_R}$ that allows RevA to solve SIS instances with respect to $\mathbf{R}$. At a high level, due to the pseudo-randomness of binary-secret LWE, we argue that $\mathbf{C}$ is statistically close to a sample from a uniform distribution, thus no adversary can learn the identity committed to in $\mathbf{C}$, which more generally maintains the anonymity properties of the VLR-HABS scheme.

To revoke an identity, RevA uses its trapdoor $\mathbf{T_R}$ for $\mathbf{R}$ to compute an extended trapdoor for $\mathbf{R}_{\mathsf{id}}$, using the ExtBasis and RandBasis algorithms from Bonsai Signatures [10], recalled in the full version [20]. These algorithms allows RevA to compute a short basis for an extended matrix if it has knowledge of a trapdoor for the input matrix $\mathbf{R}$. Here, the extended matrix is $\mathbf{R}_{\mathsf{id}}$. The RandBasis algorithm randomises the extended basis, with some loss in quality, so that the trapdoor $\mathbf{T_R}$ cannot be recovered. It then invokes SampleD to compute a small vector $\mathbf{y}$ such that $\mathbf{R}_{\mathsf{id}}\mathbf{y} = \mathbf{0}$, i.e. solving the SIS problem for $\mathbf{R}_{\mathsf{id}}$. It appends $\mathbf{y}$ to a public revocation list RevokeList. During the verification phase, the verifier obtains RevokeList from the revocation authority and computes $\mathbf{Cy} = \mathbf{BR}_{\mathsf{id}}\mathbf{y} + \mathbf{Ey}$ for each $\mathbf{y} \in$ RevokeList. If id has been revoked, then $\mathbf{R}_{\mathsf{id}}\mathbf{y} = \mathbf{0}$ for some $\mathbf{y} \in$ RevokeList and hence $\mathbf{Cy} = \mathbf{BR}_{\mathsf{id}}\mathbf{y} + \mathbf{Ey} = \mathbf{B0} + \mathbf{Ey} = \mathbf{Ey}$ where $\|\mathbf{Ey}\| \leqslant n\beta^2$. If $\|\mathbf{Cy}\| > n\beta^2$ for all $\mathbf{y} \in$ RevokeList and $\mathbf{C}$ in the signature, then the verifier is assured that the signature was not generated using a revoked id.

To show the correctness of $\mathbf{C}$ and that it contains the IDs encrypted in the ciphertext, the signer is required to generate a zero-knowledge proof. In the decomposition-extension framework for Stern-like protocols, this is done by instead letting $\mathbf{R}^* := [\mathbf{R}||\mathbf{R}_1^0||\mathbf{R}_1^{(1)}||...||\mathbf{R}_d^{(0)}||\mathbf{R}_d^{(1)}]$ and proving the g relation $\mathbf{C} = \hat{f}_{id}(\mathbf{B})\mathbf{R}^* + \mathbf{E}$. See the full version [20] for definitions and how to remove the dependency of $\mathbf{A}_{id}$ on id. This makes the resulting relation linear, and is efficiently provable using the proof in Sect. 4.2. We also note that $\mathbf{R}^*$ is now public so the prover only needs to hide $\mathbf{B}, \mathbf{E}$ and id as part of the witness.

4.2   Zero-Knowledge Protocol

We define a Stern-like protocol that will form the core of our VLR-HABS scheme. The protocol will allow a signer to convince the verifier in zero-knowledge that:

1. The warrant contains a set of committed attributes that satisfy the policy.
2. For each attribute in the warrant, the signers possess a valid delegation path.
3. The ciphertext is a correct encryption of the IDs that appear in the warrant.
4. The signer's revocation token is correctly committed via an LWE function.

The protocol is instantiated with the following public parameters: $\mathbf{A}, \mathbf{R}, \{\mathbf{A}_i^b\}_{i=1}^{ld}$, $\{\mathbf{R}_i^b\}_{i=1}^d, \mathbf{G}^*, \mathbf{P}^*, \mathbf{Q}, \{\mathbf{C}_{id}\}_{id\in\text{warr}}, \{\mathbf{f}_i\}_{i=1}^\delta, \mathbf{p}, \mathbf{u}$. The prover's witness are the vectors uid, $\mathbf{z}_0, \{\mathbf{z}_i, \mathbf{a}_i, \mathbf{e}_i\}_{i=1}^\delta, \{\text{id}\}_{id\in\text{warr}}$ and the matrices $\{\mathbf{B}_{id}, \mathbf{E}_{id}\}_{id\in\text{warr}}$. The relation is defined as:

$$\mathcal{R}_1 := \begin{cases} \mathbf{A}_{[id_1||...||id_l]}(\mathbf{z}_i) = \mathbf{a}_i \mod q_1, i \in [1,\delta] \text{ and } id_j \in \text{warr}[\mathbf{a}_i] \\ \mathbf{C}_{id} = \mathbf{BR}_{id} + \mathbf{E} \mod q_3 \text{ for id} \in \text{warr} \\ \mathbf{f}_{id} = \mathbf{P}^*\mathbf{e} + \mathbf{Q}[id_1||...||uid] \mod q_2 \text{ for every id } \in \text{warr}[\mathbf{a}_i], i \in [1,\delta] \\ \langle \mathbf{a}, \mathbf{p} \rangle = 1 \text{ where } \mathbf{a} = [\mathbf{a}_1||...||\mathbf{a}_\delta] \wedge \mathbf{A}_{uid}(\mathbf{z}_0) = \mathbf{u} \mod q_1 \end{cases}$$

Theorem 1. *Let* COM *be a statistically hiding and computationally binding string commitment scheme. Then the protocol is a zero-knowledge argument of knowledge with perfect completeness with soundness error 2/3. That is:*

- *There exists a poly-time simulator that outputs an accepting transcript that is statistically close to one produced by an honest prover with a valid witness.*
- *There exists a poly-time extractor, such that, on input of a commitment* CMT *and 3 responses* $(\text{RSP}_1, \text{RSP}_2, \text{RSP}_3)$ *corresponding to each challenge* $\{1,2,3\}$, *outputs a valid witness for the relation* $\mathcal{R}_1$.

A full description of the protocol, and proof of Theorem 1, can be found in the full version of this paper. However, in the full version of this paper [20], we discuss how the sub-relation for each building block is proven along with an overview of some techniques from a line of works by Ling et al. [27–29]. Our full protocol combines these techniques to prove the relation $\mathcal{R}_1$.

4.3   Specification of VLR-HABS

We now give high-level description of our lattice-based VLR-HABS scheme and present the formal algorithms in Figs. 5 and 6.

Setup: The setup algorithm generates the public parameters and is executed by a trusted party to initiate the scheme, it begins by setting a parameter d where 2^d will be the maximum number of AAs and Users in the scheme. It samples uniformly random matrices $\{\mathbf{A}_i^{(b)}\}_{j=0}^{ld} \hookleftarrow \mathbb{Z}_q^{n_1 \times m_1}$, $\{\mathbf{R}_j^{(b)}\}_{j=1}^d \hookleftarrow \mathbb{Z}_q^{m_3 \times k_3}$ ($b \in \{0,1\}$) that generate the public keys and revocation tokens respectively. Two further matrices are computed $(\mathbf{A}, \mathbf{R})$ with corresponding trapdoors $(\mathbf{T_A}, \mathbf{R})$ according to GenBasis(n_1, m_1, q_1) and GenBasis(n_3, m_3, q_3), respectively. The key pair $(\mathsf{sk_{RA}}, \mathsf{pk_{RA}}) := (\mathbf{T_A}, \mathbf{A})$ is that of RA and $(\mathsf{sk_{RevA}}, \mathsf{pk_{RevA}}) := (\mathbf{T_R}, \mathbf{R})$ is for the RevA. The TA also generates its key pair for IBE-GPV as $(\mathsf{sk_{TA}}, \mathsf{pk_{TA}}) := (\mathbf{T_D}, \mathbf{D}) \leftarrow$ GenBasis(n_2, m_2, q_2). Finally, it samples a vector $\mathbf{u} \in \mathbb{Z}_q^{n_1}$ that is used in the key-issuing phase of the scheme, and defines the attribute universe as $\mathbb{A} = \{\mathbf{a}_i\}_{i=1}^N$, for N total attributes. It outputs these under public parameters $\mathsf{pp} := (\mathbf{A}, \mathbf{R}, \mathbf{D}, \mathbf{u}, \{\mathbf{A}_i^{(b)}\}_{j=1}^{ld}, \{\mathbf{R}_i^{(b)}\}_{j=1}^d, \mathbb{A})$, which will be an implicit input to all algorithms.

UKGen: To join the scheme, the RA selects an identity id as a binary string of length d. It computes the corresponding public key $\mathsf{upk} := \mathbf{A}_{uid}$ as $[\mathbf{A}||\mathbf{A}_1^{id[1]}||...||\mathbf{A}_d^{id[d]}]$. It computes $\mathbf{T}_{\mathbf{A}_{uid}} \leftarrow$ RandBasis(ExtBasis$(\mathbf{T_A}, \mathbf{A}_{uid}), \mathbf{u}, \beta_1)$, and then computes the user signing key as $\mathsf{usk} = \mathbf{z}_0 \leftarrow$ SampleD$(\mathbf{T}_{\mathbf{A}_{uid}}, \mathbf{A}_{uid}, \mathbf{u}, \beta_1)$, which satisfies $\mathbf{A}_{uid}\mathbf{z}_0 = \mathbf{u}$. The key pair is issued to the user.

AKGen: For an Authority joining the scheme, it is issued an identity id $\in \{0,1\}^d$. The keys for the authorities are issued during attribute delegation as they are dependent on both the attribute and position within the hierarchy.

AttIssue: This algorithm takes as input an attribute $\mathbf{a} = \mathbf{a}$, an AA secret key ask_i, a public key apk_{i+1} for either an IA or a user, and warr containing a matrix $\mathbf{A}_i$ with corresponding trapdoor $\mathbf{T}_{\mathbf{A}_i}$. For the attribute $\mathbf{a}$, a kth level AA extends its public key $\mathbf{A}_{id_1||...||id_i} := [\mathbf{A}||\mathbf{A}_1^{id_1[1]}||...\mathbf{A}_d^{id_1[d]}||...||\mathbf{A}_{kd+1}^{id_i[1]}||...||\mathbf{A}_{(k+1)d}^{id_i[d]}]$ to a $k+1$-level entity by computing $\mathbf{A}' \leftarrow [\mathbf{A}_{(k+1)d+1}^{id_j[1]}||...||\mathbf{A}_{(k+2)d}^{id_j[d]}]$ and executing $\mathbf{T}_{\mathbf{A}_j,\mathbf{a}} \leftarrow$ RandBasis(ExtBasis$(\mathbf{T}_{\mathbf{A}_{id}}, [\mathbf{A}_{id}||\mathbf{A}']), \mathbf{a}, \beta_1)$. If it is issuing to an authority, it sets $\mathsf{skd}_i \leftarrow \mathbf{T}_{\mathbf{A}_j,\mathbf{a}}$, if it is issuing to a user, then it first computes a Bonsai signature on $\mathbf{A}_j$ with respect to $\mathbf{a}$. That is, a short vector $\mathbf{z} \leftarrow$ SampleD$(\mathbf{T}_{\mathbf{A}_j,\mathbf{a}}, \mathbf{A}_j, \mathbf{a}, \beta_1)$ and sets $\mathsf{skd}_i = \mathbf{z}$. It appends $(\mathsf{id}, \mathbf{A}_j, \mathbf{a}, \mathsf{skd}_i)$ the (possibly empty) warrant and returns warr.

Revoke: To revoke an identity, the algorithm Revoke takes as input a user identity, id. Using its secret key, $\mathsf{sk_{RevA}} = \mathbf{T_R}$, a trapdoor for $\mathbf{R}$, it sets $\mathbf{R}_{id} = [\mathbf{R}||\mathbf{R}_1^{id[1]}||...||\mathbf{R}_d^{id[d]}]$ and then computes the revocation token $\mathbf{y}$ as a short vector that satisfies $\mathbf{R}_{id}\mathbf{y} = \mathbf{0}$. It appends $\mathbf{y}$ to RevokeList.

Sign: The signing algorithm takes as input a set of attributes $\{\mathbf{a}_i\}_{i=1}^\delta$ with associated $\{\mathbf{A}_{id_i}, \mathbf{T}_{\mathbf{A}_{id_i}} = \mathbf{z}_i\}_{i=1}^\delta$, the user's secret key $\mathsf{usk} = \mathbf{z}_0$, a message m and a policy Ψ, and we denote the signer's ID as uid for clarity. Recall that for each attribute, the delegated keys are short vectors that solve $\mathbf{A}_{id_i}\mathbf{z}_i = \mathbf{a}_i$, and similarly the public value $\mathbf{u}$ proves that the signer has knowledge of usk as it solves $\mathbf{A}_{uid}\mathbf{z}_0 = \mathbf{u}$. It then prepares its revocation tokens by computing an LWE instance as, for each id $\in$ warr, $\mathbf{C}_{id} = \mathbf{BR}_{id} + \mathbf{E}$ where $\mathbf{B}$ is a binary matrix sampled from $\mathbb{B}^{m_3 \times n_3}$ and $\mathbf{E}$ is an error matrix sampled from χ. $\mathbf{B}$ must be a binary secret so that the norm is small and we can use the zero-knowledge protocol. It generates keys for a one-time signature as (osk, ovk) and encrypts the identities of the AAs in the delegation path under the Identity-based Encryption Scheme (GPV-IBE) using ovk as a pseudo-identity. To do this, it samples $\mathbf{e}_1, \mathbf{e}_2 \leftarrow \chi$ and $\mathbf{s} \hookleftarrow \mathbb{Z}_q^n$ and computes the following: $\mathbf{f}_i^{(1)} = \mathbf{Ds} + \mathbf{e}_1, \mathbf{f}_i^{(2)} = \mathbf{N}^T \mathbf{s} + \mathbf{e}_2 + \lfloor q/2 \rfloor \mathsf{id}_i$ and sets $\mathbf{f}_i = [\mathbf{f}_i^{(1)} || \mathbf{f}_i^{(2)}]$, for each $i \in [1, \delta]$. It generates the zero-knowledge argument of knowledge π, described in Sect. 4.2 for the relation $\mathcal{R}_1$. In particular, ZKAoK ensures that for each identity that appears in a delegation path for an attribute also, it appears in a corresponding ciphertext and revocation token. This is done by showing that the vectors $\mathbf{t}_{i,\mathbf{z}}^{(j)}$ and matrices $\mathbf{T}_{id,\mathbf{B}}$ belong to the sets $\mathsf{SecretExt}_\beta(d_i^{(1)})$ and $\overline{\mathsf{SecretExt}}_\beta(d_{id}^{(1)})$, respectively for a delegation path i, identity id and where the vectors d_i are the message encrypted in the ciphertext. Using the Fiat-Shamir heuristic[2]., the signer turns the interactive protocol into non-interactive and binds the message to the message, policy, revocation tokens $\mathbf{C} = \{\mathbf{C}_{id}\}_{id \in \text{warr}}$, ciphertext $\mathbf{f} := \{\mathbf{f}_i\}_{i=1}^\delta$ and proof. It computes the challenge as:

$$\mathsf{CH} = \{Ch\}_{i=1}^t = \{\mathcal{H}_1(\mathsf{m}, \Psi, \mathbf{f}, \mathbf{C}, \mathsf{ovk}, \mathsf{pp}, \mathsf{CMT}_i)\}_{i=1}^t$$

Finally, it computes a one-time signature over the proof π, ciphertext $\mathbf{f}$, message m and policy Ψ as σ_o. Since the choice of the OTS can be generic we leave the function here unspecified. However, for security and instantiation, we shall reuse the Bonsai signature scheme from [10], with use of a chameleon hash function $\mathcal{H}_2 : \mathbb{Z}_q^* \rightarrow \{0,1\}^{\tilde{m}}$. It outputs the VLR-HABS signature: $\sigma = (\mathbf{f}, \mathbf{C}, \pi, \sigma_o, \mathsf{ovk})$.

Verify: To verify a candidate signature σ, a verifier obtains the list RevokeList from the RevA, potentially offline and before the signature is presented. It parses σ as $(\mathbf{f}, \mathbf{C}, \pi, \sigma_o, \mathsf{ovk})$ and checks that π and σ_o pass verification. It then computes $\|\mathbf{C}_{id}\mathbf{y}\|$ and outputs 0 if any $\|\mathbf{C}_{id}\mathbf{y}\| \leqslant n_3 \beta_3^2$ for any $\mathbf{y} \in$ RevokeList, id $\in$ warr.

Trace: On input of a candidate VLR-HABS signature, the tracing algorithm parses σ as $(\mathbf{f}, \mathbf{C}, \pi, \sigma_o, \mathsf{ovk})$. It first verifies σ, then, using its secret key, $\mathbf{T}_D$ it can create an identity-dependent decryption key $\mathbf{S}_{\mathsf{ovk}}$ for a ciphertext $\mathbf{f}_{id}$, with which it can extract the user ID and identities of the authorities that appear in the delegation path of any attribute. This algorithm outputs $\mathbf{S}_{\mathsf{ovk}}, \{id_i\}_{i=1}^\delta$.

Judge: This algorithm is then able to verify the correctness of decryption of this IBE-GPV ciphertext. It takes as input the decryption key $\mathbf{S}_{\mathsf{ovk}}$ and checks that it is a valid key for $\mathbf{f}_i$, that is, it checks $\mathbf{DS} \stackrel{?}{=} \mathcal{H}_0(\mathsf{ovk})$ and $\|\mathbf{S}\| \leqslant \beta_2$. If this passes, it also checks the decryption is correct by evaluating $\mathbf{f} \stackrel{?}{=} \mathbf{P}^* \mathbf{e} + \mathbf{Q}id$ and outputs 1 if all checks hold, else it outputs 0. By using a one-time identity in

---

[2] As in [4], we choose to present the FS heuristic for simplicity. We note, however, that one could instantiate our scheme with the Unruh transform of [39] to achieve security in the quantum random oracle model (QROM).

our IBE scheme, we are able to bypass expensive zero-knowledge proofs in this stage and instead only require the Trace algorithm it output a verifiable key for the "identity" ovk.

Detailed Description. We provide the complete specification only for the Setup and AKGen algorithms here, and define UKGen, AttIssue, Revoke, Sign, Verify, Trace, Judge in Figs. 5 and 6.

- Setup(λ). It generates the Root Authority and Revocation Authority key-pairs as $(\mathsf{skd}_0, \mathsf{pkd}_0) := (\mathbf{T_A}, \mathbf{A}) \leftarrow \mathsf{GenBasis}(n_1, m_1, q_1)$, and $(\mathsf{sk}_{\mathrm{RevA}}, \mathsf{pk}_{\mathrm{RevA}}) := (\mathbf{T_R}, \mathbf{R}) \leftarrow \mathsf{GenBasis}(n_3, m_3, q_3)$. Next it samples random matrices $\{\mathbf{A}_i^b\}_{i=1}^{ld} \hookleftarrow \mathbb{Z}_{q_1}^{n_1 \times m_1}$ and $\{\mathbf{R}_i\}_{i=1}^{d} \hookleftarrow \mathbb{Z}_{q_3}^{n_3 \times m_3}$. During this phase, the TA keys are also computed as $(\mathsf{skd}_{TA}, \mathsf{pkd}_{TA}) = (\mathbf{T_D}, \mathbf{D}) \leftarrow \mathsf{GenBasis}(n_2, m_2, q_2)$. Define χ_2 be a β_2 bounded distribution $\mathcal{D}_{\mathbb{Z}, \alpha_2}$, and similarly let $\chi_3 = \mathcal{D}_{\mathbb{Z}, \alpha_3}$ (i.e. bounded by β_3).
- AKGen. Sample and output $\mathsf{id} \hookleftarrow \{0, 1\}^d$.

UKGen (ask_0)

0 :   Sample $\mathsf{uid} \hookleftarrow \{0, 1\}^d$

1 : $\mathbf{A}_{\mathsf{uid}} = [\mathbf{A} || \mathbf{A}_1^{\mathsf{id}[1]} || ... || \mathbf{A}_d^{\mathsf{id}[d]}]$

2 : $\mathbf{T}_{\hat{\mathbf{A}}} \leftarrow \mathsf{ExtBasis}(\mathbf{T_A}, \mathbf{A}_{\mathsf{uid}})$

3 : $\mathbf{z}_{\mathsf{uid}} \leftarrow \mathsf{SampleD}(\mathbf{T}'_{\hat{\mathbf{A}}}, \mathbf{A}_{\mathsf{uid}}, \mathbf{u}, \beta_1)$

4 : $\mathsf{id} \leftarrow \mathsf{uid}$

5 : $(\mathsf{skd}_{\mathsf{id}}, \mathsf{pkd}_{\mathsf{id}}) \leftarrow (\mathbf{z}_{\mathsf{uid}}, \mathbf{A}_{\mathsf{uid}})$

6 :   **return** $(\mathsf{id}, \mathsf{skd}_{\mathsf{id}}, \mathsf{pkd}_{\mathsf{id}})$

Revoke ($\mathbf{T_R}$, (id, RevokeList))

0 : $\mathbf{R}_{\mathsf{id}} \leftarrow [\mathbf{R} || \mathbf{R}_1^{\mathsf{id}[1]} || ... || \mathbf{R}_d^{\mathsf{id}[d]}]$

1 : $\mathbf{T}_{\mathbf{R}^*} \leftarrow \mathsf{ExtBasis}(\mathbf{T_R}, \mathbf{R}_{\mathsf{id}})$

2 : $\mathbf{y} \leftarrow \mathsf{SampleD}(\mathbf{T}'_{\mathbf{R}^*}, \mathbf{R}^*, \mathbf{0}, \beta_3)$

3 :   RevokeList $\leftarrow$ RevokeList $\cup \{\mathbf{y}\}$

4 :   **return** RevokeList

Judge (σ, warr, $\mathbf{S}_{\mathsf{ovk}}$, RevokeList)

0 :   Parse σ as

       $(\pi, \Psi, \mathsf{m}, \{[\mathbf{f}_1^{(i)} || \mathbf{f}_2^{(i)}]^T\}_{i=1}^\delta, \{\mathbf{C}_i\}_{i=1}^{l\delta})$

1 :   **if** $\exists i$ s.t. $\lfloor \mathbf{f}_2^{(i)} - \mathbf{S}_{\mathsf{ovk}} \cdot \mathbf{f}_1^{(i)} \rceil \neq \mathsf{warr}[i]$,

       return 0

2 :   **elseif** $\mathbf{DS}_{\mathsf{ovk}} \neq \mathcal{H}_0(\mathsf{ovk})$, **return** 0

3 :   **else return** 1

Trace (σ, $\mathbf{T_D}$, RevokeList)

0 :   Parse σ as $(\pi, \Psi, \mathsf{m}, \{\mathbf{f}_i\}_{i=1}^\delta, \{\mathbf{C}_i\}_{i=1}^{l\delta})$

1 :   **if** $\mathsf{Verify}(\mathbf{A}_0, (\pi, \sigma_o, \mathsf{ovk}, \{\mathbf{f}_i\}_{i=1}^\delta,$

       $\{\mathbf{C}_i\}_{i=1}^{l\delta}), \mathsf{RevokeList}) = 1$ **then**

2 : $\mathbf{S}_{\mathsf{ovk}} \leftarrow \mathsf{SampleD}(\mathbf{T_D}, \mathbf{D}, \mathcal{H}_0(\mathsf{ovk}), \beta_2)$

3 :   **for** $i \in [1, ..., \delta]$:

4 :   Parse $\mathbf{f}_i = [\mathbf{f}_i^{(1)} || \mathbf{f}_i^{(2)}]$

5 : $[\mathsf{id}_1 || ... || \mathsf{uid}] = \lfloor \mathbf{f}_i^{(1)} - \mathbf{S}_{\mathsf{ovk}} \cdot \mathbf{f}_i^{(2)} \rceil$

6 : $\mathsf{warr} = \mathsf{warr} \cup \{\mathsf{id}_1, ..., \mathsf{uid}\}$

7 :   **return** $(\mathsf{warr}, \mathbf{S}_{\mathsf{ovk}})$

8 :   **else return** $\bot$

Fig. 5. Algorithms UKGen, Revoke, Trace and Judge of our VLR-HABS construction.

AttIssue (warr$_i$, a, [pkd$_j$|upk])

---

0 :   Parse (skd$_{i,a}$, pkd$_j$) as (($\mathbf{T}_{\mathbf{A}_i,\mathbf{a}}$, $\mathbf{A}_i$, id$_i$), $\mathbf{A}_j$, id$_j$)

1 : $\mathbf{A}' \leftarrow [\mathbf{A}_{(k+1)d+1}^{\mathrm{id}_j[1]}||...||\mathbf{A}_{(k+2)d}^{\mathrm{id}_j[d]}]$

2 : $\mathbf{T}'_{\mathbf{A}^*} \leftarrow$ RandBasis(ExtBasis($\mathbf{T}_{\mathbf{A}_{\mathrm{id}}}$, [$\mathbf{A}_{\mathrm{id}}||\mathbf{A}'$]), a, β_1)

3 :   **if** $|\mathrm{id}_j| = ld$ **then**

4 : $\mathbf{z}_j \leftarrow$ SampleD($\mathbf{T}'_{\mathbf{A}^*}$, [$\mathbf{A}_i||\mathbf{A}_j$], a, β_1)

5 :   skd$_{j,\mathbf{a}} \leftarrow \mathbf{z}_j$

6 :   **else** ,   skd$_{j,\mathbf{a}} \leftarrow \mathbf{T}_{\mathbf{A}^*}$

7 :   **return** warr $=$ warr$_i \cup \{$id$_j$, $\mathbf{A}_j$, skd$_{j,\mathbf{a}}$, a$\}$

Sign ((usk, warr), pkd$_{\mathrm{id}}$, m, Ψ)

---

0 :   Parse warr as $\{$id$_{i,j}$, $\mathbf{A}_{i,j}$, $\mathbf{z}_i$, $\mathbf{a}_i\}_{i\in[1,\delta],j\in[1,l]}$ with $|\Psi| = \delta$

1 :   (ovk, osk) $\leftarrow$ OTS.KGen(λ)

2 : $\mathbf{N} := \mathcal{H}_0$(ovk), $\mathbf{s} \hookleftarrow \mathbb{Z}_q^n$, $\mathbf{e}_1 \hookleftarrow \chi_2$, $\mathbf{e}_2 \hookleftarrow \chi_2$

3 :   **foreach** $i \in [1,\delta]$ compute

4 : $\mathbf{f}_i^{(1)} = \mathbf{D}^T\mathbf{s} + \mathbf{e}_1$, $\mathbf{f}_i^{(2)} = \mathbf{N}^T\mathbf{s} + \mathbf{e}_2 + \lfloor q/2 \rfloor$id$_i$ and set $\mathbf{f}_i = [\mathbf{f}_i^{(1)}||\mathbf{f}_i^{(2)}]$

5 :   **foreach** $i \in$ warr

6 : $\mathbf{R}_i \leftarrow [\mathbf{R}||\mathbf{R}_1^{\mathrm{id}[1]}||...||\mathbf{R}_d^{\mathrm{id}[d]}]$, $\mathbf{B}_i \hookleftarrow \mathbb{B}^{k_2\times(d+1)n_2}$, $\mathbf{E}_i \hookleftarrow \chi_3^m$.
         Compute $\mathbf{C}_i \leftarrow \mathbf{B}_i\mathbf{R}_i + \mathbf{E}_i$

7 :   Set $\mathbf{f} := \{\mathbf{f}_i\}_{i=1}^{\delta}$, $\mathbf{C} := \{\mathbf{C}_i\}_{i\in\mathrm{warr}}$

8 : $\pi := (\{\mathsf{CMT}_i, \mathsf{RSP}_i, \mathsf{CH}_i\}_{i=1}^t) \leftarrow$ ZKAoK(uid, $\mathbf{z}_0$, $\{$id$_i$, $\mathbf{B}_i$, $\mathbf{E}_i\}_{i\in\mathrm{warr}}$,
                                    $\{\mathbf{e}_i, \mathbf{z}_i, \mathbf{a}_i\}_{i=1}^{\delta}$, $(\mathbf{C}, \mathbf{Q}, \mathbf{P}, \mathbf{f}, \mathrm{ovk}, \Psi, \mathrm{pp})$, $\mathcal{R}_1$)

9 : $\sigma_o \leftarrow$ OTS.Sign(osk, $\mathcal{H}_2$(m, Ψ, π, $\mathbf{f}$, $\mathbf{C}$))

10 :   **return** $\sigma \leftarrow (\pi, \sigma_o, \mathrm{ovk}, \mathbf{f}, \mathbf{C})$

Verify (pkd$_0$, σ, RevokeList)

---

0 :   Parse σ as $(\pi, \sigma_o, \mathrm{ovk}, \{\mathbf{f}_i\}_{i=1}^{\delta}, \{\mathbf{C}_i\}_{i\in\mathrm{warr}})$

1 :   **if** $\exists \mathbf{y} \in$ RevokeList and $\exists \mathbf{C}_i : i \in$ warr s.t. $\|\mathbf{C}_i\mathbf{y}\| \leqslant n_3\beta_3^2$, **return** 0

2 :   **if** ZKAoK.Verify(π, Ψ, m, $\{\mathbf{C}_i\}_{i=1}^{l\delta}$) $\neq 1$, **return** 0

3 :   **if** OTS.Verify(ovk, σ_o, $\mathcal{H}_2$(m, Ψ, π, $\mathbf{f}$, $\mathbf{C}$)) $\neq 1$, **return** 0

4 :   **else return** 1

Fig. 6. Algorithms AttIssue, Sign and Verify of our VLR-HABS construction.

5   Security, Efficiency and Extensions

In this section, we state the security theorems, followed by efficiency considerations and parameter selection for our VLR-HABS scheme. We start by giving two lemmata that we will use in the analysis of our scheme. The proofs for Lemmas 1 to 5, and Theorems 2 and 3 are given in the full version of this paper [20].

Lemma 1. *Let $\beta = \mathsf{poly}(n)$, $q \geqslant (2n\beta^2 + 1)^2$ and $m \geqslant 2n$, then for a fixed $\mathbf{y} \in \mathbb{Z}_q^m$ with $\|\mathbf{y}\|_\infty \leqslant \beta$, and a uniformly random matrix $\mathbf{C} \hookleftarrow \mathbb{Z}_q^{k \times m}$, we have $\Pr[\|\mathbf{Cy}\|_\infty \leqslant n\beta^2] \leqslant \mathsf{negl}(n)$.*

Lemma 2. *Let $\beta = \mathsf{poly}(n)$, then for $(\mathbf{R}, \mathbf{B}, \mathbf{C}, \mathbf{E}, \mathbf{y}) \in \mathbb{Z}_q^{m \times k} \times \mathbb{Z}_q^{n \times m} \times \mathbb{Z}_q^{n \times k} \times \mathbb{Z}_q^{n \times k} \times \mathbb{Z}_q^k$ such that $\mathbf{Ry} = \mathbf{0}$ with $\|\mathbf{y}\|_\infty \leqslant \beta$ and $\mathbf{C} = \mathbf{BR} + \mathbf{E}$, where $\mathbf{B}, \mathbf{R}$ are uniformly random and $\mathbf{E}$ is drawn from β-bounded distribution χ over $\mathbb{Z}_q^n$, then $\Pr[\|\mathbf{Cy}\|_\infty \leqslant n\beta^2] = 1$.*

Theorem 2. *Our* VLR-HABS *construction given in Figs. 5 and 6 is correct.*

Theorem 3. *Let* COM *be a statistically hiding and computationally binding string commitment scheme. Then our* VLR-HABS *construction given in Figs. 5 and 6 offers path anonymity, non-frameability and path traceability in the Random Oracle Model if the* $\mathsf{LWE}_{n_2, m_2, q_2, \chi_2}$, $\mathsf{LWE}_{n_3, m_3, q_3, \chi_3}$ *and* $\mathsf{SIS}_{n_5, m_5, q_5, \beta_5}$, $\mathsf{SIS}_{n_1, m_1, q_1, \beta_1}$ *and* $\mathsf{SIS}_{n_4, m_4, q_4, \beta_4}$ *problems are computationally infeasible in λ, $\mathcal{H}_0$ and $\mathcal{H}_2$ are collision resistant and $\mathcal{H}_1$ is a random oracle.*

5.1 Efficiency and Parameters

We instantiate the scheme with the parameter choices given in Table 1. We used the estimator by Albrecht et al. [2] to evaluate the estimated security of each LWE and SIS instance. For the values relating to the Bonsai signature, GPV-IBE, OTS and KTX commitment scheme COM, we directly use conditions as given in their original works. For the ZKAoK we use the parameters of the underlying commitment scheme and use a soundness parameter $t = \omega(\lambda)$. The values for n_i are assumed to be fixed and are typically a small polynomials in λ. The VLR mechanism uses values from the trapdoor delegation in [10] restricted to the conditions of Lemmas 1 and 2. Public keys are elements of $\mathbb{Z}_q^{n_1 \times m_1}$ which is quadratic in n_1. The signing operation takes $t \cdot \mathcal{O}(|\mathsf{warr}|(n_1^2 + n_2^2 + n_3^2) + n_4^2)$ steps and the length of signature is also quadratic in the parameter n_1. The revocation check that completes the verification algorithm is linear in the number of revoked users, which matches other VLR schemes such as [24] where they note this complexity for VLR seems unavoidable. The Trace and Judge algorithms are linear in $|\mathsf{warr}|$.

We briefly note some final generic changes to improve upon efficiency. Firstly, the protocol benefits from the pre-computation of offline/online signatures [36] that are naturally compatible with our one-time signature. Here, the OTS signature is produced ahead of time (potentially batched), using a chameleon hash function for $\mathcal{H}_3$, that would allow the signer to find a corresponding randomness to match the message it must sign when generating the VLR-HABS signature. Secondly, commitments in ZKAoK can be hashed prior to sending to minimise size of the signature, at the expense of additional hash computations by the signer and verifier. Thirdly, delegation of a short basis has order $\mathcal{O}(n^2)$. More efficient trapdoor delegations exist, e.g. the lattice trapdoor by Micciancio and Peikert [33], however it is not clear how to argue security as the structure of the resulting Boyen signature does not lend itself to be embedded over multiple delegations. Finding a more efficient yet compatible trapdoor could be viewed as an interesting open problem. Finally, we note using complexity assumptions and tools for ideal lattices [31] instead of integral lattices reduce most of their associated operations by about a linear factor in the security parameter.

Table 1. Parameter Selection for VLR-HABS based on its building blocks. We target 128-bit security, therefore set the soundness parameter $t = 219$. ID bit length $d = 16$, which supports 65536 entities across a hierarchy of depth $l = 3$. Note m_i' are the number of samples in LWE & SIS challenges.

Building Blocks	i	n_i	m_i'	m_i	q_i	β_i	α_i
Bonsai Signature	1	500	618	9840	2^{21}	31440	—
GPV-IBE	2	400	—	16800	2^{16}	—	10^{-4}
VLR	3	1400	1840	29440	2^{62}	—	10^{-3}
OTS	4	500	41	656	2^{21}	31440	—
COM	5	400	—	25600	2^{16}	3200	—

5.2   Revoking Attributes

We now briefly describe how to achieve attribute revocation for our VLR-HABS scheme. We observe that we can apply similar techniques to those used to revoke users. In particular, the signer, upon generating a VLR-HABS signature, also commits to the attributes as LWE instances $\mathbf{C} = \mathbf{B}\tilde{\mathbf{A}} + \mathbf{E}$, where $\tilde{\mathbf{A}}$ is the binary decomposition of an attribute concatenated with $\mathbf{R}$, $[\mathbf{R}||\mathbf{a}]$. Revocation is then performed by the authority by computing a short vector such that $\|\mathbf{C}\mathbf{y}\| \leqslant n\beta^2$. The argument ZKAoK would have to be modified to show that the attributes are correctly committed to. Minor modifications to the security properties path anonymity, non-frameability and path traceability would be required. In particular, in path anonymity we prevent the adversary from revoking an attribute used in the challenge signature, as this would allow it to trivially break path anonymity. This can be achieved by standard bookkeeping techniques and the proofs follow a similar strategy.

Revoking an attribute for a specific user is similarly possible by altering the delegation process to delegate an attribute of the form id||att (the bit-string concatenation) and further requiring the ZKAoK to link id to the identity used in $\mathbf{A}_{id}$ and $\mathbf{R}_{id}$. This could be achieved using the techniques already used in the zero-knowledge protocol. We finally note that this would require the policy to be encoded in a specific format that, intuitively, ignores the first d bits of the attribute id||att.

6 Conclusion

The VLR-HABS scheme proposed in this paper improves upon security and functionality of existing HABS constructions by proposing a lattice-based scheme which supports verifier-local revocation and a wider range of signing policies. Our scheme is based on LWE and SIS assumptions which are believed to offer post-quantum security. It supports inner-product relations which allow for conjunctive, disjunctive and threshold policies as well as polynomial evaluations of attributes. Revocation in our HABS schemes uses a novel VLR mechanism that allows revocation of signers, attributes as well as intermediate authorities. Our scheme also implies the first lattice-based (non-hierarchical) ABS scheme with these properties.

References

1. Ajtai, M.: Generating hard instances of lattice problems. In: STOC 1996. ACM (1996)
2. Albrecht, M.R., Player, R., Scott, S.: On the concrete hardness of learning with errors. J. Math. Cryptol. **9**, 169–203 (2015)
3. Ateniese, G., Song, D., Tsudik, G.: Quasi-efficient revocation of group signatures. In: Blaze, M. (ed.) FC 2002. LNCS, vol. 2357, pp. 183–197. Springer, Heidelberg (2003). https://doi.org/10.1007/3-540-36504-4_14
4. Bansarkhani, R.E., Kaafarani, A.E.: Post-quantum attribute-based signatures from lattice assumptions. Cryptology ePrint Archive, Report 2016/823 (2016). https://eprint.iacr.org/2016/823
5. Baum, C., Lin, H., Oechsner, S.: Towards practical lattice-based one-time linkable ring signatures. In: Naccache, D., et al. (eds.) ICICS 2018. LNCS, vol. 11149, pp. 303–322. Springer, Cham (2018). https://doi.org/10.1007/978-3-030-01950-1_18
6. Boneh, D., Shacham, H.: Group signatures with verifier-local revocation. In: CCS 2004. ACM (2004)
7. Brickell, E.: An efficient protocol for anonymously providing assurance of the container of a private key (2003)
8. Bringer, J., Patey, A.: Backward unlinkability for a VLR group signature scheme with efficient revocation check. In: SECRYPT, vol. 2012 (2011)
9. Camenisch, J., Neven, G., Rückert, M.: Fully anonymous attribute tokens from lattices. In: Visconti, I., De Prisco, R. (eds.) SCN 2012. LNCS, vol. 7485, pp. 57–75. Springer, Heidelberg (2012). https://doi.org/10.1007/978-3-642-32928-9_4
10. Cash, D., Hofheinz, D., Kiltz, E., Peikert, C.: Bonsai trees, or how to delegate a lattice basis. J. Cryptol. **25**(4), 601–639 (2012)
11. Cayrel, P.-L., Lindner, R., Rückert, M., Silva, R.: A lattice-based threshold ring signature scheme. In: Abdalla, M., Barreto, P.S.L.M. (eds.) LATINCRYPT 2010. LNCS, vol. 6212, pp. 255–272. Springer, Heidelberg (2010). https://doi.org/10.1007/978-3-642-14712-8_16
12. Chu, C.-K., Liu, J.K., Huang, X., Zhou, J.: Verifier-local revocation group signatures with time-bound keys. In: ASIACCS. ACM (2012)
13. Drăgan, C.-C., Gardham, D., Manulis, M.: Hierarchical attribute-based signatures. In: Camenisch, J., Papadimitratos, P. (eds.) CANS 2018. LNCS, vol. 11124, pp. 213–234. Springer, Cham (2018). https://doi.org/10.1007/978-3-030-00434-7_11

14. El Kaafarani, A., Ghadafi, E.: Attribute-based signatures with user-controlled linkability without random oracles. In: O'Neill, M. (ed.) IMACC 2017. LNCS, vol. 10655, pp. 161–184. Springer, Cham (2017). https://doi.org/10.1007/978-3-319-71045-7_9

15. El Kaafarani, A., Ghadafi, E., Khader, D.: Decentralized traceable attribute-based signatures. In: Benaloh, J. (ed.) CT-RSA 2014. LNCS, vol. 8366, pp. 327–348. Springer, Cham (2014). https://doi.org/10.1007/978-3-319-04852-9_17

16. El Kaafarani, A., Katsumata, S.: Attribute-based signatures for unbounded circuits in the ROM and efficient instantiations from lattices. In: Abdalla, M., Dahab, R. (eds.) PKC 2018. LNCS, vol. 10770, pp. 89–119. Springer, Cham (2018). https://doi.org/10.1007/978-3-319-76581-5_4

17. Escala, A., Herranz, J., Morillo, P.: Revocable attribute-based signatures with adaptive security in the standard model. In: Nitaj, A., Pointcheval, D. (eds.) AFRICACRYPT 2011. LNCS, vol. 6737, pp. 224–241. Springer, Heidelberg (2011). https://doi.org/10.1007/978-3-642-21969-6_14

18. Gardham, D.: Hierarchical attribute-based signatures. Ph.D. thesis, University of Surrey (2021)

19. Gardham, D., Manulis, M.: Hierarchical attribute-based signatures: short keys and optimal signature length. In: Deng, R.H., Gauthier-Umaña, V., Ochoa, M., Yung, M. (eds.) ACNS 2019. LNCS, vol. 11464, pp. 89–109. Springer, Cham (2019). https://doi.org/10.1007/978-3-030-21568-2_5

20. Gardham, D., Manulis, M.: Revocable hierarchical attribute-based signatures from lattices. Cryptology ePrint Archive, Report 2022/397 (2022)

21. Groth, J., Sahai, A.: Efficient non-interactive proof systems for bilinear groups. In: Smart, N. (ed.) EUROCRYPT 2008. LNCS, vol. 4965, pp. 415–432. Springer, Heidelberg (2008). https://doi.org/10.1007/978-3-540-78967-3_24

22. Herranz, J.: Attribute-based signatures from RSA. Theor. Comput. Sci. **527**, 73–82 (2014)

23. Katz, J., Sahai, A., Waters, B.: Predicate encryption supporting disjunctions, polynomial equations, and inner products. In: Smart, N. (ed.) EUROCRYPT 2008. LNCS, vol. 4965, pp. 146–162. Springer, Heidelberg (2008). https://doi.org/10.1007/978-3-540-78967-3_9

24. Langlois, A., Ling, S., Nguyen, K., Wang, H.: Lattice-based group signature scheme with verifier-local revocation. In: Krawczyk, H. (ed.) PKC 2014. LNCS, vol. 8383, pp. 345–361. Springer, Heidelberg (2014). https://doi.org/10.1007/978-3-642-54631-0_20

25. Li, J., Au, M.H., Susilo, W., Xie, D., Ren, K.: Attribute-based signature and its applications. In: ACM ASIACCS 2010, pp. 60–69. ACM (2010)

26. Libert, B., Vergnaud, D.: Group signatures with verifier-local revocation and backward unlinkability in the standard model. In: Garay, J.A., Miyaji, A., Otsuka, A. (eds.) CANS 2009. LNCS, vol. 5888, pp. 498–517. Springer, Heidelberg (2009). https://doi.org/10.1007/978-3-642-10433-6_34

27. Ling, S., Nguyen, K., Stehlé, D., Wang, H.: Improved zero-knowledge proofs of knowledge for the ISIS problem, and applications. In: Kurosawa, K., Hanaoka, G. (eds.) PKC 2013. LNCS, vol. 7778, pp. 107–124. Springer, Heidelberg (2013). https://doi.org/10.1007/978-3-642-36362-7_8

28. Ling, S., Nguyen, K., Wang, H.: Group signatures from lattices: simpler, tighter, shorter, ring-based. In: Katz, J. (ed.) PKC 2015. LNCS, vol. 9020, pp. 427–449. Springer, Heidelberg (2015). https://doi.org/10.1007/978-3-662-46447-2_19

29. Ling, S., Nguyen, K., Wang, H., Xu, Y.: Lattice-based group signatures: achieving full dynamicity with ease. In: ACNS (2017)

30. Ling, S., Nguyen, K., Wang, H., Xu, Y.: Constant-size group signatures from lattices. In: Abdalla, M., Dahab, R. (eds.) PKC 2018. LNCS, vol. 10770, pp. 58–88. Springer, Cham (2018). https://doi.org/10.1007/978-3-319-76581-5_3

31. Lyubashevsky, V., Peikert, C., Regev, O.: On ideal lattices and learning with errors over rings. In: Gilbert, H. (ed.) EUROCRYPT 2010. LNCS, vol. 6110, pp. 1–23. Springer, Heidelberg (2010). https://doi.org/10.1007/978-3-642-13190-5_1

32. Maji, H.K., Prabhakaran, M., Rosulek, M.: Attribute-based signatures. In: Kiayias, A. (ed.) CT-RSA 2011. LNCS, vol. 6558, pp. 376–392. Springer, Heidelberg (2011). https://doi.org/10.1007/978-3-642-19074-2_24

33. Micciancio, D., Peikert, C.: Trapdoors for lattices: simpler, tighter, faster, smaller. In: Pointcheval, D., Johansson, T. (eds.) EUROCRYPT 2012. LNCS, vol. 7237, pp. 700–718. Springer, Heidelberg (2012). https://doi.org/10.1007/978-3-642-29011-4_41

34. Okamoto, T., Takashima, K.: Efficient attribute-based signatures for non-monotone predicates in the standard model. In: Catalano, D., Fazio, N., Gennaro, R., Nicolosi, A. (eds.) PKC 2011. LNCS, vol. 6571, pp. 35–52. Springer, Heidelberg (2011). https://doi.org/10.1007/978-3-642-19379-8_3

35. Sakai, Y., Attrapadung, N., Hanaoka, G.: Practical attribute-based signature schemes for circuits from bilinear map. IET Inf. Secur. **12**, 184–193 (2018)

36. Shamir, A., Tauman, Y.: Improved online/offline signature schemes. In: Kilian, J. (ed.) CRYPTO 2001. LNCS, vol. 2139, pp. 355–367. Springer, Heidelberg (2001). https://doi.org/10.1007/3-540-44647-8_21

37. Su, Q., Zhang, R., Xue, R., Li, P.: Revocable attribute-based signature for blockchain-based healthcare system. IEEE Access **8**, 127884–127896 (2020)

38. Tsabary, R.: An equivalence between attribute-based signatures and homomorphic signatures, and new constructions for both. In: Kalai, Y., Reyzin, L. (eds.) TCC 2017. LNCS, vol. 10678, pp. 489–518. Springer, Cham (2017). https://doi.org/10.1007/978-3-319-70503-3_16

39. Unruh, D.: Non-interactive zero-knowledge proofs in the quantum random oracle model. In: Oswald, E., Fischlin, M. (eds.) EUROCRYPT 2015. LNCS, vol. 9057, pp. 755–784. Springer, Heidelberg (2015). https://doi.org/10.1007/978-3-662-46803-6_25

40. Wang, Q., Chen, S., Ge, A.: A new lattice-based threshold attribute-based signature scheme. In: Lopez, J., Wu, Y. (eds.) ISPEC 2015. LNCS, vol. 9065, pp. 406–420. Springer, Cham (2015). https://doi.org/10.1007/978-3-319-17533-1_28

41. Zhang, Y., Liu, X., Hu, Y., Zhang, Q., Jia, H.: Attribute-based signatures for inner-product predicate from lattices. In: Vaidya, J., Zhang, X., Li, J. (eds.) CSS 2019. LNCS, vol. 11982, pp. 173–185. Springer, Cham (2019). https://doi.org/10.1007/978-3-030-37337-5_14

42. Zhou, S., Lin, D.: Shorter verifier-local revocation group signatures from bilinear maps. In: Pointcheval, D., Mu, Y., Chen, K. (eds.) CANS 2006. LNCS, vol. 4301, pp. 126–143. Springer, Heidelberg (2006). https://doi.org/10.1007/11935070_8

Covert Authentication from Lattices

Rajendra Kumar[1]([⊠]) [iD] and Khoa Nguyen[2] [iD]

[1] Center for Quantum Technologies, National University of Singapore,
Singapore, Singapore
rjndr2503@gmail.com

[2] Institute of Cybersecurity and Cryptology, School of Computing and Information
Technology, University of Wollongong, Wollongong, Australia

Abstract. Introduced by von Ahn et al. (STOC'05), covert two-party computation is an appealing cryptographic primitive that allows Alice and Bob to securely evaluate a function on their secret inputs in a steganographic manner, i.e., even the existence of a computation is oblivious to each party - unless the output of the function is favourable to both. A prominent form of covert computation is *covert authentication*, where Alice and Bob want to authenticate each other based on their credentials, in a way such that the party who does not hold the appropriate credentials cannot pass the authentication and is even unable to distinguish a protocol instance from random noise. Jarecki (PKC'14) put forward a blueprint for designing covert authentication protocols, relying on a covert conditional key-encapsulation mechanism, an identity escrow scheme, a covert commitment scheme and a Σ-protocol satisfying several specific properties. He also proposed an instantiation based on the Strong RSA, the Decisional Quadratic Residuosity and the Decisional Diffie-Hellman assumptions. Despite being very efficient, Jarecki's construction is vulnerable against quantum adversaries. In fact, designing covert authentication protocols from post-quantum assumptions remains an open problem.

In this work, we present several contributions to the study of covert authentication protocols. First, we identify several technical obstacles in realizing Jarecki's blueprint under lattice assumptions. To remedy, we then provide a new generic construction of covert Mutual Authentication (MA) protocol, that departs from given blueprint and that requires somewhat weaker properties regarding the employed cryptographic ingredients. Next, we instantiate our generic construction based on commonly used lattice assumptions. The protocol is proven secure in the random oracle model, assuming the hardness of the Module Learning With Errors (M-LWE) and Module Short Integer Solution (M-SIS) and the NTRU problems, and hence, is potentially quantum-safe. In the process, we also develop an approximate smooth projective hashing function associated with a covert commitment, based on the M-LWE assumption. We then demonstrate that this new ingredient can be smoothly combined with existing lattice-based techniques to yield a secure covert MA scheme.

© Springer Nature Switzerland AG 2022
G. Ateniese and D. Venturi (Eds.): ACNS 2022, LNCS 13269, pp. 480–500, 2022.
https://doi.org/10.1007/978-3-031-09234-3_24

1   Introduction

The major goal of cryptography is to protect the security of the computation and communication over insecure networks. Steganography, on the other hand, aims to hide the very fact that some computation or communication has taken place. Covert cryptography is the research area that aims to simultaneously achieve the goals of both cryptography and steganography, i.e., to ensure the security of cryptographic protocols and to hide their existence from adversaries at the same time. A secure protocol is said to be covert if the communications between two parties can not be distinguished from the message flows in the public channel. Note that this is only possible when the public channel is steganographic, namely, it contains sufficient min-entropy. An example of a steganographic channel is the random channel, where messages are uniformly random over some finite ranges.

The study of covert cryptography was initiated by von Ahn et al. [40], who introduced the notion of covert two-party computation. Chandran et al. [9] subsequently generalized this notion to the multi-party setting. In these protocols, participants can compute any functionality of their inputs in a way such that no observer can distinguish the exchanged messages from random flows in the public channel, and, even protocol participants cannot determine whether the other party is following the protocol. In both constructions from [9,40], the protocols require a linear number of rounds in the circuit representations of the desired functions. In fact, Goyal and Jain [22] later showed that maliciously-secure covert computations could not be done in a constant number of rounds if there is no access to trusted parameters. However, this impossibility result can be by-passed if one assumes the existence of trusted parameters or public keys - which are mostly available in practical applications.

A prominent sub-area of covert cryptography is the study of *covert authentication*. In such protocols, two parties aim to mutually authenticate each other using verifiable certificates in a covert manner: a dishonest party who does not possess a valid certificate is not only unable to succeed in the authentication but also cannot distinguish a protocol instance from a random channel message. Jarecki [24] gave the first constant-round construction of covert mutual authentication (consisting of 5 rounds - which can be reduced to 3 rounds in the random oracle model). His protocol additionally supports the revocations of group membership, and is proven secure under the strong RSA, the DQR, and the DDH assumptions. The protocol is practically efficient, but it is vulnerable against quantum adversaries. To date, the design of covert authentication protocols based on post-quantum assumptions remains an open problem.

In this work, we aim to tackle the above discussed open question. Specifically, we study the plausibility of constructing covert authentication protocols based on lattice-based assumptions - which are among the most prominent foundations for cryptography in the post-quantum era. Lattice-based cryptography [1,18,19,21,37,38] is an emerging research direction that receives significant attention from the community. Lattices have enabled virtually any cryptographic primitives one can think of. It would be quite natural to think that it is technically straightforward to obtain a lattice-based covert authentication scheme. However, we observe that there are non-trivial challenges on the way.

In [24], Jarecki gave a blueprint to construct a covert mutual authentication (MA) protocol, based on an identity escrow scheme [28] (namely, an interactive form of group signatures [10]) and a covert conditional key encapsulation mechanism (CKEM) scheme. The latter ingredient, i.e., CKEM, can be seen as an encryption counterpart of zero-knowledge proofs (ZKP) [20] or as a generalization of smooth projective hash (SPH) functions [12] to interactive protocols. Jarecki designed a covert CKEM with the witness-extraction property (so that it would be possible to extract a group certificate in case of a forgery) via a combination of an SPH, a covert commitment scheme (i.e., one that produces uniformly random commitment values) and a Σ-protocol [11] with some special properties. The main idea is to let the prover covertly commit to his first message a as com, send response z to the challenge c from the verifier and then execute an SPH with the verifier on the statement that a, which is supposed to be recoverable based on (x, c, z), is indeed contained in com. We refer the reader to the original paper [24] for details on this generic construction.

While Jarecki's blueprint [24] can be efficiently instantiated from traditional number-theoretic assumptions, we note that there are 3 distinctions in the lattice setting: (i) Lattice-based primitives typically have to deal with noises [38], and as a consequence, it is notoriously hard to obtain exact versions of smooth projective hashing [5,25,26,42]; (ii) Existing efficient lattice-based Σ-protocols [6,16,34] normally admit a gap in soundness, namely, the language for which soundness can be achieved is a strict superset of the one used for defining zero-knowledge-ness[1]; (iii) Protocol messages in the lattices setting are not always uniformly random, e.g., they can be samples from discrete Gaussian distributions. These aspects make it challenging to realize covert MA protocols from lattice assumptions. These obstacles also inspire us to revisit Jarecki's generic construction: Can we achieve covert MA based on somewhat weaker assumptions on the underlying cryptographic ingredients?

OUR RESULTS AND TECHNIQUES. This work provides several contributions to the study of covert mutual authentication protocols. First, we revisit the notion of covertness defined in [24]. Instead of specifically requiring a uniformly random channel, we suggest a generalized formulation by assuming that the public channel messages are distributed according to a probability distribution that is efficiently and publicly sampleable. We then say that an interactive protocol is covert if its transcript can be efficiently simulated by a simulator that only has access to the public information. Second, we provide a new generic construction of covert mutual authentication, that relies on an approximate smooth projective hashing (ASPH) scheme with associated covert commitment, a key reconciliation scheme and a group authentication scheme. The first two ingredients can handle the noises as well as the soundness gap, that occur in the lattice setting,

---

[1] There exist exact lattice-based zero-knowledge proof systems with no soundness gap, e.g., [7,15,32], however, they tend to be relatively less efficient.

as discussed above. Meanwhile, the third ingredient can be seen as an interactive version of group signatures, where there is no opening authority that can break users' anonymity[2]. Hence, while our construction does not support user revocation, it can achieve a stronger security notion than the one from [24], which we call *external covertness*. This robust property guarantees that any adversary having access to all the public and private information of the protocol will not be able to distinguish between an actual protocol transcript and a simulated transcript sampled according to a given distribution.

Our next contribution is to instantiate the new generic construction from lattice assumptions. To this end, we provide a construction of ASPH based on module lattices. An ASPH scheme with covert commitment aims to compute two "nearby" hash values of the message. The first hash value is obtained by using the hashing key and the commitment, while the second one is computed using the projective key and randomness used in the commitment. Our construction is adapted from the Katz-Vaikuntanathan construction [26] that operates in general lattices. We observe that the encryption scheme used for ASPH in [26] can be replaced by a commitment scheme. The scheme's public information consists of random matrices $\mathbf{A}_1$ and $\mathbf{A}_2$ that are "tall", i.e., their numbers of rows are significantly greater than their numbers of columns. In this way, matrices $\mathbf{A}_1, \mathbf{A}_2$ do represent sparse random lattices. A commitment to a message is then a Learning-With-Errors (LWE) instance [38] of the form

$$com(m; r) := A_1 m + A_2 r + e,$$

for which the LWE secret is the message m concatenated with a random vector r. The hiding property of the scheme follows from the Module-LWE assumption [8,30]. As in [3,6], we consider a relaxed notion of binding for the employed commitment scheme, in which the set of acceptable openings could be a superset of set of honestly generated (message, randomness) pairs. More specifically, we consider the set containing the tuple (com, m, r) for which there exists a ring element z such that $\|z(com - A_1 m) - A_2 r\|$ is small. Using a technical lemma about the length of the shortest vector in the lattice generated by the random matrix, we can prove the relaxed binding property of the scheme. In the ASPH scheme to compute the first hash value h, we sample a vector f from discrete Gaussian distribution. Then, the hash value h is $f^T(com - A_1 m)$ and the projection key pk is $f^T A_2$. The second hash value h' is $pk \cdot r$. It is easy to show the correctness of the ASPH protocol. The main challenge here is to prove the Soundness, for which we need to show that when the given commitment to a message is not contained in the relaxed set then (pk, h) is statistically close to uniform over the respective domain. For this end, we use a theorem from [25] about the distribution of a matrix multiplied by a vector sampled from a Gaussian distribution. Suppose the lattice generated by the matrix has a significantly large shortest vector. In that case, the distribution of the matrix multiplied by a vector sampled from Gaussian distribution is indistinguishable from a uniform

---

[2] Alternatively, one can view group authentication as an interactive form of ring signatures [39], where there is a centralized authority who is in charge of user enrollment.

distribution. As the commitment is not contained in the relaxed set, we know that the lattice generated by the matrix $[(com - A_1 m) \ A_2]$ has a significantly large shortest vector, and by using the property, we can demonstrate the soundness of the ASPH scheme. This technical step is indeed the biggest hurdle that prevented us from directly using any of the previous lattice-based commitment schemes, such as [3,6,13,17,27,41].

An additional lattice-based technical ingredient employed in our construction is a relatively efficient group authentication (GA) scheme. A GA scheme aims to assign a certificate to group members, and enable the latter to prove their legitimate group membership via an interactive proof system. To this end, we extract a GA scheme from the lattice-based group signature of [14], which is arguably the most efficient option available to date[3]. As per Jarecki's blueprint, we need a Σ-protocol satisfying special properties for proving the relation capturing group certificate validity. However, due to the soundness gap of the protocol in [14], we are unable to prove the special soundness property on the same relation. Nevertheless, we demonstrate that special soundness holds in a relaxed manner, i.e., it holds for a superset of the relation corresponding to certificate validity, and then show that this relaxation is sufficient for our application. We note that the security notion we achieve here is stronger than the notion of certificate unforgeability considered in [24] - we refer to this property as *strong unforgeability*. Yet, the security of our construction relies on the same computational assumptions as in [14], namely, Module-LWE, Module-SIS, and NTRU.

As a summary, the generic construction and the lattice-based realization we suggest here considerably depart from the specifications of Jarecki's blueprint. We generalize the ideas of [24] and show that our modifications are sufficient to achieve covert mutual authentication in general and in the lattice setting, despite relying on somewhat weaker cryptographic ingredients. Our lattice-based protocol consists of 5 rounds and can be reduced to 3-round in the random oracle model. The scheme inherits efficiency features from the employed lattice-based building blocks [3,14,25] without a significant change in parameters.

ORGANIZATION. The rest of the paper is organized as follows. In Sect. 2, we provide our definitions and model of covertness and covert mutual authentication (MA), as well as definitions of cryptographic ingredients needed for our constructions: covert commitment schemes, approximate smooth projective hashing (ASPH), key reconciliation and group authentication (GA) protocols. In Sect. 3, we present our generic construction of covert MA. In Sect. 4, we recall some necessary background on lattices and the computational assumptions we will employ. Then, in Sect. 5, we present our lattice-based ASPH scheme on covert commitment - which is a major technical building block for instantiating our construction of covert MA based on lattices.

---

[3] Note that we can extract a GA scheme from other existing lattice-based group signature systems, such as [29,31,33], but it would be much less efficient.

2 Cryptographic Definitions and Models

2.1 Covertness and Covert Mutual Authentication

Covertness. To define the covertness of two-party protocols, we assume that the protocol runs over a public channel with periodic message flow from some probability distribution $\mathcal{T}$, which is efficiently sampleable based on the public information of the protocol. A protocol is said to be covert if the communication between two parties can not be efficiently distinguished from the message flow in the public channel. This is only possible when the public channel is steganographic, i.e., it has sufficient min-entropy. One example of steganographic channels is a random channel where messages are randomly distributed over some finite range, as used in [24].

Covert Mutual Authentication. In this work, we are interested in (implicit) mutual authentication protocols based on the membership of a given group. Such a protocol allows two certified group members to establish a random shared key if they both honestly follow the protocol.

A group involves a group manager (GM) and a polynomial (in security parameter τ) number of group members. A Mutual Authentication (MA) protocol is a triple of algorithms $(\mathbf{KG}, \mathbf{CG}, \mathbf{Auth})$. Algorithm $\mathbf{KG}(1^\tau)$ returns (mpk, msk), where msk (master secret key) is only known to the GM and mpk (master public key) is a public information. For group member with identity i, GM assigns a certificate $sk_i \leftarrow \mathbf{CG}(i, msk)$. For authentication between P_i and P_j, both parties run interactive protocol $\mathbf{Auth}$ with P_i's input $(mpk, (sk_i, i))$ and P_j's input$(mpk', (sk_j, j))$, and get keys K and K' respectively. If $mpk = mpk'$ and if (sk_i, i) and (sk_j, j) are valid group certificates under mpk, then $K = K'$, Otherwise (K, K') are independent and uniformly random numbers.

We say that an MA protocol is covert if it satisfies the properties of internal covertness and external covertness, defined as follows.

1. Internal Covertness: There exists an efficiently sampleable distribution $\mathcal{T}$, such that for any PPT adversary (excluding group manager and group members), acting as one of the parties in the authentication protocol, it is infeasible for the adversary to distinguish with non-negligible advantage whether the honest party is following the protocol or sending the messages generated according to distribution $\mathcal{T}$.

2. External Covertness: There exists an efficiently sampleable distribution $\widetilde{\mathcal{T}}$ such that for any PPT adversary (including the group manager and group members), who does not have access to the randomness used in the execution of the protocol, it is infeasible for the adversary to distinguish with non-negligible advantage between the transcript generated by the valid execution of the protocol and transcript sampled according to distribution $\widetilde{\mathcal{T}}$.

We define security games G and $\widetilde{G}$ for PPT adversaries $\mathcal{A}$ and $\widetilde{\mathcal{A}}$, denoted by $\mathcal{G}_{\mathcal{A}}(1^\tau, b)$ and $\widetilde{\mathcal{G}}_{\widetilde{\mathcal{A}}}(1^\tau, \widetilde{b})$, respectively, where game G represents the internal covertness property and game $\widetilde{G}$ represents the external covertness property.

Adversary $\mathcal{A}$ only has access to the public parameter of the protocol. In terms of known information, adversary $\widetilde{\mathcal{A}}$ is more powerful than $\mathcal{A}$ and has access to msk and the certificates sk_i's for all group members. Let u and $\widetilde{u}$ be sequences of random bits sampled from some fixed, efficiently sampleable distributions $\mathcal{T}$ and $\widetilde{\mathcal{T}}$, respectively.

- Generate $(mpk, msk) \leftarrow \mathbf{KG}(1^\tau)$. Let $N := \mathrm{poly}(\tau)$ be the number of group members and compute $sk_i \leftarrow \mathbf{CG}(msk, i)$ for $i \in [N]$.
- **Game** $\mathcal{G}_{\mathcal{A}}(1^\tau, b)$:
  1. Adversary $\mathcal{A}$ is allowed to make $\mathrm{poly}(\tau)$ number of calls to $\mathbf{Exec}(\bullet)$.
     - $\mathbf{Exec}(i)$: Execute the $\mathbf{Auth}$ protocol with input $(mpk, (sk_i, i))$, interacting with adversary $\mathcal{A}$.
  2. Adversary $\mathcal{A}$ return identity i^* of a group member.
  3. Adversary $\mathcal{A}$ is allowed to make only one call to $\mathbf{Test}(i^*)$.
     - $\mathbf{Test}(i)$: If $b = 1$, then execute $\mathbf{Auth}$ protocol with input $(mpk, (sk_i, i))$ interacting with adversary $\mathcal{A}$, and send the local output K to $\mathcal{A}$. Otherwise, send random message u sampled from the distribution $\mathcal{T}$ and send a random key to adversary $\mathcal{A}$.
  4. When $\mathcal{A}$ halts and outputs a bit b^*, the game outputs the same bit b^*.
- **Game** $\widetilde{\mathcal{G}}_{\widetilde{\mathcal{A}}}(1^\tau, \widetilde{b})$:
  1. $\widetilde{\mathcal{A}}$ is given the key pair (mpk, msk) and certificates sk_i's for all $i \in [N]$.
  2. $\widetilde{\mathcal{A}}$ returns identities i^* and j^* of two group members.
  3. Adversary $\widetilde{\mathcal{A}}$ is allowed to make only one call to $\mathbf{ExtTest}(i^*, j^*)$.
     - $\mathbf{ExtTest}(i, j)$: If $\widetilde{b} = 1$, then the challenger sends a transcript of an authentication protocol between group members i and j. Otherwise, the challenger sends a string $\widetilde{u}$ sampled from a distribution $\widetilde{\mathcal{T}}$.
  4. $\widetilde{\mathcal{A}}$ halts and outputs a bit $\widetilde{b}^*$. Game $\widetilde{G}$ outputs the same bit $\widetilde{b}^*$.

Definition 1. *An MA scheme $(\mathbf{KG}, \mathbf{CG}, \mathbf{Auth})$ is said to satisfy the internal covertness property if for any PPT adversary $\mathcal{A}$, the advantage $\varepsilon = |\Pr[\mathcal{G}_{\mathcal{A}}(1^\tau, 0) = 1] - \Pr[\mathcal{G}_{\mathcal{A}}(1^\tau, 1) = 1]|$ is negligible in τ.*

Definition 2. *An MA scheme $(\mathbf{KG}, \mathbf{CG}, \mathbf{Auth})$ is said to satisfy the external covertness property if for any PPT adversary $\widetilde{\mathcal{A}}$, the advantage $\varepsilon = |\Pr[\widetilde{\mathcal{G}}_{\widetilde{\mathcal{A}}}(1^\tau, 0) = 1] - \Pr[\widetilde{\mathcal{G}}_{\widetilde{\mathcal{A}}}(1^\tau, 1) = 1]|$ is negligible in τ.*

2.2 Covert Commitment Schemes

Let $\Pi = (\mathbf{Gen}, \mathbf{Com}, \mathbf{Verify})$ be a commitment scheme with message space $\mathcal{M}$. For security parameter λ, algorithm $\mathbf{Gen}(\lambda)$ generates the commitment public key e. For any message $m \in \mathcal{M}$, algorithm $\mathbf{Com}(m, e)$ computes the commitment c and witness r. To open the commitment c, given witness r and message m, verification algorithm $\mathbf{Verify}(c, r, m)$ outputs 1 for accept or 0 for reject.

The standard security properties of commitment schemes are binding and hiding, which can be defined in the perfect, statistical or computational sense. Here, we require the covertness property, which says that for any message $m \in \mathcal{M}$, the distribution of commitment value c over the randomness r is indistinguishable from the uniform distribution over commitment space. Note that covertness is a stronger notion than hiding, i.e., the former implies the latter.

2.3   Approximate Smooth Projective Hashing

We adapt from [26] the definitions of Approximate Smooth Projective Hash Function (ASPH). Let Ψ and Ψ^* be a binary relations on some sets $\mathcal{X}$ and $\mathcal{W}$, such that $(\mathcal{X}, \mathcal{W}) \supset \Psi^* \supseteq \Psi$. Let $\Pi = (\mathbf{Hash}, \mathbf{PHash})$ be a pair of algorithms for δ-ASPH scheme over relations Ψ and Ψ^*. Let Alice's input be x_A and Bob's input be (x_B, w). Alice computes $(pk, h) := \mathbf{Hash}(x_A; r)$ and sends the projection key pk to Bob. Bob computes the hash value $h' := \mathbf{PHash}(pk, x_B, w)$. It is a δ-ASPH scheme if it satisfies the following properties.

- Completeness: If $(x_A, w) \in \Psi$ and $x_A = x_B$ then

$$\Pr[\|h - h'\|_\infty > \delta] = \mathbf{negl}.$$

- Soundness: If $(x_A, w) \notin \Psi^*$, then (pk, h) is statistically close to uniform over the respective domain[4].
- Covertness: There exists an efficiently sampleable distribution $\$(\mathcal{U}_{pk})$ such that distribution of $pk \leftarrow \mathbf{Hash}(x)$ for any x is computationally indistinguishable from distribution $\$(\mathcal{U}_{pk})$.

2.4   Key Reconciliation Schemes

The aim of a Key Reconciliation (KR) scheme is to generate a common secret if and only if Alice and Bob have "close by" secrets. Let $q \in \mathbb{Z}^+$ and $\delta \in \mathbb{R}^+$. Suppose that Alice and Bob possess secrets d_1 and d_2, respectively, such that d_1 is uniformly random in $\mathbb{Z}_q$ and $|d_1 - d_2| \le \delta$. Then $\Pi = (\mathbf{Enc}_\delta, \mathbf{Dec}_\delta)$, where Alice and Bob run the algorithms $\mathbf{Enc}_\delta$ and $\mathbf{Dec}_\delta$, respectively, is a key reconciliation scheme if the following properties are satisfied.

- $\mathbf{Enc}_\delta(d_1; r)$ computes the secret η and f such that distribution of (η, f) is indistinguishable from uniform in some given ranges of integers.
- $\mathbf{Dec}_\delta(d_2, f)$ computes the secret η'. If $|d_1 - d_2| \le \delta$, then $\eta = \eta'$.

In this work, we employ the key reconciliation scheme from [25]. Let $t := \lfloor \log q \rfloor$ and $b := \lceil \log \delta \rceil$. The scheme proceeds as follows.

- $\mathbf{Enc}_\delta(d_1; r)$: Let $r_b = 1$ and $r_{b+1} = 0$. For all $j \in [t] \setminus \{b, b+1\}$, sample $r_j \leftarrow \{0, 1\}$. Then compute $f = d_1 + \sum_{j=0}^{t-1} 2^j r_j \mod q$ and $\eta = \sum_{j=b+2}^{t-1} 2^{j-b-2} r_j$.
- $\mathbf{Dec}_\delta(d_2, f)$: Compute $\eta' = \lfloor \frac{f - d_2 \mod q}{2^{b+2}} \rfloor$.

By construction, the distribution of the pair (f, η) is indistinguishable from uniformly random integers in $([q], [2^{t-b-2} - 1])$. We refer to [25, Section 3.2] for more details.

---

[4] In this work we use a relaxed soundness condition. We show that the Soundness property holds over the overwhelming proportion of instances.

2.5 Group Authentication Protocols

Group Authentication (GA) can be viewed as an interactive form of group signatures, in which there is no opening authority who can break group members' anonymity. A GA protocol allows Alice to convince Bob that she is a valid group member without revealing any additional information.

A GA scheme is a tuple of algorithms $(\mathbf{KG}, \mathbf{CG}, \mathbf{Ver}, \mathbf{Ver}^*, \mathbf{Com}, \Sigma)$. Let $\mathcal{C}$ be the challenge set and $\overline{\mathcal{C}} := \{c_1 - c_2 | c_1 \neq c_2 \in \mathcal{C}\}$. Algorithm $\mathbf{KG}(\lambda)$, where λ is the security parameter, generates the group public key gpk and group secret key gsk, where gpk is a public information and gsk is the private information of the Group Manager (GM). Let $\mathcal{S}$ be the set of identities of group members. For any identity $i \in \mathcal{S}$, algorithm $\mathbf{CG}(i, gsk)$ generates a certificate sk_i for group member with identity i, such that $\mathbf{Ver}(gpk, (sk_i, i)) = 1$. Let Ψ^{GA} be the committed certificate validity relation,

$$\Psi^{GA} = \Big\{((gpk, C), (sk, i, r)) \mid \mathbf{Ver}(gpk, (sk, i)) = 1 \text{ and } C = \mathbf{Com}(i; r)\Big\}.$$

Let $\mathbf{Ver}^*$ be a relaxed verification check, associated with a set $\overline{\mathcal{C}}$. Let $\widetilde{\Psi}^{GA} \supset \Psi^{GA}$ be the relaxed certificate validity relation,

$$\widetilde{\Psi}^{GA} = \Big\{(gpk, (sk, i, c)) \mid \mathbf{Ver}^*(gpk, (sk, i, c)) = 1\Big\}.$$

We call a GA scheme on relations Ψ^{GA} and $\widetilde{\Psi}^{GA}$ secure if it satisfies the following properties.

1. **Strong Unforgeablity:** For any PPT adversary $\mathcal{A}$, the probability that given gpk as input to $\mathcal{A}$, can output $(sk, i, c) \leftarrow \mathcal{A}(gpk)$ such that $(gpk, (sk, i, c)) \in \widetilde{\Psi}^{GA}$, is negligible in λ.
2. **Special-Σ Protocol:** The relations $(\Psi^{GA}, \widetilde{\Psi}^{GA})$ admits a Special-Σ-protocol.
3. **Covertness of Commitment:** The commitment scheme **Com** is covert.

3 Covert Mutual Authentication: Generic Constructions

In this section, we first describe a generic construction for covert Mutual Authentication (MA) schemes. To this end, we start with a Group Authentication (GA) scheme, then convert it into a covert MA scheme using an Approximate Smooth Projective Hashing (ASPH) with an associated covert commitment scheme and a Key Reconciliation (KR) scheme. Recall that Jarecki's generic construction [24] uses an exact smooth projective hashing. Here, in contrast, we show that ASPH is sufficient for the design of covert MA. We note that our construction does not support the revocation of group membership, but it enjoys a stronger security guarantee than the MA protocol proposed in [24], namely, external covertness. We then instantiate our construction under lattice-based assumptions, using the technical ingredients we developed in the previous sections.

3.1 Our Generic Construction of Covert MA

Our generic construction employs the following ingredients.

- A GA scheme $\Pi_{GA} = (\mathbf{KG}_{GA}, \mathbf{CG}_{GA}, \mathbf{Ver}, \mathbf{Ver}^*, \mathbf{Com}_{GA}, \Sigma)$ with Special Σ-protocol $\Sigma = (\mathbf{P}_1, \mathbf{P}_2, \mathbf{V})$ on relations Ψ^{GA} and $\widetilde{\Psi}^{GA}$ defined upon certificates generated by $\mathbf{CG}_{GA}$;
- A δ-ASPH system $\Pi_{ASPH} = (\mathbf{PG}, \mathbf{Com}, \mathbf{Hash}, \mathbf{PHash})$ with associated covert commitment scheme on relations Ψ and Ψ^*;
- A KR scheme $\Pi_{KR} = (\mathbf{Enc}_\delta, \mathbf{Dec}_\delta)$;
- A collision-resistant hash function $\mathcal{H}$.

The scheme $\Pi_{MA} = (\mathbf{KG}, \mathbf{CG}, \mathbf{Auth})$ then works as follows.

- **KG**: Given the security parameter λ, and the set of identities of group members $\mathcal{S}$, compute $(gpk, gsk) \leftarrow \mathbf{KG}_{GA}(\lambda)$ and $\pi \leftarrow \mathbf{PG}(\lambda)$. Set $mpk = (gpk, \pi)$ and $msk = gsk$.
- **CG**(gsk, i): Generate a certificate $(sk_i) \leftarrow \mathbf{CG}_{GA}(gsk, i)$ for the group member with identity $i \in \mathcal{S}$.
- **Auth**(i, j): P_i and P_j follow the authentication protocol with inputs (sk_i, i) and (sk_j, j), respectively.
  1. P_i computes $C_i \leftarrow \mathbf{Com}_{GA}(i, sk_i; r_i)$ and sends C_i to P_j.
  2. Let $x_i = (mpk, C_i)$ and $w_i = (sk_i, i, r_i)$. P_i runs Special Σ-protocol $\Sigma = (\mathbf{P}_1, \mathbf{P}_2, \mathbf{V})$ with input (x_i, w_i) and P_j with input x_i.
     (a) P_i computes $a_i \leftarrow \mathbf{P}_1(x_i, w_i; r_1)$ - the first message of the Σ-protocol. Then, it computes a commitment to $\mathcal{H}(a_i)$ as $(b_i) \leftarrow \mathbf{Com}(\mathcal{H}(a_i), r_2)$ and sends b_i to P_j.
     (b) When P_j sends back a challenge c_i, P_i computes the second message $z_i \leftarrow \mathbf{P}_2(x_i, w_i, r_1, c_i)$ and sends z_i to P_j.
     (c) P_j computes $a_i' = f_{\mathbf{V}}(x_i, c_i, z_i)$, $(h_i, pk_i) \leftarrow \mathbf{Hash}(b_i, \mathcal{H}(a_i'); r_3)$ and $(\eta_i, f_i) = \mathbf{Enc}_\delta(h_i; r_4)$. It sends (pk_i, f_i) to P_i and sets $K_j = \eta_i$.
     (d) P_i computes $h_i' = \mathbf{PHash}(pk_i, \mathcal{H}(a_i), r_2)$ and sets $K_i' = \mathbf{Dec}_\delta(f_i, h_i')$.
  3. P_j computes $C_j \leftarrow \mathbf{Com}_{GA}(j, sk_j; r_j)$ and sends C_j to P_i.
  4. Let $x_j = (mpk, C_j)$ and $w_j = (sk_j, j, r_j)$. P_j runs Special Σ-protocol $\Sigma = (\mathbf{P}_1, \mathbf{P}_2, \mathbf{V})$ with input (x_j, w_j) and P_i with input (x_j).
     (a) P_j computes $a_j \leftarrow \mathbf{P}_1(x_j, w_j; r_5)$ - the first message of the Σ-protocol. Then, it computes a commitment to $\mathcal{H}(a_j)$ as $(b_j) \leftarrow \mathbf{Com}(\mathcal{H}(a_j), r_6)$ and sends b_j to P_i.
     (b) Receiving challenge c_j from P_i, it computes the second message $z_j \leftarrow \mathbf{P}_2(x_j, w_j, r_5, c_j)$ and sends z_j to P_i.
     (c) P_i computes $a_j' = f_{\mathbf{V}}(x_j, c_j, z_j)$, $(h_j, pk_j) \leftarrow \mathbf{Hash}(b_j, \mathcal{H}(a_j'); r_7)$ and $(\eta_j, f_j) = \mathbf{Enc}_\delta(h_j; r_8)$. It sends (pk_j, f_j) to P_j and sets $K_i = \eta$.
     (d) P_j computes $h_j' = \mathbf{PHash}(pk_j, \mathcal{H}(a_j), r_6)$ and sets $K_j' = \mathbf{Dec}_\delta(f_j, h_j')$.
- The final secret key for P_i is $K_i \oplus K_i'$ and for P_j is $K_j \oplus K_j'$.

Correctness. Assume that both P_i and P_j have valid group membership certificates. First, by the special simulation property of the Special Σ-protocol, we get $a'_i = a_i$. Next, by the correctness of the ASPH scheme, we have $\|h_i - h'_i\| \leq \delta$. Then, by the correctness of the KR scheme, we obtain that $K'_i = K_j$. Similarly, we can show that $K'_j = K_i$. Hence, in the end of the protocol, P_i and P_j share the same secret key.

Theorem 1 (Internal Covertness). *The scheme $\Pi_{MA} = (KG, CG, Auth)$ satisfies the internal covertness property if $\Pi_{GA} = (KG_{GA}, CG_{GA}, Ver, Ver^*, Com_{GA})$ is a covert GA scheme, $\Pi_{ASPH} = (PG, Com, Hash, PHash)$ is a δ-ASPH with associated covert commitment scheme and $\Pi_{KR} = (Enc_\delta, Dec_\delta)$ is a KR scheme.*

In the proof, we let $\$(Com_{GA})$ be the distribution for the covertness of the commitment scheme $\mathbf{Com_{GA}}$ and $\$(Com)$ be the distribution for the covertness of commitment scheme $\mathbf{Com}$. Let $\$(\mathcal{U}_f)$ be the uniform distribution over the range of f from $\mathbf{Enc_\delta}$. Let $\$(\Sigma)$ be the distribution over the response (z_i) in Σ protocol. The distribution $\$(\mathcal{U}_{pk})$ is as defined in Sec. 2.3..

Proof. As there is a symmetry in the authentication protocol, we assume that the adversary $\mathcal{A}$ plays the role of P_j. Suppose that $\mathcal{A}$ can distinguish between $\mathcal{G}_\mathcal{A}(1^\tau, 0)$ and $\mathcal{G}_\mathcal{A}(1^\tau, 1)$ with advantage ε. Let $\mathcal{G}_\mathcal{A}(1^\tau, b, i^*)$ be a game which follows $\mathcal{G}_\mathcal{A}(1^\tau, b)$ but if adversary queries **Test**(i) for $i \neq i^*$ then it halts and outputs 1. It is easy to see that there exists an identity i^* for which adversary $\mathcal{A}$ distinguishes between $G_0 = \mathcal{G}_\mathcal{A}(1^\tau, 0, i^*)$ and $G_1 = \mathcal{G}_\mathcal{A}(1^\tau, 1, i^*)$ with advantage at least ε/N where N is the group size. In the rest of the proof, we will show that the distinguishing advantage between G_0 and G_1 is negligible by the games' succession.

Game G_2: Let G_2 be the game which follows G_1, except in all **Auth**(i, j) instances of **Exec**(i) and **Test**(i) queries, we modify by replacing P_i's message z_i in step (2)(b) by a message sampled from distribution $\$(\Sigma)$. Let $G_1(t)$ be the game that follows G_2 in the first t **Exec** queries while the remaining ones are as in G_1. The only difference in $G_1(t)$ and $G_1(t-1)$ is in the message (z_i), and the covertness of Special Σ-protocol ensures that $G_1(t)$ and $G_1(t-1)$ are indistinguishable. Hence G_2 and G_1 are indistinguishable.

Game G_3: Let G_3 be the game which follows G_2, except in all **Auth**(i, j) instances of **Exec**(i) and **Test**(i) queries, we modify by replacing P_i's message b_i in step (2)(a) by a message sampled from distribution $\$(Com)$. Similarly, the covertness of **Com** implies that G_3 and G_2 are indistinguishable.

Game G_4: Let G_4 be the game which follows G_3, except in all **Auth**(i, j) instances of **Exec**(i) and **Test**(i) queries, we modify by replacing P_i's message C_i in step (1) by a message sampled from distribution $\$(Com_{GA})$. Similarly, the covertness of $\mathbf{Com_{GA}}$ implies that G_4 and G_3 are indistinguishable.

Note that, in game G_4, the response to **Auth**(i, j) instance of **Exec**(i) and **Test**(i) queries is sampled by $\$(Com_{GA})$ in step (1), $\$(Com)$ in step (2)(a), and

$\$(\Sigma)$ in step (2)(b), and steps (3)-(4) depend only on the adversary's response. Hence, game G_4 can be easily simulated using the public information.

Game G_5: Let G_5 be the game that follows G_4 but in all $\mathbf{Auth}(i^*, j)$ instance triggered by $\mathbf{Test}(i^*)$, we replace P_i's message (pk_j, f_j) in step (4)(c) by uniformly random elements from respective domains. Let ε_1 be the advantage by which the adversary can distinguish between G_5 and G_4. The only difference in these two games is in (f_j, pk_j) and from the property of KR scheme we know that if (h_j, pk_j) is uniformly random then (f_j, pk_j) is uniformly random. So, adversary $\mathcal{A}$ can distinguish between (f_j, pk_j) from G_5 and G_4 only if (h_j, pk_j) is not uniformly random distributed in game G_4. For b_j, z_j and c_j from game G_4, if $((b_j, \mathcal{H}(a'_j)), \bullet) \notin \Psi^*$ where $a'_j = f_\mathbf{V}(x_j, c_j, z_j)$, then by the soundness property of the ASPH scheme, (h_j, pk_j) in game G_4 is statistically indistinguishable from uniformly random string and (f_j, pk_j) is also statistically indistinguishable from uniformly random string. Let ε_{ASPH} be the negligible advantage adversary can have in this. Hence with probability $\varepsilon_2 = \varepsilon_1 - \varepsilon_{ASPH}$, a random interaction in game G_4 with adversary yields (b_j, c_j, z_j) such that $((b_j, \mathcal{H}(a'_j)), \bullet) \in \Psi^*$. We fix the adversary initial randomness and run the interaction twice until adversary outputs b_j creates a fork. With atleast $\varepsilon_2^2/2$ probability, we get two transcripts $(b_j, c_j, z_j, \check{c}_j, \check{z}_j)$ such that $a' = f_\mathbf{V}(x_j, c_j, z_j)$, $\check{a}' = f_\mathbf{V}(x_j, \check{c}_j, \check{z}_j)$ and there exists r and $\check{r}$ satisfy $((b_j, \mathcal{H}(a')), r) \in \Psi^*$ and $((b_j, \mathcal{H}(\check{a}')), \check{r}) \in \Psi^*$. With probability at least $(1 - \varepsilon_3)$ (over public parameter of scheme $\mathbf{Com}$), the commitment scheme is perfectly binding over relation Ψ^*, and it thus implies that $\mathcal{H}(a') = \mathcal{H}(\check{a}')$. Let ε_{col} be the upper bound on the probability that the hash values of different a' and $\check{a}'$ produce a collision. Hence with probability $\varepsilon_4 = \frac{\varepsilon_2^2}{2} - \varepsilon_3 - \varepsilon_{col}$, adversary gets $(x_j, a', c_j, \check{c}_j, z_j, \check{z}_j)$ such that $c_j \neq \check{c}_j$ and $\mathbf{V}(x_j, a', c_j, z_j) = \mathbf{V}(x_j, a', \check{c}_j, \check{z}_j) = 1$. By the special soundness property of Special Σ protocol, the adversary can extract w such that $(x_j, w) \in \widetilde{\Psi}^{GA}$. If ε_4 is non-negligible, then it breaks the *Strong Unforgeability* of the scheme Π_{GA}. Hence, ε_4 is negligible, implying that ε_1 is also negligible, because ε_{ASPH}, ε_{col} and ε_3 are negligible.

Game G_6: For each $\mathbf{Auth}(i, j)$ query triggered by $\mathbf{Exec}(i)$ in game G_5, samples C_i are as from $\$(Com_{GA})$. Game G_6 exactly follows G_5, except that we revert this change by replacing $C_i \leftarrow \mathbf{Com}(i, sk_i)$ and by a similar argument used between G_4 and G_3, we get that G_5 and G_6 are indistinguishable.

Game G_7: For each $\mathbf{Auth}(i, j)$ query triggered by $\mathbf{Exec}(i)$ in game G_6 in step (2)(a), we sample b_i from the distribution $\$(Com)$. In game G_7, we revert this change by replacing $b_i \leftarrow \mathbf{Com}(\mathcal{H}(a_i))$. By a similar argument as used between G_3 and G_2, we get that G_6 and G_7 are indistinguishable.

Game G_8: For each $\mathbf{Auth}(i, j)$ query triggered by $\mathbf{Exec}(i)$ in game G_7 in step (2)(b), we sample z_i from the distribution $\$(\Sigma)$. In game G_8, we revert this change by replacing $z_i \leftarrow \mathbf{P}_2(x_i, w_i, r_1, c_i)$. By a similar argument as used between G_2 and G_1, we get that G_7 and G_8 are indistinguishable. Note that game G_8 is the same as G_0 and by succession of games we have shown that game G_0 and G_1 are indistinguishable. $\qquad\square$

Theorem 2 (External Covertness). *The given scheme $\Pi_{MA} = (KG, CG,$ Auth) satisfies the external covertness property if $\Pi_{GA} = (KG_{GA}, CG_{GA}, Ver,$ $Ver^*, Com_{GA})$ is a covert GA scheme, $\Pi_{ASPH} = (PG, Com, Hash, PHash)$ is a δ-ASPH with associated covert commitment scheme and $\Pi_{KR} =$ (Enc_δ, Dec_δ) is a KR scheme.*

We defer the proof to the full version.

Round Complexity. It is easy to see that step 1 and step 2(a) can be combined in one round. Similarly step 3 and step 4(a) can be combined. The **Auth** protocol can be executed in 5 rounds. In the first round, P_i sends C_i and b_i to P_j. In the second round, P_j sends c_i, C_j and b_j to P_i. In third round, P_i sends c_j and z_i to P_j. In the fourth round, P_j sends z_i and (pk_i, f_i) to P_i. In the fifth round, P_i sends (pk_j, f_j) to P_j. In the Random Oracle Model (ROM), the protocol can be executed in three rounds if c_i and c_j are computed as $c_i = \mathcal{H}'(x_i, b_i)$ and $c_j = \mathcal{H}'(x_j, b_j)$ for a hash function $\mathcal{H}'$ onto $\{0,1\}^\tau$ modeled as random oracle. The only issue comes in **Game** G_5 of Theorem 1 (Internal Covertness) where adversary fork two transcript with same commitment. By using the general forking lemma from [4], if adversary make almost $q_{\mathcal{H}'}$ hash queries then we get an algorithm that create the same two transcript with probability at least $\varepsilon_2 \cdot \left(\frac{\varepsilon_2}{q_{\mathcal{H}'}} - \frac{1}{2^\tau} \right)$. The rest of the proof of internal covertness follows as it is.

4   Some Background on Lattices

Let $d > 0$ be a power of 2 and q be a prime. Define the rings $\mathcal{R} := \mathbb{Z}[X]/(X^d + 1)$ and $\mathcal{R}_q := \mathbb{Z}_q[X]/(X^d + 1)$. For any element $z = \sum_{i=0}^{d-1} z_i X^i \in \mathcal{R}$, the ℓ_p norm of z, for $1 \le p < \infty$, is defined as $\|z\|_p := \left(\sum_i |z_i|^p \right)^{1/p}$, while its ℓ_∞ norm is defined as $\|z\|_\infty := \max_i \{|z_i|\}$. To compute the norm of an element $z \in \mathcal{R}_q$, we use the unique representation where $z_i \in \left[-\frac{q-1}{2}, \frac{q-1}{2} \right]$ for each coefficient of z. The norm definition can be naturally extended to vectors over $\mathcal{R}_q^k$.

We use lowercase bold letters to denote a column vector over $\mathcal{R}_q$ and uppercase bold letters to denote a matrix over $\mathcal{R}_q$. For a vector $\boldsymbol{x}$, its ith coordinate is denoted by x_i. For a matrix $\boldsymbol{M}$, we denote by M_j its jth column and by $M_{i,j}$ the element at its ith row and j^{th} column. For any probability distribution $\mathcal{D}$, we use notation $x \leftarrow \mathcal{D}$ to denote that x is sampled with probability $\mathcal{D}(x)$. When S is a finite set, we use notation $x \xleftarrow{\$} S$ to denote that x is sampled uniformly at random from S. For probability distributions $\mathcal{X}$ and $\mathcal{Y}$ over a countable set S, we use $\Delta(\mathcal{X}, \mathcal{Y})$ to denote the statistical distance between $\mathcal{X}$ and $\mathcal{Y}$ which is defined as

$$\Delta(\mathcal{X}, \mathcal{Y}) = \frac{1}{2} \sum_{x \in S} |\Pr[\mathcal{X} = x] - \Pr[\mathcal{Y} = x]|.$$

For any $\beta \in \mathbb{R}_{>0}$, we use S_β to denote the set of ring elements with infinity norm less than or equal to β, i.e., $S_\beta = \{a \in \mathcal{R} \mid \|a\|_\infty \le \beta\}$. We will use the following bounds [3,36]:

- If $\|f\|_\infty \leq \beta$ and $\|g\|_1 \leq \gamma$ then $\|f \cdot g\|_\infty \leq \beta\gamma$.
- If $\|f\|_2 \leq \beta$ and $\|g\|_2 \leq \gamma$ then $\|f \cdot g\|_\infty \leq \beta\gamma$.

We will use the following result about the factorization of a cyclotomic polynomial modulo a prime number.

Theorem 3. *[35, Corollary 1.2] Let $d \geq k > 1$ be a power of 2 and $q = 2k + 1$ mod $4k$ is a prime. Then the polynomial $X^d + 1$ factors as*

$$X^d + 1 = \prod_{j=1}^{k}(X^{d/k} - r_j) \quad \mathrm{mod}\ q$$

for distinct $r_j \in \mathbb{Z}_q \setminus \{0\}$, where $X^{d/k} - r_j$ is irreducible in $\mathbb{Z}_q[X]$. Furthermore any $y \in \mathbb{Z}_q[X]/(X^d + 1)$ that satisfies $0 < \|y\|_\infty \leq \frac{q^{1/k}}{\sqrt{k}}$ has an inverse in $\mathbb{Z}_q[X]/(X^d + 1)$.

Discrete Gaussian: For any $\sigma > 0$, $k \in \mathbb{Z}_{>0}$ and $\boldsymbol{y} \in \mathcal{R}^k$, for all $\boldsymbol{x} \in \mathcal{R}^k$, define $\rho_{\sigma,\boldsymbol{y}}(\boldsymbol{x}) := \exp\left(\frac{-\|\boldsymbol{x}-\boldsymbol{y}\|_2^2}{2\sigma^2}\right)$. For any discrete set $S \subseteq \mathcal{R}^k$, we extend the definition as $\rho_{\sigma,\boldsymbol{y}}(S) := \sum_{\boldsymbol{x}\in S} \exp\left(\frac{-\|\boldsymbol{x}-\boldsymbol{y}\|_2^2}{2\sigma^2}\right)$. We use $\boldsymbol{x} \leftarrow \mathcal{D}_{\sigma,\boldsymbol{y}}^k$ to denote that

$$\Pr_{U \sim \mathcal{D}_{\sigma,\boldsymbol{y}}^k}[\boldsymbol{x} = U] := \frac{\rho_{\sigma,\boldsymbol{y}}(\boldsymbol{x})}{\rho_{\sigma,\boldsymbol{y}}(\mathcal{R}^k)},$$

namely, $\boldsymbol{x}$ is sampled from $\mathcal{R}^k$ with probability proportional to $\rho_{\sigma,\boldsymbol{y}}(\boldsymbol{x})$. We omit the parameter $\boldsymbol{y}$ when $\boldsymbol{y} = \boldsymbol{0}$. We will use the following lemma from [2,3,34].

Lemma 1. *For any $\delta, \sigma \in \mathbb{R}^+$, $k, d \in \mathbb{Z}^+$,*

$$\Pr\left[\|\boldsymbol{x}\|_2 > \delta\sigma\sqrt{kd} \mid \boldsymbol{x} \leftarrow \mathcal{D}_\sigma^k\right] < \delta^{kd} \cdot \exp\left(\frac{kd(1-\delta^2)}{2}\right).$$

Computational Assumptions: We will work with a ring $\mathcal{R}_q = \mathbb{Z}_q[X]/(X^d + 1)$ (where d is a power of 2), and security of our construction is based on the hardness of module variants [8,30] of the Short Integer Solution (**SIS**) problem [1] and the Learning With Errors (**LWE**) problem [38], as well as on the hardness of the **NTRU** problem [23]. For convenience, we define the **M-SIS** problem in the ℓ_2 and the ℓ_∞ norm, and the **M-LWE** problem only in the ℓ_∞ norm.

Definition 3. *For any $n, m, q \in \mathbb{Z}^+$, $p \in \{2, \infty\}$ and $\beta \in \mathbb{R}^+$, the M-SIS$_{n,m,q,\beta}^p$ problem is defined as follows: Given $\boldsymbol{A} \xleftarrow{\$} \mathcal{R}_q^{n\times m}$, find $\boldsymbol{z} \in \mathcal{R}_q^{n+m}$ such that $[\boldsymbol{I}_n\ \boldsymbol{A}]\,\boldsymbol{z} = \boldsymbol{0}$ and $\beta \geq \|\boldsymbol{z}\|_p > 0$.*

Due to space constraint, we provide the reminder on other used computational assumptions and rejection sampling techniques in the full version.

5   Approximate Smooth Projective Hashing from M-LWE

In this section, we construct an Approximate Smooth Projective Hashing (ASPH) scheme with a covert commitment. We adapt the ideas used in the PAKE scheme by Katz and Vaikuntanathan [26], whose security relies on the **LWE** assumption. We observe that the encryption method used in [26] can also be seen as a commitment mechanism.

In Sect. 5.1, we provide several technical lemmas. Using them, we construct an **M-LWE**-based covert commitment scheme in Sect. 5.2 and a δ-ASPH scheme in Sect. 5.3.

5.1   Supporting Lemmas

In this section, we assume that q is a prime satisfying $q = 5 \mod 8$. We follow the technique from [30] to prove the following two lemmas.

Lemma 2. *Let q be a prime satisfying $q = 5 \mod 8$. For $\boldsymbol{B} \xleftarrow{\$} \mathcal{R}_q^{m \times k}$ with probability at most $q^{kd - dm/2}(1 + 4^{-md})$, we have:*

$$\min_{s \in \mathcal{R}_q^k \setminus \{0\}} \|\boldsymbol{Bs}\|_\infty < \frac{\sqrt{q}}{4}.$$

Proof. First we calculate the probability of $0 < \min_{s \in \mathcal{R}_q^k \setminus \{0\}} \|\boldsymbol{Bs}\|_\infty < \frac{\sqrt{q}}{4}$. By the union bound, we get

$$\sum_{\substack{t \in \mathcal{R}_q^m, \\ 0 < \|t\|_\infty < \sqrt{q}/4}} \sum_{s \in \mathcal{R}_q^k} \Pr_{\boldsymbol{B} \xleftarrow{\$} \mathcal{R}_q^{m \times k}} (\boldsymbol{Bs} = t) = \sum_{\substack{t \in \mathcal{R}_q^m, \\ 0 < \|t\|_\infty < \sqrt{q}/4}} \sum_{s \in \mathcal{R}_q^k} \prod_{i \leq m} \Pr_{b_i \xleftarrow{\$} \mathcal{R}_q^k} \left(b_i^T s = t_i\right).$$

From Theorem 3, we know that $X^d + 1$ factors into two irreducible polynomials $f_1 = X^{d/2} - r_1$ and $f_2 = X^{d/2} - r_2$ in $\mathcal{R}_q$. Hence by the Chinese Reminder Theorem (CRT), we have $\mathcal{R}_q \simeq \mathbb{F}_{q^{d/2}} \times \mathbb{F}_{q^{d/2}}$. The equality $b_i^T s = t_i$ holds iff it holds for both the CRT components. If s is nonzero in a CRT component then the equation holds with probability at most $q^{-d/2}$ in that component. Notice that, if t_i is non-zero then Theorem 3 implies that t_i is also non-zero in both the CRT components as $\|t_i\|_\infty \leq \sqrt{q}/4$. As $t \neq 0$, it implies that s should be non-zero on both CRT components to satisfy $b_i^T s = t_i$ for i where $t_i \neq 0$. So the probability can be upper bounded by

$$\sum_{\substack{t \in \mathcal{R}_q^m, \\ 0 < \|t\|_\infty < \sqrt{q}/4}} \sum_{s \in \mathcal{R}_q^k} \prod_{i \leq m} q^{-d} < \left(\frac{\sqrt{q}}{4}\right)^{dm} q^{kd} q^{-md}.$$

Now we only need to bound the probability of $\min_{s \in \mathcal{R}_q^k \setminus \{0\}} \|\boldsymbol{Bs}\|_\infty = 0$. Notice that, s is non-zero in at least one of the CRT component. By a simple probabilistic argument, we can also bound this probability by $q^{kd} q^{-md/2}$. Hence the result follows. $\square$

Lemma 3. *Let q be a prime satisfying $q = 5 \mod 8$. Given $B \in \mathcal{R}_q^{m \times k}$, for $a \xleftarrow{\$} \mathcal{R}_q^m$ with atmost $q^{(k+1)d - dm/2} 4^{-md}$ probability, we have*

$$\min_{z \in \mathcal{R}_q \setminus \{0\}, s \in \mathcal{R}_q^k} \|((za + Bs)^T, z)^T\|_\infty < \frac{\sqrt{q}}{4}.$$

Due to space restriction, we defer the proof of Lemma 3 to Full version.

We additionally need the following result from [25].

Theorem 4. *[25, Theorem 3] Let $\chi \in \mathbb{N}, \varepsilon > 0, B \in \mathcal{R}_q^{m \times k}$ and $\sigma > \frac{q\sqrt{\log(2d(1+1/\varepsilon))/\pi}}{\chi}$. If $\min_{s \in \mathcal{R}_q^k \setminus \{0\}} \|Bs\|_\infty \geq \chi$ then $\Delta(f^T B, \mathcal{U}) \leq 2\varepsilon$ where $f \leftarrow (\mathcal{D}_{\mathcal{R}, \sigma})^m$ and $\mathcal{U}$ is uniform distribution over $\mathcal{R}_q^{1 \times k}$.*

Let $\mathcal{M} := \left(\frac{\mathbb{Z}_q[X]}{\langle X^{d/2} - 1 \rangle}\right)^n \subset \mathcal{R}_q^n$. We will require the following lemma to prove the binding property of our commitment scheme.

Lemma 4. *For all but an at most 2^{-md} fraction of (a_0, A_1, A_2) over $(\mathcal{R}_q^m \times \mathcal{R}_q^{m \times n} \times \mathcal{R}_q^{m \times k})$, there does not exist $(c, m, r, z, m^*, r^*, z^*) \in (\mathcal{R}_q^m \times \mathcal{M} \times \mathcal{R}_q^k \times \mathcal{R}_q \times \mathcal{M} \times \mathcal{R}_q^k \times \mathcal{R}_q)$ such that $m \neq m^*$, and*

$$\max\{\|z\|_\infty, \|z(c - a_0 - A_1 m) - A_2 r\|_\infty\} \leq \frac{\sqrt{q}}{4}$$

and

$$\max\{\|z^*\|_\infty, \|z^*(c - a_0 - A_1 m^*) - A_2 r^*\|_\infty\} \leq \frac{\sqrt{q}}{4}.$$

Proof. Let $\Lambda' := [a_0 \ A_1]$. Fix some c, m, m^* such that $m \neq m^*$, and let

$$y := c - a_0 - A_1 m = c - A' \begin{bmatrix} 1 \\ m \end{bmatrix}$$

and

$$y^* := c - a_0 - A_1 m^* = c - A' \begin{bmatrix} 1 \\ m^* \end{bmatrix}.$$

Let $f_1 = \frac{\mathbb{Z}_q[X]}{\langle X^{d/2} - r_1 \rangle}, f_2 = \frac{\mathbb{Z}_q[X]}{\langle X^{d/2} - r_2 \rangle}$, where $X^{d/2} - r_1$ and $X^{d/2} - r_2$ are irreducible factors of $X^d - 1$ over $\mathbb{Z}_p$ as stated in Theorem 3. From the description of message space $\mathcal{M}$, we get that $m \neq m' \mod f_1$ and $m \neq m' \mod f_2$.

As $m \neq m^*$, we get that $\begin{bmatrix} 1 \\ m \end{bmatrix}$ and $\begin{bmatrix} 1 \\ m^* \end{bmatrix}$ are linearly independent. Therefore, for a uniformly random choice of a_0 and A_1, we have that y and y^* are uniformly random and independent. Let E_1 be the event that $\min_{\substack{s \in \mathcal{R}_q^k, z \in \mathcal{R}_q \\ s.t. \ 0 < \|z\| < \sqrt{q}/4}} \|yz + A_2 s\|_\infty \leq \sqrt{q}/4$ and E_2 be the event that $\min_{\substack{s \in \mathcal{R}_q^k, z^* \in \mathcal{R}_q \\ s.t. \ 0 < \|z^*\| < \sqrt{q}/4}} \|y^* z + A_2 s\|_\infty \leq \sqrt{q}/4$. From Lemma 3, we get $\Pr_{a_0, A_1}[E_1 \text{ and } E_2] \leq q^{2(k+1)d - md} \cdot 2^{-4md}$.

Now, using the union bound over c, m, m^*, we deduce that, with at most

$$q^{md+nd} \cdot q^{2(k+1)d-md} \cdot 2^{-4md} < q^{(k+n+1)2d} \cdot 2^{-4md} < 2^{-md},$$

probability over the uniform choice of (a_0, A_1, A_2) over $(\mathcal{R}_q^m \times \mathcal{R}_q^{m \times n} \times \mathcal{R}_q^{m \times k})$, there exists $(c, m, r, z, m^*, r^*, z^*)$ such that $m \neq m^*$ and

$$\|z(c - a_0 - A_1 m) - A_2 r\|_\infty \leq \frac{\sqrt{q}}{4}, \quad 0 < \|z\|_\infty \leq \frac{\sqrt{q}}{4}$$

and

$$\|z^*(c - a_0 - A_1 m^*) - A_2 r^*\|_\infty \leq \frac{\sqrt{q}}{4}, \quad 0 < \|z^*\|_\infty \leq \frac{\sqrt{q}}{4}.$$

$\square$

5.2   Covert Commitments from M-LWE

Let us first describe the commitment scheme.

- **PG**(λ): Given the security parameter λ, choose $k, n \in \mathbb{Z}^+$, $m > (k + n + 1) \log q \in \mathbb{Z}$, $\beta < \sqrt{q}/4 \in \mathbb{R}^+$, $a_0 \xleftarrow{\$} \mathcal{R}_q^m$, $A_1 \xleftarrow{\$} \mathcal{R}_q^{m \times n}$, and $A_2 \xleftarrow{\$} \mathcal{R}_q^{m \times k}$. Let $\mathcal{M} := \left(\frac{\mathbb{Z}_q[X]}{\langle X^{d/2} - 1 \rangle} \right)^n \subset \mathcal{R}_q^{n5}$.

- **Com**$(m; r, e)$: For a message $m \in \mathcal{M}$, sample vectors $r \xleftarrow{\$} \mathcal{R}_q^k$ and $e \leftarrow S_\beta^m$. Output the commitment

$$\text{Com}(m; r, e) = c = a_0 + A_1 m + A_2 r + e.$$

- **Ver**(c, m, r, z): Output 1 if $\|z(c - a_0 - A_1 m) - A_2 r\|_\infty \leq \frac{\sqrt{q}}{4}$, $z \in \mathcal{R}_q$, $0 < \|z\|_\infty \leq \sqrt{q}/4$, and $m \in \mathcal{M}$, otherwise output 0.

Covertness of the commitment (which implies the computational hiding property) directly relies on the **M-LWE**$_{m,k,q,\beta}$ assumption. We get the statistical binding property as a corollary of Lemma 4.

5.3 δ-ASPH Scheme

We construct a δ-**ASPH** scheme on relations

$$\Psi := \left\{ ((c, m), r, 1) \mid c \in \mathcal{R}_q^m, m \in \mathcal{M}, r \in \mathcal{R}_q^k, \|c - a_0 - A_1 m - A_2 r\| \leq \beta \right\}$$

[6] and

$$\Psi^* := \left\{ ((c, m), r, z) \mid c \in \mathcal{R}_q^m, m \in \mathcal{M}, r \in \mathcal{R}_q^k, \text{Ver}(c, m, r, z) = 1 \right\}.$$

---

[5] We choose such a message space $\mathcal{M}$ to make sure that there does not exist $m, m' \in \mathcal{M}$ such that $m \neq m'$ but either $m = m'$ mod f_1 or $m = m'$ mod f_2 where $f_1 = \frac{\mathbb{Z}_q[X]}{\langle X^{d/2} - r_1 \rangle}$, $f_2 = \frac{\mathbb{Z}_q[X]}{\langle X^{d/2} - r_2 \rangle}$. Here $X^{d/2} - r_1$ and $X^{d/2} - r_2$ are irreducible factors of $X^d - 1$ over $\mathbb{Z}_p$ as stated in Theorem 3. We are using this condition in Lemma 4.

[6] Set of commitment, message and witness generated by an honest party.

- The public parameters consist of $\beta \in \mathbb{R}^+$, $\sigma \geq 4\sqrt{q \log(2d(1 + 1/\varepsilon))/\pi}$ and $\delta := \beta(m + 1) \cdot \sigma\sqrt{2d}$.
- **Hash**$(c, m; f)$: Given commitment c and message m, first sample $f \leftarrow \mathcal{D}_\sigma^{m+1}$, then compute the hash value $h = f^T \left((c - a_0 - A_1 m)^T, 1\right)^T$ and output the projection key $pk := \left(f^T (A_2^T \ 0)^T\right)^T$.
- **PHash**(pk, m, r): Given the projection key pk, message m and witness r for commitment c, compute the hash value as $h' = pk^T \cdot r$.

Correctness. Assume that we are given c, a commitment to message m with witness r, i.e., $\|c - a_0 - A_1 m - A_2 r\|_\infty \leq \beta$. This implies that

$$h - h' = f^T \left((c - a_0 - A_1 m)^T, 1\right)^T - f^T (A_2^T \ 0)^T r$$
$$= f^T \left((c - a_0 - A_1 m - A_2 r)^T, 1\right)^T.$$

Let $f^T = (f_1, \ldots, f_{m+1})$. As vector f is from a Gaussian distribution, by Lemma 1 with probability at least $(1 - 2^{-d/7})^{m+1} \geq 1 - (m + 1) \cdot 2^{-d/7}$, we have $\forall i \in [m + 1], \|f_i\|_2 \leq \sigma\sqrt{2d}$. It implies that, with probability at least $(1 - m \cdot 2^{-d/7})$, it holds that $\|h - h'\|_\infty \leq \beta(m + 1) \cdot \sigma\sqrt{2d} = \delta$.

Soundness. Let c be a commitment and let message m be such that there does not exist (r, z) such that $\mathbf{Ver}(c, m, r, z) = 1$ i.e.

$$\forall(r, z) \in \mathcal{R}_q^{k+1} : \|z(c - a_0 - A_1 m) - A_2 r\|_\infty > \sqrt{q}/4 \text{ or } \|z\|_\infty \notin (0, \sqrt{q}/4]. \quad (1)$$

We want to show that $(h, pk) = \left(f^T \left((c - a_0 - A_1 m)^T, 1\right)^T, (f^T (A_2^T \ 0)^T)^T\right)$ is statistically indistinguishable from $\mathcal{R}_q^{k+1}$. Let $B := [A_2' \ t] \in \mathcal{R}_q^{m \times (k+1)}$ where $A_2' = [A_2^T \ 0]^T$ and $t = \left((c - a_0 - A_1 m)^T \ 1\right)^T$. Lemma 2 implies that with probability at least $(1 - 2^{-d})$, we have

$$\forall s \in \mathcal{R}_q^k \setminus \{0\}, \|A_2 s\|_\infty \geq \sqrt{q}/4 \text{ i.e. } \forall s \in \mathcal{R}_q^k \setminus \{0\}, \|A_2' s\|_\infty \geq \sqrt{q}/4. \quad (2)$$

Therefore, from Eq. 1 and 2, we get the $\forall s \in \mathcal{R}_q^{k+1} \setminus \{0\}$, $\|Bs\|_\infty \geq \sqrt{q}/4$. Hence Theorem 4 implies that $\Delta(f^T B, \mathcal{U}) \leq 2\varepsilon$, where $\mathcal{U} \xleftarrow{\$} \mathcal{R}_q^{k+1}$.

Covertness. From Eq. 2 and Theorem 4, we get that $\Delta(f^T A_2', \mathcal{U}) \leq 2\varepsilon$ where $\mathcal{U} \xleftarrow{\$} \mathcal{R}_q^k$. Hence, the covertness property follows.

Acknowledgements. We would like to thank Divesh Aggarwal for the helpful discussion, and thank the reviewers for valuable comments and suggestions.

Rajendra Kumar was supported in part by the Singapore National Research Foundation under NRF RF Award No. NRF-NRFF2013-13, the Ministry of Education, Singapore under grants MOE2012-T3-1-009 and MOE2019-T2- 1-145. Khoa Nguyen was supported in part by Vietnam National University HoChiMinh City (VNUHCM) under grant number NCM2019-18-01.

References

1. Ajtai, M.: Generating hard instances of lattice problems (extended abstract). In: STOC 1996, pp. 99–108 (1996)
2. Banaszczyk, W.: New bounds in some transference theorems in the geometry of numbers. Math. Ann. **296**(1), 625–635 (1993)
3. Baum, C., Damgård, I., Lyubashevsky, V., Oechsner, S., Peikert, C.: More efficient commitments from structured lattice assumptions. In: Catalano, D., De Prisco, R. (eds.) SCN 2018. LNCS, vol. 11035, pp. 368–385. Springer, Cham (2018). https://doi.org/10.1007/978-3-319-98113-0_20
4. Bellare, M., Neven, G.: Multi-signatures in the plain public-key model and a general forking lemma. In: CCS 2006, pp. 390–399 (2006)
5. Benhamouda, F., Blazy, O., Ducas, L., Quach, W.: Hash proof systems over lattices revisited. In: Abdalla, M., Dahab, R. (eds.) PKC 2018. LNCS, vol. 10770, pp. 644–674. Springer, Cham (2018). https://doi.org/10.1007/978-3-319-76581-5_22
6. Benhamouda, F., Krenn, S., Lyubashevsky, V., Pietrzak, K.: Efficient zero-knowledge proofs for commitments from learning with errors over rings. In: Pernul, G., Ryan, P.Y.A., Weippl, E. (eds.) ESORICS 2015. LNCS, vol. 9326, pp. 305–325. Springer, Cham (2015). https://doi.org/10.1007/978-3-319-24174-6_16
7. Bootle, J., Lyubashevsky, V., Seiler, G.: Algebraic techniques for short(er) exact lattice-based zero-knowledge proofs. In: Boldyreva, A., Micciancio, D. (eds.) CRYPTO 2019. LNCS, vol. 11692, pp. 176–202. Springer, Cham (2019). https://doi.org/10.1007/978-3-030-26948-7_7
8. Brakerski, Z., Gentry, C., Vaikuntanathan, V.: (leveled) fully homomorphic encryption without bootstrapping. In: ITCS 2012, pp. 309–325 (2012)
9. Chandran, N., Goyal, V., Ostrovsky, R., Sahai, A.: Covert multi-party computation. In: FOCS 2007, pp. 238–248 (2007)
10. Chaum, D., van Heyst, E.: Group signatures. In: Davies, D.W. (ed.) EUROCRYPT 1991. LNCS, vol. 547, pp. 257–265. Springer, Heidelberg (1991). https://doi.org/10.1007/3-540-46416-6_22
11. Cramer, R.: Modular design of secure yet practical cryptographic protocols. Ph.D. thesis, January 1997
12. Cramer, R., Shoup, V.: Universal hash proofs and a paradigm for adaptive chosen ciphertext secure public-key encryption. In: Knudsen, L.R. (ed.) EUROCRYPT 2002. LNCS, vol. 2332, pp. 45–64. Springer, Heidelberg (2002). https://doi.org/10.1007/3-540-46035-7_4
13. Damgård, I., Orlandi, C., Takahashi, A., Tibouchi, M.: Two-round n-out-of-n and multi-signatures and trapdoor commitment from lattices. In: Garay, J.A. (ed.) PKC 2021. LNCS, vol. 12710, pp. 99–130. Springer, Cham (2021). https://doi.org/10.1007/978-3-030-75245-3_5
14. del Pino, R., Lyubashevsky, V., Seiler, G.: Lattice-based group signatures and zero-knowledge proofs of automorphism stability. In: CCS 2018, pp. 574–591 (2018)
15. Esgin, M.F., Nguyen, N.K., Seiler, G.: Practical exact proofs from lattices: new techniques to exploit fully-splitting rings. In: Moriai, S., Wang, H. (eds.) ASIACRYPT 2020. LNCS, vol. 12492, pp. 259–288. Springer, Cham (2020). https://doi.org/10.1007/978-3-030-64834-3_9
16. Esgin, M.F., Steinfeld, R., Liu, J.K., Liu, D.: Lattice-based zero-knowledge proofs: new techniques for shorter and faster constructions and applications. In: Boldyreva, A., Micciancio, D. (eds.) CRYPTO 2019. LNCS, vol. 11692, pp. 115–146. Springer, Cham (2019). https://doi.org/10.1007/978-3-030-26948-7_5

17. Esgin, M.F., Zhao, R.K., Steinfeld, R., Liu, J.K., Liu, D.: MatRiCT: efficient, scalable and post-quantum blockchain confidential transactions protocol. In: ACM CCS 2019, pp. 567–584 (2019)

18. Gentry, C.: Fully homomorphic encryption using ideal lattices. In: STOC 2009, pp. 169–178 (2009)

19. Gentry, C., Peikert, C., Vaikuntanathan, V.: Trapdoors for hard lattices and new cryptographic constructions. In: STOC 2008, pp. 197–206 (2008)

20. Goldwasser, S., Micali, S., Rackoff, C.: The knowledge complexity of interactive proof-systems (extended abstract). In: STOC 1985, pp. 291–304 (1985)

21. Gorbunov, S., Vaikuntanathan, V., Wee, H.: Predicate encryption for circuits from LWE. In: Gennaro, R., Robshaw, M. (eds.) CRYPTO 2015. LNCS, vol. 9216, pp. 503–523. Springer, Heidelberg (2015). https://doi.org/10.1007/978-3-662-48000-7_25

22. Goyal, V., Jain, A.: On the round complexity of covert computation. In: STOC 2010, pp. 191–200 (2010)

23. Hoffstein, J., Pipher, J., Silverman, J.H.: NTRU: a ring-based public key cryptosystem. In: Buhler, J.P. (ed.) ANTS 1998. LNCS, vol. 1423, pp. 267–288. Springer, Heidelberg (1998). https://doi.org/10.1007/BFb0054868

24. Jarecki, S.: Practical covert authentication. In: Krawczyk, H. (ed.) PKC 2014. LNCS, vol. 8383, pp. 611–629. Springer, Heidelberg (2014). https://doi.org/10.1007/978-3-642-54631-0_35

25. Jiang, S., Gong, G., He, J., Nguyen, K., Wang, H.: PAKEs: new framework, new techniques and more efficient lattice-based constructions in the standard model. In: Kiayias, A., Kohlweiss, M., Wallden, P., Zikas, V. (eds.) PKC 2020. LNCS, vol. 12110, pp. 396–427. Springer, Cham (2020). https://doi.org/10.1007/978-3-030-45374-9_14

26. Katz, J., Vaikuntanathan, V.: Smooth projective hashing and password-based authenticated key exchange from lattices. In: Matsui, M. (ed.) ASIACRYPT 2009. LNCS, vol. 5912, pp. 636–652. Springer, Heidelberg (2009). https://doi.org/10.1007/978-3-642-10366-7_37

27. Kawachi, A., Tanaka, K., Xagawa, K.: Concurrently secure identification schemes based on the worst-case hardness of lattice problems. In: Pieprzyk, J. (ed.) ASIACRYPT 2008. LNCS, vol. 5350, pp. 372–389. Springer, Heidelberg (2008). https://doi.org/10.1007/978-3-540-89255-7_23

28. Kilian, J., Petrank, E.: Identity escrow. In: Krawczyk, H. (ed.) CRYPTO 1998. LNCS, vol. 1462, pp. 169–185. Springer, Heidelberg (1998). https://doi.org/10.1007/BFb0055727

29. Langlois, A., Ling, S., Nguyen, K., Wang, H.: Lattice-based group signature scheme with verifier-local revocation. In: Krawczyk, H. (ed.) PKC 2014. LNCS, vol. 8383, pp. 345–361. Springer, Heidelberg (2014). https://doi.org/10.1007/978-3-642-54631-0_20

30. Langlois, A., Stehlé, D.: Worst-case to average-case reductions for module lattices. Des. Codes Crypt. **75**(3), 565–599 (2014). https://doi.org/10.1007/s10623-014-9938-4

31. Libert, B., Ling, S., Nguyen, K., Wang, H.: Zero-knowledge arguments for lattice-based accumulators: logarithmic-size ring signatures and group signatures without trapdoors. In: Fischlin, M., Coron, J.-S. (eds.) EUROCRYPT 2016. LNCS, vol. 9666, pp. 1–31. Springer, Heidelberg (2016). https://doi.org/10.1007/978-3-662-49896-5_1

32. Ling, S., Nguyen, K., Stehlé, D., Wang, H.: Improved zero-knowledge proofs of knowledge for the ISIS problem, and applications. In: Kurosawa, K., Hanaoka, G. (eds.) PKC 2013. LNCS, vol. 7778, pp. 107–124. Springer, Heidelberg (2013). https://doi.org/10.1007/978-3-642-36362-7_8

33. Ling, S., Nguyen, K., Wang, H.: Group signatures from lattices: simpler, tighter, shorter, ring-based. In: Katz, J. (ed.) PKC 2015. LNCS, vol. 9020, pp. 427–449. Springer, Heidelberg (2015). https://doi.org/10.1007/978-3-662-46447-2_19

34. Lyubashevsky, V.: Lattice signatures without trapdoors. In: Pointcheval, D., Johansson, T. (eds.) EUROCRYPT 2012. LNCS, vol. 7237, pp. 738–755. Springer, Heidelberg (2012). https://doi.org/10.1007/978-3-642-29011-4_43

35. Lyubashevsky, V., Seiler, G.: Short, invertible elements in partially splitting cyclotomic rings and applications to lattice-based zero-knowledge proofs. In: Nielsen, J.B., Rijmen, V. (eds.) EUROCRYPT 2018. LNCS, vol. 10820, pp. 204–224. Springer, Cham (2018). https://doi.org/10.1007/978-3-319-78381-9_8

36. Micciancio, D.: Generalized compact knapsacks, cyclic lattices, and efficient one-way functions. Comput. Complex. 16(4), 365–411 (2007)

37. Peikert, C.: A decade of lattice cryptography. Found. Trends® Theoret. Comput. Sci. 10(4), 283–424 (2016)

38. Regev, O.: On lattices, learning with errors, random linear codes, and cryptography. In: STOC 2005, pp. 84–93 (2005)

39. Rivest, R.L., Shamir, A., Tauman, Y.: How to leak a secret. In: Boyd, C. (ed.) ASIACRYPT 2001. LNCS, vol. 2248, pp. 552–565. Springer, Heidelberg (2001). https://doi.org/10.1007/3-540-45682-1_32

40. Von Ahn, L., Hopper, N., Langford, J.: Covert two-party computation. In: STOC 2005, pp. 513–522 (2005)

41. Xie, X., Xue, R., Wang, M.: Zero knowledge proofs from ring-LWE. In: Abdalla, M., Nita-Rotaru, C., Dahab, R. (eds.) CANS 2013. LNCS, vol. 8257, pp. 57–73. Springer, Cham (2013). https://doi.org/10.1007/978-3-319-02937-5_4

42. Zhang, J., Yu, Y.: Two-round PAKE from approximate SPH and instantiations from lattices. In: Takagi, T., Peyrin, T. (eds.) ASIACRYPT 2017. LNCS, vol. 10626, pp. 37–67. Springer, Cham (2017). https://doi.org/10.1007/978-3-319-70700-6_2

Spreading the Privacy Blanket:
Differentially Oblivious Shuffling for Differential Privacy

Dov Gordon[1], Jonathan Katz[2], Mingyu Liang[1(✉)], and Jiayu Xu[3]

[1] George Mason University, Fairfax, USA
{gordon,mliang5}@gmu.com
[2] University of Maryland, College Park, USA
[3] Algorand, Boston, USA
jiayux@uci.edu

Abstract. In the *shuffle model* for differential privacy, n users locally randomize their data and submit the results to a trusted "shuffler" who mixes the results before sending them to a server for analysis. This is a promising model for real-world applications of differential privacy, as several recent results have shown that, in some cases, the shuffle model offers a strictly better privacy/utility tradeoff than what is possible in a purely local model.

A downside of the shuffle model is its reliance on a trusted shuffler, and it is natural to try to replace this with a distributed shuffling protocol run by the users themselves. While it would of course be possible to use a fully secure shuffling protocol, one might hope to instead use a more-efficient protocol having weaker security guarantees.

In this work, we consider a relaxation of secure shuffling called *differential obliviousness* that we prove suffices for differential privacy in the shuffle model. We also propose a differentially oblivious shuffling protocol based on onion routing that requires only $O(n \log n)$ communication while tolerating any constant fraction of corrupted users. We show that for practical settings of the parameters, our protocol outperforms existing solutions to the problem.

Keywords: Differential privacy · Onion routing

1 Introduction

Differential privacy [19] has become a leading approach for privacy-preserving data analysis. Traditional mechanisms for differential privacy operate in the *curator model*, where a trusted server holds all the sensitive data and releases noisy statistics about that data. To reduce the necessary trust assumptions,

D. Gordon—Work supported by NSF awards #1942575 and #1955264.
J. Katz—Work supported in part by a Facebook Privacy Enhancing Technologies Award and NSF award #1837517. Portions of this work were done while at GMU.
J. Xu—Portions of this work were done while at GMU.

G. Ateniese and D. Venturi (Eds.): ACNS 2022, LNCS 13269, pp. 501–520, 2022.
https://doi.org/10.1007/978-3-031-09234-3_25

researchers subsequently proposed the *local model* of differential privacy. Here, each user applies a local randomizer $\mathcal{R}$ to its sensitive data x_i to obtain a noisy result y_i, and then forwards y_i to a server who analyzes all the noisy data it obtains. A drawback of local mechanisms is that, in some cases, they provably require more noise (and hence offer reduced utility) than mechanisms in the curator model for a fixed level of privacy. For example, computing a differentially private mean of n users' inputs can be done with $O(1)$ noise in the centralized curator model [19] but requires $\Omega(\sqrt{n})$ noise in the local model [5,13].

A recent line of work has explored an intermediate model that provides a tradeoff between these extremes. In the *shuffle model* [4,8,16,36], users locally add noise to their data as in the local model, but also have access to a trusted entity $\mathcal{S}$ (a "shuffler") that anonymizes their data before it is forwarded to the server. That is, whereas in the local model the server obtains the ordered vector of noisy inputs $(y_1, \ldots, y_n)$, in the shuffle model the server is given only the multiset $\{y_i\} := \mathcal{S}(y_1, \ldots, y_n)$ which hides information about which element was contributed by which user. (The $\{y_i\}$ can be encrypted with the server's public key before being sent to the shuffler so the shuffler does not learn the value submitted by any user.) Balle et al. [4] analyze the result of composing a local differentially private mechanism with a shuffler, and show a setting where the shuffle model offers a strictly better privacy/utility tradeoff than what is possible in the local model.

Although the shuffle model relies on a weaker trust assumption than the curator model, it may still be undesirable to rely on a trusted shuffler who is assumed not to collude with the curator. It is thus natural to consider replacing the shuffler by a distributed protocol executed by the users themselves. Clearly, using a fully secure shuffling protocol to instantiate the shuffler preserves the privacy guarantees of the shuffle mode. However, fully secure distributed-shuffling protocols are inefficient in practice (see Sect. 1.1).

Our Contributions. We consider a relaxation of oblivious shuffling that we call *differential obliviousness*. (Prior work has considered the same or similar notions in other settings; see Sect. 1.1.) Roughly, for any honest pair of users and any pair of values y, y', a differentially oblivious shuffling protocol hides (in the same sense as differential privacy) whether the first user contributed y and the second user contributed y', or vice versa. Generalizing the results of Balle et al. [4], we analyze the privacy obtained by composing a local differentially private mechanism with any *differentially oblivious* shuffling protocol, and show that such shuffling protocols suffice to replace the trusted shuffler.

With this result in place, we then seek an efficient differentially oblivious shuffling protocol. In the context of anonymous communication, Ando et al. [1] show a differentially oblivious shuffling protocol using $O(n \log n)$ communication.[1] Their protocol is based on *onion routing*, in which each user routes its

---

[1] Ando et al. consider a "many-to-many" variant of shuffling, where each of the n users wants to send a message to a distinct recipient, in contrast to our setting where all n inputs are sent to a designated receiver. Nevertheless, their results can be applied to our setting with minor modifications, so we ignore the distinction.

message to the server via a path of randomly chosen users, with nested encryption being used to hide from each intermediate user everything about the route except for the previous and next hops. Ando et al. analyze the privacy of onion routing against an adversary who corrupts some fraction of the users in the network in addition to the server, and who is also assumed able to eavesdrop on all communication in the network. While such an adversary may be appropriate in the context of using anonymous communication to evade state-sponsored censorship, we believe it is overkill for most deployments of differential privacy that could benefit from the shuffle model. Instead, we consider a weaker adversary who can only monitor the communications of corrupted users, and analyze the differential obliviousness of onion routing in this model. Our analysis uses very different techniques from those of Ando et al., and results in better concrete parameters as well as an asymptotic improvement in the average per-user communication complexity.

As in the work of Ando et al., we can adapt our protocol to handle a malicious adversary by routing dummy messages alongside real ones and checking partway along the route whether any dummy messages have been dropped. Focusing on the application to the shuffle model, we observe that the overall privacy degrades smoothly if only a few (real) messages are dropped—a dropped message is similar to having one less user—and thus a secure protocol only needs to abort when many messages are dropped by the adversary. As a consequence, we are able to address malicious behavior with lower overhead (compared to the semi-honest setting) than Ando et al.

1.1 Related Work

Secure Shuffling. There is a long line of work studying secure shuffling protocols. We survey some of what is known, restricting attention to protocols secure against $t = \Theta(n)$ corruptions.

Fully secure shuffling can be done via secure computation of a permutation network [24,32], or by having $t + 1$ parties sequentially shuffle locally [24,29]. Either approach requires $\Omega(n^2)$ communication. While it is possible to improve the asymptotic communication complexity to $O(n \log n)$ by using $\Theta(\log n)$-size committees (cf. [9,17,31]), the concrete efficiency of that approach is unclear.

Movahedi et al. [31] considered a relaxed version of shuffling in which security may fail completely with probability $O(1/n^3)$; this can be viewed as a form of differential obliviousness. The communication complexity of their protocol is $O(n \cdot \text{polylog} \, n)$. Their protocol and that of Ando et al. [1] (discussed earlier) are the only practical protocols for shuffling we are aware of with sub-quadratic communication complexity.

Bell et al. [6] proposed a different approach for achieving a relaxed form of shuffling. Their construction requires $O(n^2)$ communication, which can be improved to $O(n \log n)$ for constant size input domains. To the best of our knowledge, it has the best concrete efficiency of any prior shuffling protocol. They are also motivated by applications to the shuffle model, but do not prove that their relaxation provides differential privacy when composed with a local differentially private mechanism. Their protocol does not provide a smooth tradeoff between privacy and performance as our approach does.

We provide a concrete comparison between our shuffling protocol and prior work in Sects. 4.4 and 5.1.

In roughly concurrent work, Bünz et al. [10] propose a differentially oblivious shuffling protocol that relies on a very strong form of trusted setup.

Anonymous Communication. Sender-anonymous communication can be used to implement oblivious shuffling. DC-nets [15] and mix networks [14], two classical approaches for anonymous communication, both require $\Omega(n^2)$ communication for security against a constant fraction of corrupted parties.

Backes et al. [3] proposed a security definition for anonymous routing inspired by differential privacy, and Kuhn et al. [25] gave a definition of security (sender-message pair unlinkability) nearly identical to our own definition of differential obliviousness. Neither of these works show new protocols realizing their definitions. Several recent anonymous communication systems [27,34,35] also define security in terms of differential privacy, but the per-user communication complexity of these systems is $\Omega(n)$. None of these works consider how anonymous-communication protocols compose with other differentially private mechanisms.

Bellet et al. [7] study "gossip" protocols that provide differential privacy. The model they consider is quite different from ours, and they focus on one-to-many communication rather than many-to-one communication as we do here.

The onion routing protocol [1,21,33] that we study in this paper is used as part of the Tor anonymous communication network (though Tor uses paths with only three intermediate nodes). Although Tor has received a lot of attention in the security community, most of that work focuses on active attacks and/or attacks that are specific to Tor. While some theoretical analyses of the anonymity provided by onion routing exist [1,2,11,18,20,26,28], none (other than the work of Ando et al. [1]) prove differential obliviousness.

Differentially Private Computation. The idea of relaxing security for distributed protocols in the context of differential privacy has appeared in a number of prior works [5,12,22,23,29,30]. Beimel et al. [5] first proposed the idea, and studied how the relaxation impacts efficiency for the problem of secure summation. He et al. [23] and Groce et al. [22] construct differentially private set-intersection protocols that are more efficient than fully secure protocols for the same task. Mazloom and Gordon [29], and Mazloom et al. [30] leverage differential privacy to make graph-parallel computations more efficient. Chan et al. [12] consider a version of differential obliviousness (defined differently from ours) in the client/server model, studying sorting, merging, and range-query data structures under that relaxation.

2   Definitions

Differential Privacy. We use the standard notion of (approximate) differential privacy. Two vectors of inputs $\mathbf{x} = (x_1, \ldots, x_n)$ and $\mathbf{x}' = (x_1', \ldots, x_n')$ are called *neighboring* if they differ at a single index; i.e., if there exists an index i such that $x_i \neq x_i'$ but $x_j = x_j'$ for $j \neq i$. Let f denote a randomized process mapping a vector of inputs $(x_1, \ldots, x_n) \in D^n$ to an output in some range R. We say that f satisfies (ϵ, δ)-*approximate differential privacy* if for all neighboring vectors $\mathbf{x}, \mathbf{x}' \in \mathbf{D^n}$ and subsets $R' \subseteq R$ we have

$$\Pr[f(\mathbf{x}) \in \mathbf{R}'] \leq e^\epsilon \cdot \Pr[\mathbf{f}(\mathbf{x}') \in \mathbf{R}'] + \delta.$$

If f satisfies $(\epsilon, 0)$-approximate differential privacy then we simply say that f is ϵ-*differentially private*. For compactness, we abbreviate these as (ϵ, δ)-DP/ϵ-DP.

Local Differential Privacy and the Randomized Response Mechanism. In the setting of local differential privacy (LDP), each user U_i applies a randomized function $\mathcal{R}$ to their own input x_i and then sends the result y_i to an untrusted server. Translating the guarantees of differential privacy to this setting, we say that $\mathcal{R}$ is (ϵ, δ)-LDP if for all $x, x' \in D$ and $R' \subseteq R$ we have

$$\Pr[\mathcal{R}(x) \in R'] \leq e^\epsilon \cdot \Pr[\mathcal{R}(x') \in R'] + \delta.$$

If $\mathcal{R}$ is $(\epsilon, 0)$-LDP then we simply say that $\mathcal{R}$ is ϵ-LDP.

Let $\gamma \in (0, 1)$ be a parameter, and let D denote a discrete domain in which users' inputs lie. The randomized response mechanism $\mathcal{R}_{\gamma, D}$ is defined as

$$\mathcal{R}_{\gamma, D}(x) = \begin{cases} x & \text{with probability } 1 - \gamma \\ y \leftarrow D & \text{with probability } \gamma \end{cases} ;$$

i.e., with probability γ a user replaces its input with a uniform value in D, and with the remaining probability leaves its input unchanged. It is not hard to show that if $\gamma \geq |D|/(e^\epsilon + |D| - 1)$ then $\mathcal{R}_{\gamma, D}$ is ϵ-LDP.

The Shuffle Model. In the *shuffle model* [4,8,16,36] each user U_i computes $y_i \leftarrow \mathcal{R}(x_i)$ as in the local model, but then sends y_i to a trusted "shuffler" $\mathcal{S}$. After receiving a message from all n users, $\mathcal{S}$ outputs the multiset (which can also be viewed as a *histogram*) $h = \{y_i\}$. If we overload notation and let $\mathcal{S}$ also denote the process of mapping a list of elements to the multiset containing those elements, then $\mathcal{R}$ defines the randomized process

$$\mathcal{S} \circ \mathcal{R}^{\otimes n} \stackrel{\text{def}}{=} \mathcal{S} \circ (\mathcal{R} \times \cdots \times \mathcal{R})(x_1, \ldots, x_n) = \mathcal{S}(\mathcal{R}(x_1), \ldots, \mathcal{R}(x_n)).$$

Balle et al. [4] showed that under certain conditions the shuffle model improves the privacy of an LDP mechanism.[2]

Theorem 1. *Let $\mathcal{R}$ be an ϵ-LDP mechanism. If $\epsilon \leq \log(n/\log(1/\delta))/2$, then $\mathcal{S} \circ \mathcal{R}^{\otimes n}$ is (ϵ', δ)-DP with $\epsilon' = O(\min\{1, \epsilon\} \cdot e^\epsilon \sqrt{\log(1/\delta)/n})$.*

For the particular case of randomized response they show

Theorem 2. *Fix values n, ϵ, δ, and D. If $\gamma \geq \max \left\{ \frac{14 \cdot |D| \log(2/\delta)}{(n-1) \cdot \epsilon^2}, \frac{27 \cdot |D|}{(n-1) \cdot \epsilon} \right\}$, then $\mathcal{S} \circ \mathcal{R}_{\gamma, D}^{\otimes n}$ is (ϵ, δ)-DP.*

---

[2] For clarity, we state a slightly looser bound than what they prove.

Differentially Private Protocols. More generally, we may consider interactive protocols executed by a server and n users, each of whom initially holds an input x_i. The server has no input, and is the only party to generate an output. We say that a protocol Π *implements* a (randomized) function f if the honest execution of Π when the users hold inputs $x_1, \ldots, x_n$, respectively, results in the server generating output distributed according to $f(x_1, \ldots, x_n)$.

In this setting, the server's view may contain more than just its output. It is also natural to consider that some of the users executing the protocol may themselves be corrupted and colluding with the server. (For simplicity, in what follows we assume semi-honest corruptions; i.e., we assume corrupted parties—including the server—follow the protocol as directed, but may then try to learn additional information based on their collective view of the protocol execution. The definitions can be extended in the obvious way to handle malicious behavior.) Given a set of parties A (that we assume by default always includes the server), we let $\mathrm{VIEW}_{\Pi,A}(x_1, \ldots, x_n)$ be the random variable denoting the joint view of the parties in A in an execution of protocol Π when the users initially hold inputs $x_1, \ldots, x_n$. Let H denote the set of users not in A; let $\mathbf{x_A}$ denote the inputs of users in A; and let $\mathbf{x_H}$ denote the inputs of users outside of A. Then:

Definition 1. *Protocol Π is (ϵ, δ)-DP for t corrupted users if for any set A containing the server and up to t users and any $\mathbf{x_A}$, the function mapping $\mathbf{x_H}$ to $\mathrm{VIEW}_{\Pi,A}(\mathbf{x_A}, \mathbf{x_H})$ is (ϵ, δ)-DP, i.e., for any neighboring $\mathbf{x_H}, \mathbf{x'_H}$ and any set V of possible (joint) views of the parties in A, we have*

$$\Pr[\mathrm{VIEW}_{\Pi,A}(\mathbf{x_A}, \mathbf{x_H}) \in \mathbf{V}] \leq e^{\epsilon} \cdot \Pr[\mathrm{VIEW}_{\Pi,A}(\mathbf{x_A}, \mathbf{x'_H}) \in \mathbf{V}] + \delta.$$

The above can be relaxed to *computational* DP as well.

One can also consider protocols operating in a hybrid world. The shuffle model is a special case of this, where the parties have access to an ideal functionality $\mathcal{S}$ implementing the shuffler. Concretely, the protocol $(\mathcal{R}_{\gamma,D} \times \cdots \times \mathcal{R}_{\gamma,D})^{\mathcal{S}}$ corresponding to the randomized response mechanism is the one in which each user locally computes $y_i \leftarrow \mathcal{R}_{\gamma,D}(x_i)$ and then sends y_i to $\mathcal{S}$, which sends the result $\{y_i\} := \mathcal{S}(y_1, \ldots, y_n)$ to the server. The fact that some of the users themselves might be corrupted, however, now needs to be taken into account. For example, the following is a corollary of Theorem 2:

Corollary 1. *Fix n, t, ϵ, δ, and D. If $\gamma \geq \max\left\{ \frac{14 \cdot |D| \log(2/\delta)}{(n-t-1) \cdot \epsilon^2}, \frac{27 \cdot |D|}{(n-t-1) \cdot \epsilon} \right\}$, then $(\mathcal{R}_{\gamma,D} \times \cdots \times \mathcal{R}_{\gamma,D})^{\mathcal{S}}$ is (ϵ, δ)-DP for t corrupted users in the $\mathcal{S}$-hybrid model.*

Shuffle Protocols. A protocol Σ run by n users and a server is a *shuffle protocol* if it implements $\mathcal{S}$, i.e., if the output generated by the server when running Σ is the multiset consisting of the users' inputs. We are interested in shuffle protocols that ensure differential privacy when used to implement the shuffle model. Note, however, that we cannot use differential privacy to analyze a shuffle protocol; no shuffle protocol is differentially private, since two neighboring inputs $\mathbf{y}, \mathbf{y'}$ lead to different outputs. Instead, we use a related definition that we call *differential* *obliviousness.* Call vectors $\mathbf{y}, \mathbf{y}'$ *neihgboring* if they differ by a transposition, i.e., there exist i, j such that $y_i' = y_j$, $y_j' = y_i$, and $y_k' = y_k$ for $k \notin \{i, j\}$ (so $\mathbf{y}'$ and $\mathbf{y}$ are identical except the elements at positions i, j are swapped). Then:

Definition 2. *Shuffle protocol Σ is (ϵ, δ)-differentially oblivious for t corrupted users if for any set A containing the server and up to t users, any $\mathbf{y_A}$, any neighboring $\mathbf{y_H}, \mathbf{y_H'}$, and any set V of possible (joint) views of the parties in A,*

$$\Pr[\text{VIEW}_{\Sigma, A}(\mathbf{y_A}, \mathbf{y_H}) \in V] \le e^{\epsilon} \cdot \Pr[\text{VIEW}_{\Sigma, A}(\mathbf{y_A}, \mathbf{y_H'}) \in V] + \delta.$$

3   Distributing the Privacy Blanket

Generalizing the result of Balle et al. [4], we show that a differentially oblivious shuffle protocol suffices for implementing the shuffle model. Specifically:

Theorem 3. *Let Σ be a shuffle protocol that is (ϵ, δ)-differentially oblivious for t corrupted users, and let $\mathcal{R}$ be an ϵ_0-LDP mechanism. For any δ' such that $\epsilon_0 \le \log((n - t)/\log(1/\delta'))/2$, protocol $(\mathcal{R}^{\otimes n})^{\Sigma}$ is $(\epsilon + \epsilon', \delta + \delta')$-differentially private for t corrupted users, where $\epsilon' = O(\max\{1, \epsilon_0\} \cdot e^{\epsilon_0} \sqrt{\log(1/\delta')/(n - t)})$.*

We prove the above in the full version of our paper; here, we focus on the particular case of randomized response. We show:

Theorem 4. *Let Σ be a shuffle protocol that is (ϵ, δ)-differentially oblivious for t corrupted users. If $(\mathcal{R}_{\gamma, D} \times \cdots \times \mathcal{R}_{\gamma, D})^{\mathcal{S}}$ is (ϵ', δ')-differentially private for t corrupted users, then $(\mathcal{R}_{\gamma, D} \times \cdots \times \mathcal{R}_{\gamma, D})^{\Sigma}$ is $(\epsilon + \epsilon', \delta + \delta')$-differentially private for t corrupted users.*

Overview of the Proof of Theorem 4. Throughout this section, we let Π denote $\mathcal{R}_{\gamma, D} \times \cdots \times \mathcal{R}_{\gamma, D}$; our goal is to prove differential privacy of Π^{Σ}. We provide a formal proof starting in the next subsection; here, we provide an overview.

Fix some neighboring inputs $\mathbf{x} = (\mathbf{x_A}, \mathbf{x_H})$ and $\mathbf{x}' = (\mathbf{x_A}, \mathbf{x_H'})$, and some set of adversarial views V. (Each view in V includes the views of the server and t corrupted users in an execution of Π^{Σ}.) Conceptually, we separate each view $v \in V$ into three components: a component v_1 reflecting the adversary's view of the input to Σ (in particular, v_1 includes the randomized inputs $\mathbf{y_A}$ of the corrupted parties); the final multiset h output by the server (which has the same distribution as the multiset that would be output by the shuffler in $\Pi^{\mathcal{S}}$ conditioned on v_1); and the view v_2 that results from execution of Σ itself.

For some first component v_1 and output multiset h, let $Y(v_1, h)$ denote the set of (possibly modified) honest inputs $\mathbf{y_H}$ to Σ that are consistent with v_1, h, and $\mathbf{x}$, and let $Y'(v_1, h)$ denote the set of $\mathbf{y_H}$ consistent with v_1, h, and $\mathbf{x}'$. Using Corollary 1 and letting $m = n - t$, we show (cf. Lemma 1):

$$\sum_{(v_1, h) : (v_1, h, v_2) \in V} \Pr[v_1 \mid \mathbf{x}] \cdot \Pr\left[\mathcal{R}_{\gamma, D}^{\otimes m}(\mathbf{x}) \in Y(v_1, h) \mid v_1\right]$$

$$\le e^{\epsilon'} \cdot \sum_{(v_1, h) : (v_1, h, v_2) \in V} \Pr[v_1 \mid \mathbf{x}'] \cdot \Pr\left[\mathcal{R}_{\gamma, D}^{\otimes m}(\mathbf{x}') \in Y'(v_1, h) \mid v_1\right] + \delta'. \tag{1}$$

(Note that $\Pr[v_1 \mid \mathbf{x}'] = \Pr[\mathbf{v_1} \mid \mathbf{x}]$ since v_1 only depends on the true inputs of the corrupted parties.) For v_1, h as above, let $V_2(v_1, h) = \{v_2 \mid (v_1, h, v_2) \in V\}$. In what is the most technical part of the proof, we then use differential obliviousness of Σ to show (cf. Lemma 5) that for any v_1, h we have

$$\Pr_{\mathbf{y_H} \leftarrow \mathbf{Y}(\mathbf{v_1}, \mathbf{h})} [v_2 \in V_2(v_1, h)] \le e^\epsilon \cdot \Pr_{\mathbf{y'_H} \leftarrow \mathbf{Y'}(\mathbf{v_1}, \mathbf{h})} [v_2 \in V_2(v_1, h)] + \delta. \tag{2}$$

The proof of the above follows from a combinatorial analysis of the two sets Y and Y'. Recall that an element in Y and an element in Y' are neighboring if they differ by a single transposition. Differential obliviousness of Σ guarantees that neighboring vectors give rise to (roughly) the same view. If we can establish a bijection between Y and Y', mapping each element of Y to a neighboring element in Y', Eq. (2) would follow immediately. Unfortunately, Y and Y' do not necessarily have the same size, and so such a bijection may not exist. Nevertheless, we show how to extend Y and Y' to multisets $[Y]$ and $[Y']$ (by duplicating certain elements) having the same size, and so that the resulting multisets preserve the probabilities of each vector (so sampling uniform $\mathbf{y_H} \in \mathbf{Y}$ gives the same distribution as sampling uniform $\mathbf{y_H} \in [\mathbf{Y}]$, and similarly for Y' and $[Y']$). We then show that there is a bijection $\phi : [Y] \to [Y']$ such that $\mathbf{y_H}$ and $\phi(\mathbf{y_H})$ are neighboring. This allows us to prove that Eq. (2) holds.

Since

$$\Pr[(v_1, h, v_2) \in V \mid \mathbf{x}] = \sum_{(v_1, h, v_2) \in V} \Pr[(v_1, h, v_2) \mid \mathbf{x}]$$

$$= \sum_{(v_1, h) : (v_1, h, v_2) \in V} \Pr[v_1 \mid \mathbf{x}] \cdot \Pr[\mathcal{R}_{\gamma, \mathbf{D}}^{\otimes \mathbf{m}}(\mathbf{x}) \in \mathbf{Y}(\mathbf{v_1}, \mathbf{h}) \mid \mathbf{v_1}]$$

$$\cdot \Pr_{\mathbf{y_H} \leftarrow \mathbf{Y}(\mathbf{v_1}, \mathbf{h})} [v_2 \in V_2(v_1, h)],$$

combining Eqs. (1) and (2) allows us to prove Theorem 4.

3.1   Notation and Preliminaries

We now formalize the preceding intuition. We assume t users are corrupted and let $m = n - t$ be the number of uncorrupted users. Fix some neighboring inputs $\mathbf{x} = (\mathbf{x_A}, \mathbf{x_H})$ and $\mathbf{x}' = (\mathbf{x_A}, \mathbf{x'_H})$, and for $i \in [m]$ let $x_{H,i}$ be the input of the ith honest user. Without loss of generality, we assume $\mathbf{x_H}$ and $\mathbf{x'_H}$ differ on the input of the mth user, and further assume that $x_{H,m} = 1$ and $x'_{H,m} = 2$.

The Adversary's View. We now make explicit the components of the adversary's view in an execution of Π^Σ on input $\mathbf{x}$. The first component of the view, which we denote by v_1, includes $\mathbf{y_A} = (\mathcal{R}_{\gamma, \mathbf{D}} \times \cdots \times \mathcal{R}_{\gamma, \mathbf{D}})(\mathbf{x_A})$, i.e., the adversary's inputs to Σ. Following Balle et al. [4], we also include in v_1 the vector $\mathbf{b} = (\mathbf{b_1}, \ldots, \mathbf{b_m})$ indicating which of the honest users' inputs are replaced by a random value, i.e., if $b_i = 0$ then $y_{H,i} = x_{H,i}$ and if $b_i = 1$ then $y_{H,i} \leftarrow D$. The second component of the adversary's view is the multiset $h = \mathcal{S}(\mathbf{y_A}, \mathbf{y_H})$ output by Σ, in which $\mathbf{y} = (\mathbf{y_A}, \mathbf{y_H})$ denotes the vector of inputs the parties provide to Σ; note that parts of $\mathbf{y_H}$ (corresponding to inputs that have not been randomized) can be deduced from v_1. The third component v_2 of the adversary's view consists of the entire view of the adversary in the execution of Σ on inputs $\mathbf{y}$. (Although v_2 determines h, we find it useful to treat h separately.)

For the rest of the proof, fix some set of views $V = \{(v_1, h, v_2)\}$. Note that views for which $b_m = 1$ are equiprobable regardless of whether the honest inputs are $\mathbf{x_H}$ or $\mathbf{x'_H}$; therefore, we assume without loss of generality that all views in V have $b_m = 0$. We let $V' = \{(v_1, h) \mid \exists v_2 : (v_1, h, v_2) \in V\}$ and, for any $(v_1, h) \in V'$, we let $V_2(v_1, h) = \{v_2 \mid (v_1, h, v_2) \in V\}$.

For some fixed v_1, h, let $Y(v_1, h)$ denote the set of honest inputs $\mathbf{y_H}$ consistent with v_1, h, and $\mathbf{x}$. That is, $Y(v_1, h)$ contains all $\mathbf{y_H} \in \mathbf{D^m}$ such that (1) for all i with $b_i = 0$, we have $y_{H,i} = x_{H,i}$ (so, in particular, $y_{H,m} = x_{H,m} = 1$), and (2) $\mathcal{S}(\mathbf{y_A}, \mathbf{y_H}) = \mathbf{h}$ (where $\mathbf{y_A}$ is fixed by v_1). Similarly, we let $Y'(v_1, h)$ denote the set of $\mathbf{y_H}$ consistent with v_1, h, and $\mathbf{x'}$.

3.2   Step 1: Using Local Differential Privacy of $\mathcal{R}_{\gamma,D}$

Lemma 1. *If $\Pi^\mathcal{S}$ is (ϵ', δ')-DP for t corrupted users, then for any set of views V and any pair of neighboring inputs $\mathbf{x}, \mathbf{x'}$, we have:*

$$\sum_{(v_1,h) \in V'} \Pr[v_1 \mid \mathbf{x}] \cdot \Pr\left[\mathcal{R}_{\gamma,\mathbf{D}}^{\otimes m}(\mathbf{x}) \in \mathbf{Y}(\mathbf{v_1}, \mathbf{h}) \mid \mathbf{v_1}\right]$$

$$\leq e^{\epsilon'} \cdot \sum_{(v_1,h) \in V'} \Pr[v_1 \mid \mathbf{x'}] \cdot \Pr\left[\mathcal{R}_{\gamma,\mathbf{D}}^{\otimes m}(\mathbf{x'}) \in \mathbf{Y'}(\mathbf{v_1}, \mathbf{h}) \mid \mathbf{v_1}\right] + \delta'.$$

The proof is given in the full version.

We also state a useful corollary. Define

$$\Delta(v_1, h) \stackrel{\text{def}}{=}$$
$$\max\left\{\Pr[\mathcal{R}_{\gamma,D}^{\otimes m}(\mathbf{x}) \in \mathbf{Y}(\mathbf{v_1}, \mathbf{h}) \mid \mathbf{v_1}] - e^{\epsilon'} \cdot \Pr[\mathcal{R}_{\gamma,D}^{\otimes m}(\mathbf{x'}) \in \mathbf{Y'}(\mathbf{v_1}, \mathbf{h}) \mid \mathbf{v_1}], \mathbf{0}\right\}.$$

Using the fact that $\Pr[v_1 \mid \mathbf{x}] = \Pr[\mathbf{v_1} \mid \mathbf{x'}]$, we then have:

Corollary 2. *If $\Pi^\mathcal{S}$ is (ϵ', δ')-DP for t corrupted users, then for any set of views V and any pair of neighboring inputs $\mathbf{x}, \mathbf{x'}$, it holds that:*

$$\sum_{(v_1,h) \in V'} \Pr[v_1 \mid \mathbf{x}] \cdot \mathbf{\Delta}(\mathbf{v_1}, \mathbf{h}) \leq \delta'.$$

3.3   Step 2: Using Differential Obliviousness of Σ

In this section we fix some $(v_1, h) \in V'$, and write Y, Y', and V_2 for $Y(v_1, h)$, $Y'(v_1, h)$, and $V_2(v_1, h)$, respectively. For simplicity, we assume both Y and Y' are non-empty; the case where one or both are empty can be addressed by Lemma 1. Recall that if $\mathbf{y_H} \in \mathbf{Y}$ then $y_{H,m} = 1$, and if $\mathbf{y'_H} \in \mathbf{Y'}$ then $y'_{H,m} = 2$.

Let $\bar{h}$ denote the multiset that remains after removing from h the multiset given by the elements of $\mathbf{y_A}$ and the multiset $\{\mathbf{x_{H,i}} \mid \mathbf{b_i} = \mathbf{0}, \mathbf{i} \neq \mathbf{m}\}$ (both of which are determined by v_1). Let c_1 be the number of 1's in $\bar{h}$, and let c_2 be the number of 2's in $\bar{h}$; note that $c_1, c_2 \neq 0$ since Y and Y' are non-empty. The following characterizes the relative sizes of Y and Y' in terms of c_1 and c_2:

Lemma 2. $\frac{|Y|}{|Y'|} = \frac{c_1}{c_2}$.

Proof. Let C be the number of ways of distributing all the elements of $\bar{h}$ that are not equal to 1 or 2 among the honest users who have changed their inputs. A vector $\mathbf{y_H}$ is consistent with v_1, h, and $\mathbf{x}$ only if a 1 is associated with the last user, and the remaining $c_1 + c_2 - 1$ elements of $\bar{h}$ that are 1 or 2 are distributed among the $c_1 + c_2 - 1$ users who remain from those who have changed their inputs. Thus,

$$|Y| = C \cdot \binom{c_1 + c_2 - 1}{c_1 - 1}.$$

Siilarly,

$$|Y'| = C \cdot \binom{c_1 + c_2 - 1}{c_2 - 1}.$$

The lemma follows.

Lemma 3. *For every $\mathbf{y_H} \in \mathbf{Y}$, there are c_2 vectors in Y' that result from transposing the final entry of $\mathbf{y_H}$ with some other entry of $\mathbf{y_H}$. Similarly, for every $\mathbf{y'_H} \in \mathbf{Y'}$, there are c_1 vectors in Y that result from transposing the final entry of $\mathbf{y'_H}$ with some other entry of $\mathbf{y'_H}$.*

Proof. We prove the first statement; the second follows symmetrically. Fix some $\mathbf{y_H} \in \mathbf{Y}$. The final entry of $\mathbf{y_H}$ is 1, and there are c_2 other entries of $\mathbf{y_H}$ that are equal to 2 and that correspond to users who have changed their inputs. Transposing the final entry of $\mathbf{y_H}$ with the entries at any of those locations gives a vector in Y'.

Mapping Between Y and Y'. Ideally, we would like to construct a bijection between Y and Y' such that a vector in Y is mapped to a vector in Y' iff they are transpositions of each other. Then for each pair of such vectors $\mathbf{y_H}$ and $\mathbf{y'_H}$, we could argue that $\mathrm{VIEW}_{\Sigma, A}(\mathbf{y_A}, \mathbf{y_H})$ and $\mathrm{VIEW}_{\Sigma, A}(\mathbf{y_A}, \mathbf{y'_H})$ must be "close" by differential obliviousness of Σ. Unfortunately, as shown in Lemma 2, the cardinalities of Y and Y' might be different, so such a bijection might not exist.

To resolve this issue, we "duplicate" vectors in Y and Y' so that the resulting multisets $[Y]$ and $[Y']$ have the same cardinality. Concretely, we let $[Y]$ be a multiset consisting of c_2 copies of each element $\mathbf{y_H} \in \mathbf{Y}$. Similarly, we let $[Y']$ be a multiset consisting of c_1 copies of each element $\mathbf{y'_H} \in \mathbf{Y'}$. Note that sampling uniformly from $[Y]$ (resp., $[Y']$) is equivalent to sampling uniformly from Y (resp., Y'). Moreover, by Lemma 2, $[Y]$ and $[Y']$ have the same size. We show:

Lemma 4. *There is a bijection $\phi : [Y] \to [Y']$ such that for every $\mathbf{y_H} \in [Y]$, the vector $\phi(\mathbf{y_H}) \in [Y']$ is a transposition of $\mathbf{y_H}$.*

Proof. Consider the bipartite graph G with vertex sets $[Y]$ and $[Y']$, where there is an edge between $\mathbf{y}_H \in [Y]$ and $\mathbf{y}'_H \in [Y]'$ iff $\mathbf{y}'_H$ results from transposing the final entry of $\mathbf{y}_H$ with some other entry of $\mathbf{y}_H$. Using Lemma 3 and the fact that every vector in Y' is included c_1 times in $[Y']$, we see that each $\mathbf{y}_H \in [Y]$ has exactly $c_1 \cdot c_2$ edges. Reasoning analogously, each $\mathbf{y}'_H \in [Y']$ has $c_1 \cdot c_2$ edges. Hall's marriage theorem implies that G has a complete matching, which is also a perfect matching since $[Y]$ and $[Y']$ have the same size. Any such matching constitutes a bijection ϕ as claimed by the lemma.

Recall that the third component of the adversary's view, v_2, is equal to $\mathrm{VIEW}_{\Sigma,A}(\mathbf{y_A}, \mathbf{y_H})$. We may now prove the main result of this section.

Lemma 5. *If Σ is (ϵ, δ)-differentially oblivious for t corrupted users:*

$$\Pr_{\mathbf{y_H} \leftarrow \mathbf{Y}}[\mathrm{VIEW}_{\Sigma,A}(\mathbf{y_A}, \mathbf{y_H}) \in \mathbf{V_2}] \le e^{\epsilon} \cdot \Pr_{\mathbf{y'_H} \leftarrow \mathbf{Y'}}[\mathrm{VIEW}_{\Sigma,A}(\mathbf{y_A}, \mathbf{y'_H}) \in \mathbf{V_2}] + \delta.$$

Proof. Let $\phi : [Y] \to [Y']$ be a bijection as guaranteed by Lemma 4. Differential obliviousness of Σ implies that for any $\mathbf{y}_H \in [Y]$:

$$\Pr\left[\mathrm{VIEW}_{\Sigma,A}(\mathbf{y_A}, \mathbf{y_H}) \in \mathbf{V_2}\right] \le e^{\epsilon} \cdot \Pr[\mathrm{VIEW}_{\Sigma,A}(\mathbf{y_A}, \phi(\mathbf{y_H})) \in \mathbf{V_2}] + \delta.$$

Recalling that $[Y]$ and $[Y']$ have the same size, we thus have

$$\Pr_{\mathbf{y_H} \leftarrow \mathbf{Y}}[\mathrm{VIEW}_{\Sigma,A}(\mathbf{y_A}, \mathbf{y_H}) \in \mathbf{V_2}] = \Pr_{\mathbf{y_H} \leftarrow [Y]}[\mathrm{VIEW}_{\Sigma,A}(\mathbf{y_A}, \mathbf{y_H}) \in \mathbf{V_2}]$$

$$= \sum_{\mathbf{y_H} \in [Y]} \frac{\Pr\left[\mathrm{VIEW}_{\Sigma,A}(\mathbf{y_A}, \mathbf{y_H}) \in \mathbf{V_2}\right]}{|[Y]|}$$

$$\le \sum_{\mathbf{y_H} \in [Y]} \frac{e^{\epsilon} \cdot \Pr[\mathrm{VIEW}_{\Sigma,A}(\mathbf{y_A}, \phi(\mathbf{y_H})) \in \mathbf{V_2}] + \delta}{|[Y]|}$$

$$= \sum_{\mathbf{y'_H} \subset [Y']} \frac{e^{\epsilon} \cdot \Pr[\mathrm{VIEW}_{\Sigma,A}(\mathbf{y_A}, \mathbf{y'_H}) \in \mathbf{V_2}] + \delta}{|[Y']|}$$

$$= e^{\epsilon} \cdot \Pr_{\mathbf{y'_H} \leftarrow \mathbf{Y'}}[\mathrm{VIEW}_{\Sigma,A}(\mathbf{y_A}, \mathbf{y'_H}) \in \mathbf{V_2}] + \delta.$$

Combining Corollary 2 and Lemma 5 allows us to prove Theorem 4. Details are given in the full version.

4   A Differentially Oblivious Shuffle Protocol

In this section, we describe a construction of a differentially oblivious shuffler. We present the protocol in Sect. 4.1 and analyze its obliviousness (for a semi-honest adversary) in Sects. 4.2 and 4.3. We compare its concrete performance to relevant prior work in Sect. 4.4. We defer a discussion of how to deal with malicious behavior to the full version.

Inputs: Each user i has input y_i.

Round 1: Each user chooses $r-1$ users $i_1, \ldots, i_{r-1} \leftarrow [n]$ uniformly and independently, and then forms the onion encryption C_r as described in the text. It sends C_r to user i_1.

Rounds $\ell = 2, \ldots, r-1$: For each ciphertext $C_{r-\ell+2}$ received in the previous round, compute $(i_\ell, C_{r-\ell+1}) := \mathsf{Dec}_{\mathsf{sk}_{i_{\ell-1}}}(C_{r-\ell+2})$ and forward $C_{r-\ell+1}$ to user i_ℓ.

Round r: For each ciphertext C_2 received in the previous round, compute $(S, C_1) := \mathsf{Dec}_{\mathsf{sk}_{i_{r-1}}}(C_2)$ and forward C_1 to the server S.

Output: S initializes $h := \emptyset$. Then, for each ciphertext C received in the previous round, compute $y := \mathsf{Dec}_{\mathsf{sk}_S}(C)$ and add y to h.

Fig. 1. A differentially oblivious shuffling protocol, parameterized by r.

4.1 A Shuffling Protocol

Recall that in our setting we have n users holding inputs $y_1, \ldots, y_n$, respectively, who would like a server (that we treat as distinct from the n users) to learn the multiset $h = \{y_i\}$. We assume the parties have public/private keys $(\mathsf{pk}_1, \mathsf{sk}_1), \ldots, (\mathsf{pk}_n, \mathsf{sk}_n)$, respectively, and that the server has keys $(\mathsf{pk}_S, \mathsf{sk}_S)$. Our protocol, which is based on onion routing [21,33], works as follows. Let r be a parameter that we fix later. Each user U chooses $r-1$ users $i_1, \ldots, i_{r-1} \leftarrow [n]$ uniformly and independently (it may be that U chooses itself), and then forms a nested ("onion") encryption of the form

$$C_r = \mathsf{Enc}_{\mathsf{pk}_{i_1}}(i_2, \mathsf{Enc}_{\mathsf{pk}_{i_2}}(i_3, \cdots (i_{r-1}, \mathsf{Enc}_{\mathsf{pk}_{i_{r-1}}}(S, \mathsf{Enc}_{\mathsf{pk}_S}(y)))\cdots)),$$

such that at each "layer" the identity of the next receiver is encrypted along with an onion encryption whose outer layer can be removed by that receiver. In the first round, U sends C_r to the first receiver i_1, who decrypts to remove the outer layer and thus obtains i_2 and an onion encryption C_{r-1} that it forwards to i_2 in the next round. This process continues for $r-1$ rounds, until in the rth round all parties send the ciphertext $\mathsf{Enc}_{\mathsf{pk}_S}(y)$ they have obtained to the server. (We assume a synchronous communication network.) See Fig. 1.

The protocol requires r rounds of communication, and the total number of ciphertexts transmitted is exactly rn. Since ciphertexts have length $O(r \log n)$, the total communication complexity is $O(r^2 n \log n)$.

4.2 Analysis of Obliviousness ($\epsilon = 0$)

We assume a semi-honest adversary who corrupts up to t users as well as the server S. The attacker has access to the state of any corrupted user, and can also determine which user sent any message that it received. However, we assume the attacker *cannot* eavesdrop on the communication between honest users, so in particular it cannot tell whether some honest user i sent a message to some other honest user j in some round. We treat encryption as ideal in our analysis of obliviousness in order to simplify our treatment.

Assume without loss of generality that users U_1, U_2 are honest and hold different inputs, and fix input vectors $\mathbf{y}$ and $\mathbf{y}'$ that are identical except the inputs of U_1 and U_2 are swapped. Let i_ℓ^1 denote the ℓth intermediate user chosen by U_1 for $1 \le \ell \le r - 1$, and set $i_0^1 = 1$; define $i_0^2, \ldots, i_{r-1}^2$ similarly. (We let round 0 refer to the beginning of the algorithm when U_1 and U_2 each hold their own input.) Say that U_1 *and* U_2 *can swap at round* j (with $0 \le j < r - 1$) if the routing paths of U_1 and U_2 both have an honest user in rounds j and $j + 1$ (i.e., for which users i_j^1, i_{j+1}^1, i_j^2, and i_{j+1}^2 are all honest). A key observation is that if there exists some j such that U_1 and U_2 can swap at round j then the distributions on the attacker's views are *identical* regardless of whether the input vector is $\mathbf{y}$ or $\mathbf{y}'$. The reason for this is that it is equally likely that the onion encryption of U_1 was routed from i_j^1 to i_{j+1}^1 and that of U_2 went from i_j^2 to i_{j+1}^2, or that the communication was "flipped" (in which case we say *the swap happened*) so that the onion encryption of U_1 was routed from i_j^1 to i_{j+1}^2 and that of U_2 went from i_j^2 to i_{j+1}^1. In other words, if there exists some j such that U_1 and U_2 can swap at round j, then perfect obliviousness is achieved. If we let $x_{t,r}$ denote the probability of this event in an execution of the protocol with parameter r when up to t users are corrupted, we have:

Theorem 5. *The protocol in Fig. 1 is* $(0, 1 - x_{t,r})$*-differentially oblivious for t corrupted users.*

Our problem is now reduced to lower bounding $x_{t,r}$. Let $p_t = (1 - t/n)^2$ be the probability that U_1 and U_2 both choose an honest user in some fixed round $j \ge 1$ when t users are corrupted. By definition, we have $x_{t,1} = 0$, and $x_{t,2} = p_t$ since both U_1 and U_2 are honest in round 0. By conditioning on the outcomes of the final two rounds, we can derive the following recurrence relation for $r > 2$:

$$x_{t,r} = p_t^2 + (1 - p_t) \cdot x_{t,r-1} + p_t \cdot (1 - p_t) \cdot x_{t,r-2}.$$

Although it is possible to solve this recurrence, it is cleaner to simply bound $x_{t,r}$ for any desired t, r. The following can be proved by induction on r:

Theorem 6. *For $r > 1$, it holds that $x_{n/3,r} \ge 1 - 0.85^r$. Thus, for $r > 1$ the protocol of Fig. 1 is $(0, 0.85^r)$-differentially oblivious for $n/3$ corrupted users.*

For $r > 1$, it holds that $x_{n/2,r} \ge 1 - 0.95^r$. Thus, for $r > 1$ the protocol of Fig. 1 is $(0, 0.95^r)$-differentially oblivious for $n/2$ corrupted users.

4.3   Analysis of Obliviousness ($\epsilon > 0$)

We show here an alternate analysis that allows us to prove (ϵ, δ)-differential obliviousness for $\epsilon > 0$. (This analysis is incomparable to the analysis of the previous section since, for fixed r, we may obtain larger ϵ but smaller δ.)

We focus again on the case where we have input vectors $\mathbf{y}$ and $\mathbf{y}'$ that are identical except that the inputs of honest users U_1 and U_2 are swapped. The observation we rely on here is that even if there is no round j where U_1 and U_2 can swap at round j, it is still possible to achieve some privacy if their inputs can be swapped via some other honest users. For example, say there is an honest user U_3 and $0 \leq j < j' < j'' < r - 1$ such that (1) U_1 and U_3 can swap at round j, (2) U_2 and U_3 can swap at round j', and (3) U_1 and U_3 can swap at round j''. Then the following events lead to the same view for the adversary: the input vector was $\mathbf{y}$ and none of the swaps happens; the input vector was $\mathbf{y}$ and (only) swaps #1 and #3 happen; or the input vector was $\mathbf{y}'$ and all three swaps happen. This gives some privacy (given a view consistent with these events, the adversary cannot determine with certainty whether the input was $\mathbf{y}$ or $\mathbf{y}'$), but the privacy is not perfect: since each swap is equally likely to happen or not, conditioned on the adversary's view being consistent with the above input $\mathbf{y}$ is twice as likely as input $\mathbf{y}'$. In this particular example the level of privacy obtained is relatively low, but privacy improves as more honest users can potentially be involved in the swaps.

In the full version we give a more detailed analysis of the ϵ, δ parameters obtained by considering swaps between multiple honest users; here we simply describe the qualitative conclusions of the analysis. Say U_1 and U_2 are *swap-compatible* if there are $0 \leq j < j' < j'' < r - 1$ such that (1) the routing path of U_1 has an honest user in rounds j and $j + 1$ as well as rounds j'' and $j'' + 1$, and (2) the routing path of U_2 has an honest user in rounds j' and $j' + 1$ (or the similar event with the roles of U_1 and U_2 interchanged). If U_1, U_2 are swap-compatible then U_1 can potentially swap with some other honest users at round j, other honest users can potentially swap with U_2 at round j', and then U_1 can again potentially swap with other honest users at round j''. For that to occur requires other honest users who can potentially swap with U_1, U_2 at the appropriate rounds; roughly speaking, the more honest users can swap with U_1, U_2, the higher privacy will be achieved for U_1, U_2.

Let δ_1 denote the probability that U_1, U_2 are not swap-compatible. Next, fix some desired value for $\epsilon > 0$. When U_1, U_2 are swap-compatible, we can derive a lower bound m on the number of other honest users that need to be able to swap with U_1, U_2 (we do not define this event more formally here) to ensure privacy bound ϵ. Letting δ_2 be the probability that there are fewer than m other honest users who can swap with U_1, U_2, we can then conclude that our protocol achieves $(\epsilon, \delta_1 + \delta_2)$-differential obliviousness. Note that δ_1 depends only on the corruption threshold and the number of rounds r, and decreases exponentially with r as in the $\epsilon = 0$ case. On the other hand, δ_2 also depends on the total number of parties n as well as the privacy parameter ϵ (since decreasing ϵ requires increasing m, which in turn increases the probability δ_2 of failing to have m other honest users who can swap with U_1, U_2).

4.4   Performance Analysis

To analyze the performance of our protocol and compare it with prior work, we assume encryption is done using the KEM-DEM paradigm, with the KEM portion having a length of 256 bits. We allocate 20 bits for user identities, which suffices for up to $n = 2^{20}$ users,[3] and we assume users' inputs are 128 bits long. The innermost ciphertext thus requires $256 + 128 = 384$ bits, and in each of the other layers we add 256 bits for the next key encapsulation plus 20 bits for the user ID. An r-layer onion ciphertext thus requires $384 + 276(r - 1)$ bits.

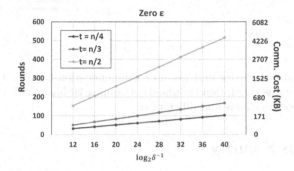

Fig. 2. Round complexity and per-user communication complexity for achieving $\epsilon = 0$ and different δ for various corruption thresholds, assuming 20-bit user IDs.

The $\epsilon = 0$ case. In Fig. 2, we give the number of rounds and per-user communication complexity needed to achieve $(0, \delta)$-differential obliviousness for several values of δ and various corruption thresholds. Note that these results are independent of the number of parties n. Our results compare favorably to prior work of Movahedi et al. [31], especially when the number of parties is large. In particular, for a corruption threshold of $t \approx n/3$ the protocol of Movahedi et al. [31] uses 500 rounds and communication of 128 MB per user when $n = 33{,}000$, and approximately 0.5–1 GB over 1,000 rounds when $n = 10^6$.

Additionally, note that δ is often set to be $10^{-4} \geq \delta \geq 10^{-6}$ in the differential privacy literature. Using that range of values, we require $r \approx 55$–83 with $n/3$ corrupted users, and our per-user communication cost is reduced to 53–119 KB.

The $\epsilon > 0$ case. In Fig. 3, we show how $\delta = \delta_1 + \delta_2$ relates to n, r, and t, and ϵ. Specifically, in Fig. 3(a) we show how the round/communication complexity depends on δ_1, and in Fig. 3(b) we show how ϵ varies with δ_2.

We can use these figures to determine how to set parameters. For example, say we have $n = 12{,}000$ users and up to $t = n/3$ corruptions, and want to determine the δ achievable for $\epsilon = 1$. From Fig. 3(b) we see that $\delta_2 \approx 2^{-23}$. Using Fig. 3(a), we see that 43 rounds suffice for $\delta_1 \approx 2^{-23}$. Thus, the protocol is $(1, 2^{-22})$-differentially oblivious with 43 rounds. Assuming 20 bits for the user IDs, this corresponds to per-user communication of 32 KB.

---

[3] In fact, these identifiers are the only part of our construction that contribute to the $O(\log n)$ multiplicative factor in the overhead.

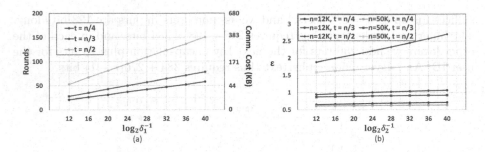

Fig. 3. (a) Round complexity and per-user communication complexity for achieving different δ_1 for various corruption thresholds, assuming 20-bit user IDs. (b) ϵ vs. δ_2 for various corruption thresholds and different n.

5 Malicious Security

We briefly discuss how to address malicious attacks affecting privacy; denial-of-service attacks and other attacks that affect correctness are out of scope. If the encryption scheme used by the protocol is non-malleable, and timestamps and identifiers are included in each layer of the onion to prevent replay attacks [11], then the only attack an adversary can carry out on the protocol of Sect. 4 is to drop messages to reduce the effective number of honest users contributing to the output histogram and thereby degrade privacy (cf. Corollary 1).

As in the work of Ando et al. [1], we can address such an attack by having honest users (1) route dummy messages alongside their real messages, (2) check partway through the shuffling that their dummy messages have not been dropped, and (3) abort the protocol if malicious behavior is detected. Compared to the work of Ando et al., however, we can achieve security against malicious behavior with much lower overhead, both because we assume the adversary cannot eavesdrop on communication between honest users and also because we focus on the eventual application of our protocol to the shuffle model. With regard to the latter point, note that although dropping even a single user's input can be catastrophic for differential obliviousness of a shuffling protocol (e.g., if $\mathbf{y}$ and $\mathbf{y}'$ are input vectors that differ by a transposition of the inputs of users 1 and 2, and the input of user 1 is dropped), dropping a few users' inputs has only a small effect on end-to-end differential privacy when the shuffle protocol is used to instantiate the shuffle model. Concretely, let $\hat{\mathcal{S}}_d$ represent an ideal shuffler that is identical to $\mathcal{S}$ except that the adversary can select d honest users whose messages are dropped. The following is a natural extension of Corollary 1:

Lemma 6. *Fix* $n, t, d, \epsilon, \delta,$ *and* D. *If* $\gamma \geq \max\left\{ \dfrac{14 \cdot |D| \log(2/\delta)}{(n-d-t-1) \cdot \epsilon^2}, \dfrac{27 \cdot |D|}{(n-d-t-1) \cdot \epsilon} \right\}$, *then* $(\mathcal{R}_{\gamma,D} \times \cdots \times \mathcal{R}_{\gamma,D})^{\hat{\mathcal{S}}_d}$ *is* (ϵ, δ)-*DP for* t *corrupted users in the* $\hat{\mathcal{S}}_d$-*hybrid model.*

It thus suffices to realize $\hat{\mathcal{S}}_d$ for small d. We describe our approach for doing so somewhat informally, and leave a detailed analysis for the full version. Let r, s be two parameters. At a high level, our modified protocol has four stages:

1. Each user U_i runs the onion-routing protocol from Sect. 4 twice, in parallel. It sends its real input y_i to the server using $r + s - 1$ intermediate hops, and sends a random dummy value to a randomly selected user R_i—called a "checker"–using $r - 1$ intermediate hops. Appropriate padding is used to make sure the onion encryptions are indistinguishable.
2. After round r, each user U_i asks R_i to respond with the random dummy value chosen by U_i. If R_i responds with the correct value, then U_i sets $\mathsf{cheat}_i := 0$; otherwise, it sets $\mathsf{cheat}_i := 1$.
3. The users run a protocol to determine whether any user set $\mathsf{cheat} = 1$. (We discuss below how this can be implemented efficiently.) If so, they all abort and do not run the next phase.
4. Parties run the onion-routing protocol on the remaining real messages.

The overall argument for why this preserves privacy is as follows. Prior to round r, the adversary cannot distinguish real onion encryptions from dummy onion encryptions. Setting parameters appropriately, we can ensure that if a malicious adversary drops d or more of the honest users' onion encryptions before round r, then with high probability at least one of those will correspond to a dummy message associated with an honest checker; in that case, cheating will be detected and all honest users will abort. This, in turn, means that the real input of an honest user will be completely hidden from the adversary by the onion encryption unless the final s intermediate users chosen by that honest user for the onion-routing of its real message are all corrupted. The probability that this occurs for some honest user is at most $n \cdot (t/n)^s$.

The above shows that if the honest users do not abort by round r, then at most d of the honest users' real messages were dropped before round r. We can thus claim privacy at round r, with the number of honest messages being at least $n - t - d$, just as we did in Sect. 4. Nothing prevents the adversary from dropping as many messages as it likes after round r, but doing so cannot degrade the privacy already achieved by round r.

Efficient Implementation of Stage 3. In stage 3 we need a distributed protocol with the property that if any honest user holds $\mathsf{cheat} = 1$ then all honest users output 1. While this can be achieved using n executions of secure broadcast, doing so would be inefficient and is overkill for our purposes; in particular, it is acceptable for us if the adversary causes disagreement among the honest users. We propose the following lightweight protocol that can be based on any multisignature scheme. Every user who holds $\mathsf{cheat} = 0$ sends a signature on some designated message M to the server. The server then combines these signatures into a single, constant-size signature, and sends it to every user. Each user locally verifies the signature it receives from the server with respect to every users' public key, and outputs 1 if verification fails (or if it does not receive any signature from the server). Note that even if all-but-one of the users are corrupted, an adversary cannot forge a valid multisignature on M unless every honest party held $\mathsf{cheat} = 0$.

5.1   Performance Analysis

We analyze the communication overhead of the malicious protocol relative to the semi-honest protocol for the same privacy guarantees. Using dummy messages incurs roughly $2\times$ overhead compared with the semi-honest protocol using the same number of rounds. (For simplicity, we do not count the communication in stages 2 and 3 which is anyway dominated by the onion routing. In fact, since dummy messages are not routed in stage 4, the communication overhead is less than $2\times$ of the semi-honest protocol with the same number of rounds.) However, since the total number of rounds must be increased in the malicious setting, the overall communication overhead is higher. (Note that the total communication complexity is quadratic in the number of rounds since the length of each onion encryption is linear in the number of rounds.)

Zero ϵ. For the values of t, δ in Fig. 2, we need to set s equal to anywhere from 5% to 52% of r. This results in a total communication overhead of 2.2–4.6$\times$ compared to the semi-honest protocol.

Non-zero ϵ. For the parameters in Fig. 3, we need to set s equal to anywhere from 30–80% of r. This results in a total communication overhead of 3.4–6.4$\times$ compared to the semi-honest protocol.

Comparison to Prior Work. For $n = 1,000,000$ users, $t = n/3$, and to achieve $(0, 2^{-40})$-differential privacy, our malicious protocol requires $r + s = 212$ rounds and 1.5 MB communication per party. In comparison, for 1,000,000 parties and $t = n/5$, we estimate[4] Bell et al. [6] costs 12 rounds and communication of 199 KB per party. While the performance of our protocol is inferior, we note that in practice, often worse privacy parameters are chosen, and our protocol would then out-perform that of Bell at al. For example, if $(1.25, 2^{-20})$-differential privacy suffices and $t = n/3$, our per-party communication cost reduces to 169 KB using only 70 rounds. If $(0.454, 2^{-20})$-differential privacy suffices and $t = n/5$, our per-party communication cost reduces to 70.9 KB using only 45 rounds.

Finally, if a DO shuffle is used in applications beyond the privacy blanket, we compare even more favorably when the input domain size is larger than $O(n^{1/3})$. Specifically, our communication cost per party grows logarithmically in the domain size, while theirs either grows linearly in the domain size, or super linearly in n.

References

1. Ando, M., Lysyanskaya, A., Upfal, E.: Practical and provably secure onion routing. In: ICALP 2018, volume 107 of LIPIcs, pp. 144:1–144:14. Schloss Dagstuhl, July 2018

---

[4] We assume the availability of PKI so we drop the cost for Merkle tree verification in their protocol. We also use their baseline solution (rather than the invertible Bloom lookup table solution) to take advantage of the small domain setting.

2. Backes, M., Goldberg, I., Kate, A., Mohammadi, E.: Provably secure and practical onion routing. In: 25th IEEE Computer Security Foundations Symposium (CSF), pp. 369–385 (2012)
3. Backes, M., Kate, A., Manoharan, P., Meiser, S., Mohammadi, E.: AnoA: a framework for analyzing anonymous communication protocols. In: 26th IEEE Computer Security Foundations Symposium (CSF), pp. 163–178 (2013)
4. Balle, B., Bell, J., Gascón, A., Nissim, K.: The privacy blanket of the shuffle model. In: Boldyreva, A., Micciancio, D. (eds.) CRYPTO 2019. LNCS, vol. 11693, pp. 638–667. Springer, Cham (2019). https://doi.org/10.1007/978-3-030-26951-7_22
5. Beimel, A., Nissim, K., Omri, E.: Distributed private data analysis: simultaneously solving how and what. In: Wagner, D. (ed.) CRYPTO 2008. LNCS, vol. 5157, pp. 451–468. Springer, Heidelberg (2008). https://doi.org/10.1007/978-3-540-85174-5_25
6. Bell, J.H., Bonawitz, K.A., Gascón, A., Lepoint, T., Raykova, M.: Secure single-server aggregation with (poly)logarithmic overhead. In: ACM CCS, pp. 1253–1269. ACM Press (2020)
7. Bellet, A., Guerraoui, R., Hendrikx, H.: Who started this rumor? Quantifying the natural differential privacy guarantees of gossip protocols. In 34th International Symposium on Distributed Computing (DISC), volume 179 of LIPIcs, pp. 8:1–8:18 (2020)
8. Bittau, A., et al.: Prochlo: strong privacy for analytics in the crowd. In: Proceedings 26th Symposium on Operating Systems Principles (SOSP), pp. 441–459 (2017)
9. Boyle, E., Goldwasser, S., Tessaro, S.: Communication locality in secure multi-party computation. In: Sahai, A. (ed.) TCC 2013. LNCS, vol. 7785, pp. 356–376. Springer, Heidelberg (2013). https://doi.org/10.1007/978-3-642-36594-2_21
10. Bünz, B., Hu, Y., Matsuo, S., Shi, E.: Non-interactive differentially anonymous router (2021). Available at https://eprint.iacr.org/2021/1242
11. Camenisch, J., Lysyanskaya, A.: A formal treatment of onion routing. In: Shoup, V. (ed.) CRYPTO 2005. LNCS, vol. 3621, pp. 169–187. Springer, Heidelberg (2005). https://doi.org/10.1007/11535218_11
12. Hubert Chan, T.-H., Chung, K.-M., Maggs, B.M., Shi, E.: Foundations of differentially oblivious algorithms. In: 30th SODA, pp. 2448–2467. ACM-SIAM (2019)
13. Chan, T.-H.H., Shi, E., Song, D.: Optimal lower bound for differentially private multi-party aggregation. In: Epstein, L., Ferragina, P. (eds.) ESA 2012. LNCS, vol. 7501, pp. 277–288. Springer, Heidelberg (2012). https://doi.org/10.1007/978-3-642-33090-2_25
14. Chaum, D.: Untraceable electronic mail, return addresses, and digital pseudonyms. Comm. ACM 24(2), 84–88 (1981)
15. Chaum, D.: The dining cryptographers problem: unconditional sender and recipient untraceability. J. Cryptol. 1(1), 65–75 (1988)
16. Cheu, A., Smith, A., Ullman, J., Zeber, D., Zhilyaev, M.: Distributed differential privacy via shuffling. In: Ishai, Y., Rijmen, V. (eds.) EUROCRYPT 2019. LNCS, vol. 11476, pp. 375–403. Springer, Cham (2019). https://doi.org/10.1007/978-3-030-17653-2_13
17. Dani, V., King, V., Movahedi, M., Saia, J.: Brief announcement: breaking the $O(nm)$ bit barrier, secure multiparty computation with a static adversary. In: 31st ACM PODC, pp. 227–228. ACM (2012)
18. Das, D., Meiser, S., Mohammadi, E., Kate, A.: Anonymity trilemma: strong anonymity, low bandwidth overhead, low latency - choose two. In 2018 IEEE Symposium on Security and Privacy, pp. 108–126. IEEE Computer Society Press (2018)

19. Dwork, C., McSherry, F., Nissim, K., Smith, A.: Calibrating noise to sensitivity in private data analysis. In: Halevi, S., Rabin, T. (eds.) TCC 2006. LNCS, vol. 3876, pp. 265–284. Springer, Heidelberg (2006). https://doi.org/10.1007/11681878_14

20. Feigenbaum, J., Johnson, A., Syverson, P.F.: Probabilistic analysis of onion routing in a black-box model. ACM Trans. Inf. Syst. Secur. 15(3), 14:1–14:28 (2012)

21. Goldschlag, D.M., Reed, M.G., Syverson, P.F.: Hiding routing information. In: Anderson, R. (ed.) IH 1996. LNCS, vol. 1174, pp. 137–150. Springer, Heidelberg (1996). https://doi.org/10.1007/3-540-61996-8_37

22. Groce, A., Rindal, P., Rosulek, M.: Cheaper private set intersection via differentially private leakage. Proc. Priv. Enhancing Technol. (PETS) 2019(3), 6–25 (2019)

23. He, X., Machanavajjhala, A., Flynn, C.J., Srivastava, D.: Composing differential privacy and secure computation: a case study on scaling private record linkage. In: ACM CCS 2017, pp. 1389–1406. ACM Press (2017)

24. Huang, Y., Evans, D., Katz, J.: Private set intersection: are garbled circuits better than custom protocols? In: NDSS 2012. The Internet Society, February 2012

25. Kuhn, C., Beck, M., Schiffner, S., Jorswieck, E.A., Strufe, T.: On privacy notions in anonymous communication (2018). Available at https://arxiv.org/abs/1812.05638

26. Kuhn, C., Beck, M., Strufe, T.: Breaking and (partially) fixing provably secure onion routing. In: 2020 IEEE Symposium on Security and Privacy, pp. 168–185. IEEE Computer Society Press (2020)

27. Lazar, D., Gilad, Y., Zeldovich, N.: Karaoke: distributed private messaging immune to passive traffic analysis. In: Proceedings 13th USENIX Conference on Operating Systems Design and Implementation, pp. 711–725. USENIX Association (2018)

28. Mauw, S., Verschuren, J.H.S., de Vink, E.P.: A formalization of anonymity and onion routing. In: Samarati, P., Ryan, P., Gollmann, D., Molva, R. (eds.) ESORICS 2004. LNCS, vol. 3193, pp. 109–124. Springer, Heidelberg (2004). https://doi.org/10.1007/978-3-540-30108-0_7

29. Mazloom, S., Dov Gordon, S.: Secure computation with differentially private access patterns. In: ACM CCS 2018, pp. 490–507. ACM Press (2018)

30. Mazloom, S., Le, P.H., Ranellucci, S., Dov Gordon, S.: Secure parallel computation on national scale volumes of data. In: USENIX Security 2020, pp. 2487–2504. USENIX Association (2020)

31. Movahedi, M., Saia, J., Zamani, M.: Secure multi-party shuffling. In: Scheideler, C. (ed.) SIROCCO 2014. LNCS, vol. 9439, pp. 459–473. Springer, Cham (2015). https://doi.org/10.1007/978-3-319-25258-2_32

32. Smart, N.P., Talibi Alaoui, Y.: Distributing any elliptic curve based protocol. In: Albrecht, M. (ed.) IMACC 2019. LNCS, vol. 11929, pp. 342–366. Springer, Cham (2019). https://doi.org/10.1007/978-3-030-35199-1_17

33. Syverson, P.F., Goldschlag, D.M., Reed, M.G.: Anonymous connections and onion routing. In: 1997 IEEE Symposium on Security and Privacy, pp. 44–54. IEEE Computer Society Press (1997)

34. Tyagi, N., Gilad, Y., Leung, D., Zaharia, M., Zeldovich, N.: Stadium: a distributed metadata-private messaging system. In: Proceedings 26th Symposium on Operating Systems Principles (SOSP), pp. 423–440. ACM Press (2017)

35. van den Hooff, J., Lazar, D., Zaharia, M., Zeldovich, N.: Vuvuzela: scalable private messaging resistant to traffic analysis. In: Proceedings 25th Symposium on Operating Systems Principles (SOSP), pp. 137–152. ACM Press (2015)

36. Erlingsson, Ú., Feldman, V., Mironov, I., Raghunathan, A., Talwar, K., Thakurta, A.: Amplification by shuffling: from local to central differential privacy via anonymity. In: SODA 2019, pp. 2468–2479 (2019)

Bootstrapping for Approximate Homomorphic Encryption with Negligible Failure-Probability by Using Sparse-Secret Encapsulation

Jean-Philippe Bossuat[1]([✉]), Juan Troncoso-Pastoriza[1],
and Jean-Pierre Hubaux[1,2]

[1] Tune Insight SA, Lausanne, Switzerland
{jean-philippe,juan,jean-pierre}@tuneinsight.com
[2] École polytechnique fédérale de Lausanne (EPFL), Lausanne, Switzerland
jean-pierre.hubaux@epfl.ch

Abstract. Bootstrapping parameters for the approximate homomorphic-encryption scheme of Cheon et al., CKKS (Asiacrypt 17), are usually instantiated using sparse secrets to be efficient. However, using sparse secrets constrains the range of practical parameters within a tight interval, as they must support a large enough depth for the bootstrapping circuit but also be secure with respect to the sparsity of their secret.

We present a bootstrapping procedure for the CKKS scheme that combines both dense and sparse secrets. Our construction enables the use of parameters for which the homomorphic capacity is based on a dense secret, yet with a bootstrapping complexity that remains the one of a sparse secret and with a large security margin. Moreover, this also enables us to easily parameterize the bootstrapping circuit so that it has a negligible failure probability that, to the best of our knowledge, has never been achieved for the CKKS scheme. When using the parameters of previous works, our bootstrapping procedures enable a faster execution with an increased precision and lower failure probability. For example, we are able to bootstrap a plaintext of $\mathbb{C}^{32768}$ in 20.2 s, with 32.11 bits of precision, 285 remaining modulus bits, a failure probability of $2^{-138.7}$, and 128 bit security.

Keywords: Fully Homomorphic Encryption · Bootstrapping · Implementation

1 Introduction

1.1 The CKKS Scheme

The CKKS scheme by Cheon et al. [10] is a *leveled* ring learning with errors (R-LWE) [23] homomorphic-encryption scheme that enables approximate arithmetic over vectors of complex numbers. Since its introduction, this scheme has

J.-P. Bossuat, J. Troncoso-Pastoriza—Part of this work was carried out at EPFL.

© Springer Nature Switzerland AG 2022
G. Ateniese and D. Venturi (Eds.): ACNS 2022, LNCS 13269, pp. 521–541, 2022.
https://doi.org/10.1007/978-3-031-09234-3_26

grown in popularity, as it is currently the most efficient for performing encrypted floating-point arithmetic. Ciphertexts are tuples of $R_Q = \mathbb{Z}_Q[X]/(X^N+1)$, with the main cryptographic parameters being the polynomial-ring degree N and its modulus Q; for a given security parameter λ and fixed N, an upper bound on Q can be derived (a smaller Q leads to a more secure instance).

A fresh CKKS ciphertext is of the form $(c_0, c_1) = (-as + m + e, a) \in R_Q^2$ for a a random polynomial, s and e low-norm secret polynomials and m a message polynomial. The decryption is obtained by evaluating $\langle (c_0, c_1), (1, s) \rangle = m + e$.

A message m is encrypted at the modulus Q (maximum *level*) and each subsequent multiplication *consumes* a *level* and reduces the size of the modulus Q. Hence, the upper bound on Q fixes the maximum homomorphic capacity of fresh ciphertexts (the maximum circuit's depth). Once a ciphertext reaches its smallest possible modulus q, it can be *bootstrapped* back to a larger modulus, thus enabling the evaluation of arbitrary-depth circuits.

1.2 Bootstrapping

The bootstrapping procedure for the CKKS scheme was first proposed by Cheon et al. [8] and can be summarized in four steps: (i) ModRaise: raise the ciphertext, currently at its smallest modulus q, back to its highest modulus Q. (ii) CoeffsToSlots: homomorphically evaluate the canonical embedding τ. (iii) EvalMod: homomorphically evaluate a modular reduction, approximated by the scaled sine function $q/(2\pi) \cdot \sin(2\pi x/q)$. (iv) SlotsToCoeffs: homomorphically evaluate τ^{-1}. The procedure outputs a ciphertext at modulus Q' with $Q > Q' > q$, the difference between Q' and q being the *residual* homomorphic capacity after the bootstrapping. Cheon et al. evaluate τ with a matrix (plaintext) × vector (encrypted) multiplication and compute the scaled sine function using the Taylor series of e^{ix} followed by an extraction of the imaginary part to retrieve $\sin(x)$.

Extensive works have since improved the efficiency of the original procedure of Cheon et al. The first improvement was proposed by Chen et al. [4]. In their work, they improved the efficiency of the homomorphic evaluation of τ by multiple orders of magnitude by adopting an FFT-like approach instead of a single matrix-vector multiplication. They also proposed a more efficient polynomial approximation by directly approximating $\sin(x)$ with a Chebyshev interpolant. In a concurrent work Cheon et al. [6] proposed a similar technique to improve the evaluation of τ.

These works were followed by efforts aimed at improving the homomorphic modular reduction, which is the most difficult step of the bootstrapping since the CKKS scheme does not support the evaluation of non-polynomial functions. Han and Ki [13] proposed a polynomial interpolation that takes into account the distribution of the message and uses a scaled cosine to enable the double angle formula, which allowed them to greatly reduce the degree of the interpolant. Lee et al. [19] proposed a modified multi-interval Remez algorithm to find the optimal minimax approximation of the scaled sine/cosine functions, and used the inverse sine function to remove the error introduced by the approximation of the ideal modular function by a trigonometric function. Lee et al. [20] proposed a polynomial interpolation that minimizes the variance of the interpolant, thus reducing the error introduced by the homomorphic evaluation of the polynomial. Jutla and Manohar [15] proposed a novel variant of the Lagrange interpolation that allowed them to directly approximate the modular reduction function, without having to rely on trigonometric functions. They also proposed [16] to use a sine series to approximate the modular reduction and achieved a much higher precision than the previous works. Lee et al. [21] proposed a polynomial approximation method for the modular reduction based on the L2-norm minimization. Similarly to Jutla and Manohar, their technique allows them to avoid using trigonometric functions and directly approximate the modular reduction.

Bossuat et al. [3] proposed a more efficient algorithm to evaluate general linear transformations and a polynomial evaluation algorithm that preserves the ciphertext scale and does not introduce rescaling errors, as well as several other smaller improvements to the bootstrapping procedure. They show that, when combined, these improvements lead to a bootstrapping an order of magnitude more efficient than the previous works. Additionally, they proposed the first practical instance of a bootstrapping with a dense secret as well as the first open source implementation [18] of the bootstrapping for the full-RNS (Residue Number System) variant of the CKKS scheme [7]. Finally, Yu and Hayato [14] proposed a more efficient way to evaluate the trace function.

Put together, these works improved the bootstrapping procedure to be orders of magnitude more efficient and precise than the original proposal by Cheon et al. However, the bootstrapping circuit has fundamentally remained unchanged since its first introduction. One of its limitations is its high sensitivity to the density h of the secret s: the larger h is (the more non-zero elements s has), the more complicated the EvalMod step is and the higher depth the bootstrapping requires. The density h also has an impact on the bootstrapping failure probability. Indeed, the magnitude of the plaintext coefficient on which the homomorphic modular reduction must be applied is a function of h, and if a single coefficient falls outside of the approximation interval (a ciphertext typically encrypts 2^{14} to 2^{16} values), the bootstrapping procedure fails and returns unusable values. Bossuat et al. [3] observed that commonly used bootstrapping parameters have a high failure probability and it is only recently that works have started to quantify and mitigate this failure probability.

For these reasons, bootstrapping procedures are instantiated with sparse secrets (with small h). But recent improvements on attacks targeting sparse secrets [9,11,24] have reduced the upper bound on the modulus Q; consequently, parameters using sparse keys must be regularly updated. Being able to mitigate this dependency on sparse secrets would therefore be an important step for the adoption and practicality of CKKS bootstrapping.

1.3   Our Contributions

In this work, we propose a *sparse-secret encapsulation* technique for the CKKS bootstrapping; the technique improves the CKKS bootstrapping security and efficiency by taking advantage of the security margin provided by using evaluation keys at a small modulus. Our main contributions can be summarized as follows:

Minimized Security-Dependency on Sparse Secrets. The *leveled* property of the CKKS scheme is tightly related to its security, as the security of an R-LWE sample is notably based on the size of its modulus Q. For a fixed ring degree N and a security parameter λ, an upper bound for Q is derived and the public keys are generated using this Q. Although R-LWE samples at modulus Q have security λ, previous works did not take into account that elements at a lower *level* have a proportionally smaller modulus, hence a larger security.

We propose a modification to the bootstrapping circuit that enables the generation of all evaluation keys using a secret that is independent from the one on which the complexity of the EvalMod step is based. Instead of the usual single secret instance, our bootstrapping instance uses an additional ephemeral secret that determines the complexity of the bootstrapping procedure. As such, the maximum modulus Q does not depend anymore on the sparse secret that defines the complexity of the EvalMod step, hence a denser secret can be used to generate the evaluation keys.

This construction has a two-fold benefit: (i) It increases the flexibility to choose bootstrapping parameters, such as ones with a denser secret and larger homomorphic capacity, as the security of all evaluation keys at the maximum modulus is based on a different secret than the one defining the circuit complexity. (ii) The dependency on the sparse secret is minimized by limiting it to an evaluation key at the smallest modulus; we show that this evaluation key also has a large security margin against attacks that target sparse (and dense) secrets.

Negligible Failure Probability. By having the EvalMod step rely on a ephemeral sparse secret of low h, we are able to greatly reduce the complexity of this step, allowing for a higher precision and a much lower failure probability. In fact, we can easily make this failure probability smaller than the security parameter $2^{-\lambda}$, which has never been achieved before, to the best of our knowledge.

Empirical Experiments and Open Source Implementation. We evaluate our contribution with empirical experiments and provide an open source implementation of this work in the Lattigo library [18].

The rest of the article is organized as follow: In Sect. 2, we introduce the used notation and recall the necessary background for the CKKS scheme and its bootstrapping; In Sect. 3, we present our core contributions; In Sect. 4, we give the security argument that our modification does not introduce any new security assumption and examine the security of our construction for concrete parameters; In Sect. 5, we empirically analyse the impact of our contribution on the noise and bootstrapping precision. In Sect. 6, we evaluate our contribution with empirical experiments and discuss the implications of our modified bootstrapping procedure.

2   Background

In this section, we introduce the notation used in the rest of this paper, as well as the necessary technical background related to our contribution.

2.1   Notation

For N, a fixed power of two, let $R_Q = \mathbb{Z}_Q[X]/(X^N + 1)$ be the cyclotomic polynomial ring over the integers modulo Q with coefficients in $[-\lfloor Q/2 \rfloor, \lfloor Q/2 \rfloor)$. Define $Y = X^{N/2n}$ for n some power of two smaller than N (a polynomial in Y is a polynomial in X with zero at coefficient degree that are not a multiple of $N/2n$). We denote single elements (polynomials or numbers) in italics, e.g., a, and vectors of such elements in bold, e.g., $\boldsymbol{a}$. We denote $a^{(i)}$ the element at position i of the vector $\boldsymbol{a}$ or the degree-i coefficient of the polynomial a. We denote $\|\cdot\|$ the infinity norm, $[\cdot]_Q$, $\lfloor \cdot \rfloor$, $\lceil \cdot \rfloor$ the reduction modulo Q, rounding to the previous and to the closest integer, respectively (coefficient-wise for polynomials), and $\langle \cdot, \cdot \rangle$ the inner product.

We define the following distributions over R_Q: χ_Q has coefficients uniformly distributed over $\mathbb{Z}_Q$. χ_h has coefficients uniformly distributed over $\{-1, 1\}$ and exactly h non-zero coefficients. χ_σ has coefficients distributed according to a centered discrete Gaussian distribution with standard deviation σ. Unless otherwise specified, σ is assumed to be 3.19 (Homomorphic Encryption Standard [1]) and sampled values are truncated to $[-\lfloor 6\sigma \rfloor, \lfloor 6\sigma \rfloor]$. We denote the act of sampling a polynomial from a given distribution χ by $\leftarrow \chi$.

An R-LWE distribution is parameterized by the tuple $\{N, Q, h, \sigma\}$ and is sampled as $(-as + e, a) \in R_Q^2$ with $s \leftarrow \chi_h$, $a \leftarrow \chi_Q$ and $e \leftarrow \chi_\sigma$. We say that a parameter set $\{N, Q, h, \sigma\}$ is λ-secure if the advantage of an adversary $\mathcal{A}$ to distinguish between the distribution $(-as + e, a) \in R_Q^2$ and the uniform distribution $U(R_Q^2)$ is bounded by $2^{-\lambda}$:

$$\text{Adv}_\mathcal{A} = |\Pr[\mathcal{A}^{(-as+e,a)} = 1] - \Pr[\mathcal{A}^{U(R_Q^2)} = 1]| \leq 2^{-\lambda}.$$

2.2   Approximate Homomorphic Encryption (CKKS)

A CKKS plaintext is a polynomial $m(Y) \in \mathbb{Z}_Q[Y]/(Y^{2n} + 1)$ (with $X^{N/2n} = Y$). We define the following plaintext encoding:

- The *coefficient* encoding, for which the message $\boldsymbol{m} \in \mathbb{R}^{2n}$ is directly encoded on $\mathbb{Z}_Q[Y]/(Y^{2n} + 1)$ as $m(Y) = \lfloor \Delta \boldsymbol{m} \rceil$, for Δ a scaling factor.
- The *slot* encoding, for which the message $\boldsymbol{m} \in \mathbb{C}^n$ is subjected to the canonical embedding $\tau : \mathbb{C}^n \to \mathbb{R}^{2n}$, which preserves the coefficient-wise complex arithmetic. The *coefficient* encoding is then applied to encode the result on $\mathbb{Z}_Q[Y]/(Y^{2n} + 1)$.

A CKKS ciphertext ct_Q^s is an R-LWE sample masking a plaintext polynomial m: $(c_0, c_1) = (-as + m + e, a) \in R_Q^2$, and the decryption circuit is its evaluation at the secret s: $\langle (c_0, c_1), (1, s) \rangle = m + e \in R_Q$.

A CKKS switching key $\mathsf{swk}_{QP}^{s \to s'}$ is a vector of R-LWE samples masking a secret s: $(-a^{(i)}s' + w^{(i)}Ps + e^{(i)}, a^{(i)}) \in R_{QP}^{2 \times \beta}$ for $1 \le i \le \beta$, $\boldsymbol{w} = (w^{(1)}, \ldots, w^{(\beta)})$ an integer basis decomposition and P a secondary modulus such that $P \approx \sum w^{(i)}$. Note that the security of the R-LWE samples used in the switching keys is based on the modulus QP. Through the public algorithm KeySwitch, $\mathsf{swk}_{QP}^{s \to s'}$ can be used to homomorphically re-encrypt a ciphertext $\mathsf{ct}^s = (c_0, c_1)$ to a ciphertext $\mathsf{ct}^{s'} = (c_0', c_1')$ by computing $(c_0', c_1') = (c_0, 0) + \lfloor P^{-1} \cdot \langle \boldsymbol{w}^{-1}(c_1), \mathsf{swk}^{s \to s'} \rangle \rceil$, where $\boldsymbol{w}^{-1}(c_1)$ denotes the decomposition of the coefficients of c_1 in base $\boldsymbol{w}$. The additional modulus P is used to control the magnitude of the error (which is $\langle \boldsymbol{w}^{-1}(c_1), \boldsymbol{e} \rangle$) added during the key-switching. The public encryption key is a switching key $\mathsf{swk}_{QP}^{0 \to s}$. In addition to the access structure management that this procedure provides, it is a fundamental building block of the CKKS scheme as it is used to ensure the correctness and compactness of the decryption circuit for several core homomorphic operations (e.g. ciphertext-ciphertext multiplication and homomorphic plaintext-slots cyclic-rotations).

2.3 Bootstrapping

The bootstrapping procedure of the CKKS scheme [8] aims at raising the ciphertext to a higher modulus to enable further homomorphic evaluation. More specifically, upon the input of a ciphertext ct_q^s such that $\langle \mathsf{ct}_q^s, (1, s) \rangle = m(Y) + e$, for s a secret with h non-zero coefficients, the CKKS bootstrapping outputs a ciphertext $\mathsf{ct}_{Q'}^s$ that decrypts to $m'(Y) = m(Y) + e'$, where $Q > Q' > q$ for Q the maximum modulus, Q' the modulus after the bootstrapping, and q the modulus before the bootstrapping. It is important to note that $\|e'\| \ge \|e\|$. This implies that, although this procedure is referred to as *bootstrapping*, its aim is not to reduce the underlying error but to enable further computations. The procedure consists of the following four steps: ModRaise, CoeffsToSlots, EvalMod, and SlotsToCoeffs. We now briefly explain them, omitting the error terms for clarity.

ModRaise: the *exhausted* ciphertext, whose modulus is q, is expressed in the modulus $Q \gg q$. Note that this step does not modify the coefficients of the ciphertext (thus has no effect on the error), as it only represent them in a different RNS basis. This yields a ciphertext that decrypts to $[c_0 + sc_1]_Q = q \cdot I(X) + m(Y) = m'(Y)$, where $q \cdot I(X) = \left[-[sc_1]_q + sc_1 \right]_Q$ is an integer polynomial that represents the extra multiples of q not removed by the reduction modulo Q (because $Q \gg q$). Note that $\|I(X)\| \le h$ (s has h non-zero coefficients).

If $2n \ne N$ (*sparse* packing), then $Y \ne X$ and $I(X)$ is not a polynomial in Y. In other words, we have multiples of q in the coefficients X that are not multiples of $N/2n$. In this case, we can map $q \cdot I(X) + m(Y)$ to $(N/2n) \cdot (q \cdot \tilde{I}(Y) + m(Y))$ by evaluating a trace-like map $X \to \sum_{i=0}^{N/2n-1} (-1)^i X^{i2n+1}$ [8] that zeroes those coefficients of X whose degree is not a multiple of $N/2n$, and multiplies the others by $N/2n$.

The remaining steps of the bootstrapping remove this unwanted $q \cdot \tilde{I}(Y)$ polynomial by homomorphically evaluating a modular reduction by q on $m'(Y)$.

CoeffsToSlots: the canonical embedding τ is homomorphically evaluated on $m'(Y)$. Indeed, $m'(Y)$ can be seen as a fresh message in the *coefficient* domain. To enable the parallel (slot-wise) evaluation, it needs to be encoded in the *slot* domain.

EvalMod: a polynomial approximation of the function $f(x) = x \mod q$ is homomorphically evaluated on $m'(Y)$, thus removing the unwanted $\tilde{I}(Y)$ polynomial.

SlotsToCoeffs: the inverse of the canonical embedding, τ^{-1}, is evaluated on $m'(Y)$ and a close approximation (recall that $||e'|| \geq ||e||$) of the original message $m(Y)$, minus the unwanted polynomial, is retrieved. After this last step, the ciphertext has modulus $Q' > q$ and we can evaluate further operations, until it reaches modulus q and a new bootstrapping is needed.

3 Proposed Technique

Our contribution is based on two observations: (i) The complexity of the EvalMod step is determined by the secret distribution of the ciphertext during the Mod-Raise step (we further specify this dependency in Sect. 3.1). (ii) The *leveled* behavior of the CKKS scheme positively affects its security. I.e., ciphertexts entering the ModRaise procedure are at a low *level*, and a sparser secret can be used for the same security.

We use these observations to modify the ModRaise step of the bootstrapping by encapsulating it between two KeySwitching procedures: The first one switches the low-*level* ciphertext to a sparser secret $\tilde{s}$ before the ModRaise and the second one, after the ModRaise, switches the high-*level* ciphertext back to a dense secret s.

We detail now the original ModRaise procedure and the improvement we bring to it.

3.1 Original ModRaise and Bootstrapping Failure Probability

The original ModRaise (see Sect. 2.3) takes a ciphertext $\mathsf{ct} = (c_0, c_1) \in R_q^2$ that decrypts to $m(Y)$, a polynomial of $2n$ coefficients, and outputs a new ciphertext $\mathsf{ct}' = (c_0', c_1') \in R_Q^2$ that decrypts to a new message of the form $q \cdot \tilde{I}(Y) + m(Y) + e$.

The infinity norm of the polynomial $\tilde{I}(Y)$ is upper-bounded by the Hamming weight h of the secret, hence the EvalMod step has to evaluate a polynomial approximation of the modular reduction in the interval $[-h, h]$. However, this upper bound h can be quite large; since $\tilde{I}(Y)$ follows an Irwin-Hall distribution [19], we have that $||\tilde{I}(Y)||$ is $\mathcal{O}(\sqrt{h})$ with high probability [8] and, in practice, a smaller probabilistic bound $K < h$ is used instead. Given that the ciphertext encrypts a message $m(Y)$ with $Y = X^{N/2n}$ under a secret $s \leftarrow \chi_h$ before the ModRaise, the exact probability $f(K, h, n) = \Pr[||\tilde{I}(Y)|| > K]$ can be computed by adapting the cumulative probability function of the Irwin-Hall distribution [3]:

$$1 - \left(\frac{2}{(h+1)!} \left(\sum_{i=0}^{\lfloor K + 0.5(h+1) \rfloor} (-1)^i \binom{h+1}{i} (K + 0.5(h+1) - i)^{h+1} \right) - 1 \right)^{2n}.$$

$$(1)$$

We refer to $f(K, h, n)$ as the *bootstrapping failure probability*, i.e. the probability that at least one coefficient of $\tilde{I}(Y)$ falls outside of the approximation interval $[-K, K]$. Indeed, when such event happens, the procedure returns unusable values. For example, if we upper bound the failure probability to $f(K, h, n) \leq 2^{-15}$ for a fixed $n = 2^{15}$ slots and variable h, then $\lim_{h \to \infty} K \approx 1.81\sqrt{h}$ [3].

Therefore, the density h of the secret has a two-fold effect on the practicality of the bootstrapping. On the one hand, the sparser the secret, the smaller the range of parameters that can securely and efficiently evaluate the bootstrapping circuit, as a smaller h implies a smaller upper-bound on the modulus Q for a fixed ring degree N and a security parameter λ. On the other hand, the denser the secret, the more *levels* are required for the EvalMod step. Indeed, this step homomorphically evaluates a modular reduction on the interval $[-K, K]$ that, as shown, is proportional to $\sqrt{h}$.

3.2 ModRaise with *Sparse-Secret Encapsulation*

We instantiate the base scheme, as well as its bootstrapping circuit, with a secret s of density h such that the R-LWE samples of the keys, under s and at modulus QP, are at least λ-secure. We then encapsulate the ModRaise step between two KeySwitch such that the ciphertext is only temporarily switched to a sparser secret $\tilde{s}$ with density $\tilde{h} < h$, with R-LWE samples under $\tilde{s}$ and at modulus $qp \ll QP$ being at least λ-secure. Consequently, the unwanted polynomial $q \cdot \tilde{I}(Y)$ depends on the distribution of $\tilde{s}$, but the bootstrapping circuit remains evaluated under s.

For this instantiation, we generate two sets of parameters $\{N, QP, h, \sigma\}$ and $\{N, qp, \tilde{h}, \sigma\}$, with $qp \ll QP$ and $\tilde{h} < h$, which are both at least λ-secure; and we sample a secret $s \leftarrow \chi_h$, as well as a secret $\tilde{s} \leftarrow \chi_{\tilde{h}}$. Let $\mathsf{swk}_{qp}^{s \to \tilde{s}}$ be a switching key at modulus qp, which can be used to publicly re-encrypt a ciphertext from the secret s to the secret $\tilde{s}$. And let $\mathsf{swk}_{QP}^{\tilde{s} \to s}$ be a switching key at modulus QP, which can be used to publicly re-encrypt a ciphertext from $\tilde{s}$ to s.

Given a ciphertext ct_q^s at modulus q encrypted under s, our proposed algorithm first key-switches ct_q^s from s to $\tilde{s}$ using $\mathsf{swk}_{qp}^{s \to \tilde{s}}$. Then, it applies the regular ModRaise algorithm that expresses its coefficients in a larger modulus. The ciphertext is now expressed in the modulus Q, but with coefficients whose norm remains unchanged and bounded by $\lfloor q/2 \rfloor$. Finally, the algorithm key-switches the ciphertext back to the key s by using $\mathsf{swk}_{QP}^{\tilde{s} \to s}$. We detail our modified ModRaise in Algorithm 1.

Algorithm 1: Encapsulated ModRaise

Input: ct_q^s, $\mathsf{swk}_{qp}^{s \to \tilde{s}}$, $\mathsf{swk}_{QP}^{\tilde{s} \to s}$
Output: ct_Q^s
1   $\mathsf{ct}_q^{\tilde{s}} \leftarrow \mathsf{KeySwitch}(\mathsf{ct}_q^s, \mathsf{swk}_{qp}^{s \to \tilde{s}})$
2   $\mathsf{ct}_Q^{\tilde{s}} \leftarrow \mathsf{ModRaise}(\mathsf{ct}_q^{\tilde{s}}, Q)$
3   $\mathsf{ct}_Q^s \leftarrow \mathsf{KeySwitch}(\mathsf{ct}_Q^{\tilde{s}}, \mathsf{swk}_{QP}^{\tilde{s} \to s})$
4   **return** ct_Q^s

Remark 1. Algorithm 1 is implementation-agnostic, and therefore compatible with both the original [10] and the full-RNS variants of the CKKS scheme proposed by Cheon et al. [7]. If the implementation of the KeySwitch begins with a modulus basis extension (for example, from Q to QP), Algorithm 1 can be optimized by merging the ModRaise step in the second KeySwitch (now from q to QP), such that it essentially becomes two consecutive key-switches.

3.3 Impact on the Evaluation-Key Generation

Our modification to the bootstrapping slightly changes how evaluation keys are generated, as we now need to generate two sets of evaluation keys instead of one:

1. A set parameterized by $\{N, QP, h, \sigma\}$ that uses a key s and comprises the encryption key, all the necessary evaluation keys for the linear transformations and homomorphic modular reduction, as well as the switching key $\mathsf{swk}_{QP}^{\tilde{s} \to s}$.
2. A set parameterized by $\{N, qp, \tilde{h}, \sigma\}$, with $qp \ll QP$ and $\tilde{h} < h$, and that uses a secret $\tilde{s}$ and comprises the switching key $\mathsf{swk}_{qp}^{s \to \tilde{s}}$.

Although we increase the number of evaluation keys by two, this is only marginal with respect to the total number of switching keys needed for the bootstrapping; this is largely dominated by the number of rotations keys needed for the linear transformations, which is in the order of a hundred for $n = 2^{15}$ slots.

Our construction allows to us to use a dense secret for s and to instantiate all the evaluation keys at a larger modulus, which will inevitably increase their size. We however stress that the increase in size of the key set is a normal behavior of the scheme as it is directly related to the homomorphic capacity of a parameter set.

In Sect. 4, we show that the modification to the ModRaise algorithm and the addition of the switching keys $\mathsf{swk}_{QP}^{\tilde{s} \to s}$ and $\mathsf{swk}_{qp}^{s \to \tilde{s}}$ does not introduce new security assumptions and that our construction is secure.

4 Security Analysis

In this section, we provide a security argument for Algorithm 1 (Sect. 3.2) that shows our modification neither changes nor introduces new security assumptions to the CKKS scheme or its original bootstrapping. We then discuss the benefit on the security of using a small ephemeral secret during the bootstrapping and estimate security of such ephemeral secrets for concrete parameters.

Note that, regardless of our proposition, users should always be aware of the security implications of using the CKKS scheme [22] as well as sparse secrets, and that they should carefully choose how it is parameterized.

4.1 Security of the Modified ModRaise

We consider an adversary $\mathcal{A}$ who has access to the public transcript of Algorithm 1:

- ct_q^s, an R-LWE sample $(-as + m + e, a) \in R_q^2$ with m a message, and security parameterized by the tuple $\{N, q, h, \sigma\}$.
- $\mathsf{swk}_{qp}^{s \to \tilde{s}}$, a switching-key composed of a set of R-LWE samples $(-a^{(i)}\tilde{s} + w^{(i)}ps + e^{(i)}, a^{(i)}) \in R_{qp}^{2 \times \beta}$ with $a^{(i)} \leftarrow R_{qp}$, $\tilde{s} \leftarrow \chi_{\tilde{h}}$, $e^{(i)} \leftarrow \chi_{\sigma}$ and $w = (w^1, \dots, w^\beta)$ a decomposition basis. The security of this set of R-LWE samples is parameterized by the tuple $\{N, qp, \tilde{h}, \sigma\}$.
- $\mathsf{swk}_{QP}^{\tilde{s} \to s}$, a switching-key composed of a set of R-LWE samples $(-a^{(i)}s + w^{(i)}P\tilde{s} + e^{(i)}, a^{(i)}) \in R_{QP}^{2 \times \beta}$ with $a^{(i)} \leftarrow R_{QP}$, $s \leftarrow \chi_h$, $e^{(i)} \leftarrow \chi_{\sigma}$ and $w = (w^1, \dots, w^\beta)$ a decomposition basis. The security of this set of R-LWE samples is parameterized by the tuple $\{N, QP, h, \sigma\}$.

$\mathcal{A}$ wins if it can distinguish $(\mathsf{ct}_q^s, \mathsf{swk}_{qp}^{s \to \tilde{s}}, \mathsf{swk}_{QP}^{\tilde{s} \to s})$ from the uniform distribution $U(R_q^2, R_{qp}^{2 \times \beta}, R_{QP}^{2 \times \beta})$ with an advantage greater than $2^{-\lambda}$. Therefore, to ensure that

$$\mathrm{Adv}_{\mathcal{A}} = |\Pr[\mathcal{A}^{(\mathsf{ct}_q^s, \mathsf{swk}_{qp}^{s \to \tilde{s}}, \mathsf{swk}_{QP}^{\tilde{s} \to s})} = 1] - \Pr[\mathcal{A}^{(R_q^2, R_{qp}^{2 \times \beta}, R_{QP}^{2 \times \beta})} = 1]| \leq 2^{-\lambda},$$

it suffices to select the parameter sets $\{N, qp, \tilde{h}, \sigma\}$ and $\{N, QP, h, \sigma\}$ to be at least λ-secure ($\{N, q, h, \sigma\}$ is naturally at least λ-secure if $\{N, QP, h, \sigma\}$ is itself λ-secure since $q \ll QP$). Regarding their joint distribution, the security argument holds under the assumption of circular security, which is already required to generate evaluation keys. For a parameterization example, we take two sets of parameters from the work of Cheon et al. [5]: $\{2^{15}, 2^{881}, 2^{14}, 3.2\}$ and $\{2^{15}, 2^{431}, 2^6, 3.2\}$; both are $\lambda = 128$-bit secure. Note that, in practice, the second set of parameters $\{N, qp, \tilde{h}, \sigma\}$ has a much smaller qp (e.g. 120 bits) than the 431 bits used in this example, because it is instantiated at the smallest possible modulus. Hence, this parameter set is actually more secure than the one that uses the dense key (see Table 1).

Table 1. Parameters' security for the low-*level* switching key. The modulus of the switching key is composed of q and an additional modulus p used during the key-switching. W denotes log(keyspace size), i.e., $\log\left(\binom{N}{h} \cdot 2^{\tilde{h}}\right)$. The asterisk * indicates that the estimator failed to provide a result and instead the security was extrapolated.

$\log(N)$	$\log(qp)$	$\tilde{h}$	W	Primal [2]	Dual [2]	Dec [2]	Hybrid-Primal [5]	Hybrid-Dual [5]
16	60+61	64	792	368.0	340.4	376.0	260.4	317.8
		32	427	222.7	192.5	226.6	168.5*	283.8
15	55+56	64	728	309.2	415.0	315.6	217.7	227.8
		32	395	187.9	191.5	319.0	140.9	162.2

4.2 Minimizing the Use of Sparse Secrets and Achieving Higher Security

Previous works on the CKKS bootstrapping assumed predefined single sparse-secret parameters and were focused on improving efficiency [4–6,8,13–16,19–21]. The use of a sparse secret was deemed necessary to make the bootstrapping sufficiently practical. Although Bossuat et al. [3] showed that using a single dense secret can also be practical, this comes at the cost of reduced efficiency and precision (due to the need to evaluate a polynomial of several hundred coefficients).

Our work changes this paradigm by, instead, proposing a higher-level change that directly removes this constraint. Although simple, our *sparse-secret encapsulation* brings a significant improvement to the security and practicality of the CKKS bootstrapping. It enables the user to instantiate the bootstrapping evaluation keys with a dense secret, which brings more freedom in making choices about the parameters and isolates the security assumption related to the sparse-secret to a single low-*level* (small modulus) key. Being at a low *level*, this key benefits from a large security margin against the most recent attacks [9,24] and will be, in practice, more secure than the evaluation keys generated with the dense secret. This result is a more practical and secure CKKS bootstrapping. Table 1 provides parameterization examples and their security for the low-*level* switching key that uses a sparse secret.

5 Empirical Noise Analysis

In this section we quantify the effect of our modification on the noise of the bootstrapping procedure. Our modification impacts the noise in two dimensions: it slightly modifies the circuit by adding additional key-switching operations and it allows the use of denser keys.

The initial noise of the CKKS scheme is well understood and numerous works have carried out noise analyses [8,10,17,20]. These works, however, keep their analysis to single operations because when operations are composed the estimation of the noise (either as a bound or an average case) becomes less and less meaningful since the initial exact noise is unknown.

For this reason, noise analysis, especially for complicated circuits such as the bootstrapping, remains heuristic and with loose bounds. This is especially true when other factors besides the initial noise have to be taken into account, such as polynomial approximations or plaintext distribution. Therefore, noise analysis for circuits is experimentally conducted in practice.

In this section, we empirically demonstrate with experiments the following propositions:

Proposition 1. *The modification to the ModRaise step only adds a small additive noise which has a negligible impact on the bootstrapping precision.*

Proposition 2. *The noise terms which are a function of the density h of the secret quickly dominate the additive noise of the bootstrapping circuit.*

5.1   Proposition 1

Our modification to the ModRaise step adds two key-switching operations, one before it and one after it. The noise introduced by the key-switching is additive and can be minimized to a rounding error if correctly parameterized [13,17,20].

The ModRaise step is followed by the CoeffsToSlots step, which homomorphically evaluates the encoding algorithm. This step is carried out by evaluating a linear transformation [8] on the ciphertext vector and for n slots requires $O(\sqrt{n})$ plaintext multiplications and $O(\sqrt{r}\log_r(n))$ rotations [12] (which are key-switching operations), for a radix $r \leq n$.

Hence, the two additional key-switching happening during the ModRaise step should only have a small negligible impact on the overall additive bootstrapping error. We verify Proposition 1 with the following empirical experiment: we compare the error of the reference circuit of Bossuat et al. [3] and the same circuit where only the ModRaise step differs. We use the exact same parameters as the one used by Bossuat et al. for all parameter sets, as well as the same secret-key density. For our modified circuit, the ModRaise step switches the secret to a different one of the same density h.

Table 2 reports the results of the experiment. We observe that there is no significant difference between the noise of the original bootstrapping of Bossuat et al. and our modified circuit. The largest differences are coming from the sets IV and V but remain small (0.09 to 0.25 bits of difference). Both can be attributed to parameters that lead to a bootstrapping instance that is more sensitive to the distribution of the initial noise (larger secret density) and/or the additive noise (smaller plaintext scale). We will see in Sect. 6.1 that the reduction in the EvalMod complexity from a smaller $\tilde{h}$ allows to entirely mitigate this small loss of precision and even increase the bootstrapping precision. Note that this experiment is performed in a worst-case scenario, that is with fresh ciphertexts. In practice, a ciphertext input to the bootstrapping procedure accumulates the error of all the previous homomorphic operations, thus the noise from the two additional key-switching, which is additive, has far lower impact.

Table 2. Impact of the modified ModRaise on the bootstrapping precision, by comparison between the results of Bossuat et al. [3] and the same bootstrapping circuit but with the modified ModRaise. Our work uses identical parameters to the ones of Bossuat et al. for all sets and our modified ModRaise switches the secret to a different secret of same density h. N is the ring degree, $\log QP$ the modulus of the switching keys, h the density of the secret, n the number of plaintext slots, K the probabilistic upper bound of $\|\tilde{I}(Y)\|$, $d_{\sin(x)}$ the degree of the scaled cosine interpolant (Han and Ki's method [13]), r the number of double angle evaluations, $d_{\arcsin(x)}$ the degree of the arcsine interpolant (Taylor series) and $\log \epsilon^{-1}$ the negative log of the error, which is interpreted as the plaintext precision.

Set [3]	$\log(N)$	$\log(QP)$	h	$\log(n)$	K	$d_{\sin(x)}$	r	$d_{\arcsin(x)}$	$\log(\epsilon^{-1})$	
									[3]	Ours
I	16	1546	192	15	25	63	2	0	25.70	25.71
				14					26.00	26.07
II	16	1547	192	15	25	63	2	7	31.50	31.51
				14					31.60	31.68
III	16	1553	192	15	25	63	2	0	19.10	19.09
				14					18.90	18.92
IV	16	1792	32768	15	325	255	4	0	16.80	16.65
				14					17.30	17.21
V	15	768	192	14	25	63	2	0	15.50	15.15
				13					15.40	15.29

5.2   Proposition 2

The error of individual homomorphic operations of the CKKS scheme has been studied and is well understood [8,10,17,20]. Notably, the error of a decrypted and decoded message in the CKKS scheme is a function of $\sqrt{h}$, h being the number of non zero elements of the secret key. Although the error related to the secret distribution can be controlled and minimized for most operations with a careful parameterization and scale management (such as addition, plaintext multiplication or key-switching), ciphertext multiplication amplifies the error at a much greater rate because their error terms are compounded. This is specifically the case for polynomial evaluation, which involves ciphertext exponentiation when computing the power basis.

We empirically verify this statement with the following experiment: we compare the precision of the bootstrapping circuit and its different individual parts for an increasing main secret density h. For the full bootstrapping circuit we use our modified ModRaise step with an ephemeral secret with $\tilde{h} = 32$ ($\lambda \approx 168$ for $N = 2^{16}$ and $\log(qp) = 121$, see Table 1 in Sect. 4). The results of this experiment are in Fig. 1.

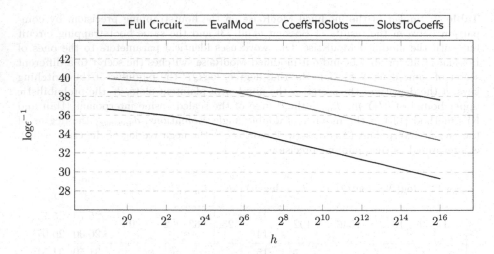

Fig. 1. Precision of the full bootstrapping circuit and its different individual steps for a secret s with variable h. The full circuit uses our modified ModRaise with an ephemeral secret $\tilde{s}$ with $\tilde{h} = 32$. The parameters are $\log N = 2^{16}$ and $\log n = 2^{15}$, an initial scale of 2^{52} and 60-bit moduli (the maximum allowed size) are used for all operations. The EvalMod parameters are $K = 10$, $d_{\sin(x)} = 30$, $r = 3$ and $d_{\arcsin(x)} = 7$. $\log \epsilon^{-1}$ is the negative log of the error, which is interpreted as the precision.

We observe that for operations involving a controlled noise augmentation (CoeffsToSlots and SlotsToCoeffs can be summarized as sums of plaintext multiplications and key-switching operations) the initial encryption noise (which includes the encoding error of both the plaintext vector and plaintext matrices) is much larger than the noise added by the homomorphic operations and the decryption process. This results in a constant precision until the noise terms related to h become dominant, which happens at around $h = 2^8$ for Coeffs-ToSlots and $h = 2^{14}$ for SlotsToCoeffs. At this point, the line starts to follow the $\sqrt{h}$ relationship (doubling h induces a loss of precision of 0.5 bits).

As expected, the EvalMod step, which is an operation involving ciphertext exponentiation, has a noise growth that quickly overcomes the initial noise with a steady $\sqrt{h}$ relationship that already starts at $h = 2^4$. We observed that increasing the degree of the interpolant actually reduced the precision instead of increasing it. This means that the expected gain in precision from the additional higher degree terms of the interpolant was actually cancelled by the error resulting from higher exponentiation to compute the additional terms of the power basis.

The precision of the full circuit follows the one of the EvalMod step with a stable offset of about 4 bits, confirming that the EvalMod step is the bottleneck of the bootstrapping circuit precision. This is not surprising, since the EvalMod step is the only non-linear part of the bootstrapping circuit. This offset is the result of the composition of the different part of the bootstrapping circuit and compounding of their errors.

The loss of precision caused by a higher secret density can be compensated by increasing the initial scale Δ if needed. However, when using the full-RNS variant of the CKKS scheme [7] this scale cannot be arbitrarily increased, since the size of the used primes is limited by machine words, which are usually of 64 bits. In practice, the maximum size of the primes is even smaller, typically of 61 bits, to enable more efficient implementations. A solution is to use multiple words per prime or multiple primes per *level*, but both will induce an overhead.

5.3 Conclusion

In this section we empirically showed that: (i) our modification to the ModRaise step has a negligible impact on the bootstrapping precision and that (ii) the noise term related to the density h of the secret quickly dominates all other terms when ciphertext multiplication is involved. Our experiments allow us to conclude that our construction, by itself, only has a negligible impact on the bootstrapping precision, and that an increased noise when using a main secret with a higher density h comes from the inherent noise of the scheme and not from our modification of the ModRaise step. These results are further confirmed with the experimental results shown in Sect. 6.

6   Evaluation

In this section, we evaluate the performance of our proposed modification against the recent work of Bossuat et al. [3], which is currently the state of art in term of *bootstrapping throughput* (number of plaintext bits bootstrapped per second). We will show that, when using the same parameters, our construction enables a more efficient and precise bootstrapping with a much lower failure probability.

We implemented our work in the Lattigo library [18]. All benchmarks were conducted on hardware with the same specifications as the one used by Bossuat et al. (Windows 10, i5-6600K CPU @ 3.50 GHz, 32 GB of RAM, single threaded), ensuring fair comparisons. All parameter sets, for all experiments, have a security $\lambda \approx 128$.

Table 3. Bootstrapping precision and failure probability when reducing the complexity of the EvalMod step. The original results of Bossuat et al. [3] are given for reference and we use the same cryptographic parameter sets for all experiments (which are identical to the ones in Table 2). n is the number of plaintext slots, h the density of the main secret, $\tilde{h}$ the density of the ephemeral secret, K the range for the approximation of the scaled sine function, $f(K, h, n)$ the failure probability function, and $\log \epsilon^{-1}$ the negative log of the error, which is interpreted as the plaintext precision. Details about the interpolant used for each set can be found in Table 4. The security of the ephemeral secret is, for $\tilde{h} = 32$, $\lambda \approx 168$ for the Sets I to IV, and $\lambda \approx 141$ for Set V (see Table 1 in Sect. 4).

Set [3]	$\log n$	h	Bossuat et al. [3]			This work				This work			
			K	$f(K,h,n)$	$\log \epsilon^{-1}$	$\tilde{h}$	K	$f(K,\tilde{h},n)$	$\log \epsilon^{-1}$	$\tilde{h}$	K	$f(K,\tilde{h},n)$	$\log \epsilon^{-1}$
I	15	192	25	-15.58	25.70	32	12	-34.11	27.32	32	16	-138.70	26.63
	14			-16.58	26.00			-35.11	27.39			-139.70	26.89
II	15	192	25	-15.58	31.50	32	12	-34.11	32.36	32	16	-138.70	32.11
	14			-16.58	31.60			-35.11	32.17			-139.70	32.04
III	15	192	25	-15.58	19.10	32	12	-34.11	19.14	32	16	-138.70	19.13
	14			-16.58	18.95			-35.11	18.92			-139.70	18.90
IV	15	32768	325	-14.90	16.80	32	12	-34.11	23.80	32	16	-138.70	23.12
	14			-15.90	17.30			-35.11	24.29			-139.70	23.62
V	14	192	25	-16.58	15.50	32	12	-34.11	15.48	32	16	-139.70	15.45
	13			-17.58	15.40			-35.11	15.66			-140.70	15.55

6.1 Better Precision, Reduced Failure Probability and Smaller Interpolant

The EvalMod step of the bootstrapping procedure evaluates a polynomial approximation of the modular reduction. The *bootstrapping failure probability* is given by the function $f(K, h, n)$ (see Eq. 1 in Sect. 3.1), with $[-K, K]$ the range of the approximation, h the density of the secret at the moment of the ModUp step and n the number of plaintext slots. If a coefficient falls outside of the range $[-K, K]$, the polynomial approximation fails and the bootstrapping procedure returns unusable values. Hence, the precision of the polynomial approximation evaluated during the EvalMod is a trade off between the degree d of the approximation (which has an impact on the number of levels consumed during this step), and the range K of the approximation (which, for a given d, determines both the precision and failure probability of the EvalMod step). So, for a fixed d, h and n, the greater K is, the smaller the failure probability, but the smaller the precision. Therefore, if h can be reduced, K can be reduced and the precision increased (up to the inherent precision of the interpolant).

Table 3 compares the precision and failure probability of the bootstrapping from the original work of Bossuat et al. [3] with ours. Additional information about the used interpolant can be found in Table 4.

We observe that, for all sets, the bootstrapping precision is either similar or improved, showing that we are able to achieve a failure probability that is many orders of magnitude smaller without compromising security or precision.

The largest improvement is for Set IV, which is not surprising since Bossuat et al. had to use a very large interpolant for their EvalMod step.

Table 4. Interpolants used for the EvalMod step of the experiments of Table 3. K is the range of the interpolation, $d_{\sin(x)}$ the degree of the scaled cosine interpolant (Han and Ki's method [13]), r the number of double angle evaluations, and $d_{\arcsin(x)}$ the degree of the arcsine interpolant (Taylor series).

Set [3]	Bossuat et al. [3]				This work				This work			
	K	$d_{\sin(x)}$	r	$d_{\arcsin(x)}$	K	$d_{\sin(x)}$	r	$d_{\arcsin(x)}$	K	$d_{\sin(x)}$	r	$d_{\arcsin(x)}$
I	25	63	2	0	12	22	3	0	16	30	3	0
II	25	63	2	7	12	24	3	7	16	30	3	7
III	25	63	2	0	12	22	3	0	16	30	3	0
IV	325	255	4	0	12	22	3	0	16	44	2	0
V	25	63	2	0	12	22	3	0	16	30	3	0

The configuration of Bossuat et al. led to a failure probability of $2^{-31.6}$ per plaintext slot ($2^{-15.6}$ for $n = 2^{15}$ slots). Our failure probability per slot is now $2^{-50.1}$ ($2^{-34.11}$ for $n = 2^{15}$ slots) for $K = 12$ and $2^{-154.7}$ ($2^{-138.7}$ for $n = 2^{15}$ slots) for $K = 16$, which is smaller than the security parameter. Note that when using Han and Ki's interpolation method, the interpolant has a minimum degree of $d_{\sin(x)} = 2(K-1)$, hence $K = 16$ is the maximum value to get a depth $\log(d + 1) \leq 5$ interpolant.

For all parameter sets except for Set IV, Bossuat et al. used $K = 25$, $d_{\sin(x)} = 63$ (the degree of the scaled sine interpolant) and $r = 2$ (the number of double angle evaluation), for a total depth of $6 + 2 = 8$. By reducing K to 12 and 16, we were originally able to reduce the interpolant degree to $d_{\sin(x)} \approx 40$ for an equivalent bootstrapping precision. In this configuration, it turns out that $d_{\sin(x)}$ is now small enough to be able to increase r to 3 and further reduce $d_{\sin(x)}$ to a value equal to or smaller than 31. This allows us to keep the same depth and precision, but with a more efficient polynomial evaluation, since each double angle evaluation only needs one multiplication.

In conclusion, Table 3 shows that, when using the parameters of Bossuat et al. in conjunction with our modified ModRaise step and a small ephemeral secret, the bootstrapping precision and failure probability can be noticeably improved.

6.2 Higher Bootstrapping Throughput

The *bootstrapping utility* is a metric that enables the evaluation of the performance of a bootstrapping circuit. It is a concept that was first introduced by Chen et al. [4] as $n \times$ Levels/Time, for n the number of plaintext slots, Levels the number of *levels* available after the bootstrapping, and Time the bootstrapping complexity represented in CPU time (single threaded). It was then expanded to the *bootstrapping throughput* by Bossuat et al. [3], which measures the number of plaintext bits bootstrapped per second as $n \times \log \epsilon^{-1} \times \log Q'/\text{Time}$, for $\log \epsilon^{-1}$ the bootstrapping precision and $\log Q'$ the number of modulus bits available after the bootstrapping. Bossuat et al. use $\log Q'$ instead of the number of remaining *levels* because this value is more representative of the actual remaining homomorphic capacity. Indeed, optimizing a homomorphic circuit often leads to a dynamic scale, in which case the notion of level does not make sense anymore.

Table 5 reports the *bootstrapping throughput* of the experiments of Table 3 (along with Table 4). This comparison between the results of Bossuat et al. and ours shows that our modification allows for better timings, even though two additional key-switching operations are added to the ModUp step.

Table 5. Comparison of the *bootstrapping throughput* [3] with $\log(\text{bits}/s) = \log(n \times \log Q' \times \log \epsilon^{-1}/\text{Time})$, where n is the number of plaintext slots, Q' the residual modulus after the bootstrapping, $\log \epsilon^{-1}$ the bootstrapping precision, and Time the CPU cost in seconds.

Set [3]	$\log(n)$	Bossuat et al. [3]				This work				Ratio
		$\log(\epsilon^{-1})$	$\log(Q')$	Time	$\log(\text{bits}/s)$	$\log(\epsilon^{-1})$	$\log(Q')$	Time	$\log(\text{bits}/s)$	bits/s
I	15	25.7	420	23.0	23.87	26.63	420	19.9	24.13	1.19×
	14	26.0	420	16.9	23.33	26.89	420	14.9	23.56	1.17×
II	15	31.5	285	23.4	23.59	32.11	285	20.2	23.82	1.17×
	14	31.6	285	16.0	23.13	32.04	285	14.5	23.30	1.12×
III	15	19.1	505	18.1	24.06	19.13	505	15.9	24.24	1.13×
	14	18.9	505	13.1	23.50	18.90	505	11.9	23.64	1.10×
IV	15	16.8	410	39.2	22.70	23.12	420	19.9	23.93	2.34×
	14	17.3	410	24.9	22.15	23.62	420	14.9	23.37	2.33×
V	14	15.5	110	7.5	21.82	15.45	110	5.9	22.17	1.27×
	13	15.4	110	6.0	21.14	15.55	110	4.5	21.57	1.34×

We observe that all parameter sets of our work have a larger *bootstrapping throughput*, with Set IV achieving a throughput that is 2.34× the one of Bossuat et al. This shows that our proposed change to the ModUp steps enables a better *bootstrapping throughput* in addition to a negligible failure probability (note that this failure probability is not taken into account in the *bootstrapping throughput*).

6.3   Dense Key Bootstrapping

In the previous sections, we evaluated the performance of our modified bootstrapping against the results of Bossuat et al., for which the parameters use a sparse secret as the main secret. In this section, we evaluate the performance of our modified bootstrapping with parameters that use a dense secret as the main secret.

By increasing the density of the main secret from 192 to $N/2$, we are able to increase $\log QP$ to ≈ 1790 for $N = 2^{16}$ and ≈ 881 for $N = 2^{15}$, thus increasing the remaining homomorphic capacity ($\log Q'$) after the bootstrapping, and still retaining a security of $\lambda \approx 128$ bits.

Table 6. *Bootstrapping throughput* [3] of various parameter sets with a $\log QP$ based on a dense secret as the main secret, with $\log(\text{bits}/s) = \log(n \times \log Q' \times \log \epsilon^{-1}/\text{Time})$, where n is the number of plaintext slots, Q' the residual modulus after the bootstrapping, $\log \epsilon^{-1}$ the bootstrapping precision, and Time the CPU cost in seconds.

$\log(N)$	$\log(QP)$	$(h, \tilde{h})$	$\log(n)$	$\log(\epsilon^{-1})$	$\log(Q')$	Time	$\log(\text{bits}/s)$
16	$1401 + 366$	$(N/2, 32)$	15	23.0	580	25.1	24.05
16	$1483 + 305$	$(N/2, 32)$	15	29.8	465	26.3	24.04
16	$1488 + 305$	$(N/2, 32)$	15	17.8	745	21.5	24.26
15	$768 + 112$	$(N/2, 32)$	14	17.3	166	7.9	22.50

Table 6 reports the result of this experiment and shows that despite the expected and unavoidable loss of precision of $0.5 \cdot \log((N/2)/192) \approx 3.7$ for $N = 2^{16}$ and ≈ 3.2 for $N = 2^{15}$ (see Sect. 5), we are still able to obtain a similar if not greater *bootstrapping throughput* than when using a sparse secret as the main secret. Timings are slightly larger than the ones reported in Table 5 because all operations are happening at a higher modulus, thus are more costly. The parameter set for $N = 2^{15}$ shows a significantly larger *bootstrapping throughput* compared to Set V of both Bossuat et al. and our work ($1.6\times$ and $1.25\times$ respectively). The reason is that this parameter set could only accommodate for a small homomorphic capacity when using a sparse secret, and the bootstrapping precision had to be deliberately tuned down to end up with a meaningful remaining homomorphic capacity after the bootstrapping. Being able to increase the homomorphic capacity also allowed us to allocate larger moduli to the bootstrapping circuit, thus increasing its precision.

Although the *bootstrapping throughput* reported in Table 6 is only slightly larger than the one shown in Table 5 (with the exception of the parameter set using $N = 2^{15}$), the parameters used in Table 6 would likely not have to be updated even if attacks on sparse secrets were improved, because these would not apply to the main secret (which is dense), and the low-level sparse secret benefits from a large security margin.

7   Conclusion

In this work, we have presented a *sparse-secret encapsulation* technique for the bootstrapping of the CKKS scheme. We have shown that by temporarily switching during the ModRaise step the low-*level* ciphertext to a sparser secret, we can optimize the efficiency-security trade-off of the bootstrapping circuit, by breaking the dependency between the sparse-secret security and the largest modulus. This enables all high-*level* evaluation keys to use a denser secret, thus to provide a greater initial homomorphic capacity and more resilience to attacks targeting sparse secrets, while still enjoying a lower-complexity bootstrapping. Moreover, our technique also enables the parameterization of the EvalMod step in an interval that is large enough to make its failure probability arbitrarily small, which, to the best of our knowledge, has never been achieved before.

When using the parameters of previous works, our experiments show that the proposed modification allows for a 128-bit secure bootstrapping with negligible failure probability, that also benefits from a greater remaining homomorphic capacity, greater precision, and smaller complexity. Moreover, when using a dense secret, our bootstrapping circuit has greater *bootstrapping throughput* than previous state-of-the-art approaches that use a sparse secret, especially for small parameters.

We believe these improvements are a major step forward for the security, stability, efficiency and reliability of the bootstrapping of the CKKS scheme, which is a necessary building block to enable high-depth arithmetic circuit evaluation under encryption.

Acknowledgments. We would like to thank Christian Mouchet for his valuable feedback. This work was supported in part by the grant #2017-201 of the ETH Domain PHRT Strategic Focal Area.

References

1. Albrecht, M.R., Player, R., Scott, S.: On the concrete hardness of learning with errors. J. Math. Cryptol. **9**(3), 169–203 (2015)
2. Albrecht, M., et al.: Homomorphic encryption security standard. Technical report. Toronto, Canada: HomomorphicEncryption.org, November 2018
3. Bossuat, J.-P., Mouchet, C., Troncoso-Pastoriza, J., Hubaux, J.-P.: Efficient bootstrapping for approximate homomorphic encryption with non-sparse keys. In: Canteaut, A., Standaert, F.-X. (eds.) EUROCRYPT 2021. LNCS, vol. 12696, pp. 587–617. Springer, Cham (2021). https://doi.org/10.1007/978-3-030-77870-5_21
4. Chen, H., Chillotti, I., Song, Y.: Improved bootstrapping for approximate homomorphic encryption. In: Ishai, Y., Rijmen, V. (eds.) EUROCRYPT 2019. LNCS, vol. 11477, pp. 34–54. Springer, Cham (2019). https://doi.org/10.1007/978-3-030-17656-3_2
5. Cheon, J.H., Son, Y., Yhee, D.: Practical FHE parameters against lattice attacks. In: IACR Cryptology ePrint Archive 2021, p. 39 (2021)
6. Cheon, J.H., Han, K., Hhan, M.: Faster homomorphic discrete Fourier transforms and improved FHE bootstrapping. In: IACR Cryptology ePrint Archive 2018, p. 1073 (2018)
7. Cheon, J.H., Han, K., Kim, A., Kim, M., Song, Y.: A full RNS variant of approximate homomorphic encryption. In: Cid, C., Jacobson Jr., M. (eds.) Selected Areas in Cryptography–SAC 2018. SAC 2018. LNCS, vol. 11349, pp. 347–368. Springer, Cham (2019). https://doi.org/10.1007/978-3-030-10970-7_16
8. Cheon, J.H., Han, K., Kim, A., Kim, M., Song, Y.: Bootstrapping for approximate homomorphic encryption. In: Nielsen, J.B., Rijmen, V. (eds.) EUROCRYPT 2018. LNCS, vol. 10820, pp. 360–384. Springer, Cham (2018). https://doi.org/10.1007/978-3-319-78381-9_14

9. Cheon, J.H., Hhan, M., Hong, S., Son, Y.: A hybrid of dual and meet-in-the-middle attack on sparse and ternary secret LWE. IEEE Access **7**, 89497–89506 (2019)

10. Cheon, J.H., Kim, A., Kim, M., Song, Y.: Homomorphic encryption for arithmetic of approximate numbers. In: Takagi, T., Peyrin, T. (eds.) ASIACRYPT 2017. LNCS, vol. 10624, pp. 409–437. Springer, Cham (2017). https://doi.org/10.1007/978-3-319-70694-8_15

11. Espitau, T., Joux, A., Kharchenko, N.: On a dual/hybrid approach to small secret LWE. In: Bhargavan, K., Oswald, E., Prabhakaran, M. (eds.) INDOCRYPT 2020. LNCS, vol. 12578, pp. 440–462. Springer, Cham (2020). https://doi.org/10.1007/978-3-030-65277-7_20

12. Han, K., Hhan, M., Cheon, J.H.: Improved homomorphic discrete Fourier transforms and FHE bootstrapping. IEEE Access **7**, 57361–57370 (2019). https://doi.org/10.1109/ACCESS.2019.2913850

13. Han, K., Ki, D.: Better bootstrapping for approximate homomorphic encryption. In: Jarecki, S. (ed.) CT-RSA 2020. LNCS, vol. 12006, pp. 364–390. Springer, Cham (2020). https://doi.org/10.1007/978-3-030-40186-3_16

14. Ishimaki, Y., Yamana, H.: Faster homomorphic trace-type function evaluation. IEEE Access **9**, 53061–53077 (2021). https://doi.org/10.1109/ACCESS.2021.3071264

15. Jutla, C.S., Manohar, N.: Modular lagrange interpolation of the mod function for bootstrapping of approximate HE. Cryptology ePrint Archive, Report 2020/1355 (2021). https://eprint.iacr.org/2020/1355

16. Jutla, C.S., Manohar, N.: Sine series approximation of the mod function for bootstrapping of approximate HE. Cryptology ePrint Archive, Report 2021/572 (2021). https://eprint.iacr.org/2021/572

17. Kim, A., Papadimitriou, A., Polyakov, Y.: Approximate homomorphic encryption with reduced approximation error. Cryptology ePrint Archive, Report 2020/1118 (2020). https://ia.cr/2020/1118

18. Lattigo 3.0.2. EPFL-LDS, January 2022. https://github.com/ldsec/lattigo

19. Lee, J.-W., Lee, E., Lee, Y., Kim, Y.-S., No, J.-S.: High-precision bootstrapping of RNS-CKKS homomorphic encryption using optimal minimax polynomial approximation and inverse sine function. In: Canteaut, A., Standaert, F.-X. (eds.) EUROCRYPT 2021. LNCS, vol. 12696, pp. 618–647. Springer, Cham (2021). https://doi.org/10.1007/978-3-030-77870-5_22, https://eprint.iacr.org/2020/552

20. Lee, Y., Lee, J., Kim, Y.S., Kang, H., No, J.S.: High-precision and low-complexity approximate homomorphic encryption by error variance minimization. Cryptology ePrint Archive, Report 2020/1549 (2020). https://eprint.iacr.org/2020/1549

21. Lee, Y., Lee, J.-W., Kim, Y.-S., No, J.-S.: Near-optimal polynomial for modulus reduction using L2-norm for approximate homomorphic encryption. IEEE Access **8**, 144321–144330 (2020). https://doi.org/10.1109/ACCESS.2020.3014369

22. Li, B., Micciancio, D.: On the security of homomorphic encryption on approximate numbers. In: Canteaut, A., Standaert, F.-X. (eds.) EUROCRYPT 2021. LNCS, vol. 12696, pp. 648–677. Springer, Cham (2021). https://doi.org/10.1007/978-3-030-77870-5_23

23. Lyubashevsky, V., Peikert, C., Regev, O.: On ideal lattices and learning with errors over rings. In: Gilbert, H. (ed.) EUROCRYPT 2010. LNCS, vol. 6110, pp. 1–23. Springer, Heidelberg (2010). https://doi.org/10.1007/978-3-642-13190-5_1

24. Son, Y., Cheon, J.H.: Revisiting the Hybrid attack on sparse and ternary secret LWE. In: IACR Cryptology ePrint Archive 2019, p. 1019 (2019)

(Commit-and-Prove) Predictable Arguments with Privacy

Hamidreza Khoshakhlagh[✉]

Aarhus University, Aarhus, Denmark
hamidreza@cs.au.dk

Abstract. Predictable arguments introduced by Faonio, Nielsen and Venturi [14] are private-coin argument systems where the answer of the prover can be predicted in advance by the verifier. In this work, we study predictable arguments with additional privacy properties. While the authors in [14] showed compilers for transforming PAs into PAs with zero-knowledge property, they left the construction of witness indistinguishable predictable arguments (WI-PA) in the plain model as an open problem. In this work, we first propose more efficient constructions of zero-knowledge predictable arguments (ZK-PA) based on trapdoor smooth projective hash functions (TSPHFs). Next, we consider the problem of WI-PA construction in the plain model and show how to transform PA into WI-PA using non-interactive witness-indistinguishable proofs.

As a relaxation of predictable arguments, we additionally put forth a new notion of predictability called *Commit-and-Prove Predictable Argument* (CPPA), where except the first (reusable) message of the prover, all the prover's responses can be predicted. We construct an efficient zero-knowledge CPPA in the non-programmable random oracle model for the class of all polynomial-size circuits. Finally, following the connection between predictable arguments and witness encryption, we show an application of CPPAs with privacy properties to the design of witness encryption schemes, where in addition to standard properties, we also require some level of privacy for the decryptors who own a valid witness for the statement used during the encryption process.

Keywords: Predictable arguments · Zero-knowledge · Witness indistinguishability · Witness encryption

1 Introduction

Interactive proofs (IPs) and arguments introduced by Goldwasser, Micali, and Rackoff [19] are cryptographic protocols that allow a prover to convince a verifier about the veracity of a public statement $x \in \mathcal{L}$, where $\mathcal{L}$ is an NP language. The interaction may consist of several rounds of communication, at the end of which the verifier decides to accept or reject the prover's claim on the membership of

H. Khoshakhlagh—Funded by the Concordium Foundation under Concordium Blockchain Research Center, Aarhus.

G. Ateniese and D. Venturi (Eds.): ACNS 2022, LNCS 13269, pp. 542–561, 2022.
https://doi.org/10.1007/978-3-031-09234-3_27

x in $\mathcal{L}$. There are two properties required for an IP, namely *completeness* and *soundness*. Completeness means that if $x \in \mathcal{L}$, the honest prover can always convince the honest verifier. Soundness means that for $x \notin \mathcal{L}$ no (even unbounded) malicious prover can convince the honest verifier that $x \in \mathcal{L}$. Argument systems are like IPs, except they are only computationally sound; i.e., it should be *computationally hard* (and not impossible) for a malicious prover to convince the verifier that $x \in \mathcal{L}$. An interactive proof is called *public-coin* if the verifier messages are uniformly and independently random, and *private-coin* otherwise.

Recently, Faonio, Nielsen and Venturi [14] introduced a new property for argument systems called *predictability*. Predictable arguments (PA) are private-coin argument systems where the answer of the prover can be predicted efficiently, given the honest verifier's (private) random coins. The prover in such arguments is deterministic and must be consistent with the unique accepting transcript throughout the entire protocol. Faonio et al. [14] formalized this notion and provided several constructions based on various cryptographic assumptions. They also considered PAs with additional privacy properties, namely a *zero-knowledge* (ZK) property, and showed two transformations from PAs into ZK-PAs, the first in the common reference string (CRS) model, and the second in the non-programmable random oracle (NPRO) model.

1.1 Our Contribution

In this paper, we study predictable arguments with privacy properties in more detail. Our results are three-fold:

First, we provide a more efficient construction of ZK-PA in the CRS model. Compared to the generic transformation of [14], the resulting argument is much more efficient although it works only for a restricted class of languages; i.e., all languages that admit SPHFs. This includes all algebraic languages described in Sect. 2.2.

Second, we answer an open problem raised in [14] and show how to construct witness indistinguishable PAs (WI-PA) in the plain model by using non-interactive witness indistinguishable (NIWI) proofs in the plain model. Informally, in order to ensure that the verifier's challenge in the first round is well-formed, we force the verifier to provide a NIWI proof for the statement that "the produced challenge is well-formed". Witness-indistinguishability follows from the soundness of the underlying NIWI and the predictability of the argument. Moreover, we provide a reduction that shows how an adversary breaking the soundness of the WI-PA can be exploited in order to violate the WI property of the underlying NIWI proof system.

Third, motivated by the fact that predictable argument (even without privacy properties) is a strong notion[1], we put forward a relaxation of predictable

---

[1] This follows by the fact that predictable arguments and witness encryption (that only exists based on strong primitives like indistinguishability obfuscation) are equivalent.

arguments, namely, commit-and-prove[2] predictable arguments (CPPA) that, except the first message of the prover, all the prover's responses can be predicted. We formalize this notion for the language of dynamic statements of form $x = (cm, C, y)$, where cm is the prover's first message, and C is an arbitrary polynomial-size circuit possibly specified by the verifier. In particular, we consider a case where the prover publishes a first message cm, after which the prover can run an unbounded number of predictable arguments for different but correlated statements (cm, C_i, y_i). In contrast to PAs for which efficient construction based on standard assumptions (even without ZK) seems out of reach, we give a construction of ZK-CPPA for any polynomial-size circuit $C \in P$ in the NPRO model using garbled circuits (GC) and oblivious transfer (OT). Our construction is very similar to the three-round zero-knowledge argument of [15] with the main difference being the reusability of the prover's first message and providing ZK in the non-UC model under milder assumptions.

Applications. To demonstrate the usefulness of (CP)PA with privacy properties, we will give its application in the context of witness encryption. We consider witness encryption schemes with a strong notion of privacy for the decryptor, wherein a malicious encryptor should not learn any information about the decryptor's witness, even after the decryptor reveals the decrypted message. Our motivating applications for this scenario are dark pools and over-the-counter (OTC) markets in which an investor (the encrypting party) is interested to communicate with only those trading parties (potential decryptors) whose financial conditions satisfy some constraint. To realize this application, a recent work by Ngo et al. [23] introduced the notion of *witness key agreement* (WKA) which allows the two sides to agree on a secret key k, given that the trading parties hold a witness that satisfies the desired relation. We show in Sect. 6.1 that the witness encryption (WE) interpretation of our ZK-CPPA construction can be used to realize this application with an efficiency improvement in some aspects.

1.2   Related Work

This paper is a follow-up to the work of Faonio et al. [14] that introduced the notion of predictable arguments of knowledge (PAoK) systems. While PAs are always honest-verifier zero-knowledge, providing zero-knowledge or even the weaker notion of witness-indistinguishability is quite challenging. In [14], the authors show a compiler for constructing ZK-PA in the CRS model and leave the construction of WI-PA in the plain model as an open problem. We answer the open problem and propose more efficient ZK-PAs in the CRS model. A related work is that of Bitansky and Choudhuri [7] who recently constructed deterministic-prover ZK arguments for NP and showed that such arguments imply ZK-PA for NP. Different from [7] who mainly focus on feasibility results and require strong

---

[2] We call our notion *commit-and-prove* PA because, roughly speaking, a prover first commits to an input (once and for all) and later proves that an opening for the commitment satisfies some properties of interest. Our name is also inspired by the phrase "commit-and-prove schemes" used in some papers, e.g., [9].

assumptions (e.g., indistinguishability obfuscation) in their construction, our work considers practical solutions in the CRS model. In another related work, Dahari and Lindell [13] studied deterministic-prover honest verifier ZK arguments in the plain model. In the same work, they also constructed full ZK arguments given that the prover has access to a pair of witnesses one of which can be used as a basis for the prover's randomness. This differs from our ZK-PA construction wherein the prover is "truly deterministic" although at the cost of requiring a trusted setup. The recent work of [10] introduced the notion of *Witness Maps*. A Unique Witness Map (UWM) is a cryptographic notion that maps all the witnesses for an NP statement to a single witness in a deterministic way. While UWMs can be seen as deterministic-prover NIWI arguments, they differ from WI-PA in several respects, making the two concepts incomparable. First, WI-PA does not require a trusted setup in the form of a common reference string, whereas UWMs are in the CRS model. Second, we consider WI-PA as an interactive protocol, whereas UWMs are non-interactive. Lastly, although UWMs are deterministic-prover, they are not necessarily predictable.

2 Preliminaries

Let PPT denote probabilistic polynomial-time. All adversaries throughout this work will be stateful. By $y \leftarrow \mathcal{A}(\mathsf{x}; r)$ we denote that $\mathcal{A}$, given input x and randomness r, outputs y. Let $\lambda \in \mathbb{N}$ be the security parameter and $\mathsf{negl}(\lambda)$ be an arbitrary negligible function. We write $a \approx_\lambda b$ if $|a - b| \leq \mathsf{negl}(\lambda)$.

2.1 Pairings

A pairing is defined by a tuple $\mathsf{bp} = (p, \mathbb{G}_1, \mathbb{G}_2, \mathbb{G}_T, \hat{e}, g_1, g_2)$ where $\mathbb{G}_1, \mathbb{G}_2, \mathbb{G}_T$ are (additive) groups of prime order p, g_1 is a generator of $\mathbb{G}_1$, g_2 is a generator of $\mathbb{G}_2$, and $\hat{e} : \mathbb{G}_1 \times \mathbb{G}_2 \to \mathbb{G}_T$ is an efficient, non-degenerate bilinear map. In particular, $\hat{e}(a \cdot g_1, b \cdot g_2) = (ab) \cdot \hat{e}(g_1, g_2)$ for any $a, b \in \mathbb{Z}_p$. We denote $[a]_t := a \cdot g_t$ for $t \in \{1, 2, T\}$ where we define $g_T = \hat{e}(g_1, g_2)$. The same notation naturally extends to matrices $[M]_t$ for $M \in \mathbb{Z}_p^{n \times m}$.

2.2 Algebraic Languages

We refer to algebraic languages as the set of languages associated to a relation that can be described by algebraic equations over abelian groups. To be more precise, let gpar be some global parameters, generated by a probabilistic polynomial-time algorithm setup.gpar which takes the security parameter λ as input. These global parameters can correspond to the description of groups involved in the construction and usually includes the description of a bilinear group. Throughout the paper, we suppose that these global parameters are implicitly given as input to each algorithm.

Let $\mathsf{lpar} = (\mathbf{M}, \boldsymbol{\theta})$ be a set of language parameters generated by a polynomial-time algorithm setup.lpar which takes gpar as input. Here, $\mathbf{M} : \mathbb{G}^\ell \mapsto \mathbb{G}^{n \times k}$ and

$\theta : \mathbb{G}^{\ell} \mapsto \mathbb{G}^n$ are linear maps such that their different coefficients are not necessarily in the same algebraic structures. Namely, in the most common case, given a bilinear group $\mathsf{gpar} = (p, \mathbb{G}_1, \mathbb{G}_2, \mathbb{G}_T, \hat{e}, [1]_1, [2]_2)$, they can belong to either $\mathbb{Z}_p$, $\mathbb{G}_1$, $\mathbb{G}_2$, or $\mathbb{G}_T$ as long as the equation $\theta(\mathbf{x}) = \mathbf{M}(\mathbf{x}) \cdot \mathbf{w}$ is "well-consistent".

Formally, for a set $\mathcal{X}_{\mathsf{lpar}}$ that defines the underlying domain, we define an algebraic language $\mathcal{L}_{\mathsf{lpar}} \subset \mathcal{X}_{\mathsf{lpar}}$ as

$$\mathcal{L}_{\mathsf{lpar}} = \left\{ \mathbf{x} \in \mathbb{G} \middle| \exists \mathbf{w} \in \mathbb{Z}_p^k : \theta(\mathbf{x}) = \mathbf{M}(\mathbf{x}) \cdot \mathbf{w} \right\} . \tag{1}$$

An algebraic language where $\mathbf{M}$ is independent of $\mathbf{x}$ and θ is the identity function is called a *linear language*.

Finally, we note that algebraic languages are as expressive as generic NP languages. This is because every binary circuit can be represented by a set of linear equations.

2.3   Smooth Projective Hash Function

Let $\mathcal{L}_{\mathsf{lpar}}$ be a NP language, parametrized by a language parameter lpar, and $\mathcal{R}_{\mathsf{lpar}} \subseteq \mathcal{X}_{\mathsf{lpar}}$ be its corresponding relation. A Smooth projective hash functions (SPHFs [12]) for $\mathcal{L}_{\mathsf{lpar}}$ is a cryptographic primitive with this property that given lpar and a statement x, one can compute a hash of x in two different ways: either by using a projection key hp and $(\mathsf{x}, \mathsf{w}) \in \mathcal{R}_{\mathsf{lpar}}$ as $\mathsf{pH} \leftarrow \mathsf{projhash}(\mathsf{lpar}; \mathsf{hp}, \mathsf{x}, \mathsf{w})$, or by using a hashing key hk and $\mathsf{x} \in \mathcal{X}_{\mathsf{lpar}}$ as $\mathsf{H} \leftarrow \mathsf{hash}(\mathsf{lpar}; \mathsf{hk}, \mathsf{x})$. The formal definition of SPHF follows.

Definition 1. *A SPHF for* $\{\mathcal{L}_{\mathsf{lpar}}\}$ *is a tuple of PPT algorithms* $(\mathsf{setup}, \mathsf{hashkg}, \mathsf{projkg}, \mathsf{hash}, \mathsf{projhash})$*, which are defined as follows:*

$\mathsf{setup}(1^{\lambda})$**:** *Takes in a security parameter* λ *and generates the global parameters* pp *together with the language parameters* lpar*. We assume that all algorithms have access to* pp*.*

$\mathsf{hashkg}(\mathsf{lpar})$**:** *Takes in a language parameter* lpar *and outputs a hashing key* hk*.*

$\mathsf{projkg}(\mathsf{lpar}; \mathsf{hk}, \mathsf{x})$**:** *Takes in a hashing key* hk*,* lpar*, and a statement* x *and outputs a projection key* hp*, possibly depending on* x*.*

$\mathsf{hash}(\mathsf{lpar}; \mathsf{hk}, \mathsf{x})$**:** *Takes in a hashing key* hk*,* lpar*, and a statement* x *and outputs a hash value* H*.*

$\mathsf{projhash}(\mathsf{lpar}; \mathsf{hp}, \mathsf{x}, \mathsf{w})$**:** *Takes in a projection key* hp*,* lpar*, a statement* x*, and a witness* w *for* $\mathsf{x} \in \mathcal{L}$ *and outputs a hash value* pH*.*

A SPHF needs to satisfy the following properties:

Correctness. It is required that $\mathsf{hash}(\mathsf{lpar}; \mathsf{hk}, \mathsf{x}) = \mathsf{projhash}(\mathsf{lpar}; \mathsf{hp}, \mathsf{x}, \mathsf{w})$ for all $\mathsf{x} \in \mathcal{L}$ and their corresponding witnesses w.

Smoothness. It is required that for any lpar and any $\mathsf{x} \notin \mathcal{L}$, the following distributions are statistically indistinguishable:

$$\left\{ (\mathsf{hp}, \mathsf{H}) : \mathsf{hk} \leftarrow \mathsf{hashkg}(\mathsf{lpar}), \mathsf{hp} \leftarrow \mathsf{projkg}(\mathsf{lpar}; \mathsf{hk}, \mathsf{x}), \mathsf{H} \leftarrow \mathsf{hash}(\mathsf{lpar}; \mathsf{hk}, \mathsf{x}) \right\}$$

$$\left\{ (\mathsf{hp}, \mathsf{H}) : \mathsf{hk} \leftarrow \mathsf{hashkg}(\mathsf{lpar}), \mathsf{hp} \leftarrow \mathsf{projkg}(\mathsf{lpar}; \mathsf{hk}, \mathsf{x}), \mathsf{H} \leftarrow_{\$} \Omega \right\} .$$

where Ω is the set of hash values.

2.4 Predictable Arguments

Predictable arguments are multi-round interactive protocols where the verifier generates a challenge (which will be sent to the prover) and at the same time it can predict the prover's response to that challenge. Here we recall the formal definition of predictable arguments (PA) [14][3].

Let $\mathcal{RG}$ be a relation generator that takes in a security parameter 1^λ and returns a polynomial-time decidable binary relation $\mathcal{R}_{\mathsf{lpar}}$. For a pair $(\mathsf{x}, \mathsf{w}) \in \mathcal{R}_{\mathsf{lpar}}$, we call x the statement and w the witness. The set of all possible relations $\mathcal{R}_{\mathsf{lpar}}$ that the relation generator $\mathcal{RG}$ (for a given 1^λ) may output is denoted by $\mathcal{RG}_\lambda$. To make the notation simple, we assume that $\mathcal{R}_{\mathsf{lpar}}$ can be described with a language parameter lpar by which λ can be deduced as well.

Definition 2 (Predictable Argument (PA)). *A predictable argument for a relation $\mathcal{R}_{\mathsf{lpar}}$ (with the corresponding language parameter lpar) is an interactive protocol between a prover P and a verifier V, which can be specified by two algorithms $\Pi_{\mathsf{pa}} - (\mathsf{Chall}, \mathsf{Resp})$ defined as follows:*

(Executed by V): $(c, b) \leftarrow \mathsf{Chall}(\mathsf{lpar}, \mathsf{x})$. The algorithm takes in lpar and a statement x, and returns a challenge c along with a predicted answer b.
(Executed by P): $a \leftarrow \mathsf{Resp}(\mathsf{lpar}, \mathsf{x}, \mathsf{w}, c)$. The algorithm takes in lpar, a pair of statement-witness (x, w) and a challenge c, and returns an answer a.
(Executed by V): If $a = b$, V returns acc; otherwise it returns rej.

We denote by $\langle \mathsf{P}(\mathsf{lpar}, \mathsf{x}, \mathsf{w}), \mathsf{V}(\mathsf{lpar}, \mathsf{x}) \rangle$ an execution between P and V with common inputs $(\mathsf{lpar}, \mathsf{x})$ and prover's secret input w. The success of the prover in convincing the verifier is denoted by $\langle \mathsf{P}(\mathsf{lpar}, \mathsf{x}, \mathsf{w}), \mathsf{V}(\mathsf{lpar}, \mathsf{x}) \rangle = \mathsf{acc}$. Also, we may call (c, b) as both the output of $\mathsf{Chall}()$, or the output of V running $\mathsf{Chall}()$. The same convention holds for a.

We require two properties for a PΛ: *completeness* and *soundness*.

- **(Perfect) Completeness.** A predictable argument has perfect completeness if for all $\lambda \in \mathbb{N}$, for all $\mathcal{R}_{\mathsf{lpar}} \in \mathcal{RG}_\lambda$, and for all $(\mathsf{x}, \mathsf{w}) \in \mathcal{R}_{\mathsf{lpar}}$

$$\Pr\left[a = b : (c, b) \leftarrow \mathsf{Chall}(\mathsf{lpar}, \mathsf{x}); a \leftarrow \mathsf{Resp}(\mathsf{lpar}, \mathsf{x}, \mathsf{w}, c) \right] = 1$$

- **ϵ-Soundness.** For all $\lambda \in \mathbb{N}$, all $\mathsf{x} \notin \mathcal{L}_{\mathsf{lpar}}$, and all PPT adversaries $\mathcal{A}$

$$\Pr\left[a = b : \mathcal{R}_{\mathsf{lpar}} \leftarrow_{\$} \mathcal{RG}_\lambda; (c, b) \leftarrow \mathsf{Chall}(\mathsf{lpar}, \mathsf{x}); a \leftarrow \mathcal{A}(\mathsf{lpar}, \mathsf{x}, c) \right] \approx_\lambda \epsilon$$

We call a PA sound if $\epsilon \in \mathsf{negl}(\lambda)$. A PA is secure if it is complete and sound. Furthermore, we say that a PA is *zero-knowledge* (ZK-PA) if there exists a PPT algorithm Sim that computes the predicted answer of any valid statement x without knowing the random coins used in $\mathsf{Chall}()$ nor any witness for x, but only knowing the challenge c. In the case of ZK in the CRS model, the algorithm takes in also a CRS trapdoor τ which is generated by a setup algorithm $(\mathsf{crs}_\tau, \tau) \leftarrow \mathsf{setup}(1^\lambda)$. For notational simplicity, we assume that in this case lpar contains crs_τ as well.

---

[3] We define PAs as one-round protocols. As shown in [14], this is without loss of generality as every ρ-round PA can be squeezed into a one-round PA.

Zero-Knowledge

$(\mathsf{crs}_\tau, \tau) \leftarrow \mathsf{setup}(1^\lambda); (\mathsf{x}, \mathsf{w}, c) \leftarrow \mathcal{A}(\mathsf{crs}_\tau, \tau);$

if $\mathcal{R}_{\mathsf{lpar}}(\mathsf{x}, \mathsf{w}) = 0,$ then return 0;

$b \leftarrow_\$ \{0, 1\};$ if $b = 0$ then $a \leftarrow \mathsf{Resp}(\mathsf{lpar}, \mathsf{x}, \mathsf{w}, c);$ else $a \leftarrow \mathsf{Sim}(\mathsf{lpar}, \mathsf{x}, \tau, c);$

$b' \leftarrow \mathcal{A}(a);$

return $b = b';$

Fig. 1. Experiment for the definition of Zero-knowledge

- **Zero-Knowledge.** A predictable argument Π is zero-knowledge if there exists a PPT simulator Sim such that for all PPT adversary $\mathcal{A}$, $\Pr[\mathsf{Exp}^{\mathsf{zk}}_{\Pi,\mathsf{Sim}}(\mathcal{A}, \lambda) = 1] \approx_\lambda \frac{1}{2}$, where $\mathsf{Exp}^{\mathsf{zk}}_{\Pi,\mathsf{Sim}}(\mathcal{A}, \lambda)$ is depicted in Fig. 1.

In this work, we also consider a weaker version of zero-knowledge, called *witness indistinguishability* (WI) which informally states that the adversarial verifier cannot identify which witnesses are held by the prover.

- **Witness-Indistinguishability.** A predictable argument Π is statistically witness indistinguishable if for any adversary $\mathcal{A}$, for any common statement x, for any witnesses $\mathsf{w}_1, \mathsf{w}_2$ such that $(\mathsf{x}, \mathsf{w}_1) \in \mathcal{R}_{\mathsf{lpar}}, (\mathsf{x}, \mathsf{w}_2) \in \mathcal{R}_{\mathsf{lpar}}$, the following holds:

$$\langle \mathsf{P}(\mathsf{lpar}, \mathsf{x}, \mathsf{w}_1), \mathcal{A}(\mathsf{lpar}, \mathsf{x}) \rangle \approx_\lambda \langle \mathsf{P}(\mathsf{lpar}, \mathsf{x}, \mathsf{w}_2), \mathcal{A}(\mathsf{lpar}, \mathsf{x}) \rangle$$

2.5 Oblivious Transfer

A 2-round oblivious transfer (OT) is a protocol between a receiver and a sender and consists of three polynomial-time algorithms $\Pi_{\mathsf{OT}} = (\Pi^R_{\mathsf{OT}}, \Pi^S_{\mathsf{OT}}, \Pi^O_{\mathsf{OT}})$ defined as follows:

First round. The receiver generates the first message $m^R \leftarrow \Pi^R_{\mathsf{OT}}(b; r^R)$ for the selection bit $b \in \{0, 1\}$ and random tape $r^R \in \{0, 1\}^{\mathsf{poly}(\lambda)}$.

Second round. For the input messages (x^0, x^1), where $x^l \in \{0, 1\}^{\mathsf{poly}(\lambda)}$ for $l \in \{0, 1\}$, the sender generates the second message $m^S \leftarrow \Pi^S_{\mathsf{OT}}(m^R, (x^0, x^1); r^S)$ using random tape $r^S \in \{0, 1\}^{\mathsf{poly}(\lambda)}$.

Output. The receiver computes the output $x = \Pi^O_{\mathsf{OT}}(m^S, b, r^R)$.

In this work, we are interested in OT protocols that are *correct* and securely implement the standard ideal OT functionality $\mathcal{F}_{\mathsf{OT}}$ in the presence of malicious adversaries. Moreover, we require an additional property called *sender-extractability* [15], which at a high-level means that the randomness of the sender is sufficient to reconstruct its input. The formal definition of this property and $\mathcal{F}_{\mathsf{OT}}$ can be found in the full version [22].

2.6   Garbled Circuits

We recall the definition of garbling schemes formalized in [3]. At a high-level, a garbling scheme consists of four algorithms $\mathsf{GC} = (\mathsf{Garble}, \mathsf{Encode}, \mathsf{Eval}, \mathsf{Decode})$ defined as follows: Garble takes a circuit C and outputs a garbled circuit $\mathbf{C}$, encoding information e, and decoding information d. Encode takes an input e and x, and outputs a garbled input X. Eval takes as input a garbled circuit $\mathbf{C}$, and a garbled input X and outputs a garbled output Y. Finally, Decode takes d and a garbled output Y, and outputs a plain output y. In this work, we also assume an extra verification algorithm Verify that takes $(C, \mathbf{C}, e)$ as input and outputs 1 if this triple is valid.

A garbling scheme GC should satisfy *correctness* and the following security properties: *authenticity* which informally captures the unforgeability of the output of a garbled circuit evaluations, and *verifiability* that ensures the existence of an algorithm Verify that takes a circuit C, a (possibly maliciously generated) garbled circuit $\mathbf{C}$, and encoding information e, and outputs 1 if $\mathbf{C}$ is a valid garbling of C. The formal definition of these properties can be found in the full version [22].

3   More Efficient ZK-PA

PAs have deterministic provers and hence by an impossibility result from Goldreich and Oren [18] cannot be zero-knowledge in the plain model for non-trivial languages. Faonio *et al.* [14] circumvented this impossibility and provided two constructions by using setup assumptions. Their first construction in the CRS model is based on the natural idea of adding a NIZK proof of knowledge π for the "well-formedness" of the challenge generated by the challenger. Although this gives a generic compiler for constructing ZK-PAs from PAs, here we investigate designing out-of-the-box ZK-PA protocols with concrete efficiency. We give a construction in the CRS model which is based on the notion of Trapdoor Smooth Projective Hash Functions (TSPHFs).

3.1   TSPHF-Based ZK-PAs in the CRS Model

As shown in [14], PAs can be constructed from SPHFs, but since the projection key in SPHFs can be generated in a malicious way, they can provide only honest-verifier zero-knowledge property and it is not clear how to construct ZK-PA from standard SPHFs directly. Benhamouda *et al.* [4] defined the notion of *trapdoor SPHFs* (TSPHFs) as an extension of SPHF in which one can verify the correctness of the projection key generation. More in details, a TSPHF comes with three additional algorithms (tsetup, verHP, thash). tsetup outputs a CRS crs_τ with a trapdoor τ. The trapdoor τ can be used by thash to compute the hash value of any statement x (only by knowing public hp). The algorithm verHP takes in a key hp and the CRS crs_τ, and outputs 1 if hp is a valid projection key. The properties a TSPHF must verify are the same as SPHF, except the smoothness property is

---

- Setup(1^λ): Run $(\mathsf{crs}_\tau, \tau) \leftarrow \mathsf{tsetup}(1^\lambda)$ and return $(\mathsf{crs}_\tau, \tau)$.
- Chall(lpar, x):
  - Run $\mathsf{hk} \leftarrow_\$ \mathsf{hashkg}(\mathsf{lpar})$ and $\mathsf{hp} \leftarrow \mathsf{projkg}(\mathsf{lpar}; \mathsf{hk}, \mathsf{x})$.
  - Compute $\mathsf{H} \leftarrow \mathsf{hash}(\mathsf{lpar}; \mathsf{hk}, \mathsf{x})$.
  - Return $(c, b) := (\mathsf{hp}, \mathsf{H})$.
- Resp(lpar, x, w, c): For $c := \mathsf{hp}$, check if $\mathsf{verHP}(\mathsf{crs}_\tau, \mathsf{hp}) = 1$, then run $\mathsf{pH} \leftarrow \mathsf{projhash}(\mathsf{lpar}; \mathsf{hp}, \mathsf{x}, \mathsf{w})$ and return $a := \mathsf{pH}$.
- Sim(lpar, x, τ, c): Parse $c := \mathsf{hp}$ and return $\mathsf{tH} \leftarrow \mathsf{thash}(\mathsf{lpar}; \mathsf{hp}, \mathsf{x}, \tau)$.

Fig. 2. ZK-PA Π_{zkpa} from TSPHFs.

no longer statistical but computational as hp should now contain enough information to compute the hash of any statement. Moreover, a TSPHF should satisfy zero-knowledge property which informally states that for any statement x with valid witness w, the projected hash value $\mathsf{pH} \leftarrow \mathsf{projhash}(\mathsf{lpar}; \mathsf{hp}, \mathsf{x}, \mathsf{w})$ should be indistinguishable from the trapdoor hash value $\mathsf{tH} \leftarrow \mathsf{thash}(\mathsf{lpar}; \mathsf{hp}, \mathsf{x}, \tau)$. For a more formal definition of TSPHFs, We refer the reader to [4].

In this section, we show the connection between ZK-PAs and TSPHFs [6], namely we construct ZK-PA for a relation $\mathcal{R}_{\mathsf{lpar}}$ given a TSPHF for the same relation. Different from [14], the relation $\mathcal{R}_{\mathsf{lpar}}$ here is identical. This is because [14] considers the connection for the knowledge-sound PAs (and extractable SPHFs) whereas here we only consider soundness and (computational) smoothness. As a direct result of this, we obtain ZK-PA for all languages that admit TSPHFs (i.e., *algebraic languages*).

3.2 Construction of ZK-PA from TSPHFs

Let $\Pi_{\mathsf{tsphf}} = (\mathsf{setup}, \mathsf{tsetup}, \mathsf{hashkg}, \mathsf{projkg}, \mathsf{hash}, \mathsf{projhash}, \mathsf{verHP}, \mathsf{thash})$ be a TSPHF for $\mathcal{L}_{\mathsf{lpar}}$. The construction of $\Pi_{\mathsf{zkpa}} = (\mathsf{Setup}, \mathsf{Chall}, \mathsf{Resp}, \mathsf{Sim})$ in the CRS model is given in Fig. 2. Due to space constraints, the proof of the next theorem is deferred to the full version [22].

Theorem 1. *If the TSPHF Π_{tsphf} is correct, (computationally) smooth and zero-knowledge, then Π_{zkpa} in Fig. 2 is secure and zero-knowledge.*

Instantiation and Efficiency Evaluation. Given the above connection, one can now obtain a secure ZK-PA for any algebraic language $\mathcal{L}_{\mathsf{lpar}}$ with $\mathsf{lpar} = (\mathbf{M}, \boldsymbol{\theta})$ (see Eq. 1) in the bilinear setting based on the efficient construction of TSPHF in [6] (see full version [22] for details). The resulting ZK-PA is sound under the DDH assumption in $\mathbb{G}_2$ (See [6], Appendix E.3 for the security proof). To evaluate efficiency, we note that compared to the original construction of ZK-PA in [14], the above construction is more efficient as it only has one more group element in the challenge c (compared to the non-zk construction of PA), whereas the idea of adding a NIZK proof for the well-formedness of c in [14] has at least a linear overhead in the size of c^4.

Remark 1. Recently, Abdolmaleki et al. [1] show how one can use non-blackbox techniques to construct a subversion-resistant variant of smooth projective hash functions. Following a similar approach directly yields the construction of ZK-PA in the plain model, thus giving another way to circumvent the [18] impossibility using non-blackbox techniques. The recent work of [7] also construct ZK-PA for all NP. Their construction, however, mainly focuses on a *feasibility* result rather than efficiency, and requires strong assumptions such as indistinguishability obfuscation. Moreover, while the zero-knowledge simulator in their construction is non-black-box which is inherent in the plain model, we rather focus on more efficient constructions in the CRS model.

4   Witness-Indistinguishable Predictable Arguments

Due to a classical impossibility result [18], a prerequisite for constructing 2-message ZK proof systems based on black-box techniques is a common reference string (CRS)—a string generated by a trusted party to which both prover and verifier have access. Requiring such a trust model may however be overkill for some applications where a weaker notion of privacy such as witness indistinguishability (WI) is sufficient. Weaker than ZK property, this property states that for any two possible witnesses w_1, w_2, an adversary cannot distinguish proofs generated by w_1 from the proofs generated by w_2. Given a PA $\Pi_{pa} = (\mathsf{Chall}, \mathsf{Resp})$ for an NP language $\mathcal{L}$, we show how to construct a WI-PA $\Pi_{wipa} = (\mathsf{Chall}', \mathsf{Resp}')$ for the same language. At first it may seem that regardless of which witness is used by the prover when running Resp, it has the same functionality since all the witnesses return the same (predicted) answer. This argument is however not true: while for an honestly-generate challenge, Resp behaves the same regardless of which valid witness is used, this might not be true for maliciously generated challenges. To circumvent this issue, the key idea is to require the verifier to prove that the challenge is indeed generated from a proper run of Chall with some randomness. This should be done without breaking the soundness, meaning the secret coins of the verifier should be kept hidden from the prover. To this end, we will use a NIWI proof system as an ingredient, through which the verifier proves the following statement: there exists a random string α, such that $c = \mathsf{Chall}(\mathsf{lpar}, x; \alpha)$. The prover first checks if the NIWI proof verifies and if so, computes the predicted answer as before.

Since we use a NIWI proof system in the plain model as an ingredient of our construction, below we recall the definition of WI for such proof systems. We note that a construction of NIWI in the plain model for all NP languages and based on standard assumptions is presented in [21].

---

[4] Here we are assuming that the security of the construction should remain under standard and falsifiable assumptions as it is easy to construct succinct NIZKs based on non-falsifiable assumptions.

- Chall'(lpar, x): the verifier computes $(c, b) \leftarrow$ Chall(lpar, x; α) and sends the challenge c along with a NIWI proof π for the existence of α such that c is the first output of Chall(lpar, x; α).
- Resp'(lpar, x, w, c, π): the prover first checks the NIWI proof π. If π verifies, the prover computes $a \leftarrow$ Resp(lpar, x, w, c) and returns a.

Fig. 3. Construction of WI-PA

Definition 3. *Let* $\Pi_{\mathsf{niwi}} = (\mathcal{P}_{\mathsf{niwi}}, \mathcal{V}_{\mathsf{niwi}})$ *be a non-interactive proof system for a language* $\mathcal{L}_{\mathsf{lpar}}$. *We say that* Π_{niwi} *is computationally witness-indistinguishable if for all* $(\mathsf{x}, \mathsf{w}_1, \mathsf{w}_2)$ *such that* $(\mathsf{x}, \mathsf{w}_1) \in \mathcal{R}_{\mathsf{lpar}}$ *and* $(\mathsf{x}, \mathsf{w}_2) \in \mathcal{R}_{\mathsf{lpar}}$, *and for all PPT adversaries* $\mathcal{A}$,

$$\Pr\left[\mathcal{A}(\pi) = 1 \; : \; \pi \leftarrow \mathcal{P}_{\mathsf{niwi}}(\mathsf{lpar}, \mathsf{x}, \mathsf{w}_1)\right] \approx_\lambda \Pr\left[\mathcal{A}(\pi) = 1 \; : \; \pi \leftarrow \mathcal{P}_{\mathsf{niwi}}(\mathsf{lpar}, \mathsf{x}, \mathsf{w}_2)\right]$$

4.1 Our Construction

Let $\Pi_{\mathsf{pa}} = (\mathsf{Chall}, \mathsf{Resp})$ be a predictable argument for language $\mathcal{L}_{\mathsf{lpar}}$, and Π_{niwi} be a non-interactive computational WI proof system in the plain model for the language of statements c for which there exists α such that $c = \mathsf{Chall}(\mathsf{lpar}, \mathsf{x}; \alpha)$. We construct a WI-PA $\Pi_{\mathsf{wipa}} = (\mathsf{Chall}', \mathsf{Resp}')$ for $\mathcal{L}_{\mathsf{lpar}}$ as depicted in Fig. 3. The completeness of the construction follows straightforwardly from the completeness of Π_{pa}. We prove soundness and WI in the next theorem.

Theorem 2. *The construction in Fig. 3 is a statistical witness-indistinguishable predictable argument in the plain model.*

Proof. **Soundness.** Let $\mathsf{x} \notin \mathcal{L}_{\mathsf{lpar}}$ and $\mathcal{A}$ be an efficient adversary that breaks soundness of Π_{wipa} by convincing the honest verifier V with non-negligible probability ε. I.e., $\varepsilon(n) \geq \frac{1}{p(n)}$ for some polynomial p and for infinitely many n's. Denoting this set by N, we restrict ourselves to $n \in N$ from now on. This indicates that there exists a first message c from V on which $\mathcal{A}$ convinces V with probability at least ε. Fix this challenge c and the corresponding answer b computed by V. Define a set S as follows:

$$S = \left\{ b : \Pr\left[\mathcal{A}(\mathsf{lpar}, \mathsf{x}, c) = b | (c, b) \leftarrow \mathsf{Chall}(\mathsf{lpar}, \mathsf{x})\right] \geq \frac{\varepsilon}{2} \right\}$$

Fix some $b_0 \in S$ and define $S_0 \subseteq S$ as

$$S_0 = \left\{ b \in S : \Pr\left[\mathcal{A}(\mathsf{lpar}, \mathsf{x}, c) = b | (c, b_0) \leftarrow \mathsf{Chall}(\mathsf{lpar}, \mathsf{x})\right] \geq \frac{\varepsilon}{4} \right\}.$$

Since $b_0 \in S$, we have that $\Pr\left[\mathcal{A}(\mathsf{lpar}, \mathsf{x}, c) = b_0 | (c, b_0) \leftarrow \mathsf{Chall}(\mathsf{lpar}, \mathsf{x})\right] \geq \frac{\varepsilon}{2}$ and therefore $|S_0| \cdot \frac{\varepsilon}{4} \leq 1 - \frac{\varepsilon}{2}$, which consequently implies that $|S_0| \leq \frac{4}{\varepsilon}$. Now, the fact that ε is non-negligible indicates that S_0 is bounded by a polynomial. On the other hand, we have that $\Pr[b \in S] \geq \frac{\varepsilon}{2}$, and that S is exponential in the security parameter λ. This means that there should exist $b_1 \in S$ such that $b_1 \notin S_0$. We now construct a non-uniform PPT adversary $\mathcal{B}$ that breaks the witness-indistinguishability of Π_{niwi}. Let $aux = (\alpha_0, \alpha_1, b_0, b_1)$ be such that $(c, b_0) \leftarrow \mathsf{Chall}(\mathsf{lpar}, \mathsf{x}; \alpha_0)$ and $(c, b_1) \leftarrow \mathsf{Chall}(\mathsf{lpar}, \mathsf{x}; \alpha_1)$. Given aux as advice, $\mathcal{B}$ proceeds as follows: it first returns $(c, (b_0, \alpha_0), (b_1, \alpha_1))$ to the WI challenger and obtains a proof π. Next, $\mathcal{B}$ calls $\mathcal{A}$ on input (π, c) and returns i when it receives b_i from $\mathcal{A}$. Note that for π that is computed using (r_0, b_0), $\mathcal{A}$ returns b_1 with probability at most $\frac{\varepsilon}{4}$, whereas for π computed by (r_1, b_1), $\mathcal{A}$ returns b_1 with probability at least $\frac{\varepsilon}{2}$. This makes $\mathcal{B}$ a successful adversary in breaking WI.

WI. Let V^* be an adversary against WI property of Π_{wipa} and $(\mathsf{x}, \mathsf{w}_1, \mathsf{w}_2)$ be such that $(\mathsf{x}, \mathsf{w}_1), (\mathsf{x}, \mathsf{w}_2) \in \mathcal{R}_{\mathsf{lpar}}$. It follows from (statistical) soundness of the NIWI proof that V^*'s first message is computed correctly with overwhelming probability. This together with predictability of the argument indicates that the answer from the prover is unique regardless of which witness is used and thus completes the proof. □

5 Commit-and-Prove Predictable Arguments

We study a relaxed notion of predictability in interactive argument systems which consists of two phases: In phase 1 (commitment phase), the prover commits to its witness once for all and sends the commitment to the verifier. In phase 2 (challenge-response phase), the prover and the verifier engage in a predictable argument protocol, where the verifier's challenges may depend on the commitment in such a way that the prover's responses can be predicted by the verifier. The type of relations we consider are of the following form: a statement $\mathsf{x} = (\mathsf{cm}, C, y)$ and a witness (w, d) are in the relation (i.e., $(\mathsf{x}, (\mathsf{w}, \mathsf{d})) \in \mathcal{R}$) iff "cm commits to w by randomness d, and $C(\mathsf{w}) = y$". Here C is a circuit in some polynomial-size circuit class $\mathcal{C}$ and y is the expected output of the circuit.

Definition 4 (Commit-and-Prove Predictable Arguments). *Let $\mathcal{C}$ be a class of polynomial-sized circuits. A commit-and-prove predictable argument for $\mathcal{C}$ is a multi-round protocol (between a prover P and a verifier V) which consists of three algorithms $\Pi_{\mathsf{cppa}} = (\mathsf{Commit}, \mathsf{Chall}, \mathsf{Resp})$:*

Commitment phase *(executed by P): $\mathsf{cm} \leftarrow \mathsf{Commit}(\mathsf{w}; \mathsf{d})$ on input a value w, generates a commitment cm by using some randomness d.*
Interaction phase. *Each round proceeds as follows:*
 - *(**Executed by** V): $(c, b) \leftarrow \mathsf{Chall}(\mathsf{cm}, C, y)$ on input a statement (cm, C, y) such that $C \in \mathcal{C}$, generates a challenge c and a predicted answer b.*
 - *(**Executed by** P): $a \leftarrow \mathsf{Resp}(\mathsf{cm}, C, \mathsf{w}, \mathsf{d}, c)$ on input a commitment cm, a circuit $C \in \mathcal{C}$, the committed value w, the randomness d, returns a response a.*
V accepts the proof iff $a = b$ in all rounds.

We call a CPPA as a ρ-round CPPA if the interaction phase consists of ρ rounds. A CPPA should satisfy *completeness* and *soundness* as defined below:

(Perfect) Completeness. An honest prover with a statement $\mathsf{x} = (\mathsf{cm}, C, y)$ and witness (w, d) such that (w, d) opens the commitment (i.e., $\mathsf{cm} = \mathsf{Commit}(\mathsf{w}; \mathsf{d})$), and $C(\mathsf{w}) = y$ can always convince the verifier with over-whelming probability. More precisely, a CPPA has perfect completeness if for all $\lambda \in \mathbb{N}$, for all $C \in \mathcal{C}$, and for all $(\mathsf{x} = (\mathsf{cm}, C, y), (\mathsf{w}, \mathsf{d})) \in \mathcal{R}$

$$\Pr\left[a = b \ : \ (c, b) \leftarrow \mathsf{Chall}(\mathsf{cm}, C, y); a \leftarrow \mathsf{Resp}(\mathsf{cm}, C, \mathsf{w}, \mathsf{d}, c) \right] = 1$$

ϵ-**Soundness.** For all $\lambda \in \mathbb{N}$, and all (stateful) PPT adversaries $\mathcal{A} = (\mathcal{A}_1, \mathcal{A}_2)$

$$\Pr\left[\begin{array}{ll} a = b \wedge & (\mathsf{w}, \mathsf{d}, C, y) \leftarrow \mathcal{A}_1(1^\lambda); \mathsf{cm} \leftarrow \mathsf{Commit}(\mathsf{w}; \mathsf{d}) \\ C(\mathsf{w}) \neq y & (c, b) \leftarrow \mathsf{Chall}(\mathsf{cm}, C, y); a \leftarrow \mathcal{A}_2(\mathsf{w}, \mathsf{d}, C, y, c) \end{array} \right] \approx_\lambda \epsilon$$

We call a CPPA sound if $\epsilon \in \mathsf{negl}(\lambda)$. A CPPA is secure if it is correct and sound. Similar to PAs, one can show that CPPAs can also be made extremely laconic in terms of both round complexity and proof complexity. Specifically, the same technique in [14] can be used to collapse any ρ-round CPPA into a single round CPPA.

In this work, we only focus on CPPA protocols with the zero-knowledge property. A CPPA is *zero-knowledge* (ZK-CPPA) if there exists a PPT algorithm Sim that computes the predicted answer of any valid statement x without knowing the random coins used by Chall() nor any witness for x, but only knowing the challenge c. Since our construction of ZK-CPPA is in the non-programmable random oracle (NPRO) model, we define this property in this model.

Definition 5 (Zero-knowledge CPPA in the NPRO model). *We say that a CPPA* (Commit, Chall, Resp) *for a class of circuits $\mathcal{C}$ satisfies the zero-knowledge property in the NPRO model if for any PPT adversary $\mathcal{A}$, there exists a PPT simulator Sim such that for all PPT distinguisher $\mathcal{D}$, for all $(\mathsf{x}, \mathsf{w}) \in \mathcal{R}$, and all auxiliary inputs $z \in \{0, 1\}^*$, we have:*

$$\max_{\mathcal{D}, z} \left| \Pr[\mathcal{D}^H(\mathsf{x}, \tau, z) = 1 : \tau \leftarrow (\mathsf{P}^H(\mathsf{x}, \mathsf{w}) \leftrightarrows \mathcal{A}^H(\mathsf{x}, z))] \right.$$

$$\left. - \Pr[\mathcal{D}^H(\mathsf{x}, \tau, z) = 1 : \tau \leftarrow \mathsf{Sim}^H(\mathsf{x}, z)] \right| \leq \mathsf{negl}(|\mathsf{x}|)$$

Where P and $\mathcal{A}$ are respectively the prover and the (malicious) verifier running the CPPA protocol, and $\mathsf{P}^H(\mathsf{x}, \mathsf{w}) \leftrightarrows \mathcal{A}^H(\mathsf{x}, z)$ denotes the random variable corresponding to a protocol transcript on input (x, w).

We now give our construction of ZK-CPPA for all polynomial-size circuits P in the NPRO model. The construction is similar to the three-round ZK protocol of [15], with the difference that the first message in our protocol is reusable. Moreover, here we only focus on providing ZK property as defined above, whereas the construction of [15] shows ZK in the UC model.

5.1 ZK-CPPA Based on Garbled Circuits and Oblivious Transfer

Let $\mathsf{GC} = (\mathsf{Garble}, \mathsf{Encode}, \mathsf{Eval}, \mathsf{Decode}, \mathsf{Verify})$ be a garbled circuit with correctness, authenticity, and verifiability, and $\Pi_{\mathsf{OT}} = (\Pi_{\mathsf{OT}}^R, \Pi_{\mathsf{OT}}^S, \Pi_{\mathsf{OT}}^O)$ be a sender-extractable oblivious transfer protocol that realizes $\mathcal{F}_{\mathsf{OT}}$. At a high level, the construction proceeds as follows. The prover P with witness $\mathsf{w} = (\mathsf{w}_1, \ldots, \mathsf{w}_n) \in \{0,1\}^n$ plays the role of the receiver in n instances of the OT protocol and commits to its witness bits by providing w_j as input to the j-th instance of Π_{OT}. Let $m_j^R \leftarrow \Pi_{\mathsf{OT}}^R(\mathsf{w}_j; r_j^R)$ and define cm and d as the set of $\{m_j^R\}_{j \in [n]}$ and $\{r_j^R\}_{j \in [n]}$, respectively. For a circuit-value pair (C, y) of the verifier's choice, let $\hat{C}$ be a circuit that realizes the following relation $\mathcal{R}$: $\mathcal{R}(\mathsf{x} = (\mathsf{cm}, C, y), (\mathsf{w}, \mathsf{d})) = 1$ iff (w, d) open cm and $C(\mathsf{w}) = y$. The verifier V constructs a GC $\mathbf{C}$ for $\hat{C}$ and sends it along with the second message of the OT as the challenge c. Moreover, V sets the predicted answer b to be the output 1-key k^1 of the final gate in the circuit. Now, P with a valid witness (w, d) evaluates $\mathbf{C}$ and sends the obtained garbled output $a = \mathsf{k}^1$ as the predicted answer. It is not hard to see that this construction results in a CPPA. To additionally ensure ZK property, we follow the same approach as [15] by enforcing V to also provide a ciphertext $ct = H(\mathsf{k}^1) \oplus r$, where H is a random oracle and r is the randomness used by V to produce the second message of the OT. When P computes k^1, she first recovers r and then computes all the labels by executing the extractor Ext guaranteed by the sender-extractability property. Finally, P verifies if the garbled circuit has been constructed correctly and if so, she sends the predicted answer $a = \mathsf{k}^1$ to V. The resulting protocol Π_{cppa} is described in Fig. 4. The proof idea is similar in spirit to the proof of Theorem 4.2 in [15]. We give a proof sketch here.

Theorem 3. *Let GC be a correct, authentic, and verifiable garbling scheme, Π_{OT} be a sender-extractable OT protocol that securely implements $\mathcal{F}_{\mathsf{OT}}$, and H be a random oracle. The protocol Π_{cppa} in Fig. 4 is a secure and zero-knowledge commit-and-prove predictable argument as defined in Definitions 4 and 5.*

Proof (Sketch). Completeness follows straightforwardly by the correctness property of the underlying OT and the garbling scheme.

In order to show soundness, let us consider a PPT adversary $\mathcal{A} = (\mathcal{A}_1, \mathcal{A}_2)$ and assume that $(\mathsf{w}, \mathsf{d}, C, y)$ is a tuple returned by $\mathcal{A}_1$ that corresponds to a false statement. That is, $\mathsf{x} = (\mathsf{cm}, C, y)$, where $\mathsf{cm} = \mathsf{Commit}(\mathsf{w}; \mathsf{d})$ and $C(\mathsf{w}) \neq y$. We show that for $(c, b) \leftarrow \mathsf{Chall}(\mathsf{cm}, C, y)$, if $\mathcal{A}_2$ having c can compute the predicted answer b, then one can either break the sender security of the underlying OT protocol, or the authenticity of the garbling scheme. To show this reduction, we first note that b is the correct label k^1. Now, given that $C(\mathsf{w}) \neq y$, there can be two cases where $\mathcal{A}_2$ can output k^1 with non-negligible probability. In the first case, $\mathcal{A}_2$ outputs k^1 by the ability of computing invalid labels $\mathsf{k}_j^{1-\mathsf{w}_j}$ that does not correspond to its committed value. It is not hard to see that such $\mathcal{A}_2$ can be used to break OT sender security. The reduction $\mathcal{B}$ proceeds as follows: $\mathcal{B}$ first computes a garbled circuit $\mathbf{C}$ and sends the labels to the OT challenger. Next, it extracts $\mathcal{A}_2$'s input w and forwards it as the choice bits of the receiver. The OT challenger computes the sender's message either by invoking a real sender, or by invoking the simulator, and sends it to the reduction who further forwards to $\mathcal{A}_2$ together with $\mathbf{C}$ and a random T. Now, since $\mathcal{A}_2$ can compute k^1 only in the real execution of Π_{OT}, a successful $\mathcal{A}_2$ with non-negligible probability ϵ implies that $\mathcal{B}$ can distinguish the real and simulated view of the OT protocol with probability at least ϵ. In the second case, where $\mathcal{A}_2$ does not use invalid labels but computes the correct k^1, it is straightforward to construct an adversary $\mathcal{B}$ that breaks the authenticity of the underlying garbling scheme by forging k^1 for a given garbled circuit $\mathbf{C}$.

We now argue that Π_{cppa} is zero-knowledge in the NPRO model. Let V^* be a PPT adversary against the ZK property. We construct an efficient simulator Sim that simulates the protocol as follows. Sim observes V^*'s calls to the random oracle, so that for every query $H(u)$ made by V^*, Sim records u in a set L. To simulate the first message, Sim invokes the simulator of Π_{OT} for the corrupt receiver. Upon receiving V^*'s message c, Sim parses c as $(\mathbf{C}, \{m_j^S\}_{j \in [n]}, T)$ and defines the set $\tilde{R} = \{H(u) \oplus T | u \in L\}$. For any $r \in \tilde{R}$ parsed as $r = r_1 || \dots || r_n$, Sim computes $(k_j^0, k_j^1) \leftarrow \mathsf{Ext}(m_j^R, m_j^S, r_j^S)$ for $j \in [n]$ and checks if $\mathsf{Verify}(\hat{C}, \mathbf{C}, \{k_j^0, k_j^1\}_{j \in [n]}) = 1$. If there exists such $r \in \tilde{R}$, the simulator sends Y to V^*, where $Y \in L$ is so that $r = H(Y) \oplus T$. Otherwise, Sim aborts the protocol. The output of the simulator is perfectly indistinguishable from the real distribution and this completes the proof. $\square$

6   Applications: Witness Encryption with Decryptor Privacy

Besides being a notion of theoretical interest, we also show the applications of (commit-and-prove) predictable arguments with zero-knowledge or witness-indistinguishability property in the context of witness encryption. Witness encryption (WE) is a powerful notion of encryption introduced by Garg et al. [17]. A WE scheme for an NP relation $\mathcal{R}_{\mathsf{lpar}}$ allows to encrypt a message m with respect to a statement x as $ct \leftarrow \mathsf{WE.Enc}(\mathsf{lpar}, m, \mathsf{x})$. The ciphertext can be decrypted as $m \leftarrow \mathsf{WE.Dec}(ct, \mathsf{w})$ for any w such that $(\mathsf{x}, \mathsf{w}) \in \mathcal{R}_{\mathsf{lpar}}$. Security guarantees that no adversary should learn any non-trivial information about m if $\mathsf{x} \notin \mathcal{L}_{\mathsf{lpar}}$, where $\mathcal{L}_{\mathsf{lpar}}$ is the language corresponding to $\mathcal{R}_{\mathsf{lpar}}$. More formally, we say that a WE is secure if it is complete and sound as defined below:

- **Completeness.** A WE has completeness if for all $\lambda \in \mathbb{N}$, for all $\mathcal{R}_{\mathsf{lpar}} \in \mathcal{RG}_\lambda$, for all m, and for all $(\mathsf{x}, \mathsf{w}) \in \mathcal{R}_{\mathsf{lpar}}$

$$\Pr[\mathsf{Dec}(\mathsf{Enc}(\mathsf{lpar}, \mathsf{x}, m), \mathsf{w}) = m] \geq 1 - \mathsf{negl}(\lambda)$$

If the probability is 1, we say WE is perfectly complete.
- **Soundness.** A WE has soundness if for all $\lambda \in \mathbb{N}$ and all PPT adversaries $\mathcal{A}$, there exists a negligible function $\mathsf{negl}(\lambda)$ such that for any m_0, m_1

$$\Pr\left[\begin{array}{c} \mathcal{R}_{\mathsf{lpar}} \leftarrow_\$ \mathcal{RG}_\lambda; \mathsf{x} \leftarrow \mathcal{A}(\mathsf{lpar}); b \leftarrow_\$ \{0,1\}; \\ ct \leftarrow \mathsf{Enc}(\mathsf{lpar}, \mathsf{x}, m_b); b' \leftarrow \mathcal{A}(\mathsf{lpar}, \mathsf{x}, ct) \end{array} : \begin{array}{c} b = b' \wedge \mathsf{x} \notin \mathcal{L}_{\mathsf{lpar}} \\ \wedge |m_0| = |m_1| \end{array} \right] \approx_\lambda \mathsf{negl}(\lambda)$$

- **Oracles and Primitives**: A correct, authentic, and verifiable garbling scheme $\mathsf{GC} = (\mathsf{Garble}, \mathsf{Encode}, \mathsf{Eval}, \mathsf{Decode})$, a sender-extractable 2-round OT Π_{OT}, and a hash function $H : \{0,1\}^* \to \{0,1\}^{\mathsf{poly}(\lambda)}$ modeled as a random oracle.
- **P's private input**: $\mathsf{w} \in \{0,1\}^n$, where $n = \mathsf{poly}(\lambda)$.
- **Commitment Phase**: P plays the role of the receiver in n instances of Π_{OT} and computes $(\mathsf{cm}, \mathsf{d})$ as follows:
  1. Sample uniformly random r_j^R from $\{0,1\}^\lambda$, and compute $m_j^R \leftarrow \Pi_{\mathsf{OT}}^R(\mathsf{w}_j; r_j^R)$ for $j \in [n]$.
  2. Define $\mathsf{cm} = \{m_j^R\}_{j \in [n]}$ and $\mathsf{d} = \{r_j^R\}_{j \in [n]}$.
- **Common inputs**: A security parameter λ, and a statement $\mathsf{x} = (\mathsf{cm}, C, y)$, where C is a polynomial-size circuit.
- **Challenge**: Let $\hat{C}$ be a circuit that realizes the following relation $\mathcal{R}$: $\mathcal{R}(\mathsf{x} = (\mathsf{cm}, C, y), (\mathsf{w}, \mathsf{d})) = 1$ iff (w, d) opens cm and $C(\mathsf{w}) = y$. V plays the role of the sender in n instances of Π_{OT} and computes a pair (c, b) of challenge-predicted answer as follows:
  1. Compute $(\mathbf{C}, e, d) \leftarrow \mathsf{Garble}(1^\lambda, \hat{C})$, where $e := \{k_j^0, k_j^1\}_{j \in [n]}$, and $d := (k^0, k^1)$.
  2. For $j \in [n]$, sample uniformly random r_j^S from $\{0,1\}^\lambda$, and compute $m_j^S = \Pi_{\mathsf{OT}}^S(k_j^0, k_j^1, m_j^R; r_j^S)$.
  3. Compute $T = H(k^1) \oplus r^S$, where $r^S = r_1^S || \ldots || r_n^S$.
  4. Define $c = (\mathbf{C}, \{m_j^S\}_{j \in [n]}, T)$ and $b = k^1$, and send c to P.
- **Response**: P proceeds as follows:
  1. Execute $k_j^{\mathsf{w}_j} = \Pi_{\mathsf{OT}}^O(m_j^S, \mathsf{w}_j, r_j^R)$ for $j \in [n]$.
  2. Execute $Y = \mathsf{Eval}(\mathbf{C}, \{k_j^{\mathsf{w}_j}\}_{j \in [n]})$.
  3. Recover $r^S = H(Y) \oplus T$, and parse $r^S = r_1^S || \ldots || r_n^S$.
  4. Reconstruct sender's inputs $(k_j^0, k_j^1) \leftarrow \mathsf{Ext}(m_j^R, m_j^S, r_j^S)$ for $j \in [n]$. Abort if the extractor fails for some $j \in [n]$.
  5. Send the predicted answer $a = Y$ if $\mathsf{Verify}(\hat{C}, \mathbf{C}, \{k_j^0, k_j^1\}_{j \in [n]}) = 1$; and abort otherwise.
- V accepts the proof iff $a = b$.

Fig. 4. ZK-CPPA Π_{cppa} based on GC and OT

While being a very powerful notion, existing constructions of WE are not satisfactory, as they are either based on strong assumptions such as indistinguishability obfuscation and multilinear maps [11,16,17,20], or based on new and unexplored algebraic structures [2].

As noted in [14], predictable arguments imply witness encryption as one can encrypt a bit m by generating a challenge-answer pair (c, b) for the PA and define the ciphertext as $(c, b \oplus m)$. Viceversa, a PA can be constructed from WE by encrypting a random bit m and then asking the prover to return m.

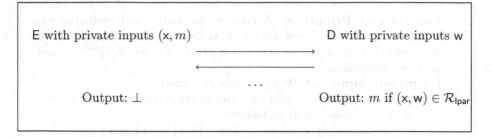

E with private inputs (x, m) D with private inputs w

Output: $\perp$ Output: m if $(x, w) \in \mathcal{R}_{\mathsf{lpar}}$

Fig. 5. Functionality of a WE scheme with decryptor privacy for a relation $\mathcal{R}_{\mathsf{lpar}}$

Furthermore, it is not hard to show that commit-and-prove predictable arguments are also equivalent to a variant of witness encryption studied in [5,8]. It is therefore interesting to see the applications of predictable arguments with privacy in the context of witness encryption. While the standard definition of witness encryption requires the above properties, for some applications explained below, we may require some level of privacy for the decryptor as well. In other words, we may ask for a WE scheme that mimics the following functionality (See Fig. 5): the functionality is parameterized by a message space $\mathcal{M}$ and an NP relation $\mathcal{R}_{\mathsf{lpar}}$. An encryptor E with private inputs $m \in \mathcal{M}$ and bitstring x interacts with a decryptor D with private input w, at the end of which D outputs m iff $(x, w) \in \mathcal{R}$. Note that this is different from standard WE wherein the decryptor aims to obtain the message internally without revealing it to the environment. Here instead, the decrypted message is revealed to the encryptor which may break the privacy of the decryptor. Since the encryptor knows the plaintext when running the encryption algorithm, one may wonder how the decrypted message can leak some information about the decryptor's witness. In the full version [22], we provide an example to illustrate this scenario.

6.1 Application: Dark Pools

We now justify our model of WE with decryptor privacy. In our model, we are assuming that the decryptor D sends back the decrypted message to the encryptor E whereas in all previous works, the communication is non-interactive (i.e., "one-shot") in the sense that there is only one message ct from E to D. Our motivating applications are *dark pools* and *over-the-counter* markets. Dark pools are anonymized trading platforms that allow parties to place invisible orders such that each party can only know their own orders. Such pools allow the investors to communicate only to those whose transaction conditions satisfy some constraints. At the same time, they should also guarantee that investors do not learn any information about traders' secret information.

In a recent work, Ngo et al. [23] introduced a new cryptographic primitive called *Witness Key Agreement* (WKA) as a tool to make this possible. In the dark pool scenario, a WKA allows a party E to securely agree on a secret key with another party D who owns a secret witness satisfying some arithmetic relation.

More precisely, in the presence of a public bulletin board or a public blockchain, a WKA addresses the following problem: given n parties who have committed to their secret inputs w, and published the commitments cm anonymously on the blockchain, an investor E wants to agree on a key k with any party whose committed secret w satisfies some relation; i.e., $C(w) = y$, where C is an arbitrary arithmetic circuit specified by E. Similar to NP relations defined in Sect. 5, one can set x = (cm, C, y) and let $\mathcal{R}$ be defined such that $\mathcal{R}(x, (w, d)) = 1$ iff cm commits to w (with decommitment d) and $C(w) = y$. Once the secret key k is recovered by the legitimate party (i.e., any party with valid witness (w, d) such that $\mathcal{R}(x, (d, w)) = 1$), they together with the investor can secure their communication from any external party by using k.

We now demonstrate how our construction of ZK-CPPA can be used as a drop-in replacement for a witness key agreement. At a high level, the protocol proceeds as follows. All parties first commit to their secret values w via cm $\leftarrow$ Commit(w; d), and publish the resulting commitments cm. Later, an investor who wish to communicate only with participants whose secret satisfy $C(w) = y$ (for some arbitrarily chosen circuit C and value y) considers the following relation: $\mathcal{R}(x = (cm, C, y), (w, d)) = 1$ iff $C(w) = y$, and cm = Commit(w; d). Let us assume that $x_i = (cm_i, C, y)$ is the statement corresponding to party i. The investor now encrypts the secret key k under all such statements x_i[5]. It is not hard to see that only the prover with the valid witness (w_i, d_i) can decrypt the ciphertext. Moreover, since the construction is ZK, the decrypted message k says nothing about (w_i, d_i), even if the ciphertext is generated maliciously.

Efficiency and Comparison with [23]. In [23], the authors propose a WKA construction based on a type of *Succinct Zero-Knowledge Non-Interactive Argument of Knowledge Proof System* (zk-SNARK) from non-interactive linear proof systems (NILP), where the verifier is designated. The construction at a high-level is as follows. A designated verifier—playing the role of the investor— first broadcasts a CRS as a challenge for the relation $\mathcal{R}$ of interest. Next, a prover publishes a partial zk-SNARK proof as a response for the committed value that satisfies $\mathcal{R}$. Finally, the verifier using the partial proof can derive a shared secret key with the prover.

We now compare our proposed construction for WKA with that of [23]. In contrast to our scheme which is ZK, the construction of [23] only provides honest-verifier ZK. Moreover, the WKA in [23] requires an expensive trusted setup which should be invoked every time an investor E_i asks for the preprocessing of a new CRS corresponding to the relation $\mathcal{R}_i$ of E_i's interest. On the other hand, the major downside of our scheme is that the size of the ciphertext grows linearly with the number of parties in the system as the investor should encrypt the message under every existing commitment in the system, whereas the size of ciphertext in [23] is independent of the number of parties. This suggests that there might well be a trade-off between the size of the ciphertext and the required

---

[5] We again emphasize that we see the notions of PA and WE (and their "commit-and-prove" variants) interchangeably here, as the implication from one to another is straightforward and shown in [14].

number of trusted setups and our construction performs better when the number of parties is small.

7   Conclusion and Open Problems

In this work, we study predictable arguments with privacy properties and show their application to the construction of witness encryption schemes that require decryptor's privacy. We also introduce CPPAs that provide a weakening of predictability and give an efficient construction using garbled circuits techniques. While we construct CPPA in the random oracle model, an interesting open question is whether PA also exists in this model. Another theoretical question left open by our work is to show if WI deterministic-prover argument (WI-DA) implies WI-PA. While zero-knowledge deterministic-prover argument (ZK-DA) was characterized in a recent work by Bitansky and Choudhuri in [7], where they showed that ZK-DA implies ZK-PA, it would be interesting to do the same characterization for the weaker notion of witness indistinguishability. Finally, finding more applications for CPPA would be an interesting question.

References

1. Abdolmaleki, B., Khoshakhlagh, H., Lipmaa, H.: Smooth zero-knowledge hash functions. IACR Cryptology ePrint Archive, Report 2021/653 (2021)
2. Bartusek, J., Ishai, Y., Jain, A., Ma, F., Sahai, A., Zhandry, M.: Affine determinant programs: a framework for obfuscation and witness encryption, pp. 82:1–82:39 (2020)
3. Bellare, M., Hoang, V.T., Rogaway, P.: Foundations of garbled circuits, pp. 784–796 (2012)
4. Benhamouda, F., Blazy, O., Chevalier, C., Pointcheval, D., Vergnaud, D.: New techniques for SPHFs and efficient one-round PAKE protocols. In: Canetti, R., Garay, J.A. (eds.) CRYPTO 2013. LNCS, vol. 8042, pp. 449–475. Springer, Heidelberg (2013). https://doi.org/10.1007/978-3-642-40041-4_25
5. Benhamouda, F., Lin, H.: Mr NISC: multiparty reusable non-interactive secure computation. In: Pass, R., Pietrzak, K. (eds.) TCC 2020. LNCS, vol. 12551, pp. 349–378. Springer, Cham (2020). https://doi.org/10.1007/978-3-030-64378-2_13
6. Benhamouda, F., Pointcheval, D.: Trapdoor smooth projective hash functions. Cryptology ePrint Archive, Report 2013/341 (2013). https://eprint.iacr.org/2013/341
7. Bitansky, N., Choudhuri, A.R.: Characterizing deterministic-prover zero knowledge. In: Pass, R., Pietrzak, K. (eds.) TCC 2020. LNCS, vol. 12550, pp. 535–566. Springer, Cham (2020). https://doi.org/10.1007/978-3-030-64375-1_19
8. Campanelli, M., David, B., Khoshakhlagh, H., Konring, A., Nielsen, J.B.: Encryption to the future: a paradigm for sending secret messages to future (anonymous) committees. Cryptology ePrint Archive, Report 2021/1423 (2021). https://eprint.iacr.org/2021/1423
9. Campanelli, M., Fiore, D., Querol, A.: LegoSNARK: modular design and composition of succinct zero-knowledge proofs, pp. 2075–2092 (2019)

10. Chakraborty, S., Prabhakaran, M., Wichs, D.: Witness maps and applications. In: Kiayias, A., Kohlweiss, M., Wallden, P., Zikas, V. (eds.) PKC 2020. LNCS, vol. 12110, pp. 220–246. Springer, Cham (2020). https://doi.org/10.1007/978-3-030-45374-9_8

11. Chen, Y., Vaikuntanathan, V., Wee, H.: GGH15 beyond permutation branching programs: proofs, attacks, and candidates. In: Shacham, H., Boldyreva, A. (eds.) CRYPTO 2018. LNCS, vol. 10992, pp. 577–607. Springer, Cham (2018). https://doi.org/10.1007/978-3-319-96881-0_20

12. Cramer, R., Shoup, V.: Universal hash proofs and a paradigm for adaptive chosen ciphertext secure public-key encryption. In: Knudsen, L.R. (ed.) EUROCRYPT 2002. LNCS, vol. 2332, pp. 45–64. Springer, Heidelberg (2002). https://doi.org/10.1007/3-540-46035-7_4

13. Dahari, H., Lindell, Y.: Deterministic-prover zero-knowledge proofs. Cryptology ePrint Archive, Report 2020/141 (2020). https://eprint.iacr.org/2020/141

14. Faonio, A., Nielsen, J.B., Venturi, D.: Predictable arguments of knowledge. In: Fehr, S. (ed.) PKC 2017. LNCS, vol. 10174, pp. 121–150. Springer, Heidelberg (2017). https://doi.org/10.1007/978-3-662-54365-8_6

15. Ganesh, C., Kondi, Y., Patra, A., Sarkar, P.: Efficient adaptively secure zero-knowledge from garbled circuits. In: Abdalla, M., Dahab, R. (eds.) PKC 2018. LNCS, vol. 10770, pp. 499–529. Springer, Cham (2018). https://doi.org/10.1007/978-3-319-76581-5_17

16. Garg, S., Gentry, C., Halevi, S., Raykova, M., Sahai, A., Waters, B.: Candidate indistinguishability obfuscation and functional encryption for all circuits, pp. 40–49 (2013)

17. Garg, S., Gentry, C., Sahai, A., Waters, B.: Witness encryption and its applications, pp. 467–476 (2013)

18. Goldreich, O., Oren, Y.: Definitions and properties of zero-knowledge proof systems. J. Cryptol. 7(1), 1–32 (1994)

19. Goldwasser, S., Micali, S., Rackoff, C.: The knowledge complexity of interactive proof systems. SIAM J. Comput. 18(1), 186–208 (1989)

20. Goyal, R., Koppula, V., Waters, B.: Lockable obfuscation, pp. 612–621 (2017)

21. Groth, J., Ostrovsky, R., Sahai, A.: Non-interactive Zaps and new techniques for NIZK. In: Dwork, C. (ed.) CRYPTO 2006. LNCS, vol. 4117, pp. 97–111. Springer, Heidelberg (2006). https://doi.org/10.1007/11818175_6

22. Khoshakhlagh, H.: (Commit-and-Prove) predictable arguments with privacy. Cryptology ePrint Archive, Report 2022/377 (2022). https://eprint.iacr.org/2022/377

23. Ngo, C.N., Massacci, F., Kerschbaum, F., Williams, J.: Practical witness-key-agreement for blockchain-based dark pools financial trading. In: Borisov, N., Diaz, C. (eds.) FC 2021. LNCS, vol. 12675, pp. 579–598. Springer, Heidelberg (2021). https://doi.org/10.1007/978-3-662-64331-0_30

MPC

Communication-Efficient Proactive MPC for Dynamic Groups with Dishonest Majorities

Karim Eldefrawy[1], Tancrède Lepoint[5], and Antonin Leroux[2,3,4](✉)

[1] SRI International, Menlo Park, USA
karim.eldefrawy@sri.com, iacr@tancre.de
[2] DGA, Paris, France
[3] LIX, CNRS, Ecole Polytechnique, Institut Polytechnique de Paris, Paris, France
antonin.leroux@polytechnique.org
[4] INRIA, Palaiseau, France
[5] New York, USA

Abstract. Secure multiparty computation (MPC) has recently been increasingly adopted to secure cryptographic keys in enterprises, cloud infrastructure, and cryptocurrency and blockchain-related settings such as wallets and exchanges. Using MPC in blockchains and other distributed systems highlights the need to consider dynamic settings. In such dynamic settings, parties, and potentially even parameters of underlying secret sharing and corruption tolerance thresholds of sub-protocols, may change over the lifetime of the protocol. In particular, stronger threat models – in which *mobile* adversaries control a changing set of parties (up to t out of n involved parties at any instant), and may eventually corrupt *all n parties* over the course of a protocol's execution – are becoming increasingly important for such real world deployments; secure protocols designed for such models are known as Proactive MPC (PMPC).

In this work, we construct the first efficient PMPC protocol for *dynamic* groups (where the set of parties changes over time) secure against a *dishonest majority* of parties. Our PMPC protocol only requires $O(n^2)$ (amortized) communication per secret, compared to existing PMPC protocols that require $O(n^4)$ and only consider static groups with dishonest majorities. At the core of our PMPC protocol is a new efficient technique to perform multiplication of secret shared data (shared using a bivariate scheme) with $O(n\sqrt{n})$ communication with security against a dishonest majority without requiring pre-computation. We also develop a new efficient bivariate batched proactive secret sharing (PSS) protocol for dishonest majorities, which may be of independent interest. This protocol enables multiple dealers to contribute different secrets that are efficiently shared together in one batch; previous batched PSS schemes required all secrets to come from a single dealer.

T. Lepoint—Part of this work was performed while at SRI International and Google.

G. Ateniese and D. Venturi (Eds.): ACNS 2022, LNCS 13269, pp. 565–584, 2022.
https://doi.org/10.1007/978-3-031-09234-3_28

1   Introduction

Dynamic MPC settings, where parties and parameters of the underlying secret sharing and sub-protocols can change during the execution of the protocol, have attracted a lot of attention in the past years. Some of these settings consider very powerful adversaries who can compromise dishonest majorities, i.e., active/malicious or passive/semi-honest parties that may add up to a majority. Additionally, for long-lived computation and better security guarantees, stronger threat models in which *mobile* adversaries [7,10] control a changing set of parties (up to t out of the n parties at any instant), and may eventually corrupt *all n parties* over the course of a protocol's execution or lifetime of confidential inputs, are becoming increasingly attractive in the real world deployments of MPC. MPC protocols withstanding such *mobile* adversaries are typically called Proactive MPC (PMPC) [7,10].

Table 1. Overview of features and limitations of proactive secret sharing (PSS) and proactive MPC (PMPC) protocols.

	Type	Batching	Dynamic Groups	Dishonest Majority	Fair Reconstruct	Subprotocols Communication (amortized)
[1]	PMPC	✓	✗	✗	✗	$O(1)$
[2]	PSS/PMPC	✓	✓	✗	✗	$O(1)$
[3]	PSS only	✗	✗	✓	✓	$O(n^4)$
[5]	PMPC	✗	✗	✓	✓	$O(n^4)$
[4]	PSS only	✓	✓	✓	✓	$O(n^2)$
This work	PMPC	✓	✓	✓	✓	$O(n^2)$

Related work in proactive secret sharing (PSS) and PMPC, and the different settings considered, is listed in Table 1. In the *honest majority setting*, the early work of Baron, Eldefrawy, Lampkins, and Ostrovsky [1] introduces the framework to construct PMPC from PSS by computing the circuit layer by layer and (proactively) redistributing the parties' secret shares after each layer. The PMPC protocol handles batching (i.e., the secret sharing contains many secrets operated on in a coefficient-wise manner) and static groups in the honest majority setting. In a follow-up work, Baron, Eldefrawy, Lampkins, and Ostrovsky [2] consider then the setting of dynamic groups. The study of PSS and PMPC in the dishonest majority setting starts with the work of Dolev, Eldefrawy, Lampkins, Ostrovsky, and Yung [3], in which they present a PSS scheme (without batching) for static groups. Feasibility of constructing PMPC withstanding a dishonest majority of parties was then demonstrated by Eldefrawy, Ostrovsky, Park, and Yung in [5]. The subprotocols in the last two works have communication complexity $O(n^4)$, which significantly hinders their practicality. The schemes from [3] and [5] have the additional property of ensuring fair reconstruction with the gradual sharing model from Hirt, Lucas and Maurer [8]. The PSS scheme from [3] was later revisited by Eldefrawy, Lepoint, and Leroux [4]: they present an efficient PSS scheme with batching, fair reconstruct with no complexity overhead and dynamic groups, with security against mixed adversaries that can compromise a majority of parties, but leave as future work to extend it to a full PMPC protocol. This naturally brings us to formulate the following open problem:

> *Can we develop a communication-efficient PMPC protocol that handles batching, with amortized communication $O(n^2)$ or less, for dynamic groups, and with security against mixed adversaries that can compromise a majority of parties?*

1.1 Contributions

In this work, we affirmatively answer this question by constructing an efficient PMPC protocol with four key properties: (i) batching, (ii) suitability for dynamic groups (iii) security against a majority of active/malicious or passive/semi-honest corruptions, and allowing (iv) fair reconstruct with no complexity overhead in the mixed adversarial setting proposed by Hirt, Lucas, and Maurer [8]. Our protocol achieves computational security and the efficiency is enabled by only requiring $O(n^2)$ (amortized) communication per secret when batching $O(n)$ secrets. Our communication model assumes a broadcast channel and pairwise secure channels. Concretely, we make the following contributions:

1. We develop the *first* efficient fair PMPC for dishonest majorities and dynamic groups, with $O(n^2)$ (amortized with batches of size $\ell = n-2$) communication (in both broadcast and secure channels). Our new PMPC protocol protects secrecy of the inputs when active and passive corruptions are less than $n - 3 - \sqrt{\ell}$ at any time of the protocol. Additionally, the computation is *fair* if the number of active corruption is less than k and the number of passive corruption is less than $\min(n-k-\sqrt{\ell}, 2(n-k)-\ell)$ during the reconstruction, for $1 \leq k \leq n/3$ (cf. Theorem 1).
2. We develop a new efficient bivariate batched proactive secret sharing (PSS) Share protocol for dishonest majorities that enables multiple dealers to contribute different secrets that are shared together in one batch. Previous batched PSS schemes in the dishonest majority setting required all secrets to come from one dealer.
3. At the core of the protocol is a new efficient sub-protocol for multiplying secret-shared data (using a bivariate sharing of degree $d = n-2$ for batches of size d) with $O(n\sqrt{n})$ amortized communication, and secure when the number of corruptions (either active or passive) is less than $n - 3 - \sqrt{n-2}$ without requiring pre-computation (cf. Theorem 2). The techniques developed to this effect might be of independent interest.

1.2   Technical Overview

Previous PMPC protocols [5], proven secure in the dishonest majority setting and for static groups, builds on top of the proactive secret sharing scheme of [3] by augmenting it with protocols for adding and multiplying shares to perform computation on the secret shares following the same (arithmetic) PMPC blueprint as proposed in [1]. While additions are computed locally, multiplications require using the standard GMW MPC protocol [6], so as to obtain a proactive secret sharing of the multiplication of two secrets. The asymptotic communication efficiency of [5] is the same as that of [3], i.e. $O(n^4)$.

Similarly, we develop our new PMPC protocol for dynamic groups with dishonest majorities on top of a recent PSS protocol [4] for the dishonest majority setting. However, the PSS of [4] differs significantly from that of [3], and extending [4] to an efficient PMPC protocol with (amortized) communication $O(n^2)$ requires care and new techniques; the rest of this section summarizes the main intuition behind our construction.

Let us briefly recall the PSS construction of [4]. Secrets $s_1, \ldots, s_\ell$ are secret shared among n participants $P_1, \ldots, P_n$ by a dealer, which construct a bivariate polynomial g such that:

- $g(x, \cdot)$ and $g(\cdot, y)$ are of degree at most $d \leq n - 1$;
- the secrets are embedded as $g(\beta_i, \beta_i) = s_i$ for distinct β_i's;
- the secret share of party P_i is the polynomial $g(\alpha_i, \cdot)$, for distinct α_i's.

This sharing naturally supports additions: party P_i will be able to locally add its secret shares $g(\alpha_i, \cdot)$ (where g is the bivariate polynomial for $s_1, \ldots, s_\ell$) and $g'(\alpha_i, \cdot)$ (where g' is the bivariate polynomial for $s'_1, \ldots, s'_\ell$) to obtain a secret sharing of the sum of the secrets $(s_1 + s'_1, \ldots, s_\ell + s'_\ell)$.

Contribution 1: Efficient Multi-dealer Batched Sharing Protocol. We point here a subtle feature which was not present in [3,5] and that usually does not manifest in the standard PSS functionality and was also lacking from [4]. Multi-dealer batched sharing allows us to use the batching techniques (and the resulting improvement in communication complexity) for computations where each participant has $O(1)$ secrets, something impossible with single-dealer sharing protocols because each participant has to do at least one sharing for its secrets. We obtain this multi-dealer sharing with a simple adaptation of techniques used in [4]. It suffices that all the dealers generate a classical Shamir sharing for each of their secrets and then a bivariate sharing for the whole batch is obtained by combining these univariate polynomials into a bivariate polynomial. Additionally, performing addition and multiplication on batch of secrets require permuting the secrets between consecutive layers to align them. Thus, the underlying PSS needs to be secure even when some of the shared secrets have been leaked to the adversary.

Contribution 2: Efficient Multiplication of Shared Secrets for Groups with Dishonest Majorities. This protocol is at the core of our contributions enabling the construction of our new communication-efficient PMPC protocol. In fact, our `Mult` protocol achieves even better than the minimal requirement of $O(n^2)$ with an amortized communication complexity of $O(n\sqrt{n})$ against up to approximately $n - \sqrt{n}$ actively corrupted participant. This improvement of $\sqrt{n}$ over the standard quadratic complexity for multiplication without precomputation in the dishonest majority setting may be of independent interest. It has the following blueprint:

1. The participants have shares for two "bivariate" secret sharings g, g' containing both ℓ secrets to be multiplied together. First, g is transformed into $\ell^{\frac{1}{2}}$ "univariate" secret sharings $f_1(\alpha_i), \ldots, f_{\ell^{\frac{1}{2}}}(\alpha_i)$, where each f_j is of degree d and contains $\ell^{\frac{1}{2}}$ secrets (and similarly for g'). This step is done by each party generating a random polynomial and using the Lagrange interpolation formula to embed the secrets from g.
2. Then, $\ell^{\frac{1}{2}}$ "blinding" bivariate polynomials h_j of degree d such that $h_j(\beta_i, \beta_i) = 0$, are generated. This step follows the classical approach of generating blinding polynomials: each party generates a random polynomial evaluating in 0 in the β_i's.
3. Next, $\ell^{\frac{1}{2}}$ bivariate polynomials $g_j^* = f_j(x) f_j'(y) + h_j(x, y)$ are computed, and party P_i learns $g_j^*(\alpha_i, \cdot)$. Note that h_j "blinds" the product of the polynomials f_j and f_j' (except in (β_i, β_i) where g_j^* will evaluate into the product of the secrets. This step uses the secure multiplication protocol introduced in [9] in the context of threshold ECDSA.
4. Against active corruptions, correctness of the computation is verified using additively homomorphic commitments. To verify the correctness of the multiplication operations involved in the computation of g_j^*, the participants reveal $g_j^*(\text{rand}_j, \cdot)$ for some random values rand_j. This reduces the security threshold by one while preventing an adversary to deviate from the protocol undetected.
5. Finally, all the $\ell^{\frac{1}{2}}$ bivariate secret sharings $g_j^*(\alpha_i, \cdot)$ are recombined into a single bivariate sharing $g''(\alpha_i, \cdot)$ that embeds the $\ell = \ell^{\frac{1}{2}} \cdot \ell^{\frac{1}{2}}$ secrets.

1.3 Paper Outline

The rest of the paper is organized as follows. Section 2 overviews preliminaries required for the paper. Section 3 revisits the PSS scheme of [4] for the setting of PMPC and introduces a new multi-dealer batched share sub-protocol. Section 4 presents the ideal functionality and concrete instantiation of our new PMPC protocol for dynamic groups with dishonest majorities. Section 5 focuses on each subprotocols of the overall PMPC protocol and proves their security; the formal security proofs for the PMPC protocol are provided in the full version.

2   Preliminaries

Notation. Throughout the paper, we consider a set of n parties $\mathcal{P} = \{P_1, ..., P_n\}$, connected by pairwise synchronous secure channels and authenticated broadcast channels. $\mathcal{P}$ want to securely perform computations over a finite field $\mathbb{F} = \mathbb{Z}_q$ for a prime q.

For integers a, b, we denote $[a, b] = \{k : a \leq k \leq b\}$ and $[b] = [1, b]$.[1] We denote by $\mathbb{P}_k$ the set of polynomials of degree k exactly over $\mathbb{F}$. When a variable v is drawn randomly from a set S, we denote $v \leftarrow S$.

2.1   Adversary Model

In this section, we briefly recall the *proactive* security model and the mixed adversary setting used in this work. For a more precise exposition, we refer the reader to [5, Sect. 2]. The adversary in this model is considered to be a *mobile* adversary that can adaptively decide which parties to (passively or actively) corrupt between predefined "refresh phases" of the protocol. The computation is thus divided into "operation phases"; for example, the circuit representing the computation can be expressed as layers followed by "refresh phases" in which a refresh protocol is performed to prevent the adversary from learning too much information. The adversary can retain all the states of a corrupted party, but once a party is uncorrupted the adversary cannot learn future states of such a previously corrupted party unless it re-corrupts the party. At any point in time, we assume that at any point during the execution protocol, the adversary controls at most N parties (passively or actively); N is called the corruption threshold, and when $N \geq n/2$, we are in the dishonest majorities setting. Finally, note that in the proactive security model, a party can be uncorrupted either because the adversary willingly releases control of said party to compromise another party while not violating the corruption threshold, or because the party was proactively rebooted to a pristine state (hence the term of proactive security); henceforth, the adversary loses control over the party. In both cases, the uncorrupted party can recover its shares with the help of the other parties using a recovery protocol, and can continue participating in the computation.

2.2   Commitment Scheme

A commitment scheme [11] is a classical cryptographic primitive. The commitment to a message $m \in \mathbb{F}_p$ under randomness $r \in \mathbb{F}_p$ is written $C(m, r)$. The opening information $o(m, r)$ can be revealed to enable a verifier to check whether $C(m, r)$ was indeed a valid commitment to m. A commitment scheme is *computationally hiding* if $C(m, r)$ does not reveal information to a computationally bounded attacker. It is *perfectly binding* if a commitment $C(m_1, r)$ can never be opened with $o(m_2, r')$ when $m_1 \neq m_2$.

---

[1] In particular, if $a > b$, we have $[a, b] = \emptyset$.

In this paper, we use an additively homomorphic commitment scheme, i.e., there is an operation $\star$ such that $C(m_1, r_1) \star C(m_2, r_2) = C(m_1 + m_2, r_1 + r_2)$. In particular, we instantiate our protocols with the computationally hiding and perfectly binding commitment scheme $(g^m h^r, g^r) \in G^2$ where G is a group of prime order p with generator g. This protocol is secure under the hardness of the DDH problem. For any element $(g_1, g_2) \in G^2$, there exists a unique value m and randomness r such that $(g_1, g_2) = C(m, r)$. This fact will help us simplify some protocols and proofs.

Finally, we naturally extend the definition to commitments on polynomials by providing a vector of commitments for the coefficients of the polynomial. For a polynomial f, we denote by $C(f, R_f)$ the commitment to f.

2.3 Shares and Sharings

In the following, we will use two kinds of secret sharings: univariate and bivariate. In both cases, the term *sharing* is used to denote a polynomial (either univariate or bivariate). The secrets are stored in the evaluations of this sharing on publicly known points. In this context, one *share* will always refer to the information held by one participant (the evaluation of the sharing on one point in the univariate setting, or a univariate polynomial in the bivariate setting). Hence, a univariate share is a point, while a bivariate share is a univariate polynomial. With these conventions and the notations of Sect. 2.2, the meaning of a commitment to a *share* or to a *sharing* is clear.

More precisely, when talking about univariate sharing we refer to the classical Shamir secret sharing. Thus, a sharing f of degree d for the batch of secrets $s_1, \ldots, s_\ell$ between n participants is a univariate polynomial f of degree d that satisfies $f(\beta_j) = s_j$ for all $j \in [\ell]$ and each party P_r share is the evaluation $f(\alpha_r)$ for a set of public values $\beta_1, \ldots, \beta_\ell, \alpha_1, \ldots, \alpha_n$. In that case, it can be shown that the corruption threshold for secrecy on the $s_1, \ldots, s_\ell$ is $d + 1 - \ell$.

For the bivariate sharing, we use the construction introduced in [4]. A bivariate sharing g of degree d is a bivariate polynomial of degree d in both variables with $g(\beta_j, \beta_j) = s_j$ for $j \in [\ell]$. In that case, the share of the participant P_r is the univariate polynomial $g(\alpha_r, \cdot)$. For efficiency reasons in the PSS from [4], it is also possible that P_r end up with the knowledge of the univariate polynomial $g(\cdot, \alpha_r)$. It was shown in [4] that the corruption threshold is $d + 1 - \sqrt{\ell}$ for secrecy. Usually, we choose the biggest value possible for d. First, it is clear from the way the sharings are distributed that d must be smaller or equal to $n - 1$. In the case of proactive secret sharing, we also require $d \leq n - 2$ because the PSS functionality from [3, 4] requires to perform regularly a Recover protocol where $d + 1$ participants will cooperate to recover the shares of another party. Since, there are no other constraint we usually take $d = n - 2$. In the rest of the article, we often use the fact that $d \approx n$ implicitly. When concrete security thresholds are given, either we state the formula with d or replace d by the value $n - 2$. In terms of the number of secrets ℓ, the PSS from [4] requires $\ell \leq d$ and we keep this restriction in this paper.

2.4   Polynomials and Degrees of Freedom

In this section, we introduce the notion of *degree of freedom* with respect to a set of equations for a polynomial. This definition will prove useful to clarify and formalize some statements later. For the rest of this paragraph we fix f to be a polynomial of degree d (either univariate or bivariate) over a field k. We define an equation on f as an equality of the following form

$$\sum_{x \in X} f(x) = C \tag{1}$$

where X is a finite set of points ($X \subset k$ if f is univariate and $X \subset k^2$ if f is bivariate) and $C \in k$. In the special case where $X = \{x\}$, we call this the *evaluation equation* on x.

A system of equations on f is composed of several such equations as follows:

Definition 1. *A system of equations E on f is a finite set of equations*

$$E = \left\{ \sum_{x \in X_i} f(x) = C_i \right\}_{i \in \mathcal{I}}$$

where $X_i \subset k$ and $C_i \in k$ for all $i \in \mathcal{I} \subset \mathbb{N}$. When $\exists i$ such that $x \in X_i$ we write $f(x) \in E$.

Since polynomials of given degree d are elements of a finite vector space, it makes sense to talk about *independent equations* (in the classical sense). Hence, the dimension of a system of equations is the number of independent equations in that system. This is a terminology that we will use throughout this paper.

Definition 2. *Let E be a system of equations as per Definition 1. The degree of freedom of f with respect to E is the dimension of E subtracted from the dimension of f and is denoted by $d_f(E)$.*

In Definition 2, by dimension of f, we mean the dimension of the space in which f lives in (the dimension is $d+1$ for univariate polynomials of degree d and $(d+1)^2$ for bivariate polynomials of degree d). Another definition of the dimension could be the maximum size of an independent system of equations on f; we note that the degree of freedom is always a positive integer.

We now illustrate how this terminology helps formulate some security statements. Let us consider a univariate sharing f of m secrets and a set of corrupted parties $\{P_1, \cdots, P_t\}$ by an adversary $\mathcal{A}$. From the corruption, $\mathcal{A}$ learns the share $f(\alpha_r)$ of all corrupted parties P_r. This can be seen as a set of t equations on f. Provided, that no other equations is leaked on f, the adversary has gathered a system of t independent equations. Thus, the degree of freedom of f with respect to the system of $\mathcal{A}$ is $d + 1 - t$. We have perfect secrecy on the m secrets if m is smaller than this degree of freedom. Intuitively, this notion of degree of freedom relates to the number of secrets that can be hidden inside a polynomial. It comes especially handy when dealing with bivariate polynomials as we do in this article.

3   Proactive Secret Sharing

Constructing MPC from PSS is a natural and well-established approach. In this work, we build upon the PSS from [4] to obtain efficient PMPC. Before introducing our new generic PMPC protocol (see Sect. 4), we need to adapt slightly the scheme from [4].

In fact, the issue is not with the protocols from [4] per se, but rather with the proofs and security thresholds. In the PMPC framework, operations are performed component-wise on batch of secrets, creating a sharing of $s_1 \star t_1, \ldots, s_\ell \star t_\ell$ from sharing of $s_1, \ldots, s_\ell$ and $t_1, \ldots, t_\ell$ (for the desired operation $\star$). In a generic arithmetic circuit, there is no guarantee that all the secrets are aligned before each layer of computation. That is why it is standard to use a `Permute` protocol to realign the secrets before each round. As a result, the participants will produce some sharings where secrets coming from different participants might end up in the same batch. This is why we need to ensure secrecy in the setting of a batched sharing where some of the secrets are known to the adversary. In [4] where the `Share` is always performed by a single dealer and the batch of secrets are not reorganized, this situation never happens. Thus, the proofs from [4] need to be updated to show that the protocols retain the desired security in this case. We postpone this analysis to the full version of this paper due to lack of space.

In Protocol 1, we introduce an extension of the `Share` protocol to the case of multiple dealers, allowing several participants to cooperate and generate a common secret sharing of their secrets. To add more flexibility, we also make possible to add secrets in an existing sharing when the threshold for the maximal number of secrets have not been reached. This extension is quite natural given what we said above and allows us to obtain the improvement on the communication complexity due to batching even in situations where each participant has $O(1)$ secrets (which would not be possible in a single-dealer setting since each participant has to produce at least one sharing).

In the protocol below, when $\ell_1 = 0$, we assume that there is no bivariate secret sharing g. We build our `Share` protocol upon the building-block `Recover` which is part of the PSS from [4]. It can be used by $d + 1$ participants having shares for a bivariate sharing g of degree d to distribute a set of shares for g to another participant.

The security for Protocol 1 is stated in Lemma 1. In all the protocols in this work, we highlight the $\boxed{\text{critical steps using boxes}}$, as the full protocols includes (standard) use of commitments and openings to resist against malicious/mixed adversaries.

Protocol 1. `Share` protocol

INPUT: A subset of dealer participants $\mathcal{P}_D \subset \{P_1, \ldots, P_n\}$. A partition $\cup_{P_r \in \mathcal{P}_D} S_r$ for $\{s_{\ell_1+1}, \ldots, s_{\ell_2}\}$ where each P_r knows the elements of S_r. A bivariate secret sharing g with commitment $C(g, R_g)$ for the batch of secrets $\{s_1, \ldots, s_{\ell_1}\}$.

OUTPUT: Distributes a bivariate sharing g' for the secrets $\{s_1, \ldots, s_{\ell_2}\}$.

1. For each $P_r \in \mathcal{P}_D$ and each $s_j \in S_r$, $\boxed{P_r \text{ samples } g_j, R_{g_j} \leftarrow \mathbb{P}_d}$ such that $\boxed{g_j(\beta_j) = s_j}$ and broadcasts the commitments $C(g_j, R_{g_j})$.

2. For all $r' \in [d+1]$, and $s_j \in S_r$ each $\boxed{P_r \in \mathcal{P}_D \text{ sends}}$ $\boxed{o(g_j(\alpha_{r'}), R_{g_j}(\alpha_{r'})) \text{ to } P_{r'}}$. The receiver $P_{r'}$ broadcasts a bit indicating if the opening is correct. For each share for which an irregularity was reported, P_r broadcasts the opening. If the opening is correct, $P_{r'}$ accepts the value, otherwise P_r is disqualified and added to the set of corrupted parties B. The protocols aborts and each party outputs B.

3. Each $P_r \in \{P_1, \ldots, P_n\}$ $\boxed{\text{samples } q_{r,j}, R_{q_{r,j}} \leftarrow \mathbb{P}_d}$ with $\boxed{q_{r,j}(\beta_j) = 0}$ for all $j \in [\ell_1 + 1, \ell_2]$.

4. For all $r \in [n]$, $r' \in [d+1]$, and $s_j \in S_r$ each $\boxed{P_r \text{ sends}}$ $\boxed{o(q_{r,j}(\alpha_{r'}), R_{q_{r,j}}(\alpha_{r'})) \text{ to } P_{r'}}$. The receiver $P_{r'}$ broadcasts a bit indicating if the opening is correct. For each share for which an irregularity was reported, P_r broadcasts the opening. If the opening is correct, $P_{r'}$ accepts the value, otherwise P_r is disqualified and added to the set of corrupted parties B. The protocols aborts and each party outputs B.

5. Each $P_r \in \{P_1, \ldots, P_{d+1}\}$ $\boxed{\text{samples } g_r, R_{g_r} \leftarrow \mathbb{P}_d}$ such that $\boxed{g_r(\beta_j) = g_j(\alpha_r) + \sum_{u=1}^{n} q_{u,j}(\alpha_r)}$ for all $j \in [\ell_1 + 1, \ell_2]$ and $\boxed{g_r(\beta_j) = g(\alpha_r, \beta_j)}$ (and the same for R_{g_r} with respect to the polynomials $R_{g_j}, R_{q_{u,j}}, R_g$) for all $j \in [\ell_1]$. P_r broadcasts the commitments g_r, R_{g_r}.
   Note that this implicitly defines g' a random bivariate polynomial of degree d with $g'(\alpha_r, \cdot) = g_r(\cdot)$.

6. For all $r \in [d+1]$ and $j \in S_r$, each party locally compute the commitments $C(g_r(\beta_j), R_{g_r}(\beta_j))$, $C(g_j(\alpha_r), R_{g_j}(\alpha_r))$ and $C(q_{u,j}(\alpha_r), R_{q_{u,j}}(\alpha_r))$ for all $u \in [n]$ before verifying the relation

$$C(g_r(\beta_j), R_{g_r}(\beta_j)) = C(g_j(\alpha_r), R_{g_j}(\alpha_r)) \star_{u=1}^{n} C(q_{u,j}(\alpha_r), R_{q_{u,j}}(\alpha_r)).$$

7. For $r' \in [d+2, n]$, $\{P_1, \ldots, P_{d+1}\} \cup \{P_{r'}\}$ perform $\boxed{\text{Recover on } g'}$.

We write t_P (resp. t_A) for the number of passively (resp. actively) corrupted participants. Lemma 1 informally summarizes the security of Protocol 1 but should not be considered as a formal security statement. In the full version of this article, we use several such preliminary lemmas to *formally prove* Theorem 2.

Lemma 1 *(Informal). Let g be a bivariate sharing for ℓ_1 secrets $s_1, \ldots, s_{\ell_1}$ such that the adversary knows $\ell_1' \leq \ell_1$ of those shared secrets (and no other information aside from the prescribed shares) and let $s_{\ell_1+1}, \ldots, s_{\ell_2}$ be new secrets among which $\ell_2' - \ell_1 \leq \ell_2 - \ell_1$ values are known to the adversary. When $\ell_1 + \ell_2 \leq d$ and $t_P, t_A \leq d+1-\sqrt{\ell}$, the **Share** protocol above is correct and preserves secrecy* *of the $(\ell_2 - \ell_2') + (\ell_1 - \ell_1')$ secrets unknown to the adversary under the hardness of DDH. Additionally, apart from the shares of corrupted participants and the secrets already known, the adversary does not learn any other evaluation of the sharing g'.*

A proof for Lemma 1 can be obtained with ideas similar to the ones used in [4] to prove security of their PSS scheme.

Communication Complexity: the above protocol requires $O(dn(\ell_2 - \ell_1))$ communication. Thus, it yields an amortized communication complexity of $O(n^2)$ when $d \approx n$.

4 Communication-Efficient Proactive MPC (PMPC) for Dynamic Groups with Dishonest Majorities

We follow the standard blueprint that develops PMPC based on PSS (e.g., [1,5]) for arithmetic circuit. An arithmetic circuit can be divided into consecutive layers (each consisting of additions or multiplications) such that the outputs of a layer are only used once in the next layer.[2]

The outline of our PMPC protocol (Protocol 2) is similar to the one of [5]. We provide a brief summary below and refer the reader to [5] for more details. Our PMPC protocol consists of 8 sub-protocols listed below with a quick summary of their purpose. We put the tag (PSS, denoting Proactive Secret Sharing) to indicate protocols that are not introduced in this work; for those we use the construction from [4].

- **Share**: Takes a batch of secrets and produces a secret sharing. (Protocol 1)
- **Refresh**: Rerandomizes a secret sharing. (PSS)
- **Recover**: Produces a share of an existing sharing. (PSS)
- **Redistribute**: Changes the number of participants for a sharing. (PSS)
- **Reconstruct**: Takes shares of a secret sharing and recovers the secrets. (PSS)
- **Add**: Performs component-wise additions of two sharings.
- **Mult**: Performs component-wise multiplications of two sharings.
- **Permute**: Takes a set of secret sharings and applies a permutation on all the secrets.

The main idea is to use secret sharings to keep the inputs private: several **Share** are performed at the beginning to create secret sharings of the inputs and all the remaining computations are performed using such secret sharings until the last layer of the circuit where **Reconstruct** is used to compute the outputs. **Refresh** and **Recover** are the two sub-protocols that make the scheme (proactively) secure against mobile adversaries. In our adversarial model, we assume that the adversary can only change the set of corrupted participants during the

---

[2] Multiple uses can be handled easily by duplicating some sharings according to the circuit's requirement but we avoid them entirely to simplify the explanations.

Refresh phase. Therefore, the frequency of **Refresh** executions can be adjusted and provides a tradeoff between security and efficiency. For maximal security it can be performed after every other sub-protocol. For simplicity in Protocol 2, we refresh at every layer of the arithmetic circuit computation, and more precisely we denote R the set of layers λ after which we perform a **Refresh** operation (see Step 3e). **Recover** is used when parties are "decorrupted" and reset to a pristine default state after which they need to obtain shares to participate in the computation. The goal of **Redistribute** is to handle dynamic groups. These five protocols constitutes the PSS from [4]. We extend their PSS scheme with **Add** and **Mult** protocols to evaluate the gates of the arithmetic circuits to be computed over the secret sharings. Since our PMPC protocol works with batches of secrets, we also introduce a **Permute** protocol that permutes the underlying shared secrets to align them correctly to perform **Add** and **Mult**.

To handle dynamic groups, we assume for simplicity that the dynamic changes are planned before the execution of the protocol. The **Redistribute** will be performed between consecutive layers of computations. The set $\mathcal{L}_\lambda$ is the set of leaving parties after the execution of layer λ. Similarly, $\mathcal{N}_\lambda$ is the set of new parties after layer λ. Due to the batching, there is also a need to reorder the secrets before performing the layer computation (see the full version of the paper). S_λ is the set of secrets after execution of layer $\lambda - 1$ (i.e., after the arrival of $\mathcal{N}_\lambda$ and departure of $\mathcal{L}_\lambda$) σ_λ is the permutation to be performed on S_λ before the computation of layer λ. S_1 is just the set of inputs and σ_1 is the identity.

Protocol 2. PMPC for Dynamic Groups with Dishonest Majorities

INPUT: An arithmetic circuit C of depth d_C that has inputs $x_1, \ldots, x_n$ where each x_i is a vector of m_i values of input for the participant P_i. R is the set of layers after which a refresh phase is to be performed.

OUTPUT: $n + k$ values $y_1, \ldots, y_{n+k}$ for some $k \in \mathbb{N}$ where the total set of parties participating in the computation of C is $\{P_1, \ldots, P_{n+k}\}$. Each y_i is either the output values of the circuit Y or a special symbol $\perp$ indicating that P_i do not receive any output. We denote $\mathcal{O}$ the set of parties with non-$\perp$ output.

1. The participants label all the secrets involved in the computation and group them in batches of size ℓ. Then, the participants perform several execution of **Share** to distribute sharings of all the secrets. After this point, all the values on the input wires of C that involves participant $P_1, \ldots, P_n$ are shared among all the other parties. In particular, all the input wires of the first layer of C are shared.
2. Run the **Refresh** protocol. This corresponds to one refresh phase.
3. For each circuit layer $\lambda = 1, \ldots, d_C$:
   (a) A permutation σ_λ of all the shared secrets is performed with the protocol **Permute** to align the secrets involved in all the gates of the layer λ.

(b) For each batch of addition or multiplication gates in layer λ: Compute a sharing of a batch of outputs using `Add` or `Mult`.

(c) The set of leaving participant $\mathcal{L}_\lambda$ exits the execution of the protocol using the `Redistribute` protocol. Then, the set of new parties $\mathcal{N}_\lambda$ is introduced with a new execution of `Redistribute`.

(d) All the participants may perform multiple executions of `Share` so that all the inputs of the gates of the layer $\lambda + 1$ are shared among the parties, possibly rewriting over the old secrets that will not be reused during the rest of the computation.

(e) If $\lambda \in R$, run the `Refresh` protocol.

4. At the end of the previous step, the parties are supposed to have a sharing for all the value in the output Y. We also assume that all the parties P_i with $y_i \neq \perp$ are among the set of parties at this time of the protocol. The parties in $\mathcal{O}$ perform a `Permute` protocol to regroup the output values in a set of bivariate sharings.

5. The `Reconstruct` protocol is performed several times so that all the values in Y are revealed to all $P_r \in \mathcal{O}$.

6. Two special operations may be ran during the execution of the protocol.
   - Upon receiving a message `Help!` from a party P_r, all the parties execute several times `Recover` to provide P_r sharings of all the secret values required for the later computations of the protocol. If the procedure occurs after the sharing by P_r of the value ρ_r, the other parties also reveal to P_r their share of the sharing so that P_r can compute the value ρ_r for himself.
   - If one of the participant exits the protocol without prior agreement, the remaining parties perform `Redistribute` in the corrupted mode to distribute all secrets between them with a proper sharing.

Remark 1. For easy of exposition, we assumed that all the outputs (represented by the set Y) are revealed to all the participants in $\mathcal{O}$. In reality, the protocols often require that each participant obtain a different output. We can apply standard techniques to modify Protocol 2 in order to handle this functionality. For a given sharing containing several outputs that are to be revealed to different participants it suffices that each of these participants generate a new sharing of zeroes and a random value at the index of the desired output. Then, each of these sharings can be added to the initial sharing with `Add`. Finally, the participants perform `Reconstruct` on the sharing obtained after all the operations. Thus, the participants will learn values $s_1 + \rho_1, \ldots, s_\ell + \rho_\ell$ where the ρ_i are the random values. The participants that is supposed to get the value s_i will be able ρ_i since he was the one to generate it, but the other participants will not learn anything on s_i.

In the full version, we prove Theorem 1, which shows that Protocol 2 securely realizes the ideal functionality $\text{IDEAL}^{\mathcal{Z},\mathcal{S},\mathcal{F}_{PMPC}}$ (also defined in the full version). The thresholds are computed by taking $d = n - 2$ (which is the maximum possible value).

Theorem 1. *For a circuit $\mathcal{C}$ where the minimum number of participants is n_0. When the size batch is $\ell = n_0 - 2$, and assuming the hardness of DDH, the protocol Π^{PMPC} introduced in Protocol 2 securely realizes the ideal process $\text{IDEAL}_{unfair}^{Z,S,\mathcal{F}_{PMPC}}$ against any adversary bounded at any given time by the multi-threshold $T(\ell) = \{(n-3-\sqrt{\ell}, n-3-\sqrt{\ell})\}$ with n the number of participants at that time. Additionally, when the adversary is also bounded by the multi-threshold $T_f(\ell) = \{(k, \min(n-k-\sqrt{\ell}, 2(n-k)-\ell, 1 \leq k \leq n/3\}, \Pi^{PMPC}$ securely realizes $\text{IDEAL}_{fair}^{Z,S,\mathcal{F}_{PMPC}}$.*

5 Subprotocols for PMPC

In Sects. 5.1 to 5.4, we introduce the sub-protocols used in the Mult protocol described at a high level in Sect. 1.2. Next, we introduce the full multiplication protocol in Sect. 5.5. We defer the treatment of reordering the secrets to the full version as it follows essentially from previous work.

5.1 Bivariate to Univariate Sharing

The subprotocol from this section efficiently transforms a (bivariate) secret sharing of a batch of ℓ secrets $s_1, \ldots, s_\ell$ into several univariate sharings of smaller size. For simplicity, we treat the case where $\ell = vm$ and construct v univariate sharings of m secrets each. This procedure is described in Protocol 3.

We denote g the bivariate sharing of degree d and $(f_k)_{k \in [v]}$ the univariate sharings of degree d. We write $I_k = [(k-1)m + 1, km]$ and each f_k will be a sharing for s_j for all $j \in I_k$. We also denote $\Pi_r(x) = \prod_{\substack{u \in [d+1] \\ u \neq r}} \frac{x - \alpha_u}{\alpha_r - \alpha_u}$ for the Lagrange polynomial.

Protocol 3. `ReshareBivariateToUnivariate`

INPUT: A set $\mathcal{P} = \{P_1, \ldots, P_n\}$ holding a bivariate sharing for a batch of $\ell = mv$ secrets $s_1 = g(\beta_1, \beta_1), \ldots, s_\ell = g(\beta_\ell, \beta_\ell)$ and the commitment to this sharing $C(g, R_g)$.

OUTPUT: For all $k \in [v]$, each party P_r holds its share of the univariate sharing for the batch of secrets $\{s_j\}_{j \in I_k}$ along with a commitment $C(f_k, R_{f_k})$ to that sharing.

1. For $k \in [v]$:
   (a) For $r \in [d+1]$, P_r samples polynomials $\boxed{q_r, R_{q_r} \leftarrow \mathbb{P}_d}$ such that

   $$g(\alpha_r, \beta_j)\Pi_r(\beta_j) = q_r(\beta_j), \quad R_g(\alpha_r, \beta_j)\Pi_r(\beta_j) = R_{q_r}(\beta_j), \quad \forall j \in I_k.$$

   P_r broadcast $C(q_r, R_{q_r})$.
   (b) For all $j \in I_k$, each participant computes locally $C(q_r(\beta_j), R_{q_r}(\beta_j))$ and $C(g(\alpha_r, \beta_j), R_g(\alpha_r, \beta_j))$ and verifies that

   $$C(q_r(\beta_j), R_{q_r}(\beta_j)) = \Pi_r(\beta_j) \cdot C(g(\alpha_r, \beta_j), R_g(\alpha_r, \beta_j))$$

If the verification fails, P_r is added to the list of corrupted participant B. The protocol aborts and each participant outputs B.

(c) For $r \in [d+1]$ and $r' \in [n]$, P_r sends $\boxed{o(q_r(\alpha_{r'}), R_{q_r}(\alpha_{r'})) \text{ to } P_{r'}}$. The receiver $P_{r'}$ broadcasts a bit indicating if the opening is correct. For each share for which an irregularity was reported, P_r broadcasts the opening. If the opening is correct, $P_{r'}$ accepts the value, otherwise P_r is disqualified and added to the set of corrupted parties B. The protocols aborts and each party outputs B.

(d) Each party P_r sets its share as $\boxed{f_k(\alpha_r) = \sum_{u=1}^{d+1} q_u(\alpha_r)}$ and locally compute the commitment to f_k.

5.2   Blinding Bivariate Mask Generation

The goal of the BlindingBivariateGeneration protocol is for the participants to share and generate a bivariate sharing h of the m values $0, \ldots, 0$. Hence, it will verify $h(\beta_j, \beta_j) = 0$ for $j \in I$, where $I \subset [\ell]$ has size m (typically the I_k defined for Protocol 3). This sharing will be used to blind some values during the multiplication protocol and that is why we will sometimes call this sharing a blinding mask. As this protocol is designed to be used during the multiplication, we need that h verifies some very specific conditions on its values and their distribution to the participants. This condition depends on some threshold t and is very ad hoc but will allow us to quantify the "amount of randomness" we need from the blinding mask. We write $C_{\mathtt{mult}}(t)$ this condition. For a subset $T \subset [n]$, we write E_T the biggest system of independent equations gathered by an adversary $\mathcal{A}$ corrupting each P_r for $r \in T$. The condition $C_{\mathtt{mult}}(t)$ can be expressed as follows:

Definition 3. *A bivariate sharing h of degree d for m secrets is said to satisfy the condition $C_{\mathtt{mult}}(t)$ for $t \leq n$ if for every subset $T \subset [n]$ of size t:*

- *For any $u \notin T$, the degree of freedom of $h(\alpha_u, \cdot)$ with respect to the adversary's knowledge is $d + 2 - m$.*
- *For a system of equation E on h, let us write $X_E = \{x, \exists y \text{ such that } h(x, y) \in E\}$. For any $u \notin T$, any value z and any system of equations E such that $\#X_E \leq d-t$ and $\alpha_u \notin X_E$, the evaluation equation of $h(\alpha_u, z)$ is independent of $E \cup E_T$.*

Protocol 4. BlindingBivariateGeneration

INPUT: A set of index $I \subset [\ell]$ of size m.

OUTPUT: A bivariate sharing of $0, \ldots, 0$ at the points $(\beta_j)_{j \in I}$ is distributed to the parties along with the commitment to this sharing.

1. $\boxed{\text{For } r \in [n], P_r \text{ samples } q_r, R_{q_r} \leftarrow \mathbb{P}_d \text{ such that } q_r(\beta_j) = 0 \text{ for } j \in I}$ and broadcast the commitment $C(q_r, R_{q_r})$.

2. For $j \in I$, each P_r broadcasts the openings $o(0, R_{q_r}(\beta_j))$. If one of the opening is not correct, the corresponding participant is added to the list of corrupted participant B.

3. For $r \in [n]$, $r' \in [n]$, $\boxed{P_r \text{ sends to } P_{r'}}$ the opening $\boxed{o(q_r(\alpha_{r'}), R_{q_r}(\alpha_r))}$. If the opening is not correct, the corresponding participant is added to the list of corrupted participant B.

4. For $r' \in [n]$, $P_{r'}$ computes $q(\alpha_{r'}) = \sum_{r=1}^n q_r(\alpha_{r'})$, $R_q(\alpha_{r'}) = \sum_{r=1}^n R_{q_r}(\alpha_{r'})$, and locally compute the commitment $C(q, R_q)$.

5. $\boxed{\text{For } r \in [d+1], P_r \text{ samples } h(\alpha_r, \cdot), R_h(\alpha_r, \cdot) \leftarrow \mathbb{P}_d \text{ such that}}$

$\boxed{h(\alpha_r, \beta_j) = q(\alpha_r), R_h(\alpha_r, \beta_j) = R_q(\alpha_r)}$ and broadcast the commitment $C(h(\alpha_r, \cdot), R_h(\alpha_r, \cdot))$.

(*Note that this implicitly defines random bivariate polynomials h, R_h of degree d.*)

6. For $j \in I$ and $r \in [d+1]$, parties locally compute $C(h(\alpha_r, \beta_j), R_h(\alpha_r, \beta_j))$, $C(q(\alpha_r), R_q(\alpha_r))$ and check if $C(h(\alpha_r, \beta_j), R_h(\alpha_r, \beta_j)) = C(q(\alpha_r), R_q(\alpha_r))$. If one commitment does not satisfy the equation, the corresponding participant is added to the list of corrupted participant B.

7. For $r' \in [d+2, n]$, $\{P_1, \ldots, P_{d+1}\} \cup \{P_{r'}\}$ perform $\boxed{\text{Recover on } h}$.

5.3   Bivariate Product

The BivariateProduct protocol aims at creating a bivariate sharing $g^\star$ for the multiplication of the secrets contained in two univariate sharings f, f' under the blinding bivariate mask h. To distribute $g^\star(x, y) = f(x)f'(y) + h(x, y)$, each pair of participants is going to interact. The core of this exchange is a zero-knowledge multiplication protocol, denoted ZK-Mult, described in the full version and based on [9, Sect. 6.2]. When composed with the key generation KeyGen of the Paillier encryption, this protocol ZK-mult securely realizes the $\mathcal{F}_{prod}$ functionality (see Fig. 1). The protocol is performed by two participants P_1, P_2 where the input for P_1 is a key pair for the Paillier encryption scheme and a value x while P_2 has input the corresponding public key and two values y, δ. At the end of the protocol, P_1 learns $x \cdot y + \delta$. This subprotocol will be repeated to compute product of polynomials.

$\mathcal{F}_{prod}$ interacts with two parties P_1 and P_2.
Upon reception of x from P_1 and y, δ from P_2, $\mathcal{F}_{prod}$ sends $xy + \delta$ to P_1 and the special symbol $\perp$ to P_2.

Fig. 1. Functionality $\mathcal{F}_{prod}$

Protocol 5. BivariateProduct

INPUT: A set I of indices of size m and a set $\mathcal{P} = \{P_1, \ldots, P_n\}$ of participants holding two univariate sharings f, f' to batches $(s_i)_{i \in I}$, $(s'_i)_{i \in I}$ of m secrets and one bivariate sharing h to m zeroes and the commitments to these sharings $C(f, R_f), C(f', R_{f'}), C(h, R_h)$.

OUTPUT: The bivariate sharing of $g^\star(x, y) = f(x)f'(y) + h(y, x)$ and the commitment $C(g^\star, R_{g^\star})$ (with $R_{g^\star}(x, y) = f(x)R_{f'}(y) + R_h(y, x)$).

1. For all $r \in [n]$ and $r' \in [d+1]$,
   (a) P_r samples $(pk_r, sk_r), (pk_{r,R}, sk_{r,R}) \leftarrow$ KeyGen, produces two NIZK proofs of key generation and broadcasts all the public keys and corresponding proofs.
   (b) $P_{r'}$ verifies the proofs and if one of the verification fails, P_r is added to the set of corrupted participants.
   (c) $\boxed{P_r \text{ and } P_{r'} \text{ perform ZK-Mult}}$ on inputs $pk_r, sk_r, f(\alpha_r)$ for P_r and $pk_r, f'(\alpha_{r'}), h(\alpha_{r'}, \alpha_r)$ for $P_{r'}$. $\boxed{P_r \text{ obtains output } g^\star(\alpha_r, \alpha_{r'})}$.
   (d) $\boxed{P_r \text{ and } P_{r'} \text{ perform ZK-Mult}}$ on inputs $pk_{r,R}, sk_{r,R}, f(\alpha_r)$ for P_r and $pk_{r,R}, R_{f'}(\alpha_{r'}), R_h(\alpha_{r'}, \alpha_r)$ for $P_{r'}$. $\boxed{P_r \text{ obtains output } R_{g^\star}(\alpha_r, \alpha_{r'})}$.
   (e) P_r computes locally the commitments $C(f'(\alpha_{r'}), R_{f'}(\alpha_{r'}))$ and $C(h(\alpha_{r'}, \alpha_r), R_h(\alpha_{r'}, \alpha_r))$ and checks that

   $$C(g^\star(\alpha_r, \alpha_{r'}), R_{g^\star}(\alpha_r, \alpha_{r'})) =$$

   $$\left(f(\alpha_r) \cdot C(f'(\alpha_{r'}, R_{f'}(\alpha_{r'}))) \right) \star C(h(\alpha_{r'}, \alpha_r), R_h(\alpha_{r'}, \alpha_r))$$

   If the verification fails, $P_{r'}$ is added to the list of corrupted participants B.

2. $\boxed{P_r \text{ broadcast}}$ the commitment $\boxed{C(g^\star(\alpha_r, \cdot), R_{g^\star}(\alpha_r, \cdot))}$ for all $r \in [d+1]$.

5.4 Random Evaluation for Commitment Verification

The goal of Protocol 6 is to generate a random value **rand** used to ensure correctness of the shared commitments in Protocol 5 by revealing $f(\mathbf{rand})$ in clear.

Protocol 6. CommitmentVerification

INPUT: Two univariate sharings f, f' and one bivariate sharings h distributed among a set $\mathcal{P} = \{P_1, \ldots, P_n\}$. Another bivariate sharing $g^\star(x, y) = f(x)f'(y) + h(y, x)$ distributed among the participant along with the commitment $C(g, R_g)$ for some bivariate polynomials g, R_g

OUTPUT: A bit $b \in \{0, 1\}$.

1. For $r \in [n]$, $\boxed{P_r \text{ samples } v_r, R_{v_r} \leftarrow \mathbb{F}}$ and broadcast $C(v_r, R_{vr})$.

2. For $r \in [n]$, $\boxed{P_r \text{ broadcasts } o(v_r, R_{v_r})}$. If the verification fails, P_r is added to the list of corrupted participant B.
   Then, every party computes $\boxed{\text{rand} = \sum_{u=1}^n v_u}$. If rand is any values of the protocol (α_r or β_j), go back to step 1.

3. For $r \in [n]$, $\boxed{P_r \text{ samples } \hat{f}_r, R_{\hat{f}_r} \leftarrow \mathbb{P}_d}$ such that $\boxed{\hat{f}_r(\text{rand}) = 0}$ and broadcasts $C(\hat{f}_r, R_{\hat{f}_r})$.

4. For $r \in [n]$, $\boxed{P_r \text{ sends to all } P_{r'}}$ the opening to $\boxed{o(\hat{f}_r(\alpha_{r'}), R_{\hat{f}_r}(\alpha_{r'}))}$.
   The receiver P_r broadcasts a bit indicating if the opening is correct. For each share for which an irregularity was reported, P_r broadcasts the opening. If the opening is correct, $P_{r'}$ accepts the value, otherwise P_r is disqualified and added to the set of corrupted parties B. The protocols aborts and each party outputs B.

5. Each P_r broadcasts the openings $o(0, R_{\hat{f}_r}(\text{rand}))$. If one of the opening is not correct, the corresponding participant is added to the list of corrupted participant B.

6. Set $\hat{f} = f + \sum_{u=1}^n \hat{f}_u$ and $R_{\hat{f}} = R_f + \sum_{u=1}^n R_{\hat{f}_u}$. For $r \in [n]$,
   $\boxed{P_r \text{ broadcasts the opening } o(\hat{f}(\alpha_r), R_{\hat{f}}(\alpha_r))}$.

7. For all $r \in [n]$, each party computes locally $C(\hat{f}(\alpha_r), R_{\hat{f}}(\alpha_r))$ and verifies that the opening is correct. If the verification fails, P_r is added to the list of corrupted participant B.

8. Each party computes the values $\boxed{\hat{f}(\text{rand}) \text{ by interpolation}}$.

9. For all $r' \in [d+1]$, each participants computes locally the commitments $C(f'(\alpha_{r'}), R_{f'}(\alpha_{r'}))$, $C(h(\alpha_{r'}, \alpha_r), R_h(\alpha_{r'}, \alpha_r))$ and $C(g(\text{rand}, \alpha_{r'}), R_g(\text{rand}, \alpha_{r'}))$ and checks that

$$C(g(\text{rand}, \alpha_{r'}), R_g(\text{rand}, \alpha_{r'})) =$$

$$\Big(f(\text{rand}) \cdot C(f'(\alpha_{r'}, R_{f'}(\alpha_{r'}))) \Big) \star C(h(\alpha_{r'}, \alpha_r), R_h(\alpha_{r'}, \alpha_r))$$

   If one of the verifications fails the participants broadcasts a 0, otherwise it broadcasts a 1.

10. If one 0 was broadcasted in the previous step, the protocols outputs $b = 0$, otherwise it outputs $b = 1$.

5.5   The Multiplication Protocol

We are now ready to introduce the whole protocol performing the multiplication of two bivariate sharings g, g' containing ℓ secrets each. The output g'' is a bivariate sharing for the ℓ pair-wise products of secrets in g, g'. We have also a value m which must respect the bound $m \leq d - t_P$ to obtain security. For simplicity we assume that $\ell = mv$. The generalization for any ℓ is straightforward.

Protocol 7. Mult

INPUT: A set $\mathcal{P} = \{P_1, \ldots, P_n\}$ holding two bivariate sharings g, g' for two batches of $\ell = mv$ secrets $s_1, \ldots, s_\ell$ and $s'_1, \ldots, s'_\ell$ and the commitment to these sharings $C(g, R_g), C(g', R_{g'})$.

OUTPUT: Each party holds its shares for the bivariate sharing g'' for the batch of ℓ secrets $s_1 s'_1, \ldots, s_\ell s'_\ell$ along with the commitment $C(g'', R_{g''})$

1. The participants perform $\boxed{\texttt{ReshareBivariateToUnivariate on } g}$ and $\boxed{g'}$. We write $(f_k)_{k \in [v]}$ and $(f'_k)_{k \in [v]}$ the outputs of the two executions.
2. For $k \in [v]$,
    1. Set $I_k = [1 + (k-1)m, km]$ and execute $\boxed{\texttt{BlindingBivariate}}$ $\boxed{\texttt{Generation}}$ on input I_k. We write h_k the bivariate sharing obtained in output.
    2. Participants perform $\boxed{\texttt{BivariateProduct}}$ on the sharings f_k, f'_k, h_k and set I_k to obtain $g^\star_k$ a bivariate sharing with a bivariate commitment $C(g_k, R_{g_k})$.
    3. Participants execute $\boxed{\texttt{CommitmentVerfication}}$ on sharings $f_k, f'_k, h_k, g^\star_k$. If the output is 0, the protocol aborts and each party outputs B the set of corrupted participants.
    4. P_r $\boxed{\text{interpolates } g^\star_k(\alpha_r, \beta_j)}$ for $j \in I_k$.
3. For $r \in [d+1]$, $\boxed{P_r \text{ samples } g''(\alpha_r, \cdot), R_{g''}(\alpha_r, \cdot) \leftarrow \mathbb{P}_d}$ with $\boxed{g''(\alpha_r, \beta_j) = g^\star_k(\alpha_r, \beta_j)}$ and $R_{g''}(\alpha_r, \beta_j) = R_{g^\star_k}(\alpha_r, \beta_j)$ for all $k \in [v]$ and $j \in I_k$ and broadcast the commitment $C(g'', R_{g''})$.
    (Note that this implicitly defines a bivariate polynomial g'' of degree d.)
4. For all $r \in [d+1]$, each participant $P_{r'}$ computes $C(g_k(\alpha_r, \beta_j), R_{g_k}(\alpha_r, \beta_j))$ and $C(g''(\alpha_r, \beta_j), R_{g''}(\alpha_r, \beta_j))$ and checks equality for all $k \in [v]$ and $j \in I_k$. If one of the verification fails for index r, P_r is added to the set of corrupted participants B. The protocol aborts and each participant outputs B.
5. For $r' \in [d+2, n]$, $\{P_1, \ldots, P_{d+1}\} \cup \{P_{r'}\}$ perform $\boxed{\texttt{Recover on } g''}$.

Communication Complexity: The complexity of $\texttt{ReshareBivariateToUni}$ $\texttt{variate}$ is $O(n^2 v)$ and $O(n^2)$ for $\texttt{BlindingBivariateGeneration}$, $\texttt{Bivariate}$ $\texttt{Product}$ and $\texttt{CommitmentVerification}$. Thus, the overall complexity of the two first steps is $O(n^2 v)$. The final $\texttt{Recover}$ step is performed in $O(n^2)$ when $n - d = O(1)$. Overall, this is $O(n^2 v)$ and $O(n^2/m)$ amortized. When $\ell = n - 2$ and $m \approx \sqrt{\ell}$, we obtain the claimed amortized complexity of $O(n\sqrt{n})$.

Theorem 2. *When $\ell \leq d$ and $m = \lceil \sqrt{\ell} \rceil$ and assuming the hardness of DDH, the protocol Π^{MULT} introduced in Protocol 7 securely realizes the ideal process*

IDEAL$_{mixed}^{\mathcal{Z},\mathcal{S},\mathcal{F}_{MULT,\ell}}$ against any adversary bounded by the multi-threshold $T(\ell)$ where we have $T(\ell) = \{(d - 1 - \sqrt{\ell}, d - 1 - \sqrt{\ell})\}$.

The ideal functionality IDEAL$_{mixed}^{\mathcal{Z},\mathcal{S},\mathcal{F}_{MULT,\ell}}$ and the proof of Theorem 2 can be found in the full version.

References

1. Baron, J., Eldefrawy, K., Lampkins, J., Ostrovsky, R.: How to withstand mobile virus attacks, revisited. In: PODC, pp. 293–302. ACM (2014)
2. Baron, J., Defrawy, K.E., Lampkins, J., Ostrovsky, R.: Communication-optimal proactive secret sharing for dynamic groups. In: Malkin, T., Kolesnikov, V., Lewko, A.B., Polychronakis, M. (eds.) ACNS 2015. LNCS, vol. 9092, pp. 23–41. Springer, Cham (2015). https://doi.org/10.1007/978-3-319-28166-7_2
3. Dolev, S., ElDefrawy, K., Lampkins, J., Ostrovsky, R., Yung, M.: Proactive secret sharing with a dishonest majority. In: Zikas, V., De Prisco, R. (eds.) SCN 2016. LNCS, vol. 9841, pp. 529–548. Springer, Cham (2016). https://doi.org/10.1007/978-3-319-44618-9_28
4. Eldefrawy, K., Lepoint, T., Leroux, A.: Communication-efficient proactive secret sharing for dynamic groups with dishonest majorities. In: Conti, M., Zhou, J., Casalicchio, E., Spognardi, A. (eds.) ACNS 2020. LNCS, vol. 12146, pp. 3–23. Springer, Cham (2020). https://doi.org/10.1007/978-3-030-57808-4_1
5. Eldefrawy, K., Ostrovsky, R., Park, S., Yung, M.: Proactive secure multiparty computation with a dishonest majority. In: Catalano, D., De Prisco, R. (eds.) SCN 2018. LNCS, vol. 11035, pp. 200–215. Springer, Cham (2018). https://doi.org/10.1007/978-3-319-98113-0_11
6. Goldreich, O., Micali, S., Wigderson, A.: How to play any mental game or a completeness theorem for protocols with honest majority. In: Aho, A.V. (ed.) STOC, pp. 218–229. ACM (1987)
7. Herzberg, A., Jarecki, S., Krawczyk, H., Yung, M.: Proactive secret sharing or: how to cope with perpetual leakage. In: Coppersmith, D. (ed.) CRYPTO 1995. LNCS, vol. 963, pp. 339–352. Springer, Heidelberg (1995). https://doi.org/10.1007/3-540-44750-4_27
8. Hirt, M., Maurer, U., Lucas, C.: A dynamic tradeoff between active and passive corruptions in secure multi-party computation. In: Canetti, R., Garay, J.A. (eds.) CRYPTO 2013. LNCS, vol. 8043, pp. 203–219. Springer, Heidelberg (2013). https://doi.org/10.1007/978-3-642-40084-1_12
9. Lindell, Y., Nof, A.: Fast secure multiparty ECDSA with practical distributed key generation and applications to cryptocurrency custody. In: ACM Conference on Computer and Communications Security, pp. 1837–1854. ACM (2018)
10. Ostrovsky, R., Yung, M.: How to withstand mobile virus attacks (extended abstract). In: PODC, pp. 51–59. ACM (1991)
11. Pedersen, T.P.: Non-interactive and information-theoretic secure verifiable secret sharing. In: Feigenbaum, J. (ed.) CRYPTO 1991. LNCS, vol. 576, pp. 129–140. Springer, Heidelberg (1992). https://doi.org/10.1007/3-540-46766-1_9

PSI-Stats: Private Set Intersection Protocols Supporting Secure Statistical Functions

Jason H. M. Ying[1,2]([✉]), Shuwei Cao[2,3], Geong Sen Poh[2,3], Jia Xu[2,3], and Hoon Wei Lim[2,3]

[1] Seagate Technology, Singapore, Singapore
jasonhweiming.ying@seagate.com
[2] NUS-Singtel Cyber Security R&D Laboratory, Singapore, Singapore
[3] Trustwave, Singapore, Singapore

Abstract. Private Set Intersection (PSI) enables two parties, each holding a private set to securely compute their intersection without revealing other information. This paper considers settings of secure statistical computations over PSI, where both parties hold sets containing identifiers with one of the parties having an additional positive integer value associated with each of the identifiers in her set. The main objective is to securely compute some desired statistics of the associated values for which its corresponding identifiers occur in the intersection of the two sets. This is achieved without revealing the identifiers of the set intersection. In this paper, we present protocols which enable the secure computations of statistical functions over PSI, which we collectively termed *PSI-Stats*. Implementations of our constructions are also carried out based on simulated datasets as well as on actual datasets in the business use cases that we defined, in order to demonstrate practicality of our solution. *PSI-Stats* incurs 5× less monetary cost compared to the current state-of-the-art circuit-based PSI approach due to Pinkas *et al.* (EUROCRYPT'19). Our solution is more tailored towards business applications where monetary cost is the primary consideration.

Keywords: Private set intersection · Homomorphic encryption · Statistical functions

1 Introduction

Private set intersection (PSI) enables two parties to learn the intersection of their sets without exposing other elements (identifiers or items) that are not within this intersection. This has wide-ranging applications in data sharing, private contact discovery, private proximity testing [29], privacy-preserving ride-sharing [20], botnet detection [28] and human genomes testing [5]. We highlight a number of notable work that have been achieved in this domain in Sect. 6.

The main problem statement of our work can be simply described as follows. Sender A and receiver B hold sets of identifiers with receiver B additionally

© Springer Nature Switzerland AG 2022
G. Ateniese and D. Venturi (Eds.): ACNS 2022, LNCS 13269, pp. 585–604, 2022.
https://doi.org/10.1007/978-3-031-09234-3_29

holds positive integer values associated with each of the identifiers. Denote the sets held by A, B to be X and Y respectively. The objective is for B to learn the desired statistical output function of some collection (dependent on X) of the associated values, while preserving certain private information about their respective sets. More formally, B seeks to learn the value $F_D(X,Y)$, where D is the decisional rule and F is the desired statistical function computed over D. To preserve privacy, A does not learn Y and $D(X,Y)$ while B does not learn X, $D(X,Y)$ and $|D(X,Y)|$. In our context, D is the private set intersection (PSI) of the identifiers contained in X and Y. These settings arise in numerous business and practical applications.

1.1   Our Contributions

We present *PSI-Stats* to address this main problem statement. *PSI-Stats* is a collection of protocols to support the secure computations of statistical functions over PSI. These include a myriad of frequently applied standard statistical functions such as various generalized means, standard deviation, variance, etc. The proposed protocols achieve the privacy requirements outlined in the problem statement. The main contributions are summarized here.

- *PSI-Stats* can be enabled to securely compute multiple related statistical functions within a single executed protocol with minimal additional communication and computational overhead, while maintaining the privacy guarantees as defined in the main problem statement. Our techniques are also applicable to non-symmetric functions such as weighted arithmetic mean.
- It is undesirable in many instances for receiver B to know both the intersection cardinality and the output functionality as the combination of these can reveal some information about the intersection set. To address this issue, one key contribution of our work is to restrict any such inference information to the absolute possible bare minimum. This is achieved by hiding the intersection cardinality from receiver B and thus only the desired output functionality (and nothing more) is revealed to him.
- We carried out extensive experiments of our protocols to determine their practicality and feasibility. Our test input sizes range from small to large. The experimental results demonstrate that *PSI-Stats* is practical and scales well for large input sizes. We also conducted experimental comparisons of our protocols with the current state-of-the-art circuit-based PSI protocol due to Pinkas *et al.* [34]. Our protocols incur 5× less monetary cost and 5.2× less communication overhead.

In an interactive protocol, there are three factors in the overall measurement of efficiency: the first relates to the communication overhead, the second relates to the computational cost and the third relates to the number of communication rounds (or round complexity). The work in this paper does not claim to outperform circuit-based PSI protocols across all the three factors above. As an example, the current state-of-the-art for circuit-based PSI protocols is the very recent work of Pinkas *et al.* [34] which we reckon to potentially attain the lowest computational cost (after the necessary circuit modifications in order to accommodate outputs of statistical functions).

A goal of our work aims to present protocols with minimal communication overhead based upon well-established, time-tested hardness assumptions while concurrently ensuring that running times remain practical. To that end, the *PSI-Stats* protocols in this paper incur the lowest communication overhead over all circuit-based types (inclusive of the most recent state-of-the-art [34]) by several factors. In that regard, *PSI-Stats* is especially relevant in settings where communication cost comes at a premium or instances where bandwidth is limited.

Circuit-based PSI approaches can generally be instantiated by either Yao's garbled circuit protocol [41] or the GMW protocol [19]. While Yao's protocol provides a constant round complexity, the GMW protocol is typically the overall preferred option as it has several advantages over the former. A comprehensive comparison between Yao's protocol and the GMW protocol can be found in [39]. However for circuit-based PSI under the GMW family, the round complexity is dependent on the circuit depth which increases with increasing set sizes and/or increasing bit-length of items. This can potentially be a bottleneck in high latency networks. By contrast, the *PSI-Stats* protocols operate with a low constant round complexity of 3, independent of the input set sizes *and* the bit-length of items.

To the best of our knowledge, alternative approaches to solve the main problem statement beyond circuit-based methods are either less efficient in our context or employ the usage of computationally intensive homomorphic encryption schemes, such as [7,9]. We resolve the problem without resorting to the machinery of such expensive approaches. It should be noted that our protocols reveal the intersection size to sender A. However, this does not enable sender A to apply any inference attack based on the associated values held by receiver B as they all safeguarded by homomorphic encryptions in our protocols. On the other hand, such attacks are relevant if this intersection cardinality is revealed to receiver B as discussed. Hence, it is crucial that this information is hidden from receiver B which our protocols attain.

2 Preliminaries

The security model in this paper operates in the semi-honest setting. In this model, adversaries can attempt to obtain information from the execution of the protocol but they are unable to perform any deviations from the intended protocol steps. The semi-honest model is typically suited in scenarios where execution of the software is ensured through software attestation or business restrictions, without any assumption that an external untrusted party is unable to obtain the transcript of the protocol upon completion. Indeed, the majority of the research in related domains also focus on solutions in the semi-honest model. Hereinafter, we shall simply refer to mean as being arithmetic mean while references to other generalized means will be stated explicitly.

In this paper, we say an integer x is l-bit (length) if $x \in \mathbb{Z} \cap [2^{l-1}, 2^l - 1]$ and x is at most l-bit (length) if $x \in \mathbb{Z} \cap [0, 2^l - 1]$. The standard ceiling function is given by $\lceil . \rceil$, where $\lceil x \rceil$ represents the smallest integer greater than or equal to x. The nearest integer function is denoted by $\lfloor . \rceil$, log refers to the natural logarithm, and e is the standard mathematical constant (i.e. the base of the natural logarithm). The participants' setting and notations in the description of our protocols in this paper is identical. We provide it here to serve as a convenient common reference.

Notations

a_i, b_i: identifiers.
A holds $X = \{a_1, a_2, \ldots, a_m\}$.
B holds $Y = \{(b_1, t_1), (b_2, t_2), \ldots, (b_n, t_n)\}$, $t_i \in \mathbb{Z}^+$.
$Y' = \{b_1, b_2, \ldots, b_n\}$.
$E(.)$: Paillier encryption of a 3072-bit modulus.
$h(.)$: SHA-256 hash function.
G: a multiplicative group of integers of large prime order.

---

3   Private Set Intersection-Mean

This section describes a protocol to correctly output only the intersection mean (i.e. without disclosing intersection-sum nor intersection cardinality to B). There are numerous flexible applications for the intersection mean functionality apart from the secure computation over numerical values. For instance, records in a dataset can be encoded as 0 or 1 to represent entries of a binary attribute such as "gender". The arithmetic mean of these encoded values can thus directly provide the percentages of "females" and "males" which belong in the intersection of the two datasets. We provide concrete recommendations for the appropriate sizes of the various parameter values for use in our protocols which we also show to provide strong security guarantees satisfying statistical indistinguishability.

PROTOCOL 1 (Private Set Intersection-Mean)

Input: A inputs set X; B inputs set Y.
Output: A outputs $|X \cap Y'|$, B outputs intersection mean.

1. **Setup:** A and B jointly agree on E, a hash function h and a group G of large prime order. B generates a public-private key pair of E, announces the public key and keeps the private key to herself.
2. **A's encryption phase:** A
(a) selects a random private exponent $k_1 \in G$;
(b) computes $h(a_i)^{k_1}$.
A sends $h(a_i)^{k_1}$ to B.
3. **B's encryption phase:** B
(a) selects a random private exponent $k_2 \in G$;
(b) computes $h(a_i)^{k_1 k_2}$;

(c) computes $\{h(b_j)^{k_2}, E(t_j)\}$.

B returns $h(a_i)^{k_1 k_2}$ in shuffled order to A. B sends $\{(h(b_j)^{k_2}, E(t_j)\}$ to A.

4. **Matching & homomorphic computations:** A

(a) computes $\{h(b_j)^{k_2 k_1}, E(t_j)\}$;

(b) computes the set I of intersection indices where

$$I = \{j : h(a_i)^{k_1 k_2} = h(b_j)^{k_2 k_1} \text{ for some } i\};$$

(c) samples a uniformly random 1024-bit value of r.

(d) selects uniformly random integer values of r_1, r_2, where $0 \le r_1 \le 2^{128} - 1$, $2^{511} \le r_2 \le 2^{512} - 1$ with r_1 satisfying

$$r_1 \equiv r \bmod k$$

where $k = |I|$.

(e) additive homomorphically computes

$$E\left(r_2 + \frac{r - r_1}{k} \sum_{i \in I} t_i\right).$$

A sends r and $E\left(r_2 + \frac{r-r_1}{k} \sum_{i \in I} t_i\right)$ to B.

5. **B's decryption phase:** B performs decryptions of the ciphertext received from A and computes (division over real numbers)

$$\frac{1}{|I|} \sum_{i \subset I} t_i \approx \frac{1}{r}\left(r_2 + \frac{r - r_1}{k} \sum_{i \in I} t_i\right).$$

Theorem 1. *Protocol 1 correctly outputs the intersection mean (and which can also be made arbitrarily close to the exact value).*

3.1   On the Chosen Sizes of r, r_1, r_2

The larger the value of r, the closer the approximation of output $\mathcal{M}'$ is to the exact mean value $\mathcal{M}$. Moreover, this approximation can be made arbitrary close for arbitrary large values of r (along with corresponding large parameter sizes of E). In practice, a sufficiently large value of r already provides a very tight approximation. The size choices of r_1, r_2 are 128 bits and 511 bits respectively to prevent exhaustive search attacks. After the sizes of r_1, r_2 are set, the size of r can be chosen to sufficiently overwhelm r_1, r_2. In our case, we set r to be of size 1024-bit which is sufficient for $\mathcal{M}'$ to $\mathcal{M}$ to be extremely close. In particular,

$$|\mathcal{M} - \mathcal{M}'| < 2^{-512}\mathcal{M} \tag{1}$$

which suffices for all practical intent.

3.2   Flexibility of Protocol

It should be noted that the exact mean value in fact reveals additional information about the sum or cardinality. For instance, if the mean is an integer $\mathcal{M}$ then it follows that the sum is divisible by $\mathcal{M}$. More generally, if the mean is a rational number $\frac{a}{b}$ with $\gcd(a,b) = 1$, then the sum is divisible by a and the cardinality is divisible by b. As discussed in the preliminary section, we do not consider such implicit information which can be deduced from the output functionality. Nevertheless, Protocol 1 has the added benefit of flexibility which enables the adjustment of varying degrees of approximation tightness if one wishes to circumvent the above issues. This can be achieved by adjusting the size of a randomly sampled r. The approximation weakens with decreasing sizes of r. More generally, for a random sample r of x-bit, $x \geq 515$, the difference yields

$$|\mathcal{M} - \mathcal{M}'| < 2^{512-x}\mathcal{M}. \tag{2}$$

3.3   Security Analysis

The security arising from the communication in Step 2 and Step 3 follows from the validity of the Decisional Diffie-Hellman assumption as well as the hardness of the Decisional Composite Redisuosity Problem. Hence, the remaining security and privacy aspects to consider occur in Step 4 where B receives r and $E\left(r_2 + \frac{r-r_1}{k}\sum_{i \in I} t_i\right)$. Since r is sampled uniformly at random from a collection of 1024-bit integers, B is unable to distinguish r from a random uniformly selected 1024-bit integer. As before, denote $\mathcal{M}$ to be the exact value of the intersection mean. Thus, B obtains $r_2 + \frac{r-r_1}{k}\sum_{i \in I} t_i = r_2 + (r - r_1)\mathcal{M}$. Moreover, only r and $\mathcal{M}$[1] are known to B and thus only effectively can compute $r_2 - r_1\mathcal{M}$ which we show in the following is statistically indistinguishable from a uniformly sampled 512-bit integer. This serves the purpose of hiding the cardinality and intersection sum. We begin with a standard security definition.

Definition 1. *Let X and Y be two distributions over $\{0,1\}^n$. The statistical distance of X and Y, denoted by $\Delta(X,Y)$ is defined to be*

$$\Delta(X,Y) = \max_{U \subseteq \{0,1\}^n} |Pr[X \in U] - Pr[Y \in U]|$$

$$= \frac{1}{2}\sum_{v \in Supp(X) \cup Supp(Y)} |Pr[X = v] - Pr[Y = v]|. \tag{3}$$

X is ϵ statistically indistinguishable from Y if $\Delta(X,Y) \leq \epsilon$.

---

[1] Technically only $\mathcal{M}'$, which is a close approximation to $\mathcal{M}$ can be computed by B. In essence, this distinction is largely irrelevant in this specific context as we evaluate a stronger security setting than required where B has the knowledge of both $\mathcal{M}$ and $\mathcal{M}'$.

In particular, we show that $r_2 - r_1 \mathcal{M}$ is statistically indistinguishable from uniformly distributed 512-bit integers, when $\mathcal{M}$ is a fixed positive integer. It can be assumed here that the intersection mean $\mathcal{M}$ is at most 80-bit in all practical settings. Denote random variables $R_1 = \mathrm{unif}[0, c]$ and $R_2 = \mathrm{unif}[a, b]$ to be the discrete uniform distributions over $\mathbb{Z} \cap [0, c]$ and $\mathbb{Z} \cap [a, b]$ respectively such that $c\mathcal{M} \ll a \ll b$. We first establish the following.

Theorem 2.
$$\Delta(R_2 - R_1 \mathcal{M}, R_2) = \frac{c\mathcal{M}}{2(b - a + 1)}. \tag{4}$$

In Protocol 1, $a = 2^{511}$, $b = 2^{512} - 1$, $c = 2^{128} - 1$ and $\mathcal{M}$ is assumed to be at most 80-bit. Hence in Protocol 1,

$$\Delta(R_2 - R_1 \mathcal{M}, R_2) \leq 2^{-300}. \tag{5}$$

This shows that $r_2 - r_1 \mathcal{M}$ is 2^{-300} statistically indistinguishable from uniformly distributed 512-bit integers when $\mathcal{M}$ is a positive integer. Here, we simply apply 80-bit as a concrete upper bound of $\mathcal{M}$ in all practical use cases. It can in fact be way larger than 80-bit subject to the corresponding constraints of (5). In cases where $\mathcal{M} = \frac{a}{b}$ is a non-integer positive rational number such that $a \ll r_2$, a similar argument can be applied to show that $r_2 b - r_1 a$ is statistically indistinguishable from uniformly distributed 512-bit integers which are multiplied by a factor of b.

3.4   Geometric Mean

Our method can be adapted to output the intersection geometric mean functionality without revealing the intersection size to B. One application arises in the computation of the Atkinson index [4] of income inequality which is a function of both the geometric mean and arithmetic mean. Another such instance of the geometric mean can arise in Econometrics as specified by the generalized Cobb-Douglas production function [14], where its inputs can represent working hours of labourers and each exponent is the reciprocal of the number of inputs.

The geometric mean of a data set $\{t_1, t_2, \ldots, t_k\}$ is given by $\left(\prod_{i=1}^{k} t_i \right)^{\frac{1}{k}}$. A natural line of approach is to replace additive homomorphic encryption with a multiplicative homomorphic encryption (e.g. RSA [38]) in view of the multiplicative structure of the output. This works perfectly fine if the intersection size is exposed to B. However, in the security model where the intersection size is kept secret from B, there is no known efficient public-key based protocol utilizing multiplicative homomorphic encryption which can achieve this with reasonable accuracy. We present a method to attain this desired functionality using ideas based on our earlier approach for arithmetic mean.

Without being overly verbose, we do not detail the fully fledged protocol but instead highlight the crucial steps. Suppose $t_i \in [1, t + 1]$. We first seek an injective function $f_c : t_i \rightarrow \lfloor c \log t_i \rceil$ for some positive integer constant c. Here $\lfloor . \rceil$ denotes the nearest integer function in accordance with the most recent IEEE Standard for floating-point arithmetic [1]. The value of c is chosen by B, the party who holds the list of associated values. We show that f_c can be constructed by taking $c \geq t + 1$.

Theorem 3. f_c is injective $\forall\, c \geq t + 1$.

The injectivity condition is stipulated to ensure that no two distinct values of t_i's correspond to the same image under f_c. The protocol for the intersection geometric mean proceeds by replacing t_i with $\lfloor c \log t_i \rceil$ given in Protocol 1. One other difference lies in the final decryption step performed by B. More specifically in the final step, B obtains the intersection geometric mean by computing

$$e^{\frac{1}{cr}\left(r_2+\frac{r-r_1}{k}\sum_{i\in I}\lfloor c\log t_i\rceil\right)} \approx e^{\frac{1}{c|I|}\sum_{i\in I}\lfloor c\log t_i\rceil} \approx e^{\frac{1}{|I|}\sum_{i\in I}\log t_i} = \left(\prod_{i\in I}t_i\right)^{\frac{1}{|I|}}. \tag{6}$$

In general, larger values of c provide a greater precision. In practice, such large values of c can always be chosen since the modulus of the Paillier encryption is much larger than $\max\{\log t_i\}$. The proofs of correctness and security mirror that of the intersection mean.

3.5   Extensions to Variance and Standard Deviation

Our techniques presented in this section can be further extended to compute various other statistical functions of the associated values in the intersection. The general overall idea is for B to receive the values of nth-order moment about the origin in order to compute the nth central moment (without knowledge of the intersection size). Let R be a random variable. In our context, R can be considered to be the discrete uniform distribution over the associated values in the intersection. The nth-order moment about the origin μ'_n is defined to be $\mu'_n = \mathbb{E}[R^n]$. The nth central moment μ_n is defined to be $\mu_n = \mathbb{E}[(R - \mathbb{E}[R])^n]$. For example, the mean in this case is $\mu'_1 = \mathbb{E}[R]$. Variance and standard deviation provide a measure of the amount of dispersion of a list of values. A low standard deviation indicates that the values tend to be clustered around its mean, while a high standard deviation indicates that the values are dispersed over a wider range of values. In step 3 of the protocol, B sends both $E(t_j)$ and $E(t_j^2)$ to A. This enables A to return values of $\mathbb{E}[R]$ and $\mathbb{E}[R^2]$ to B. The variance can then be simply computed by $\mathrm{Var}(R) = \mathbb{E}[R^2] - (\mathbb{E}[R])^2$ and standard deviation $\sigma = \sqrt{\mathrm{Var}(R)}$. At the end of this protocol, B outputs the mean and standard deviation (or variance). At the same time, B's knowledge of $\mathbb{E}[R^2]$ during this process does not reveal any additional information since that quantity can be derived from any generic protocol which outputs the mean and standard deviation (or variance). The protocols for the skewness and kurtosis output functionalities can be similarly constructed.

4   Intersection-Sum with Approximate Composition

Trivially, the intersection sum output S reveals that there are less than l elements (or identifiers) in the intersection with associated values greater than $\frac{S}{l}$. In many scenarios, B wishes to know more about the composition of the sum. In particular, given the intersection sum, B wishes to have an estimate of the number of elements in the intersection with associated value of at most $\hat{t}$ (i.e. its approximate sum composition). This information cannot be captured merely by the knowledge of intersection sum. To that end, we present two protocols, labelled as type 1 and 2 which enable the output of intersection sum along with its approximate sum composition.

PROTOCOL 2 (Sum Composition type 1)

Input: A inputs set X; B inputs set Y.

Output: A outputs $|X \cap Y'|$, B outputs $\sum_{i \in I} t_i$ and an upper bound for $\sum_{i \in I} \frac{1}{t_i}$, where I is the set of indices of $b_i \in X \cap Y'$.

1. **Setup:** Identical to Protocol 1.
2. A'**s encryption phase:** Identical to Protocol 1.
3. B'**s encryption phase:** B
(a) selects a random private exponent $k_2 \in G$;
(b) computes $h(a_i)^{k_1 k_2}$;
(c) computes $\{h(b_j)^{k_2}, E(t_j)\}$.
B returns $h(a_i)^{k_1 k_2}$ in shuffled order to A. B sends $\{h(b_{\sigma(j)})^{k_2}, E(t_{\sigma(j)})\}_{j=1}^{n}$ to A, where σ is a permutation of j such that $t_{\sigma(j)} \geq t_{\sigma(j+1)}$. B sends M to A where

$$M \geq \max \left\{ \frac{t_{\sigma(j)}}{t_{\sigma(j+1)}} \right\}.$$

4. **Matching & homomorphic computations:** A
(a) computes $\{(h(b_j)^{k_2 k_1}, E(t_j)\}$;
(b) computes the set I of intersection indices where

$$I = \{j : h(a_i)^{k_1 k_2} = h(b_j)^{k_2 k_1} \text{ for some } i\};$$

(c) additive homomorphically computes $E\left(\sum_{i \in I} t_i\right)$;
(d) samples uniformly random r, r_1, r_2 from a sufficiently large set of positive integers such that $r \gg r_1, r_2$ and $\frac{r_1}{r_2} \geq k$, where $k = |I|$;
(e) computes $r_1 + rk(M^k - 1)$ and additive homomorphically computes

$$E\left(r_2 + r(M - 1)\sum_{i=1}^{k} M^{i-1} t_i'\right),$$

where $\{t'_i\}_{i=1}^k$ is a permutation of $\{t_i\}_{i \in I}$ s.t. $t'_{i+1} \leq t'_i$.

A sends $E\left(\sum_{i \in I} t_i\right)$, $E\left(r_2 + r(M-1)\sum_{i=1}^k M^{i-1}t'_i\right)$ and $r_1 + rk(M^k - 1)$

to B.

5. **B's decryption phase:** B performs decryptions of the ciphertexts received

from A to obtain $\sum_{i \in I} t_i$ and an upper bound for $\sum_{i \in I} \frac{1}{t_i}$ given by

$$\sum_{i \in I} \frac{1}{t_i} \leq \frac{r_1 + rk(M^k - 1)}{r_2 + r(M-1)\sum_{i=1}^k M^{i-1}t'_i}.$$

Theorem 4. *Protocol 2 outputs* $\sum_{i \in I} t_i$ *and an upper bound for* $\sum_{i \in I} \frac{1}{t_i}$.

4.1   Applicability of Sum Composition

Let the sum composition measure T be denoted to be

$$T = \frac{r_1 + rk(M^k - 1)}{r_2 + r(M-1)\sum_{i=1}^k M^{i-1}t'_i}. \tag{7}$$

Theorem 5. *There are less than l elements in the intersection with associated integer values of at most $\hat{t}$ where $\hat{t} \in \mathbb{Z}^+$ satisfying $\hat{t} < \frac{l}{T}$.*

For instance when $l = 1$, it can be established that there are no small associated integer values under $\frac{1}{T}$ contained in the set intersection. In other words, every element in the intersection has an associated value of at least $\frac{1}{T}$. It should be noted that the applicability of this measure of sum composition is dependent on the distribution of the associated values held by B. Generally, this output functionality is more useful when the spread of associated values is sufficiently large. In practice, B who holds the associated values can decide whether to initiate these two protocols based on his dataset. Type 1 enables the transmission of an approximate sum composition without any substantial increase in communication over the intersection-sum. However, that requires B to reveal an upper bound of M to A. We describe a type 2 protocol where communication cost is not an overriding consideration without disclosing an upper bound of M to A. Type 2 also results in a tighter output approximation compared to type 1. A key ingredient involves an injective mapping of the set of reciprocals of positive integers to the set of positive integers which preserves addition. Denote f_c to be such an injective map such that $f_c : t_i \rightarrow \left\lceil \frac{c}{t_i} \right\rceil$ for a suitable large constant c.

PROTOCOL 3 (Sum Composition type 2)

Input: A inputs set X; B inputs set Y.

Output: A outputs $|X \cap Y'|$, B outputs $\sum_{i \in I} t_i$ and an upper bound for $\sum_{i \in I} \frac{1}{t_i}$, where I is the set of indices of $b_i \in X \cap Y'$.

1. **Setup:** Identical to Protocol 1.
2. **A's encryption phase:** Identical to Protocol 1.
3. **B's encryption phase:** B
(a) selects a random private exponent $k_2 \in G$;
(b) computes $h(a_i)^{k_1 k_2}$;
(c) computes $\{h(b_j)^{k_2}, E(t_j), E(f_c(t_j))\}$.
B returns $h(a_i)^{k_1 k_2}$ in shuffled order to A. B sends $\{h(b_j)^{k_2}, E(t_j), E(f_c(t_j))\}$ to A.
4. **Matching & homomorphic computations:** A
(a) computes $\{h(b_j)^{k_2 k_1}, E(t_j), E(f_c(t_j))\}$;
(b) computes the set I of intersection indices where

$$I = \{j : h(a_i)^{k_1 k_2} = h(b_j)^{k_2 k_1} \text{ for some } i\};$$

(c) additive homomorphically computes

$$E\left(\sum_{i \in I} t_i\right) \quad \text{and} \quad E\left(\sum_{i \in I} f_c(t_i)\right).$$

A sends $E\left(\sum_{i \in I} t_i\right)$ and $E\left(\sum_{i \in I} f_c(t_i)\right)$ to B.

5. **B's decryption phase:** B performs decryptions of the ciphertexts received from A to obtain $\sum_{i \in I} t_i$ and an upper bound for $\sum_{i \in I} \frac{1}{t_i}$ given by

$$\sum_{i \in I} \frac{1}{t_i} \leq \frac{1}{c} \sum_{i \in I} f_c(t_i).$$

Theorem 6. *Protocol 3 outputs $\sum_{i \in I} t_i$ and an upper bound for $\sum_{i \in I} \frac{1}{t_i}$.*

4.2 On the Selection of c

Suppose the values of t_i's are bounded by x bits. We show that taking c to be of size $2x + 1$ bits admits f_c to be injective. Indeed, let t_i, t_j be two distinct associated values. Without loss of generality, assume $t_i < t_j$, Then

$$\left| \frac{c}{t_i} - \frac{c}{t_j} \right| = c \left(\frac{t_j - t_i}{t_i t_j} \right) \geq 1 \tag{8}$$

since c is of size $2x + 1$ bits. It follows that

$$\left| \frac{c}{t_i} - \frac{c}{t_j} \right| \geq 1 \Rightarrow \left[\frac{c}{t_i} \right] \neq \left[\frac{c}{t_j} \right] \tag{9}$$

which proves injectivity.

4.3   Comparisons Between Type 1 and Type 2

Table 1. Recommended RSA key length from NIST

security level (κ)	80	112	128	192	256
RSA key length	1024	2048	3072	7680	15360

The NIST report [6] details the recommended RSA key length (in bits) to achieve a κ-bit security as given in Table 1. In the case of E being the Paillier encryption, a 2048-bit length modulus corresponds to a 112-bit security level. This translates to a ciphertext of length 4096-bit for Paillier encryption. Thus, this increase in communication overhead is approximately in the region of $4096n$ bits. On the other hand for large intersection sizes, type 2 is more practical and has a lower computational cost.

5   Implementation and Performance

We implemented *PSI-Stats* in C++. The benchmark machine is desktop workstation running on a single-thread with an Intel Core i7-7700 CPU @ 3.60 GHz and 28 GB RAM. The bandwidth is 4867 Mbps with round-trip time of 0.02 ms. The respective input sizes m, n are equal and the comparisons are based on the running time (in seconds) as well as communication cost (in MB). All experiments apart from the UCI and Kaggle datasets are run at full intersection sizes (i.e. intersection size $= m = n$). We set the value of $c = 10^9$ for the geometric mean protocol. In running Protocol 1, we also provide the readers with the results of the actual generalized means alongside the outputs that it obtained from the execution of the protocol. The output generalized means values given in the tables are all rounded down to the nearest whole number.

We apply similar parameters as with the experiments conducted in [22]. The elements/identifiers in the generated datasets are 128-bit strings, with associated values being at most 32 bits long (the specific testing range is set between 1 to 100). The sum of the associated values is also bounded by 32 bits. The input set

Table 2. Performance of Private Intersection-arithmetic mean protocol.

	Time(s)			Comm.[MB]	Actual Value	Output (rounded down)
Input Size	Offline	Online	Total			
1000	1.46	0.49	1.95	0.4997	51.31	51
2000	2.84	0.94	3.78	0.9994	48.91	48
3000	4.22	1.41	5.63	1.4991	51.76	51
4000	5.6	1.87	7.47	1.9988	44.525	44
5000	6.96	2.33	9.29	2.4985	48.835	48
10000	14.3	4.8	19.1	4.9976	51.64	51
50000	69.3	23.4	92.7	24.988	48.45	48
100000	142	48	190	49.976	50.83	50

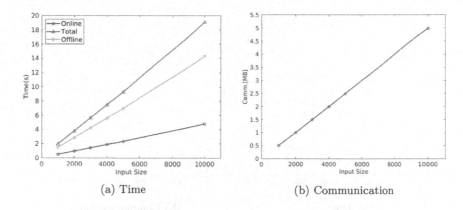

(a) Time   (b) Communication

Fig. 1. Performance on Arithmetic Mean

sizes range from 1000 to 100000. An elliptic curve with 256-bit group elements constitute the group G. The hash function SHA-256 is utilized for h. The Paillier encryption involves the product of two 768 bit primes which yields a plaintext space of 1536 bits and ciphertext of length 3072 bits.

In addition, we have segmented the total time into disjoint durations of the offline and online phases. The offline phase refers to the pre-computation process where the parties can perform offline computations of their respective individual dataset even before the initial round of communication commences. The online phase begins from the initial round of communication to the end of the protocol. In practice, the online phase duration generally provides a more relevant indicator of practical performance as opposed to the total time taken. The results are presented in Tables 2 and 3, and illustrated in Figs. 1 and 2, which highlight that both the running time and communication cost in our protocols are linear with respect to the input size.

Table 3. Performance of Private Intersection-geometric mean protocol.

| Input Size | Time(s) | | | Comm.[MB] | Actual Value | Output (rounded down) |
	Offline	Online	Total			
1000	1.53	0.52	2.05	0.4997	37.84	37
2000	2.93	0.99	3.92	0.9994	38.07	38
3000	4.31	1.48	5.79	1.4991	36.71	36
4000	5.88	1.91	7.79	1.9988	36.58	36
5000	7.01	2.38	9.39	2.4985	42.288	42
10000	15.2	5.2	20.4	4.9976	44.28	44
50000	70	24.2	94.2	24.988	43.04	43
100000	151	52	203	49.976	37.13	37

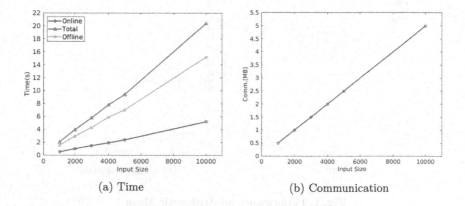

(a) Time   (b) Communication

Fig. 2. Performance on Geometric Mean

Table 4. Performance of PSI-Stats on a UCI repository dataset.

| Input Size | Time(s) | | | Comm.[MB] | Actual Mean | Output (rounded down) |
	Offline	Online	Total			
45211	63.17	20.78	83.95	22.591	1422.65	1422

Table 5. Performance of PSI-Stats on a Kaggle dataset.

| Input Size | Time(s) | | | Comm.[MB] | Actual Mean | Output (rounded down) |
	Offline	Online	Total			
30000	45.6	15.6	61.2	14.992	1422.65	1422

We also select a couple of actual datasets to conduct our experiments. The dataset [27] taken from the UCI ML repository [12] relates to marketing campaigns of a Portuguese banking institution. This dataset consists of a pair of sets: one of which is a proper subset of the other. We extract the attribute of interest corresponding to the yearly bank balance of bank's clients. A holds the smaller set of size 4521 while B holds the larger set of size 45211. To simulate a practical setting, each input (representing a client) is assigned a *kojin bangō* which is a unique 12-digit ID number issued to residents in Japan for taxation purpose. Other identifiers such as the Social Security Number issued in the United States can also be similarly assigned. The set size of A is then increased to 45211 to match that of B by generating a distinct *kojin bang* for each new client. Consequently, the set size is 45211 for both parties and the intersection corresponds to the original smaller set of size 4521. Related figures in the computation of mean yearly balance of common clients between these two parties via *PSI-Stats* are presented in Table 7. The second dataset involves spending from a mall taken from Kaggle [2] which has an input size of 30000. We use the column labelled "payment 2" as the set of corresponding associated values. The performance of *PSI-Stats* of selected functionalities on the Kaggle dataset is recorded in Table 5.

5.1   Comparisons with Circuit-Based PSI Protocols

The main direct competitor to *PSI-Stats* is a general-purpose circuit-based PSI. One advantage of *PSI-Stats* compared to existing circuit based approaches is that it incurs the lowest communication overhead. This is particular crucial in low bandwidth settings or where communication cost is at a premium. In this regard, we demonstrate the comparisons in two aspects. The first evaluation is based on the monetary cost to run the protocols on an external cloud server which is dependent on the computation and the communication cost. This provides a fair universal comparison of protocols with varying computation and communication cost. Such a mode of comparison was first introduced in [32] and also applied in [8]. For this purpose, our reference cloud server is the Amazon Web Service (AWS) with the reference price model[2] of (0.005 USD/hr, 0.08 USD/GB). The second evaluation is based on the run times of protocols when conducted at a bandwidth setting of 1 Mbps with a round-trip time of 0.02 ms.

The current most efficient state-of-the-art circuit-based PSI protocol is the recent work of Pinkas *et al.* [34]. While there are two main approaches for the generic secure two-party computation of Boolean circuits, the GMW approach is the better performing over Yaos garbled circuit on the balance of both communication and computational cost. Since one of our evaluations is based upon monetary cost, we shall use the GMW approach of [34] to serve as a benchmark in the comparisons of *PSI-Stats* with circuit-based PSI approaches. We run the "no stash" protocol of [34] along with the arithmetic mean protocol of *PSI-Stats*. The results are reflected in Tables 6 and 7. It should be emphasized that

---

[2] https://aws.amazon.com/ec2/spot/pricing.   https://aws.amazon.com/cloudfront/pricing/.

Table 6. Comparisons of monetary cost (in cents)

	Pinkas et al. [34]			PSI-Stats		
Input Size	Time(s)	Comm.[MB]	Cost(cents)	Time(s)	Comm.[MB]	Cost(cents)
5000	0.649	13.6	0.1063	9.29	2.5	0.0208
10000	1.042	26.3	0.2056	19.1	5.0	0.0417
20000	2.077	52.9	0.4136	37.7	10.0	0.0833
30000	3.105	79.2	0.6192	56.3	15.0	0.1249
2^{20}	107.96	2702	21.12	1902	524	4.36

Table 7. Comparisons of run time at network bandwidth setting of 1 Mbps.

	Pinkas et al. [34]			PSI-Stats	
Input Size	Time(s)	Comm. [MB]	Input Size	Time(s)	Comm. [MB]
5000	113.48	13.6	5000	29.1	2.5
10000	222.60	26.3	10000	58.3	5.0
20000	444.01	52.9	20000	119.1	10.0
30000	666.23	79.2	30000	174.8	15.0
300,000	6529	776	2^{20}	6113	524

the "no stash" protocol outputs the set intersection (without payload) as compared to the arithmetic mean of the set intersection given in the running times of *PSI-Stats*. Substantial modifications have to be incorporated to the "no stash" protocol to support secure post-processing of the output of the set intersection (e.g. statistical functions) which incur additional communication and computational overheads. Nevertheless, the results of [34] in Tables 6 and 7 serve well as a lower bound reference for the output functionality of arithmetic mean. Moreover, to optimize the efficiency when running the protocol of [34], we compute in Matlab the minimal number of mega-bins B required such that each mega-bin contains at most $max_b \leq 1024$ elements with probability under 2^{-40} for various set sizes n. The probability that there exists a bin with at least max_b elements given in [34] is bounded above by

$$B \sum_{i=max_b}^{3n} B^{-i} \binom{3n}{i} \left(1 - \frac{1}{B}\right)^{3n-i}.$$

Our computed minimum values of B are 19, 38, 75, 113 for $n = 5000, 10000, 20000, 30000$ respectively.

From the experimental results, *PSI-Stats* has a lower communication overhead by an average factor of 5.2× and incurs 5× less monetary cost compared to [34] as evidenced by Table 6. The results of Table 7 also demonstrates a much lower run time in a network bandwidth setting of 1 Mbps. Moreover, when the round-trip time is increased from 0.02 ms to 100 ms, the run time of [34] increases by 3.2 s and 3.84 s for set sizes of 2^{12} and 2^{16} respectively. In contrast, the run time increase for *PSI-Stats* is merely 0.3 s. Since the complexities of *PSI-Stats* scale linearly with respect to computation and communication, the comparison of monetary cost ratio is expected to be maintained at 5× for larger datasets.

6   Related Work

6.1   Existing PSI Protocols

An early PSI protocol is based upon the Diffie Hellman paradigm [26] which is also applicable in elliptic curve cryptography. A similar idea can be traced back to [40]. A method based on oblivious polynomial evaluation was introduced in [16,17]. An approach via blind RSA was presented in [11]. All the above methods are based on public-key cryptography.

Oblivious transfer (OT) extension was first introduced in [23]. The main objective of an OT extension is to enable the computation a large number of OT based off a smaller number along with symmetric cryptographic operations to achieve better running times. This technique engendered numerous OT-based PSI protocols. The notion of garbled bloom filter based on OT extension was coined in [13] and utilized to perform PSI. The main idea is to allow one of the parties to learn the bit-wise AND of two Bloom filters via OT. This outcome results in a valid Bloom filter for the set intersection. That was subsequently optimized to some extent in [36]. There are a number of other notable OT-based schemes presented in [18,25,30,33,36,37]. The particular work of [25] is based on an OT extension protocol found in [24].

Recently, threshold PSI protocols have been proposed [42,43]. The earlier work [42] leaks the intersection size, while the subsequent work [43] has no such leakage. Instead of revealing computation results of associated values, they suppress the output if the intersection set does not satisfy the agreed policy.

Generic multi-party protocols such as garbled circuits can also be used to compute PSI. The first such protocol involving garbled circuit appeared in [21] which was later improved in [36]. Other notable circuit-based PSI protocols are presented in [15,33–35]. The protocol of [10] can incorporate several approaches of 2PC beyond garbled circuits. Circuit-based approaches can typically serve for generic computation purposes. On the other hand, they result in larger communication overheads as compared to other custom-based PSI protocols.

The most related existing work in relation to this paper is that of Ion *et al.* [22] which considers the single special case where F is the sum. It should be noted that any natural attempts to convert the computation of sum to arithmetic mean by sending the set intersection size to the receiving party B violates the privacy requirements of the problem statement since the additional knowledge of cardinality can induce an inference attack. In contrast, our work here provides solutions to a large class of statistical functions F without this drawback. By doing so our protocols provide more flexible and comprehensive utilities.

7   Conclusion

We present *PSI-Stats* which supports the secure computations of various statistical functions in a privacy-preserving manner. The benefit of *PSI-Stats* having a substantially lower monetary cost and communication cost compared to circuit based PSI approaches is desirable in many business applications. This is also relevant in environments of low network bandwidths. We have noted from our experiments that the run time of all of our protocols is dominated by the time taken to perform encryption of each associated value. As such, *PSI-Stats* is highly parallelizable and the performance can be further enhanced when multi-threading is enabled. In addition, *PSI-Stats* can easily be extended to enable statistical outputs only if the size of the intersection set exceeds a pre-defined threshold value. In instances where the intersection set of the identifiers between the two parties is null or under a specified threshold size, party A can call for an early abort of the protocol. This feature has also appeared in [42] where a secret key cannot be recovered if the size is not reached, thereby prompting an abort.

Acknowledgements. We thank Sherman Chow and the anonymous reviewers for their helpful comments, as well as Benny Pinkas, Thomas Schneider, Oleksandr Tkachenko and Avishay Yanai for initially providing us with their codes of the implementation in [34]. This work was supported by the NUS-NCS Joint Laboratory for Cyber Security, Singapore.

References

1. IEEE 754-2019 - IEEE Standard for Floating-Point Arithmetic. standards.ieee.org
2. Kaggle. https://www.kaggle.com/uciml/default-of-credit-card-clients-dataset
3. Agrawal, R., Evfimievski, A., Srikant, R.: Information sharing across private databases. In: Proceedings of the 2003 ACM SIGMOD International Conference on Management of Data, pp. 86–97 (2003)
4. Atkinson, A.B.: On the measurement of inequality. J. Econ. Theor. **2**(3), 244–263 (1970)
5. Baldi, P., Baronio, R., Cristofaro, E.D., Gasti, P., Tsudik, G.: Countering GATTACA: efficient and secure testing of fully-sequenced human genomes. In: ACM Conference on Computer and Communications Security, pp. 691–702 (2011)
6. Barker, E.: Recommendation for key management part 1: general (revision 4). NIST Spec. Publ. **800**(57), 1–147 (2016)
7. Boneh, D., Goh, E.-J., Nissim, K.: Evaluating 2-DNF formulas on ciphertexts. In: Theory of Cryptography Conference, pp. 325–341 (2005)
8. Chase, M., Miao, P.: Private set intersection in the internet setting from lightweight oblivious prf. In: Annual International Cryptology Conference, CRYPTO 2020, pp. 34–63 (2020)
9. Cheon, J.H., Kim, A., Kim, M., Song, Y.: Homomorphic encryption for arithmetic of approximate numbers. In: ASIACRYPT 2017, pp. 409–437 (2017)
10. Ciampi, M., Orlandi, C.: Combining private set-intersection with secure two-party computation. In: International Conference on Security and Cryptography for Networks, pp. 464–482 (2018)

11. De Cristofaro, E., Tsudik, G.: Practical private set intersection protocols with linear complexity. In: Sion, R. (ed.) FC 2010. LNCS, vol. 6052, pp. 143–159. Springer, Heidelberg (2010). https://doi.org/10.1007/978-3-642-14577-3_13
12. Dheeru, D., Taniskidou, E.K.: UCI Machine Learning Repository (2017)
13. Dong, C., Chen, L., Wen. Z.: When private set intersection meets big data: an efficient and scalable protocol. In: Proceedings of the 2013 ACM SIGSAC Conference on Computer and Communications Security, CCS 2013, pp. 789–800 (2013)
14. Durlauf, S.N., Blume, L.E.: The New Palgrave Dictionary of Economics, vol. 6 (2008)
15. Falk, B.H., Noble, D., Ostrovsky, R.: Private set intersection with linear communication from general assumptions. In: Proceedings of the 18th ACM Workshop on Privacy in the Electronic Society, pp. 14–25 (2019)
16. Freedman, M.J., Hazay, C., Nissim, K., Pinkas, B.: Efficient set intersection with simulation-based security. J. Cryptol. **29**(1), 115–155 (2016)
17. Freedman, M.J., Nissim, K., Pinkas, B.: Efficient private matching and set intersection. In: Cachin, C., Camenisch, J.L. (eds.) EUROCRYPT 2004. LNCS, vol. 3027, pp. 1–19. Springer, Heidelberg (2004). https://doi.org/10.1007/978-3-540-24676-3_1
18. Garimella, G., Mohassel, P., Rosulek, M., Sadeghian, S., Singh, J.: Private set operations from oblivious switching. In: Garay, J.A. (ed.) PKC 2021. LNCS, vol. 12711, pp. 591–617. Springer, Cham (2021). https://doi.org/10.1007/978-3-030-75248-4_21
19. Goldreich, O., Micali, S., Wigderson, A.: How to play any mental game. In: Proceedings of the 19th Annual ACM Symposium on Theory of Computing, pp. 218–229 (1987)
20. Hallgren, P., Orlandi, C., Sabelfeld, A.: PrivatePool: privacy-preserving ridesharing. In: 2017 IEEE 30th Computer Security Foundations Symposium (CSF), pp. 276–291 (2017)
21. Huang, Y., Evans, D., Katz, J.: Private set intersection: are garbled circuits better than custom protocols? In: Network and Distributed System Security, NDSS 2012 (2012)
22. Ion, M., et al.: On deploying secure computing: private intersection-sum-with-cardinality. In: IEEE European Symposium on Security and Privacy, EuroS&P 2020, pp. 370–389 (2020)
23. Ishai, Y., Kilian, J., Nissim, K., Petrank, E.: Extending oblivious transfers efficiently. In: Boneh, D. (ed.) CRYPTO 2003. LNCS, vol. 2729, pp. 145–161. Springer, Heidelberg (2003). https://doi.org/10.1007/978-3-540-45146-4_9
24. Kolesnikov, V., Kumaresan, R.: Improved OT extension for transferring short secrets. In: Canetti, R., Garay, J.A. (eds.) CRYPTO 2013. LNCS, vol. 8043, pp. 54–70. Springer, Heidelberg (2013). https://doi.org/10.1007/978-3-642-40084-1_4
25. Kolesnikov, V., Kumaresan, R., Rosulek, M., Trieu, N.: Efficient batched oblivious PRF with applications to private set intersection. In: Proceedings of the 2016 ACM SIGSAC Conference on Computer and Communications Security, CCS 2016, pp. 818–829 (2016)
26. Meadows, C.: A more efficient cryptographic matchmaking protocol for use in the absence of a continuously available third party. In: Symposium on Security and Privacy, S&P 1986, pp. 134–137 (1986)
27. Moro, S., Laureano, R., Cortez, P.: Using data mining for bank direct marketing: an application of the CRISP-DM methodology. In: Proceedings of the European Simulation and Modelling Conference, ESM 2011, pp. 117–121 (2011)

604   J. H. M. Ying et al.

28. Nagaraja, S., Mittal, P., Hong, C., Caesar, M., Borisov, N.: BotGrep: finding P2P bots with structured graph analysis. In: USENIX Security Symposium, pp. 95–110 (2010)
29. Narayanan, A., Thiagarajan, N., Lakhani, M., Hamburg, M., Boneh, D.: Location privacy via private proximity testing. In: NDSS, vol. 11 (2011)
30. Orrù, M., Orsini, E., Scholl, P.: Actively secure 1-out-of-N OT extension with application to private set intersection. In: Handschuh, H. (ed.) CT-RSA 2017. LNCS, vol. 10159, pp. 381–396. Springer, Cham (2017). https://doi.org/10.1007/978-3-319-52153-4_22
31. Paillier, P.: Public-key cryptosystems based on composite degree residuosity classes. In: Stern, J. (ed.) EUROCRYPT 1999. LNCS, vol. 1592, pp. 223–238. Springer, Heidelberg (1999). https://doi.org/10.1007/3-540-48910-X_16
32. Pinkas, B., Rosulek, M., Trieu, N., Yanai, A.: SpOT-Light: lightweight private set intersection from sparse OT extension. In: Boldyreva, A., Micciancio, D. (eds.) CRYPTO 2019. LNCS, vol. 11694, pp. 401–431. Springer, Cham (2019). https://doi.org/10.1007/978-3-030-26954-8_13
33. Pinkas, B., Schneider, T., Segev, G., Zohner, M.: Phasing: private set intersection using permutation-based hashing. In: 24th USENIX Security Symposium, USENIX Security 2015, pp. 515–530 (2015)
34. Pinkas, B., Schneider, T., Tkachenko, O., Yanai, A.: Efficient circuit-based PSI with linear communication. In: Ishai, Y., Rijmen, V. (eds.) EUROCRYPT 2019. LNCS, vol. 11478, pp. 122–153. Springer, Cham (2019). https://doi.org/10.1007/978-3-030-17659-4_5
35. Pinkas, B., Schneider, T., Weinert, C., Wieder, U.: Efficient circuit-based PSI via Cuckoo hashing. In: Nielsen, J.B., Rijmen, V. (eds.) EUROCRYPT 2018. LNCS, vol. 10822, pp. 125–157. Springer, Cham (2018). https://doi.org/10.1007/978-3-319-78372-7_5
36. Pinkas, B., Schneider, T., Zohner, M.: Faster private set intersection based on OT extension. In: USENIX Security Symposium, vol. 14, pp. 797–812 (2014)
37. Pinkas, B., Schneider, T., Zohner, M.: Scalable private set intersection based on OT extension. ACM Trans. Priv. Secur. (TOPS) **21**(2), 1–35 (2018)
38. Rivest, R.L., Shamir, A., Adleman, L.: A method for obtaining digital signatures and public-key cryptosystems. Commun. ACM **21**(2), 120–126 (1978)
39. Schneider, T., Zohner, M.: GMW vs. Yao? Efficient secure two-party computation with low depth circuits. In: Sadeghi, A.-R. (ed.) FC 2013. LNCS, vol. 7859, pp. 275–292. Springer, Heidelberg (2013). https://doi.org/10.1007/978-3-642-39884-1_23
40. Shamir, A.: On the power of commutativity in cryptography. In: de Bakker, J., van Leeuwen, J. (eds.) ICALP 1980. LNCS, vol. 85, pp. 582–595. Springer, Heidelberg (1980). https://doi.org/10.1007/3-540-10003-2_100
41. Yao, A.C.C.: How to generate and exchange secrets. In: 27th Annual Symposium on Foundations of Computer Science, SFCS 1986, pp. 162–167 (1986)
42. Zhao, Y., Chow, S.S.M.: Are you the one to share? Secret transfer with access structure. Proc. Priv. Enhancing Technol. **2017**(1), 149–169 (2017)
43. Zhao, Y., Chow, S.S.M.: Can you find the one for me? In: Proceedings of the Workshop on Privacy in the Electronic Society, pp. 54–65 (2018)

Efficient Oblivious Evaluation Protocol and Conditional Disclosure of Secrets for DFA

Kittiphop Phalakarn[1](✉), Nuttapong Attrapadung[2], and Kanta Matsuura[1]

[1] The University of Tokyo, Tokyo, Japan
{kittipop,kanta}@iis.u-tokyo.ac.jp
[2] National Institute of Advanced Industrial Science and Technology, Tokyo, Japan
n.attrapadung@aist.go.jp

Abstract. In oblivious finite automata evaluation, one party holds a private automaton, and the other party holds a private string of characters. The objective is to let the parties know whether the string is accepted by the automaton or not, while keeping their inputs secret. The applications include DNA searching, pattern matching, and more. Most of the previous works are based on asymmetric cryptographic primitives, such as homomorphic encryption and oblivious transfer. These primitives are significantly slower than symmetric ones. Moreover, some protocols also require several rounds of interaction. As our main contribution, we propose an oblivious finite automata evaluation protocol via conditional disclosure of secrets (CDS), using one (potentially malicious) outsourcing server. This results in a constant-round protocol, and no heavy asymmetric-key primitives are needed. Our protocol is based on a building block called "an oblivious CDS scheme for deterministic finite automata" which we also propose in this paper. In addition, we propose a standard CDS scheme for deterministic finite automata as an independent interest.

Keywords: Finite automata · Conditional disclosure of secrets · Multi-client verifiable computation · Secure multi-party computation

1 Introduction

In a problem of oblivious finite automata evaluation, one party holds a private automaton, and the other party holds a private string of characters. The objective is to let the parties know whether the string is accepted by the automaton or not, while keeping their inputs secret.

The applications include DNA matching, string searching, password format validation, spam email detection, log files audition, and more. As stated in [39], DNA technology can help us predict a probability that a patient will develop a specific disease, and predict the result of the therapy. However, revealing personal DNA sequence to public can be harmful. An undesired parental relationship can be discovered, or an employee may be rejected to work with a company due to a

© Springer Nature Switzerland AG 2022
G. Ateniese and D. Venturi (Eds.): ACNS 2022, LNCS 13269, pp. 605–625, 2022.
https://doi.org/10.1007/978-3-031-09234-3_30

probability to develop some diseases. Thus, DNA matching should be performed in an oblivious way. This is also applied to other sensitive information such as passwords, email contents, and log files.

As an example, a patient may want to know if there is any anomaly in his or her DNA sequence. Since the DNA sequence can be considered as private information, the patient should not reveal his or her DNA in clear. On the other hand, a doctor has the anomaly pattern modeled with regular language. The pattern can be considered as a valuable research insight, and should also be kept secret. To let one or both of the parties know whether the DNA sequence matches the pattern, oblivious finite automata evaluation is perfectly suitable here. As another example, an email message and a malware pattern can be considered as sensitive information. To obliviously check whether the email contains a malware or not, the oblivious finite automata evaluation can also be used in the same way.

However, almost all of the previous works are constructed based on public key cryptographic primitives, such as homomorphic encryption and oblivious transfer (OT). These asymmetric-key operations (e.g. exponentiation) are some orders of magnitude slower than the symmetric-key operations. In addition, some of the previous works require several rounds of interaction.

On the other hand, generic secure multi-party computation protocol can also be used, but their performance can be worse compared to specifically designed methods. Executing string matching algorithm with Yao's garbled circuit protocol [29,41] can be inefficient due to the number of comparisons involved in the dynamic programming technique. Using information-theoretic protocol is also possible [11,21], but the process will be interactive, and the round complexity will depend on the size of the circuit, which can be large in this case.

A verifiable oblivious finite automata evaluation protocol in an outsourced setting is also an open problem stated in [42].

1.1   Our Contributions

In this paper, we propose an oblivious finite automata evaluation protocol via conditional disclosure of secrets (CDS). This results in a constant-round protocol, and no heavy asymmetric-key primitives are needed. We claim three contributions of our work as follows.

Oblivious CDS for DFA. We present the first CDS scheme for the class of deterministic finite automata (DFA). DFA allows to compute satisfiability for regular languages, and therefore is suitable for the aforementioned applications (e.g., DNA matching). Previous work on CDS were proposed for some other classes; for example, equality, inner product predicate [15], and set intersection [7]. To the best of our knowledge, we are the first to consider CDS for DFA.

As a short introduction to (standard) CDS scheme for DFA, the scheme involves two senders and a receiver. One sender has a DFA, the other sender has an input string, and the receiver knows both the DFA and the input string. The two senders also have a common secret and a common randomness which are not known to the receiver. Each sender can send only one message to the receiver without any communication with the other sender. The goal of the CDS scheme for DFA is to let the receiver know the secret if and only if the automaton accepts the input string.

In this paper, we propose an *oblivious* CDS scheme for DFA. The main difference between the oblivious CDS and the standard CDS is the information leaked to the receiver. In the standard CDS, the receiver knows the automaton and the string, and knows whether the automaton accepts the string or not, while the receiver in the oblivious CDS will not know. Thus, oblivious CDS is more suitable for privacy-preserving applications.

Oblivious DFA Evaluation Protocol via CDS. We propose an oblivious DFA evaluation protocol using the oblivious CDS scheme for DFA as a building block. The advantage of our protocol is that it is constant-round and non-interactive. Using CDS as the underlying scheme can be seen as a trade-off between adding one (potentially malicious) outsourcing server and using asymmetric cryptographic primitives.

Standard CDS for DFA. As an independent interest, we also propose a standard CDS scheme for DFA. To the best of our knowledge, converting CDS for other computation classes to CDS for DFA is not straightforward; ours is the first explicit construction for such CDS for DFA.

1.2   Our Approaches

One of our goals is to achieve a constant-round protocol for oblivious finite automata evaluation. Previous protocols [14,35,42] that perform in constant rounds for a similar task all use the idea of garbled circuits and require asymmetric-key primitives such as homomorphic encryption or oblivious transfer. Intuitively, these asymmetric-key primitives play an essential role in hiding private inputs from one party to the other party in the two-party settings.

Our approach to mitigate the need for asymmetric-key primitives is to utilize an additional (potentially malicious) outsourcing server. We observe that oblivious CDS [7] fits wells in this context as it allows an outsourcing server to compute a function obliviously without knowing the inputs or the result. Moreover, known oblivious CDS schemes do not require costly asymmetric-key operations. However, all the previous CDS constructions do not support the class of finite automata (even for standard CDS schemes). To this end, we hence propose the first oblivious CDS for DFA.

We adapt the garbled circuit techniques from Frikken [14] to construct our oblivious CDS for DFA. The construction includes a pseudorandom function (PRF). We then use our oblivious CDS as a building block for our oblivious DFA evaluation protocol, based on the multi-client verifiable computation framework of Bhadauria and Hazay [7]. Note that the CDS schemes in [7] consider predicates of equality and set intersection, which are different from DFA.

For the standard CDS, we extend the techniques in the ABE context from [2] that convert DFA into span programs, and adapt to the CDS context. Our construction of standard CDS is information theoretic. (Our oblivious CDS may imply a standard CDS, but that construction will require a PRF.)

1.3 Related Works

While previous studies on oblivious evaluation for DFA were somewhat peaking about 10 years ago or more [8,14,35] (with recent improvements such as [42] being somewhat less major), there are some renewed interests very recently (in 2019–2021) in secure computation regarding DFA (and a related class, namely, NC1), in the context of ABE in top conference papers such as [1,2,22,23,28]. These reflect theoretical and practical interests towards secure DFA computations. We hope that our work offers practical improvements for oblivious DFA evaluation as our protocol is the first explicit constant-round protocol that does not require expensive public-key operations.

In this subsection, we briefly describe related works as follows.

Oblivious Finite Automata Evaluation. The problem of oblivious DFA evaluation was first studied by Troncoso-Pastoriza et al. [39]. Their protocol is based on additive secret sharing, homomorphic encryption, and oblivious transfer. At the start of each round (corresponding to each character in the input string), both parties hold shares of the current state of the automaton. Homomorphic encryption and oblivious transfer are then applied in order to compute the shares of the next state. It is obvious that the number of communication rounds is linear in the length of the input string. The protocol also requires $O(|x||Q|)$ modular exponentiations (where $|x|$ is the length of the input string and $|Q|$ is the total number of states of the DFA), which can be a performance drawback.

The second work proposed by Frikken [14] tried to reduce the number of rounds by using the idea of Yao's garbled circuit [41]. They also reduce the number of modular exponentiations to $O(|x|)$. It is shown in [14] that their protocol is 2 to 3 orders of magnitude faster than [39]. However, the protocol is still based on oblivious transfer.

The first protocol that is secure against malicious adversaries is proposed by Gennaro et al. [18]. It is based on public-key encryption and zero knowledge proof of knowledge. The protocol requires several rounds of interactions. Another work that discussed the security in malicious setting is the work of Mohassel et al. [35]. Using similar idea from [14], they proposed an oblivious evaluation protocol for DFA with alphabets $\{0,1\}$. The protocol is based on OT extension [26] against malicious adversaries.

Laud and Willemson [27] modeled the transition function as a polynomial, and then evaluate it privately using arithmetic black box (ABB) model. This ABB model can be realized by either secret sharing, homomorphic encryption, or other primitives. If information theoretic primitive such as secret sharing is used, the protocol is also information theoretic. However, performing secure multiplication on secret shares requires several rounds of interactions.

More previous works include the work of Di Crescenzo et al. [13] which is based on conditional transfer protocol, and the work of Zhao et al. [42] which considers a setting with additively shared input string.

Oblivious Finite Automata Evaluation with Outsourcing Servers. The protocol proposed by Blanton and Aliasgari [8] generalizes the work of [39] to the

Table 1. Comparison between oblivious DFA evaluation protocols

Protocol	Primitives	Use Asym.	Parties	Round	Comm. Cost	Security
Troncoso et al. [39]	SS, HE, OT	Y	2	$O(|x|)$	$O(|x|(|Q| + |\Sigma|))$	SH
Frikken [14]	OT, PRF	Y	2	$O(1)$	$O(|x||Q||\Sigma|)$	SH
Gennaro et al. [18]	HE, ZK	Y	2	$O(|x|)$	$O(|x||Q||\Sigma|)$	M
Mohassel et al. [35]	OT, PRG	Y	2	$O(1)$	$O(|x||Q||\Sigma|)$	M
Laud&Willemson [27]	ABB	Y/N	2+	$O(|Q||\Sigma|)$	$O(|x||Q||\Sigma|)$	SH/M
Crescenzo et al. [13]	PRF	Y	2	$O(|x||Q||\Sigma|)$	$O(|x||Q||\Sigma|)$	SH
Zhao et al. [42]	HE, PRG	Y	2	$O(1)$	$O(|x||Q||\Sigma|)$	SH
Blanton&Aliasgari [8]	SS, OT	Y	4+	$O(|x|)$	$O(|x||Q||\Sigma|)$	SH
Wei&Reiter [40]	HE	Y	3	$O(|x|)$	$O(|x||Q||\Sigma|)$	SH, M*
Ours (Section 4)	PRF	N	3	$O(1)$	$O(|x||Q||\Sigma|)$	SH, M†

Asym: Asymmetric-key Primitives   SS: Secret Sharing   HE: Homomorphic Encryption
OT: Oblivious Transfer   PRF: Pseudorandom Function   PRG: Pseudorandom Generator
ZK: Zero-Knowledge Proof   ABB: Arithmetic Black Box (can be implemented from SS or HE)
SH: Semi-honest M: Malicious   Y/N and SH/M: Depend on the building block
*Client can be semi-honest, server can be malicious
†String and automaton holders can be semi-honest, outsourcing server can be malicious

outsourced setting. To keep all the inputs private, their work uses a secret sharing technique to outsource the automaton and the input string to two computing servers. These servers are assumed to be semi-honest. Oblivious transfer is used as a building block. In the case that we want to outsource the inputs to more than two servers, threshold homomorphic encryption must be applied.

Another work in outsourced setting is proposed by Wei and Reiter [40]. In their protocol, a client with a DFA wants to execute it on encrypted string stored on a cloud server. They model the transition function as a polynomial, and then evaluate it privately using homomorphic encryption. The decryption key from the string owner is shared between the client and the cloud server.

We note that almost all of the previous works (including both with and without outsourcing servers) are based on asymmetric cryptographic primitives. Some also require several round of communication and interaction. Comparison between the oblivious evaluation protocols is presented in Table 1.

CDS. Conditional disclosure of secrets (CDS) was firstly proposed in [19] as a building block for symmetrically private information retrieval system (SPIR). Their CDS supports the condition equivalent to monotone access structure of a secret sharing scheme. CDS is also used to construct priced oblivious transfer (i.e., SPIR with cost for each item) in [3]. In addition, CDS is used to reduce share size of secret sharing schemes [4–6,30,32]. Some works tried to relate CDS to attribute-based encryption (ABE) [15]. Recently, the work of [7] proposed new variants of CDS, including private CDS and oblivious CDS. The CDS schemes of [7] are for equality and set intersection classes. The main application of these variants is a multi-client verifiable computation protocol. We list some CDS schemes in the literature in Table 2 (note that this list is not exhaustive). To the best of our knowledge, there is no known CDS for DFA until our work.

Table 2. Comparison between CDS schemes

CDS Scheme	Type	Functionalities	Security
Gertner et al. [19]	Standard	Monotone access structure	Info. theoretic
Gay et al. [15]	Standard	Equality, Inner product, Index predicate, Prefix, Disjointness	Info. theoretic
Liu et al. [31]	Standard	Index predicate	Info. theoretic
Bhadauria&Hazay [7]	Oblivious	Equality	Info. theoretic
Bhadauria&Hazay [7]	Private	Equality, Inequality, Set intersection cardinality	Computational
Ours (Section 3)	Oblivious	DFA	Computational
Ours (Section 5)	Standard	DFA	Info. theoretic

Multi-client Verifiable Computation. Gennaro et al. [17] was the first to propose the definition of verifiable computation protocol. Their construction, based on Yao's garbled circuit, is only for two parties, a client and an outsourcing server. The definition was then generalized to multi-client setting by Choi et al. in [9]. Using non-interactive key exchange (NIKE) protocol, their protocol is secure against malicious server, and semi-honest clients. Gordon et al. [24] later strengthened the security guarantee to malicious clients setting, using homomorphic encryption and attribute-based encryption as building blocks. It can be seen that the existing verifiable computation protocols at that time are quite complex. Recently, Bhadauria and Hazay [7] proposed two-client verifiable computation protocol based on various types of CDS. Some of the advantages provided by CDS are simplicity of the verification, and no need for asymmetric-key primitives.

1.4   Organization

After reviewing preliminaries in Sect. 2, we propose an oblivious CDS scheme for DFA in Sect. 3. An oblivious DFA evaluation protocol via CDS is presented in Sect. 4. As an independent interest, we propose a standard CDS scheme for DFA in Sect. 5. Finally, Sect. 6 concludes the paper. Proofs are provided in the full version.

2   Preliminaries

In this section, we review related background knowledge, including finite automata, conditional disclosure of secrets, and multi-clients verifiable computation. Definitions of PRF, coin-tossing protocol, and monotone span program are standard, and are provided in the full version. Matrices are denoted with bold capitals. We denote $\{1, \ldots, n\}$ and $\{a, a+1, \ldots, b\}$ with $[n]$ and $[a, b]$, respectively. The symbol $\approx$ denotes standard indistinguishability between two distributions, which can be information theoretic or computational depending on the case.

2.1   Finite Automata

In this paper, we consider deterministic finite automata (DFA), which is a special case of nondeterministic finite automata (NFA).

A deterministic finite automaton is defined by a 5-tuple $M = (Q, \Sigma, \Delta, q_0, F)$ where Q is a finite set of states, Σ is a finite set of all possible alphabets, $\Delta : Q \times \Sigma \rightarrow Q$ is a transition function which outputs the next state from the current state and the given alphabet, $q_0 \in Q$ is an initial state, and $F \subseteq Q$ is a set of accepting states. (In case of a nondeterministic finite automaton, the transition function is generalized to $\Delta : Q \times \Sigma \rightarrow 2^Q$.) In this work, we assume that states are numbered from 1 to $|Q|$ where $q_0 = 1$, and Σ can be numbered from 0 to $|\Sigma| - 1$. In Sect. 5, we also assume that there is only one accepting state, $F = \{|Q|\}$. Any DFA can be transformed to satisfy these conditions.[1]

A string of alphabets $x = x_0 x_1 \cdots x_{n-1} \in \Sigma^n$ is accepted by the automaton M if there is a sequence of states $q_0 q_1 \cdots q_n$ such that $q_i = \Delta(q_{i-1}, x_{i-1})$ for all $i \in [n]$, and $q_n \in F$. We say $M(x) = 1$ if M accepts x, and $M(x) = 0$ otherwise.

2.2   Conditional Disclosure of Secrets

In our paper, we only focus on 3-party CDS, where Alice and Bob are senders, and Claire is a receiver. Alice has an input a from the domain A, a secret s from $\{0,1\}^\kappa$, and a randomness r from the domain R. Bob has an input b from the domain B, the same secret s, and the same randomness r. For the standard CDS, Claire only knows the inputs a and b. Everyone agrees on a function $f : A \times B \rightarrow \{0,1\}$. Each of Alice and Bob can send only one message to Claire without any communication to each other. The goal of the scheme is to let Claire learn the secret s if $f(a,b) = 1$, and let Claire learn nothing otherwise. The definition of CDS is as follows.

Definition 1 (CDS). *Let* $f : A \times B \rightarrow \{0,1\}$ *be a condition,* $s \in \{0,1\}^\kappa$ *be a secret, and* $r \in R$ *be a randomness chosen randomly with uniform distribution. Let* $\mathsf{Enc_A}$ *and* $\mathsf{Enc_B}$ *be PPT encoding algorithms, and* Dec *be a deterministic decoding algorithm. The correctness and secrecy properties must hold as follows.*

Correctness: For all inputs $(a,b) \in A \times B$ *where* $f(a,b) = 1$,

$$Pr[\mathsf{Dec}(a, b, \mathsf{Enc_A}(a, s, r), \mathsf{Enc_B}(b, s, r)) \neq s] \leq \mathsf{negl}(\kappa).$$

Secrecy: There exists a polynomial time algorithm Sim *such that for every input* $(a,b) \in A \times B$ *where* $f(a,b) = 0$ *and a secret* $s \in \{0,1\}^\kappa$, *the following distributions are indistinguishable.*

$$\{\mathsf{Sim}(a,b)\}_{a \in A, b \in B} \approx \{\mathsf{Enc_A}(a, s, r), \mathsf{Enc_B}(b, s, r)\}_{a \in A, b \in B}.$$

One useful variant of CDS called as **oblivious CDS** is proposed in [7]. In this setting, Claire does not know a and b. Informally explained, Claire learns a value at the end of the scheme, but Claire will not know whether the condition is satisfied, or whether the decoded value is equal to the secret. The definition of the oblivious CDS from [7] is as follows. For the definition of secrecy of oblivious CDS, we use indistinguishability based definition, which is equivalent to the real-ideal definition in [7].

---

[1] This can be done by adding one special character marking the end of the string.

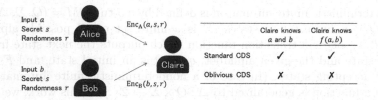

Fig. 1. Standard CDS and oblivious CDS

Definition 2 (Oblivious CDS). *Let* $f : A \times B \to \{0,1\}$ *be a condition,* $s \in \{0,1\}^\kappa$ *be a secret, and* $r \in R$ *be a randomness chosen randomly with uniform distribution. Let* $\mathsf{Enc_A}$ *and* $\mathsf{Enc_B}$ *be PPT encoding algorithms, and* Dec *be a deterministic decoding algorithm. The properties must hold as follows.*

Correctness: For all inputs $(a,b) \in A \times B$ *where* $f(a,b) = 1$,

$$Pr[\mathsf{Dec}(\mathsf{Enc_A}(a,s,r), \mathsf{Enc_B}(b,s,r)) \neq s] \leq \mathsf{negl}(\kappa).$$

Indistinguishability: There exists a polynomial time algorithm Sim *such that for every input* $(a,b) \in A \times B$ *and a secret* $s \in \{0,1\}^\kappa$, *the following distributions are indistinguishable.*

$$\{\mathsf{Sim}(1^{|a|}, 1^{|b|}, \mathsf{Dec}(\mathsf{Enc_A}(a,s,r), \mathsf{Enc_B}(b,s,r)))\}_{a \in A, b \in B}$$
$$\approx \{\mathsf{Enc_A}(a,s,r), \mathsf{Enc_B}(b,s,r)\}_{a \in A, b \in B}.$$

The diagram of the standard and oblivious CDS is shown in Fig. 1.

2.3 Multi-client Verifiable Computation

Similar to [7,9], we consider a multi-client verifiable computation (MVC) setting where a set of clients outsources the computation to an untrusted computing server. We focus on a non-interactive setting where clients do not interact with each other after the setup phase. In our work, we consider a setting with semi-honest clients and a malicious server (assume no collusion). The clients should follow the protocol perfectly, while the outsourcing server may try to change the computation result. The definition of MVC from [7,9] is as follows.

Definition 3 (MVC). *Consider a setting where each client has an input* α_i, *and the goal is to compute* $f(\alpha_1, \ldots, \alpha_m)$. *The MVC protocol consists of four algorithms.*

- $\delta \leftarrow \mathsf{Setup}$: *Generate a common random string* δ *for all clients.*
- $(\widetilde{\alpha}_i, \tau_i) \leftarrow \mathsf{Input}(\alpha_i, \delta, 1^\lambda)$: *For each client, using* α_i, δ, *and security parameter* 1^λ *as inputs, this algorithm outputs an encoded input* $\widetilde{\alpha}_i$ *and the decoding secret* τ_i *kept private by the client.*
- $(\beta_1, \ldots, \beta_m) \leftarrow \mathsf{Compute}(f, \widetilde{\alpha_1}, \ldots, \widetilde{\alpha_m})$: *Using the function description and the encoded inputs, the computing server executes this algorithm to generate encoded outputs* β_i.

$\mathsf{PrivClient}^{\gamma}_{A,i}(1^{\lambda}) :$

$(\alpha^0_1, \ldots, \alpha^0_m), (\alpha^1_1, \ldots, \alpha^1_m) \leftarrow A_0(1^{\lambda})$
  where $\alpha^0_i = \alpha^1_i$
  and $f(\alpha^0_1, \ldots, \alpha^0_m) = f(\alpha^1_1, \ldots, \alpha^1_m)$
$\delta \leftarrow \mathsf{Setup}$
$(\widetilde{\alpha_j}, \tau_j) \leftarrow \mathsf{Input}(\alpha^{\gamma}_j, \delta, 1^{\lambda})$ for all $j \in [m]$
$(\beta_1, \ldots, \beta_m) \leftarrow \mathsf{Compute}(f, \widetilde{\alpha_1}, \ldots, \widetilde{\alpha_m})$
$\gamma' \leftarrow A_1(\beta_i, \tau_i)$
return γ'

$\mathsf{PrivServer}^{\gamma}_{A}(1^{\lambda}) :$

$(\alpha^0_1, \ldots, \alpha^0_m), (\alpha^1_1, \ldots, \alpha^1_m) \leftarrow A_0(1^{\lambda})$
$\delta \leftarrow \mathsf{Setup}$
$(\widetilde{\alpha_j}, \tau_j) \leftarrow \mathsf{Input}(\alpha^{\gamma}_j, \delta, 1^{\lambda})$ for all $j \in [m]$
$\gamma' \leftarrow A_1(\widetilde{\alpha_1}, \ldots, \widetilde{\alpha_m})$
return γ'

Fig. 2. Privacy for multi-client verifiable computation

– $y \cup \{\bot\} \leftarrow \mathsf{Verify}(\beta_i, \tau_i)$: *For each client, using β_i and τ_i as inputs, this algorithm generates an output y (which supposes to be $f(\alpha_1, \ldots, \alpha_m)$), or outputs a symbol $\bot$ in case that the server attempted to cheat.*

We are interested in the protocol that is sound and private.

Soundness: For all inputs $(\alpha_1, \ldots, \alpha_m)$ and a malicious server A, let $\delta \leftarrow \mathsf{Setup}$, $(\widetilde{\alpha_i}, \tau_i) \leftarrow \mathsf{Input}(\alpha_i, \delta, 1^{\lambda})$, $(\beta_1, \ldots, \beta_m) \leftarrow A(f, \widetilde{\alpha_1}, \ldots, \widetilde{\alpha_m})$, and $y \cup \{\bot\} \leftarrow \mathsf{Verify}(\beta_i, \tau_i)$ for all $i \in [m]$. It must hold that

$$Pr[y \neq f(\alpha_1, \ldots, \alpha_m)] \leq negl(\lambda).$$

Privacy Against the Clients: We consider a setting with adversarial i-th client. From the security game in Fig. 2, the MVC is private against the client if

$$|\Pr[\mathsf{PrivClient}^0_{A,i}(1^{\lambda}) = 1] - \Pr[\mathsf{PrivClient}^1_{A,i}(1^{\lambda}) = 1]| \leq negl(\lambda).$$

Privacy Against the Server: We consider a setting with adversarial server. From the security game in Fig. 2, the MVC is private against the server if

$$|\Pr[\mathsf{PrivServer}^0_A(1^{\lambda}) = 1] - \Pr[\mathsf{PrivServer}^1_A(1^{\lambda}) = 1]| \leq negl(\lambda).$$

3   Oblivious CDS for DFA

In this section, we propose an oblivious CDS scheme for DFA, which is used as a building block to construct an oblivious DFA evaluation protocol in the next section.

In the setting of an oblivious CDS scheme for DFA, Alice has a private DFA M, Bob has a private input string x, and both have a common secret s and a common randomness r. On the other hand, Claire does not have any inputs. The condition is defined as $f(M, x) = 1$ if M accepts x, and $f(M, x) = 0$ otherwise. At the end of the scheme, Claire should learn the secret if and only if M accepts x. Our construction is based on the idea of garbled transition matrix from [14]. The proposed scheme is shown in Fig. 3.

Oblivious CDS scheme for DFA

Input:

- Alice has a DFA $M = (Q, \Sigma, \Delta, q_0, F)$, a secret s, and a randomness r.
- Bob has an input string $x = x_0 x_1 \cdots x_{n-1}$, a secret s, and a randomness r.
- Claire has no input.

Algorithm:

1. For each $t \in [0, n-1]$, Alice randomly generates a state permutation function $\pi_t : Q \to Q$ and a character permutation function $\phi_t : \Sigma \to \Sigma$ from the randomness r.
2. For each $t \in [0, n-1]$, Alice extracts a garbled state key $k^{\text{state}}_{t, \pi_t(q)}$ for each $q \in Q$, and a garbled character key $k^{\text{char}}_{t, \phi_t(\sigma)}$ for each $\sigma \in \Sigma$ from the randomness r.
3. For each $t \in [0, n-2]$, $q \in Q$, and $\sigma \in \Sigma$, Alice randomly generates a garbled transition matrix element

$$g_{t, \pi_t(q), \phi_t(\sigma)} = H(k^{\text{state}}_{t, \pi_t(q)}, k^{\text{char}}_{t, \phi_t(\sigma)}) \oplus (k^{\text{state}}_{t+1, \pi_{t+1}(\Delta(q, \sigma))} || \pi_{t+1}(\Delta(q, \sigma))).$$

For each $q \in Q$, and $\sigma \in \Sigma$, Alice generates a garbled transition matrix element of the last step. If $\Delta(q, \sigma) \in F$, then

$$g_{n-1, \pi_{n-1}(q), \phi_{n-1}(\sigma)} = H(k^{\text{state}}_{n-1, \pi_{n-1}(q)}, k^{\text{char}}_{n-1, \phi_{n-1}(\sigma)}) \oplus (w || mw + s)$$

where w and m are generated from the randomness r. If $\Delta(q, \sigma) \notin F$, then

$$g_{n-1, \pi_{n-1}(q), \phi_{n-1}(\sigma)} = H(k^{\text{state}}_{n-1, \pi_{n-1}(q)}, k^{\text{char}}_{n-1, \phi_{n-1}(\sigma)}) \oplus (c || d)$$

where (c, d) is a random point not on the line $P(\chi) = m\chi + s$. This point (c, d) is not known to Bob.
4. Alice sends the garbled transition matrix $\{g_{t, \pi_t(q), \phi_t(\sigma)}\}_{t, q, \sigma}$ and the garbled state key of the first state $k^{\text{state}}_{0, \pi_0(q_0)}$ together with $\pi_0(q_0)$ to Claire.
5. For each $t \in [0, n-1]$, Bob generates the character permutation function $\phi_t : \Sigma \to \Sigma$, and extracts the garbled character key $k^{\text{char}}_{t, \phi_t(x_t)}$ from the randomness r in the same way as Alice.
6. Bob randomly chooses a point $(z, mz + s)$ where $z \neq w$ is totally random, and m is generated from the randomness r. Note that Alice does not know this point, and this point is different from Alice's point.
7. Bob sends $(\phi_t(x_t), k^{\text{char}}_{t, \phi_t(x_t)})$ for each $t \in [0, n-1]$, and $(z, mz + s)$ to Claire.
8. For each $t \in [0, n-1]$, Claire, with current permuted state $\pi_t(q)$, permuted character $\phi_t(x_t)$, garbled state key $k^{\text{state}}_{t, \pi_t(q)}$, and garbled character key $k^{\text{char}}_{t, \phi_t(x_t)}$, computes the next permuted state and state key

$$(k^{\text{state}}_{t+1, \pi_{t+1}(\Delta(q, x_t))} || \pi_{t+1}(\Delta(q, x_t))) = g_{t, \pi_t(q), \phi_t(x_t)} \oplus H(k^{\text{state}}_{t, \pi_t(q)}, k^{\text{char}}_{t, \phi_t(x_t)}),$$

and in the last round discovers

$$(i || j) = g_{n-1, \pi_{n-1}(q), \phi_{n-1}(x_{n-1})} \oplus H(k^{\text{state}}_{n-1, \pi_{n-1}(q)}, k^{\text{char}}_{n-1, \phi_{n-1}(x_{n-1})}).$$

9. Claire interpolates the points (i, j) from the garbled matrix and $(z, mz + s)$ from Bob to find the y-intercept. Claire outputs this value as s'.

Fig. 3. Oblivious CDS scheme for DFA

As an overview, the scheme can be divided into two parts. In the first part, Alice generates a garbled version of the DFA M, and Bob generates keys corresponding to the input string x. Claire, who receives the garbled transition matrix and keys, can recover an intermediate result embedded inside the garbled matrix. This recovered intermediate result depends on the condition of M and x. We use state permutation functions to hide the automaton structure, and use character permutation functions to hide the input string. The suitable state and character permutations can be as simple as $\pi_t(i) = ((i + u_t) \bmod |Q|) + 1$ and $\phi_t(i) = (i + v_t) \bmod |\Sigma|$ where u_t and v_t are random shift values. Since Claire can only decode the value corresponding to the state at each step, and cannot know whether the final state is an accepting state or not, Claire does not know anything from the intermediate result of the garbled matrix.

In the second part, Claire decodes the secret from the intermediate result. The intermediate result that Claire can recover will be a point on a 2D plane. Before sending messages to Claire, Alice and Bob agree on the same linear equation $P(\chi) = m\chi + s$ where m is generated from the common randomness. If the automaton accepts the input string, Claire will recover a random point on this line. If not, Claire will recover a random point not on this line. Bob also sends the other random point on this line to Claire. Finally, Claire uses two points from the garbled matrix and from Bob to decode the secret via interpolation.

The scheme is secure in the sense that Claire cannot learn anything about the inputs and the result. See the following theorem.

Theorem 1. *Assume that H is a secure PRF. The oblivious CDS for DFA in Fig. 3 satisfies correctness and indistinguishability as per Definition 2.*

4   Oblivious DFA Evaluation via CDS

In this section, we present an oblivious DFA evaluation protocol via CDS. The protocol shown in Fig. 4 is based on the multi-client verifiable computation framework from [7]. In short, we execute two oblivious CDS schemes for DFA M and $\overline{M}$, where $\overline{M}$ is the complement DFA of M. Since exactly one condition must be satisfied, Claire can recover the secret for that condition (but Claire will not know which one). Security then follows from the underlying oblivious CDS. The protocol is secure against semi-honest Alice and Bob, and malicious Claire. Here, Claire can be considered as an untrusted outsourcing server.

There is a reason why we have to execute two oblivious CDS schemes for DFA M and $\overline{M}$. If Alice and Bob execute only one oblivious CDS scheme for the DFA M, Claire may output a random value, and then Alice and Bob may conclude that the DFA does not accept the input string. When the oblivious CDS schemes for both M and $\overline{M}$ are executed, it is difficult for Claire to change the result, since either $s_1 = s_1'$ or $s_2 = s_2'$ must be satisfied, but not both. The protocol in Fig. 4 satisfies the following theorem.

Theorem 2. *Assume that H in Fig. 3 is a secure PRF. The oblivious DFA evaluation protocol in Fig. 4 is a sound and private MVC as per Definition 3.*

Oblivious DFA evaluation protocol via CDS

Input:

- Alice has a DFA $M = (Q, \Sigma, \Delta, q_0, F)$.
- Bob has an input string $x = x_0 x_1 \cdots x_{n-1}$.
- Claire has no input.

Algorithm:

1. $\delta = (s_1, s_2, r_1, r_2) \leftarrow$ Setup : Alice and Bob get common secrets (s_1, s_2) and common randomness (r_1, r_2) from a coin-tossing protocol or a public source of randomness. These values are not known to Claire.
2. $(\widetilde{\alpha_i}, \tau_i) \leftarrow$ Input$(\alpha_i, \delta, 1^\lambda)$: Alice and Bob execute the oblivious CDS scheme (Figure 3) for the DFA M and the input string x using the secret s_1 and the randomness r_1. They also execute the oblivious CDS scheme (Figure 3) for the DFA $\overline{M} = (Q, \Sigma, \Delta, q_0, Q - F)$ and the input string x using the secret s_2 and the randomness r_2. Here, $\widetilde{\alpha_1}$ and $\widetilde{\alpha_2}$ are CDS messages, and $\tau_1 = \tau_2 = (s_1, s_2)$.
3. $(\beta_1, \beta_2) \leftarrow$ Compute$(f, \widetilde{\alpha_1}, \widetilde{\alpha_2})$: Claire computes the output values s_1' and s_2' from both CDS schemes. Here, $\beta_1 = \beta_2 = (s_1', s_2')$.
4. $y \cup \{\perp\} \leftarrow$ Verify(β_i, τ_i) : If $s_1 = s_1'$, both Alice and Bob output "$M(x) = 1$". If $s_2 = s_2'$, both of them output "$M(x) = 0$". Otherwise, output $\perp$.

Fig. 4. Oblivious DFA evaluation protocol via CDS

Application. It is not difficult to see how this protocol can be used for DNA matching and other applications. In this case, Alice holds a pattern modeled with a DFA[2], and Bob holds a DNA sequence. Firstly, they generate common secrets and randomness. Next, Alice generates the garbled transition matrices of the DFA and its complement, while Bob transforms the DNA sequence into garbled character keys, according to the oblivious CDS scheme for DFA. After the oblivious CDS schemes for DFA are executed, Alice and Bob conclude their result based on Claire's outputs.

4.1 Complexity Analysis

We now briefly analyze round complexity, communication complexity, and computational complexity of our protocol in Fig. 4. See Table 1 for more details.

Round Complexity. In Fig. 4, two CDS can be executed in parallel. Each of Alice and Bob then send one message to Claire, and Claire sends the results back. The total number of rounds is 2, which is a constant. Our protocol can also be considered as non-interactive.

---

[2] The method in [38] can be used to transform a pattern p to a finite automaton $LEV_d(p)$ accepts the language $L_d(p)$ contains all strings with Levenshtein distance at most d from p. It is shown in [39] that a finite automaton for a language $\Sigma^* L_d(p) \Sigma^*$ will not have too many states.

Table 3. Numbers of operations for oblivious DFA evaluation protocols

Protocol	Automaton Holder		String Holder		Outsourcing Server	
	Asym. Comp.	Sym. Comp.	Asym. Comp.	Sym. Comp.	Asym. Comp.	Sym. Comp.
Troncoso et al. [39]	$O(|x||Q||\Sigma|)$	$O(|x||\Sigma|+|Q|)$	$O(|x||Q|)$	$O(|x|)$	-	-
Frikken [14]	$O(|x|)$	$O(|x||Q||\Sigma|)$	$O(|x|)$	$O(|x|)$	-	-
Gennaro et al. [18]	$O(|Q|(|x|+|\Sigma|))$	-	$O(|x||Q|)$	-	-	-
Mohassel et al. [35]	$O(|x|)$	$O(|x|(|Q|+|\Sigma|))$	$O(|x|)$	$O(|x|)$	-	-
Laud&Willemson [27]	-	$O(|x||Q||\Sigma|)$	-	$O(|x|)$	-	-
Crescenzo et al. [13]	$O(|x||Q||\Sigma|)$	$O(|Q|)$	$O(|x||Q||\Sigma|)$	-	-	-
Zhao et al. [42]	$O(|x|)$	$O(|x||Q|)$	$O(|x|)$	$O(|x|)$	-	-
Blanton&Aliasgari [8]	-	-	-	-	$O(|x|)$	$O(|x||Q||\Sigma|)$
Wei&Reitor [40]	$O(|x||Q||\Sigma|)$	-	$O(|x||\Sigma|(|Q|+|\Sigma|))$	-	-	-
Ours	-	$O(|x||Q||\Sigma|)$	-	-	-	$O(|x|)$

- : Negligible compare to other operations

Table 4. Numbers of operations for protocols with outsourcing servers

Protocol	Automaton Holder	Outsourcing Server
Blanton&Aliasgari [8]	-	1-out-of $|\Sigma|$ OT $\times 2$
		1-out-of-$|Q||\Sigma|$-OT $\times 2|x|$
		1-out-of-$|Q|$-OT $\times 2$
Ours	PRF $\times 2|x||Q||\Sigma|$	PRF $\times 2|x|$

Communication Complexity. The largest part of the communication is the garbled transition matrices. Thus, the communication complexity is $O(|x||Q||\Sigma|)$.

Computational Complexity. We trade-off a usage of asymmetric-key operations with one outsourcing server. Hence, the protocol can be more efficient compared to the previous works with heavy usage of homomorphic encryption and oblivious transfer (OT).

We briefly compare numbers of operations of the oblivious DFA evaluation protocols in Table 3. Some of the works have at least $O(|x||Q||\Sigma|)$ asymmetric computation, and some have a bit lower asymmetric computation as at least $O(|x|)$. Ours requires zero asymmetric computation. Although [27] also requires zero asymmetric computation (depend on the building block), it requires $O(|Q||\Sigma|)$ rounds (see Table 1), while ours has constant rounds.

We compare protocols with outsourcing servers in Table 4. Blanton et al. [8] uses $2|x|$ applications of 1-out-of-$|Q||\Sigma|$-OT, while our protocol uses $2|x||Q||\Sigma|$ applications of PRF. Since OT typically uses public-key operations such as modular exponentiations (e.g., [10,16]), while PRF can be based on symmetric ones such as block ciphers or keyed one-way hash functions (e.g., [12,20]) which are several orders of magnitude more efficient than public-key operations [36], this suggests that ours should be fundamentally faster than [8]. In more details, according to the state-of-the-art schemes for fast 1-out-of-n OT in [10,16,33,34], running m applications of 1-out-of-n OT requires $O(m)$ modular exponentiations and $O(nm)$ overall time. This suggests that [8] requires $O(|x|)$ asymmetric-key operations and $O(|x||Q||\Sigma|)$ symmetric operations. On the other hand, ours uses $2|x||Q||\Sigma|$ applications of PRF.

We note also that even looking at less-dominant computation part in OT (besides its public-key operations), running one OT application itself typically already requires more than one applications of PRF. Theoretically justified by [25], OT is an expensive operation compared to the evaluation of a PRF or a PRG. The OT protocol in [36] also uses a PRF as a building block. This also confirms that ours protocol should be fundamentally faster than [8].

5   CDS for DFA

As an independent interest, we propose a standard CDS for DFA in this section. In the setting of a standard CDS scheme for DFA, Alice has a DFA M, a secret s, and a randomness r, while Bob has an input string x, the same secret s, and the same randomness r. Claire knows both M and x, but does not know s or r. Claire can learn s if and only if $M(x) = 1$, and learn nothing else if $M(x) = 0$. As an overview of our construction, we transform the automaton and the input string into monotone span programs using a method from [2], and then construct a CDS scheme for those span programs. The transformations are applied to both automaton and input string in order to polynomially bound the size of the span program. Note that the standard CDS for DFA in this section does not require a PRF.[3] Complexity analysis of our standard CDS for DFA is in the full version.

5.1   Transform an Input String to a MSP

The following transformation from an input string to a MSP is from [2]. We extend it in order to support any size of alphabets. An input string x is transformed to a MSP $(\boldsymbol{L}_x, \rho_x)$, and a DFA M is transformed to a set of attributes S_M. A universe of attributes for DFA is denoted as

$$\mathcal{U}_M = \{(\sigma, i, j) : i, j \in [Q_{max}], \sigma \in \Sigma\} \cup \{\text{``Size} = i\text{''} : i \in [Q_{max}]\} \cup \{\text{``Dummy''}\}$$

where Q_{max} is a maximum number of states that all parties agree on. Each attribute can be represented by an integer using the following mapping.

$$\text{``Dummy''} \mapsto 0, \quad (\sigma, i, j) \mapsto 2|\Sigma|((i+j)^2 + j) + 2\sigma, \quad \text{``Size} = i\text{''} \mapsto 2i + 1$$

A DFA $M = (Q, \Sigma, \Delta, q_0, F)$ is transformed into a set of attributes

$$S_M = \{\text{``Dummy''}\} \cup \{(\sigma, i, j) \in \Sigma \times Q^2 : j = \Delta(\sigma, i)\} \cup \{\text{``Size} = |Q|\text{''}\}.$$

To transform an input string $x = x_0 x_1 \ldots x_{n-1}$ with length $|x| = n$ to a MSP, we define the following matrices as in [2].

- $\boldsymbol{I}_n$ denotes $n \times n$ identity matrix.
- $\boldsymbol{g}_n$ and $\boldsymbol{0}_n$ denote column vectors $(1, \ldots, 1)^\top$ and $(0, \ldots, 0)^\top$ of size n.
- $\boldsymbol{0}_{m \times n}$ denotes a zero matrix of size $m \times n$.

---

[3] In practice, PRF can be used to reduce the size of the common randomness.

Table 5. Submatrix $[V_n || W_n]^{(\sigma)}$ associated with σ (refer to Table 4 in [2]) and a MSP (L_x, ρ_x) from an input string x (refer to Table 5 in [2])

$$- \ V_n = I_n \otimes g_n = \begin{bmatrix} g_n & 0_n & \cdots & 0_n \\ 0_n & g_n & \cdots & 0_n \\ \vdots & \vdots & \ddots & \vdots \\ 0_n & 0_n & \cdots & g_n \end{bmatrix} \text{ of size } n^2 \times n.$$

- $W_n = -g_n \otimes I_n = [-I_n || \ldots || -I_n]^\top$ of size $n^2 \times n$.
- For each $\sigma \in \Sigma$, define $[V_n || W_n]^{(\sigma)}$ associated with σ as shown in Table 5 (left). Each row is corresponding to (σ, i, j) for all $i, j \in [n]$.

The MSP matrix L_x with labeling function ρ_x is shown in Table 5 (right). We refer to the following theorem proved in [2].

Theorem 3. *Using the method above, let (L_x, ρ_x) be a MSP constructed from an input string x, and S_M be a set of attributes constructed from a DFA M. We have (L_x, ρ_x) accepts S_M if and only if $M(x) = 1$ and $|Q| \leq n$.*

5.2 Transform a DFA to a MSP

Similar to the previous subsection, we also transform a DFA to a MSP. We refer to the transformation from a DFA to a MSP from [2] with an extension to support any size of alphabets. A universe of attributes for input strings is denoted as

$$\mathcal{U}_x = \{(i, \sigma) : i \in [0, n_{max}], \sigma \in \Sigma\} \cup \{\text{"Length} = i\text{"} : i \in [n_{max}]\} \cup \{\text{"Dummy"}\}$$

where n_{max} is a maximum length of input string that all parties agree on. Each attribute can be represented by an integer using the following mapping.

$$\text{"Dummy"} \mapsto 0, \quad (i, \sigma) \mapsto (|\Sigma| + 1)i + \sigma + 1, \quad \text{"Length} = i\text{"} \mapsto (|\Sigma| + 1)(i + 1)$$

An input string $x = x_0 x_1 \ldots x_{n-1}$ is transformed into a set of attributes

$$S_x = \{\text{"Dummy"}\} \cup \{(i, x_i) : i \in [0, n-1]\} \cup \{\text{"Length} = n\text{"}\}.$$

Table 6. A MSP $(\boldsymbol{L}_M, \rho_M)$ from a DFA M (refer to Table 2 in [2])

		1	−10...0	0...0	0...0	...	0...0	0...0
"Dummy"	↦	1	−10...0	0...0	0...0	...	0...0	0...0
"$x_0 = 0$"	↦	$0_{|Q|}$	$I_{|Q|}$	$Y^{(0)}$	$0_{|Q|\times|Q|}$	⋯	$0_{|Q|\times|Q|}$	$0_{|Q|\times|Q|}$
"$x_0 = 1$"	↦	$0_{|Q|}$	$I_{|Q|}$	$Y^{(1)}$	$0_{|Q|\times|Q|}$	⋯	$0_{|Q|\times|Q|}$	$0_{|Q|\times|Q|}$
⋮		⋮	⋮	⋮	⋮	⋱	⋮	⋮
"$x_0 = |\Sigma| - 1$"	↦	$0_{|Q|}$	$I_{|Q|}$	$Y^{(|\Sigma|-1)}$	$0_{|Q|\times|Q|}$	⋯	$0_{|Q|\times|Q|}$	$0_{|Q|\times|Q|}$
"$x_1 = 0$"	↦	$0_{|Q|}$	$0_{|Q|\times|Q|}$	$I_{|Q|}$	$Y^{(0)}$	⋯	$0_{|Q|\times|Q|}$	$0_{|Q|\times|Q|}$
⋮		⋮	⋮	⋮	⋮	⋱	⋮	⋮
"$x_{|Q|-1} = |\Sigma| - 1$"	↦	$0_{|Q|}$	$0_{|Q|\times|Q|}$	$0_{|Q|\times|Q|}$	$0_{|Q|\times|Q|}$	⋯	$I_{|Q|}$	$Y^{(|\Sigma|-1)}$
"Length = 1"	↦	0	0...0	0...01				
"Length = 2"	↦	0		0...0	0...01			
⋮		⋮				⋱		
"Length = $|Q|$"	↦	0					0...0	0...01

To transform a DFA $M = (Q, \Sigma, \Delta, q_0, F)$ to a MSP matrix, we define a submatrix $\boldsymbol{Y}^{(\sigma)}$ for each $\sigma \in \Sigma$ with size $|Q| \times |Q|$ in the same way as [2]. The cell of $\boldsymbol{Y}^{(\sigma)}$ at position (i, j) is -1 if $j = \Delta(i, \sigma)$, and is 0 otherwise. The MSP matrix $\boldsymbol{L}_M$ with a labeling function ρ_M is shown in Table 6. We refer to the following theorem proved in [2].

Theorem 4. *Using the method above, let $(\boldsymbol{L}_M, \rho_M)$ be a MSP constructed from a DFA M, and S_x be a set of attributes constructed from an input string x. We have $(\boldsymbol{L}_M, \rho_M)$ accepts S_x if and only if $M(x) = 1$ and $n \leq |Q|$.*

5.3   CDS for MSP

A CDS scheme for MSP is proposed in Fig. 5. In this setting, Alice has a MSP $(\boldsymbol{L}, \rho)$, a secret s, and a randomness r. Bob has a set of attributes S, the same secret s, and the same randomness r. Claire has only $(\boldsymbol{L}, \rho)$ and S. The idea is that Alice performs a dot product between the MSP and a secret vector, masks the results with random values, and then sends to Claire. At the same time, Bob sends the random values corresponding to the set of attributes. If the set of attributes satisfies the MSP, masked random values can be cancelled out, and the secret can be recovered. The method can be considered as a linear secret sharing based on MSP.

From the scheme, Claire will only learn the values from rows corresponding to the set of attributes. Correctness and security then follow from linear secret sharing of MSP. We have the following theorem.

CDS scheme for MSP

Input:

- Alice has a MSP $(L \in \mathbb{Z}_p^{\ell \times m}, \rho)$, a secret s, and a randomness r.
- Bob has a set of attributes $S = \{u_1, \ldots, u_n\}$, a secret s, and a randomness r.
- Claire has the MSP (L, ρ), and the set of attributes S.

Algorithm:

1. Alice randomly generates an m-element vector $v = (v_1, \ldots, v_m)$ such that the first element is $v_1 = s$.
2. For each $i \in [\ell]$, let L_i (the i-th row of L) be the j-th row that is associated with the attribute u. Alice calculates $w_i = L_i \cdot v + r_{u,j}$ where $r_{u,j}$ is extracted from the randomness r. Alice then sends $\{w_i\}_{i \in [\ell]}$ to Claire.
3. For each $u \in S$, Bob extracts $\{r_{u,j}\}_{j \in [\ell_{max}]}$ from the randomness r in the same way as Alice, where ℓ_{max} is the maximum number of rows that can be associated to an attribute. Bob then sends $\{r_{u,j}\}_{u \in S, j \in [\ell_{max}]}$ to Claire.
4. For each L_i that can map to an attribute in S, Claire computes $(L_i \cdot v)$ from $w_i - r_{u,j}$. If (L, ρ) accepts S, then there exists a vector ω such that $\omega \cdot L_S = (1, 0, \ldots, 0)$. Claire can calculate s from $\omega \cdot (L_S \cdot v)$.

Fig. 5. CDS scheme for MSP

Theorem 5. *The CDS scheme for MSP proposed in Fig. 5 is correct and secure. That is when (L, ρ) accepts S, we have $Pr[Dec((L, \rho), S, \mathsf{Enc_A}((L, \rho), s, r), \mathsf{Enc_B}(S, s, r)) = s] = 1$. And when (L, ρ) does not accept S, there exists a simulator Sim such that $\{\mathsf{Sim}((L, \rho), S)\} \approx \{\mathsf{Enc_A}((L, \rho), s, r), \mathsf{Enc_B}(S, s, r)\}$.*

5.4 CDS for DFA

We are now ready to use the building blocks from previous subsections to construct a CDS scheme for DFA. The scheme is shown in Fig. 6. Alice and Bob first transform a DFA and an input string into MSPs and sets of attributes. After that, they execute two CDS schemes for MSP in parallel. If the automaton accepts the input string, Claire will learn the secret of the CDS scheme. Correctness and security follow from the schemes in previous subsections. We have the following theorem.

Theorem 6. *The CDS scheme for DFA proposed in Fig. 6 is correct and secure. That is when a DFA M accepts an input string x, it holds that $Pr[Dec(M, x, \mathsf{Enc_A}(M, s, r), \mathsf{Enc_B}(x, s, r)) = s] = 1$. And when M does not accept x, there exists a simulator Sim such that $\{\mathsf{Sim}(M, x)\} \approx \{\mathsf{Enc_A}(M, s, r), \mathsf{Enc_B}(x, s, r)\}$.*

CDS scheme for DFA

Input:

- Alice has a DFA $M = (Q, \Sigma, \Delta, q_0, F)$, a secret s, and randomness (r_1, r_2).
- Bob has an input string $x = x_0 x_1 \ldots x_{n-1}$, a secret s, and randomness (r_1, r_2).
- Claire has the finite automaton M, and the input string x.

Algorithm:

1. Alice generates $(\boldsymbol{L}_M, \rho_M)$ and S_M from M.
2. Bob generates $(\boldsymbol{L}_x, \rho_x)$ and S_x from x.
3. Alice and Bob execute two CDS schemes with inputs $((\boldsymbol{L}_M, \rho_M), S_x, s, r_1)$ and inputs $((\boldsymbol{L}_x, \rho_x), S_M, s, r_2)$ at the same time.
4. If M accepts x, then Claire can recover the secret s.

Fig. 6. CDS scheme for DFA

6 Concluding Remarks

In this paper, we propose an oblivious CDS scheme for DFA. Then we use it as a building block to construct an oblivious DFA evaluation protocol. We also propose a standard CDS scheme for DFA as an independent interest.

Some of the previous works considered oblivious CDS schemes for NFA, including [27, 37]. We believe that our work could be extended for those situations. For the works considered NFA, although there exists an algorithm to convert a NFA into a DFA, the number of states in the result DFA can be exponentially large. Thus, these schemes can have an advantage in this case.

At this point, we do not know how to construct an oblivious (or even a standard) CDS scheme for NFA without using asymmetric-key operations. Using the method in Sect. 3 can leak the structure of the NFA to Claire. This is because at each step, Claire will have more than one state keys, and may know which states have transitions to the same state. Extending the method from [2] to the NFA setting is also not trivial. We left this problem as future work.

In addition, it is interesting to extend our protocol to a setting with malicious Alice and Bob. It is also interesting to try constructing oblivious evaluation protocols for pushdown automata and Turing machine. The difficulty is how to keep track of the memory obliviously. Moreover, we would like to try constructing oblivious protocols via CDS for Moore machine and Mealy machine as well. Although, we can embed the output information into the garbled transition matrix in the same way as [14], the output from this revised protocol will not be verifiable and not be secure against malicious Claire anymore.

Acknowledgments. Nuttapong Attrapadung was partly supported by JSPS KAKENHI Kiban-A Grant Number 19H01109. Kanta Matsuura was partially supported by JSPS KAKENHI Grant Number 17KT0081.

References

1. Agrawal, S., Maitra, M., Yamada, S.: Attribute based encryption (and more) for nondeterministic finite automata from LWE. In: Boldyreva, A., Micciancio, D. (eds.) CRYPTO 2019. LNCS, vol. 11693, pp. 765–797. Springer, Cham (2019). https://doi.org/10.1007/978-3-030-26951-7_26
2. Agrawal, S., Maitra, M., Yamada, S.: Attribute based encryption for deterministic finite automata from DLIN. In: Hofheinz, D., Rosen, A. (eds.) TCC 2019. LNCS, vol. 11892, pp. 91–117. Springer, Cham (2019). https://doi.org/10.1007/978-3-030-36033-7_4
3. Aiello, B., Ishai, Y., Reingold, O.: Priced oblivious transfer: how to sell digital goods. In: Pfitzmann, B. (ed.) EUROCRYPT 2001. LNCS, vol. 2045, pp. 119–135. Springer, Heidelberg (2001). https://doi.org/10.1007/3-540-44987-6_8
4. Applebaum, B., Beimel, A., Farràs, O., Nir, O., Peter, N.: Secret-sharing schemes for general and uniform access structures. In: Ishai, Y., Rijmen, V. (eds.) EUROCRYPT 2019. LNCS, vol. 11478, pp. 441–471. Springer, Cham (2019). https://doi.org/10.1007/978-3-030-17659-4_15
5. Applebaum, B., Beimel, A., Nir, O., Peter, N.: Better secret sharing via robust conditional disclosure of secrets. In: Proceedings of the 52nd Annual ACM SIGACT Symposium on Theory of Computing, pp. 280–293 (2020)
6. Beimel, A., Peter, N.: Optimal linear multiparty conditional disclosure of secrets protocols. In: Peyrin, T., Galbraith, S. (eds.) ASIACRYPT 2018. LNCS, vol. 11274, pp. 332–362. Springer, Cham (2018). https://doi.org/10.1007/978-3-030-03332-3_13
7. Bhadauria, R., Hazay, C.: Multi-clients verifiable computation via conditional disclosure of secrets. In: Galdi, C., Kolesnikov, V. (eds.) SCN 2020. LNCS, vol. 12238, pp. 150–171. Springer, Cham (2020). https://doi.org/10.1007/978-3-030-57990-6_8
8. Blanton, M., Aliasgari, M.: Secure outsourcing of DNA searching via finite automata. In: Foresti, S., Jajodia, S. (eds.) DBSec 2010. LNCS, vol. 6166, pp. 49–64. Springer, Heidelberg (2010). https://doi.org/10.1007/978-3-642-13739-6_4
9. Choi, S.G., Katz, J., Kumaresan, R., Cid, C.: Multi-client non-interactive verifiable computation. In: Sahai, A. (ed.) TCC 2013. LNCS, vol. 7785, pp. 499–518. Springer, Heidelberg (2013). https://doi.org/10.1007/978-3-642-36594-2_28
10. Chou, T., Orlandi, C.: The simplest protocol for oblivious transfer. In: Lauter, K., Rodríguez-Henríquez, F. (eds.) LATINCRYPT 2015. LNCS, vol. 9230, pp. 40–58. Springer, Cham (2015). https://doi.org/10.1007/978-3-319-22174-8_3
11. Cramer, R., Damgård, I., Maurer, U.: General secure multi-party computation from any linear secret-sharing scheme. In: Preneel, B. (ed.) EUROCRYPT 2000. LNCS, vol. 1807, pp. 316–334. Springer, Heidelberg (2000). https://doi.org/10.1007/3-540-45539-6_22
12. Desai, A., Hevia, A., Yin, Y.L.: A practice-oriented treatment of pseudorandom number generators. In: Knudsen, L.R. (ed.) EUROCRYPT 2002. LNCS, vol. 2332, pp. 368–383. Springer, Heidelberg (2002). https://doi.org/10.1007/3-540-46035-7_24
13. Di Crescenzo, G., Coan, B., Kirsch, J.: Privacy-preserving deterministic automata evaluation with encrypted data blocks. In: Garcia-Alfaro, J., Navarro-Arribas, G., Hartenstein, H., Herrera-Joancomartí, J. (eds.) ESORICS/DPM/CBT -2017. LNCS, vol. 10436, pp. 275–294. Springer, Cham (2017). https://doi.org/10.1007/978-3-319-67816-0_16

14. Frikken, K.B.: Practical private DNA string searching and matching through efficient oblivious automata evaluation. In: Gudes, E., Vaidya, J. (eds.) DBSec 2009. LNCS, vol. 5645, pp. 81–94. Springer, Heidelberg (2009). https://doi.org/10.1007/978-3-642-03007-9_6

15. Gay, R., Kerenidis, I., Wee, H.: Communication complexity of conditional disclosure of secrets and attribute-based encryption. In: Gennaro, R., Robshaw, M. (eds.) CRYPTO 2015. LNCS, vol. 9216, pp. 485–502. Springer, Heidelberg (2015). https://doi.org/10.1007/978-3-662-48000-7_24

16. Genç, Z.A., Iovino, V., Rial, A.: The simplest protocol for oblivious transfer - revisited. Inf. Process. Lett. **161**, 105975 (2020)

17. Gennaro, R., Gentry, C., Parno, B.: Non-interactive verifiable computing: outsourcing computation to untrusted workers. In: Rabin, T. (ed.) CRYPTO 2010. LNCS, vol. 6223, pp. 465–482. Springer, Heidelberg (2010). https://doi.org/10.1007/978-3-642-14623-7_25

18. Gennaro, R., Hazay, C., Sorensen, J.S.: Text search protocols with simulation based security. In: Nguyen, P.Q., Pointcheval, D. (eds.) PKC 2010. LNCS, vol. 6056, pp. 332–350. Springer, Heidelberg (2010). https://doi.org/10.1007/978-3-642-13013-7_20

19. Gertner, Y., Ishai, Y., Kushilevitz, E., Malkin, T.: Protecting data privacy in private information retrieval schemes. In: Proceedings of the 30th Annual ACM Symposium on Theory of Computing, pp. 151–160 (1998)

20. Goldreich, O., Goldwasser, S., Micali, S.: How to construct random functions. J. ACM (JACM) **33**(4), 792–807 (1986)

21. Goldwasser, S., Ben-Or, M., Wigderson, A.: Completeness theorems for non-cryptographic fault-tolerant distributed computing. In: Proceedings of the 20th STOC, pp. 1–10 (1988)

22. Gong, J., Waters, B., Wee, H.: ABE for DFA from k-Lin. In: Boldyreva, A., Micciancio, D. (eds.) CRYPTO 2019. LNCS, vol. 11693, pp. 732–764. Springer, Cham (2019). https://doi.org/10.1007/978-3-030-26951-7_25

23. Gong, J., Wee, H.: Adaptively secure ABE for DFA from k-Lin and more. In: Canteaut, A., Ishai, Y. (eds.) EUROCRYPT 2020. LNCS, vol. 12107, pp. 278–308. Springer, Cham (2020). https://doi.org/10.1007/978-3-030-45727-3_10

24. Gordon, S.D., Katz, J., Liu, F.-H., Shi, E., Zhou, H.-S.: Multi-client verifiable computation with stronger security guarantees. In: Dodis, Y., Nielsen, J.B. (eds.) TCC 2015. LNCS, vol. 9015, pp. 144–168. Springer, Heidelberg (2015). https://doi.org/10.1007/978-3-662-46497-7_6

25. Impagliazzo, R., Rudich, S.: Limits on the provable consequences of one-way permutations. In: Proceedings of the 21st Annual ACM Symposium on Theory of Computing, pp. 44–61 (1989)

26. Ishai, Y., Kilian, J., Nissim, K., Petrank, E.: Extending oblivious transfers efficiently. In: Boneh, D. (ed.) CRYPTO 2003. LNCS, vol. 2729, pp. 145–161. Springer, Heidelberg (2003). https://doi.org/10.1007/978-3-540-45146-4_9

27. Laud, P., Willemson, J.: Universally composable privacy preserving finite automata execution with low online and offline complexity. IACR Cryptol. ePrint Arch. **2013**, 678 (2013)

28. Lin, H., Luo, J.: Compact adaptively secure ABE from k-Lin: beyond NC^1 and towards NL. In: Canteaut, A., Ishai, Y. (eds.) EUROCRYPT 2020. LNCS, vol. 12107, pp. 247–277. Springer, Cham (2020). https://doi.org/10.1007/978-3-030-45727-3_9

29. Lindell, Y., Pinkas, B.: A proof of security of Yao's protocol for two-party computation. J. Cryptol. **22**(2), 161–188 (2009)

30. Liu, T., Vaikuntanathan, V.: Breaking the circuit-size barrier in secret sharing. In: Proceedings of the 50th Annual ACM SIGACT Symposium on Theory of Computing, pp. 699–708 (2018)

31. Liu, T., Vaikuntanathan, V., Wee, H.: Conditional disclosure of secrets via non-linear reconstruction. In: Katz, J., Shacham, H. (eds.) CRYPTO 2017. LNCS, vol. 10401, pp. 758–790. Springer, Cham (2017). https://doi.org/10.1007/978-3-319-63688-7_25

32. Liu, T., Vaikuntanathan, V., Wee, H.: Towards breaking the exponential barrier for general secret sharing. In: Nielsen, J.B., Rijmen, V. (eds.) EUROCRYPT 2018. LNCS, vol. 10820, pp. 567–596. Springer, Cham (2018). https://doi.org/10.1007/978-3-319-78381-9_21

33. Mansy, D., Rindal, P.: Endemic oblivious transfer. In: Proceedings of the 2019 ACM SIGSAC Conference on Computer and Communications Security, pp. 309–326 (2019)

34. McQuoid, I., Rosulek, M., Roy, L.: Minimal symmetric PAKE and 1-out-of-n OT from programmable-once public functions. In: Proceedings of the 2020 ACM SIGSAC Conference on Computer and Communications Security, pp. 425–442 (2020)

35. Mohassel, P., Niksefat, S., Sadeghian, S., Sadeghiyan, B.: An efficient protocol for oblivious DFA evaluation and applications. In: Dunkelman, O. (ed.) CT-RSA 2012. LNCS, vol. 7178, pp. 398–415. Springer, Heidelberg (2012). https://doi.org/10.1007/978-3-642-27954-6_25

36. Naor, M., Pinkas, B.: Computationally secure oblivious transfer. J. Cryptol. **18**(1), 1–35 (2005)

37. Sasakawa, H., Harada, H., duVerle, D., Arimura, H., Tsuda, K., Sakuma, J.: Oblivious evaluation of non-deterministic finite automata with application to privacy-preserving virus genome detection. In: Proceedings of the 13th Workshop on Privacy in the Electronic Society, pp. 21–30 (2014)

38. Schulz, K.U., Mihov, S.: Fast string correction with Levenshtein automata. Int. J. Doc. Anal. Recogn. **5**(1), 67–85 (2002)

39. Troncoso-Pastoriza, J.R., Katzenbeisser, S., Celik, M.: Privacy preserving error resilient DNA searching through oblivious automata. In: Proceedings of the 14th ACM Conference on Computer and Communications Security, pp. 519–528 (2007)

40. Wei, L., Reiter, M.K.: Third-party private DFA evaluation on encrypted files in the cloud. In: Foresti, S., Yung, M., Martinelli, F. (eds.) ESORICS 2012. LNCS, vol. 7459, pp. 523–540. Springer, Heidelberg (2012). https://doi.org/10.1007/978-3-642-33167-1_30

41. Yao, A.C.: Protocols for secure computations. In: 23rd Annual Symposium on Foundations of Computer Science, pp. 160–164. IEEE (1982)

42. Zhao, C., Zhao, S., Zhang, B., Jing, S., Chen, Z., Zhao, M.: Oblivious DFA evaluation on joint input and its applications. Inf. Sci. **528**, 168–180 (2020)

Efficient and Tight Oblivious Transfer from PKE with Tight Multi-user Security

Saikrishna Badrinarayanan[1], Daniel Masny[2($\boxtimes$)], and Pratyay Mukherjee[3]

[1] Snap Inc., Mountain View, USA
[2] Meta Inc., Menlo Park, USA
daniel.masny@rub.de
[3] Swirlds Labs, Richardson, USA

Abstract. We propose an efficient oblivious transfer in the random oracle model based on public key encryption with pseudorandom public keys. The construction is as efficient as the state of art though it has a significant advantage. It has a tight security reduction to the multi-user security of the underlying public key encryption. In previous constructions, the security reduction has a multiplicative loss that amounts in at least the amount of adversarial random oracle queries. When considering this loss for a secure parameter choice, the underlying public key encryption or elliptic curve would require a significantly higher security level which would decrease the overall efficiency.

Our OT construction can be instantiated from a wide range of assumptions such as DDH, LWE, or codes based assumptions as well as many public key encryption schemes such as the NIST PQC finalists. Since tight multi-user security is a very natural requirement which many public key encryption schemes suffice, many public key encryption schemes can be straightforwardly plugged in our construction without the need of reevaluating or adapting any parameter choices.

1 Introduction

An oblivious transfer (OT) [Rab81,EGL82] is an interactive protocol between two parties called a sender and a receiver. At the end of the protocol, the sender outputs two messages m_0, m_1 while the receiver outputs b, m_b for a choice bit b. Security requires that the sender does not learn b and the receiver does not learn m_{1-b}. OT is a fundamental building block in cryptography [Kil88], particularly in secure multi-party computation (MPC) [Yao82,Yao86,CvT95,IPS08, IKO+11,BL18,GS18], which allows mutually distrusting parties to securely perform joint computations on their privately held data. MPC has a plethora of applications in practice, for example, in securely training machine learning models (e.g. [MR18]), private set intersection (e.g. [KKRT16,PRTY20]) etc. In fact, a significant body of practically efficient MPC protocols do rely primarily on the primitive of OT (e.g. [NNOB12,KOS16]), which makes *efficient secure OT* an important and very natural objective.

Part of the work was done while the authors were at Visa Research.

© Springer Nature Switzerland AG 2022
G. Ateniese and D. Venturi (Eds.): ACNS 2022, LNCS 13269, pp. 626–642, 2022.
https://doi.org/10.1007/978-3-031-09233-3_31

Within the last years, there has been significant progress in making OT more efficient. Chou and Orlandi [CO15] proposed a very efficient OT in the random oracle model [BR93, CGH98] based on the DDH assumption. It turned out, that it does not achieve UC security [GIR17, HL17], but only stand-alone security. Masny and Rindal [MR19] proposed an OT from public key encryption (PKE) with pseudorandom public keys that is as well very efficient but also UC secure and can be instantiated from a variety of assumptions such as LWE or code based assumptions. The construction makes it very easy to plug in PKE schemes such as the NIST PQC candidates [SAB+20, DKR+20, CDH+20, ABC+20] which is a significant advantage over more tailored construction of OT based on DDH [CSW20], LWE [PVW08, BD18, BDK+20] or McEliece [DvMN08, DNM12]. McQuoid, Rosulek and Roy [MRR20, MRR21] gave a more modular analysis of this approach, extended it to PKEs with pseudorandom ciphertexts (PKE B) as well as increased the efficiency when multiple OTs are run in parallel. Masny and Watson [MW21] increased the efficiency by leveraging a PKI.

This approach works as follows. Using a specific query pattern to a random oracle, a receiver can freely chose one public key while a second public key will be completely determined by the random oracle. At the same time, a sender can reproduce the same queries and public keys and then encrypt one OT string under each of the public keys. Though he will not be able to determine which of the keys has been freely chosen by the receiver. At the same time, the receiver can only recover the string under the freely chosen public key but not the other. Unfortunately, this approach has some drawbacks, namely the receiver could repeat the query pattern to the random oracle until he finds a public keys that might be easier to break than the average public key and then try to recover both strings. Typically, a PKE is hard to break for a random public key with overwhelming probability and therefore it should not cause an issue. Nevertheless, it limits how tightly one can prove the security of the OT protocol based on a PKE scheme.

This drawback can be resolved by using a PKE that is tightly secure in the multi-user setting. Tight multi user security has received significant attention in the context of key exchange, PKE and signatures [Hås88, BBM00, HJ12, Zav12, BHJ+15, KMP16, CKMS16, GKP18, GJ18, PR20, LLGW20, JKRS21]. Bellare, Boldyreva and Micali [BBM00] showed that ElGamal is tightly secure even when multiple challenge ciphertexts are given to the adversary. There are numerous works that focus on tight multi-user secure PKE [Hås88, HJ12, Zav12, CKMS16, GKP18]. The tightness requirement does not put significant restrictions on known PKEs. Tight multi-user security is a very natural property that a PKE should typically have since usually the security of all users and not just of a single user needs to be considered. Non-tightness would demand an increase in the bit security level of a PKE when used across many users which would render the PKE significantly less efficient.

Unfortunately, using a tightly secure PKE in the multi user setting is not sufficient. The security analysis of [MR19, MRR20, MRR21] also involves reprogramming the random oracle and guessing which query a malicious receiver will later use during the OT protocol. This comes at the cost of a security loss which is multiplicative in the amount of adversarial random oracle queries. This issue seems to requires a more in-depth analysis of this approach of constructing OT and opens the question whether a similar construction could achieve tight security. In this paper, we answer the following question:

Can we construct efficient OT that is tightly secure in the ROM from public-key encryption?

1.1 Our Contribution

We propose a new construction of OT in the random oracle model which can be proven tightly secure based on the multi-user security of the underlying PKE. This approach follows the paradigm of Masny and Rindal [MR19, MRR20, MRR21, MW21] by specifying a pattern of random oracle queries which allows a malicious receiver to choose one public key freely while a second one is determined by the random oracle.

We use a mild notion of multi-user security which is weaker than the notion proposed in previous literature such as [BBM00]. In our notion, we require that an adversary receives n user public keys and then decides for which he wants to see a challenge ciphertext. The notion of [BBM00] allows an adversary to see challenge ciphertext for all of the public keys. Nevertheless, there are many PKEs that even achieve the stronger notion of [BBM00] with a tight security proof under the DDH or LWE [Reg05] assumption. We recap the most basic PKEs and their tight reductions to DDH and LWE in Sect. 3. The results extend straightforwardly to code based schemes, the ring or module LWE [LPR10, BGV12, LS15] setting or elliptic curves.

For our OT, we require a second property that is the pseudorandomness of the public keys. This requirement is the same as in [MR19] we the exception that it holds tightly based on the underlying assumption even when n keys are seen. We recap this property as well in Sect. 3 for the PKEs of interest.

In Fig. 1, we compare our result with previous works. Since the main difference of our construction to [MR19] is how the random oracle is used, the efficiency of our OT is very similar to [MR19]. On one hand, we need to compute 3 additional hash evaluations. The hash evaluations are standard evaluations mapping onto $\{0, 1\}^*$ and when using elliptic curves, not to curve points. On the other hand, we are actually, similar to [MRR20] able to reduce the communication complexity on the receivers side from $2|\mathsf{pk}|$ ([MRR20]) to $|\mathsf{pk} + 2\lambda|$. In particular when instantiating the OT with lattice or code based schemes [SAB+20, DKR+20, CDH+20, ABC+20] which have rather long keys, this is a significant reduction. Even when instantiating the OT with ElGamal encryption, we need to sample one random group element less which requires an exponentiation. In the elliptic curve setting, our construction is compatible with the performance optimizations of [MRR21] and would therefore be competitive with the currently fastest implementations of UC OT reported in [MRR21]. Further, our OT is based on a PKE with pseudorandom public keys (PKE A), which,

	UC	Loss	Model	Com($\mathcal{R}$)	Com($\mathcal{S}$)
[CO15]	✗	-	ROM	$\log|G|$	$\log|G|$
[MR19]	PKE A	$O(q)$	ROM	$2|\mathsf{pk}|$	$2|\mathsf{ct}|$
[CSW20]	DDH	$O(q^2)$	ROM,CRS	$2\log|G|$	$\log|G|$
[MRR20]	PKE B	$O(q^2)$	ROM	$|\mathsf{ct}|+\lambda$	$|\mathsf{pk}|$
[MRR20]*	PKE A	$O(q)$	ROM	$|\mathsf{ct}|+\lambda$	$|\mathsf{pk}|$
[MRR21]	PKE B	$O(q)$	Ideal Cipher	$|\mathsf{ct}|+\lambda$	$|\mathsf{pk}|$
[MRR21]*	PKE A	$O(1)$	Ideal Cipher	$|\mathsf{ct}|+\lambda$	$|\mathsf{pk}|$
Ours	PKE A	$O(1)$	ROM	$|\mathsf{pk}|+2\lambda$	$2|\mathsf{ct}|$

Fig. 1. We compare our construction with previous works. The depicted loss assumes tight multi-user security of the underlying PKE. We emphasize that the listed works realize different OT functionalities and therefore the comparison between the communication should be interpreted with caution. PKE A stands for PKE with pseudorandom public keys and PKE B stands for PKE with uniform ciphertexts. q is the amount of adversarial random oracle queries (hash evaluations). [MRR20]*, [MRR21]* are slight adaptations of the original works to make them compatible with the PKE A setting.

unlike PKEs with uniform ciphertexts (PKE B), can be efficiently instantiated with post-quantum PKEs, e.g. from codes or lattices. We could also use our techniques to construct an OT from a PKE with pseudorandom ciphertexts (PKE B), though it is unclear whether the tightness would still hold and it might require stronger assumptions such as the interactive DDH assumption [MR19] or oracle assumptions [BCJ+19, MRR21].

As shown in Fig. 1, our OT is currently the only OT among the most efficient OTs that is tightly secure in the random oracle model. The main challenge is typically security against a malicious receiver. Previous works suffer at least a loss of $O(q)$ where q is the amount of adversarial hash evaluations. For a conservative parameter choice, previous works need to start with a significantly higher security level of the PKE or elliptic curve which negatively impacts efficiency and communication complexity or alternatively, use a stronger model such as the ideal cipher model as in case of [MRR21]*.

We emphasize that Fig. 1 states the loss for [MRR20]* and [MRR21]* when using a PKE with tight multi user security. Using (plain) single user secure PKE, the loss increases by a factor of q. This also holds for the loss stated for [MR19].

1.2   Technical Overview

We follow an approach by Masny and Rindal [MR19]. They construct a two round OT in which the receiver starts by sending a message r_0, r_1 from this message the sender can derive two public keys under which he encrypts the two OT strings. The public keys are $\mathsf{pk}_0 := r_1 + \mathsf{H}(r_0)$ and $\mathsf{pk}_1 := r_0 + \mathsf{H}(r_1)$. When following this approach, proving security against a malicious sender is typically easy since the random oracle can be programmed such that the simulator knows the secret keys for both public keys which can then be used to extract the malicious sender's string. The more challenging part is to prove security against a malicious receiver $\mathcal{R}^*$. Given that $\mathcal{R}^*$ makes only two random oracle queries, r_0 and r_1, the simulator can observe the first query, let it be r_b. Then, b is the extracted choice bit. Further, when the second query is made, the simulator could pick a public key pk^* of its choice and program the oracle H such that $\mathsf{H}(r_{1-b}) := pk^* - r_b$ and thus $pk_{1-b} = pk^*$. If $\mathcal{R}^*$ learns information about the OT string s_{1-b}, he would then break the security of the PKE.

Unfortunately, when the malicious receiver makes many queries, it is not clear how to program $\mathsf{H}(r_{1-b})$ since any of the q previous queries $\tilde{r}_1, \ldots, \tilde{r}_q$ could be the r_b query. This would lead to the potential public keys $pk_{1-b,1} := \tilde{r}_1 + \mathsf{H}(r_{1-b}), \ldots, pk_{1-b,q} := \tilde{r}_q + \mathsf{H}(r_{1-b})$. We could guess $j \in [q]$ such that $r_b = \tilde{r}_j$ but this would cause a loss of q.

Before explaining our construction, we first take an intermediate step. The MR OT has similarities with a sequential OR proof [RST01, AOS02]. Instead we could follow the parallel OR proof paradigm [CDS94]. The public keys would be then derived from a message r, c_0, c_1 and defined as $pk_0 := r + \mathsf{H}(c_0)$ and $pk_1 := r + \mathsf{H}(c_1)$. This construction has similarities with the McQuoid, Rosulek and Roy OT [MRR20]. As an additional constraint, we ask that $\hat{\mathsf{H}}(r) = c_0 + c_1$, where $\hat{\mathsf{H}}$ is a second random oracle. When proving security against $\mathcal{R}^*$, whenever $\mathcal{R}^*$ makes a query to $\hat{\mathsf{H}}$, the simulator samples a random $\hat{c}$ and programs $\mathsf{H}(\hat{c} + c_j) = pk_j^* - r$ for any previous query c_j to H for a public key of its choice. Since $\hat{c}$ is uniform, it is very unlikely that H has been programmed on this input for a previous query. Now we could just rely on the multi-user security of the PKE rather than trying to guess which of the previous queries corresponds to r_b. Nevertheless, $\mathcal{R}^*$ could first query $\hat{\mathsf{H}}$ for r and then query H for c_0, c_1 such that $\hat{\mathsf{H}}(r) = c_0 + c_1$. This would cause an issue in the programming strategy which assumes that the adversary queries first c_0 or c_1 to H. Further, this strategy does not seem to help $\mathcal{R}^*$ since by using a guessing strategy, we could show that by the security of the PKE, $\mathcal{R}^*$ cannot learn any of the OT strings. However, it seems that we cannot show this via a tight reduction.

We resolve the issue via the following approach. We let the receiver send (r, c_0, c_1) and the public keys are defined as $pk_0 := r + \hat{\mathsf{H}}(\hat{c}_0)$ and $pk_1 := r + \hat{\mathsf{H}}(\hat{c}_1)$, where $\hat{c}_0 := c_1 + \mathsf{H}(r, c_0)$ and $\hat{c}_1 := c_0 + \mathsf{H}(r, c_1)$. $\hat{c}_0$ and $\hat{c}_1$ could be seen as the r_0, r_1 values of the MR OT. But rather than using them directly, we apply an additional random oracle on them as "correlation breaker". A PKE scheme is typically not tightly secure in a setting where an adversary A can first suggest q shifts $\tilde{r}_1, \ldots, \tilde{r}_q$, then receives public key pk and finally tries to break IND-CPA security under public key $pk - \tilde{r}_j$ where $j \in [q]$ is chosen by A. Though a correlation robust hash function $\hat{\mathsf{H}}$ [IKNP03] is tailored to such a setting and maps all inputs $pk - r_1, \ldots, pk - r_q$ to strings that do not collide as long as pk is uniform and independent of $\tilde{r}_1, \ldots \tilde{r}_q$. In our setting, we need something stronger than correlation robustness since we also need programmability such that we can program these disjunct strings to different public keys. Fortunately, a random oracle provides both properties such that for any choice of r, c_0, c_1 among the random oracle queries of $\mathcal{R}^*$, at least one of the public keys pk_0 and pk_1 will correspond to a programmed key chosen by the simulator. When q is the total amount of random oracle queries, there are at most q^2 choices for r, c_0, c_1 among the queries. This is due to the fact, that for any $b \in \{0, 1\}$, c_b is uniquely defined by r and c_{1-b}. Therefore, there will be at most q^2 choices of public keys pk_0, pk_1 and hence the multi-user security of PKE for q^2 user is sufficient to prove security against a malicious receiver.

For the proof, it would sufficient to just hash r_0, r_1 of the MR OT, though in the actual protocol, we need to allow the receiver to control one of the public keys. For this reason we introduce r to the protocol. Interestingly, our protocol could be seen as a combination of sequential and parallel OR proof techniques.

2 Preliminaries

Notation. For $n \in \mathbb{N}$, we use $[n]$ to denote the set $\{1, \ldots, n\}$. We use λ to denote the security parameter. And $x \leftarrow \mathcal{X}$, $x \leftarrow X$ to sample x from a distribution $\mathcal{X}$ or uniformly random from a set X.

Let Π be a protocol between two parties $\mathcal{S}$ and $\mathcal{R}$. For two (interactive) algorithms $\mathcal{S}', \mathcal{R}'$ that do not necessarily follow the protocol description of Π, we use $[\mathcal{S}', \mathcal{R}']_\Pi$ to denote the interaction between $\mathcal{S}'$ and $\mathcal{R}'$ in protocol Π, where $\mathcal{S}'$ takes the role of $\mathcal{S}$ and $\mathcal{R}'$ the role of $\mathcal{R}$. For an environment D, we use $\mathsf{D}([\mathcal{S}', \mathcal{R}']_\Pi)$ to denote an interaction of D with $\mathcal{S}', \mathcal{R}'$ who interact in Π. Here, we follow the simple UC framework of [CCL15].

For a cyclic group $\mathcal{G}$ of order $p \in \mathbb{N}$ with generator g, we use $[\![1]\!]$ to denote g and for $a, b \in \mathbb{N}$, $[\![a]\!] + b[\![1]\!] = [\![a + b]\!]$. For $a, b \in \mathbb{Z}_q^\eta$, we use $\langle a, b \rangle$ to denote the inner product between a and b. For an oracle $\mathcal{O}$ and an algorithm A, we use $\mathsf{A}^\mathcal{O}$ to denote A when A has query access to $\mathcal{O}$.

Cryptographic Assumptions

We recap the DDH and LWE problems below. Since we consider the UC setting, we need to consider non-uniform algorithms which receive an auxiliary input.

Definition 1 (Decisional Diffie-Hellman (DDH)). *A ppt algorithm* A *solves the decisional Diffie-Hellman (DDH) problem for a group $\mathcal{G}$ of order $p \in \mathbb{N}$ with generator $[\![1]\!]$ with probability ϵ if for any polynomial auxiliary input z,*

$$| \Pr[\mathsf{A}(z, [\![1]\!], [\![a]\!], [\![b]\!], [\![ab]\!]) = 1] - \Pr[\mathsf{A}(z, [\![1]\!], [\![a]\!], [\![b]\!], [\![c]\!]) = 1]| \geq \epsilon,$$

where $a, b, c \leftarrow \mathbb{Z}_p$.

Definition 2 (Learning with Errors (LWE)). *A ppt algorithm* A *solves the Learning with Errors (LWE) problem for parameters $q, \eta \in \mathbb{N}$ and noise distribution $\mathcal{X}$ with probability ϵ if for any polynomial auxiliary input z*

$$| \Pr[\mathsf{A}^{\mathcal{O}_{\mathsf{LWE}}}(z) = 1] - \Pr[\mathsf{A}^{\mathcal{O}_{\mathsf{U}}}(z) = 1]| \geq \epsilon,$$

where $\mathcal{O}_{\mathsf{LWE}}$ is a oracle that outputs samples of the form $a, \langle a, s \rangle + e$ with $a \leftarrow \mathbb{Z}_q^\eta$, $e \leftarrow \mathcal{X}$ and each sample uses the same secret $s \leftarrow \mathbb{Z}_q^\eta$. $\mathcal{O}_{\mathsf{U}}$ is the oracle that outputs a, u with $a \leftarrow \mathbb{Z}_q^\eta$, $u \leftarrow \mathbb{Z}_q$.

Public Key Encryption. We define public key encryption and its multi-user security below. We emphasize that we consider a setting with only a single challenge ciphertext which is a weaker security notion than the commonly used multi-user security setting in which an adversary receives a challenge ciphertext for each public key.

Definition 3 (Public Key Encryption). *A public key encryption (PKE) is a triplet of algorithms* (Gen, Enc, Dec) *and a message space* M *with the following syntax.*

Gen: *Takes as input* 1^λ *and outputs a key pair* (sk, pk).
Enc: *Takes as input* pk *and a message* m ∈ M *and outputs a ciphertext* ct.
Dec: *Takes as input* sk *and a ciphertext* ct *and outputs a message* m.

We require correctness and M-IND-CPA *security.*

Correctness: *For any* m ∈ M

$$\Pr[\mathsf{Dec}(\mathsf{sk}, \mathsf{Enc}(\mathsf{pk}, \mathsf{m})) = \mathsf{m}] \geq 1 - \mathsf{negl},$$

where (sk, pk) ← Gen(1^λ).
n-**Multi-User IND-CPA** (M-IND-CPA): *For any ppt adversary* A := (A_1, A_2) *and any polynomial auxiliary input* z

$$| \Pr[\mathsf{A}_2(\mathsf{st}, \mathsf{ct}_0^*) = 1] - \Pr[\mathsf{A}_2(\mathsf{st}, \mathsf{ct}_1^*) = 1]| \leq \mathsf{negl},$$

where for all $i \in [n]$, ($\mathsf{sk}_i, \mathsf{pk}_i$) ← Gen($1^\lambda$), (st, i^*, m_0, m_1) ← $A_1(z, \mathsf{pk}_1, \ldots, \mathsf{pk}_n)$ *and for all* $b \in \{0, 1\}$ ct_b^* ← Enc(pk_{i^*}, m_b).

In addition to the multi-user IND-CPA security, we also need that public keys are indistinguishable from uniform in the multi-user setting.

Definition 4 (PKE with Pseudorandom Public Keys). *For* $n \in \mathbb{N}$, *we call a PKE scheme* n-*multi-user public key indistinguishable* (M-IND-PK) *over group* G *if for any ppt* A *and polynomial auxiliary input* z

$$| \Pr[\mathsf{A}(z, \mathsf{pk}_1, \ldots, \mathsf{pk}_n) = 1] - \Pr[\mathsf{A}(z, u_1, \ldots, u_n) = 1]| \leq \mathsf{negl},$$

where for all $i \in [n]$, ($\mathsf{sk}_i, \mathsf{pk}_i$) ← Gen($1^\lambda$) *and* u_i ← G.

Oblivious Transfer. We use the simplified UC framework which is sufficient for full UC [CCL15]. Below, we define UC secure OT.

Definition 5 (Ideal Oblivious Transfer Functionality). *An ideal OT functionality* $\mathcal{F}_{\mathsf{OT}}$ *interacts with two ppt parties* S *and* R *as follows.* $\mathcal{F}_{\mathsf{OT}}$ *takes* s_0, s_1 *from* S. $\mathcal{F}_{\mathsf{OT}}$ *takes* b *from* R *and returns* s_b.

Definition 6 (Oblivious Transfer). *We call a protocol* Π *between two ppt parties, a sender* S *and a receiver* R, *oblivious transfer (OT) if at the end of the protocol they have established a correlation in which* S *holds strings* (s_0, s_1) *and* R *holds* (b, s_b). *For security, we require two properties with respect to a functionality* $\mathcal{F}_{\mathsf{OT}}$.

Security Against a Malicious Sender: *For any ppt adversary* A, *there exists a ppt adversary* A' *such that for any ppt environment* D *and any polynomial size auxiliary input* z

$$|\Pr[D(z, [A, \mathcal{R}]_\Pi) = 1] - \Pr[D(z, [A', \mathcal{F}_{OT}]_\Pi) = 1]| = \mathsf{negl},$$

where all algorithms receive input 1^λ. $\mathcal{R}$ *additionally receives input* b.

Security Against a Malicious Receiver: *For any ppt adversary* A, *there exists a ppt adversary* A' *such that for any ppt environment* D *and any polynomial size auxiliary input* z

$$|\Pr[D(z, [\mathcal{S}, A]_\Pi) = 1] - \Pr[D(z, [\mathcal{F}_{OT}, A']_\Pi) = 1]| = \mathsf{negl},$$

where all algorithms receive input 1^λ.

3   Public Key Encryption in the Multi User Setting

We use this section to recap commonly known public key encryption schemes that are tightly secure in the multi-user setting. As a proof of concept, we consider ElGamal, Regev encryption and dual Regev encryption.

Definition 7 (ElGamal). *The ElGamal PKE over group* $\mathcal{G}$ *with order* $p \in \mathbb{N}$ *and generator* $[\![1]\!]$ *with message space* $\mathsf{M} := \mathcal{G}$ *has the following syntax.*

$\mathsf{Gen}([\![1]\!]) \to (\mathsf{pk}, \mathsf{sk})$: *Sample* $x \leftarrow \mathbb{Z}_p$ *and output* $\mathsf{pk} := [\![x]\!]$ *and* $\mathsf{sk} := x$.
$\mathsf{Enc}([\![1]\!], \mathsf{pk}, \mathsf{m}) \to (\mathsf{ct}_1, \mathsf{ct}_2)$: *Sample* $r \leftarrow \mathbb{Z}_p$ *and output* $\mathsf{ct}_1 := [\![r]\!]$, $\mathsf{ct}_2 := r\mathsf{pk}+\mathsf{m}$.
$\mathsf{Dec}([\![1]\!], \mathsf{sk}, \mathsf{ct}) \to \mathsf{m}$: *Output* $\mathsf{m} := \mathsf{ct}_2 - \mathsf{sk} \cdot \mathsf{ct}_1$.

It is straightforward to see that ElGamal is perfectly correct. Let us recap that it is tightly secure in the multi-user setting. Due to the fact that the public keys are uniform over $\mathcal{G}$, ElGamal is perfectly n-M-IND-PK secure.

Lemma 1. *Let* $\mathcal{G}$ *be of prime order and DDH be* ϵ *hard over* $\mathcal{G}$ *and* n *polynomial, then ElGamal over* $\mathcal{G}$ *is* 2ϵ n-M-IND-CPA *secure.*

Proof. The proof follows straightforwardly from the random selfreducibility of the DDH assumption. The reduction for parameter $d \in \{0, 1\}$ receives a DDH challenge $[\![a]\!], [\![b]\!], [\![c]\!]$ and samples for all $i \in [n]$ $r_i \leftarrow \mathbb{Z}_p$. It forwards z and $\mathsf{pk}_1 := r_1[\![a]\!], \ldots, \mathsf{pk}_n := r_n[\![a]\!]$ to A that tries to break ElGamal. When A send $i^*, \mathsf{m}_0, \mathsf{m}_1$, the reduction sends $\mathsf{ct} := ([\![b]\!], r_i[\![c]\!] \cdot \mathsf{m}_d)$. The reduction outputs the output of A.

When $[\![c]\!] = [\![ab]\!]$, ct is an encryption of m_d, i.e. $\mathsf{ct} := \mathsf{ct}_d$, while when c is uniform, ct encrypts a uniform message, i.e. $\mathsf{ct} := \mathsf{ct}_U$. If A distinguishes ct_d from ct_U with probability ϵ', the reduction solves DDH with probability ϵ'. Assuming that DDH is ϵ hard, A cannot distinguish ct_d from ct_U with $\epsilon' > \epsilon$ for any $d \in \{0, 1\}$ and it cannot distinguish ct_0 from ct_1 with $\epsilon' > 2\epsilon$.   □

Definition 8 (Regev Encryption [Reg05]). *Regev encryption with the parameters* $q, \eta, m \in \mathbb{N}$ *with* $m \geq \eta \log q$ *and message space* $\{0,1\}^m$ *has the following syntax.*

$\mathsf{Gen}(1^\lambda) \rightarrow (\mathsf{pk}, \mathsf{sk})$: *Sample* $s \leftarrow \mathbb{Z}_q^\eta$, $A \leftarrow \mathbb{Z}_q^{m \times \eta}$, $e \leftarrow \mathcal{X}^m$ *and output* $\mathsf{pk} :=$
$(A, As + e)$ *and* $\mathsf{sk} := s$.
$\mathsf{Enc}(\mathsf{pk}, \mathsf{m}) \rightarrow (\mathsf{ct}_1, \mathsf{ct}_2)$: *Sample* $R \leftarrow \{0,1\}^{m \times m}$ *and output* $\mathsf{ct}_1 := R\mathsf{pk}_1$, $\mathsf{ct}_2 :=$
$R\mathsf{pk}_2 + \mathsf{m}\lfloor \frac{q}{2} \rfloor$.
$\mathsf{Dec}(\mathsf{sk}, \mathsf{ct}) \rightarrow \mathsf{m}$: *Compute* $\hat{\mathsf{m}} := \mathsf{ct}_2 - \mathsf{ct}_1 \cdot \mathsf{sk}$ *and output* $\mathsf{m} := |\lfloor \frac{2}{q} \hat{\mathsf{m}} \rceil|$.

For a proper choice of q, m and $\mathcal{X}$, Regev encryption will be correct.

Lemma 2. *Let LWE be* ϵ *hard and* n *polynomial, then Regev encryption is* 2ϵ
n-*M-IND-CPA and* ϵ n-*M-IND-PK secure.*

Proof. We first show M-IND-CPA security. The reduction for parameter $d \in$
$\{0,1\}$ receives access to an oracle $\mathcal{O}$ that it uses to generate A_i, b_i for all $i \in [n]$.
It sets $\mathsf{pk}_i := (A_i, b_i + A_i s_i)$ for $s_i \leftarrow \mathbb{Z}_q^\eta$ and forwards them to A. After A sends
(i^*, m_0, m_1), the reduction samples $R \leftarrow \{0,1\}^{m \times m}$ and sends $\mathsf{ct} := (RA_i, R(b_i + A_i s_i) + \mathsf{m}\lfloor \frac{q}{2} \rceil)$. The reduction outputs the output of A.

When $\mathcal{O} = \mathcal{O}_{\mathsf{LWE}}$, ct is an encryption of m_d, i.e. $\mathsf{ct} := \mathsf{ct}_d$, while when $\mathcal{O} = \mathcal{O}_{\mathsf{U}}$,
ct is by the leftover hash lemma uniform, i.e. $\mathsf{ct} := \mathsf{ct}_{\mathsf{U}}$. If A distinguishes ct_d from
ct_{U} with probability ϵ', the reduction solves LWE with probability ϵ'. Assuming
that LWE is ϵ hard, A cannot distinguish ct_d from ct_{U} with $\epsilon' > \epsilon$ for any
$d \in \{0,1\}$ and it cannot distinguish ct_0 from ct_1 with $\epsilon' > 2\epsilon$.

Let us now consider the M-IND-PK security. The reduction defines pk_i as
previously. When $\mathcal{O} = \mathcal{O}_{\mathsf{LWE}}$, then pk_i is a proper public key and when $\mathcal{O} = \mathcal{O}_{\mathsf{U}}$,
then the public key is uniform. If A can distinguish them, it solves LWE.   □

Definition 9 (Dual Regev Encryption [GPV08]). *Dual Regev encryption
with the parameters* $q, \eta, m \in \mathbb{N}$ *with* $m \geq \eta \log q$ *and message space* $\{0,1\}^m$ *has
the following syntax.*

$\mathsf{Gen}(1^\lambda) \rightarrow (\mathsf{pk}, \mathsf{sk})$: *Sample* $R \leftarrow \{0,1\}^{m \times m}$, $A \leftarrow \mathbb{Z}_q^{m \times \eta}$ *and output* $\mathsf{pk} :=$
(A, RA) *and* $\mathsf{sk} := R$.
$\mathsf{Enc}(\mathsf{pk}, \mathsf{m}) \rightarrow (\mathsf{ct}_1, \mathsf{ct}_2)$: *Sample* $s \leftarrow \mathbb{Z}_q^n$, $e_1, e_2 \leftarrow \mathcal{X}^m$, $R' \leftarrow \{0,1\}^{m \times m}$ *and
outputs* $\mathsf{ct}_1 := \mathsf{pk}_1 \cdot s + e_1$, $\mathsf{ct}_2 := \mathsf{pk}_2 \cdot s + R'e_2 + \mathsf{m}\lfloor \frac{q}{2} \rceil$.
$\mathsf{Dec}(\mathsf{sk}, \mathsf{ct}) \rightarrow \mathsf{m}$: *Compute* $\hat{\mathsf{m}} := \mathsf{ct}_2 - \mathsf{sk} \cdot \mathsf{ct}_1$ *and output* $\mathsf{m} := |\lfloor \frac{2}{q} \hat{\mathsf{m}} \rceil|$.

Correctness follows in the same way as in Regev encryption. By the leftover
hash lemma, the public key is statistically indistinguishable from uniform and
therefore dual Regev encryption is M-IND-PK secure.

Lemma 3. *Let LWE be* ϵ *hard and* n *polynomial, then dual Regev encryption is*
2ϵ n-*M-IND-CPA secure.*

Proof. The reduction for parameter $d \in \{0,1\}$ receives access to an oracle $\mathcal{O}$
that it uses to generate A_i, b_i for all $i \in [n]$. It sets $\mathsf{pk}_i := (A_i, R_i A_i)$ for $R_i \leftarrow$

$\{0,1\}^{m \times m}$ and forwards them to A. After A sends (i^*, m_0, m_1), the reduction sends $\mathsf{ct} := (b_i, R_i b_i + \mathsf{m} \lfloor \frac{q}{2} \rceil)$. The reduction outputs the output of A.

When $\mathcal{O} = \mathcal{O}_{\mathsf{LWE}}$, ct is an encryption of m_d, i.e. $\mathsf{ct} := \mathsf{ct}_d$, while when $\mathcal{O} = \mathcal{O}_{\mathsf{U}}$, ct is by the leftover hash lemma (with leakage Re_2) uniform, i.e. $\mathsf{ct} := \mathsf{ct}_{\mathsf{U}}$. If A distinguishes ct_d from ct_{U} with probability ϵ', the reduction solves LWE with probability ϵ'. Assuming that LWE is ϵ hard, A cannot distinguish ct_d from ct_{U} with $\epsilon' > \epsilon$ for any $d \in \{0,1\}$ and it cannot distinguish ct_0 from ct_1 with $\epsilon' > 2\epsilon$. $\square$

We remark that our security proofs for multi user security require more LWE samples than the proofs of the standard PKE security notions. We emphasize that there are well known techniques to generate many LWE samples from a fixed amount of LWE samples [Reg05,ILL89]. Since such a rerandomization increases the noise level, one needs to start with a lower noise level which decreases the hardness of LWE slightly such that the approximation factor of the underlying SVP instance increases by a factor of $\tilde{O}(n^{1/2})$.

4   Oblivious Transfer from PKE

Theorem 1. *Let PKE be a* M-IND-CPA *and* M-IND-PK *secure and correct. Then Protocol 2 is a UC secure OT in the ROM.*

Proof. Given the correctness of PKE, an honest sender and receiver will establish correlation $(s_0, s_1), (b, s_b)$ with overwhelming probability.

We now focus on security against a malicious sender.

Lemma 4. *Let PKE be ϵ_u 1-M-IND-PK secure. Then, for any ppt adversary A, there exists a ppt adversary A' such that for any ppt environment D and any polynomial size auxiliary input z*

$$| \Pr[\mathsf{D}(z, [\mathsf{A}, \mathcal{R}]_{\Pi}) = 1] - \Pr[\mathsf{D}(z, [\mathsf{A}', \mathcal{F}_{\mathsf{OT}}]_{\Pi}) = 1]| \le \epsilon_u,$$

where all algorithms receive input 1^λ. $\mathcal{R}$ additionally receives input b.

Proof. We construct a receiver $\mathcal{R}'$ follows the description of $\mathcal{R}$ by sampling $(\mathsf{pk}_b, \mathsf{sk}_b) \leftarrow \mathsf{Gen}(1^\lambda)$, $\hat{c}_b \leftarrow \{0,1\}^\lambda$, $c_b \leftarrow \{0,1\}^\lambda$, computing $r := \mathsf{pk}_b - \hat{\mathsf{H}}_b(\hat{c}_b)$, $c_{1-b} := \hat{c}_b \oplus H(r, c_b)$. Unlike $\mathcal{R}$, $\mathcal{R}'$ computes $\hat{c}_{1-b} := c_b \oplus \mathsf{H}_{1-b}(r, c_{1-b})$, samples $(\mathsf{pk}_{1-b}, \mathsf{sk}_{1-b}) \leftarrow \mathsf{Gen}(1^\lambda)$ and programs $\hat{\mathsf{H}}_{1-b}(\hat{c}_{1-b}) := \mathsf{pk}_{1-b} - r$. Otherwise, $\mathcal{R}'$ follows the description of $\mathcal{R}$.

Notice that in case of $\mathcal{R}$, $r + \hat{\mathsf{H}}_{1-b}(\hat{c}_{1-b})$ is uniform while in case of $\mathcal{R}'$, it has the distribution of a public key generated by Gen. If D can distinguish $[\mathsf{A}, \mathcal{R}']$ from $[\mathsf{A}, \mathcal{R}]$, then D can be used to break the 1-M-IND-PK security of PKE with probability ϵ_u as follows. The reduction receives a 1-M-IND-PK challenge pk and sets $\mathsf{pk}_{1-b} := \mathsf{pk}$. When pk is uniform, it simulates $\mathcal{R}$ and otherwise $\mathcal{R}'$. Therefore,

$$| \Pr[\mathsf{D}(z, [\mathsf{A}, \mathcal{R}]_{\Pi}) = 1] - \Pr[\mathsf{D}(z, [\mathsf{A}, \mathcal{R}']_{\Pi}) = 1]| \le \epsilon_u.$$

Oblivious Transfer Protocol

Primitives:
- PKE scheme $(\mathsf{Gen}, \mathsf{Enc}, \mathsf{Dec})$ with pseudorandom public keys in G.
- Random oracles
  - $\mathsf{H}_0, \mathsf{H}_1 : \mathsf{G} \times \{0,1\}^\lambda \rightarrow \{0,1\}^\lambda$.
  - $\hat{\mathsf{H}}_0, \hat{\mathsf{H}}_1 : \{0,1\}^\lambda \rightarrow \mathsf{G}$.

Common input: 1^λ.
Sender $\mathcal{S}$ input: s_0, s_1.
Receiver $\mathcal{R}$ input: $b \in \{0,1\}$.

1. $\mathcal{R}$ samples $(\mathsf{pk}_b, \mathsf{sk}_b) \leftarrow \mathsf{Gen}(1^\lambda), \hat{c}_b \leftarrow \{0,1\}^\lambda, c_b \leftarrow \{0,1\}^\lambda$, computes
   - $r := \mathsf{pk}_b - \mathsf{H}_b(\hat{c}_b)$
   - $c_{1-b} := \hat{c}_b \oplus \mathsf{H}_b(r, c_b)$
   and sends (r, c_0, c_1).
2. $\mathcal{S}$ computes
   - $\hat{c}_0 := c_1 \oplus \mathsf{H}_0(r, c_0), \hat{c}_1 := c_0 \oplus \mathsf{H}_1(r, c_1)$,
   - $\mathsf{pk}_0 := r + \hat{\mathsf{H}}_0(\hat{c}_0), \mathsf{pk}_1 := r + \hat{\mathsf{H}}_1(\hat{c}_1)$,
   - $\mathsf{ct}_0 := \mathsf{Enc}(\mathsf{pk}_0, s_0), \mathsf{ct}_1 := \mathsf{Enc}(\mathsf{pk}_1, s_1)$,
   and sends $(\mathsf{ct}_0, \mathsf{ct}_1)$.
3. $\mathcal{R}$ computes $s_b := \mathsf{Dec}(\mathsf{sk}_b, \mathsf{ct}_b)$.

Fig. 2. Oblivious Transfer in the Random Oracle Model. $(+, -)$ are used to denote the operations in G. $\oplus$ is the xor operation over $\{0,1\}^*$.

Based on $\mathcal{R}'$, we can construct an adversary A' which interacts with A, relays all interaction between A and D and needs to submit s_0 and s_1 to $\mathcal{F}_{\mathsf{OT}}$. A' follows the process of $\mathcal{R}'$ when constructing r, c_0, c_1 that defines pk_0 and pk_1. As $\mathcal{R}'$, A' knows both, sk_0 and sk_1 which A' uses to decrypt ct_0 and ct_1 to obtain s_0 and s_1. Since, A' follows the description of $\mathcal{R}'$, it leads to the same interaction between A and D. Therefore

$$\Pr[\mathsf{D}(z, [\mathsf{A}, \mathcal{R}']_\Pi) = 1] = \Pr[\mathsf{D}(z, [\mathsf{A}', \mathcal{F}_{\mathsf{OT}}]_\Pi) = 1],$$

which concludes the proof of the lemma. $\square$

We conclude the theorem with the following lemma that establishes security against a malicious receiver.

Lemma 5. *Let PKE be ϵ_u q^2-M-IND-PK and ϵ_t q^2-M-IND-CPA secure. Then, for any ppt adversary A making at most q random oracle queries to H_0, H_1, $\hat{\mathsf{H}}_0$ and $\hat{\mathsf{H}}_1$ combined, there exists a ppt adversary A' such that for any ppt environment D and any polynomial size auxiliary input z*

$$|\Pr[\mathsf{D}(z, [\mathcal{S}, \mathsf{A}]_\Pi) = 1] - \Pr[\mathsf{D}(z, [\mathcal{F}_{\mathsf{OT}}, \mathsf{A}']_\Pi) = 1]| \leq \epsilon_u + \epsilon_t + \frac{q^2}{2^\lambda},$$

where all algorithms receive input 1^λ.

Proof. For simplicity, we assume that when A sends r, c_0, c_1 during the protocol to the sender, it has queried the random oracles for $H_0(r, c_0)$, $H_1(r, c_1)$, $\hat{H}_0(\hat{c}_0)$ and $\hat{H}_1(\hat{c}_1)$. We can assume this without loss of generality by making at most 4 additional queries and setting the amount of queries to $\hat{q} = q + 4$. Since this is not significant for our overall bound, we identify $\hat{q}$ with q in the following. We also assume without loss of generality that A queries an oracle only once per input.

We define three intermediate algorithms $\mathcal{S}_1, \mathcal{S}_2, \mathcal{S}_3$ playing the role of sender $\mathcal{S}$. $\mathcal{S}_1$ is identical to $\mathcal{S}$ except that it simulates random oracles H_0, H_1 as follows. For all $i \in [q]$ and $j \in [q]$ (where q is the amount of queries), it samples $\mathsf{pk}_{i,j} \leftarrow G$. Whenever A makes a query $r_i, c_{i,d}$ to H_d for $i \in [q]$ and $d \in \{0,1\}$, $\mathcal{S}_1$ samples $H_d(r_i, c_{i,d}) \leftarrow \{0,1\}^\lambda$ and does the following for any $j \in [q]$ with $j < i$ for which the jth query is a query $r_j, c_{j,1-d}$ to H_{1-d} with $r_j = r_i$.

1. Compute $\hat{c}_{i,j,d} := c_{j,1-d} \oplus H_d(r_i, c_{i,d})$.
2. If $\hat{H}_d(\hat{c}_{i,j,d})$ is defined (through programming or a query), abort. Otherwise, program $\hat{H}_d(\hat{c}_{i,j,d}) := \mathsf{pk}_{i,j} - r_i$.

Afterwards, $\mathcal{S}_1$ answers the query with $H_d(r_i, c_{i,d})$.

When A sends r, c_0, c_1, $\mathcal{S}_1$ computes $\mathsf{pk}_0, \mathsf{pk}_1$ in the same way as $\mathcal{S}$. $\mathcal{S}_1$ defines b^* such that $\mathsf{pk}_{1-b^*} = \mathsf{pk}_{i,j}$ for a $i \in [q]$ and $j \in [q]$. If no such b^*, i, j exists, $\mathcal{S}_1$ aborts. Otherwise, it concludes the protocol according to the description of $\mathcal{S}$.

Let us now consider whether an environment D can distinguish $[A, \mathcal{S}]$ from $[A, \mathcal{S}_1]$. Since $\mathsf{pk}_{i,j}$ are uniform in G, the output distribution of $\hat{H}_d$, in particular for every point $\hat{H}_d(\hat{c}_{i,j,d}) := \mathsf{pk}_{i,j} - r_i$ is uniform over G, in both settings. Other than that, $\mathcal{S}_1$ differs from $\mathcal{S}$ by two abort conditions - one during queries to H_d and one after seeing (r, c_0, c_1). Let us assume that $\mathcal{S}_1$ aborts during a query to H_d. This implies that either A has queried $\hat{H}_d$ for $\hat{c}_{i,j,d} = c_{j,1-d} \oplus H_d(r_i, c_{i,d})$ for an $j \in [q]$ or there exists a $j \in [q]$ and a $j' \in [q] \setminus \{j\}$ with $c_{j,1-d} \oplus H_d(r_i, c_{i,d}) = c_{j',1-d} \oplus H_d(r_i, c_{i,d})$. In the former case, A would predict $H_d(r_i, c_{i,d}) = c_{j,1-d} \oplus \hat{c}_{i,j,d}$ which happens for each query with probability at most $\frac{q}{2^\lambda}$. In the latter case, $c_{j,1-d} = c_{j',1-d}$ and thus A would make the same query twice which we have excluded w.l.o.g. since every adversary queries any input at most once.[1]

The second abort condition never triggers for the following reason. Since A sends r, c_0, c_1, he will query r, c_0 to H_0 and r, c_1 to H_1. Let $b^* \in \{0,1\}$ such that A makes query r, c_{b^*} before r, c_{1-b^*}. When A makes query c_{1-b^*}, c_{b^*} will therefore be defined and $\mathcal{S}_1$ will program $\hat{H}_{1-b^*}(c_{b^*} \oplus H_d(r, c_{1-b^*})) = \mathsf{pk}_{i,j} - r$ for some $i, j \in [q]$. By the definition of pk_{1-b^*}, $\mathsf{pk}_{1-b^*} = \mathsf{pk}_{i,j}$. Thus, we obtain the bound

$$|\Pr[D(z, [\mathcal{S}, A]_\Pi) = 1] - \Pr[D(z, [\mathcal{S}_1, A]_\Pi) = 1]| \leq \frac{q^2}{2^\lambda}.$$

---

[1] In case an adversary is allowed to query inputs multiple time, $\mathcal{S}_1$ would simply not try to program the oracle on an input that the adversary has queried already and send the output that is consistent with the previous query for that input.

$\mathcal{S}_2$ is identical to $\mathcal{S}_1$ except that it samples $(\mathsf{pk}_{i,j}, \mathsf{sk}_{i,j}) \leftarrow \mathsf{Gen}(1^\lambda)$ for any $i, j \in [q]$. If there is an environment D that can distinguish $[\mathsf{A}, \mathcal{S}_2]$ from $[\mathsf{A}, \mathcal{S}_1]$, then we can break the q^2-M-IND-PK security, i.e. public keys are hard to distinguish from uniform, of PKE as follows. The reduction receives q^2 challenge public keys $\widehat{\mathsf{pk}}_{i,j}$ for $i, j \in [q]$. Instead of sampling $\mathsf{pk}_{i,j}$, it sets $\mathsf{pk}_{i,j} := \widehat{\mathsf{pk}}_{i,j}$.

When the challenge public keys are uniform, the reduction simulates $\mathcal{S}_1$ and otherwise (when the challenge public keys are distributed according to Gen) $\mathcal{S}_2$. Therefore,

$$| \Pr[\mathsf{D}(z, [\mathcal{S}_1, \mathsf{A}]_\Pi) = 1] - \Pr[\mathsf{D}(z, [\mathcal{S}_2, \mathsf{A}]_\Pi) = 1]| \le \epsilon_u.$$

Our next intermediate sender $\mathcal{S}_3$ follows the description of $\mathcal{S}_2$ except that after receiving r, c_0, c_1 from A, it defines $\mathsf{ct}_{1-b^*} := \mathsf{Enc}(\mathsf{pk}_{1-b^*}, 0)$. If there is an environment D that can distinguish $[\mathsf{A}, \mathcal{S}_2]$ from $[\mathsf{A}, \mathcal{S}_3]$, we can break the q^2-M-IND-CPA security of PKE as follows. The reduction receives q^2 challenge public keys $\widehat{\mathsf{pk}}_{i,j}$ for $i, j \in [q]$. As previously, it sets $\mathsf{pk}_{i,j} := \widehat{\mathsf{pk}}_{i,j}$. It then follows the description of $\mathcal{S}_2$ until it defines b^* and can compute $\mathsf{pk}_{1-b^*} = \mathsf{pk}_{i,j}$ for some $i, j \in [q]$. The reduction sends $((i, j), \mathsf{m}_0 := s_{1-b^*}, \mathsf{m}_1 := 0)$ to the M-IND-CPA challenger and receives back ct^*. It then sets $\mathsf{ct}_{1-b^*} := \mathsf{ct}^*$. When ct^* encrypts s_{1-b^*}, the reduction simulates $\mathcal{S}_2$ and otherwise $\mathcal{S}_3$. Therefore,

$$| \Pr[\mathsf{D}(z, [\mathcal{S}_2, \mathsf{A}]_\Pi) = 1] - \Pr[\mathsf{D}(z, [\mathcal{S}_3, \mathsf{A}]_\Pi) = 1]| \le \epsilon_t.$$

Based on $\mathcal{S}_3$, we can define A$'$ which interacts with A, relays all interaction between A and D and submits b^* to $\mathcal{F}_{\mathsf{OT}}$ and then receives s_{b^*} which is used to generate ct_{b^*}. Since A$'$ follows the description of $\mathcal{S}_3$, it leads to the same interaction between A and D. Therefore, we can conclude the lemma with

$$\Pr[\mathsf{D}(z, [\mathcal{S}_3, \mathsf{A}]_\Pi) = 1] = \Pr[\mathsf{D}(z, [\mathcal{F}_{\mathsf{OT}}, \mathsf{A}']_\Pi) = 1].$$

$\square$

Lemmas 4 and 5 are sufficient to establish Theorem 1. $\square$

Acknowledgements. We thank James Bartusek for a discussion that led to the techniques presented in this paper.

References

[ABC+20] Albrecht, M.R.: Classic McEliece. Technical report, National Institute of Standards and Technology (2020). https://csrc.nist.gov/projects/post-quantum-cryptography/round-3-submissions

[AOS02] Abe, M., Ohkubo, M., Suzuki, K.: 1-out-of-n signatures from a variety of keys. In: Zheng, Y. (ed.) ASIACRYPT 2002. LNCS, vol. 2501, pp. 415–432. Springer, Heidelberg (2002). https://doi.org/10.1007/3-540-36178-2_26

[BBM00] Bellare, M., Boldyreva, A., Micali, S.: Public-key encryption in a multi-user setting: security proofs and improvements. In: Preneel, B. (ed.) EUROCRYPT 2000. LNCS, vol. 1807, pp. 259–274. Springer, Heidelberg (2000). https://doi.org/10.1007/3-540-45539-6_18

[BCJ+19] Bradley, T., Camenisch, J., Jarecki, S., Lehmann, A., Neven, G., Xu, J.: Password-authenticated public-key encryption. In: Deng, R.H., Gauthier-Umaña, V., Ochoa, M., Yung, M. (eds.) ACNS 2019. LNCS, vol. 11464, pp. 442–462. Springer, Cham (2019). https://doi.org/10.1007/978-3-030-21568-2_22

[BD18] Brakerski, Z., Döttling, N.: Two-message statistically sender-private OT from LWE. In: Beimel, A., Dziembowski, S. (eds.) TCC 2018. LNCS, vol. 11240, pp. 370–390. Springer, Cham (2018). https://doi.org/10.1007/978-3-030-03810-6_14

[BDK+20] Büscher, N., et al.: Secure two-party computation in a quantum world. In: Conti, M., Zhou, J., Casalicchio, E., Spognardi, A. (eds.) ACNS 2020. LNCS, vol. 12146, pp. 461–480. Springer, Cham (2020). https://doi.org/10.1007/978-3-030-57808-4_23

[BGV12] Brakerski, Z., Gentry, C., Vaikuntanathan, V.: (Leveled) fully homomorphic encryption without bootstrapping. In: Goldwasser, S. (ed.) ITCS 2012, pp. 309–325. ACM, January 2012

[BHJ+15] Bader, C., Hofheinz, D., Jager, T., Kiltz, E., Li, Y.: Tightly-secure authenticated key exchange. In: Dodis, Y., Nielsen, J.B. (eds.) TCC 2015. LNCS, vol. 9014, pp. 629–658. Springer, Heidelberg (2015). https://doi.org/10.1007/978-3-662-46494-6_26

[BL18] Benhamouda, F., Lin, H.: k-round multiparty computation from k-round oblivious transfer via garbled interactive circuits. In: Nielsen, J.B., Rijmen, V. (eds.) EUROCRYPT 2018. LNCS, vol. 10821, pp. 500–532. Springer, Cham (2018). https://doi.org/10.1007/978-3-319-78375-8_17

[BR93] Bellare, M., Rogaway, P.: Random oracles are practical: a paradigm for designing efficient protocols. In: Denning, D.E., Pyle, R., Ganesan, R., Sandhu, R.S., Ashby, V. (eds.) ACM CCS 1993, pp. 62–73. ACM Press, November 1993

[CCL15] Canetti, R., Cohen, A., Lindell, Y.: A simpler variant of universally composable security for standard multiparty computation. In: Gennaro, R., Robshaw, M. (eds.) CRYPTO 2015. LNCS, vol. 9216, pp. 3–22. Springer, Heidelberg (2015). https://doi.org/10.1007/978-3-662-48000-7_1

[CDH+20] Chen, C., et al.: NTRU. Technical report, National Institute of Standards and Technology (2020). https://csrc.nist.gov/projects/post-quantum-cryptography/round-3-submissions

[CDS94] Cramer, R., Damgård, I., Schoenmakers, B.: Proofs of partial knowledge and simplified design of witness hiding protocols. In: Desmedt, Y.G. (ed.) CRYPTO 1994. LNCS, vol. 839, pp. 174–187. Springer, Heidelberg (1994). https://doi.org/10.1007/3-540-48658-5_19

[CGH98] Canetti, R., Goldreich, O., Halevi, S.: The random oracle methodology, revisited (preliminary version). In: 30th ACM STOC, pp. 209–218. ACM Press, May 1998

[CKMS16] Chatterjee, S., Koblitz, N., Menezes, A., Sarkar, P.: Another look at tightness II: practical issues in cryptography. Cryptology ePrint Archive, Report 2016/360 (2016). https://eprint.iacr.org/2016/360

[CO15] Chou, T., Orlandi, C.: The simplest protocol for oblivious transfer. In: Lauter, K., Rodríguez-Henríquez, F. (eds.) LATINCRYPT 2015. LNCS, vol. 9230, pp. 40–58. Springer, Cham (2015). https://doi.org/10.1007/978-3-319-22174-8_3

[CSW20] Canetti, R., Sarkar, P., Wang, X.: Efficient and round-optimal oblivious transfer and commitment with adaptive security. In: Moriai, S., Wang, H. (eds.) ASIACRYPT 2020. LNCS, vol. 12493, pp. 277–308. Springer, Cham (2020). https://doi.org/10.1007/978-3-030-64840-4_10

[CvT95] Crépeau, C., van de Graaf, J., Tapp, A.: Committed oblivious transfer and private multi-party computation. In: Coppersmith, D. (ed.) CRYPTO 1995. LNCS, vol. 963, pp. 110–123. Springer, Heidelberg (1995). https://doi.org/10.1007/3-540-44750-4_9

[DKR+20] D'Anvers, J.-P., et al.: SABER. Technical report, National Institute of Standards and Technology (2020). https://csrc.nist.gov/projects/post-quantum-cryptography/round-3-submissions

[DNM12] David, B.M., Nascimento, A.C.A., Müller-Quade, J.: Universally composable oblivious transfer from lossy encryption and the McEliece assumptions. In: Smith, A. (ed.) ICITS 2012. LNCS, vol. 7412, pp. 80–99. Springer, Heidelberg (2012). https://doi.org/10.1007/978-3-642-32284-6_5

[DvMN08] Dowsley, R., van de Graaf, J., Müller-Quade, J., Nascimento, A.C.A.: Oblivious transfer based on the McEliece assumptions. In: Safavi-Naini, R. (ed.) ICITS 2008. LNCS, vol. 5155, pp. 107–117. Springer, Heidelberg (2008). https://doi.org/10.1007/978-3-540-85093-9_11

[EGL82] Even, S., Goldreich, O., Lempel, A.: A randomized protocol for signing contracts. In: Chaum, D., Rivest, R.L., Sherman, A.T. (eds.) CRYPTO 1982, pp. 205–210. Plenum Press, New York (1982)

[GIR17] Genç, Z.A., Iovino, V., Rial, A.: "The simplest protocol for oblivious transfer" revisited. Cryptology ePrint Archive, Report 2017/370 (2017). https://eprint.iacr.org/2017/370

[GJ18] Gjøsteen, K., Jager, T.: Practical and tightly-secure digital signatures and authenticated key exchange. In: Shacham, H., Boldyreva, A. (eds.) CRYPTO 2018. LNCS, vol. 10992, pp. 95–125. Springer, Cham (2018). https://doi.org/10.1007/978-3-319-96881-0_4

[GKP18] Giacon, F., Kiltz, E., Poettering, B.: Hybrid encryption in a multi-user setting, revisited. In: Abdalla, M., Dahab, R. (eds.) PKC 2018. LNCS, vol. 10769, pp. 159–189. Springer, Cham (2018). https://doi.org/10.1007/978-3-319-76578-5_6

[GPV08] Gentry, C., Peikert, C., Vaikuntanathan, V.: Trapdoors for hard lattices and new cryptographic constructions. In: Ladner, R.E., Dwork, C. (eds.) 40th ACM STOC, pp. 197–206. ACM Press, May 2008

[GS18] Garg, S., Srinivasan, A.: Two-round multiparty secure computation from minimal assumptions. In: Nielsen, J.B., Rijmen, V. (eds.) EUROCRYPT 2018. LNCS, vol. 10821, pp. 468–499. Springer, Cham (2018). https://doi.org/10.1007/978-3-319-78375-8_16

[Hås88] Håstad, J.: Solving simultaneous modular equations of low degree. SIAM J. Comput. 17(2), 336–341 (1988)

[HJ12] Hofheinz, D., Jager, T.: Tightly secure signatures and public-key encryption. In: Safavi-Naini, R., Canetti, R. (eds.) CRYPTO 2012. LNCS, vol. 7417, pp. 590–607. Springer, Heidelberg (2012). https://doi.org/10.1007/978-3-642-32009-5_35

[HL17] Hauck, E., Loss, J.: Efficient and universally composable protocols for oblivious transfer from the CDH assumption. Cryptology ePrint Archive, Report 2017/1011 (2017). https://eprint.iacr.org/2017/1011

[IKNP03] Ishai, Y., Kilian, J., Nissim, K., Petrank, E.: Extending oblivious transfers efficiently. In: Boneh, D. (ed.) CRYPTO 2003. LNCS, vol. 2729, pp. 145–161. Springer, Heidelberg (2003). https://doi.org/10.1007/978-3-540-45146-4_9

[IKO+11] Ishai, Y., Kushilevitz, E., Ostrovsky, R., Prabhakaran, M., Sahai, A.: Efficient non-interactive secure computation. In: Paterson, K.G. (ed.) EUROCRYPT 2011. LNCS, vol. 6632, pp. 406–425. Springer, Heidelberg (2011). https://doi.org/10.1007/978-3-642-20465-4_23

[ILL89] Impagliazzo, R., Levin, L.A., Luby, M.: Pseudo-random generation from one-way functions (extended abstracts). In: 21st ACM STOC, pp. 12–24. ACM Press, May 1989

[IPS08] Ishai, Y., Prabhakaran, M., Sahai, A.: Founding cryptography on oblivious transfer - efficiently. In: Wagner, D. (ed.) CRYPTO 2008. LNCS, vol. 5157, pp. 572–591. Springer, Heidelberg (2008). https://doi.org/10.1007/978-3-540-85174-5_32

[JKRS21] Jager, T., Kiltz, E., Riepel, D., Schäge, S.: Tightly-secure authenticated key exchange, revisited. In: Canteaut, A., Standaert, F.-X. (eds.) EUROCRYPT 2021. LNCS, vol. 12696, pp. 117–146. Springer, Cham (2021). https://doi.org/10.1007/978-3-030-77870-5_5

[Kil88] Kilian, J.: Founding cryptography on oblivious transfer. In: 20th ACM STOC, pp. 20–31. ACM Press, May 1988

[KKRT16] Kolesnikov, V., Kumaresan, R., Rosulek, M., Trieu, N.: Efficient batched oblivious PRF with applications to private set intersection. In: Weippl, E.R., Katzenbeisser, S., Kruegel, C., Myers, A.C., Halevi, S. (eds.) ACM CCS 2016, pp. 818–829. ACM Press, October 2016

[KMP16] Kiltz, E., Masny, D., Pan, J.: Optimal security proofs for signatures from identification schemes. In: Robshaw, M., Katz, J. (eds.) CRYPTO 2016. LNCS, vol. 9815, pp. 33–61. Springer, Heidelberg (2016). https://doi.org/10.1007/978-3-662-53008-5_2

[KOS16] Keller, M., Orsini, E., Scholl, P.: MASCOT: faster malicious arithmetic secure computation with oblivious transfer. In: Weippl, E.R., Katzenbeisser, S., Kruegel, C., Myers, A.C., Halevi, S. (eds.) ACM CCS 2016, pp. 830–842. ACM Press, October 2016

[LLGW20] Liu, X., Liu, S., Gu, D., Weng, J.: Two-pass authenticated key exchange with explicit authentication and tight security. In: Moriai, S., Wang, H. (eds.) ASIACRYPT 2020. LNCS, vol. 12492, pp. 785–814. Springer, Cham (2020). https://doi.org/10.1007/978-3-030-64834-3_27

[LPR10] Lyubashevsky, V., Peikert, C., Regev, O.: On ideal lattices and learning with errors over rings. In: Gilbert, H. (ed.) EUROCRYPT 2010. LNCS, vol. 6110, pp. 1–23. Springer, Heidelberg (2010). https://doi.org/10.1007/978-3-642-13190-5_1

[LS15] Langlois, A., Stehlé, D.: Worst-case to average-case reductions for module lattices. Des. Codes Crypt. 75(3), 565–599 (2014). https://doi.org/10.1007/s10623-014-9938-4

[MR18] Mohassel, P., Rindal, P.: ABY^3: a mixed protocol framework for machine learning. In: Lie, D., Mannan, M., Backes, M., Wang, X. (eds.) ACM CCS 2018, pp. 35–52. ACM Press, October 2018

[MR19] Masny, D., Rindal, P.: Endemic oblivious transfer. In: Cavallaro, L., Kinder, J., Wang, X., Katz, J. (eds.) ACM CCS 2019, pp. 309–326. ACM Press, November 2019

[MRR20] McQuoid, I., Rosulek, M., Roy, L.: Minimal symmetric PAKE and 1-out-of-N OT from programmable-once public functions. In: Ligatti, J., Ou, X., Katz, J., Vigna, G. (eds.) ACM CCS 2020, pp. 425–442. ACM Press, November 2020

[MRR21] McQuoid, I., Rosulek, M., Roy, L.: Batching base oblivious transfers. IACR Cryptol. ePrint Arch. **2021**, 682 (2021)

[MW21] Masny, D., Watson, G.J.: A PKI-based framework for establishing efficient MPC channels. In: Kim, Y., Kim, J., Vigna, G., Shi, E. (eds.) CCS 2021: 2021 ACM SIGSAC Conference on Computer and Communications Security, Virtual Event, Republic of Korea, 15–19 November 2021, pp. 1961–1980. ACM (2021)

[NNOB12] Nielsen, J.B., Nordholt, P.S., Orlandi, C., Burra, S.S.: A new approach to practical active-secure two-party computation. In: Safavi-Naini, R., Canetti, R. (eds.) CRYPTO 2012. LNCS, vol. 7417, pp. 681–700. Springer, Heidelberg (2012). https://doi.org/10.1007/978-3-642-32009-5_40

[PR20] Pan, J., Ringerud, M.: Signatures with tight multi-user security from search assumptions. In: Chen, L., Li, N., Liang, K., Schneider, S. (eds.) ESORICS 2020. LNCS, vol. 12309, pp. 485–504. Springer, Cham (2020). https://doi.org/10.1007/978-3-030-59013-0_24

[PRTY20] Pinkas, B., Rosulek, M., Trieu, N., Yanai, A.: PSI from PaXoS: fast, malicious private set intersection. In: Canteaut, A., Ishai, Y. (eds.) EUROCRYPT 2020. LNCS, vol. 12106, pp. 739–767. Springer, Cham (2020). https://doi.org/10.1007/978-3-030-45724-2_25

[PVW08] Peikert, C., Vaikuntanathan, V., Waters, B.: A framework for efficient and composable oblivious transfer. In: Wagner, D. (ed.) CRYPTO 2008. LNCS, vol. 5157, pp. 554–571. Springer, Heidelberg (2008). https://doi.org/10.1007/978-3-540-85174-5_31

[Rab81] Rabin, M.O.: How to exchange secrets by oblivious transfer. Technical report, Harvard University (1981)

[Reg05] Regev, O.: On lattices, learning with errors, random linear codes, and cryptography. In: Gabow, H.N., Fagin, R. (eds.) 37th ACM STOC, pp. 84–93. ACM Press, May 2005

[RST01] Rivest, R.L., Shamir, A., Tauman, Y.: How to leak a secret. In: Boyd, C. (ed.) ASIACRYPT 2001. LNCS, vol. 2248, pp. 552–565. Springer, Heidelberg (2001). https://doi.org/10.1007/3-540-45682-1_32

[SAB+20] Schwabe, P., et al.: CRYSTALS-KYBER. Technical report, National Institute of Standards and Technology (2020). https://csrc.nist.gov/projects/post-quantum-cryptography/round-3-submissions

[Yao82] Yao, A.C.-C.: Protocols for secure computations (extended abstract). In: 23rd FOCS, pp. 160–164. IEEE Computer Society Press, November 1982

[Yao86] Yao, A.C.-C.: How to generate and exchange secrets (extended abstract). In: 27th FOCS, pp. 162–167. IEEE Computer Society Press, October 1986

[Zav12] Zaverucha, G.M.: Hybrid encryption in the multi-user setting. Cryptology ePrint Archive, Report 2012/159 (2012). https://eprint.iacr.org/2012/159

Efficient Two-Party Exponentiation from Quotient Transfer

Yi Lu[1,2(✉)], Keisuke Hara[2,3], Kazuma Ohara[2], Jacob Schuldt[2], and Keisuke Tanaka[1]

[1] Tokyo Institute of Technology, Tokyo, Japan
lu.y.ai@m.titech.ac.jp, keisuke@c.titech.ac.jp
[2] National Institute of Advanced Industrial Science and Technology (AIST), Tokyo, Japan
{hara-keisuke,ohara.kazuma,jacob.schuldt}@aist.go.jp
[3] Yokohama National University, Yokohama, Japan

Abstract. Secure multi-party computation (MPC) allows participating parties to jointly compute a function over their inputs while keeping them private. In particular, MPC based on additive secret sharing has been widely studied as a tool to obtain efficient protocols secure against a dishonest majority, including the important two-party case. In this paper, we propose a two-party protocol for an exponentiation functionality based on an additive secret sharing scheme. Our proposed protocol aims to securely compute a public base exponentiation $a^x \bmod p$ for some prime p, where the exponent $x \in \mathbb{Z}_p$ is a (shared) secret and the base $a \in \mathbb{Z}_p$ is public. Our protocol is based on a new simple but efficient approach involving quotient transfer that allows the parties to perform the most expensive part of the computation locally, and requires 3 rounds and 4 invocations of multiplication. As an intermediate primitive for our efficient two-party exponentiation protocol, we propose an efficient modulus conversion protocol. This protocol might be of independent interest.

1 Introduction

1.1 Background

Secure multi-party computation (MPC) allows a set of parties to compute an arbitrary function of their inputs without revealing the private inputs to each other, except for what can be obtained from the output of the function. While MPC is applicable in many different settings, a line of research which has attracted a lot of attention recently, is the application of MPC in the area of machine learning (*e.g.*, see [RSC+19, MLS+20, CVA18, KRC+20, AA20, CCPS19, BCP+20, CRS20]). One of the technical issues when combining MPC and deep learning is that deep learning require various operations which are difficult to implement in MPC efficiently (*e.g.*, division, reciprocal operation, square root, and exponentiation).

Exponentiation in MPC. In this paper, we deal with how to implement an exponentiation functionality in MPC based on secret sharing. Exponentiation is frequently used function in machine learning, and is also useful e.g. for protecting secret keys

© Springer Nature Switzerland AG 2022
G. Ateniese and D. Venturi (Eds.): ACNS 2022, LNCS 13269, pp. 643–662, 2022.
https://doi.org/10.1007/978-3-031-09234-3_32

in distributed systems such as Blockchain. In the latter context, MPC is used to generate discrete logarithm-based digital signatures while distributing the secret key, which is referred to as a threshold signatures or distributed signatures [GGN16,Lin17, WWW+14].

Exponentiation MPC protocols for different settings have been proposed so far. The first one is *public base*: the base is public and the exponent is secret; the second one is *public exponent*: the base is private and the exponent is public; and last one is *private exponentiation*: both the base and the exponent are privately held. In this paper, we focus on the public base variant. This variant shows up in many real-world applications. For example, in the deep learning setting mentioned above, it is frequently required that the value e^x is computed, where e is Napier's constant.

In the following, in order to clarify our goal, we highlight three properties of exponentiation MPC protocols: (based on) additive secret sharing/Shamir's secret sharing, honest-majority/dishonest-majority, and with/without bit-decomposition. Firstly, we note that our goal is to construct an efficient public base exponentiation protocol *without using bit-decomposition* based on *additive secret sharing* in the *dishonest-majority* setting.

Additive Secret Sharing vs. Shamir's Secret Sharing. When constructing MPC protocols based on secret sharing, we mainly have two types of secret sharing: additive secret sharing and Shamir's secret sharing.

Additive secret sharing [ISO] is defined over a finite additive group $(\mathbb{G}, +)$. In additive secret sharing for n parties, a secret $x \in \mathbb{G}$ will be randomly divided into $[x]^1, \ldots, [x]^n$ such that $[x]^1 + \cdots + [x]^n = x$, where n is the number of parties. The defined group for additive secret sharing determines the element form of shares and type of circuit on which parties want to perform.

Compared with Shamir's secret sharing, which is based on polynomial interpolation, one of the advantages of MPC based on additive secret sharing is the compatibility with "dishonest-majority" MPC frameworks. In other words, MPC based on additive secret sharing can be easily integrated with existing dishonest-majority MPC frameworks [DPSZ12,DKL+13,KPR18,ALSZ15,KOS16], and thus can utilize the ecosystems of these frameworks such as other efficient MPC protocols or cheater detection functionality. This is explained in more detail below.

Dishonest-Majority vs. Honest-Majority. Honest/dishonest-majority is a criteria of MPC security regarding the number of corrupted parties among all participants. We call a MPC protocol secure against an honest (resp. dishonest) majority if the number of corrupted parties are less than (resp. equal or more) than half of the total number of parties. Note that security in the dishonest-majority setting is much harder to achieve than in the honest-majority setting. In the fully information-theoretic setting, there exists an impossibility result showing that MPC for arbitrary functions cannot be constructed in the dishonest-majority setting [BGW88]. To achieve security against a dishonest majority, the previous works often introduce some computational assumptions, or the "online/offline" paradigm described below.

A Bit-Decomposition-Based Approach. A common approach for realizing some MPC functionalities is to firstly compute a binary representation of the input in secret-shared form, and then construct a MPC protocol for the evaluation of the functionality in question via a Boolean circuit or a "mixed" Boolean and arithmetic circuit. The first step is known as *bit-decomposition*, and the usefulness of this approach was illustrated by Damgård et al. in [DFK+06] who proposed MPC protocols for equality testing, comparison, and exponentiation. Concretely, in a bit-decomposition protocol, a secret shared input $[x]_p$ is converted to a bit-wise sharing $[x_0]_p, \cdots, [x_{\ell-1}]_p$, such that $x = \sum_{i=0}^{\ell-1} x_i 2^i$, where the input $x \in \mathbb{Z}_p$ for some prime p.

Making use of bit-decomposition in the public base setting allows the adaptation of the well-known "square-and-multiply" algorithm (also referred to as "exponentiation by squaring" or "binary exponentiation") to the MPC setting. More specifically, considering a public base a and a secret shared exponent $[x]_p$, using bit-decomposition the secret shared bit representation $[x]_B = [x_0]_p \cdots [x_{\ell-1}]_p$, where $\sum_{i=0}^{\ell-1} 2^i x_i, x_i \in \{0, 1\}$ can be obtained. Then, using the square-and-multiply algorithm, the shares $[a^x]_p$ can be obtained from this equation:

$$a^x = a^{\sum_{i=0}^{i-1} 2^i x_i} = \prod_{i=0}^{\ell-1} a^{2^i x_i} = \prod_{i=0}^{\ell-1} (x_i a^{2^i} + 1 - x_i)$$

While a protocol based on this can be implemented in $\mathcal{O}(1)$ rounds, $\mathcal{O}(\ell \log \ell)$ invocations of the underlying multiplication MPC protocol is required[1] due to the cost of bit-decomposition. The relatively high cost in terms multiplications is a disadvantage of this approach.

To avoid this, previous works [NX11, AAN18] focused on how to construct public base exponentiation protocol without relying on bit-decomposition techniques. In particular, Aly, Abidin, and Nikova [AAN18] proposed a highly efficient public base exponentiation protocol and it requires only 3 rounds and 6 invocations of multiplication. While their protocol is efficient, it depends on Shamir's secret sharing scheme.[2]

Online/Offline Paradigm and Additive Sharing. The online/offline paradigm using preprocessed random shares called "Beaver triple" or "multiplication triple" [Bea92] is a well-known and easy way to implement multiplication in the dishonest-majority setting. These dishonest-majority protocols consist of a preprocessing phase for generating Beaver triples (called the "offline phase") and a MPC protocol for the function to be computed which consumes Beaver triples (called the "online phase"). To the best of our knowledge, all known efficient offline protocols generating Beaver triples are designed for additive secret sharing, such as protocols using homomorphic encryption [DPSZ12, DKL+13, KPR18], or oblivious transfer [ALSZ15, KOS16]. Therefore,

---

[1] Since the multiplication MPC protocol is dominant in the communication, the communication complexity of MPC is usually measured by the number of invocation of multiplication.

[2] To construct an exponentiation protocol over additive secret sharing, we could consider utilizing share conversion between Shamir and Additive secret sharing. However, [AAN18] additionally assumes the base and the exponent are shared by different moduli, which implies an additional modulus conversion is needed. These aspects make this approach more expensive.

MPC based on additive secret sharing is useful in that it is easily integrated with these protocols.

On the other hand, the BGW protocol [BGW88], which is a well-known MPC protocol based on the Shamir's secret sharing scheme, is limited in its scope to the honest majority setting (that is, the number of corrupted parties is bounded by $n/2$).

1.2   Our Contribution

Based on the above motivation, we propose a new public base exponentiation protocol without bit-decomposition based on additive secret sharing with the following three contributions.

New Framework for Exponentiation Protocol. At first, we propose a new framework for exponentiation constructed via a *quotient transfer* (QT) functionality.[3] In this framework, we realize a constant round public base exponentiation protocol based on an additive secret sharing scheme.

Efficient Exponentiation Protocol Based on Constrained QT Protocol. For obtaining an efficient exponentiation protocol in our framework, we propose a limited QT protocol (which we denote a *constrained* QT protocol) without relying on bit-decomposition. Here, *constrained* means that our QT protocol only works for even integers as input. Since we bypass the use of a bit-decomposition protocol, we succeed in reducing the complexity of our QT protocol. Combining our framework and constrained QT protocol, we obtain an efficient public base exponentiation protocol based on additive secret sharing.

Note that our exponentiation protocol has the limitation that inputs should be less than half of the underlying modulus. That is, compared to the existing exponentiation protocols, an additional condition $2x < p$ is required for our protocol, where x is the input and p is the modulus of the underlying group. We believe that this limitation is not significant for many practical applications.

Modulus Conversion Protocol Based on Constrained QT Protocol. In order to utilize our constrained QT protocol effectively, the secret shared exponent must be multiplied by two to ensure it is even, which in turn leads to the requirement that the public base is a quadratic residue in the group over which the exponent is shared. To address this limitation, we also propose a new modulus conversion protocol that enables the efficient conversion of additive shares over a prime field to additive shares over a different prime field. Using this we can ensure that the public base is always a quadratic residue via an appropriate conversion before running our exponentiation protocol. The modulus conversion protocol is likewise based on our constrained QT protocol, and to the best of our knowledge, outperforms existing protocols. This might be of independent interest.

As the most important advantage, our resulting exponentiation protocol requires only 3 rounds and 4 invocations of multiplication even in the case that we need our

---

[3] QT was implicitly defined by [KIM+18]. In addition, in [OWIO19], a part of their protocol can be seen as a QT protocol based on bit-decomposition, even though they did not directly highlight this as a QT protocol.

Table 1. Comparison between two-party (public base) exponentiation protocols.

Protocol	Tool[§]	DM frame. comp.[¶]	BD[⋆]	Rounds	Multiplication[†]	
[DFK+06]	Linear	Yes	Yes	119	$\mathcal{O}(\ell \log \ell)$	50176
[NX11]*	Linear	Yes	No	20	$\mathcal{O}(\ell)$	10508
[AAN18]	Shamir's	No	No	3	$\mathcal{O}(1)$	6
This work (with conversion)[§]	Additive	Yes	No	3	$\mathcal{O}(1)$	4
This work (w/o conversion)[§]	Additive	Yes	No	2	$\mathcal{O}(1)$	3

§ In this column, "Linear" stands for (general) linear secret sharing, "Shamir's" stands for Shamir's secret sharing, and "Additive" stands for additive secret sharing. We note that a secret sharing scheme is called linear if the reconstruction procedure of the scheme is a linear mapping. Linear secret sharing includes Shamir's secret sharing and additive secret sharing.

¶ In this column, we note whether each protocol is compatible with dishonest-majority (DM) frameworks.

⋆ In this column, we point out whether each protocol requires bit-decomposition (BD) or not.

* The proposed protocol is a private exponent type protocol, not a public base type protocol. As the former implies the later, in our comparison, we use their private exponent type protocol as a public base type.

† We consider the case $\ell = 64$ when estimating the number of multiplications.

§ Here, we consider two cases: whether we need modulus conversion or not. As mentioned in Sect. 1.2, in our protocol, if the public base does not have quadratic residue, we require an additional modulus conversion. In this case, when our modulus conversion is used, we need additional 1 round and 1 invocation of multiplication.

modulus conversion protocol as subroutine. Moreover, if modulus conversion is not required, our exponentiation protocol only requires 2 rounds and 3 invocations of multiplication. We furthermore note that our modulus conversion protocol requires only 1 round and 1 invocation of multiplication.

1.3 Existing Exponentiation Protocols Without Bit-Decomposition

In this section, we compare the efficiency of the existing exponentiation protocols and summarize the comparison in Table 1. Up until now, as mentioned in Sect. 1.1, there have been a few works on exponentiation protocols not relying on a bit-decomposition protocol.

In 2011, Ning and Xu [NX11] introduced private exponentiation type protocols without bit-decomposition. As a result, they obtain a protocol with 20 rounds and $164 \cdot \ell + 12$ invocations of multiplication for a public base, where ℓ is the number of message bits. In particular, when we consider $\ell = 64$, the number of invocations of multiplication is 10508.

Recently, Aly, Abidin, and Nikova [AAN18] simplified Ning et al.'s protocol, and reduced the communication complexity and the number of invocations of multiplication based on the Shamir's secret sharing scheme. They also constructed a new public exponent exponentiation protocol. Regarding the public base exponentiation protocol, the number of rounds is 3 and the number of multiplication invocations is $3(1 + \lfloor \log(n) \rfloor)$, where n means the number of parties. In particular, in the two-party setting (that is, $n = 2$), the number of invocations of multiplication is 6. We note that their protocol needs to use different moduli in the groups of base and exponentiation in order to ensure correctness. This is a drawback when considering composition with other protocols (not only in theoretical sense but also in an implementation). Compared to their protocol, our protocol has same modulus in the groups of base and exponentiation.

In Table 1, we compare our work with the results by Ning et al. and Aly et al. in the two-party setting (all protocols without bit-decomposition), and the result by [DFK+06] which uses bit-decomposition. There, ℓ denotes the bit-length of the input. In the rows "[DFK+06]" and "[NX11]", we consider the case $\ell = 64$ when estimating the number of multiplications.

Although we obtain an efficient constant-round MPC protocol for an exponentiation functionality in the two-party setting, it is still an open problem to extend our protocol to the three or (more general) n-party setting. The main difficulty is to extend our QT protocol to the n-party setting efficiently. See Sect. 3.3 for the details.

1.4   Technical Overview

In the following, we will outline the main ideas behind our constructions.

Local Exponentiation. The main idea behind our approach is to make the computing parties do most of the computation locally. In particular, the exponentiation itself is done locally based on the shares of the exponent x. Let us for a moment assume that the two parties hold shares $[x]_p^1, [x]_p^2 \in \mathbb{Z}_p$, respectively, and that $[x]_p^1 + [x]_p^2 = x$ *over the integers* i.e. no reduction modulo p is required to recover x. In this case, the parties can directly compute $y_i = a^{[x]_p^i} \bmod p$, which will satisfy $o = y_1 \cdot y_2 \bmod p = a^{[x]_p^1 + [x]_p^2} \bmod p = a^x \bmod p$. Shares of o can be obtained by letting each party compute a sharing of y_i, send one share to the other party[4], and let both parties interact in a standard multiplication protocol to compute $[o]_i$.

However, a standard secure sharing of x requires a potential reduction modulo p when adding the shares i.e. $[x]_p^1 + [x]_p^2 = x \bmod p$ which implies $[x]_p^1 + [x]_p^2 = x + t \cdot p$ for $t \in \{0, 1\}$ over the integers. In other words, the above value o will in this case be of the form $o = a^x \cdot a^{tp}$. Here, $a^{tp} = a^t \bmod p$ due to Fermat's little theorem, and we observe that the term a^t can be eliminated from o assuming the parties can compute (shares of) t by multiplying o with the multiplicative inverse a^{-1} conditioned on the value of t.

Efficient Quotient Transfer. The above approach assumes that the parties can efficiently compute the value t. This was implicitly defined by Kikuchi et al. [KIM+18] as a QT protocol. Note, however, that the efficiency of this protocol is crucial in the above approach to exponentiation, and basing the QT protocol on e.g. bit-decomposition as done by [OWIO19], will defy the purpose of this approach.

We propose a simple but efficient approach to a QT protocol constrained to even inputs. Specifically, we observe that if the input x is even, the value of t can be determined by the least significant bits of the shares $[x]_p^1$ and $[x]_p^2$, as $t = 1$ implies that

---

[4] In our actual exponentiation protocol given in Algorithm 1, each party *locally* sets the shares $[y_i]_p^i = y_i$ and $[y_i]_p^{1-i} = 0$ (and does not send their shares to each other) in order to optimize the round complexity.

$[x]_p^1 + [x]_p^2$ over the integers must be odd as the prime p is likewise odd, whereas $t = 0$ implies that $[x]_p^1 + [x]_p^2$ over the integers must be even (as the input is likewise even). Hence, the QT protocol can in this case be implemented via the appropriate comparison of the least significant bits of the shares $[x]_p^1$ and $[x]_p^2$. To make use of this constrained QT protocol in the computation of an exponentiation, we simply multiply input x by 2, and compute $\sqrt{a}^{2x}$.

Modulus Conversion. The above assumes that an appropriate value $\sqrt{a}$ can be computed i.e. that a is a quadratic residue modulo the prime p. Note that since p is prime, half of all elements in $\mathbb{Z}_p$ are quadratic residues, and if this is the case for a, the above approach works. However, if a is a quadratic non-residue, a different approach is required. We address this case by simply converting the shares of x in $\mathbb{Z}_p$ to shares in $\mathbb{Z}_{p'}$ for a prime p' for which a *is* a quadratic residue.

Similar to the above, for this to work, an efficient modulus conversion protocol is required. We obtain this by observing that our QT protocol allows the shares of q to be drawn from $\mathbb{Z}_{p'}$ as opposed to $\mathbb{Z}_p$ which the shares of the input x belongs to, which in turn, allows us to construct a very efficient modulus conversion protocol (the details are given in Sect. 3.2). Note that the restriction that the input x is even can easily be overcome by firstly multiplying x by 2, doing the conversion, and then multiply the result by 2^{-1}, which are both local operations. In comparison to the efficient conversion protocol by [KIM+18], which is based on bit-wise processing of the input, our protocol is simpler and more efficient. Concretely, while the modulus conversion protocol [KIM+18] requires $\mathcal{O}(\log p')$ rounds and $\mathcal{O}(\log p')$ invocations of multiplication, our protocol requires only 1 round and 1 invocation of multiplication.

2 Preliminaries

In this section, we review some preliminaries.

2.1 Notations

In this paper, we use the following notations. $x \leftarrow X$ denotes sampling an element x from a finite set X uniformly at random. $y \leftarrow \mathcal{A}(x; r)$ denotes that a probabilistic algorithm $\mathcal{A}$ outputs y for an input x using a randomness r, and we simply denote $y \leftarrow \mathcal{A}(x)$ when we need not write an internal randomness explicitly. λ denotes a security parameter. A function $f(\lambda)$ is a negligible function in λ, if $f(\lambda)$ tends to 0 faster than $\frac{1}{\lambda^c}$ for every constant $c > 0$. $\mathrm{negl}(\lambda)$ denotes an unspecified negligible function. PPT stands for probabilistic polynomial time. p and p' denote safe prime numbers. n denotes the number of parties. Let $[x]_p$ denote a secretly shared input $x \in \mathbb{Z}_p$. Let P be the set of n parties and P_i the i-th party for $i = 1, \cdots, n$. The operation $+$ is a normal addition over integers. The congruence relation $a = kp + b$ is represented as $a \equiv b(\bmod p)$, where a, b, k, and p are integers.

2.2 Additive Secret Sharing

In this section, we introduce the definition of additive secret sharing. In general, an additive secret sharing scheme is defined over finite additive groups. Among them, we consider the case over $\mathbb{Z}_p$ (the set of integers modulo p). An additive secret sharing scheme over $\mathbb{Z}_p$ consists of the following two algorithms **Share** and **Reconstruct**.

- **Share** : Given a value $x \in \mathbb{Z}_p$ as input, this algorithm outputs shares $[x]_p = ([x]_p^1, \ldots, [x]_p^n)$ of x such that $[x]_p^1 + [x]_p^2 + \cdots + [x]_p^n \equiv x (\bmod\, p)$, where $[x]_p^i$ denotes P_i's share. All shares are distributed uniformly at random in $\mathbb{Z}_p$ under the constraint that they sum to x. In the following, we use the notation $[x]_p \leftarrow$ **Share**(x).
- **Reconstruct** : Given all n shares $[x]_p$ as input, this algorithm outputs a value $x = ([x]_p^1 + \cdots + [x]_p^n) \bmod p$.

Note that the requirement on the random distribution of shares implies that only given access to $n - 1$ shares in $[x]_p$, the value x is information theoretically hidden.

An additive secret sharing scheme supports the following computations on shares.

- **Local operation** : Given shares $[a]_p, [b]_p$ and a scalar $\alpha \in \mathbb{Z}_p$, the parties can generate shares of $[a + b]_p, [\alpha a]_p$, and $[\alpha + a]_p$ using only local operations.
- **Multiplication** : Given shares $[a]_p$ and $[b]_p$, we assume the parties can generate $[ab]_p$ by invoking an ideal multiplication functionality $\mathcal{F}_{\mathrm{Mul}}([a]_p, [b]_p)$. This might be implemented using a multiplication protocol based on Beaver triples [Bea92]. In the following, we use the notation $[ab]_p \leftarrow [a]_p \cdot [b]_p$ to denote $[ab]_p \leftarrow \mathcal{F}_{\mathrm{Mul}}([a]_p, [b]_p)$.

2.3 A Model of Secure Two-Party Computation

In this section, we formally introduce two-party computation. A two-party computation is specified by a (possibly probabilistic) procedure referred to as a *functionality*. Denote $f : (\{0, 1\}^*)^2 \rightarrow (\{0, 1\}^*)^2$ as the two-ary functionality. Specifically, each party P_i can obtain distinct outputs $f_i(\mathbf{x})$ in general, where $f = (f_0, f_1)$ and $\mathbf{x} = (x_1, x_2)$ is a pair of inputs.

Definition of Security. The security of MPC is formalized by simulation-based security definitions. Roughly speaking, if there exist simulators who can generate the view of each party in the execution from given inputs and outputs, an MPC protocol is called *secure*. This formalization implies that each party learns nothing about other users' inputs from the execution of the protocol, except for the information that can be derived from outputs.

Definition 1 (Computational Indistinguishability). *Two probability ensembles $X = \{X(a, n)\}_{a \in \{0,1\}^*, n \in \mathbb{N}}$ and $Y = \{Y(a, n)\}_{a \in \{0,1\}^*, n \in \mathbb{N}}$ are said to be computationally indistinguishable, denoted by $X \stackrel{c}{\approx} Y$, if for any non-uniform PPT algorithm $\mathcal{D}$ there exists a negligible function $\mathrm{negl}(\lambda)$ such that for every $a \in \{0, 1\}^*$ and every $n \in \mathbb{N}$,*

$$\left| \Pr_{X \leftarrow x}[\mathcal{D}(X(a, n)) = 1] - \Pr_{Y \leftarrow y}[\mathcal{D}(Y(a, n)) = 1] \right| = \mathrm{negl}(\lambda).$$

Definition 2 (Security). *Let* $f : (\{0,1\}^*)^2 \to (\{0,1\}^*)^2$ *be a 2-ary functionality and let* π *be a two-party protocol for computing* f. *Let* $\mathbf{x} = (x_0, x_1)$ *be a pair of inputs. Let* $\mathsf{View}_i^\pi(\mathbf{x}, \lambda)$ *be the view of the party* P_i *during an execution of a protocol* π *on the input* $\mathbf{x}$ *and* λ. *Let* $\mathsf{Output}^\pi(\mathbf{x})$ *be the output of all parties from an execution of* π. *We say that a protocol* π *securely computes* f *in the presence of semi-honest adversaries, if there exist PPT algorithms* $\mathcal{S}_1$ *and* $\mathcal{S}_2$ *such that*

$$\{(\mathcal{S}_1(1^\lambda, x_1, f_1(\mathbf{x})), f(\mathbf{x}))\}_{\mathbf{x}, \lambda} \overset{c}{\approx} \{(\mathsf{View}_1^\pi(\mathbf{x}, \lambda), \mathsf{Output}^\pi(\mathbf{x}, \lambda))\}_{\mathbf{x}, \lambda}$$

and

$$\{(\mathcal{S}_2(1^\lambda, x_2, f_2(\mathbf{x})), f(\mathbf{x}))\}_{\mathbf{x}, \lambda} \overset{c}{\approx} \{(\mathsf{View}_2^\pi(\mathbf{x}, \lambda), \mathsf{Output}^\pi(\mathbf{x}, \lambda))\}_{\mathbf{x}, \lambda},$$

where $x_1, x_2 \in \{0,1\}^*$ *and* $|x_1| = |x_2|$.

In addition, we say that π *securely computes* f *in the presence of semi-honest adversaries in the* $\mathcal{F}$-*hybrid model if* π *contains ideal calls to a trusted party computing a certain functionality* $\mathcal{F}$.

Remark 1 (On Local Computations). Note that the functionalities with only a *local computation* (*i.e.*, a computation which needs no communication among parties) obviously satisfy the above Definition 2, since the view of such functionality is only the information that can be obtained from shares. Such a view leaks no information regarding inputs due to the security of the underlying secret sharing scheme.

Universal Composability Framework. A stronger notion of security typically considered for MPC can be obtained via the Universal Composability (UC) framework, which is a general framework allowing arbitrary MPC protocols to be represented and analyzed. Protocols that are proven secure in the UC framework have the property that they maintain their security when run in parallel and concurrently with other secure and insecure protocols. In [KLR10], Kushilevitz, Lindell, and Rabin showed that under certain circumstances, stand-alone security as defined above (Definition 2), implies security in the UC framework:

Theorem 1 (Theorem 1.5 in [KLR10]). *Every protocol that is secure in the stand-alone model and has start synchronization and a straight-line black-box simulator is UC-secure under concurrent general composition (universal composition).*

In the above theorem, a "straight-line" simulator means that a non-rewinding simulator, and "start synchronization" means that the inputs of all parties are fixed before the execution begins (also called as "input availability"). All of the protocols considered in this paper satisfies these conditions, and hence, Theorem 1 ensures that we obtain UC-security of our protocols.

2.4 Quotient Transfer Functionality

We now introduce the quotient transfer (QT) functionality $\mathcal{F}_{\mathrm{QT}}$ for a two-party protocol. This functionality plays a central role in our construction of an exponentiation protocol. Let $[a]_p = ([a]_p^1, [a]_p^2)$. Here, we have a value t satisfying $[a]_p^1 + [a]_p^2 = a + t \cdot p$ ($t \in \{0, 1\}$) over the integers. We define the QT functionality as

$$[t]_{p'} \leftarrow \mathcal{F}_{\mathrm{QT}}([a]_p, p').$$

Note that, if $[a]_p^1 + [a]_p^2 < p$, then $t = 0$, else $t = 1$. We emphasize that although the individual shares $[a]_p^i$ are elements in $\mathbb{Z}_p$, the addition considered above is over the integers.

2.5 Modulus Conversion Functionality

We introduce the modulus conversion functionality $\mathcal{F}_{\mathrm{Conv}}$. A modulus conversion functionality is a functionality that converts a share in $\mathbb{Z}_p$ into one in $\mathbb{Z}_{p'}$ (with $p \neq p'$). Let $x \in \mathbb{Z}_p$. We define $\mathcal{F}_{\mathrm{Conv}}$ as

$$[x]_{p'} \leftarrow \mathcal{F}_{\mathrm{Conv}}([x]_p, p').$$

2.6 Exponentiation Functionality

Here, we introduce a (public base) exponentiation functionality $\mathcal{F}_{\mathrm{EXP}}$. Let p be some prime. Let $a \in \mathbb{Z}_p$ and $x \in \mathbb{Z}_p$. We define $\mathcal{F}_{\mathrm{EXP}}$ as

$$[a^x \bmod p]_p \leftarrow \mathcal{F}_{\mathrm{EXP}}(a, [x]_p).$$

Note that, as we will consider additive secret sharing of x over $\mathbb{Z}_p$, we define the above exponentiation functionality for $x \in \mathbb{Z}_p$, whereas the exponent space typically considered for exponentiation in $\mathbb{Z}_p$ would be restricted to $\mathbb{Z}_{\phi(p)} = \mathbb{Z}_{p-1}$. However, the functionality remains well-defined for the extension $x \in \mathbb{Z}_p$.

3 Our Exponentiation Protocol

In this section, we propose our exponentiation protocol. We first introduce a new framework for an exponentiation protocol in Sect. 3.1. Then, we provide a modulus conversion protocol using a QT protocol in Sect. 3.2. Next, we provide a constrained QT protocol without bit-decomposition which only works on even numbers in Sect. 3.3. In the end, we introduce a concrete construction of our framework of an exponentiation protocol using our constrained QT protocol and modulus conversion protocol (which is also obtained by our constrained QT protocol) in Sect. 3.4.

3.1 A New Framework for Exponentiation Protocol

In this section, we provide our new framework for an exponentiation protocol. Before describing our framework formally, we give its overview.

In the public base exponentiation setting, a naive idea for computing $a^x \bmod p$ is that each party P_i ($i \in \{0, 1\}$) locally computes $a^{[x]_p^i} \bmod p$ and invokes a multiplication protocol to get a value $a^{[x]_p^0 + [x]_p^1} \bmod p$. Here, a subtle point is that $[x]_p^0 + [x]_p^1$ is not always equal to x since there is a situation that $[x]_p^0 + [x]_p^1 = x + p$ holds. That is, we have the case $a^{[x]_p^0 + [x]_p^1} \bmod p = a^{x+p} \bmod p = (a^x \cdot a^p) \bmod p$ and in this case, we should eliminate the term $a^p \bmod p$ to get a correct result $a^x \bmod p$. In order to solve this problem, we utilize a QT functionality $\mathcal{F}_{QT}$. By using $\mathcal{F}_{QT}$, we can know the secret shared values $[t]_p$ such that $[x]_p^0 + [x]_p^1 = x + t \cdot p$ and eliminate the term $a^p \bmod p$ correctly. Formally, our new framework Π_{EXP} for $\mathcal{F}_{EXP}$ is described in Algorithm 1.

Algorithm 1. Our framework for exponentiation protocol Π_{EXP}

Input: $a, [x]_p$
Output: $[o]_p$
1: Each $P_i (i \in \{0, 1\})$ locally computes $y_i = a^{[x]_p^i} \bmod p$
2: Each $P_i (i \in \{0, 1\})$ locally sets $[y_i]_p^i = y_i$ and $[y_i]_p^{1-i} = 0$
3: $[d]_p \leftarrow [y_0]_p \cdot [y_1]_p$
4: $[t]_p \leftarrow \mathcal{F}_{QT}([x]_p, p)$
5: $[o_1]_p \leftarrow (1 - [t]_p)[d]_p,$
6: $[o_2]_p \leftarrow [t]_p [d]_p$
7: $[o]_p \leftarrow [o_1]_p + [o_2]_p (a)^{-p}$

Correctness. Here, we show the correctness of our framework of an exponentiation protocol Π_{EXP}.

Theorem 2. Π_{EXP} *is correct in* $(\mathcal{F}_{Mul}, \mathcal{F}_{QT})$-*hybrid model.*

The protocol Π_{EXP} is aimed at correctly computing $a^x \bmod p$, where $a \in \mathbb{Z}_p$ and $x \in \mathbb{Z}_p$. Each party P_i firstly computes $a^{[x]_p^i} \bmod p$ and sets $[y_i]_p^i = y_i$ and $[y_i]_p^{1-i} = 0$ locally, then utilizes a multiplication MPC protocol to compute $(a^{[x]_p^0}) \bmod p \cdot (a^{[x]_p^1}) \bmod p = a^{[x]_p^0 + [x]_p^1} \bmod p$. Here, we need to handle two cases for the value x. Concretely, we have $[x]_p^0 + [x]_p^1 = x + t \cdot p$ ($t \in \{0, 1\}$). In the following proof, we have the correct value a^x in both of the cases $[x]_p^0 + [x]_p^1 \leq p$ and $[x]_p^0 + [x]_p^1 > p$.

Proof of Theorem 2. Let $a \in \mathbb{Z}_p$ and $x \in \mathbb{Z}_p$. Regarding the secret value x, we have the following two cases.

- In the case of $[x]_p^0 + [x]_p^1 \leq p$ (that is, we have $t = 0$ and $[x]_p^0 + [x]_p^1 = x$), each P_i locally computes $a^{[x]_p^i} \bmod p$, sets $[y_i]_p^i = y_i$ and $[y_i]_p^{1-i} = 0$, and uses $\mathcal{F}_{Mul}$ to compute d. From the correctness of $\mathcal{F}_{Mul}$, we have $d = a^{[x]_p^0 + [x]_p^1} \bmod p = a^x \bmod p$. Moreover, from the correctness of $\mathcal{F}_{QT}$, we get $t = 0$. Therefore, $o_1 = d, o_2 = 0$, and $o = a^x \bmod p$ hold.
- In the case of $[x]_p^0 + [x]_p^1 > p$ (that is, we have $t = 1$ and $[x]_p^0 + [x]_p^1 = x + p$), each P_i locally computes $a^{[x]_p^i} \bmod p$, sets $[y_i]_p^i = y_i$ and $[y_i]_p^{1-i} = 0$, and uses $\mathcal{F}_{Mul}$ to compute d. From the correctness of $\mathcal{F}_{Mul}$, we have $d = a^{[x]_p^0 + [x]_p^1} \bmod p = a^{x+p} \bmod p$. Moreover, from the correctness of $\mathcal{F}_{QT}$, we get $t = 1$. Therefore, $o_1 = 0, o_2 = d \cdot (a)^{-p} \bmod p = (a)^{x+p} \cdot (a)^{-p} \bmod p = a^x \bmod p$, and $o = a^x \bmod p$ hold. $\qquad\square$ **(Theorem** 2**)**

Security. Then, we prove the security of our new framework.

Theorem 3. Π_{EXP} *can securely compute* $\mathcal{F}_{\text{EXP}}$ *in* $(\mathcal{F}_{\text{Mul}}, \mathcal{F}_{\text{QT}})$-*hybrid model.*

Proof of Theorem 3. We construct a separate simulator for each party (S_0 for the P_0's view and S_1 for the P_1's view, as in Definition 2). Consider the case that P_1 is corrupted. The view of P_1 can be written as:

$$\text{View}_1^{\Pi_{\text{EXP}}}(a, [x]_p) = ([d]_p^1, [t]_p^1, [o_2]_p^1, [o_1]_p^1, r),$$

where $[d]_p = [y_0]_p \cdot [y_1]_p$, $y_i = a^{[x]_p^i} \bmod p$ for $i \in \{0, 1\}$, $[y_i]_p^i = y_i$ and $[y_i]_p^{i-1} = 0$ for $i \in \{0, 1\}$, and r is a randomness used by P_1. We need to show that the simulator S_1 can generate the view of P_1. In the protocol, P_1 receives an input consisting of values a and $[x]_p^1$. Then, S_1 is given $(a, [x]_p^1, [o]_p^1)$ and works as follows:

1. S_1 chooses a uniform randomness r from $\mathbb{Z}_p$.
2. S_1 chooses a uniformly distributed random number $[d]_p^1$, $[t]_p^1$, and $[o_2]_p^1$ from $\mathbb{Z}_p$.
3. S_1 computes $[o_1]_p^1 = [o]_p^1 - [o_2]_p^1 \cdot a^{-1}$.
4. S_1 outputs $([d]_p^1, [t]_p^1, [o_2]_p^1, [o_1]_p^1, r)$.

Due to the security of the underlying additive secret sharing scheme, $[d]_p^1, [t]_p^1, [o_2]_p^1$, and r are uniformly at random in $\mathbb{Z}_p$. Moreover, since the shares of $[o]_p^1$ and $[o_2]_p^1$ are distributed randomly conditioned on $[o]_p^1 = [o_1]_p^1 + [o_2]_p^1 \cdot a^{-1}$, which is same as in the real execution. Thus, the distribution of $([d]_p^1, [t]_p^1, [o_2]_p^1, [o_1]_p^1)$ output by S_1 is equal to one which are given for P_1. Furthermore, due to the correctness of Π_{EXP} (shown in Theorem 2), the output of $\Pi_{\text{EXP}}(a, [x]_p)$ is equal to the output of functionality $\mathcal{F}_{\text{EXP}}(a, [x]_p)$. Hence, we have

$$\{(S_1(a, [x]_p^1, [o]_p^1), \mathcal{F}_{\text{EXP}}(a, [x]_p))\} \stackrel{c}{\approx} \{(\text{View}_1^{\Pi_{\text{EXP}}}(a, [x]_p), \Pi_{\text{EXP}}(a, [x]_p))\}$$

Similar with above, in the case that P_0 is corrupted, we can also construct S_0 which can simulate the view of P_0. Therefore, Π_{EXP} securely computes $\mathcal{F}_{\text{EXP}}$ in $(\mathcal{F}_{\text{Mul}}, \mathcal{F}_{\text{QT}})$-hybrid model. $\qquad \square$ **(Theorem 3)**

Remark 2 (Existing (Inefficient) Protocols over Our Framework). As mentioned in Sect. 1.2, we can realize Π_{EXP} using existing primitives. Specifically, a part of the previous work [OWIO19] can be seen as a QT protocol, even though they did not explicitly define this as a QT protocol. However, since their protocol is based on bit-decomposition, the resulting Π_{EXP} suffers from a large multiplication cost.

Efficiency of Our Exponentiation Framework. Here, we give an analysis for the efficiency (round complexity and the number of invocations of multiplication) of our exponentiation framework. In the analysis for round complexity, an important point is that we can execute some procedures simultaneously in Π_{EXP}. Concretely, since the computation in the functionality $\mathcal{F}_{\text{QT}}$ (Step. 4) does not depend on the previous steps, $\mathcal{F}_{\text{QT}}$ can be executed with previous procedures in a parallel way. Taking into account this optimization, the round complexity of Π_{EXP} is $\max(r_{\text{QT}}, r_{\text{Mul}}) + r_{\text{Mul}}$, where r_{QT} and r_{Mul} represent the round complexity of $\mathcal{F}_{\text{QT}}$ and $\mathcal{F}_{\text{Mul}}$ respectively. Also, the number of invocations of multiplication is $i_{\text{QT}} + 2 \cdot i_{\text{Mul}}$, where i_{QT} and i_{Mul} represent the number of invocations of multiplication of $\mathcal{F}_{\text{QT}}$ and $\mathcal{F}_{\text{Mul}}$ respectively.

3.2   A Modulus Conversion Protocol Using Quotient Transfer Functionality

In this section, we provide a modulus conversion protocol which can change $x \in \mathbb{Z}_p$ to $x \in \mathbb{Z}_{p'}$. This modulus conversion protocol consists of the QT functionality and a transfer formula. By using the QT functionality, we can know the secret shared values $[t]_{p'}$ such that $[x]_p^0 + [x]_p^1 = x + t \cdot p$. Then, the transfer formula change x into $x \in \mathbb{Z}_{p'}$ by eliminating the influence of overflow. Formally, our modulus conversion protocol is described in Algorithm 2.

Algorithm 2. Our modulus conversion protocol Π_{Conv}

Input: $[x]_p, p'$
Output: $[x]_{p'}$
  1: $[t']_{p'} \leftarrow \mathcal{F}_{\text{QT}}([x]_p, p')$
  2: Each $P_i(i \in \{0, 1\})$ sets $[x]_{p'}^i = [x]_p^i - [t']_{p'}^i \cdot p$
  3: Output $[x]_{p'}$

Correctness. Firstly, we prove the correctness of Π_{Conv}.

Theorem 4. Π_{Conv} *is correct in* $\mathcal{F}_{\text{QT}}$*-hybrid model.*

Proof of Theorem 4. From the correctness of $\mathcal{F}_{\text{QT}}$, we can obtain a correct $t' \in \{0, 1\}$ satisfying $[x]_p^0 + [x]_p^1 = x + t' \cdot p$. Next, we obtain $[x]_{p'}^0 = [x]_p^0 - [t']_{p'}^0 \cdot p$ and $[x]_{p'}^1 = [x]_p^1 - [t']_{p'}^1 \cdot p$. Then, we have the following equation

$$[x]_{p'}^0 + [x]_{p'}^1 = [x]_p^0 - [t']_{p'}^0 \cdot p + [x]_p^1 - [t']_{p'}^1 \cdot p \bmod p'$$
$$= [x]_p^0 + [x]_p^1 - ([t']_{p'}^0 + [t']_{p'}^1) \cdot p \bmod p'$$
$$= x + t' \cdot p - ([t']_{p'}^0 + [t']_{p'}^1) \cdot p \bmod p'$$

Here, since we have $[t']_{p'}^0 + [t']_{p'}^1 = t'$ when $[t']_{p'}^0 + [t']_{p'}^1 \leq p'$ holds and $[t']_{p'}^0 + [t']_{p'}^1 = t' + p'$ when $[t']_{p'}^0 + [t']_{p'}^1 > p'$ holds, $[t']_{p'}^0 + [t']_{p'}^1 \bmod p'$ equals to t'. Then, $t' \cdot p - ([t']_{p'}^0 + [t']_{p'}^1) \cdot p$ is equal to 0 over modulus p'. Thus, we have $[x]_{p'}^0 + [x]_{p'}^1 = x \bmod p'$ and get shares $[x]_{p'}^0$ and $[x]_{p'}^0$ satisfying that the sum of them is equal to x over $\mathbb{Z}_{p'}$. Therefore, Π_{Conv} is correct in $\mathcal{F}_{\text{QT}}$-hybrid model.   □ **(Theorem 4)**

Security. Then, we prove the security of Π_{Conv}.

Theorem 5. Π_{Conv} *is UC-secure in* $\mathcal{F}_{\text{QT}}$*-hybrid model.*

Proof of Theorem 5. We construct a separate simulator for each party (S_0 for the P_0's view and S_1 for the P_1's view, as in Definition 2). Consider the case that P_1 is corrupted. The view of P_1 can be written as:

$$\text{View}_1^{\Pi_{\text{Conv}}}([x]_p, p') = ([t]_{p'}^1, r),$$

where r is a randomness used by P_1. We need to show that the simulator S_1 can generate the view of P_1. In the protocol, P_1 receives an input consisting of values $[x]_p^1$ and p'. Then, S_1 is given $([x]_p^1, [x]_{p'}^1, p')$ and works as follows:

1. S_1 chooses a uniform randomness r from $\mathbb{Z}_p$.
2. S_1 chooses uniformly distributed random $[t]_{p'}^1$ from $\mathbb{Z}_{p'}$.
3. S_1 outputs $([t]_{p'}^1, r)$.

Due to the security of the underlying additive secret sharing scheme, r and $[t]_{p'}^1$ are uniformly at random in $\mathbb{Z}_{p'}$ in the real execution. Thus, the distribution of $[t]_{p'}^1$ output by S_1 is equal to one which are given for P_1. Furthermore, due to the correctness of Π_{EXP} (shown in Theorem 4), the output of $\Pi_{\text{Conv}}([x]_p, p')$ is equal to the output of functionality $\mathcal{F}_{\text{Conv}}([x]_p, p')$. Hence, we have

$$\{(S_1(p', [x]_p^1, [t]_{p'}^1), \mathcal{F}_{\text{Conv}}([x]_p, p'))\} \overset{c}{\approx} \{(\text{View}_1^{\Pi_{\text{Conv}}}([x]_p, p'), \Pi_{\text{Conv}}([x]_p, p'))\}$$

Similar with above, in the case that P_0 is corrupted we can also construct S_0 which can simulate the view of P_0. Therefore, Π_{Conv} securely computes $\mathcal{F}_{\text{Conv}}$ in $(\mathcal{F}_{\text{Mul}}, \mathcal{F}_{\text{Conv}})$-hybrid model. Moreover, from Theorem 1, Π_{Conv} is also UC-secure in $\mathcal{F}_{\text{QT}}$-hybrid model, and thus Theorem 5 holds. □ **(Theorem 5)**

Efficiency of Our Modulus Conversion Protocol. Here, we give an analysis of the efficiency (round complexity and the number of invocations of multiplication) of our modulus conversion protocol Π_{Conv}. The round complexity is r_{QT}, where r_{QT} represents the round complexity of $\mathcal{F}_{\text{QT}}$. Also, the number of invocations of multiplication is i_{QT}, where i_{QT} represents the number of invocations of multiplication of $\mathcal{F}_{\text{QT}}$.

As mentioned in Sect. 3.3, both of the round complexity r_{QT} and the number of invocations of multiplication i_{QT} of our constrained QT protocol are 1. Thus, our modulus conversion protocol requires only 1 round and 1 invocation of multiplication. Compared to the most efficient modulus conversion protocol [KIM+18] which requires $\mathcal{O}(\log p')$ rounds and $\mathcal{O}(\log p')$ invocations of multiplication, we can see that our modulus conversion protocol is more efficient.

3.3 A Constrained Quotient Transfer Protocol Without Bit-Decomposition

In this section, we provide our constrained QT protocol without the bit-decomposition protocol. Our core idea is that we can check whether $[x]_p^0 + [x]_p^1$ is bigger than p or not by using only the least significant bit (LSB) of the shares of even inputs. Namely, our QT protocol securely computes $\mathcal{F}_{\text{QT}}$ if the input is an even number. Note that this restriction does not occur any problem when used in our exponentiation protocol. More specifically, the input of our exponentiation protocol is not restricted to even numbers. See Sect. 3.4 for the details.

We propose our constrained QT protocol as described in Algorithm 3. Let p and p' be odd primes. Regarding an input for Algorithm 3, let x be an even and b_i the LSB of $[x]_p^i$ for $i \in \{0,1\}$.

Algorithm 3. Our Constrained Quotient Transfer Protocol Π_{QT}

Input: $[x]_p, p'$
Output: $[t]_{p'}$
1: Each $P_i(i \in \{0,1\})$ locally computes $b_i = \mathrm{LSB}([x]_p^i)$.
2: Each $P_i(i \in \{0,1\})$ locally sets $[b_i]_{p'}^i = b_i$ and $[b_i]_{p'}^{1-i} = 0$.
3: $[t]_{p'} = [b_0]_{p'} + [b_1]_{p'} - 2 \cdot [b_0]_{p'} \cdot [b_1]_{p'}$
4: Output $[t]_{p'}$

Remark 3 (On an extension to n-party setting). We can easily extend our two-party QT protocol into n-party protocol by executing the LSB checking (Step 3 in Algorithm 3) n times for an input x for judging how many times x exceeds the underlying modulus p. However, this naive approach requires n invocations of multiplication and the resulting protocol is not efficient. It is an interesting open question to extend our QT protocol into n-party setting efficiently (which derives an efficient constant-round n-party MPC protocol for an exponentiation functionality based on additive secret sharing).

Correctness. Here, we prove the correctness of Π_{QT}.

Theorem 6. *If the input x is even, Π_{QT} is correct in $\mathcal{F}_{\mathrm{Mul}}$-hybrid model.*

Proof of Theorem 6. Since x is even and p is prime, the last bit of x must be 0 and the last bit of p must be 1. Since $[x]_p^0 + [x]_p^1 = x + t \cdot p$ ($t \in \{0,1\}$) holds, $\mathrm{LSB}([x]_p^0) \oplus \mathrm{LSB}([x]_p^1)$ have two cases. If $[x]_p^0 + [x]_p^1 = x$ holds, then $\mathrm{LSB}([x]_p^0) \oplus \mathrm{LSB}([x]_p^1) = 0$ holds. Otherwise, $\mathrm{LSB}([x]_p^0) \oplus \mathrm{LSB}([x]_p^1) = 1$ holds. Thus, the value of $\mathrm{LSB}([x]_p^0) \oplus \mathrm{LSB}([x]_p^1)$ is equal to the value t. Moreover, due to the correctness of $\mathcal{F}_{\mathrm{Mul}}$, we can see that $[b_0]_{p'} + [b_1]_{p'} - 2 \cdot [b_0]_{p'} \cdot [b_1]_{p'}$ computes the shares of $t = \mathrm{LSB}([x]_p^0) \oplus \mathrm{LSB}([x]_p^1)$ over $\mathbb{Z}_{p'}$ in Step 3. Therefore, if the input x is even, Π_{QT} is correct in $\mathcal{F}_{\mathrm{Mul}}$-hybrid model.   □ **(Theorem 6)**

Security. Then, we prove the security of Π_{QT}.

Theorem 7. Π_{QT} *is UC-secure in $\mathcal{F}_{\mathrm{Mul}}$-hybrid model.*

Proof of Theorem 7. We construct a separate simulator for each party (S_0 for the P_0's view and S_1 for the P_1's view, as in Definition 2). Consider the case that P_1 is corrupted. The view of P_1 can be written as:

$$\mathrm{View}_1^{\Pi_{\mathrm{QT}}}([x]_p) = ([c]_{p'}^1, r),$$

where $[c]_{p'} = [b_1]_{p'} \cdot [b_0]_{p'}$, $b_i = \text{LSB}([x]_p^i)$ for $i \in \{0, 1\}$, $[b_i]_{p'}^i = b_i$ and $[b_i]_{p'}^{1-i} = 0$ for $i \in \{0, 1\}$, and r is a randomness used by P_1.

We need to show that a simulator can generate the view of the P_1. In the protocol, P_1 receives an input consisting of values $([x]_p^1, p')$. Then, S_1 is given $([x]_p^1, [t]_{p'}^1, p')$ and works as follows:

1. S_1 chooses a uniform randomness r from $\mathbb{Z}_{p'}$.
2. S_1 generates $b_1 = \text{LSB}([x]_p^1)$.
3. S_1 sets $[b_1]_{p'}^1 = b_1$ and $[b_0]_{p'}^1 = 0$.
4. S_1 computes $[c]_{p'}^1 = ([b_1]_{p'}^1 + [b_0]_{p'}^1 - [t]_{p'}^1) \cdot 2^{-1}$.
5. S_1 outputs $[c]_{p'}^1$ and r.

Since the randomness r is uniformly at random in $\mathbb{Z}_{p'}$ and the share $[c]_{p'}^1$ is distributed randomly conditioned on $[t]_{p'}^1 = [b_0]_{p'}^1 + [b_1]_{p'}^1 - 2 \cdot [c]_{p'}^1$, which are same as in the real execution. Thus, the distribution of $([c]_{p'}^1, r)$ output by S_1 is equal to one which are given for P_1. Furthermore, due to the correctness of $\mathbf{\Pi}_{\text{QT}}$ (shown in Theorem 6), the output of $\mathbf{\Pi}_{\text{QT}}([x]_p, p')$ is equal to the output of functionality $\mathcal{F}_{\text{QT}}([x]_p, p')$. Hence, we have

$$\{(S_1([x]_p^1, [t]_{p'}^1, p'), \mathcal{F}_{\text{QT}}([x]_p, p')\} \overset{c}{\approx} \{(\text{View}_1^{\mathbf{\Pi}_{\text{QT}}}([x]_p, p'), \mathbf{\Pi}_{\text{QT}}([x]_p, p')\}.$$

Similar with above, in the case that P_0 is corrupted, we can also construct S_0 which can simulate the view of P_0.

Therefore, $\mathbf{\Pi}_{\text{QT}}$ securely computes $\mathcal{F}_{\text{QT}}$ in $\mathcal{F}_{\text{Mul}}$-hybrid model. Moreover, from Theorem 1, $\mathbf{\Pi}_{\text{QT}}$ is also UC-secure in $\mathcal{F}_{\text{Mul}}$-hybrid model, and thus Theorem 7 holds.

□ (**Theorem 7**)

Efficiency of Our Constrained QT Protocol. Here, we give an analysis of the efficiency (round complexity and the number of invocations of multiplication) of our constrained QT protocol $\mathbf{\Pi}_{\text{QT}}$. The round complexity is r_{Mul}, where r_{Mul} represents the round complexity of $\mathcal{F}_{\text{Mul}}$. Also, the number of invocations of multiplication is i_{Mul}, where i_{Mul} represents the number of invocations of multiplication of $\mathcal{F}_{\text{Mul}}$.

3.4   A Concrete Protocol in Our Framework

In this section, we propose our concrete protocol $\mathbf{\Pi}'_{\text{EXP}}$ based on our framework $\mathbf{\Pi}_{\text{EXP}}$ for the exponentiation functionality $\mathcal{F}_{\text{EXP}}$. Here, $\mathbf{\Pi}_{\text{EXP}}$ is realized by the concrete $\mathbf{\Pi}_{\text{Conv}}$ in Sect. 3.2 using our constrained QT protocol $\mathbf{\Pi}_{\text{QT}}$ in Sect. 3.3, and we denote this protocol $\mathbf{\Pi}'_{\text{EXP}}$ which is described in Algorithm 4. In the following, let $a \in \mathbb{Z}_p$ and $x \in \mathbb{Z}_p$. As mentioned in Sect. 1.2, since we need to ensure the inputs are always even, our concrete exponentiation protocol requires a condition $2x < p$ for inputs x. We note that regarding the output $[o]_{p'}$ in Algorithm 4, if we want to convert it back to shares in $\mathbb{Z}_p$ (as opposed to in $\mathbb{Z}_{p'}$), we just need to apply modulus conversion to it again.

Remark 4 (On the selection of modulus p'). In Algorithm 4, we assume that a prime p' is known such that there exists an element b satisfying $b = \sqrt{a}$ in $\mathbb{Z}_{p'}$. Note that for a prime p, half of elements in $\mathbb{Z}_p$ have square roots in $\mathbb{Z}_p$, and if this is the case for a, the element $b \in \mathbb{Z}_p$ can be found via standard algorithms. In other words, for

---

Algorithm 4. Our concrete exponentiation protocol Π'_{EXP}

Input: $a, [x]_p, p'$
Output: $[o]_{p'}$
 1: $b := \sqrt{a}$, where $b \in \mathbb{Z}_{p'}$
 2: $[2x]_p \leftarrow 2[x]_p$
 3: **if** $p \neq p'$ **then**
 4:   $[2x]_{p'} \leftarrow \Pi_{\mathrm{Conv}}([2x]_p, p')$
 5:   $v := [2x]_{p'}$
 6: **else**
 7:   $v := [2x]_p$
 8: **end if**
 9: Output $[o]_{p'} \leftarrow \Pi_{\mathrm{EXP}}(b, v)$

---

a randomly chosen a, the probability that setting $p' = p$ is sufficient, where p is the prime underlying the additive sharing of x, is $1/2$. However, if no square root for a exists in $\mathbb{Z}_p$, a different prime p' must be used. An appropriate p' might be found simply by trying a random prime p', test whether a has a square root in $\mathbb{Z}_{p'}$, and if not, try a new random prime p'. Under the assumption that an element $a \in \mathbb{Z}_{p'}$ has a square root in $\mathbb{Z}_{p'}$ with probability $1/2$ for a randomly chosen p', this approach will efficiently find an appropriate p' with overwhelming probability. We note that since a is assumed to be public, finding an appropriate p' can be done before the exponentiation protocol is executed, and might be based on publicly available information for commonly used values of a and p.

Correctness. Here, we prove the correctness of our protocol Π'_{EXP}.

Theorem 8. Π'_{EXP} *correctly computes* $\mathcal{F}_{\mathrm{EXP}}$ *in* $(\mathcal{F}_{\mathrm{QT}}, \mathcal{F}_{\mathrm{Conv}}, \mathcal{F}_{\mathrm{Mul}})$-*hybrid model if* $2x < p'$ *holds.*

Before showing our formal proof, we give some subtle points which happens in the proof. The difference with the protocol Π_{EXP} is that, x is extended to $2x$ in Π'_{EXP} since Π_{QT} can only work over even numbers. (Here, since we need to compute $2x$ exactly without reducing in p', $2x < p'$ is required.) Thus, we compute $\sqrt{a}^{2x}$ instead of a^x directly, where $[2x]^0_{p'} + [2x]^1_{p'} = 2x + t \cdot p'$ ($t \in \{0, 1\}$). In the following, it is confirmed that both in the two cases, we can obtain correct result $a^x \bmod p$ in the end of Π'_{EXP}.

Proof of Theorem 8. Here, we consider the case that $p \neq p'$ holds. (In the case of $p = p'$, we just need to skip the process of Π_{Conv}.) First, Π_{Conv} changes $2x \in \mathbb{Z}_p$ to $2x \in \mathbb{Z}_{p'}$. In Π_{Conv} on input $2x$, from the correctness of Π_{QT} and the fact that the input $2x$ is an even number, we can get a correct value $t \in \{0, 1\}$ satisfying $[2x]^0_{p'} + [2x]^1_{p'} = 2x + t \cdot p'$. From the correctness of Π_{Conv}, we obtain $[2x]^0_{p'}$ and $[2x]^1_{p'}$, where $[2x]^0_{p'} + [2x]^1_{p'} = 2x \bmod p'$. Moreover, each party P_i computes $y_i = b^{[2x]^i_{p'}} \bmod p$ and shares y_i to each other, where $b^2 \equiv a (\bmod p)$. Thus, from the correctness of Π_{EXP} and the correctness of Π_{QT}, we can obtain a (correct) output $o = b^{[2x]^0_{p'} + [2x]^1_{p'}} \bmod p = a^x \bmod p$. □ **(Theorem 8)**

Security. Finally, we prove the security of Π'_{EXP}.

Theorem 9. Π'_{EXP} *securely computes* $\mathcal{F}_{\text{EXP}}$ *in* $(\mathcal{F}_{\text{QT}}, \mathcal{F}_{\text{Conv}}, \mathcal{F}_{\text{Mul}})$*-hybrid model.*

Proof of Theorem 9. From the UC-security of the underlying Π_{Conv} (Theorem 5), Π_{QT} (Theorem 7), and the underlying multiplication protocol, we can easily see that Π'_{EXP} securely computes $\mathcal{F}_{\text{EXP}}$.   □ **(Theorem 9)**

Efficiency of Our Concrete Exponentiation Protocol. Here, we give an analysis of the efficiency (round complexity and the number of invocations of multiplication) of our concrete exponentiation protocol Π'_{EXP}.

Firstly, we estimate the round complexity of Π'_{EXP}. Recall that the round complexity of our exponentiation framework, modulus conversion protocol, and constrained QT protocol is $\max(r_{\text{QT}}, r_{\text{Mul}}) + r_{\text{Mul}}$, r_{QT}, and r_{Mul} respectively, where r_{QT} and r_{Mul} represent the round complexity of $\mathcal{F}_{\text{QT}}$ and $\mathcal{F}_{\text{Mul}}$ respectively. That is, instantiating our exponentiation framework and modulus conversion protocol by our constrained QT protocol, the round complexity is $2 \cdot r_{\text{Mul}}$ and r_{Mul}, respectively. In the case that we need to convert the modulus p to another p', since Π'_{EXP} calls one modulus conversion protocol and one exponentiation framework, the round complexity of our concrete exponentiation protocol is $3 \cdot r_{\text{Mul}}$. In contrast, if we do not need to convert the modulus p to another p', since Π'_{EXP} calls only one exponentiation framework, the round complexity of our concrete exponentiation protocol is $2 \cdot r_{\text{Mul}}$. By using a standard multiplication protocol, the round complexity of the multiplication protocol r_{Mul} is 1. Thus, the round complexity of our concrete exponentiation protocol is 3 in the former cast and 2 in the latter case.

Secondly, we estimate the number of invocations of multiplications of Π'_{EXP}. Recall that the number of invocations of multiplications of our exponentiation framework, modulus conversion protocol, and constrained QT protocol is $i_{\text{QT}} + 2 \cdot i_{\text{Mul}}$, i_{QT}, and i_{Mul}, respectively. That is, instantiating our exponentiation framework and modulus conversion protocol by our constrained QT protocol, the number of invocations of multiplications is 3 and 1, respectively.

4   Conclusion

In this paper, we give a new two-party exponentiation protocol based on an additive secret sharing scheme which is compatible with well-known dishonest-majority MPC frameworks. The efficiency of our protocol is characterized by two cases. If we need modulus conversion in our protocol, it requires 3 rounds and 4 invocations of MPC multiplication. In contrast, it requires only 2 rounds and 3 invocations of MPC multiplication if we do not need modulus conversion. The core techniques for obtaining our protocol are two-fold. One is an efficient constrained quotient transfer protocol which only works on even numbers without bit-decomposition. The other is an efficient modulus conversion protocol based on the above efficient quotient transfer protocol. We believe that these two primitives might be of independent interest and could have further applications. We leave it as future work to construct efficient unconstrained QT protocols that will remove the limitation $2x < p$ in our concrete protocol and investigate how to extend our protocol to support non-integer values such as fixed-point numbers.

Acknowledgements. A part of this work was supported by JST SPRING JPMJSP2106, JST OPERA JPMJOP1612, JST CREST JPMJCR2113, JSPS KAKENHI JP19H01109, JP21H04879, and MIC JPJ000254.

References

[ISO] ISO/IEC 19592-2:2017(en) Information technology - Security techniques - Secret sharing - Part 2: Fundamental mechanisms (2017)

[AA20] Arpita, P., Ajith, S.: BLAZE: blazing fast privacy-preserving machine learning. In: Proceedings 2020 Network and Distributed System Security Symposium, pp. 459–480 (2020)

[AAN18] Aly, A., Abidin, A., Nikova, S.: Practically efficient secure distributed exponentiation without bit-decomposition. In: Meiklejohn, S., Sako, K. (eds.) FC 2018. LNCS, vol. 10957, pp. 291–309. Springer, Heidelberg (2018). https://doi.org/10.1007/978-3-662-58387-6_16

[ALSZ15] Asharov, G., Lindell, Y., Schneider, T., Zohner, M.: More efficient oblivious transfer extensions with security for malicious adversaries. In: Oswald, E., Fischlin, M. (eds.) EUROCRYPT 2015. LNCS, vol. 9056, pp. 673–701. Springer, Heidelberg (2015). https://doi.org/10.1007/978-3-662-46800-5_26

[BCP+20] Byali, M., Chaudhari, H., Patra, A., Suresh, A.: FLASH: fast and robust framework for privacy-preserving machine learning. In: Proceedings on Privacy Enhancing Technologies, pp. 459–480 (2020)

[Bea92] Beaver, D.: Efficient multiparty protocols using circuit randomization. In: Feigenbaum, J. (ed.) CRYPTO 1991. LNCS, vol. 576, pp. 420–432. Springer, Heidelberg (1992). https://doi.org/10.1007/3-540-46766-1_34

[BGW88] Ben-Or, M., Goldwasser, S., Wigderson, A.: Completeness theorems for non-cryptographic fault-tolerant distributed computation (extended abstract). In: 20th ACM STOC, pp. 1–10. ACM Press, May 1988

[CCPS19] Chaudhari, H., Choudhury, A., Patra, A., Suresh, A.: ASTRA: high throughput 3PC over rings with application to secure prediction. In: Proceedings of the 2019 ACM SIGSAC Conference on Cloud Computing Security Workshop, pp. 81–92 (2019)

[CRS20] Chaudhari, H., Rachuri, R., Suresh, A.: Trident: efficient 4PC framework for privacy preserving machine learning. In: Proceedings on 27th Annual Network and Distributed System Security Symposium (2020)

[CVA18] Chiraag, J., Vinod, V., Anantha, C.: GAZELLE: a low latency framework for secure neural network inference. In: Proceedings of the 27th USENIX Conference on Security Symposium, pp. 1651–1668 (2018)

[DFK+06] Damgård, I., Fitzi, M., Kiltz, E., Nielsen, J.B., Toft, T.: Unconditionally secure constant-rounds multi-party computation for equality, comparison, bits and exponentiation. In: Halevi, S., Rabin, T. (eds.) TCC 2006. LNCS, vol. 3876, pp. 285–304. Springer, Heidelberg (2006). https://doi.org/10.1007/11681878_15

[DKL+13] Damgård, I., Keller, M., Larraia, E., Pastro, V., Scholl, P., Smart, N.P.: Practical covertly secure MPC for dishonest majority - or: breaking the SPDZ limits. In: Crampton, J., Jajodia, S., Mayes, K. (eds.) ESORICS 2013. LNCS, vol. 8134, pp. 1–18. Springer, Heidelberg (2013). https://doi.org/10.1007/978-3-642-40203-6_1

[DN03]   Damgård, I., Nielsen, J.B.: Universally composable efficient multiparty computation from threshold homomorphic encryption. In: Boneh, D. (ed.) CRYPTO 2003. LNCS, vol. 2729, pp. 247–264. Springer, Heidelberg (2003). https://doi.org/10.1007/978-3-540-45146-4_15

[DPSZ12]   Damgård, I., Pastro, V., Smart, N., Zakarias, S.: Multiparty computation from somewhat homomorphic encryption. In: Safavi-Naini, R., Canetti, R. (eds.) CRYPTO 2012. LNCS, vol. 7417, pp. 643–662. Springer, Heidelberg (2012). https://doi.org/10.1007/978-3-642-32009-5_38

[GGN16]   Gennaro, R., Goldfeder, S., Narayanan, A.: Threshold-optimal DSA/ECDSA signatures and an application to bitcoin wallet security. In: Manulis, M., Sadeghi, A.-R., Schneider, S. (eds.) ACNS 2016. LNCS, vol. 9696, pp. 156–174. Springer, Cham (2016). https://doi.org/10.1007/978-3-319-39555-5_9

[KIM+18]   Kikuchi, R., Ikarashi, D., Matsuda, T., Hamada, K., Chida, K.: Efficient bit-decomposition and modulus-conversion protocols with an honest majority. In: Susilo, W., Yang, G. (eds.) ACISP 2018. LNCS, vol. 10946, pp. 64–82. Springer, Cham (2018). https://doi.org/10.1007/978-3-319-93638-3_5

[KLR10]   Kushilevitz, E., Lindell, Y., Rabin, T.: Information-theoretically secure protocols and security under composition. SIAM J. Comput. 39(5), 2090–2112 (2010)

[KOS16]   Keller, M., Orsini, E., Scholl, P.: MASCOT: faster malicious arithmetic secure computation with oblivious transfer. In: Weippl, E.R., Katzenbeisser, S., Kruegel, C., Myers, A.C., Halevi, S. (eds.) ACM CCS 2016, pp. 830–842. ACM Press, October 2016

[KPR18]   Keller, M., Pastro, V., Rotaru, D.: Overdrive: making SPDZ great again. In: Nielsen, J.B., Rijmen, V. (eds.) EUROCRYPT 2018. LNCS, vol. 10822, pp. 158–189. Springer, Cham (2018). https://doi.org/10.1007/978-3-319-78372-7_6

[KRC+20]   Kumar, N., Rathee, M., Chandran, N., Gupta, D., Rastogi, A., Sharma, R.: CrypTFlow: secure TensorFlow inference. In: Proceedings 2020 IEEE Symposium on Security and Privacy, pp. 336–353 (2020)

[Lin17]   Lindell, Y.: Fast secure two-party ECDSA signing. In: Katz, J., Shacham, H. (eds.) CRYPTO 2017. LNCS, vol. 10402, pp. 613–644. Springer, Cham (2017). https://doi.org/10.1007/978-3-319-63715-0_21

[MLS+20]   Mishra, P., Lehmkuhl, R., Srinivasan, A., Zheng, W., Popa, R.A.: Delphi: a cryptographic inference service for neural networks. In: Proceedings of the 29th USENIX Conference on Security Symposium, pp. 2505–2522 (2020)

[NX11]   Ning, C., Xu, Q.: Constant-rounds, linear multi-party computation for exponentiation and modulo reduction with perfect security. In: Lee, D.H., Wang, X. (eds.) ASIACRYPT 2011. LNCS, vol. 7073, pp. 572–589. Springer, Heidelberg (2011). https://doi.org/10.1007/978-3-642-25385-0_31

[OWIO19]   Ohara, K., Watanabe, Y., Iwamoto, M., Ohta, K.: Multi-party computation for modular exponentiation based on replicated secret sharing. IEICE Trans. Fundam. Electron. Commun. Comput. Sci. 102(9), 1079–1090 (2019)

[RSC+19]   Sadegh Riazi, M., Samragh, M., Chen, H., Laine, K., Lauter, K., Koushanfar, F.: XONN: XNOR-based oblivious deep neural network inference. In: Proceedings of the 28th USENIX Conference on Security Symposium, pp. 1501–1518 (2019)

[WWW+14]   Wang, Y., Wong, D.S., Wu, Q., Chow, S.S.M., Qin, B., Liu, J.: Practical distributed signatures in the standard model. In: Benaloh, J. (ed.) CT-RSA 2014. LNCS, vol. 8366, pp. 307–326. Springer, Cham (2014). https://doi.org/10.1007/978-3-319-04852-9_16

Efficient Compiler to Covert Security with Public Verifiability for Honest Majority MPC

Thomas Attema[1,2,3], Vincent Dunning[1(✉)], Maarten Everts[4,5], and Peter Langenkamp[1]

[1] TNO, Applied Cryptography and Quantum Algorithms,
The Hague, The Netherlands
{thomas.attema,vincent.dunning,peter.langenkamp}@tno.nl
[2] CWI, Cryptology Group, Amsterdam, The Netherlands
[3] Leiden University, Mathematical Institute, Leiden, The Netherlands
[4] University of Twente, Services and Cyber Security, Enschede, The Netherlands
maarten.everts@utwente.nl
[5] Linksight, Utrecht, The Netherlands

Abstract. We present a novel compiler for transforming arbitrary, passively secure MPC protocols into efficient protocols with covert security and public verifiability in the honest majority setting. Our compiler works for protocols with any number of parties > 2 and treats the passively secure protocol in a black-box manner.

In multi-party computation (MPC), covert security provides an attractive trade-off between the security of actively secure protocols and the efficiency of passively secure protocols. In this security notion, honest parties are only required to detect an active attack with some constant probability, referred to as the *deterrence rate*. Extending covert security with *public verifiability* additionally ensures that any party, even an external one not participating in the protocol, is able to identify the cheaters if an active attack has been detected.

Recently, Faust et al. (EUROCRYPT 2021) and Scholl et al. (Preprint 2021) introduced similar covert security compilers based on computationally expensive time-lock puzzles. At the cost of requiring an honest majority, our work avoids the use of time-lock puzzles completely. Instead, we adopt a much more efficient *publicly verifiable secret sharing* scheme to achieve a similar functionality. This obviates the need for a trusted setup and a general-purpose actively secure MPC protocol. We show that our computation and communication costs are orders of magnitude lower while achieving the same deterrence rate.

Keywords: Multi-Party Computation · Compiler · Covert Security · Honest Majority

© Springer Nature Switzerland AG 2022
G. Ateniese and D. Venturi (Eds.): ACNS 2022, LNCS 13269, pp. 663–683, 2022.
https://doi.org/10.1007/978-3-031-09234-3_33

1   Introduction

Multi-party computation (MPC) is a subfield of cryptography allowing a set of mutually distrusting parties to jointly compute functions over their inputs without revealing anything but the outcome of the computation.

This way, nothing more can be deduced about the inputs of other parties than what could be deduced from the outcome of the computation alone. Traditionally, two types of adversaries have been considered in MPC; *passive* and *active* adversaries. Passive adversaries try to deduce as much private information as possible but follow the protocol honestly. Active adversaries are additionally allowed to arbitrarily deviate from the protocol, which might also compromise the correctness of the outcome. In general, passively secure protocols are fast but might not be considered secure in many realistic scenarios unless there is a good reason to assume that an untrusted party will not deviate from the protocol. Actively secure protocols are very secure in this regard, but active security comes at the cost of increasing the communication and computation complexity.

As a trade-off between the benefits of these two notions, *covert* security was introduced by Aumann and Lindell in 2007 [3]. Instead of safeguarding the protocol against an active attack, the idea of this notion is that it is sufficient to only detect the attack with a certain probability called the *deterrence rate* ϵ. Usually the deterrence rate can be chosen arbitrarily, thus providing a dynamic trade-off between the efficiency and security of passively and actively secure protocols, respectively. Goyal, Mohassel and Smith [13] presented a covertly secure version of garbled-circuit based MPC protocols [5] and Damgard et al. [9] introduced a cheap cut-and-choose approach for an efficient and covertly secure offline phase for the SPDZ protocol [11], replacing costly zero-knowledge proofs required for active security. While this notion has led to promising results, in 2012 Asharov and Orlandi [2] observed that it might not be sufficient for practical applications. If a party detects a cheating attempt, there is in general no way of proving that another party has acted maliciously. Therefore they introduced the extended notion of *publicly verifiable* covert security. This property equips the parties with a mechanism to generate a *certificate* that proves a cheating attempt to *anyone*, including external parties not participating in the MPC protocol. Even though this notion looks promising for wider use in practice, relatively little research has been done in this area. The only concrete protocols in this security model have been presented in [2,15,16].

Another line of research is the trade-off between the number of corruptions a protocol can tolerate and efficiency, again giving up some security by tolerating less corruptions to achieve a more efficient protocol. A popular relaxation in literature is the assumption of an *honest majority*, meaning that more than half of the parties are guaranteed to behave honestly. Concrete protocols with active security and only sublinear overhead in the honest majority model have been presented in [6,14].

To ease the development of MPC with stronger security guarantees, *compilers* were introduced. Compilers allow for a modular approach to cryptographic protocol design; they provide a generic transformation from protocols with certain (security) properties to protocols with stronger properties. For instance, covert/active security compilers take as input a passively secure MPC protocol and output a protocol with covert/active security. The focus of this work will be on compiling passively secure protocols into efficient protocols with covert security and public verifiability for *any* passively secure protocol with an arbitrary number of parties $n > 2$.

Many MPC protocols proceed as follows. They first run an input independent pre-processing phase to set up some correlated randomness, e.g., Beaver triples [4]. Because this phase can be executed before the secret input values are available, it is also referred to as the offline phase. This pre-processing allows the actual computation, the online phase, to be executed very efficiently. Since actively secure online phases nowadays are quite efficient already, we specifically target our compiler towards the more expensive pre-processing protocols. As was proven in [10], combining a covertly secure pre-processing protocol with public verifiability and an actively secure online phase yields an overall protocol with covert security and public verifiability. Therefore, our compiler could for example be used to replace the actively secure pre-processing step of the SPDZ protocol with a covertly secure one from our compiler and combine it with the actively secure online phase of SPDZ [11] to improve the overall efficiency.

Typically, covert security is obtained by a cut-and-choose strategy where the passively secure protocol is simply executed multiple times after which some of these executions are "opened" to verify the behavior of the parties. An important predicament to overcome for public verifiability is the prevention of a *detection-dependent abort*. This means that an adversary should not be able to prevent the generation of a certificate once it sees its cheating attempt is going to be detected. The first covert security compiler *without* public verifiability was presented by Damgård, Geisler and Nielsen in 2010 [8]. Their approach is based on the assumption of an honest majority of participants. A covert security compiler *with* public verifiability, secure against *any* number of corruptions, was first presented by Damgård et al. in 2020 [10]. They presented two compilers in the 2-party case; one for input-independent protocols and one for input-dependent protocols. Furthermore, they sketch how to extend their approach to arbitrary numbers of parties. To prevent a detection-dependent abort, detecting active attacks is done by letting each party independently and obliviously choose which executions it wants to verify. To guarantee for a constant number of k executions that at least one execution remains closed, the number of executions that can be chosen by each party (and hence the deterrence rate) decreases for increasing numbers of parties. Concretely, each party can choose at most $\frac{k-1}{n}$ executions and thus obtains $\epsilon = \frac{k-1}{kn}$.

Constructions with a constant deterrence rate for any number of parties have been presented by Faust et al. [12] and concurrently by Scholl et al. [19]. Both works follow a *shared coin toss* (SCT) strategy. With this strategy, the parties together toss a coin to determine which executions will be verified by everyone guaranteeing maximal deterrence rates regardless of the amount of parties. To prevent a detection-dependent abort, both [12] and [19] use time-lock puzzles (TLP) to lock the potential evidence before the coin toss such that the honest parties are guaranteed its availability in case the adversary aborts after seeing the outcome of the coin toss. A TLP hides a secret message and solving the TLP reveals this message. Moreover, solving a TLP is guaranteed to require a fixed amount of work. A TLP therefore guarantees that a message is hidden for a fixed amount of time and that it can be revealed after this fixed amount of time.

However, the time-locks introduce strict timing assumptions which introduce subtle issues in practice when used for this application. The entire security against a detection-dependent abort in these works relies on the assumption that the TLP is hidden for a few synchronous communication rounds. In theory, the synchronous communication model ensures that the parties communicate in fixed rounds through a global clock. In practice, this is typically realized by picking a certain *timeout* after which all messages for a round should have been received. With the TLP approach, if the amount of work required for solving the TLP is picked too low, an adversary has a higher probability of solving the TLP early and perform a detection-dependent abort. On the other hand, by picking a larger amount of work, the complexity for the honest parties to solve the TLP becomes undesirably high. The TLPs only need to be solved in case of misbehavior, so using an extremely complex puzzle could be acceptable to decrease the probability of the adversary solving the TLP too early. However, since we cannot make assumptions about the power of the adversary, it is still impossible to guarantee the security of the TLP and thus secrecy of the underlying message for a small number of communication rounds.

Furthermore, both TLP approaches require the availability of a general-purpose, actively secure MPC protocol to realize a trusted setup and implement an ideal functionality that constructs the TLP. This seems counterintuitive in a setting where the goal is to increase the security of a passively secure protocol through compilation. Furthermore, these functionalities prove to be very costly.

1.1   Contributions

In this work, we introduce a novel and efficient covert security compiler with public verifiability in the honest majority setting.

Our approach is based on the covert security compilers with public verifiability presented in [10,12,19]. We adapt their constructions and use a *publicly verifiable secret sharing scheme (PVSS)* to replace the costly time-lock puzzles (TLP). Compared to [10], our compilers yield much higher deterrence rates in the multi-party setting. This is achieved by following a *shared coin toss (SCT)* strategy, similar to the compilers of [12,19]. More precisely, for any number of executions of the passive protocol k, a deterrence rate of $1 - \frac{1}{k}$ can be achieved independent of the number of parties n. The public verifiability of the compilers of [12,19] is based on the use of TLPs to ensure availability of potential evidence after the coin toss. In contrast, we adopt a PVSS to distribute the evidence among all the parties. Due to the honest-majority assumption, the PVSS can be instantiated such that the adversary corrupting less than $n/2$ parties cannot reconstruct this secret evidence prematurely, while the honest parties are able to reconstruct. The prior works of [12,19] do however provide security against a dishonest majority.

With our adaptation, we remove the need for a trusted setup and an actively secure puzzle generation. We show that as a result, both the computation and communication complexity of our compiler decrease by multiple orders of magnitude. Moreover, an efficient and secure TLP instantiation for the purpose of achieving public verifiability, requires an accurate estimation of the adversary's computational resources. Therefore, in this application, it is inherently difficult to instantiate a TLP appropriately. For these reasons, our approach, avoiding TLPs altogether, provides security against a more realistic adversary model.

Our compiler makes black-box use of the passively secure protocol and can therefore enhance the security of *any* passively secure protocol, including future protocols. In [14] and [6], active security is obtained by adapting a specific secret-sharing based protocol and requires a stronger security notion than plain passive security. Therefore, these protocols are incomparable to our compiler.

1.2   Technical Overview

Covert Security. Covert security is obtained in a similar fashion to related constructions, where active cheating is usually detected by some cut-and-choose mechanism. More precisely, the passively secure protocol is executed k times after which $t < k$ executions are opened to verify the behavior of the parties. Opening an execution is done by revealing the randomness used by each party during an execution of the protocol. Note that in this work we are specifically targeting input-independent protocols and hence the behavior of a party is completely determined by the (publicly known) protocol description and the randomness used. Given the randomness of the other parties, each party can replay the protocol execution and verify the behavior of the other parties during the actual protocol execution. If no deviations are detected, the result of one of the unopened executions can then be picked as the output of the protocol. However, this approach still allows a dishonest party to decide which randomness to reveal *after* learning which executions are to be opened, i.e., there is no guarantee that the revealed randomness was used during the executions. To prevent this, the parties are required to commit to their randomness before the protocol execution. This technique was introduced by Hong et al. [15] and is also referred to as *derandomization*. After the k parallel executions, the parties perform a joint coin toss outputting an integer $1 \leq i \leq k$ indicating the protocol execution that is to be used as output. The remaining $k - 1$ executions are opened and the parties verify each other's behavior.

Public Verifiability. Public verifiability is obtained by making each party accountable for its messages by letting them *sign* all the messages they send during the protocol executions. If it is later detected that a party has sent an incorrect message, anyone can verify that this party must have sent the malicious message. It is essential to prevent a so-called *detection-dependent abort*, meaning an adversary cannot prevent the generation of a certificate once it sees it is going to be detected. To prevent this, we "lock" the randomness used by sharing it among all parties using a PVSS *before* the coin toss. If an adversary aborts after the coin toss, the parties have enough shares to reconstruct the randomness and verify behavior anyways. Here the honest majority assumption is required to guarantee enough honest shares for reconstructing each randomness while the adversary cannot get hold of enough shares to reconstruct the randomness used in the output execution.

Note that we can not simply accuse a party who aborts at this stage as there is no publicly verifiable evidence of this (such as a signature of a party on a malicious message). An external party who wishes to verify the protocol execution can not distinguish between an actual, active attack or an accident such as a network failure. Therefore, this straightforward approach could lead to an honest party unjustly being punished or is deniable by an adversary who can claim that he was not at fault.

Public Verifiability from PVSS. By using a PVSS, the parties are guaranteed to be able to proof that an active attack occurred. To this end the parties can first use the PVSS to verify all the randomness shares distributed by each party before the coin toss. In case the verification of some share fails, anyone can verify that the adversary attempted to cheat by distributing inconsistent shares. If the verifications succeed, the shares are guaranteed to reconstruct to a well-defined value, namely the randomness of the distributor. The distributor is furthermore committed to this randomness by a proof of correct distribution. This verification can be performed without interaction with the distributor or any of the other parties. Therefore, verification can also be done by external parties, making it publicly verifiable.

In case an adversary aborts after the coin toss, the parties can combine their shares to reconstruct the randomness of the adversary. During this reconstruction phase, each party is required to also publish a proof of correct decryption. This way, the honest parties can combine only correct shares to reconstruct the value originally distributed. Furthermore, an adversary cannot 'incriminate' an honest party by publishing a different share than distributed by the honest party. As an additional benefit of the PVSS strategy, the protocol can still continue and succeed in case an otherwise honest party is not able to deliver this information in time.

2 Preliminaries

Our compiler uses several building blocks. As cryptographic building blocks, the compiler uses a commitment scheme (Com, Open) and a signature scheme (Gen, Sign, Verify). Throughout this work, the commitment scheme is assumed to be non-interactive, but our compiler could trivially be instantiated with an interactive commitment scheme as well. Committing to a message m with randomness r will be denoted by $(c, d) \leftarrow \text{Com}(m; r)$, where c is the resulting commitment and $d = (m, r)$ the opening information. Opening a commitment is then denoted with $m' \leftarrow \text{Open}(c, d)$. For a correct opening, we get that $m' = m$ and $m' = \perp$ otherwise. The commitment scheme should satisfy the *hiding* and *binding* properties.

The signature scheme should be *existentially unforgeable against chosen message attacks*. Before the protocol execution, all parties are expected to generate a public-private key pair (pk, sk) using Gen and register their public key. Signing a message m using a private key sk is denoted as $\sigma \leftarrow \text{Sign}_{sk}(m)$. Verifying a signature using the corresponding public key is denoted as accept, $\perp \leftarrow \text{Verify}_{pk}(m, \sigma)$.

2.1 Multi-party Computation

The goal of Multi-Party Computation (MPC) protocols is to allow a group of n participants $\mathcal{P} = P_1, \ldots, P_n$ to compute a shared function f over their private inputs $x_1, \ldots, x_n$ while keeping their inputs hidden from each other. This group of participants can be divided in two sets: *honest* participants and *corrupt* participants. The honest participants will strictly follow the protocol description while corrupt participants are assumed to be under the influence of a central adversary.

In general for an MPC protocol to be considered secure, it needs to satisfy two requirements: *privacy* and *correctness*. Privacy means that an adversary is not able to learn more than what it can deduce from its own inputs and the output of the protocol. Particularly the adversary should not be able to gain any additional information about the inputs of the honest parties. Correctness means that the outcome of the protocol received by the honest parties should be correct. To reason about the security of such a protocol in the presence of an adversary, we follow the standard real/ideal world paradigm to show that our protocol in the real world is indistinguishable from an ideal execution of the same functionality. Informally, this paradigm specifies an ideal Functionality $\mathcal{F}$ and proofs that the MPC protocol Π implements exactly this ideal execution and is thus as secure as the ideal world.

In this work we assume that the adversary $\mathcal{A}$ with auxiliary input z can statically corrupt a set $\mathbb{A} \subset \mathcal{P}$ of the parties with $|\mathbb{A}| < \frac{n}{2}$. Furthermore, let $\Pi : (\{0,1\}^*)^n \rightarrow (\{0,1\}^*)^n$ be the real-world protocol computing functionality f taking one input per party $\{x_1, x_2, \ldots, x_n\} = \overline{x}$ and returning one output to each party. We define the outputs of the honest parties and $\mathcal{A}$ in a real-world execution of Π as $\text{REAL}_\lambda[\mathcal{A}(z), \mathbb{A}, \Pi, \overline{x}]$, where λ is the security parameter.

In the passive security model, an ideal world adversary $\mathcal{S}$ is assumed to try to deduce as much information as possible while honestly participating in the protocol. On the other hand, active adversaries may arbitrarily deviate from the protocol in order to try to deduce more information or break the correctness of the outcome.

Covert Security. The idea of covert security is to assume an adversary who *is* capable of performing an active attack, but a certain probability of being caught cheating is enough to refrain him from doing so. This probability of being caught is called the *deterrence rate* ϵ.

In this work, we follow the strongest definition for covert security originally defined by Aumann and Lindell [3] called *strong explicit cheat (SECF)*. The ideal functionality for calculating a function f in the presence of covert adversaries according to this definition will be called $\mathcal{F}_{\text{covert}}$. This functionality allows S to perform cheating like an active adversary. With a probability of ϵ, $\mathcal{F}_{\text{covert}}$ informs all the parties of a cheating attempt. With a probability of $1 - \epsilon$, a cheating attempt is successful in which case S learns the inputs of all the parties and may decide their outputs. For readability of our protocols, we slightly alter the original SECF definition to not require *identifiable abort*. Due to the honest majority assumption this can, however, easily be obtained by adding a byzantine agreement at the end of the protocol. The formal definition of $\mathcal{F}_{\text{covert}}$ can be found in the full version of this paper [1].

The joint distribution of the outputs of the honest parties and the ideal-world adversary S (with auxiliary input z) is denoted as $\texttt{IDEAL}_\lambda^\epsilon[S(z), \mathbb{A}, \mathcal{F}_{\text{covert}}, \bar{x}]$. Covert security can now be defined as follows, where $\overset{c}{\equiv}$ denotes computationally indistinguishable:

Definition 1 (Covert security with deterrence rate ϵ). *A protocol Π securely computes $\mathcal{F}_{covert}$ with deterrence rate ϵ if for every real-world adversary $\mathcal{A}$, we can find an ideal-world adversary S such that for all security parameters $\lambda \in \mathbb{N}$:*

$$\left\{ IDEAL_\lambda^\epsilon[S(z), \mathbb{A}, \mathcal{F}_{covert}, \bar{x}] \right\}_{\bar{x}, k \in \{0,1\}^*} \overset{c}{\equiv} \left\{ REAL_\lambda[\mathcal{A}(c), \mathbb{A}, \Pi, \bar{x}] \right\}_{\bar{x}, k \in \{0,1\}^*}.$$

Public Verifiability. As an extension to covert security, the notion of *publicly verifiable* covert security (PVC) was proposed by Asharov and Orlandi in 2012 [2]. This form of security provides the parties with a mechanism to generate a publicly verifiable *certificate* in case cheating is detected. This certificate proves to *anyone* that a certain party attempted to cheat during the protocol.

We use the approach of [15] where a Judge algorithm is added to a real-world protocol Π. If, in the execution of Π, cheating is detected, the protocol outputs a certificate cert. The Judge algorithm verifies this certificate and outputs the public key (the "identity") of the cheater if it is valid. The vector of public keys is defined as $\vec{pk} = (pk^1, \ldots, pk^n)$, corresponding to the P_is. Furthermore, we have extracted the verification procedure of the protocol to a separate Blame algorithm. Blame takes the view of a party P_i, returns a certificate cert and outputs $\texttt{corrupted}_j$ in case party P_j is found to be cheating. Formally, we define covert security with public verifiability as:

Definition 2 (Covert security with deterrence rate ϵ and public verifiability). *A protocol $(\Pi, Blame, Judge)$ securely computes $\mathcal{F}_{covert}$ with a deterrence rate of ϵ and public verifiability if the following three conditions hold:*

- *Covert security: Π is secure against a covert adversary according to Definition 1 for covert security with deterrence rate ϵ. Additionally, Π might now output cert in case cheating is detected.*

- **Public Verifiability:** *If an honest party P_i detects cheating by another party P_j and outputs* cert *in an execution of Π, then* Judge$(\bar{pk}, \mathcal{F}, $cert$) = pk^j$ *except with negligible probability.*
- **Defamation-Freeness:** *If party P_i is honest and executes Π in the presence of an adversary $\mathcal{A}$, then the probability that $\mathcal{A}$ creates* cert* *such that* Judge$(\bar{pk}, \mathcal{F}, $cert$^*) = pk^i$ *is negligible.*

2.2 Publicly Verifiable Secret Sharing

Verifiable secret sharing (VSS) [7] is an extension of regular secret-sharing that provides additional security against active attacks. VSS protects honest parties against malicious participants by equipping the secret sharing scheme with mechanisms to (i) verify that they received consistent shares from an untrusted dealer and (ii) verify that they received the correct shares from the other parties during reconstruction. With *publicly* verifiable secret sharing (PVSS) [18, 21], properties (i) and (ii) can be verified by *anyone*, also parties outside the secret sharing protocol, without any interaction. In general, a PVSS can be instantiated from any secret sharing scheme with an arbitrary access structure $\mathcal{A}$. For this work, a threshold access structure such as realized with Shamir's secret sharing scheme [20] is sufficient. In this work, we require the PVSS to satisfy the definition first presented by Schoenmakers [18], which adds an additional proof of correct decryption:

Definition 3 (PVSS Scheme). *A PVSS scheme with a set of players $\mathcal{P}$ and access structure $\mathcal{A} \subseteq \mathcal{P}$ consists of the following three algorithms:*

- $(E_i(s_i)_{i \in \mathcal{P}}, $dproof$) \leftarrow$ Distribute(s): *The distribution algorithm takes as input a secret s and publishes a set of encrypted shares $E_i(s_i)_{i \in \mathcal{P}}$ and some public distribution proof* dproof.
- true *or* $\perp \leftarrow$ Verify$($dproof$, E_i(s_i))$: *The verification algorithm takes as input a distribution proof and an encrypted share $E_i(s_i)$ and outputs* true *if $E_i(s_i)$ encrypts a valid share s_i of s according to* dproof.
- $s' \leftarrow$ Reconstruct$(\{$rproof$_i, s_i\}_{i \in A})$: *The reconstruction algorithm takes a set of decrypted shares $s_i, i \in A$ and corresponding decryption proofs of some subset $A \subseteq \mathcal{P}$ and outputs the reconstructed value s'. In case $A \in \mathcal{A}$, we call A a qualified subset and as a result, $s' = s$ if the verifications of the encrypted shares succeeded according to the proofs.*

Here, it is assumed that we already have a registered public key of all the participants. Instead of generating and distributing the secrets directly, a dealer publishes encrypted shares $E_j(s_j)$ with the known public keys of each party P_j. Furthermore, the dealer publishes a string dproof which shows that each E_j encrypts a consistent share s_j. This proof also commits the dealer to the value of the secret s and guarantees that no one can wrongly claim to have received a wrong share since anyone can verify this. In this work we will abuse notation and let Verify$($dproof$, E_i(s_i)_{P \in \mathcal{P}})$ denote the verification of all shares destined for the parties in P of the same secret s. Now, true is interpreted as all verifications succeeding while $\perp$ means at least one verification failed. If the reconstruction succeeds, we are guaranteed that this is the original secret s. During the reconstruction phase, the parties decrypt and publish their shares s_j from $E_j(s_j)$ along with a string $\mathtt{rproof}_j$ which shows that they performed the decryption correctly. Using these, the other parties can now exclude the shares of participants who failed to decrypt correctly. If enough decryptions $(t+1)$ pass the verification, the parties can reconstruct the original secret successfully.

We require the PVSS to satisfy the *correctness*, *soundness* and *privacy* security guarantees.

Definition 4 (Correctness). *If a dealer honestly follows the* Distribute *algorithm to publish the encrypted shares $E_i(s_i)_{i \in P}$ and a public proof* dproof, *then the outcome of* Verify(dproof, $E_i(s_i)$) *is guaranteed to be* true. *Furthermore, if during reconstruction a party P_i honestly decrypts $E_i(s_i)$, publishes its share s_i and honestly generates the proof* $\mathtt{rproof}_i$, *then another honest party receiving the decrypted share s_i and* $\mathtt{rproof}_i$ *accepts this share. Finally, a qualified subset $A \subseteq P$ is guaranteed to reconstruct the original secret s if the dealer and the parties in A honestly follow the* Distribute *and* Reconstruct *protocols.*

Definition 5 (Soundness). *If* Verify(dproof, $E_i(s_i)$) $==$ true, *then for all qualified subsets $A_1, A_2 \subset P$, the following holds:*

$$\mathtt{Reconstruct}(\{\mathtt{rproof}_i, s_i\}_{i \in A_1}) == \mathtt{Reconstruct}(\{\mathtt{rproof}_i, s_i\}_{i \in A_2}).$$

Furthermore, if a malicious party submits a fake share during reconstruction, verification of this share fails with an overwhelming probability.

Definition 6 (Privacy). *An adversary corrupting a set of participants A such that $|A| < t$ should not be able to learn anything about the secret s from the shares s_i with $i \in A$.*

3   Building Blocks

In this section, we will introduce the basic building blocks of our PVC compiler. The PVC compiler uses a public bulletin board and a public coin tossing functionality. Furthermore, our compiler slightly modifies the passively secure protocol execution.

Public Bulletin Board. For public communication required by the PVSS, we model an ideal functionality $\mathcal{F}_{\mathsf{bb}}$, which represents a public bulletin board. A formal description of this Functionality can be found in the full version of this paper [1]. The public bulletin board functionality guarantees that the honest parties agree on all the messages that have been sent. In practice, this functionality could be realized using the *echo broadcast* protocol of [17].

$\mathcal{F}_{\text{coin}}$ Ideal coin-tossing functionality

- Consider a number of parties $P_1, P_2, \ldots, P_n$
- If $\mathcal{F}_{\text{coin}}$ receives a message (flip) from P_i, it stores (flip, P_i) in memory if it is not stored in memory yet.
- Once $\mathcal{F}_{\text{coin}}$ has stored all the messages (flip, P_i) for $i \in [n]$, $\mathcal{F}_{\text{coin}}$ picks a random value $r \in_R \{0,1\}^\lambda$ and sends (flip, r) to all the parties.

Coin Tossing. An ideal functionality $\mathcal{F}_{\text{coin}}$ receives ok_i from each party $P_i, i \in [n]$ and outputs a random λ-bit string r to all the parties. The adversary should not be able to influence the outcome of the coin-tossing protocol. Therefore, we require a coin-tossing protocol with security against an active adversary $\mathcal{A}$.

Passively Secure Protocol. The compiler presented in this work is designed to compile an arbitrary input-independent protocol Π_{pass} with passive security. Furthermore, we require the parties to agree on a public transcript that is the same in case of an honest execution, to compare to expected executions later on. To obtain such transcripts, we assume a fixed ordering in the messages and that every party can see each message sent during an execution of the protocol. In case Π_{pass} is secure against $n - 1$ corruptions, we can simply broadcast every message since the adversary was allowed to see each message anyways. Otherwise, we need to keep the messages hidden by broadcasting symmetric-key encrypted messages instead, as presented in [10]. To ease notation, we will assume Π_{pass} to be secure against $n - 1$ corruptions but adding symmetric-key encryption for an arbitrary number of corruptions could be realized in a straightforward way by simply opening the keys in the execution opening protocol as well.

4   PVC Compiler

In this section we will present the main compiler Π_{comp} for transforming an arbitrary n-party MPC protocol Π_{pass} with passive security and no private inputs into an n-party MPC protocol with covert security and public verifiability. This compiler uses a commitment scheme, a signature scheme, a publicly-verifiable secret sharing scheme (PVSS) and an actively secure coin tossing protocol. We assume that every party already has registered a public key at the start of the protocol. Roughly speaking, Π_{comp} works in four separate phases: *seed generation, protocol execution, evidence creation* and *execution opening and verification*. In the seed generation phase, the parties set up k seeds from which they derive their randomness during the k executions of Π_{pass}. In the protocol execution phase, Π_{pass} is executed k times. In the evidence creation phase, the parties use the PVSS to secret share their seed openings to all the other parties and sign the information so that they can be held accountable later on. Finally, in the execution opening and verification phase, the parties toss a coin to select $k - 1$ executions, open the randomness seeds for these $k - 1$ executions and verify the behavior of the other parties. If no cheating is detected, the parties output

---

Π_{seed} Seed generation procedure

This protocol works with an arbitrary number n of parties $\mathcal{P} = \{P_1, P_2, \ldots, P_n\}$. To generate uniformly random seeds for every party, the parties execute the following steps:

1. Party P_i samples uniformly random a private seed $\text{seed}^i_{\text{priv}}$, generates $(c^i, d^i) \leftarrow \text{Com}(\text{seed}^i_{\text{priv}})$ and sends c^i to the other parties.
2. For each $j \in [n]$, P_i samples a uniformly random public seed share $\text{seed}^{(i,j)}_{(\text{pub})}$ and sends $\text{seed}^{(i,j)}_{(\text{pub})}$ to all the other parties.
3. Each party calculates the public seeds $\text{seed}^i_{\text{pub}}$ for each P_i as $\bigoplus_{j=0}^n \text{seed}^{(i,j)}_{\text{pub}}$.
4. If the parties have not received all the expected messages before some predefined timeout, the parties send abort to all the other parties and output abort. Otherwise, P_i outputs $(\text{seed}^i_{\text{priv}}, d^i, \{\text{seed}^j_{\text{pub}}, c^j\}\}_{j \in [n]})$.

---

their output in the unopened execution. Otherwise, they output the obtained certificate. A formal description of Π_{comp} can be found in the full version of this paper [1].

Seed Generation. In order to guarantee covert security for *any* passively secure protocol Π_{pass}, we need to be guaranteed that the used randomness is picked uniformly at random. To achieve this, we run an actively secure seed generation procedure Π_{seed} for each of the executions of Π_{pass}. A formal description of this procedure can be found in Π_{seed}.

In the seed generation procedure, each party P_i picks a private seed $\text{seed}^i_{\text{priv}}$ for itself and publicly commits to this seed. Together all the parties generate a public seed for each party P_i by first picking a public seed *share* and defining the public seed $\text{seed}^i_{\text{pub}}$ for P_i as the sum of the shares of all the parties. During the executions of Π_{pass}, the parties derive randomness from a seed that is the XOR of the private and public seed, and is thus uniformly random.

Protocol Execution. In the protocol execution phase, the parties run the passively secure protocol k times in parallel and obtain an output y^i_j and transcript trans^i_j for each of the executions. In these executions, every party sends each message to every other party and *signs* each message to hold them accountable.

Evidence Creation. In the evidence creation phase, the parties are required to generate publicly verifiable, encrypted shares for the opening information of *all* of the k randomness seeds used:

$$(\{E_h(d_h)^{(i,j)}\}_{h \in [n]}, \text{dproof}^i_j) \leftarrow \text{PVSS.Distribute}(d^i_j).$$

and publicly broadcast these using $\mathcal{F}_{\text{bb}}$. This ensures availability of all the used randomness seeds after the coin toss for verification by the honest parties. In case the adversary aborts after seeing the coin toss, the honest parties can reconstruct its seeds using these shares, which are guaranteed to be correct if the PVSS verifications succeed. Furthermore, the parties sign the tuple:

$$\texttt{evidence}_j = (i, j, \{c_j^l, \texttt{dproof}_j^l\}_{l \in [n]}, \texttt{trans}_j)$$

With which they can be held accountable later on.

In the next sections, we will explain the subprotocols Π_{open}, $\Pi_{\text{reconstruct}}$ and Blame executed in the *execution opening and verification* phase.

4.1   Execution Opening

After executing k parallel instantiations of the passively secure MPC protocol, the parties will run Π_{open} to open the seeds used in $k - 1$ of these executions. Before Π_{open} is executed, the parties have already published encrypted shares of the opening information of all of their seeds. In Π_{open}, the parties then verify these encrypted shares using the PVSS. If a verification fails, the parties generate a certificate and abort. If all verifications succeed, the parties jointly toss a coin to select the executions to open. At this point, it is too late for an adversary to abort since its seed openings have already been correctly distributed. Now, either the parties simply open all the seeds used in these executions (the optimistic case) or engage in $\Pi_{\text{reconstruct}}$ to reconstruct missing seeds (the pessimistic case). Note that we cannot simply indicate parties who fail to open their seeds as malicious since we are not able to generate a publicly verifiable certificate of this as an external judge is not able to distinguish between an active attack or an accidental abort. As an additional benefit, the PVSS strategy gives us a form of fault-tolerance. By being able to verify the executions in case of an abort, the protocol can still continue and succeed in case an otherwise honest party was accidentally not able to deliver this information in time.

4.2   Seed Reconstruction

If reconstructions are required, the parties engage in an execution of $\Pi_{\text{reconstruct}}$. This protocol starts by the parties announcing to everyone which seeds they are missing. For every missing message received, the parties decrypt their own share of the published share encryptions of the corresponding seed opening. This share together with a publicly verifiable proof of correct decryption is then published on the bulletin board. Using these proofs, these parties can then pool together $t + 1$ shares of which the proofs are valid to reconstruct the correct seed opening. Due to the honest majority, we have that $t < \frac{n}{2}$, which guarantees that the honest parties can reconstruct missing seed openings in case an adversary refuses to distribute them. Finally the parties output a complete set of all seed openings $\mathcal{D}_i$. Note that in an honest execution of the PVC protocol, the parties already have a complete set after Π_{open} and thus $\Pi_{\text{reconstruct}}$ can be skipped. Using all the seeds, the parties can now verify the behavior of all the other parties in the opened executions. This procedure has been extracted to a separate Blame algorithm.

Π_{open}   Protocol for opening a set of executions

At the start of the protocol, all the parties know the encrypted seed shares $\{E_h(d_h)^{(i,j)}\}$ of every party $P_i, i \in [n]$ in every execution $j \in [k]$ for every party $P_h, h \in [n]$ as well as the corresponding proofs $\texttt{dproof}_j^i$. Furthermore, the parties have the signatures σ_j^i together with corresponding evidence tuples $\texttt{evidence}_j$. Finally, each party P_i holds a set of private seed openings $\{d_1^i, d_2^i, \ldots, d_k^i\}$, a set of outputs $\{y_1^i, y_2^i, \ldots, y_k^i\}$ and a set of transcripts $\{\texttt{trans}_1^i, \texttt{trans}_2^i, \ldots, \texttt{trans}_k^i\}$. To open $k-1$ protocol executions, do the following:

Share Verification:

1. First, the parties use the $\texttt{Verify}$ algorithm of the PVSS to check the validity of all the shares to generate the set:

$$M = \left\{ (l, m) \in ([n], [k]) : \text{PVSS.Verify}(\texttt{dproof}_m^l, E_h(d_h)_{h \in [n]}^{(l,m)}) = \bot \right\}.$$

If any of the parties obtain $M \neq \varnothing$, choose the tuple $(l, m) \in M$ with minimal l and m, calculate the certificate $\texttt{cert}_{\text{invs}} = \left(pk_l, \texttt{evidence}_m, E_j(d_j)_{j \in [n]}^{(l,m)}, \sigma_m^l \right)$ and output $\texttt{corrupted}_l$.

Joint Coin Tossing Phase:

2. If all the verifications succeed, each party P_i sends $(\texttt{flip})$ to $\mathcal{F}_{\text{coin}}$, receives $(\texttt{flip}, r)$ and calculates the joint coin toss as $\texttt{coin} = r \mod k$.
3. Now, the parties exchange the set of seeds they have used in the $k-1$ executions according to the coin toss such that each party P_i obtains:

$$\mathcal{D}_i = \{d_j^h : h \in [n], j \in [k] \setminus \texttt{coin}\}$$

   Optimistic case: Each party P_i generates $\phi_j^i \leftarrow \texttt{Sign}(d_j^i)$ for all of its seed openings $\{d_j^i\}_{j \in [k] \setminus \texttt{coin}}$ and sends (ϕ_j^i, d_j^i) to all the other parties. Each party P_i verifies the signatures and constructs $\mathcal{D}_i$.
   Pessimistic case: If a number of parties P_j fails to publish their seed shares and/or valid signatures within a given amount of time, the parties engage in an execution of $\Pi_{\text{reconstruct}}$ to obtain $\mathcal{D}_i$.

Output:

4. Finally, each party outputs $(\mathcal{D}_i, \texttt{coin})$.

4.3   Blame Algorithm

In the $\texttt{Blame}$ algorithm, the behavior of the parties is verified and a certificate is generated in case cheating was detected. This $\texttt{Blame}$ algorithm takes the view of a party as input. First, the $\texttt{Blame}$ algorithm verifies the seed openings of all the parties. If the seed opening was obtained via reconstruction, an *invalid opening (1)* certificate is returned. In case the seed opening was given directly by the adversary, and *invalid opening (2)* certificate is generated. To ensure the parties

---

Protocol $\Pi_{\text{reconstruct}}$

At the start of the protocol, the encrypted seed openings, shares $\{E_h(d_h)^{(i,j)}\}$ of every party $P_i, i \in [n]$ in every execution $j \in [k]$ meant for every party $P_h, h \in [n]$ as well as the corresponding proof strings dproof_j^i are publicly known. The parties recover the seed openings they are missing in the following way:

Missing seeds announcement:

1. Each party P_i starts with a (non-complete) set of seed openings $\mathcal{D}_i$. Assume P_i did not receive the seed openings d_m^l of some party P_l in some execution m. Call the set of tuples (l, m) of missing seed openings $\mathcal{E}_i$.
2. For every tuple $(l, m) \in \mathcal{E}_i$, P_i sends a message $\text{missing}_{(l,m)}^i$ to all the other parties.

Missing seed reconstruction:

3. For every $\text{missing}_{(l,m)}^j$ message received by P_i, P_i performs the following steps:
   - If $m == \text{coin}$, skip this message.
   - Otherwise, P_i decrypts its corresponding share d_i from $E_i(d_i)^{(l,m)}$, computes the string $\text{rproof}_{(l,m)}^i$ and sends $(\text{send}, (d_i, \text{rproof}_{(l,m)}^i), i)$ to $\mathcal{F}_{\text{bb}}$.
4. For every tuple $(l, m) \in \mathcal{E}_i$, P_i does the following:
   - For every message received from $\mathcal{F}_{\text{bb}}$ of the form $((d_j, \text{rproof}_{(l,m)}^j), j)$, P_i verifies the $\text{rproof}_{(l,m)}^j$.
   - Once $t + 1$ of the received proofs are successfully verified, P_i reconstructs the seed opening d_m^l from the $t + 1$ shares and adds this to $\mathcal{D}_i$.

Output:

5. Finally, P_i outputs the set of seed openings $\mathcal{D}_i$.

---

agree on which party cheated, the one with the lowest party- and execution id is picked. If all the seeds can be opened correctly, the Blame algorithm simulates the executions using the randomness seeds obtained in the previous step, resulting in *expected* transcripts. If for any execution the actual transcript does not match with the expected transcript, the first party deviating from the protocol is identified and a *deviation certificate* is generated.

4.4   Judge Algorithm

The Judge algorithm takes a certificate and verifies it to confirm that the accused party actually cheated. If the verification succeeds, the public key of the cheater is output and otherwise $\perp$ is outputted. This algorithm does not require any communication with the parties and can thus be run by third parties as well. We assume the judge has access to the messages publicly stored via $\mathcal{F}_{\text{bb}}$. The judge performs a number of steps depending on the certificate type. If the certificate does not match any of the four templates, $\perp$ is returned. Regardless of which certificate type it receives, it first verifies the signature of the accused party

---

Algorithm Blame(view)

The Blame algorithm takes as input the view **view** of a party, which consists of:

- Public coin **coin**
- All the seed commitments and openings $\{c_j^i, d_j^i\}_{i \in [n], j \in [k] \setminus \texttt{coin}}$
- Encrypted seed shares $\{E_h(d_h)^{(i,j)}\}_{h, i \in [n], j \in [k]}$
- The set $\mathcal{E}$ of tuples of seed openings obtained via reconstruction
- PVSS proofs for distribution $\{\texttt{dproof}_j^i\}_{i \in [n], j \in [k]}$ and reconstruction $\{\texttt{rproof}_{(l,m)}^j\}_{j \in [n], (l,m) \in \mathcal{E}}$
- Public keys $\{pk_j\}_{j \in [n]}$, signatures $\{\sigma_j^i\}_{i \in [n], j \in [k]}$ and $\{\phi_j^i\}_{i \in [n], j \in [k]}$
- Additional information $\{\texttt{evidence}_j\}_{j \in [k]}$

To verify the behavior of the parties, do:

1. Open the private seeds of all the parties $P_i, i \in [n]$ in each execution $j \in [k] \setminus \texttt{coin}$ as $\mathbf{seed}_{(j,\text{priv})}^i \leftarrow \texttt{Open}(c_j^i, d_j^i)$.
2. Construct the set $S = \{(l,m) \in ([n], [k] \setminus \texttt{coin}) : \mathbf{seed}_{(l,\text{priv})}^i == \bot\}$. If S is not empty, pick the tuple (l, m) with the lowest l, m and produce an invalid opening certificate:
   - If $(l,m) \in \mathcal{E}$: set
     $$\texttt{cert}_{\text{invo1}} = (pk_l, \texttt{evidence}_m, \{d_j, \texttt{rproof}_{(l,m)}^j\}_{j \in [n]}, \{E_j(d_j)^{(l,m)}\}_{j \in [n]}, \sigma_m^l).$$
   - **Otherwise**: set $\texttt{cert}_{\text{invo2}} = (pk_l, \texttt{evidence}_m, d_m^l, \phi_m^l, \sigma_m^l)$

   And output $(l, \texttt{cert}_{\text{invo(1/2)}})$.
3. If all the verifications succeeded, set $\mathbf{seed}_j^i = \mathbf{seed}_{(j,\text{priv})}^i \oplus \mathbf{seed}_{(j,\text{pub})}^i$. As the randomness seed of each party P_i in each execution $j \in [k]$.
4. Re-run each execution j of Π_{pass} for $j \in [k] \setminus \texttt{coin}$ by simulating party P_i using random seed $\mathbf{seed}_j^i$ to obtain each transcript $\mathbf{trans}_j'$.
5. Using $\texttt{evidence}_j$, construct the set $S = \{m : \mathbf{trans}_m \neq \mathbf{trans}_m'\}$. If S is not empty, pick the lowest m and find the party P_l that sends the first message in $\mathbf{trans}_m$ which is inconsistent with the expected message from $\mathbf{trans}_m'$ and construct a protocol deviation certificate
   $$\texttt{cert}_{\text{dev}} = (pk_l, \texttt{evidence}_m, \{d_m^i\}_{i \in [n]}, \sigma_m^l),$$
   and output $(l, \texttt{cert}_{\text{dev}})$. Otherwise, output $(\cdot, \bot)$.

---

on the **evidence**. If this signature is invalid, we can never be sure that the information was communicated by the accused party and thus $\bot$ is returned.

4.5   Security

To prove that the compiler presented above satisfies Definition 2 for covert security with public verifiability, we first state the guarantees in Theorem 1 and then prove that our compiler satisfies the requirements of *covert security (with deterrence rate ϵ), public verifiability* and *defamation-freeness* separately.

Algorithm Judge(cert)

We assume the judge knows the function Π_{pass} to be computed. To check a certificate, do:

- If $\text{Verify}(\text{evidence}_m, \sigma_m^l) = \bot$, output $\bot$.
- Else, interpret evidence_m as $\left(i, m, \{\text{seed}_{(m,\text{pub})}^l, c_m^l, \text{dproof}_m^l\}_{l \in [n]}, \text{trans}_m^i\right)$.

Depending on the type of certificate, do:

invs:
- $\text{cert}_{\text{invs}} = (pk_l, \text{evidence}_m, E_j(d_j)_{j \in [n]}^{(l,m)}, \sigma_m^l)$.
- If $\text{PVSS.Verify}(\text{dproof}_m^l, E_j(d_j)_{j \in [n]}^{(l,m)}) = \bot$, output pk_l. Otherwise, output $\bot$.

invo1:
- $\text{cert}_{\text{invo1}} = (pk_l, \text{evidence}_m, \{d_j, \text{rproof}_{(l,m)}^j\}_{j \in [n]}, \{E_j(d_j)^{(l,m)}\}_{j \in [n]}, \sigma_m^l)$.
- If $\text{PVSS.Verify}(\text{dproof}_m^l, E_j(d_j)_{j \in [n]}^{(l,m)}) = \bot$, output $\bot$.
- Verify $t + 1$ of the $\text{rproof}_{(l,m)}^j$'s and use the corresponding d_j's to reconstruct d_m^l. If no $t+1$ valid shares are available, output $\bot$.
- If $\text{Open}(c_m^l, d_m^l) \neq \bot$, output $\bot$. Otherwise, output pk_l.

invo2:
- $\text{cert}_{\text{invo2}} = (pk_l, \text{evidence}_m, d_m^l, \phi_m^l, \sigma_m^l)$.
- If $\text{Verify}_{pk_l}(d_m^l, \phi_m^l) = \bot$, output $\bot$.
- If $\text{Open}(c_m^l, d_m^l) \neq \bot$, output $\bot$. Otherwise, output pk_l.

dev:
- $\text{cert}_{\text{dev}} = (pk_l, \text{evidence}_m, \{d_j^i\}_{i \in [n], j \in [k] \backslash \text{coin}}, \sigma_m^l)$.
- For every party P_i and execution m, open $\text{seed}_{(m,\text{priv})}^i \leftarrow \text{Open}(c_m^i, d_m^i)$ and calculate $\text{seed}_m^i = \text{seed}_{(m,\text{priv})}^i \oplus \text{seed}_{(m,\text{pub})}^i$.
- Re-run execution m of Π_{pass} by simulating each party P_i using random seed seed_m^i to obtain transcript trans_m'.
- If $\text{trans}_m' == \text{trans}_m$, output $\bot$.
- If the first party that sends an incorrect message in trans_m' is indeed P_l, output pk_l. Otherwise, output $\bot$.

Otherwise:
- If the certificate does not match any of the four formats, output $\bot$.

Theorem 1. *Suppose the PVSS (Distribute, Verify, Reconstruct) satisfies the privacy, correctness and soundness properties with a threshold $t < n/2$. Furthermore, assume the commitment scheme (Com, Open, Verify) is binding and hiding. Let the signature scheme (Gen, Sign, Verify) be existentially unforgeable under chosen plaintext attacks. Finally, assume Π_{coin} implements $\mathcal{F}_{coin}$ with active security. If Π_{pass} is passively secure, the compiler $COMP_{PVC} = (\Pi_{comp}, \Pi_{open}, \Pi_{reconstruct})$ with the additional algorithms Blame and Judge is covertly secure with public verifiability against $t < \frac{n}{2}$ corruptions with deterrence rate $\epsilon = 1 - \frac{1}{k}$.*

Intuitively, an adversary can try to cheat in a number of ways in the resulting protocol Π_{PVC}. First, it can do so by causing the seed openings of its own seeds to fail. This could be achieved by either (i) distributing inconsistent shares in step 3 of Π_{comp} or (ii) sending an incorrect opening in step 3 of Π_{open}. Cheating strategy (i) is easily detected by the verification algorithm of the PVSS scheme, which anyone can verify. Furthermore, the proofs of correct decryption ensure that the adversary cannot announce a wrong share and the honest parties will always obtain the correct seed openings. Cheating strategy (ii) is noticed when any of the seed openings fail. In this case, the adversary has already published a signature on the commitment *and* on the opening which means anyone can see that the opening fails and the adversary must have sent this.

Furthermore, an adversary can attempt to cheat by deviating from the protocol description in any of the protocol executions. Since the protocol is run without private inputs, deviating means sending a message that is inconsistent with the protocol description and the committed randomness. If all of the seed openings succeeded, the parties can detect this when simulating the protocol executions later on. Since everyone knows the commitment and the opening, everyone knows the randomness that should have been used. Furthermore, the commitments to the seeds have been signed and thus an adversary cannot deny that he has sent an inconsistent message. A formal proof of this theorem can be found in the full version of this paper [1].

5   Computation and Communication Complexity

In this section, we analyze the computation and communication complexity of our compiler. For concreteness, we assume that the PVSS used for our compiler is the scheme presented by Schoenmakers [18], but stress that our compiler will work with any PVSS satisfying Definition 3. As our compiler simply executes the passively secure protocol k times while signing the messages, the computational complexity of the protocol execution phase is roughly k times the passively secure protocol. Note that the k executions are independent of each other and can therefore fully be executed in parallel, preserving the round complexity of the passively secure protocol. In terms of communication, each party needs to be able to see each message sent during the protocol execution. Therefore, the communication complexity of the compiler increases with a factor of $n-1$. Note that this is inherent to all currently known constructions for compilers in our setting [10,12,19].

The main difference in terms of complexity between our work and previous works lies in the execution opening and verification phase, where the goal is to open $k-1$ executions while preventing a detection-dependent abort. The total number of exponentiations required to distribute the seed openings of k executions with n parties and verify the distributed seeds of all the parties is given in Table 1. Furthermore, the number of exponentiations required for decryption and reconstruction in case of an aborting adversary is given as well. Here, m is the amount of missing messages in total while e is the amount of missing seeds of a single party. The total number of group elements communicated via $\mathcal{F}_{\text{bb}}$ in the execution opening phase of our protocol is given in Table 2. In an honest execution, every party uses the PVSS to distribute its seeds and then simply opens its seeds. If a party refuses to do this, for m distinct seeds missing, the parties need to publish their decrypted shares together with a proof of correct decryption.

5.1   Comparison with Prior Work

In contrast to our approach, the deterrence rate ϵ of [10] is inversely proportional to the number of parties n. For this reason, we focus on comparing our construction with the TLP approach of Faust et al. [12]. More specifically, we focus on comparing the execution opening and verification phase. In our case, this is realized by Π_{open} and possibly $\Pi_{\text{reconstruct}}$ while the work of [12] uses a maliciously secure TLP generation functionality for this.

Table 1. Computation complexity as number of modular exponentiations.

Step	Comp. Complexity
Distribution	$\frac{n^2+3n+4}{2} \cdot k$
Verification	$(\frac{n^2}{2} + 4n) \cdot (kn - k)$
Decryption	$3 \cdot m$
Reconstruction	$(4 \cdot n + \frac{n}{2}) \cdot e$

Table 2. Communication complexity as number of field elements communicated per party.

Step	Comm. Complexity
Distribution	$k \cdot (\frac{n}{2} + 2n + 1)$
Opening	$2 \cdot k$
Reconstruction	$2 \cdot m$

Note that their puzzle generation does not include the solving of a TLP. The puzzle generation always has to be executed but the parties only need to solve a TLP in case of an abort. They present an estimation for the total number of AND gates for the circuit of this puzzle generation functionality. This circuit has a linear complexity in the number of parties, while our seed distribution introduces a cubic computational complexity. However, the complexity of their functionality is dependent on the length of the RSA modulus N in the terms: $192|N|^3 + 112|N|^2 + 22|N|$. To illustrate the effects of both complexities, we present a concrete example. Take an honest execution of the protocol with $n = 5$, $t = 2$, $k = 2$ and thus $\epsilon = \frac{1}{2}$. With a security parameter of 128 bits, our approach costs approximately 10^8 bit operations while the circuit of [12] requires in the order of 10^{12} AND gates to be maliciously evaluated for an RSA modulus of 2048 bits.

In terms of communication complexity, our solution is linearly dependent on the number of parties and in the above scenario, the opening phase would require around 31 group elements to be communicated via $\mathcal{F}_{\text{bb}}$. Assuming $\mathcal{F}_{\text{bb}}$ is naively implemented using an echo-broadcast protocol, this would require each party to send $(n-1)^2 + 3n + 3$ messages per group element. In the above example, this would mean each party has to communicate around 8000 bytes with 64-bit messages. Instantiating [12] with the actively secure protocol of Yang et al. [22] requires 193 bytes per party per multiplication triple. This would thus require in the order of 10^{14} bytes to be communicated. Altogether, we expect our construction to outperform the earlier works in practical scenarios.

Acknowledgements. The research activities that led to this result were funded by ABN AMRO, CWI, De Volksbank, Rabobank, TMNL, PPS-surcharge for Research and Innovation of the Dutch Ministry of Economic Affairs and Climate Policy, TNO's Appl. AI programme and the Vraaggestuurd Programma Cyber Security & Resilience, part of the Dutch Top Sector High Tech Systems and Materials program.

References

1. Full version of this paper. IACR ePrint 2022/454
2. Asharov, G., Orlandi, C.: Calling out cheaters: covert security with public verifiability. In: Wang, X., Sako, K. (eds.) ASIACRYPT 2012. LNCS, vol. 7658, pp. 681–698. Springer, Heidelberg (2012). https://doi.org/10.1007/978-3-642-34961-4_41
3. Aumann, Y., Lindell, Y.: Security against covert adversaries: efficient protocols for realistic adversaries. In: Vadhan, S.P. (ed.) TCC 2007. LNCS, vol. 4392, pp. 137–156. Springer, Heidelberg (2007). https://doi.org/10.1007/978-3-540-70936-7_8
4. Beaver, D.: Efficient multiparty protocols using circuit randomization. In: Feigenbaum, J. (ed.) CRYPTO 1991. LNCS, vol. 576, pp. 420–432. Springer, Heidelberg (1992). https://doi.org/10.1007/3-540-46766-1_34
5. Beaver, D., Micali, S., Rogaway, P.: The round complexity of secure protocols (extended abstract). In: 22nd ACM STOC, pp. 503–513 (1990)
6. Boyle, E., Gilboa, N., Ishai, Y., Nof, A.: Efficient fully secure computation via distributed zero-knowledge proofs. In: ASIACRYPT 2020, Part III, pp. 244–276 (2020)
7. Chor, B., Goldwasser, S., Micali, S., Awerbuch, B.: Verifiable secret sharing and achieving simultaneity in the presence of faults (extended abstract). In: 26th FOCS, pp. 383–395 (1985)
8. Damgård, I., Geisler, M., Nielsen, J.B.: From passive to covert security at low cost. In: Micciancio, D. (ed.) TCC 2010. LNCS, vol. 5978, pp. 128–145. Springer, Heidelberg (2010). https://doi.org/10.1007/978-3-642-11799-2_9
9. Damgård, I., Keller, M., Larraia, E., Pastro, V., Scholl, P., Smart, N.P.: Practical covertly secure MPC for dishonest majority – or: breaking the SPDZ limits. In: Crampton, J., Jajodia, S., Mayes, K. (eds.) ESORICS 2013. LNCS, vol. 8134, pp. 1–18. Springer, Heidelberg (2013). https://doi.org/10.1007/978-3-642-40203-6_1
10. Damgård, I., Orlandi, C., Simkin, M.: Black-box transformations from passive to covert security with public verifiability. In: Micciancio, D., Ristenpart, T. (eds.) CRYPTO 2020. LNCS, vol. 12171, pp. 647–676. Springer, Cham (2020). https://doi.org/10.1007/978-3-030-56880-1_23
11. Damgård, I., Pastro, V., Smart, N., Zakarias, S.: Multiparty computation from somewhat homomorphic encryption. In: Safavi-Naini, R., Canetti, R. (eds.) CRYPTO 2012. LNCS, vol. 7417, pp. 643–662. Springer, Heidelberg (2012). https://doi.org/10.1007/978-3-642-32009-5_38
12. Faust, S., Hazay, C., Kretzler, D., Schlosser, B.: Generic compiler for publicly verifiable covert multi-party computation. In: Canteaut, A., Standaert, F.-X. (eds.) EUROCRYPT 2021. LNCS, vol. 12697, pp. 782–811. Springer, Cham (2021). https://doi.org/10.1007/978-3-030-77886-6_27

13. Goyal, V., Mohassel, P., Smith, A.: Efficient two party and multi party computation against covert adversaries. In: Smart, N. (ed.) EUROCRYPT 2008. LNCS, vol. 4965, pp. 289–306. Springer, Heidelberg (2008). https://doi.org/10.1007/978-3-540-78967-3_17

14. Goyal, V., Song, Y., Zhu, C.: Guaranteed output delivery comes free in honest majority MPC. In: Micciancio, D., Ristenpart, T. (eds.) CRYPTO 2020. LNCS, vol. 12171, pp. 618–646. Springer, Cham (2020). https://doi.org/10.1007/978-3-030-56880-1_22

15. Hong, C., Katz, J., Kolesnikov, V., Lu, W., Wang, X.: Covert security with public verifiability: faster, leaner, and simpler. In: Ishai, Y., Rijmen, V. (eds.) EUROCRYPT 2019. LNCS, vol. 11478, pp. 97–121. Springer, Cham (2019). https://doi.org/10.1007/978-3-030-17659-4_4

16. Kolesnikov, V., Malozemoff, A.J.: Public verifiability in the covert model (Almost) for free. In: Iwata, T., Cheon, J.H. (eds.) ASIACRYPT 2015. LNCS, vol. 9453, pp. 210–235. Springer, Heidelberg (2015). https://doi.org/10.1007/978-3-662-48800-3_9

17. Reiter, M.K.: Secure agreement protocols: reliable and atomic group multicast in rampart. In: ACM CCS 1994, pp. 68–80 (1994)

18. Schoenmakers, B.: A simple publicly verifiable secret sharing scheme and its application to electronic voting. In: Wiener, M. (ed.) CRYPTO 1999. LNCS, vol. 1666, pp. 148–164. Springer, Heidelberg (1999). https://doi.org/10.1007/3-540-48405-1_10

19. Scholl, P., Simkin, M., Siniscalchi, L.: Multiparty computation with covert security and public verifiability. IACR Cryptol. ePrint Archive, p. 366 (2021)

20. Shamir, A.: How to share a secret. Commun. Assoc. Comput. Mach. **22**(11), 612–613 (1979)

21. Stadler, M.: Publicly verifiable secret sharing. In: Maurer, U. (ed.) EUROCRYPT 1996. LNCS, vol. 1070, pp. 190–199. Springer, Heidelberg (1996). https://doi.org/10.1007/3-540-68339-9_17

22. Yang, K., Wang, X., Zhang, J.: More efficient MPC from improved triple generation and authenticated garbling. In: ACM CCS 2020, pp. 1627–1646 (2020)

How Byzantine is a Send Corruption?

Karim Eldefrawy[1], Julian Loss[2], and Ben Terner[3(✉)]

[1] SRI International, Menlo Park, CA, USA
karim.eldefrawy@sri.com
[2] University of Maryland, College Park, MD, USA
[3] UC Irvine, Irvine, CA, USA
bterner@uci.edu

Abstract. Consensus protocols enable n parties, each holding some input string, to agree on a common output even in the presence of corrupted parties. Recent work has pushed to understand the problem when a majority of parties may be corrupted thus providing higher resilience, and under various forms of corruptions. Zikas, Hauser, and Maurer introduced a model in which *receive-corrupt* parties may not receive messages sent to them, and *send-corrupt* parties may have their sent messages dropped. Otherwise, receive-corrupt and send-corrupt parties behave honestly and their inputs and outputs are constrained by the security definitions. Zikas, Hauser, and Maurer gave a perfectly secure, linear-round protocol for $n > t_{\mathsf{rcv}} + t_{\mathsf{snd}} + 3t_{\mathsf{byz}}$, where t_{rcv}, t_{snd}, and t_{byz} represent thresholds on receive-, send-, and byzantine-corruptions.

We present the first expected constant-round protocol in the general corruption model tolerating $n > t_{\mathsf{rcv}} + 2t_{\mathsf{snd}} + 2t_{\mathsf{byz}}$. In comparison, all current sublinear round consensus protocols fail if there exists even a single party which cannot communicate with some honest parties, but whose output must be consistent with the honest parties. While presenting our protocol, we explore the pathology of send-corruptions and characterize the difficulty of dealing with them in sublinear-round protocols. As an illustrative and surprising example (even though not in sublinear rounds), we show that the classical Dolev-Strong broadcast protocol degrades from tolerating $t_{\mathsf{byz}} < n$ corruptions in the byzantine-only model to $t_{\mathsf{byz}} < n/2 - t_{\mathsf{snd}}$ when send-corrupt parties' outputs must be consistent with honest parties; we also show why other recent dishonest-majority broadcast protocols degrade similarly.

We prove that our new consensus protocol achieves an optimal threshold of $n > t_{\mathsf{rcv}} + t_{\mathsf{snd}} + 2t_{\mathsf{byz}}$ when we constrain the adversary to either drop all or none of a sender's messages in a round (we denote this model by spotty send corruptions). To our knowledge, our protocol for the spotty send corruption model is thus the first sublinear-round consensus protocol for a majority of online faulty parties *in any model*. Because we are unable to prove optimality of our protocol's corruption budget in the general case, we leave open the question of optimal corruption tolerance for both send-corruptions and byzantine-corruptions.

Keywords: Consensus · byzantine agreement · constant rounds · dishonest majority

G. Ateniese and D. Venturi (Eds.): ACNS 2022, LNCS 13269, pp. 684–704, 2022.
https://doi.org/10.1007/978-3-031-09234-3_34

1   Introduction

Consensus protocols, also known as byzantine agreement protocols, enable n parties, each holding some input value, to agree on common outputs even in the presence of byzantine corrupted parties. However, the byzantine model often does not reflect the real world; in practice, crashing a party, or even forcing inconsistent uplink or downlink behavior, is much easier than corrupting it.

A line of work has explored mixed models in which both crash faults and byzantine faults are permitted. Garay and Perry [11] and Altmann, Fitzi, and Maurer [4] show that byzantine agreement is possible if and only if $n > t_{cra} + 3t_{byz}$. In the asynchronous model, Backes and Cachin [5] showed that broadcast within the mixed model is possible if and only if $n > 2t_{cra} + 3t_{byz}$. Kursawe [15] developed a consensus protocol for the same bound assuming a public key infrastructure (PKI). Recently, Wan et al. [21,22] showed round efficient broadcast protocols for dishonest majorities. Zikas, Hauser and Maurer [23] gave a protocol in the error-free synchronous model for $n > t_{rcv} + t_{snd} + 3t_{byz}$, where t_{rcv} bounds the number of receive corruptions, t_{snd} bounds the number of send corruptions, and t_{byz} bounds the number of byzantine corruptions.

Faulty Parties With Consistent Outputs. Zikas, Hauser and Maurer introduced parties which may be faulty *but the faulty processors' outputs must be consistent with honest parties' outputs* because they otherwise behave honestly. In all other corruption models, the output of any faulty party need not be considered by the definition. We show that the duality of a send-corrupt party whose outputs must nonetheless be consistent with honest parties introduces new challenges for achieving consensus in sublinear rounds. *It is currently not known how to push corruption tolerance for sublinear-round broadcast to the dishonest majority setting, and for sublinear-round consensus we do not know how to do better than treating a send-corrupt party as fully byzantine.* However, treating the otherwise-honest party in this way also forfeits any guarantees on its output.

1.1   Send and Receive Corruptions: Honest-but-Faulty

Send-corrupt parties participate in a protocol as honest parties do, but an adversary has the power to determine which messages sent by a send-corrupt party are delivered and which are not. Nevertheless, they still listen to the protocol and their outputs must be consistent with the honest parties' outputs.

Receive-corrupt parties may cease to receive messages, but the messages they send are delivered. A receive-corrupted party may detect that it is receive-corrupted if it does not receive messages that it is expecting. If a receive-corrupted party detects that it is corrupted, then – as in [23] – the party enters a *zombie* state. A zombie party stops sending and receiving messages, and outputs $\perp$, becoming the functional equivalent to a crashed party in the common literature. If a receive-corrupted party has not detected that it is corrupt then it may continue to participate, and we require that its output agrees with the honest parties' outputs, even though it may not receive all protocol messages.

Zombies and Live Parties. Because send-corrupted and receive-corrupted parties may still continue to participate without intentionally deviating from the protocol, our definitions require that their outputs (if they produce outputs) are consistent with those of the honest parties. We call all honest, send-corrupt, and non-zombie receive-corrupt parties *live parties*; this denotes that the party continues to (try to) participate as if it were an honest party.

We use the convention that whenever a party becomes a zombie, it sends a special message (zombie) to all other parties. Upon receiving such a message, a party deducts one from its count of n the number of parties, as well as deducts one from its threshold for the number of receive-corrupted parties. Note that send-corrupt parties may fail to send their zombie declarations, and receive-corrupt parties may fail to receive other parties' declarations.

1.2 The Pathology of Send Corruptions

We consider two forms of send corruptions, one more pathological than the other.

1. *Standard send corruption:* In the general case (denoted as simply a send corruption) as in [23], the adversary may adaptively drop any of a send-corrupt party's outgoing messages in any round.
2. *Spotty send corruption:* In a weaker case, an adversary adaptively drops either *all or none* of a send-corrupt party's outgoing messages in a round.

Pathology of a (Standard) Send Corruption. Our standard model of a send corruption permits the adversary to selectively drop messages by send-corrupting a party. Because this behavior is a subset of a byzantine corruption, one would expect that corruption bounds follow directly from the byzantine case. We show that this is not the case in general. In our model, a send-corrupt party may receive a message that would change its output *and fail to inform any honest party about the message.*

As an illustrative example (embodying a common technique), the Dolev-Strong broadcast protocol requires that if some honest party – whose output is constrained by definition – receives a message, then all other honest parties will receive that message before the protocol terminates. But as we show in Sect. 3.1, Dolev-Strong breaks down in our model because a send-corrupt party may receive a message that would change its output but fail to forward it.

In the extreme case, divide an execution into sets such that S contains all send-corrupt parties and H contains all honest parties, and let $|S| > |H|$. Then it may be the case that *a majority of parties cannot communicate with the honest parties*, but all of their outputs must be consistent. For this reason, it appears very difficult to tolerate more send-corrupt parties than honest parties. Any such construction must ensure that sufficiently many parties are "aware" of a message to allow it to influence the output. Specifically, we do not know how to generate and use information that an honest party has *not* received a message sent by a send-corrupt party. On the other hand, impossibility proofs that depend on partitioning techniques also fail in this model because it is impossible to completely separate the send-corrupt group from the honest group, since send-corrupt parties always receive all of the honest parties' messages.

Pathology of a Spotty Send Corruption. We argue that although our "spotty" send corruption is limited in some ways, it is still rich enough to force popular techniques for synchronous consensus to fail. In particular, it is unclear how to construct a protocol that employs leader election in order to reach constant expected round complexity in our model. Specifically, a strongly rushing adversary as described above can wait for a leader to be elected – and even to send messages that attest to its election (e.g., based on a VRF, as in [12,19]) – then spotty-corrupt the party, and force it to fail as leader for the duration of its tenure. While in the purely byzantine model this attack can be mitigated by using threshold signatures (see, e.g., [2,16]), this approach completely fails in our model, as electing a leader would most likely elect one of the t_{snd} send-corrupt parties (since t_{snd} can be much larger than the number of honest parties). For this reason, recent protocols for dishonest majority broadcast that rely on the player-replaceable paradigm, such as [6] and [1] fail in our model.

1.3   Contributions

We provide the first systematic treatment of the pathology of send-corruptions, and show that considering send-corrupt parties as "nearly" honest in the definition *either completely breaks or substantially deteriorates the corruption tolerance of both classical and recent broadcast protocols.*

We then provide an expected constant-round byzantine agreement protocol that is secure in the strongly adaptive setting against t_{snd} send-corruptions, t_{rcv} receive corruptions, and t_{byz} byzantine corruptions where $t_{rcv} + 2t_{snd} + 2t_{byz} < n$. Our protocol builds consensus from graded consensus and a common coin [8,14], with subtle adaptations for our corruption model, with a parallelization of the implementation of FixReceive from [23]. When send-corruptions are *spotty*, we show our protocol achieves optimal corruption tolerance of $t_{rcv} + t_{snd} + 2t_{byz} < n$.

To our knowledge, our protocol for the spotty send model is the first sublinear-round consensus protocol for a majority of online faulty parties *in any model.*

1.4   Comparison with Related Work and Obvious Solutions

Recent Advances in Dishonest-Majority Broadcast. One might expect that because dishonest-majority broadcast protocols tolerate $n > t_{byz}$ corruptions, they are sufficient for building a consensus protocol tolerating $n > t_{snd} + 2t_{byz}$ corruptions via folklore reductions (which we discuss in detail in the full version), which would achieve better corruption tolerance than our construction in Sect. 4. We show that this is not true and that recent advances in dishonest-majority for adaptive adversaries by Wan et al. [21,22] also fail in our model.

The work of Wan et al. [22] provides an expected constant-round protocol for dishonest majority broadcast under a weakly adaptive adversary. However, their "Trust Graphs" assume that only byzantine parties do not send messages, and any party that fails to send a message can be excluded. This fails in our model because send-corrupt parties must be consistent with honest parties.

Another recent work [21] uses time-lock puzzles to provide a round-efficient broadcast protocol in the presence of dishonest majority and a strongly adaptive adversary. However, the approach also fails because honest parties may never learn the puzzles sent by send-corrupt parties. It is possible to construct an execution in which honest parties solve a set of puzzles T, and the send-corrupt parties solve another set of time-lock puzzles $T' = T \cup S$, where S are puzzles that are never distributed to the honest parties. However, our definitions require that send-corrupt parties' outputs match those of the honest parties.

Adapting ZHM [23] to an Expected Constant-Round Protocol. A natural attempt to achieve sub-linear round consensus tolerating $n > t_{\mathsf{rcv}} + t_{\mathsf{snd}} + 3t_{\mathsf{byz}}$ is to adapt the protocol by Zikas, Hauser and Maurer (ZHM) [23] to an expected constant-round protocol using the standard construction [8,14] via graded consensus and a common coin protocol. The ZHM protocol depends on the phase-king paradigm [10]; it must run long enough to guarantee that the king is honest in at least one round. To achieve expected constant-rounds, phase king is replaced with a common coin; however, all common coin constructions that we know require some threshold scheme. Threshold schemes work in our model when $n - t_{\mathsf{rcv}} > 2(t_{\mathsf{snd}} + t_{\mathsf{byz}})$, meaning there are more honest parties than send-corrupt or byzantine parties. In the dishonest majority setting where send-corrupt plus byzantine parties outnumber honest parties, the construction suffers from the partitioning attack described above: a group of send-corrupt parties reach the threshold independently of and without knowledge of honest parties, and honest parties therefore output a different coin than send-corrupt parties. The ZHM construction and corruption bound therefore fail in sublinear rounds.

Expected Constant-Round Consensus Protocols. There are a number of expected constant-round consensus protocols for the honest-majority setting that consider only byzantine faults. Feldman and Micali [8] gave an expected constant-round scheme for $n > 3t_{\mathsf{byz}}$. Katz and Koo [14] later gave a protocol tolerating $n > 2t_{\mathsf{byz}}$, assuming a PKI and signatures. Micali [18] gave another simple protocol assuming $n > 3t_{\mathsf{byz}}$. Abraham et al. [2] gave the most efficient scheme and tolerate a strongly rushing, adaptive adversary for $n > 2t_{\mathsf{byz}}$.

Mixed Corruption Models. In Table 1 we overview the results most relevant to our work: consensus protocols in mixed corruption models. We include a construction by modifying Dolev-Strong broadcast (Sect. 3.1) via the reduction of consensus to broadcast.

To our knowledldge, our "spotty" send-corrupt protocol exceeds the corruption bounds of all comparable models with "exotic" corruptions, who always require that a majority of online nodes are honest. For example, recent work has generalized crash corruptions into "sleepy" [20] or "sluggish" [13] faults. In the

Table 1. Comparison with relevant consensus protocols in mixed corruption models. $\widehat{R}$ indicates the round complexity R is given in expectation; otherwise worst-case round complexity is always the round complexity. DS denotes Dolev-Strong.

Protocol	Faults	# Rounds
Modified DS (Sect. 3.1)	Send & Byz: $2t_{snd} + 2t_{byz} < n$	$O(n)$
GP [11]	Crash & Byz: $t_{cra} + 3t_{byz} < n$	$O(n)$
ZHM [23]	Receive, Send, Byz: $t_{snd} + t_{rcv} + 3t_{byz} < n$	$O(n)$
This paper	Receive, Spotty Send, Byz: $t_{rcv} + t_{snd} + 2t_{byz} < n$	$\widehat{O(1)}$
This paper	Receive, Send, Byz: $t_{rcv} + 2t_{snd} + 2t_{byz} < n$	$\widehat{O(1)}$

sluggish model [13], a (mobile) sluggish party can be temporarily disconnected from honest parties due to network partition, but can later rejoin. While disconnected, messages sent by or to a party are delayed until the party is reconnected. However, in that work it is (inherently) required that at least half of the parties are not sluggish and participate in the protocol at all times, and the adversary is static. This is a sharp contrast to our model, which allows a majority of dishonest parties and an adaptive adversary. Abraham et al. [3], also in the sluggish model, require a majority of online parties to be honest at all times.

In the "sleepy" model [20], the adversary can make parties "fall asleep" and later wake them up (i.e., temporarily crash them) at which point all messages that they missed are delivered at once, potentially along with adversarially-inserted messages. In their model, a protocol requires only that a majority of the *awake* parties are honest, which closely resembles our result. However, there are no send-or-receive-corruptions, meaning all awake parties are full participants in the protocol, so their sends always succeed and no incoming messages are dropped; this avoids the difficulties studied in this paper.

Malkhi et al. [17] consider yet another mixed model of corruption, but require that a majority of online players behave honestly. The protocol of Garay and Perry [11] runs in $O(n)$ round complexity, but only works when $n > 3t_{byz} + t_{cra}$.

1.5   Paper Outline

The rest of the paper is organized as follows: Section 2 covers preliminaries and definitions required in the rest of this paper. Section 3 discusses the pathology of send corruptions by illustrating how common paradigms for broadcast fail for send-corrupt parties. Section 4 introduces our new expected constant-round consensus protocol for send and receive corruptions.

In the full version, we include the following appendices. In Appendix A, we provide the proofs of the protocols in Sect. 4. In Appendix B, we show that the construction in Sect. 4 has improved corruption tolerance in the spotty send model, and prove its optimality. In Appendix C we recall the classical protocol by Dolev and Strong for authenticated broadcast. In Appendix D we give a (folklore) construction of consensus from broadcast that completes the reduction of optimal fault tolerance for consensus in the presence of (general) send corruptions to optimal fault tolerance of broadcast in the presence of send corruptions.

2 Model and Definitions

We consider a set of n parties $\mathcal{P} = \{p_1, \ldots, p_n\}$ who may send and receive messages over a network. A protocol specifies the messages that parties send to each other, how they change their internal states, and how they produce their outputs. An execution of a protocol proceeds in a series of time steps, in which in each step each party first receives messages and then sends messages. We assume that all parties start an execution at the same time and have internal clocks that advance at the same rate.

Network. We assume that the network is managed by an adversary that is constrained by synchronization requirements. Parties are connected via peer-to-peer authenticated channels. We assume a synchronous network; this means that any message sent at time t must be delivered to its intended recipient at time $t + 1$ (unless message delivery is attacked by the adversary, as described below).

Corruptions. The adversary may adaptively corrupt parties that participate in an execution. We allow an adversary to corrupt a party in one of three modes, which we describe in the following. A party that is not corrupted must follow the protocol specification and is called *honest*. Once a party is corrupted, it may not become honest again.

A *receive* corruption allows the adversary to selectively drop messages sent to the party. A *send* corruption allows the adversary to selectively drop messages sent by the party. A *byzantine* corruption allows the adversary to control all messages sent by the party and view its internal state. We categorize send corruptions in two types:

1. A (standard) send corruption allows the adversary to adaptively drop arbitrary messages sent by the party without constraint.
2. A *spotty* corruption allows the adversary to adaptively drop all messages sent by a spotty party p at some time by issuing an instruction (drop, p) to the network. Specifically, the drop instruction is constrained such that *all messages* must be dropped if any message is dropped. Because all messages sent by a party at some time must either be delivered or dropped, we say that the adversary must *uniformly* drop or deliver messages for the party.

Recall that a party that detects it is corrupted declares itself a zombie; it does this by outputting zombie. We call a party *live* if it is not byzantine-corrupted and has not declared itself a zombie – all honest parties and send corrupt parties are live, and receive corrupt parties that have not become zombies are live. We note that the adversary does not need to corrupt both a sender and a receiver in order to drop a message between them; it suffices for the adversary to corrupt only one of them. We also do not require that the sets of send-corrupt and receive-corrupt parties are disjoint. However, any party that is both send-corrupt and receive-corrupt is counted toward both thresholds.

Strongly Rushing Adversary. We consider an adversary that is *strongly rushing*, similar to that of [1,2], but we extend it to drop messages from send-corrupt parties. In our model, a *strongly rushing* adversary is permitted to read messages that are sent by an honest party over the network and then choose to corrupt the party in the same time step. If the adversary chooses to send-corrupt the party, then it can drop messages sent by the party in that step; similarly, if the adversary chooses to receive-corrupt the party, then it can drop messages sent to the party in that step. In either case, the party is send- or receive-corrupted from that step forth. If the adversary chooses to byzantine corrupt a party in some step, it removes all messages sent by the party at that time step. The adversary then chooses what messages the party sends in that step, and to which parties it sends what messages. The corrupted party is byzantine corrupted from that time forth.

2.1 Digital Signatures and Coin Flipping

Our constructions require the use of a digital signature scheme. In particular, we assume that parties have access to a public key infrastructure (PKI) for a digital signature scheme, meaning each party is aware of a set of public keys $\{\mathsf{pk}_1, \ldots, \mathsf{pk}_n\}$, where pk_i is associated with p_i for $i \in [n]$. We consider that all parties choose their own public and private keys; in particular, some parties may adversarially choose their key pairs. Our constructions will assume an idealized signature scheme for which signatures are perfectly unforgeable; with signature schemes that achieve unforgeability against computationally bounded adversaries, our protocols achieve security except with negligible probability.

Our construction requires the use of an unbiasable coin flipping protocol Π^{coin}. We assume idealized access to such a primitive, as if implemented by an ideal functionality that takes no input (or more formally, takes as input the empty string) and delivers a uniformly random bit to all parties. Such a coin flipping protocol may be instantiated (assuming a trusted setup) by augmenting threshold signatures [16] (using threshold $t_{\mathsf{byz}} + 1$, see below) with a protocol for reliable sends in our model, such as FixReceive ([23], or ours below). At a high level, we require that: (A) Until at least one live party queries Π^{coin} in the r-th invocation, the output for that invocation is uniformly distributed for the adversary. (B) All live parties output the same value in Π^{coin}.

2.2 Defining Broadcast and Consensus

We provide new definitions for the considered mixed model by adapting the standard definitions of consensus protocols and constraining the behavior of all live parties, including send-corrupt parties and receive-corrupt parties that have not become zombies. Note that our definitions quantify over all the inputs of live parties that participate starting at the beginning of an execution, and over the outputs of only parties that are not zombies by the end of the execution.

Towards the definitions, we introduce thresholds on the number of corruptions that we permit the adversary to make per execution. We use t_{snd}, t_{rcv}, and t_{byz} to denote thresholds on the number of send, receive, and byzantine corruptions, respectively, in an execution. We introduce the following definition of an execution in which some parties may be corrupted in order to facilitate the definitions of our consensus problems.

Definition 1 ($(t_{snd}, t_{rcv}, t_{byz})$-Compliant Execution). *For a protocol Π, we say that an execution of Π is $(t_{snd}, t_{rcv}, t_{byz})$ compliant if at most t_{snd}, t_{rcv}, and t_{byz} parties are send-corrupted, receive-corrupted, and byzantine-corrupted, respectively, in the execution.*

Broadcast. In a broadcast protocol, a dealer $D \in \mathcal{P}$ wishes to send a message $m \in \{0,1\}^*$ to the parties in $\mathcal{P}$. Each party $p \in \mathcal{P}$ outputs a message $m' \in \{0,1\}^* \cup \{\bot\}$, subject to the following constraints:

Definition 2 (Broadcast). *Let Π be a protocol for parties $\mathcal{P} = \{p_1, \ldots, p_n\}$ in which a distinguished party $D \in \mathcal{P}$ holds an input $m \in \{0,1\}^*$. Π is a Broadcast protocol if the following properties hold except with negligible probability.*

1. *$(t_{snd}, t_{rcv}, t_{byz})$-**Validity:** Π is $(t_{snd}, t_{rcv}, t_{byz})$-valid if in every $(t_{snd}, t_{rcv}, t_{byz})$-compliant execution in which D is honest or receive corrupt (but not send-corrupt), every live party outputs m.*

2. *$(t_{snd}, t_{rcv}, t_{byz})$-**Consistency:** Π is $(t_{snd}, t_{rcv}, t_{byz})$-consistent if in every $(t_{snd}, t_{rcv}, t_{byz})$-compliant execution in which any live party outputs $m' \in \{0,1\}^* \cup \{\bot\}$, every live party outputs m'.*

3. *$(t_{snd}, t_{rcv}, t_{byz})$-**Termination:** Π is $(t_{snd}, t_{rcv}, t_{byz})$-terminating if in every $(t_{snd}, t_{rcv}, t_{byz})$-compliant execution, every live party outputs some $m' \in \{0,1\}^* \cup \{\bot\}$ and terminates within finitely many steps.*

If Π is $(t_{snd}, t_{rcv}, t_{byz})$-valid, $(t_{snd}, t_{rcv}, t_{byz})$-consistent, and $(t_{snd}, t_{rcv}, t_{byz})$-terminating then we call it $(t_{snd}, t_{rcv}, t_{byz})$-secure.

Consensus. In a (binary) consensus protocol, each party has an input $b \in \{0,1\}$. Each party is expected to output a bit $v \in \{0,1\}$.

Definition 3 (Consensus). *Let Π be protocol for parties $\mathcal{P} = \{p_1, \ldots, p_n\}$ in which each party has an input $b \in \{0,1\}$. Π is a Consensus protocol if the following properties hold except with negligible probability.*

1. *$(t_{snd}, t_{rcv}, t_{byz})$-**Validity:** Π is $(t_{snd}, t_{rcv}, t_{byz})$-valid if in every $(t_{snd}, t_{rcv}, t_{byz})$-compliant execution in which all live parties have the same input $b \in \{0,1\}$, all honest parties output b.*

2. $(t_{snd}, t_{rcv}, t_{byz})$-**Consistency:** Π is $(t_{snd}, t_{rcv}, t_{byz})$-consistent *if in every* $(t_{snd}, t_{rcv}, t_{byz})$-*compliant execution in which any live party outputs* v, *every live party outputs* v.

3. $(t_{snd}, t_{rcv}, t_{byz})$-**Termination:** Π is $(t_{snd}, t_{rcv}, t_{byz})$-terminating *if in every* $(t_{snd}, t_{rcv}, t_{byz})$-*compliant execution, every live party outputs* $v \in \{0, 1\}$ *and terminates within finitely many steps.*

If Π is $(t_{snd}, t_{rcv}, t_{byz})$-*valid,* $(t_{snd}, t_{rcv}, t_{byz})$-*consistent, and* $(t_{snd}, t_{rcv}, t_{byz})$-*terminating then we call it* $(t_{snd}, t_{rcv}, t_{byz})$-*secure.*

3   On the Difficulty of Optimal Corruption Tolerance for Send-Corrupt Parties

In this section we discuss the pathology of "standard" send corruptions with respect to current techniques in the literature, and describe why send corruptions appear as deleterious as full byzantine corruptions. Although our focus is on consensus protocols, we consider techniques for both consensus and broadcast; the two are related by a (folklore) reduction, which we discuss in the full version.

We remark that there is evidence for the difficulty of send corruptions in the classical literature. The impossibility proof by Dolev and Strong [7] that any deterministic broadcast protocol requires at least $t_{byz} + 1$ rounds (for at most t_{byz} byzantine corruptions) requires only dropping messages sent by parties that otherwise act honestly. It follows immediately that any deterministic broadcast protocol requires at least $t_{snd} + 1$ rounds (or more generally, at least $t_{snd} + t_{byz} + 1$ rounds). Moreover, there has been recent work by Chan, Pass, and Shi [6] to extend the lowerbound by Dolev and Strong to randomized protocols. Because their adaptation also requires only dropping sent messages, their lowerbound also directly transfers to the send-corrupt model.

In Sect. 3.1, we show that the Dolev-Strong broadcast protocol fails as written when considering send corruptions. We modify the protocol and show that without new ideas, its corruption threshold degrades from $n > t_{byz}$ (in the original model) to $n > 2(t_{snd} + t_{byz})$. In Sect. 3.2, we visit recent techniques for security against strongly rushing, adaptive adversaries and show that these also fail to yield a corruption threshold better than $n > 2t_{snd} + 2t_{byz}$ (which our construction in Sect. 4 achieves) when requiring send-corrupt parties' outputs to be consistent with honest parties' outputs.

3.1   Modifying Dolev-Strong Broadcast

As an example of the pathology of send-corruptions, we now recall the classical authenticated broadcast protocol by Dolev and Strong [7]. Because the protocol is canon, we defer the original to the full version but review it here.

The protocol uses a data structure that we will call a sig-chain. A 1-sig-chain is a pair (m, σ), where σ is a signature on string m. For $i > 1$, an i-sig-chain is a pair (m, σ), where m is an $(i - 1)$-sig-chain and σ is a signature on m. A *valid* i-sig-chain is a sig-chain with the property that no two signatures in the sig-chain are computed using the same key. An i-sig-chain *contains* a message m' if m' is the message of the 1-sig-chain on which the sig-chain is built.

The protocol operates as follows: In the first round, the dealer creates a 1-sig-chain containing its input and sends the sig-chain to all parties. In every subsequent round i, any party that received a valid $i - 1$ chain in the previous round that did not contain a signature that it had computed creates an $i - 1$ sig-chain by appending its own signature to the chain. It then sends the i-sig-chain to all parties. In any round i, if a party receives a valid i-sig-chain, then it adds the message m contained in the sig-chain to a set of candidate outputs. If the set of candidate outputs contains only one candidate at the end, then the party outputs that message. Otherwise it outputs $\perp$.

Where Dolev-Strong Fails. In the send-corruption model, the Dolev-Strong protocol fails because it is possible for send-corrupt parties to output some message m while honest parties output $\perp$. Consider an execution in which the parties are partitioned into three sets: H contains all of the honest parties, S contains all send-corrupt parties, and B contains all byzantine parties. Let the dealer be send-corrupt. It is possible that in this execution, the send-corrupt parties communicate only with parties in $S \cup B$. Then send-corrupt and byzantine parties can collectively build a $t_{byz} + 1$-chain containing m and no honest parties ever receives the dealer's message or any sig-chain containing the message. But this violates consistency.

Modifications. In order to resolve this problem, we must make two modifications to the protocol. First, a party must receive an $t_{snd} + t_{byz} + 1$-sig-chain for any message that it will output; no chain of less than $t_{snd} + t_{byz} + 1$ length may add a message to the set of candidate outputs. (This additionally requires that the protocol is run for $t_{snd} + t_{byz} + 1$ rounds.) Second, we update the bounds to require that $n > 2t_{snd} + 2t_{byz}$. A majority of honest parties is necessary to ensure that honest parties can always build a $t_{snd} + t_{byz} + 1$-sig-chain without the assistance of byzantine or send-corrupt parties, which is necessary for validity.

We present our modified Dolev-Strong protocol Π^{modDS} in Fig. 1.

Theorem 1. Π^{modDS} *is a* (t_{snd}, t_{byz})*-secure broadcast protocol for* $n > 2t_{snd} + 2t_{byz}$.

Proof. The proof is similar to the original by Dolev and Strong, subject to modifications described above. Validity follows from the fact that when $n > 2t_{snd} + 2t_{byz}$ and the dealer is honest, the honest parties build a $(t_{snd} + t_{byz} + 1)$ sig-chain, and that no sig-chain can exist containing some m' that the dealer did not send. Consistency follows from the fact that if a $(t_{snd} + t_{byz} + 1)$ sig-chain exists, then some honest party's signature must be included. It follows that if any honest party output m, then all honest parties receive a $(t_{snd} + t_{byz} + 1)$ sig-chain containing m. Assume that some honest party receives a $(t_{snd} + t_{byz} + 1)$ sig-chain containing m and another honest party receives a $(t_{snd} + t_{byz} + 1)$ sig-chain containing m'.

Protocol 1 Modified Dolev Strong Broadcast Protocol Π^{modDS}

Shared Setup: Public Key Infrastructure (PKI) for a signature scheme.

Inputs: The dealer $D \in \mathcal{P}$ has an input $m \in \{0,1\}^*$.

Outputs: Each party $p \in \mathcal{P}$ outputs a value $m' \in \{0,1\}^* \cup \{\bot\}$.

Local Variable: Each party $p \in \mathcal{P}$ maintains a local variable S, which is a set initialized to $\{\}$.

Protocol: The protocol begins at time 0 and proceeds in rounds. Each round party p proceeds as follows:

1. **Round 1: Dealer's Messages** The Dealer D signs its input $\sigma \leftarrow \mathsf{sign}_{\mathsf{sk}}(m)$ and sends (m, σ) to all parties.
2. **Sig Chains:** For every round i from 2 to $t_{\mathsf{snd}} + t_{\mathsf{byz}} + 1$: For every valid $(i-1)$-sig-chain c that p received at the end of round $i-1$ in which none of the signatures were constructed by p, p computes $\sigma \leftarrow \mathsf{sign}_{\mathsf{sk}}(c)$ and sends (σ, c) to all parties.
3. **Output:** For every valid $(t_{\mathsf{snd}} + t_{\mathsf{byz}} + 1)$-sig-chain c that p received at the end of round $t_{\mathsf{snd}} + t_{\mathsf{byz}} + 1$, let m' be the message contained by c and update $S = S \cup \{m'\}$. If $|S| = 1$, then p outputs the element $m' \in S$. If $|S| \neq 1$, then p outputs $\bot$.

Fig. 1. Modified Dolev-Strong Broadcast Protocol Π^{modDS}

Then both sig-chains must include an honest signature, and therefore there must be $(t_{\mathsf{snd}} + t_{\mathsf{byz}} + 1)$ sig-chain containing m and m' in the view of every honest party. It follows that every honest and send-corrupt party outputs $\bot$.

Can Dolev-Strong Be Fixed to Support $n > t_{\mathsf{snd}} + t_{\mathsf{byz}}$? We have shown that without new ideas, Dolev-Strong cannot be updated to tolerate $n > t_{\mathsf{snd}} + t_{\mathsf{byz}}$ (which it is easy to prove is an optimal corruption budget). However, we cannot rule out such a threshold. In the pathological execution described above, honest parties do not send any messages if they do not receive any valid sig-chains. However, honest parties may send messages in each round containing $\bot$, indicating "I have not received a message," which conveys that the party's sent message *was not dropped*. This provides more information to the protocol, but we do not know how to use such a technique to improve broadcast.

3.2 Recent Techniques for Adaptive, Strongly Rushing Adveraries

Recent techniques for byzantine agreement and broadcast against a strongly rushing adversary also fail when requiring consistency between send-corrupt parties' outputs and honest parties' outputs. For example, the byzantine agreement protocol by Abraham et al. [2] and the broadcast protocol by Wan et al. [21] achieve security against a strongly adaptive adversary by effectively committing to any leader's messages early in the protocol, and then revealing a leader in a later round. This thwarts strongly rushing adaptive adversaries because by the time a leader is elected, it is too late to corrupt the leader and remove the messages it has sent.

In the partitioning attack, send-corrupt parties are able to send messages to each other but not to the honest parties, and they are able to reach signature thresholds on messages that no honest party ever receives. For example, in [2], messages often require $b + 1$ distinct signatures (implying at least one honest party signed a message) in order to be recognized by an honest party. But when there are more send-corrupt parties than honest parties, any threshold number of signatures that honest parties must be able to attain on their own must also be attainable by send-corrupt parties only. This can cause send-corrupt parties to adopt a different leader in some step than the honest parties. Similarly, in [21], send-corrupt parties' puzzles may never be delivered to honest parties. When honest parties choose a leader based on the solutions to a set of time-lock puzzles, send-corrupt parties may make a decision based on a larger set than the honest parties, and their decisions may differ. This form of attack is prevented by the implicit echoing assumption in [21], but it does not carry into the send-corrupt model. In our model, this attack is thwarted by requiring the number of honest parties be greater than $2(t_{\mathsf{snd}} + t_{\mathsf{byz}})$, as thresholds on the number of signatures can enforce that some honest party signs a message.

4   Constant-Round Synchronous Consensus for $n > t_{\mathsf{rcv}} + 2t_{\mathsf{snd}} + 2t_{\mathsf{byz}}$

We now present a protocol for consensus in synchronous networks in the presence of send corruptions, receive corruptions, and byzantine corruptions where digital signatures are available. We prove that the protocol is $(t_{\mathsf{snd}}, t_{\mathsf{rcv}}, t_{\mathsf{byz}})$-secure for $n > t_{\mathsf{rcv}} + 2t_{\mathsf{snd}} + 2t_{\mathsf{byz}}$. In the full version, we show the same protocol is $(t_{\mathsf{snd}}, t_{\mathsf{rcv}}, t_{\mathsf{byz}})$-secure for $n > t_{\mathsf{rcv}} + t_{\mathsf{snd}} + 2t_{\mathsf{byz}}$ when send corruptions are *spotty*, and that corruption budget is optimal.

Towards presenting our consensus protocol, we first present protocols for weak broadcast, weak consensus, and graded consensus. Each protocol is used as a building block in our ultimate consensus protocol. Due to space constraints, we defer the proofs of most of our protocols to the full version. Before introducing these building blocks, we introduce another protocol for reliable sending when all parties send messages to each other.

4.1   All-to-All FixReceive

Our All-to-All FixReceive protocol is similar to FixReceive from [23], tuned for the common scenario in which all parties attempt to send a message to all other parties. The parties forward all unique messages that they receive, in order to ensure that every party either receives message that was sent, or detects that it is receive-corrupted. The parties output all unique messages that they receive.

A party detects whether it is receive-corrupt based on the number of messages it receives; if so, it becomes a zombie and notifies the other parties. We prove that a receive-corrupt party that does not become a zombie must receive a message from another honest or send-corrupt party. We then prove that if some honest party attempts to send a message m via the protocol, then every non-zombie party must receive that message. The proofs are deferred to the full version.

Protocol 2 All-To-All FixReceive Protocol $\Pi^{FR}(t_{\mathsf{snd}}, t_{\mathsf{rcv}}, t_{\mathsf{byz}})$

Inputs: Each party $p \in \mathcal{P}$ has an input $m \in \{0,1\}^*$.

Outputs: Each party $p \in \mathcal{P}$ outputs some message for every other party in $\mathcal{P}$, or outputs zombie.

Protocol: The protocol proceeds in two rounds, in which every party sends its input m to every other party, and then parties forward the unique messages they have received, as follows:

1. **Send Messages:** Each party sends its signed input m to every other party.
2. **Replay:** Every party forwards every unique message that it received in Round 1 to every other party. If a party did not receive any unique messages in Round 1, it sends $\perp$ to every other party.
3. **Output:** If a party p does not receive more than $n - t_{\mathsf{snd}} - t_{\mathsf{byz}}$ messages (including $\perp$) in either round, it sends zombie to all parties and outputs zombie. Otherwise, p outputs the set of unique messages that it received in Round 2.

Fig. 2. All-to-all FixReceive Protocol Π^{FR}

Lemma 1 (Zombies in Π^{FR}). *Any party p becomes a zombie during Π^{FR} only when it is receive-corrupt. If p does not become a zombie then it received a message from at least one honest or send-corrupt party.*

Lemma 2 (Honest and Receive-Corrupt Send to All). *If an honest party or receive-corrupt party (but not send-corrupt) sends a message m using Π^{FR}, then every live party receives m or becomes a zombie.*

4.2 Weak Broadcast

Our first building block is a weak broadcast primitive. In a weak broadcast protocol, a dealer $D \in \mathcal{P}$ wishes to send a message $m \in \{0,1\}^*$ to the parties in $\mathcal{P}$. Each party $p \in \mathcal{P}$ outputs a message $m' \in \{0,1\}^* \cup \{\perp\}$, subject to the following constraints:

Definition 4 (Weak Broadcast). *Let Π be a protocol for parties $\mathcal{P} = \{p_1, \ldots, p_n\}$ and a distinguished party $D \in \mathcal{P}$ holds an input $m \in \{0,1\}^*$. Π is a* Weak Broadcast *protocol if the following properties hold except with negligible probability.*

1. $(t_{\mathsf{snd}}, t_{\mathsf{rcv}}, t_{\mathsf{byz}})$-**Validity:** *$\Pi$ is $(t_{\mathsf{snd}}, t_{\mathsf{rcv}}, t_{\mathsf{byz}})$-valid if in every $(t_{\mathsf{snd}}, t_{\mathsf{rcv}}, t_{\mathsf{byz}})$-compliant execution in which D is honest or receive corrupt (but not send-corrupt), every live party outputs m.*
2. $(t_{\mathsf{snd}}, t_{\mathsf{rcv}}, t_{\mathsf{byz}})$-**Unanimity:** *$\Pi$ is $(t_{\mathsf{snd}}, t_{\mathsf{rcv}}, t_{\mathsf{byz}})$-unanimous if in every $(t_{\mathsf{snd}}, t_{\mathsf{rcv}}, t_{\mathsf{byz}})$-compliant execution in which D is live, either every live party outputs $m \in \{0,1\}^*$ or every live party outputs $\perp$.*
3. $(t_{\mathsf{snd}}, t_{\mathsf{rcv}}, t_{\mathsf{byz}})$-**Consistency:** *$\Pi$ is $(t_{\mathsf{snd}}, t_{\mathsf{rcv}}, t_{\mathsf{byz}})$-consistent if in every $(t_{\mathsf{snd}}, t_{\mathsf{rcv}}, t_{\mathsf{byz}})$-compliant execution in which any honest party outputs $m' \in \{0,1\}^*$, every live party outputs m' or $\perp$.*

Protocol 3 Weak Broadcast Protocol Π^{WB}

Shared Setup: Public Key Infrastructure for a signature scheme, every party knows the identity of the dealer and its public key pk.

Inputs: The dealer $D \in \mathcal{P}$ has an input $m \in \{0,1\}^*$.

Outputs: Each party $p_i \in \mathcal{P}$ outputs a value $m' \in \{0,1\}^* \cup \{\bot\}$.

Protocol: The protocol begins at time 0 and proceeds in rounds, in which each round lasts for Δ time. Each round party p proceeds as follows:

1. **Dealer's Messages:** The Dealer D signs its input $\sigma \leftarrow \mathsf{sign}_{\mathsf{sk}}(m)$ and sends (deal, m, σ) to all parties, where σ is the signature on m using its secret signing key sk.
2. **Echo Dealer's Value:** Parties run Π^{FR} based on the messages they received from D. If p received a message from D, let (m', σ) be the message and signature that p received. p inputs (echo, m', σ) to Π^{FR}. Otherwise, p inputs (echo, $\bot, \bot$) to Π^{FR}.
3. **Replay:** Parties again run Π^{FR} based on the messages they received in the previous round, where each party provides all of the unique messages it received in the previous Π^{FR} as input.
4. **Verification and Output:** If p did not output any messages signed with D's key from the first run of Π^{FR}, then it outputs $\bot$. If in the outputs of the second run of Π^{FR}, p receives any two pairs (m'_i, σ_i) and (m'_j, σ_j) such that $m'_i \neq m'_j$ but $\mathsf{ver}_{\mathsf{pk}}(\sigma_i) = 1$ and $\mathsf{ver}_{\mathsf{pk}}(\sigma_j) = 1$, then p outputs $\bot$. Otherwise, p outputs the unique message m' that it received in the first run of Π^{FR} whose signature verifies with D's public key.

Fig. 3. Weak broadcast protocol Π^{WB}

4. $(t_{\mathsf{snd}}, t_{\mathsf{rcv}}, t_{\mathsf{byz}})$**-Termination:** Π is $(t_{\mathsf{snd}}, t_{\mathsf{rcv}}, t_{\mathsf{byz}})$-*terminating if in every* $(t_{\mathsf{snd}}, t_{\mathsf{rcv}}, t_{\mathsf{byz}})$-*compliant execution, every live party outputs some* $m' \in \{0,1\}^* \cup \{\bot\}$ *and terminates within finitely many steps.*

If Π *is* $(t_{\mathsf{snd}}, t_{\mathsf{rcv}}, t_{\mathsf{byz}})$-*valid,* $(t_{\mathsf{snd}}, t_{\mathsf{rcv}}, t_{\mathsf{byz}})$-*consistent, and* $(t_{\mathsf{snd}}, t_{\mathsf{rcv}}, t_{\mathsf{byz}})$-*terminating then we call it* $(t_{\mathsf{snd}}, t_{\mathsf{rcv}}, t_{\mathsf{byz}})$-*secure. If* Π *is additionally* $(t_{\mathsf{snd}}, t_{\mathsf{rcv}}, t_{\mathsf{byz}})$-*unanimous, then we call it* $(t_{\mathsf{snd}}, t_{\mathsf{rcv}}, t_{\mathsf{byz}})$-*secure with unanimity.*

Our protocol for weak broadcast is presented in Fig. 3. It follows a standard construction, adapted for our corruption model by invoking Π^{FR} to distribute messages. It permits a designated *dealer* to send an arbitrary message m to all parties, with the guarantee that every party outputs either m or $\bot$.

Lemma 3 (Security of Weak Broadcast Π^{WB}). *Protocol* $\Pi^{\mathsf{WB}}(t_{\mathsf{snd}}, t_{\mathsf{rcv}}, t_{\mathsf{byz}})$ *is a* $(t_{\mathsf{snd}}, t_{\mathsf{rcv}}, t_{\mathsf{byz}})$-*secure weak broadcast protocol for* $n > t_{\mathsf{snd}} + t_{\mathsf{rcv}} + 2t_{\mathsf{byz}}$.

Proof. The proof is deferred to the full version.

We provide an additional statement about the outputs of Π^{WB} when the dealer is corrupt but not byzantine. Specifically, consistency holds over the outputs of all live parties when the dealer is send-corrupt (and not only when some honest party outputs $m \neq \bot$).

Lemma 4. *When the dealer is send-corrupt, if one live party outputs $m \neq \perp$, then every live party outputs $m' \in \{m, \perp\}$*

Proof. Follows directly from unforgeability of the idealized signature scheme.

4.3   Weak Consensus

We use weak consensus as a stepping stone to achieve consensus. In a weak consensus protocol, all honest parties have an input $b \in \{\perp, 0, 1\}$, and all honest parties are expected to output a value $v \in \{\perp, 0, 1\}$, subject to the following:

Definition 5. (Weak Consensus). *Let Π be a protocol for parties $\mathcal{P} = \{p_1, \ldots, p_n\}$ in which every party $p \in \mathcal{P}$ has an input $b \in \{0, 1\}$. Π is a Weak Consensus protocol if the following properties hold except with negligible probability.*

1. $(t_{\mathsf{snd}}, t_{\mathsf{rcv}}, t_{\mathsf{byz}})$-**Validity:** Π *is* $(t_{\mathsf{snd}}, t_{\mathsf{rcv}}, t_{\mathsf{byz}})$-valid *if in every* $(l_{\mathsf{snd}}, l_{\mathsf{rcv}}, l_{\mathsf{byz}})$-*compliant execution in which all honest parties have the same input b and no live parties have input $1 - b$, all honest parties output b.*
2. $(t_{\mathsf{snd}}, t_{\mathsf{rcv}}, t_{\mathsf{byz}})$-**Consistency:** Π *is* $(t_{\mathsf{snd}}, t_{\mathsf{rcv}}, t_{\mathsf{byz}})$-consistent *if in every* $(t_{\mathsf{snd}}, t_{\mathsf{rcv}}, t_{\mathsf{byz}})$-*compliant execution in which any live party outputs $v \in \{0, 1\}$, no live party outputs $1 - v$.*
3. $(t_{\mathsf{snd}}, t_{\mathsf{rcv}}, t_{\mathsf{byz}})$-**Termination:** Π *is* $(t_{\mathsf{snd}}, t_{\mathsf{rcv}}, t_{\mathsf{byz}})$-terminating *if in every* $(t_{\mathsf{snd}}, t_{\mathsf{rcv}}, t_{\mathsf{byz}})$-*compliant execution, every live party outputs $v \in \{\perp, 0, 1\}$ and terminates within finitely many steps.*

If Π is $(t_{\mathsf{snd}}, t_{\mathsf{rcv}}, t_{\mathsf{byz}})$-valid, $(t_{\mathsf{snd}}, t_{\mathsf{rcv}}, t_{\mathsf{byz}})$-consistent, and $(t_{\mathsf{snd}}, t_{\mathsf{rcv}}, t_{\mathsf{byz}})$-terminating then we call it $(t_{\mathsf{snd}}, t_{\mathsf{rcv}}, t_{\mathsf{byz}})$-secure.

We present our weak consensus protocol Π^{WC} in Fig. 4. The protocol is an adaptation of the reduction from Weak Consensus to Weak Broadcast [9], and proceeds in two synchronous rounds. First, in parallel, each party signs its protocol input and sends its signed input to all parties. Second, upon receiving all other parties' inputs, each party attempts to generate a *certificate* in favor of some output value. A certificate for a bit u is a set of $n - t_{\mathsf{snd}} - t_{\mathsf{rcv}} - t_{\mathsf{byz}}$ unique, valid signatures on u. If a party is able to generate a certificate, it sends the certificate to all other parties.

A party outputs a bit v only if it meets three conditions: (1) it must generate a certificate in the beginning of the second round; (2) it must receive at least $n - t_{\mathsf{snd}} - t_{\mathsf{rcv}} - t_{\mathsf{byz}}$ valid certificates from distinct parties; (3) it must not receive a valid certificate for $1 - v$ from any other party. Otherwise it outputs $\perp$.

Intuitively, validity of the protocol is guaranteed by the fact that if all live parties have input b, then all honest parties will be able to construct a certificate for b, and there will not be enough corrupt parties to construct a certificate for $1 - b$. Consistency is guaranteed by the fact that if two live parties are able to generate certificates for opposite values, then they must share their certificates with each other, and then both output $\perp$.

Lemma 5. (Security of Π^{WC}). *Protocol $\Pi^{\mathsf{WC}}(t_{\mathsf{snd}}, t_{\mathsf{rcv}}, t_{\mathsf{byz}})$ is a $(t_{\mathsf{snd}}, t_{\mathsf{rcv}}, t_{\mathsf{byz}})$-secure Weak Consensus protocol in synchronous networks for $n > t_{\mathsf{rcv}} + \frac{3}{2} t_{\mathsf{snd}} + 2 t_{\mathsf{byz}}$.*

Proof. The proof is deferred to the full version.

Protocol 4 Weak Consensus $\Pi^{\mathsf{WC}}(t_{\mathsf{cra}}, t_{\mathsf{byz}})$

Shared Setup: Public Key infrastructure for a signature scheme.
Inputs: Each party $p \in \mathcal{P}$ has an input $b \in \{\bot, 0, 1\}$ and a secret signing key for the signature scheme.
Outputs: Each party $p \in \mathcal{P}$ outputs a value $v \in \{\bot, 0, 1\}$.
Protocol: The protocol begins at time 0 and proceeds in rounds, in which each round lasts for Δ time. Each party p_i proceeds as follows:

1. **Sign Inputs:** In parallel, each party signs its input bit and sends its signed input to all other parties.
2. **Construct Certificates and WB:** Each party collects all of the signed input bits from the other parties. If there is a $v \in \{0, 1\}$ for which $n - t_{\mathsf{snd}} - t_{\mathsf{rcv}} - t_{\mathsf{byz}}$ valid signed messages are received, p constructs a *certificate* composed of $n - t_{\mathsf{snd}} - t_{\mathsf{rcv}} - t_{\mathsf{byz}}$ signatures from distinct parties on v. The parties then invoke n weak broadcasts in parallel, in which p_i is the dealer in the ith weak broadcast, and p_i provides its certificate as input if it has one; otherwise p_i provides $\bot$ as its input.
3. **Output:** Each party receives any certificates sent to it in Round 2. If p constructed a certificate for some v in round 2 AND p has received at least $n - t_{\mathsf{snd}} - t_{\mathsf{rcv}} - t_{\mathsf{byz}}$ certificates for v by the end of round 2 from distinct parties AND p has not received a valid certificate for $1 - v$, then p outputs v. Otherwise, p outputs $\bot$.

Fig. 4. Weak Consensus Protocol Π^{WC}

4.4   Graded Consensus

We define an additional weakened form of consensus called *graded consensus*, which was originally introduced by Feldman and Micali [8]. In a graded consensus protocol, each party has an input $b \in \{0, 1\}$. Each party is expected to output a pair $(v, g) \in \{0, 1\}^2$, where v is the output bit and g is a *grade*.

Definition 6 (0/1 Graded Consensus). *Let Π be a protocol for parties $\mathcal{P} = \{p_1, \ldots, p_n\}$ where each party has input $b \in \{\bot, 0, 1\}$. Π is a 0/1 Graded Consensus protocol if the following properties hold except with negligible probability.*

1. *$(t_{\mathsf{snd}}, t_{\mathsf{rcv}}, t_{\mathsf{byz}})$-**Validity:** Π is $(t_{\mathsf{snd}}, t_{\mathsf{rcv}}, t_{\mathsf{byz}})$-valid if in every $(t_{\mathsf{snd}}, t_{\mathsf{rcv}}, t_{\mathsf{byz}})$-compliant execution in which all honest parties have the same input $b \in \{0, 1\}$ and no live parties have input $1 - b$, all live parties output $(b, 1)$.*
2. *$(t_{\mathsf{snd}}, t_{\mathsf{rcv}}, t_{\mathsf{byz}})$-**Consistency:** Π is $(t_{\mathsf{snd}}, t_{\mathsf{rcv}}, t_{\mathsf{byz}})$-consistent if in every $(t_{\mathsf{snd}}, t_{\mathsf{rcv}}, t_{\mathsf{byz}})$-compliant execution in which any live party outputs $(v, 1)$, every live party outputs $(v, g) \in \{0, 1\}^2$.*

Protocol 5 Graded Consensus $\Pi^{\mathsf{GC}}(t_{\mathsf{snd}}, t_{\mathsf{rcv}}, t_{\mathsf{byz}})$

Inputs: Each party $p \in \mathcal{P}$ has an input $b \in \{\bot, 0, 1\}$

Outputs: Each party $p \in \mathcal{P}$ outputs a pair $(v, g) \in \{0, 1\}^2$

Protocol: The protocol begins at time 0 and proceeds in synchronous rounds, labeled below, where each round lasts long enough for its corresponding subprotocol to complete. Each party p proceeds as follows:

1. **Weak Consensus:** Run Π^{WC} with b as input. Let b' denote the output of Π^{WC}.
2. **Weak Broadcast:** In parallel, all parties invoke n copies of $\Pi^{\mathsf{WB}}(t_{\mathsf{snd}}, t_{\mathsf{rcv}}, t_{\mathsf{byz}})$, where p_j is the dealer in the jth copy. p_j uses the value b' as its input to Π^{WB}. For $u \in \{\bot, 0, 1\}$, let n_u denote the number of weak broadcasts for which p outputs u.
3. **Output:**
   - Assign $v \leftarrow u \in \{0, 1\}$ for which $n_u > n_{1-u}$. Break ties by assigning $v \leftarrow 1$.
     Assign $g \leftarrow 1$ if $n_v \geq n - t_{\mathsf{byz}} - t_{\mathsf{rcv}} - t_{\mathsf{snd}}$. Else $g \leftarrow 0$. Output (v, g)

Fig. 5. Graded consensus protocol Π^{GC}

*3. $(t_{\mathsf{snd}}, t_{\mathsf{rcv}}, t_{\mathsf{byz}})$-**Termination:** Π is $(t_{\mathsf{snd}}, t_{\mathsf{rcv}}, t_{\mathsf{byz}})$-terminating if in every $(t_{\mathsf{snd}}, t_{\mathsf{rcv}}, t_{\mathsf{byz}})$-compliant execution, every live party outputs $(v, g) \in \{0, 1\}^2$ and terminates within finitely many steps.*

If Π is $(t_{\mathsf{snd}}, t_{\mathsf{rcv}}, t_{\mathsf{byz}})$-valid, $(t_{\mathsf{snd}}, t_{\mathsf{rcv}}, t_{\mathsf{byz}})$-consistent, and $(t_{\mathsf{snd}}, t_{\mathsf{rcv}}, t_{\mathsf{byz}})$-terminating then we call it $(t_{\mathsf{snd}}, t_{\mathsf{rcv}}, t_{\mathsf{byz}})$-secure.

Our graded consensus protocol Π^{GC} is presented in Fig. 5; it is an adaptation to our fault model of the reduction of graded consensus to weak broadcast discussed by Fitzi [9]. Specifically, Π^{GC} proceeds in synchronous rounds in which two subprotocols are invoked. First, parties invoke a weak consensus protocol, using their protocol inputs as input to the weak consensus protocol. Second, in parallel, all parties weak broadcast their outputs from the weak consensus protocol. Parties determine their outputs based on the weak broadcasts they receive. First, a party sets the bit v to the value $u \in \{0, 1\}$ for which it received more weak broadcasts carrying u than $1 - u$. Second, a party sets its grade g to 1 if it receives than $n - t_{\mathsf{byz}} - t_{\mathsf{rcv}} - t_{\mathsf{snd}}$ weak broadcasts carrying bit v, and sets its grade to 0 otherwise. It then outputs (v, g). Intuitively, each party outputs a bit v based on the majority of weak broadcasts that it has received. A party outputs grade 1 if it has received a large enough majority of weak broadcasts carrying v that it is guaranteed no other honest party has received a majority of weak broadcasts carrying $1 - v$. The proof follows from a quorum argument.

Lemma 6 (Security of Π^{GC}). *Protocol $\Pi^{\mathsf{GC}}(t_{\mathsf{snd}}, t_{\mathsf{rcv}}, t_{\mathsf{byz}})$ is a $(t_{\mathsf{snd}}, t_{\mathsf{rcv}}, t_{\mathsf{byz}})$-secure graded consensus protocol in synchronous networks for $n > t_{\mathsf{rcv}} + 2t_{\mathsf{snd}} + 2t_{\mathsf{byz}}$.*

Proof. The proof is deferred to the full version.

4.5   Expected Constant-Round Consensus

In Fig. 6 we present Π^*, our expected constant-round protocol for consensus. The protocol follows the standard coin-loop paradigm to go from graded consensus to byzantine agreement. To ensure termination, the protocol ensures that when a party terminates, it holds a certificate that it can send to all parties in order to make them terminate with the same value.

Theorem 2 (Main Theorem). $\Pi^*(t_{snd}, t_{rcv}, t_{byz})$ *is a* $\Pi^*(t_{snd}, t_{rcv}, t_{byz})$-*secure consensus protocol in synchronous networks for* $n > t_{rcv} + 2t_{snd} + 2t_{byz}$, *where a common coin primitive is available.*

Proof. The proof is deferred to the full version.

Protocol 6 Expected Constant-Round Protocol $\Pi^*(t_{snd}, t_{rcv}, t_{byz})$

Common Setup: The parties have access to a public key infrastructure for some signature scheme.

Inputs: Each party $p \in \mathcal{P}$ has an input $b \in \{0, 1\}$

Outputs: Each party $p \in \mathcal{P}$ outputs some $b' \in \{0, 1\}$

Internal Variable: Each party maintains a variable $v \in \{0, 1\}$ which is initialized to b. For each $u \in \{0, 1\}$, each party also maintains a set D_u of distinct (decide, u) messages that it has received.

Protocol: The protocol begins at time 0 and proceeds in synchronous rounds. Each party p proceeds as follows:

- **Loop** starting with iteration $i = 0$ until terminating:
  1. **Subround A (Graded Consensus):** Run $\Pi^{GC}(t_{snd}, t_{rcv}, t_{byz})$ with v as input. Let (u, g) denote p's output of Π^{GC}.
  2. **Subround B (Common Coin):** Invoke a common coin protocol Π^{coin} and assign to ψ_i the output.
  3. **Conditional Update:** If $g = 0$, then update $v \leftarrow \psi_i$. If $g = 1$, then update $v \leftarrow u$.
  4. **Conditional Decision:** If $g = 1$ and $v = \psi_i$: sign (decide, v), send the signed message to all parties, and output v.
  5. **Certificate Send:** All parties invoke Π^{FR}, where any party that has generated or received a *certificate* since the last invocation of Π^{FR} provides the certificate as input, and terminates after Π^{FR}. Any party that does not have a certificate inputs $\perp$.
- **Certificate:** Upon receiving a signed (decide, u) message from any party, add the message to D_u. When D_u contains at least $t_{byz} + 1$ messages from distinct parties, construct a *certificate* of $t_{byz} + 1$ (decide, u) messages from distinct parties. Upon receiving a certificate, output u (if have not already output).

Fig. 6. Expected constant-round consensus protocol Π^*

References

1. Abraham, I., et al.: Communication complexity of byzantine agreement, revisited. In: Proceedings of the 2019 ACM Symposium on Principles of Distributed Computing, pp. 317–326 (2019)
2. Abraham, I., Devadas, S., Dolev, D., Nayak, K., Ren, L.: Synchronous byzantine agreement with expected $O(1)$ rounds, expected $O(n^2)$ communication, and optimal resilience. In: Goldberg, I., Moore, T. (eds.) FC 2019. LNCS, vol. 11598, pp. 320–334. Springer, Cham (2019). https://doi.org/10.1007/978-3-030-32101-7_20
3. Abraham, I., Malkhi, D., Nayak, K., Ren, L., Yin, M.: Sync hotstuff: simple and practical synchronous state machine replication. Cryptology ePrint Archive, Report 2019/270 (2019). https://eprint.iacr.org/2019/270
4. Altmann, B., Fitzi, M., Maurer, U.: Byzantine agreement secure against general adversaries in the dual failure model. In: Jayanti, P. (ed.) DISC 1999. LNCS, vol. 1693, pp. 123–139. Springer, Heidelberg (1999). https://doi.org/10.1007/3-540-48169-9_9
5. Backes, M., Cachin, C.: Reliable broadcast in a computational hybrid model with byzantine faults, crashes, and recoveries. In: DSN, pp. 37–46. IEEE Computer Society (2003)
6. Hubert Chan, T.-H., Pass, R., Shi, E.: Round complexity of byzantine agreement, revisited. In: IACR Cryptology ePrint Archive, 2019, p. 886 (2019)
7. Dolev, D., Raymond Strong, H.: Authenticated algorithms for byzantine agreement. SIAM J. Comput. **12**(4), 656–666 (1983)
8. Feldman, P., Micali, S.: An optimal probabilistic protocol for synchronous byzantine agreement. SIAM J. Comput. **26**(4), 873–933 (1997)
9. Fitzi, M.: Generalized communication and security models in byzantine agreement. PhD thesis, ETH Zurich, 3 2003. Reprint as, vol. 4 of ETH Series in Information Security and Cryptography. Hartung-Gorre Verlag, Konstanz (2003). ISBN 3-89649-853-3
10. Garay, J.A., Katz, J., Koo, C.-Y., Ostrovsky, R.: Round complexity of authenticated broadcast with a dishonest majority. In: FOCS, pp. 658–668. IEEE Computer Society (2007)
11. Garay, J.A., Perry, K.J.: A continuum of failure models for distributed computing. In: Segall, A., Zaks, S. (eds.) WDAG 1992. LNCS, vol. 647, pp. 153–165. Springer, Heidelberg (1992). https://doi.org/10.1007/3-540-56188-9_11
12. Gilad, Y., Hemo, R., Micali, S., Vlachos, G., Zeldovich, N.: Algorand: scaling byzantine agreements for cryptocurrencies. In: SOSP, pp. 51–68. ACM (2017)
13. Guo, Y., Pass, R., Shi, E.: Synchronous, with a chance of partition tolerance. Cryptology ePrint Archive, Report 2019/179 (2019). https://eprint.iacr.org/2019/179
14. Katz, J., Koo, C.-Y.: On expected constant-round protocols for byzantine agreement. In: Dwork, C. (ed.) CRYPTO 2006. LNCS, vol. 4117, pp. 445–462. Springer, Heidelberg (2006). https://doi.org/10.1007/11818175_27
15. Kursawe, K.: Distributed protocols on general hybrid adversary structures (2004)
16. Libert, B., Joye, M., Yung, M.: Born and raised distributively: fully distributed non-interactive adaptively-secure threshold signatures with short shares. In: PODC, pp. 303–312. ACM (2014)
17. Malkhi, D., Nayak, K., Ren, L.: Flexible byzantine fault tolerance. arXiv preprint arXiv:1904.10067 (2019)
18. Micali, S.: Byzantine agreement, made trivial (2017)

19. Micali, S., Rabin, M.O., Vadhan, S.P.: Verifiable random functions. In: FOCS, pp. 120–130. IEEE Computer Society (1999)
20. Pass, R., Shi, E.: The sleepy model of consensus. In: Takagi, T., Peyrin, T. (eds.) ASIACRYPT 2017. LNCS, vol. 10625, pp. 380–409. Springer, Cham (2017). https://doi.org/10.1007/978-3-319-70697-9_14
21. Wan, J., Xiao, H., Devadas, S., Shi, E.: Round-efficient byzantine broadcast under strongly adaptive and majority corruptions. In: Pass, R., Pietrzak, K. (eds.) TCC 2020. LNCS, vol. 12550, pp. 412–456. Springer, Cham (2020). https://doi.org/10.1007/978-3-030-64375-1_15
22. Wan, J., Xiao, H., Shi, E., Devadas, S.: Expected constant round byzantine broadcast under dishonest majority. In: Pass, R., Pietrzak, K. (eds.) TCC 2020. LNCS, vol. 12550, pp. 381–411. Springer, Cham (2020). https://doi.org/10.1007/978-3-030-64375-1_14
23. Zikas, V., Hauser, S., Maurer, U.: Realistic failures in secure multi-party computation. In: Reingold, O. (ed.) TCC 2009. LNCS, vol. 5444, pp. 274–293. Springer, Heidelberg (2009). https://doi.org/10.1007/978-3-642-00457-5_17

Blockchain

Babel Fees via Limited Liabilities

Manuel M. T. Chakravarty[1]([✉]), Nikos Karayannidis[2], Aggelos Kiayias[3,4],
Michael Peyton Jones[5], and Polina Vinogradova[6]

[1] IOHK, Utrecht, The Netherlands
manuel.chakravarty@iohk.io
[2] IOHK, Athens, Greece
nikos.karagiannidis@iohk.io
[3] IOHK, Edinburgh, Scotland
[4] University of Edinburgh, Edinburgh, Scotland
akiayias@inf.ed.ac.uk
[5] IOHK, London, England
michael.peyton-jones@iohk.io
[6] IOHK, Ottawa, Canada
polina.vinogradova@iohk.io

Abstract. Custom currencies (ERC-20) on Ethereum are wildly popular, but they are second class to the primary currency Ether. Custom currencies are more complex and more expensive to handle than the primary currency as their accounting is not natively performed by the underlying ledger, but instead in user-defined contract code. Furthermore, and quite importantly, transaction fees can only be paid in Ether. In this paper, we focus on being able to pay transaction fees in custom currencies. We achieve this by way of a mechanism permitting *short term liabilities* to pay transaction fees in conjunction with offers of custom currencies to compensate for those liabilities. This enables block producers to accept custom currencies in exchange for settling liabilities of transactions that they process.

We present formal ledger rules to handle liabilities together with the concept of *babel fees* to pay transaction fees in custom currencies. We also discuss how clients can determine what fees they have to pay, and we present a solution to the knapsack problem variant that block producers have to solve in the presence of babel fees to optimise their profits.

1 Introduction

Custom currencies, usually following the ERC-20 standard, are one of the most popular smart contracts deployed on the Ethereum blockchain. These currencies are however second class to the primary currency Ether. Custom tokens are not natively traded and accounted for by the Ethereum ledger; instead, part of the logic of an ERC-20 contract replicates this transfer and accounting functionality. The second class nature of custom tokens goes further, though: transaction processing and smart contract execution fees can only be paid in Ether—even by users who have got custom tokens worth thousands of dollars in their wallets.

The above two limitations and the disadvantages they introduce seem hard to circumvent. After all, it seems unavoidable that custom tokens must be issued

© Springer Nature Switzerland AG 2022
G. Ateniese and D. Venturi (Eds.): ACNS 2022, LNCS 13269, pp. 707–726, 2022.
https://doi.org/10.1007/978-3-031-09234-3_35

by a smart contract and interacting with a smart contract requires fees in the primary currency. Still, recent work addressing the first limitation, showed that it can be tackled: by introducing *native custom tokens* (see e.g., [6]) it is possible to allow custom tokens to reuse the transfer and accounting logic that is already part of the underlying ledger. This is achieved without the need for a global registry or similar global structure via the concept of *token bundles* in combination with *token policy scripts* that control minting and burning of custom tokens. Nevertheless, even with native custom tokens, transaction fees still need to be paid in the primary currency of the underlying ledger.

To the best of our knowledge the only known technique to tackle the second limitation is in the context of Ethereum: the *Ethereum Gas Station Network (GSN).*[1] The GSN attempts to work around this inability to pay fees with custom tokens by way of a layer-2 solution, where a network of relay servers accepts fee-less *meta-transactions* off-chain and submits them, with payment, to the Ethereum network. In return for this service, the GSN may accept payment in other denominations, such as custom tokens. Meta-transactions have the downside that in order to remove trust from intermediaries, custom infrastructure in *every* smart contract that wants to accept transactions via the GSN is needed. This has the serious downside that GSN users are only able to engage with the subset of the ledger state that explicitly acknowledges the GSN network. Beyond reducing the scope of GSN transactions, this introduces additional complexity on smart contract development including the fact that participating smart contracts must be pre-loaded with funds to pay the GSN intermediaries for their services.

Motivated by the above, we describe a solution that lifts this second limitation of custom tokens entirely and without requiring any modification to smart contract design. More specifically, we introduce the concept of *babel fees,* where fee payment is possible in any denomination that another party values sufficiently to pay the actual transaction fee in the primary currency. Our requirements for babel fees go beyond what GSN offers and are summarized as follows: (1) participants that create a babel fee transaction should be able to create a normal transaction, which will be included in the ledger exactly as is (i.e., no need for meta-transactions or specially crafted smart contract infrastructure) and (2) the protocol should be non-interactive in the sense that a single message from the creator of a transaction to the participant paying the fee in the primary currency should suffice. In other words, we want transaction creation and submission to be structurally the same for transactions with babel fees as for regular transactions.

Our implementation of babel fees is based on a novel ledger mechanism, which we call *limited liabilities.* These are negative token amounts (debt if you like) of strictly limited lifetime. Due to the limited lifetime of liabilities, we prevent any form of inflation (of the primary currency and of custom tokens).

Transactions paid for with babel fees simply pay their fees with primary currency obtained by way of a liability. This liability is combined with custom tokens offered to any party that is willing to cover the liability in exchange for receiving the custom tokens. In the first instance, this allows block producers to

---

[1] https://docs.opengsn.org/.

process transactions with babel fees by combining them with a second fee paying transaction that covers the liability and collects the offered custom tokens. More generally, more elaborate matching markets can be set up.

We describe native custom tokens and liabilities in the context of the UTXO ledger model. However, our contribution is more general and we sketch in the unabridged version [7, Appendix C] how it can be adapted for an account-based ledger. In summary, this paper makes the following contributions:

- We introduce the concept of *limited liabilities* as a combination of negative values in multi-asset token bundles with batched transaction processing (Sect. 2).
- We introduce the concept of *babel fees* on the basis of limited liabilities as a means to pay transaction fees in tokens other than a ledger's primary currency (Sect. 2).
- We present formal ledger rules for an UTXO multi-asset ledger with limited liabilities (Sect. 3).
- We present a concrete spot market scheme for block producers to match babel fees (Sect. 4).
- We present a solution to the knapsack problem that block producers have to solve to maximise their profit in the presence of babel fees (Sect. 5).

We discuss related work in Sect. 6.

2   Limited Liabilities in a Multi-asset Ledger

To realise babel fees by way of liabilities, we require a ledger that supports multiple *native* assets—i.e., a number of tokens accounted for by the ledger's builtin accounting. Moreover, one of these native tokens is the *primary currency* of the ledger. The primary currency is used to pay transaction fees and may have other administrative functions, such as staking in a proof-of-stake system.

2.1   Native Custom Assets

To illustrate limited liabilities and Babel fees by way of a concrete ledger model, we use the UTXO$_{ma}$ ledger model [6]—an extension of Bitcoin's *unspent transaction output (UTXO)* model to natively support multiple assets.[2] For reference, we list the definitions of that ledger model in the unabridged paper [7, Appendix A], with the exception of the ledger rules that we discuss in the following section. To set the stage, we summarise the main points of the ledger model definitions in the following.

We consider a ledger l to be a list of transactions $[t_1, \ldots, t_n]$. Each of these transactions consists of a set of inputs *is*, a list of outputs *os*, a validity interval *vi*, a forge field *value$_{forge}$*, a set of asset policy scripts *ps*, and a set of signatures *sigs*. Overall, we have

---

[2] The UTXO$_{ma}$ ledger model is in-production use in the Cardano blockchain.

$$t = (inputs : is, outputs : os, validityInterval : vi,$$

$$forge : value_{forge}, scripts : ps, sigs : sigs)$$

The inputs refer to outputs of transactions that occur earlier on the ledger—we say that the inputs *spend* those outputs. The outputs, in turn, are pairs of addresses and values: $(addr : a, value : v)$, where $addr$ is the hash of the public key of the key pair looking that output and $value$ is the *token bundle* encoding the multi-asset value carried by the output. We don't discuss script-locked outputs in this paper, but they can be added exactly as described in [5].

Token bundles are, in essence, finite maps that map an asset ID to a quantity—i.e., to how many tokens of that asset are present in the bundle in question. The asset ID itself is a pair of a hash of the policy script defining the asset's monetary policy and a token name, but that level of detail has no relevance to the discussion at hand. Hence, for all examples, we will simply use a finite map of assets or tokens to quantities—e.g., $\{wBTC \mapsto 0.5, MyCoin \mapsto 5, nft \mapsto 1\}$ contains 0.5 wrapped Bitcoin, five *MyCoin* and one *nft*.

The *forge* field in a transaction specifies a token bundle of minted (positive) and burned (negative) tokens. Each asset occurring in the forge field needs to have its associated policy script included in the set of policy scripts ps. Moreover, the *sigs* fields contains all signatures signing the transaction. These signatures need to be sufficient to unlock all outputs spent by the transaction's inputs is. Finally, the validity interval specifies a time frame (in an abstract unit of ticks that is dependent on the length of the ledger) in which the transaction may be admitted to the ledger.

We call the set of all outputs that (1) occur in a transaction in ledger l and (2) are not spent by any input of any transaction in l the ledger's UTXO set—it constitutes the ledger's state.

2.2 Limited Liabilities

In a UTXO, the value for a specific token in a token bundle is always positive. In other words, the value component of a UTXO is always a composition of assets. It cannot include a debt or liability. We propose to *locally* change that.

Liabilities. We call a token in a token bundle that has a negative value a *liability*. In other words, for a token bundle *value* and asset a, if $value(a) < 0$, the bundle *value* includes an a-liability.

Transaction Batches. In order to prevent liabilities appearing on the ledger proper, we do not allow the state of a fully valid ledger to contain UTXOs whose value includes a liability. We do, however, permit the addition of multiple transactions *at once* to a valid ledger, as long as the resulting ledger is again fully valid; i.e., it's UTXO set is again free of liabilities. We call a sequence of multiple transactions ts, which are being added to a ledger at once, a *transaction batch*. A transaction batch may include transaction outputs with liabilities as long as those liabilities are resolved by subsequent transactions in the same batch.

Consider the following batch of two transactions:

$$t_1 = (inputs : is,$$
$$outputs : [(addr : \emptyset, value : \{T_1 \mapsto -5, T_2 \mapsto 10\}),$$
$$(addr : \kappa_1, value : \{T_1 \mapsto 5\})],$$
$$validityInterval : vi, forge : 0, scripts : \{\}, sigs : sigs)$$
$$t_2 = (inputs : \{(outputRef : (t_1, 0), key : \emptyset), i_{T_1}\},$$
$$outputs : [(addr : \kappa_2, value : \{T_2 \mapsto 10\})],$$
$$validityInterval : vi, forge : 0, scripts : \{\}, sigs : sigs')$$

The first output of transaction t_1 may be spend by anybody ($addr = \emptyset$). It contains both a liability of $-5T_1$ and an asset of $10T_2$. The second transaction t_2 spends that single output of t_1 and has a second input i_{T_1}, which we assume consumes an output containing $5T_1$, which is sufficient to cover the liability.

Overall, we are left with $5T_1$ exposed in t_1's second output and locked by κ_1 as well as $10T_2$, which t_2 exposes in its single output, locked with the key κ_2. Both transactions together take a fully valid ledger to a fully valid ledger as the liability is resolved within the transaction batch.

We have these two facts: (a) we have one transaction resolving the liability of another and (b) liabilities are not being permitted in the state of a fully valid ledger. Consequently, transaction batches with internal liabilities are either added to a ledger as a whole or all transactions in the batch are rejected together. This in turn implies that, in a concrete implementation of liabilities in a ledger on a blockchain, the transactions included in one batch always need to go into the same block. A single block, however, may contain several complete batches.

Pair Production. Liabilities in batches enable us to create transactions that temporarily (i.e., within the batch) inflate the supply of a currency. For example, consider a transaction t with two outputs o_1 and o_2, where o_1 contains $5000\,TT$ and o_2 contains $-5000\,TT$. While value is being preserved, we suddenly do have a huge amount of T at our disposal in o_1. In loose association with the somehow related phenomenon in quantum physics, we call this *pair production*—the creation of balancing positive and negative quantities out of nothing.

As all liabilities are confined to one batch of transactions only, this does not create any risk of inflation on the ledger. However, in some situations, it can still be problematic as it may violate invariants that an asset's policy script tries to enforce. For example, imagine that T is a *role token* [5] - i.e., a non-fungible, unique token that we use to represent the capability to engage with a contract. In that case, we surely do not want to support the creation of additional instances of the role token, not even temporarily.

In other words, whether to permit pair production or not depends on the asset policy of the produced token. Hence, we will require in the formal ledger rules, discussed in Sect. 3, that transactions producing a token T always engage T's asset policy to validate the legitimacy of the pair production.

2.3 Babel Fees

Now, we are finally in a position to explain the concrete mechanism underlying babel fees. The basic idea is simple: assume a transaction t that attracts a fee of x C (where C is the ledger's primary currency), which we would like to pay in custom currency T. We add an additional *babel fee output* o_{babel} with a liability to $t : o_{babel} = \{C \mapsto -x, T \mapsto y\}$. This output indicates that we are willing to pay y T to anybody who pays the x C in return. Hence, anybody who consumes o_{babel} will receive the y T, but will at the same time have to compensate the liability of $-x$ C. The two are indivisibly connected through the token bundle. Thus, we may view a token bundle that combines a liability with an asset as a representation of an atomic swap.

The transaction t can, due to the liability, never be included in the ledger all by itself. The liability $-x$ C does, however, make a surplus of x C available inside t to cover t's transaction fees.

To include t in the ledger, we need a counterparty to whom y T is worth at least x C. That counterparty batches t with a fee paying transaction t_{fee} that consumes o_{babel}. In addition, t_{fee} will have to have another input from which it derives the x C together with its own transaction fee, all out of the counterparty's assets. The transaction t_{fee} puts the y T, by itself, into an unencumbered output for subsequent use by the counterparty. Finally, the counterparty combines t and t_{fee} into a transaction batch for inclusion into the ledger.

In Sect. 4, we will outline a scheme based on Babel fees and fee paying transactions, where block producing nodes act as fee paying counterparties for transactions that offer Babel fees in the form of custom tokens that are valuable to those block producer. They do so, on the fly, in the process of block production.

2.4 Other Uses Liabilities and Liabilities on Account-Based Ledgers

Due to space constraints, we relegate a discussion of other uses of liabilities to the unabridged paper [7, Appendix B], which, in Appendix C, also describes how limited liabilities can be realised on an account-based ledger.

3 Formal Ledger Rules for Limited Liabilities

In this section, we formalise the concept of limited liabilities by building on the UTXO_{ma} ledger; i.e., the UTXO ledger with custom native tokens as introduced in existing work [6]. To add support for limited liabilities, we modify the ledger rules in three ways:

1. The original UTXO_{ma} rules are defining ledger validity by adding transactions to the ledger one by one. We extend this by including the ability to add transactions in *batches*; i.e., multiple transactions at once.
2. We drop the unconditional per-transaction ban on negative values in transaction outputs and replace it by the weaker requirement that there remain no negative values at the fringe of a batch of transactions. In other words,

liabilities are confined to occur inside a batch and are forced to be resolved internally in the batch where they are created.

3. We amend the rules about the use of policy scripts such that the script of a token T is guaranteed to be run in every transaction that increases the *supply* of T.

In this context, the supply of a token T in a given transaction t is the amount of T that is available to be locked by outputs of t. If that supply is larger than the amount of T that is consumed by all inputs of t taken together, then we regard t as increasing the supply. This may be due to forging T or due to pair production (as discussed in Sect. 2.2).

3.1 Validity

In the original UTXO$_{ma}$ ledger rules, we extend a ledger l with one transaction t at a time. In the UTXO$_{ll}$ ledger rules (UTXO$_{ma}$ with limited liabilities), we change that to add transactions in a two stage process that supports the addition of batches of transactions ts with internal liabilities:

1. We modify the definition of the *validity* of a transaction t in a ledger l from UTXO$_{ma}$, such that it gives us *conditional validity* of t in l for UTXO$_{ll}$ as defined in Fig. 1.
2. We define validity of a batch of one or more transactions ts by way of the conditional validity of the individual $t \in ts$ together with the *batch validity* of ts in ledger l.

We describe the details of these two stages in the following.

3.2 Stage 1: Conditional Validity

Conditional validity in UTXO$_{ll}$ is defined very much like full validity in UTXO$_{ma}$. Figure 1 defines the conditions for transactions and ledgers to be conditionally valid, which are mutually dependent. The definitions in Figs. 1 and 2 are based on the ledger formalisation introduced for UTXO$_{ma}$ [6]. We do not repeat this formalisation here to favour conciseness, but summarise it in the unabridged paper [7, Appendix A].

Definition 1 (Conditional validity of transactions and ledgers). *A transaction $t \in$ Tx is conditionally valid for a conditionally valid ledger $l \in$ Ledger during tick currentTick if t abides by the conditional validity rules of Fig. 1, using the auxiliary functions summarised in Fig. 2.*

A ledger $l \in$ Ledger, in turn, is conditionally valid if either l is empty or l is of the form $t::l'$ with l' being a conditionally valid ledger and t being conditionally valid for l'.

Figure 1 highlights the two changes that we are making to the UTXO$_{ma}$ rules: firstly, we struck out Rule (2), and secondly, we changed Rule (8) in two

1. **The current tick is within the validity interval**

$$\mathsf{currentTick} \in t.validityInterval$$

2. ~~**All outputs have non-negative values**~~

$$\text{For all } o \in t.outputs,\ o.value \geq 0$$

3. **All inputs refer to unspent outputs**

$$\{i.outputRef : i \in t.inputs\} \subseteq \mathsf{unspentOutputs}(l).$$

4. **Value is preserved**

$$t.forge + \sum_{i \in t.inputs} \mathsf{getSpentOutput}(i, l) = \sum_{o \in t.outputs} o.value$$

5. **No output is locally double spent**

$$\text{If } i_1, i \in t.inputs \text{ and } i_1.outputRef = i.outputRef \text{ then } i_1 = i.$$

6. **All inputs validate**

$$\text{For all } i \in t.inputs, \text{ there exists } sig \in t.sigs, \mathsf{verify}(i.key, sig, \mathsf{txId}(t))$$

7. **Validator scripts match output addresses**

$$\text{For all } i \in t.inputs, \ \mathsf{keyAddr}(i.key) = \mathsf{getSpentOutput}(i, l).addr$$

8. **Forging**
   ♦ A transaction which changes the supply —i.e., $\mathsf{changedSupply}(t, l) \neq \{\}$— is only valid if either:
   (a) the ledger l is empty (that is, if it is the initial transaction).
   (b) ♦ for every policy ID $h \in \mathsf{changedSupply}(t, l)$, there exists $s \in t.scripts$ with $h = \mathsf{scriptAddr}(s)$.

9. **All scripts validate**

$$\text{For all } s \in t.scripts,$$
$$[\![s]\!](\mathsf{scriptAddr}(s), t, \{\mathsf{getSpentOutput}(i, l) \mid i \in t.inputs\}) = \mathsf{true}$$

Fig. 1. Conditional validity of a transaction t in a ledger l permitting liabilities

places marked with ♦. The removal of Rule (2) permits liabilities in the first place. Outputs may now contain negative values and, if they do, the associated transaction is merely conditionally valid. Full validity is now conditional on resolving all liabilities from other transactions that are added in the same batch.

Moreover, the change to Rule (8) ensures that transactions that change the supply of a token under a policy s with script address h do run the policy script s, regardless of whether the change in supply is due to a non-empty forge field $t.forge$ or due to pair production. In either case, the script is guaranteed an

– output references provided by a transaction
unspentTxOutputs : Tx → Set[OutputRef]
unspentTxOutputs(t) $=$ {(txId(t), 1), . . . , (txId(id), |$t.outputs$|)}

– a ledger's UTXO set
unspentOutputs : Ledger → Set[OutputRef]
unspentOutputs([]) $=$ {}
unspentOutputs($t :: l$) $=$ (unspentOutputs(l) \ $t.inputs$) ∪ unspentTxOutputs(t)

– the outputs spent by the given set of transaction inputs
getSpentOutput : Input × Ledger → Output
getSpentOutput(i, l) $=$ $l$lookupTx($l, i.outputRef.id$).$outputs[i.outputRef.index]$

– policy IDs of assets whose amount varies
policiesWithChange : $Quantities$ × $Quantities$ → Set[PolicyID]
policiesWithChange(val_1, val_2) $=$ {$a.pid \mid a \in$ supp($val_1 - val_2$)}

– policy IDs whose supply changed in the transaction
changedSupply : Tx × Ledger → Set[PolicyID]
changedSupply(t, l) $=$
  policiesWithChange($\sum_{o \in \text{getSpentOutput}(t.inputs)} o.value^+, \sum_{o \in t.outputs} o.value^+$) ∪
  policiesWithChange($\sum_{o \in \text{getSpentOutput}(t.inputs)} o.value^-, \sum_{o \in t.outputs} o.value^-$)
  where
      $value^+(a) =$ **if** $value(a) > 0$ **then** $value(a)$ **else** 0
      $value^-(a) =$ **if** $value(a) < 0$ **then** $value(a)$ **else** 0

Fig. 2. Auxiliary validation functions

opportunity to validate that the increase in supply abides by the rules enforced by the token policy. In other words, transactions that contain supply changes that violate the associated token policy are guaranteed to be rejected.

Changed Supply. The change in supply is computed with the help of the function changedSupply(t, l) (defined in Fig. 2) that, for a given ledger l, determines all policy script hashes h that control an asset whose supply is changed by the transaction t. Such a change may be due to the minting or burning of assets in the transactions forge field $t.forge$ or it may be due to pair production, as discussed in Sect. 2.2. The function changedSupply spots supply changes by comparing the quantity of assets and asset liabilities in the inputs and outputs of a transaction. It uses the helper functions $value^+$ and $value^-$ to filter all positive (assets) and negative (liabilities), respectively, out of a token bundle.

Script Validation. Rule (8) uses the set of hashes of policy scripts computed by changedSupply to check that all the corresponding scripts are included in the $t.scripts$ field. The scripts in $t.scripts$ are exactly those that Rule (9) executes.

Note that the primary currency of the ledger may require a special case in this rule. The total supply of the primary currency may be constant as part of the ledger implementation, and therefore its minting policy will always fail to validate, even in the case of producing and consuming transient debt. This may be addressed in (among others) one of the following ways: either modify the policy to specifically allow pair production of the primary currency, or modify this rule to not check the primary currency policy at all.

3.3   Stage 2: Batch Validity

For a ledger to be valid, we require that it is conditionally valid and that its state (i.e., the set of unspent outputs) does not contain any negative quantities.

Definition 2 (Ledger validity). *A ledger l : Ledger is* (fully) valid *if l is conditionally valid and also, for all, $o \in$ unspentOutputs$(l), o.value \geq 0$.*

On that basis, we define the validity of a batch of transactions ts for a valid ledger l.

Definition 3 (Validity of a batch of transactions). *A batch of transactions ts : List[Tx] is* (fully) valid *for a valid ledger l : Ledger if ts ++ l is a fully valid ledger.*

4   Implementing Babel Fees

In this section, we describe a concrete spot market, where users can exchange custom tokens via the babel fees mechanism described in Sect. 2.3. This spot market comprises a set of *sellers* $\mathbb{S} = \{s_1, s_2, ..., s_n\}$ and a set of *buyers*[3] $\mathbb{B} = \{b_1, b_2, ..., b_m\}$. Sellers sell bundles of custom tokens to buyers, who in return provide primary tokens to cover the fees incurred by the transactions submitted by the sellers to the network.

4.1   Babel Offers

In this context, a transaction with a babel fee output (as per Sect. 2.3) essentially constitutes an offer—specifically, the offer to obtain a specified amount of custom tokens by paying the liability in primary tokens included in the babel fee output. We define such offers as follows.

Definition 4. *We define a* babel offer *to be a tuple of the form:*

$$BabelOffer \stackrel{\text{def}}{=} (Tx_{id}, TName, TAmount, Liability)$$

where Tx_{id} is a unique identifier of the transaction containing the babel fee output, $TName$ is a string corresponding to the name of a custom token, $TAmount$

---

[3] Buyers in this market are the *block issuers* of the blockchain.

is a positive integer $\in \mathbb{Z}^+$ corresponding to the amount of tokens offered and Liability is a negative integer $\in \mathbb{Z}^-$ corresponding to the amount in primary tokens that has to be paid for obtaining the tokens.

Sellers produce such babel offers, which are then published to the network and are visible to all buyers.

4.2 Exchange Rates

In our model, we assume that the spot market of babel offers operates in distinct rounds.[4] In every round, a buyer is selected from the set $\mathbb{B}$ at random. The selected buyer has the opportunity to accept some of the outstanding offers by paying the corresponding liabilities. The rational buyer chooses the offers that maximise her utility function, which we elaborate in Sect. 5.

In order to help sellers to make attractive offers, we assume that every buyer i, $i = 1, 2, ..., m$ publishes a list $L_i[(T_j, XR_j)]$ of exchange rates XR_j for every exchangeable custom token T_j, $j = 1, ..., k$. The list of exchange rates from all buyers $BL[i] = L_i$, $i = 1, ..., m$ is available to all sellers $s \in \mathbb{S}$. Note that the buyer can set $XR_j = +\infty$ if they don't accept the token.

Given a specific babel offer $g = (t_g, (\text{token}_A, \text{amount}_A, \text{liability}_A))$ offering an amount of a custom token token_A, and assuming that there is only a single buyer b with a published exchange rate for token_A equal to $XR_A = \frac{\text{token}_A}{\text{primary token}}$, an attractive offer should adhere the inequality: $\text{amount}_A \geq |\text{liability}_A| XR_A$. Naturally, an offer gets more attractive to the degree that excess tokens are offered over the minimum needed to meet the exchange rate for the liability.

4.3 Coverage

To generalise to the case where m possible buyers express an interest in token_A, we need to consider the following question: how many token_A does a seller need to offer to ensure that $P\%$ buyers consider the offer attractive?

The seller has to choose the cheapest P_{th} percentile from the available exchange rates listed for token_A, which by definition is satisfied by an effective exchange rate that is greater than $P\%$ of the published exchange rates. In other words, for the offer g from above to be attractive to $P\%$ of buyers, the seller needs to choose the amount for token_A as follows:

$$\text{amount}_A \geq |\text{liability}_A| percentile(P, \text{token}_A, BL) \tag{1}$$

where $percentile(P, \text{token}_A, BL)$ is the lowest exchange rate for token_A, such that it is still greater than $P\%$ of the exchange rates listed for that token in the exchange rate table BL. In this case, we say that the offer g has $P\%$ *coverage*.

For example, assume a liability of 0.16 primary tokens and a set of 10 buyers with the following published exchange rates for token_A, $BL_{\text{token}_A} = \{1.63, 1.38, 3.00, 1.78, 2.00, 1.81\}$. If a seller wants to ensure that more than 70%

---

[4] In practice this can be the block-issuing rounds.

of the buyers will consider her offer, she computes the 70th percentile of the exchange rates, which is 2.00. Thus, the seller knows that she has to offer at least $0.16 \times 2.00 = 0.32$ of $token_A$.

4.4 Liveness

Consider a babel offer that is published to the network and assume that there is *at least one party* b_i (buyer) that is attracted by this offer. The interested party will then create a transaction batch t_{xb} (see Sect. 2.2) that covers the liability and will publish it to the network with the expectation that this will (eventually) be included into a block and be published in the ledger implemented by the blockchain. Therefore, it is crucial to ensure *censorship resilience* for our Babel offers and show that our spot market for Babel offers enjoys the property of *liveness* [10].

If b_i is selected as a block issuer, then she will include the transaction batch in the block she will create and thus liveness is preserved. However, if b_i is never selected as a block issuer (or is selected with a very low probability), then we must ensure the accepted offer will eventually be included into the blockchain. In the following analysis, we distinguish between two cases: a) The case where all buyers are acting rationally (but not maliciously) and b) the case where a percent of the buyers are controlled by a malicious adversary party. Our detailed analysis is presented in the paper's unabridged version [7, Appendix D] and has shown that our spot market indeed enjoys liveness, if the buyers are rational players trying to maximize their profit. Moreover, in the case of adversary players, if honest majority holds and a Babel offer attracts at least one honest player, then the accepted offer will be (eventually) published in the blockchain and thus liveness is preserved.

5   Transaction Selection for Block Issuers

A block issuer constructs a block of transactions by choosing from a set of available transactions called the *mempool*. A rational block issuer tries to maximize her utility. In our case, we assume that this utility is a value, corresponding to the amount of primary currency earned by this block. These earnings come from the transaction fees paid either in primary currency or custom tokens. Hence we assume the existence of a utility function of the form: $utility::CandidateBlock \rightarrow Value$, where $CandidateBlock$ is a list of transactions $CandidateBlock \overset{\text{def}}{=} List[CandidateTransaction]$ and $Value$ is an amount $\in \mathbb{Z}^+$ of primary currency at the lowest denomination.

5.1   The Value of Babel Offers

A candidate transaction residing in the mempool and waiting to be included in a block can be either a (single) transaction or a transaction batch (see Sect. 2.2). In the following, we define the concept of a *candidate transaction*:

Definition 5. *A candidate transaction residing in the mempool is defined as quadruple:*

$$Candidate\,Transaction \stackrel{\text{def}}{=} (Tx_{id},\ Value,\ Liability,\ Size)$$

where Tx_{id} is a unique identifier of a transaction (or a transaction batch) in the mempool, Value for the case of transactions corresponds to the transaction fees expressed in the primary currency, while for the case of transaction batches, it corresponds to the total value of the obtained custom tokens expressed as an amount in the primary currency. In the case of transaction batches, Liability $\in \mathbb{Z}^-$ is the amount expressed in the primary currency that has to be paid for covering this liability. In the case of transactions, it equals zero. Finally, Size is the total size of the transaction, or the transaction batch as a whole, expressed in bytes.

We assume the existence of a function that can transform a Babel offer (Definition 4) into a candidate transaction batch: $batchVal::BabelOffer \rightarrow CandidateTransaction$. We need this function in order to be able to express the value of the obtained custom tokens in primary currency, so that Babel offers are comparable to the transaction fees of conventional transactions. Any such conversion function might be chosen by the block issuer based on her business logic of how to evaluate a specific offer. In particular, one reasonable approach to defining the conversion function is the following:

$$Value = \sum_{\forall token \in BabelOffer} TAmount \frac{nominalVal}{|Liability\ per\ token|} nominalVal$$

$$= \sum_{\forall token \in BabelOffer} \frac{(TAmount \times nominalVal)^2}{|Liability|}$$

The nominal value of the token, $nominalVal$, is essentially the current rate $\frac{primary\ currency}{custom\ token}$; i.e., it expresses what amount of primary currency one custom token is worth. Therefore, if the exchange rate between a custom token T and the primary currency A is 3:1, then $\mathtt{nominalVal} = 0.33A$. Of course, this rate is dynamic and it is determined by market forces just like with fiat currencies and Bitcoin fees. We assume that this information is available to the block producer, when they need to select candidate transactions from the mempool to include in a new block. In fact, block issuers can publish exchange rates for specific tokens they consider acceptable (as discussed in see Sect. 4). Intuitively, the higher the nominal value, the more valuable the token is to the block issuer.

Hence, whenever a block issuer tries to assemble a block they face the following optimization problem:

Definition 6. *The transaction selection problem $TxSelection(n, S_B, M, R)$ is the problem of filling a candidate block of size S_B, with a subset $B_n \subseteq M$ of n available candidate transactions $M = \{tx_1, tx_2, ..., tx_n\}$, where we use $B_n \subseteq \{1, 2, .., n\}$, without spending more than a reserve R of available primary currency on liabilities, in such a way that $utility(B_n) \geq utility(B'_n) \ \forall$ block $B'_n \subseteq M$. Every candidate transaction $tx_i = (i, v_i, l_i, s_i)$, for $i = 1, ..., n$ is defined according to Definition 5 and has a fixed liability l_i and size s_i in bytes. We assume that the value of a candidate transaction that corresponds* *to a Babel offer is not fixed; instead, it decreases (just as its desirability) as we select candidate transactions offering the same custom token for the block. Thus, the value v_i of a candidate transaction is expressed as a function of what has already been selected for the block, $v_i(B_{i-1}) : CandidateBlock \rightarrow Value$, where $B_{i-1} \subseteq \{1, 2, ..., i-1\}$ and $v_i(\emptyset) = v_{io}$ is the initial value of the offer and $0 \leq v_i(B_{i-1}) \leq v_{oi}$. Finally, the* utility *function that we want to maximize is defined as utility* $= \sum_{i \in B_n} v_i(B_{i-1})$, *where B_{i-1} is the solution to the* $TxSelection(i-1, S_B - \sum_{j=i}^{n} s_j, M - \{i, ..., n\}, R - \sum_{j=i}^{n} l_j)$ *problem.*

5.2 Dynamic Programming

We start with the presentation of an optimal solution to the transaction selection problem. It is a variation of the dynamic programming solution to the 0–1 knapsack problem [9]. It is important to note that we want conventional transactions and transaction batch offers to be comparable *only* with respect to the value offered and their size. We do not want to view liability as another constraint to the knapsack problem, because this would favor zero liability candidate transactions (i.e., conventional transactions) over Babel offers. The liability aspect of the offer has already been considered in the value calculation of the conversion function from a `BabelOffer` to a `CandidateTransaction`, as shown in the indicative conversion formula above.

5.3 Optimal Algorithm of the Transaction Selection Problem

The optimal algorithm presented in Algorithm 1 proceeds as follows. Initially, we order the candidate transactions of M in descending order of their (initial) value per size ratio $v_{io}/s_i, i = 1, 2, ...n$. We maintain an array $U[i], i = 1, 2, ...n$. Each entry $U[i]$ is a list of tuples of the form (t_s, t_v, r, b). A tuple (t_s, t_v, r, b) in the list $U[i]$ indicates that there is a block B assembled from the first i candidate transactions that uses space exactly $t_s \leq S_B$, has a total value exactly $utility(B) = t_v \leq \sum_{i=1}^{n} v_{oi}$, has a residual amount of primary currency to be spent on liabilities exactly $r \leq R$ and has a *participation bit* b indicating if transaction i is included in B, or not.

This list does not contain all possible such tuples, but instead keeps track of only the most efficient ones. To do this, we introduce the notion of one tuple *dominating* another one; a tuple (t_s, t_v, r, b) dominates another tuple (t'_s, t'_v, r', b'), if $t_s \leq t'_s$ and $t_v \geq t'_v$; that is, the solution indicated by the tuple (t_s, t_v, r, b) uses no more space than (t'_s, t'_v, r', b'), but has at least as much value. Note that domination is a transitive property; that is, if (t_s, t_v, r, b) dominates (t'_s, t'_v, r', b') and (t'_s, t'_v, r', b') dominates (t''_s, t''_v, r'', b''), then (t_s, t_v, r, b) also dominates (t''_s, t''_v, r'', b''). We will ensure that in any list, no tuple dominates another one; this means that we can assume each list $U[i]$ is of the form $[(t_{s1}, t_{v1}, r_1, b_1), ..., (t_{sk}, t_{vk}, r_k, b_k)]$ with $t_{s1} < t_{s2} < ... < t_{sk}$ and $t_{v1} < t_{v2} < ... < t_{vk}$. Since every list $U[i], i = 1, 2, ..., n$ does not include dominating tuples and also the sizes of the transactions are integers and so are their values, then we can see that the maximum length of such a list is $min(S_B + 1, V_o + 1)$, where $V_o = \sum_{i=1}^{n} v_{oi}$.

Algorithm 1 starts out with the initialization of list $U[1]$ (line 2) and then iterates through all $n-1$ transactions (lines 3–10). In each iteration j, we initially set $U[j] \longleftarrow U[j-1]$ after turning off the participation bit in all tuples (lines 4–5). Then for each tuple $(t_s, t_v, r, b) \in U[j-1]$, we also add the tuple $(t_s + s_j, t_v + v_j(B_{j-1}), r - l_j, 1)$ to the list, if $t_s + s_j \le S_B \wedge r - l_j \ge R$; that is, if by adding transaction j to the corresponding subset, we do not surpass the total available size S_B and do not deplete our reserve R for liabilities (lines 6–9). Note that the value of transaction j at this point is determined by the contents of the corresponding block B_{j-1} through the function call $v_j(B_{j-1})$. To this end, in lines 14–22 we provide a function that returns the block corresponding to a specific tuple. We finally remove from $U[j]$ all dominated tuples by sorting the list with respect to their space component, retaining the best value for each space total possible, and removing any larger space total that does not have a corresponding larger value (line 10). We return the maximum total value from the list $U[n]$ along with the corresponding block B_n (lines 11–13).

Algorithm 1: Transaction selection algorithm for a block (Optimal Solution).

Input: A set M of candidate transactions $M = \{tx_1, tx_2, ..., tx_n\}$, where
$\quad\quad tx_i = (i, v_i(B_{i-1}), l_i, s_i)$ for $i = 1, ..., n$ according to Definition 5
Input: An amount of primary currency available for covering liabilities, called the reserve R.
Input: An available block size S_B
Input: A utility function $util = \sum_{i \in B_n} v_i(B_{i-1})$
Output: $(B, util(B), res)$: A candidate block $B \subseteq M$ such that
$\quad\quad util(B) > util(B') \forall B' \subseteq M$, the value of this block $(util(B))$ and a residual
$\quad\quad$ amount res from the reserve R such that $res \ge 0$

```
   /* Assume array U[i]: Array[List[(Size, Value, Liability, Bit)]], i = 1,...n    */
 1 order transactions in M in descending order of v_io/s_i, i = 1, 2..., n
 2 U[1] ⟵ [(0, 0, R, 0), (s_1, v_1o, R − l_1, 1)]
 3 for j = 2 to n do
 4     baseList ⟵ copy list U[j − 1] with zero participation bits for all tuples
 5     U[j] ⟵ baseList
 6     foreach (t_s, t_v, r, b) ∈ baseList do
 7         if t_s + s_j ≤ S_B ∧ r − l_j ≥ R then
 8             B_{j−1} ⟵ getBlock(U, j − 1, t_s)
 9             Add tuple (t_s + s_j, t_v + v_j(B_{j−1}), r − l_j, 1) to U[j]
10     Remove dominating pairs from list U[j]
11 (S_final, V_max, residual, b) ⟵ max_{(s,v,r)∈U[n]}(v)
12 B_n ⟵ getBlock(U, n, S_final)
13 return (B_n, V_max, residual)
   // ------------------------------------------------------------
14 getBlock(U: Array[List[(Size, Value, Liability, Bit)]], n:Tx_id, t_sn: Size) return
   CandidateBlock
15 B ⟵ []
16 t_s ⟵ t_sn
17 for i = n down to 1 do
18     (t_si, t_vi, r_i, b_i) ⟵ getTuple(U[i], t_s)
19     if b_i == 1 then
20         B ⟵ i : B  // ":" is list construction
21         t_s ⟵ t_s − t_si
22 return B
```

Theorem 1. *Algorithm 1 correctly computes the optimal value for the transaction selection problem.*

The proof of the theorem is contained in the unabridged paper [7, Appendix E].

5.4 Polynomial Approximation

Since we iterate through all available n transactions and in each iteration we process a list of length $min(S_B + 1, V_o + 1)$, where $V_o = \sum_{i=1}^{n} v_{oi}$, we can see that Algorithm 1 takes $O(n \ min(S_B, V_o))$ time. This is not a polynomial-time algorithm, since we assume that all input numbers are encoded in binary; thus, the size of the input number S_B is essentially $log_2 S_B$, and so the running time $O(nS_B)$ is exponential in the size of the input number S_B, not polynomial. Based on the intuition that if the maximum value V_o was bounded by a polynomial in n, the running time will indeed be a polynomial in the input size, we now propose an approximation algorithm for the transaction selection problem that runs in polynomial time and is based on a well-known fully polynomial approximation scheme of the 0–1 knapsack problem [13].

The basic intuition of the approximation algorithm is that if we round the (integer) values of the candidate transactions to $v_i'(B_{i-1}) = \lfloor v_i(B_{i-1})/\mu \rfloor$, where $0 \le v_i'(B_{i-1}) \le \lfloor v_{io}/\mu \rfloor = v_{io}'$ and run Algorithm 1 with values v_i' instead of v_i, then by an appropriate selection of μ, we could bound the maximum value $V_o' = \sum_{i=1}^{n} v_{io}'$ by a polynomial in n and return a solution that is at least $(1 - \epsilon)$ times the value of the optimal solution (OPT). In particular, if we choose $\mu = \epsilon v_{omax}/n$, where v_{omax} is the maximum value of a transaction; that is, $v_{omax} = max_{i \in M}(v_{oi})$. Then, for the total maximum value V_o', we have $V_o' = \sum_{i=1}^{n} v_{io}' = \sum_{i=1}^{n} \lfloor \frac{v_{io}}{\epsilon v_{omax}/n} \rfloor = O(n^2/\epsilon)$. Thus, the running time of the algorithm is $O(n \ min(S_B, V_o')) = O(n^3/\epsilon)$ and is bounded by a polynomial in $1/\epsilon$. Algorithm 2 contains our approximate algorithm for the transaction selection problem. Essentially, we run Algorithm 1 for the problem instance TxSelection(n, S_B, M', R), where $M' = \{tx_1', tx_2', ..., tx_n'\}$, and $tx_i' = (i, v_i'(B_{i-1}), l_i, s_i)$ for $i = 1, ..., n$ We can now prove that this algorithm returns a solution whose value is at least $(1 - \epsilon)$ times the value of the optimal solution.

Theorem 2. *Algorithm 2 provides a solution which is at least $(1 - \epsilon)$ times the value of OPT.*

The proof of the theorem is in the unabridged paper [7, Appendix F].

6   Related Work

Babel fees are enabled by swap outputs based on limited-lifetime liabilities. These swaps, once being proposed (as part of a complete transaction), can be resolved unilaterally by the second party accepting the swap as elaborated in the unabridged paper [7, Appendix B].

Algorithm 2: Transaction selection algorithm for a block (Approximate Solution).

Input: A set M of candidate transactions $M = \{tx_1, tx_2, ..., tx_n\}$, where
$\quad tx_i = (i, v_i(B_{i-1}), l_i, s_i)$ for $i = 1, ..., n$ according to Definition 5
Input: An amount of primary currency available for covering liabilities, called the reserve R.
Input: An available block size S_B
Input: A utility function $util = \sum_{i \in B_n} v_i(B_{i-1})$
Input: The acceptable error ϵ from the optimal solution, where $0 < \epsilon < 1$
Output: $(B, util(B), res)$: A candidate block B such that $util(B) > util(B') \forall B' \subseteq M$, the
$\qquad$ value of this block $(util(B))$ and a residual amount res from the reserve R such
$\qquad$ that $res \geq 0$

1 $v_o max \longleftarrow max_{i \in M}(v_{oi})$
2 $\mu \longleftarrow \epsilon v_{omax}/n$
3 $v_i'(B_{i-1}) \longleftarrow \lfloor v_i(B_{i-1})/\mu \rfloor$ for $i = 1, 2, ..., n$
4 run Algorithm 1 for the problem instance $\texttt{TxSelection}(n, S_B, M', R)$, where
$\quad M' = \{tx_1', tx_2', ..., tx_n'\}$, and $tx_i' = (i, v_i'(B_{i-1}), l_i, s_i)$ for $i = 1, ..., n$

Atomic Swaps and Collateralized Loans. Atomic swaps (which may be used to pay for fees) often go via an exchange, including for Ethereum ERC-20 tokens [15] and Waves' custom natives [22], as well as multi-blockchain exchanges based on atomic swaps [12,14]. These exchanges come in varying degrees of decentralisation. Atomic swaps are also used for swapping or auctioning assets across chains [11,16]. Our proposal is fully decentralized and single-chain. It allows transactions carrying swap or fee-coverage offers to be disseminated directly via the blockchain network (because they are fully-formed transactions), without any off-chain communication.

A notable difference between our swap mechanism and some layer-2 DEX solutions, such as Ethereum's Uniswap [21] and SwapDEX [19], is that these require proof of liquidity (i.e. assets locked in a contract), as well as contract-fixed exchange rates. Our proposal enables users to accept the optimal number of exchange offers without an obligation to have liquidity or to accept them. Users are also free to choose and change their exchange rates at any time, without on-chain actions.

Our limited-lifetime liabilities are a sort of loan, but one that is resolved before it is even recorded on the ledger. There is also work on ledger-based loans [4,20], but this leads to rather different challenges and mechanisms. In particular, the liabilities we propose do not require collateral backing (as they are resolved within a single batch). Moreover, unlike either atomic swaps or collateralized loans, our mechanism requires no actions from the user after submitting a swap offer or fee-less transaction to the network.

These mechanisms, while having some capacity to address some of the same shortcomings as the babel fees mechanism, are usually a combination of off-chain solutions and layer-2 (via smart contracts) are quite different from the single-chain, ledger-integrated proposal we provided.

Child Pays for Parent. The UTXO model enforces a partial ordering on transactions that can be taken advantage of to encourage block producers to include less desirable (smaller-fee) transactions in a block by also disseminating a higher-fee transaction that depends on the undesirable transaction. This is known as a child-pays-for-parent technique [17]. Like ours, it deals with fully formed transactions, and requires no further input from the author of the small-fee transaction. The solution we propose, however, is geared towards a ledger model where transaction validation rules enforce a minimum fee, so any transaction that does not pay it (via liabilities or directly) will be rejected regardless of whether a high-fee transaction depends on it.

Ethereum. Ethereum's Gas Station Network (GSN) [1] infrastructure consists of (a) a network of nodes listening for meta-transactions (transaction-like requests to cover transaction fees), which turn these requests into complete transactions, with fees covered by the relay node, and (b) an interface that contracts must implement in order for the relay nodes to use this contract's funds to subsidize the transaction fees.

Babel fees are simpler as they don't require the following (all of which the GSN relies on): (1) disseminating of partially formed (meta-)transactions on a separate network, (2) adding infrastructure, such as relays, relay hubs, and a separate communication network, (3) any changes to smart contracts to allow them to participate, (4) submitting transactions to make or update fee-covering or exchange offers, (5) any further action from the user after submitting a transaction that requires its fees to be covered, and (6) pre-paying for the fee amounts contracts are able to cover.

Another solution for processing transactions without any primary currency included to cover fees, called Etherless Ethereum Tokens, is proposed in [3]. This approach includes a formal composability framework (including formal proofs of important properties), requires notably less gas consumption, and offers a much more seamless user experience than the GSN. However, it still relies on the off-chain dissemination of meta-transactions, and requires changes to smart contracts to opt in to participation, as well as fix an exchange rate.

Algorand. Algorand is an account-based cryptocurrency which supports custom native tokens. It provides users with a way to perform atomic transfers (see [2]). An atomic transfer requires combining unsigned transactions into a single group transaction, which must then be signed by each of the participants of each of the transactions included. This design allows users to perform, in particular, atomic swaps, which might be used to pay fees in non-primary currencies.

As with our design, the transactions get included into the ledger in batches. Unlike Babel fees, however, incomplete transactions cannot be sent off to be included in the ledger without any further involvement of the transaction author.

Debt Representation in UTXO Blockchains. There are similarities between the debt representation proposal presented in [8] and the mechanism we propose, the main one being the idea of representing debt as special inputs on an UTXO ledger. Unlike the debt model we propose, the model presented in that paper allows debt to be recorded in a persistent way on the ledger. As we prevent liabilities to ever enter the ledger state, we side step the main issues discussed in [8], including the need for managing permissions for issuing debt on the ledger, and therefore also for the trust users may be obligated to place in the debt issuer, and vice-versa. The possibility of unresolved debt remaining on the ledger (and therefore inflation) is a concern that needs to be taken seriously in this case.

Debt recorded on the ledger state (and outside a transaction batch) enables functionality that we cannot support with limited liabilities. Moreover, if a debt-creating transaction is complete and ready to be applied to the ledger, all nodes are able to explicitly determine the validity of this transaction. This way, these transaction can be relayed by the existing network, without any special consideration for their potential to be included in a batch, and by who.

Another key difference between the two proposals is that ours assumes an underlying multi-asset ledger, so that the debt-outputs have another major interpretation—they also serve as offers for custom token fee coverage, as well as swaps. Finally, the ledger we propose treats debt outputs and inputs in a uniform way, rather than in terms of special debt transactions and debt pools, which result in potentially complicated special cases.

Stellar DEX. The Stellar system [18] supports a native, ledger-implemented DEX to provide swap functionality (and therefore, custom token fee payment).

In the Stellar DEX, offers posted by users are stored on the ledger. A transaction may attempt an exchange of any asset for any other asset, and will fail if this exchange is not offered. This approach requires submitting transactions to manage a user's on-chain offers, and also requires all exchanges to be exact—which means no overpaying is possible to get one's bid selected. A transaction may attempt to exchange assets that are not explicitly listed as offers in exchange for each other on the DEX. The DEX, in this case, is searched for a multi-step path to exchanging these assets via intermediate offers. This is not easily doable using the approach we have presented.

A DEX of this nature is susceptible to front-running. In our case, block issuers are given a permanent advantage in resolving liability transactions over non-block-issuing users. Among them, however, exactly one may issue the next block, including the liabilities they resolved.

References

1. Weiss, Y., Tirosh, D., Forshtat, A.: EIP-1613: Gas stations network (2018). https://eips.ethereum.org/EIPS/eip-1613
2. Algorand Team: Algorand Developer Documentation (2021). https://developer.algorand.org/docs/
3. Andrews, J., Ciampi, M., Zikas, V.: Etherless ethereum tokens: simulating native tokens in ethereum. Cryptology ePrint Archive, Report 2021/766 (2021). https://ia.cr/2021/766

4. Black, M., Liu, T., Cai, T.: Atomic loans: cryptocurrency debt instruments (2019)
5. Chakravarty, M.M.T., et al.: Native custom tokens in the extended UTXO model. In: Margaria, T., Steffen, B. (eds.) ISoLA 2020. LNCS, vol. 12478, pp. 89–111. Springer, Cham (2020). https://doi.org/10.1007/978-3-030-61467-6_7
6. Chakravarty, M.M.T., et al.: UTXO$_{ma}$: UTXO with multi-asset support. In: Margaria, T., Steffen, B. (eds.) ISoLA 2020, Part III. LNCS, vol. 12478, pp. 112–130. Springer, Cham (2020). https://doi.org/10.1007/978-3-030-61467-6_8
7. Chakravarty, M.M.T., Karayannidis, N., Kiayias, A., Peyton Jones, M., Vinogradova, P.: Babel fees via limited liabilities. arXiv:2106.01161 (2021)
8. Chiu, M., Kalabić, U.: Debt representation in UTXO blockchains. In: Financial Cryptography and Data Security 2021 (2021)
9. Cormen, T.H., Leiserson, C.E., Rivest, R.L., Stein, C.: Introduction to Algorithms, 3rd edn. The MIT Press, Cambridge (2009)
10. Garay, J., Kiayias, A., Leonardos, N.: The bitcoin backbone protocol: analysis and applications. In: Oswald, E., Fischlin, M. (eds.) EUROCRYPT 2015. LNCS, vol. 9057, pp. 281–310. Springer, Heidelberg (2015). https://doi.org/10.1007/978-3-662-46803-6_10
11. Herlihy, M.: Atomic cross-chain swaps (2018)
12. IDEX Team: IDEX documentation (2021). https://docs.idex.io/
13. Kellerer, H., Pferschy, U., Pisinger, D.: Knapsack Problems. Springer, Heidelberg (2004). https://doi.org/10.1007/978-3-540-24777-7
14. Komodo Team: AtomicDEX documentation (2021). https://developers.komodoplatform.com/basic-docs/atomicdex/
15. Kyber Team: Kyber: An On-Chain Liquidity Protocol (2019). https://files.kyber.network/Kyber_Protocol_22_April_v0.1.pdf
16. Prestwich, J.: Cross-chain auctions via bitcoin double spends (2018). https://medium.com/summa-technology/summa-auction-bitcoin-technical-7344096498f2
17. Project, B.: Developer guides (2020). https://developer.bitcoin.org/devguide/
18. Stellar Development Foundation: Stellar Development Guides (2020). https://developers.stellar.org/docs/
19. SWAPDEX Team: SWAPDEX: Decentralized Finance is the Future (2020). https://swapdex.net/whitepaper/SWAPDEX.pdf
20. Team, M.: The maker protocol: MakerDAO's multi-collateral Dai (MCD) system. https://makerdao.com/en/whitepaper/. Accessed 26 May 2021
21. Team, U.: Uniswap whitepaper (2019). https://hackmd.io/@HaydenAdams/HJ9jLsfTz#%F0%9F%A6%84-Uniswap-Whitepaper
22. Waves.Exchange Team: Waves. Exchange Documentation (2021). https://docs.waves.exchange/en/waves-exchange/

FAST: Fair Auctions via Secret Transactions

Bernardo David[1], Lorenzo Gentile[1(✉)], and Mohsen Pourpouneh[2]

[1] IT University of Copenhagen, Copenhagen, Denmark
bernardo@bmdavid.com, lorg@itu.dk
[2] Copenhagen University, Copenhagen, Denmark
mohsen@ifro.ku.dk

Abstract. Sealed-bid auctions are a common way of allocating an asset among a set of parties but require trusting an auctioneer who analyses the bids and determines the winner. Many privacy-preserving computation protocols for auctions have been proposed to eliminate the need for a trusted third party. However, they lack *fairness*, meaning that the adversary learns the outcome of the auction before honest parties and may choose to make the protocol fail without suffering any consequences. In this work, we propose efficient protocols for both first and second-price sealed-bid auctions with fairness against rational adversaries, leveraging *secret* cryptocurrency transactions and public smart contracts. In our approach, the bidders jointly compute the winner of the auction while preserving the privacy of losing bids and ensuring that cheaters are financially punished by losing a *secret* collateral deposit. We guarantee that it is never profitable for rational adversaries to cheat by making the deposit equal to the bid plus the cost of running the protocol, *i.e.*, once a party commits to a bid, it is guaranteed that it has the funds and it cannot walk away from the protocol without forfeiting the bid. Moreover, our protocols ensure that the winner is determined and the auction payments are completed even if the adversary misbehaves so that it cannot force the protocol to fail and then rejoin the auction with an adjusted bid. In comparison to the state-of-the-art, our constructions are both more efficient and furthermore achieve stronger security properties, *i.e.*, fairness. Interestingly, we show how the second-price can be computed with a minimal increase of the complexity of the simpler first-price case. Moreover, in case there is no cheating, only collateral deposit and refund transactions must be sent to the smart contract, significantly saving on-chain storage.

Keywords: Cryptographic Protocols · Multiparty Computation · Financial Cryptography · Auctions · Sealed-Bid · First-Price · Second-Price · Fairness · Blockchain

B. David—This work was supported by the Concordium Foundation and by the Independent Research Fund Denmark with grants number 9040-00399B (TrA^{2}C) and number 9131-00075B (PUMA).
L. Gentile—This work was supported by the Concordium Foundation.
M. Pourpouneh—This work was supported by the Center for Blockchains and Electronic Markets funded by the Carlsberg Foundation under grant no. CF18-1112.

© Springer Nature Switzerland AG 2022
G. Ateniese and D. Venturi (Eds.): ACNS 2022, LNCS 13269, pp. 727–747, 2022.
https://doi.org/10.1007/978-3-031-09234-3_36

1   Introduction

Auctions are a common way of allocating goods or services among a set of parties based on their bids, *e.g.*, bandwidth spectrum, antiques, paintings, and slots for advertisements in the context of web search engines or social networks [17]. In the simplest form, there is a single indivisible object, and each bidder has a *private valuation* for the object. One of the main desirable properties in designing an auction is *incentive compatibility*, that is the auction must be designed in a way that the participating parties can maximize their expected utilities by bidding their true valuations of the object. According to design, the auction can be categorized into open auctions, and sealed-bid auctions [31].

We focus on the case of sealed-bid auctions, constructing protocols where parties holding a private bid do not have to rely on trusted third parties to ensure bid privacy. In a sealed bid auction, each bidder communicates her bid to the auctioneer privately. Then, the auctioneer is expected to declare the highest bidder as the winner and not to disclose the losing bids. In particular, in the sealed-bid *first-price* auction, the bidder submitting the highest bid wins the auction and pays what she bids, while in the sealed-bid *second-price* auction (*i.e.*, the Vickrey auction [41]) the bidder submitting the highest bid wins the auction but pays the amount of the second-highest bid [30]. It is well-known that in the second-price auctions bidding truthfully is a dominant strategy, but no dominant strategy exists in the case of first-price auctions. Moreover, while in both first-price and second-price auctions, a dishonest auctioneer may disclose the losing bids, the second-price auction, in particular, highly depends on trusting the auctioneer. Indeed, a dishonest auctioneer may substitute the second-highest bid with a bid that is slightly smaller than the first bid to increase her revenue. Therefore, it may not be possible or expensive to apply it in certain scenarios. As a result, constructing cryptographic protocols for auctioneer-free and transparent auction solutions is of great interest.

1.1   Our Contributions

In this paper, we propose Fair Auctions via Secret Transactions (FAST), in which there is no trusted auctioneer and where rational adversaries are always incentivized to complete protocol execution through a *secret* collateral deposit. The proposed protocol is such that each party can make sure the winning bid is the actual bid submitted by the winning party, and malicious parties can be identified, financially punished and removed from the execution (guaranteeing a winner is always determined). Our contributions are summarized as follows:

- We propose using *secret* collateral deposits dependent on private bids inputs to ensure that the optimal strategy is for parties to complete the protocol.
- (Sect. 3) We propose methods for implementing a financial punishment mechanism based on secret deposits and standard public smart contracts, which can be used to ensure the fair execution of our protocols.

– (Sects. 4) We propose cheater identifiable and publicly verifiable sealed bid auction protocols compatible with our secret deposit approach and more efficient than the state-of-the-art [3]. Our protocols are guaranteed to terminate, finding the winner, and paying the seller even if cheating occurs.

To achieve fairness in an auction setting, we require each party to provide a *secret* deposit of an amount of cryptocurrency equal to the party's private bid plus the cost of executing the protocol. In case a party is found to be cheating, a smart contract automatically redistributes cheaters' deposits among the honest parties, the cheater is eliminated and the remaining parties re-execute the protocol using their initial bids/deposits. Having a bid-dependent deposit guarantees that it is always more profitable to execute the protocol honestly than to cheat (as analyzed in Sect. 5).

However, previous works that considered the use of cryptocurrency deposits for achieving fairness (e.g. [2,6,8,9,18,29]) crucially rely on deposits being public, thus using the same approach would reveal information about the bid. To overcome this, we propose using secret deposits that keep the value of the deposit secret until cheating is detected. Moreover, this ensures that the parties have sufficient funds to bid for the object (*e.g.*, in a second-price auction, a party could bid very high just to figure out what is the second-highest price is and then claim her submitted bid was just a mistake). Our protocols are publicly verifiable, *i.e.* it is possible to prove to the smart contract (and to any third party verifier) that a party has cheated.

In relation to previous works (discussed in Sect. 1.3), we emphasize that:

– While using deposits to achieve fairness represents a well-known technique, previous works considered public deposits only.
– Public deposits are not suitable for applications such as sealed-bid auctions since in order to achieve fairness, bid-dependent deposits are required, and public deposits would reveal information about the bid. For this reason, we introduce secret deposits, which represent a novel technique.
– From a sealed bid auction perspective, our protocol improves the state-of-the-art both in terms of efficiency and security guarantees, i.e., it achieves fairness (while in previous works the adversary may learn the outcome of the auction before honest parties and abort without suffering any consequences).
– No previous work in this setting considers adaptive adversaries since it would drastically increase the complexity of the protocol. For this reason, we focus on the static adversary case only.

1.2 Our Techniques

We start with a first-price sealed-bid auction protocol that builds on a simple passively secure protocol similar to that of SEAL [3] and compile it to achieve active security. However, we not only obtain an actively secure protocol but also add cheater identification and public verifiability properties. We use these properties to add our financial punishment mechanism with secret deposits to this protocol. Even though our protocol achieves stronger security guarantees than SEAL (*i.e.*, sequential composability and fairness guarantees), it is more efficient than the SEAL protocol as shown in Sect. 6.

A Toy Example: Our protocol uses a modified version of the *Anonymous Veto Protocol* from [25] as a building block. The anonymous veto protocol allows a set of n parties $\mathcal{P}_1, \ldots, \mathcal{P}_n$ to anonymously indicate whether they want to veto or not on a particular subject by essentially securely computing the logical-OR function of their inputs. In this protocol, each party $\mathcal{P}_i$ has an input bit $d_i \in \{0, 1\}$ with 0 indicating no veto and 1 indicating veto, and they wish to compute $\bigvee_{i=1}^{n} d_i$.

As proposed in [3], this simple anonymous veto protocol can be used for auctions by having parties evaluate their bids bit-by-bit, starting from the most significant bit and proceeding to execute the veto protocol for each bit in the following way: 1. Until there is no veto, all parties only veto (input $d_i = 1$ in the veto protocol) if and only if the current bit of their bid is 1; 2. After the first veto, a party only vetoes if the bit of her bid in the last time a veto happened was 1 *and* the current bit is also 1. In other words, in this toy protocol, parties stop vetoing once they realize that there is another party with a higher bid (*i.e.*, there was a veto in a round when their own bit were 0) and the party with the highest bid continues vetoing according to her bid until the last bit. Therefore, the veto protocol output represents the highest bid. However, a malicious party can choose not to follow the protocol, altering the output.

Achieving Active Security with Cheater Identification and Public Verifiability: To achieve active security with cheater identification and public verifiability, we depart from a simple passively secure protocol and compile it into an active secure protocol using NIZKs following an approach similar to that of [26,29]. This ensures that at every round of the protocol all parties' inputs are computed according to the protocol rules, including previous rounds' inputs and outputs. However, since the generic techniques from [26,29] yield highly inefficient protocols, we carefully construct tailor-made efficient non-interactive zero-knowledge proofs for our specific protocol, ensuring it to be efficient.

Incentivizing Correct Behaviour with Secret Deposits: In order to create incentives for parties to behave honestly, a deposit based on their bids is required. However, a public deposit would leak information about the parties' bids, which have to be kept secret. Hence, we do secret deposits as discussed below and keep the amount secret unless a party is identified as a cheater, in which case the cheater's deposit is distributed among the honest parties. The cheater is then eliminated and the protocol is re-executed with the remaining parties using their initial bids/deposits so that a winner is determined. This makes it rational not to cheat both in the case of first and second-price auctions, *i.e.*, cheating always implies a lower utility than behaving honestly (see Sect. 5).

Achieving On-Chain Efficiency: In order to minimize the amount of on-chain communication, an approach based on techniques from [5] is adopted. Every time a message is sent from a given party to the other parties, all of them sign the message received and send the signature to each other. Communication is only done on-chain (through the smart contract) in case of suspected cheating.

Secret Deposits to Public Smart Contracts: Since we use secret deposits based on confidential transactions [35], we need a mechanism to reveal the value of cheating parties' deposits to the smart contract so it can punish cheaters. We do that by secret sharing trapdoor information used to reveal this value using a publicly verifiable secret sharing (PVSS) scheme [15] that allows us to prove in zero-knowledge both that the shares are valid and that they contain the trapdoor for a given deposit. These shares are held by a committee that does not act unless cheating is detected, in which case the committee members are reimbursed for reconstructing the trapdoor with funds from the cheater's deposit itself. We discuss this approach in Sect. 3. Providing alternative methods for holding these deposits is an important open problem.

1.3 Related Work

Research on secure auctions started by the work of Nurmi and Salomaa [38] and Franklin and Reiter [23] in the late 1900s. However, in these first constructions, the auctioneers open all bids at the end of the protocol, which reveals the losing bids to all parties. Since then, many sealed bid auction protocols have been proposed to protect the privacy of the losing bids, e.g., [1,4,27,32,33]. However, in most of these protocols, privacy is obtained by distributing the computation of the final outcome to a group of auctioneers.

A lot of work has been done to remove the role of the trusted parties, e.g., by Brandt [11]. In these protocols, the bidders must compute the winning bid in a joint effort through emulating the role of the auctioneer. Moreover, the seller plays a role in the auction and it is assumed that the seller has no incentive to collude with other bidding parties. However, later by Dreier *et al.* [22] it was pointed out that if the seller and a group of bidding parties collude with each other, then they can learn the bids of other parties. Besides weak security guarantees, the main drawback of the protocol proposed by Brandt [11] is that it has exponential computational and communication complexities.

There have been implementations of auctions including [10], which have been deployed in practice for the annual sugar beets auction in Denmark. Other works [36] have considered the use of rational cryptography in enhancing privacy. Finally, the current state-of-the-art in protocols for secure First-Price Sealed-Bid Auctions was achieved in SEAL [3], which we compare with our protocols in detail in Sect. 6. To the best of our knowledge, none of these works considers incentives for the parties to complete the protocol or punishment for cheaters.

An often desired feature of Secure Multiparty Computation (MPC) is that if a cheating party obtains the output, then all the honest parties should do so as well. Protocols that guarantee this are also called *fair* and are known to be impossible to achieve with dishonest majorities [16]. Recently, Andrychowicz et al. [2] (and independently Bentov & Kumaresan [8]) initiated a line of research that aims at incentivizing fairness in MPC by imposing cryptocurrency-based financial penalties on misbehaving parties. A line of work [9,18] culminating in [6] improved the performance of this approach with respect to the amount of on-chain storage and size of the collateral deposits from each party, while others obtained stronger notions of fairness [29]. However, all of these works focus on using *public* collateral deposits for incentivizing fairness, which is not possible for our application. Moreover, they rely on general-purpose MPC, while we provide a highly optimized specific purpose protocol for auctions with financial incentives. The protocols of [21,24] are also based on cryptocurrencies. The work of [24] is the closest to ours as it leverages a cryptocurrency to ensure fairness, but it relies on SGX trusted execution enclaves.

2   Preliminaries

Let $y \xleftarrow{\$} F(x)$ denote running the randomized algorithm F with input x and implicit randomness, obtaining the output y. When the randomness r is specified, we use $y \leftarrow F(x; r)$. For a set $\mathcal{X}$, let $x \xleftarrow{\$} \mathcal{X}$ denote x chosen uniformly at random from $\mathcal{X}$; and for a distribution $\mathcal{Y}$, let $y \xleftarrow{\$} \mathcal{Y}$ denote y sampled according to the distribution $\mathcal{Y}$. We denote concatenation of two values x and y by $x|y$. We denote negligible functions as $\mathrm{negl}(x)$. We denote two *computationally indistinguishable* ensembles $X = \{X_{\kappa,z}\}_{\kappa \in \mathbb{N}, z \in \{0,1\}^*}$ and $Y = \{Y_{\kappa,z}\}_{\kappa \in \mathbb{N}, z \in \{0,1\}^*}$ of binary random variables by $X \approx_c Y$. For a field $\mathbb{F}$ we denote by $\mathbb{F}[X]_{\leq m}$ the vector space of polynomials in $\mathbb{F}[X]$ of degree at most m.

2.1   Security Model and Setup Assumptions

We prove our protocol secure in the real/ideal simulation paradigm with sequential composition. This paradigm is commonly used to analyse cryptographic protocol security and provides strong security guarantees, namely that several instances of the protocol can be executed in sequence while preserving their security. To prove security, a real world and an ideal world are defined and compared. In the real world, the protocol π is executed with the parties, some of which are corrupted and controlled by the adversary $\mathcal{A}$. In the ideal world, the protocol is replaced by an ideal functionality $\mathcal{F}$ and a simulator $\mathcal{S}$ interacts with it. The ideal functionality $\mathcal{F}$ describes the behaviour that is expected from the protocol and acts as a trusted entity. A protocol π is said to securely realize the ideal functionality $\mathcal{F}$, if for every polynomial-time adversary $\mathcal{A}$ in the real world, there is a polynomial-time simulator $\mathcal{S}$ for the ideal world, such that the two worlds cannot be distinguished. In more detail, no probabilistic polynomial-time distinguisher $\mathcal{D}$ can have a non-negligible advantage in distinguishing the concatenation of the output of the honest parties and of the adversary $\mathcal{A}$ in the real world from the concatenation of the output of the honest parties (which come directly from $\mathcal{F}$) and of the simulator $\mathcal{S}$ in the ideal world. More details about this model are in [14]. Our protocol uses the Random Oracle Model (ROM). Note that adopting the UC model, as an alternative, requires to use UC-secure NIZK (instead of those described subsequently), but reduces the efficiency of the protocol. Also, previous works consider the sequential composability model only.

Adversarial Model: We consider *malicious* adversaries that may deviate from the protocol in any arbitrary way. Moreover, we consider the *static* case, where the adversary is only allowed to corrupt parties before protocol execution starts and parties remain corrupted (or not) throughout the execution. Moreover, we assume that parties have access to synchronous communication channels, *i.e.*, all messages are delivered within a given round with a known maximum delay.

Decisional Diffie Hellman (DDH) Assumption: The DDH problem consists in deciding whether $c = ab$ or $c \xleftarrow{\$} \mathbb{Z}_p$ in a tuple (g, g^a, g^b, g^c) where g is a generator of a group $\mathbb{G}$ of order p, and $a, b \xleftarrow{\$} \mathbb{Z}_p$. The DDH assumption states that the DDH problem is hard for every *PPT* distinguisher. It is well known that the DDH assumption implies the Discrete Logarithm assumption.

2.2 Building Blocks

Pedersen Commitments: Let p and q be large primes such that q divides $p-1$ and let $\mathbb{G}$ be the unique subgroup of $\mathbb{Z}_p^*$ of order q. All the computations in $\mathbb{G}$ are operations modulo p, however we omit the mod p to simplify the notation. Let g, h denote random generators of $\mathbb{G}$ such that nobody knows the discrete logarithm of h base g, *i.e.*, a value w such that $g^w = h$. The Pedersen commitment scheme [40] to an $s \in \mathbb{Z}_q$ is obtained by sampling $t \xleftarrow{\$} \mathbb{Z}_q$ and computing $, (s,t) = g^s h^t$. Hence, the commitment $, (s,t)$ is a value uniformly distributed in $\mathbb{G}$ and opening the commitment requires to reveal the values of s and t. The Pedersen commitments are additively homomorphic, *i.e.*, starting from the commitment to $s_1 \in \mathbb{Z}_q$ and $s_2 \in \mathbb{Z}_q$, it is possible to compute a commitment to $s_1 + s_2 \in \mathbb{Z}_q$, *i.e.*, $, (s_1, t_1) \cdot , (s_2, t_2) = , (s_1 + s_2, t_1 + t_2)$.

Simplified UTXO Model: In order to focus on the novel aspects of our protocol, we represent cryptocurrency transactions under a simplified version of the Bitcoin UTXO model [37]. For the sake of simplicity, we only consider operations of the "Pay to Public Key" (P2PK) output type, which we later show how to realize while keeping the values of transactions private. The formal description of the adopted simplified UTXO model is discussed in the full version [20].

Confidential Transactions: In the case of confidential transactions [35] the input and output amounts are kept secret using Pedersen commitments. However, in order to achieve public verifiability, the transactions contain a zero-knowledge proof that the sum of the inputs is equal to the sum of the outputs, and that all the outputs are between $[0, 2^l - 1]$ (which can be computed with Bullet Proofs [12]). Note that the input set In in confidential transactions can also be public, (*i.e.* In $= \{(\mathtt{id}_1, \mathtt{in}_1), \ldots, (\mathtt{id}_m, \mathtt{in}_m)\}$), as long as the outputs are kept private. In particular, confidential transactions can be formally defined by modifying the simplified UTXO model described above as follows:

- **Representing inputs and outputs:** Set In is defined as In $= \{(\mathtt{id}_1, \mathrm{com}(\mathtt{in}_1, r_{\mathtt{in}_1})), \ldots, (\mathtt{id}_m, \mathrm{com}(\mathtt{in}_m, r_{\mathtt{in}_m}))\}$ and set Out is defined as Out $= \{(\mathrm{com}(\mathtt{out}_1, r_{\mathtt{out}_1}), Addr_1), \ldots, (\mathrm{com}(\mathtt{out}_n, r_{\mathtt{out}_n}), Addr_n)\}$.

- **Generate Transaction with** In, Out: Compute $\frac{\prod_{j=1}^{n} \text{com}(\text{out}_j, r_{\text{out}_j})}{\prod_{i=1}^{m} \text{com}(\text{in}_i, r_{\text{in}_i})} = \text{com}$

$(0, \sum_{j=1}^{n} r_{\text{out}_j} - \sum_{i=1}^{m} r_{\text{in}_i})$ with $r_{\text{in}_i}, r_{\text{out}_j} \xleftarrow{\$} \mathbb{Z}_q$, include in the transaction the randomness $\sum_{j=1}^{n} r_{\text{out}_j} - \sum_{i=1}^{m} r_{\text{in}_i}$ and the range proofs π guaranteeing that $\text{out}_1, \cdots, \text{out}_n$ are between $[0, 2^l - 1]$. The resulting transaction is then represented by $\text{tx} = (\text{id}, \text{In}, \text{Out}, \text{Sig}, \sum_{j=1}^{n} r_{\text{out}_j} - \sum_{i=1}^{m} r_{\text{in}_i}, \pi)$.

- **Validate a Transaction** tx: Compute $\frac{\prod_{j=1}^{n} \text{com}(\text{out}_j, r_{\text{out}_j})}{\prod_{i=1}^{m} \text{com}(\text{in}_i, r_{\text{in}_i})} = \text{com}(s, t)$ and check if the obtained commitments is equal to $\text{com}(0, \sum_{j=1}^{n} r_{\text{out}_j} - \sum_{i=1}^{m} r_{\text{in}_i})$, guaranteeing that $\sum_{i=1}^{m} \text{in}_i = \sum_{j=1}^{n} \text{out}_j$, then check the validity of the range proofs π.

- **Spend a transaction output** Out: Parse $\text{Out} = (\text{com}(\text{out}_i, r_{\text{out}_i}), Addr_i)$. To spend Out, the commitment $\text{com}(\text{out}_i, r_{\text{out}_i}) = g^{\text{out}_i} h^{r_{\text{out}_i}}$ has to be opened by revealing out_i and r_{out_i}. Values out_i and r_{out_i} are included in a regular UTXO transaction and they are described in the full version [20]. Later on, this UTXO transaction can be validated by checking that $\text{out}_i, r_{\text{out}_i}$ is a valid opening of $\text{com}(\text{out}_i, r_{\text{out}_i})$ and following the steps of a regular UTXO transaction validation.

- **Spend a transaction output** Out **with a NIZKPoK of** r_{out_i}: Alternatively, an output $\text{Out} = (\text{com}(\text{out}_i, r_{\text{out}_i}), Addr_i)$ for which only out_i and $\hat{h} = h^{r_{\text{out}_i}}$ (but not r_{out_i}) are known can be spent if a NIZK π' proving knowledge of r_{out_i} is also available. Notice that knowing out_i is sufficient for validating the regular UTXO transaction created using Out as an input. Moreover, it can be checked that $g^{\text{out}_i} h^{r_{\text{out}_i}} = \text{com}(\text{out}_i, r_{\text{out}_i})$ given out_i and $\hat{h} = h^{r_{\text{out}_i}}$, while the proof π' guarantees that $\hat{h} = h^{r_{\text{out}_i}}$ is well formed.[1] Values out_i, $h^{r_{\text{out}_i}}$ and the proof π' are included in a regular UTXO transaction generated and they are described in the full version [20]. Later on, this UTXO transaction can be validated by checking that $g^{\text{out}_i} h^{r_{\text{out}_i}} = \text{com}(\text{out}_i, r_{\text{out}_i})$, checking that π' is valid and following the steps of a regular UTXO transaction validation.

Publicly Verifiable Secret Sharing (PVSS): In our work, we use the PVSS protocol π_{PVSS} from [15]. A PVSS protocol allows for a dealer to distribute encrypted shares to a set of parties in such a way that only one specific party can decrypt a share but any third party verifier can check that all shares are valid. Later on, each party can decrypt its corresponding share to allow for reconstruction while showing to any third-party verifier that the decrypted share corresponds to one of the initial encrypted shares. A deposit committee $\mathcal{C} = \{\mathcal{C}_1, \ldots, \mathcal{C}_m\}$ will execute this protocol verifying and decrypting shares provided as part of our secret deposit mechanism (further discussed in Sect. 3). Since the parties in $\mathcal{C}$ executing π_{PVSS} must have public keys registered as part of a setup phase, we capture this requirement in $\mathcal{F}_{SC}$ as presented in Sect. 2.2.

---

[1] In fact, showing such a proof of knowledge π' of r_{out_i} together with $h^{r_{\text{out}_i}}$ and out_i makes it easy to adapt reduction of the binding property of the Pedersen commitment scheme to the Discrete Logarithm assumption. Instead of obtaining r_{out_i} from the adversary, the reduction simply extracts it from π'.

NIZK for PVSS Share Consistency CC**:** As part of our secret deposit mechanism (further discussed in Sect. 3), we will use a NIZK showing that shares computed with the PVSS protocol π_{PVSS} from [15] encode secrets g^m and h^r that are terms of a Pedersen commitment $c = g^m h^r$. Formally, given generators $g_1, \ldots, g_n, g, h$ of a cyclic group $\mathbb{G}_q$ of prime order q, pairwise distinct elements $\alpha_1, \ldots, \alpha_n$ in $\mathbb{Z}_q$ and a Pedersen commitment $c = g^m h^r$ known by prover and verifier, for $p(x)$ and m, r known by the prover, this NIZK is used to prove that $(\hat{\sigma}_1, \ldots, \hat{\sigma}_n) \in \left\{ \left(g_1^{p(\alpha_1)}, \ldots, g_n^{p(\alpha_n)} \right) : p \in \mathbb{Z}_q[X], p(-1) = g^m, p(-2) = h^r \right\}$.
We denote this NIZK by $CC((g_i)_{i \in [n]}, (\alpha_i)_{i \in [n]}, g, h, c, (\hat{\sigma}_i)_{i \in [n]})$. Notice that this NIZK can be constructed using the techniques from [13] and integrated with the NIZK $LDEI$ (Low-Degree Exponent Interpolation) defined in π_{PVSS} [15].

Modelling a Stateful Smart Contract: We employ a stateful smart contract functionality $\mathcal{F}_{\mathsf{SC}}$ similar to that of [18] in order to model the smart contract that implements the financial punishment mechanism for our protocol. For the sake of simplicity, we assume that each instance of $\mathcal{F}_{\mathsf{SC}}$ is already parameterized by the address of the auctioneer party who will receive the payment for the auctioned good, as well as by the identities (and public keys) of the parties in a secret deposit committee $\mathcal{C}$ that will help the smart contract to open secret deposits given by parties in case cheating is detected. We also assume that $\mathcal{F}_{\mathsf{SC}}$ has a protocol verification mechanism pv for verifying the validity of protocol messages. For description of the $\mathcal{F}_{\mathsf{SC}}$ see the full version [20].

3 Secret Deposits in Public Smart Contracts

When using secret deposits as in our application, it is implied that there exists a secret trapdoor that can be used to reveal the value of such deposits (and transfer them). However, since we base our financial punishment mechanism on a standard public smart contract, we cannot expose the trapdoor to the smart contract. Instead, we propose that a committee $\mathcal{C} = \{\mathcal{C}_1, \ldots, \mathcal{C}_m\}$ with $m/2 + 2$ honest members[2] holds this trapdoor in a secret shared form. This committee does not act unless a cheating party needs to be punished and the trapdoor needs to be reconstructed to allow the smart contract to transfer her collateral deposit. In this case, the committee can be reimbursed from the collateral funds. We present a practical construction following this approach. Proposing methods for keeping custody of such secret deposits is left as an important open problem.

A Possible Solution: A feasible but not practical approach to do this would be storing the trapdoor with the mechanism proposed in [7], where a secret is kept by obliviously and randomly chosen committees by means of a proactive secret sharing scheme where each current committee "encrypts the secret to the future" in such a way that the next committee can open it. However, it is also necessary

---

[2] We need $m/2 + 2$ honest members to instantiate our packed publicly verifiable secret sharing based solution where two group elements are secret shared with a single share vector.

to ensure that the secrets actually correspond to the trapdoor for the parties' deposits. Providing such proofs with the scheme of [7] would require expensive generic zero-knowledge techniques (or a trusted setup for a zk-SNARK).

Protocol Π_C

Let $C = \{C_1, \ldots, C_m\}$ be the deposit committee members and $pk_{C_1}, \ldots, pk_{C_m}$ and $sk_{C_1}, \ldots, sk_{C_m}$ be their public keys and private keys, used to run π_{PVSS}, respectively. Moreover, let $pk'_{C_1}, \ldots, pk'_{C_m}$ and $sk'_{C_1}, \ldots, sk'_{C_m}$ be their public keys and private keys, used for signatures, respectively. The following steps are executed by $C_j \in C$:

- **Setup verification:** Upon receiving (SETUP, $sid, P_i, tx_i, pk_i, (\hat{\sigma}_{i1}, \ldots, \hat{\sigma}_{im})$, $LDEI_i, CC_i$) from P_i, C_j checks that tx_i is valid, verifies the shares $(\hat{\sigma}_{i1}, \ldots, \hat{\sigma}_{im})$ correctness with respect to the committee public keys $pk_{C_1}, \ldots, pk_{C_m}$ using the verification procedure of π_{PVSS} through $LDEI_i$ and verifies NIZK CC_i. If all the checks pass, compute the hashes $SH1_i = \mathcal{H}(tx_i, pk_i)$ and $SH2_i = \mathcal{H}((\hat{\sigma}_{i1}, \ldots, \hat{\sigma}_{im}), LDEI_i, CC_i)$ and the signature $Sig_{C_j,i} = sig_{sk'_{C_j}}(SH1_i|SH2_i)$, then send (SETUP-VERIFICATION, $sid, Sig_{C_j,i}$) to P_i.

- **Share decryption:** Upon receiving (OPEN, sid, P_i) from $\mathcal{F}_{SC}$, C_j uses the share decryption procedure from π_{PVSS} on $\hat{\sigma}_{ij}$, obtaining $\tilde{\sigma}_{ij}, DLEQ_{ij}$. and sending (SHARE-DECRYPTION, $sid, (\hat{\sigma}_{i1}, \ldots, \hat{\sigma}_{im}), LDEI_i, CC_i, \tilde{\sigma}_{ij}, DLEQ_{ij})$) to $\mathcal{F}_{SC}$.

Fig. 1. Protocol Π_C

A Protocol Based on PVSS: As an alternative, we propose leveraging the structure of our confidential transaction based deposits to secret share their openings with a recent efficient publicly verifiable secret sharing (PVSS) scheme called Albatross [15]. Notice that the secret amount information b_i in these deposits is represented as a Pedersen commitment $g^{b_i} h^{r_i}$ and that the Albatross PVSS scheme also allows for sharing a group element g^s, while proving in zero-knowledge discrete logarithm relations involving g^s in such a way that they can be verified by any third party with access to the public *encrypted* share. Hence, we propose limiting the bid b_i bit length in such a way that we can employ the same trick as in *lifted ElGamal* and have each party P_i share both g^{b_i} and h^{r_i} with the Albatross PVSS while proving that their public encrypted shares correspond to a secret deposit $g^{b_i} h^{r_i}$. The validity of this claim can be verified by the committee C itself or the smart contract during Stage 1 - Setup. Later on, if b_i needs to be recovered, C can reconstruct g^{b_i}, brute force b_i (because it has a restricted bit-length) and deliver it to the smart contract while proving it has been correctly computed from the encrypted shares. As we explain in Sect. 2, recovering b_i and g^{r_i} along with the proofs of share validity is sufficient for transferring the secret deposit.

In Fig. 1, we present Protocol Π_C followed by the committee $C = \{C_1, \ldots, C_m\}$ and executed as part of Protocols Π_{FPA} described in Sect. 4. The interaction of the other parties $P = \{P_1, \ldots, P_n\}$ executing Protocols Π_{FPA} and Π_{SPA} with the committee C is described as part of Stage 1 - Setup of these protocols.

Selecting Committees: In order to focus on the novel aspects of our constructions, we assume that the smart contract captured by $\mathcal{F}_{SC}$ described in the full version [20] is parameterized by a description of the committee $\mathcal{C} = \{\mathcal{C}_1, \ldots, \mathcal{C}_m\}$ and the public keys corresponding to each committee member. Notice that in practice this committee can be selected by the smart contract from the set of parties executing the underlying blockchain consensus protocol. The problem of selecting committees in a permissionless blockchain scenario has been extensively addressed in both Proof-of-Stake *e.g.* [19,28] and Proof-of-Work [39] settings.

4 First-Price Auctions

In this section, we introduce our protocol for first-price auctions (while the case of second-price auctions is addressed in the full version [20]). We consider a setting with n parties $\mathcal{P}_1, \ldots, \mathcal{P}_n$, where each party $\mathcal{P}_i$ has a l-bit bid $b_i = b_{i1}|\ldots|b_{il}$, where b_{ir} denotes the r-th bit of party $\mathcal{P}_i$'s bid.

Functionality $\mathcal{F}_{FPA}$

$\mathcal{F}_{FPA}$ operates with an auctioneer $\mathcal{P}_{AUC}$, a set of parties $\mathcal{P} = \{\mathcal{P}_1, \ldots, \mathcal{P}_n\}$ who have bids $b_1, \ldots, b_n$ as input and where $b_i = b_{i1}|\ldots|b_{il}$ is the bit representation of b_i, as well as an adversary $\mathcal{S}_{FPA}$. $\mathcal{F}_{FPA}$ is parameterized by a bid bit-length l and keeps an initially empty list bids.

- **Setup (Bid Registration):** Upon receiving (BID, sid, coins($b_i + work$)) from $\mathcal{P}_i$ where $b_i \in \{0,1\}^l$ and $work$ is the amount required to compensate the cost of running the protocol for all the other parties, $\mathcal{F}_{FPA}$ appends b_i to bids.
- **First-Price Auction:** After receiving (BID, sid, coins($b_i + work$)) from all parties in $\mathcal{P}$, for $r = 1, \ldots, l$ $\mathcal{F}_{FPA}$ proceeds as follows:
  1. Select b_{wr}, *i.e.*, the r-th bit of the highest bid b_w in the list bids.
  2. Send (ROUND-WINNER, sid, b_{wr}) to all parties and $\mathcal{S}_{FPA}$.
  3. Check if $b_{wr} = 1$ and $b_{ir} = 0$ for $i = 1, \ldots, n \neq w$. If so, let $r_w = r$, that is the first position where b_w has a bit 1 and the second highest bid b_{w2} has a bit 0, and send (LEAK-TO-WINNER, sid, r_w) to $\mathcal{P}_w$.
  4. Send (ABORT?, sid) to $\mathcal{S}_{FPA}$. If $\mathcal{S}_{FPA}$ answers with (ABORT, sid, $\mathcal{P}_i$) where $\mathcal{P}_i$ is corrupted, remove b_i from bids, remove $\mathcal{P}_i$ from $\mathcal{P}$, send (ABORT, sid, $\mathcal{P}_i$, coins($\frac{b_i + work}{|\mathcal{P}|}$)) where $|\mathcal{P}|$ is the number of remaining parties to all other parties in $\mathcal{P}$, set again $r = 1$ and go to Step 1. If $\mathcal{S}_{FPA}$ answers with (PROCEED, sid), if $r = l$ go to Payout, else increment r by 1 and go to Step 1.
- **Payout:** Send (REFUND, sid, $\mathcal{P}_w$, coins($b_i + work$)) to all parties $\mathcal{P}_i \neq \mathcal{P}_w$, send (REFUND, sid, coins($work$)) to $\mathcal{P}_w$, send coins(b_w) to $\mathcal{P}_{AUC}$, and halt.

Fig. 2. Functionality $\mathcal{F}_{FPA}$

Modelling Fair Auctions: First, we introduce an ideal model for fair auctions that we will use to prove the security of our protocol. For the sake of simplicity, when discussing this model, we use coins(n) to indicate n currency tokens being transferred where n is represented in binary, instead of describing a full UTXO transaction. Our ideal functionality $\mathcal{F}_{FPA}$ is described in Fig. 2. This functionality models the fact that the adversary may choose to abort but all it may learn is that it was the winner and the most significant bit where its bid differs from the second-highest bid. Regardless of adversarial actions, an auction result is always obtained and the auctioneer (*i.e.*, the party selling the asset) is always paid. The second-price case is presented in the full version [20].

The Protocol: In Figs. 3, 4, 5 and 6, we construct a Protocol Π_{FPA} that realizes $\mathcal{F}_{FPA}$. This protocol is executed by n parties $\mathcal{P}_1, \ldots, \mathcal{P}_n$, where each party $\mathcal{P}_i$ has a l-bit bid $b_i = b_{i1} | \ldots | b_{il}$ and a deposit committee $\mathcal{C} = \{\mathcal{C}_1, \ldots, \mathcal{C}_m\}$ that helps open secret deposits from corrupted parties in the Recovery Stage. The protocol consists of 4 main stages plus a recovery stage, which is only executed in case of suspected (or detected) cheating. In the first stage, every party i sends to the smart contract a secret deposit, whose structure will be explained in detail later. In the second and third stages, all parties jointly compute the maximum bid (bit-by-bit) by using an anonymous veto protocol that computes a logical OR on private inputs. To this aim, the parties start from the most significant bit position. Then, they apply the anonymous veto protocol according to their bits b_{ir}, with 0 representing a no veto and 1 representing a veto. If the outcome of the veto protocol (*i.e.*, the logical-OR of the the inputs) is 1, then each party $\mathcal{P}_i$ with input $b_{ir} = 0$ figures out that there is at least another party $\mathcal{P}_k$ whose bid b_k is higher than b_i and $\mathcal{P}_i$ discovers that she cannot win the auction. Therefore, from this point on, $\mathcal{P}_i$ stops vetoing, disregarding her actual bit b_{ir} in the next rounds. Otherwise, $\mathcal{P}_i$ is expected to keep vetoing or not according to her bit b_{ir}. Finally, in Stage 4 the winning party $\mathcal{P}_w$ executes the payment to the auctioneer (*i.e.*, the party selling the asset). Throughout all stages, the parties must provide proofs that they have correctly computed all protocol messages. If a party is identified as dishonest at any point, the Recovery Stage has to be executed.

Security Analysis: It is clear that this protocol correctly computes the highest bid. The ideal smart contract enforces payment once a winner is determined and punishments otherwise. The security of this protocol is formally stated in the following theorem. A game-theoretical analysis is presented in Sect. 5, where it is shown that the best strategy for any rational party is to follow the protocol.

Theorem 1. *Under the DDH Assumption, Protocol Π_{FPA} securely computes $\mathcal{F}_{FPA}$ in the $\mathcal{F}_{SC}$-hybrid, random oracle model against a malicious static adversary $\mathcal{A}$ corrupting all but one parties $\mathcal{P}_i \in \mathcal{P}$ and $m/2 - 2$ parties $\mathcal{C}_i \in \mathcal{C}$.*

Due to space limits, we leave the full proof to the full version [20].

5   Rational Strategies

In this section, we consider the incentives of parties in our protocols. Note that the set of bidders is fixed through the execution, *i.e.*, once the execution has started, even if it is required to re-execute the protocol, no new bid can be

---

Protocol Π_{FPA} (Off-chain messages exchange)

Protocol Π_{FPA} is executed with n parties $\mathcal{P} = \{\mathcal{P}_1, \ldots, \mathcal{P}_n\}$, where each party $\mathcal{P}_i$ has a l-bit bid $b_i = b_{i1}|\ldots|b_{il}$ and a deposit committee $\mathcal{C} = \{\mathcal{C}_1, \ldots, \mathcal{C}_m\}$. Parties $\mathcal{P}, \mathcal{C}$ interact among themselves and with a smart contract $\mathcal{F}_{\mathsf{SC}}$.

Off-chain messages exchange: To minimize the communication with the smart contract, an approach based on [5] is adopted. Let r be a generic round of the protocol, then each party $\mathcal{P}_i$ actually proceeds as follows when sending her messages:

- **Round$_r$:** each $\mathcal{P}_i$ sends $msg_{r,i}$, $sig_{sk_i}(msg_{r,i})$ to all the other parties;
- **Round$_{r+1}$:** all the other parties $\mathcal{P}_k$ for $k \in \{1, \ldots, n\} \setminus i$ sign the message received from party i and send $msg_{r,i}$, $sig_{sk_k}(msg_{r,i})$ to all the other parties, allowing them to check if party i sent no conflicting messages. Then, each party repeats from the instructions described in the previous round;
- **Conflicting messages:** in case $\mathcal{P}_i$ sends conflicting messages $msg_{r,i} \neq msg'_{r,i}$ to parties $\mathcal{P}_k \neq \mathcal{P}_{k'}$, $\mathcal{P}_k$ or $\mathcal{P}_{k'}$ send to the smart contract $msg_{r,i}$, $sig_{sk_i}(msg_{r,i})$ and $msg'_{r,i}$, $sig_{sk_i}(msg'_{r,i})$ as a proof that $\mathcal{P}_i$ was dishonest;
- **Evidence of a message:** in case it has to be proven that a message $msg_{r,i}$ has been sent by party $\mathcal{P}_i$ in round r, the other parties send to the smart contract the signatures $sig_{sk_1}(msg_{r,i}), \ldots, sig_{sk_n}(msg_{r,i})$ along with the message $msg_{r,i}$.

Fig. 3. Protocol Π_{FPA} (Off-chain messages exchange)

submitted, and it is therefore not possible to gain from the leaked information. Moreover, in case there is a cheating party, the protocols refund the honest parties with her deposit.

We now consider the utility of each party from participating in the protocol. The utility function of a generic party $\mathcal{P}_i$ in the first-price auction is $u_i^{FPA}(b_1, \ldots, b_n) = v_i - b_i$ if $b_i > \max_{j \neq i} b_j$ and 0 otherwise, while in the second-price auction is instead $u_i^{SPA}(b_1, \ldots, b_n) = v_i - \max_{j \neq i} b_j$ if $b_i > \max_{j \neq i} b_j$ and 0 otherwise, where v_i represents the $\mathcal{P}_i$'s private valuation of what is at stake in the auction. It is known that in the first-price auctions the optimal strategy for each rational party depends on their beliefs regarding other party's valuations, while in the second-price auction the optimal strategy for each party is to bid an amount equal to her valuation regardless of the strategy of other parties [31,34], i.e., $b_i = v_i$.

In case a party $\mathcal{P}_i$ is honest, she always gets her deposit $work$ back. Then, if she is the winner, she gets what is at stake in the auction and pays b_i, while if she is not the winner, she gets her entire deposit $b_i + work$ back. Therefore, by following the protocol each rational party has a non-negative utility, i.e., $u_i(b_1, \ldots, b_n) \geq 0$. However, if a party cheats her deposit $b_i + work$ is distributed among honest parties. Therefore, the utility of a cheating party, regardless of whether her bid is the highest or not, is $u_i(b_1, \ldots, b_n) = -(b_i + work) < 0$, which is strictly negative. Therefore, cheating is a dominated strategy for each party, i.e., regardless of what other players do it always results in a lower utility.

Protocol Π_{FPA} (Stage 1)

Stage 1 - Setup: Deposit committee parties $C_k \in C$ first execute the Setup Verification step of Π_C from Figure 1. All parties P_i proceed as follows:

1. P_i sends a secret deposit containing their bid b_i, change *change* and a fee *work* to the smart contract through a confidential transaction (as described in Section 2.2). Let $Addr_i$ be the address associated to party i and $Addr_s$ be the address associated to the smart contract, P_i proceeds as follows:

   (a) P_i sends (PARAM, sid) to $\mathcal{F}_{SC}$, receiving (PARAM, sid, g, h, pk_{C_1}, ..., pk_{C_m}).

   (b) P_i computes the bit commitments as $c_{ir} = g^{b_{ir}} h^{r_{ir}}$, with $r_{ir} \xleftarrow{\$} \mathbb{Z}_q$, to each bit b_{ir} of b_i, and the bid commitment as $c_i = \prod_{r=1}^{l} c_{ir}^{2^{l-r}} = g^{b_i} h^{\sum_{r=1}^{l} 2^{l-r} r_{ir}}$. Let r_{b_i} be equal to $\sum_{r=1}^{l} 2^{l-r} r_{ir}$. Then, c_i can be rewritten as $c_i = g^{b_i} h^{r_{b_i}} = \text{com}(b_i, r_{b_i})$.

   (c) Define sets $\text{In} = \{(\text{id}_i, \text{in}_i)\}$ and $\text{Out} = \{(c_i, Addr_s), (work, Addr_s), (\text{com}(change_i, r_{change_i}), Addr_i)\}$, where $c_i = \text{com}(b_i, r_{b_i})$ is the commitment to the bid b_i previously computed at Step 1, *work* is the amount required to compensate the cost of running the protocol for all the other parties in $\mathcal{P}$ and in C, $change = \text{in}_i - b_i - work$ and $r_{change} \xleftarrow{\$} \mathbb{Z}_q$. Note that, in this case case, in_i and *work* are public, while b_i and *change* are private.

   (d) Compute $r_{out} = r_{b_i} + r_{change_i}$, so as to allow the other parties later to verify that the sum of the inputs is equal to the sum of the outputs, *i.e.* $c_i \cdot \text{com}(change, r_{change}) \stackrel{?}{=} \text{com}(\text{in}_i - work, r_{out})$.

   (e) Compute proofs $(\pi_{b_i}, \pi_{change})$ showing that $b_i, change \in [0, 2^l - 1]$, set $\text{tx}_i = (\text{id}, \text{In}, \text{Out}, \text{Sig}, r_{b_i} + r_{change_i}, \pi)$.

   (f) Compute the shares $(\hat{\sigma}_{i1}, ..., \hat{\sigma}_{im}, LDEI_i)$ of g^{b_i} and $h^{r_{b_i}}$ using the distribution procedure from π_{PVSS} with $pk_{C_1}, ..., pk_{C_m}$ received in step (a).

   (g) Compute $CC_i \leftarrow CC((pk_{C_j})_{j \in [m]}, (j)_{j \in [m]}, g, h, c_i, (\hat{\sigma}_j)_{j \in [m]})$ to prove consistency among the shares $(\hat{\sigma}_{i1}, ..., \hat{\sigma}_{im})$ and the commitment terms g^{b_i} and $h^{r_{b_i}}$ from $c_i = g^{b_i} h^{r_{b_i}}$.

   (h) Send (SETUP, sid, P_i, tx_i, pk_i, $(\hat{\sigma}_{i1}, ..., \hat{\sigma}_{im})$, $LDEI_i$, CC_i) to each $C_j \in C$.

   (i) Upon receiving (SETUP-VERIFICATION, sid, $Sig_{C_j,i}$) from all $C_j \in C$, compute $SH1_i = \mathcal{H}(\text{tx}_i, pk_i)$ and $SH2_i = \mathcal{H}((\hat{\sigma}_{i1}, ..., \hat{\sigma}_{im}), LDEI_i, CC_i)$ and send (SETUP, sid, P_i, tx_i, pk_i, $SH1_i$, $SH2_i$, $Sig_{C_1,i}, ..., Sig_{C_m,i})$) to $\mathcal{F}_{SC}$. If a party $C_a \in C$ does not send this message, proceed to the Recovery Stage.

2. P_i samples $x_{ir} \xleftarrow{\$} \mathbb{Z}_q$ and computes $X_{ir} = g^{x_{ir}}$ for $r = 1, ..., l$, sending $c_{i1}, \cdots, c_{il}, X_{i1}, \cdots, X_{il}$ to all other parties.

3. Upon receiving all messages $c_{j1}, \cdots, c_{jl}, X_{j1}, \cdots, X_{jl}$ from other parties P_j, P_i computes $Y_{jk} = \prod_{m=1}^{j-1} X_{mk} / \prod_{m=j+1}^{n} X_{mk}$ for $j = 1, ..., n, k = 1, ..., l$, and verifies for each other party P_j that $c_j = \prod_{k=1}^{l} c_{jk}^{2^{l-k}}$ for $j \in \{1, ..., n\} \setminus i$. If this verification fails or a message is not received, proceed to the Recovery Stage.

Fig. 4. Protocol Π_{FPA} (Stage 1)

The above analysis shows that it is not rational for an adversary $\mathcal{A}$ controlling a single party to deviate from the protocol. Next, we show that it is also the case for an adversary $\mathcal{A}$ controlling more than one party. Let P_i, P_j be two parties controlled by $\mathcal{A}$ and let $v_{\mathcal{A}}$ be the valuation of the adversary for what is at stake

---

Protocol Π_{FPA} (Stages 2 and 3)

Stage 2 - Before First Veto: All parties $\mathcal{P}_i$, starting from the most significant bit b_{i1} and moving bit-by-bit to the least significant bit b_{il} of their bid $b_i = b_{i1}|\ldots|b_{il}$, run in each round r the anonymous veto protocol until the outcome is a veto (*i.e.*, $V_r \neq 1$) for the first time. Therefore each party $\mathcal{P}_i$ proceeds as follows:

1. Compute v_{ir} as follows: if $b_{ir} = 0$ then $v_{ir} = Y_{ir}^{x_{ir}}$; if $b_{ir} = 1$ then $v_{ir} = g^{\bar{r}_{ir}}$ where $\bar{r}_{ir} \xleftarrow{\$} \mathbb{Z}_q$. Then generate NIZK proving that v_{ir} has been correctly computed $BV_{ir} \leftarrow BV\{b_{ir}, r_{ir}, x_{ir}, \bar{r}_{ir} \mid (\frac{c_{ir}}{g^{b_{ir}}} = c_{ir} = h^{r_{ir}} \wedge v_{ir} = Y_{ir}^{x_{ir}} \wedge X_{ir} = g^{x_{ir}}) \vee (\frac{c_{ir}}{g^{b_{ir}}} = \frac{c_{ir}}{g} = h^{r_{ir}} \wedge v_{ir} = g^{\bar{r}_{ir}})\}$, sending a message (v_{ir}, BV_{ir}) to all parties.
2. Upon receiving all messages (v_{kr}, BV_{kr}) from other parties $\mathcal{P}_k$, $\mathcal{P}_i$ checks the proofs BV_{kr} for $k \in \{1, \ldots, n\} \backslash i$ and, if all checks pass, computes $V_r = \prod_{k=1}^n v_{kr}$ and then goes to Stage 3 if $V_r \neq 1$ (at least one veto), otherwise follows the steps in Stage 2 again until the round $r = l$. Note that, unless all the bids are equal to 0, at some point the condition $V_r \neq 1$ is satisfied. If a message is not received from party $\mathcal{P}_k$ or if BV_{kr} is invalid, proceed to the Recovery Stage.

Stage 3 - After First Veto: Let $\hat{r}$ denote the last round at which there was a veto (*i.e.*, $V_{\hat{r}} \neq 1$). All parties $\mathcal{P}_i$, starting from $b_{i\hat{r}+1}$ and moving bit-by-bit to the least significant bit b_{il} of their bid $b_i = b_{i1}|\ldots|b_{il}$, run in each round $r > \hat{r}$ the anonymous veto protocol taking into account both the input bit b_{ir} and the declared input bit d_{ir}, defined as the value that satisfies the logical condition $(b_{ir} = 0 \wedge d_{ir} = 0) \vee (b_{ir} = 1 \wedge d_{i\hat{r}} = 1 \wedge d_{ir} = 1) \vee (b_{ir} = 1 \wedge d_{i\hat{r}} = 0 \wedge d_{ir} = 0)$, *i.e.*, each party $\mathcal{P}_i$ vetoes at round r iff she also vetoed at round $\hat{r}$ (*i.e.*, $d_{i\hat{r}} = 1$), and her current input bit $b_{ir} = 1$. Therefore, each $\mathcal{P}_i$ proceeds as follows:

1. Compute v_{ir} as follows: if $b_{ir} = 0$, then $v_{ir} = Y_{ir}^{x_{ir}}$; if $d_{i\hat{r}} = 1 \wedge b_{ir} = 1$, then $v_{ir} = g^{\bar{r}_{ir}}$ where $\bar{r}_{ir} \xleftarrow{\$} \mathbb{Z}_q$; if $d_{i\hat{r}} = 0 \wedge b_{ir} = 1$, then $v_{ir} = Y_{ir}^{x_{ir}}$. Then generate NIZK proving that v_{ir} has been correctly computed $AV_{ir} \leftarrow AV\{b_{ir}, r_{ir}, x_{ir}, \bar{r}_{i\hat{r}}, \bar{r}_{ir}, x_{i\hat{r}} \mid (\frac{c_{ir}}{g^{b_{ir}}} = c_{ir} = h^{r_{ir}} \wedge v_{ir} = Y_{ir}^{x_{ir}} \wedge X_{ir} = g^{x_{ir}}) \vee (\frac{c_{ir}}{g^{b_{ir}}} = \frac{c_{ir}}{g} = h^{r_{ir}} \wedge d_{i\hat{r}} = g^{\bar{r}_{i\hat{r}}} \wedge v_{ir} = g^{\bar{r}_{ir}}) \vee (\frac{c_{ir}}{g^{b_{ir}}} = \frac{c_{ir}}{g} = h^{r_{ir}} \wedge d_{i\hat{r}} = Y_{i\hat{r}}^{x_{ir}} \wedge X_{i\hat{r}} = g^{x_{i\hat{r}}} \wedge v_{ir} = Y_{ir}^{x_{ir}} \wedge X_{ir} = g^{x_{ir}})\}$, sending a message (v_{ir}, AV_{ir}) to all parties.
2. Upon receiving all messages (v_{kr}, AV_{kr}) from other parties $\mathcal{P}_k$, $\mathcal{P}_i$ checks the proofs AV_{kr} for $k \in \{1, \ldots, n\} \backslash i$ and, if all checks pass, computes $V_r = \prod_{k=1}^n v_{kr}$, following the steps in Stage 3 again until round $r = l$. If a message is not received from party $\mathcal{P}_k$ or if AV_{kr} is invalid, proceed to the Recovery Stage.

Fig. 5. Protocol Π_{FPA} (Stages 2 and 3)

in the auction. Without loss of generality let $b_i > b_j$. If $\mathcal{A}$ does not deviate from the protocol, then her utility is either 0 (in case neither b_i nor b_j is the winning bid) or $v_\mathcal{A} - b_i$ (in case b_i is the winning bid). Instead, if $\mathcal{A}$ deviates from the protocol by making $\mathcal{P}_i$ dropout, in case b_j is not the second-highest bid, then her utility is $-(work + b_i)$. If b_j is the second-highest bid, $\mathcal{A}$ gets what is at stake in the auction but her utility is $v_\mathcal{A} - (b_i + work + b_j)$. Therefore $\mathcal{A}$ always prefers to behave honestly.

Protocol Π_{FPA} (Stages 4 and Recovery)

Stage 4 - Output: At this point, each party $\mathcal{P}_i$ knows the value of V_r for each round $r = 1, \cdots, l$ and the protocol proceeds as follows:

1. $\mathcal{P}_i$ computes the winning bid as $b_w = b_{w1}|\cdots|b_{wl}$, such that $b_{wr} = 1$ if $V_r \neq 1$ and $b_{wr} = 0$ if $V_r = 1$, and sends b_w to all other parties (causing all parties $\mathcal{P}_k$ to sign b_w and send $sig_{sk_k}(b_w)$ to each other). We denote by $\mathcal{P}_w$ the winning party (*i.e.* the party whose bid is b_w).

2. $\mathcal{P}_w$ opens the commitment to her bid $com(b_w, r_{b_w})$ towards the smart contract by sending (OUTPUT, $sid, \mathcal{P}_w, b_w, r_{b_w}, \{sig_{sk_k}(b_w)\}_{k \in [n]}$) to $\mathcal{F}_{SC}$.

3. If $\mathcal{P}_w$ does not open her commitment or if multiple parties open their commitments, $\mathcal{P}_i$ proceeds to the Recovery Stage.

4. Finally, all parties who honestly completed the execution of the protocol receive a refund of their deposit from the smart contract, apart from the winning party, who only receives a refund equivalent to the *work* funds.

Recovery Stage: Parties $\mathcal{C}_i \in \mathcal{C}$ listen to $\mathcal{F}_{SC}$ and execute the Share Decryption step of $\Pi_{\mathcal{C}}$ from Figure 1 if requested. In case a party $\mathcal{P}_i \in \mathcal{P}$ is suspected of cheating, the Recovery stage is executed as follows to identify the cheater depending on the exact suspected cheating:

– **Missing message or signatures**: a message msg_{ri} or a signature $sig_{sk_i}(msg_{r-1,i'})$, on a message $msg_{r-1,i'}$ by $\mathcal{P}_i'$, expected to be sent in round r by $\mathcal{P}_i$ is not received by $\mathcal{P}_k$. Then, $\mathcal{P}_k$ sends to $\mathcal{F}_{SC}$ the message (RECOVERY-MISSING, $sid, msg, \{sig_{sk_k}(msg)\}_{k \in [n]}$), where msg is the last message signed by all parties and waits for $\mathcal{F}_{SC}$ to request the missing message. In that way, $\mathcal{P}_i$ is expected to send msg_{ri} or $sig_{sk_i}(msg_{r-1,i'})$ to $\mathcal{F}_{SC}$. If no action is taken, $\mathcal{P}_i$ is identified as a cheater.

– **Conflicting messages or Invalid message**: In round r, $\mathcal{P}_i$ sends conflicting messages $msg_{ri}, sig_{sk_i}(msg_{ri})$ and $msg_{ri}', sig_{sk_i}(msg_{ri}')$ to different parties $\mathcal{P}_k$ and $\mathcal{P}_k'$. In this case, $\mathcal{P}_k$ and $\mathcal{P}_k'$ set the conflicting messages as a proof of cheating $\pi_c = (msg_{ri}, sig_{sk_i}(msg_{ri}), msg_{ri}', sig_{sk_i}(msg_{ri}'))$. Otherwise, $\mathcal{P}_i$ sends an invalid message $msg_{ri}, sig_{sk_i}(msg_{ri})$ to $\mathcal{P}_k$ (*i.e.* the message does not follow the structure described in the protocol for messages in round r), $\mathcal{P}_k$ uses this message as a proof of cheating $\pi_c = (msg_{ri}, sig_{sk_i}(msg_{ri}))$. $\mathcal{P}_k$ sends (RECOVERY-CHEAT, $sid, \mathcal{P}_i, \pi_c$) to the smart contract and $\mathcal{P}_i$ is identified as a cheater.

Every party $\mathcal{P}_i$ identified as a cheater loses her whole deposit ($b_i + work$), which is distributed to the other parties by $\mathcal{F}_{SC}$, and the protocol continues as follows:

– **Re-execution (unknown b_w)**: in case b_w has not been computed, the protocol is re-executed from Stage 2 excluding the parties identified as cheaters.

– **Complete payment (known b_w but unknown $\mathcal{P}_w$)**: in case b_w has been computed but $\mathcal{P}_w$ does not send (OUTPUT, $sid, \mathcal{P}_w, b_w, r_{b_w}, \{sig_{sk_k}(b_w)\}_{k \in [n]}$) to $\mathcal{F}_{SC}$, all $\mathcal{P}_i \in \mathcal{P}$ compute a NIZK $NW_i \leftarrow NW\{x_{i1}, \ldots, x_{il} \mid (V_1 = 1 \wedge v_{i1} = Y_{i1}^{x_{i1}}) \vee \ldots \vee (V_l = 1 \wedge v_{i1} = Y_{i1}^{x_{i1}})\}$ showing that they are not the winner. Then they send to $\mathcal{F}_{SC}$ (RECOVERY-PAYMENT, sid, NW_i). The winner $\mathcal{P}_w$ (in case it is identified) or all parties $\mathcal{P}_i$ who do not act (in case $\mathcal{P}_w$ is not identified) are identified as dishonest and lose their deposits, which are distributed among the honest parties.

Fig. 6. Protocol Π_{FPA} (Stages 4 and Recovery)

Note that *it is necessary to have the deposit amount at least equal to the bid.* Indeed, let d be any deposit amount smaller than b_i. Then the utility of $\mathcal{A}$ by making $\mathcal{P}_i$ drop out the protocol is $v_{\mathcal{A}} - (d + work + b_j)$, while it is $v_{\mathcal{A}} - b_i$ by behaving honestly. Therefore, in case $d + work + b_j < b_i$, $\mathcal{A}$ prefers to deviate from the protocol to increase her utility. A similar argument shows that in the second-price auction, $\mathcal{A}$ always prefers to act honestly.

6 Complexity Analysis and Comparison to Other Protocols

In this section, we present concrete estimates for the computational and communication complexity of our first and second-price auction protocols, *i.e.*, Π_{FPA} and Π_{SPA}, respectively. We show that, in the first-price case, Π_{FPA} is more efficient than the state-of-the-art protocol SEAL [3]. In the second-price case, we show that Π_{SPA} only incurs a small overhead (dominated by re-executing one round) over Π_{FPA}. Note that the complexity of Stages 2 and 3 is based on the NIZK constructions available in the full version [20].

Table 1. First-price auction computational complexity comparison in terms of exponentiations performed by a party $\mathcal{P}_i \in \mathcal{P}$: n is the number of parties, l is the total number of rounds in Stages 2 and 3 (*i.e.*, bit-length of bids), τ is the number of rounds in Stage 2.

	Stage 1	Stage 2	Stage 3	Total
FAST	$nl + l + 8\log l + 2$	$\tau(8 + 10n)$	$(l - \tau)(19 + 22n)$	$23nl + 20l + 8\log l - 11\tau - 12n\tau + 2$
SEAL [3]	$11l + 12nl$	$\tau(17 + 20n)$	$(l - \tau)(33 + 36n)$	$48nl + 44l - 16\tau - 16n\tau$

Table 2. First price auction communication complexity comparison in terms of transmitted bits by a party $\mathcal{P}_i \in \mathcal{P}$: n is the number of parties, l is the total number of rounds in Stages 2 and 3 (*i.e.*, the bit-length of bids), τ is the number of rounds of Stage 2, $|\mathbb{G}|$ and $|\mathbb{Z}_q|$ indicate the bit-length of elements $g \in \mathbb{G}$ and $z \in \mathbb{Z}_q$ respectively, κ id the security parameter, as defined in Sect. 2.

	Stage 1	Stage 2	Stage 3	Total
FAST	$n((2l + 10)|\mathbb{G}| + 3\kappa + 4\log l)$	$n\tau(|\mathbb{G}| + 6|\mathbb{Z}_q|)$	$n(l - \tau)(|\mathbb{G}| + 11|\mathbb{Z}_q|)$	$n(|\mathbb{G}|(3l + 10) + |\mathbb{Z}_q|(11l - 5\tau) + 3\kappa + 4\log l)$
SEAL [3]	$17nl|\mathbb{G}|$	$23n\tau|\mathbb{G}|$	$36n(l - \tau)|\mathbb{G}|$	$(53nl - 13n\tau)|\mathbb{G}|$

The First-Price Case: A concrete estimate of computational complexity is shown in Table 1 and one for communication complexity is shown in Table 2.

We estimate these concrete complexities in terms of the number of exponentiations performed by a party $\mathcal{P}_i$ and of the number of bits transmitted by a party $\mathcal{P}_i$ in an execution of protocol Π_{FPA}, respectively. Moreover, we compare the complexity of our protocol with SEAL [3], which is the current state-of-the-art protocol for first-price sealed-bid auctions. In a similar way to our protocol, SEAL requires all parties to jointly compute the maximum bid bit-by-bit and is subdivided into a Stage 1 devoted to the setup, a Stage 2 identifying the rounds of the protocol before the first veto and a Stage 3 identifying the rounds of the protocol after the first veto. Hence, we highlight the differences in terms of complexity stage by stage. Note that, in order to make the communication complexities of the two protocols comparable, both of them have been expressed in terms of $|\mathbb{G}|$. Finally, FAST has an additional Stage 4 guaranteeing that the payment from the winning party $\mathcal{P}_w$ to the auctioneer is executed. On the other hand, SEAL does not guarantee this property. In particular, Stage 4 requires 1 exponentiation per party and has a communication complexity equal to $2(n-1)|\mathbb{G}|$.

The Second-Price Case: The computational and communication complexities of the proposed second-price auction are still linear in the number of agents. That is, assuming that at round r, there is a party who is the only one that is vetoing, then the parties have to re-run the rth round with one less party. More precisely, by following the notation of Table 1 and 2, let τ be the number of rounds in Stage 2, then the computational complexity of Stage 1 and Stage 2 is similar to the first-price auction, that is $nl + l + 8\log l + 2$ for Stage 1, and $8\tau + 10n\tau$ for Stage 2. Let r, be the number of rounds until there is only a single party who is veto-ing. Therefore the computational complexity of Stage 3 is $19r + 22nr$ until there is only a single veto. After this, the parties have to run the protocol with one less party, i.e., $n-1$ parties. Depending on the bid structure of the remaining $n-1$ parties, the protocol is either in Stage 2 or Stage 3. Let τ' denote the number of rounds until the remaining $n-1$ parties get a veto. Then the computational complexity for these τ' rounds would be $8\tau' + 10(n-1)\tau'$, and for the remaining $l - (\tau + \tau' + r)$ it would be $19(l - (\tau + \tau' + r)) + 22(n-1)(l - (\tau + \tau' + r))$. Using the same notation, a similar argument follows for the communication complexity per party in the case of the second-price auction.

References

1. Abe, M., Suzuki, K.: M + 1-st price auction using homomorphic encryption. In: Naccache, D., Paillier, P. (eds.) PKC 2002. LNCS, vol. 2274, pp. 115–124. Springer, Heidelberg (2002). https://doi.org/10.1007/3-540-45664-3_8
2. Andrychowicz, M., Dziembowski, S., Malinowski, D., Mazurek, L.: Secure multiparty computations on bitcoin. In: 2014 IEEE Symposium on Security and Privacy, pp. 443–458. IEEE Computer Society Press, May 2014
3. Bag, S., Hao, F., Shahandashti, S.F., Ray, I.G.: Seal: sealed-bid auction without auctioneers. IEEE Trans. Inf. Forensics Secur. **15**, 2042–2052 (2019)

4. Baudron, O., Stern, J.: Non-interactive private auctions. In: Syverson, P. (ed.) FC 2001. LNCS, vol. 2339, pp. 364–377. Springer, Heidelberg (2002). https://doi.org/ 10.1007/3-540-46088-8_28

5. Baum, C., David, B., Dowsley, R.: A framework for universally composable publicly verifiable cryptographic protocols. IACR Cryptol. ePrint Arch. **2020**, 207 (2020)

6. Baum, C., David, B., Dowsley, R.: Insured MPC: efficient secure computation with financial penalties. In: Bonneau, J., Heninger, N. (eds.) FC 2020. LNCS, vol. 12059, pp. 404–420. Springer, Cham (2020). https://doi.org/10.1007/978-3-030-51280-4_22

7. Benhamouda, F., et al.: Can a public blockchain keep a secret? In: Pass, R., Pietrzak, K. (eds.) TCC 2020. LNCS, vol. 12550, pp. 260–290. Springer, Cham (2020). https://doi.org/10.1007/978-3-030-64375-1_10

8. Bentov, I., Kumaresan, R.: How to use bitcoin to design fair protocols. In: Garay, J.A., Gennaro, R. (eds.) CRYPTO 2014. LNCS, vol. 8617, pp. 421–439. Springer, Heidelberg (2014). https://doi.org/10.1007/978-3-662-44381-1_24

9. Bentov, I., Kumaresan, R., Miller, A.: Instantaneous decentralized poker. In: Takagi, T., Peyrin, T. (eds.) ASIACRYPT 2017. LNCS, vol. 10625, pp. 410–440. Springer, Cham (2017). https://doi.org/10.1007/978-3-319-70697-9_15

10. Bogetoft, P., Damgård, I., Jakobsen, T., Nielsen, K., Pagter, J., Toft, T.: A practical implementation of secure auctions based on multiparty integer computation. In: Di Crescenzo, G., Rubin, A. (eds.) FC 2006. LNCS, vol. 4107, pp. 142–147. Springer, Heidelberg (2006). https://doi.org/10.1007/11889663_10

11. Brandt, F.: Fully private auctions in a constant number of rounds. In: Wright, R.N. (ed.) FC 2003. LNCS, vol. 2742, pp. 223–238. Springer, Heidelberg (2003). https://doi.org/10.1007/978-3-540-45126-6_16

12. Bünz, B., Bootle, J., Boneh, D., Poelstra, A., Wuille, P., Maxwell, G.: Bulletproofs: short proofs for confidential transactions and more. In: 2018 IEEE Symposium on Security and Privacy, pp. 315–334. IEEE Computer Society Press, May 2018

13. Camenisch, J., Stadler, M.: Proof systems for general statements about discrete logarithms. Technical Report/ETH Zurich, Department of Computer Science, vol. 260 (1997)

14. Canetti, R.: Security and composition of multiparty cryptographic protocols. J. Cryptol. **13**(1), 143–202 (2000)

15. Cascudo, I., David, B.: ALBATROSS: publicly AttestabLe BATched randomness based on secret sharing. In: Moriai, S., Wang, H. (eds.) ASIACRYPT 2020. LNCS, vol. 12493, pp. 311–341. Springer, Cham (2020). https://doi.org/10.1007/978-3-030-64840-4_11

16. Cleve, R.: Limits on the security of coin flips when half the processors are faulty (extended abstract). In: 18th ACM STOC, pp. 364–369. ACM Press, May 1986

17. Cramton, P., et al.: Spectrum auctions. In: Handbook of Telecommunications Economics, vol. 1, pp. 605–639 (2002)

18. David, B., Dowsley, R., Larangeira, M.: Kaleidoscope: an efficient poker protocol with payment distribution and penalty enforcement. In: Meiklejohn, S., Sako, K. (eds.) FC 2018. LNCS, vol. 10957, pp. 500–519. Springer, Heidelberg (2018). https://doi.org/10.1007/978-3-662-58387-6_27

19. David, B., Gaži, P., Kiayias, A., Russell, A.: Ouroboros praos: an adaptively-secure, semi-synchronous proof-of-stake blockchain. In: Nielsen, J.B., Rijmen, V. (eds.) EUROCRYPT 2018. LNCS, vol. 10821, pp. 66–98. Springer, Cham (2018). https:// doi.org/10.1007/978-3-319-78375-8_3

20. David, B., Gentile, L., Pourpouneh, M.: FAST: fair auctions via secret transactions. Cryptology ePrint Archive, Report 2021/264 (2021). https://ia.cr/2021/264

21. Deuber, D., Döttling, N., Magri, B., Malavolta, G., Thyagarajan, S.A.K.: Minting mechanism for proof of stake blockchains. In: Conti, M., Zhou, J., Casalicchio, E., Spognardi, A. (eds.) ACNS 2020. LNCS, vol. 12146, pp. 315–334. Springer, Cham (2020). https://doi.org/10.1007/978-3-030-57808-4_16

22. Dreier, J., Dumas, J.-G., Lafourcade, P.: Brandt's fully private auction protocol revisited. J. Comput. Secur. **23**(5), 587–610 (2015)

23. Franklin, M.K., Reiter, M.K.: The design and implementation of a secure auction service. IEEE Trans. Softw. Eng. **22**(5), 302–312 (1996)

24. Galal, H.S., Youssef, A.M.: Trustee: full privacy preserving Vickrey auction on top of ethereum. In: Bracciali, A., Clark, J., Pintore, F., Rønne, P.B., Sala, M. (eds.) FC 2019. LNCS, vol. 11599, pp. 190–207. Springer, Cham (2020). https://doi.org/10.1007/978-3-030-43725-1_14

25. Hao, F., Zieliński, P.: A 2-round anonymous veto protocol. In: Christianson, B., Crispo, B., Malcolm, J.A., Roe, M. (eds.) Security Protocols 2006. LNCS, vol. 5087, pp. 202–211. Springer, Heidelberg (2009). https://doi.org/10.1007/978-3-642-04904-0_28

26. Ishai, Y., Ostrovsky, R., Zikas, V.: Secure multi-party computation with identifiable abort. In: Garay, J.A., Gennaro, R. (eds.) CRYPTO 2014. LNCS, vol. 8617, pp. 369–386. Springer, Heidelberg (2014). https://doi.org/10.1007/978-3-662-44381-1_21

27. Juels, A., Szydlo, M.: A two-server, sealed-bid auction protocol. In: Blaze, M. (ed.) FC 2002. LNCS, vol. 2357, pp. 72–86. Springer, Heidelberg (2003). https://doi.org/10.1007/3-540-36504-4_6

28. Kiayias, A., Russell, A., David, B., Oliynykov, R.: Ouroboros: a provably secure proof-of-stake blockchain protocol. In: Katz, J., Shacham, H. (eds.) CRYPTO 2017. LNCS, vol. 10401, pp. 357–388. Springer, Cham (2017). https://doi.org/10.1007/978-3-319-63688-7_12

29. Kiayias, A., Zhou, H.-S., Zikas, V.: Fair and robust multi-party computation using a global transaction ledger. In: Fischlin, M., Coron, J.-S. (eds.) EUROCRYPT 2016. LNCS, vol. 9666, pp. 705–734. Springer, Heidelberg (2016). https://doi.org/10.1007/978-3-662-49896-5_25

30. Klemperer, P.: Auctions: Theory and Practice. Princeton University Press, Princeton (2004)

31. Krishna, V.: Auction Theory. Academic Press, Cambridge (2009)

32. Kurosawa, K., Ogata, W.: Bit-slice auction circuit. In: Gollmann, D., Karjoth, G., Waidner, M. (eds.) ESORICS 2002. LNCS, vol. 2502, pp. 24–38. Springer, Heidelberg (2002). https://doi.org/10.1007/3-540-45853-0_2

33. Lipmaa, H., Asokan, N., Niemi, V.: Secure Vickrey auctions without threshold trust. In: Blaze, M. (ed.) FC 2002. LNCS, vol. 2357, pp. 87–101. Springer, Heidelberg (2003). https://doi.org/10.1007/3-540-36504-4_7

34. Mas-Colell, A., Whinston, M.D., Green, J.R., et al.: Microeconomic Theory, vol. 1. Oxford University Press, New York (1995)

35. Maxwell, G.: Confidential transactions (2016). https://people.xiph.org/~greg/confidential_values.txt

36. Miltersen, P.B., Nielsen, J.B., Triandopoulos, N.: Privacy-enhancing auctions using rational cryptography. In: Halevi, S. (ed.) CRYPTO 2009. LNCS, vol. 5677, pp. 541–558. Springer, Heidelberg (2009). https://doi.org/10.1007/978-3-642-03356-8_32

37. Nakamoto, S.: Bitcoin: a peer-to-peer electronic cash system (2008)

38. Nurmi, H., Salomaa, A.: Cryptographic protocols for Vickrey auctions. Group Decis. Negot. **2**(4), 363–373 (1993). https://doi.org/10.1007/BF01384489

39. Pass, R., Shi, E.: Hybrid consensus: efficient consensus in the permissionless model. In: Richa, A.W. (ed.) 31st International Symposium on Distributed Computing, DISC 2017, volume 91 of LIPIcs, Vienna, Austria, 16–20 October 2017, pp. 39:1–39:16. Schloss Dagstuhl - Leibniz-Zentrum für Informatik (2017)
40. Pedersen, T.P.: Non-interactive and information-theoretic secure verifiable secret sharing. In: Feigenbaum, J. (ed.) CRYPTO 1991. LNCS, vol. 576, pp. 129–140. Springer, Heidelberg (1992). https://doi.org/10.1007/3-540-46766-1_9
41. Vickrey, W.: Counterspeculation, auctions, and competitive sealed tenders. J. Finance 16(1), 8–37 (1961)

Astrape: Anonymous Payment Channels with Boring Cryptography

Yuhao Dong[(✉)], Ian Goldberg, Sergey Gorbunov, and Raouf Boutaba

University of Waterloo, Waterloo, ON N2L 3G1, Canada
yd2dong@uwaterloo.ca

Abstract. The increasing use of blockchain-based cryptocurrencies like Bitcoin has run into inherent scalability limitations of blockchains. Payment channel networks, or PCNs, promise to greatly increase scalability by conducting the vast majority of transactions outside the blockchain while leveraging it as a final settlement protocol. Unfortunately, first-generation PCNs have significant privacy flaws. In particular, even though transactions are conducted off-chain, anonymity guarantees are very weak. In this work, we present Astrape, a novel PCN construction that achieves strong security and anonymity guarantees with simple, black-box cryptography, given a blockchain with flexible scripting. Existing anonymous PCN constructions often integrate with specific, often custom-designed, cryptographic constructions. But at a slight cost to asymptotic performance, Astrape can use any generic public-key signature scheme and any secure hash function, modeled as a random oracle, to achieve strong anonymity, by using a unique construction reminiscent of onion routing. This allows Astrape to achieve provable security that is "generic" over the computational hardness assumptions of the underlying primitives. Astrape's simple cryptography also lends itself to more straightforward security proofs compared to existing systems.

Furthermore, we evaluate Astrape's performance, including that of a concrete implementation on the Bitcoin Cash blockchain. We show that despite worse theoretical time complexity compared to state-of-the-art systems that use custom cryptography, Astrape operations on average have a very competitive performance of less than 10 ms of computation and 1 KB of communication on commodity hardware. Astrape explores a new avenue to secure and anonymous PCNs that achieves similar or better performance compared to existing solutions.

1 Introduction

1.1 Payment Channel Networks

Blockchain cryptocurrencies are gaining in popularity and becoming a significant alternative to traditional government-issued money. For instance, over 300,000 Bitcoin transactions alone [2] are processed every day. Unfortunately,

---

An extended version of this paper, and its accompanying source code, is available [12].

© Springer Nature Switzerland AG 2022
G. Ateniese and D. Venturi (Eds.): ACNS 2022, LNCS 13269, pp. 748–768, 2022.
https://doi.org/10.1007/978-3-031-09234-3_37

such high demand inevitably leads to well-known scalability barriers [8]. Bitcoin, for instance, processes less than 10 transactions every second [20], far less than a reasonable global payment system.

Payment channels [11] are a common technique to scale cryptocurrency transactions. In a nutshell, Alice and Bob open a payment channel by submitting a single transaction to the blockchain, locking up a sum of cryptocurrency from both of the parties. They can then pay each other by simply mutually signing a division of the locked money. Additional blockchain transactions are required only when the channel is closed by submitting an up-to-date signed division, unlocking the latest balances of Alice and Bob. This allows most activity to remain off-chain, while retaining the blockchain for final settlement: as long as the blockchain is secure, nobody can steal funds. More importantly, payment channels can be organized into *payment-channel networks* (PCNs) [20], where users without any open channels between them can pay each other through intermediaries.

1.2   Anonymity in PCNs

Unfortunately, "first-generation" PCNs based on the HTLC (hash time-locked contract), such as Lightning Network [11], have a significant problem—poor anonymity [18]. In the worst case, HTLC payments are as transparently linkable as blockchain payments [18], threatening the improved privacy that is often cited [23,24] as a benefit of PCNs. Furthermore, naive implementations fall victim to subtle fee-stealing attacks, like the "wormhole attack" [19], that threaten economic viability.

A sizable body of existing work on fixing PCN security and privacy exists. On one hand, specialized constructions achieve strong anonymity in specific settings, such as Bolt [14] for hub-based PCNs on the Zcash blockchain, providing for indistinguishability of two concurrent transactions even when all intermediaries are malicious. On the other hand, general solutions for all PCN topologies, like Fulgor [18] and the AMHL (Anonymous Multi-hop Locks) family [19], achieve a somewhat weaker, topology-dependent notion of anonymity: *relationship anonymity* [6,17]. This property, common to onion-routing and other anonymous communication protocols, means that two concurrent transactions cannot be distinguished as long as they share at least one honest intermediary.

1.3   Why Boring Cryptography?

Unfortunately, there remains a shortcoming common to all existing anonymous PCN constructions—custom, often number-theoretic and sometimes complex cryptographic primitives. No existing anonymous PCN construction limits itself to the bare-bones cryptographic primitives used in HTLC—black-box access to a generic signature scheme and hash function. For example, AMHL uses either homomorphic one-way functions or special constructions that exploit the mathematical structure of ECDSA or Schnorr signatures and Tumblebit uses a custom cryptosystem based on the RSA assumption. Blitz [5], though relying on an ostensibly black-box signature scheme, requires it to have a property[1] that rules out many post-quantum signature schemes.

However, it is unclear that relationship anonymity requires sophisticated techniques. Relationship anonymity appears to be relatively "easy" elsewhere. Well-understood anonymous constructs like onion routing and mix networks exist for communication with no more than standard primitives used in secure communication (symmetric and asymmetric encryption). Of course, communication is probably easier—indeed some go beyond relationship anonymity with only simple cryptography—but it seems plausible that PCNs can use similarly elementary primitives to achieve anonymity.

Furthermore, "boring" cryptography has practical advantages. For one, non-standard cryptography poses significant barriers to adoption. Reliable and performant implementations of novel cryptographic functions are difficult to obtain, and tight coupling between a PCN protocol and a particular cryptographic construction makes swapping out primitives impossible. With use of black-box cryptography, a system is *generic over cryptographic hardness assumptions*—instead of assuming that, say, the RSA or discrete-log problems are hard, we only need to assume that there exists, for example, *some* secure signature scheme and *some* secure hash function.

Thus, we believe that efficient yet privacy-preserving PCNs that only use well-understood and easily replaced black-box cryptographic primitives are crucial to usable PCNs. In fact, AMHL's authors already proposed that "an interesting question related to [anonymous PCN constructions] is under which class of hard problems such a primitive exists" [19] that they conjecturally answered with linear homomorphic one-way functions.

1.4   Our Contributions

In this paper, we present Astrape,[2] a PCN protocol that limits itself to "boring", generic cryptography already used in HTLC, yet achieves strong relationship anonymity. Despite achieving comparable security, privacy, and performance to other anonymous PCN constructions, Astrape does not introduce any cryptographic constructs other than those used in HTLC. This is accomplished using a novel construct reminiscent of onion routing that avoids the use of any form of zero-knowledge verification.

2   Background and Related Work

2.1   First-Generation PCNs with HTLC

An extremely useful property of payment channels is that they can be used to construct *payment channel networks* (PCNs) [8,10,20], allowing users without

---

[1] In particular, the ability for any party, given any public key, to generate new public keys that correspond to the same private key yet are unlinkable to the previous public key. This is crucial to the "stealth addresses" that Blitz's pseudonymous privacy rests upon.

[2] Greek for "lightning", pronounced "As-trah-pee".

channels directly between each other to pay each other via intermediaries. At the heart of any PCN is a *secure multi-hop transaction* mechanism—some way of Alice paying Bob to pay Carol without any trust in Bob. Most PCNs implement this using a smart contract known as the *Hash Time-Lock Contract* (HTLC). An HTLC is parameterized over a *sender* Alice, the *recipient* Bob, a deadline t, and a *puzzle* s. It locks up a certain amount of money, unlocking it according to the following rules:

- The money goes to Bob if he produces π where $H(\pi) = s$ before time t, where H is a secure hash function.
- Otherwise, the money goes to Alice.

We can use HTLC to construct secure multi-hop transactions. Consider a sender U_0 wishing to send money to a recipient U_n through untrusted intermediaries $U_1, \ldots, U_{n-1}$. At first, U_0 will generate a random π and $s = H(\pi)$, while sending the pair (π, s) to U_n over a secure channel. U_0 can then lock money in a HTLC parameterized over U_0, U_1, s, t_1, notifying U_1. U_1 would send an HTLC over U_1, U_2, s, t_2, notifying U_2, and so on. The deadline must become earlier at each step—$t_1 > t_2 > \cdots > t_n$—this ensures that in case of an uncooperative or malicious intermediary, funds always revert to the sender.

The payment eventually will be routed to U_n, who will receive an HTLC over U_{n-1}, U_n, s, t_n. The recipient will claim the money by providing π; this allows U_{n-1} to claim money from U_{n-2} using the same π, and so on, until all outstanding HTLC contracts are fulfilled. U_0 has successfully sent money to U_n, while the preimage resistance of H prevents any intermediary from stealing the funds.

2.2 Hub-Based Anonymous Payment Channels

Unfortunately, HTLC has an inherent privacy problem—a common identifier $s = H(\pi)$ visible to all nodes in the payment path [14, 18, 19]. This motivates *anonymous* PCN design. *Hub-based* approaches form the earliest kind of anonymous PCN design. Here, the shape of the network is limited to a star topology with users communicating with a centralized hub. Some solutions are highly specialized, such as Green and Miers' Bolt [14], which relies on the Zcash blockchain's zero-knowledge cryptography. Other solutions, such as Tumblebit [15] and the more recent A2L [22], provide more general solutions that work on a wide variety of blockchains.

Hub-based PCN constructions tackle the difficult problem of providing unlinkability between transactions despite the existence of only a single untrusted intermediary. It is therefore unsurprising that specialized cryptography is needed to protect anonymity. On the other hand, observations of real-world PCNs like the Lightning Network, as well as economic analysis [13], show that actual PCNs often have intricate topologies without dominating hubs. General, topology-agnostic solutions are thus more important to deploying private PCNs in practice.

2.3 Relationship-Anonymous Payment Channels

Unlike hub-based approaches, where no intermediaries are trusted, general private PCN constructions target *relationship anonymity*. This concept, shared with onion routing and other anonymous communication protocols, assumes at least one honest intermediary. Thus intermediaries are in fact crucial to relationship-anonymous PCNs' privacy properties. Like most hub-based approaches, relationship-anonymous payment channels do not by themselves deal with information leaked by side channels such as timing and value.

The earliest solution to PCN privacy in this family was probably Fulgor and Rayo [18], a closely related pair of constructions that can be ported to almost all HTLC-based PCNs. Fulgor/Rayo combines a "multi-hop HTLC" contract with out-of-band ZKPs to remove the common identifier across payment hops.

In a later work, Malavolta et al. [19] introduced *anonymous multi-hop locks* (AMHL), a rigorous theoretical framework for analyzing private PCN contracts. The AMHL paper provided a concrete instantiation using linear homomorphic one-way functions (hOWFs), as well as a conjecture that hOWFs are necessary for implementing anonymous PCNs. They also presented a variant that uses a clever encoding of homomorphic encryption in ECDSA to be used in ECDSA-based cryptocurrencies like Bitcoin. The latter "scriptless" variant was generalized in later work to a notion of adaptor signatures [4], where a signature scheme like ECDSA is "mangled" in such a way that a correct signature reveals a secret based on a cryptographic condition. The authors of AMHL also discovered "wormhole attacks" on HTLC-based PCNs. These attacks exploit a fundamental flaw in the HTLC construction to allow malicious intermediaries to steal transaction fees from honest ones, a problem that AMHL's anonymity techniques also solve.

More recently, Blitz [5] introduced *one-phase* payment channels that support multi-hop payments without a two-phase separation of coin creation and spending, improving performance and reliability. Blitz also achieves stronger anonymity than HTLC, but its notion of anonymity is strictly weaker than the relationship anonymity of AMHL and Fulgor/Rayo. Other relationship-anonymous systems consider powerful adversaries that control most nodes and achieve indistinguishability of concurrent transactions, but Blitz considers local adversaries controlling a single intermediary and limits itself to hiding the rest of the path from this intermediary.

3   Our Approach

As we argued in Sect. 1.3, all of these existing solutions share an undesirable reliance on either custom cryptographic constructions or primitives with special properties, like Blitz's stealth-address signature schemes. This causes inflexibility, difficult implementation, and an inability to respond to cryptanalytic breakthroughs like practical quantum computing.

Astrape is our solution to this problem. We show with a novel design that avoids the zero-knowledge verification paradigm, anonymous and atomic multi-hop transactions can be constructed with nothing but the two building blocks of HTLCs—hashing and signatures. Unlike existing work, no specific assumptions about the structure of the hash function or signature scheme are made, allowing

Astrape to be easily ported to different concrete cryptographic primitives and its security properties to "fall out" from those of the primitives. This also allows Astrape to achieve high performance on commodity hardware using standard cryptographic libraries.

3.1 Generalized Multi-hop Locks

In our discussion of Astrape, we avoid describing the concrete details of a specific payment channel network and cryptocurrency. Instead, we introduce an abstract model—generalized multi-hop locks. This model readily generalizes to different families of payment channel networks.

We model a *sender*, U_0, sending money to a *receiver*, U_n, through intermediaries $U_1, \ldots, U_{n-1}$. We assume a "source routing" model, where the graph of all valid payment paths in the network is publicly known and the sender can choose any valid path to the recipient. After an *initialization* phase where the sender may securely communicate parameters to each hop, each user U_i where $i < n$ *creates* a *coin* and notifies U_{i+1}. This coin is simply a contract ℓ_{i+1} known as a *lock script*, that essentially releases money to U_{i+1} given a certain key k_{i+1}. We call this lock the *right lock* of U_i and the *left lock* of U_{i+1}.

Finally, the payment completes once all coins created in the protocol have been unlocked and spent by fulfilling their lock scripts. Typically, this happens through a chain reaction where the recipient's left lock ℓ_n is unlocked, allowing U_{n-1} to unlock its left lock, etc.

Formally, we model a GMHL over a set of participants U_i as a tuple of four PPT algorithms $\mathbb{L} = (\mathsf{Init}, \mathsf{Create}, \mathsf{Unlock}, \mathsf{Vf})$, defined as follows:

Definition 1. *A GMHL* $\mathbb{L} = (\mathsf{Init}, \mathsf{Create}, \mathsf{Unlock}, \mathsf{Vf})$ *consists of the following polynomial-time protocols:*

1. $\langle s_0^I, \ldots, (s_n^I, k_n) \rangle \Leftarrow \langle \mathsf{Init}_{U_0}(1^\lambda, U_1, \ldots, U_n), \mathsf{Init}_{U_1}, \ldots, \mathsf{Init}_{U_n} \rangle$: *the initialization protocol, started by the sender* U_0, *that takes in a security parameter* 1^λ *and the identities of all hops* U_i *and returns an initial state* s_i^I *to all users* U_i. *Additionally, the recipient receives a key* k_n.
2. $\langle (\ell_i, s_{i-1}^R), (\ell_i, s_i^L) \rangle \Leftarrow \langle \mathsf{Create}_{U_{i-1}}(s_{i-1}^I), \mathsf{Create}_{U_i}(s_i^I) \rangle$: *the coin-creating protocol run between two adjacent hops* U_{i-1} *and* U_i, *creating the "coin sent from* U_{i-1} *to* U_i". *This includes a lock representation* ℓ_i *as well as additional state on both ends — unlocking the lock represented by* ℓ_i *releases the money.*
3. $k_i \Leftarrow \mathsf{Unlock}_{U_i}(\ell_{i+1}, (s_i^I, s_i^L, s_i^R), k_{i+1})$: *the coin-spending protocol, run by each intermediary* U_i *where* $i < n$, *obtains a valid unlocking key* k_i *for the "left lock"* ℓ_i *given its "right lock"* ℓ_{i+1}, *its unlocking key* k_{i+1} *(already verified by* Vf *below), and* U_i's *internal state.*
4. $\{0, 1\} \Leftarrow \mathsf{Vf}(\ell, k)$: *given a lock representation* ℓ *and an unlocking key* k, *return 1 iff the* k *is a valid solution to the lock* ℓ

As an example, a formalization of HTLC in the GMHL model can be found in the extended version of this paper [12, App. A].

Generalizability to Non-PCN Systems. We note here that GMHL makes no mention of typical PCN components such as channels, the blockchain, etc. This is because GMHL is actually agnostic of *how* exactly the locks are evaluated and enforced. In a typical PCN, these locks will be executed within bilateral payment channels, falling back to a public blockchain for final settlement.

However, other enforcement mechanisms can be used. Notably, all the locks could simply be contracts directly executing on a blockchain. In this way, any anonymous PCN formulated in the GMHL model is equivalent to a specification for a provably anonymous *on-chain, multi-hop coin tumbling service* that can anonymize entirely on-chain payments by routing them through multiple intermediaries.

Comparison to existing work. GMHL is an extension of *anonymous multi-hop locks*, the model used in the eponymous paper by Malavolta et al. [19]. In particular, AMHL defines an anonymous PCN construction in terms of the operations KGen, Setup, Lock, Rel, Vf, four of which correspond to GMHL functions.

Although AMHL's model is useful, we could not use it verbatim. This is largely because AMHL's original definition [19] also included its security and privacy properties, while we wish to be able to use the same framework in a purely *syntactic* fashion to discuss PCNs with other security and anonymity goals.

Nevertheless, GMHL can be considered as AMHL, reworded and used in a more general context. As we will soon see, Astrape's desired security and privacy properties are actually very similar to those of AMHL, though we will consider other systems formulated in the GMHL framework along the way. Astrape can be considered an alternative implementation of the same "anonymous multi-hop locks" [19] construct.

3.2   Security and Execution Model

Now that we have a model to discuss PCN constructions, we can discuss our security model, as well as a model of the GMHL execution environment in which Astrape will execute.

Active Adversary. We use a similar adversary model to that of AMHL [19]. That is, we model an adversary $\mathcal{A}$ with access to a functionality corrupt(U_i) that takes in the identifier of any user U_i and provides the attacker with the complete internal state of U_i. The adversary will also see all incoming and outgoing communication of U_i. corrupt(U_i) will also give the adversary active control of U_i, allowing it to impersonate U_i when communicating with other participants.

Anonymous Communication. We assume there is a secure and anonymous message transmission functionality $\mathcal{F}_{\text{anon}}$ that allows any participant to send messages to any other participant. Messages sent by an honest (non-corrupted) user with $\mathcal{F}_{\text{anon}}$ hide the identity of the sender and cannot be read by the adversary, although the adversary may arbitrarily delay messages.

There are many ways of implementing $\mathcal{F}_{anon}$, the exact choice of which is outside the scope of this paper. One solution recommended by existing work [18,19] is an onion-routing circuit constructed over the same set of users U_i, constructed with a provably private protocol like Sphinx [9]. Public networks such as Tor may also be used to implement $\mathcal{F}_{anon}$.

Exposed Lock Activity. In contrast to communication, *lock activity*—the content of all locks being created, as well as the unlocking keys during unlocking—is not secure. This is because in practice, lock activity often happens on public media like blockchains. We pessimistically assume that the adversary can see all lock activity, while a non-adversary only sees lock activity concerning locks that it sends and receives.

Liveness and Timeouts. We assume that every coin lock ℓ_i comes with an appropriate timeout that will return money to U_{i-1} (i.e., able to be unlocked by a signature from U_{i-1} after the timeout) if U_i does not take action. We also assume that each left lock ℓ_i's deadline is at least δ later than that of the right lock ℓ_{i+1}, where δ is an upper bound on network latency between honest parties, even under disruption by the adversary. In the most common setting of a PCN consisting of bilateral payment channels backed by a blockchain, this is essentially a blockchain censorship-resistance assumption. With a liveness assumption, we can then omit timeout handling from the description of the protocol, in line with related work (such as AMHL [19]).

Infallible Lock Execution. We formulate Astrape in the GMHL model, and assume the existence of a mechanism that will guarantee that cryptocurrency locks are always correctly executed in the face of arbitrary adversarial activity. In practice, both bilateral payment channels falling back to a general-purpose public blockchain (like Ethereum) and direct use of this blockchain are good approximations of this mechanism.

Lock Functionality. We assume that inside our on-chain contracts we are able to use at least the following operations:

- *Concatenation*, producing a bitstring $x||y$ of length $|n+m|$ from two bitstrings x, y, where x has length n and y has length m.
- *Bitwise XOR*, producing a bitstring $x \oplus y$ from two bitstrings x, y

as well as the cryptographic hash function H defined below. An implication of this assumption is that PCNs on blockchains with highly restricted scripting languages, like Bitcoin, cannot use Astrape.

Cryptographic Assumptions. One of Astrape's main goals is to make minimal cryptographic assumptions. We assume only:

- *Generic cryptographic hash function.* We assume a hash function H, modeled as a random oracle for the purpose of security proofs, producing λ bits of output, where 1^λ is the security parameter. We use the random oracle both as a pseudorandom function and as a commitment scheme, which is well known [7] to be secure.

- *Generic signature scheme.* We assume a secure signature scheme that allows for authenticated communication between any two users U_i and U_j.

3.3   Security and Privacy Goals

Against the adversary we described above, we want to achieve the following security and privacy objectives:

Relationship Anonymity. Given two simultaneous payments between different senders $S_{\{0,1\}}$ and receivers $R_{\{0,1\}}$ with payment paths of the same length intersecting at the same position at at least one honest intermediate user, an adversary corrupting all of the other intermediate users cannot determine, with probability non-negligibly better than $1/2$ (guessing), whether S_0 paid R_0 and S_1 paid R_1, or S_0 paid R_1 and S_1 paid R_0. This is an established standard for anonymity in payment channels [18,19] and is analogous to similar definitions for anonymous communication [6,21]. It is important to note that the adversary is not allowed to corrupt the sender—senders always know who they are sending money to.

Balance Security. For an honest user U_i, if its right lock ℓ_i is unlocked, U_i must always be able to unlock its left lock ℓ_{i-1} even if all other users are corrupt. Combined with the timeouts mentioned in our security model, this guarantees that no intermediary node can lose money even if everybody else conspires against it.

Wormhole Resistance. We need to be immune to the *wormhole attack* on PCNs, where malicious intermediaries steal fees from other intermediaries. The reason why is rather subtle [19], but for our purposes this means that given an honest sender and an honest intermediary U_{i+1}, ℓ_i cannot be spent by U_i until U_{i+1} spends ℓ_{i+1}. Intuitively, this prevents honest intermediaries from being "left out".

4   Construction

4.1   Core Idea: Balance Security + Honest-Sender Anonymity

Unlike existing systems that utilize the mathematical properties of some cryptographic construction to build a secure and anonymous primitive, Astrape is constructed out of two separate *broken* constructions, both of which use boring cryptography and are straightforward to describe:

- **XorCake**, which has relationship anonymity but lacks balance security if the sender U_0 is malicious

- **HashOnion** which has balance security, but *loses relationship anonymity* in the Unlock phase. That is, an adversary limited only to observing Init and Create cannot break relationship anonymity, but an adversary observing Unlock can.

The key insight here is that if we can combine XorCake and HashOnion in such a way to ensure that HashOnion's Unlock phase *can only reveal information when the sender is malicious*, we obtain a system, Astrape, that has both relationship anonymity and balance security. This is because the definition of relationship anonymity assumes an honest sender: if the sender is compromised, it can always simply tell the adversary the identity of its counterparty, breaking anonymity trivially. It is important to note that such a composition *does not in any way weaken anonymity* compared to existing "up-front anonymity" systems like AMHL, even in the most pessimistic case.[3]

We now describe XorCake and HashOnion, and their composition into Astrape.

4.2 XorCake: Anonymous but Insecure Against Malicious Senders

Let us first describe XorCake's construction. XorCake is an extremely simple construction borrowed from "multi-hop HTLC", a building block of Fulgor [18]. It has relationship anonymity, but not balance security against malicious senders.

Recall that in GMHL, the sender (U_0) wishes to send a sum of money to the recipient (U_n) through $U_1, \ldots, U_{n-1}$. At the beginning of the transaction, the sender samples n independent λ-bit random strings $(r_1, \ldots, r_n)$. Then, for all $i \in 1, \ldots, n$, she sets n values $s_i = H(r_i \oplus r_{i+1} \oplus \cdots \oplus r_n)$, where H is a secure hash function. That is, s_i is simply the hash of the XOR of all the values r_j for $j \geq i$. U_0 then uses the anonymous channel $\mathcal{F}_{\text{anon}}$ to provide U_n the values (r_n, s_n) and all the other U_i with (r_i, s_i, s_{i+1}).

Then, for each pair of neighboring nodes (U_i, U_{i+1}), U_i sends U_{i+1} a coin encumbered by a regular HTLC ℓ_{i+1} asking for the preimage of s_{i+1}. U_n knows how to unlock ℓ_n, and the solution would let U_{n-1} unlock ℓ_{n-1}, and so on. That is, each lock ℓ_i is simply an HTLC contract asking for the preimage of s_i.

In the extended version [12, App. A], we give the formal definition of XorCake in the GMHL framework.

XorCake by itself satisfies relationship anonymity. A full proof is available in the Fulgor paper from which XorCake was borrowed [19], but intuitively this is because r_i will be randomly distributed over the space of possible strings because H behaves like a random oracle. This means that unlike in HTLC, no two nodes U_i and U_j can deduce that they are part of the same payment path unless they are adjacent.

---

[3] In a sense then, Astrape has "pseudo-optimistic" anonymity. Its design superficially suggests an optimistic construction with an anonymous "happy path" and a non-anonymous "unhappy path", but the latter non-anonymity is illusory—the sender can always prevent the "unhappy" path from deanonymizing the transaction even if all other parties are malicious.

State-Mismatch Attack. Unfortunately, *XorCake does not have balance security.* Consider a malicious sender who follows the protocol correctly, except for sending an incorrect r_i to U_i. (Note that U_i cannot detect that r_i is incorrect given a secure hash function.) Then, when ℓ_{i+1} is unlocked, ℓ_i cannot be spent! In an actual PCN such as the Lightning Network, all coins "left" of U_i will time out, letting the money go back to U_0. U_0 paid U_n with U_i's money instead of her own. We call this the "state-mismatch attack", and because of it, XorCake is not a viable PCN construction on its own. In Fulgor, XorCake was combined with out-of-band zero-knowledge proofs of the correctness of r_i, but as we will see shortly, Astrape can dispense with them.

4.3   HashOnion: Secure but Eventually Non-anonymous

We now present HashOnion, a PCN construction that has balance security but not relationship anonymity. Note that unlike HTLC, HashOnion's non-anonymity stems entirely from information leaked in the Unlock phase, a property we will leverage to build a fully anonymous construction combining HashOnion and XorCake.

At the beginning of the transaction, U_0 generates random values s_i for $i \in \{1, \ldots, n\}$, then "onion-like" values x_i, recursively defined as $x_i = H(s_i \| x_{i+1})$, $x_n = H(s_n \| 0^\lambda)$.

Essentially, x_i is a value that commits to all s_j where $j \geq i$. An onion-like commitment is used rather than a "flat" commitment (say, a hash of all s_j where $j \geq i$) as it is crucial for balance security, as we will soon see.

For all intermediate nodes $0 < i < n$, the sender sends (x_{i+1}, s_i) to U_i, while for the destination, the sender sends s_n. Then, each intermediary U_{i-1} sends to its successor U_i a lock ℓ_i, which can be only be unlocked by some $k_i = (s_i, \ldots, s_n)$ where $H(s_i \| H(s_{i+1} \| H(\ldots H(s_n \| 0^\lambda)))) = x_i$. U_{i-1} constructs this lock from the x_i it received from the sender. Finally, during the unlock phase, the recipient U_n solves ℓ_n with $k_n = (s_n)$. This allows each U_i to spend ℓ_i, completing the transaction.

For balance security, we need to show that with a solution $k_{i+1} = (s_{i+1}, \ldots, s_n)$ to ℓ_{i+1}, and s_i, we can always construct a solution to ℓ_i . This is obvious: we just add s_i to the solution: $k_i = (s_i, s_{i+1}, \ldots, s_n)$.

One subtle problem is that U_i needs to make sure that its left lock is actually the correct ℓ_i and not some bad ℓ_i' parameterized over some $x_i' \neq H(s_i \| x_{i+1})$. Otherwise, its right lock might get unlocked with a solution that does not let it unlock its left lock. Fortunately, this is easy: given s_i, x_{i+1} from the sender, U_i can just check that its left lock, parameterized over some x_i, matches $x_i = H(s_i \| x_{i+1})$ before sending out ℓ_{i+1} (parameterized with x_{i+1}) to the next hop. Thus, every user can make sure that if its right lock is unlocked, so can its left lock, so balance security holds.

We also see that although the unlocking procedure breaks relationship anonymity by revealing all the s_i, before the unlock happens, HashOnion does have relationship anonymity. This is because the adversary cannot connect the different x_i as long as one s_i remains secret—that of the one honest intermediary.

4.4   Securing XorCake+HashOnion

We now move on to composing XorCake and HashOnion. We do so by creating a variant of HashOnion that embeds XorCake and recognizes an *inconsistency witness*. That is, this variant of HashOnion will unlock only when given a combination of values that proves an attempt by the sender to execute a state-mismatch attack for XorCake.

To construct such a lock, after generating the XorCake parameters, U_0 creates n λ-bit values x_i recursively:

$$x_n = o_n, \qquad x_i = H(\overbrace{r_i||s_i||s_{i+1}}^{\text{XorCake parameters}}||o_i||x_{i+1})$$

where o_i is a random nonce sampled uniformly from all possible λ-bit values.[4] The intuition here is that x_i *commits* to all the information U_0 would give to all hops U_j where $j \geq i$.

Afterwards, the sender then uses $\mathcal{F}_{\text{anon}}$ to send $(o_i, x_i, x_{i|1})$, in addition to the XorCake parameters (r_i, s_i, s_{i+1}), to every hop i. Every hop U_i checks that all the parameters are consistent with each other.

We next consider what will happen if the sender attempts to fool an intermediate hop U_i with a state-mismatch attack. U_{i+1} would unlock its left lock ℓ_{i+1} by giving k_{i+1} where $H(k_{i+1}) = s_{i+1}$ but $H(r_i \oplus k_{i+1}) \neq s_i$. This then causes U_i to fail to unlock its left lock.

But this attempt allows U_i to generate a cryptographic witness verifiable to anybody knowing x_i: λ-bit values $k_{i+1}, r_i, s_i, s_{i+1}, o_i, x_{i+1}$ where:

$$H(k_{i+1}) = s_{i+1}, H(r_i \oplus k_{i+1}) \neq s_i, H(r_i||s_i||s_{i+1}||o_i||x_{i+1}) = x_i$$

This inconsistency witness proves that the preimage of s_{i+1} XOR-ed with r_i does not equal the preimage of s_i, demonstrating that the values given to U_i are inconsistent and that U_0 is corrupt. Since U_{i-1} knows x_i, U_i can therefore prove that it was a victim of a state-mismatch attack to U_{i-1}.

Since x_i commits to *all* XorCake initialization states "rightwards" of U_i, U_i, in cooperation with U_{i-1}, can also produce a witness that U_{i-2} can verify using x_{i-1}. This is simply a set of λ-bit values $k_{i+1}, r_{i-1}, s_{i-1}, r_i, s_i, s_{i+1}, x_i, o_i, o_{i-1}, x_{i+1}$ where:

$$H(k_{i+1}) = s_{i+1}, H(r_i \oplus k_{i+1}) \neq s_i,$$

$$H(r_i||s_i||s_{i+1}||o_i||x_{i+1}) = x_i, H(r_{i-1}||s_{i-1}||s_i||o_{i-1}||x_i) = x_{i-1}$$

We can clearly extend this idea all the way back to U_1—given a witness demonstrating a state-mismatch attack against U_i, U_{i-1} can verify the witness and generate a similar one verifiable by U_{i-2}, and so on. This forms the core construction that Astrape uses to fix XorCake's lack of balance security.

---

[4] $||$ denotes concatenation. In our case, it is possible to unambiguously separate concatenated values, since we only ever concatenate λ-bit values.

4.5   Complete Construction

We now present the complete construction of Astrape, as formalized in Fig. 1 within the GMHL framework. Note that we use the notation $\mathsf{Tag}[x_1, \ldots, x_n]$ to represent a n-tuple of values with an arbitrary "tag" that identifies the type of value.

---

function $\mathsf{Init}_{U_0}^{\mathsf{AS}}(1^\lambda, U_1, \ldots, U_n)$
Upon invocation by U_0:
  generate λ-bit random numbers $\{r_1, \ldots, r_n\}$
  $x_n \leftarrow$ random λ-bit number
  for i **in** $n-1, \ldots, 1$ **do**
    $s_i \leftarrow H(r_i \oplus r_{i+1} \oplus \cdots \oplus r_n)$
    $o_i \leftarrow$ random λ-bit number
    if $i < n$ **then**
      $x_i \leftarrow H(r_i \| s_i \| s_{i+1} \| o_i \| x_{i+1})$
  for i **in** $1, \ldots, n$ **do**
    if $i = n$ **then**
      send $s_n^I = (k_n = \mathsf{HSoln}[r_n], s_n)$ to U_n
    else
      send $s_i^I = (r_i, s_i, s_{i+1}, x_i, x_{i+1}, o_i)$ to U_i

function $\mathsf{Create}_{U_i}^{\mathsf{AS}}(s_i^I = (r_i, s_i, s_{i+1}, x_i, x_{i+1}, o_i))$
Upon invocation by U_i, where $i < n$:
  if $x_i \neq H(r_i \| s_i \| s_{i+1} \| o_i \| x_{i+1})$ **then**
    abort *bad initial state*
  if $i > 0$ **then**
    wait for $\ell_i = \mathsf{Astrape}[\hat{x}_i, \hat{s}_i]$ to be created
    if $\hat{x}_i \neq x_i$ or $\hat{s}_i \neq s_i$ **then**
      abort *invalid left lock*
  return $\ell_{i+1} = \mathsf{Astrape}[x_{i+1}, s_{i+1}]$

function $\mathsf{Unlock}_{U_i}^{\mathsf{AS}}(\ell_{i+1}, s_i^I, k_{i+1})$
Upon invocation by U_i, where $i < n$:
  $\Gamma_i \leftarrow r_i \| s_i \| s_{i+1} \| o_i$
  parse $s_i^I = (r_i, s_i, s_{i+1}, x_i, x_{i+1}, o_i)$
  if parse $k_{i+1} = \mathsf{HSoln}[\kappa_{i+1}]$ **then**
    if $H(r_i \oplus \kappa_{i+i}) = s_i$ **then**
      return $k_i = \mathsf{HSoln}[r_i \oplus \kappa_{i+1}]$
    else
      return $k_i = \mathsf{WSoln}[\kappa_{i+1}, x_{i+1}, \{\Gamma_i\}]$
  else
    parse $k_{i+1} = \mathsf{WSoln}[\kappa_j, x_j, \{\Gamma_{i+1}, \ldots, \Gamma_j\}]$
    return $k_i = \mathsf{WSoln}[\kappa_j, x_j, \{\Gamma_i, \Gamma_{i+1}, \ldots, \Gamma_j\}]$

function $\mathsf{Vf}^{\mathsf{AS}}(\ell, k)$
  parse $\ell = \mathsf{Astrape}[x, s]$
  if parse $k = \mathsf{HSoln}[\kappa]$ **then**
    return 1 iff $H(\kappa) = s$ ▷ *"normal" case*
  else if parse $k = \mathsf{WSoln}[\kappa, \chi, \{\Gamma_i, \ldots, \Gamma_j\}]$ **then**
    if $\exists i$ s.t. $\Gamma_i.\mathrm{length} \neq 4\lambda$ bits **then**
      return 0
    parse $\Gamma_j = r_j \| s_j \| s_{j+1} \| o_j$
    if $H(r_j \oplus \kappa) = s_j$ **then**
      return 0   ▷ *state good*
    $\hat{x} \leftarrow H(\Gamma_i \| H(\Gamma_{i+1} \| \ldots H(\Gamma_j \| \chi)))$
    return 1 iff $\hat{x} = x$ ▷
  "inconsistency" case

Fig. 1. Astrape as a GMHL protocol

Initialization. In the first phase, represented as Init in GMHL, the sender U_0 first establishes communication to the n hops $U_1, \ldots, U_n$, the last one of which is the receiver. When talking to intermediaries and the recipient, U_0 uses our abstract functionality $\mathcal{F}_{\mathrm{anon}}$.

The sender then generates random λ-bit strings $(r_1, \ldots, r_n)$ and $(o_1, \ldots, o_n)$, deriving $s_i = H(r_i \oplus r_{i+1} \oplus \cdots \oplus r_n)$ and $x_i = H(r_i \| s_i \| s_{i+1} \| o_i \| x_{i+1}); x_n = H(o_n)$. She then sends to each intermediate hop U_i the tuple $s_i^I = (r_i, s_i, s_{i+1}, x_i, x_{i+1}, o_i)$ and gives the last hop U_n the initial state $s_n^I = (r_n, s_n)$ and the unlocking key $k_n = \mathsf{HSoln}[r_n]$.

Creating the Coins. We now move on to Create, where all the coins are initially locked. U_0 then sends U_1 a coin encumbered with a lock represented as

$\ell_1 = \mathsf{Astrape}[x_1, s_1]$. When each hop U_i receives a correctly formatted coin from its previous hop U_{i-1}, it sends the next hop U_{i+1} a coin with a lock $\ell_{i+1} = \mathsf{Astrape}[x_{i+1}, s_{i+1}]$. Note that U_i checks whether its left lock is consistent with the parameters it received from U_0; this ensures that when U_i's right lock unlocks later, U_i can always construct a solution for its left lock. If the checks fail, Create aborts, and all of the locks will eventually time out (see Sect. 3.2), returning money to the sender.

As specified in Vf, each of these locks ℓ_i can be spent either through solving a XorCake-type puzzle to find the preimage of s_i (the "normal" case) or by presenting an inconsistency witness with a HashOnion-type witness demonstrating x_i's commitment to inconsistent data (the "inconsistency" case). After all the transactions with Astrape-encumbered coins are sent, U_n can finally claim its money, triggering the next phase of the protocol.

Unlocking the Coins. The last step is Unlock. After receiving the final coin from U_{n-1}, the recipient unlocks its lock ℓ_n by providing to Vf the preimage of the HTLC puzzle: $k_n = \mathsf{HSoln}[r_n]$—this is the only way an honest recipient can claim the money in a payment originating from an honest sender. Each intermediate node U_i reacts when its right lock ℓ_{i+1} is unlocked with key k_{i+1}:

- If U_{i+1} solved the HTLC puzzle with $k_{i+1} = \mathsf{HSoln}[\kappa_{i+1}]$, construct $\kappa_i = r_i \oplus \kappa_{i+1}$
  - If $H(\kappa_i) = s_i$, this means that there is no state-mismatch attack happening. We unlock our left lock with $k_i = \mathsf{HSoln}[\kappa_i]$.
  - Otherwise, there must be an attack happening. We construct a witness and create a key that embeds the witness verifiable with x_i. This gives us $k_i = \mathsf{WSoln}[\kappa_{i+1}, x_{i+1}, \{\Gamma_i\}]$, where $\Gamma_i = r_i||s_i||s_{i+1}||o_i$.
- Otherwise, U_{i+1} demonstrated that the sender attempted to defraud some U_j, where $j > i$ unlocked ℓ_{i+1} by presenting an inconsistency witness $k_{i+1} = \mathsf{WSoln}[\kappa_j, x_j, \{\Gamma_{i+1}, \Gamma_{i+2}, \ldots, \Gamma_j\}]$.
  - We can simply construct $k_i = \mathsf{WSoln}[\kappa_j, x_j, \{\Gamma_i, \Gamma_{i+1}, \ldots, \Gamma_j\}]$ where $\Gamma_i = r_i||s_i||s_{i+1}||o_i$. This transforms the witness verifiable with x_{i+1} to a witness verifiable with x_i.

Note that both cases are covered by Vf—it accepts and verifies both "normal" unlocks with HSoln-tagged tuples, and "inconsistency" unlocks with WSoln. Thus, even though Astrape is a composition of XorCake and HashOnion, the final construction fully "inlines" the two into the same flow of initialization, coin creation, and unlocking, with no separate procedure to process inconsistency witnesses. Unlocking continues backwards towards the sender until all the locks created in the previous step are unlocked. We have balance security—node U_i can unlock its left lock ℓ_i if and only if node U_{i+1} has unlocked ℓ_{i+1}, so no intermediaries can lose any money.

Security proofs, as well as a discussion on side-channel and griefing attacks, can be found in the extended version [12, §5].

5   Blockchain Implementation

Astrape is easy to implement on blockchains with Turing-complete scripting languages, like Ethereum, as well as layer-2 PCNs such as Raiden built on these blockchains, but blockchains without Turing-complete scripts involve two main challenges.

First, these blockchains typically do not allow recursion or loops in lock scripts. This means that we cannot directly implement the Vf function. Instead, we must "unroll" Vf to explicitly check for witnesses to inconsistencies in the parameters given to U_i, U_{i+1}, etc. So for an n-hop payment the size of every lock script grows to $\Theta(n)$. In practice, the mean path length in the Lightning Network is currently around 5 (see our measurements in Sect. 6.4), and privacy-focused onion routing systems such as Tor or I2P typically use 3 to 5 hops. We believe linear-length script sizes are not a significant concern for Astrape deployment. An Astrape deployment can simply pick an arbitrary maximum for the number of hops supported and achieve reasonable worst-case performance.

The second issue is more serious: some blockchains have so little scripting that Astrape cannot be implemented. Astrape requires an "append-like" operation || that can take in two bytestrings and combine them in a collision-resistant manner. Unfortunately, the biggest blockchain Bitcoin has disabled all string-manipulation opcodes. Whether an implementation based solely on the 32-bit integer arithmetic that Bitcoin uses is possible is an interesting open question.

6   Comparison with Existing Work

In this section, we compare Astrape with existing PCN constructions. First, we compare Astrape's design choices and features with that of other systems, showing that it explores a novel design space. Then, we evaluate Astrape's concrete performance. We compare Astrape's performance with that of other PCN constructions, both anonymous and non-anonymous. Finally, we explore Astrape's performance on a real-world network graph from the Lightning Network.

6.1   Design Comparison

In Table 1, we compare Astrape's properties with those of existing

Table 1. Comparison of different PCNs

	Topology	Anon[a]	Efficient[b]	Crypto
HTLC	Mesh	No	Yes	Sig. + hash
Tumblebit	Hub	Yes	No	Custom RSA
Bolt	Hub	Yes	Yes	NIZKP
Teechain	Hub	Yes	Yes	Trusted comp
Fulgor/Rayo	Mesh	Yes	No	ZKP
AMHL$_{van}$[c]	Mesh	Yes	Yes	Homom. OWF
AMHL$_{ecd}$	Mesh	Yes	Yes	ECDSA, Homom. enc
AMHL$_{sch}$	Mesh	Yes	Yes	Schnorr sigs
Blitz	Mesh	Weak[d]	Yes	SA[e] sig. + hash
Astrape	Mesh	Yes	Yes	Sig. + hash

a   Relationship anonymity
b   Roughly comparable performance to HTLC. For example, ZKPs requiring many orders of magnitude more computation time than HTLC are not considered "efficient".
c   AMHL is a family of three closely related constructions. We denote by *van, ecd, sch* the "vanilla", ECDSA, and Schnorr implementations respectively.
d   See discussion in Section 2.3.
e   A "stealth-address" signature scheme; i.e., a signature scheme where any party knowing a public key can generate unlinkably different public keys that correspond to the same private key.

Table 2. Resource usage of different PCN systems (n hops, c-byte HTLC contract, d-byte Astrape contract); AHML variants van,ecd,sch as in Table 1

	Plain HTLC	Fulgor/ Rayo	AMHL	Astrape (Bitcoin Cash)	Astrape
Comput. time (ms)	< 0.001	$\approx 200n$	$\approx n$ (van) $\approx 3n$ (ecd) $\approx 3n$ (sch)	$\approx 0.7n$	$\approx 0.25n$
Comm. size (bytes)	$32n$	$1650000n$	$32 + 96n$ (van) $416 + 128n$ (ecd) $256 + 128n$ (sch)	$192n$	$192n$
Lock (bytes)	$32 + c$	$32 + c$	$32 + c$	$108 + 39 \cdot n$	$64 + d$
Unlock, normal case (bytes)	32	32	32 (van) / 64	32	32
Unlock, worst case (bytes)	32	32	32 (van) / 64	$64 + 128 \cdot n$	$64 + 128 \cdot n$

payment channel networks. We see that except for HTLC, which does not achieve anonymity, all previous PCN networks use cryptographic constructions specialized for their use case. Furthermore, only more recent constructions achieve efficiency comparable to HTLC. It is thus clear that Astrape is the first and only PCN construction that works on all PCN topologies, achieves strong anonymity, and performs at high efficiency, while using the same simple cryptography as HTLC.

6.2 Implementation and Benchmark Setup

To demonstrate the feasibility and performance of our construction, we developed a prototype implementation in the Go programming language. We implemented all the cryptographic constructions of Astrape inside a simulated GMHL model. We used the libsodium library's implementation of the ed25519 [16] signature scheme and blake2b [3] hash function. In addition, we generated script locks in Bitcoin Cash's scripting language to illustrate script sizes for scripting languages with no loops. The Bitcoin Cash scripts, written in the higher-level CashScript language, can be found in the extended version [12, App. B].

All tests were done on a machine with a 3.2 GHz Intel Core i7 and 16 GB RAM. Network latency is not simulated, as this is highly application dependent. These conditions are designed to be maximally similar to those under which Fulgor [18] and AMHL [19] were evaluated, allowing us to compare the results directly.

6.3 Resource Usage

Our first set of tests compares Astrape's resource usage to that of other PCN constructions. We compare both a simulation of Astrape and a concrete implementation using Bitcoin Cash's scripting language to traditional HTLC, Fulgor/Rayo, and all three variants of AMHL.

We summarize the results in Table 2, where n refers to the number of hops, c to the size of an HTLC contract, and d to the size of an Astrape contract. We copy results for Fulgor/Rayo [18] and AMHL (ECDSA) [19] from their original sources, which use an essentially identical setup.

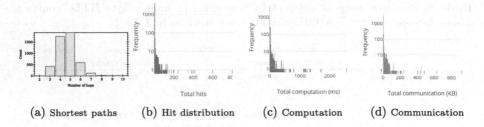

| (a) Shortest paths | (b) Hit distribution | (c) Computation | (d) Communication |

Fig. 2. Overhead distribution

Computation Time. We measure computation time, with communication and other overhead ignored. The time measured is the sum of the CPU time taken by each hop, for all steps of the algorithm. We note that by eschewing non-standard cryptographic primitives, Astrape achieves lower computation times across the board compared to Fulgor/Rayo and AMHL.

Communication Overhead. We also measure the communication overhead of each system. This is defined as all the data that needs to be communicated *other than the locks and their opening solutions.* For example, in Astrape, this includes all the setup information sent from U_0, while in AMHL this includes everything exchanged during the Setup, Lock, and Rel [19] phases. We see that Astrape has by far the least communication overhead of all the anonymous PCN constructions. Note especially the extreme overhead of the zero-knowledge proofs used in Fulgor/Rayo.

Lock Overhead. The last measure is *per-coin* lock overhead—the size of each lock script (the "lock size") and that of the information required to unlock it (the "unlock size"). This is a very important component of a system's resource usage, since lock and unlock sizes directly translate into transaction fees in blockchain cryptocurrencies. Astrape's performance differs in two important ways.

First of all, Astrape's Vf function is expressed in a recursive manner. In blockchains like Bitcoin Cash that support neither recursion nor loops in their scripting language, we must "unroll" the Vf implementation. This causes lock sizes to be linear in the number of hops. In blockchains with general-purpose scripting languages, though, lock size is generally constant. Second, the worst-case unlock size is larger for Astrape. When the sender is malicious and all coins have to be spent by invoking HashOnion, we need n parameters $(\Gamma_1, \ldots, \Gamma_n)$ to unlock each coin for an n-hop payment. However, despite this asymptotic disadvantage, we believe that Astrape nevertheless offers competitive lock performance. This is because payment routes are quite short in practice, as we will shortly see.

6.4   Statistical Simulation

Finally, we simulate the performance of Astrape on the network graph of the
Lightning Network (LN).

Setup. We set up a mainnet Lightning Network node using the lnd [1] reference
implementation. We then used the lncli describegraph command to capture the
network topology of Lightning Network in February 2021. This gives us a graph
of 9566 nodes and 72164 edges. Finally, we randomly sample 5,000 pairs of nodes
in the network and calculate the shortest paths between them. This gives us a
randomly sampled set of real-life payment paths.

Path Statistics. As we have previously shown, paths more than 10 hops long
still have fairly small overhead even with non-recursive lock scripts, but much
longer paths will cause rather large unlock sizes. We examine whether the graph
topology will force payments to grow too long; Fig. 2a illustrates the distribution
of lengths for our 5,000 randomly selected payment paths. On average, a payment
path was 5.12 hops long, though the Lightning Network specification allows up
to 20 hops. This indicates that shortest payment paths long enough to pose
seriously ballooning worst-case overhead are practically nonexistent.

Total Scalability. One important attribute we wish to explore with the LN topology is the total scalability of the network—how fast can a PCN process transactions as a whole.

To do so, we keep track of how many times each node appears, or is "hit", in
our 5,000 randomly selected payment routes. On average, this is 2.99, but the vast
majority of nodes are hit only once, while a few nodes are hit hundreds of times.
The distribution of hits is plotted in Fig. 2b as a log-linear histogram. We then
look at the *distribution of overhead* in the network for both computation and
communication. This is by calculating the total computation and communication
cost for each node "hit" by the 1,000 random payments, using values from the
Bitcoin Cash implementation.

Computation cost is plotted in Fig. 2c. We see that the most heavily loaded
node in the entire network did around 2,000 ms of computation to process 1,500
transactions. This indicates that the largest hubs in a PCN with the current
Lightning Network topology will be able to process around 750 transactions a
second per CPU core. Such a throughput is orders of magnitude higher than that
of typical blockchains and is within reach of many traditional payment systems.
We note that this is only the maximum throughput of a *single CPU core*—in
practice hubs likely have multicore machines, and with many hubs the total LN
throughput will be many times this number.

Communication cost is plotted in Fig. 2d. We pessimistically assume that
all payments are settled through HashOnion. Even so, the total network load
averages to only about 3.58 KB per node. The largest hubs' total load still do
not exceed 1 MB. This illustrates that the bottleneck is actually computation,
not communication.

In summary, we see that Astrape's worst-case asymptotic performance poses no barriers to the total throughput of an Astrape-powered payment channel network. PCNs can enjoy the superb scalability associated with them just as easily with Astrape-powered privacy and security.

7   Conclusion

First-generation payment channel networks and other trust-minimizing intermediarized cryptocurrency payment systems lack strong privacy and security guarantees. Existing research, although solving the privacy and security problems, tend to rely on custom cryptographic primitives that cannot be easily swapped with alternatives based on different computational hardness assumptions.

We presented Astrape, a novel PCN construction that breaks this conundrum. Astrape is the first PCN that achieves relationship anonymity and balance security with only black-box access to generic conventional cryptography. It relies on a general idea of using non-anonymous post-hoc inconsistency witnesses to achieve balance security, while avoiding any information leaks when senders are not corrupt. This allows Astrape to avoid dealing with the zero-knowledge verification used to achieve balance security in existing relationship-anonymous PCNs without sacrificing any anonymity or security properties.

Furthermore, we demonstrate that Astrape is practical to deploy in the real world. Performance is superior on average to existing private PCNs, even on blockchains that are unsuitable for free-form smart contracts. We also showed that Astrape achieves high scalability on a real-world payment channel network graph.

Acknowledgement. We thank the reviewers and Sherman Chow for helping to improve this paper. We thank NSERC for Discovery Grant RGPIN-07014 and Create 498002-2017. This research was undertaken, in part, thanks to funding from the Canada Research Chairs program.

References

1. Lightning Network Daemon (2019). https://github.com/lightningnetwork/lnd
2. Blockchain Charts (2021). https://www.blockchain.com/charts. Accessed 1 Apr 2022
3. Aumasson, J.-P., Neves, S., Wilcox-O'Hearn, Z., Winnerlein, C.: BLAKE2: simpler, smaller, fast as MD5. In: Jacobson, M., Locasto, M., Mohassel, P., Safavi-Naini, R. (eds.) ACNS 2013. LNCS, vol. 7954, pp. 119–135. Springer, Heidelberg (2013). https://doi.org/10.1007/978-3-642-38980-1_8
4. Aumayr, L., et al.: Bitcoin-compatible virtual channels. In: 2021 IEEE Symposium on Security and Privacy (SP), pp. 901–918. IEEE (2021)
5. Aumayr, L., Monero-Sanchez, P., Maffei, M.: Blitz: secure multi-hop payments without two-phase commits. In: 30th USENIX Security Symposium (2021)
6. Backes, M., Kate, A., Manoharan, P., Meiser, S., Mohammadi, E.: AnoA: a framework for analyzing anonymous communication protocols. In: 2013 IEEE 26th Computer Security Foundations Symposium, pp. 163–178. IEEE (2013)

7. Camenisch, J., Drijvers, M., Gagliardoni, T., Lehmann, A., Neven, G.: The wonderful world of global random oracles. In: Nielsen, J.B., Rijmen, V. (eds.) EUROCRYPT 2018. LNCS, vol. 10820, pp. 280–312. Springer, Cham (2018). https://doi.org/10.1007/978-3-319-78381-9_11

8. Croman, K., et al.: On scaling decentralized blockchains. In: Clark, J., Meiklejohn, S., Ryan, P.Y.A., Wallach, D., Brenner, M., Rohloff, K. (eds.) FC 2016. LNCS, vol. 9604, pp. 106–125. Springer, Heidelberg (2016). https://doi.org/10.1007/978-3-662-53357-4_8

9. Danezis, G., Goldberg, I.: Sphinx: a compact and provably secure mix format. In: 30th IEEE Symposium on Security and Privacy, pp. 269–282. IEEE (2009)

10. Decker, C., Russell, R., Osuntokun, O.: eltoo: a simple layer2 protocol for bitcoin (2018). https://blockstream.com/eltoo.pdf

11. Decker, C., Wattenhofer, R.: A fast and scalable payment network with bitcoin duplex micropayment channels. In: Pelc, A., Schwarzmann, A.A. (eds.) SSS 2015. LNCS, vol. 9212, pp. 3–18. Springer, Cham (2015). https://doi.org/10.1007/978-3-319-21741-3_1

12. Dong, Y., Goldberg, I., Gorbunov, S., Boutaba, R.: Astrape: anonymous payment channels with boring cryptography (2022). https://github.com/nullchinchilla/astrape-paper/

13. Engelmann, F., Kopp, H., Kargl, F., Glaser, F., Weinhardt, C.: Towards an economic analysis of routing in payment channel networks. In: Proceedings of the 1st Workshop on Scalable and Resilient Infrastructures for Distributed Ledgers, pp. 1–6 (2017)

14. Green, M., Miers, I.: Bolt: anonymous payment channels for decentralized currencies. In: Proceedings of the 2017 ACM SIGSAC Conference on Computer and Communications Security, pp. 473–489. ACM (2017)

15. Heilman, E., Alshenibr, L., Baldimtsi, F., Scafuro, A., Goldberg, S.: TumbleBit: an untrusted bitcoin-compatible anonymous payment hub. In: Network and Distributed System Security Symposium (2017)

16. Josefsson, S., Liusvaara, I.: Edwards-Curve Digital Signature Algorithm (EdDSA). RFC 8032, January 2017. https://doi.org/10.17487/RFC8032, https://rfc-editor.org/rfc/rfc8032.txt

17. Lai, R.W.F., Cheung, H.K.F., Chow, S.S.M., So, A.M.-C.: Another look at anonymous communication. In: Phan, R.C.-W., Yung, M. (eds.) Mycrypt 2016. LNCS, vol. 10311, pp. 56–82. Springer, Cham (2017). https://doi.org/10.1007/978-3-319-61273-7_4

18. Malavolta, G., Moreno-Sanchez, P., Kate, A., Maffei, M., Ravi, S.: Concurrency and privacy with payment-channel networks. In: Proceedings of the 2017 ACM SIGSAC Conference on Computer and Communications Security, pp. 455–471. ACM (2017)

19. Malavolta, G., Moreno-Sanchez, P., Schneidewind, C., Kate, A., Maffei, M.: Anonymous multi-hop locks for blockchain scalability and interoperability. In: NDSS (2019)

20. McCorry, P., Möser, M., Shahandasti, S.F., Hao, F.: Towards bitcoin payment networks. In: Liu, J.K., Steinfeld, R. (eds.) ACISP 2016. LNCS, vol. 9722, pp. 57–76. Springer, Cham (2016). https://doi.org/10.1007/978-3-319-40253-6_4

21. Pfitzmann, A., Hansen, M.: A terminology for talking about privacy by data minimization: anonymity, unlinkability, undetectability, unobservability, pseudonymity, and identity management (2010)

22. Tairi, E., Moreno-Sanchez, P., Maffei, M.: A2L: anonymous atomic locks for scalability and interoperability in payment channel hubs. In: 42nd IEEE Symposium on Security and Privacy (2021)
23. Van Wirdum, A.: How the lightning network layers privacy on top of bitcoin (2016). https://bitcoinmagazine.com/articles/how-the-lightning-network-layers-privacy-on-top-of-bitcoin-1482183775. Accessed 1 Apr 2022
24. Yousaf, H., et al.: An empirical analysis of privacy in the lightning network (2021)

Block-Cyphers

A White-Box Speck Implementation Using Self-equivalence Encodings

Joachim Vandersmissen[1(✉)], Adrián Ranea[2], and Bart Preneel[2]

[1] atsec information security, Austin, USA
joachim@atsec.com
[2] imec-COSIC, KU Leuven, Leuven, Belgium
{adrian.ranea,bart.preneel}@esat.kuleuven.be

Abstract. In 2002, Chow et al. initiated the formal study of white-box cryptography and introduced the CEJO framework. Since then, various white-box designs based on their framework have been proposed, all of them broken. Ranea and Preneel proposed a different method in 2020, called *self-equivalence encodings* and analyzed its security for AES. In this paper, we apply this method to generate the first academic white-box SPECK implementations using self-equivalence encodings. Although we focus on SPECK in this work, our design could easily be adapted to protect other add-rotate-xor (ARX) ciphers. Then, we analyze the security of our implementation against key-recovery attacks. We propose an algebraic attack to fully recover the master key and external encodings from a white-box SPECK implementation, with limited effort required. While this result shows that the linear and affine self-equivalences of SPECK are insecure, we hope that this negative result will spur additional research in higher-degree self-equivalence encodings for white-box cryptography. Finally, we created an open-source Python project implementing our design, publicly available at https://github.com/jvdsn/white-box-speck. We give an overview of five strategies to generate output code, which can be used to improve the performance of the white-box implementation. We compare these strategies and determine how to generate the most performant white-box SPECK code. Furthermore, this project could be employed to test and compare the efficiency of attacks on white-box implementations using self-equivalence encodings.

Keywords: White-box cryptography · Self-equivalence · SPECK

1 Introduction

Traditionally, honest parties use cryptographic algorithms in combination with cryptographic keys to encrypt or decrypt messages. However, there are situations in which these keys must remain hidden in software, even from the party performing the encryption or decryption. In this case, the adversary has full control over the execution environment. As such, the implementation is a "white box" to the adversary. White-box cryptography is used to protect these implementations

© Springer Nature Switzerland AG 2022
G. Ateniese and D. Venturi (Eds.): ACNS 2022, LNCS 13269, pp. 771–791, 2022.
https://doi.org/10.1007/978-3-031-09234-3_38

against key-recovery attacks. From an attacker's perspective, reverse engineering and extracting a protected implementation of a cipher is less convenient compared to simply redistributing the keys. This implementation might also be restricted to a specific computing platform. As a result, white-box cryptography is a widely deployed method to protect private keys in the mobile banking industry and for digital rights management (DRM).

In 2002, Chow et al. initiated the formal study of white-box cryptography in their seminal work [19]. They introduced the *White-Box Attack Context*, also called the *white-box model*. The white-box model has three main properties:

- The attacker is a privileged user on the same host as the cryptographic algorithm, with complete access to the implementation.
- The attacker can dynamically execute the cryptographic algorithm.
- At any point before, during, or after the execution, the attacker is able to view and modify the internal details of the implementation.

On top of this, they introduced the first academic framework (commonly called the CEJO framework) to generate protected implementations in the white-box model, based on the AES block cipher [21]. Shortly after publishing their work on AES, Chow et al. also applied their method to the protection of the DES block cipher [20]. Concurrently, a practical side-channel attack on the white-box DES implementation was published by Jacob et al., using Differential Fault Analysis [27]. However, this attack was not applicable to the AES implementation protected using the CEJO framework. Still, it would take only two years for the initial AES implementation to be broken; in 2004, Billet et al. designed a practical key-recovery attack by analyzing the composition of the AES lookup tables [8].

The publication of these papers sparked more interest in the topic of white-box cryptography, with many new constructions based on DES [31] and AES [2,28,29,41,42] appearing over the years. Unfortunately, all of these implementations have been broken, using both algebraic attacks [22,24,26,30,34,40] and attacks based on side-channel analysis [12,13,16]. All of these designs improved upon or were inspired by the CEJO framework. Consequently, this framework has been analyzed extensively.

On the other hand, the work of Chow et al. also spurred research into entirely different types of constructions, using modified cipher designs [18] or completely new white-box ciphers [9,14,15]. Often this includes different security goals, such as *incompressibility* or *one-wayness* [11]. Some of these new designs have enjoyed limited success, while others were quickly broken [23,35].

In 2016, McMillion et al. used a type of permutations called *self-equivalences* to construct a toy white-box implementation of AES [33]. A self-equivalence of a function is a pair of permutations which can be applied to the start and end of that function without changing the original behavior. McMillion et al. divided AES into substitution and permutation (affine) layers. Then, they computed the self-equivalences of the substitution layers and applied these self-equivalence encodings to the affine layers directly preceding and succeeding the substitution layer. The resulting white-box implementation (also called a *self-equivalence implementation*) is a composition of substitution layers and encoded affine layers containing the round keys. In the same work, they also presented a practical attack to recover the cryptographic key from such implementations.

The work of McMillion et al. received little attention, and was only recently picked up Ranea and Preneel [36]. They analyzed the white-box security of substitution-permutation network (SPN) ciphers protected using self-equivalence encodings. They proposed a generic attack on such implementations, and proved that it is possible to recover the key from self-equivalence implementations of traditional SPN ciphers, if the S-box does not have differential and linear approximations with probability one. As cryptographically strong S-boxes are designed to resist differential [6] and linear [32] cryptanalysis, they showed that self-equivalence encodings are unsuitable to protect this class of traditional SPN ciphers. On the other hand, they also indicated that self-equivalence encodings might be of interest to protect ciphers with a better self-equivalence structure.

One possible class of interesting ciphers are add-rotate-xor (ARX) ciphers, whose rounds consist of the three basic operations the name implies: modular addition, bitwise rotation, and bitwise XOR. Because ARX ciphers do not rely on cryptographically strong S-boxes to provide nonlinearity, they are not susceptible to the attack described by Ranea and Preneel. Furthermore, in [37], it was found that the n-bit modular addition has a number of self-equivalences exponential in n. As a result, ciphers employing the modular addition as their only source of nonlinearity are a promising target for research in white-box cryptography based on self-equivalence encodings.

1.1   Contributions

In this paper, we introduce the first academic method to protect SPECK implementations using self-equivalence encodings. Let n be the SPECK word size, and m the number of key words, that is, the key size divided by n [3]. We start by rewriting the SPECK encryption function E_k as a substitution-permutation network (SPN), a composition of affine layers AL and substitution layers SL, with the first and last affine layer having a special structure. To obtain the self-equivalence implementation $\overline{E_k}$, we apply self-equivalence encodings of SL to each of the affine layers. Notably, this design could also be applied to protect other ARX ciphers.

Then, we define the set of linear self-equivalences of SL as $SE_L(SL)$ and the set of affine self-equivalences of SL as $SE_A(SL)$. Using a result from [37], we can determine that $SE_L(SL)$ contains $3 \times 2^{2n+2}$ elements and $SE_A(SL)$ contains $3 \times 2^{2n+8}$ elements. To encode an affine layer, self-equivalences are randomly sampled from $SE_L(SL)$ or $SE_A(SL)$. Provided that n is large enough, it would be impossible for an attacker to brute force the self-equivalence encodings of an encoded affine layer.

However, we found that it is possible to efficiently recover the linear self-equivalence encodings from an encoded affine layer by computing the Gröbner basis of a system of equations. An attacker can then easily compute the round keys, external encodings, and the SPECK master key. Additionally, we also analyzed the security of affine self-equivalence encodings. We show that an attacker can recover the affine self-equivalence encodings from an encoded affine layer up to one free variable. Consequently, the attacker only has to try 2^{m+1} possible configurations to break the white-box SPECK implementation. As m is at most 4 in practice, only $2^5 = 32$ configurations need to be guessed.

We tested these attacks using our Python implementation on consumer hardware. For $n = 64$, the largest SPECK word size available, we found that it took only 16.08 and 42.00 s to break the self-equivalence implementations when linear and affine self-equivalence encodings were used, respectively. Unfortunately, we conclude that these self-equivalence encodings are trivially insecure in the white-box model. Still, we hope that our method can be extended using higher-degree self-equivalences in the future to produce a secure white-box SPECK implementation.

We also created a Python implementation of our white-box SPECK method, capable of generating correct white-box SPECK code. This allows us to compare the performance impact of our design to an unprotected SPECK implementation. Because this impact is significant, we extend the program with strategies to generate more performant code. These strategies improve the execution speed of the matrix-vector product, one of the core functions in our implementations, and reduce the disk space required to store the binary matrices and vectors. We believe that these code generation strategies can be of independent interest to improve the performance of other mathematical computations relying on the storage of matrices and the computation of a matrix-vector product. In particular, these improvements could be applied to self-equivalence implementations of other ARX ciphers.

Finally, we compare an unprotected, reference SPECK implementation, an unoptimized white-box SPECK implementation, and the code generated by the different code generation strategies for three different SPECK variants: SPECK32/64, SPECK64/128, and SPECK128/256. The results show that the bit-packed and SIMD code generation strategies provides the most efficient code, both in terms of disk space usage and execution time. However, these strategies still pale in comparison to the unprotected, reference SPECK implementation, which is 5.4 times smaller and 24.8 times faster than the most efficient white-box implementations.

White-box cryptography is a hard problem, and over the years many white-box designs have been proposed and broken. While many new designs are based on the CEJO framework [20], we attempt to build on the comparatively recent method using self-equivalences [33]. Even though the results show our design is insecure for SPECK, we hope that this work can still be a useful stepping stone in the study of self-equivalence encodings for white-box cryptography.

A full version of this paper, which includes attack results and performance details for additional SPECK configurations, can be found at [39].

Outline. In Sect. 2, we define some preliminary notation and concepts that will be reused throughout this text. We introduce our approach to apply self-equivalence encodings to SPECK in Sect. 3. Then, in Sect. 4, we will analyze the security of our white-box SPECK implementation using linear and affine self-equivalence encodings. In Sect. 5, we give an overview of our Python project to generate white-box SPECK implementations using self-equivalence encodings and a comparison of five additional strategies to improve the performance of the generated code. Lastly, Sect. 6 contains the conclusions and future work.

2 Preliminaries

In general, lowercase symbols in this paper refer to numbers and vectors, while uppercase symbols are used to denote functions and matrices. In particular, E and D will be used to denote encryption and decryption functions, respectively. On top of this, we use E_k and D_k to refer to encryption and decryption functions with a hard coded key, k.

Finite fields with q elements are written as $\mathbb{F}_q$. We will only work with the finite field over two elements, $\mathbb{F}_2$. Vectors over this field are called binary vectors, while matrices over $\mathbb{F}_2$ are called binary matrices. More specifically, binary vectors in the vector space $\mathbb{F}_2^n$ are called n-bit vectors. The addition in $\mathbb{F}_2$ is denoted using $\oplus$, and we extend this to the addition of n-bit vectors by pairwise addition of each element. Finally, as a shorthand, we will sometimes replace $\oplus c$ by $\oplus_c$ if c is a constant.

A function $A : \mathbb{F}_2^n \mapsto \mathbb{F}_2^m$ is called an (n, m)-bit function. If $n = m$, then we simply call these functions n-bit functions. We use $\circ$ to refer to the composition of functions.

An important operation in this paper is the *modular addition*, defined as the addition of two numbers x and y, modulo some power of two. We use $\boxplus$ to refer to the modular addition, and $\boxminus$ to refer to its inverse, the *modular subtraction*. Lastly, $x \ggg \alpha$ denotes a right bitwise circular shift of x by α positions and $x \lll \beta$ denotes a left bitwise circular shift of x by β positions.

2.1 Self-equivalences

We briefly introduce the definition of linear and affine self-equivalences, and its matrix and matrix-vector forms.

Definition 1 (Linear self-equivalence, [10]). *Let F be an (n, m)-bit function. Let A be an n-bit linear permutation and B be an m-bit linear permutation. If $F = B \circ F \circ A$, we call the pair (A, B) a linear self-equivalence of F.*

Because A and B are linear functions, they could be given in the form of $n \times n$ and $m \times m$ matrices, respectively. In that case, we say (A, B) is a linear self-equivalence of F in matrix form.

Definition 2 (Affine self-equivalence, [10]). *Let F be an (n, m)-bit function. Let A be an n-bit linear permutation, a an n-bit constant, B an m-bit linear permutation, and b an m-bit constant. Together, (A, a) and (B, b) describe affine permutations. If $F = (\oplus_b \circ B) \circ F \circ (\oplus_a \circ A)$, we call the pair $((A, a), (B, b))$ an affine self-equivalence of F, or just a self-equivalence of F.*

Similarly, A, a, B, and b could be given in the form of $n \times n$ and $m \times m$ matrices, and vectors of length n and m, respectively. In that case, we say $((A,a),(B,b))$ is an (affine) self-equivalence of F in matrix-vector form. Of course, linear self-equivalences are also affine self-equivalences, with a and b equal to the zero vector.

In this paper, we will mostly work with the matrix and matrix-vector forms of self-equivalences. This allows us to precisely specify the self-equivalences we are using, as well as manipulate these matrices and vectors using basic linear algebra.

2.2 Speck

SPECK is a family of lightweight block ciphers proposed by the National Security Agency in 2013 [3]. In particular, SPECK was designed with a focus on performance in software. In this paper, we also use "the SPECK (block) cipher" to refer to the general design of the SPECK family.

The SPECK family consists of ten different instances, depending on the *block size* and *key size* parameters. The block size refers to the size in bits of the input, internal state, and output. These values always consist of two words, x and y, with bit size n. The key size refers to the size in bits of the master key k, which consists of m key words, with bit size n. We use the block size and key size in a shorthand notation to refer to specific SPECK instances. For example, SPECK128/256 refers to a SPECK instance with block size 128 and key size 256.

3 Self-equivalences and Speck

This section describes how self-equivalences can be used to create a white-box implementation of SPECK[1]. Being an ARX cipher, the SPECK encryption function is commonly written as a composition of the basic operations: modular addition, bitwise rotation, and bitwise XOR. However, to properly use self-equivalences in our design, SPECK needs to be rewritten as a repeated composition of non-linear and affine layers, similar to a substitution-permutation network (SPN). In the case of SPECK, the non-linear layers will contain the modular addition, and the affine layers contain the bitwise rotation, bitwise XOR, and round keys.

Then, we introduce the definition of an *encoding*: a permutation applied to the start or the end of a function F, to hide the original behavior of F. Encodings can be applied to the round functions of a block cipher to create *encoded implementations*, a type of white-box implementations [19].

We use a special type of encodings, based on self-equivalences of the modular addition, to encode the affine layers of SPECK. The start of the first affine layer and the end of the last affine layer are encoded using random permutations, called *external encodings*. When these encodings are applied to all affine layers

---

[1] Our method will focus on protecting the SPECK encryption function, but this design could easily be adapted to the SPECK decryption function.

of SPECK, we obtain a *self-equivalence implementation*, a different type of white-box implementations [36]. Note the difference with encoded implementations: in an encoded implementation, entire round functions are encoded; in a self-equivalence implementation, only the affine layers are encoded.

Let us start by rewriting the SPECK encryption function as a substitution-permutation network (SPN). First, we define the encryption function of an SPN.

Definition 3 (SPN encryption function). *Let E_k be an encryption function which takes a plaintext m and encrypts this plaintext using key k to produce ciphertext c. Then E_k represents the encryption function of a substitution-permutation network if E_k can be decomposed in affine layers AL and substitution layers SL as follows:*

$$E_k = AL^{(n_r)} \circ SL \circ \cdots \circ AL^{(2)} \circ SL \circ AL^{(1)} \ .$$

In addition, we call $SL \circ AL^{(r)}$ an SPN encryption round $E^{(r)}$.

We can now show that the SPECK encryption function can also be written as a combination of SPN encryption rounds. Let E_k be the encryption function of the SPECK cipher consisting of n_r rounds with word size n. E_k can be decomposed into affine layers AL and substitution layers SL:

$$E_k = AL^{(n_r)} \circ SL \circ \cdots \circ AL^{(1)} \circ SL \circ AL^{(0)}$$

with:

$$SL(x, y) = (x \boxplus y, y),$$
$$AL^{(0)}(x, y) = (x \ggg \alpha, y),$$
$$AL^{(r)}(x, y) = ((x \oplus k^{(r)}) \ggg \alpha, (x \oplus k^{(r)}) \oplus (y \lll \beta)), \text{ for } 1 \le r \le n_r - 1,$$
$$AL^{(n_r)}(x, y) = (x \oplus k^{(n_r)}, (x \oplus k^{(n_r)}) \oplus (y \lll \beta)) \ .$$

This result is also shown visually in Fig. 1. Here, two SPECK rounds are shown in sequence, with the dotted lines indicating the affine layers separated by modular additions. Evidently, this can be extended to n_r SPECK rounds, resulting in $n_r + 1$ affine layers, where layer 0 and n_r have a special structure.

In the previous definitions of AL, the SPECK state consists of two n-bit variables x and y. However, the self-equivalences of SL are $2n$-bit affine permutations, which operate on vectors of length $2n$ with elements in $\mathbb{F}_2$. To be able to apply these self-equivalences to AL, we need rewrite AL as $2n$-bit affine permutations operating on a $2n$-bit state vector xy:

$$AL^{(0)} = R_\alpha,$$
$$AL^{(r)} = R_\alpha \circ X \circ L_\beta \circ \oplus_{k'^{(r)}}, \text{ for } 1 \le r \le n_r - 1,$$
$$AL^{(n_r)} = X \circ L_\beta \circ \oplus_{k'^{(n_r)}} \ .$$

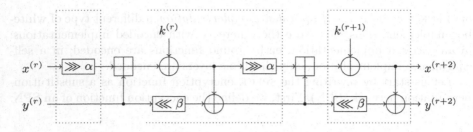

Fig. 1. Diagram of two SPECK encryption rounds, with affine layers indicated using dotted lines.

Here, xy contains the bits of x and y in little-endian order, R_α represents a right circular shift of x by α bits, L_β represents a left circular shift of y by β bits, and X represents the bitwise XOR operation such that $y = x \oplus y$. Finally, $k'^{(r)}$ is a vector of length $2n$ containing the key bits of the round key $k^{(r)}$ in the first n positions and zero in the last n positions.

To protect the key material in $AL^{(r)}$, we need to encode the affine layers. Let us first introduce the definitions of an encoding.

Definition 4 (Encoding, [36]). *Let F be an (n, m)-bit function and let (I, O) be a pair of n-bit and m-bit permutations, respectively. The function $\overline{F} = O \circ F \circ I$ is called an encoded F, and I and O are called the input and output encoding, respectively.*

In our design, the encodings I and O will mainly be self-equivalences of SL when an affine layer is encoded. Therefore, we call these encodings *self-equivalence encodings*. However, the input encoding of the first affine layer and the output encoding of the last affine layer must be random affine permutations, called the external encodings. It is critical to the security of white-box implementations that these external encodings are generated at random and kept secret from the attacker. Without external encodings, our design would be trivially insecure [19]. Now, we define the encoded affine layers.

Definition 5 (Encoded affine layer, [36]). *Let $AL^{(r)}$ be an affine layer of the SPECK cipher, with $1 \leq r \leq n_r$. Then we call $\overline{AL^{(r)}}$ an encoded affine layer, with:*

$$\overline{AL^{(r)}} = (\oplus_{o^{(r)}} \circ O^{(r)}) \circ AL^{(r)} \circ (\oplus_{i^{(r)}} \circ I^{(r)}),$$

where $((O^{(r)}, o^{(r)}), (I^{(r+1)}, i^{(r+1)}))$ is a self-equivalence of the SPECK substitution layer SL, and $(I^{(1)}, i^{(1)})$ and $(O^{(n_r)}, o^{(n_r)})$ are random affine permutations.

Note that $AL^{(0)}$ will not be encoded: this affine layer does not contain any key material, so it can be skipped.

If the self-equivalences composed with each $AL^{(r)}$ are sampled randomly from a set of self-equivalences, the unencoded affine layer $AL^{(r)}$ can not be recovered without knowledge of $(I^{(r)}, i^{(r)})$ and $(O^{(r)}, o^{(r)})$. This effectively hides the round keys inside the affine layers, and is the basis of our method to protect SPECK implementations using self-equivalence encodings. Moreover, this process could easily be adapted to other ARX ciphers. When all affine layers of a SPECK encryption function are encoded using self-equivalence encodings and external encodings, we obtain a self-equivalence implementation of SPECK.

Definition 6 (Self-equivalence implementation, [36]). *Let E_k be the encryption function of the* SPECK *cipher consisting of n_r rounds with word size n. We call $\overline{E_k}$ a self-equivalence implementation of* SPECK, *with:*

$$\overline{E_k} = \overline{AL^{(n_r)}} \circ SL \circ \cdots \circ \overline{AL^{(1)}} \circ SL \circ AL^{(0)} \ .$$

We can show that a self-equivalence implementation of SPECK, $\overline{E_k}$, is functionally equivalent to E_k, up to the external encodings. Due to the self-equivalence property, the intermediate encodings are canceled:

$$\begin{aligned}
\overline{E_k} &= \overline{AL^{(n_r)}} \circ SL \circ \cdots \circ \overline{AL^{(1)}} \circ SL \circ AL^{(0)} \\
&= (\oplus_{o^{(n_r)}} \circ O^{(n_r)}) \circ AL^{(n_r)} \circ SL \circ \cdots \circ AL^{(1)} \circ (\oplus_{i^{(1)}} \circ I^{(1)}) \circ SL \circ AL^{(0)} \\
&= (\oplus_{o^{(n_r)}} \circ O^{(n_r)}) \circ AL^{(n_r)} \circ SL \circ \cdots \circ AL^{(1)} \circ SL \circ AL^{(0)} \circ (\oplus_{i'^{(1)}} \circ I'^{(1)}) \\
&= (\oplus_{o^{(n_r)}} \circ O^{(n_r)}) \circ E_k \circ (\oplus_{i'^{(1)}} \circ I'^{(1)}) \ .
\end{aligned}$$

This property is also illustrated in Fig. 2, for two encryption rounds. The dashed lines indicate the substitution layer SL surrounded by its self-equivalence, which can simply be reduced to SL. The encoded affine layers $\overline{AL^{(r)}}$ and $\overline{AL^{(r+1)}}$ are marked by dotted lines.

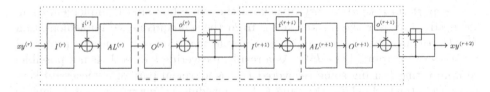

Fig. 2. Diagram of two SPECK SPN encryption rounds encoded using self-equivalences.

3.1   Self-equivalences of SL

We use the method described in [37] to generate the self-equivalences of SL. This allows us to randomly sample both linear and affine self-equivalences. For more information, we refer the reader to Sect. 5.2 of [37].

We call the sets of linear and affine self-equivalences generated using this method $SE_L(SL)$ and $SE_A(SL)$, respectively. When $n > 2$, $|SE_L(SL)| = 3 \times 2^{2n+2}$ and $|SE_A(SL)| = 3 \times 2^{2n+8}$. This is important for the security of our method to protect SPECK implementations: the number of self-equivalences should be as high as possible to prevent a simple brute-force key-recovery attack.

For $n = 64$, the largest SPECK word size, this would result in 3×2^{130} and 3×2^{136} possibilities for linear and affine self-equivalences, respectively, enough to resist a naive brute-force attack. In the next section, we introduce a more extensive security analysis of self-equivalence encodings and show an attacker can still recover self-equivalences without resorting to brute-force.

4   Security Analysis

This section analyzes the security of our white-box SPECK design. The security of white-box implementations can be expressed in many different ways. Most commonly, the goal of the attacker is to extract the cryptographic key from a provided implementation (*key extraction*). However, other security notions include *one-wayness* and *incompressibility*. A detailed analysis of white-box cryptography security goals is presented by Bock et al. in [11]. In this paper, we focus on the fundamental white-box security feature: resistance to key-recovery attacks.

In our analysis, we will evaluate the security of our white-box SPECK method from an algebraic perspective. Although self-equivalence encodings are generated at random, they are not completely random linear or affine transformations. We will try to exploit the additional structure of $SE_L(SL)$ and $SE_A(SL)$ to reduce the brute-force search space of possible self-equivalence encodings and recover key bits. Moreover, to fully compromise the security, we will also need to recover the external encodings from the white-box implementation. Unlike the attack introduced by Ranea and Preneel in [36], which is based on *equivalence problems* and not applicable to SPECK, we analyze self-equivalence equations in bits. In the broader context of the white-box model, our approach is quite simple: we only require access to the encoded affine layers of the implementation.

To perform a key-recovery attack on the white-box SPECK implementation, we need to recover the master key k from the self-equivalence implementation $\overline{E_k}$. Unfortunately, the self-equivalence implementation only contains protected versions of the round keys, $k^{(r)}$. As a result, recovering k directly is not possible, so computing k using some recovered $k^{(r)}$ is a crucial part of a successful key-recovery attack. Luckily, the SPECK key schedule is invertible, and k can be computed easily, using only the m first round keys. Let n be the SPECK word size, and m the number of key words, that is, the key size divided by n [3]. Suppose $k^{(1)}, \ldots, k^{(m)}$ are known, then compute:

$$l^{(r+m-1)} = (k^{(r)} \lll \beta) \oplus k^{(r+1)}$$

$$l^{(r)} = ((l^{(r+m-1)} \oplus r) \boxminus k^{(r)}) \lll \alpha .$$

Combining $l^{(m-1)}, \ldots, l^{(1)}$, and $k^{(1)}$, we obtain the master key k.

Note that this approach can be extended to reconstruct k using any sequence of m consecutive round keys, by working backwards to compute the preceding $k^{(r)}$ and $l^{(r)}$ values.

4.1   Security Analysis of Linear Self-equivalences

We start the analysis of the white-box method for SPECK by looking at a variant where all encodings, both self-equivalence encodings and external encodings, are linear. Although linear encodings are significantly weaker than affine encodings in terms of security, they are also conceptually easier to understand. Furthermore, the analysis of this weaker version might give us some initial insights in the security of a more secure variant using affine encodings.

In this section, we will focus on a single intermediate affine layer of an encoded SPECK encryption function $\overline{E_k}$. For the sake of convenience, we repeat the definition of an encoded affine layer for round r (see Definition 5) here:

$$\overline{AL^{(r)}} = (\oplus_{o^{(r)}} \circ O^{(r)}) \circ AL^{(r)} \circ (\oplus_{i^{(r)}} \circ I^{(r)}) \tag{1}$$

Because we only consider linear encodings for now, $i^{(r)}$ and $o^{(r)}$ are zero vectors. Consequently, Eq. (1) can be simplified to:

$$\overline{AL^{(r)}} = O^{(r)} \circ AL^{(r)} \circ I^{(r)} \tag{2}$$

This encoded affine layer will be stored as a combination of an encoded matrix $\overline{M^{(r)}}$ and an encoded vector $\overline{v^{(r)}}$:

$$\overline{M^{(0)}} = M^{(0)},$$
$$\overline{v^{(0)}} = v^{(0)},$$
$$\overline{M^{(r)}} = O^{(r)} M^{(r)} I^{(r)}, \text{ for } 1 \le r \le n_r,$$
$$\overline{v^{(r)}} = O^{(r)} v^{(r)}, \text{ for } 1 \le r \le n_r .$$

For each round r, $M^{(r)}$ represents the known linear operations of the affine layer, while $v^{(r)}$ is the constant of the affine layer. However, as $v^{(0)}$ does not contain any key material, this round is not protected using self-equivalences.

To hide the key material in $v^{(r)}$, $(O^{(r)}, I^{(r+1)})$ need to be randomly generated linear self-equivalences of SL. If the self-equivalences are generated using the method from [37], then $SE_L(SL)$ can be parameterized by a bit vector c of length $2n + 5$, where n is the SPECK word size. We do not describe the full parametrization for $SE_L(SL)$ here, instead, it can be found in the Python project code. For any encoded matrix $\overline{M^{(r)}}$, $c^{(r-1)}$ and $c^{(r)}$ fully define $I^{(r)}$ and $O^{(r)}$, respectively. In other words, if it is possible to recover these bit vectors, an attacker can re-generate $I^{(r)}$ and $O^{(r)}$, peel off the self-equivalence encodings, and compute the round keys and external encodings.

We will now describe a method to recover $c^{(r-1)}$ and $c^{(r)}$ for any intermediate round r. Let X and Y be the matrix forms of the unknown self-equivalence encodings, $I^{(r)}$ and $O^{(r)}$, respectively. Combining this with the definition of $\overline{M^{(r)}}$, we obtain the following equation:

$$\overline{M^{(r)}} = Y M^{(r)} X \tag{3}$$

As $I^{(r)}$ and $O^{(r)}$ are generated using the method from [37], each entry in the matrices X and Y is parameterized by $c^{(r-1)}$ and $c^{(r)}$ respectively. Furthermore, $M^{(r)}$ and $\overline{M^{(r)}}$ are the $2n \times 2n$ matrices known to the attacker. By looking at each entry of these matrices individually, Eq. (3) can be written as a system of $(2n)^2$ equations in $2 \times (2n + 5)$ unknowns, the bits in $c^{(r-1)}$ and $c^{(r)}$. Let α_i be the unknowns corresponding to X and β_i the unknowns corresponding to Y. Now, let R be the Boolean polynomial ring in these variables, that is:

$$R = \mathbb{F}_2[\alpha_i, \beta_i]/\langle \alpha_i^2 + \alpha_i, \beta_i^2 + \beta_i \rangle, \text{ for } 1 \leq i \leq 2n + 5 .$$

Of course, depending on the density of X, Y, and $M^{(r)}$, many of these equations might not include any α_i or β_i variables. However, by computing the Gröbner basis G of the ideal defined by these equations in R, it is possible to uniquely determine the values of α_i and β_i. We verified this experimentally for every SPECK word size. This in turn reveals the values of $c^{(r-1)}$ and $c^{(r)}$.

An attacker can use this method to recover $c^{(r)}$ for $\overline{M^{(r+1)}}$ and $1 \leq r \leq m$, where m is the number of SPECK key words. The attacker then re-generates the self-equivalences $(O^{(r)}, I^{(r+1)})$. Because $v^{(r)}$ is always publicly known, the attacker can compute

$$(O^{(r)})^{-1}\overline{v^{(r)}} = (O^{(r)})^{-1}O^{(r)}v^{(r)}$$
$$= v^{(r)}$$

to obtain the round keys $k^{(r)}$ for $r = 1, 2, \ldots, m$.

Similarly, an attacker can recover $c^{(1)}$ from $\overline{M^{(2)}}$ and re-generate the self-equivalence $(O^{(1)}, I^{(2)})$. As with $v^{(r)}$, $M^{(1)}$ is always publicly known, so the attacker can compute

$$(O^{(1)}M^{(1)})^{-1}\overline{M^{(1)}} = (O^{(1)}M^{(1)})^{-1}O^{(1)}M^{(1)}I^{(1)}$$
$$= I^{(1)}$$

to obtain the input external encoding $I^{(1)}$.

Finally, an attacker can recover $c^{(n_r-1)}$ from $\overline{M^{(n_r-1)}}$ and re-generate the self-equivalence $(O^{(n_r-1)}, I^{(n_r)})$. The attacker then computes

$$\overline{M^{(n_r)}}(M^{(n_r)}I^{(n_r)})^{-1} = O^{(n_r)}M^{(n_r)}I^{(n_r)}(M^{(n_r)}I^{(n_r)})^{-1}$$
$$= O^{(n_r)}$$

to obtain the output external encoding $O^{(n_r)}$.

Note that it is not possible to recover $c^{(1)}$ from $\overline{M^{(1)}}$ or $c^{(n_r-1)}$ from $\overline{M^{(n_r)}}$. Because $M^{(1)}$ and $M^{(n_r)}$ are multiplied by respectively $I^{(1)}$ and $O^{(n_r)}$, random affine permutations, Eq. (3) does not hold.

The most expensive operation in this attack is computing the Gröbner basis for $4n^2$ equations in $2 \times (2n + 5)$ variables. Unfortunately, it is notoriously difficult to estimate the time complexity required to compute the Gröbner basis.

Instead, we implemented this attack in Python [1] using SageMath [38] and the POLYBORI framework [17]. We executed this implementation using a single core on a laptop with an AMD Ryzen 7 PRO 3700U CPU, running Linux 5.15.5. The attack took only 16.08 s to recover the master key and external encodings from a white-box SPECK128/256 instance. The full results for every SPECK instance can be found in [39], Appendix A.

Clearly, it is feasible to execute this attack using even modest consumer hardware. We conclude that a white-box SPECK implementation using only linear encodings is insecure against key-recovery attacks, even with relatively limited capabilities. In particular, it is not necessary to inspect or modify the execution of the white-box implementation. Furthermore, recovering the encodings is possible using only the information revealed by a single encoded affine layer.

4.2   Security Analysis of Affine Self-equivalences

Knowing that a white-box SPECK implementation using only linear encodings is insecure, we can try to extend this attack to the full design using affine encodings. We start by updating the equations for $\overline{M^{(r)}}$ and $\overline{v^{(r)}}$ with affine self-equivalence encodings $(I^{(r)}, i^{(r)})$ and $(O^{(r)}, o^{(r)})$:

$$\overline{M^{(0)}} = M^{(0)},$$
$$\overline{v^{(0)}} = v^{(0)},$$
$$\overline{M^{(r)}} = O^{(r)} M^{(r)} I^{(r)}, \text{ for } 1 \leq r \leq n_r,$$
$$\overline{v^{(r)}} = O^{(r)}(v^{(r)} \oplus M^{(r)} i^{(r)}) \oplus o^{(r)}, \text{ for } 1 \leq r \leq n_r .$$

Once again, we will try to recover the coefficients used to generate a random affine self-equivalence $((O^{(r)}, o^{(r)}), (I^{(r+1)}, i^{(r+1)}))$. In this case, if the self-equivalences are generated using the method from [37], then $SE_A(SL)$ can be parameterized by a bit vector c of length $2n + 11$, where SPECK n is the word size. We previously showed that $c^{(r)}$ can easily be recovered from $\overline{M^{(r)}}$ when only linear encodings are used. However, we found that some coefficients are exclusively used in the constants $i^{(r)}$ and $o^{(r)}$. As a result, we also need to use the definition of $\overline{v^{(r)}}$ to recover the full value of $c^{(r)}$. Furthermore, to simplify our implementation, we will simultaneously recover the bit vector $k^{(r)}$, the round key bits for round r.

Instead of uniquely determining $c^{(r-1)}$, $c^{(r)}$, and $k^{(r)}$ for a round r, we will describe a method to generate possible configurations for these coefficients and key bits. Let (X, x) and (Y, y) be the matrix-vector forms of the unknown self-equivalence encodings, $(I^{(r)}, i^{(r)})$ and $(O^{(r)}, o^{(r)})$, respectively. First, we apply the definition of $\overline{M^{(r)}}$ again to obtain $(2n)^2$ equations, similar to the first step in the attack on linear self-equivalences (Eq. (3)). Let α_i be the unknowns corresponding to (X, x), β_i the unknowns corresponding to (Y, y), and R_1 the Boolean polynomial ring in these variables, that is:

$$R_1 = \mathbb{F}_2[\alpha_i, \beta_i]/\langle \alpha_i^2 + \alpha_i, \beta_i^2 + \beta_i \rangle, \text{ for } 1 \leq i \leq 2n + 11 .$$

Computing the Gröbner basis G_1 of the ideal defined by these equations in R_1 reveals the values of $4n + 15$ unknowns, slightly less than the total number, $2 \times (2n + 11)$. Now, let z represent the vector $v^{(r)}$, unknown to the attacker. Combining this with (X, x) and (Y, y) and the definition of $\overline{v^{(r)}}$, we obtain the following equation:

$$\overline{v^{(r)}} = Y(z \oplus M^{(r)}x) \oplus y \tag{4}$$

In this case, x is parametrized by $c^{(r-1)}$, whereas Y and y are parametrized by $c^{(r)}$. Furthermore, recall that $v^{(r)}$ contains $k^{(r)}$, the n unknown round key bits. As $M^{(r)}$ and $\overline{v^{(r)}}$ are known to the attacker, Eq. (4) can be written as a system of $2n$ equations in $2 \times (2n + 11) + n$ unknowns. As before, let α_i be the unknowns corresponding to (X, x) and β_i the unknowns corresponding to (Y, y). We now also introduce γ_j to denote the unknowns corresponding to z. Let R_2 the Boolean polynomial ring in these variables, that is:

$$R_2 = R_1[\gamma_j]/\langle \gamma_j^2 + \gamma_j \rangle, \text{ for } 1 \leq j \leq n \ .$$

However, because the values of $4n+15$ unknowns were revealed by G_1, we also define the quotient ring $Q = R_2/G_1$. Finally, we again compute the Gröbner basis G_2 of the ideal defined by the equations of $\overline{v^{(r)}}$ in Q. This uniquely determines the values of all but one of the unknowns, resulting in two possible configurations for $c^{(r-1)}$, $c^{(r)}$, and $k^{(r)}$.

An attacker can then follow the same process described in Sect. 4.1 to recover the possible round keys and external encodings $I^{(1)}$ and $O^{(n_r)}$. In total, 2^{m+1} possible configurations must be enumerated, with m the number of key words. Because m is at most 4 for SPECK, this exponential function is no problem in practice. We implemented this attack in Python [1] using SageMath [38] and POLYBORI [17] and executed it using the same setup used for linear encodings. Now the attack took 42.00 s to recover the master key and external encodings from a white-box SPECK128/256 instance. Again, the full results can be found in [39], Appendix A.

Although this attack is certainly more expensive than the one for linear encodings, the master key and external encodings are still easily extracted in practice. Consequently, we must conclude that our white-box SPECK method is insecure in the white-box model. However, a higher level of security might be achieved by using quadratic, cubic, and even quartic self-equivalences.

5   Implementation

In previous sections, we discussed the theoretical foundations of our method to construct white-box SPECK implementations. To research the practical viability of this method, we also implemented a program to generate white-box SPECK code. This project is publicly available in our GitHub repository[2]. Our program

---

[2] https://github.com/jvdsn/white-box-speck.

to generate white-box SPECK implementations[3] is written in Python, a free and open source programming language [1]. We chose Python because its source code is completely portable across platforms, programming in Python is comparatively simple, and it is possible to interact with SageMath using a language interface [38]. SageMath is a free and open source mathematics package, which is used extensively for mathematical computations throughout the project.

Our program generates white-box SPECK implementations in four major steps. First, the program takes the block size $2n$ and master key k as input. Using the SPECK key schedule, k is transformed into round keys $k^{(r)}$, and $M^{(r)}$ and $v^{(r)}$ (see Sect. 4.1) are computed. Then, for each round r, random self-equivalence encodings are generated to encode $M^{(r)}$ and $v^{(r)}$. In this step, the random external encodings are also generated and applied to round 1 and n_r. Finally, using $\overline{M^{(r)}}$ and $\overline{v^{(r)}}$, the program generates the output code, a white-box SPECK implementation and its inverse external encodings.

Currently, this output code is exclusively C source code. We chose the C programming language because it is widely used, provides fast low-level memory control, and contains a convenient interface for single instruction, multiple data (SIMD) functions. However, our project could easily be adapted to return source or compiled code for other programming languages.

The generated C code follows the same intuitive pattern as simple SPN cipher implementations. For each round, a modular addition and affine transformation are performed, except for the final round, which consists only of the affine transformation. Because the white-box SPECK encryption algorithm operates on vectors of bits instead of integers, the input x and y has to be converted to bits first. Similarly, the state vector xy has to be converted back to integers after encryption. No key expansion is necessary, as the round keys $k^{(r)}$ are encoded in the affine layers.

The encryption function relies on five subroutines: functions to convert to and from bits, a function to perform the modular addition on xy, a function to perform the matrix-vector product, and a function to perform the vector addition. Conversion to and from binary is done big-endian. The other three functions use a standard textbook implementation. For example, the modular addition simply performs the addition with carry algorithm on each individual bit, ignoring the final carry to perform the modular reduction. In the case of the matrix-vector product, two **for** loops are used to compute the resulting vector. For the vector addition, the generated code performs an XOR operation for each bit in the vector. We call this the default code generation strategy; in the next section we will consider techniques to implement these functions more efficiently.

Finally, apart from the definitions and implementations of these subroutines, the required data (matrices $\overline{M^{(r)}}$ and vectors $\overline{v^{(r)}}$) will also have to be stored in the C source code. A straightforward way of storing a matrix in C is to use

---

[3] Our project currently only supports the generation of white-box SPECK encryption code. However, the existing project could easily be modified to also generate white-box SPECK decryption implementations. When discussing the generated code in this section, we always refer to SPECK encryption.

a two-dimensional array: storing each row as an array of the elements in an enclosing array to represent the full matrix. A vector can be stored by simply using a single one-dimensional array. In total, $n_r + 1$ two-dimensional arrays and $n_r + 1$ one-dimensional arrays are generated by the default code generation strategy.

5.1   Code Generation Strategies

Although the method described previously generates correct and functional C code, this code is far from optimal. We introduce five additional code generation strategies to improve the efficiency of the generated C code.

Sparse matrix code generation Because the entries of $\overline{M^{(r)}}$ are in $\mathbb{F}_2$, one could consider storing only the nonzero entries to save disk space. The other entries are then implicitly known to be 0. We call this the *sparse matrix representation*. In addition to reducing the disk space used by the generated C code, using the sparse matrix representation also simplifies the matrix-vector product. Similar to the sparse matrix representation, we can also use a *sparse vector representation* for the vectors $v^{(r)}$. The vector addition can also be modified to take advantage of the sparse vector representation.

Inlined code generation Before the C code is generated, the contents of $\overline{M^{(r)}}$ and $\overline{v^{(r)}}$ are already known. Therefore, it is possible to generate $n_r + 1$ different functions for the matrix-vector product and for the vector addition. In the case of the matrix-vector products, these functions will only contain the array operations for the nonzero entries in the matrix. Similarly, the functions for the vector additions only modify the positions for the nonzero entries in the vector. In this way, the data is inlined in the function implementations.

Bit-packed code generation The C standard library contains data types to store 16-bit, 32-bit, and 64-bit unsigned integers. Instead of storing the bits individually in an integer data type, we can use these larger data types to store multiple bits simultaneously, bit-packing n bits in an n-bit unsigned integer. This will considerably reduce the disk space usage and improve the execution time of the generated C code. When $n = 24$ or $n = 48$, the data must be stored in 32-bit or 64-bit unsigned integers, respectively.

Inlined bit-packed code generation This code generation strategy combines the previous two strategies. n bits are bit-packed in an n-bit unsigned integer, and used in $n_r + 1$ different functions for the matrix-vector product and for the vector addition. Compared to the inlined strategy, this method has the advantage of the state vector xy being bit-packed. Compared to the bit-packing method, we might expect a performance improvement as a result of the loop unrolling in the inlined functions.

SIMD code generation We extend the bit-packed code generation with instructions from the Advanced Vector Extensions (AVX) and Advanced Vector Extensions 2 (AVX2) instruction sets. Single instruction, multiple data (SIMD) allows algorithms to operate on multiple pieces of data, called vectors, at the same time. For example, sixteen 16-bit integers could be combined into a 256-bit SIMD vector, which could then be manipulated using SIMD instructions. For the sake of simplicity, our implementation does not consider $n = 24$ and $n = 32$.

5.2   Comparison

To provide a comprehensive comparison of the SPECK encryption performance for the unprotected and self-equivalence implementations, we tested three different variants: SPECK32/64, SPECK64/128, and SPECK128/256. We did not test the block sizes 48 and 96, as these parameters are not supported by all code generation strategies. For every variant, we used the keys from the original SPECK test vectors to perform the encryptions [3]. However, the choice and length of key should not have an impact on the performance of the self-equivalence implementations. Furthermore, to ensure a fair comparison, the same affine self-equivalence encodings were used when generating C code using different strategies. We give an overview of the results for each of the three variants, the full details of the experiments can be found in [39], Appendix B.

In the case of SPECK32/64, the unprotected reference implementation takes up 16 320 bytes of disk space, with the smallest self-equivalence implementation, the bit-packed implementation, using only 19 552 bytes of disk space. To compare the performance, 1 000 000 random encryptions were performed upon execution of the program. On average, the unprotected implementation finished this in 0.22 s at 4.0 GHz, reaching a throughput of 220 cycles per byte (c/b). The most efficient self-equivalence implementation, again the bit-packed implementation, is considerably slower, taking on average 2.26 s, which results in a throughput of 2260 c/b.

Because unprotected implementations do not store matrices and vectors which depend on the block size, the required disk space for the unprotected SPECK64/128 implementation stays the same. The smallest self-equivalence implementations are the SIMD and bit-packed implementations, using 31 072 and 31 080 bytes respectively. For a block size of 64 bits, 300 000 encryptions were executed, which results in an average execution time of 0.08 s for the unprotected implementation. This is equivalent to a throughput of 133 c/b. Here, the SIMD strategy also produces the fastest code (1.31 s, 2183 c/b), however bit-packed code is only slightly behind (1.51 s, 2517 c/b).

Finally, for SPECK128/256 implementations, the sparse matrix representation requires a similar amount of disk space on average (95 345.6 bytes) compared to the bit-packed (88 760 bytes) or SIMD (88 752 bytes) implementations. While code generated using these strategies still takes up six times the amount of disk space of an unprotected implementation, it still improves on the default self-equivalence implementation with a reduction of 85%. For this block size, the number of random encryption iterations was set to 100 000. The experimental results show an average throughput of 125 c/b for the unprotected implementation, while the bit-packed code is the most performant self-equivalence implementation, reaching a throughput of 2825 c/b on average.

6   Conclusion

In this work, we introduced the first academic method to protect white-box SPECK implementations using self-equivalence encodings. We showed that these encodings can be applied to SPECK rounds, ostensibly hiding the round keys in encoded affine layers. Similar techniques could be used to protect other ARX ciphers, such as SALSA20 [5], CHACHA20 [4], or THREEFISH [25]. We also analyzed the security of our design against key-recovery attacks. We presented practical attacks to fully recover the self-equivalence encodings and external encodings of a self-equivalence implementation, showing that our method is completely insecure in the white-box model. Finally, we created a Python project to generate self-equivalence implementations using our method. We used this project to calculate the impact of our method on the performance of SPECK. Furthermore, we were able to compare five additional strategies to generate output C code, and determined an overall optimal strategy: bit-packed code generation.

One possible area for future research is the generation of self-equivalences. In this paper, we only employed linear and affine self-equivalences. Extending this design to quadratic, cubic, or higher-degree self-equivalences could result in more secure white-box implementations. Alternatively, the security of our current method could be analyzed using several approaches in the white-box model. In particular, we did not consider the known techniques based on side-channel analysis, such as differential fault analysis [7] and differential computation analysis [12]. Our Python project could be used to test and compare the efficiency of several attacks on white-box implementations using self-equivalence encodings.

Acknowledgements. Joachim Vandersmissen would like to thank atsec information security for its support. Adrián Ranea is supported by a PhD Fellowship from the Research Foundation - Flanders (FWO). The authors would like to thank the anonymous reviewers for their comments and suggestions.

References

1. Welcome to python.org. https://www.python.org/
2. Baek, C.H., Cheon, J.H., Hong, H.: White-box AES implementation revisited. J. Commun. Netw. **18**(3), 273–287 (2016)
3. Beaulieu, R., Shors, D., Smith, J., Treatman-Clark, S., Weeks, B., Wingers, L.: The SIMON and SPECK families of lightweight block ciphers. IACR Cryptol. ePrint Arch, p. 404 (2013)
4. Bernstein, D.J.: ChaCha, a variant of Salsa20. In: Workshop Record of SASC, vol. 8, pp. 3–5 (2008)
5. Bernstein, D.J.: The Salsa20 family of stream ciphers. In: Robshaw, M., Billet, O. (eds.) New Stream Cipher Designs. LNCS, vol. 4986, pp. 84–97. Springer, Heidelberg (2008). https://doi.org/10.1007/978-3-540-68351-3_8
6. Biham, E., Shamir, A.: Differential cryptanalysis of the full 16-round DES. In: Brickell, E.F. (ed.) CRYPTO 1992. LNCS, vol. 740, pp. 487–496. Springer, Heidelberg (1993). https://doi.org/10.1007/3-540-48071-4_34

7. Biham, E., Shamir, A.: Differential fault analysis of secret key cryptosystems. In: Kaliski, B.S. (ed.) CRYPTO 1997. LNCS, vol. 1294, pp. 513–525. Springer, Heidelberg (1997). https://doi.org/10.1007/BFb0052259

8. Billet, O., Gilbert, H., Ech-Chatbi, C.: Cryptanalysis of a white box AES implementation. In: Handschuh, H., Hasan, M.A. (eds.) SAC 2004. LNCS, vol. 3357, pp. 227–240. Springer, Heidelberg (2004). https://doi.org/10.1007/978-3-540-30564-4_16

9. Biryukov, A., Bouillaguet, C., Khovratovich, D.: Cryptographic Schemes Based on the ASASA Structure: Black-Box, White-Box, and Public-Key (Extended Abstract). In: Sarkar, P., Iwata, T. (eds.) ASIACRYPT 2014. LNCS, vol. 8873, pp. 63–84. Springer, Heidelberg (2014). https://doi.org/10.1007/978-3-662-45611-8_4

10. Biryukov, A., De Cannière, C., Braeken, A., Preneel, B.: A toolbox for cryptanalysis: linear and affine equivalence algorithms. In: Biham, E. (ed.) EUROCRYPT 2003. LNCS, vol. 2656, pp. 33–50. Springer, Heidelberg (2003). https://doi.org/10.1007/3-540-39200-9_3

11. Bock, E.A., Amadori, A., Brzuska, C., Michiels, W.: On the security goals of white-box cryptography. IACR Trans. Cryptogr. Hardw. Embed. Syst. 2020(2), 327–357 (2020)

12. Bock, E.A., et al.: White-box cryptography: don't forget about grey-box attacks. J. Cryptol. 32(4), 1095–1143 (2019)

13. Alpirez Bock, E., Brzuska, C., Michiels, W., Treff, A.: On the ineffectiveness of internal encodings - revisiting the DCA attack on white-box cryptography. In: Preneel, B., Vercauteren, F. (eds.) ACNS 2018. LNCS, vol. 10892, pp. 103–120. Springer, Cham (2018). https://doi.org/10.1007/978-3-319-93387-0_6

14. Bogdanov, A., Isobe, T.: White-box cryptography revisited: space-hard ciphers. In: CCS, pp. 1058–1069. ACM (2015)

15. Bogdanov, A., Isobe, T., Tischhauser, E.: Towards practical whitebox cryptography: optimizing efficiency and space hardness. In: Cheon, J.H., Takagi, T. (eds.) ASIACRYPT 2016. LNCS, vol. 10031, pp. 126–158. Springer, Heidelberg (2016). https://doi.org/10.1007/978-3-662-53887-6_5

16. Bos, J.W., Hubain, C., Michiels, W., Teuwen, P.: Differential computation analysis: hiding your white-box designs is not enough. In: Gierlichs, B., Poschmann, A.Y. (eds.) CHES 2016. LNCS, vol. 9813, pp. 215–236. Springer, Heidelberg (2016). https://doi.org/10.1007/978-3-662-53140-2_11

17. Brickenstein, M., Dreyer, A.: PolyBoRi: a framework for Gröbner-basis computations with boolean polynomials. J. Symb. Comput. 44(9), 1326–1345 (2009)

18. Bringer, J., Chabanne, H., Dottax, E.: White box cryptography: another attempt. IACR Cryptol. ePrint Arch., p. 468 (2006)

19. Chow, S., Eisen, P., Johnson, H., Van Oorschot, P.C.: White-box cryptography and an AES implementation. In: Nyberg, K., Heys, H. (eds.) SAC 2002. LNCS, vol. 2595, pp. 250–270. Springer, Heidelberg (2003). https://doi.org/10.1007/3-540-36492-7_17

20. Chow, S., Eisen, P., Johnson, H., van Oorschot, P.C.: A white-box DES implementation for DRM applications. In: Feigenbaum, J. (ed.) DRM 2002. LNCS, vol. 2696, pp. 1–15. Springer, Heidelberg (2003). https://doi.org/10.1007/978-3-540-44993-5_1

21. Daemen, J., Rijmen, V.: The advanced encryption standard process. In: The Design of Rijndael. Information Security and Cryptography, 2nd edn. Springer, Heidelberg (2002). https://doi.org/10.1007/978-3-662-04722-4_1

22. De Mulder, Y., Roelse, P., Preneel, B.: Cryptanalysis of the Xiao – Lai white-box AES implementation. In: Knudsen, L.R., Wu, H. (eds.) SAC 2012. LNCS, vol. 7707, pp. 34–49. Springer, Heidelberg (2013). https://doi.org/10.1007/978-3-642-35999-6_3

23. De Mulder, Y., Wyseur, B., Preneel, B.: Cryptanalysis of a perturbated white-box AES implementation. In: Gong, G., Gupta, K.C. (eds.) INDOCRYPT 2010. LNCS, vol. 6498, pp. 292–310. Springer, Heidelberg (2010). https://doi.org/10.1007/978-3-642-17401-8_21

24. Derbez, P., Fouque, P., Lambin, B., Minaud, B.: On recovering affine encodings in white-box implementations. IACR Trans. Cryptogr. Hardw. Embed. Syst. **2018**(3), 121–149 (2018)

25. Ferguson, N., et al.: The Skein hash function family. Submission to NIST (round 3) 7(7.5), 3 (2010)

26. Goubin, L., Masereel, J.-M., Quisquater, M.: Cryptanalysis of white box DES implementations. In: Adams, C., Miri, A., Wiener, M. (eds.) SAC 2007. LNCS, vol. 4876, pp. 278–295. Springer, Heidelberg (2007). https://doi.org/10.1007/978-3-540-77360-3_18

27. Jacob, M., Boneh, D., Felten, E.: Attacking an obfuscated cipher by injecting faults. In: Feigenbaum, J. (ed.) DRM 2002. LNCS, vol. 2696, pp. 16–31. Springer, Heidelberg (2003). https://doi.org/10.1007/978-3-540-44993-5_2

28. Karroumi, M.: Protecting white-box AES with dual ciphers. In: Rhee, K.-H., Nyang, D.H. (eds.) ICISC 2010. LNCS, vol. 6829, pp. 278–291. Springer, Heidelberg (2011). https://doi.org/10.1007/978-3-642-24209-0_19

29. Lee, S., Choi, D., Choi, Y.J.: Conditional re-encoding method for cryptanalysis-resistant white-box AES. ETRI J. **37**(5), 1012–1022 (2015)

30. Lepoint, T., Rivain, M., De Mulder, Y., Roelse, P., Preneel, B.: Two attacks on a white-box AES implementation. In: Lange, T., Lauter, K., Lisoněk, P. (eds.) SAC 2013. LNCS, vol. 8282, pp. 265–285. Springer, Heidelberg (2014). https://doi.org/10.1007/978-3-662-43414-7_14

31. Link, H.E., Neumann, W.D.: Clarifying obfuscation: improving the security of white-box DES. In: ITCC (1), pp. 679–684. IEEE Computer Society (2005)

32. Matsui, M.: Linear cryptanalysis method for DES cipher. In: Helleseth, T. (ed.) EUROCRYPT 1993. LNCS, vol. 765, pp. 386–397. Springer, Heidelberg (1994). https://doi.org/10.1007/3-540-48285-7_33

33. McMillion, B., Sullivan, N.: Attacking white-box AES constructions. In: SPRO@CCS, pp. 85–90. ACM (2016)

34. Michiels, W., Gorissen, P., Hollmann, H.D.L.: Cryptanalysis of a generic class of white-box implementations. In: Avanzi, R.M., Keliher, L., Sica, F. (eds.) SAC 2008. LNCS, vol. 5381, pp. 414–428. Springer, Heidelberg (2009). https://doi.org/10.1007/978-3-642-04159-4_27

35. Minaud, B., Derbez, P., Fouque, P., Karpman, P.: Key-recovery attacks on ASASA. J. Cryptol. **31**(3), 845–884 (2018)

36. Ranea, A., Preneel, B.: On self-equivalence encodings in white-box implementations. In: Dunkelman, O., Jacobson, Jr., M.J., O'Flynn, C. (eds.) SAC 2020. LNCS, vol. 12804, pp. 639–669. Springer, Cham (2021). https://doi.org/10.1007/978-3-030-81652-0_25

37. Ranea, A., Vandersmissen, J., Preneel, B.: Implicit white-box implementations: White-boxing ARX ciphers. IACR Cryptol. ePrint Arch. (2022)

38. The Sage Developers: SageMath, the Sage Mathematics Software System (Version 9.4) (2021). https://www.sagemath.org

39. Vandersmissen, J., Ranea, A., Preneel, B.: A white-box speck implementation using self-equivalence encodings (full version). IACR Cryptol. ePrint Arch. (2022)
40. Wyseur, B., Michiels, W., Gorissen, P., Preneel, B.: Cryptanalysis of white-box DES implementations with arbitrary external encodings. In: Adams, C., Miri, A., Wiener, M. (eds.) SAC 2007. LNCS, vol. 4876, pp. 264–277. Springer, Heidelberg (2007). https://doi.org/10.1007/978-3-540-77360-3_17
41. Xiao, Y., Lai, X.: A secure implementation of white-box AES. In: 2009 2nd International Conference on Computer Science and its Applications, pp. 1–6. IEEE (2009)
42. Yoo, J., Jeong, H., Won, D.: A method for secure and efficient block cipher using white-box cryptography. In: ICUIMC, pp. 89:1–89:8. ACM (2012)

Improved Differential-Linear Attack with Application to Round-Reduced Speck32/64

Feifan Wang[1,2] and Gaoli Wang[1,2(✉)]

[1] Shanghai Key Laboratory of Trustworthy Computing,
East China Normal University, Shanghai 200062, China
glwang@sei.ecnu.edu.cn
[2] State Key Laboratory of Cryptology, P.O. Box 5159, Beijing 100878, China

Abstract. Since the differential-linear cryptanalysis was introduced by Langford and Hellman in 1994, there have been many works inheriting and developing this technique. It has been used to attack numerous ciphers, and in particular, sets the record for Serpent, ICEPOLE, Chaskey, 8-round AES, and so on. In CRYPTO 2020, Beierle *et al.* showed that the data complexity of differential-linear attack can be significantly reduced by generating enough right pairs artificially. In this paper, we manage to find the property in the differential propagation of modular addition. Based on this, we can select special bits to flip to produce right pairs in a certain differential-linear attack. For application, we focus on the differential-linear attack of the ARX cipher Speck32/64. With the differential-linear trail we concatenate, we construct 9-round and 10-round distinguishers with the correlation of $2^{11.58}$ and $2^{14.58}$, respectively. Then we use enough flipped bits to reduce the complexity of the key recovery attack. As a result, we can use only 2^{25} chosen plaintexts to attack 14-round Speck32/64 with the time complexity of about 2^{62}, which has a slight improvement than before. To our best knowledge, this is the first differential-linear attack of the Speck family.

Keywords: Differential-linear cryptanalysis · ARX · Speck32/64

1 Introduction

ARX ciphers are one popular category in symmetric key primitives. ARX is short for three operations: addition modulo 2^n, word-wise rotation and XOR. There are many famous examples of ARX-based designs such as block ciphers FEAL [29], Speck [6], stream ciphers Salsa20 [10], ChaCha [9], MAC algorithms Chaskey [27], Siphash [3] and hash functions Skein [19], BLAKE [4]. Due to the simple composition of the design, ARX constructions are quite friendly for software implementation. With the extensive design and use of ARX ciphers, their security analysis has caught cryptanalysts' attention in recent years.

When it comes to the security of ARX ciphers, the two best known techniques in symmetric cryptography—differential cryptanalysis [11] and linear

© Springer Nature Switzerland AG 2022
G. Ateniese and D. Venturi (Eds.): ACNS 2022, LNCS 13269, pp. 792–808, 2022.
https://doi.org/10.1007/978-3-031-09234-3_39

cryptanalysis [26] have to be taken into consideration. In previous works, the differential and linear properties of the only non-linear operation—modular addition in ARX ciphers had been well understood [23,31].

However, because of the mutual promotion between designers and cryptanalysts, like the *wide-trail strategy* [16] in AES, there also exists a *long-trail strategy* [17] in designing ARX-based ciphers. Because of this, the pure differential attack or linear attack fails to achieve outstanding results in many cases when analyzing long rounds of ARX ciphers. Luckily, for this case, differential-linear cryptanalysis, which was introduced by Langford and Hellman [21] in 1994, shows its advantage.

Informally, the differential-linear analysis combines a differential characteristic with probability p for the first s rounds and a linear characteristic with correlation q for the next t rounds, resulting in a differential-linear characteristic covering $r+t$ rounds with correlation pq^2 and an attack with the data complexity of roughly $p^{-2}q^{-4}$.

From several recent works [15,24], we have seen the potential of differential-linear attack in ARX ciphers. One of the most prominent results is the improved differential-linear framework on ARX primitives presented by Beierle *et al.* [7], who cleverly observe that the complexity of a differential-linear attack can be reduced immediately, if the attacker could construct enough right pairs for the differential part.

Inspired by their work, we study the differential properties of the modular addition, and find that the differential propagation has a decreasing nature under certain restrictions. Based on this unique property, we can determine the special bits in the specified differential characteristic and using them to generate enough right pairs for free. As a demonstration, we apply this method to attack round-reduced Speck32/64.

Related Works. Among many ARX-based ciphers, the Speck family is one of the most attractive primitives for researchers. Since it was published in 2013, it has received numerous analyses from the cryptographic community. Due to the limitation of space, we only list those representative works here. Abed *et al.* [1] presented the results of the Speck family against the differential attack and rectangle attack. At the same time, Biryuov *et al.* [12] applied another advanced search strategy to find better differential characteristics than before. In [18], Dinur proposed a sub-cipher attack and carried out the key recovery attack based on the best differential by that time. In [32], Yao et al. provided the results of all variants of Speck against the linear attack. In [25], Liu *et al.* analyzed the security of Speck against the rotational cryptanalysis with xored constants proposed in [2]. Most recently, as a suitable target instance, many works based on machine learning have been applied to the Speck family [8,20].

Even though there have been so many works related, the differential-linear attack has not been used to evaluate the security of the Speck family so far.

Our Contributions. In this paper, we first study the differential propagation in the modular addition. By extending the definition of the xor differential to the bit level and combining a simple proposition of differential weight, we observe that there is a monotonous property in the differential propagation.

Then we show that we can improve the data complexity of a certain differential-linear attack by using those bits which we call valid flipped bits. As proof of this, we present one concrete example and one generic example in the differential of modular addition with 8-bit inputs and outputs.

Next, we introduce our new differential-linear attack on round-reduced Speck 32/64. With regard to the differential-linear characteristic, we apply a restrictive search strategy and obtain a 7-round optimal trail as a result. Combined with the short differential, we can construct effective distinguishers on 9-round and 10-round Speck32/64. We find 21 and 24 valid flipped bits for them, respectively.

Finally, with the above improvements and a trivial 1-round filter, we can mount 13-round and 14-round key recovery attacks with improved data complexity and improved time complexity. For comparison, we summarize our attack and some other results in Table 1.[1]

Table 1. Summary of attacks on Speck32/64

Rounds Attacked /	Time	Data	Memory	Type of Attack
11	2^{38}	$2^{14.5}$	-	Neural Differential [20]
11	$2^{46.68}$	$2^{30.07}$	$2^{37.1}$	Rectangle [1]
12	$2^{60.22}$	$2^{30.87}$	-	Linear [32]
13	2^{57}	2^{25}	2^{22}	Differential [18]
13	2^{59}	2^{22}	2^{39}	Differential-linear(Sec 4.4)
14	2^{63}	2^{31}	2^{22}	Differential [18]
14	$2^{62.47}$	$2^{30.47}$	2^{22}	Differential [30]
14	2^{62}	2^{25}	2^{39}	Differential-linear(Sec 4.4)

Organization of the Paper. The rest of the paper is organized as follows: Sect. 2 provides the description of Speck and recalls some relevant definitions and propositions on the differential properties of ARX ciphers. Section 3 revisits the differential-linear cryptanalysis and explains our improvement on it. Section 4 describes our new results on round-reduced Speck32/64. Section 5 draws the conclusion finally.

2   Preliminaries

For any $x \in \mathbb{F}_2^n$, we denote by $x[i]$ the i-th bit of x, where $x[n-1]$ represents the most significant bit(MSB). And we use $x[0:n]$ to denote the n-bit string x. Thus we can obtain that $x = \sum_{i=0}^{n-1} x[i]2^i$. Further, a n-bit string with few 1

---

[1] Source code about our experiment can be found in https://github.com/regnik/speck_dl_analysis.

is simply denoted as $x\{i, j, k\}$ according to the location of bit 1 in x. We denote by $\neg x$ the bit-wise inverse of value x. Furthermore, we denote by $\oplus$ the bit-wise xor, $+$ the addition modulo 2^n and $\ggg$ the word-wise rotation. We also denote the correlation of a random variable X as $Cor(X) = 2 \cdot Pr[X = 0] - 1$.

2.1 Description of Speck

Speck is a family of block ciphers designed by the U.S. National Security Agency in 2013. It has 10 versions due to different block size $2n$ and key size mn. For example, Speck32/64 refers to the variant of the Speck family with block size 32 bits and key size 64 bits.

The Speck family takes two n-bit words as input and outputs two n-bit words after a sequence of T rounds.

The round function is defined as

$$x_{i+1} = ((x_i \ggg \alpha) + y_i) \oplus k_i$$
$$y_{i+1} = (y_i \lll \beta) \oplus x_{i+1}$$

The key schedule of Speck generates successive round keys by the same function as the round function from the master key, which is defined as

$$l_{i+m-1} = (k_i + (l_i \ggg \alpha)) \oplus i$$
$$k_{i+1} = (k_i \lll \beta) \oplus l_{i+m-1}$$

The rotation constants (α, β) is $(7, 2)$ for Speck32 and $(8, 3)$ for the other variants. For intuitiveness, Fig. 1 describes the round function and key schedule of Speck. For more details, one can refer to [6].

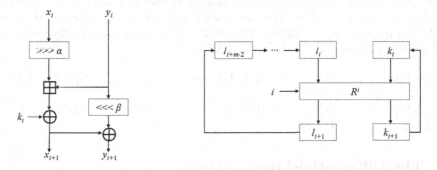

Fig. 1. Left: The Round Function of Speck. Right: The Key Schedule of Speck. R^i is the round function where i acts as $k[i]$.

2.2   The Differential Properties of ARX Ciphers

For the differential properties of ARX ciphers, we just need to pay attention to the only non-linear operation addition modulo 2^n. We follow the notions in the previous work[13,23]. We denote by xdp^+ the XOR-differential probability of addition modulo 2^n.

Definition 1. (xdp^+ [13]) Let α, β, γ be fixed n-bit differences. Then the XOR-differential probability of addition modulo 2^n, denoted by $xdp^+(\alpha, \beta \longmapsto \gamma)$, where α,β are input differences and γ is output difference, is defined as:

$$xdp^+(\alpha, \beta \longmapsto \gamma) = 2^{-2n} \cdot \# \{(x,y) : ((x \oplus \alpha) + (y \oplus \beta)) \oplus (x + y) = \gamma\}.$$

Proposition 1. (weight of $(\alpha, \beta \longmapsto \gamma)$ [23]) Let α, β, γ be fixed n-bit differences. The weight of the differential $(\alpha, \beta \longmapsto \gamma)$ denoted by $w(\alpha, \beta \longmapsto \gamma)$ can be computed as:

$$w(\alpha, \beta \longmapsto \gamma) = -log_2(xdp^+) = h(\neg eq(\alpha, \beta \longmapsto \gamma)),$$

where $eq(x,y,z) = (\neg x \oplus y) \wedge (\neg x \oplus z)$ and $h(x)$ denotes the numbers of non-zero bit in x except the MSB.

If we extend the Definition 1 at a bit level, more precisely, we limit the two input differences to a single active bit, with the aid of Proposition 1, let $\alpha = 2^i, \beta = 2^i, \gamma = 0$, then we can obtain $xdp^+(2^i, 2^i \longmapsto 0) = 1/2$; let $\alpha = 2^i, \beta = 2^i, \gamma = 2^{i+1}$, then we can obtain $xdp^+(2^i, 2^i \longmapsto 2^{i+1}) = 1/2^2$; let $\alpha = 2^i, \beta = 2^i, \gamma = 2^{i+1}+2^{i+2}$, then we can obtain $xdp^+(2^i, 2^i \longmapsto 2^{i+1}+2^{i+2}) = 1/2^3$... Based on this, we can observe the following property:

Proposition 2. (Monotonicity of $xdp^+[i]$) Let $\alpha \{i\}$, $\beta \{i\}$ be fixed n-bit differences with only one non-zero bit located at the i-th LSB of α, β. And $\varnothing$ denotes no difference. Then the probability with which the differential bit $\alpha[i]$ and $\beta[i]$ propagate to the output differential bit of γ is monotonically decreasing following the direction i to the second MSB:

$$xdp^+[\{i\}, \{i\} \longmapsto \varnothing] > xdp^+[\{i\}, \{i\} \longmapsto \{i+1\}] > \cdots > xdp^+[\{i\}, \{i\} \longmapsto \{i+1, i+2, \cdots, n-2\}]$$
$$xdp^+[\{i\}, \varnothing \longmapsto \{i\}] > xdp^+[\{i\}, \varnothing \longmapsto \{i, i+1\}] > \cdots > xdp^+[\{i\}, \varnothing \longmapsto \{i, i+1, i+2, \cdots, n-2\}]$$

3   The Differential-Linear Attack

3.1   Langford and Hellman's Differential-Linear Cryptanalysis Revisited

Let E be a cipher which we can divide into two sub parts E_1 and E_2 such that $E = E_2 \circ E_1$. The attacker applies a differential trail $\delta_i \xrightarrow{E_1} \delta_m$ and a linear approximation $\Gamma_m \xrightarrow{E_2} \Gamma_o$ and then explores the particular link between the ciphertexts.

Specifically, suppose that the differential trail holds with probability p, that is to say,

$$Pr\left[E_1(x) \oplus E_1(x \oplus \delta_i) = \delta_m\right] = p.$$

Further, suppose that the linear approximation has a correlation q,[2] that is to say,

$$Cor\left[\Gamma_m \cdot x \oplus \Gamma_o \cdot E_2(x)\right] = q.$$

Under the assumption that $E_1(x)$ and $E_2(x)$ are independent, we have

$$Cor\left[\Gamma_o \cdot E(x) \oplus \Gamma_o \cdot E(x \oplus \delta_i)\right] = pq^2.$$

Thus, if p, q are large enough, the attacker can distinguish the cipher E from a random permutation by preparing $O(p^{-2}q^{-4})$ chosen plaintexts.

3.2 Differential-Linear Cryptanalysis with Experimental Middle Part

Note that the above analysis is heuristic due to the assumption of the independence of the sub parts. However, the sub parts and the whole cipher are not independent in some cases. To estimate the complexity of the analysis more accurate, the experimental middle part is naturally added. Consequently, the cipher E is divided into three sub parts E_1, E_2 and E_m such that $E = E_2 \circ E_m \circ E_1$. Here, the middle part E_m should be experimentally evaluated. Suppose we have the middle differential-linear approximation $\delta_m \xrightarrow{E_m} \Gamma_m$ with correlation r, that is to say,

$$Cor\left[\Gamma_m \cdot E_m(x) \oplus \Gamma_m \cdot E(x \oplus \delta_m)\right] = r.$$

Then, we have

$$Cor\left[\Gamma_m \cdot E_m(E_1(x)) \oplus \Gamma_m \cdot E_m(E_1(x \oplus \delta_i))\right] = pr.$$

Finally, we can obtain that

$$Cor\left[\Gamma_o \cdot E(x) \oplus \Gamma_o \cdot E(x \oplus \delta_i)\right] = prq^2.$$

For a formal explanation of the middle differential-linear trail, one can refer to a recent work which proposed the Differential-Linear Connectivity Table (DLCT) [5].

In this paper, we apply the latter of the above two structures. (see Fig. 2) Specially, we adopt the similar strategy in [7,22] to determine the middle part. We limit us to search for the differential-linear characteristics with one active input bit and one active output bit firstly. Then under the certain active bit, we search for the differential characteristics before and the linear characteristics after, respectively. And it is natural to concatenate these three part according to this structure finally.

---

[2] In some literature, the linear approximation is measured by bias. Note that for a specific linear approximation, the correlation is twice the bias. And the analysis holds also.

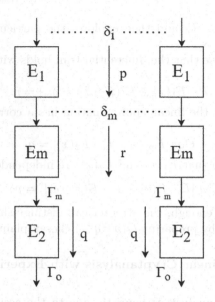

Fig. 2. Differential-linear structure with the experimental middle part

3.3   Improvement upon the Differential Part for ARX Ciphers

For a usual differential-linear attack, the adversary needs to use $O(p^{-2}r^{-2}q^{-4})$ chosen plaintexts to construct a valid distinguisher at first. It means that, at the end of the differential part, the adversary has to collect $O(r^{-2}q^{-4})$ right pairs. In other words, the complexity of the attack comes largely from the procedure of generating eligible plaintext pairs. Yet, for a typical ARX cipher, we can significantly improve this by exploiting the properties we observe in Sect. 2. This has been discussed before in [7]. Here, we revisit and further extend the idea.

Let us be given a cipher E. We have obtained the first sub part $E_1:\mathbb{F}_2^n \to \mathbb{F}_2^n$ and have found a differential characteristic $\delta_i \longrightarrow \delta_m$ with probability p. This means, among all $x \in \mathbb{F}_2^n$, there expects to be $2^n \cdot p$ pairs satisfying the trail. We observe the ciphertexts of the pairs $(x, x \oplus \delta_i)$ to filter those dissatisfying the given differential trail with probability p. However, a lot of repetitive work has been done in this stage. Actually, the right pairs $x \in \mathbb{F}_2^n$ have a particular structure which is ignored by us. If we are given a right pair, we can generate many other right pairs by doing minor modifications. This can be naturally applied to reduce the data complexity in a classical differential-linear attack. We use χ to cover all values of x which defines a right pair $(x, x \oplus \delta_i)$. Our goal is, given one $x \in \chi$, one can collect enough other elements from χ. In particular, if we consider only those pairs in χ, the expected correlation would increase to rq^2, with a gain of p than before. We call those bits which keep independent of the given differential

---

Algorithm 1: Finding valid flipped bits

Input: input difference δ_i, output difference δ_m, sample space N, lower bound
     of probability $\mathcal{B}$
Output: indexes of valid flipped bits

1   Initialize counter $c = 0$ and $r[0:n-1] = 0$;
2   **for** $i = 1:N$ **do**
3 | Randomly pick a valid input x ;
4 | **if** $E_1(x) \oplus E_1(x \oplus \delta_i) = \delta_m$ **then**
5 | | increase c;
6 | | **for** $j = 0:n-1$ **do**
7 | | | Flip the j-th bit of the original x, denoted by $\hat{x}$;
8 | | | **if** $E_1(\hat{x}) \oplus E_1(\hat{x} \oplus \delta_i) = \delta_m$ **then**
9 | | | | increase $r[j]$;
10 | | | **end**
11 | | **end**
12 | **end**
13 **end**
14 **for** $j = 0:n-1$ **do**
15 | $p[j] = r[j]/c$;
16 | **if** $p[j] \geqslant \mathcal{B}$ **then**
17 | | save j;
18 | **end**
19 **end**

"valid flipped bits". Note that the number of valid flipped bits should be enough. In particular, denote this number by b, we require $2^b > r^{-2}q^{-4}$.

Since it is hard to know the complete distribution of right pairs, we start with a trivial analysis. Assume that E_1 can be easily described by two independent parts, called E_1^0 and E_1^1. Among them, $E_1 : \mathbb{F}_2^n \to \mathbb{F}_2^n, E_1^0/E_1^1 : \mathbb{F}_2^m \to \mathbb{F}_2^m$ and $n = 2m$. We now have a differential $\alpha \xrightarrow{E_1^0} \beta$ with probability p, so we can extend it to the differential $0, \alpha \xrightarrow{E_1} 0, \beta$, which holds the same probability. This suggests that we have found m valid flipped bits and thus we can generate 2^m right pairs freely with only one known right pair. However, only a few ciphers can be treated in this way. For most ciphers, we need to use an automatic search. The basic idea is shown in Algorithm 1. In detail, the algorithm firstly takes sample pairs as input, then filters out the wrong pairs, and finally returns the probability that a right pair keeps right when flipping each bit itself. We will concern those bits with high probabilities to construct the subspace.

In CRYPTO 2020, Beierle *et al.* used this trivial technique during the differential part and some other ideas to significantly improve the cryptanalysis results of two typical ARX ciphers—Chakey and ChaCha. In their work, ChaCha is the case that can be simply divided into two independent input parts so that the

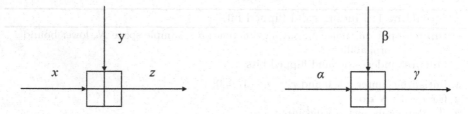

Fig. 3. The 8-bit addition example. x, y, z are 8 bit inputs and outputs, while α, β, γ are 8 bit input differences and output differences.

subspace of flipped bits can be naturally found, while Chaskey is dependent on the experiment with the aid of automatic search. They set the lower bound of probability to 0.95. We are not aware of the rationality, but we consider it to be generated iteratively after numerous trials. In this paper, we develop a new technique to help us find more valid flipped bits. We study the conditions in the propagation of the differential. Moreover, we are able to know the exact effect of each bit on the given differential.

Considering an simple addition model cipher with two 8-bit input and one 8-bit output (see Fig. 3), let us be given a valid differential trail $\alpha, \beta \longrightarrow \gamma$. We call one valid input (x, y) and another valid input $(x \oplus \alpha, y \oplus \gamma)$ a pair. And a pair which satisfies $(x + y) \oplus ((x \oplus \alpha) + (y \oplus \beta)) = \gamma$ is called a right pair. We consider the carry bits c. For $z = x + y$, we define $c[0] = 0$ and $c[i + 1] = (x[i] \wedge y[i]) \vee (x[i] \wedge c[i]) \vee (y[i] \wedge c[i])$. Following the notions in Sect. 2.2, we start our analysis with a concrete example.

Example 1. $\alpha\{3\}, \beta\{3, 6\} \to \gamma\{6\}$. For this example, one case is shown in Fig. 4. From the example, we can see that $\alpha[3]$ and $\beta[3]$ jointly lead to $\varnothing$ in $\gamma[3]$. In detail, the difference in $\alpha[3]$ and $\beta[3]$ is eliminated because $0 + 1 = 1 + 0$ and none of them generate carry to $z[4]$. If $x[3]$ on the left is changed to value 1, this phenomenon will not happen. The value of $x[3]$ and $y[3]$ can be regarded as the first condition to generate the given differential. We can also see that $\beta[6]$ leads to $\gamma[6]$. Intuitively, this may give us another condition. Since $z[6] = x[6] \oplus y[6] \oplus c[6]$, the difference on this position comes from $x[6]$, $y[6]$ and $c[6]$ together. We can observe that the value of $y[6]$ has no effect on the difference while the value of $x[6]$ does. For any right pair satisfying this differential, if we change $x[3]$ or $x[6]$, the pair would not stay right since the modification in the two positions has broken the conditions with which the difference can propagate. Moreover, due to the carry bit, for $x[0 : 5]$ and $y[0 : 5]$, we have to concern about how the value of the location affects $c[6]$. With the aid of the proposition in Sect. 2, we can easily evaluate these things. When we change $x[5]$, it has a probability of 50% that the pair keeps right. Because $xdp^+[5, \varnothing \to 5] = 1/2$, in other words, the probability that the change does not disturb the output difference is $1/2$.

And obviously, if we flip $x[7]$, this differential will be unaffected. With respect to each bit of the input, we are able to compute the probability that flipping this bit would not make the right pair incorrect. We also summarize the experimental results in Fig. 5. And it seems that the experiment fits our expectations well. Note that our result is tested upon a sample space of 2^{16}.

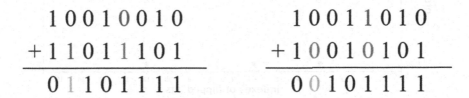

Fig. 4. One right pair of $\alpha\{3\}, \beta\{3,6\} \rightarrow \gamma\{6\}$.

From the example above, we can extend it to a more generic situation with detailed analysis. Note that the MSB of modular addition is one fixed valid flipped bit. We will ignore it in the following analysis. Then we can observe some interesting properties in several typical differentials. For a differential $\alpha\{i\}, \beta\{i\} \rightarrow \varnothing$, the right pair should satisfy $x[i] \neq y[i]$. If we flip any position except $x[i]$ or $y[i]$, it will have no effect on the original difference, which means that we can find 14 valid flipped bits for this specific differential. For a differential $\alpha\{i\}, \beta\{i\} \rightarrow \gamma\{i+1\}$, the right pair should not only satisfy $x[i] = y[i]$, but also satisfy $x[i+1] = y[i+1]$. And we can find 12 valid flipped bits. For a differential $\alpha\{i\}, \varnothing \rightarrow \gamma\{i\}$, we need to limit the output difference to the only active bit so that the right pair should satisfy $y[i] = c[i]$. Thus we can naturally find $(7-i+1) + [7-(i+1)+1] = 15 - 2i$ valid flipped bits. Since $c[i]$ is affected by the bit before i, we will destroy this condition when we change $x[0 : i-1]$ and $y[0 : i]$ with corresponding probability. If we flip $x[j](0 \leq j \leq i)$, the probability will be the same as the probability that $\alpha[j]$ will not propagate to $\gamma[i]$.

3.4 Improvement upon the Differential-Linear Distinguisher

With the improvement upon the differential part, we can construct a differential-linear distinguisher with lower cost than before. In particular, if we can generate enough right pairs for the differential part, then we can use these pairs to distinguish the cipher with lower data complexity, which would work as follows (the notions follow the analysis before in this paper):

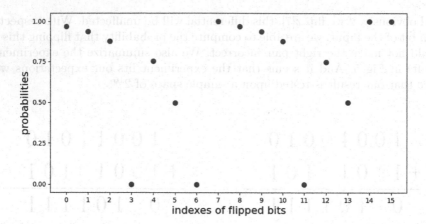

Fig. 5. The probabilities that the pair stays right when index[i] is flipped, where x covers 0–7 and y covers 8–15.

1. Collect enough right pairs (x, x').
2. Compute
$$Cor[\Gamma_o \cdot E(x) \oplus \Gamma_o \cdot E(x')].$$
3. If we can observe the correlation of rq^2 with $O(r^{-2}q^{-4})$ pairs, we consider this distinguisher to be effective.

4   Differential-Linear Attack on Round-Reduced Speck32/64

4.1   The Overview of Our Attack

We now give an overview of our attack. First, we divide the cipher into three sub parts. For Speck32/64, E_1 covers 1 or 2 rounds, E_m covers 7 rounds and E_2 covers 1 round. And we search the appropriate trails for the three parts, respectively. Then, we try to find special bits to flip in the differential and reduce the data complexity of the whole attack. Finally, we give the complete key recovery attack of the round-reduced Speck32/64.

4.2   Searching for Appropriate Trails

To determine the exact number of rounds which is covered by three sub parts, it is natural to list all the possible combinations of $E = E_2 \circ E_m \circ E_1$ and find all the valuable differential and linear trails, respectively. However, it costs too much time to select the winner from all the combinations due to the limited computation. In fact, by observing many good differential trails and good linear trails, we can find that most of them have a special internal difference with only one active bit, which is called "hourglass structure" in [22]. So for the middle part of our attack, we restrict ourselves to evaluate the differential-linear trail with a single active input bit and a single active output bit. In other words, we evaluate all the correlations of $Cor(E_1(x)[j] \oplus E_m(x \oplus 2^i)[j]$. Then, when the middle part has been determined, the output difference and the input mask of the two remaining parts would be fixed accordingly. By traversing all the differential trails with this output difference and linear trails with this input mask, the differential-linear distinguisher would be constructed.

For Speck32/64, we have observed the following 7-round differential-linear trail denoted by DL with correlation $r = 2^{-7.58}$:

$$0x1000 \quad 0000 \longrightarrow 0x0001 \quad 0000$$

Under the restriction of output difference, we have two differential characteristics denoted by $D1$ and $D2$:

Notation	Input Difference	Output Difference	rounds covered	Probability(log_2)
D1	0x000a 0400	0x1000 0000	1	-2
D2	0x8440 8102	0x1000 0000	2	-5

Under the restriction of input mask, we have observed 1-round linear trail denoted by L with the correlation of 2^{-1}:

$$0x0001 \quad 0000 \longrightarrow 0x0e00 \quad 0c00$$

Note that this linear trail is derived from the classical linear approximation in the modular addition. Based on the analysis of Sect. 3, we can immediately obtain two differential-linear distinguishers: 9-round distinguisher $D1 - DL - L$ with the correlation of about $2^{-11.58}$, 10-round distinguisher $D2 - DL - L$ with the correlation of about $2^{-14.58}$.

4.3   Flipping Special Bits in Differential Characteristics

To improve the complexity of the distinguisher listed above, we now examine the valid flipped bits in the differential trails. For $D1$, we can apply the results of example directly. Then we can easily find $x[3:6]$ and $y[13:15]$ as flipped bits with probability 1. And after computing all the probabilities, we choose 14 more bits ranked in the front, which are $x[7:13]$ and $y[0:6]$. Since the probability of the flipped bits is not 1, we need to determine the exact probability that we can get such a right pair that we can generate 2^{21} pairs from it. By the experiment, we test it to be $2^{-0.095}$. Using the Algorithm 1 and set the bound to be 0.95, we can obtain the same results. For $D2$, there are no trivial flipped bits with probability 1. Thus we use the Algorithm 1 directly and set the bound to be 0.7. We still can not find enough valid flipped bits. But for the first round of $D2$, we can find 24 valid flipped bits with probability 1, which are $x[0:6]$, $x[10:14]$, $y[1]$, $y[4:7]$ and $y[9:15]$.

4.4   Extending the Distinguishes to Key Recovery

We first show that for Speck32/64, there has a natural 1-round filter with which we can check one input pair whether to be the right pair of given 1-round differential without any information on key bits. Since under the single-key setting, it is obvious that $(x_i \ggg \alpha + y_i) \oplus ((x'_i \ggg \alpha + y'_i) = (x_i \ggg \alpha + y_i) \oplus k_i \oplus ((x'_i \ggg \alpha + y'_i) \oplus k_i$. This means that we can filter wrong pairs before for free and we apply this trivial tip in following attacks.

Then, the distinguishers (see Fig. 6) can be extended to a key-recovery attack by adding one round before and three rounds behind so that we can mount 13-round and 14-round practical attacks to round-reduced Speck32/64, respectively, as follows:

9-Round Distinguisher for the 13-Round Key Recovery Attack. We now have a 9-round differential-linear trail:

$$\delta_i = 0x000a \quad 0400 \xrightarrow{1r} 0x1000 \quad 0000 \xrightarrow{8r} 0e00 \quad 0c00 = \Gamma_o$$

We describe the attack as follows:

1. Collect $2^2 \cdot 2^{0.095}$ pairs of plaintexts (P_i, P'_i) s.t. their difference after the first round are equal to δ_i. This procedure is consistent with the step mentioned in [1].
2. For each pair, partially encrypt it and check it whether to be a right pair of the differential. Note that this does not need any guess on $k[1]$. There expects one pair to remain after this step. If so, keep it and generate 2^{21} pairs by 21 valid flipped bits we examined.
3. Request the ciphertexts (C_i, C'_i) of these pairs under the unknown master key.
4. Initialize a list of 2^{37} counters to zeros. For each (C_i, C'_i), try all the possible values of the 37 key bits $k_{10}[0:4], k_{11}, k_{12}$, partially decrypt (C_i, C'_i) to the intermediate state corresponding to the output mask of our differential-linear distinguisher. Compute the xor sum of the subset of bits contained in Γ_o, if the values in both pairs are equal, increase the current counter.
5. Sort the counter by the correlation. The right subkey is expected to be in the first 2^{37-a} values of the list, where a is the bit advantage we can obtain.

The attack needs the data complexity of about $2 \cdot 2^{21} = 2^{22}$. Using the formula[3] in [28] and under such data complexity, we have 2 bit advantages and the success possibility is about 89%. The time complexity which is dominated by step 4 is $2^{22} \cdot 2^{37} = 2^{59}$. Also, the attack needs $2^{37} \cdot 4 = 2^{39}$ times of memory access.

---

[3] The formula was adapted to differential-linear cryptanalysis in [14] and we use the adapted version here.

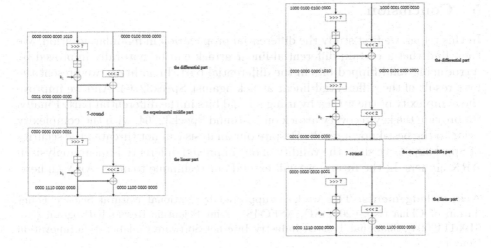

Fig. 6. Our new distinguishers

10-round distinguisher for the 14-round key recovery attack. We now have a 10-round differential-linear trail:

$$\delta_i = 0x8440 \quad 8102 \xrightarrow{1r} 0x000a \quad 0400 \xrightarrow{1r} 0x1000 \quad 0000 \xrightarrow{8r} 0x0e00 \quad 0c00 = \Gamma_o$$

With little modification, we describe the attack as follows:

1. Collect 2^3 pairs of plaintexts (P_i, P_i') s.t. their difference after the first round are equal to δ_i. This procedure is consistent with the step mentioned in [1].
2. For each pair, partially encrypt it and check it whether to be a right pair of the differential $0x84408102 \longrightarrow 0x000a0400$. Again, this procedure does not need any guess on $k[1]$. There expects one pair to remain after this step as well. If so, keep it and generate 2^{24} pairs by 24 valid flipped bits we examined.
3. Request the ciphertexts (C_i, C_i') of these pairs under the unknown master key.
4. Initialize a list of 2^{37} counters to zeros. For each (C_i, C_i'), try all the possible values of the 37 key bits $k_{11}[0:4], k_{12}, k_{13}$, partially decrypt (C_i, C_i') to the intermediate state corresponding to the output mask of our differential-linear distinguisher. Compute the xor sum of the subset of bits contained in Γ_o, if the values in both pairs are equal, increase the current counter.
5. Sort the counter by the correlation. The right subkey is expected to be in the first 2^{37-a} values of the list, where a is the bit advantage we can obtain.

This attack needs the data complexity of $2 \cdot 2^{24} = 2^{25}$, and the time complexity which is dominated by the key guess in step 4 is about $2 \cdot 2^{24} \cdot 2^{37} = 2^{62}$. Again, using the formula in [28] and under such data complexity, we have 1 bit advantages and the success possibility is about 91%. Also, the attack needs $2^{37} \cdot 4 = 2^{39}$ times of memory access.

5 Conclusion

In this paper, we first study the differential propagation in modular addition. We then find that a certain differential-linear attack can be naturally improved by introducing valid flipped bits in the differential part. In addition, we present the first result of the differential-linear attack against Speck32/64. And we improve the complexity of the attack by using special bits in the differential part. Finally, we provide the key recovery attack on 14-round Speck32/64, with the complexity prior to the best-known result. Despite our analysis can not threaten the security of Speck32/64, we show the validity of our improved differential-linear analysis in ARX ciphers. In the future, we will extend our technique to other ARX ciphers.

Acknowledgements. This work is supported by National Natural Science Foundation of China (No. 62072181), NSFC-ISF Joint Scientific Research Program (No. 61961146004), Shanghai Trusted Industry Internet Software Collaborative Innovation Center.

References

1. Abed, F., List, E., Lucks, S., Wenzel, J.: Differential cryptanalysis of round-reduced SIMON and SPECK. In: Cid, C., Rechberger, C. (eds.) FSE 2014. LNCS, vol. 8540, pp. 525–545. Springer, Heidelberg (2015). https://doi.org/10.1007/978-3-662-46706-0_27
2. Ashur, T., Liu, Y.: Rotational cryptanalysis in the presence of constants. IACR Trans. Symmetric Cryptol. **2016**(1), 57–70 (2016)
3. Aumasson, J.-P., Bernstein, D.J.: SipHash: a fast short-input PRF. In: Galbraith, S., Nandi, M. (eds.) INDOCRYPT 2012. LNCS, vol. 7668, pp. 489–508. Springer, Heidelberg (2012). https://doi.org/10.1007/978-3-642-34931-7_28
4. Aumasson, J.P., Henzen, L., Meier, W., Phan, R.C.W.: Sha-3 proposal Blake. Submission to the NIST SHA-3 Competition (Round 2) (2008)
5. Bar-On, A., Dunkelman, O., Keller, N., Weizman, A.: DLCT: a new tool for differential-linear cryptanalysis. In: Ishai, Y., Rijmen, V. (eds.) EUROCRYPT 2019. LNCS, vol. 11476, pp. 313–342. Springer, Cham (2019). https://doi.org/10.1007/978-3-030-17653-2_11
6. Beaulieu, R., Shors, D., Smith, J., Treatman-Clark, S., Weeks, B., Wingers, L.: The SIMON and SPECK families of lightweight block ciphers. Cryptology ePrint Archive, Report 2013/404 (2013). https://eprint.iacr.org/2013/404
7. Beierle, C., Leander, G., Todo, Y.: Improved differential-linear attacks with applications to ARX ciphers. In: Micciancio, D., Ristenpart, T. (eds.) CRYPTO 2020. LNCS, vol. 12172, pp. 329–358. Springer, Cham (2020). https://doi.org/10.1007/978-3-030-56877-1_12
8. Benamira, A., Gerault, D., Peyrin, T., Tan, Q.Q.: A deeper look at machine learning-based cryptanalysis. In: Canteaut, A., Standaert, F.-X. (eds.) EUROCRYPT 2021. LNCS, vol. 12696, pp. 805–835. Springer, Cham (2021). https://doi.org/10.1007/978-3-030-77870-5_28
9. Bernstein, D.J.: ChaCha, a variant of Salsa 20 (2008). http://cr.yp.to/chacha.html
10. Bernstein, D.J.: The Salsa20 family of stream ciphers. In: Robshaw, M., Billet, O. (eds.) New Stream Cipher Designs. LNCS, vol. 4986, pp. 84–97. Springer, Heidelberg (2008). https://doi.org/10.1007/978-3-540-68351-3_8

11. Biham, E., Shamir, A.: Differential cryptanalysis of DES-like cryptosystems. In: Menezes, A.J., Vanstone, S.A. (eds.) CRYPTO 1990. LNCS, vol. 537, pp. 2–21. Springer, Heidelberg (1991). https://doi.org/10.1007/3-540-38424-3_1

12. Biryukov, A., Roy, A., Velichkov, V.: Differential analysis of block ciphers SIMON and SPECK. In: Cid, C., Rechberger, C. (eds.) FSE 2014. LNCS, vol. 8540, pp. 546–570. Springer, Heidelberg (2015). https://doi.org/10.1007/978-3-662-46706-0_28

13. Biryukov, A., Velichkov, V., Le Corre, Y.: Automatic search for the best trails in ARX: application to block cipher SPECK. In: Peyrin, T. (ed.) FSE 2016. LNCS, vol. 9783, pp. 289–310. Springer, Heidelberg (2016). https://doi.org/10.1007/978-3-662-52993-5_15

14. Blondeau, C., Leander, G., Nyberg, K.: Differential-linear cryptanalysis revisited. J. Cryptol. 30(3), 859–888 (2017)

15. Broll, M., et al.: Further improving differential-linear attacks: applications to chaskey and serpent. Cryptology ePrint Archive, Report 2021/820 (2021). https://eprint.iacr.org/2021/820

16. Daemen, J., Rijmen, V.: The Design of Rijndael: AES - The Advanced Encryption Standard. Information Security and Cryptography, Springer, New York (2002)

17. Dinu, D., Perrin, L., Udovenko, A., Velichkov, V., Großschädl, J., Biryukov, A.: Design strategies for ARX with provable bounds: SPARX and LAX. In: Cheon, J.H., Takagi, T. (eds.) ASIACRYPT 2016. LNCS, vol. 10031, pp. 484–513. Springer, Heidelberg (2016). https://doi.org/10.1007/978-3-662-53887-6_18

18. Dinur, I.: Improved differential cryptanalysis of round-reduced speck. In: Joux, A., Youssef, A. (eds.) SAC 2014. LNCS, vol. 8781, pp. 147–164. Springer, Cham (2014). https://doi.org/10.1007/978-3-319-13051-4_9

19. Ferguson, N., et al.: The Skein hash function family. Submission to the NIST SHA-3 Competition (Round 2) (2009)

20. Gohr, A.: Improving attacks on round-reduced Speck32/64 using deep learning. In: Boldyreva, A., Micciancio, D. (eds.) CRYPTO 2019. LNCS, vol. 11693, pp. 150–179. Springer, Cham (2019). https://doi.org/10.1007/978-3-030-26951-7_6

21. Langford, S.K., Hellman, M.E.: Differential-linear cryptanalysis. In: Desmedt, Y.G. (ed.) CRYPTO 1994. LNCS, vol. 839, pp. 17–25. Springer, Heidelberg (1994). https://doi.org/10.1007/3-540-48658-5_3

22. Leurent, G.: Improved differential-linear cryptanalysis of 7-round Chaskey with partitioning. In: Fischlin, M., Coron, J.-S. (eds.) EUROCRYPT 2016. LNCS, vol. 9665, pp. 344–371. Springer, Heidelberg (2016). https://doi.org/10.1007/978-3-662-49890-3_14

23. Lipmaa, H., Moriai, S.: Efficient algorithms for computing differential properties of addition. In: Matsui, M. (ed.) FSE 2001. LNCS, vol. 2355, pp. 336–350. Springer, Heidelberg (2002). https://doi.org/10.1007/3-540-45473-X_28

24. Liu, Y., Sun, S., Li, C.: Rotational cryptanalysis from a differential-linear perspective: practical distinguishers for round-reduced FRIET, Xoodoo, and Alzette. Accepted by EUROCRYPT 2021. Cryptology ePrint Archive, Report 2021/189 (2021). https://eprint.iacr.org/2021/189

25. Liu, Y., Witte, G.D., Ranea, A., Ashur, T.: Rotational-XOR cryptanalysis of reduced-round SPECK. IACR Trans. Symmetric Cryptol. 2017(3), 24–36 (2017)

26. Matsui, M.: Linear cryptanalysis method for DES cipher. In: Helleseth, T. (ed.) EUROCRYPT 1993. LNCS, vol. 765, pp. 386–397. Springer, Heidelberg (1994). https://doi.org/10.1007/3-540-48285-7_33

27. Mouha, N., Mennink, B., Van Herrewege, A., Watanabe, D., Preneel, B., Verbauwhede, I.: Chaskey: an efficient MAC algorithm for 32-bit microcontrollers. In: Joux, A., Youssef, A. (eds.) SAC 2014. LNCS, vol. 8781, pp. 306–323. Springer, Cham (2014). https://doi.org/10.1007/978-3-319-13051-4_19
28. Selçuk, A.A.: On probability of success in linear and differential cryptanalysis. J. Cryptol. **21**(1), 131–147 (2008)
29. Shimizu, A., Miyaguchi, S.: Fast data encipherment algorithm FEAL. In: Chaum, D., Price, W.L. (eds.) EUROCRYPT 1987. LNCS, vol. 304, pp. 267–278. Springer, Heidelberg (1988). https://doi.org/10.1007/3-540-39118-5_24
30. Song, L., Huang, Z., Yang, Q.: Automatic differential analysis of ARX block ciphers with application to SPECK and LEA. In: Liu, J.K., Steinfeld, R. (eds.) ACISP 2016. LNCS, vol. 9723, pp. 379–394. Springer, Cham (2016). https://doi.org/10.1007/978-3-319-40367-0_24
31. Wallén, J.: Linear approximations of addition modulo 2^n. In: Johansson, T. (ed.) FSE 2003. LNCS, vol. 2887, pp. 261–273. Springer, Heidelberg (2003). https://doi.org/10.1007/978-3-540-39887-5_20
32. Yao, Y., Zhang, B., Wu, W.: Automatic search for linear trails of the SPECK family. In: Lopez, J., Mitchell, C.J. (eds.) ISC 2015. LNCS, vol. 9290, pp. 158–176. Springer, Cham (2015). https://doi.org/10.1007/978-3-319-23318-5_9

Deep Neural Networks Aiding Cryptanalysis: A Case Study of the Speck Distinguisher

Norica Băcuieți[1,2]($\boxtimes$), Lejla Batina[3], and Stjepan Picek[3,4]

[1] ETH Zürich, Zürich, Switzerland
[2] Politehnica University of Timișoara, Timișoara, Romania
noricabacuieti@gmail.com
[3] Radboud University, Nijmegen, The Netherlands
[4] Delft University of Technology, Delft, The Netherlands
{lejla.batina,stjepan.picek}@ru.nl

Abstract. At CRYPTO'19, A. Gohr proposed neural distinguishers for the lightweight block cipher Speck32/64, achieving better results than the state-of-the-art at that point. However, the motivation for using that particular architecture was not very clear; therefore, in this paper, we study the depth-10 and depth-1 neural distinguishers proposed by Gohr [7] with the aim of finding out whether smaller or better-performing distinguishers for Speck32/64 exist.

We first evaluate whether we can find smaller neural networks that match the accuracy of the proposed distinguishers. We answer this question in the affirmative with the depth-1 distinguisher successfully pruned, resulting in a network that remained within one percentage point of the unpruned network's performance. Having found a smaller network that achieves the same performance, we examine whether its performance can be improved as well. We also study whether processing the input before giving it to the pruned depth-1 network would improve its performance. To this end, convolutional autoencoders were found that managed to reconstruct the ciphertext pairs successfully, and their trained encoders were used as a preprocessor before training the pruned depth-1 network. We found that, even though the autoencoders achieved a nearly perfect reconstruction, the pruned network did not have the necessary complexity anymore to extract useful information from the preprocessed input, motivating us to look at the feature importance to get more insights. To achieve this, we used LIME, with results showing that a stronger explainer is needed to assess it correctly.

Keywords: Neural distinguisher · Feature importance · Speck · Pruning

1 Introduction

Traditional symmetric cryptanalysis shows small improvements over time, and people started considering alternative ways to improve it. Since deep learning

© Springer Nature Switzerland AG 2022
G. Ateniese and D. Venturi (Eds.): ACNS 2022, LNCS 13269, pp. 809–829, 2022.
https://doi.org/10.1007/978-3-031-09234-3_40

has recently attracted much attention due to the significant advances in research areas such as computer vision and speech recognition, it did not take long until researchers also started to consider Deep Neural Networks (DNNs) in the area of cryptography. DNNs are a family of non-linear machine learning classifiers that, given a dataset and a loss function, try to learn the optimal hyperparameters minimizing the loss. Using DNNs, A. Gohr was the first to achieve better results than that time's state-of-the-art, revolutionizing cryptanalysis, i.e., the study of cryptographic systems with the purpose of finding weaknesses [7]. Encouraged by Gohr's results, more papers followed that built upon his work, e.g., [9].

Starting from Gohr's neural networks, the purpose of this paper is to investigate whether there exists a smaller or better-performing neural network for executing a better *distinguishing attack*. Generally, in a distinguishing attack against a cryptographic primitive (a cipher in our case), the adversary tries to *distinguish* between (or *classify*) encrypted data and random data, thus helping in the cryptanalysis of the cipher. Specifically, if an adversary manages to distinguish the output of a cipher from random data faster than a brute force key search, this is considered a break for the cipher. Thus, the cipher cannot be considered secure enough to ensure the confidentiality of the encrypted information. These distinguishing attacks can be *differential*, in which case we talk about differential cryptanalysis, that is, cryptanalysis with regards to bitwise differences in the inputs given to the cipher [5]. In a differential attack, the non-random properties of the ciphertext pair produced by the cipher when given a plaintext pair with some known input difference are exploited for various purposes, one of which is distinguishing. Those differential attacks further branch into *purely differential attacks*, where the adversary uses only the ciphertext pair's bitwise difference, and *general differential attacks*, where the information from the complete ciphertext pair is used [7]. Our work will focus on general differential distinguishing attacks on the lightweight iterated block cipher Speck32/64 achieved by neural networks.

Motivation. While the application of neural networks in cryptanalysis evidently brings good practical results, it is also important to provide some theoretical support. Otherwise, the improvements make limited sense, as one cannot obtain guidance for the design and analysis of cryptanalytic primitives. Thus, it becomes important to study the behavior of neural network distinguishers and the interpretability and explainability of such solutions. Unfortunately, deep learning explainability is a difficult problem that is not solved in general. Still, some observations are possible, especially from the perspective of the neural network size and the feature importance.

Recently, either a rather sophisticated technique exploited Speck's internal state values obtained through brute force key search [4] or a model that required k times more data was deployed [10]. On the contrary, to make the analysis simpler, our paper remains in the low data setting. Concretely, only the plaintext inputs and ciphertext outputs are known. In addition, the same training/test size and data format as in Gohr's work is kept for comparison. Concretely, we want to find out whether:

1. A smaller, equally-good-performing distinguisher can be obtained by systematically pruning Gohr's distinguishers to the bare minimum needed to achieve their current performance.
2. Preprocessing the input will improve the performance of Gohr's (pruned) distinguishers.

Main Contributions. We show that the state-of-the-art on neural distinguisher can be improved and that there are still multiple avenues to explore. We demonstrate these with the following contributions, which, to the best of our knowledge, are the first studies in the setting of neural differential distinguishers.

1. We evaluate the Lottery Ticket Hypothesis [6] on neural Speck distinguishers to see whether a smaller or better-performing network can be obtained, finding out that this is the case. Indeed, the Lottery Ticket Hypothesis states there are subnetworks that match or even outperform the accuracy of the original network. To obtain such subnetworks, we conduct pruning based on average activations equal to zero.
2. We successfully strip the currently best neural distinguisher for Speck (the depth-1 distinguisher), presenting a smaller network whose accuracy remains around one percentage point of the depth-1 distinguisher's.
3. We successfully train autoencoders that achieve a nearly perfect reconstruction of the given ciphertext pairs and study the performance of the proposed (and pruned) Speck distinguishers when autoencoders do a prior feature engineering.
4. We study the importance of the inputs using Local Interpretable Model-agnostic Explanations (LIME) [15] to gain insights into the (pruned) distinguishers' behavior, which might aid in the improvement of future preprocessing methods.

2 The Speck Family of Block Ciphers

2.1 Notations and Conventions

In this paper, the bitwise eXclusive-OR operation will be denoted by $\oplus$, the bitwise AND operation by $\wedge$, modular addition modulo 2^n by $\boxplus$, a left or right bitwise rotation by $\lll$ and $\ggg$, respectively, and the concatenation of two-bit strings a and b will be denoted by $a \parallel b$. Furthermore, the Hamming weight hw of a bit string is given by the number of ones present in it.

2.2 Speck Block Cipher

The lightweight iterated block cipher Speck was designed by Beaulieu et al. for the US National Security Agency (NSA) with the intent of being efficient in software implementations on micro-controllers [3]. At its core, it is comprised of three basic functions: modular **A**ddition (modulo 2^k), bitwise **R**otation, and bitwise e**X**clusive-OR of k-bit words, thus being an ARX construction. Since it is an *iterated* block cipher, it has a round function (that is iterated), which, in the case of Speck, is a simple Feistel structure. The round function $F: \mathbb{F}_2^k \times \mathbb{F}_2^{2k}$ takes as input a k-bit subkey K and the cipher's internal state that consists of two k-bit words denoted as L_i and R_i, and computes the cipher's next internal state as:

$$L_{i+1} = ((L_i \gg \alpha) \boxplus R_i) \oplus K \tag{1}$$

$$R_{i+1} = (R_i \lll \beta) \oplus L_{i+1} \tag{2}$$

Here, i and $i{+}1$ represent the current, respectively, next round, and α and β are constants specific to each member of the Speck cipher family. Regarding the subkeys used, they are generated with a non-linear key schedule from a master key using the above-described round function as the main operation, but with details that change from one Speck member to another.

As the key schedule will not be studied in this paper, please refer to [3] for additional information. Concretely, for the Speck member studied in this paper, the block size n is 32 bits, the word size k is 16 bits, the key size m is 64 bits, α is 7, β is 2, and the round function is applied maximally 22 times to compute a ciphertext output from the plaintext input.

2.3 The Setup

For the implementation of the Speck32/64 cipher and distinguishers studied, as well as for the algorithms needed for generating the datasets with a given input difference and evaluating the results, this paper refers to the code provided by the author of [7] here[1]. For all experiments, a training set of size 10^7, a test set of size 10^6, and a batch size of $5\,000$ were used as in the previous related work [7]. Finally, the experiments were run on an RTX 3090, and the code that was used to conduct the experiments, as well as some figures, can be found in the associated repository[2].

3 Related Works on Neural Speck Distinguishers

Since the release of the lightweight block cipher Speck, differential and neural distinguishers have been used to cryptanalyze it. First, at CRYPTO'19, Gohr proposed such distinguishers, focusing on the input difference $\Delta_{in} = 0x0040/0000$ [1]. The author defined *real pairs* as being ciphertext pairs (C, C') resulting from encrypting plaintext pairs (P, P') where $P \oplus P' = \Delta_{in}$, and *random pairs* being ciphertext pairs (C, C') resulting from encrypting plaintext pairs (P, P') where there is no fixed input difference. Then, the author aimed to distinguish the *real pairs* from the *random pairs*, deploying several methods that are described below. In the process, the author compared the performance of a purely differential distinguisher to a neural distinguisher for 5 to 8 rounds, showing that the neural distinguisher outperforms the purely differential one. Those

---

[1] https://github.com/agohr/deep_speck.
[2] https://github.com/NoricaBacuieti/TheSpeckAttack.

distinguishers were denoted D_r and N_r for differential and neural distinguishers for Speck reduced to $r \in \{5, 6, 7, 8\}$ rounds, respectively.

Purely Differential Distinguisher. First, the entire difference distribution table (DDT) of Speck for the input difference Δ_{in} was computed under the Markov assumption [13]. Then, to distinguish real ciphertext pairs from random ones, the author first assumed that random ciphertext pair differences, i.e., $\Delta_{out} = C \oplus C'$, are distributed according to the uniform distribution. Next, the author took the corresponding transition probability $P(\Delta_{in} \rightarrow \Delta_{out})$ from the DDT, classifying the ciphertext pair difference as *real*, if $P(\Delta_{in} \rightarrow \Delta_{out}) > \frac{1}{2^{32}-1}$, and as *random* otherwise. For more details, please refer to [7].

Gohr's Neural Distinguisher. The proposed deep neural network is a residual network consisting of three types of blocks: an *initial convolution, convolutional blocks*, and a *prediction head*. Concretely, they are:

1. Block 1: the initial convolution consisting of a 1D-CNN layer with kernel size 1, 32 channels, padding, and stride of size 1, followed by batch normalization and a ReLU activation layer.
2. Block 2-i: the convolutional one-to-ten residual blocks/units, each residual block consisting of two 1D-CNN layers with kernel size 3, 32 channels and padding, and stride of size 1, each followed by batch normalization and a ReLU activation layer. These layers are then followed by an additional layer where the input of this block is also added to its output and passed to the input of the subsequent block. This last operation makes the block, and thus also the network, residual, the input that skips all those layers being called a residual connection.
3. Block 3: the prediction head consisting of two dense layers, having 64 neurons and followed by batch normalization and a ReLU activation layer each, closing with a dense layer of one neuron using a sigmoid activation function.

The neural distinguishers give a score between 0 and 1, where a score greater than or equal to 0.5 classifies the sample as a real pair; otherwise, it is classified as random. Using this setup, neural distinguishers were trained for Speck reduced to 5 and 6 rounds, but different approaches were taken for Speck reduced to 7 and 8 rounds. For Speck reduced to 7 rounds, *key search* was used to improve the accuracy of the neural distinguisher. For more details, the method described can be found in [7].

Moving to the neural distinguisher for 8 rounds, since the previously mentioned approach did not improve this distinguisher's performance, the neural distinguisher for 8 rounds was obtained from the seven-round neural distinguisher using the staged training method. Again, more details can be found in [7].

Obtaining superior results compared to purely differential distinguishers indicated that the neural distinguishers learn more than differential cryptanalysis. It thus motivated A. Gohr to conduct *the real differences experiment* with the goal to distinguish real ciphertext pairs (C, C') drawn from the real distribution (again obtained from the $\Delta_{in} = \text{0x0040/0000}$ difference) from masked real ciphertext pairs $(C \oplus M, C' \oplus M)$ where M is a random 32-bit value. By conducting this experiment, Gohr wanted to show that the previously obtained neural distinguishers (without retraining) offer comparable results to key search. The results for both the real-vs-random, as well as for the real differences experiment, can be found in [7].

Inspired by A. Gohr's work, Benamira et al. [4] went further and developed an approach to estimate the property learned by Gohr's deep neural network. Concretely, they replaced Gohr's three building blocks with the following steps:

1. Changing (C, C') into $I = (\Delta L, \Delta V, V_0, V_1)$, where $\Delta L = C_l \oplus C_l'$ is the addition modulo 2 between the left parts of C and C', and $V_i = L_i \oplus R_i$ is the difference between the two parts of the internal state at round i.
2. Changing the 512-feature vector [4] of the DNN into a feature vector of probabilities $F = (P(Real \mid I_{M1}) P(Real \mid I_{M2}) \cdots P(Real \mid I_{Mm}))^T$.
3. Changing the final dense layer of the third building block into the Light Gradient Boosting Machine (LGBM) [12] model.

The authors defined an *output distribution table* (ODT) directly on the values $(\Delta L, \Delta V, V_0, V_1)$ instead of the DDT of the ciphertext pair difference $(C_l \oplus C_l', C_r \oplus C_r')$. Then, they used the ODT to define a *masked output distribution table* (M-ODT). This M-ODT is a compressed ODT where the input is not $I = (\Delta L, \Delta V, V_0, V_1)$, but $I_M = (\Delta L \wedge M_1, \Delta V \wedge M_2, V_0 \wedge M_3, V_1 \wedge M_4)$, where $M \in \mathcal{M}_{hw}$, $M = (M_1, M_2, M_3, M_4)$ is an ensemble of four 16-bit masks, each having the Hamming weights hw (later set to 16 and 18). Then, by considering several masks, they defined the set of relevant masks of $\mathcal{M}_{hw}$ as R_M, being able to compute for each input I the probability $P(Real \mid I_M)$, $\forall M \in R_M$ [4]. Having those defined, they developed a three-step approach for recognizing the output of Speck reduced to 5 and 6 rounds as follows:

1. Extract the masks from Gohr's DNN with dataset 1.
2. Construct the M-ODT with dataset 2.
3. Train the LGBM classifier from the probabilities stored in the M-ODT with dataset 3.

Through this approach, they obtained results similar to Gohr's DNN, thus showing that they have successfully modeled the DNN's property. The results can be seen in [4].

They concluded by explaining how to improve A. Gohr's results by means of creating batches of ciphertext inputs instead of pairs. They used two approaches for training and evaluating the M-ODT distinguisher: one where each element of the batch is given a score by the distinguisher and then takes the median of the results, and the other one where the whole batch is considered as a single input. For both methods, they obtained a 100% accuracy on 5 and 6 rounds, as well as on 7 rounds with the first method [4].

More recently, taking inspiration from both the works mentioned above, Hou et al. [10] first developed an algorithm based on SAT, which returns input differences of high-probability differential characteristics. They proposed an alternative format for the training and test data, where they would group k ciphertext differences in a matrix and regard it as one sample, and they used this type of sample to train the ResNet. Concretely, they tried it either with the same input difference as A. Gohr or a better one as chosen by their SAT-based algorithm. Using this new data format in combination with the input differences suggested by their algorithm, they managed to obtain an accuracy of 88.19% and 56.49% for Speck reduced to 7 and 8 rounds, respectively, which is superior to A. Gohr's results. More details can be found in [10].

4   The Network Under Lens

First, A. Gohr's network containing ten blocks of type 2 and its performance on Speck reduced to 7 and 8 rounds will be examined. Following this, the Lottery Ticket Hypothesis using two different pruning methods: one-shot pruning and iterative pruning will be evaluated for this depth-10 distinguisher, analyzing the results. After that, Gohr's best network, the depth-1 distinguisher, containing one block of type 2, will be examined in detail to see whether even this already small network can be further pruned. For this purpose, the Lottery Ticket Hypothesis will be evaluated for this network, followed by a computation of the average percentage of activations equal to zero and pruning of the network.

4.1   The Initial Network

First, we aim to reproduce the results given in [7] with the depth-10 neural distinguisher for Speck reduced to 5 and 6 rounds. In addition, we also want to see its performance for Speck reduced to 7 and 8 rounds by following the same training method as opposed to the approaches used in [7]. After having trained and evaluated the distinguishers five times, the results can be seen in Table 1.

Table 1. Accuracies of the depth-10 Neural distinguishers for Speck32/64 reduced to 5, 6, 7, and 8 rounds in the real-vs-random experiment.

Distinguisher	Accuracy	TPR	TNR
N_5	$0.927 \pm 1.46 \times 10^{-4}$	$0.901 \pm 3.92 \times 10^{-4}$	$0.953 \pm 5.86 \times 10^{-4}$
N_6	$0.787 \pm 3.90 \times 10^{-4}$	$0.719 \pm 9.66 \times 10^{-4}$	$0.855 \pm 7.45 \times 10^{-4}$
N_7	$0.611 \pm 4.17 \times 10^{-4}$	$0.551 \pm 1.98 \times 10^{-3}$	$0.671 \pm 1.90 \times 10^{-3}$
N_8	$0.500 \pm 7.53 \times 10^{-5}$	$0.368 \pm 3.55 \times 10^{-1}$	$0.632 \pm 3.55 \times 10^{-1}$

From these results, one can see that for Speck reduced to 5 and 6 rounds, the results could be reproduced. What is more, for Speck reduced to 7 rounds, the distinguisher gave a similar accuracy to the one in [7], where the author used the approach mentioned in Sect. 3. Perhaps, the more sophisticated approach [7] was used more for seeing whether it would improve the distinguisher's accuracy, but since the improvement is insignificant, we will use the same training approach as for the first two distinguishing cases. When looking at the N_8 distinguisher, the improvement achieved by using the approach mentioned in Sect. 3 managed to make the neural distinguisher slightly better than the differential distinguisher. However, it is not considerable compared to the N_8 distinguisher trained using the same approach as for Speck reduced to 5 and 6 rounds. Since the N_8 distinguisher without the training approach mentioned above is no better than random guessing, even though results will be given for it as well, the decisions will be based on the results of the other three distinguishers.

With this, we turn to the next section, where we will look at the Lottery Ticket Hypothesis and the results obtained by effectuating the steps needed for evaluating it for the depth-10 and depth-1 versions of this distinguisher.

4.2   The Lottery Ticket Hypothesis

The *Lottery Ticket Hypothesis* (LTH) was first proposed by Frankle and Carbin in [6]. It was proposed after finding that appropriately initialized pruned networks are capable of training effectively while achieving a comparable accuracy to the original network in a similar number of training epochs. It reads as follows:

A randomly initialized dense neural network contains a subnetwork initialized such that - when trained in isolation - it can match the test accuracy of the original network after training for at most the same number of iterations.

Thus, the reasons behind evaluating the LTH is to see whether:

1. Some subnetworks perform similar to the baseline network for each of the four distinguishers, and how much the performance decreases as the network becomes more sparse. The goal is to get an idea of the trade-off between the network's size and its performance.
2. There are winning tickets and whether their performance is significantly better than the baseline network.
3. Similar conclusions to the ones in [6] can be drawn. Those are:
   - Iterative pruning finds winning tickets that match the accuracy of the baseline network at smaller network sizes than one-shot pruning.
   - Winning tickets are 10% (or less) to 20% of the baseline network's size.

As mentioned, these subnetworks are obtained by pruning, and in the following subsections, two pruning strategies will be put under test for the LTH: *one-shot pruning* and *iterative pruning*.

The Winning Tickets. According to [6], after having pruned the trained baseline network of the smallest-magnitude weights, we are ready to define what a *winning ticket* is. A *winning ticket* is a subnetwork that, when trained in isolation after having had the remaining weights reinitialized with the weights of the baseline network *prior to training*, will provide classification accuracy equivalent or superior to the baseline networks.

Frankle and Carbin have repeated the experiments with random initialization of the pruned network. However, the randomly initialized pruned network no

longer matched the trained (unpruned) baseline network's performance eviden-
tiating that the pruned networks need to be appropriately initialized. Therefore,
the pruning strategies will be defined to reinitialize the remaining weights of the
pruned network to the weights of the unpruned network prior to training.

One-shot pruning. In one-shot pruning, the baseline network is trained once, $p\%$
of the weights are pruned, and then the remaining weights are reinitialized to the
weights of the baseline network prior to training. The process will be repeated
for several values of $p\%$ to see the possible changes in the performance of the
distinguisher. Please refer to [6] for the pseudocode and further details.

Iterative pruning. In iterative pruning, we again start from a baseline network
that is trained once. But unlike in one-shot pruning, where we start from the
same pretrained weights θ_0 each time we repeat the process with a different value
of $p\%$, now, at each pruning trial $i \in \{1, t\}$, $p\%$ of the *remaining* weights are
pruned. Again, since there is no indication of what an appropriate value for $p\%$
would be, one would have to try different values. However, if the improvement
of the winning tickets' performance will not be significant, the experiments will
be run just for one value of $p\%$. For more details, please refer to [6].

Results. Here, the results that were obtained by evaluating the LTH for the N_5,
N_6, N_7, and N_8 distinguishers based on the depth-10 neural network are given.
Experiments with both one-shot pruning (depicted in *yellow*) as well as iterative
pruning (depicted in *green*) were conducted and compared to the results obtained
for the (unpruned) baseline model (depicted in **black**). Specifically, for each
distinguisher, accuracy was computed and compared to those obtained with the
baseline network. The experiment was run five times per pruning ratio for each
pruning method, the results were averaged, and the minimum and maximum at
each pruning trial were indicated. The accuracies can be seen in Fig. 1.

For both pruning methods, there were 9 pruning trials, where:

1. For one-shot pruning: 10%, 20%, 30%, 40%, 50%, 60%, 70%, 80%, and 90%,
   respectively, of the network was pruned.
2. For iterative pruning: 20% of the remaining network's weights was pruned
   per trial.

Looking at the results of the four distinguishers, two things can be observed
immediately: at least up to 90% of the depth-10 network can be pruned without
losing (on average) performance, and there are winning tickets that even slightly
outperform (on average) the baseline network. Therefore, it can be empirically
confirmed that the LTH does indeed find subnetworks (winning tickets) that will
provide classification accuracy equivalent or superior to the baseline network.

Then, looking at the findings of the authors in [6], they have found that
iterative pruning finds winning tickets that match the accuracy of the baseline
network at smaller network sizes than does one-shot pruning. In addition, they
have also found that the winning tickets are 10% (or less) to 20% of the baseline network's size. These findings could not be entirely confirmed by the results

above nor by the ones presented in the next subsection where the depth-1 network (which can be regarded as an already 90% pruned version of this depth-10 network) is examined. First, iterative pruning does not seem to be superior to one-shot regarding finding winning tickets that match the accuracy of the baseline network at smaller network sizes. Looking at the results, iterative pruning is either outperformed by one-shot pruning or is just barely outperforming one-shot pruning. Perhaps more trials per pruning ratio are needed to be firm in this sense. However, since iterative pruning is, as noted by the authors of [6] costly, the conclusion is left that both pruning methods perform similarly concerning finding winning tickets at smaller network sizes. Second, the results presented above and in the next subsection show that winning tickets can be found, in general, at every pruning ratio by both pruning methods.

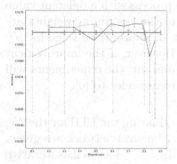

(a) The *accuracy* of N_5 after pruning $p\%$ of the network.

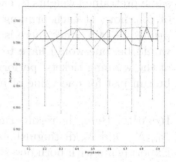

(b) The *accuracy* of N_6 after pruning $p\%$ of the network.

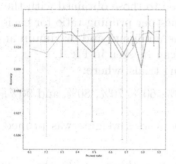

(c) The *accuracy* of N_7 after pruning $p\%$ of the network.

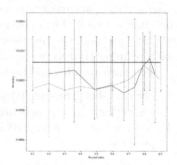

(d) The *accuracy* of N_8 after pruning $p\%$ of the network.

Fig. 1. The accuracys obtained after evaluating the LTH for the depth-10 N_5, N_6, N_7, and N_8 distinguishers.

While, on the one hand, we have looked at whether similar conclusions to the ones in [6] could be drawn, on the other hand, some of their conclusions were directly considered when running the experiments. First, while the globally smallest-magnitude weights were pruned in both pruning methods, the authors also experimented with pruning the smallest weights per layer with the same ratio, finding that for ResNet-18 and VGG-19, global pruning finds smaller winning tickets. They explained that some layers have far more parameters than others and that when all layers are pruned with the same ratio, the smaller layers become bottlenecks. Since in the depth-10 baseline network, some layers presented a similar difference of parameters as in the network studied by them, the experiments were run directly with the globally smallest-magnitude weights pruning approach to avoid the pitfall of having such bottlenecks.

Second, the authors have also found that the value from which the learning rate starts matters for the LTH's success. When starting from a higher learning rate for Resnet-18 and VGG-19, the performance of the networks obtained with iterative pruning was no better than that of randomly reinitialized pruned networks (random guessing). However, they have found that at a lower learning rate, the subnetworks remain within one percentage point of the baseline network's accuracy. Although they do not give intuition behind this result, since the point of the LTH is to find subnetworks that match or outperform the baseline network's performance, it makes sense to choose a (lower) learning rate that would allow the model to learn a more optimal set of weights. The baseline network proposed by A. Gohr already started with a small learning rate of 0.002 which further decreased to 0.0001, and as seen, iterative pruning did indeed find winning tickets.

4.3   The Smaller Network

Having seen that at least 90% of the depth-10 network can be pruned (even with some minor improvement on average), we now turn to the best network A. Gohr has found, namely, the version with only one block of type 2, the depth-1 network. Again, first, we will try to reproduce the results Gohr obtained for Speck reduced to 5 and 6 rounds, and then see the distinguisher's performance on Speck reduced to 7 and 8 rounds using the same training approach as for the first two distinguishing cases. After having trained and evaluated the distinguishers five times, the results can be seen in Table 2.

Table 2. Accuracies of the depth-1 Neural distinguishers for Speck32/64 reduced to 5, 6, 7, and 8 rounds in the real-vs-random experiment.

Distinguisher	Accuracy	TPR	TNR
N_5	$0.927 \pm 1.46 \times 10^{-4}$	$0.897 \pm 1.06 \times 10^{-3}$	$0.954 \pm 8.45 \times 10^{-4}$
N_6	$0.783 \pm 1.39 \times 10^{-4}$	$0.717 \pm 1.34 \times 10^{-3}$	$0.850 \pm 1.11 \times 10^{-3}$
N_7	$0.608 \pm 9.91 \times 10^{-4}$	$0.542 \pm 3.99 \times 10^{-3}$	$0.674 \pm 4.56 \times 10^{-3}$
N_8	$0.500 \pm 1.52 \times 10^{-4}$	$0.51 \pm 1.92 \times 10^{-1}$	$0.489 \pm 1.92 \times 10^{-1}$

As expected from the results of the previous subsection, as well as from the results that Gohr obtained for the depth-1 N_5 and N_6 distinguishers, the accuracy of the depth-1 N_5 and N_6 distinguishers remained similar to the depth-10 distinguisher's. What is more, the accuracy of the N_7 distinguisher decreased by only around one percentage point, which can be considered as an insignificant decrease. Having seen that reducing the depth-10 network to depth-1 does not affect the distinguishers' performance significantly, the next question raised was whether the depth-1 network can be pruned even more at an insignificant performance loss. The LTH with the two pruning methods was evaluated again for this depth-1 network to determine whether this is the case. The accuracies can be seen in Fig. 2. Those show, again, that one could prune even 90% of this small network without losing (on average) in terms of performance. Therefore, in the next subsections, we will look at the importance of each major part of this smaller network and how it affects the performance of the distinguishers.

4.4   How Much Smaller Can We Go?

To find the answer to this question, we will first look at the activation map of each layer of the four neural distinguishers to see how much they learn at each layer. The idea is that if we see completely black activation maps, nothing is learned at that layer so that it can be pruned entirely. However, if there is only some activation present, some channels/neurons of that layer can be pruned, and how much it can be pruned in such cases needs to be determined through experiments. In this paper, results will be given for two cases that show that the performance is marginally affected even when the depth-1 network is pruned significantly.

To compute the activation maps, the keract[3] [14] library was used, and they can be seen in the associated repository. For each of the four distinguishers, the five activation maps were computed, where A_1, A_2, and A_3 correspond to the activation maps of the three convolutional layers, and A_4 and A_5 correspond to the activation maps of the two dense layers. However, since the results were similar, just the activation maps of the N_5 distinguisher are given.

After examining them, the findings confirm the results obtained with the LTH, according to which even this small network can be further pruned. Concretely, the A_1 activation maps have around 13–15 channels with no activation or an insignificant number of activations, the A_2 activation maps have 12–18 such channels, and the A_3 activation maps, 6–10 channels. Then, looking at the A_4 and A_5 activation maps, there are around 10 and 20–25 neurons, respectively, that show some activation.

Now, even though these were the activation maps for just one input value each, the results were similar for all three distinguishers, so we go to the next step where we prune. As mentioned, besides having some maps with no activation, which will not influence the performance of the distinguishers, some maps have almost no activation but with a/some large activation value/s. First, to confirm that the performance will not be affected, a network from which the minimum number of empty channels/neurons will be removed from each layer will be trained.

---

[3] https://pypi.org/project/keract/4.4.0/.

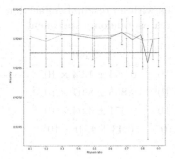

(a) The *accuracy* of N_5 after pruning $p\%$ of the network.

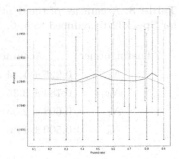

(b) The *accuracy* of N_6 after pruning $p\%$ of the network.

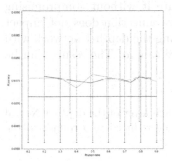

(c) The *accuracy* of N_7 after pruning $p\%$ of the network.

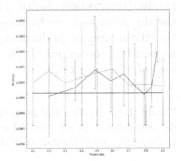

(d) The *accuracy* of N_8 after pruning $p\%$ of the network.

Fig. 2. The accuracys obtained after evaluating the LTH for the depth-1 N_5, N_6, N_7, and N_8 distinguishers.

Then, going to the other extreme, the maximum number of empty channels/neurons over all three distinguishers for each layer will be pruned to see how much the performance is affected and whether a finer-grained pruning approach is needed. To conduct these experiments, the kerassurgeon[4] library will be used. However, since it does not support residual connections, we will first see whether they have a significant impact on the performance of the distinguishers. After training the depth-1 distinguishers with no residual connection, the results can be seen in Table 3.

As can be seen, the accuracy of the distinguishers did not decrease, which indicates that a residual connection is not necessary. This was also expected since the use of residual connections is to allow the training of very deep neural networks. In a nutshell, those residual connections mitigate the vanishing gradients and accuracy saturation problems by allowing an alternate path for gradients to flow through and allowing the model to learn an identity function [8]. This ensures that the higher layers will perform at least as well as the lower (deeper)

---

[4] https://pypi.org/project/kerassurgeon/.

Table 3. Accuracies of the depth-1 Neural distinguishers with no residual connection for Speck32/64 reduced to 5, 6, 7, and 8 rounds in the real-vs-random experiment.

Distinguisher	Accuracy	TPR	TNR
N_5	$0.925 \pm 1.44 \times 10^{-4}$	$0.897 \pm 1.30 \times 10^{-3}$	$0.954 \pm 1.24 \times 10^{-3}$
N_6	$0.784 \pm 3.35 \times 10^{-4}$	$0.714 \pm 5.68 \times 10^{-4}$	$0.855 \pm 8.07 \times 10^{-4}$
N_7	$0.608 \pm 2.55 \times 10^{-3}$	$0.542 \pm 6.00 \times 10^{-3}$	$0.671 \pm 4.94 \times 10^{-3}$
N_8	$0.500 \pm 1.36 \times 10^{-4}$	$0.57 \pm 4.48 \times 10^{-1}$	$0.43 \pm 4.50 \times 10^{-1}$

layers. However, since we have such a small network, the benefits of using a residual connection vanish, allowing us to eliminate it without compromising the distinguishers' performance. Since the residual connection does not impact the distinguishers' performance, we will start pruning the depth-1 network with no residual connection to see how much smaller we can go. The results can be seen in Tables 4, 5, 6, 7.

Table 4. Accuracies and pruned channels/neurons of each layer of the depth-1 Neural distinguisher with no residual connection for Speck32/64 reduced to 5 rounds in the real-vs-random experiment for different APoZ values.

APoZ	Accuracy	C1	C2	C3	D1	D2
1	$0.925 \pm 1.58 \times 10^{-4}$	6.4	2	2	2.6	3.4
0.9	$0.924 \pm 1.50 \times 10^{-3}$	6.2	9.6	11	24.6	3.2
0.8	$0.920 \pm 1.76 \times 10^{-2}$	6	14	23.2	45.6	6.6
0.7	$0.904 \pm 3.05 \times 10^{-2}$	11.6	20.4	28.4	53.6	10.6

Table 5. Accuracies and pruned channels/neurons of each layer of the depth-1 Neural distinguisher with no residual connection for Speck32/64 reduced to 6 rounds in the real-vs-random experiment for different APoZ values.

APoZ	Accuracy	C1	C2	C3	D1	D2
1	$0.785 \pm 9.06 \times 10^{-4}$	6.4	6	2.2	2.2	4.4
0.9	$0.783 \pm 3.02 \times 10^{-3}$	5.4	11.2	14.4	21.8	7
0.8	$0.780 \pm 1.32 \times 10^{-2}$	3.6	15	21.8	40.4	10.4
0.7	$0.737 \pm 1.48 \times 10^{-2}$	10	20	28.6	56	30.4

Using kerassurgeon, each of the four distinguishers' layers were pruned based on the average percentage of activations equal to zero (APoZ) described in [11]. In the tables, the accuracies for each distinguisher and the average number of channels/neurons that were pruned from each of the five layers are presented.

Table 6. Accuracies and pruned channels/neurons of each layer of the depth-1 Neural distinguisher with no residual connection for Speck32/64 reduced to 7 rounds in the real-vs-random experiment for different APoZ values.

APoZ	Accuracy	C1	C2	C3	D1	D2
1	$0.607 \pm 3.23 \times 10^{-3}$	8.2	15	12.2	16.2	27.8
0.9	$0.608 \pm 1.23 \times 10^{-3}$	6.8	17.2	17.8	26.2	31.4
0.8	$0.601 \pm 8.78 \times 10^{-3}$	6.6	20.2	24.8	40.8	35.6
0.7	$0.597 \pm 5.25 \times 10^{-3}$	12	25.6	27.4	49.6	43

Table 7. Accuracies and pruned channels/neurons of each layer of the depth-1 Neural distinguisher with no residual connection for Speck32/64 reduced to 8 rounds in the real-vs-random experiment for different APoZ values.

APoZ	Accuracy	C1	C2	C3	D1	D2
1	$0.500 \pm 2.80 \times 10^{-4}$	0.8	0	0	2.2	15.4
0.9	$0.500 \pm 2.32 \times 10^{-4}$	2.2	0.2	1.2	2.4	20.2
0.8	$0.500 \pm 3.23 \times 10^{-4}$	2.2	1.2	2	11.8	24
0.7	$0.500 \pm 1.09 \times 10^{-4}$	5.6	8.4	7	17.2	32.6

As suspected, the depth-1 network can be even further pruned without significantly impacting the distinguishers' performance. One can see that when the channels/neurons that had the APoZ value greater or equal to 0.7 were removed from the N_6 distinguisher, the accuracy decreased by five percentage points. In contrast, for greater cutoff values, the accuracy decreased by less than one percentage point. Now, seeing that the depth-1 network can be pruned, we will decide how much to prune the network before moving to the next section.

Since we saw the accuracy decreasing for an APoZ value greater or equal to 0.7, we look at the number of channels/neurons pruned above this cutoff across the first three distinguishers. Two experiments were run where the distinguishers' layers were pruned in two ways: one in which the smallest (for an APoZ value equal to 1) and one in which the largest (for an APoZ value equal to 0.8) number of channels/neurons per layer across all three distinguishers was pruned. The processes were called min-pruning and max-pruning, and the results can be seen in Tables 8 and 9.

Table 8. Accuracies of the min-pruned depth-1 Neural distinguishers with no residual connection for Speck32/64 reduced to 5, 6, 7, and 8 rounds in the real-vs-random experiment.

Distinguisher	Accuracy	TPR	TNR
N_5	$0.923 \pm 1.67 \times 10^{-3}$	$0.890 \pm 3.52 \times 10^{-3}$	$0.955 \pm 5.11 \times 10^{-4}$
N_6	$0.782 \pm 6.27 \times 10^{-4}$	$0.713 \pm 1.19 \times 10^{-3}$	$0.850 \pm 6.12 \times 10^{-4}$
N_7	$0.605 \pm 1.75 \times 10^{-3}$	$0.546 \pm 3.70 \times 10^{-3}$	$0.664 \pm 4.26 \times 10^{-3}$
N_8	$0.500 \pm 1.99 \times 10^{-4}$	$0.54 \pm 5.36 \times 10^{-1}$	$0.44 \pm 2.50 \times 10^{-1}$

Table 9. Accuracies of the max-pruned depth-1 Neural distinguishers with no residual connection for Speck32/64 reduced to 5, 6, 7, and 8 rounds in the real-vs-random experiment.

Distinguisher	Accuracy	TPR	TNR
N_5	$0.915 \pm 1.41 \times 10^{-3}$	$0.875 \pm 1.54 \times 10^{-3}$	$0.955 \pm 1.50 \times 10^{-3}$
N_6	$0.770 \pm 4.24 \times 10^{-3}$	$0.691 \pm 8.84 \times 10^{-3}$	$0.848 \pm 1.37 \times 10^{-4}$
N_7	$0.596 \pm 7.70 \times 10^{-3}$	$0.543 \pm 7.40 \times 10^{-3}$	$0.648 \pm 1.63 \times 10^{-2}$
N_8	$0.500 \pm 1.65 \times 10^{-4}$	$0.54 \pm 2.83 \times 10^{-1}$	$0.460 \pm 2.83 \times 10^{-1}$

While the performance was expected not to be impacted in the first case, the second one was done more of sheer curiosity to see how the performance would change. As expected, in the first case, the performance remained within one percentage point, but, in the second case, the performance surprisingly remained again within one percentage point. For all experiments conducted in this paper (unless otherwise specified), the results are the average of five trials, which was considered appropriate given the time some of the experiments took (see the associated repository for details). However, the results might differ a bit if more trials per experiment would be conducted. Nevertheless, we keep the max-pruned network where we remove 7 channels from C1, 21 from C2, 25 from C3, 46 neurons from D1, and 36 from D2.

Finally, satisfied that we could even further prune the depth-1 network with no residual connection while the performance remained within one percentage point, we will move to the next section.

5   Visualizing the Important Features

In this section, we will look at whether a prior feature engineering will improve the performance of our distinguishers and whether all 64 input bits are needed for classification. A trained encoder will be used to preprocess the input, and regarding the assessment of the feature importance, LIME will be used. Finally, the experiments will be conducted on the max-pruned depth-1 network with no residual connection (also referred to as *pruned network*).

5.1   Feature Engineering Using an Autoencoder

Here, we will look at whether prior input engineering will improve the performance and, for this purpose, autoencoders of various compression capacities have been trained. An autoencoder is a neural network that learns to reproduce its input to its output, and it comprises of two parts: an encoder and a decoder. The encoder compresses the input to a latent representation, that is, an encoding that contains all the important information needed to represent the input, and the decoder takes this latent representation, trying to reconstruct the input [2]. The reason for choosing autoencoders to perform feature engineering was that autoencoders learn such a latent representation that ignores noise, anticipating that the network's performance would improve by bringing the useful features forward. The autoencoders corresponding to the results presented in Tables 10, 11, and 12 consist of one, two, and three blocks, respectively, each block being comprised of:

1. A 1D-CNN layer with kernel size 3, 32 channels, padding and stride of size 1, followed by a batch normalization and a ReLU activation layer.
2. A 1D-MaxPooling/1D-UpSampling layer with pool-size/size 2.

Table 10. Accuracies of the one-block autoencoder for Speck32/64 reduced to 5, 6, 7, and 8 rounds in the real-vs-random experiment.

Distinguisher	Accuracy	TPR	TNR
N_5	$0.999 \pm 2.10 \times 10^{-6}$	$0.999 \pm 4.41 \times 10^{-5}$	$0.999 + 4.72 \times 10^{-6}$
N_6	$0.999 \pm 4.94 \times 10^{-6}$	$0.999 \pm 3.26 \times 10^{-5}$	$0.999 \pm 2.60 \times 10^{-5}$
N_7	$0.999 \pm 1.25 \times 10^{-5}$	$0.999 \pm 4.83 \times 10^{-5}$	$0.999 \pm 5.58 \times 10^{-5}$
N_8	$0.999 \pm 2.38 \times 10^{-5}$	$0.999 \pm 1.11 \times 10^{-4}$	$0.999 \pm 1.44 \times 10^{-4}$

Table 11. Accuracies of the two-block autoencoder for Speck32/64 reduced to 5, 6, 7, and 8 rounds in the real-vs-random experiment.

Distinguisher	Accuracy	TPR	TNR
N_5	$0.999 \pm 1.00 \times 10^{-6}$	$0.999 \pm 6.54 \times 10^{-7}$	$0.999 \pm 1.53 \times 10^{-6}$
N_6	$0.999 \pm 3.68 \times 10^{-7}$	$0.999 \pm 3.83 \times 10^{-7}$	$0.999 \pm 4.82 \times 10^{-6}$
N_7	$0.999 \pm 2.31 \times 10^{-6}$	$0.999 \pm 2.76 \times 10^{-6}$	$0.999 \pm 2.32 \times 10^{-6}$
N_8	$0.999 \pm 5.93 \times 10^{-6}$	$0.999 \pm 6.03 \times 10^{-6}$	$0.999 \pm 5.99 \times 10^{-6}$

Table 12. Accuracies of the three-block autoencoder for Speck32/64 reduced to 5, 6, 7, and 8 rounds in the real-vs-random experiment.

Distinguisher	Accuracy	TPR	TNR
N_5	$0.889 \pm 1.98 \times 10^{-2}$	$0.893 \pm 1.86 \times 10^{-2}$	$0.885 \pm 2.20 \times 10^{-2}$
N_6	$0.895 \pm 2.30 \times 10^{-2}$	$0.904 \pm 1.96 \times 10^{-2}$	$0.886 \pm 2.94 \times 10^{-2}$
N_7	$0.871 \pm 1.11 \times 10^{-2}$	$0.861 \pm 3.61 \times 10^{-2}$	$0.881 \pm 2.70 \times 10^{-2}$
N_8	$0.896 \pm 4.03 \times 10^{-2}$	$0.879 \pm 5.69 \times 10^{-2}$	$0.914 \pm 3.39 \times 10^{-2}$

A prior reshaping and permutation of the input were also performed as in [7]. Concretely, starting from four 16-bit strings, the encoder of the one-block autoencoder compressed them into four 8-bit strings, the encoder of the two-block autoencoder compressed them into four 4-bit strings, and the encoder of the three-block autoencoder compressed them into four 2-bit strings. The results show that a convolutional encoder manages to learn a latent representation of the input that allows the convolutional decoder to reconstruct it almost perfectly for the one and two-block cases and reasonably well for the three-block case. Having seen these results, the pretrained encoders that were trained on a separate training set were added as a preprocessing step to the pruned network, and training was again performed to see the effect. Performance close to the one we already saw (or even a slightly better one) was expected. However, preliminary runs show quite the contrary. Even though the pretrained one and two-block encoders were used as a preprocessing step (as they were the most promising ones), the results do not show an improvement in the performance of the distinguishers. What is more, not even comparable results to the ones we already saw for the pruned network earlier are obtained.

For instance, for the pruned network with a one-block encoder as a preprocessor, the N_5 distinguisher's accuracy was 88%, and for the pruned network with a two-block encoder as a preprocessor, it was 82%. It seems that, even though the encoder managed to learn an efficient latent representation, once the input was transformed/engineered by the encoder, the pruned network did not have the complexity to decompose the engineered input and recombine it in a useful way. Having this intuition, the one-block encoder was added as a preprocessor to the original depth-10 network, and, when looking at the results of the N_5 distinguisher, the accuracy indeed improved compared to the time when the pruned network was used; namely, it reached a 92% accuracy. As suspected, when adding an encoder to perform feature engineering, the network that does the classification needs indeed to be complex enough to extract useful information from the latent representation.

5.2   Feature Visualization with LIME

Next, we will look closer at the input features and their importance to try to gain insights into the (pruned) distinguishers' behavior, which might aid in the improvement of future preprocessing methods. We will do this using one of the state of the art explanation techniques called Local Interpretable Model-agnostic Explanations (LIME) [15]. In short, according to [15], LIME explains the predictions of any classifier in an interpretable and faithful manner by learning an interpretable model locally around the prediction. Using it, the feature importances for all four distinguishers were computed, giving explanations for the five best predictions belonging to class 1 (fixed difference) and class 0 (random difference). In the associated repository, results are given just for the five best predictions of class 1 of the N_5 and N_6 distinguishers as the feature importance was similar. LIME with a submodular pick was also run [15]. However, even though it selected the instances judiciously, the results were similar to what was obtained so far, thus not contributing to a greater understanding of the distinguishers' behavior. From the figures given in the associated repository, we see that the importance of each feature is insignificant and that it varies from distinguisher to distinguisher (even from instance to instance). It seems that there is no clear local region that would have a considerable impact on the classification. Now, LIME already samples from both the vicinity of the instance and further away from it. Still, it is possible that even larger regions need to be considered for the important features to become evident to the explainer.

Then, even though for Speck reduced to 5 rounds, the distinguisher performs quite well, the explainer suggests that removing any (even all of the 64 features) will insignificantly affect the classifier's performance. Having obtained those results even for a fairly good distinguisher and after seeing the type of explainer LIME currently uses, it might well be that the *linear* explanation model will not be able to explain the distinguishers' behavior as there might be no linear boundary to begin with. For now, as LIME could not identify the important features, the conclusion is left that all of the 64 inputs are important.

6   Conclusions and Future Work

In this paper, the distinguisher proposed by A. Gohr [7] was under a study to find a better performing or smaller distinguisher for Speck32/64. To this end, the Lottery Ticket Hypothesis has been evaluated for the first time for the distinguisher mentioned above, discovering that even the depth-1 version can be further pruned without significantly compromising the performance, empirically confirming the hypothesis anew. Then, based on the conclusions of prior experiments, the depth-1 network was successfully pruned to potentially aid in the process of explaining its behavior, besides having seen how pruning the suggested limit would affect the performance.

Next, it has been studied whether a prior feature engineering would result in a performance gain. In the process, convolutional autoencoders of various compression capacities that successfully reconstructed the inputs were for the first time discovered, using their trained encoders as a preprocessor prior to training the pruned depth-1 network. Results have shown that even though convolutional autoencoders manage to learn a latent representation that they can nearly perfectly decode when passing the encoded inputs to the pruned depth-1 network, the network's performance decreased. This led to suspicion that the pruned network did not have the necessary complexity to extract useful information from the encoded inputs, which was later confirmed by additional experiments.

As a follow-up, intending to explain the distinguisher's behavior, the classification explainer LIME was for the first time deployed in this setting. Results showed that, despite the pruned depth-1 distinguisher performing reasonably well, LIME considered that none of the 64 inputs impacted the classification outcome. This suggests that a stronger explainer than the one LIME currently uses is needed, suspecting two possible causes (mentioned in Sect. 5) for LIME's current results that are yet to be studied.

One direction for future work would be to train the most recent networks used for image recognition to see whether a better performance can be achieved.

Then, since there are still instances classified with high confidence as belonging to the opposite class, a second suggestion would be to look at ensemble learning to see whether it could alleviate the problem. Moreover, since the evaluation of the LTH revealed that the depth-1 neural distinguisher could be further pruned, it would be interesting to consider evaluating it for different neural distinguishers. Finally, combining the SAT-based algorithm [10] with the framework presented in [16] for extending the differential attack to more rounds would be interesting as well.

References

1. Abed, F., List, E., Lucks, S., Wenzel, J.: Differential cryptanalysis of round-reduced Simon and Speck. In: Cid, C., Rechberger, C. (eds.) FSE 2014. LNCS, vol. 8540, pp. 525–545. Springer, Heidelberg (2015). https://doi.org/10.1007/978-3-662-46706-0_27
2. Bank, D., Koenigstein, N., Giryes, R.: Autoencoders. CoRR abs/2003.05991 (2020). https://arxiv.org/abs/2003.05991
3. Beaulieu, R., Treatman-Clark, S., Shors, D., Weeks, B., Smith, J., Wingers, L.: The Simon and speck lightweight block ciphers. In: 2015 52nd ACM/EDAC/IEEE Design Automation Conference (DAC), pp. 1–6 (2015). https://doi.org/10.1145/2744769.2747946
4. Benamira, A., Gerault, D., Peyrin, T., Tan, Q.Q.: A deeper look at machine learning-based cryptanalysis. In: Canteaut, A., Standaert, F.-X. (eds.) EURO-CRYPT 2021. LNCS, vol. 12696, pp. 805–835. Springer, Cham (2021). https://doi.org/10.1007/978-3-030-77870-5_28
5. Biham, E., Shamir, A.: Differential cryptanalysis of des-like cryptosystems, vol. 4, pp. 2–21 (1990). https://doi.org/10.1007/3-540-38424-3_1
6. Frankle, J., Carbin, M.: The lottery ticket hypothesis: training pruned neural networks. CoRR abs/1803.03635 (2018). http://arxiv.org/abs/1803.03635
7. Gohr, A.: Improving attacks on round-reduced speck32/64 using deep learning. In: Boldyreva, A., Micciancio, D. (eds.) CRYPTO 2019. LNCS, vol. 11693, pp. 150–179. Springer, Cham (2019). https://doi.org/10.1007/978-3-030-26951-7_6
8. He, K., Zhang, X., Ren, S., Sun, J.: Identity mappings in deep residual networks. In: Leibe, B., Matas, J., Sebe, N., Welling, M. (eds.) ECCV 2016. LNCS, vol. 9908, pp. 630–645. Springer, Cham (2016). https://doi.org/10.1007/978-3-319-46493-0_38
9. Hou, Z., Ren, J., Chen, S.: Cryptanalysis of round-reduced simon32 based on deep learning. IACR Cryptol. ePrint Arch. 2021, 362 (2021)
10. Hou, Z., Ren, J., Chen, S.: Improve neural distinguisher for cryptanalysis. Cryptology ePrint Archive, Report 2021/1017 (2021). https://ia.cr/2021/1017
11. Hu, H., Peng, R., Tai, Y., Tang, C.: Network trimming: a data-driven neuron pruning approach towards efficient deep architectures. CoRR abs/1607.03250 (2016). http://arxiv.org/abs/1607.03250
12. Ke, G., et al.: LightGBM: a highly efficient gradient boosting decision tree. In: Proceedings of the 31st International Conference on Neural Information Processing Systems, pp. 3149–3157. NIPS 2017, Curran Associates Inc., Red Hook, NY, USA (2017)
13. Lai, X., Massey, J.L., Murphy, S.: Markov ciphers and differential cryptanalysis. In: Davies, D.W. (ed.) EUROCRYPT 1991. LNCS, vol. 547, pp. 17–38. Springer, Heidelberg (1991). https://doi.org/10.1007/3-540-46416-6_2

14. Remy, P.: Keract: a library for visualizing activations and gradients (2020). https:// github.com/philipperemy/keract
15. Ribeiro, M.T., Singh, S., Guestrin, C.: Why should i trust you? explaining the predictions of any classifier. In: Proceedings of the 22nd ACM SIGKDD International Conference on Knowledge Discovery and Data Mining, pp. 1135–1144. KDD 2016, Association for Computing Machinery, New York, NY, USA (2016). https://doi. org/10.1145/2939672.2939778, https://doi.org/10.1145/2939672.2939778
16. Yadav, T., Kumar, M.: Differential-ml distinguisher: machine learning based generic extension for differential cryptanalysis. Cryptology ePrint Archive, Report 2020/913 (2020). https://ia.cr/2020/913

Post-quantum Cryptography

Carry-Less to BIKE Faster

Ming-Shing Chen[1]💿, Tim Güneysu[2,3]💿, Markus Krausz[2](✉)💿,
and Jan Philipp Thoma[2]💿

[1] Academia Sinica, Taipei, Taiwan
mschen@crypto.tw
[2] Ruhr University Bochum, Bochum, Germany
{tim.guneysu,markus.krausz,jan.thoma}@rub.de
[3] DFKI GmbH, Cyber-Physical Systems, Bremen, Germany

Abstract. Recent advances in the development of quantum computers manifest the urge to initiate the transition from classic public key cryptography to quantum secure algorithms. Therefore, NIST has initiated a post-quantum cryptography standardization process which is currently in its third and final round. One of the Key Encapsulation Mechanism (KEM) candidates is BIKE. In this paper we optimize the algorithm to achieve new speed-records for constant-time implementations of BIKE with parameter set `bike1l` on two different embedded architectures. For the ARM Cortex-M4 we leverage the performance benefit of bit-polynomial multiplication in radix-16 to outperform existing implementations. We explore different algorithmic approaches on the RISC-V-based VexRiscv platform and implement parts of the standard RISC-V Bitmanip Extension to measure its impact on BIKE. Our results indicate boundaries and trade-offs between different approaches for bit-polynomial multiplication beyond the BIKE use-case.

Keywords: NIST PQC Standardization · Constant-Time
Implementation · Cortex-M4 · RISC-V · Polynomial Multiplication

1 Introduction

The NIST standardization process was initiated in 2017 in the face of the ongoing development in quantum computing which threatens the security of traditional public key cryptography like RSA. Currently, the standardization is in its third and (presumably) final round. The set out goal is to standardize one or more Key Encapsulation Mechanisms (KEM) and Digital Signature Schemes (DSS) from the remaining 9 KEMs (4 finalists and 5 alternate candidates) and 6 DSSs (3 finalists and 3 alternate candidates). The code-based BIKE [2] scheme has been selected as an alternate KEM candidate. Compared to other quantum secure KEM schemes (see Table 7 for performance numbers) that are mostly lattice-based, the code-based BIKE is relatively slow. This leads to challenges in the deployability, especially in embedded environments where the much faster, quantum-insecure algorithms need to be replaced for long-term security.

© Springer Nature Switzerland AG 2022
G. Ateniese and D. Venturi (Eds.): ACNS 2022, LNCS 13269, pp. 833–852, 2022.
https://doi.org/10.1007/978-3-031-09234-3_41

In this paper, we tackle the performance problem by optimizing a key operation in BIKE: polynomial multiplication in $\mathbb{F}_2[x]$, also named bit-polynomial multiplication in the following, and equivalent to carry-less multiplication. Foundations to our work were laid by Brent et al. [9] in 2008, who implemented and improved state-of-the-art bit-polynomial multiplication algorithms and evaluated the performance for varying input sizes on the Intel Core 2 processor.

We evaluate various algorithmic approaches for bit-polynomial multiplication in the context of BIKE on two widespread architectures. The ARM Cortex-M4 is the reference platform for embedded benchmarks of PQC schemes selected by the NIST. Much effort has already been put into optimizing BIKE for the Cortex-M4. However, the implementation presented in this work outperforms even the previous fastest and highly optimized implementation [12] which utilizes the FFT. Our second evaluation platform is the RISC-V soft-core VexRiscv. The modular, plugin-based design allows us to directly measure the impact of a dedicated carry-less multiplication instruction. By implementing two different versions, one that is based on integer multiplication and the radix-16 form, and the other using a hardware accelerated carry-less multiplication instruction, we can explore the design space and trade-offs in terms of performance and area requirements. Additionally we port the optimized FFT based implementation for the VexRiscv to evaluate its performance against our two implementations using variants of Karatsuba and Toom-Cook.

1.1   Related Work

In 2021, Chen et al. [12] presented two optimized implementations for BIKE, one tailored for the Intel Haswell architecture and one for the ARM Cortex-M4. Besides other optimizations, they adopted two different strategies for accelerating bit-polynomial multiplication. Their implementation for the x86 Haswell used the carry-less multiplication (`pclmulqdq`) instruction for a base multiplier. On top of that they used multiple stages of Karatsuba and finally one stage of Bernstein's [6] five-way recursive multiplication algorithm. Their implementation of the Cortex-M4, however, used a FFT based multiplication algorithm. Although the M4 platform does not come with the carry-less multiplication instruction, the question arises whether the length of polynomials in BIKE is long enough for the FFT based multiplication to show its complexity supremacy on the M4 platform.

Classic McEliece is another quantum-safe, code-based KEM scheme that was submitted to the NIST's post-quantum cryptography standardization process. Recently, Chen and Chou [11] presented an optimized, constant-time implementation for Classic McEliece on the Cortex-M4 platform. They showed that the polynomial multiplication in small finite fields, $\mathbb{F}_{2^{12}}$ and $\mathbb{F}_{2^{13}}$, can be performed with integer multiplication by representing data in the radix-16 representation. In this paper we investigate the radix-16 multiplication approach for BIKE.

The open source RISC-V ISA has been utilized to develop co-processors [14] and accelerators [27] to speed up post-quantum cryptography. Pircher et al. [25] accelerated Classic McEliece with RISC-V's vector instruction extension. Similar to their work, we explore RISC-V's Instruction Set Extensions (ISE) for accelerating BIKE's performance on the VexRiscv core.

1.2 Contribution

To summarize, in this work we make multiple contributions.

- We develop a constant-time implementation for BIKE on the Cortex-M4 which outperforms Chen et al. [12] by accelerating the bit-polynomial multiplication. We present an optimized multiplication based on integer multiplication and the radix-16 format. We show how to perform shift operations in the radix-16 format efficiently, to reduce the overhead of transformations during the multiplications. We profile different variants of Karatsuba and Toom-Cook to determine the optimal algorithm and implementation for the given setting.
- We provide the fastest constant-time implementation for BIKE for the VexRiscv, and with this the first version optimized for the RISC-V ISA. Our fastest implementation is more than three times faster than the **portable** implementation provided by the BIKE team. We evaluate three different variants: one based on the radix-16 format, one based on additional instructions and supplementary we port the FFT implementation by Chen et al. for the M4 to the RISC-V ISA.
- We extend the VexRiscv with carry-less multiplication and conditional move instructions as proposed by the standard RISC-V ISA extension for bitmanipulation to evaluate the performance impact of the ISE for BIKE. Our carry-less multiplication implementation is parameterized by a window size and thus allows a finer choice for the area-performance trade-off.

2 BIKE

In this section we briefly recap the specification of BIKE [2], a code-based key encapsulation mechanism, in the version it was submitted to the third round of NIST's Post-Quantum Cryptography standardization process.

Figure 1 depicts BIKE's algorithms for key generation, encapsulation and decapsulation. A secret key (h_0, h_1, σ), with $(h_0, h_1) \in \mathcal{R}^2$ and $|h_0| = |h_1| = w/2$ together with a public key h is generated by the key generation algorithm. With the public key h as input, the encapsulation algorithm outputs a session key K and a ciphertext c where the session key is encapsulated. The decapsulation algorithm on the other hand takes the secret key (h_0, h_1, σ) and the ciphertext c as inputs and either generates the session key K or outputs $\bot$.

In the encapsulation and decapsulation, three different hash functions based on Keccak are used: **H**, **K** and **L** with the following domains and ranges.

KeyGen: $() \mapsto (h_0, h_1, \sigma), h$	**Encaps**: $h \mapsto K, c$
Output: $(h_0, h_1, \sigma) \in \mathcal{H}_w \times \mathcal{M}, h \in \mathcal{R}$	Input: $h \in \mathcal{R}$
1: $h_0, h_1 \xleftarrow{\$} \mathcal{H}_w$	Output: $K \in \mathcal{K}, c \in \mathcal{R} \times \mathcal{M}$
2: $h = h_1 \cdot h_0^{-1}$	1: $m \xleftarrow{\$} \mathcal{M}$
3: $\sigma \xleftarrow{\$} \mathcal{M}$	2: $e_0, e_1 \leftarrow \mathbf{H}(m)$
	3: $c = (e_0 + e_1 \cdot h, m \oplus \mathbf{L}(e_0, e_1))$
	4: $K \leftarrow \mathbf{K}(m, c)$

Decaps: $(h_0, h_1, \sigma), c \mapsto K$
Input: $((h_0, h_1), \sigma) \in \mathcal{H}_w \times \mathcal{M}, c = (c_0, c_1) \in \mathcal{R} \times \mathcal{M}$
Output: $K \in \mathcal{K}$
1: $e' \leftarrow \mathrm{decoder}(c_0 h_0, h_0, h_1)$ $\triangleright e' \in \mathcal{R}^2 \cup \{\perp\}$
2: $m' = c_1 \oplus \mathbf{L}(e')$ $\triangleright$ with the convention $\perp = (0, 0)$
3: **if** $e' = \mathbf{H}(m')$ **then** $K \leftarrow \mathbf{K}(m', c)$, **else** $K \leftarrow \mathbf{K}(\sigma, c)$

Fig. 1. BIKE's key generation, encapsulation, and decapsulation.

- **H**: $\{0,1\}^\ell \to \{0,1\}^{2r}_{[t]}$,
- **K**: $\{0,1\}^{r+2\ell} \to \{0,1\}^\ell$,
- **L**: $\{0,1\}^{2r} \to \{0,1\}^\ell$,

The computation time spent during the encapsulation is mostly determined by the costs for the multiplication of $e_1 \cdot h$ in $\mathcal{R}$. The inversion of h_0 during the key generation invokes several multiplications in $\mathcal{R}$, so does the decoding algorithm `decoder` that is used during the decapsulation.

A multiplication in the ring $\mathcal{R} = \mathbb{F}_2[x]/(x^r - 1)$ consists of a polynomial multiplication in $\mathbb{F}_2[x]$, i.e., bit-polynomial multiplication and a reduction modulo the irreducible polynomial $x^r - 1$. Since the reduction simply shifts the terms of degree $\geq r$ to the lower degree part, the bit-polynomial multiplication dominates the computing time of multiplications in $\mathcal{R}$. Altogether one can observe that the multiplication is an essential factor for the performance of BIKE and thus the focus of our optimizations in this paper.

For a detailed specification and security analysis of BIKE we refer the reader to the BIKE's team official communication website [2].

System Parameters. BIKE can be instantiated with three different parameter sets, each fulfilling a different security level as proposed by the NIST. Table 1 lists the three sets, denoted as `bikel1`, `bikel3`, and `bikel5` and their corresponding parameters r, w, t, and ℓ. Parameter r determines the size of the polynomials and is therefore the key parameter for our optimizations.

3 Evaluation Platforms

For this work we are using two different evaluation platforms. The first is the `STM32f4-Discovery` development board featuring an ARM Cortex-M4 processor. The second platform is the VexRiscv soft-core, that we used due to its modular design.

Table 1. Parameter Sets of BIKE.

Parameter Set	r	w	t	ℓ
bike1	12323	142	134	256
bike3	24659	206	199	256
bike5	40973	274	264	256

3.1 The ARM Cortex-M4

Our first evaluation target is the ARM Cortex-M4, a 32-bit RISC processor that was already used as a representative for microcontrollers in numerous publications about efficient implementations of post-quantum cryptography [18].

We choose the STM32f4-Discovery development board as our working platform, identical to the pqm4 benchmarking project [17]. The STM32f4-Discovery board comes with the STM32F407VGT6 microcontroller, including the ARM Cortex-M4 with the floating-point unit. The microcontroller has 192-KB of SRAM and 1-MB of flash memory and can be clocked with up to 168 MHz.

The M4 implements the ARMv7E-M ISA and provides the programmer with thirteen 32-bit general-purpose registers. A further register can be used for computations when the content of the link register is preserved on the stack.

In this work, we use the multiply-and-accumulate instruction (umlal) exceedingly. The instruction 'umlal rdLo, rdHi, rn, rm' multiplies two 32-bit integers in rn and rm and then adds the 64-bit product to the values of two 32-bit registers (rdHi,rdLo) in one clock cycle. Important to note is that many of the instructions on the M4 allow to shift one of the operands without latency overhead.

Single 32-bit memory access usually takes 2 cycles. However, loading n 32-bit words can be as fast as $n+1$ cycles, when consecutive loads can be pipelined and no cache misses occur. Storing n 32-bit words takes only n cycles in the best case. The optional floating-point unit comes with 32 additional 32-bit registers that can also be used to store intermediate values. With a latency of one cycle to move data between a general-purpose and a floating-point register, the floating-point registers exhibit a faster access time than the RAM.

We use the pqm4 [17] framework in version 6435b29 to benchmark our implementation. It is important to note that the pqm4 framework benchmarks implementations at 24 MHz to have zero wait states when accessing code or data in the flash memory. Our code is compiled with the arm-noneeabi-gcc-10.2.1 compiler.

3.2 The VexRiscv

VexRiscv [24] is a modular 32-bit RISC-V processor that features a 5-stage pipeline with bypassable execute- and memory stage, i.e. results may be forwarded through the pipeline if an instruction does not utilize the respective stage. VexRiscv is written in the hardware description language SpinalHDL [23] and features a versatile plugin system which allows defining custom CPU extensions. Similar to the Cortex-M4, most instructions are executed in one cycle. We use the default *GenFull* configuration of VexRiscv that implements the RISC-V base integer instructions (I) combined with the standard RISC-V Instruction Set Extensions (ISE) for integer multiplication and division (M) and atomic instructions (A). *GenFull* features a dynamic target branch predictor with 4096 kB of cache memory for data and instructions respectively. For the VexRiscv we compile our code with `clang` version 13.0.0.

RISC-V is an open and modular ISA with a small set of base integer instructions (RV32I/ RV64I) that can be expanded with standard ISA extensions or non-standard custom extensions. The RISC-V ISA provides 31 general purpose registers for the programmer (x1-x31).

The RISC-V Bitmanip (B) extension [3] is close to becoming ratified and includes many instructions that will be useful for cryptographic implementations. Besides advanced logic and bit permutation instructions it includes a conditional move instruction (`cmov`) that allows a branchless, constant-time selection of a value without arithmetic detours. One subset of the bit-manipulation extension is the Zbc extension that defines carry-less multiplications. Equivalent to the integer multiplication instructions, there is one instruction for computing the lower half of the product (`clmul`) and one for the upper half (`clmulh`). Carry-less multiplication corresponds to the multiplication of polynomials in $\mathbb{F}_2[x]$, also named bit-polynomial multiplication in this paper. The pseudocode is shown in Fig. 2.

```
u32 clmul(u32 rs1, u32 rs2){        u32 clmulh(u32 rs1, u32 rs2){
   u32 x = 0;                          u32 x = 0;
   for (int i=0; i<32; i++){           for (int i=1; i<32; i++){
      if ((rs2 >> i) & 1)                 if ((rs2 >> i) & 1)
         x ^= rs1 << i;                       x ^= rs1 >> (32-i);
   }                                   }
   return x;                           return x;
}                                   }
```

Fig. 2. Pseudocode for the `clmul` (left) and `clmulh` (right) instructions.

Implementing `clmul` and `cmov`. We implement the aforementioned instructions to VexRiscv using the plugin system. Our implementation of `clmul` features a configurable window size that defines how many bits of the input registers are processed in each clock cycle. This allows us to explore trade-offs between area consumption and execution performance later on. Since the overall input size is 32 bits, we allow window sizes of $w = 2^i$ with $i \in \{2, ..., 5\}$. The instruction therefore has a latency of $32/w$ clock cycles in the execution stage. During that time, the execution stage is blocked and cannot be used by other instructions (VexRiscv does not support SMT).

The cmov instruction is computationally much less complex then clmul, however, the instruction format requires an additional register encoded to the opcode of the instruction. Therefore, the VexRiscv *RegFile*-plugin needs to be modified and the decoding position of *rs3* within the op-code needs to be defined in the RISC-V ISA definition. The *cmov*-plugin itself is fairly simple as it sets the target register *rd* to *rs1* or *rs3* depending on the value of *rs2*. The logic is implemented in the execute stage.

We use the cmov instruction as a counterpart to the sel of the Cortex-M4 for the Barrel shifter that is used in the decoder in BIKE (See Chap. 4 in [11]). Without the cmov, a constant-time arithmetic solution requires three instructions instead.

The RISC-V bit-manipulation extension in general induces a comparatively large area overhead as reported in the draft standardization [3, Fig. 3.1]. Table 2 shows the area utilization of our ISA extensions for several choices of w on a Xilinx Artix-7 FPGA (xc7a200tfbg484-3) using Vivado 2021.1 and the area-optimized synthesis and implementation strategies. The clmul-w configurations also include the cmov extension while the original version is built using the unmodified GenFull configuration without any plugins. The FF utilization decreases with increasing w since the less intermediate values need to be buffered for large window sizes. All designs could be placed with 160 MHz (±5 MHz).

Table 2. Vexriscv area footprint of the hardware implementation for the conditional move instruction and carryless multiply with different window sizes (clmul-w). The clmul-w configurations also include cmov.

	Original	cmov	clmul-4	clmul-8	clmul-16	clmul-32
LUT	1831	1954	2140	2169	2306	2459
FF	1634	1675	1747	1746	1737	1669

4   Bit-Polynomial Multiplication

Depending on the size of the polynomial (a degree $n-1$ polynomial in $\mathbb{F}_2[x]$ has the size of n bits) the fastest algorithm for a multiplication varies. Depending on the architecture, the base multiplication (e.g. word size) is either done with a dedicated instruction or the window method. This base multiplication can be lifted by a divide-and-conquer algorithm to an intermediate size. For polynomials of very large size, an FFT based approach offers the fastest asymptotic runtime.

Brent et al. [9] examined the performance of bit-polynomial multiplication algorithms on the Intel Core 2 processor. In particular, they report that the FFT based approach first outperforms the Karatsuba/Toom-Cook algorithms at a polynomial size of 2461×64-bit words (157504 bits). They report 3295×64-bit words (210880 bits) as the biggest size where a Karatsuba/Toom-Cook variant runs faster than the FFT based multiplications. However their results are not directly transferable to other architectures, as the available instructions differ, which can lead to clearly different costs for the base multiplications. For example Brent et al. use Intel's SSE extension with 128-bit SIMD instructions, whereas the embedded platforms we use in this work, natively only offer 32-bit instructions. Game-changing instructions like a clmul on the other hand lower the cost of the base multiplication considerably. The different costs for the base multiplication for Karatsuba/Toom-Cook algorithms can considerably move the threshold where FFT based approaches become faster.

4.1 Single-Word Polynomial Multiplication

Multiplication of polynomials with the size of a word (32-bit for the processors we used in this work) is most efficient with a dedicated instruction. In 2008 Intel introduced [15] an instruction for carry-less multiplication to accelerate cryptographic computations. Such an instruction is also available on other architectures like PowerPC, Sparc or ARMv8.

However, embedded processors like the Cortex-M4 are usually not equipped with such an instruction. In this case the window method [9] is the fastest known algorithm. To compute the multiplication of two polynomials $c = a \cdot b$ the window algorithm, parameterized with the window size s, precomputes in the first step a table with 2^s entries. The table consists of the multiples of b by all polynomials of degree smaller than s. In the next step the algorithm iterates over a looking at s bits at a time and composes the product c out of the precomputed values. However, we note this method is not suitable for architectures with data cache since it queries the table with values from the input operand, which is vulnerable to cache-timing side-channel attacks [5].

The window algorithm is used in the **portable** implementation, we also used it in our hardware implementation of the carry-less multiplication instruction for RISC-V.

4.2 Multiplication for Intermediate-Sized Polynomials

For polynomials of medium size it is beneficial to apply a divide-and-conquer algorithm that divides the polynomial in smaller parts.

Karatsuba. The well known Karatsuba [19] algorithm breaks down the multiplication of two polynomials into three half-size multiplications and can be recursively applied until the size of the base multiplication (usually word size) is reached.

To multiply two polynomials $F = F_0 + F_1 t^n$ and $G = G_0 + G_1 t^n$ of degree $2n$, the Karatsuba algorithm reduces the task into three multiplications with polynomials of degree n. After multiplying $F_0 G_0$, $(F_0 + F_1)(G_0 + G_1)$ and $F_1 G_1$ the product FG can be determined by computing.

$$F_0 G_0 + ((F_0 + F_1)(G_0 + G_1) - F_0 G_0 - F_1 G_1) t^n + F_1 G_1 t^{2n}$$

Recursively applied, the Karatsuba algorithm requires $O(n^{\log_2 3})$ base multiplications.

Karatsuba Variants. Weimerskirch and Paar [30] provided a generalization of Karatsuba for polynomial multiplication of arbitrary degree and recursive use. In 2005, Montgomery [21] developed Karatsuba variants for multiplication of polynomials with five, six and seven terms k in contrast to the two terms of the classic Karatsuba algorithm.

In 2009, Bernstein [6] improved the Karatsuba algorithm for $k = 2$ by reducing the number of required additions and named it the refined Karatsuba:

$$(1 - t^n)(F_0 G_0 - F_1 G_1 t^n) + (F_0 + F_1)(G_0 + G_1)t^n.$$

Speaking in terms of compiler optimizations, this is basically an improvement by a common subexpression elimination. In the same paper Bernstein introduced an optimized recursive multiplication algorithm for polynomials with $k = 3$.

Bernstein's five-way algorithm [6] computes the product $H = FG$ of two polynomials $F_0 + F_1 x^n + F_2 x^{2n}$ and $G_0 + G_1 x^n + G_2 x^{2n}$ of degree $3n$ by using

$$H = U + H(\infty)(x^{4n} + x^n) + \frac{U + V + H(\infty)(x^4 + x)}{x^2 + x}(x^{2n} + x^n)$$

with

$$U = H(0) + (H(0) + H(1))z \text{ and } V = H(x) + (H(x) + H(x+1))(x^n + x).$$

It requires five multiplications of polynomials of degree n:

$$H(0) = F_0 \cdot G_0,$$
$$H(1) = (F_0 + F_1 + F_2) \cdot (G_0 + G_1 + G_2),$$
$$H(x) = (F_0 + F_1 x + F_2 x^2) \cdot (G_0 + G_1 x + G_2 x^2),$$
$$H(x+1) = ((F_0 + F_1 + F_2) + F_1 x + F_2 x^2) \cdot ((G_0 + G_1 + G_2) + G_1 x + G_2 x^2),$$
$$H(\infty) = F_2 \cdot G_2.$$

Toom-Cook. The Toom-Cook [13] algorithm is a generalization of the Karatsuba algorithm and is modular in the number of terms k the polynomials are divided into. With $k = 2$ the Toom-Cook algorithm corresponds to Karatsuba, with e.g. $k = 3$ the Toom-Cook algorithm divides the input polynomials into three terms and reduces the number of smaller multiplications from nine to five, compared to the schoolbook method. This leads to an asymptotic runtime of $O(n^{\log_3 5})$. With growing parameter k the overhead of the algorithm becomes bigger and thus limits its usage. In practice [7,9], Toom-Cook with $k = 2$ (TC2), $k = 3$ (TC3) and $k = 4$ (TC4) are used for efficient intermediate size multiplication. Bernstein's five-way algorithm corresponds to Toom-Cook with $k = 3$.

The usage of Toom-Cook multiplication in $\mathbb{F}_2[x]$ comes with special characteristics. TC3 for example requires five evaluation points, but $\mathbb{F}_2[x]$ only offers the two elements 0, 1 and the point ∞. However, it is possible to use any power of the variable x as an additional evaluation point [9]. The disadvantage of this method is that the size of the polynomials for some of the submultiplications increases slightly. This makes an implementation more complicated for example compared to the classic Karatsuba, where a polynomial with a size $n = 2^l$ can be neatly divided into l (recursive) layers. Bodrato [7] showed that any Toom-Cook algorithm in $\mathbb{F}_2[x]$ with $k > 2$ requires at least one division. For smaller polynomial sizes, this for example can make Montgomery's Karatsuba variants - that do not require a division - faster, despite the slower asymptotic runtime. Brent et al. provide a word aligned variant of Toom-Cook with $k = 3$ (TC3W) that uses $0, 1, 2^w, 2^{-w}$ and ∞ as evaluation points (with word-size w). The advantage of this variant is that all suboperations including divisions operate at word-size granularity and thus, no bitshifts are required. This is especially beneficial for our radix-16 approach as explained in the next chapter.

4.3 Multiplication for Large Polynomials

In 1971 Schönhage and Strassen [28] demonstrated how to multiply large integers in $O(n \log n \log \log n)$ by using the FFT. Cantor and Kaltofen [10] later generalized this method to arbitrary polynomials. To perform a multiplication based on a FFT, one first transforms the two input polynomials into the FFT domain, computes the actual multiplication in the FFT domain, and transforms the product back to the original domain for the result by an inverse FFT. For multiplications that share an operand, the shared polynomial is kept in the FFT domain. This reduces the number of necessary transformations and thus the costs. The reduction step during a multiplication in the ring $\mathbb{F}_2[x]/(x^r - 1)$ requires the back transformation of the bit-polynomial multiplication result, even for consecutive dependent multiplications.

Chen et al. [12] used a Frobenius Additive FFT (FAFFT) for the bit-polynomial multiplication in BIKE on the Arm Cortex-M4 platform. We ported their implementation to the RISC-V architecture for comparisons.

5   Bit-Polynomial Multiplication in the Radix-16 Representation

Bit-Polynomial Multiplication via Integer Multiplication. An uncommon option to implement bit-polynomial multiplication uses integer multiplication in combination with data in a radix-16 representation. With the radix-16 representation, one expresses a degree-7 polynomial $a = \sum_{i=0}^{7} a_i x^i \in \mathbb{F}_2[x]$ as a

32-bit integer $a_0 + a_1 2^4 + a_2 2^8 + \cdots + a_7 2^{28}$. Multiplying polynomials $a \cdot b \to c$ in this form with integer multiplication yields:

$$(a_0 + a_1 \cdot 2^4 + a_2 \cdot 2^8 + \cdots + a_7 \cdot 2^{28}) \cdot (b_0 + b_1 \cdot 2^4 + b_2 \cdot 2^8 + \cdots + b_7 \cdot 2^{28})$$

$$= a_0 b_0 + (a_1 b_0 + a_0 b_1) \cdot 2^4 + (a_2 b_0 + a_1 b_1 + a_0 b_2) \cdot 2^8 + \cdots + (a_7 b_7) \cdot 2^{56}$$

an integer where the bit of index $4i$ is exactly c_i, and thus after masking out the other indices remains c in radix-16 representation. Chen and Chou [11] presented the multiplication in radix-16 formats and applied it to multiplication in $\mathbb{F}_{2^{12}}$ and $\mathbb{F}_{2^{13}}$, i.e., polynomials of 12 and 13 bits. In this work, we present the techniques for extending the method to bit-polynomial multiplication in BIKE, including the optimization of 32-bit base multiplication, data conversion, logic shift operation, and building multiplications for polynomials of various sizes in the following.

Table 3. Performing an 8-bit bit-polynomial multiplication with 32-bit integer multiplication in radix-16 form.

00010001000100010001000100010001 × 00010001000100010001000100010001
0001 0001 0001 0001 0001 0001 0001 0001
0001 0001 0001 0001 0001 0001 0001 0001
0001 0001 0001 0001 0001 0001 0001 0001
0001 0001 0001 0001 0001 0001 0001 0001
0001 0001 0001 0001 0001 0001 0001 0001
0001 0001 0001 0001 0001 0001 0001 0001
0001 0001 0001 0001 0001 0001 0001 0001
0001 0001 0001 0001 0001 0001 0001 0001
0000 0001 0010 0011 0100 0101 0110 0111 1000 0111 0110 0101 0100 0011 0010 0001

Base Multiplication in Radix-16 Form. Table 3 shows an example of an 8-bit bit-polynomial multiplication with a 32-bit integer multiplication using the radix-16 form. Even during a multiplication of two radix-16 values with all bits set, the carry bits do not propagate. Furthermore this example demonstrates that the lower half of the multiplication result can be added to the higher half (both residing in a 32-bit register) without a prior reduction. One can see that the pairwise sum of each nibble is capped at eight and therefore does not lead to a carry propagation to the next nibble. This observation allows the use of the powerful multiply-with-accumulate instruction (umlal) of the Cortex-M4 during the combination of 16 8-bit bit-polynomial multiplications to perform one 32-bit multiplication.

The radix-16 format quadruples the size of a polynomial during computation, to avoid this memory overhead when storing polynomials, we pack four bytes in radix-16 format in one register by shifting byte i, i bits to the left.

To perform one 32-bit bit-polynomial multiplication we therefore extract four bytes for each operand, perform 16 integer multiplications with reductions in between and pack the result in two 32-bit registers. For the Cortex-M4 we are able to express this operation with only 46 instructions, by using the umlal instruction as explained before and the barrel-shifter. For our RISC-V implementation we need 89 instructions for the same operation, because not only of the missing barrel-shifter and multiply-with-accumulate instruction, but also are multiplications of 32-bit values expressed with two instructions, one for the lower half and one for the upper half of the result.

Data Conversion for the Radix-16 Representation. Similar to a polynomial multiplication via a FFT, the input and output polynomials have to be transformed to and from the radix-16 representation for the multiplication.

Since an 8-bit polynomial is stored in a 32-bit register in the radix-16 representation, a straight-forward approach would increase the memory footprint by factor four. Even more importantly, it would multiply the number of memory instructions for a bit-polynomial multiplication by four. One can however store four 8-bit polynomials in radix-16 representation in one 32-bit register.

Figure 3 shows the steps of data movement in a 32-bit register for converting data to the radix-16 representation. The leftmost table shows the original data, and the fields represent register bits ordered from right to left and top to bottom. The converting method is modified from the matrix transpose algorithm. In each step, we swap the data in blue with the data in green. The first step swaps two 2×4 matrices. The second step swaps off-diagonal 2×2 matrices in two 4×4 matrices. The last step swaps off-diagonal elements in all 2×2 matrices. In the rightmost table, the data has been split into 4 lanes (columns). The original data in bits 0 to 7 move to the first lane, bits 8 to 15 move to the third lane, and so on.

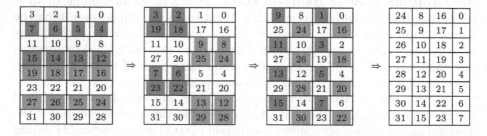

Fig. 3. Swap steps for converting 32-bit data to the radix-16 representation.

Logic Shift for the Radix-16 Data. Analog to the FFT based bit-polynomial multiplication, the multiplication with the radix-16 form becomes more efficient when intermediate results of consecutive multiplications remain in the radix-16 representation. The divide-and-conquer algorithms that lift our base multiplication to the size that is required for BIKE introduce additional operations during the smaller multiplications however.

Some operations, e.g. addition in $\mathbb{F}_2[x]$ that correspond to a xor operation, can be applied to the polynomials in radix-16 representation without any adaptation. But other operations, in particular logic shifting, require a radix-16 specific implementation that can be costly.

Figure 4 shows an example of a shift-left-by-1 for data in the radix-16 representation. In the figure, bits in registers are ordered from right to left and top to bottom. Four lanes in a 32-bit register are shown as four rows. We use the multiply-with-accumulate instruction (umlal) of the Cortex-M4 to perform the shift operations for radix-16 data. For shifting left by i, we set one operand to be the constant $2^{i \cdot 4}$ and the other operand is the data to be shifted. After the umlal instruction, the register holding the lower part of the product contains the almost shifted result. Some data has been moved to the higher part of the product, and hence we spend extra operations to move them to the correct positions. While applying the same idea for the shift-right operation, we set the constant to be $2^{32-4 \cdot i}$ and collect the main part of the shift resulting in the higher part of the product.

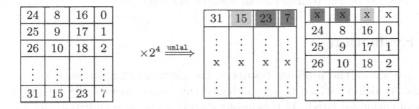

Fig. 4. Shift left by 1 in radix-16 representation.

Lifting the 32-Bit Base-Multiplication with Karatsuba and Toom-Cook. The portable implementation [2] of the BIKE team uses the refined Karatsuba recursively to lift its base multiplication to 16384 bits for bike11, however only 12323-bit polynomial multiplication is required by bike11. The optimized BIKE implementation for the x86 by Chen et al. [12] improves this algorithmic approach by using one layer of Bernstein's five-way Karatsuba at the top: the base multiplication is lifted to 4096-bit with the same refined Karatsuba and then combined to 12288 bits with the five-way Karatsuba. With a small overhead they further lift it to 12350 bits.

For our implementations we first followed the algorithmic approach by Chen et al. and combined it with radix-16 specific operations in $\mathbb{F}_2[x]$ that allows us to keep the subpolynomials in the radix-16 form for the entire multiplication, except for the one division in Bernstein's five-way Karatsuba. As already mentioned in Sect. 4, the word-aligned Toom-Cook 3 (TC3W) algorithm that divides a polynomial in three terms and requires five submultiplications just as Bernstein's five-way Karatsuba, does not require radix-16 specific operations. This is, because all operations in this algorithm operate on word-size granularity at which the radix-16 format does not differ from the normal representation of bit-polynomials. The drawback of this algorithm is the small increase of the size of the polynomials for the submultiplications. Beyond that we tested the usefulness of TC4 for bit-polynomial multiplication with sizes relevant for BIKE on our embedded platforms.

We also adapted the gf2x library [8] by Brenet et al. for bare-metal application on our evaluation platforms, it includes implementations of TC3, TC3W, TC4 and Karatsuba (including variants by Weimerskirch et al. and Montgomery) optimized for $\mathbb{F}_2[x]$. Based on nine pretuned base multiplications for polynomials of the size from one to nine words (32-bit) that we partially optimized in assembly, we benchmarked the cycles for each Toom-Cook variant and the refined Karatsuba for all polynomial sizes, up to the size required by BIKE. The optimal algorithm for each size is fed back to the implementation. The testing showed that TC3W slightly outperforms Bernstein's five-way Karatsuba for our case and is the optimal choice for the first layers until the refined Karatsuba is used. TC3W is first used for an input size of 19×32-bit words (608 bits), the refined Karatsuba is latest used for a size of 129×32-bit words (4128 bits). TC4 did not show better results for our specific setting.

6 Evaluation

Figure 5 shows the profiling results of the `portable` implementation of BIKE on the VexRiscv, which clearly indicate the importance of the bit-polynomial multiplication for BIKE. In this implementation the base multiplication function contributes 36.41% of the overall computation time of the KEM, and more than half of the time is spent in the full-size multiplication.

6.1 Comparisons of Multipliers

To directly compare the different approaches for bit-polynomial multiplication for BIKE, we measure the cycles spent on the Cortex-M4 for one multiplication including all transformations if necessary. Table 4 shows our measurements comparing this work with the `portable` implementation [2] of the BIKE team and the FFT based implementation by Chen et al. [12]. Recall that in the `bike11` parameter set, polynomials are 12323 bit long and in the `bike13` parameter set 24659 bit.

The `portable` implementation is based on Karatsuba and the window algorithm as its building block in C. The FFT based approach considerably outperforms the `portable` version for the two parameter sets `bike11` and `bike13` and is more than two times faster on the M4. Yet, our approach based on the radix-16 representation has an about 23% smaller cycle count than the FFT approach for `bike11`. For `bike13` on the other hand, the asymptotic smaller runtime causes

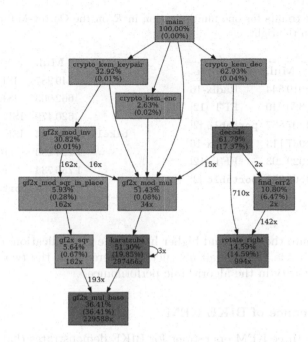

Fig. 5. Profiling of the `portable` implementation of BIKE on the VexRiscv using [4]. Functions with less than 2% impact on the overall execution time are omitted.

the FFT based multiplication to be slightly faster. These findings eliminate the radix-16 approach for any other parameter set than `bike1l`. For the further evaluation we thus concentrate on `bike1l` only. A relevant conclusion of these experiments is also that the boundary that defines whether the Karatsuba and Toom-Cook approach or the FFT approach is most efficient is at around 24659 bits on the Cortex-M4.

Important to note is the impact of the transformations that is small for radix-16, but very distinct for the FFT approach. Chen et al. report a reduction of about 30% in cycle consumption for one multiplication when one input transformation is omitted. In this case the FFT multiplication is faster than our approach, which becomes apparent at BIKE's decoder.

For the VexRiscv we see in Table 4 that the Instruction Set Extension (ISE) allows an implementation that clearly outperforms all other multiplication approaches and is more than seven times faster than the `portable` version provided by the BIKE team, even in the configuration with the smallest area footprint.

Interesting is the performance of the radix-16 implementation on the VexRiscv: Different to the Cortex-M4, the multiplication in radix-16 is not faster than the FFT based approach. The main reason for this are the different integer multiplication instructions. On the Cortex-M4 we can add a value to a 64-bit multiplication result in one cycle, on the VexRiscv we need two instructions

Table 4. Cycle counts for one multiplication in $\mathcal{R}$ on the Cortex-M4 on the left and the VexRiscv on the right.

	Mul.	Imple.
	1 019 544	Radix-16
bike1	1 320 940	FFT [12]
	2 897 887	portable [2]
	2 937 113	Radix-16
bike3	2 929 293	FFT [12]
	9 606 051	portable [2]

	Mul.	Imple.
	749 287	ISE (w=4)
	662 963	ISE (w=8)
	620 479	ISE (w=16)
bike1	598 744	ISE (w=32)
	2 224 293	Radix-16
	1 756 734	FFT [12]
	5 313 565	portable [2]

alone to compute the lower and higher half of the multiplication, each of which consumes one cycle. This small instruction difference in the two architectures causes the disparity in the algorithmic performance.

6.2   Performance of BIKE KEM

Measuring the three KEM operations for BIKE demonstrates that our radix-16 multiplication approach beats the current fastest implementations of BIKE on the Cortex-M4 (Table 5). For the `bike1` parameter set we observe an improvement in cycles of about 13% for the key generation and about 7% for the encapsulation. The decapsulation is about 3% slower than the FFT based approach. This is due to the many multiplications in the decoder where input transformations can be omitted and thus the FFT based multiplications are faster. For an implementation where code size is insignificant, one could use the FFT based multiplication for the decoder and our radix-16 multiplication in the key generation and encapsulation to achieve the best overall performance.

Table 5. Cycle counts for BIKE on the Cortex-M4.

	Key Gen	Encaps	Decaps	Imple.
	21 137 291	2 989 187	50 832 769	Radix-16
bike1	24 935 033	3 253 379	49 911 673	FFT [12]
	65 414 337	4 824 059	114 592 442	portable [2]

For the VexRiscv we provide three different implementations, one is based on the multiplication in radix-16 representation and derived from our Cortex-M4 implementation. The second implementation is a portation of the FFT based approach from Chen et al., and enables us to compare the performance of the different algorithmic foundations also on the VexRiscv. The third implementation uses the `clmul` and `cmov` instruction, that are included in the RISC-V ISA extension B. The distinct performance advantage of the additional instruction comes with higher costs in hardware area though. As described in Sect. 3.2, our `clmul` implementation can be configured with different window sizes w to allow a tradeoff, between area and performance.

As expected, the FFT based approach is much faster than the `portable` implementation on the VexRiscv, the key generation is about 58%, the encapsulation 44% and the decapsulation 48% faster, as shown in Table 6. The multiplication in radix-16 can not compete with the multiplication based on the FFT as shown in Sect. 6.1, and the corresponding BIKE implementation behaves accordingly.

When the `clmul` and `cmov` instructions are added to the VexRiscv, the tables clearly turn again. Our implementation with the additional instruction compared to the one based on the FFT saves more than 46% during key generation and about 19% during encapsulation and decapsulation, in the smallest setting. More than 2.5 million cycles can be saved in the key generation alone, when the implementation of the `clmul` instruction is switched from a window size of 4, to a window size of 32. We also measured the impact of both instructions individually, the `cmov` instruction alone is responsible for a reduction of about ten million cycles in the decapsulation.

Table 6. Cycle counts for BIKE on the VexRiscv.

	Key Gen	Encaps	Decaps	Imple.
	18 189 581	4 234 986	72 917 099	ISE (w=4)
	16 726 630	4 149 304	71 623 427	ISE (w=8)
	15 993 482	4 105 239	70 978 980	ISE (w=16)
bikel1	15 627 784	4 085 334	70 659 901	ISE (w=32)
	46 301 780	6 396 252	107 814 753	Radix-16
	34 275 830	5 264 852	88 810 190	FFT [12]
	111 916 192	9 483 762	160 643 740	portable [2]

6.3 Comparison with Other NIST Post-quantum Candidates

The `pqm4` [17] includes implementations for most of the KEMs that are candidates in the third round of the post-quantum standardization process by NIST. We are not aware of any implementation of the code-based KEM HQC [20] for the Cortex-M4. For Classic McEliece [1], the third code-based KEM that is still a candidate in the standardization process, an optimized constant-time implementation for the Cortex-M4 exists [11].

Despite our optimizations, BIKE is outperformed by KEMs based on ideal lattices on the Cortex-M4, similar to other platforms. BIKE is in most cases clearly faster than FrodoKEM [22] (based on standard lattices) and SIKE [16] (based on isogenies), as the numbers in Table 7 show. Compared to the numbers reported by Chen and Chou [11], the key generation in our BIKE implementation is more than 73 times faster than the one in McEliece. However, the encapsulation is about 6 times, and the decapsulation about 2 times slower.

A RISC-V counterpart to the `pqm4` framework, called `pqriscv` is available on github, but only as work-in-progress. By the time of writing this paper, there are no post-quantum implementations included that could be used to compare the performance with our work.

Table 7. Cycle counts of the 3rd-round KEMs on the Cortex-M4. All numbers are from pqm4 [17] commit-6841a6b (ecxl. `bike1l` and `mceliece348864`).

Scheme (Implementation)	Level	Key Gen	Encaps	Decaps
`bike1l` (this work, radix-16)	1	21 137 291	2 989 187	50 832 769
`mceliece348864` (m4f) [11]	1	1 589 600 267	482 594	2 291 003
`frodokem640aes` (m4)	1	48 348 105	47 130 922	46 594 383
`kyber512` (m4)	1	463 343	566 744	525 141
`kyber768` (m4)	3	763 979	923 856	862 176
`lightsaber` (m4f)	1	361 687	513 581	498 590
`saber` (m4f)	3	654 407	862 856	835 122
`ntruhps2048509` (m4f)	1	79 658 656	564 411	537 473
`ntruhps2048677` (m4f)	3	143 734 184	821 524	815 516
`sikep434` (m4)	1	48 264 129	78 911 465	84 276 911
`sikep610` (m4)	3	119 480 622	219 632 058	221 029 700

7 Conclusion

Besides providing the fastest implementation of BIKE for two architectures, this work presents an interesting case study about bit-polynomial multiplication. Our measurements underline that besides the size of the polynomial, also the architecture and the algorithmic embedding of the multiplication are an important factor to be considered in the pursuit of optimal performance. Not only game-changing instruction like a carry-less multiplication instruction can make the difference, but also a two-part integer multiplication instruction versus a one-cycle multiply-and-accumulate instruction. The small performance penalty of our Cortex-M4 implementation in the decoder of BIKE against the FFT based approach highlights the impact of the algorithmic embedding.

Furthermore, we present an informative example of how RISC-V's adaptability allows variable solutions for cryptographic implementations.

While our implementation is safe against timing-side-channels by adhering to the constant-time policy, it is not hardened against power-side-channel attacks. A recent work [29] introduces a possible power-side-channel attack against BIKE and exploits the arithmetic move. The application of `cmov` instructions instead of arithmetic moves should reduce the leakage, but we did not validate this as it is out of scope for this paper. Of course, this simple modification alone is far from a full power-side-channel protection, which is an interesting target for future work.

Acknowledgements. Some of this work was done while Ming-Shing Chen was working at Ruhr University Bochum, funded by the Deutsche Forschungsgemeinschaft (DFG, German Research Foundation) under Germany's Excellence Strategy - EXC 2092 CASA - 390781972. The work of Markus Krausz and Jan Philipp Thoma was funded by the German Federal Ministry of Education and Research (BMBF) under the project "QuantumRISC" (ID 16KIS1038) [26] and project "PQC4MED" (ID 16KIS1044).

References

1. Albrecht, M., et al.: Classic McEliece (2017). https://classic.mceliece.org/
2. Aragon, N., et al.: BIKE–bit flipping key encapsulation (2017). https://bikesuite. org/
3. Bachmeyer, J., et al.: RISC-V Bit-Manipulation ISA-extensions. https://github. com/riscv/riscv-bitmanip/releases/download/1.0.0/bitmanip-1.0.0.pdf
4. Becker, L.A.: VexRiscv-Profiler: a measurement tool for the vexriscv. https:// github.com/neunzehnhundert97/VexRiscv-Profiler
5. Bernstein, D.J.: Cache-timing attacks on AES (2005)
6. Bernstein, D.J.: Batch binary edwards. In: Halevi, S. (ed.) CRYPTO 2009. LNCS, vol. 5677, pp. 317–336. Springer, Heidelberg (2009). https://doi.org/10.1007/978-3-642-03356-8_19
7. Bodrato, M.: Towards optimal Toom-cook multiplication for univariate and multivariate polynomials in characteristic 2 and 0. In: Carlet, C., Sunar, B. (eds.) WAIFI 2007. LNCS, vol. 4547, pp. 116–133. Springer, Heidelberg (2007). https:// doi.org/10.1007/978-3-540-73074-3_10
8. Brent, R., Gaudry, P., Thomé, E., Zimmermann, P.: gf2x-1.3.0 (2021). https:// gitlab.inria.fr/gf2x/gf2x
9. Brent, R.P., Gaudry, P., Thomé, E., Zimmermann, P.: Faster multiplication in GF(2)[x]. In: van der Poorten, A.J., Stein, A. (eds.) ANTS 2008. LNCS, vol. 5011, pp. 153–166. Springer, Heidelberg (2008). https://doi.org/10.1007/978-3-540-79456-1_10
10. Cantor, D.G., Kaltofen, E.: On fast multiplication of polynomials over arbitrary algebras. Acta Inform. **28**(7), 693–701 (1991)
11. Chen, M.S., Chou, T.: Classic McEliece on the ARM Cortex-M4. IACR Trans. Cryptogr. Hardw. Embed. Syst. **2021**(3), 125–148 (2021). https://doi.org/10. 46586/tches.v2021.i3.125-148, https://tches.iacr.org/index.php/TCHES/article/view/8970
12. Chen, M.S., Chou, T., Krausz, M.: Optimizing BIKE for the intel Haswell and ARM Cortex-M4. IACR Trans. Cryptogr. Hardw. Embed. Syst. **2021**(3), 97–124 (2021). https://doi.org/10.46586/tches.v2021.i3.97-124, https://tches.iacr. org/index.php/TCHES/article/view/8969
13. Cook, S.A., Aanderaa, S.O.: On the minimum computation time of functions. Trans. Am. Math. Soc. **142**, 291–314 (1969)

14. Fritzmann, T., Sharif, U., Müller-Gritschneder, D., Reinbrecht, C., Schlichtmann, U., Sepulveda, J.: Towards reliable and secure post-quantum co-processors based on RISC-V. In: 2019 Design, Automation Test in Europe Conference Exhibition (DATE), pp. 1148–1153 (2019). https://doi.org/10.23919/DATE.2019.8715173
15. Gueron, S., Kounavis, M.: Carry-less multiplication and its usage for computing the GCM mode. white paper, Intel Corporation (2008)
16. Jao, D., et al.: SIKE (2017). https://sike.org/
17. Kannwischer, M.J., Rijneveld, J., Schwabe, P., Stoffelen, K.: PQM4: post-quantum crypto library for the ARM Cortex-M4. https://github.com/mupq/pqm4
18. Kannwischer, M.J., Rijneveld, J., Schwabe, P., Stoffelen, K.: pqm4: testing and benchmarking NIST PQC on ARM Cortex-M4. IACR Cryptology ePrint Archive 2019, 844 (2019). https://eprint.iacr.org/2019/844
19. Karatsuba, A.: Multiplication of multidigit numbers on automata. In: Soviet Physics Doklady, vol. 7, pp. 595–596 (1963)
20. Melchor, C.A., et al.: Hamming quasi-cyclic (HQC). NIST PQC Round 2, 4–13 (2018)
21. Montgomery, P.L.: Five, six, and seven-term Karatsuba-like formulae. IEEE Trans. Comput. 54(3), 362–369 (2005)
22. Naehrig, M., et al.: FrodoKEM (2017). https://frodokem.org/
23. Papon, C.: Spinalhdl. https://github.com/SpinalHDL/SpinalHDL
24. Papon, C.: Vexriscv–32 bit RISC-V processor. https://github.com/SpinalHDL/VexRiscv
25. Pircher, S., Geier, J., Zeh, A., Mueller-Gritschneder, D.: Exploring the RISC-V vector extension for the Classic McEliece post-quantum cryptosystem. In: 2021 22nd International Symposium on Quality Electronic Design (ISQED), pp. 401–407. IEEE (2021)
26. QuantumRISC: Quantumrisc–next generation cryptography for embedded systems (2020). https://www.quantumrisc.org/
27. Roy, D.B., Fritzmann, T., Sigl, G.: Efficient hardware/software co-design for post-quantum crypto algorithm SIKE on ARM and RISC-V based microcontrollers. In: Proceedings of the 39th International Conference on Computer-Aided Design, pp. 1–9 (2020)
28. Schönhage, A., Strassen, V.: Schnelle multiplikation grosser zahlen. Computing 7(3), 281–292 (1971)
29. Sim, B.Y., Kwon, J., Choi, K.Y., Cho, J., Park, A., Han, D.G.: Novel side-channel attacks on quasi-cyclic code-based cryptography. IACR Transactions on Cryptographic Hardware and Embedded Systems, pp. 180–212 (2019)
30. Weimerskirch, A., Paar, C.: Generalizations of the Karatsuba algorithm for efficient implementations. IACR Cryptol. ePrint Arch. 2006, 224 (2006)

Faster Kyber and Dilithium
on the Cortex-M4

Amin Abdulrahman[1,2]($\boxtimes$), Vincent Hwang[3,4]($\boxtimes$), Matthias J. Kannwischer[3]($\boxtimes$), and Amber Sprenkels[5]($\boxtimes$)

[1] Ruhr University Bochum, Bochum, Germany
amin.abdulrahman@mpi-sp.org
[2] Max Planck Institute for Security and Privacy, Bochum, Germany
[3] Academia Sinica, Taipei, Taiwan
matthias@kannwischer.eu
[4] National Taiwan University, Taipei, Taiwan
[5] Digital Security Group, Radboud University, Nijmegen, The Netherlands
amber@electricdusk.com

Abstract. This paper presents faster implementations of the lattice-based schemes Dilithium and Kyber on the Cortex-M4. Dilithium is one of three signature finalists in the NIST post-quantum project (NIST PQC), while Kyber is one of four key-encapsulation mechanism (KEM) finalists.

Our optimizations affect the core polynomial arithmetic involving number-theoretic transforms in both schemes. Our main contributions are threefold: We present a faster signed Barrett reduction for Kyber, propose to switch to a smaller prime modulus for the polynomial multiplications cs_1 and cs_2 in the signing procedure of Dilithium, and apply various known optimizations to the polynomial arithmetic in both schemes. Using a smaller prime modulus is particularly interesting as it allows using the Fermat number transform resulting in especially fast code.

We outperform the state-of-the-art for both Dilithium and Kyber. For Dilithium, our NTT and iNTT are faster by 5.2% and 5.7%. Switching to a smaller modulus results in speed-up of 33.1%–37.6% for the relevant operations (sum of the base multiplication and iNTT) in the signing procedure. For Kyber, the optimizations results in 15.9%–17.8% faster matrix-vector product which is a core arithmetic operation in Kyber.

Keywords: Dilithium · Kyber · NIST PQC · Fermat Number Transform · Number-Theoretic Transform · Arm Cortex-M4

1 Introduction

Lattice-based cryptography appears to be the most promising family of post-quantum replacements needed for public-key cryptography broken by Shor's algorithm [Sho94]. As lattice-based key encapsulation schemes and digital signatures provide reasonable key, ciphertext, and signature sizes and have particularly good performance on a variety of platforms, they are expected to be standardized soon. One of such standardization efforts is the NIST PQC [Nat] project

© Springer Nature Switzerland AG 2022
G. Ateniese and D. Venturi (Eds.): ACNS 2022, LNCS 13269, pp. 853–871, 2022.
https://doi.org/10.1007/978-3-031-09234-3_42

aiming to find replacements for NIST's standards for key establishment and digital signatures as early as 2024. NIST PQC is nearing the end of its third round with announcements due in early 2022. Among the third round finalists in the competitions are 5 lattice-based schemes including the three key-encapsulation mechanisms (KEMs) Kyber, NTRU, and Saber as well as the digital signature schemes Dilithium, and Falcon. As there are only two other finalists (Classic McEliece and Rainbow) that are not lattice-based, which both have excessively large keys, it appears very likely that some of the lattice-based schemes are going to be selected for standardization unless there are cryptanalytic breakthroughs.

Lattice-based cryptography is particularly suitable for microcontrollers as the key material is still of manageable size and computational performance is particularly fast with encapsulation and decapsulation in a few milliseconds while signing and verification times in the tens to hundreds of milliseconds. NIST has designated the Arm Cortex-M4 as the primary microcontroller optimization target for NIST PQC, and, hence, it has received the most attention so far.

It appears that the number-theoretic transforms are cores of all high-speed implementations of lattice-based crypto for the Cortex-M4. It is either prescribed in the specification of Dilithium, Falcon, and Kyber, or maintains to be the fastest polynomial multiplication methods in Saber, NTRU [CHK+21], and NTRU Prime [ACC+20].

In this work, we focus on Kyber and Dilithium on the Cortex-M4. They are both part of the "Cryptographic Suite for Algebraic Lattices (CRYSTALS)" and are both designed to benefit from the NTT. We show that even though implementations have been improving for many years, we can still significantly improve the involved arithmetic.

Contributions. The contribution of this work is threefold. Firstly, we apply various known techniques from work on the Cortex-M4 optimizing Saber, NTRU, and NTRU Prime. While the techniques are already known, they have so far not been applied to Kyber and Dilithium. This includes (1) the use of Cooley–Tukey butterflies for the inverse NTT of both Kyber and Dilithium previously proposed for Saber in [ACC+21]; (2) the use of floating point registers for caching values in the NTT of Dilithium and Kyber which was first proposed in the context of NTTs for NTRU Prime in [ACC+20]. This allows to merge more layers of the NTT and reduce memory access time for loading twiddle factors; (3) we make use of the "asymmetric multiplication" proposed in [BHK+21] which eliminates some duplicate computation in the base multiplication of Kyber at the cost of extra stack usage; and (4) we use an idea from [CHK+21] to improve the accumulation in the matrix-vector product of Kyber by using a 32-bit accumulator allowing to eliminate some modular reductions at the cost of more stack usage.

Secondly, we present a faster Cortex-M4 instruction sequence to implement a signed Barrett reduction on packed 16-bit values applicable to the Kyber NTT. This immediately improves the Barrett reduction code proposed in [BKS19] from 8 cycles to 6 cycles per packed reduction.

Thirdly, we propose to use a different implementation for computing the product cs_1 as well as cs_2 in Dilithium. Since both c and s_1/s_2 have very small absolute values, we can switch to a much smaller modulus q' that allows efficient computation of the product. For Dilithium2 and Dilithium5, we make use of the Fermat prime $q' = 257$, which allows using a particularly fast variant of the NTT called the Fermat number transform (FNT), similar to [LMPR08] for SWIFFT. Furthermore, [LMPR08] implements FNT on an Intel processor while we implement FNT on the Cortex-M4 and make use of its barrel shifter. For Dilithium3 the FNT does not work as $\mathbf{s}_1$ and $\mathbf{s}_2$ have larger values. We instead use an incomplete NTT with $q' = 769$ which is still much faster than computing it modulo the original Dilithium prime. To best of our knowledge, we are the first to propose using a smaller modulus for these multiplications within Dilithium.

Code. Our code is open-source and available at https://github.com/Faster KyberDilithiumM4/FasterKyberDilithiumM4. We will publish the code alongside the paper under a CC0 copyright waiver.

Structure. Section 2 recalls the preliminaries regarding Kyber, Dilithium, and the Cortex-M4. In Sect. 3 and Sect. 4, we describe the optimizations applied to Kyber and Dilithium, respectively. Lastly, in Sect. 5, we present the performance results and compare them to previous work.

2 Preliminaries

This section introduces the cryptographic schemes Kyber and Dilithium, which are both part of the Cryptographic Suite for Algebraic Lattices (CRYSTALS). Furthermore we give a brief introduction into the polynomial multiplication using the NTT, revisit the Barrett reduction and present relevant details considering our target platform, the Arm Cortex-M4.

2.1 Notation

For a prime q and a power of two n, we denote the polynomial ring $\mathbb{Z}_q[X]/(X^n + 1)$ by $\mathcal{R}_q$. An element $a \in \mathcal{R}_q$ is represented by a coefficient vector $a_i \in \mathbb{Z}_q$, such that $a = \sum_{i=0}^{n-1} a_i X^i$. We denote polynomials using lower-case letters (e.g., a), vectors of polynomials using lower-case boldfaced letters (e.g., $\mathbf{a}$), and matrices of polynomials using upper-case boldfaced letters (e.g., $\mathbf{A}$). We symbolize polynomials, vectors, and matrices inside NTT-domain using $\hat{a}$, $\hat{\mathbf{a}}$, and $\hat{\mathbf{A}}$, respectively.

Following the definitions from [BDK+20, ABD+20], for an odd q we define the result of the central reduction $r' = r \bmod {}^{\pm}q$ as the unique element in $[-\frac{q-1}{2}, \frac{q-1}{2}]$ satisfying $r' \equiv r \bmod q$. Similarly, we define the result of $r' = r \bmod {}^{+}q$ as the unique element in $[0, q)$ satisfying $r' \equiv r \bmod q$. For scenarios in which the range of the reduction result does not matter, we write $r' = r \bmod q$.

The function sampleUniform($\cdot$) samples coefficients for polynomials, vectors of polynomials, or matrices of polynomials from a uniformly random distribution. In case a seed is given as the argument, the output is pseudorandomly generated from the seed.

2.2 Polynomial Multiplications Using the NTT

The NTT is a variant of the discrete Fourier transform (DFT) defined over finite fields and is commonly used for efficient polynomial multiplications. The efficiency of this strategy is based on the fact that a polynomial multiplication inside NTT domain amounts to the coefficient-wise multiplication of the two polynomials. Specifically, the negacyclic NTT is used for multiplying polynomials in $\mathbb{Z}_q[X]/(X^n + 1)$.

Computing the negacyclic NTT can be viewed as the evaluation of a polynomial at powers of a primitive n-th root of unity ζ_n for the polynomial ring $\mathcal{R}_q$ with q prime. Additionally, multiplying all coefficients a_i of $a \in \mathcal{R}_q$ by powers of a $2n$-th root of unity $\zeta_{2n} = \sqrt{\zeta_n}$ is called "twisting" [Ber01].

This comes down to computing

$$\text{NTT}(a) = \hat{a} = \sum_{i=0}^{n-1} \hat{a}_i X^i \text{ with } \hat{a}_i = \sum_{j=0}^{n-1} a_j \zeta_{2n}^j \zeta_n^{ij}$$

for the forward transform (NTT) and

$$\text{iNTT}(\hat{a}) = a = \sum_{i=0}^{n-1} a_i X^i \text{ with } a_i = n^{-1} \zeta_{2n}^{-i} \sum_{j=0}^{n-1} \hat{a}_j \zeta_n^{-ij}$$

for the inverse transform (iNTT) [AB74]. The powers of the roots of unity used during the computation of the NTT are also frequently called "twiddle factors".

For computing the NTT itself efficiently, fast Fourier transform (FFT) algorithms, which only require $\Theta(n \log n)$ operations, are commonly used. This algorithm was first described by Gauss in 1805 [Gau66] but it is also oftentimes credited to Cooley and Tukey who published the same algorithm in 1965 [CT65]. The basic idea of the algorithm is to split the computation of a length n NTT into, most commonly, two separate number-theoretic transforms (NTTs) with an input size of $n/2$ each. Formally, we compute the isomorphism $\mathcal{R}_q \to \prod_i \mathbb{Z}_q[X]/(X - \zeta_{2n}^i)$ for $i = 1, 3, 5, \ldots, n - 1$ as given by the Chinese Remainder Theorem (CRT), as also explained in [BDK+20, Section 2.2]. For example, in the first instance we map $\mathbb{Z}_q[X]/(X^n + 1)$ to $\mathbb{Z}_q[X]/(X^{n/2} - \zeta_{2n}^{n/2}) \times \mathbb{Z}_q[X]/(X^{n/2} + \zeta_{2n}^{n/2})$. This splitting is usually repeated for $\log_2 n$ iterations, called "NTT layers", where the results of the i-th layer are the remainders of polynomials $a \mod (X^{2^{i-1}} \pm \zeta_{2n}^j)$ for some j. Computing these remainders involves $n/2$ so-called butterfly operations per layer. The CooleyTukey (CT) butterfly, consisting of one addition, one subtraction, and one multiplication in $\mathbb{Z}_q$, is depicted in Fig. 1a.

While the CT algorithm is frequently used for computing the NTT, the Gentleman–Sande FFT algorithm is commonly deployed for computing the iNTT. In contrast to this, we use the CT algorithm for the computation of the NTT and its inverse. A depiction of the GS butterfly is Fig. 1b.

Using this method, the product of $f, g \in \mathcal{R}_q$ can be efficiently computed as $\text{iNTT}(\text{NTT}(f) \circ \text{NTT}(g))$, where $\circ$ indicates the base multiplication of two polynomials. In case the NTT is computed on $\log n$ layers, base multiplication is equal to

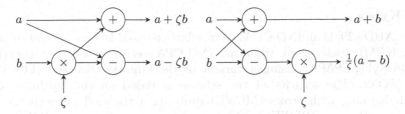

(a) Cooley–Tukey butterfly   (b) Gentleman–Sande butterfly

Fig. 1. NTT butterfly operations

coefficient-wise multiplication requiring only n multiplications. In case the NTT is computed on $l < \log n$ layers, yielding 2^l polynomials mod $x^m - \omega$ for $m = \frac{n}{2^l}$ and ω a power of a root of unity, it is called an "incomplete" NTT. For this scenario, the base multiplication corresponds to pairwise $m \times m$ schoolbook multiplications. This idea was initially introduced in [LS19] for the case of the modulus not supporting an NTT on $\log n$ layers, but is also applied for performance reasons in several other implementations, for example, [ABCG20, CHK+21, ACC+21].

2.3   Fermat Number Transform

The Fermat number transform (FNT) is a special case of NTT in that the modulus is a Fermat number $F_t := 2^{2^t} + 1$. It was introduced in [SS71] for large integer multiplications and in [AB74, AB75] for digital convolutions. In this paper, we implement FNT for negacyclic convolution. For arbitrary F_t as the modulus, cyclic transformations of sizes dividing 2^{t+2} are supported [AB74, AB75]. For computing a negacyclic transformation of size $n = 2^{t+1}$ and $\zeta_{2n} = \sqrt{2}$, the first split becomes

$$\mathbb{Z}_{F_t}[X]/(X^n - 2^{2^t}) \cong \mathbb{Z}_{F_t}[X]/(X^{\frac{n}{2}} - 2^{2^{t-1}}) \times \mathbb{Z}_{F_t}[X]/(X^{\frac{n}{2}} + 2^{2^{t-1}})$$
$$= \mathbb{Z}_{F_t}[X]/(X^{\frac{n}{2}} - 2^{2^{t-1}}) \times \mathbb{Z}_{F_t}[X]/(X^{\frac{n}{2}} - 2^{2^{t-1}(1 + 2)}).$$

After applying t layers, all of the polynomial rings are of the form $\mathbb{Z}_{F_t}[x]/(X^{\frac{n}{2^t}} - 2^j)$ where j is an odd number. Since $\zeta_{2n}^2 = 2$, we can apply one more split. Furthermore, if F_t is a prime, then we can compute cyclic transformations of sizes up to $2^{2^t} = F_t - 1$ and negacyclic transformations up to $2^{2^t - 1}$. Since the twiddles in initial t layers are powers of two, we can multiply with the twiddles using shift operations which is much cheaper than explicit multiplications on many platforms. Note that the only known prime Fermat numbers are $F_0 = 3$, $F_1 = 5$, $F_2 = 17$, $F_3 = 257$, $F_4 = 65\,537$. Out of those, only F_3 and F_4 appear promising for the use in Dilithium. They allow to compute 3 or 4 layers using only shifts.

2.4   Kyber

Kyber [ABD+20] is an IND-CCA2-secure lattice-based key-encapsulation mechanism(KEM) constructed from an IND-CPA secure public-key encryption scheme Kyber.CPAPKE using a variant of the Fujisaki–Okamoto (FO) transform [FO99]. The security of the scheme is based on the hardness of the module-learning with errors (MLWE) problem, a trade-off between the ring-learning with errors(RLWE) problem and learning with errors (LWE) problem [ABD+20, Section 1.5]. Kyber is one of four round-three KEM-finalists in the NIST PQC [Nat] next to Saber [DKRV20], NTRU [CDH+20], and Classic McEliece [ABC+20].

Parameters. Kyber uses $q = 3329$ as its prime and n is chosen to be 256. Thus, it operates on $\mathcal{R}_q = \mathbb{Z}_{3329}[X]/(X^{256} + 1)$ [ABD+20, Section 1.4]. The specification defines three different security levels of Kyber, namely Kyber-512 ($k = 2, \eta_1 = 3$), Kyber-768 ($k = 3, \eta_1 = 2$), and Kyber-1024 ($k = 4, \eta_1 = 2$) [ABD+20, Section 1.4]. Due to the fact that q and n remain constant across the three parameter sets, almost all possible optimizations apply to all variants. For the specification of Kyber, we refer to [ABD+20] and omit the description.

Number Theoretic Transform. Since polynomial multiplication is among the most costly operations for Kyber, the polynomial ring has been chosen, such that Kyber can profit from efficient polynomial multiplication using the NTT.

For $q = 3329$, as deployed in Kyber, no primitive 512-th but only primitive 256-th roots of unity exist for $\mathcal{R}_q$ with the first one being $\zeta_n = 17$ [ABD+20]. This means that the defining polynomial of $\mathcal{R}_q$ ($X^{256} + 1$) factors into 128 polynomials of degree one and not into 256 polynomials of degree zero. Therefore, the result of the NTT of $f \in \mathcal{R}_q$ is a vector of 128 polynomials of degree one. Thus, in contrast to Sect. 2.2, the coefficients $\hat{a}_i$ inside NTT domain are given by

$$\hat{a}_{2i} = \sum_{j=0}^{127} a_{2j}\zeta_n^{(2\mathrm{br}_7(i)+1)j}, \text{ and } \hat{a}_{2i+1} = \sum_{j=0}^{127} a_{2j+1}\zeta_n^{(2\mathrm{br}_7(i)+1)j}$$

as defined in [ABD+20]. The function br_7 computes the bit reversal of a 7-bit integer on its argument.

The absence of a primitive 512-th root of unity also has an impact on the base multiplication of two polynomials inside NTT domain: Instead of coefficient-wise multiplication, we need to perform schoolbook multiplications of size 2×2, i.e., we need to compute 128 products $\mathrm{mod}(X^2 - \zeta_n^{2\mathrm{br}_7(i)+1})$ [ABD+20].

2.5   Dilithium

Dilithium [DKL+18, BDK+20] is a lattice-based digital signature scheme based on the "Fiat-Shamir with Aborts" approach [Lyu09]. Its security is based on the hardness of the modular short integer solution (MSIS) and MLWE problems and it is currently among the three signature-finalists in the NIST PQC project [Nat], next to Falcon [FHK+20] and Rainbow [CDK+20].

Parameters. Dilithium deploys the prime $q = 8380417 = 2^{23} - 2^{13} + 1$ and operates on the polynomial ring $\mathcal{R}_q = \mathbb{Z}_q[X]/(X^n + 1)$ with $n = 256$. The two parameters q and n are the same across all parameter sets.

Dilithium offers three different parameter sets, namely Dilithium2, Dilithium3, and Dilithium5, which target the three NIST security levels 2, 3, and 5. More details on the differences between the three parameter sets can be obtained from Table 1. The matrix dimension is given by (k, l), the bounds for sampling the secret key by η, the number of ± 1 in the challenge polynomial c is τ, and #reps refers to the expected number of repetitions during the rejection sampling in the signature generation process [BDK+20]. The parameters γ_1 and γ_2 define the range for the coefficient $\mathbf{y}$ and the low-order rounding range [BDK+20].

Table 1. Overview of Dilithium's parameter sets [BDK+20]

Scheme	NIST level	(k,l)	η	τ	γ_1	γ_2	#reps	$\lvert pk \rvert$	$\lvert sig \rvert$
Dilithium2	2	$(4,4)$	2	39	2^{17}	$(q-1)/88$	4.25	1312 B	2420 B
Dilithium3	3	$(6,5)$	4	49	2^{19}	$(q-1)/32$	5.1	1952 B	3293 B
Dilithium5	5	$(8,7)$	2	60	2^{19}	$(q-1)/32$	3.85	2592 B	4595 B

We refer to [BDK+20] for the specification of Dilithium and omit the description.

Number Theoretic Transform. Since the main algebraic operations used by Dilithium are polynomial multiplications, Dilithium's ring was chosen in such a way that the NTT can be applied [BDK+20]. In contrast to Kyber, for the Dilithium ring, a $2n$-th primitive root of unity $r = 1753$ exists [BDK+20] and thus it is possible to compute a complete NTT with eight layers as described in Sect. 2.2. This allows for base multiplication by coefficient-wise multiplication.

2.6 Barrett Reduction

The Barrett reduction [Bar87] is an efficient algorithm for reductions in $\mathbb{Z}_q$. Besides its performance, one advantage is that it can be easily implemented in constant-time. A variant of the Barrett reduction that operates on signed integers has been presented in [Sei18, Algorithm 5] which has also been deployed in a previous implementation of Kyber [ABCG20]. Algorithm 2.1 is an illustration.

Algorithm 2.1: Signed Barrett Reduction [ABCG20]

Input : q with $0 < q < \frac{\beta}{2}, 2 \nmid q$ and a with $-\frac{\beta}{2} \leq a < \frac{\beta}{2}$
Output: r with $r = a \pmod q, 0 \leq r \leq q$

1 $v \leftarrow \lfloor \frac{2^{\log(q)-1} \cdot \beta}{q} \rfloor$ ▷ precomputed
2 $t \leftarrow \lfloor \frac{av}{2^{\log(q)-1} \cdot \beta} \rfloor$ ▷ signed high product and arithmetic right shift
3 $t \leftarrow tq \bmod \beta$ ▷ signed low product
4 **return** $r \leftarrow a - t$

2.7   Arm Cortex-M4

The target platform for our implementation is the Arm Cortex-M4(F), which is a NIST-recommended evaluation platform for the candidates of the NIST PQC project. The Arm Cortex-M4 is based on the Armv7E-M instruction set architecture with 14 usable 32-bit general purpose registers. Additionally, on the Cortex-M4F, there are 32 single-precision floating-point registers [ARM11].

The instruction set also provides a number of powerful digital signal processing (DSP) instructions which allow to perform arithmetic operation on two half words or four bytes at the same time and have proven themselves to be beneficial in numerous implementations [BKS19,ABCG20,KMSRV18] of Kyber [ABD+20], and Saber [DKRV20]. In particular, the instructions smul{b,t}{b,t} multiply specific halfwords and smla{b,t}{b,t} multiply specific halfwords and accumulate the product to the specified accumulator. Additionally, the instructions smuad{,x} perform two halfword-multiplications and add up their products, while smlad{,x} perform two halfword-multiplications and add up their products which is then added to an accumulator. All of these instructions take one cycle to execute. Moreover, the Cortex-M4 can compute the 64-bit product of two 32-bit values (optionally, with accumulation) in a single cycle. Furthermore, the Cortex-M4 provides a barrel shifter for shifting or rotating the second operand for certain instructions with no additional cost.

On the Cortex-M4, store instructions always take a single cycle, while a sequence of independent loads takes $n + 1$ cycles. Using the vldm instruction, it is possible to directly load data from the memory into the floating point registers. This also consumes $n + 1$ cycles for n data words.

3   Improvements to Kyber Implementations

For Kyber, we propose several optimizations for implementing NTT and iNTT and some speed optimizations to the matrix-vector product at the cost of a higher stack usage. We provide one implementation with all optimizations and one with only the optimizations that do not impact the stack usage.

We base our implementations on [ABCG20] and the implementation in the pqm4 [KRSS19] project. In the following we focus on our contributions and omit details of the numerous optimizations present in previous implementations.

3.1   NTT

Caching in FPU Registers. For Kyber, on the layers 7–4, 15 twiddle factors are required and re-used multiple times throughout the iterations. By using the floating-point registers for caching the twiddle factors, the number of cycles for memory loads are reduced. This technique has been proven to be beneficial in past work [ACC+20, CHK+21, ACC+21]. In our implementations, we load the 15 twiddle factors (packed into eight registers) into the floating-point registers once with `vldm` instruction in nine cycles. Then, in each iteration the twiddle factors are fetched from the floating-point registers with `vmov` in a single cycle each.

On the three remaining layers, it is not beneficial to make use of the floating point registers because in each of the 16 iterations at least one unique twiddle factor per layer is required, meaning none of the twiddle factors are re-used.

Better Layer Merging. In our implementations we make use of the common optimization strategy of merging layers of the NTT computation [GOPS13]. The idea behind this strategy is to load multiple coefficients at once such that more than one layer of NTT can be computed at a time. This reduces the number of memory operations required at the cost of taking up more registers. The state-of-the-art implementation of Kyber [ABCG20] also deploys this strategy merging layers 7–5 and 4–2 while computing layer 1 separately.

By making use of the floating point registers, we instead implement the NTT by merging layers 7–4 and 3–1. Layers 7–4 can be merged by first computing three layers of NTT on each $(a_1, a_3, a_5, a_7, a_9, a_{11}, a_{13}, a_{15})$ and $(a_0, a_2, a_4, a_6, a_8, a_{10}, a_{12}, a_{14})$ and then combining their results. First, the NTT on $(a_1, a_3, \ldots, a_{15})$ is computed and each of the layer 5 outputs is multiplied by the corresponding twiddle factors of the fourth layer. Then, $(a_1, a_3, \ldots, a_{15})$ are moved to the floating point registers for later use. After that, the polynomials $(a_0, a_2, \ldots, a_{14})$ are loaded and the NTT is computed on them. Finally, we `vmov` $(a_0, a_2, \ldots, a_{14})$ one at a time and compute the final add-sub. In summary, this requires 128 additional `vmov`s, whereas a separate layer requires 128 loads and 128 stores.

3.2   Inverse NTT

The most significant change we apply to the inverse NTT is the switch from Gentleman–Sande butterflies to Cooley Tukey butterflies. Therefore, all of the optimizations mentioned in the context of the NTT also apply to the inverse NTT.

Switch to CT-Butterflies. In previous implementations of Kyber for the Arm Cortex-M4, the NTT was always implemented using CT butterflies, while the inverse NTT was implemented using GS butterflies, which is a commonly seen pattern for implementations using the NTT in general. Opposed to that, we implement the inverse NTT using CT butterflies in order to avoid the necessity of intermediate modular reductions by limiting the coefficients' growths, as for example suggested in [Sei18, Section 2.1] or implemented for Saber in [ACC+21].

Algorithm 3.1: Packed Barrett Reduction [BKS19]	**Algorithm 3.2:** Improved Packed Barrett Reduction
Input : $a = (a_t \| a_b)$	**Input** : $a = (a_t \| a_b)$
Output: $c = (c_t \| c_b) \bmod {}^{\pm}q$	**Output:** $c = (c_t \| c_b) \bmod {}^{\pm}q$
1 smulbb $t_0, a, \lfloor \frac{2^{26}}{q} \rceil$	1 smlawb $t_0, -\lfloor \frac{2^{32}}{q} \rfloor, a, 2^{15}$
2 smultb $t_1, a, \lfloor \frac{2^{26}}{q} \rceil$	2 smlabt t_0, q, t_0, a
3 asr $t_0, t_0, \#26$	3 smlawt $t_1, -\lfloor \frac{2^{32}}{q} \rfloor, a, 2^{15}$
4 asr $t_1, t_1, \#26$	4 smulbt t_1, q, t_1
5 smulbb t_0, t_0, q	5 add $t_1, a, t_1, \text{lsl } \#16$
6 smulbb t_1, t_1, q	6 pkhbt $c, t_0, t_1, \text{lsl } \#16$
7 pkhbt $t_0, t_0, t_1, \text{lsl } \#16$	
8 usub16 r, a, t_0	

Using CT butterflies for the inverse NTT requires to do additional twisting during the computation of the last layer but the total number of multiplications does generally not increase because multiplications in the same amount can be omitted during the butterfly operations ("light butterflies"). One side effect of this approach is that some coefficients will grow larger than in the forward NTT because the multiplications in the butterflies always include reductions and now the operands of the addition and subtraction in the butterfly are not always limited by this. To counteract, we insert two modular multiplications on the fourth layer to limit the growth of the coefficients to be in $(-9q, 9q)$, at most after the fourth layer. By detailed range analysis, we found that on the last three layers we need 20 additional reductions on packed arguments in total.

Moreover, the Montgomery multiplication during the twisting removes the need of a separate Barrett reduction of every coefficient at the end of the last layer. This saves 256 Barrett reductions.

Note that due to the new structure of the iNTT the input coefficients' absolute values need to be smaller than q.

3.3   Faster Barrett Reduction

Similar to previous implementations, we deploy the Barrett reduction to reduce the coefficients. The Barrett reduction of two 16-bit integers packed in one 32-bit register has been previously implemented [BKS19] as shown in Algorithm 3.1. Using the smlaw{b,t} instructions as in Algorithm 3.2, the cycle count of one Barrett reduction is reduced by one. This means for reducing a packed argument, two cycles are saved. In contrast to the implementation from Algorithm 3.1, the technique presented in Algorithm 3.2 requires two Barrett constants which are both different from the previous one. Moreover, using this optimization removes the guarantee of the reduction's result being in $[0, q)$, instead it will result in $[-\frac{q-1}{2}, \frac{q-1}{2}]$ for an odd q. Therefore, its output must not be passed to one of the packing or compression functions because they assume the input to be in $[0, q)$.

This means, it may not be used in the `poly_reduce` function but it can be used inside the NTT and iNTT.

3.4 Matrix-Vector Product

For speed optimization of the matrix-vector product, we implement two techniques. Both of them require additional stack space and therefore, if a low memory footprint is a concern, the applicability needs to be checked. Further, we re-implement the C function for the computation of the matrix-vector product in assembly which allows us to significantly lower the number of function calls required by efficiently using the registers and making use of macros. We proceed similarly for the inner product in the decryption.

Asymmetric Multiplication. For the computation of the matrix-vector product $\mathbf{As}$ in Kyber, we compute $\mathrm{iNTT}(\hat{\mathbf{A}} \circ \mathrm{NTT}(\mathbf{s}))$. During this computation, every row of $\hat{\mathbf{A}}$ needs to be multiplied by $\hat{\mathbf{s}}$. Therefore it is a common strategy to cache the result of $\hat{\mathbf{s}}$ instead of recomputing it for every row of $\hat{\mathbf{A}}$ [BKS19]. Using a trick for integer multiplication presented in [BDL+11,BHK+21] extended the aforementioned concept for which incomplete NTTs are deployed.

Recall that the Kyber NTT is incomplete, i.e., 7 instead of 8 layers are computed, and therefore the product of two polynomials inside NTT-domain $\hat{a} \circ \hat{s} = \hat{c}$ consists of 128 2×2 schoolbook multiplications. For computing $\hat{c}_{2i} + \hat{c}_{2i+1}X = (\hat{a}_{2i} + \hat{a}_{2i+1}X)(\hat{s}_{2i} + \hat{s}_{2i+1}X) \bmod (X^2 - \zeta^{2\mathrm{br}_7(i)+1})$, we have $\hat{c}_{2i} = \hat{a}_{2i}\hat{s}_{2i} + \hat{a}_{2i+1}\hat{s}_{2i+1}\zeta^{2\mathrm{br}_7(i)+1}$ and $\hat{c}_{2i+1} = \hat{a}_{2i}\hat{s}_{2i+1} + \hat{s}_{2i}\hat{a}_{2i+1}$.

The idea behind the proposal from [BHK+21, Section 4.2] is that during the computation of $\hat{\mathbf{A}} \circ \hat{\mathbf{s}}$, each polynomial of $\hat{\mathbf{s}}$ is used k times which means that the computation of $\hat{s}_{2i+1}\zeta^{2\mathrm{br}_7(i)+1}$ is repeated k times. This can be avoided by caching the intermediate results of $\hat{s}_{2i+1}\zeta^{2\mathrm{br}_7(i)+1}$ in a separate vector $\hat{\mathbf{s}}'$.

We implement two separate variants for the base multiplication, one of which is only used for the first row of the matrix in the matrix-vector product, while the other one is used for all of the following ones. The first variant computes the same base multiplication as before except that it stores the result of $\hat{s}_{2i+1}\zeta^{2\mathrm{br}_7(i)+1}$ separately. This comes at the cost of two additional stores and one additional load from the stack for the argument containing the address of $\hat{\mathbf{s}}'$ per two polynomial multiplications. The second variant saves two `smultb` instructions, two montgomery reductions, and the load of one twiddle factor per two polynomials by loading the cached values instead. The precomputed vector can also be re-used in the inner product following the matrix-vector multiplication in encryption.

Better Accumulation. We also make use of an improved accumulation strategy in the matrix-vector product as presented in [CHK+21]. For the computation of one element of the output vector in a matrix-vector product, a total number of k base multiplications as well as $k - 1$ accumulating additions are required. Instead of reducing each coefficient directly after the base multiplication before accumulating, we delay this step until all three base multiplication results have been accumulated. We also implement this technique for the computation of the inner product. For the implementation, we define three variants of the caching and non-caching base multiplication functions each: One that takes 16-bit input values and writes to a 32-bit output array, one that takes unreduced 32-bit input values and writes to a 32-bit output array, as well as one function that also takes unreduced 32-bit input values but outputs reduced and packed coefficients in a 16-bit integer array. For the second type of the function, the operation on 32-bit values also allows for usage of `smla{b,t}` instead of `smul{b,t}` such that no extra addition is required for the accumulation, compared to the case when computing on packed 16-bit coefficients.

Due to the small size of the Kyber prime, the sum will never overflow a signed 32-bit integer: For the matrix-vector products in Kyber using asymmetric multiplication, possible vector-inputs are the output of an NTT which is in $[-\frac{q-1}{2}, \frac{q-1}{2}]$ or the cached Montgomery multiplication result from the asymmetric multiplication which is in $(-q, q)$. The coefficients of the matrix generated using the on-the-fly approach from [BKS19] are smaller than q. Therefore, the maximum result for one of the multiplications is $\in (-q^2, q^2)$. For k accumulations with $k \in \{2, 3, 4\}$, we get a maximum absolute intermediate value of $kq^2 = 4q^2 < 2^{31}$.

4   Improvements to Dilithium Implementations

For Dilithium we deploy similar strategies for optimizing the NTT and iNTT as for Kyber and optimize the multiplication of c and s_1, as well as c and s_2.

4.1   NTT and Inverse NTT

For the NTT, we merge the layers as 7–5, 4–2, 1–0 to reduce the number of memory operations. This differs from the previous implementation [GKS20, GKOS18] where layers 7–6, 5–4, 3–2, and 1–0 are merged. For the iNTT, we similarly switch to CT-butterflies and merge as in the NTT.

Switch to CT-Butterflies. Just as for Kyber, we switch to CT butterflies for the computation of the iNTT. Further, we make use of a technique introduced in [ACC+21, Appendix D] which computes light butterflies with one less reduction. As opposed to the Kyber, the coefficients' growth due to the light butterflies is not of concern for the Dilithium since values up to $256q$ fit in a 32-bit register.

4.2   Small NTTs for Dilithium

In the signature generation of Dilithium, we recall that the polynomial c consists of τ ± 1's and $256 - \tau$ 0's, and all polynomials in s_1 and s_2 consist of elements in $[-\eta, \eta]$. The absolute values of the coefficients in cs_1 and cs_2 are bounded by $\tau\eta$, and the computation can be regarded as in $\mathbb{Z}_{q'}$ for $q' > 2\tau\eta$ [CHK+21, Section 2.4.6]. As far as we know, all implementations choose $q' = 8380417$ and employ the NTT defined for Dilithium. However, since only the correct cs_1 and cs_2 are required, there is some freedom for choosing q'. The parameters $\tau \cdot \eta$ are $39 \cdot 2 = 78$ for, $49 \cdot 4 = 196$ for Dilithium3, and $60 \cdot 2 = 120$ for Dilithium5. Consequently, we choose the Fermat number $q' = F_3 = 257$ for Dilithium2 and Dilithium5, and $q' = 769$ for Dilithium3. Alternatively, one can also re-use the Kyber prime $q' = 3329$ for any of the parameters in case re-using the code is of interest. We have also experimented with the Fermat number $q' = F_4 = 65537$ for Dilithium3. However, this did not result in in a speed-up compared to $q' = 769$.

FNT for Dilithium2 and Dilithium5. For $q' = 257 = 2^8 + 1$, we have FNT defined over $\mathbb{Z}_{257}[X]/(X^{256}+1)$. We implement the forward transformation with 7 layers of CT butterflies. Since the input coefficients for c, s_1, and s_2 are at most in $[-\eta, \eta]$, we only need very few reductions. Recall that a CT butterfly maps (a, b) to $(a + \omega b, a - \omega b)$, we can implement it with mla and mls. Furthermore, we can also take a closer look at the initial layers. Since $-1 \equiv 2^8$ (mod 257), the first layer can be written as $\mathbb{Z}_{257}[X]/(X^{256} + 1) \cong \mathbb{Z}_{257}[X]/(X^{128} - 2^4) \times \mathbb{Z}_{257}[X]/(X^{128} + 2^4)$ and the corresponding CT butterfly maps (a, b) to $(a + 2^4 b, a - 2^4 b)$. We denote such computation as $\texttt{CT\_FNT}(a, b, 4)$. Notice that without loading twiddle factors, we can implement $\texttt{CT\_FNT}(a, b, \texttt{logW})$ efficiently with barrel shifter as illustrated in Algorithm 4.1.

Let iFNT be the inverse of FNT. We first observe that the inverse of 2^k can be written as $2^{-k} \equiv 2^{16-k} \equiv -2^{8-k}$ (mod $2^8 + 1$). There are two places where we need to multiply by an inverse of a power of two: (i) the inverses corresponded to the butterflies with $\omega = 2^{\texttt{logW}}$ in CT_FNT, and (ii) the scaling by 128^{-1} at the end of iFNT. We denote $\texttt{CT\_iFNT}(a, b, \texttt{logW})$ as the function mapping (a, b) to $(a - 2^{\texttt{logW}}b, a + 2^{\texttt{logW}}b) = (a + 2^{8+\texttt{logW}}b, a - 2^{8+\texttt{logW}}b)$ and implement it with barrel shifter as shown in Algorithm 4.2. Clearly, if $\texttt{CT\_FNT}(a, b, k)$ computes $(a + 2^k b, a - 2^k b)$, then $\texttt{CT\_iFNT}(a, b, 8 - k)$ computes $(a + 2^{-k}b, a - 2^{-k}b)$ which can be used in iFNT. We compute iFNT with four layers of GS butterflies followed by three layers of CT butterflies. During the GS butterflies, since the twiddle factors are also very small, we can replace some of the mul, add, and sub with mla and mls. For CT butterflies, since the twiddle factors are powers of two, we implement them with Algorithm 4.2. Lastly, at the end of CT butterflies, we merge the twisting by powers of two with the multiplication by 128^{-1}.

NTT over 769 for Dilithium3. For Dilithium3, since the maximum absolute value of cs_1 and cs_2 is bounded by $\tau\eta = 4 \cdot 49 = 196$, we cannot use $q' = 257 < 2 \cdot 196$. We therefore choose $q' = 769$ and modify the NTT and iNTT from Kyber. Except for discarding most of the Barrett reductions, the code is the same.

Recall that for the NTT in Kyber, we require the output to be in $[-\frac{q'}{2}, \frac{q'}{2}]$ for the secret key. However, for Dilithium3, since we are only using 16-bit NTT for computing cs_1 and cs_2, we can remove the Barrett reductions at the end and allow elements growing up to $7q'$ in absolute value.

Algorithm 4.1: CT_FNT(a, b, logW).	**Algorithm 4.2:** CT_iFNT(a, b, logW).
Input : (a,b) = (a, b) **Output:** (a,b) = $(a + 2^{\log W} b, a - 2^{\log W} b)$ 1 add a, a, b, lsl #logW 2 sub b, a, b, lsl #(logW+1)	**Input** : (a,b) = (a, b) **Output:** (a,b) = $(a - 2^{\log W} b, a + 2^{\log W} b)$ 1 sub a, a, b, lsl #logW 2 add b, a, b, lsl #(logW+1)

For the iNTT, replacing with $q' = 769$ allows us to postpone the Barrett reductions by one layer and reduce the number of Barrett reductions by half. At the end of iNTT, we replace the 16-bit Montgomery multiplication with straight multiplication and 32-bit Barrett reduction. By using 32-bit Barrett reduction, the result is within $[-384, 384]$ if the product is in $[-113025697, 113025697]$. Since $\log_2(\frac{113025697}{384}) \approx 18.17$, we derive values in $[-384, 384]$ by applying 32-bit Barrett reduction to the product of any signed 16-bit value and any constant from $[-384, 384]$. The downside for using 32-bit Barrett reduction is a slightly higher register pressure, but overall it is more favorable because we don't need to reduce them again. This is different from the 16-bit NTT in [ACC+21]. They implemented the twist with Montgomery multiplication and then reduced the result to $[-384, 384]$ with an additional 32-bit Barrett reduction.

5 Results

In this section, we present the implementations results of Kyber and Dilithium.

5.1 Benchmarking Setup

Our concrete hardware target is the STM32F4DISCOVERY with the STM32-F407VG MCU, which also is the target of previous publications concerning implementations of post-quantum schemes on microcontrollers. It comes with 1 MiB of flash memory, and 192 KiB of RAM.

Our benchmarking setup is based on pqm4 [KRSS19]. During the benchmarks, we clock the microcontroller at 24 MHz in order to avoid wait states during memory operations. We compile the code using arm-none-eabi-gcc version 10.2.1 with the -O3 option. Regarding the Keccak implementation, we make use of the code provided in pqm4. For the randomness generation we rely on the microcontroller's hardware random number generator (RNG).

We compare our Kyber implementations to the code currently present in pqm4 which is based on the work in [ABCG20] and [BKS19]. Similarly, we compare our implementations of Dilithium (2 and 3) to the code in pqm4 which is based on [GKS20]. For Dilithium5, pqm4 does not currently have an implementation due to a lack of stack space. We apply some of the stack optimizations of [GKS20] to our implementations, especially to make Dilithium5 work as well. It is important to note that the parameters of Kyber and Dilithium were changed at the start of the third round of the NISTPQC competition. The numbers presented here reflect the round 3 versions contained in pqm4. Those are optimizations from the original papers ported to the third round parameters. The performance results for the full schemes do not match the original publications.

5.2   Performance of NTT-Related Functions

In Table 2, we present the cycle counts for the transformations we deploy in our implementations of Kyber and Dilithium. For the Kyber NTT, we achieve a speedup of 12.6%. Regarding the Kyber iNTT, we obtain a speedup of up-to 21.3%. Note that for the stack-optimized variant an additional reduction is required before the iNTT because of the absence of asymmetric multiplication.

We achieve a speedup of 5.2% for the Dilithium NTT, and 5.7% for the iNTT. For the small NTTs the metric we are optimizing is $(k + l) \cdot$ NTT + #reps · (NTT + $(k + l) \cdot$ (basemul + iNTT)). As most of the small NTT are computed outside of the loop, we moved some of the reductions into the NTT resulting in a faster basemul. Note that for $q = 257$ and $q = 769$ the NTT and iNTT have very close performance, but the basemul differs. This results in the FNT being advantageous for Dilithium2 and Dilithium5. For (basemul + iNTT), we achieve a speedup of 37.6% for $q = 257$, and 33.1% for $q = 769$ compared to $q = 8380417$ from [GKS20]. We also compare our $q = 769$ implementation to an existing one by [ACC+21], because theoretically, their 6-layer approach could also be used as well. Since the computation is dominated by (basemul + iNTT), we find that our 7-layer approach is faster. We also carefully examine the code by [ACC+21], and find that the last 32-bit Barrett reduction is performed outside the reported iNTT, so the speedup is more.

Table 3 contains the result for our benchmarks of the MVP and inner product (IP) functions as deployed in Kyber. For the MVP, we consider the MVP as it is computed in the key generation. The MVP in the encryption is similar but contains k NTTs less. Note that in the actual implementation of Kyber, the MVP is interleaved with the on-the-fly generation of the matrix. For ease of comparison, we additionally provide benchmarks for a stripped down variant of the MVP excluding the hashing. Regarding our benchmarks, we count the caching for the asymmetric multiplication towards the MVP although the IP for the encryption also benefits of this pre-computation. For the same reasons as for the MVP, the benchmarks of our IP functions only include the NTTs, the base multiplications, and deserialization, if applicable. For the speed optimized MVP implementation, we get speedups between 15.9% and 17.8% (excl. hashing). The stack optimized variant, achieves speedups between 12.1% and 12.5%. We achieve speedups of 26.9%–31.7% (enc) and 21.6%–23.3% (dec) for the speed optimized inner product, while for the stack variant we obtain speedups of 4%–6.3% and 17.3%–18.9%, respectively. We observe that for larger k, the speed optimization strategy gives increasingly lower cycle counts due to asym. multiplication.

Table 2. Cycle counts for transformation operations of Kyber and Dilithium. NTT and iNTT correspond to the schemes default transformations, i.e., $q = 3329$ for Kyber and $q = 8380417$ for Dilithium. The NTT with $q = 257$ is deployed for Dilithium2 and Dilithium5, and the NTT with $q = 769$ is used used for Dilithium3.

	Prime	Implementation	NTT	iNTT	basemul
Kyber	$q = 3329$	[ABCG20]	6852	6979	2317
		This work	5992	5491/6282[a]	1613[b]
Dilithium	$q = 8380417$	[GKS20]	8540	8923	1955
		This work	8093	8415	1955
	$q = 257$	This work	5524	5563	1225
	$q = 769$	[ACC+21] (6-layer)	4852	4817	2966
		This work	5200	5537	1740

[a] First value is for speed-optimization, second for stack-optimization.
[b] Asymmetric basemul as used in the IP (enc). As the basemul in the MVP and IP consists of individual function calls, the cycle count is not straight forward to measure.

Table 3. Cycle counts for matrix-vector and inner products used in Kyber.

implementation	variant	operation	Kyber-512	Kyber-768	Kyber-1024
pqm4		Matrix-Vector Product[a]	66291	127634	209517
		Matrix-Vector Product[b]	226580	484077	840498
		Inner Product (enc)	11978	14696	17429
		Inner Product (dec)	29888	41910	53792
This work	speed	Matrix-Vector Product[a]	55746	106380	172152
		Matrix-Vector Product[b]	211606	457213	796349
		Inner Product (enc)	8762	10331	11898
		Inner Product (dec)	23425	32354	41275
	stack	Matrix-Vector Product[a]	58028	112503	184149
		Matrix-Vector Product[b]	214053	463590	808206
		Inner Product (enc)	11218	13877	16733
		Inner Product (dec)	24722	34167	43619

[a] Measurement excluding the hashing.
[b] Measurement including the hashing.

5.3 Performance of Schemes

Per Table 4, we achieve speedups of 3.3%–4.2%, 3.1%–3.6%, and 5.1%–5.2% for the key generation, encapsulation, and decapsulation our speed optimized variant. As to be expected due to the caching of intermediate values for speed optimizations, our speed implementation has a higher stack usage. Our stack implementations use essentially the same stack as previous work.

Table 5 contains the results for Dilithium. We achieve consistent speedups for all parameter sets. The absolute savings due to our optimizations are clearly seen, particularly in signing. The speedup for signing ranges from 1.5% to 5.6%. In

Table 4. Cycle counts and stack usage for Kyber for the key generation, encapsulation, and decapsulation. Cycle counts are averaged over 100 executions.

implementation	variant		Kyber-512		Kyber-768		Kyber-1024	
			cc	stack [B]	cc	stack [B]	cc	stack [B]
pqm4, [ABCG20]		K	458k	2 220	745k	3 100	1 188k	3 612
		E	553k	2 308	899k	2 780		3 292	3 292
		D	513k	2 324	839k	2 804	1 294k	3 324
This work	speed	K	443k	4 272	718k	5 312	1 138k	6 336
		E	536k	5 376	870k	6 416	7 432	7 432
		D	487k	5 384	796k	6 432	1 227k	7 448
	stack	K	444k	2 220	724k	2 736	1 149k	3 256
		E	540k	2 308	879k	2 808	3 328	3 328
		D	492k	2 324	807k	2 824	1 246k	3 352

relative terms, the impact of our optimizations on the full Kyber and Dilithium seem relatively small compared to the speedups we gain for the polynomial arithmetic. This is due to dominance of the hashing operations as thoroughly analyzed in previous work [KRSS19].

Table 5. Cycle counts and stack usage for Dilithium. K, S, and V correspond to the key generation, signature generation, and signature verification. Cycle counts are averaged over 10000 executions.

implementation	variant		Dilithium2		Dilithium3		Dilithium5	
			cc	stack [B]	cc	stack [B]	cc	stack [B]
pqm4, [GKS20]		K	1 602k	38k	2 835k	61k	4 836k	98k
		S	4 336k	49k	6 721k	74k	9 037k	115k
		V	1 579k	36k	2 700k	58k	4 718k	93k
This work	speed	K	1 596k	8 508	2 827k	9 540	4 829k	11 696
		S	4 093k	49k	6 623k	69k	8 803k	116k
		V	1 572k	36k	2 692k	58k	4 707k	93k

Acknowledgments. This work has been supported by the European Commission through the ERC Starting Grant 805031 (EPOQUE), the Sinica Investigator Award AS-IA-109-M01, and the Taiwan Ministry of Science and Technology Grant 109-2221-E-001-009-MY3. We thank Bo-Yin Yang for sharing the idea of 16-bit Barrett reductions.

References

[AB74] Agarwal, R.C., Burrus, C.S.: Fast convolution using Fermat number transforms with applications to digital filtering. IEEE Trans. Acoust. Speech Signal Process. **22**(2), 87–97 (1974)

[AB75] Agarwal, R.C., Burrus, C.S.: Number theoretic transforms to implement fast digital convolution. Proc. IEEE **63**(4), 550–560 (1975)

[ABC+20] Albrecht, M.R., et al.: Classic McEliece. Submission to the NIST Post-Quantum Cryptography Standardization Project Nat (2020). https://classic.mceliece.org/

[ABCG20] Alkim, E., Bilgin, Y.A., Cenk, M., Gérard, F.: Cortex-M4 optimizations for R, MLWE schemes. IACR Trans. Cryptogr. Hardw. Embed. Syst. **2020**(3), 336–357 (2020)

[ABD+20] Avanzi, R., et al.: CRYSTALS-Kyber: algorithm specifications and supporting documentation (version 3.0). Submission to round 3 of the NIST post-quantum project Nat, October 2020

[ACC+20] Alkim, E., et al.: Polynomial multiplication in NTRU prime: comparison of optimization strategies on cortex-M4. IACR Trans. Cryptogr. Hardw. Embed. Syst. **2021**(1), 217–238 (2020)

[ACC+21] Abdulrahman, A., Chen, J.P., Chen, Y.J., Hwang, V., Kannwischer, M.J., Yang, B.Y.: Multi-moduli NTTs for saber on Cortex-M3 and Cortex-M4. Cryptology ePrint Archive, Report 2021/995 (2021). https://ia.cr/2021/995

[ARM11] ARM: Cortex-M4 Devices Generic User Guide. ARM, August 2011

[Bar87] Barrett, P.: Implementing the Rivest Shamir and Adleman public key encryption algorithm on a standard digital signal processor. In: Odlyzko, A.M. (ed.) CRYPTO 1986. LNCS, vol. 263, pp. 311–323. Springer, Heidelberg (1987). https://doi.org/10.1007/3-540-47721-7_24

[BDK+20] Bai, S., et al.: CRYSTALS-dilithium: algorithm specifications and supporting documentation (version 3.0). Submission to round 3 of the NIST post-quantum project Nat, October 2020

[BDL+11] Bernstein, D.J., Duif, N., Lange, T., Schwabe, P., Yang, B.-Y.: High-speed high-security signatures. In: Preneel, B., Takagi, T. (eds.) CHES 2011. LNCS, vol. 6917, pp. 124–142. Springer, Heidelberg (2011). https://doi.org/10.1007/978-3-642-23951-9_9

[Ber01] Bernstein, D.J.: Multidigit multiplication for mathematicians (2001)

[BHK+21] Becker, H., Hwang, V., Kannwischer, M.J., Yang, B.Y., Yang, S.Y.: Neon NTT: faster dilithium, Kyber, and saber on Cortex-A72 and Apple M1. Cryptology ePrint Archive, Report 2021/986 (2021). https://ia.cr/2021/986

[BKS19] Botros, L., Kannwischer, M.J., Schwabe, P.: Memory-efficient high-speed implementation of Kyber on Cortex-M4. In: Buchmann, J., Nitaj, A., Rachidi, T. (eds.) AFRICACRYPT 2019. LNCS, vol. 11627, pp. 209–228. Springer, Cham (2019). https://doi.org/10.1007/978-3-030-23696-0_11

[CDH+20] Chen, C., et al.: NTRU. Submission to the NIST Post-Quantum Cryptography Standardization Project Nat (2020). https://ntru.org/

[CDK+20] Chen, M., et al.: Rainbow. Submission to round 3 of the NIST post-quantum project Nat (2020)

[CHK+21] Chung, C.M.M., et al.: NTT multiplication for NTT-unfriendly rings: new speed records for Saber and NTRU on Cortex-M4 and AVX2. IACR Trans. Cryptogr. Hardw. Embed. Syst. **2021**(2), 159–188 (2021)

[CT65] Cooley, J.W., Tukey, J.W.: An algorithm for the machine calculation of complex Fourier series. Math. Comput. **19**(90), 297–301 (1965)

[DKL+18] Ducas, L., et al.: CRYSTALS-dilithium: a lattice-based digital signature scheme. IACR Trans. Cryptogr. Hardw. Embed. Syst. **2018**(1), 238–268 (2018)

[DKRV20] D'Anvers, J.P., Karmakar, A., Roy, S.S., Vercauteren, F.: SABER. Submission to round 3 of the NIST post-quantum project Nat (2020)

[FHK+20] Fouque, P.A., et al.: FALCON. Submission to round 3 of the NIST postquantum project Nat (2020). https://falcon-sign.info/

[FO99] Fujisaki, E., Okamoto, T.: Secure integration of asymmetric and symmetric encryption schemes. In: Wiener, M. (ed.) CRYPTO 1999. LNCS, vol. 1666, pp. 537–554. Springer, Heidelberg (1999). https://doi.org/10.1007/3-540-48405-1_34

[Gau66] Gauss, C.F.: Theoria Interpolationis Methodo Nova Tractata. Nachlass **3**, 265–330 (1866)

[GKOS18] Güneysu, T., Krausz, M., Oder, T., Speith, J.: Evaluation of lattice-based signature schemes in embedded systems. In: 2018 25th IEEE International Conference on Electronics, Circuits and Systems (ICECS), pp. 385–388 (2018)

[GKS20] Greconici, D.O.C., Kannwischer, M.J., Sprenkels, A.: Compact dilithium implementations on Cortex-M3 and Cortex-M4. IACR Trans. Cryptogr. Hardw. Embed. Syst. **2021**(1), 1–24 (2020)

[GOPS13] Güneysu, T., Oder, T., Pöppelmann, T., Schwabe, P.: Software speed records for lattice-based signatures. In: Gaborit, P. (ed.) PQCrypto 2013. LNCS, vol. 7932, pp. 67–82. Springer, Heidelberg (2013). https://doi.org/10.1007/978-3-642-38616-9_5

[KMSRV18] Karmakar, A., Mera, J., Roy, S.S., Verbauwhede, I.: Saber on ARM: CCA-secure module lattice-based key encapsulation on ARM. IACR Trans. Cryptogr. Hardw. Embed. Syst. **2018**(3), 243–266 (2018)

[KRSS19] Kannwischer, M.J., Rijneveld, J., Schwabe, P., Stoffelen, K.: pqm4: testing and benchmarking NIST PQC on ARM Cortex-M4. In: Second NIST PQC Standardization Conference (2019)

[LMPR08] Lyubashevsky, V., Micciancio, D., Peikert, C., Rosen, A.: SWIFFT: a modest proposal for FFT hashing. In: Nyberg, K. (ed.) FSE 2008. LNCS, vol. 5086, pp. 54–72. Springer, Heidelberg (2008). https://doi.org/10.1007/978-3-540-71039-4_4

[LS19] Lyubashevsky, V., Seiler, G.: NTTRU: truly fast NTRU using NTT. IACR Trans. Cryptogr. Hardw. Embed. Syst. **2019**(3), 180–201 (2019)

[Lyu09] Lyubashevsky, V.: Fiat-Shamir with aborts: applications to lattice and factoring-based signatures. In: Matsui, M. (ed.) ASIACRYPT 2009. LNCS, vol. 5912, pp. 598–616. Springer, Heidelberg (2009). https://doi.org/10.1007/978-3-642-10366-7_35

[Nat] National Institute of Standards and Technology: Post-Quantum Cryptography Standardization Project. Accessed 04 Apr 2021

[Sei18] Seiler, G.: Faster AVX2 optimized NTT multiplication for Ring-LWE lattice cryptography. Report 2018/039 (2018)

[Sho94] Shor, P.W.: Algorithms for quantum computation: discrete logarithms and factoring. In: FOCS 1994, pp. 124–134. IEEE (1994)

[SS71] Schönhage, A., Strassen, V.: Schnelle Multiplikation großer Zahlen. Computing **7**(3–4), 281–292 (1971)

Quantum-Resistant Software Update Security on Low-Power Networked Embedded Devices

Gustavo Banegas[1]([✉]), Koen Zandberg[2], Emmanuel Baccelli[2,3], Adrian Herrmann[3], and Benjamin Smith[1]

[1] Inria and Laboratoire d'Informatique de l'École Polytechnique,
Institut Polytechnique de Paris, Palaiseau, France
`gustavo@cryptme.in, smith@lix.polytechnique.fr`
[2] Inria Saclay, Palaiseau, France
{`koen.zandberg,emmanuel.baccelli`}`@inria.fr`
[3] Freie Universität Berlin, Berlin, Germany
`adrian.herrmann@fu-berlin.de`

Abstract. As the Internet of Things (IoT) rolls out today to devices whose lifetime may well exceed a decade, conservative threat models should consider adversaries with access to quantum computing power. The IETF-specified SUIT standard defines a security architecture for IoT software updates, standardizing metadata and cryptographic tools— digital signatures and hash functions—to guarantee the update legitimacy. SUIT performance has been evaluated in the pre-quantum context, but not yet in a post-quantum context. Taking the open-source implementation of SUIT available in RIOT as a case study, we survey post-quantum considerations, and quantum-resistant digital signatures in particular, focusing on low-power, microcontroller-based IoT devices with stringent memory, CPU, and energy consumption constraints. We benchmark a range of pre- and post-quantum signature schemes on a range of IoT hardware including ARM Cortex-M, RISC-V, and Espressif (ESP32), which form the bulk of modern 32-bit microcontroller architectures. Interpreting our benchmarks in the context of SUIT, we estimate the real-world impact of transition from pre- to post-quantum signatures.

Keywords: Post-quantum · Security · IoT · Microcontroller · Embedded Systems

1 Introduction

Decades of experience with the Internet and networked software has shown that *you can't secure what you can't update*. Meanwhile, recent technological and societal trends have fuelled the massive deployment of cyberphysical systems; these

G. Banegas and K. Zandberg—Equally contributed to this work.
This work was funded by the European Commission through H2020 SPARTA, https://www.sparta.eu/.

© Springer Nature Switzerland AG 2022
G. Ateniese and D. Venturi (Eds.): ACNS 2022, LNCS 13269, pp. 872–891, 2022.
https://doi.org/10.1007/978-3-031-09234-3_43

systems are increasingly pervasive, and we are increasingly dependent on their functionalities. A so-called Internet of Things (IoT) emerges, weaving together an extremely wide variety of machines (embedded software and hardware) which are required to cooperate via the network, at large scale.

Unpatched devices—or worse, unpatchable devices—quickly become liabilities. Exploits weaponizing compromised IoT devices are demonstrated time and again, sometimes spectacularly as with botnets such as Mirai [7]. However, the cure can become a disease: software updates are themselves an attack vector. Legitimate software updates laced with malware can compromise the updated device [46]. Once IoT devices are deployed, up and running, it thus becomes crucial to understand how, and when, software embedded in IoT devices is updated; how software updates are secured; and what level of security is provided.

In this paper, we study the impact of the pre- to post-quantum transition on IoT software updates, assuming that we want to maintain 128-bit conventional security (matching current internet security standards) while reaching NIST Level 1 post-quantum security. We aim to answer the following questions:

- *How do the practical costs of pre- and post-quantum security compare?*
- *What is the footprint of post-quantum security, relative to typical low-power operating system footprints?*
- *What are the potential alternatives for post-quantum signature schemes to secure IoT software updates, and which hash functions should be used?*

1.1 Low-Power IoT and Post-quantum Cryptography

Low-Power IoT Characteristics. One prominent and highly challenging component of IoT deployments consists in integrating low-power, resource-constrained IoT devices into the distributed system. These devices are typically based on low-cost microcontrollers (e.g., ARM Cortex M, RISC-V, ESP), interconnected via low-power radio or wired communication. An estimated 250 billion microcontrollers are in use today around the globe [31]. Compared to microprocessor-based devices, microcontrollers aim for a different trade-off: They offer much smaller capacity in computing, networking, memory [17], in order to achieve radically lower energy consumption and a tiny price tag (¡$1 unit price). It is not uncommon to have a total memory budget of 64 KB of RAM and 500 KB of ROM (flash) for the whole embedded system software—including drivers, crypto libraries, OS kernel, network stack and application logic. Nonetheless, the functionalities and services provided by constrained microcontroller-based devices are as crucial as those of less constrained elements in the cyberphysical system.

Post-quantum Cryptography. Post-quantum cryptosystems are designed to run on contemporary hardware, yet resist adversaries equipped with both classical and quantum computers. Many signature schemes claim post-quantum security, some old and some new, but until now none has seen wide deployment. Recent research in post-quantum cryptography has revolved around the National Institute of Standards and Technology (NIST) Post-Quantum Cryptography project [47], which will select a limited number of candidate schemes for standardization. This process is currently in its third round; draft standards are expected by 2024.

Post-quantum Security for Low-Power IoT. Let's get back to the motto *you can't secure what you can't update (securely).* In our quest for post-quantum security, the first priority is to guarantee the legitimacy of software updates received via the network on low-power IoT devices. The crucial cryptographic tool here is a digital signature. Open standards targeting IoT security (such as the IETF [52]) specify a variety of signature schemes to secure software updates on low-power devices, including one scheme (LMS [41]) that offers quantum resistance.

Implementation Approaches. Cryptographic implementations are often developed to tackle specific problems, such as speed or size. Most implementations take advantage of special instructions or hardware, but this narrows their applicability to specific architectures, which does not fully reflect the reality of IoT. Usually, operating systems (OS) must support more than one architecture.

Typically, new cryptographic algorithm implementations are demonstrated as stand-alone applications—a key first step in proving feasibility. But in practice, the OS does not have only the cryptography package: it has other modules, a network stack, and the kernel.

Focusing on portability and wide deployment, our experimental work did not use any tuned assembly, or platform-specific instructions: we only modified the implementations to fit real-life conditions, such as those imposed by RIOT for our use-case (for example: not dedicating the entire stack to crypto).

1.2 Contributions and Outline

In this paper, we:

- review the SUIT specification for secure software updates on low-power IoT devices, using its open-source implementation in the RIOT operating system as a case study;
- show how crypto primitives including digital signatures and hash functions are used in compliance with SUIT;
- analyze post-quantum considerations for SUIT-compliant hash functions, which we benchmark on low-power 32-bit microcontrollers;
- survey post-quantum signature schemes, and derive a selection of schemes most applicable for the secure IoT software update use case;
- benchmark signatures on heterogeneous low-power IoT hardware based on popular 32-bit microcontrollers (ARM Cortex-M, RISC-V and ESP32);
- compare the performance of post-quantum signature schemes (LMS, Falcon, and Dilithium) against typical pre-quantum schemes (Ed25519 and secp256); and
- conclude on the cost of post-quantum security, and outline perspectives for low-power IoT.

We begin with a survey of related work in Sect. 2. In Sect. 3, we set out our case study: we describe SUIT software updates, categorise typical software update types, detail pre-quantum cryptographic considerations and begin to identify the main issues for the transition to post-quantum cryptography. We focus on post-quantum signature schemes in Sect. 4, explaining our choice of candidate schemes for benchmarking. Our experimental results appear in Sect. 5; we interpret their impact in the context of SUIT software updates in Sect. 6, before concluding in Sect. 7.

2   Related Work

The performance of pre-quantum digital signature schemes in the context of secure software updates on various Cortex-M microcontrollers is evaluated in [55]. Various NIST candidate post-quantum schemes are compared as component algorithms in TLS 1.3 in [51], analyzing performance, security, and key and signature sizes, as well as the impact of post-quantum authentication on TLS 1.3 handshakes in realistic network conditions, while [38] shows a real life experiment with clients using two post-quantum schemes: an isogeny-based algorithm (SIKE) and a lattice-based algorithm (HRSS). More recently, another experiment with different schemes was conducted by Cloudflare [20,49].

For pure post-quantum cryptographic implementation work targeting microcontrollers, [18] evaluates the performance of stateful LMS on Cortex-M4 microcontrollers, while pqm4 [35] aims to implement and benchmark NIST candidate schemes on Cortex-M4, with M4 assembly subroutines plugged into some of the PQClean implementations. (Note that among the NIST candidate signature schemes, PQClean implements only Dilithium, Falcon, Rainbow, and SPHINCS+; of these, pqm4 implements only Dilithium and Falcon.) Software verifying SPHINCS, RainbowI, GEMSS, Dilithium2, and Falcon-512 signatures in Cortex-M3 using less than 8 KB of RAM is presented in [28].

Many post-quantum signature schemes use standard SHA3 hashing under the hood. SHA3 performance in hardware (FGPA) has been studied [29,34,36], but surprisingly few studies focus on SHA3 performance in software on low-power microcontrollers. Some prior work exists: [11] and [37] focus on 8-bit microcontrollers, while [30] compares the performance of Keccak variants on 32-bit ARM Cortex-M microcontrollers.

3   Case Study: Low-Power Software Updates with SUIT

The IETF's Software Updates for Internet of Things (SUIT) specifications [43, 44] define a security architecture, standard metadata and cryptographic schemes able to secure IoT software updates, applicable on microcontroller-based devices. An open-source implementation of the SUIT workflow is available in RIOT [54], a common operating system for low-power IoT devices [10] which we use as base for our case study.

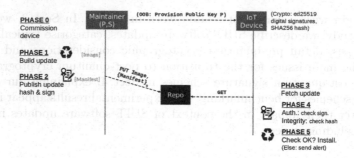

Fig. 1. SUIT secure software update workflow.

3.1 SUIT Workflow

Figure 1 shows the SUIT workflow. In the preliminary *Phase 0*, the authorized maintainer flashes the IoT device with commissioning material: the bootloader, initial image, and authorized crypto material. Once the IoT device is commissioned, up and running, we iterate a cycle of Phases 1–5, whereby the authorized maintainer can build a new image (*Phase 1*), hash and sign the corresponding standard metadata (the so-called SUIT manifest, *Phase 2*) and transfer to the device over the network via a repository (e.g. a CoAP resource directory). The IoT device fetches the update and SUIT manifest from the repository (*Phase 3*), and verifies the signature (*Phase 4*). Upon successful verification, the new software is installed and booted (*Phase 5*); otherwise, the update is dropped.

The cryptographic tools needed for software updates in general, and SUIT in particular, are a digital signature scheme and a hash function. The digital signature authenticates (a hash of) the software update binary.

We distinguish four broad categories for low-power IoT software updates, defining the following four prototypical use cases:

- **U1**: Software module update (≈ 5 KB)
- **U2**: Small firmware update without crypto libraries (≈ 50 KB)
- **U3**: Small firmware update including crypto libraries (≈ 50 KB)
- **U4**: Large firmware update (≈ 250 KB)

We will see that the costs and recommendations for post-quantum SUIT are different for each of these typical updates.

3.2 Security Features of SUIT

The metadata and the cryptographic primitives specified by SUIT can mitigate attacks exploiting software updates [42]. To give three simple examples:

- *Tampered/Unauthorized Firmware Update Attacks:* Adversaries may try to update the IoT device with a modified, intentionally flawed firmware image. To counter this threat, SUIT specifies the use of digital signatures on a hash of the image binary and the metadata, to ensure the integrity of both.

- *Firmware Update Replay Attacks:* Adversaries may replay a valid, but old (known-to-be-flawed) update. To mitigate this threat, SUIT metadata includes a sequence number that is increased with each new firmware update.
- *Firmware Update Mismatch Attacks:* Adversaries may send an authentic update to an incompatible device. To counter this, SUIT specifies the inclusion of device-specific conditions, to be verified before installing a firmware image.

3.3   Hash Functions with SUIT

The metadata of the update (the SUIT Manifest [43]) includes a cryptographic hash of the software update binary. The SUIT standard specification [43] allows the use of SHA-2 or SHA-3, with 224-, 256-, 384-, or 512-bit output.

Post-quantum Considerations. There are few quantum attacks against SHA-2 and SHA-3 in the literature. Grover's algorithm may be parallelized to find hash preimages [12]; this attack applies to both Merkle–Damgård hashes (e.g. SHA-2) and Sponge-based hashes (e.g. SHA-3). For collision resistance, the state-of-the-art in quantum collision search does not drastically reduce the complexity with respect to classical algorithms [21]. On the other hand, classical attacks for SHA-2 might become a reality, as shown in [25].

Low-Power IoT Considerations. Low-power systems must run hash functions quickly, using as little power as possible; minimal memory (RAM and flash) usage is also desirable. In this context, since we aim for 128-bit security, the two functions we should consider for SUIT are SHA-256 and SHA3-256.

Table 1 compares the memory usage and speed of three hash function implementations on an ARM Cortex M4 microcontroller: RIOT's default implementation of SHA-256, a compact implementation of SHA3-256 optimized to minimize flash memory, and an implementation of SHA3-256 optimized for speed on Cortex M4 ARMv7M architectures. Stack is roughly equivalent across the different implementations, but speed and flash vary widely: SHA3-256 can offer slightly faster execution than SHA-256, but at the price of a 10× larger flash footprint. For a flash footprint similar to SHA-256, the comparative speed of SHA3-256 diminishes drastically for larger inputs. For more detailed analysis of different Keccak variants on microcontrollers, see [30].

Table 1. SHA2 and SHA3 performance on an ARM Cortex-M4 microcontroller.

Hash function	Flash (B)	Stack (B)	Time (KTicks) to hash			
			64B	100B	1024B	10240B
SHA-256 (RIOT OS)	1008	384	277	278	1943	17933
SHA3-256 Compact	1692	404	1336	1342	10402	98448
SHA3-256 fast-ARMv7M	11548	284	223	228	1672	15732

Conclusions. Based on our analysis, there are no *direct* post-quantum aspects to consider here. Rather, the choice hash function should be driven by low-power criteria, and by other *indirect* post-quantum aspects detailed below. Recall the four prototypical use cases from Sect. 3.1. In **U1** and **U2**, the updated software does not include the hash function implementation (the cryptographic tools are external, e.g., in a bootloader). In such cases, the flash memory overhead for the hash function is of no concern, and SHA3-256 (optimized for speed) is the best choice. In **U3** and **U4**, however, the update includes the cryptographic tools and the hash function code; thus, a tradeoff appears. For small firmware updates as in **U3**, a 10 KB flash overhead represents a significant 25% bump in what needs to be stored on the device and transmitted over the network. As updates are infrequent, execution speed may be considered less of a priority, and thus both SHA-256 and flash-optimized SHA3-256 are valid options. For larger updates as in **U4**, the storage and transfer overhead is negligible, so speed-optimized SHA3-256 is the best option again.

Let us now consider a complementary perspective: most post-quantum signature scheme proposals use SHA-3 in their constructions. Indeed, candidates for the upcoming NIST post-quantum signature standard are required to be SHA-3/SHAKE compatible, because that is the current US standard. Since space for code on IoT devices is very limited, factorization is typically desirable: using a single hash function for both hashing and signing reduces the flash footprint.

For these reasons, SHA3-256 is the primary choice in our case-study.

3.4 Digital Signatures with SUIT

The SUIT architecture relies on the software update distributor (the authorized maintainer in Fig. 1) issuing a long-term public-private key pair used to generate and verify digital signatures on IoT software updates. The public key is pre-installed on the IoT device(s) to be updated during commissioning (*Phase 0*).

Digital signature use in SUIT is specified in the COSE standard [48], which defines how to sign and encrypt compact (CBOR) binary serialized objects. For the 128-bit classical security level, COSE specifies the elliptic-curve signature schemes Ed25519 and ECDSA on NIST P-256. These schemes offer very small public (and private) keys at 32B each, and 64B signatures.

To give some concrete perspective, Table 2 shows the memory footprint of SUIT and related software components using Ed25519, compared to the whole software embedded on the IoT device. This measurement uses the open-source RIOT implementation on the Nordic nRF52840 Development Kit, a popular low-power IoT board based on an ARM Cortex-M4 microcontroller. The flash memory footprint of this firmware is 52.5 KB; the RAM (stack) usage is 16.3 KB.

In this typical pre-quantum configuration, the crypto represents a small part of the flash footprint: under 15% of a ≈50 KB total. The elliptic-curve signature adds 15% to the size of the SUIT manifest metadata and less than 0.1% to the data that must be transferred over the network, counting the manifest and the firmware binary as depicted in Table 2.

Table 2. Network transfer cost and decomposition of SUIT firmware update (for nRF52840 Dev Kit) using minimal metadata with Ed25519+SHA-256.

	SUIT		OS firmware				
	Metadata	Signature	**Total**	Crypto	Kernel Modules	Network Modules	OTA
Size (B)	419	64	52485	7161	17039	20113	8172

Post-quantum Considerations. Elliptic-curve schemes are advantageous because they provide high security guarantees even though keys and signatures are very small. However, the security of elliptic-curve signatures is guaranteed by the hardness of the elliptic-curve Discrete Logarithm Problem, which can be solved efficiently on large quantum computers using Shor's algorithm [13,32,50].

It is important to note that a breakthrough in quantum computing at a time T will not affect the security of elliptic-curve signatures generated before T, but it would certainly destroy the security of any elliptic-curve signatures generated after T. In our use case, the distributor's key pair has a very long planned lifetime, possibly equal to that of the devices to be updated; securely updating the key itself will be impossible, or at least undesirable. We therefore need to build-in resistance to the quantum threat in anticipation of such a development.

Low-Power IoT Considerations. The range of post-quantum signature schemes considered as potential replacements for elliptic-curve signatures is wide and diverse, and the idiosyncrasies that distinguish the various schemes are exaggerated by the constraints of low-power IoT devices. However, all of these schemes have public key and signature sizes that are one or two orders of magnitude larger than the elliptic-curve equivalents. Post-quantum signatures are therefore far from drop-in replacements; they represent a significant research challenge for microcontroller and IoT implementations.

Nevertheless, the IETF recently began standardizing alternative signature schemes with COSE/SUIT for post-quantum security, such as LMS [41]. In the next sections, we survey alternative quantum-resistant schemes, comparing their performance against state-of-the-art pre-quantum schemes in SUIT.

4   Post-quantum Digital Signatures

The signature schemes that we consider target at least NIST Level 1 for *post-quantum security*. This is the basic security level proposed by NIST as part of its Post-Quantum Cryptography (PQC) Standardization Project [47]. Level 1 security includes both 128 bits of classical security, and an equivalent level of security with respect to some model of quantum computation. That is, an adversary should require on the order of 2^{128} operations to gain any non-negligible advantage when attacking the scheme, even if this adversary benefits from quantum computing power. The 128-bit security level is now standard in mainstream internet applications requiring long-term security.

4.1   Post-quantum Signature Paradigms

We can classify the post-quantum signatures into the underlying hard problems that guarantee their security:

Hash-Based Signatures. Hash-based signatures are among the oldest digital signature schemes. Their security is based on the difficulty of inverting cryptographic hash functions. The security assumptions have been well studied, which gives an academic maturity to the problem. Hash-based signatures tend to offer very fast verification, though this comes at the cost of very large signatures.

Lattice-Based Signatures. These schemes are based on hard problems in Euclidean lattices, and related problems like Learning With Errors (LWE). These schemes offer fast signing and verification, but have relatively large signatures.

Multivariate Signatures. The security of "multivariate" schemes is based on the difficulty of solving certain low-degree polynomial systems in many variables. A recent analysis in [16] has brought their security levels into question.

Isogeny-Based Signatures. Isogeny-based cryptosystems are based on the difficulty of computing unknown isogenies between elliptic curves. Recent isogeny-based signature schemes such as SQISign [26] inherit small parameter sizes from conventional elliptic-curve cryptography (ECC), making them interesting for microcontroller applications, but they also inherit and increase ECC's burden of heavy algebraic calculations, which makes for very slow runtimes. These signature schemes have not yet been subjected to extensive security analysis.

Code-Based Signatures. Code-based cryptosystems are based on the difficulty of hard problems from the theory of error-correcting codes. The McEliece key exchange scheme [40] is among the oldest of all public-key cryptosystems. Code-based signatures, on the other hand, are much less well-established.

Zero-Knowledge-Based Signatures. A new category of post-quantum signatures uses Zero-Knowledge (ZK) techniques, combining algorithms from symmetric cryptography with a technique known as Multi-Party Computation In The Head.

Summary. Table 3 compares signature and key sizes, and maturity of security analysis of various post-quantum signature scheme proposals, summarizing the "pros" and "cons" of each paradigm according to our requirements.

4.2   Selection of Candidates

When choosing candidate signature schemes, we must consider key and signature sizes, runtime performance, and maturity with respect to security analysis. While the relatively compact parameters of some isogeny- and code-based signature schemes may make them interesting for future work targeting microcontrollers,

Table 3. Overview of post-quantum signature candidates. "Security analysis" reflects the maturity of analysis of the scheme: here we consider the age of the scheme, recent attacks, and how well-studied the underlying hard problem is.

Paradigm	Scheme	Security Analysis	Sizes (B)		
			Signature	Public Key	Private Key
Hash-based	LMS [41]	mature	4756	60	64
	SPHINCS+-128f [8]	mature	17088	32	64
Lattice-based	Dilithium [9]	less mature	2528	1312	2420
	Falcon [27]	less mature	1281	897	666
MQ-based	RainbowI [23]	not mature	66	157800	101200
	GeMSS [19]	not mature	417416	14520	48
Isogeny-based	SQISign [26]	not mature	204	64	16
Code-based	WAVE [24]	not mature	1625	≈13000000	N/R
Zero-knowledge-based	Picnic3-L1 [22]	not mature	13802	34	17

at present these schemes are far from theoretical maturity. The true security level of the NIST multivariate and ZK-based candidates is a subject of current debate, though their extremely large keys and/or signatures would likely eliminate them from consideration for our applications in any case.

The NIST PQC project has dominated research in post-quantum cryptography in recent years. Its candidate cryptosystems are a natural first port of call for credible post-quantum signature algorithms, since they have had the benefit of concerted analysis from the cryptographic community—especially the Round 3 proposals, which are candidates for standardization in the coming years. However, these are not the only algorithms that we should consider. For example, among hash-based signature schemes, we might compare the older LMS scheme (which is not a NIST candidate) with the newer SPHINCS+ scheme (which is a NIST Round 3 alternate). LMS has smaller computational requirements, but the signer must maintain some state between signatures; SPHINCS+ is a heavier scheme, but it is stateless. Statelessness is an advantage for general applications. In our use case, however, statefulness is natural (it corresponds naturally to the version number on the software update), and easier to maintain—so the lighter LMS is a more natural choice.

Post-quantum Choices. For the reasons above, we chose to focus our efforts on three post-quantum signature algorithms: LMS, Dilithium, and Falcon, representing the hash-based and lattice-based categories. LMS has 60B public keys and 4756-byte signatures. Dilithium II, targeting NIST security level 2, has 1312B public keys and 2420B signatures. Falcon-512, targeting NIST security level 1, has 897B public keys and 666B signatures.

Pre-quantum Choices. To make a meaningful comparison with pre-quantum algorithms, we selected two elliptic-curve schemes: the Ed25519 [15,33] scheme, and the historic standard ECDSA based on the secp256 curve [45]. These schemes offer particularly small 32B public keys and 64B signatures.

5   Benchmarks

5.1   Hardware Testbed Setup

Our benchmarks were run on popular, commercial, off-the-shelf IoT hardware, representative of the landscape of modern 32-bit microcontroller architectures:

- **ARM Cortex-M4**: the **Nordic nRF52840 Development Kit** provides a typical ARM Cortex-M4 microcontroller running at 64 MHz, with 256 KB RAM, 1 MB flash, and a 2.4 GHz radio transceiver compatible with both IEEE 802.15.4 and Bluetooth Low-Energy.
- **Espressif ESP32**: the **WROOM-32 board** (ESP32 module with the ESP32-D0WDQ6 chip on board) provides two low-power Xtensa® 32-bit LX6 microprocessors with integrated Wi-Fi and Bluetooth, operating at 80 MHz, with 520 KB RAM, 448 KB ROM and 16 KB RTC SRAM.
- **RISC-V**: the **Sipeed Longan Nano GD32VF103CBT6** Development Board provides a RISC-V 32-bit core running at 72 MHz with 32 KB RAM and 128 KB flash.

IoT-Lab [6] provides this hardware for reproducibility on open access testbeds.

5.2   Software Setup

We used RIOT [5] as a base for our benchmarks.

Pre-quantum Implementations. We used three different libraries, all currently supported in RIOT.

Ed25519: For Ed25519, we used two libraries: **C25519** (provided in [1]) and **Monocypher** [53]. Both contain constant-time finite-field arithmetic based on public-domain implementations [14]. One difference between Monocypher and C25519 is that Monocypher uses precomputed tables to speed up the computation of elliptic curve points.

ECDSA: For ECDSA, we used Intel's **Tinycrypt** library [2], which is designed to provide cryptographic standards for constrained devices. ECDSA differs from Ed25519 both in some specific details of the signature algorithm and in using the NIST standard p256 curve instead of Curve25519.

Post-quantum Implementations. We re-used publicly available code after making some small modifications to fit the hardware requirements.

LMS: For LMS, we used the Cisco implementation [3], removing calls to `malloc` since it can lead to memory fragmentation [39], and in such low level can be dangerous and slow.[1] This change might lead to some small improvements in performance, since the kernel already knows the address at compile-time rather than only at runtime. For our benchmark, we used the smallest parameters proposed in [41, Section 5]: that is, SHA-2 with 256-bit output for the hash function (since we tried to keep the code as close as possible to [3]) with tree height 5, and 32 bytes associated with each node. For the LMOTS, we use 32 bytes and 4 bits of width for Winternitz coefficients. We remove the OpenSSL call from the original code and change for a implementation of SHA256 provided in their repository [3]. Furthermore, we are using HSS with 2 layers. These parameters satisfy the life cycle of updates: in particular, the key lifetime will never be surpassed by the amount of updates.

Dilithium: We prepared two Dilithium implementations based on PQClean [4].

- **Dynamic Dilithium** is the basic PQClean implementation. The first step in *signing* and *verifying* is to expand a random seed given in the public key into a large matrix (cf. [9, Sec. 3.1]).

- **Static Dilithium** modifies the PQClean implementation to precompute the matrix and store it in the flash memory. This makes signing and verification both faster, though it also requires more flash and reduces flexibility, since signatures can only be verified against the flashed key.

Falcon: We used the Falcon implementation provided by PQClean [4], without any significant structural modifications.

Parameter Sizes. Table 4 gives the sizes (in bytes) of the private key, public key, and signature for each of these schemes.

Table 4. Key and signature sizes for benchmarked signature schemes.

	Algorithm	Private Key (B)	Public Key (B)	Signature (B)
Pre-quantum	Ed25519	32	32	64
	ECDSA p256	32	32	64
Post-quantum	Falcon	1281	897	666
	Dilithium	2528	1312	2420
	LMS (RFC8554)	64	60	4756

5.3   Pre- and Post-quantum Signature Benchmarks

Tables 5, 6, and 7 present our benchmarking results on our three target architectures: Cortex-M, ESP32 and RISC-V. For each implementation we give the total

---

[1] More details about dynamic allocation in embedded devices are available from https://github.com/RIOT-OS/RIOT/blob/master/CODING_CONVENTIONS. md.

flash memory used by the library, and for the signing and verification operations we list the running time in milliseconds and in thousands of "ticks" (computed from the hardware clock and time spent), and the stack required.

We see that Monocypher's Ed25519 is the fastest for signing among all the candidates, on all three boards. (Since the RISC-V board has only 32 KB RAM, the Falcon and Dilithium signing algorithms could not be run there.) Falcon offers the fastest verification on all three boards, followed by Static Dilithium.

6   The Impact of Post-quantum in SUIT/COSE

6.1   The Cost of Post-quantum Security

How do post-quantum security costs compare to typical pre-quantum security costs? A toe-to-toe comparison between pre- and post-quantum signatures must consider public key and signature sizes, running time, and memory requirements.

Table 4 shows that post-quantum algorithms always have larger public key and signature sizes, generally by well over an order of magnitude. Compared with standard elliptic-curve signature schemes, Falcon's public keys are 28× larger and its signatures are 10.4× larger; Dilithium's public keys are 41× larger than elliptic-curve keys, and its signatures are 38× larger. LMS avoids this spectacular

Table 5. Signature benchmarks: ARM Cortex-M (nRF52840 Dev. Kit).

	Algorithm	Flash (B)	Sign			Verify		
			Time (ms)	(KiloTicks)	Stack (B)	Time (ms)	(KiloTicks)	Stack (B)
Pre-quantum	Ed25519 (C25519)	5106	845	54111	1180	1953	125012	1300
	Ed25519 (Monocypher)	13852	17	1136	1420	40	2599	1936
	ECDSA p256 (Tinycrypt)	6498	294	18871	1084	313	20037	1024
Post-quantum	Falcon	57613	1172	75020	42240	15	1004	4744
	Dilithium (Dynamic)	11664	465	29788	51762	53	3407	36058
	Dilithium (Static)	26672	135	8655	35240	23	1510	19504
	LMS (RFC8554)	12864	9224	590354	13212	123	7908	1580

Table 6. Signature benchmarks: Espressif ESP32 (WROOM-32 board).

	Algorithm	Flash (B)	Sign			Verify		
			Time (ms)	(KiloTicks)	Stack (B)	Time (ms)	(KiloTicks)	Stack (B)
Pre-quantum	Ed25519 (C25519)	5608	921	73690	1312	2165	173205	1440
	Ed25519 (Monocypher)	17238	21	1709	1536	60	4864	2160
	ECDSA p256 (Tinycrypt)	6869	333	26696	1296	374	29948	1216
Post-quantum	Falcon	60358	1172	93824	42504	16	1322	4920
	Dilithium (Dynamic)	12397	87	7036	51954	43	3508	36242
	Dilithium (Static)	27197	121	9694	35412	21	1706	19620
	LMS (RFC8554)	15177	7583	606674	13488	101	8141	1808

growth in public key sizes, with keys only 1.875× larger than elliptic-curve public keys; but its signatures are a massive 74.3× larger than elliptic-curve signatures.

Looking at running time, as we saw in Sect. 5, post-quantum signatures have their advantages and disadvantages. Signature verification is considerably faster across all the IoT devices that we tested. Signing is generally slower. A comparison of the signing algorithms in Table 5 shows that the fastest post-quantum algorithm runs in 135 ms, which is 7.94× slower than Ed25519 (Monocypher). But the tables are turned when we compare signature verification algorithms: The fastest pre-quantum algorithm runs in 40 ms, which is 2.65× slower than post-quantum Falcon. Efficient verification is a required and valuable feature (in all scenarios), but in this setting, it comes at the price of an increase in stack and flash memory.

Looking at memory requirements, we see that post-quantum flash requirements can grow to over 11× the smallest pre-quantum flash. Similarly, post-quantum algorithms impose a considerable increase in stack memory.

Table 7. Signature benchmarks: RISC-V (Sipeed Longan Nano board). *Falcon flash only contains the verification algorithm. Static Dilithium flash contains the verification algorithm and hard-coded public key.*

	Algorithm	Flash (B)	Sign		Verify	
			Time (ms)	Stack (KiloTicks) (B)	Time (ms)	Stack (KiloTicks) (B)
Pre-quantum	Ed25519 (C25519)	6024	956	68883 1312	2242	161475 1440
	Ed25519 (Monocypher)	17328	16	1194 1376	41	3013 1920
	ECDSA p256 (Tinycrypt)	7452	270	19489 1224	308	22192 1112
Post-quantum	Falcon	11122	—	— —	13	975 4756
	Dilithium (Dynamic)	—	—	— —	—	— —
	Dilithium (Static)	25148	—	— —	17	1237 19572
	LMS (RFC8554)	15889	9105	655614 13352	122	8808 1736

6.2   The Cost of Post-quantum SUIT/COSE

What is the footprint of quantum-resistant security, relative to typical low-power operating system footprints? As a concrete example: consider a firmware update for RIOT on the nRF52840dk. In the classification of Sect. 3.1, the update is

- type **U2**, where the update does *not* include the cryptographic libraries binary (i.e., these tools are external, e.g., in a bootloader), or
- type **U3**, where the update includes the cryptographic libraries binary.

We want to add quantum resistance to SUIT/COSE by changing the cryptographic algorithms from Ed25519 and SHA256 to Falcon, LMS, or Dilithium, and SHA3-256.

Impact on the SUIT Manifest. In practical terms, the size of the SUIT manifest increases according to the new signature size. In Sect. 2 we saw that the SUIT manifest with pre-quantum Ed25519 (or ECDSA) has total size $419+64 = 483B$. Moving to post-quantum signatures, this total becomes

- Falcon: $419 + 666 = 1085B$, a $\approx 2.24\times$ increase;
- Dilithium: $419 + 2420 = 2839B$, a $\approx 5.87\times$ increase; and
- LMS: $419 + 4756 = 5175B$, a $\approx 9.84\times$ increase.

Impact on SUIT Software Update Performance. Now consider the crucial aspect of network transfer costs, and the memory resources required to actually apply the firmware update on the IoT device. Table 8 uses our measurements to evaluate the relative cost of the entire SUIT software update process. We see that impact of switching to quantum-resistant security in SUIT varies widely in terms of network transfer costs, ranging from negligible increase ($\sim 1\%$) to major impact ($3\times$ more), depending on the software update use case.

6.3   Post-quantum Signatures for IoT

What are the potential alternatives for post-quantum digital signature schemes to secure IoT software updates? There are many possible deployments of IoT, and several possible scenarios for IoT software updates. It is safe to assume that the authorized maintainer, responsible for updating the firmware, has powerful hardware. Hence, the computational burden of signing is not the main concern here. On the other hand, a constrained device will be responsible for signature verification in Phases 3, 4, and 5 of the SUIT workflow in Fig. 1.

Table 8. Relative costs for SUIT with quantum resistance (ARM Cortex M4).

SUIT	Flash	Stack	Data Transfer	
			U2	U3
base w. Ed25519 / SHA256	52.4KB	16.3KB	47KB	53KB
with Falcon / SHA3-256	+120%	+18%	+1.1%	+120%
with LMS / SHA3-256	+34%	+1.2%	+9%	+43%
with Dilithium / SHA3-256	+30%	+210%	+4.3%	+34%

As we have seen above, the cryptography package does not run standalone in the board: it must coexist with several other modules (including kernel, network stack, and libraries), and the application itself.

One challenge that we faced in deploying the schemes was sharing stack memory (and SRAM memory). For example, on our RISC-V platform (recall Table 7) the total RAM memory budget available was 32 kB for the whole system—which is very small, but not an uncommon budget. We could not run Dilithium to sign or verify within these limits, because it consumed all of the stack. In fact, we needed to adapt stack use for all of the post-quantum algorithms we used.

Execution speed is another challenge. Slow signature verification may impact real-time applications if special care is not taken. Typically, on low-power IoT devices, there is no parallel computing. For instance, RIOT OS uses a preemptive multithreading paradigm, where a single thread is running at any given time. If signature verification takes a long time, running in a high-priority thread, then the system blocks on this task until completion. It is therefore necessary to carefully tune the priority of the crypto verification thread so as not to stop other functionally essential tasks, especially if signature verification is slow.

6.4   Real-World Usability of Post-quantum Signatures

Let us revisit the four prototypical software update categories from Sect. 3.1, and consider the choice of postquantum signatures for each.

In use cases **U1** (a small module update) and **U2** (small firmware update without crypto libraries), the package contains the software update and the signature. Hence, speed and signature size are more important than flash size. In these cases, **Falcon** has an advantage over LMS and Dilithium.

The use case **U3** (small firmware update with crypto libraries) is more complicated, with flash playing a much more crucial role. Since we must transfer the update with crypto over a low-power network, the package size has a higher impact on energy costs. As a point of reference, it takes 30–60 s to transfer 50 KB on a low-power IEEE802.15.4 radio link, depending on link quality and network load (assuming non-extreme cases). This is to compare with plus-or-minus 2 s of computation speed difference for signature verification among the candidate cryptosystems. In this case, as shown in Table 8, **LMS** presents the best tradeoff between flash size, network transfer costs, verification time, and stack size.

In use case **U4** (larger updates), the large network transfer costs overwhelm the other costs, reducing the comparative advantages of one post-quantum signature over another.

From the point of view of cryptographic maturity, LMS is the safest choice. As noted in Sect. 4.2, hash-based problems have received extensive cryptanalysis from the cryptographic community, while the security of structured lattice-based schemes like Falcon is less well-understood. Nevertheless, compared to the pre-quantum state of the art, LMS imposes a significant increase in signature size and running time, which has a major impact on SUIT performance. Thus, despite its relative lack of maturity, the performance characteristics of Falcon make it extremely tempting for applications with smaller updates.

Deployment of Post-quantum Security. On a positive note: even though it necessitates increased data transfer, flash, and stack, post-quantum security can be deployed on today's IoT hardware (i.e. tomorrow's legacy hardware). In a nutshell: we can upgrade to quantum-resistant software update security on heterogeneous legacy IoT hardware without vast changes in portable C code.

It is clear that we will need to pay a price in the transition of pre-quantum to post-quantum algorithms. However, operating systems (for low powered devices such as RIOT) can already offer the tools to verify quantum-resistant signatures.

7 Conclusion

We have made an experimental study of the transition from pre- to post-quantum cryptography applied to securing software updates on low-power IoT devices, taking an open-source implementation of the IETF standard SUIT as concrete case study. We compare the performance of standard pre-quantum and selected post-quantum candidates for the required cryptographic schemes (signatures and hashing), in the same environment (RIOT) on three low-power IoT platforms (ARM Cortex-M, RISC-V, and ESP32) representative of the current landscape of 32-bit microcontrollers. We show that upgrading from classical 128-bit security to NIST Level 1 post-quantum security is indeed achievable today on these platforms, and we derive recommendations based on our performance analysis. We also characterize the toll of the pre- to post-quantum transition on memory footprints and network transfer costs in the IoT software update process.

Future Work. The priority remains to stabilize the current versions of post-quantum signatures before pushing their implementations to common low-power embedded software platforms such as RIOT. Meanwhile, NIST has yet to determine the new post-quantum signature standard; should new candidates be included in a new call, more analysis will be necessary.

References

1. Curve25519 and Ed25519 for low-memory systems, October 2017. https://www.dlbeer.co.nz/oss/c25519.html
2. TinyCrypt Cryptographic Library, July 2018. https://github.com/01org/tinycrypt
3. LMS Hash-Based Signature Implementation (2021). https://github.com/cisco/hash-sigs/
4. PQClean (2021). https://github.com/PQClean/PQClean
5. RIOT Operating System (2021). http://www.riot-os.org
6. Adjih, C., et al.: FIT IoT-LAB: a large scale open experimental IoT testbed. In: 2015 IEEE 2nd World Forum on Internet of Things (WF-IoT), pp. 459–464 (2015)
7. Antonakakis, M., et al.: Understanding the Mirai Botnet. In: 26th USENIX Security Symposium (USENIX Security 17), Vancouver, BC, pp. 1093–1110. USENIX Association, August 2017
8. Aumasson, J.P., et al.: SPHINCS+ stateless hash-based signatures. https://sphincs.org/
9. Avanzi, R., et al.: CRYSTALS/Dilithium. https://pq-crystals.org/
10. Baccelli, E., et al.: RIOT: an open source operating system for low-end embedded devices in the IoT. IEEE Internet Things J. 5(6), 4428–4440 (2018)

11. Balasch, J., et al.: Compact implementation and performance evaluation of hash functions in ATtiny devices. In: Mangard, S. (ed.) CARDIS 2012. LNCS, vol. 7771, pp. 158–172. Springer, Heidelberg (2013). https://doi.org/10.1007/978-3-642-37288-9_11

12. Banegas, G., Bernstein, D.J.: Low-communication parallel quantum multi-target preimage search. In: Adams, C., Camenisch, J. (eds.) SAC 2017. LNCS, vol. 10719, pp. 325–335. Springer, Cham (2018). https://doi.org/10.1007/978-3-319-72565-9_16

13. Banegas, G., Bernstein, D.J., van Hoof, I., Lange, T.: Concrete quantum cryptanalysis of binary elliptic curves. IACR Trans. Cryptogr. Hardw. Embed. Syst. **2021**(1), 451–472 (2021)

14. Bernstein, D.J.: Curve25519: new Diffie-Hellman speed records. In: Yung, M., Dodis, Y., Kiayias, A., Malkin, T. (eds.) PKC 2006. LNCS, vol. 3958, pp. 207–228. Springer, Heidelberg (2006). https://doi.org/10.1007/11745853_14

15. Bernstein, D.J., Duif, N., Lange, T., Schwabe, P., Yang, B.-Y.: High-speed high-security signatures. J. Cryptogr. Eng. **2**, 77–89 (2012)

16. Beullens, W.: Improved cryptanalysis of UOV and rainbow. IACR Cryptol. ePrint Arch. **2020**, 1343 (2020)

17. Bormann, C., Keranen, A., Ersue, M.: RFC 7228: terminology for constrained node networks. IETF Request For Comments (2014)

18. Campos, F., Kohlstadt, T., Reith, S., Stöttinger, M.: LMS vs XMSS: comparison of stateful hash-based signature schemes on ARM Cortex-M4. In: Nitaj, A., Youssef, A. (eds.) AFRICACRYPT 2020. LNCS, vol. 12174, pp. 258–277. Springer, Cham (2020). https://doi.org/10.1007/978-3-030-51938-4_13

19. Casanova, A., Faugère, J.C., Macario-Rat, G., Patarin, J., Perret, L., Ryckeghem, J.: GeMSS: a GrEat multivariate short signature. https://www-polsys.lip6.fr/Links/NIST/GeMSS.html

20. Celi, S., Wiggers, T.: KEMTLS: post-quantum TLS without signatures, January 2020. https://blog.cloudflare.com/kemtls-post-quantum-tls-without-signatures/

21. Chailloux, A., Naya-Plasencia, M., Schrottenloher, A.: An efficient quantum collision search algorithm and implications on symmetric cryptography. In: Takagi, T., Peyrin, T. (eds.) ASIACRYPT 2017. LNCS, vol. 10625, pp. 211–240. Springer, Cham (2017). https://doi.org/10.1007/978-3-319-70697-9_8

22. Chase, M., et al.: Picnic: a family of post-quantum secure digital signature algorithms. https://eprint.iacr.org/2017/279

23. Chen, M.S., et al.: Rainbow signature. https://www.pqcrainbow.org/

24. Debris-Alazard, T., Sendrier, N., Tillich, J.-P.: Wave: a new family of trapdoor one-way preimage sampleable functions based on codes. In: Galbraith, S.D., Moriai, S. (eds.) ASIACRYPT 2019. LNCS, vol. 11921, pp. 21–51. Springer, Cham (2019). https://doi.org/10.1007/978-3-030-34578-5_2

25. Dobraunig, C., Eichlseder, M., Mendel, F.: Analysis of SHA-512/224 and SHA-512/256. In: Iwata, T., Cheon, J.H. (eds.) ASIACRYPT 2015. LNCS, vol. 9453, pp. 612–630. Springer, Heidelberg (2015). https://doi.org/10.1007/978-3-662-48800-3_25

26. De Feo, L., Kohel, D., Leroux, A., Petit, C., Wesolowski, B.: SQISign: compact post-quantum signatures from quaternions and isogenies. In: Moriai, S., Wang, H. (eds.) ASIACRYPT 2020. LNCS, vol. 12491, pp. 64–93. Springer, Cham (2020). https://doi.org/10.1007/978-3-030-64837-4_3

27. Fouque, P.A., et al.: Falcon: fast-Fourier lattice-based compact signatures over NTRU. https://falcon-sign.info

28. Gonzalez, R., et al.: Verifying post-quantum signatures in 8 kB of RAM. In: Cheon, J.H., Tillich, J.-P. (eds.) PQCrypto 2021 2021. LNCS, vol. 12841, pp. 215–233. Springer, Cham (2021). https://doi.org/10.1007/978-3-030-81293-5_12
29. Guo, X., Huang, S., Nazhandali, L., Schaumont, P.: Fair and comprehensive performance evaluation of 14 second round SHA-3 ASIC implementations. In: The Second SHA-3 Candidate Conference. Citeseer (2010)
30. Herrmann, A.: The challenge of security in IoT - a study of cryptographic sponge functions and an implementation for RIOT, vol. 3. https://github.com/emmanuelsearch/Keccak-Bachelor-Thesis/raw/main/thesis.pdf
31. Collins, H.L.: Why TinyML is a giant opportunity. https://venturebeat.com/2020/01/11/why-tinyml-is-a-giant-opportunity/
32. Häner, T., Jaques, S., Naehrig, M., Roetteler, M., Soeken, M.: Improved quantum circuits for elliptic curve discrete logarithms. In: Ding, J., Tillich, J.-P. (eds.) PQCrypto 2020. LNCS, vol. 12100, pp. 425–444. Springer, Cham (2020). https://doi.org/10.1007/978-3-030-44223-1_23
33. Josefsson, S., Liusvaara, I.: Edwards-Curve Digital Signature Algorithm (EdDSA). RFC 8032 (2017)
34. Jungk, B., Apfelbeck, J.: Area-efficient FPGA implementations of the SHA-3 finalists. In: 2011 International Conference on Reconfigurable Computing and FPGAs, pp. 235–241. IEEE (2011)
35. Kannwischer, M.J., Rijneveld, J., Schwabe, P., Stoffelen, K.: PQM4: post-quantum crypto library for the ARM Cortex-M4. https://github.com/mupq/pqm4
36. Kaps, J.P., et al.: Lightweight implementations of SHA-3 candidates on FPGAs. In: Bernstein, D.J., Chatterjee, S. (eds.) INDOCRYPT 2011. LNCS, vol. 7107, pp. 270–289. Springer, Heidelberg (2011). https://doi.org/10.1007/978-3-642-25578-6_20
37. Kim, Y.B., Choi, H., Seo, S.C.: Efficient implementation of SHA-3 hash function on 8-Bit AVR-based sensor nodes. In: Hong, D. (ed.) ICISC 2020. LNCS, vol. 12593, pp. 140–154. Springer, Cham (2021). https://doi.org/10.1007/978-3-030-68890-5_8
38. Kwiatkowski, K., Valenta, L.: The TLS post-quantum experiment, October 2019. https://blog.cloudflare.com/the-tls-post-quantum-experiment/
39. Labrosse, J.J.: Chapter 15 - real-time kernels. In: Ganssle, J. (ed.) The Firmware Handbook, Embedded Technology, pp. 211–229. Newnes, Burlington (2004)
40. McEliece, R.J.: A public-key cryptosystem based on algebraic coding theory. DSN Progress Report, vol. 42–44, pp. 114–116 (1978)
41. McGrew, D., Curcio, M., Fluhrer, S.: RFC 8554: Leighton-Micali hash-based signatures. IETF Request for Comments, April 2019
42. Moran, B., Tschofenig, H., Birkholz, H.: A manifest information model for firmware updates in IoT devices. Internet-Draft draft-ietf-suit-information-model-12, Internet Engineering Task Force, May 2021. Work in Progress
43. Moran, B., Tschofenig, H., Birkholz, H., Zandberg, K.: A CBOR-based serialization format for the software updates for Internet of Things (SUIT) Manifest. Internet-Draft draft-ietf-suit-manifest-12, Internet Engineering Task Force, February 2021. Work in Progress
44. Moran, B., Tschofenig, H., Brown, D., Meriac, M.: A firmware update architecture for Internet of Things. RFC 9019, April 2021
45. National Institute of Standards and Technology. FIPS186-4: Digital signature standard (DSS). https://doi.org/10.6028/NIST.FIPS.186-4
46. Newman, L.H.: Inside the unnerving supply chain attack that corrupted CCleaner. Wired (2018)

47. NIST: Post-Quantum Cryptography Project. https://csrc.nist.gov/projects/post-quantum-cryptography
48. Schaad, J.: CBOR Object Signing and Encryption (COSE). RFC 8152, July 2017
49. Schwabe, P., Stebila, D., Wiggers, T.: Post-quantum TLS without handshake signatures. In: Ligatti, J., Ou, X., Katz, J., Vigna, G. (eds.) CCS '20: 2020 ACM SIGSAC Conference on Computer and Communications Security, Virtual Event, USA, 9–13 November 2020, pp. 1461–1480. ACM (2020)
50. Shor, P.W.: Algorithms for quantum computation: discrete logarithms and factoring. In: 35th Annual Symposium on Foundations of Computer Science, Santa Fe, New Mexico, USA, 20–22 November 1994, pp. 124–134. IEEE Computer Society (1994)
51. Sikeridis, D., Kampanakis, P., Devetsikiotis, M.: Post-quantum authentication in TLS 1.3: a performance study. In: 27th Annual Network and Distributed System Security Symposium, NDSS 2020, San Diego, California, USA, 23–26 February 2020. The Internet Society (2020)
52. Tschofenig, H., Baccelli, E.: Cyberphysical security for the masses: a survey of the internet protocol suite for Internet of Things security. IEEE Secur. Privacy **17**(5), 47–57 (2019)
53. Vaillant, L.: Monocypher. https://monocypher.org/
54. Zandberg, K., Schleiser, K.: SUIT Reference Implementation. RIOT (2020). http://api.riot-os.org/group_sys_suit.html
55. Zandberg, K., Schleiser, K., Acosta, F., Tschofenig, H., Baccelli, E.: Secure firmware updates for constrained IoT devices using open standards: a reality check. IEEE Access **7**, 71907–71920 (2019)

Post-quantum ID-Based Ring Signatures from Symmetric-Key Primitives

Maxime Buser[✉], Joseph K. Liu, Ron Steinfeld, and Amin Sakzad

Faculty of Information Technology, Monash University, Melbourne, Australia
{maxime.buser,joseph.liu,ron.steinfeld,amin.sakzad}@monash.edu

Abstract. Ring signatures and ID-based cryptography are considered promising in terms of application. A ring signature authenticates messages while the author of the message remains anonymous. ID-based cryptographic primitives suppress the need for certificates in public key infrastructures (PKI). In this work, we propose a generic construction for post-quantum ID-based ring signatures (IDRS) based on symmetric-key primitives from which we derive the first two constructions of IDRS. The first construction named PicRS utilizes the Picnic digital signature to ensure its security while the second construction XRS is motivated by the stateful digital signature XMSS instead of Picnic, allowing a signature size reduction. Both constructions have a competitive signature size when compared with state-of-the-art lattice-based IDRS. XRS can achieve a competitive signature size of 889 KB for a ring of 4096 users while the fully stateless PicRS achieves a signature size of 1.900 MB for a ring of 4096 users. In contrast, the shortest lattice-based IDRS achieves a signature size of 335 MB for the same ring size.

Keywords: ID-based ring signature · Applied post-quantum cryptography · Symmetric-key primitives

1 Introduction

Ring signatures [28] are currently considered one of the most valuable cryptographic primitives to ensure privacy. They allow a member of a group (i.e. ring) to anonymously sign a message on behalf of a group in a spontaneous manner. This spontaneity allows signers to form a group of their own choice and to generate an anonymous signature. According to their great promise in providing authenticity and anonymity, ring signatures have attracted a lot of interest from the research community.

ID-based Ring Signature (IDRS): ID-based cryptography [29] was introduced in 1984 to erase the need for certificates in public key infrastructures (PKI). ID-based cryptography utilizes a public key which is the identity of the user, for example, an identity can be an email address or a name. In this framework, a trusted third party named the private key generator (PKG) is required. PKG

© Springer Nature Switzerland AG 2022
G. Ateniese and D. Venturi (Eds.): ACNS 2022, LNCS 13269, pp. 892–912, 2022.
https://doi.org/10.1007/978-3-031-09234-3_44

uses the identity of a user and his private key to generate the secret signing key of the corresponding identity. The interest in combining both ID-based cryptography and ring signature is undeniable as proven by the works [4, 15, 16, 20, 23, 32]. As explained by Chow et al. [16], the main advantage of ID-based Ring signature (IDRS) over "traditional" ring signatures in PKI is that IDRS provides better spontaneity. PKI's ring signatures can only form a ring with users that requested certificates for their public keys while in IDRS signers can form a ring using users' identities even if they did not request their secret signing keys to PKG. Additionally, IDRS may significantly reduce the communication overhead in sending the list of ring public keys to the verifier along with the signature for PKI's RS. The ring IDs may be much shorter and may even be implicitly known by the verifier (e.g. all employees of a certain organization/department).

Post-quantum IDRS: In 2016, the post-quantum (PQ) standardization process was launched by NIST and generated considerable attention from researchers. This also motivates to design post-quantum IDRS as this would provide primitives which ensure anonymity without requiring any certificates. There exist different PQ candidates to design quantum-safe cryptographic primitives. Lattice-based cryptography is currently the most investigated candidate due to its promise of flexibility. There are currently multiple lattice-based IDRS; the first one by Wang [30] and more recent works by Zhao et al. [33], Wei et al. [31] and Cao et al. [12]. To the best of our knowledge, those are the only quantum-safe IDRS.

In this work, we will focus on another promising candidate: symmetric-key primitives, for example hash functions or block ciphers. These are old primitives providing the advantage of a well-studied and well-understood security. Another advantage is that the security of a symmetric-key-based protocol depends only on the integrated primitives and not on any assumed hard problem. This means that, if a symmetric-key primitive has been broken, it can simply be replaced and the design would still be secure. On the contrary, if the hardness assumption of lattice-based constructions has been broken, then all schemes relying on this assumption are not secure anymore. The recent design of zero-knowledge proof systems obtained from symmetric-key primitives opens up new directions. Zero-knowledge proof systems as ZKBoo [21], ZKB++ [13], KKW [26], ZK-STARK [6], Aurora [7] and Ligero++ [9] allow a user to prove the knowledge of a secret witness w such that $C(w) = 1$, where C is a public circuit similar to hash functions. For all these aforementioned reasons, our work studies PQ IDRS constructed based on symmetric-key primitives only.

1.1 Contributions

The contributions of this work can be presented in the following three parts:

Generic Post-quantum ID-Based Ring Signatures (Sect. 3): We designed a circuit C (see Sect. 3.1) to allow signers to execute a zero-knowledge proof that they own a witness w such that $C(w) = 1$. C is divided into two sub-circuits: C_1 and C_2. C_1 proves the membership of the signer to the ring through

Table 1. PicRS and XRS comparisons. PQ = post-quantum, N = ring size, ✓ = proven, (✓) = assumed, h = XMSS tree height

IDRS	PQ candidate	$\|\sigma\|$ (Asympt.)	Max. N (Asympt.)	IDRS.Setup time	$\|SID\|$ (KB)	NIZK	PQ	H	(est.)$\|\sigma\|$(MB)		
									$N=2^6$	$N=2^{12}$	$N=2^{20}$
PicRS	Symmetric	$\mathcal{O}(\log N)$	unli.	$\mathcal{O}(1)$	167	KKW	✓	LowMC	169.964	170.153	170.406
								SHA3	3619	3622	3626
						Ligero++	(✓)	SHA3	2.046	2.046	2.047
								MiMC	1.902	1.902	1.903
								Poseidon	1.898	1.899	1.900
XRS	Symmetric	$\mathcal{O}(\log N)$	2^{20}	$\mathcal{O}(2^h)$	4.899	KKW	✓	LowMC	12.487	12.680	12.930
								SHA3	332.300	335.266	339.211
						Ligero++	(✓)	SHA3	1.490	1.491	1.493
								MiMC	0.973	0.976	0.979
								Poseidon	0.885	0.889	0.893
[33]	Lattice	$\mathcal{O}(N)$	unli	-	615000	-	✓	-	5	335	32243

an accumulator (see Definition 4) and C_2 proves the knowledge of a signing secret key generated by the private key generator PKG. In our generic IDRS construction, the signing private key for the identity ID is a digital signature of ID generated by PKG, therefore C_2 proves the knowledge of a valid digital signature. Both C_1 and C_2 are linked through an "AND" logical gate ($C = C_1 \cdot C_2$). The generic circuit is illustrated in Fig. 1.

Applicable Post-quantum ID-Based Ring Signatures Named PicRS and XRS from the Generic Construction (Sect. 4): We implemented sub-circuit C_1 with a Merkle Accumulator (Sect. 4.1) to prove the membership to the ring. sub-circuit C_2 can be initiated in two different ways:

(1) PKG uses Picnic digital signature [13], which means that a signer needs to prove the knowledge of a valid Picnic signature. We designed circuit Picnic.C presented in Sect. 4.2, Algorithm 1 and Fig. 3 to prove this statement.
(2) PKG uses the stateful digital signature XMSS [24], which means that a signer needs to prove the knowledge of a valid XMSS signature. We designed circuit XMSS.C presented in Sect. 4.2, Algorithm 2 and Fig. 4 to prove this statement.

Picnic.C allows to design the first IDRS PicRS, where a signer uses circuit $C =$ PicRS.$C =$ Merkle.$C(= C_1) \cdot$ Picnic.$C(= C_2)$ to generate a signature. The second implementation named XRS ensues from circuit XMSS.C. In XRS, a signer uses circuit $C =$ XRS.$C =$ Merkle.$C(= C_1) \cdot$ XMSS.$C(= C_2)$ to generate a signature. While PicRS is stateless for the signer and PKG, XRS is still stateless for the signer but requires PKG to keep an updated state to the stateful nature of XMSS. The PicRS's PKG can generate an unlimited number of signing secret keys and therefore handle an unlimited number of users, while there is a cap for the maximum number of users in XRS (e.g. 2^{20} users).

Applicable Constructions Analysis and Optimization (Sect. 5): We evaluate our constructions with two different zero-knowledge proof systems: KKW

[26], Ligero++ [9]. Each of them is tested with the standard hash function SHA3 and, additionally with the following non-standard hash functions to optimize the signature size: LowMC [3], MiMC [2] and Poseidon [22]. We optimize the complexity of circuit Picnic.C and XMSS.C by testing different parameters for Picnic and XMSS to achieve the best possible signature size. In theory, both schemes have a signature size that grows logarithmically ($\mathcal{O}(\log N)$) with the size of the ring represented by N. This is an improvement when compared with lattice-based IDRSs [30,31,33] or [12], whose signature size grows linearly ($\mathcal{O}(N)$) with the ring size, making them unsuitable for large rings. In practice, PicRS and XRS signature sizes are nearly constant because proving the knowledge of a valid Picnic (PicRS) or XMSS (XRS) signature is the bottleneck of both signature sizes. PicRS achieves a size of 1.900 MB while XRS requires only 889 KB for a ring of 4096 members. Table 1 demonstrates that these sizes are competitive when compared to the current state-of-the-art of lattice-based IDRS introduced by Zhao et al. [33], which is the only work proposing concrete parameters and allowing us to estimates their signature sizes.

1.2 Overview of Techniques

At the heart of our generic IDRS, we utilize a non-interactive zero-knowledge proof system (NIZK) based on symmetric-key primitives, which allows us to prove the knowledge of a witness w such that, for a public circuit C, we have $C(w) = 1$. Traditional digital signatures, for example Picnic [13], run the NIZK on a circuit related to the underlying one-way function as in the original zero-knowledge proof based signature schemes like Picnic [13] New challenges arise in IDRS as distinct from a traditional digital signature, namely, the generated proof needs to include a part of the IDRS signature involves the "verification" circuit for the signing secret key generation (i.e. verification algorithm of a standard signature by the key generation authority). This means that optimising the size of the verification circuit for the underlying signature is critical for our IDRS signature size and we focused our efforts in this direction.

In our generic IDRS construction, a signer with an identity ID owns a witness that is the signing secret key SID. SID is a digital signature (see Definition 2), generated by PKG, using its ID as a message. A signer will use the NIZK proving procedure on circuit C to generate a signature of a message m. C is designed to prove that he knows a valid SID, in other words, a valid digital signature generated by PKG for an ID belonging to the ring L. Circuit C takes as inputs (i.e. the witness) the signer's identity ID, the corresponding signing secret key SID and the list of identities L (i.e. the ring). More formally, the signer will prove the knowledge of (ID, SID, L) such that $C(\text{ID}, \text{SID}, \text{L}) = 1$. C, summarized in Fig. 1, is composed of two main sub-circuits named C_1 and C_2, which are used to prove the membership in the ring and to prove the knowledge of a valid digital signature.

We construct applicable constructions by defining and optimizing circuit C and both its sub-circuits C_1 and C_2. C_1 is implemented as Merkle.C which is constructed on top of a Merkle accumulator [10,17,26] and a multiplexer (see

Sect. 4.1) to hide the position of the identity into the accumulator. C_2 can be implemented with the verification procedure of the Picnic digital signature or the verification algorithms of the stateful XMSS digital signature. XRS follows the same idea but, instead of having a valid picnic signature as SID, each user owns an XMSS signature. The proof of knowledge of a valid signature will be done through circuit XMSS.$C(= C_2)$. As the stateful nature of XMSS, XMSS.C requires the use of multiplexers (see Eq. 1) to hide the state and, so, provide anonymity.

1.3   Outline of the Paper

This paper is structured as follows. Section 2 formally defines IDRS. Section 3 presents the generic construction. Section 4 introduces both possible instances PicRS and XRS. Section 5 concludes the paper with a full evaluation of the two applicable constructions. Appendix A defines the cryptographic primitives used in this work.

2   Definition of ID-Based Ring Signature (IDRS)

We now formally define an ID-based ring signature. In IDRS, there is a private key generator (PKG), which is a trusted identity generating the signing secret keys of users. Only users who have received a signing secret key SID from PKG can generate a valid and anonymous signature.

Definition 1 (ID-based ring signature).   *An ID-based ring signature is defined by the tuple of algorithms:* IDRS = (IDRS.Setup, IDRS.KeyGen, IDRS.Sign, IDRS.Verify)

- (mpk, msk, param) ← IDRS.Setup(1^λ): *This algorithm takes as input the security parameters λ, it produces the master public key* mpk, *the master secret key* msk *and the public parameters* param. *This procedure is executed by the private key generator (PKG).*
- SID ← IDRS.KeyGen(ID, msk): *This algorithm takes as input an identity* ID ∈ $\{0, 1\}^*$ *and the master secret key* msk, *it outputs the signer's secret signing key* SID. *This procedure is executed by the private key generator PKG and the result is transmitted to the user with the identity* ID.
- σ ← IDRS.Sign(m, L, ID, SID, mpk, param): *This algorithm takes as input the message m, a list L of N identities, the identity of the signer* ID, *the signing secret key* SID *of the member* ID, *where* ID ∈ L, *the master public key* mpk *and the public parameters* param. *It outputs a ring signature σ.*
- 0/1 ← IDRS.Verify(m, L, σ, mpk, param): *This algorithm takes as input a ring signature σ, a message m, the ring list L, the master public key* mpk *and the public parameters* param. *It outputs 1 if σ is valid and generated by one* ID ∈ L, *0 otherwise.*

A secure ID-based ring signature achieves unforgeability and anonymity which are defined in the full version [11].

3 Generic Construction for ID-Based Ring Signature from Symmetric-Key Primitives

This section introduces our proposed generic construction of IDRS based on symmetric-key primitives. A key part of our proposal is that symmetric-key based zero-knowledge proof systems (NIZK) give us the ability to prove the knowledge of an input (i.e. witness) w of a circuit C such that $C(w) = 1$. In an IDRS, the signer needs to demonstrate that (1) he owns a secret key generated by the central authority PKG and that (2) his identity belongs to the rings. This requires a circuit C that proves both statements.

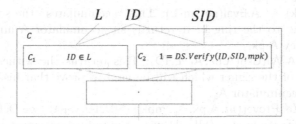

Fig. 1. Generic circuit C

The basic idea behind our generic IDRS is that the PKG possesses a digital signature (see Definition 2) key pair as master public mpk and private key msk (i.e. mpk = DS.pk, msk = DS.sk). Then, each user with an identity ID requests a signing key SID to PKG which generates a digital signature DS.σ taking the identity ID as the message or, in other words, PKG computes SID $\leftarrow$ DS.Sign(ID, msk). To sign a message m, a user in possession of a signing secret key generated by PKG proves the knowledge through a NIZK (see Definition 3) of SID associated with an identify ID belonging to the ring L (i.e. ID $\in$ L). We designed a generic circuit C (see Fig. 1) which proves the validity of both statements. C is divided into two sub-circuits" C_1 to prove ID $\in$ L and C_2 to prove $1 = $ DS.Verify(ID, SID, mpk). C_1 and C_2 are associated with "AND" gate to form the overall circuit C.

3.1 Generic IDRS Algorithms

We now formally define the algorithms for our generic construction of IDRS, which follows Definition 1.

(mpk, msk, param) $\leftarrow$ IDRS.Setup(1^λ) : This algorithm is executed by PKG and performs the following steps:
- (mpk, msk) $\leftarrow$ DS.KeyGen(1^λ) (see Definition 2)
- param $\leftarrow$ A.Gen(1^λ) (See Definition 4)
- **Return** (mpk, msk)

SID ← IDRS.KeyGen(ID, msk): This algorithm is executed by PKG on the request of the user with the identity ID. It computes a digital signature DS.σ using the ID as the message. The digital signature DS.σ is transmitted to the user ID with and becomes his signing secret key SID. This procedure executes the following steps:

  – SID ← DS.Sign(ID, msk) (see Definition 2)
  – **Return** SID

σ ← IDRS.Sign(m, L, ID, SID, mpk, param): This procedure takes as inputs the message m, the set of N identities L, in other words the ring, the signing secret key SID = DS.σ and the master public key and the public parameters param which the initial public key of an empty accumulator. This executes the following steps:

  – (A$_L$, A.pk) ← A.Eval(param, L): This "accumulates" the set of identities belonging to the ring L. It returns an accumulator A and its updated public key A.pk.
  – w$_{ID}$ ← A.WitGen(A.pk, A$_L$, L, ID): This returns the witness w$_{ID}$ for the identity of the signer which will be used to prove that his ID is included in the accumulator A$_L$.
  – π ← NIZK.Prove((m, A.pk, A$_L$, mpk), (SID, ID, w$_{ID}$)) (see Definition 3) The secret witness is w = (SID, ID, w$_{ID}$), the public statement is composed of the message m, the accumulator public key A.pk, the accumulator build on the ring A$_L$ and PKG public key mpk (x = (m, A.pk, A$_L$, mpk)). The tuple (x, w) ∈ R if and only if the following statements stand:
    (1) 1 = A.Verify(A.pk, A$_L$, w$_{ID}$, ID): This is equivalent to prove ID ∈ L, so it will be proven through sub-circuit C_1 (See Fig. 1).
    (2) 1 = DS.Verify(ID, SID, mpk): This will be proven through sub-circuit C_2 (See Fig. 1).
    Both statements will be separately proven through the sub-circuits C_1 and C_2 which are linked together with a "AND" gate to form the whole circuit C ((See Fig. 1)) and assure that they are both valid. The message to be signed, m, is embedded by integrating it to the Fiat-Shamir transform[1] [19] to generate the challenge.
  – σ ← π
  – **Return** σ

0/1 ← IDRS.Verify(m, L, σ, mpk, param): This algorithm takes as inputs the message m, the list of identities L and a ring signature σ. It verifies the validity of σ by executing the following steps:

  – π ← σ
  – (A$_L$, A.pk) ← A.Eval(param, L): The verifier construct the accumulator for the set of identities belonging to the ring L. It returns an accumulator A$_L$ and its updated public key A.pk.
  – **Return** NIZK.Verify((m, A.pk, A$_L$, mpk), π): This returns 1 if the proof π is valid for circuit C.

---

[1] Fiat-Shamir transform converts an interactive protocol into a non-interactive protocol. It generates the challenge c as an outputs of H ($c = H(r, m)$), where m is the message to be signed in IDRS, instead of receiving it from the verifier.

3.2 Security Analysis

The security of our generic IDRS depends on the symmetric-key primitives used, namely a EU-CMA secure digital signature scheme DS (see Definition 2), a secure accumulator A presented in Definition 4, a cryptographic hash function H and a secure NIZK NIZK (see Definition 3). All security proofs are presented in the full version of the paper [11].

Theorem 1 (Unforgeability). *Let* IDRS *be the construction provided in Sect. 3.1 with a cryptographic hash function H, a EUC-CMA secure digital signature scheme* DS, *a secure accumulator* A *and a secure non-interactive zero-knowledge proof system* NIZK. *Then,* IDRS *achieves unforgeability.*

Theorem 2 (Anonymity). *Let* IDRS *be the construction provided in Sect. 3.1 with a cryptographic hash function H, a EUC-CMA secure digital signature scheme* DS, *a secure accumulator* A *and a secure non-interactive zero-knowledge proof system* NIZK. *Then,* IDRS *achieves anonymity.*

4 IDRS: Applicable Constructions

This section introduces possible applicable constructions of the generic IDRS presented in Sect. 3. Section 4.1 starts with a presentation of the practical construction of sub-circuit C_1 and discusses its security while Sect. 4.2 is dedicated to presenting possible constructions of sub-circuit C_2 and also discusses their security. The section ends with the summary of two possible implementations of the generic IDRS. We assume that hash functions H output a string of 2λ bits where λ is the post-quantum security level.

4.1 Sub-circuit C_1

Sub-circuit C_1 (see Fig. 1) aims to prove the first statement $1 = $ A.Verify(A.pk, A_L, w_{ID}, ID) which is equivalent to prove ID $\in$ L or, in other words, that the identity ID of the signer belongs to the ring L. As previously stated, we use an accumulator to prove the membership to the ring. Applying NIZK based on symmetric-key primitives requires that the verification of a valid witness, A.Verify algorithm, can be expressed as a one-way circuit. This leads us to circuit Merkle.C, derived from the Merkle accumulator.

Merkle Accumulator and Circuit Merkle.C: The Merkle accumulator respects Definition 4 and "accumulates" the set of identities L as a Merkle tree [27]. Each identity of the ring L is a leaf in a Merkle tree. A Merkle tree is a binary tree in which each internal node is the hash of both its children. The accumulator's public key A.pk is the tree root as illustrated in Fig. 2a.

The membership proof consists of demonstrating the knowledge of the path from the leaf associated with the signer identity to the root of the tree. This can be represented as a circuit Merkle.$C(w_{ID}, ID) = $ A.pk, where A.pk is the Merkle root and w_{ID} is the authentication path for the identity ID composed of internal nodes of the Merkle accumulator/tree and $\log N$ bits, which indicate the direction of the path. Merkle.C is formally presented in Algorithm 2 and is composed of $\log N$ calls of hash function H, where N is the ring size. Additionally, at each level of the Merkle accumulator, Merkle.C goes through a multiplexer μ which is defined as follows:

$$\mu(x, y, b) = \begin{cases} (x, y) & \text{if } b = 0, \\ (y, x) & \text{if } b = 1. \end{cases} \tag{1}$$

μ orders the inputs of H depending on the path coming from left or right in the tree. μ hides the path's direction from ID to the root A.pk, hence ensuring anonymity to our IDRS. μ can be written as a circuit $\mu(x, y, b) = (\bar{b} \cdot x + b \cdot y, \bar{b} \cdot y + b \cdot x)$. Figure 2a depicts an example of a Merkle accumulator and Merkle.C: the corresponding witness for ID is $w_{ID} = ((w_1, 1), (w_2, 0))$, where the Merkle.$C(w_{ID}, ID) = H(\mu(H(\mu(ID, w_1, 1)), w_2, 0))$. Without the multiplexer, the position of the ID would be identifiable from the path meaning that the anonymity could not be provided. Merkle.C is presented in Algorithm 2.

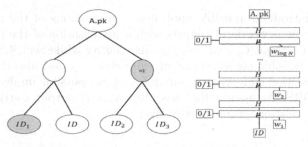

(a) Example: Merkle accumulator (b) Merkle.C repre-
with $N = 4$, $n1 = H(ID_2, ID_3)$ sentation

Fig. 2. Merkle Accumulator and circuit Merkle.C

In conclusion, Merkle.C plays the role of sub-circuit C_1 in our general circuit (see Fig. 1) to prove that the membership to the ring can be replaced in application by circuit Merkle.C presented in this section. The complexity of Merkle.C grows logarithmically with the number of identities in the ring.

Security and One-Wayness Merkle.C**:** As the security presented in Sect. 3.2 shows, we require a secure accumulator A, in our case, a secure Merkle accumulator which comes from the properties of the hash function H (see Definition 5). The collision-freeness of the accumulator comes directly from the collision resistance property of H. This means that it is computationally infeasible to construct the same accumulator from two different sets of ring members. Merkle.C's one-wayness ensues from the one-wayness of the hash function H. This circuit is a Merkle tree with a public root. It should be computationally infeasible to recover any of the leaves from the root and this is achieved because the root is an output of the hash function H, which is a one-way function.

4.2   Sub-circuit C_2

C_2 (see Fig. 1) aims to prove the validity of signing secret key SID, namely to prove that $1 = $ DS.Verify(ID, SID, mpk). Therefore, the verification procedure of the digital signature scheme is to be expressed as a one-way circuit. The current state-of-the-art of digital signatures based on symmetric-key primitives gives us two possible digital signatures: The stateless Picnic signature and the stateful XMSS signature, which meet the requirements to fulfil Theorem 1 and 2. Both schemes were chosen because they are considered as standard post-quantum signature (XMSS) or as alternative candidate (Picnic) by the NIST standardization process. It is important that it exist other alternatives [1]. We provide the pseudo-code of both circuits Picnic.C and XMSS.C in Algorithm 1 and 2 to present a clear evaluation later in this work. A more detailed explanation of both circuits is available in the full version of the paper [11].

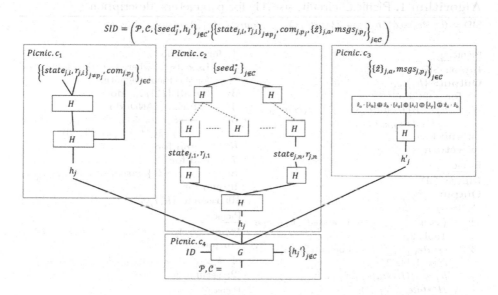

Fig. 3. Circuit Picnic.C

Circuit Picnic.C: The goal of this circuit is to prove that the signer possesses a valid Picnic signature generated by PKG. Picnic and a detailed description of its parameters are presented in the full version of the paper [11]. More formally, the signer proves the knowledge of SID such that $1 = $ Picnic.Verify(ID, SID, mpk) with the NIZK.Prove procedure and circuit Picnic.C. Circuit Picnic.C takes as inputs
$$\text{SID} = (\mathcal{C}, \mathcal{P}, \{\text{seed}_j^*, h_j'\}_{j \notin C}, \{\{state_{j,i}, r_{i,j}\}_{i \neq p_j}, com_{j,p_j}, \{\hat{z}_{j,a}\}, msgs_{j,p_j}\}_{j \in C})$$

(the Picnic signature) and the signer identity ID. To facilitate the understanding of the circuit, we present a high-level picture of Picnic.C in Fig. 3 and we divide it into four sub-circuits Picnic.c_1, Picnic.c_2, Picnic.c_3 and Picnic.c_4. Each sub-circuit executes a specific step of the Picnic verification procedure and is presented in Algorithm 1.

One-Wayness and Security of Picnic.C: The unforgeability of Picnic have been proven in [13,26] and therefore provides the desired security according to Theorem 1 and 2. The one-wayness of Picnic.C ensues from the one-wayness of the four sub-circuit presented in Algorithm 1. The one-wayness of Picnic.c_1 depends on the one-wayness of the cryptographic hash function H. Indeed, each step involves only the calls of the hash function H therefore it is computationally infeasible to invert Picnic.c_1. Picnic.c_2 provides also one-wayness for the same reason. Picnic.c_3 one-wayness depends on the one-wayness of the following equation $(\hat{z}_a \cdot [\lambda_b] \oplus \hat{z}_b \cdot [\lambda_a] \oplus [\lambda_c] \oplus [\lambda_\gamma] \oplus \hat{z}_a \cdot \hat{z}_b)$ on which the NIZK is executed. This six inputs equation has a 50% chance to output 0, which makes it one-way. Picnic.c_4's one-wayness follows directly from the one-wayness of hash function G.

Algorithm 1. Picnic.C circuit, see [11] for parameters' description

$\mathrm{SID} = (\mathcal{C}, \mathcal{P}, \{\mathrm{seed}_j^*, h_j'\}_{j \notin \mathcal{C}}, \{\{state_{j,i}\}_{i \neq p_j}, com_{j,p_j}, \{\hat{z}_{j,a}\}, msgs_{j,p_j}\}_{j \in \mathcal{C}})$

Picnic.c_1
Input: SID
Output: $\{h_j\}_{j \in \mathcal{C}}$
1: **for** $j \in \mathcal{C}$ **do**
2:   $h_j = H(H(state_{j,1}, r_{j,1}), \ldots, com_{j,p_j},$
     $.., H(state_{j,n}, r_{j,n}))$
3: **end for**
4: **return** $\{h_j\}_{j \in \mathcal{C}}$

Picnic.c_2
Input: SID
Output: $\{h_j\}_{j \notin \mathcal{C}}$
1: **for** $j \notin \mathcal{C}$ **do**
2:   $\{\mathrm{seed}_j^{(i)}\}_{i=1}^n \leftarrow \mathrm{Tree}(\mathrm{seed}_j^*, n)$ (See Table 2)
3:   $(state_{i,j}, r_{i,j}) \leftarrow \mathrm{ComputeState(seed)}$ (See Table 2)
4:   $h_j = H(H(state_{j,1}, r_{j,1}), \ldots,$
     $H(state_{j,n}, r_{j,n}))$
5: **end for**
6: **return** $\{h_j\}_{j \notin \mathcal{C}}$

Picnic.c_3
Input: SID
Output: b

1: **for** $j \in \mathcal{C}$ **do**
2:   Execute C, where C is the circuit used for the Picnic signature.
3:   **for all** $\{P_i\}_{i \neq p_j}$ **do**
4:     **for** $x \in [\mathrm{AND}]$ **do**
5:       $(\hat{z}_a \cdot [\lambda_b] \oplus \hat{z}_b \cdot [\lambda_a] \oplus [\lambda_c] \oplus [\lambda_\gamma] \oplus$
       $\hat{z}_a \cdot \hat{z}_b)^{(j,i,x)}$ (see Fig. 3)
6:     **end for**
7:   **end for**
8:   $h_j' = H(\{\hat{z}_j\}, msgs_{j,1}, \ldots, msgs_{j,n})$
9: **end for**
10: **return** $\{h_j'\}_{j \in \mathcal{C}}$

Picnic.c_4
Input: $\{h_j\}_{j \in \mathcal{C}}, \{h_j'\}_{j \in \mathcal{C}}, \{h_j, h_j'\}_{j \notin \mathcal{C}}, \mathrm{ID}$
Output: b
1: $b = (\mathcal{C}, \mathcal{P}) \overset{?}{=} G(\mathrm{ID}, h_1, h_1', \ldots, h_M, h_M')$
2: **return** b

Picnic.C
Input: SID, ID
Output: 0/1
1: $b = \mathrm{Picnic}.c_4(\mathrm{Picnic}.c_1(\mathrm{SID}),$
   $\mathrm{Picnic}.c_2(\mathrm{SID}), \mathrm{Picnic}.c_3(\mathrm{SID}), \mathrm{ID})$
2: **return** b

This important to notice that in Picnic, G computes the challenge (Fiat-Shamir transform) and is modelled as random oracle. Hence, producing NIZKs for calls to a random oracle which is not possible, but in practice G is initialized as an hash function which makes PicRS possible.

Table 2. Additional Functions and parameters summary

$r \leftarrow \mathsf{MT}(\mathcal{S})$	This circuit constructs a Merkle root r of binary tree from a set of leaves $\mathcal{S}$. This circuit executes H for $|\mathcal{S}| - 1$ times
$\{leaf_i\}_{i=1}^{2^{leaves}} \leftarrow \mathsf{Tree}(seed, depth)$	This circuit takes as input a seed $seed$ and an integer $depth$ indicating the number of the binary tree leaves. This procedure calls $2 \cdot (leaves - 1)$ executions of H
$(state, r) \leftarrow \mathsf{ComputeState}(seed)$	This circuit takes as input a $seed$ and outputs the tuple $(state, r)$. This circuit executes one Π
$\cdot$	the multiplication/"AND" gates in circuits
$+$	the addition/"OR" gates in circuits

XMSS.C Circuit: We define circuit XMSS.C that will be used to prove the knowledge of a valid SID such that $1 = \mathsf{XMSS.Verify}(\mathsf{ID}, \mathsf{SID}, \mathsf{mpk})$. We divided circuit XMSS.C into two sub-circuits XMSS.c_1 and XMSS.c_2 presented in Algorithm 2 and presented in more detail in the full paper [11]. It is crucial to highlight lines 1 and 3 in Algorithm 2 for sub-circuit XMSS.c_2. These lines execute the XMSS path verification but we added a multiplexer (the same as the one used for the Merkle accumulator presented in Sect. 4.1). This addition ensures the anonymity as it hides the position of the WOTS$^+$.pk in PKG's XMSS tree, as such providing unlinkability between two signatures generated by the same signer. To ease the understanding, we also provide a high-level representation of XMSS.C in Fig. 4.

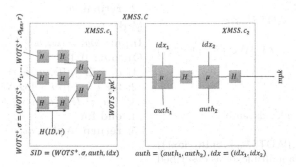

Fig. 4. XMSS.C

One-Wayness and Security of XMSS.C**:** XMSS.C is composed of two sub-circuits presented in Algorithm 2. The one-wayness of XMSS.C ensues directly from the unforgeability of XMSS used by PKG and of the one-wayness of the hash function. Indeed according to [24], the security of XMSS depends on the one-wayness of the hash function, it is computationally infeasible to compute the WOTS$^+$ public key from the XMSS tree root which is mpk. As it is computationally infeasible to invert XMSS.c_2 from mpk and also infeasible XMSS.c_2. The information leaked by the stateful nature of XMSS is hidden by integrating the multiplexer μ to circuit XMSS.c_2. Because of the multiplexer, the position of the WOTS$^+$ signature in PKG's XMSS tree is hidden and avoids the possibility to link two signatures generated by the same signer.

4.3   Applicable Post-quantum IDRSs from Symmetric-Key Primitives

This section introduced three possible circuits: Merkle.C, which can take the role of C_1, Picnic.C and XMSS.C, which can both be implemented as C_2. From these circuits, we can implemented two different IDRSs.

Post-quantum IDRS from Picnic Named PicRS**:** PicRS follows the generic construction presented in Sect. 3.1 and uses Picnic as digital signature DS. This

---

Algorithm 2. XMSS.C circuit, see [11] for parameters' description

SID = (WOTS$^+$.σ, idx, auth)

XMSS.c_1

Input: ID, WOTS$^+$.σ
Output: WOTS$^+$.pk$'$
1: $md = (md_1, \ldots, md_{len_1}) \leftarrow H(\text{ID}, r)$
2: $c = (md_1, \ldots, md_{len_2}) \leftarrow \sum_{i=1}^{len_1}(\text{Wint} - 1 - md_i)$
3: $md = (md \| c)$
4: **for** $1 \leq i \leq$ len **do**
5:     WOTS$^+$.pk$'_i$ = $H^{\text{Wint} - md_i}(\text{WOTS}^+.\sigma_i)$
6: **end for**
7: WOTS$^+$.pk$'$ = MT($\{$WOTS$^+$.pk$'_i\}_{i=1}^{len}$) (see Table 2)
8: **return** WOTS$^+$.pk$'$

XMSS.c_2

Input: WOTS$^+$.pk$'$, idx, auth
Output: b
1: $h_1 \leftarrow H(\mu(\text{WOTS}^+.\text{pk}, \text{auth}_1, \text{idx}_1))$
   {Where μ is a multiplexer as described in Sect. 4.1 and presented in 1}

2: **for** $1 \leq i \leq h$ **do**
3:     $hash_i = H(\mu(h_{i-1}, \text{auth}_i, \text{idx}_i))$
4: **end for**
5: **return** $hash_h ==$ mpk

XMSS.C

Input: SID
Output: 0/1
1: $b = $ XMSS.c_2(XMSS.c_1(SID))
2: **return** b

Merkle.C

Input: w$_{\text{ID}}$ = (w$_i$, b_i)$_{i=1}^{\log N}$, A.pk
Output: 0/1
1: $a_1 = H(\mu(\text{ID}, \text{w}_1, b_1))$
2: **for** $i = 2$ to $i = \log N$ **do**
3:     $a_i = H(\mu(a_{i-1}, \text{w}_i, b_i))$
4: **end for**
5: **return** A.pk $= a_{\log N}$

---

means that the master public and private keys mpk and msk are set to msk = Picnic.sk and mpk = Picnic.pk and each user with an identity ID owns a signing secret key SID = Picnic.σ such that $1 = $ Picnic.Verify(ID, SID, mpk). In PicRS, the general circuit C (see Fig. 1) named PicRS.C is where the signer executes the NIZK proof. We have circuit $C = $ PicRS.C where $C = $ PicRS.$C = $ Merkle.$C \cdot$ Picnic.C. PicRS security comes from the EU-CMA security of Picnic proven in [14], from the properties of the Merkle accumulator and from the one-wayness of circuits Merkle.C and Picnic.C discussed in Sect. 4.3.

Post-quantum IDRS from Picnic XMSS Named XRS: The idea of the XMSS-based IDRS construction is similar to the PicRS construction but the Picnic digital signature is replaced with the XMSS signature. This means that in XRS, each signer executes NIZK on circuit $C = $ XRS.$C = $ Merkle.$C \cdot$ XMSS.C, where XMSS.C will prove the knowledge of a valid XMSS signature (i.e. $1 = $ XMSS.Verify(ID, SID, mpk)). XRS security comes from the EU-CMA security of XMSS proven in [24], from the properties of the Merkle accumulator and from the one-wayness of circuits Merkle.C and XMSS.C discussed in Sect. 4.3.

5   Evaluation

This section analyzes the signature sizes of both applicable constructions PicRS and XRS for a post-quantum security level of $\lambda = 128$ bits. We evaluate both constructions using two different non-interactive zero-knowledge proof systems (NIZK): KKW [26] and Ligero++ [9]. We chose to work with these NIZKs because, on the one hand, KKW is considered the current state-of-the-art of symmetric-key based NIZK. It has been analyzed in the QROM model, it is considered by NIST as an alternate candidate for the standardization process [1] and provides all the security properties that our constructions require. On the other hand, Ligero++ has been less studied and its post-quantum security is only assumed, but according to the literature it achieves the most competitive proof size for large circuits when compared to other works as Aurora [7] or ZK-STARK [6], which could be promising NIZK's alternative. KKW is optimized to work on binary circuits while Ligero++ is optimized for arithmetic circuits. We implemented our schemes using different hash functions which are either considered as binary or as arithmetic circuits. We use the standard hash function SHA3 but we also tested our constructions with other hash functions which have an optimized complexity that decreases the overall size of the circuit and of the signature. The complexity of all circuits are expressed in terms of "number of H executions" and we consider an execution of the compression function $H(x, y) = z$ with $x, y, z \in \{0, 1\}^{2\lambda}$. If H has n inputs, the number of counted execution is $n - 1$.

In the rest of this section, we discuss the complexity of circuit Merkle.C. We then start the discussion on optimizing circuit Picnic.C and XMSS.C in order to have the shortest signature possible for PicRS and XRS. We express the complexity in terms of number of hash executions. We conclude the paper with a comparison between both schemes and a comparison with the current state-of-the-art of post-quantum IDRS constructed with lattices and some final recommendations.

Merkle.C **Complexity.** The complexity of Merkle.C, which is used to "accumulate" all identities in the ring L increases logarithmically ($\mathcal{O}(\log N)$) with the size of the ring. This ensues from the Merkle tree structure of the accumulator (see Sect. 4.1). The complexity of circuit Merkle.C can be expressed as |Merkle.C| = $\log N \cdot (|H| + |\mu|)$, where $|H|$ is the complexity of the hash function H, $|\mu|$ is the complexity of the multiplexer (see Eq. 1), and N the ring size. Merkle.C is implemented in both constructions, therefore this discussion is valid for both PicRS and XRS.

5.1 PicRS Signature's Size

The signature size of PicRS depends on the complexity of the circuit PicRS.C = Merkle.C · Picnic.C (see Sect. 4.3). To analyze the PicRS signature size, we need to investigate circuit Picnic.C described in Sect. 4.2 and in Algorithm 1. We optimize the complexity circuit Picnic.C by testing different parameters, proposed in their last paper [25], for the Picnic digital signature used by PKG. We express the complexity of Picnic.C in function of executions of hash functions H and G, of number of multiplication and addition gates. We consider that an execution of H has two inputs and therefore the number of calls of H grows linearly with the number of inputs.

Table 3. Picnic.C's complexity for different Picnic parameters n, M, and τ. It shows the number of executions for the hash function H and G, the multiplication (Mult.) and addition (Add.) gates

Picnic			Circuits complexity								
			Picnic.c_1	Picnic.c_2	Picnic.c_3			Picnic.c_4	Picnic.C			
n	M	τ	H	H	H	Mult.	Add.	G	H	G	Mult.	Add.
3	438	438	1752	0	5256	2680560	244831488	1	7008	1	2680560	244831488
16	604	68	2040	1673392	4352	3121200	285077760	1	1679784	1	3121200	285077760
64	803	50	6300	2495442	12800	9639000	880387200	1	2514542	1	9639000	880387200

Table 3 demonstrates that Picnic.C achieves its optimal circuit size for the Picnic scheme with the parameters $n = 3$, $\tau = 438$, and $M = 438$. This comes principally from the fact that such an instance does not need to execute subcircuit Picnic.c_2 as $M = \tau$. Therefore, for the rest of the analysis of PicRS, we use Picnic parameters ($n = 3$, $\tau = 438 = M$) as the digital signature for PKG. Table 1 shows the signature sizes of PicRS for different ring sizes with different hash functions and NIZKs.

5.2 XRS Signature's Size

XRS signature size depends on the complexity of circuit XRS.C composed of subcircuits XMSS.C and Merkle.C (see Sect. 4.3) on which the NIZK.Prove algorithm is executed. In this part, we focus on the specific sub-circuit XMSS.C and its internal sub-circuit XMSS.c_1, which is composed of len·Wint+len−1 executions of the hash function H and the second sub-circuit XMSS.c_2 consisting of h calls to H and the multiplexer μ. Table 4 presents the complexity of circuit XMSS.C with different parameters for the XMSS scheme used by PKG to generate all secret signing keys. We used parameters proposed by XMSS's original paper [24]. Our results demonstrates that XMSS should be implemented with the parameters Wint $= 4$, len $= 133$, and $h = 20$ to optimize the complexity of XMSS. It is important to note that 2^h is the maximum number of SID that can be generated by PKG in this case. The detailed reason of setting $h = 20$ is presented in Sect. 5.3.

Table 4. XMSS.C circuit sizes for each sub-circuit for different Wint and len.

XMSS			Circuits complexity		
Wint	len	h	|XMSS.c_1|	|XMSS.c_2|	|XMSS.C|
4	133	20	$665 \cdot |H|$		$\mathbf{685 \cdot |H| + 20 \cdot |\mu|}$
16	67	20	$1139 \cdot |H|$	$20 \cdot (|H| + \mu)$	$1159 \cdot |H| + 20 \cdot |\mu|$
64	44	20	$2880 \cdot |H|$		$2900 \cdot |H| + 20 \cdot |\mu|$

After optimizing the complexity of the XMSS.C, we evaluate the signature size of XRS for different group sizes and with different NIZKs and hash functions. The details of XRS features and results are presented in Table 1.

5.3   PicRS vs XRS

Choice of NIZK: As presented in Table 1, our implementations using Ligero++ as a NIZK are the best options when targeting a signature size optimization. It works better for large circuits as its proof size grows logarithmically with the circuit size while KKW grows linearly with the number of multiplication gates in the circuit. For this reason, our Ligero++-based implementations can use the standard hash function SHA3 and still achieve a decent signature size while our KKW-based implementation requires a specifically designed hash function (LowMC) to be competitive. To the best of our knowledge, KKW is optimized for binary circuits similar to LowMC while Poseidon and MiMC are arithmetic circuits that work over larger finite fields, which makes them unpractical for KKW. However, KKW has been submitted to the NIST standardization process [1], thus giving stronger security guarantees than the other Ligero++. Ligero++ was only published recently and its post-quantum security has been assumed as it relies on known post-quantum paradigms, but it has not been proven.

Signature Size: Table 1 summarizes the performance of both schemes in terms of signature size. XRS clearly outperforms PicRS due to the lower complexity of circuit XMSS.C (see Table 4) used in XRS compared to Picnic.C (see Table 3) implemented in PicRS. Even if in theory both signature sizes should increase logarithmically with the ring size, we observe that both schemes provide a nearly constant signature size because the circuit complexity of PicRS.C and XRS.C depends mainly on Picnic.C and XMSS.C. Picnic.C represent 99% of PicRS.C complexity and XMSS.C 95% of XRS.C's complexity for the largest ring $N = 2^{20}$. Because of Ligero++ proof size that increases only logarithmically with the circuit size while KKW's one increases linearly with the number of multiplication gates, PicRS and XRS implemented with Ligero++ have a signature size "more constant" than the ones implemented with KKW (see Table 1). A possible optimization for XRS could be replacing the WOTS$^+$ scheme by a few-time signature scheme named FORS [8] in the XMSS scheme used by PKG, which should further reduce the signature size for XRS. However, this assumption requires a formal security analysis.

PKG Characteristic: In PicRS, PKG enjoys the stateless feature of Picnic and therefore does not need to update his secret key after a signature as it is required for XRS. The main advantage of PicRS over XRS is that PKG can theoretically generate an infinite number of signing secret keys, so can handle an infinite number of users, while XRS is limited to 2^h users. Our implementation showed in Table 1 sets $h = 20$ due to the computation complexity of generating a XMSS tree (e.g. IDRS.Setup algorithm) which is grows exponentially with h.

Comparison with Lattice-Based IDRS: Table 1 also highlights the competitiveness of XRS and PicRS when it comes to signature sizes compared with lattice-based IDRS. It is important to highlight that none of the lattice-based works gave a precise signature size. We estimated the signature size of Zhao et al. [33] work according to their formula. We fixed their parameters to $n = 1000$ (n is their security parameters for the short integer solution problem (SIS)), $q = 2^{40}$, $w = 3$ and $k = 41$. Their estimated size is presented in Table 1. Regardless of the difference of the actual signature size, XRS and PicRS enjoy a nearly constant signature while all current state-of-the-art of lattice constructions [12,30,33], [31] have a signature size increasing linearly with the ring size N. Therefore, all of our implementations shown in Table 1 are more suitable for large rings than the lattice-based IDRS. Investigating the traditional state-of-the-art lattice-based ring signature designed by Esgin et al. [18] could be a promising future work to improve the competitiveness of lattice-based IDRS.

Final Recommendations and Conclusion: Table 1 shows that XRS implemented with Ligero++ is our most promising construction when an optimized signature size is desired. It achieves a competitive signature size with hash functions Poseidon, MiMC and even with the standard hash SHA3. ZK-STARK [6] and Aurora [7] could be a alternative to Ligero++, they both achieve a proof size slightly larger than Ligero++, but are still competitive. As illustrated in Table 1, XRS outperforms PicRS with a smaller signature size and a smaller SID that comes from the difference in size between XMSS and Picnic. It is also important to highlight that our possible constructions have been evaluated theoretically and it would be interesting to investigate the applicability with an implementation. According to KKW [26] Ligero++ [9] original papers the circuit's complexity influences running and the memory complexity of the signing and verification algorithms. This increases the advantage of XRS over PicRS. Therefore, our final recommendation would be to use XRS implemented either with Poseidon and Ligero++ to achieve the best compromise between proof size and security or with KKW combined with LowMC to ensure post-quantum security.

A   Definitions

This section defines the algorithms of the used primitives, their related security definitions are presented in the full version [11].

Definition 2 (Digital signature). *A digital signature scheme* DS *is composed by the following algorithms:*

$(\mathsf{DS.pk}, \mathsf{DS.sk}) \leftarrow \mathsf{DS.KeyGen}(1^\lambda)$: *This takes as input the security parameter* λ *and outputs the keypair* (DS.pk, DS.sk).

$\mathsf{DS}.\sigma \leftarrow \mathsf{DS.Sign}(m, \mathsf{DS.sk})$: *This takes as inputs a message* m *to be signed and a secret key* DS.sk. *It outputs a valid digital signature* $\mathsf{DS}.\sigma$.

$0/1 \leftarrow \mathsf{DS.Verify}(m, \mathsf{DS}.\sigma, \mathsf{DS.pk})$: *This takes as inputs the signed message* m, *a digital signature* $\mathsf{DS}.\sigma$, *and the public key* DS.pk. *It outputs* 1 *if* $\mathsf{DS}.\sigma$ *is valid and* 0, *otherwise.*

Definition 3 (Non-interactive zero-knowledge proof system (NIZK)). *Non-interactive zero-knowledge proof system (NIZK) [5] aims to prove that a public statement* x *and a private witness* w *belong to a defined relation* R *(i.e.* $(x, w) \in R$). *We also let* $\mathcal{L}_R = \{x | \exists w \text{ s.t. } (x, w) \in R\}$. *A* NIZK *consists of the following three algorithms:*

$\mathsf{crs} \leftarrow \mathsf{NIZK.Setup}(1^\lambda)$: *This generates the common reference string* crs *from the security parameters* λ.

$\pi \leftarrow \mathsf{NIZK.Prove}(\mathsf{crs}, x, w)$: *This generates a proof* π *for the common reference string* crs, *the statement* x *and the witness* w *that satisfies the relation* R *(to be more specific, we have* $(x, w) \in R$).

$0/1 \leftarrow \mathsf{NIZK.Verify}(\mathsf{crs}, x, \pi)$: *This returns* 1 *if the proof* π *based on the common reference string* crs *and the public statement* x *is valid,* 0 *otherwise.*

Remark 1. In this paper, we omit the use of the common reference string crs.

Definition 4 (Accumulator). *An accumulator [10]* A *is defined by the following algorithms:*

$\mathsf{A.pk} \leftarrow \mathsf{A.Gen}(1^\lambda)$: *The setup algorithm takes as input the security parameter* λ *and outputs the public key* A.pk.

$(\mathsf{A}_\mathcal{X}, \mathsf{A.pk}) \leftarrow \mathsf{A.Eval}(\mathsf{A.pk}, \mathcal{X})$: *The evaluation algorithm takes as inputs the public key* A.pk *and the set* $\mathcal{X}$ *and outputs the accumulator* $\mathsf{A}_\mathcal{X}$ *and an updated public key* A.pk *for the new accumulated set* $\mathcal{X}$.

$w_{x_i} / \bot \leftarrow$ A.WitGen(A.pk, $A_{\mathcal{X}}, \mathcal{X}, x_i$): *The witness generation algorithm takes as inputs the public key A.pk, the accumulator $A_{\mathcal{X}}$, the set $\mathcal{X}$, and an element x_i. It outputs the witness w_{x_i} if $x_i \in \mathcal{X}$ and $\bot$ otherwise.*

$0/1 \leftarrow$ A.Verify(A.pk, $A_{\mathcal{X}}, w_{x_i}, x_i$): *The verification algorithm takes as inputs the public key A.pk, the accumulator $A_{\mathcal{X}}$, the witness w_{x_i}, and the element x_i. It outputs 1 if w_{x_i} is a valid witness for $x_i \in \mathcal{X}$ and 0 otherwise.*

Definition 5 (Cryptographic Hash function). *A cryptographic hash function*

$$H : \{0,1\}^* \to \{0,1\}^{2\lambda} \tag{2}$$

takes as input a message a of any length and outputs the hash value b of length 2λ bits. A cryptographic hash function fulfills the three following properties:

- *Pre-image resistance (one-wayness): given a hash value b, where $b = H(a)$ for a uniformly random $a \in \{0,1\}^*$ it is computationally infeasible (in polynomial-time) to find a such that $b = H(a)$.*
- *Second Pre-image Resistance: knowing a pair $(a_0, H(a_0))$ for a uniformly random $a_0 \in \{0,1\}^*$ it is computationally infeasible to find another input $a_1 \in \{0,1\}^*$ such that $H(a_1) = H(a_0)$.*
- *Collision Resistance: it is computationally infeasible to find two different inputs a_0 and a_1 such that $a_0 \neq a_1$ resulting with the same hash value $b = H(a_0) = H(a_1)$*

References

1. Alagic, G., et al.: Status report on the second round of the NIST post-quantum cryptography standardization process. NIST Technical Report, July 2020
2. Albrecht, M., Grassi, L., Rechberger, C., Roy, A., Tiessen, T.: MiMC: efficient encryption and cryptographic hashing with minimal multiplicative complexity. In: Cheon, J.H., Takagi, T. (eds.) ASIACRYPT 2016. LNCS, vol. 10031, pp. 191–219. Springer, Heidelberg (2016). https://doi.org/10.1007/978-3-662-53887-6_7
3. Albrecht, M.R., Rechberger, C., Schneider, T., Tiessen, T., Zohner, M.: Ciphers for MPC and FHE. In: Oswald, E., Fischlin, M. (eds.) EUROCRYPT 2015. LNCS, vol. 9056, pp. 430–454. Springer, Heidelberg (2015). https://doi.org/10.1007/978-3-662-46800-5_17
4. Au, M.H., Liu, J.K., Yuen, T.H., Wong, D.S.: ID-based ring signature scheme secure in the standard model. In: Yoshiura, H., Sakurai, K., Rannenberg, K., Murayama, Y., Kawamura, S. (eds.) IWSEC 2006. LNCS, vol. 4266, pp. 1–16. Springer, Heidelberg (2006). https://doi.org/10.1007/11908739_1
5. Backes, M., Hanzlik, L., Schneider-Bensch, J.: Membership privacy for fully dynamic group signatures. In: ACM CCS, vol. 2019, pp. 2181–2198 (2019)
6. Ben-Sasson, E., Bentov, I., Horesh, Y., Riabzev, M.: Scalable, transparent, and post-quantum secure computational integrity. IACR Cryptol. ePrint Arch. **2018**, 46 (2018)
7. Ben-Sasson, E., Chiesa, A., Riabzev, M., Spooner, N., Virza, M., Ward, N.P.: Aurora: transparent succinct arguments for R1CS. In: Ishai, Y., Rijmen, V. (eds.) EUROCRYPT 2019. LNCS, vol. 11476, pp. 103–128. Springer, Cham (2019). https://doi.org/10.1007/978-3-030-17653-2_4

8. Bernstein, D.J., Hülsing, A., Kölbl, S., Niederhagen, R., Rijneveld, J., Schwabe, P.: The SPHINCS+ signature framework. In: ACM CCS, vol. 2019, pp. 2129–2146 (2019)
9. Bhadauria, R., Fang, Z., Hazay, C., Venkitasubramaniam, M., Xie, T., Zhang, Y.: Ligero++: a new optimized sublinear IOP. In: ACM CSS, pp. 2025–2038 (2020)
10. Boneh, D., Eskandarian, S., Fisch, B.: Post-quantum EPID signatures from symmetric primitives. In: Matsui, M. (ed.) CT-RSA 2019. LNCS, vol. 11405, pp. 251–271. Springer, Cham (2019). https://doi.org/10.1007/978-3-030-12612-4_13
11. Buser, M., Liu, J.K., Steinfeld, R., Sakzad, A.: Post-quantum ID-based ring signatures from symmetric-key primitives. Cryptology ePrint Archive, Report 2022/416 (2022). https://ia.cr/2022/416
12. Cao, C., You, L., Hu, G.: Fuzzy identity-based ring signature from lattices. Secur. Commun. Netw. **2021**, 9 p. (2021). Article ID 6692608. https://doi.org/10.1155/2021/6692608
13. Chase, M., et al.: Post-quantum zero-knowledge and signatures from symmetric-key primitives. In: ACM CCS, pp. 1825–1842. ACM (2017)
14. Chase, M., et al.: Picnic: post quantum signatures (2020). https://github.com/microsoft/Picnic
15. Chow, S.S.M., Lui, R.W.C., Hui, L.C.K., Yiu, S.M.: Identity based ring signature: why, how and what next. In: Chadwick, D., Zhao, G. (eds.) EuroPKI 2005. LNCS, vol. 3545, pp. 144–161. Springer, Heidelberg (2005). https://doi.org/10.1007/11533733_10
16. Chow, S.S.M., Yiu, S.-M., Hui, L.C.K.: Efficient identity based ring signature. In: Ioannidis, J., Keromytis, A., Yung, M. (eds.) ACNS 2005. LNCS, vol. 3531, pp. 499–512. Springer, Heidelberg (2005). https://doi.org/10.1007/11496137_34
17. Derler, D., Hanser, C., Slamanig, D.: Revisiting cryptographic accumulators, additional properties and relations to other primitives. In: Nyberg, K. (ed.) CT-RSA 2015. LNCS, vol. 9048, pp. 127–144. Springer, Cham (2015). https://doi.org/10.1007/978-3-319-16715-2_7
18. Esgin, M.F., Zhao, R.K., Steinfeld, R., Liu, J.K., Liu, D.: MatRiCT: efficient, scalable and post-quantum blockchain confidential transactions protocol. In: ACM CCS, vol. 2019, pp. 567–584 (2019)
19. Fiat, A., Shamir, A.: How to prove yourself: practical solutions to identification and signature problems. In: Odlyzko, A.M. (ed.) CRYPTO 1986. LNCS, vol. 263, pp. 186 194. Springer, Heidelberg (1987). https://doi.org/10.1007/3 540 47721 7_12
20. Gamage, C., Gras, B., Crispo, B., Tanenbaum, A.S.: An identity-based ring signature scheme with enhanced privacy. In: 2006 Securecomm and Workshops, pp. 1–5. IEEE (2006)
21. Giacomelli, I., Madsen, J., Orlandi, C.: ZKBoo: faster zero-knowledge for Boolean circuits. In: USENIX Security, pp. 1069–1083 (2016)
22. Grassi, L., Khovratovich, D., Rechberger, C., Roy, A., Schofnegger, M.: POSEIDON: a new hash function for zero-knowledge proof systems. In: USENIX Security (2021)
23. Herranz, J., Sáez, G.: New identity-based ring signature schemes. In: Lopez, J., Qing, S., Okamoto, E. (eds.) ICICS 2004. LNCS, vol. 3269, pp. 27–39. Springer, Heidelberg (2004). https://doi.org/10.1007/978-3-540-30191-2_3
24. Hülsing, A., Butin, D., Gazdag, S., Mohaisen, A.: XMSS: extended hash-based signatures. In: Crypto Forum Research Group Internet-Draft (2015). draft-irtf-cfrg-xmss-hash-based-signatures-01
25. Kales, D., Zaverucha, G.: Improving the performance of the picnic signature scheme. IACR Cryptol. ePrint Arch. **2020**, 427 (2020)

26. Katz, J., Kolesnikov, V., Wang, X.: Improved non-interactive zero knowledge with applications to post-quantum signatures. In: ACM CCS, vol. 2018, pp. 525–537 (2018)

27. Merkle, R.C.: A certified digital signature. In: Brassard, G. (ed.) CRYPTO 1989. LNCS, vol. 435, pp. 218–238. Springer, New York (1990). https://doi.org/10.1007/0-387-34805-0_21

28. Rivest, R.L., Shamir, A., Tauman, Y.: How to leak a secret. In: Boyd, C. (ed.) ASIACRYPT 2001. LNCS, vol. 2248, pp. 552–565. Springer, Heidelberg (2001). https://doi.org/10.1007/3-540-45682-1_32

29. Shamir, A.: Identity-based cryptosystems and signature schemes. In: Blakley, G.R., Chaum, D. (eds.) CRYPTO 1984. LNCS, vol. 196, pp. 47–53. Springer, Heidelberg (1985). https://doi.org/10.1007/3-540-39568-7_5

30. Wang, J.: Identity-based ring signature from lattice basis delegation. Tsinghua University, Beijing (2008)

31. Wei, B., Du, Y., Zhang, H., Zhang, F., Tian, H., Gao, C.: Identity based threshold ring signature from lattices. In: Au, M.H., Carminati, B., Kuo, C.-C.J. (eds.) NSS 2014. LNCS, vol. 8792, pp. 233–245. Springer, Cham (2014). https://doi.org/10.1007/978-3-319-11698-3_18

32. Zhang, F., Kim, K.: ID-based blind signature and ring signature from pairings. In: Zheng, Y. (ed.) ASIACRYPT 2002. LNCS, vol. 2501, pp. 533–547. Springer, Heidelberg (2002). https://doi.org/10.1007/3-540-36178-2_33

33. Zhao, G., Tian, M.: A simpler construction of identity-based ring signatures from lattices. In: Baek, J., Susilo, W., Kim, J. (eds.) ProvSec 2018. LNCS, vol. 11192, pp. 277–291. Springer, Cham (2018). https://doi.org/10.1007/978-3-030-01446-9_16

Author Index

Printed in the United States
by Baker & Taylor Publisher Services

Printed in the United States
by Baker & Taylor Publisher Services